DISCARD

The Development of Ethics

The Development of Ethics

A Historical and Critical Study

Volume I: From Socrates to the Reformation

TERENCE IRWIN

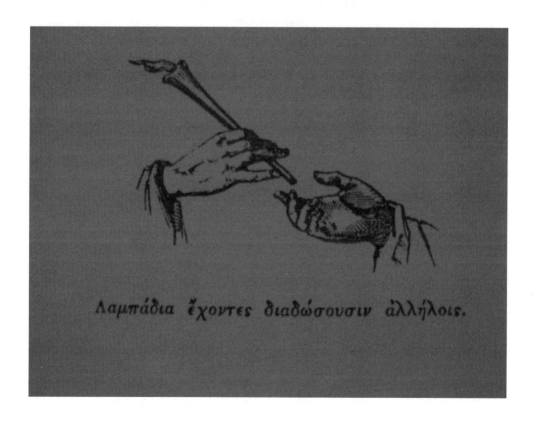

OXFORD
UNIVERSITY PRESS

OXFORD

UNIVERSITY PRESS

Great Clarendon Street, Oxford OX2 6DP

Oxford University Press is a department of the University of Oxford.
It furthers the University's objective of excellence in research, scholarship,
and education by publishing worldwide in

Oxford New York

Auckland Cape Town Dar es Salaam Hong Kong Karachi
Kuala Lumpur Madrid Melbourne Mexico City Nairobi
New Delhi Shanghai Taipei Toronto

With offices in

Argentina Austria Brazil Chile Czech Republic France Greece
Guatemala Hungary Italy Japan Poland Portugal Singapore
South Korea Switzerland Thailand Turkey Ukraine Vietnam

Oxford is a registered trade mark of Oxford University Press
in the UK and in certain other countries

Published in the United States
by Oxford University Press Inc., New York

British Library Cataloguing in Publication Data

Data available

Library of Congress Cataloging in Publication Data

Data available

Typeset by Laserwords Private Limited, Chennai, India
Printed in Great Britain
on acid-free paper by
Biddles Ltd., King's Lynn, Norfolk

ISBN 978-0-19-824267-3

1 3 5 7 9 10 8 6 4 2

In Memoriam

Henry Ernest Irwin

1915–2006

PREFACE

This book was originally intended to be a companion to *The Development of Logic*, by William and Martha Kneale, published by Oxford in 1962. I undertook it at the suggestion of Angela Blackburn, who was at that time editor for Philosophy at the Press, and with the encouragement of Sir Anthony Kenny, who was at that time the Delegate to the Press for Philosophy. I was doubtful whether I could match the learning, acuity, clarity, and brevity of Kneale and Kneale, and my doubts have certainly been vindicated. To say nothing of the first three features of Kneale and Kneale, I have not been able to achieve their brevity. On the contrary, the work has expanded to three volumes, and in this respect resembles a Victorian novel.

The three-volume novel has not been universally admired. In *The Importance of Being Earnest*, Miss Prism offers a rather unsuccessful defence:

MISS PRISM. Do not speak slightingly of the three-volume novel, Cecily. I wrote one myself in earlier days.
CECILY. Did you really, Miss Prism? How wonderfully clever you are! I hope it did not end happily? I don't like novels that end happily. They depress me so much.
MISS PRISM. The good ended happily, and the bad unhappily. That is what Fiction means.
CECILY. I suppose so. But it seems very unfair.

According to the incisive literary critic Lady Bracknell, Miss Prism's work was 'a three-volume novel of more than usually revolting sentimentality'. Though Henry James is less direct than Lady Bracknell, he none the less denounces some Victorian novels as 'large, loose, baggy monsters, with their queer elements of the accidental and the arbitrary' (Preface to *The Tragic Muse*).

I have not sought to draw precisely the moral described by Miss Prism, but I have a reasonably optimistic attitude to the history of ethics, and I don't know whether I have avoided revolting sentimentality. Some readers, if they get through the whole book, may well take Henry James's view. But perhaps some reasons can be given to explain why it is looser and baggier than Kneale and Kneale, and may not be free of queer elements of the accidental and the arbitrary.

Kneale and Kneale decided, quite reasonably, to devote most space to logic after 1879, and to treat the previous history relatively briefly. Any similar decision about the history of ethics would be misguided, Even if we supposed that, say, moral philosophy made a great advance in 1874 with Sidgwick's *Methods of Ethics*, we could hardly understand or evaluate Sidgwick's achievement without a comparison with his predecessors. More important, good reasons can be given for doubting whether Sidgwick in the 19th century, or Kant or Hume in the 18th, or Hobbes in the 17th, made the sort of advance that would justify us in relegating their predecessors to a relatively minor role.

Many people teaching the history of moral philosophy, or teaching moral philosophy from a historical point of view, would probably want to include some 'pre-modern' moralist, usually Aristotle, in their presentation of the area. Alasdair MacIntyre said he wanted to include the Greeks in his *Short History of Ethics* for the sake of undergraduates confined to the 'treadmill' of Hume, Kant, Mill, and Moore (Preface). Fewer people, however, have taken it to be equally important to discuss moral philosophy between Aristotle and Hobbes. I have tried to do something to encourage the closer study of moral philosophy between the 4th century BC and the 17th century AD, This choice has greatly increased the size of the book.

One might well argue, however, that my treatment of this important period is still too short. While I have given some space to Aquinas and to Suarez, the treatment of Augustine, Scotus, and Ockham is quite brief, and many important people (including Neoplatonists, Church Fathers, Abelard, and less well-known mediaeval writers) are omitted. The decision to omit them reflects my aim (explained further in the Introduction) of concentrating on the development of an Aristotelian outlook, but it may have been mistaken. At any rate, I hope this part of the book will encourage some more people to pursue the study of mediaeval moral philosophy far enough to discover how little of it I have covered.

A further reason for the length of this book is my aim of expounding different views fully enough to show what can be said for and against them. This is not meant to be a neutral exposition that refrains from evaluation; I also try to defend, object, or revise, where it seems appropriate. Success in these tasks would demand would need a clear understanding of all the major questions in moral philosophy, not to mention the relevant questions in other areas of philosophy. Readers who understand the questions better than I do will no doubt discover many errors in interpretation and judgment. But perhaps they will be encouraged to improve the account that I offer.

Some parts of this book (e.g., the chapters on Aristotle, Hume, Kant, Mill) cover very familiar ground and express views on questions that many others have discussed in detail. Other parts (e.g., the chapters on Suarez, Cudworth, Balguy, Price) discuss moralists who have received far less attention from moral philosophers writing in English. I have tried, as far as possible, to ignore the familiarity or unfamiliarity of a particular author. I have not refrained from going over familiar issues; nor have I discussed someone at greater length simply because he has attracted more attention from other critics. Readers may well find, therefore, that the discussion of Kant (e.g.) is rather thin, in so far as it overlooks some of the questions, elaborations, and complications that have resulted from later philosophical criticism. This uneven character (as it may seem) of different parts of the book reflects my attempt to allocate space to different people according to their importance in the argument, not according to the degree of attention they have attracted.

Though the three volumes are being published separately, they have been conceived as a single study. The division simply results from the excessive length of the book. The volumes begin at reasonably natural places (the second with Suarez, the third with Kant), but I would not want the reader to attach any particular philosophical significance to these divisions.

One inconvenience for the reader results from the separate publication of the volumes. I have not inserted cross-references to later volumes, in case the sections are re-numbered in the final stages of revision. Instead I have inserted references to the works of later philosophers. When readers have the later volumes in their hands, they should be able to find some relevant discussion by looking at the chapters that discuss these later works.

The notes and bibliography are intended to give the necessary information reasonably briefly. It seemed to me difficult and unnecessary to try to separate 'original sources' from 'secondary sources' (where ought Sidgwick's *Outlines*, for instance, to be placed?), and so I have gathered them all in a single alphabetical list. Readers who consult the list of abbreviations should be able to cope with the notes and bibliography.

I have been working intermittently on this book since 1990 or so, but it expresses an interest, beginning in the early 1970s, in the history of ethics. I mainly owe this interest to the teaching and advice of Gregory Vlastos, and to some conversations with John Rawls. Hence many of the papers I have published have provided matter, more or less proximate, for the following chapters. I have also learned from many people during this time I have been working on this book. Some of them are the helpful and well-informed people who, on hearing about the project, asked me questions of the form: 'And what are you going to say about X?'. In some cases I had to say 'Who?', and in some cases 'Nothing'. The present length of the book is partly the result of such questions. To many reasonable questions of the same form I would still have to say what Dr Johnson said about an entry in his dictionary: 'Ignorance, madam, pure ignorance.' But in some cases I discovered that X was worth reading and discussing, and moreover that Y, discussed by X, also deserved attention, and so on.

I have received comments from a number of helpful and acute anonymous referees. For Volume 1 in particular, I am pleased to be able to thank Gareth Matthews and Richard Kraut by name. Among those whose work I have learned most from I would include Richard Kraut, John Cooper, Julia Annas, and Alasdair MacIntyre.

In trying to construct some reasonably clear lines of argument, I have been helped considerably by the patient, intelligent, and thoughtful students, both undergraduate and graduate, at Cornell who have heard and discussed some of the main ideas in this book in many courses on the history of ethics. The tenacity of those who have lasted through a whole academic year, and not just one term, has been especially encouraging. Though the book contains too much to squeeze into a 28-week academic year, these students have probably been the readers I have had in mind most often.

Since I have taught in the Sage School of Philosophy at Cornell for quite a few years, I have absorbed—no doubt incompletely—many aspects of the philosophical outlook of my colleagues. If I have any slight grasp of any relevant questions in metaphysics and epistemology, I owe much of it to Richard Boyd and Sydney Shoemaker. My temerarious efforts in the study of mediaeval philosophy were encouraged by the models of scholarship and philosophical imagination provided by Norman Kretzmann and Scott MacDonald. If I have any slight grasp of moral philosophy, I owe much of it to Nicholas Sturgeon. Though he will certainly find that many things I say are false, confused, or superficial, anything that approaches truth or clarity probably results from his influence. I owe so much, in so many ways, to Gail Fine that I will not even try to describe it in detail.

The writing of this book might have taken even longer had I not been able to work on it during several periods of leave, which I owe to Cornell University, the National Endowment for the Humanities, and the Guggenheim Foundation. In 2004 I was fortunate to spend a month at the Rockefeller Foundation Study Centre in Bellagio. I spent some of the leave in Oxford, where I found more things to write about by exploring some of the resources of the Bodleian Library, and where I especially learned from discussion with David Charles.

The finishing of a long book written over many years involves a number of indispensable but tedious tasks. Fortunately, I have been helped in these tasks by the careful attention of Yurii Cohen. It would be too much to hope that he has succeeded completely in removing the effects of my errors and oversights, but he has worked hard and diligently in the interests of readers who would like citations and cross-references to be accurate and relevant.

I mentioned that Oxford University Press suggested this book to me. For this reason and for many others, it is a duty and a pleasure to thank the Delegates and officers of this admirable institution that has done so much to advance classical and philosophical learning. In particular, Peter Momtchiloff has been a source of wise advice and patient encouragement over a number of years, to me as to many other philosophers.

The design on the title page is based on Plato, *Republic* 328a. I owe it to William Whewell, who used it in several of his books on ethics, including those on the history of ethics (which I will come to in the later volumes). Since Whewell was not only a considerable moral philosopher, and a leader in the revival of the English universities in the 19th century, but also one of the first people in modern England to take up the systematic study of the history of ethics, including Plato, from a philosophical point of view. He could justly claim to have passed on the torch that had reached him from Plato.

Faculty of Philosophy
University of Oxford
June 2007

SUMMARY CONTENTS

CONTENTS

Contents

Contents

ABBREVIATIONS

This list includes only the most frequently used abbreviations, and those that might puzzle a reader. I have tried to cite primary texts from the sources that will be fairly readily available. Greek and Latin texts appearing in the OCT, BT, Loeb, PG, and PL series are listed with a reference to the relevant series, but without further details.

I have mentioned only a few of the available translations and editions.

Acronyms are normally used for the titles of books, journals, and collections. Short titles are used for articles and essays.

Page references include 'p.' only in cases where it might avoid ambiguity.

A letter after a number (e.g., 'Reid, *EAP* 755 H') usually indicates the relevant edition.

Annotated translations and editions are usually listed under the editor's name.

Ac. = Cicero, *Academica*

ACPQ = *American Catholic Philosophical Quarterly*

AP = *Ancient Philosophy*

Aquinas, *in EN* (etc.) = Aquinas' commentaries on Aristotle and on Biblical books

Arr. = Epicurus, ed. Arrighetti

Articles, *see* English Articles

AV = Bible (1611)

BCP = *Book of Common Prayer*

BF = Aquinas, Blackfriars edn.

BT = Bibliotheca Teubneriana. Greek and Latin texts. Leipzig: Teubner (later Stuttgart: Teubner and Stuttgart: K. G. Saur

CAG = *Commentaria in Aristotelem Graeca*

CD = Augustine, *De Civitate Dei*

Cic. = Cicero

CSEL = *Corpus Scriptorum Ecclesiasticorum Latinorum*

CUAP = Catholic University of America Press (Washington, DC)

CUP = Cambridge University Press (Cambridge, London, New York)

D or Denz. = Denziger, *Enchiridion Symbolorum*

DK = Diels-Kranz, *Fragmente der Vorsokratiker*

DL = Diogenes Laertius

EK = *Poseidonius, Fragments*, ed. Edelstein and Kidd

EN = Aristotle, *Ethica Nicomachea (Nicomachean Ethics)*

F. = Cicero, *De Finibus*

Fat. = Alexander, *De Fato*, or Cicero, *De Fato*

FS = *Franciscan Studies*

G = Kant, *Groundwork*

HUP = Harvard University Press (Cambridge, Mass.)

JHP = Journal of the History of Philosophy

JP = Journal of Philosophy

KpV = Kant, *Critique of Practical Reason*

L = Aquinas, Leonine edn.

Loeb = Loeb Classical Library (Greek and Latin texts with facing English translations, of varying quality). Cambridge, Mass: HUP, and London: Heinemann

LS = Long and Sedley, *The Hellenistic Philosophers*

LXX, *see* Bible, Septuaginta

M = Aquinas, Marietti edns.

M = Sextus Empiricus, *Adversus Mathematicos*

Mal. = Aquinas, *De Malo*

NP = Plutarch, *Non posse suaviter vivere secundum Epicurum*

NRSV, *see* Bible. New Revised Standard Version

OCT = Oxford Classical Texts (Scriptorum Classicorum Bibliotheca Oxoniensis). Greek and Latin texts (OUP)

Off. = Cicero, *De Officiis*

OO = *Opera Omnia*, various authors

OO = Scotus, *Opera Omnia*, ed. Wadding

OP = Scotus, *Opera Philosophica*

OSAP = Oxford Studies in Ancient Philosophy

OT = Ockham, *Opera Theologica*

OUP = Oxford University Press (including Clarendon Press and books published in Oxford, London, and New York)

P = Aquinas, Parma edn.

P = Sextus Empiricus, *Pyrrhoneae Hypotyposes*

PAS = Proceedings of the Aristotelian Society

PBACAP = Proceedings of the Boston Area Colloquium in Ancient Philosophy

PG = Patrologiae Graecae Cursus Completus, ed. Migne. Greek texts of early Christian writers

PHP = Galen, *De Placitis Hippocratis et Platonis*

Phr. = Phronesis

PL = Patrologiae Latinae Cursus Completus, ed. Migne. Latin texts of early Christian writers

Plu. = Plutarch

PR = Philosophical Review

PUP = Princeton University Press (Princeton)

QM = Scotus, *Quaestiones . . . in Metaphysica*

RTAM = Recherches de théologie ancienne et mediévale

Sent = *Sententiae* or *Scriptum super Sententiis* (various authors)

SG = Aquinas, *Summa Contra Gentiles*

SPAS = Proceedings of the Aristotelian Society, Supplementary Volumes

SR = Plutarch, *De Stoicorum Repugnantiis*

SR = Socraticorum Reliquiae, ed. Giannantoni

ST = Aquinas, *Summa Theologiae*

Stob. = Stobaeus

SVF = *Stoicorum Veterum Fragmenta*, ed. von Arnim
Sx = Sextus Empiricus
TD = Cicero, *Tusculan Disputations*
TDNT = *Theological Dictionary of the New Testament*, ed. Kittel
U = Usener, *Epicurea*
UCP = University of California Press (Berkeley and Los Angeles)
V = Scotus, *Opera Omnia*, Vatican edn.
Ver = Aquinas, *De Veritate*
VM = Plutarch, *De Virtute Morali*
Vulg., *see* Bible
W = *Duns Scotus on the Will and Morality*, ed. Wolter

1.

INTRODUCTION

1. Scope

Different people might easily write quite different books called 'The Development of Ethics' and might make quite different and reasonable decisions about what to include, what to omit, and especially about what to treat more briefly or more fully. If I were to give this book an ampler title, on the pattern of some titles in the 17th and 18th centuries, I might have chosen something like this:

The Development of Ethics
being a selective historical and critical study of
moral philosophy in the Socratic tradition
with special attention to
Aristotelian naturalism
its formation, elaboration, criticism, and defence

The different parts of this title indicate some of the omissions and emphases that determine the scope of this book.

In calling it a critical study I mean that it includes philosophical discussion as well as description and exegesis. In speaking of moral philosophy I mean that I have not tried to write a history of moral practices, or of everything that might be included under ethical thought. I have tried both to write about moral philosophy and to engage in moral philosophy through discussion of its history.

'Moral philosophy' refers to the discipline practised by (among others) Socrates, Chrysippus, Aquinas, Kant, Sidgwick, and Rawls. It is distinct, though not sharply distinct and not always distinct in the same way, from such closely related disciplines as metaphysics, epistemology, and other areas of philosophy; cosmology, theology, religion, and casuistry; natural science, social anthropology, economics, sociology, and cultural and intellectual history. No doubt moral philosophers have conceived their tasks quite differently at different times, but I believe their conceptions are close enough to justify us in speaking of one discipline. This belief needs to be tested by examination of the historical evidence.

The moral philosophers whom I have chosen for extended discussion belong to the Socratic tradition and discuss different aspects of Aristotelian naturalism. I will now try to explain these particular emphases.

2. The Socratic Tradition

To describe the Socratic tradition, I begin with a familiar passage from Aristotle on the method of moral philosophy:

As in the other cases we must set out the appearances, and first of all go through the puzzles (*aporiai*). In this way we must prove the common beliefs about these ways of being affected—ideally, all the common beliefs, but if not all, most of them, and the most important. For if the objections are solved, and the common beliefs are left, it will be an adequate proof. (*EN* 1145b2–7)[1]

Aristotle places himself in the Socratic tradition by endorsing the critical examination of common moral beliefs in order to identify the puzzles and difficulties they raise. In Plato's early dialogues Socrates raises these puzzles through systematic cross-examination of ordinary beliefs. Plato and Aristotle follow him in trying to find an account of the basic principles of morality that will resolve the puzzles and preserve 'most and the most important' among the common beliefs.

According to this view, the moral philosopher should be responsive to the relevant phenomena, which in this case are the common beliefs and convictions about the evaluation of actions and persons. A reasonable theory will try to explain them, either by giving reasons for believing them to be true, or by explaining why they seem plausible even though they are false. Aristotle does not commit the philosopher to uncritical endorsement of the appearances. He requires us to explore the relevant puzzles, to see the genuine difficulties that they raise, and seeks to solve them by reference to the 'most and the most important' common beliefs; he does not promise to retain all common beliefs, or to follow common views about which are most important.

This procedure involves revision and reconstruction of the common beliefs that we begin from. We find a clear statement of this side of the Socratic procedure in Sidgwick:

For we conceive it as the aim of a philosopher, as such, to do somewhat more than define and formulate the common moral opinions of mankind. His function is to tell men what they ought to think, rather than what they do think: he is expected to transcend Common Sense in his premises, and is allowed a certain divergence from Common Sense in his conclusions. It is true that the limits of this deviation are firmly, though indefinitely, fixed: the truth of a philosopher's premises will always be tested by the acceptability of his conclusions: if in any important point he be found in flagrant conflict with common opinion, his method is likely to be declared invalid. Still, though he is expected to establish and concatenate at least the main part of the commonly accepted moral rules, he is not necessarily bound to take them as the basis on which his own system is constructed. Rather, we should expect that the history of Moral Philosophy—so far at least as those whom we may call orthodox thinkers are concerned—would be a history of attempts to enunciate, in full breadth and clearness, those primary intuitions of Reason, by the scientific application of which the common moral thought of mankind may be at once systematized and corrected. (*ME* 373–4)

---

[1] For discussion see §67.

Sidgwick commits himself to a doctrine of 'primary intuitions of reason' that Aristotle does not mention. But the two statements of method are none the less similar enough to suggest a statement of method in moral philosophy.

In identifying the 'most important' among the common beliefs, we may hope to find the basic principles that Sidgwick calls the 'primary intuitions of reason'. The differences between different moral philosophers reflect (among other things) different judgments about which principles are 'most important'—the ones we can justifiably rely on in order to systematize and to correct other appearances. Different philosophers may be expected to appeal to other aspects of their philosophical outlook, as well as to (for instance) their scientific or theological outlook. Because of these different standards for selecting the most important appearances, moral philosophy is necessarily open to the influence of other branches of philosophy, and other sources of relevant knowledge or belief. But that does not entirely dissolve the method of ethics into any other method for acquiring knowledge. For moral philosophy, as Aristotle understands it, is ultimately responsible to the appearances; a theory succeeds only if it resolves the specific puzzles in moral appearances and vindicates the main body of the appearances it discusses.

In discussing the history of moral philosophy, I focus on the philosophers who more or less follow the Socratic pattern of moral argument. I present them as participants in a collective effort to apply this method to the past and present of moral philosophy. Among the views to be criticized, reconciled, or reconstructed, later moralists include the reflexions of their predecessors as well as the moral beliefs of their contemporaries. Aristotle recognizes that Socratic dialectical inquiry has this historical dimension.[2] Sidgwick's statement shows how later moralists treat their predecessors as interlocutors in the Socratic conversation.

But I do not simply intend to describe a collective Socratic inquiry in its historical aspect. I also try to evaluate it, and therefore to take part in it. In this respect I do not draw a sharp distinction between the method of a historian of moral philosophy and the method of a moral philosopher. It is more difficult to engage in a constructive conversation with an interlocutor whose starting point differs widely from one's own than to argue with someone with whom one already has a lot in common. But if one can find common ground with interlocutors who begin from widely different presuppositions, one may have grounds for greater confidence in the conclusions reached from this common ground.

The approach I have just described represents a widespread view of ethics and its history; and so I do not leave many people out by concentrating on those who share this view. But since different people accept it and practise it to different degrees, I say more about those who practise it more, and I say more about the historical and dialectical aspects of their views. For example, I lay special emphasis on the assessments of Greek moral philosophy by Augustine, Aquinas, Hobbes, Kant, Hegel, Sidgwick, Green, and Nietzsche, not because these moralists think of themselves primarily as historians, but because their historical reflexions show us how they participate in the historical side of Socratic dialectic.

---

[2] Aristotle practises this historical side of dialectical inquiry most explicitly in *Metaphysics* i, iii, in his discussion of the history of metaphysical speculation.

3. Aristotelian Naturalism

The Socratic approach to moral philosophy provides the main methodological theme of this book. Aristotelian naturalism provides the main substantive theme. The two themes are connected; for Aristotle believes that his naturalist theory is the most plausible conclusion from Socratic inquiry.

He defends an account of the human good as happiness (*eudaimonia*), consisting in the fulfilment of human nature, expressed in the various human virtues. His position is teleological, in so far as it seeks the basic guide for action in an ultimate end, eudaemonist, in so far as it identifies the ultimate end with happiness, and naturalist, in so far as it identifies virtue and happiness in a life that fulfils the nature and capacities of rational human nature. This is the position that I describe as 'Aristotelian naturalism', or 'traditional naturalism'. We can follow one significant thread through the history of moral philosophy by considering how far Aristotle is right, and what his successors think about his claims.

In describing Arisotle's position as 'naturalist', and in discussing various attempts to clarify and defend 'naturalism', I am using these terms with the sense I have just given them. I do not rely on the various other senses that they have acquired in the philosophy of recent centuries. Naturalism, as I understand it, does not commit itself to the claims about the definability of moral properties that Moore calls 'naturalist'. Nor does it assert that we should try to understand morality without reference to any immanent or transcendent God or gods. The relation between Aristotelian naturalism and other claims that have been described as 'naturalist' is a reasonable topic for discussion, and I will eventually have something to say about it.

In order to explore reflexion on Aristotelian naturalism, I have given some space to those who examine it in order to improve and to defend it. That is why some parts of mediaeval moral philosophy, especially Aquinas, are more prominent than some readers might expect them to be. Aquinas offers the best statement of the Aristotelian approach to moral philosophy and of Aristotelian naturalism.[3] The best way to examine this approach and this naturalist position is to reflect on Aquinas' version of them. For this reason, my chapters on Aristotle omit some questions that one might expect to see discussed there; I postpone them until I discuss Aquinas and his critics.

Even if Aquinas' position were not a reasonable version of an Aristotelian position, it would deserve attention in its own right. The criticisms that have sometimes been taken to rule it out as a defensible account of morality are ill founded. To justify this claim, I discuss the criticisms, defences, and revisions of Aquinas in later Scholastic views on morality and natural law, and especially in the views of Suarez and his critics.

To explore later expositions and defences of Aristotelian naturalism I also discuss Butler at some length. In some ways he is the central (though not the most important) figure in this whole book, because he offers an explicit defence of traditional naturalism, as he conceives it, and connects it to concerns that are usually regarded as typical of modern moral

---

[3] I lay less emphasis on the non-Aristotelian, un-Aristotelian, and anti-Aristotelian elements that are present in Aquinas' outlook because of Platonist and Christian influence. This does not mean that I think the Platonist or Christian aspects of Aquinas unimportant; but, for reasons I will try to make clear, I do not think they undermine the basically Aristotelian character of Aquinas' position.

philosophy. We may sometimes find it difficult to connect the topics discussed by Aristotle with those that preoccupy Hume, or Sidgwick, or Rawls, and we may be tempted to regard the preoccupations of the later moralists as typically 'modern'. The relevant connexions are much easier to see if we reflect on later Scholastics and on Butler's continuation of their arguments.

The aim of pursuing the defences of Aristotelian naturalism also explains the prominence of Green and Bradley in the treatment of post-Kantian moral philosophy. In Sidgwick's view, Green is wasting his time in trying to reconcile Aristotle with Kant. If we try to explore the history of reflexion on Aristotelian naturalism, we may be able to see whether Sidgwick's view is right. To clarify some of the issues raised by Sidgwick and Green, I examine both their views of the Greeks and their views of each other.

4. Critics of Aristotelian Naturalism

Aristotle advises us to identify puzzles and difficulties in the views we are exploring and trying to defend. Following his advice, I consider objections to Aristotelian naturalism, and discuss the non-Aristotelian or anti-Aristotelian views that seek to correct the errors and omissions of the Aristotelian outlook. We can compile a reasonably full and instructive case against Aristotle by attending to Epicureans, Cyrenaics, and Sceptics in ancient philosophy, to the Christian views that form an Augustinian and anti-Aristotelian tradition,[4] to the criticisms of Aquinas by Scotus and Ockham, and to the trends in moral philosophy that originate in Hobbes and Hume.

One might describe these criticisms as a series of nails in the coffin of Aristotelian naturalism. According to one view, the criticisms are so cogent that enlightened moralists are right to discard the Aristotelian view in favour of a thoroughly modern approach to ethics. I hope that readers who take this view of the history of ethics will none the less find it useful to consider what I have to say about the debates between Aristotelian naturalism and its critics. But I also hope that readers will hesitate to take this view. I do not think the critics have the best of the argument. Since I do not think they dislodge Aristotelian naturalism, it is all the more important to try to present their position fairly and sympathetically, so that one can see where they have raised legitimate points that a defender of Aristotle ought to concede, where their criticisms rest on misunderstanding, and where Aristotelian naturalism has a reasonable answer to them.

If we are trying to trace this debate, Kant raises some particularly important questions. One might regard Kantian ethics as the biggest nail in the coffin of Aristotelian naturalism. From some points of view, his deontological, autonomist, and constructivist outlook on morality stands in sharp contrast with the teleological, naturalist, and realist outlook of Aristotle. I am not convinced by this interpretation of Kant and of his relation to Aristotle. I am more inclined to argue that Kant's emphasis on rational autonomy is an unintentional defence of traditional naturalism against Hobbesian and Humean critics. Hence I try to see

---

[4] I speak of 'an' rather 'the' Augustinian tradition, to indicate that I do not think the Augustinian outlook as a whole necessarily opposes Aristotle.

why one might want to put Kant on one side or the other (or on neither) of the dispute about Aristotelian naturalism. Since my view about Kant and Aristotle is quite similar to Green's, I develop my thoughts on Kant partly in the chapters on Kant and partly in the chapter on Green.

Though Aristotelian naturalism provides the main themes of this book, it does not constrain its scope very narrowly; not everything is part of a discussion of the Aristotelian position. Nor have I designed the book as a whole as an extended argument in favour of Aristotelian naturalism. Still, the main idea of exploring questions related to Aristotelian naturalism constrains the scope and scale of the book; it partly explains why many philosophers who might deserve extended discussion in a history of ethics are omitted or treated very briefly. I hope that readers who do not agree about the centrality of Aristotelian naturalism will none the less find something to interest them in this book.

5. Beginning and End

These remarks about the main themes and lines of argument explain why I begin and end where I do. The beginning is fairly easy to explain. A proper discussion of moral thought and practice would have to begin well before Socrates, but a discussion of moral philosophy may reasonably begin with its first moral philosopher (as far as we know).

It is more difficult to decide where to end. One the one hand, omission of the 20th century might give the false impression that it does not continue the debates that I have been describing. On the other hand, the sources are all too plentiful, and it is too soon for us to tell which are more and less important. Readers should not expect, therefore, to find a full discussion of all the issues that have arisen in moral philosophy since Sidgwick's *Methods of Ethics*; still less should they expect a systematic account of all the sources that discuss these issues.

I have decided to stop with one fairly recent work in moral philosophy that ought (in both the predictive and the normative sense) still to be read in the 22nd century: Rawls's *Theory of Justice*. Apart from its importance in social and political philosophy, Rawls's book contributes significantly to the discussion of Socratic method, Aristotelian naturalism, and the connexions and contrasts between Kantian and idealist ethics. A discussion of these aspects of Rawls, therefore, makes a reasonable conclusion for my discussion.

But even though I have taken 1971 and *A Theory of Justice* for my terminus, I have not stuck to it rigidly. More recent work has thrown so much light on the questions discussed by Sidgwick and his successors that it forms a natural part of the story of moral philosophy from the later 19th century. But the reader should not expect a full account of the past century, and should expect only a few sketches of the past quarter-century.

6. Progress, Optimism, and Pessimism

If we approach the history of ethics from the point of view I have described, what do we learn? Is moral philosophy a rational and progressive discipline? Before we consider this question directly, it is helpful to distinguish, very roughly, four different approaches to the history of ethics, so that I can describe my view in comparison with them.

(1) According to one extreme non-historical conception of ethics, there is no particular reason, besides convention or convenience or purely doxographical interest, for a historical treatment. If moral theories are defensible by arguments available to anyone who thinks carefully about the subject, and no more appropriate at one time than another, then the history of ethics simply gives us a list of the positions that have been held. While it may be historically interesting to see how one position develops out of, or in reaction to, another, this sort of fact does not tell us anything about the philosophical merits of the position itself.

(2) According to another extreme conception, a moral theory cannot be assessed timelessly, and there are no timelessly appropriate questions that different moral theories try to answer. There are different questions and problems raised by different historical and cultural circumstances, and moral theories cannot intelligibly be assessed except by their success or failure in dealing with these historically-conditioned problems. The moral virtues and principles that may seem to be constant throughout the history of ethics are really products of different backgrounds, circumstances, and traditions; and it is an illusion to think there is one set of problems to be studied or described in a history of ethics.

(3) On a third view, it might seem plausible to speak of the 'evolution' of ethics, suggesting that we can see in the history of ethics a gradual approach to the principles that we have now discovered. On this view, we should be able to distinguish the 'progressive' and 'reactionary' elements in the moral thinking of previous historical periods, and show how they evolved towards the present assured results. The history of science is sometimes written from this point of view.

(4) A fourth view might look for unity rather than evolution in the history of ethics. On this view, deeper examination of the apparently various and conflicting tendencies in ethical theory will reveal some considerable degree of agreement on the main principles; and this degree of agreement will constitute some argument for the principles. This view differs from the first in so far as it does not assume that philosophers are all addressing the same questions, so that we can evaluate their views in the way we would evaluate a debate among our contemporaries. The historian's task is to discover the relatively permanent principles expressed in different intellectual and cultural embodiments.

This sketch of some extreme positions may suggest some appropriate questions. Elements of these positions are present in some influential accounts of the history of ethics. The most successful and satisfactory history of ethics in English is Sidgwick's *Outlines*, which is written from the third point of view, displaying the evolution of moral theory towards utilitarianism. The best-known recent history in English, Alasdair MacIntyre's *Short History*, tends towards the second view; and he takes a similar view in his major works on moral theory, *After Virtue* and *Whose Justice? Which Rationality?*[5] A less extreme version of this view underlies Jerome

---

[5] See MacIntyre, *AV* 11: 'We all too often still treat the moral philosophers of the past as contributors to a single debate with a relatively unvarying subject-matter, treating Plato and Hume and Mill as contemporaries both of ourselves and of each other. This leads to an abstraction of these writers from the cultural and social milieus in which they lived and thought and so the history of their thought acquires a false independence from the rest of the culture. Kant ceases to be part of the history of Prussia, Hume is no longer a Scotsman. For from the standpoint of moral philosophy as *we* conceive it these characteristics have become irrelevances. Empirical history is one thing, philosophy quite another.'

Schneewind's more recent major work on the history of modern moral philosophy; he often warns us against assuming that the history of ethics consists of a series of efforts to answer the same questions.[6] The fourth view may be found in T. H. Green's discussion of Greek ethics in *Prolegomena*.

I am most inclined to agree with the fourth view. I believe we can usefully trace the discussions I have mentioned through the history of ethics, and that we learn something about the philosophical merits and resources of different positions by considering successive efforts to attack and to defend them, and to combine one position with another.

Reflexion on this history does not necessarily lead to a 'Whig interpretation' (inspired by Macaulay's view on the development of the British constitution). I do not believe that moral philosophy has made continuous progress, or that all discarded theories belong in the dustbin. Historians of philosophy have the opportunity, and perhaps even the obligation, to point out occasions when a particular assumption or line of argument was abandoned for insufficient reasons, even when, or perhaps especially when, those insufficient reasons still influence us. The history of ethics displays more than one example of premature abandonment. Moralists of the 17th and 18th centuries were not always right about which parts of the mediaeval and Aristotelian outlook they should reject. Similarly, 20th century moralists have not always been right about which aspects of Hegelian idealism should be abandoned.

While I do not take an optimistic view about steady progress and improvement, I write from an optimistic point of view in one respect: I assume that if a particular philosophical position is widely criticized or widely dismissed by successors who were aware of it, this is not the result of foolish or uninteresting errors by the successors, but the result of some significant weaknesses in the position itself. For this reason I try to consider sympathetically the explicit and implicit objections that have been raised against different positions, on the assumption that they deserve consideration. This is why I devote some space to criticisms of the Aristotelian position of Aquinas, and, later, to criticisms of Kant and of utilitarianism. I proceed on the assumption that, whether or not the criticisms are strictly accurate, they point to some important issues that can legitimately be raised about these different positions.

In saying that I approach the history of ethics with some degree of optimism, I mean that I assume we can criticize an earlier theory constructively from the point of view of a later theory, and that in many cases a defender of an earlier theory can reasonably be expected to learn something from the criticisms of later theorists. This assumption is to some extent self-vindicating, since it requires us to focus on the aspects of theories that allow communication and mutual criticism, in contrast to those that do not. I have not, for instance, emphasized the deep and obvious differences between the general intellectual

---

[6] In this book I display some sympathy with what Schneewind calls 'the Socrates story': 'Although we have not reached agreement about the basis of morality, we know the tasks that we moral philosophers should undertake. We are trying to answer the question Socrates raised: how to live. People have always had opinions on the matter, but it is very hard to get an indubitable answer based on an undeniable foundation' (*IA* 535–6). I am also somewhat sympathetic to what he calls the 'single-aim view' of the history of moral philosophy (548). Schneewind introduces the Socrates story and the single-aim view in order to criticize them. I am more inclined to think that each of them alludes to true views about the history of ethics. I do not accept either of them, however, as Schneewind states them, since he includes in them a number of claims that I would reject (e.g., the search for an indubitable answer or an undeniable foundation).

outlook of Aristotle and Aquinas, or of Aquinas and Hobbes, or of Hobbes and Rawls; I do not mean that these difference are unimportant, but I assume that they are not all-important. For I assume that the different theories are mutually comprehensible far enough to allow fruitful criticism and replies.

But this optimistic assumption is not wholly self-vindicating. For when we examine details, we may find that our expectation of constructive mutual criticism is unfulfilled. To fulfil our expectation, we must show that different theories actually allow mutual criticism. Fruitful mutual criticism is what we expect or hope for in dispute and disagreement among contemporary philosophers. An optimistic approach to communication among past philosophers suggests that the same expectation is fulfilled when we turn to them.

To treat past philosophers as though they were contemporaries engaged in a debate would be hopelessly un-historical if we pretended that the task of understanding them is the same as the task of understanding one of our contemporaries or that they should be judged by the standards we apply to our contemporaries. If we are to understand what they are saying, or how it bears on what other people are saying, we have to reflect on what they are trying to say, within the assumptions and options available to them. We ought not to focus on the ways in which they have failed to profit from reflexion on the later theories that were unknown to them. Our task is to look for the best statement we can find of their essential points, and of their bearing on points raised by later philosophers. In speaking of 'best statement' and 'essential points' we have to rely on philosophical judgment. That is why historians of philosophy cannot do without philosophy, if they try to discuss constructive mutual criticism. Nor can they do without specifically historical study, if they try to grasp what philosophers have to say to one another across historical divisions.

This degree of optimism does not imply that the critic is always right, or that a later theory is, all things considered, an improvement over an earlier theory. The history of ethics shows regress as well as progress. But to argue that the history of ethics takes some wrong turnings is not to take the reactionary view that we ought to ignore, as far as we can, the later views and try to stick firmly with the earlier position, as it was originally formulated. Here also I proceed on an optimistic assumption, that criticism usually identifies genuine weakness, or incompleteness in a moral theory, and that the theory needs to be modified and restated so as to take account of later developments. I argue, for instance, that the Aristotelian position and the Kantian position are not mutually antagonistic, and that a proper modification of the Aristotelian position ought to incorporate some of the major Kantian claims.

Some readers may regard this suggestion as a sign of unintelligent syncretism, betraying failure to grasp the basic differences between these different theories. It may seem more sensible to conclude either that it is mere nostalgia to defend Aristotle and Aquinas, or that the Aristotelian and Kantian positions offer us a clear choice that is not to be disguised by eirenic attempts to blur the conflict between them. Philosophers who try eirenic combinations sometimes appear to be well-meaning muddlers.[7] We will want to decide whether this verdict is justified.

---

[7] It would not be too unfair to summarize Sidgwick's view of Green in *EGSM* in these terms.

7. What this Book is Not

Now that I have tried to give some idea of the point of view underlying this book, it is only fair to warn readers that they will not find in it some things that they might expect in a book with this title.

(1) It is not comprehensive. I do not try to cover every ethical view or every moral philosopher worth discussing. Nor have I tried to give a full picture of the influence of different ethical theories by discussing, or even mentioning, their less well-known exponents. This is intended to be mainly a book about major philosophers and their major works. Sometimes I have something to say about less familiar figures, when they raise some point of special interest; but these references are a small and rather unsystematic selection from the wealth of material that would provide a basis for a comprehensive history.

(2) This is not the sort of history that looks primarily for causal explanations. If I wanted to explain why philosophers accepted or rejected Aristotelian naturalism at different times, I would have to consider intellectual, social, and institutional influences that I generally ignore. The discovery of these influences is a task for an intellectual historian. I have looked for only one sort of causal influence. Appreciation or partial appreciation of the philosophical merits or defects of a particular position may be one causal influence in its acceptance or rejection. We will not be able to recognize this influence unless we can identify philosophical merits or defects; and we cannot identify them without exercising philosophical judgment. A philosophical study of the history of ethics may help us to identify this possible causal influence.

(3) This book is not a 'Cantabrigian' history, in so far as it does not share the approach of some important and illuminating work in intellectual history by members of the University of Cambridge and by authors who have published with Cambridge University Press. Two recent and distinguished Cantabrigian works are *The Cambridge History of Seventeenth-Century Philosophy* and Schneewind's *The Invention of Autonomy*. Cantabrigian history of philosophy attends to contemporary context, cultural presuppositions, social and institutional influences—all the things I have said I do not emphasize. One motive for writing Cantabrigian history might be the belief that a historical study of the sort I have undertaken is not worthwhile. But a Cantabrigian historian need not believe this. The Cantabrigian approach and my approach are not competitors; they should supplement each other and offer some mutual illumination.[8]

---

[8] In *MP* xxiv Schneewind defends Cantabrigian history, contrasting it with the view of (e.g.) Prior in *LBE* that moral philosophers are concerned with persistent questions arising out of 'reflexion on ideas that are always involved in morality'. He mentions the Euthyphro Argument as an example. He does not deny the possibility of philosophical history discussing these persistent questions; he agrees that we can reach 'some useful analyses and arguments' by this means. He points out correctly that this sort of philosophical history may miss the different significance that (e.g.) the Euthyphro Argument may have had for philosophers in different periods. One might reply, however, that if we concentrate on the different significance that this argument has for philosophers in different periods, we may miss the persistent philosophical questions that they and we are addressing. Schneewind does not explicitly commit himself to the superiority of Cantabrigian history over the philosophical exploration of persistent philosophical questions (though an incautious reader might get the impression that he prefers Cantabrigian history).

8. Level and Organization

This book is not designed only for those who already know the relevant texts. I hope some will read it who are beginning their study of the history of ethics, or of some of the main historical texts. For this reason expert readers will sometimes find some of the discussion elementary and familiar. But it is not a substitute for reading the texts, and it will not be very useful to readers who want a brief survey. Though I have tried not to presuppose extensive acquaintance with philosophy, some parts of the book are fairly detailed, and may try the patience of less experienced readers. But they should be able to skip the more detailed sections without too much loss.

Though I have found that the book expanded to a greater length than I initially expected, many readers will rightly find some of the discussion superficial, inconclusive, and repetitive. Superficiality and inconclusiveness are no doubt partly the result of my own philosophical limitations, but they are partly the result of efforts to be reasonably brief (surprising as that may seem). Though I have argued for some conclusions and against others, I have not argued fully for firm conclusions on the main issues I have explored. But I hope I have at least suggested some points that are worth considering.

Repetition is perhaps easier to justify, or at least to excuse. I have not gone as far as I could have gone in eliminating repetition, because it seemed to me on reflexion that the repetition is in some ways part of the point of the book. For instance, some questions initially raised about Aristotle return in Aquinas, Kant, Green, and Rawls. But they do not return in exactly the same form. A history ought to make clear both the old and the new elements in successive discussions of continuing themes.

I have tried to stay close enough to the texts to make it clear what I am talking about, so that readers can look up the sources for themselves. I have also provided a fair number of quotations in the footnotes. I began to add these when I was discussing relatively less accessible texts, so that readers could look at a little of the evidence without having to go to a research library. But it would be odd to give the impression that less accessible writers deserve quotation more than better-known writers do; and so I have added passages from more accessible authors as well. Reading these quotations is not a substitute for reading the full text; but I would be pleased if some readers found the quotations interesting enough to encourage them to go to the full text.

References and quotations take up most of the footnotes. I have included some references to secondary literature. But it will be obvious to the expert reader that I have not offered even a systematic selection of relevant references. I have tried to acknowledge the works I have learnt from, but I could certainly have learnt much more if I had read more.

I have eventually preferred a chronological arrangement of the chapters. After trying a more thematic arrangement, I decided that it might create some difficulties for readers trying to find their way around. At least readers who want to find what I have to say about Aristotle or Hume will have some idea of where to look for continuous accounts of each of them—though, as I remarked, they will not find everything about Aristotle (for instance) in the chapters on Aristotle. But though each chapter is generally devoted to just one philosopher, I have not stuck rigidly to this rule. Sometimes I discuss some predecessors or critics in a chapter that mainly discusses one philosopher (see, e.g. the chapters on Scotus, or Pufendorf, or Mill). And I have included some thematic chapters (e.g., on the Reformation, and on the British moralists) where it seemed appropriate to discuss themes that might be illustrated by a brief treatment of several philosophers.

Though I have followed a chronological order, I have not marked divisions into large or small historical periods. I have not made the division between ancient, mediaeval, and modern prominent in my discussion. Nor have I tried to give any general description of (for instance) the outlook of the Scientific Revolution or the Enlightenment. I am rather doubtful about whether these large historical divisions are very useful for thinking about the history of moral philosophy. If, for instance, we consider the sequence of arguments about natural law that runs from Aquinas to Pufendorf, I do not think it is useful to look for a division between mediaeval and modern contributions to the debate.

This example will illustrate my reluctance to organize the book around periods or large themes. Readers might perhaps have preferred some more historical or thematic structure. But perhaps I have given them some material that deserves to be considered in thinking about the right structure for presenting different aspects of the history of thought. To my mind, the history of moral philosophy is quite continuous, without radical revolutions or shifts in paradigms. But perhaps it would be wiser to confine this claim to the aspects of moral philosophy that I have studied in this book.

2

SOCRATES

9. The Founder of Moral Philosophy?

Ever since moral philosophers have recognized that they practise a distinct philosophical discipline, many have recognized Socrates as its founder. After a brief mention of Pythagoras, Aristotle introduces Socrates; he is the first moralist whom Aristotle discusses systematically.[1] Mill agrees with Aristotle in treating Socrates as his first colleague in moral philosophy.[2]

Even if Socrates is the first moral philosopher, he is not the first person to think seriously and rationally about morality. Even if we ignore the Hebrew Scriptures, or the ethical reflexions of Chinese writers, and confine ourselves to the Greeks, Socrates is not the first to ask questions about morality. On the contrary, his inquiries presuppose a reflective, questioning attitude to morality that was already familiar in some areas of Greek society. The Athenian tragic dramatists and historians not only raise moral and political questions, but also present explicit moral and political debates about the questions they present.

What, then, makes it reasonable to regard Socrates as the founder of a tradition of philosophical reflexion on morality? We can best answer this question by examining the methods and doctrines that Plato treats as distinctive of Socrates.

Socrates does not confine his inquiries to experts in morality; in fact, he is disappointed in his search for experts in this area. He asks whether people who make moral judgments know about morality, and he finds that they do not. Nor does he claim that he has the sort

---

[1] 'The first who undertook to discuss virtue was Pythagoras, but not correctly; for by deriving the virtues from numbers he did not apply the proper treatment to the virtues, since justice is not a square number. Socrates succeeded him, and spoke better and more fully about these things, but he did not do it correctly either. For he used to make the virtues into sciences, and this is impossible. For the sciences all involve reason, and reason is found in the intellectual part of the soul. And so, in his view, all the virtues turn out to be in the rational part of the soul. The result is that in making the virtues into sciences he does away with the non-rational part of the soul, and thereby does away also with passion and character; so that on this point he has not treated the virtues correctly' (Aristotle, *MM* 1182a15–23). Even if the *MM* is spurious, its view of Socrates is parallel to *EE* 1216b2–10.

[2] 'From the dawn of philosophy, the question concerning the summum bonum, or, what is the same thing, concerning the foundation of morality, has been accounted the main problem in speculative thought, has occupied the most gifted intellects . . . And after more than two thousand years . . . neither thinkers nor mankind at large seem nearer to being unanimous on the subject, than when the youth Socrates listened to the old Protagoras, and asserted (if Plato's dialogue be grounded on a real conversation) the theory of utilitarianism against the popular morality of the so-called sophist.' (Mill, *U*1.§1). See Schneewind on the 'Socrates story' (quoted in §6).

of knowledge that other people lack. He claims to engage in co-operative inquiries directed towards finding moral knowledge.

He takes the mark of moral knowledge to be the ability to say what a virtue is; hence his characteristic question is 'What is it?' He allows that people recognize temperate, brave, and just actions, and he asks what temperance, bravery, and justice are. He takes himself to be asking about the virtues (*aretai*)—states of persons that underlie and explain their brave (etc.) actions. He inquires especially into the virtues that were later called 'cardinal'—wisdom, temperance, bravery, and justice.[3]

Though Socrates does not claim to know the answers to his questions, he believes he can say something about the right sort of answer. In fact, he accepts a series of surprising claims about the virtues. His contemporaries and successors regarded his views as 'paradoxes', contradicting common moral beliefs.[4] They appear paradoxical to modern readers as well as to ancient. In his view, a true account of a virtue should show that all the virtues are really the same virtue, which is knowledge of the good. Knowledge of the good is also knowledge of the 'fine' (*kalon*) and morally right, and knowledge of the agent's own welfare or happiness (*eudaimonia*). Once we know what promotes our own good, we will act on our knowledge. This knowledge of the good, which is also virtue, is sufficient for happiness.

Socrates commits himself to three main paradoxes: (1) Knowledge of what is good for me is sufficient for action. (2) The virtues that promote my good are the moral virtues. (3) These virtues are sufficient for happiness. All of these Socratic paradoxes conflict with the prevalent outlook of modern moral philosophy. Sidgwick mentions the second Socratic paradox as the major division between ancient and modern outlooks. Here Socrates rejects the 'dualism of practical reason', as Sidgwick calls it, because he affirms that the demands of morality cannot conflict with the agent's own good.[5]

As Sidgwick suggests, the reaction of ancient moralists to Socrates' paradoxes is different from the reaction of modern moralists. Plato and Aristotle reject both the first and the third paradox, but still maintain the second. The Epicureans and Stoics are more sympathetic to the Socratic position. The Stoics offer the most elaborate defence of all three paradoxes; but it is not clear that the positions they defend are precisely those of Socrates.

Even these few remarks may suggest that if we understand the reactions of the ancient moralists to Socrates' views, we will understand some of the central elements in their theories. It will help us to understand these reactions if we first try to see what Socrates means by his paradoxical claims, and why he believes them.

What are we to take as sources for Socrates' views? Our main ostensible source consists of the Platonic dialogues in which Socrates is a principal speaker. But ancient readers do not treat all these dialogues as evidence for Socrates' views. Diogenes and Aristippus claim to be followers of Socrates, but they have harsh words for Plato and his doctrines. Aristotle

---

[3] On the cardinal virtues see §328. In the *Euthd.* Socrates mentions temperance, justice, and bravery as virtues; then he adds wisdom (279b4–c2). Sometimes he mentions piety as a fifth virtue (*Pr.* 329c2–330a2). These are the only virtues that Socrates discusses in the earliest Platonic dialogues, though they are not the only traits generally recognized as virtues by his contemporaries (see *M.* 74a4–6; 79a3–5 (*panta ta toiauta*); 88a6–b1). The tendency to pick out some of the recognized virtues as primary does not begin with Socrates; but earlier sources do not show any clear agreement about which virtues are primary.

[4] See Cicero, *Parad.* 4, quoted at §161n7.   [5] See Sidgwick, *OHE* 197.

attributes some of the doctrines found in the Platonic dialogues to Socrates, and others to Plato. The Stoics criticize Plato, but not Socrates, on some ethical questions.

The division that these readers mark, explicitly or implicitly, between Socrates and Plato can be understood on the assumption that they agree with Aristotle's judgment about which doctrines are Socratic and which are Platonic. He often contrasts Socrates' ethical theory with Plato's. He ascribes a purely cognitive view of virtue to Socrates, but never to Plato.[6] He believes that Plato agrees with him in distinguishing rational from non-rational parts of the soul, and in drawing conclusions for the account of virtue (*EN* 1104b11–13; 1138b5–14). Even if Aristotle were mistaken in his judgment, it would be close enough to the judgment of other ancient readers to deserve our attention. It is reasonable, then, to examine Socrates' ethics by treating Aristotle as a reliable guide to the Socratic elements in the Platonic dialogues.[7]

10. Method

Socrates believes that his inquiries are important for morality. They are not intended simply to satisfy our intellectual curiosity about the character of our moral beliefs. He suggests that if we claim to have the virtues, we ought to be able to answer his questions about them, and that if we do not try to answer his questions, we ought not to count ourselves as virtuous at all. Willingness to try to answer the Socratic questions is a mark of serious concern about one's moral character.[8] Both he and his interlocutors fail morally, therefore, when they cannot say what the virtues are.

Socrates finds that other people are too confident in their ability to answer Socratic questions; Meno assures Socrates that it is easy to say what virtue is (*M.* 71e), and other interlocutors display the same over-confidence. They are right to suppose that they can easily recognize brave or just action types (standing firm in battle, paying one's debts),[9] but they rashly infer that this is all they need to do in order to answer Socrates' questions. Their inference is rash because Socrates is not asking for a description of virtuous actions, but looking for the virtue that underlies them.

Though the interlocutors give the wrong sort of answers to his questions, Socrates does not dismiss their answers completely. He believes his interlocutors have reasonable beliefs that they can revise constructively, so as to approach a better account of virtue. His inquiries do not simply expose the ignorance of the interlocutors, but also make progress.

---

[6] See especially Aristotle, *MM* 1182a15–26 (quoted above); 1183b8–18; *EE* 1216b3–25; 1229a14–16; 1230a7–10; 1246b32–6.

[7] For good accounts of the evidence on Socrates see Ross, 'Problem'; Vlastos, *SIMP*, chs. 2–3. For Socrates and Hellenistic ethics see Long, 'Socrates'. A brief and forceful statement of a case against ascribing different ethical views to Socrates and Plato is Shorey, 'Ethics'.

[8] 'I will say, as I usually do, to anyone I meet: "My excellent man, you are an Athenian and belong to a city that is the greatest and has the highest reputation for wisdom (*sophia*) and strength. Aren't you ashamed to be taking care to gain as much wealth, reputation, and honour as you can, and while you have no care or concern for wisdom (*phronêsis*) and truth and for the best condition of your soul?" And if any of you disputes this and says he does care, I will not let him go immediately or leave him, but I will question him, test him, and cross-examine him; and if he seems to me not to possess virtue, but to say he does, I will denounce him for giving least weight to the things of greatest value and giving more weight to less valuable things' (*Ap.* 29d–30a).

[9] See *La.* 190e4–6; *Ch.* 159b1–6; *R.* 331c1–8.

Why is Socrates so confident that, even though he and his interlocutors lack knowledge of the virtues, they can improve their moral beliefs by considering and revising their attempted accounts of the virtues? He believes that when we practise Socratic inquiry, our answers to different questions form patterns. When we discover conflicts in our moral beliefs, we systematically prefer to retain a favoured set of beliefs, and we adjust our other beliefs to suit them. Epictetus the Stoic describes this process as the 'articulation' of our preconceptions.[10] We need to articulate our preconceptions so that we apply them consistently and rationally to particular situations, instead of relying on the conflicting judgments that we reach if we do not articulate our preconceptions.

Socrates believes that his method of inquiry is self-confirming; interlocutors who engage in the search for accounts of the virtues tend to agree that this is an appropriate form of inquiry. They agree that it is reasonable to look for an answer to the question 'What is F?', on the assumption that there is some single informative answer that applies to all and only the genuine cases of F, and that allows us to decide whether unfamiliar cases are genuine cases of F (*La.* 190d7–192b8; *Eu.* 5c8–7a3).

One might be surprised that Socrates and his interlocutors persist in this form of inquiry after Socrates has been proved right in his claim that they cannot answer his questions. It is not clear why they should agree that there is a single informative answer, or why they should be disturbed at their failure to find one. Perhaps Socrates overlooks the possibility that some terms should be understood through a series of analogies and connexions that cannot be captured in a single informative formula.[11] Meno suggests that there may be nothing more to an account of virtue than a description of the different types of virtue (*M.* 71e–72a). Why is it so easy for Socrates to convince him that they should still be looking for a single account of the 'one form' (72c) of virtue?

11. What is a Socratic Definition?

To see whether Socrates' expectations are reasonable, it will help to ask what he is looking for in his search for an answer to his 'What is F?' question. He expects a definition of the F to tell us not only what F things all have in common, but also to tell us the one F 'by which' F things are F, or that 'makes' them all F, or 'because of which' they are all F (*Eu.* 6d9–e1; *M.* 72c6–d1). We may call this Socrates' 'explanatory' demand.

The explanatory demand is different from the demand that a definition supply necessary and sufficient conditions. Sometimes Socrates refutes a proposed definition of F by showing that it does not cover all and only the examples of F. But in the *Euthyphro* he distinguishes the explanatory demand from a demand for necessary and sufficient conditions. For he rejects Euthyphro's suggestion that the pious can be defined as what the gods love, even though he concedes that the predicates 'pious' and 'god-beloved' are coextensive. To refute

---

[10] See Epict. ii 17.7–11, quoted and discussed at §165n28. Long, *ESSGL* offers an extended comparison of Epictetus with Socrates.

[11] Wittgenstein, *BB* 20.

Euthyphro's proposed definition, Socrates argues that the gods do not love the pious because it is god-beloved, and that therefore Euthyphro's proposal fails the explanatory demand (*Eu.* 10d1–11b1).[12]

Socrates and Euthyphro agree that pious things, as such, differ from god-beloved things, as such, because pious things, as such, have something in common beyond the fact that the gods love them. Because they differ in this way, the pious and the god-beloved are entirely different (*pantapasin heteron*, 11a4). The pious has some property, distinct from being god-beloved, because of which it is loved, whereas the god-beloved, as such, has no such property. Socrates alludes to this property by saying that the pious is 'of a sort to be loved' or 'of a character to be loved'; by having this character it is suitable to be loved antecedently to being actually loved.[13]

The dialogue does not explore the consequences of denying the point on which Socrates and Euthyphro agree. If Euthyphro were to answer Socrates by denying that the gods love the pious because it is pious, he would deny that the gods love pious actions for any reason; the fact that they love them makes them appropriate actions, but they do not love them on the basis of their appropriateness. If this account of the pious were extended to other moral properties, it would express a voluntarist account of moral properties, treating them as the products of will and choice rather than independent norms for will and choice. Plato does not explore this voluntarist account of the relation of morality to the divine will, but the *Euthyphro* suggests both what such an account would have to say and why one might be inclined to reject it.

How do we recognize the relevant explanatory difference between the pious and the god-beloved? We might try two possible answers: (1) An appeal to meaning. A correct

---

[12] His argument is this:

1. The god-beloved is god-beloved because the gods love it, and it is not the case that the gods love the god-beloved because it is god-beloved (10d9–10, e5–7).
2. The gods love the pious because it is pious, and it is not the case that the pious is pious because the gods love it. (10d1–7, e2–3).
3. Hence the pious and the god-beloved are not identical.
4. Hence the pious is not correctly defined as what the gods love.

Two helpful treatments are: Cohen, 'Piety', and Sharvy, 'Analysis'.

Socrates does most to support the first step of the argument. He appeals to simple logical, perhaps even grammatical, considerations (10a1–d12). To support (1) he appeals to a simpler case:

1a. x is being-carried (*pheromenon*) because x is carried (*pheretai*), and it is not the case that x is carried because x is being-carried.

Socrates expresses his point by claiming that the participial form ('being-carried' or 'a being-carried thing') is to be understood through the passive form ('is carried'), and that the converse is not true. His point is easier to grasp in English if we use the passive and active forms:

1b. x is carried because S carries x and it is not the case that S carries x because x is carried.

In (1) Socrates applies the pattern illustrated in (1b) to the case of 'god-beloved' (*theophiles*).

The general claim illustrated in (1) and (1b) is easy to accept. It is plausible to claim that carried or seen things, as such, have no nature in common beyond the fact that someone carries or sees them; what makes them carried or seen is simply the fact that someone carries or sees them. Similarly, then, loved things, as such, have nothing in common beyond the fact that someone loves them.

[13] 'For the one (sc. the god-beloved), because it is loved, is of a sort to be loved (*hoion phileisthai*), but the other (sc. the pious), because it is of a sort to be loved, is loved because of that' (11a4–6).

definition of the pious would say what 'pious' means. But we can see that 'pious' does not mean the same as 'god-beloved'; for it is not self-contradictory (even though it is false) to say that x is pious but the gods do not love x, whereas it is self-contradictory to say that x is god-beloved but the gods do not love x. The proposed definition of the pious as the god-beloved is therefore (we may say) 'logically inadequate', because the denial of the proposed definition is not self-contradictory. (2) An appeal to moral judgment. It would be unacceptable to suppose that the gods could make something pious simply by loving it; if it is to be an appropriate object of their love, it must already be pious. Hence the proposed definition of piety is 'morally inadequate'; to know that an action has the property mentioned in the proposed definition is not thereby to have given sufficient reason for concluding that it is pious.

These two ways of grasping the asymmetry imply two different ways of distinguishing the pious and the god-beloved. According to the logical argument, the god-beloved and the pious are different concepts, because the meanings of the terms are different. This difference in meaning is established by appeal to what is and is not self-contradictory. According to the moral argument, we do not establish difference of properties by appeals to meanings and to analytic truths, but by appeal to the different explanatory roles identified by moral judgments. A definition that is morally adequate might apparently be logically inadequate, since the denial of such a definition might not be self-contradictory. A morally adequate definition of the pious would not analyse the concept 'pious'; it would give an account of the property of piety. Even if the concepts of the pious and the god-beloved were different, it would not follow that they pick out different properties.[14]

Though some of the concepts used in drawing this distinction between logical and moral argument arouse familiar philosophical controversies, the distinction itself is difficult to avoid. A familiar modern meta-ethical illustration concerns the status of an account of rightness as what maximizes utility. We might attack the truth of this account either (a) by arguing that is not self-contradictory to claim that an action is right but does not maximize utility, or (b) by arguing that some actual or possible actions are right whether or not they maximize utility. These different objections are relevant to different sorts of accounts. The first is relevant to a question about the concept 'right', whereas the second is relevant to a question about the property of rightness.[15]

The *Euthyphro* does not make it completely clear whether Socrates is concerned with concepts or with properties. The discussions in other dialogues, however, suggest that he wants a morally adequate definition. He does not simply rely on his interlocutors' judgments about what is or is not self-contradictory; he seems to rely on their moral judgment. He assumes that moral judgments about actions and people rest on rational principles, and that we can do something to articulate these principles. This may not be true about all classification. A greengrocer puts tomatoes with vegetables, rhubarb with fruits, and peanuts with nuts, even though a botanist classifies them differently. To understand the greengrocer's arrangement, we need to refer to facts about our tastes; if our tastes changed

[14] For present purposes, I assume that concepts are, or necessarily correspond to, meanings, and that this is not true of properties.

[15] It is useful to keep this distinction in mind in discussing Moore, *PE*, and Ross, *RG*, who do not attend to it.

so that we treated rhubarb as a vegetable and tomatoes as fruit, we would not be making a mistake. Socrates assumes that our judgments about which actions are brave or just are not like the greengrocer's judgments; they do not rest on taste or convention. They rest on some reasonable criteria that virtuous actions can be shown to meet, if they are really virtuous.

If our judgments rest on reasonable criteria, we can see why Socrates persists in looking for an account of the virtues. His persistence reflects confidence in the capacity of his interlocutors. He assumes that when they make firm, confident, and considered judgments about examples of virtuous action, and these judgments conflict with the definition they have proposed, we should reject the definition and stick to their judgments about examples.[16] If these judgments were merely thoughtless responses such as one might give to an opinion poll, they would not inspire much confidence. But Socrates assumes that they reflect our implicit and partial grasp of the rational standards appropriate for judgments about the virtues.

12. Basic Moral Principles

But even if our judgments tend to display these patterns, and tend to converge on a favoured set of beliefs, we may wonder whether these facts justify us in believing that we have reached the truth, or at least are progressing towards it. To see whether Socrates has any reasonable basis for his confidence, we may consider what conclusions he thinks he reaches, and what grounds they rest on.

Though interlocutors begin with examples of virtuous actions, they soon agree that they should be looking for a state of character that underlies them. They agree with Socrates in calling this state a 'virtue' (aretê). 'Aretê" is the abstract noun corresponding to the adjective 'agathos' ('good'), and so the assumption that bravery (e.g.) is a virtue makes it an aspect of a person's goodness. But if we try to say in purely behavioural terms what makes a person good in the relevant ways, we face counter-examples. Though some actions are typical and characteristic of a given virtue, they do not exhaust the content of a virtue (Ch. 159b7–160d4). Bravery, for instance, is a state of character that is often embodied in standing firm in battle, but may on some occasions be embodied in other types of action; the brave person may withdraw when there is no point in standing firm, or it is more urgent to resist an attack elsewhere (La. 191d3–e2).

We understand why it is difficult to find a purely behavioural account of a virtue once we understand our demands on virtuous action. Interlocutors agree with Socrates that all virtuous action is 'fine' (kalon), 'good' (agathon), and 'beneficial' (ôphelimon). If an action is shameful or harmful, it cannot be virtuous, and a state of an agent producing such an action cannot be a virtue (Ch. 160e7–11; La. 192b9–d9). This is part of Socrates' reason for believing that virtue must be knowledge (since he takes knowledge of the good to be necessary and sufficient for a fine and beneficial state of character). Once we impose this condition, we find it difficult to find simple behavioural rules, or simple cognitive or affective dispositions, that

---

[16] In using 'considered judgments' I follow Rawls, 'Outline'. His description of these judgments agrees with Socrates' implicit conception.

count as virtuous. We may be tempted to identify bravery with endurance, until we notice that endurance is not always fine and beneficial, but is sometimes shameful and harmful (*La.* 192c–d).

To see whether this is a plausible demand on virtues, we need to see what Socrates and his interlocutors mean by saying that virtues must be fine and beneficial. The earliest Platonic dialogues do not offer us an explicit discussion of the fine. The *Gorgias* suggests that the fine can be understood as being either pleasant or beneficial; roughly speaking, the aesthetic uses of '*kalon*' are taken to involve pleasure, and the moral uses are taken to involve benefit (*Gorg.* 474d–475a). This account, however, does not help much if we have no idea of what sort of pleasure or benefit is relevant (cf. *R.* 505b–d).

Some passages in the dialogues suggest that 'fine', 'good', and 'just' mark the general area of morality. These are the questions that arouse disputes that cannot be settled by accepted methods of measurement (*Eu.* 7c10–d5); and Socrates assumes that living well involves living justly and finely (*Cri.* 48c9–10). When Socrates refuses to consider questions of his own survival, but insists he has overriding reason to obey the god's instruction to engage in philosophy, he says that the only thing to consider is whether he is acting as a good man should, and whether what he is doing is just; he praises Achilles who considered only the fine and just in deciding what to do (*Ap.* 28b3–d6).[17] In this case Socrates suggests that 'just', 'good', and 'fine' would all be apt descriptions of the kind of action that he chooses in preferring to go on philosophizing rather than consider his own safety. He takes the same view of other just actions he has performed at some risk to his safety, in refusing to take part in arresting Leon on the orders of the Thirty, and in objecting to the irregular trial of the generals after the battle at Arginusae (*Ap.* 32a4–33a5). These cases suggest that Socrates' use of 'fine' is quite similar to Aristotle's description of the common conception of the fine, connecting it especially with following impartial standards rather than one's narrow interest; according to this conception, it is especially fine to sacrifice one's own interest for the good of one's friends or one's community.[18]

It is reasonable, then, even if it is controversial, for Socrates and his interlocutors to assume that a virtue must be fine and beneficial. While we may recognize all sorts of virtues (or excellences; *aretai*) that make us good at pursuing different ends, we have a special conception of the virtues of a human being as such (as opposed to an athlete, a carpenter, or a knife). The virtue of a knife is what we reasonably want a knife to be like for cutting. The virtue of a human being is what we reasonably want a human being to be like; since we reasonably want each other to contribute to a common good, the common good and the fine determine the content of the virtues.

Socrates' next condition tries to ensure that all virtues meet the appropriate conditions for being fine and beneficial. He claims that each virtue is identical to the knowledge of good and evil. In this claim he assumes that the fine is included within the good; this is reasonable if he identifies the fine with the common good. He assumes further that the virtues require one and the same body of knowledge about good and evil. He does not admit one body of knowledge about bravery, another about temperance, and so on. If he allowed distinct sciences to belong to different virtues, we might acquire bravery without the other virtues.

---

[17] Partly quoted at n34 below.　　[18] For Aristotle's view see §116.

Socrates, however, denies that we can do this, and so he accepts the reciprocity of the virtues (each virtue requires each of the others) and the unity of the virtues (the supposedly distinct virtues constitute one and the same virtue).

He denies that the virtues are separable because he assumes that each of them is fine and beneficial. A supposedly brave action that did not take account of the considerations that belong to (for instance) justice would not be fine and beneficial, and hence would not be brave. A thief or murderer who willingly faces danger in the pursuit of his ends is fearless, but not brave, if bravery is a virtue, an aspect of human goodness. Sometimes Plato expresses this point by saying that if bravery is separate from wisdom, it is not always beneficial (*M.* 88b1–c4; *Euthd.* 281b4–e5). Since Socrates believes that bravery is essentially a virtue, he concludes that virtue is always beneficial, and therefore is not separate from wisdom and the other virtues. If the considerations that belong to all the virtues are relevant in principle to deciding about actions that belong to any one of the virtues, we cannot have any virtue without knowledge of the overall good.

This is Socrates' argument for the reciprocity of the virtues. Though we may initially be surprised that an apparently brave or temperate person cannot have this one virtue without also being just or wise, Socrates' demand fits our belief that the virtues are not merely resources or talents or capacities to be used well or badly, but are themselves aspects of the human goodness that allows us to use other things well. Socrates' successors have good reason for accepting his claims about the reciprocity of the virtues. Though they differ on other questions from Socrates and from one another, Plato, Aristotle, the Stoics, and Aquinas all accept his doctrine of reciprocity.[19]

Socrates, however, does not confine himself to the reciprocity of the virtues. He also affirms their identity, claiming that each of the allegedly distinct virtues is really the same knowledge of good and evil. He reaches this conclusion in the *Laches*, and defends it at length in the *Protagoras*.[20] Since he assumes that a brave person acts bravely, his identification of virtue with knowledge implies that knowledge is sufficient for virtuous action. This implication conflicts with the common belief that we can know one action is best and still choose another. Socrates needs some further argument to show that knowledge is sufficient, and not just necessary, for virtue and virtuous action.

These basic principles control Socrates' inquiries in the earliest Platonic dialogues, and help the inquiries make progress. Socrates assumes that a normal and reasonable interlocutor will accept these principles, and will accept or reject claims about the virtues to the extent that they seem to agree or disagree with the principles. Application of these principles, then, helps us to see which of our more specific judgments about the virtues are or are not acceptable.

This degree of progress, however, does not yet take us to the goal Socrates is aiming at—an account of a virtue that would allow us to decide whether a given action is or is not virtuous. To reach his goal, we need to say more specifically what the science of good and evil tells us; what sorts of goods and evils are relevant, and how do we know which actions

---

[19] See §49, §117, §185, and §325.

[20] See *La.* 199d–e; *Pr.* 349a4–c5; 361b1–3. Vlastos agrees that Socrates identifies all the virtues with knowledge of good and evil, but he denies that Socrates believes all the virtues are the same virtue. See 'Unity', and *SS* ch. 5. For some discussion see Irwin, *PE* §28–9, 59.

are good and evil? We also need to explain why we need nothing more than knowledge; why does virtue not require non-cognitive conditions that make our knowledge effective?

Socrates stimulates further thought among his successors because he does not answer these questions in great detail. While he sketches the form of a theory of the virtues, he does not do much to fill it in; and so he leaves it to his successors to take his suggestions in different directions, resulting in conflicting theories that might all reasonably claim to be Socratic. But he does not leave us completely in the dark about his own views. The Socratic dialogues offer some further suggestions about what his principles imply and about why we should believe them.

13. Knowledge of the Good: Eudaemonism

In some places Socrates explains how he understands the claim that virtue must be beneficial; he takes the relevant benefit to be the good of the virtuous agent. At the end of the *Charmides* he assumes that if Charmides has any reason for cultivating temperance, temperance benefits him, and that if it benefits him, he will be happy (*Ch.* 175d5–176a5).[21] No reason is given for this assumption. We might agree that temperance is a self-regarding virtue, and that Charmides benefits from having well-ordered desires, self-knowledge, and the other aspects of temperance that are mentioned in the dialogue. But it does not seem to be purely self-regarding. Socrates also takes it to include order and moderation in political life, and we might suppose that this is virtuous because it is beneficial to the community. Why assume that it could never require some sacrifice of the individual's interest to the common good?

Socrates makes the grounds of his assumption clearer in the *Euthydemus*. He presents a 'protreptic' discourse (*Euthd.* 278c5–d5) designed to show Cleinias 'that he ought to cultivate wisdom and virtue' (278d2–3). This starting point is different from the one that Socrates usually assumes in his inquiries; in asking what a virtue is, he and his interlocutor assume that it is worth cultivating, but they do not examine their assumption. To show that the assumption is warranted, Socrates asks whether we all want to 'do well' (*Euthd.* 278e3–6), or to 'be happy' (*eudaimonein*, 280b6),[22] and he assumes that the answer is obvious. Since happiness is our ultimate aim, we should look for the sources and means of happiness; these are the different goods.

The assumption that happiness (*eudaimonia*) is the ultimate end for action is not a paradoxical Socratic claim. According to Aristotle's account of common ethical views, we all agree that our ultimate end is happiness.[23] The main ethical question is not about whether we take happiness as the ultimate end, but about how to achieve happiness.[24]

[21] 'Happy' here translates *makarios*, which is usually treated as equivalent to *eudaimôn*, or as referring to a superlative form of *eudaimonia* (such as the gods enjoy; cf. Aristotle, *EE* 1215a10–11; b13).

[22] On the relation between 'doing well' (*eu prattein*) and being happy cf. Aristotle, *EN* 1095a17–20.

[23] 'For practically every person individually and for everyone in common there is a goal that all aim at in whatever they choose and avoid; and this . . . is happiness (*eudaimonia*) and its parts' (Aristotle, *Rhet.* 1360b4–7).

[24] *Eudaimonia* is often taken to include more than a mental state; many Greeks supposed that being rich, prosperous, and successful were ways of being *eudaimôn*, not simply means to a feeling of happiness. For this reason, 'prosperity', 'well-being', and 'welfare' suggest aspects of *eudaimonia* that might be concealed by the rendering 'happiness'. On *eudaimonia* and happiness see Sidgwick, *ME* 92–3f Ackrill, 'Eudaimonia' 23–4f Kraut, 'Conceptions'; Dybikowski, 'Happiness'.

But however obvious the eudaemonist starting point may seem, it needs some clarification. Some of the many questions that arise about it are these: (1) What makes it obviously correct? Is it just empirically obvious that we want happiness, just as it is obvious that we all want food and physical safety? Or does it reflect some non-empirical necessity? (2) Socrates suggests that happiness is not only an ultimate end, something to be chosen for its own sake, but also the ultimate end, implying that no other ends are equally ultimate. What justifies the second suggestion? (3) Is eudaemonism a claim about the explanation of action, asserting that all action aims at one's own happiness? Or is it a claim about justification, asserting that all rational action aims at one's happiness, or that one ought to take happiness as one's ultimate end?[25] (4) How are we to understand the character of happiness? If we claim to pursue three ends for their own sakes, do we (according to the eudaemonist) pursue an ultimate end, the sum of these three ends, and is this purely aggregative end happiness? Or does Socrates intend happiness to have more structure than this, so that it is not a purely aggregative end? (5) If we are eudaemonists, what kinds of aims or motives do we take to be psychologically impossible or rationally unjustified? We might suppose that some people are capable of disinterested self-sacrifice, so that they prefer other people's interest over their own. People also seem to be capable of disinterested malice, so that they want to harm someone else even if they will gain nothing by it. Are these counter-examples to eudaemonism, so that a eudaemonist must show that they are impossible? Or should we understand eudaemonism so that it allows such actions?

We need not try to answer all these questions on Socrates' behalf. It is worth our while to raise them in order to show how his eudaemonist claims provide his successors—from Plato to Aquinas—with topics for discussion. Aristotle is the first to recognize that Socrates' demand for a definition is relevant to happiness also. 'What is happiness?' is a question that Socrates passes over and that Plato considers only implicitly; but it is Aristotle's first question in the *Ethics*.[26] It is easy to see why Aristotle might suppose that a systematic treatment of the question is overdue.

14. Why Virtue is Necessary for Happiness

Socrates presents a list of commonly-recognized goods that are regarded as means to happiness. He mentions wealth; health, beauty, and other bodily advantages; good birth; positions of power and honour in one's own city; temperance, justice, and bravery; wisdom; and good fortune (*Euthd.* 279a1–c8).[27] Socrates takes all these elements in the list to be generally agreed, except for the virtues and wisdom.

He disagrees, however, with this common list of means to happiness. Common sense is uncertain about whether we really need virtue and wisdom; it is tempting to believe that if we had all the other goods, we would be happy, even if we lacked virtue and wisdom. This is the temptation that underlies Polus' claim in the *Gorgias* that the dissolute, cruel, and ruthless

---

[25] This division between explanatory (or 'exciting') and justifying reasons is partly derived from Hutcheson, *IMS* 121.

[26] See §69.

[27] Aristotle presents a similar list of goods (*Rhet.* 1360b19–23) that are generally supposed to secure the 'self-sufficiency' (*autarkeia*, 1360b14, 24) and 'security' (*asphaleia*, 1360b15, 28) that are needed for happiness.

tyrant Archelaus who has achieved worldly success has thereby achieved happiness (*Gorg.* 470c4–471d2). We might believe this and still believe that for most people the virtues are the best policy. Socrates, however, denies that Archelaus is happy; the virtues are necessary for everyone, not simply the best bet for most people.

To explain why we need the virtues, Socrates argues that we achieve happiness not by the mere possession of various goods, but only by the correct use of them (*Euthd.* 280b7–d7). Though we may grant that we are better off, other things being equal, with more of the recognized goods than with less, they may still make us worse off if we use them unwisely. We may squander our wealth, or use it to ruin our health; our great power may expose us to greater danger unless we know how to use it. But if we have the wisdom to use it correctly, we are also more resilient if we are unlucky and lose some of the recognized goods. Hence we should recognize wisdom as a necessary condition of happiness.

This step connects Socrates' argument about happiness with his inquiries into the virtues. The search for an account of each virtue leads us to agree that each virtue must be fine and beneficial, and that therefore each must be identified with the same science (*epistêmê*) or craft (*technê*) of goods and evils that ensures the correct co-ordination of all the considerations that seem (before we pursue Socratic inquiry) to belong to different virtues. Since Socrates believes for these reasons that the different virtues are to be identified with the single science of good and evil, he takes his argument about wisdom to show that the virtues are necessary for happiness.

This conclusion is all that Socrates needs to complete his protreptic task of showing that we have reason to cultivate wisdom and virtue. But it does not give us very clear practical advice. If we agree that the mere accumulation of assets does not secure happiness, because foolish people can misuse them, we may agree that wisdom is necessary for happiness, and that since this wisdom is knowledge of good and evil, it is virtue. But agreement on this point does not commit us to Socrates' assumption that the relevant virtues include bravery, temperance, and justice (279b4–c1).[28] How are we to tell that wisdom prescribes these virtues? A wise tyrant might apparently secure his position by sensible and prudent plans that are none the less unjust and cowardly, and that simply arrange for the satisfaction of his dissolute tastes.

To answer this question, we need to say more about the character of happiness. We can see (according to Socrates) that happiness is not to be defined as 'the sum of wealth, health . . . (and a list of other assets)'. We might, then, try to define it as 'the sum of wealth . . . (etc.) in so far as it is guided by wisdom'. But if the relevant sort of wisdom is to be defined as knowledge of what promotes happiness, we are trying to define happiness as 'the sum of wealth . . . (etc.) in so far as it is guided by knowledge of what promotes happiness'. Since the definiens contains an unanalysed mention of happiness, we still have not found a definition.

We would have a more satisfactory account of happiness and of virtue if we could say more about the content of the wisdom that guides us in the use of other goods. Socrates' comments so far suggest that wisdom is a productive science. Just as carpentry allows us to

---

[28] At this point in the *Euthd.* Socrates simply secures Cleinias' agreement on the point (recognized as disputable) that these recognized virtues are goods. We have to turn to other dialogues to see that Socrates believes they are goods.

use wood, saws, and nails correctly so that we produce a table rather than a jagged mass of wood with protruding nails, wisdom (we might suppose) allows us to use other goods to produce happiness rather than an unstable, chaotic, and precarious way of life.

Socrates, therefore, might try to tell us more about the product of wisdom. If we reflect on our reasons for thinking a successful but foolish person lacks happiness, we may learn how wisdom contributes to happiness. Archelaus' lack of moderation may expose him to danger. Croesus' great wealth made him presumptuous, so that he took the oracle to mean he would destroy someone else's great empire and not his own.[29] These cases may suggest that the wise person is the one who knows how to achieve both worldly success and security, and when to pursue one at the expense of the other.[30] Many Greeks valued the achievements that result from facing danger and taking risks, and for that very reason were sharply aware of the instability that may transform someone from an object of envy and admiration to an object of pity. This recognition of instability and danger suggests that we need wisdom to deal with dangerous situations.

If Socratic wisdom fits this pattern, it is a 'craft of life'.[31] It will help us to identify the way of life that strikes the right balance (to express it roughly) between success, security, and stability. A sensible person recognizes that we cannot pursue any one of these unreservedly without damaging the others, and thereby damaging our well-being. It would be worth our while to find the skills, dispositions, and traits of character that secure the right balance.

Socrates does not disavow this conception of wisdom. Nor, however, does he unequivocally endorse it. To grasp some of the complications in his position, we need to consider some of his further claims in the *Euthydemus* about virtue and happiness.

15. Why is Virtue Sufficient for Happiness?

One of the recognized goods that promote happiness is good fortune (*eutuchia, Euthd.* 279c4–8). Our previous reflexions on the sources and means of happiness make it seem obvious that good fortune should be included; for since happiness requires security and stability, it seems to need favourable external conditions that are not wholly in the agent's control. To begin with, we seem to need the appropriate sort of 'antecedent' good fortune, in the provision of the right sorts of resources—wealth, health, social position. But even if we have these and use them wisely, we also seem to need 'subsequent' good fortune; however talented, industrious, rich, and famous I may be, I cannot eliminate the possibility that some event over which I have no control will ruin me. This argument implies that even if wisdom and virtue are necessary for happiness, they are not sufficient. If we take security to be necessary for happiness, and we see the dangers that attend the actions and achievements that produce happiness, we may readily infer that we need good fortune—understood as favourable external circumstances—if we are to be secure in our enjoyment of the appropriate achievements (Aristotle, *Rhet.* 1360b28–9).

---

[29] Herodotus, i 53.
[30] On security cf. Aristotle, *Rhet.* 1360a25–9; Epicurus, *KD* 7, 13, 14 = DL x 141, 143; §158–9 below.
[31] For this Stoic expression see §178.

Socrates, however, rejects this conclusion. In his view, good fortune is already secured by wisdom, and does not require favourable external circumstances as well (*Euthd.* 279c9–d9).

Unlike the claims we have considered so far, this claim is not merely controversial, but paradoxical. Some people might deny that happiness requires virtue, understood as the craft of life. But once we notice that we need some wisdom to use external assets correctly, we may come to agree that happiness, as we normally conceive it, needs wisdom and virtue. Still, external circumstances that a wise person cannot completely control seem to affect one's happiness.

It is not clear why Socrates denies that happiness depends on external conditions beyond the control of wisdom. He argues that the wise person has better fortune than the unwise (280a4–5), and that wisdom can never go wrong, but must always succeed (280a7–8), so that wisdom always makes us fortunate (280a6). We might interpret this argument so as to make it sound. Socrates is right to claim that wisdom makes us more successful than the lack of it, so that it always contributes to our good fortune. But if we interpret the argument this way, it does not show that good fortune does not require external circumstances. Even if wisdom always makes us more successful than we would otherwise be, it does not follow that wisdom guarantees complete success in achieving our ends; we may be unlucky, and the success achieved by wisdom may not guarantee complete success. A skilful general may always succeed in finding the most astute strategy and tactics, but an unpredictable thunderstorm in the desert may none the less cause his defeat.

A different way to take this argument departs further from the common conception of happiness. Socrates may be asserting that the only success that should matter to a wise person is the sort that is secured by wisdom. On this view, the skilful general will not care if he loses the battle, as long as it was not his lack of skill that caused the defeat; nor will we care about events in our life that do not reflect a lack of wisdom in planning it. Socrates, therefore, identifies happiness with actions and events that are subject to wisdom, but he does not explain why we ought to revise the common conception of happiness in this way.

To show that external circumstances do not matter for happiness, Socrates claims that wisdom is the only good (281e4–5). He argues that other recognized goods are not goods in themselves without wisdom, but when wisdom uses them they become better than their opposites (281d6–e1). The force of this argument turns on the sense of 'in themselves'.[32] Socrates might mean that health (for instance) is not always good for us when it is separated from wisdom ('in itself'), but becomes good when it is used wisely. Alternatively he might mean that health itself is not good; the only good is the use of health (and other things) by wisdom.

This second interpretation of 'in itself' is needed if this argument is to support Socrates' claim that external circumstances are irrelevant to happiness. For if other recognized goods become good when they are properly used by wisdom, and if some of them depend on external circumstances, external circumstances may determine whether we have or lack certain goods. But if the only good is the wise use of whatever recognized goods we have, external circumstances do not affect happiness.

---

[32] The two most plausible accounts of this argument and of 'in themselves' (*auta kath'hauta*) are offered by Vlastos, *SIMP* 228–30, 305–6, and Long, 'Hellenistic' 25–9. For further discussion of this passage see §37.

This argument, therefore, offers two conceptions of happiness and two conceptions of the relation of virtue to happiness. If Socrates retains the common conception of happiness, he has a reasonable argument to show that virtue and wisdom are necessary for happiness, but no case to show that they are sufficient for it. If he maintains that they are sufficient for happiness, he needs to reject the common conception of happiness, and to maintain that only what we can control matters to our happiness.

The first of these two views anticipates the Platonic and Aristotelian view of virtue and happiness. The second anticipates the views of the Stoics and Epicureans, who modify common views of happiness in order to show that virtue is sufficient for happiness. Resolution of the obscurities in Socrates' argument reveals some of the major divisions in later Greek moral philosophy.

16. Wisdom and its Product

The conclusion that wisdom is the only good leads Socrates into a further difficulty. Since the product of wisdom has to be good, and we have found that wisdom is the only good, the product of wisdom has to be wisdom itself, and we are no nearer to finding out what this wisdom makes us wise about (292a4–e7). The discussion ends without an explicit solution to this puzzle.

Can we solve this puzzle with Socratic resources? We might plausibly doubt Socrates' claim that the previous argument has shown that wisdom is the only good. The argument has considered only the different goods that promote happiness, and has not considered happiness itself; hence it has shown (at most) that wisdom is the only genuine instrumental good. But we do not expect the product of wisdom to be an instrumental good; we expect it to be the non-instrumental good of happiness. In that case, we have no reason to conclude that the product of wisdom is wisdom itself. Further reflexion on the nature of happiness may still tell us what sort of wisdom is the productive craft that produces happiness. This solution retains the assumption that wisdom is a productive craft.

Alternatively, we might agree that wisdom is the only good, but deny that the conclusion is unsatisfactory. The discussion leaves us puzzled if we insist on treating happiness as a product of wisdom that is distinct from the exercise of wisdom itself, in the way that a chair is distinct from the exercise of the carpenter's craft. But we dissolve this puzzle if we deny that wisdom is a productive craft.[33] For if wisdom is the only good, and happiness is a good, wisdom is identical to happiness. Happiness, therefore, is not some further condition that results from the guidance of our life by wisdom; it simply consists in this guidance by wisdom.

In the *Euthydemus* Socrates does not endorse either of these solutions of the final puzzle about wisdom and happiness. As we saw in reviewing the previous argument, the different interpretations of his position anticipate the views of his successors. The purely instrumental conception of wisdom as a productive craft is part of the Epicurean view of virtue and happiness. The non-productive view is common to Plato, Aristotle, and the Stoics. But Plato and Aristotle do not take this view to justify the identification of wisdom with happiness; only the Stoics embrace the identification.

---

[33] Moreau, *CIP* 188, defends this interpretation of the argument.

17. The Supremacy of Virtue

We have examined part of a protreptic discourse in the *Euthydemus*; Socrates simply sets out some theses about happiness and virtue without his usual cross-examination. We might wonder how seriously he takes these theses, and whether other dialogues offer us any help in resolving the questions of interpretation that arise in the protreptic discourse.

A question about virtue and happiness arises from Socrates' defence of his own moral choices. He argues that when one course of action is required by the fine and the just, one should pay no attention to any considerations on the other side; in particular one should not attend to the danger of imprisonment or death.[34] Socrates claims to have taken this attitude when he was pressed to arrest Leon illegally and to allow the illegal trial of the generals (*Ap.* 32a4–33a5).[35] But he does not say whether the danger of imprisonment and death provides rational considerations against acting justly. Does just action sometimes require us to sacrifice real goods? If Socrates is a eudaemonist, and he believes that wealth, health, and safety are goods that may conflict with virtue, he believes that we are always better off acting virtuously than we would be if we protected these other goods at the expense of the virtues; hence he accepts the supremacy of virtue.

Does he believe, then, that virtue is the supreme good, in the sense just explained, but not the only good? If he believed this, we might expect that in the *Apology* he would acknowledge that virtue costs him something, by imposing a loss of other goods. But he does not concede that virtue costs him anything. Similarly, in the *Crito*, he faces a decision about whether or not to try to avoid the death sentence by escaping from prison. To decide the question, the only considerations he allows are considerations of justice (*Cri.* 48b3–c2). He allows no consideration to compete with the requirements of justice, and so he decides the question about what to do by concentrating on the question about what is just; we might expect that he would tell us to observe the requirements of justice even though we lose other goods.

This is not how he presents his choice, however. In the *Apology* he assures the jury that nothing is bad for a good man (*Ap.* 41c8–d2). Similarly, in the *Crito* he tells Crito that what matters is not living but living well, and that living well, living finely, and living justly, are the same (*Cri.* 48b5–11). If he believes this, he believes that virtue is sufficient for happiness; whatever virtuous people lose, they lose no goods that are necessary for their happiness. Nothing is bad for them because nothing deprives them of happiness, as long as they are virtuous. Socrates, therefore, accepts the more extreme view presented in the *Euthydemus*, that external circumstances do not matter at all for happiness. He believes that virtue is not simply supreme over other goods, but is sufficient by itself for happiness.

Does he also accept the extreme claim that virtue is the only good, because it is the wise use of whatever assets we may have? This conclusion does not follow from the sufficiency of virtue for happiness. We can reach it only if we assume that happiness is comprehensive, because it includes all goods; on that assumption, if virtue is both necessary and sufficient for happiness, virtue is the only good, or else it is sufficient for the presence of all other

---

[34] 'You are mistaken, sir, if you think that a man who is any use at all ought to take account of the risks of life or death, and ought not to consider only this one thing whenever he acts—whether he is doing just or unjust actions, and the actions of a good man or a bad' (*Ap.* 28b5–9). See Vlastos, *SIMP* 209–10.

[35] See §12 above.

goods. But if happiness is not comprehensive, virtue might be sufficient for happiness even if it does not guarantee the presence of all goods.

Does Socrates believe that happiness is comprehensive? If he did not, it is difficult to see how he could claim that nothing is bad for a good man. If a good man could lose some genuine goods, apparently this would be bad for him, even if it did not deprive him of happiness. If Socrates denies this, he has to claim that the loss of genuine goods is not bad for a good person who remains happy. But it is difficult to see why we should agree that nothing bad happens to me if I lose some good I had and could use well, or fail to gain some good that I could use well. Socrates' claim that nothing is bad for a good man is easier to defend if he believes that virtue is sufficient for happiness and happiness is comprehensive, so that virtue is sufficient for the presence of all genuine goods.

18. Does Happiness give a Reason for being Virtuous?

If Socrates believes that virtue is either supreme in relation to other elements of happiness or sufficient by itself for happiness, he takes a controversial position. But to decide how controversial it is, and what is controversial about it, we should look more closely at what he means. When he claims that virtue is supreme in happiness or sufficient for happiness, does he (1) simply describe the virtuous person's commitment to virtue, or does he (2) give a reason for accepting this commitment?

According to the first view, virtuous people believe that they should give practical priority to virtue, as Socrates does, and their belief that virtue is supreme in happiness (or sufficient for happiness) simply follows from that choice to give it practical priority. Someone is a general because he has been appointed general; we would misunderstand the character of military rank if we tried to explain why someone has been appointed general by the fact that he is a general, as though it were some prior reason-giving fact. Similarly, the supremacy of virtue results from the fact that the virtuous person prefers it, and is not a prior fact that gives reasons for that preference.[36]

According to the second view, the place of virtue in happiness is a reason-giving fact that explains and justifies the virtuous person's preference for virtue. It is similar to being qualified for being a general rather than to being a general. Though someone is a general because of an act of appointment, he is suitable for being a general not because of an act of appointment, but because of features prior to any act of appointment; that is why it is possible to make good and bad appointments to the rank. Similarly, one might say, the virtuous person makes the correct choice in preferring virtue over other real or supposed goods, and facts about happiness explain why this is the correct choice.

Which of these views does Socrates take? Does he regard the relation of virtue to happiness as a prior reason-giving fact or not? The protreptic discourse in the *Euthydemus* takes it for granted that practical reason begins with the desire for happiness; we take different alleged goods seriously to the extent that we take them to contribute to happiness. Here, then, happiness seems to be a source of reasons for being virtuous. But we might argue that this

---

[36] McDowell, 'Role', defends this view of *eudaimonia* in Socrates, Plato, and Aristotle.

is simply protreptic; it is meant to persuade Cleinias to take virtue and wisdom seriously, but not to describe the virtuous person's point of view. Socrates' remarks about happiness in connexion with his own actions are less easy to interpret one way or the other. When he tells Crito that living well is what matters most and that living well, living justly, and living finely are the same, we might take him simply to be reporting his choice to give priority to justice. In that case, he does not intend the claim about happiness to give a reason for believing that one ought never to act unjustly.

This, however, is not the most immediately plausible way to understand Socrates' remarks in the *Crito*. He begins by reminding Crito of their previous agreements about living well and about the relation between living well, finely, and justly. Once these points are agreed, he infers that they ought to restrict their discussion to questions of justice (*Cri.* 48b5–d5). This order would be misleading if the primary fact is Socrates' decision to act justly whatever the cost and if the relation of justice to happiness is simply the effect of his decision. It seems no less misleading for Socrates to assure the jurors that nothing is bad for a good man if he simply means that if we prefer virtue over other supposed goods, it follows that nothing is bad for us. He seems to be assuring them that virtuous people do not lose as much as other people think they lose; but if he means that for those who put virtue first, other losses do not matter, he is not addressing their main concern. If some people care so much about one good that they do not mind the loss of any others, it does not follow that they can suffer no harm; they may simply have warped preferences.

These are good reasons for supposing that Socrates intends his remarks about happiness to give a reason for his preference for virtue. On the other side, one must acknowledge that he does not say what features of happiness and virtue show that virtue is supreme in happiness or sufficient for happiness. His silence is easy to explain if he does not intend his appeal to happiness to justify his preference for virtue. We might expect a justification to argue that happiness has certain properties, and then to argue that virtue, alone or more than anything else, has these same properties. Since Socrates does not offer a justification of this form, we might infer that he does not intend any justifying role for his appeals to happiness.

Socrates' silence on these points helps us to see why Aristotle takes the question 'What is happiness?' to be the first one that a moral theorist should discuss. We will need to ask later whether Aristotle intends the answer to this question to show how facts about happiness are reason-giving facts. But at least he should allow us to be clearer on a question that Socrates raises but does not clearly answer.

19. What Sort of Virtue is Supreme in Happiness?

However we understand them, Socrates' claims about the supremacy or sufficiency of virtue are controversial; for they give practical priority to some state of the agent rather than to external circumstances. In his view, it matters more whether we have the appropriate sorts of beliefs and aims than whether we have the opportunities, assets, and circumstances that most people take to be characteristic of happiness. But we might suppose that this is the only controversial element in his claims. Once we grant that, perhaps it is trivial to claim that virtue is supreme in happiness; for 'virtue' simply refers to whatever knowledge we need to use external assets wisely. If some internal condition is supreme, it does not seem controversial to add that virtue is supreme.

If this is what Socrates means, he commits himself to a potentially revisionary account of the virtues. If we were to discover that the wisdom needed for happiness requires actions that are quite different from those we normally recognize as brave, temperate, and just, we would have to conclude that we were wrong to believe that these recognized virtues are real virtues.

If Socrates had to accept this conclusion, the consequences of his eudaemonism might conflict with his method of moral investigation. His discussions with interlocutors assume that he and they can agree on genuine examples of virtuous action; it is because temperance (e.g.) is a genuine virtue that we can infer that temperance is knowledge of good and evil. But if it turned out that temperance is not a genuine virtue, we would have reason to distrust the agreements between Socrates and his interlocutors. In that case, should we stick to the implications of eudaemonism, or should we stick to Socratic method? Since Socrates does not consider the possible conflict between his different lines of argument, he does not say which should be preferred in case of conflict.

But he does not even admit all the points that would make the conflict possible. For in claiming that virtue is supreme in happiness, he does not seem to intend the relatively uncontroversial point (in the sense explained above) that knowledge about happiness is supreme in happiness. He intends the far more controversial point that bravery, temperance, and justice are supreme. He does not consider the possibility that a clearer understanding of happiness would show that these recognized cardinal virtues are not real virtues.

To see that Socrates takes the recognized cardinal virtues to be supreme, we need only notice the prominence of justice in his defence of his actions and choices. We have seen that he believes nothing should be considered in opposition to the demands of justice, and that justice requires us to stay at whatever post our superior assigns to us (*Ap.* 28d7–29b7).[37] Socrates does not entirely agree with the common conception of justice; he argues that the mere fact that you have harmed me does not make it just for me to harm you.[38] But the virtue that he calls 'justice' overlaps enough with the recognized virtue to justify him in claiming to be talking about the same virtue. In claiming that justice requires us to keep agreements that have been justly undertaken, Socrates appeals to some common views of justice (*Cri.* 50a2–3), not to some conception of his own that depends on his distinctive views about happiness.

Once we see that Socrates means to defend justice as commonly conceived, we can see what he means in connecting justice to happiness. He suggests to Crito that justice is good for our soul in the way that health is a recognized good for the body. Just as it is not worth living with a body that is ruined by disease, it is not worth living with a soul that is ruined by injustice (*Cri.* 47d7–48a1). If Socrates were using 'justice' and 'virtue' simply to refer to knowledge of good and evil, without any commitment to its prescribing recognized just actions, his claim that it is not worth living with an unjust and vicious soul would be fairly uncontroversial. But this is not the claim he intends; he intends the more controversial claim

---

[37] Part of the context is quoted in n34 above.
[38] On the interpretation of Socrates' views about retaliation in the *Cri.* see Irwin, *PE* §31.

that it is not worth living if we lack the cardinal virtue of justice, requiring us to keep just agreements, to refrain from wanton injury to other people, to remain at the post where we are placed by a superior, and so on. The virtues that are supreme in happiness, in his view, are the recognized cardinal virtues.

Is he justified in ignoring the possibility that we are radically wrong in believing that the cardinal virtues are really virtues? He would be justified if he did not believe that an appeal to happiness gives reasons to be virtuous. If our view about the content of happiness simply reflects our preference for the cardinal virtues, it cannot undermine this preference. But, as we have seen, Socrates seems to intend claims about happiness to give reasons. Equally, he seems to intend the claim that justice is analogous to health in the soul, and that it is not worth living without justice, to give reasons for being just. If he prefers justice, but does not treat happiness as the rational basis of his preference, he gives Crito his argument in the wrong order.

If, then, he intends facts about happiness to give reasons for being virtuous, Socrates does not seem justified in ignoring the possibility that we are wrong to value the cardinal virtues. To find reason-giving facts, we need to have some account of the content of happiness that does not simply reflect our preference for the cardinal virtues; hence we leave open the logical possibility that our account of happiness will show that we are wrong to prefer the cardinal virtues. To show that this possibility is not realized, we need to give an account of the content of happiness.

20. Integrity and Socratic Virtue

Socrates' silence on these questions does not simply mark a point at which his theory is incomplete. It also marks a practical weakness in his position. He does not, as far as we can see, simply intend to announce to the Athenians that he cares most about justice, and that he will not consider anything that would divert him from this concern. If that were his position, he would display consistency and integrity in acting on his choices, but he would not show that his choices are reasonable. He intends to show, however, that his choices are reasonable, and more reasonable than the choices of someone who chose to save his skin or accumulate wealth and power at the expense of justice; such people might also display consistency, but Socrates believes they have made a mistake, by harming their soul, and hence their prospects of happiness. To show that he is right, he needs to say more about why a plausible conception of happiness supports the cardinal virtues.

We might admit that this is a legitimate question to raise about the argument Socrates offers. For protreptic purposes—we might argue—he treats happiness as a source of reasons, by treating it as an end distinct from virtue and treating virtue as a means to happiness. For these purposes he treats virtue as a productive goal-directed craft, though the *Euthydemus* suggests that this conception of virtue raises difficulties. In his other remarks on virtue and happiness—we might suggest—he does not entirely escape from this productive and teleological conception.

Still, we might argue, this conception of virtue does not capture Socrates' real convictions. According to one view, he really values integrity and consistency above everything, and he does not regard happiness as an external source of reasons.[39] Since Socrates does not claim knowledge about virtue, he does not claim to know any facts that warrant his moral choices and decisions. He discovers that morality is not primarily a matter of knowing facts, but a matter of decision and conviction. The sort of knowledge that he lacks turns out to be irrelevant to morality.

This picture of Socrates makes him appear to be a sort of existentialist who refuses to make moral values responsive to objective facts.[40] But it is not simply a modern picture of Socrates. The Cynics may have understood him in the same way, by taking integrity and consistency to extremes.[41] According to this view, the virtuous person is not the one who has grasped all the relevant reason-giving facts about ends, but the one who sticks consistently to his choice of ends in his choice of actions. Ordinary people fall short of virtue because they are inconsistent, half-hearted, compromising, and vacillating in their choices and decisions.

A case can be made for the selective interpretation and development of Socrates' position that leads to Cynicism. We will be inclined to suppose that this is the authentic Socratic insight if we believe it is misguided to expect an account of happiness to give us reasons for choosing virtue over vice. But since most Greek moralists do not agree with the Cynics on this point, it is worth our while to see what sorts of reasons they can offer by appeal to an account of happiness.

21. The Nature of Happiness: Socratic Hedonism

In the dialogues we have discussed so far, Socrates' inquiries and arguments lead him to controversial claims that he does not defend. He argues that the different virtues are all knowledge of the good, and that virtue is sufficient for happiness, but he does not defend these claims further.

We can now usefully turn to dialogues in which these Socratic claims are defended, and especially to the *Protagoras* and *Gorgias*. It is not clear whether these dialogues present the views of Socrates, or Plato's first attempts to defend Socrates' views. The views they present are closer to those of the Socratic dialogues than to the outlook of the dialogues that match Aristotle's description of Platonic, as opposed to Socratic, doctrines. At any rate, it is appropriate to consider them as defences of the Socratic views we have discussed.

The final puzzle of the *Euthydemus* arose from unsuccessful efforts to say what the product of the knowledge of good and evil would be. We can solve this puzzle if we can give a more determinate account of the content of happiness. The *Protagoras* offers this more

---

[39] On Socratic integrity see Versenyi, *SH* 168, commenting on Socrates' trial and death: 'Remaining true to himself, on his own by his own effort, he achieves all that a man could ever want: the good life . . . the great man is still supremely self-sufficient. All that really matters depends on him alone.'

[40] As Versenyi's discussion in *SH* suggests, this might be described as an existentialist conception of Socrates.

[41] See §39.

determinate account by defending a hedonist account of the good.[42] This aspect of the dialogue recommends it to Grote and Mill, who take Socrates to anticipate one element of their hedonistic utilitarianism.[43]

Socrates argues for hedonism (*Pr.* 353b–354e) in the course of his argument against incontinence, which is part of his argument for the unity of the virtues. For the moment, we can postpone consideration of these other two arguments and concentrate on his explanation and defence of hedonism. He begins from an assumption that both Protagoras and most people ('the many', 351c3; 352b3) accept, that pleasure is a good in some circumstances, but not in others. Socrates acknowledges that most people reject hedonism, because they believe that in some circumstances one ought not to choose pleasure, but one ought to choose the more painful option. But he defends hedonism by undermining these apparent counter-examples, and showing that they can be explained by the hedonist position that they appear to undermine.

To see what Socrates defends, we need to consider different claims about the relation of the good and the pleasant:

1. Goodness is pleasure, i.e., x's being good consists essentially in x's pleasure (x's being pleasant).
2. One's good is one's happiness (*eudaimonia*), i.e., one's good in one's life as a whole.
3. Happiness is achieved by the predominance[44] of pleasure in one's life as a whole.
4. x's being good on the whole = x's being pleasant = x's yielding pleasure rather than pain on the whole.

The first of these theses may be called generic hedonism, since it allows different specific versions. 'Consists essentially' is meant to indicate that this is a stronger thesis than the mere biconditional claim that something is good if and only if it is pleasant. The specific version of hedonism that Socrates defends depends on his acceptance of the second claim, which is a eudaemonist account of the good for a person. This hedonist eudaemonism explains Socrates' acceptance of the third and fourth theses. The fourth thesis commits him to the claim—initially surprising, but intelligible in the light of his explanation—that sometimes having a tooth extracted (e.g.) is pleasant, even though it causes short-term pain, because it is a means to longer-term pleasure.[45]

Hedonist eudaemonism allows Socrates to explain most people's rejection of generic hedonism. He argues that they reject it because they do not think clearly about the implications of hedonist eudaemonism. Sometimes we say that x is painful and y is pleasant, but x is better than y. Socrates argues that in these cases we do not really believe that the

---

[42] Critics disagree about the degree to which Plato means to convey his endorsement of hedonism in the *Protagoras*. I generally agree with Gosling and Taylor, *GP* 58–68.

[43] Grote, *POCS* ii 208, suggests that the hedonism of the *Pr.* solves the puzzle in the *Euthd.*: 'Good is the object of the Regal or political intelligence; but what is Good? . . . There is only one dialogue in which the question is answered affirmatively, in clear and unmistakable language, and with considerable development—and that is, the Protagoras: where Sokrates asserts and proves at length, that Good is at the bottom identical with pleasure, and Evil with pain . . . . ' For Mill see n2 above.

[44] The relevant notion of predominance is not precise. A life that was barely more pleasant than painful would scarcely be *eudaimôn*. Socrates seems to assume that pleasure must exceed pain by a large margin, but he does not say how large it must be. In contrast to pleasure (and happiness, as English philosophers sometimes speak of it), happiness is not a quantity that can come in small or large amounts.

[45] This extended use of 'pleasant' and 'painful' is assumed in the argument at 355b–356a.

preferred alternative is less pleasant all things considered, but only that it offers less pleasure in the short term; we believe it is better because it offers more pleasure in the long term. If we take a bitter medicine, or face a danger, we believe the 'painful' course of action will yield more pleasure than pain, and the 'pleasant' course of action will yield more pain than pleasure, given their total effects. Socrates believes he has now refuted the common view that pleasure itself is sometimes good and sometimes bad; he affirms that pleasure itself, rather than good pleasure, is the end. We may say that he maintains 'unqualified hedonism'.[46]

By generalizing his hedonist explanation, Socrates convinces the many that they pursue pleasure as good and avoid pain as evil (354c3–5). In pursuing x rather than y as good we pursue x because we believe that x yields greater overall pleasure than y (354b5–d3). Hence we pursue pleasure as the good and avoid pain as evil. 'Pleasant' and 'good' are two names for the same thing. Socrates does not claim that the two terms are synonymous; his 'What is it?' question does not seek to analyse concepts, but to identify explanatory properties, and in this case he claims that the feature that explains why things are good is their pleasantness, which is the same property as their goodness.[47] This identification reduces good to pleasure; we regard things as good because we suppose they are pleasant, whereas we do not regard things as pleasant because we suppose they are good. Hedonism is not an alternative to eudaemonism; it is an account of the good that eudaemonism takes to be our ultimate end.[48]

Socrates may not be the first to defend hedonist eudaemonism. A similar position may plausibly be ascribed to Democritus, though we do not know who influences whom. Democritus identifies the good with pleasure, and recognizes that some pleasures are not advantageous.[49] He probably uses eudaemonist reflexion on the future effects of these pleasures, as Socrates does, in order to decide which are not advantageous. Like Socrates, he seems to take the eudaemonist assumption to be obviously correct.

22. Hedonism and Socratic Virtue

Socrates can now offer an apparently clear and determinate answer to the question that the *Euthydemus* did not answer: what is the content of the science of good and evil? He argues that it is a 'measuring craft' that accurately counts the overall pleasure and pain resulting from a given action, so that we are not misled into thinking that the pains we suffer now are greater than those we will suffer tomorrow; temporal closeness causes us to exaggerate pains and pleasures just as spatial closeness causes us to think things are bigger than they really are, and so we need a measuring craft to make sure we are not misled by our short-sighted point of view (356c4–357b4).

The science of good and evil does not tell us that we ought to adopt a prudent outlook on our lives, so that we try to maximize the good in our life as a whole. It assumes that

---

[46] On unqualified hedonism see §29.   [47] On concepts and properties see §11 above.

[48] Contrast the views of Aristippus, §30, and Epicurus, §145, who make the pursuit of pleasure motivationally prior to the pursuit of happiness.

[49] For Democritus' views see DK 68 B74, B188, B191; Stob. ii 7.3 = A167. On Democritus' hedonism see Taylor, *ALD* 233, 'Pleasure'; and §32.

we already accept that outlook. The mistake that we make if we lack the measuring craft is not that we become indifferent to our lives as a whole, but that we exaggerate the impact of short-term pleasures and pains. Socrates assumes that we all follow Sidgwick's 'axiom of prudence', according to which 'hereafter *as such* is to be regarded neither less nor more than now'.[50] His description of the measuring craft shows how completely he takes the eudaemonist outlook for granted. He does not consider the possibility of desires that might not respond to beliefs about the good for our lives as a whole.

Socrates' account of the measuring craft helps us to see why wisdom is what we need for the proper use of external resources and circumstances. Even if we have all the resources we could wish, we may still harm ourselves if we do not predict accurately the longer-term effects of different courses of action on our prospects of pleasure and pain. With the help of hedonism, the knowledge of good and evil is no longer obscure and imprecise; it is a determinate and achievable body of knowledge that we can apply for obvious practical benefit.

This comparison with the *Euthydemus* shows us how the theory in the *Protagoras* might reasonably appeal to someone who seeks to defend Socratic claims about the knowledge of good and evil. Plato, therefore, may seriously maintain the hedonism of the *Protagoras* as part of his defence of Socratic ethics. Grote and Mill have a good reason to treat the dialogue as a partial anticipation of utilitarianism. The anticipation is only partial, since (as Grote emphasizes) Socrates does not defend the universalistic hedonism that identifies the good with the maximum pleasure of everyone affected.[51] He introduces hedonism to support eudaemonism, and so he identifies one's own good with one's own maximum pleasure.

The virtues all manifest the measuring craft that discovers one's own maximum overall pleasure. Hence Socrates suggests that the brave person is the one who sees that the immediate pain for him involved in facing danger is outweighed by the long-term pleasure for him resulting from (say) winning the battle. The temperate person will be the one who sees that the pleasure resulting from finishing the bottle of wine now is outweighed by the pain of tomorrow's hangover. Socrates does not say how this analysis might be applied to justice; but we might suggest that the just person sees that the immediate pleasure resulting from breaking this promise to repay what he owes is outweighed by the longer-term pain resulting from other people's distrust.

This sketch of an analysis of the virtues is the basis of Epicurus' moral theory.[52] He agrees with Socrates' strategy for defending hedonism, arguing that opposition to hedonism results from a superficial judgment about comparative pleasures. Once we understand the character and temporal effects of different pleasures and pains, we see that an accurate assessment of pleasures and pains recommends the cardinal virtues to us, and that those who oppose pleasure to morality have simply miscalculated pleasures and pains. Epicurus' ideas in turn are one source of Hobbes's account of the psychological basis of morality.

These later developments of hedonism show that the *Protagoras* introduces a significant and influential element of ethical reflexion. It is not surprising that Plato regards it as a plausible defence of Socrates' claims about happiness and virtue.

---

[50] See Sidgwick, *ME* 380–1.   [51] See Grote, *POCS* ii 309–13.   [52] See §157.

23. Objections to Hedonism: The *Gorgias*

Plato not only shows how hedonism might support Socratic ethics, but also argues that Socrates has good reason to reject hedonism. In the *Gorgias* Callicles, Socrates' main opponent, is a hedonist, and Socrates argues against him. This dispute about hedonism arises from a discussion of questions that the *Protagoras* alludes to, but does not discuss, about the relation between justice and the other virtues.

The *Gorgias* discusses the connexion between Socrates' moral views and his way of life. It concentrates especially on a question that earlier dialogues largely pass over, about the connexion between Socrates' eudaemonism and his defence of justice. In the earlier dialogues Socrates assumes that if we correctly grasp our happiness and the means to it, we will decide in favour of justice even if it involves the dangers that it involves for Socrates. He re-affirms this claim in the *Gorgias*, maintaining against Polus that virtue, including justice, is both necessary and sufficient for happiness (*Gorg.* 470c9–e11). Callicles is dissatisfied with Socrates' case for justice, and defends the contrary view that if we understand the nature and sources of our happiness, we will reject other-regarding justice.[53]

Callicles defends this attack on justice by appeal to a hedonist conception of happiness (494b7–495e2). We achieve happiness by maximizing our pleasure, and we increase our pleasure by increasing the strength and urgency of the appetites that we satisfy; hence we achieve happiness by cultivating the largest possible appetites and ensuring that we have the resources to satisfy them. This policy conflicts with justice because the pursuit of the resources we need to satisfy our expanded appetites gives us reason to treat other people unjustly.

As Callicles presents it, the conflict between justice and maximum satisfaction is the result of empirical facts about scarce resources. If these resources were unlimited, we would not need to act unjustly. One might, however, strengthen Callicles' position by assuming that we have appetites that are more directly opposed to justice. If we want to dominate and control others, or to torture or humiliate them, we will act unjustly (in Callicles' view) even if we have all the resources we need.[54] Hence a hedonist conception of happiness implies that we have reason to satisfy these desires at the expense of justice. While a hedonist conception does not require us to form these desires, it requires us to satisfy them if we have them.

Callicles treats hedonism as a version of eudaemonism; he offers a plan for the conduct of one's life as a whole. He points out that the rational conduct of one's life requires some virtues; the superior people need bravery to pursue their maximum satisfaction over time despite short-term dangers or difficulties (491a7–b4). If they have this virtue, they will not be deterred by social disapproval or conventional scruples from carrying out their plan. This is the conception of bravery that belongs to the hedonic measuring craft described in the *Protagoras*; the brave person looks beyond the short-term hazard to the longer-term pleasure.

---

[53] I speak of 'other-regarding justice' to pick out what Callicles calls 'conventional justice' (justice by *nomos*). For reasons I will not discuss, he takes himself to defend 'natural justice' (justice by *phusis*), which requires the stronger to dominate the weaker; see 482c4–484c3. For simplicity, I will speak of Callicles as opposing justice. On nature and convention see §133.

[54] It is not clear whether Hobbes (e.g., in *L*.17.1) intends to recognize essentially competitive motives of this sort.

But Callicles rejects the hedonist defence of temperance; he denies that a sensible person has any reason to moderate his appetites, as long as he can find the resources to satisfy them.

Socrates argues that Callicles' hedonism is inconsistent with the belief that bravery is a virtue. He observes that in battles the coward gets at least as much pleasure as the brave person gets; and so it seems that bravery is no more effective than cowardice in securing pleasure (497d8–499b3). Hedonism does not justify Callicles in preferring bravery over cowardice.[55]

We might protest that Socrates or Plato is being obtuse (perhaps deliberately) in suggesting that this sort of counter-example could refute the hedonist defence of bravery. It seems to ignore the point that the *Protagoras* underlines in its discussion of the measuring craft. Socrates' example shows that the coward gains more short-term pleasure than the brave person, because he is so relieved when the danger is past. But he gains this short-term pleasure only at the cost of longer-term pain, when the enemy attacks successfully because he deserts his post. Socrates' objection seems to reflect the misleading short-term point of view that the measuring craft corrects.

It is unlikely that Plato simply overlooks this appeal to the measuring craft. Not only does the *Protagoras* emphasize the measurement of short-term and long-term pleasures, but Callicles also relies on it in explaining why the superior person needs bravery; bravery gives us the long-term view that sets aside conventional scruples and other obstacles to our maximizing the satisfaction of our desires.

But this appeal to the measuring craft does not answer Socrates' basic objection. Hedonism does not say that the good consists in the pleasure that we gain from an impartial view of short-term and long-term pleasure; it says that the good consists in maximum pleasure. The *Protagoras* assumes that we maximize pleasure by taking the point of view of the measuring science. But this assumption is not obviously correct, and Callicles' account of the good shows why it may not be correct. He has argued that we increase our pleasure if we increase the craving that is satisfied by the pleasure. The coward seems to embody this principle; for since he does not try to inhibit his fears by thinking of the future pleasures that result from facing danger, he is more sensitive to danger than the brave person would be, and so he gains greater pleasure if the danger has passed. The less we think about future compensations, and the more sensitive we are to present dangers, the greater are the pleasures that come from short-term relief. Maximum pleasure may not result from concentration on longer-term pleasure.

24. Hedonism without Prudence?

Even if these arguments cast doubt on the consistency of Callicles' position, why should they lead him to abandon hedonism? If he cannot consistently both accept hedonism and recognize bravery as a virtue, why should he not retain hedonism and deny that bravery is a virtue?

---

[55] White, 'Prudence' 142–50, suggests that Callicles' version of hedonism reflects the view that only the present matters in assessment of one's well-being. On the Cyrenaic view see §31.

Socrates' argument suggests that the rejection of bravery would be the rejection of rational planning. If we had the coward's outlook, we would see no point in making plans for the future, and we would make no effort to carry them out in the face of obstacles. We would not be concerned about ourselves as temporally-extended rational agents. But Callicles' initial picture of the superior person presupposes the value of temporally-extended rational agency. He advises us to take control of our own lives, to set our own goals, and not simply to absorb the outlook of the inferior people around us, who are too lazy, cowardly, and scrupulous to execute the plans that express their own rational agency. He does not see, until Socrates points it out to him, that this concern for rational planning conflicts with his hedonist account of the good. Plato does not treat Callicles unfairly, therefore, in presenting him as abandoning hedonism rather than his advocacy of bravery.

This interpretation of the discussion between Callicles and Socrates should make us less surprised that Plato defends hedonism in the *Protagoras* but attacks it in the *Gorgias*.[56] The attack in the *Gorgias* results from closer consideration of the defence in the *Protagoras*. The defence of the measuring craft in the *Protagoras* assumes that concern for rational agency is consistent with hedonism. The *Gorgias* raises doubts about that assumption. To share these doubts, we need not agree with Callicles' view that everyone always maximizes pleasure by maximizing appetites. If some desires and pleasures fit Callicles' pattern, maximizing pleasure conflicts with concern for rational agency.

Perhaps, then, the measuring craft that Callicles should accept attaches less importance to rational agency than the *Protagoras* assumes. Instead of active planning and execution of our rational plans, perhaps we should take a more passive attitude to events and allow ourselves to be moved by the fears and pleasures that brave and temperate people try to restrain or to remove. The appropriate sort of measurement for a hedonist will reject the recognized virtues that the *Protagoras* advocates. Socrates does not discuss this version of hedonist eudaemonism. Though we can see why it does not appeal to Callicles, might it reasonably appeal to someone who lacks his concern for rational agency?

This question leads to a further possible implication of Socrates' objections. The hedonist position we have suggested to cope with the objections to Callicles maintains eudaemonism without concern for rational agency. But is this a reasonable position? Our preference for long-term over short-term benefits is reasonable if we think of ourselves as continuing rational agents who try to carry out our plans and aims in our actions. Since these plans and aims take time, we have a good reason to think about the longer term. But if we entirely abandon any concern for rational agency, have we any reason to take the long-term view characteristic of eudaemonism?

Though Socrates does not pursue this line of argument, it suggests that a hedonist eudaemonist has no easy answer to him. The *Gorgias*, therefore, suggests a conflict between eudaemonism and hedonism. In identifying our good with our happiness, we think of it as a good for a temporally extended rational agent who cares about his life as a whole, and who values rational planning for his life. This sort of agent cares about the security and stability that are recognized features of happiness. The *Protagoras* assumes that eudaemonism

---

[56] Gosling and Taylor, GP 70–5, believe that the argument in the *Gorg.* neither refutes hedonism nor is intended to refute it. Hence they attribute to Socrates a view similar to Epicurean hedonism. See §156.

supports hedonism, but the *Gorgias* casts doubt on that assumption. If we reject the attitude of Callicles' coward, we value rational agency over maximum pleasure; hence we accept a non-hedonist good.

Neither Socrates nor Callicles considers the rejection of eudaemonism. But we might wonder about what sort of theory we could defend if we accepted hedonism without eudaemonism. We can answer that question by considering the Cyrenaic position. Aristippus is a hedonist, but he seems to believe that hedonism conflicts with eudaemonism. He takes the view that Socrates and Callicles do not mention, and defends non-eudaemonist hedonism. The arguments we have discussed help to explain why Aristippus believes that this is a reasonable conclusion for a follower of Socrates to defend.

25. An Adaptive Conception of Happiness

The hedonism of the *Protagoras* offers a more determinate conception of happiness than we find in earlier dialogues, and so allows us to see how Socrates might defend the cardinal virtues as means to happiness. But such a defence seems to raise more difficulties than it solves. We have seen difficulties that arise from the criticism of hedonism in the *Gorgias*. But, even apart from these difficulties, it is not clear how hedonism supports Socrates' claim that virtue is sufficient for happiness. The measuring craft of the *Protagoras* tells us what we should do to improve our prospects for future pleasure; but it does not assure us that if we exercise it we will achieve maximum pleasure regardless of external circumstances.

Perhaps Plato is silent about this question because he thinks it is easy to answer. He might reply that Socrates gains so much pleasure from being just, and would find it so intolerable to act unjustly, that the measuring craft will always tell him to be just. This reply, however, is only an apparent defence of hedonism. If it has to appeal to the special pleasures of the virtuous person, it does not tell us why we have reason to be virtuous; for even if he maximizes the sort of pleasure he cares about, he may not maximize the pleasures that other people care about, and hence consideration of pleasure alone does not justify us in being virtuous. We may believe that the pleasures of the virtuous person are better than other people's; but if we take this view, we concede the point that Socrates urges against hedonism. If the only pleasures that it is good to maximize are good pleasures, we cannot identify the good with the maximization of pleasure; hence we must reject hedonism.

The questions about virtue and happiness are especially relevant to the *Gorgias*, since this dialogue highlights Socrates' conviction that virtue is sufficient for happiness. Even if Plato undermines Callicles' reasons for rejecting that conviction, we may still wonder whether Socrates is right. Do we learn anything about happiness that would convince us that the virtuous person is happy?

Socrates suggests a conception of happiness that opposes Callicles' view. Callicles holds an 'expansive' conception, so that he identifies happiness with maximum satisfaction. Socrates suggests that happiness does not consist in maximization, but in the fit between desire and satisfaction. According to Callicles, the stronger my desire for food, the greater my happiness in satisfying it; but according to Socrates, I am equally happy in satisfying a strong or a mild desire. If happiness consists in the fit between desire and satisfaction, I have reason to cultivate desires that are easy to satisfy rather than ones that are demanding and difficult to satisfy. This is what Socrates means in suggesting to Callicles that those who lack nothing are the happy people (492d3–4). Though Callicles replies that this conception of happiness implies that stones and corpses are happy (492e5–6), Socrates prefers it to Callicles' expansive conception (492e7–494a5). He holds an 'adaptive' conception of happiness, since it implies that one achieves happiness by adapting one's desires to the means available for fulfilling them.

This conception of happiness may support Socrates' belief that virtue is sufficient for happiness. If we assume that desires are plastic enough to allow us to form or to remove them when the resources are or are not available for satisfying them, and if we assume that virtue is the knowledge of how to match our desires with the available resources, virtuous people will form the desires that they can satisfy, and hence will be happy. This is why Socrates believes that if Callicles recognizes the falsity of his expansive conception of happiness and admits that we need an orderly soul with orderly desires, he is committed to accepting Socrates' view that the virtuous person is happy (506c5–507c7). If the adaptive conception were not assumed, Socrates would have a reason to assert that virtue (understood as psychic order) is necessary for happiness; but the adaptive conception gives him a reason to assert that it is also sufficient.

Though this is a plausible case for ascribing the adaptive conception to Socrates, the *Gorgias* does not develop it at length. None the less, it is worth our while to notice it, since it is another Socratic suggestion with an important afterlife. If we hold an adaptive conception and we fit our desires to the available resources, we can claim to be self-sufficient (*autarkês*) and independent of changes in external conditions. The Cynics give a clear example—even a reductio ad absurdum—of this ideal of self-sufficiency. But it also influences Epicurus, who affirms that virtuous people are happy precisely because they adapt themselves to smaller or larger external resources; they neither refuse to enjoy abundance nor regret scarcity.[57]

26. Is Virtue Identical to Happiness?

If the *Gorgias* relies on an adaptive conception of happiness, it does not commit Plato to the claim that virtue itself is identical to happiness. If the virtuous person differs from other people in knowing how to match desires to opportunities for satisfaction, virtue may still be understood as a productive craft; its product is the satisfaction and self-sufficiency that constitutes happiness.

We might, however, try a different explanation of Socrates' claim that the virtuous person is happy. We might take him to mean that virtue is identical to happiness, so that virtuous people are happy by the very fact that they are virtuous, not because virtue shows them how to fit their desires to available opportunities. We suggested a quasi-existentialist defence of this view: the virtuous person simply chooses his values, but his virtue assures his happiness because he does not count anything as worthwhile in opposition to virtue, and he sticks to this resolution with integrity and consistency. The *Gorgias* may offer a different sort of

---

[57] See §154.

defence. Socrates replies to Callicles' conception of happiness by defending rational order in the soul; he identifies the virtues with different aspects of this rational order.

One might defend rational order as a means to happiness because it helps us to adapt our desires to opportunities. But Socrates' reply to Callicles suggests a different defence. Callicles' refusal to abandon his claim that bravery is a virtue suggests that he values the rational control of his life; the value of this rational control cannot be explained by its usefulness for maximizing pleasure. One may also doubt whether its value can be explained by its usefulness in adapting desires to opportunities. If we believe that rational control is non-instrumentally good, and if we identify virtue with rational control, we have a reason to believe that virtue is non-instrumentally good.

In the *Gorgias* Plato does not offer this account of the value of virtue. His defence of the sufficiency of virtue seems to rest on an adaptive conception of happiness. But it is useful to notice that the dialogue supplies some elements of a case for attributing non-instrumental value to virtue. Though the Socratic dialogues do not develop such a case, they provide a starting point for the arguments that Plato offers in the *Republic*, and for the arguments that Aristotle and the Stoics develop from Plato.

27. Reason and Desire

We have now explored one of Socrates' controversial claims, his assertion that virtue is sufficient for happiness. We postponed discussion of his other main controversial claim, that knowledge of the good is sufficient for virtue. This claim underlies his assertion that all the virtues are really just one virtue, the knowledge of good and evil. The claim seems paradoxical, however. It seems obvious to us, as Socrates acknowledges, that we can sometimes believe that one action is better, but choose to do something else because we desire the worse action more strongly than the better action.

Socrates does not deny that we may believe that one action is just and still prefer to do what we believe to be unjust, and similarly for the other virtues. But he believes that we act against our beliefs about what is virtuous only because we do not recognize that virtue is in our interest. The virtuous person has knowledge of the good; such knowledge gives us understanding of why particular actions are good for us, and of why virtuous actions are virtuous. Knowledge is sufficient for virtue because knowledge that x is better for me than y is sufficient for me to choose x over y. Socrates believes this because of his eudaemonism; since we aim at our ultimate good, we choose one thing over another in accordance with our beliefs about what promotes our happiness.

In these claims Socrates recognizes the flexibility of human choices and aims. In choosing to take a medicine, we do not choose it because it is aspirin, but because it seems to us to be good for our health (*Gorg.* 467c5–468c8).[58] This belief does not bind us unconditionally to taking aspirin; for if we come to believe that the benefit to our health is relatively slight, and some other drug will benefit us more, we will prefer the other drug, and if we come to believe that in this particular situation health matters less than some other good, we will

---

[58] Among discussions of this passage see Santas, *S* 223–5; Penner, 'Desire'; McTighe, 'Desire'; Segvic, 'Intellectualism'.

prefer the other good. This is what Socrates means in the *Euthydemus* when he remarks that we do not simply accumulate goods, but use them for ends that we take to promote our ultimate good.

It is relatively easy to understand and to accept Socrates' view that we have desires of this sort. Indeed, we might say that because we have these desires we have a will, and are not simply moved by impulses and appetites. It is more difficult, however, to see why he supposes that this is true of all our desires. The Socratic dialogues do not make it clear why he denies that we have any desires that are unresponsive to beliefs about the good. These unresponsive desires are the source of 'incontinent' actions (as Aristotle describes them). Though Socrates does not use Aristotle's term, he recognizes that other people believe in such actions, in which we are 'overcome' by pleasure, anger, and other non-rational impulses (*Pr.* 352b2–c7). According to Aristotle, Socrates rejects the possibility of incontinence because he thinks it would be 'terrible' if knowledge were present, but one of these other impulses moved us (*EN* 1145b22–7). Why does Socrates not allow that this happens?

We can understand his reasons a little better from the way in which he describes the belief in incontinence. He suggests that if there is incontinence, knowledge does not rule us, but is 'dragged around like a slave' by these different impulses (*Pr.* 352c1–2). This description suggests that Socrates regards incontinent action as a form of compulsion in which it is not up to us to do what we do. This suggestion is relevant when he comes to describe the belief in incontinence more fully. He claims that it is ridiculous to say, as most people do, that someone knowing that bad things are bad none the less does them, when it is open (*exon*) to him not to do them, because he is overcome by pleasures (355a7–b3). Believers in incontinence, then, claim both that we are overcome and that it is up to us not to choose the action we choose.

Socrates may suggest that these different parts of the description of incontinence are inconsistent. If I do something that it is up to me not to do, I do it freely and voluntarily; but I do not do it freely and voluntarily if I am compelled to do it by some force that drags me around. Hence believers in incontinence imply that I both do and do not act voluntarily when I act incontinently.[59] Socrates believes that I act voluntarily only if I act on my belief about what is best; hence, if incontinent action is voluntary, it is action on belief about what is best, contrary to the claim that it involves choice of what I know to be worse.

Socrates does not exploit this suggestion that belief in incontinence involves these contradictory implications about voluntariness. He does not say what has to be true if it is 'open' to the incontinent agent not to choose the incontinent action. Nor does he set out his own views about what it takes to act voluntarily. He simply concludes that we do not 'willingly' (*hekôn*) choose what we believe to be worse (358c6–d4).

His attack on incontinence relies on hedonism. To show that we do not really choose what we believe to be worse, he analyses the description that most people offer of what happens in incontinent choices. He takes them to say that we choose what we believe to be worse because we are overcome by pleasure. He assumes that to be 'overcome' by the pleasure of x is to take x to be pleasanter than y. On this understanding of 'overcome', hedonism is relevant; for if Socrates' version of hedonism is true, believing that x is pleasanter than y is

---

[59] Cf. §104.

the same as believing that x is better than y. Hence we cannot believe that x is pleasanter than y without believing that x is better than y, and hence we cannot be incontinent.[60]

The weakness in this argument results from Socrates' analysis of 'overcome by pleasure'. Believers in incontinence have no reason to agree that we are overcome by the pleasure of x only if we believe x is pleasanter than y. On the contrary, they will answer that we are often attracted by this immediate pleasure of x so that we form a stronger desire for x even though we recognize that x offers us less overall pleasure than y offers. The truth of hedonism is irrelevant to any argument against this conception of being overcome. Hence Socrates' argument about pleasure does not directly address the main point on which he disagrees with believers in incontinence.

Socrates' views about incontinence imply that non-rational desires—those that are not responsive to beliefs about the overall good—have no role in the explanation of voluntary action. That is why he turns directly from his argument against incontinence to his defence of the unity of the virtues. He explains why, contrary to Protagoras' initial view (351a4–b2), the individual virtues do not require distinct sorts of training and habituation to strengthen or weaken different sorts of non-rational desires. The allegedly non-rational appetites that concern temperance and the allegedly non-rational fears that concern bravery are not in fact non-rational, but they are all responsive to our knowledge of good and evil; hence this knowledge is both necessary and sufficient for each virtue, and we have no ground for treating them as distinct virtues (360d1–361c2).

If, then, we do not accept Socrates' argument against incontinence, we lose his grounds for identifying virtue with knowledge and for believing in the unity of virtue. Since Plato and Aristotle reject his argument against incontinence, they also reject his account of the virtues. But they agree with him in not taking the possibility of incontinence for granted; they do not simply assume that it is perfectly intelligible to say that we are overcome by pleasures or non-rational desires. To explain how incontinence is possible they try to respond to Socrates' doubts about how we can be incontinent without being compelled.

Among Socrates' successors the Stoics come closest to accepting his views on incontinence, just as they come closest to accepting his views on virtue and happiness. They recognize that his views need elaboration and complication in order to answer the objections raised by Plato and Aristotle. But they believe Socrates is basically right in his paradoxical claims. To clarify, explain, and defend Socrates' claims, we need to examine the later history of Greek ethics.

[60] Socrates' argument is discussed by Vlastos, 'Acrasia'; Taylor, *PP*, ad loc; Irwin, *PE* §58.

3

THE CYRENAICS

28. The 'One-Sided' Socratics

Since we have drawn our evidence on Socrates from the early Platonic dialogues, it would be natural to turn from Socrates directly to Plato's middle and late dialogues, where Plato presents the defensible core (as he sees it) of Socratic doctrine. But if we went directly to Plato, we might miss some of the discussion of Socrates that explains the direction of Plato's reflexions. Plato was not the only disciple of Socrates who thought he could expound and defend the Socratic position. His evaluation of Socrates is easier to appreciate if we compare it with other versions of Socratic ethics.

In Plato's lifetime Aristippus, a disciple of Socrates, defended at least some aspects of the hedonist position that came to be known as Cyrenaic. At the same time Antisthenes defended the sufficiency of virtue for happiness, and understood this doctrine to exclude hedonism. His views were taken to extremes by Diogenes the Cynic. Later critics were surprised that moralists with such sharply opposed views could all claim to defend a Socratic position. Augustine comments that the disagreement among Socrates' self-styled disciples reflects some indeterminacy in Socrates' own views about the good.[1]

Some have called the Cyrenaics and Cynics 'the incomplete Socratics',[2] conveying the suggestion that they saw only one side of Socrates, and presumably that Plato and Aristotle saw both sides, and so reached a more accurate picture of him. This suggestion may not be quite fair to the one-sided Socratics. Socrates' views may have been indefinite enough to make each 'incomplete' construal of him a defensible way of tying up some loose ends that Socrates left. We might well think Plato and Aristotle showed better judgment than either the Cyrenaics or the Cynics showed about what is philosophically defensible in Socrates; but it does not follow that the position they reach is historically closer to Socrates.

---

[1] 'Since the highest good did not appear evidently in Socrates' discussions, where he considered, put forward, and destroyed everything, each of them took from those discussions what he thought fit, and placed the ultimate good wherever it seemed best to him ... The Socratics differed so much about this end that—though it is scarcely to be believed that the followers of one teacher could do this—some of them, such as Aristippus, said that the highest good is pleasure, while others, such as Antisthenes, said that it is virtue' (Augustine, CD viii 3d–e).

[2] Zeller, PG ii 1, 232, calls them the 'unvolkommenen Sokratiker' and speaks of their 'one-sided' conception of Socrates' philosophical endeavours (233). Only Plato avoided their one-sidedness by reaching a deeper understanding of the point of Socrates' inquiries (237, 387–8).

We do not know enough about the one-sided Socratics to trace in detail the historical connexions between their views and specific Platonic and Aristotelian texts. We have only unreliable reports of their views, and it is difficult to attribute specific views to the contemporaries of Socrates. Some modern critics believe that the Cyrenaic and Cynic positions really belong to post-Aristotelian ethics, rather than to the lifetime of Socrates and Plato.[3]

These difficulties in the sources do not justify us in ignoring the one-sided Socratics when we try to understand Socrates and Plato. For if these Socratics are contemporaries of Plato, Plato may reflect on their views in forming his own ethical outlook, and especially in making up his mind about Socrates' views. But how can we tell whether the doctrines that our sources ascribe to the Cynics and Cyrenaics are contemporary with Plato or belong only to the history of Hellenistic ethics?

We may be able to throw some light on this question if we examine the later Platonic dialogues with the views of the Socratics in mind. The reasonable suggestion that Plato sometimes discusses views held by his contemporaries has fallen out of favour because it has been taken to unreasonable extremes by interpreters who have seen (for instance) Antisthenes behind almost every line in Plato's later dialogues.[4] While it is hazardous to rely on the dialogues to reconstruct views for which we have rather little external evidence, it is not always implausible. If we find that a view that Plato discusses in a late dialogue reflects an intelligible development of views in the Socratic dialogues, and also fits our other evidence about the Cynics or Cyrenaics, we have some reason to infer that Plato is discussing a view of his Cynic or Cyrenaic contemporaries.

This is not the only possible conclusion; we might prefer to conclude that it is Plato who develops and discusses possible Socratic views, and that the Cynics and Cyrenaics prefer the view that Plato opposes to the one he endorses. On this account, the one-sided Socratic views are later criticisms of Plato, rather than contemporary views that Plato criticizes. But even if this account is correct, we may legitimately compare Plato's views with the one-sided Socratic views; they may throw light on each other, even if we cannot be sure of the historical order. If we can show that the one-sided Socratic views are relevant to issues that Plato discusses in the dialogues, we can at least dismiss the suggestion that these views could not have been formulated in Plato's lifetime.

Some attention to the one-sided Socratics, setting out from the early Platonic dialogues, will help us to answer some questions about the historical reliability of these dialogues. If the Socratic views defended by the one-sided Socratics are intelligible in the light of Plato's early dialogues, we have reason to believe that the early dialogues give us an accurate picture of Socrates' views. The reason is not conclusive; Plato may have misled some of his successors into believing that the early dialogues present Socrates' views, and so they may have mistakenly believed that their own views were expansions of Socrates' views. But we might well doubt whether people who were not shy about criticizing Plato would be so ready to take his word for it about Socrates.

---

[3] See n7 below. For a helpful account of the one-sided Socratics in the Hellenistic context see Long, 'Legacy'.

[4] Guthrie, *HGP* iii 347n2, comments severely, but not unfairly, on the 'Antisthenes-cult', referring to the excesses of some earlier critics.

A further reason for considering Plato's position with the views of the one-sided Socratics in mind is that we can perhaps see whether Plato's interpretation and modification of Socrates is reasonable, by comparison with the views of these other reflexions on Socrates. It may be helpful to imagine Aristippus, Antisthenes, Diogenes, and Plato reflecting on the views of Socrates, and reaching different conclusions about what Socrates meant, and about what needs to be changed to make a defensible position on a Socratic basis. We can see that these successors of Socrates have different views about which elements of Socrates are the sound Socratic basis, and which need to be abandoned, supplemented, or modified. Then we may be able to see who makes the most reasonable decisions on these questions.

29. Aristippus and the *Protagoras*

The elder Aristippus was a disciple of Socrates who criticized Plato for his departures from Socrates.[5] His doctrine is a version of hedonism; the way of life he advocates seems quite different both from the Cynic exaggeration of Socrates' behaviour and from Socrates' behaviour as we learn of it in Plato and Xenophon. In Xenophon's *Memorabilia* Socrates warns Aristippus not to fall into errors that would separate him from Socrates; especially he warns him to pay less attention to immediate pleasures.[6] Some modern critics are reluctant to ascribe hedonist views to an immediate disciple of Socrates; they believe that Cyrenaic philosophical doctrine was formulated by the second Aristippus, the grandson of the contemporary of Socrates. Moreover, some later Cyrenaics seem to respond directly to Epicurus, and it is not clear how many Cyrenaic views belong to them rather than to Aristippus the Socratic (the grandfather).[7]

We should not be surprised, however, that a disciple of Socrates defends hedonism and identifies the good with pleasure.[8] For Aristippus follows the *Protagoras* in maintaining

[5] On Aristippus as a Socratic see Aristotle, *Rhet.* 1398b30–3: 'When Aristippus heard Plato saying something in a rather authoritative tone (*epangeltikôteron*) (as Aristippus thought), he said to Plato, "Well, but our friend <said> nothing of that sort", meaning Socrates.' It is not clear if 'nothing of that sort' means (a) no view of that sort, so that Aristippus attacks Plato's view, or (b) nothing in that dogmatic tone, so that Aristippus attacks Plato's non-Socratic confidence. In the context (a) makes Aristotle's point better. On Aristippus as a companion of Socrates see also DL ii 60, iii 36.

[6] The most important passage is the long conversation in *Mem.* ii 1, which includes Prodicus' story of the Choice of Heracles (ii 1.21–34). Xenophon's account assumes that Aristippus accepts eudaemonism (see 1.11, 26). But both Socrates' advice and the story of Heracles deal with the importance of postponing immediate gratification for the sake of greater pleasure in the future. Socrates concludes by warning Aristippus to attend to what concerns his future life (34). Xenophon may realize that Aristippus tends to neglect the long-term prudential attitude that is characteristic of the hedonism in the *Protagoras*. Such 'neglect' has a special point if Aristippus accepts Cyrenaic objections to hedonistic prudence. If that is so, then Xenophon might provide some indirect, but early, evidence of Aristippus' anti-eudaemonism.

[7] Critics differ about how many Cyrenaic doctrines belong to Aristippus the Socratic, how many to his daughter Arete, and how many to her son, also called Aristippus, who was 'taught by his mother' (*mêtrodidaktos*). According to one view, Aristippus the Socratic endorsed hedonism as a way of life, but only the later Aristippus provided the philosophical basis. This view rests primarily on the frail support of Eusebius, *PE* xiv 763d–764a (perhaps not derived from Aristocles; on Eusebius' possible sources see Chiesara, *AM* xxviii–xxx). Cf. Mannebach, *ACF* 114–17; Giannantoni, *C*74–115; Guthrie, *HGP* iii 494–7; Giannantoni, *SR* iii 164–9; Tsouna-McKirahan, 'Socratic origins' 377–82.

[8] 'Those who adhered to the views of Aristippus and were called Cyrenaics held the following view: They established two affections (*pathê*), pain and pleasure, taking one of them, pleasure, to be a smooth motion, and the other, pain, to be a rough motion. In their view, one pleasure is not superior to (or "different from"; *diapherein*) from another, nor is one at all pleasanter than another. One affection is welcome, and the other repellent, to all animals. However, the bodily pleasure that they take to be the end (according to Panaetius in his book on the philosophical schools) is not the

unqualified hedonism.[9] Socrates defends this unqualified hedonism by appeal to hedonist eudaemonism.[10] He takes eudaemonism to be obviously true (cf. *Euthd.* 278e3–6; 280b5–6; 282a1–2), and he defends hedonism by arguing that happiness consists in the predominance of pleasure over pain in our life as a whole (*Pr.* 353c9–354e2). When he says that pleasure is the end (*telos*, 354b7), he does not mean that pleasure rather than happiness is the ultimate end. He takes happiness to be the end, and argues that happiness consists in pleasure, not in the pleasure of the moment (*en tô(i) parachrêma*, 353d1), but in pleasure summed over one's whole life.

This eudaemonist defence of unqualified hedonism allows Socrates to draw some of the distinctions that we can draw if we discriminate between good and bad pleasures. He does not accept all pleasures as good on the whole, because some of them have bad future effects. Hence he makes room for the recognized virtues, even though they sometimes require us to forgo short-term pleasures. Virtue is knowledge because we need a science of measuring pleasures and pains for 'the salvation of life' (*sôtêria tou biou*, 356d4–5); 'life' refers to one's life as a whole. The supposedly distinct virtues are all to be identified with this science of measurement.

The *Gorgias* rejects the unqualified hedonism of the *Protagoras*; it distinguishes good from bad pleasures and recommends the pursuit only of good pleasures (*Gorg.* 499c–500a). Plato defends this selective recommendation of pleasure in his later dialogues, and Aristotle agrees with him. The selective view rejects unqualified hedonism, since it does not identify the good with pleasure. The goodness and badness of pleasure does not consist simply in the hedonic consequences of different pleasures; it rests on some prior facts about the goodness and badness of the objects of different pleasures.

30. Hedonism without Eudaemonism

Though Aristippus returns to the unqualified hedonism of the *Protagoras*, he does not return to Socrates' eudaemonist defence of unqualified hedonism. [11] For he affirms that pleasure is the end, but denies that happiness is the end. Happiness, in his view, is a collection of pleasures, and is worth pursuing only for the sake of the momentary pleasures that compose it.[12] He is a hedonist of the present, and so he denies that our ultimate end is pleasure maximized over a whole life.

static pleasure taken in (or "following on", *epi*) the removal of pains—a sort of undisturbed condition (*anochlêsia*), which Epicurus accepts and takes to be the end' (DL ii 87). Epicurus: see §151, on DL x 136.

[9] 'Further, pleasure is a good, even if it comes about from the most unseemly things (according to Hippobotus in his book on the philosophical schools); for even if the action is unthinkable, still the pleasure is choiceworthy because of itself and good' (DL ii 88). Cf. Plato, *Pr.* 351b7-e7.

[10] See §21 on hedonism.

[11] The connexion between Aristippus and the *Protagoras* is stressed by Grote, *POCS* i, 199–201. Grote remarks that Aristippus does not appear to emphasize the importance of practical wisdom in planning for maximum pleasure in one's life as a whole. This silence in Aristippus is intelligible if he has doubts about eudaemonism.

[12] 'Moreover, in their view, the end differs from happiness. For the end is particular pleasure, whereas happiness is a collection made out of particular pleasures, among which are counted together both past and future pleasures. Particular pleasure is choiceworthy because of itself. Happiness, on the other hand, is choiceworthy not because of itself, but because of the particular pleasures....' (DL ii 87-8). 'The Annicerians <i.e. followers of Anniceris> in the Cyrenaic succession set down no definite end of the whole of life, but claimed that there is a special end for each action—the

Since Aristippus rejects the eudaemonist aspects of Socrates' hedonism, he allows only a reduced role to the measuring science. If we aim at pleasure in our life as a whole, we need some knowledge of the longer-term hedonic effects of different actions, and some knowledge of our future aims and preferences. This sort of knowledge may reasonably be attributed to temperate and brave people. But if our temporal horizon is shorter, and we are only concerned with what will give us most pleasure here and now, foresight of future effects and of our future preferences does not help us as much. That is why Aristippus believes that wisdom does not always do better than folly in securing pleasure, and allows that some virtues are found in foolish people.[13] By this he may mean that temperance and bravery do not always go with the ability to secure short-term pleasures, and so may belong to 'foolish' people who are not very good at securing these pleasures.

We cannot tell whether Aristippus intends his rejection of eudaemonism to reply to the *Protagoras*, or the *Protagoras* defends Socrates against Aristippus. At any rate, it is useful to compare these alternative statements of hedonism. Since the Socratic view that makes happiness the ultimate end is the dominant assumption in Greek ethics, Aristippus' rejection of the eudaemonist assumption is especially worth examining. Does he challenge an assumption that others thoughtlessly take for granted, or does the assumption rest on a reasonable basis that he fails to appreciate?

31. For and against Eudaemonism

Our evidence on Aristippus does not include an argument against eudaemonism. But we can perhaps see why he might reject it if we consider Plato's argument against hedonism in the *Gorgias*. We distinguished a less radical from a more radical objection to hedonist eudaemonism. Socrates' less radical argument claims that a hedonist eudaemonist cannot advocate the virtues, including bravery and temperance, that require active planning, resolution, and execution of our rational plans. His more radical argument suggests that hedonists cannot reasonably be eudaemonists; for if they do not care about rational agency, they cannot explain why we should care about our lives as a whole. Socrates intends this argument to refute hedonism, since he assumes that we will accept eudaemonism.

Aristippus, however, seems to draw the opposite conclusion. He rejects the adaptive strategy for happiness, since it rejects intense pleasures that are more difficult for us to do without. The objection to these pleasures rests on considerations about the future; the intense pleasures cause us greater pain if we cannot enjoy them, and even if we can enjoy

---

pleasure resulting from the action' (Clement, *Strom.* ii 21, 130.7–8). 'Aristippus welcomed the experience of pleasure (*hêdupatheia*), and said it is the end, and that happiness is founded on it. And he said that it was for a single time only (*monochronos*). Like prodigal people, he thought that neither the memory of past gratifications nor the expectation of future ones was anything to him, but he discerned the good by the single present time alone. He regarded having been gratified and being about to be gratified as nothing to him, on the ground that the one no longer is and the other is not yet and is unclear—just like what happens to self-indulgent people, who suppose that only what is present benefits them' (Athenaeus, xii 544a–b).

[13] 'In their view, it is not true that every wise person has a pleasant life, or that every bad person has a painful life, but it is true only for the most part. It is enough if we bring on even one pleasure at a time with enjoyment. . . . . Some of the virtues are present in foolish people as well <as wise people>' (DL ii 91).

them, we suffer greater disturbance until we can enjoy them again. Aristippus answers this objection by rejecting the eudaemonist assumption that underlies it. Socrates' argument depends on our preferring long-term over short-term satisfaction. It does not refute someone who is indifferent to long-term satisfaction.

Aristippus expresses indifference to long-term satisfaction by asserting that happiness is worth while only because of particular pleasures that compose it, and denies that memory and anticipation of pleasures have any value.[14] He is not concerned about the past or future self that has a whole life to plan for. If we plan for our good in a temporally-extended life, we show that we have some concern for ourselves as temporally-extended beings, and so we might naturally expect to be pleased or displeased by what has happened or will happen to ourselves in the past or the future. Aristippus, however, argues that memory and anticipation do not matter. The only good is the present stimulation of the soul; memory gives us at best a faint trace of past stimulation, and anticipation matters to us only if we care about the future.

In distinguishing pleasure from happiness, and denying that happiness is really the end or the good, Aristippus shows how it is natural to understand *eudaimonia*, and why the identification of pleasure with *eudaimonia* is not to be taken for granted. He thinks of happiness as extending over a temporally-extended life, and describes it as a collection of pleasures, which we want only for the sake of the particular pleasures composing it.

This may seem a rather peculiar claim; for why should we not value the collection of pleasures if we value the individual items in the collection? Aristippus might compare this case with other cases where we might choose a collection even though we value only the individual items, and not the collection as a whole. Perhaps I want to buy a miscellaneous and ill-matched collection of paintings at a sale. Each one of them is valuable to me, because I already have a large gallery of paintings, and each painting in the collection would fit somewhere at widely scattered places in the gallery. But I might say that I attach no value to the collection in itself, as such; what I value is this Rembrandt, this Degas, and so on, as individual paintings, not the collection as a whole. This would be even clearer if I attached no value at all to most of the collection, and I bought it simply because it was the only way to buy the particular Watteau I had always been looking for. If, as Aristippus thinks, I am concerned only about the present, I might accept a happy life if it is the safest way to secure what I want in the present.

The rejection of eudaemonism opposes the predominant view of Aristippus' contemporaries and his successors. Aristotle implies that eudaemonism is generally taken for granted; people generally agree that the final good is to be identified with happiness, which is also to be identified with 'living well' (*eu zēn*) and 'doing well' (*eu prattein*) (*EN* 1095a15–20). Aristotle remarks that, in contrast to this point of general agreement, people disagree about what happiness is.

If Aristotle's remark tempts us to suppose that there is no room for disagreement about whether the final good is happiness, then Aristippus should change our minds. For he believes that pleasure is the ultimate good, choiceworthy (*haireton*) for its own sake, and that anything else is choiceworthy for the sake of it; but he denies that this ultimate good is happiness.

---

14 See n12 above.

32. Epistemological and Metaphysical Objections to Eudaemonism

If Aristippus claims that we have no reason to care about happiness unless we care about our future, he implies that the ultimate basis of reasons lies in our desires. If this is his objection, he should concede that if we care about our future, we have reason to care about happiness. On this view, it is neither reasonable nor unreasonable to care about our future; the basic desire is the foundation of reasonable and unreasonable choices. We might rely on this aspect of Aristippus' views to understand passages in which he describes a prudent attitude to pleasure.[15]

Some of his remarks, however, suggest that he intends a broader attack on the pursuit of happiness, claiming that people who care about it are misguided. In the *Euthydemus* Socrates takes it for granted that we all pursue happiness. Aristotle follows him in taking the ultimate status of happiness to be a feature of common beliefs. He argues that the good must be complete and self-sufficient; and he infers that since happiness satisfies these criteria, it is the final good (1097a34–b6, b15–21). This argument helps to fix the points where Cyrenaics reject eudaemonism. If the Cyrenaics deny that happiness is the final good, then they must claim either (i) that Aristotle is wrong about the criteria for the good, or (ii) that Aristotle is right about the criteria, but wrong in thinking that happiness meets them, or (iii) that Aristotle is wrong on both counts.

Aristippus accepts the Platonic and Aristotelian belief that the good is complete,[16] but he believes that only pleasure meets this condition.[17] He also maintains that pleasure is self-sufficient, in that nothing can be added to it to make a greater good. Aristotle, following Plato, believes that we can add something to pleasure (1172b26–35). But he forms this belief from the standpoint of 'the many and the wise', who have formed the common beliefs about goodness.

To show that Aristotle is wrong, Aristippus appeals to something more fundamental than common beliefs: our initial 'affections' or 'passions' (*pathê*). Pleasure and pain are introduced because they are passions. He treats the passions as the basis for beliefs about good and evil because they are prior to education and rational belief.[18] Aristotle mentions the hedonist Eudoxus, who believes that this argument from the primitive character of pleasure give us a good reason to believe that pleasure is the good.[19] Philebus relies on a related fact about pleasure, that it is common to all animals (*Phil.* 11b4–6; 60a7–b1). Since pleasure is an aspect of sensory experience (*aisthêsis*; cf. *Tht.* 156b), it belongs to animals and young children; it is our starting point for forming beliefs about good and evil.

---

[15] See, e.g., Stob. *Ecl.* iii 17.17 = SR 98: 'The one who masters pleasure is not the one who abstains from it, but the one who uses it, but is not carried away (*ekpheromenos*), just as <the one who masters> a ship or a horse is not the one who does not use it, but the one who leads it where he wishes.' Cf. DL ii 69 = SR 87; Tarrant, 'Socratic theories' 124; Tsouna-McKirahan, 'Origins'.

[16] Plato and Aristotle represent the belief that the good is complete as widely shared (even though most people do not see its implications). Aristippus need not be influenced by Plato or Aristotle in particular.

[17] Cf. Clement, *Strom.* ii 21, 178.43 = Usener, *Epicurea* §450 (referring to the Cyrenaics without further attribution).

[18] 'A proof (*pistis*) that pleasure is the end is the fact that we find it akin to us without any decision (*aprohairetôs* . . .ô(i)keiôsthai*) from our childhood, and that once we get it we seek for nothing in addition, and that we avoid nothing as much as the opposite of pleasure, pain' (DL ii 88).

[19] Aristotle, *EN* 1172b9–25. Cf. 1153b25–32; 1094a1–3 (probably referring to Eudoxus).

Aristotle accepts the primitive, sensory, universal, and undisputed character of pleasure as a reason to believe that it is a good (1172b35–1173a2). But he does not take this to show that pleasure is the good. Aristippus' claim that our initial affections represent pleasure rather than happiness as the good is plausible. Non-rational animals and young children lack (he assumes) a conception of their lives as a whole and are not concerned for their longer-term satisfaction. But Aristotle believes that rational agents pursue happiness as the good once they are mature enough to form a conception of a good for their lives rather than a good for the moment.

Aristippus agrees with Aristotle in believing it is possible to desire something other than pleasure; but he claims that people reject pleasure only because of some perversion (DL ii 89). What sort of perversion or mistake turns us from pleasure to happiness? Aristippus supposes that facts about initial affections show that happiness is not the ultimate end. Why should we agree with this inference from facts about initial affections? Why not agree with Plato, Aristotle, and the Stoics that a conception of one's life as an object for rational deliberation and choice is a basic feature of adult rational agency?

Cyrenaics oppose eudaemonism for broader epistemological reasons. They trust exclusively in our affections, and are sceptics about everything else.[20] One aspect of this austere attitude is the Cyrenaics' scepticism about the existence of any external world. Their doubts rest on grounds that are familiar in early modern philosophy, but hard to parallel in Plato and Aristotle. They rely on an argument from conflicting appearances. Protagoras (in Plato's *Theaetetus*) argues that if you find the drink bitter to the taste, and I find it sweet, the drink in itself cannot be either bitter or sweet. Aristippus uses conflicting appearances to argue that we cannot say anything about the properties of the drink; we can only say what our affections are like (see, e.g., Plato, *Tht.* 156a–157c).

Sensory affection, according to the Cyrenaics, underlies our grasp of the end for action, as well as our grasp of reality.[21] Their reason for distrusting any non-sensory claims about the external world applies to practical beliefs as well. As Aristotle admits, once we go beyond pleasure to happiness and non-hedonic goods, we face conflicting appearances. People disagree about which things are goods,[22] and hence about what constitutes happiness. They agree in the name they use for the final good, calling it 'happiness', but they disagree on the content of happiness (*EN* 1095a17–22). But if we are enjoying some pleasure we are in no doubt at the time that this is good.

---

[20] 'The Cyrenaics say that the criteria are the affections; they alone are grasped, and are undeceiving, whereas none of the things that produce the affections is graspable (grasped? *katalêpton*) or undeceiving. For, they say, it is possible to say without being deceived or refuted that we are being whitened or sweetened; but we cannot affirm whether the thing producing the affection is white or sweet. . . . Hence, if one must speak the truth, only the affection is apparent to us; the external thing that produces the affection perhaps exists, but is not apparent to us' (Sx, M190–4). Plutarch discusses Cyrenaic epistemology at *Col.* 1120c–d. He suggests that while the Epicureans reject Cyrenaic scepticism, they really have no escape from it within their own assumptions (1120–1121e).

[21] '. . . It seems that what these people say about ends corresponds to what they say about criteria. For the affections also extend as far as the ends. For some affections are pleasant, some painful, others intermediate, and, in their view, the painful ones are evil and their end is pain, the pleasant ones are good and their undeceiving end is pleasure, and the intermediate ones are neither good nor evil and their end is what is neither good nor evil, an affection intermediate between pleasure and pain. . . . Of all things, then, the affections are criteria and ends, and, they say, we live by following these, relying on obviousness (or 'evidence', *enargeia*) and approval (*eudokêsis*)—on obviousness in relation to the other affections, and on approval in relation to pleasure' (Sx. M199–200).

[22] The discussion between Aristippus and Socrates in Xenephon, *Mem.* iii 8.1–7 suggests that Aristippus tries to expose conflicting beliefs about goods. Socrates argues that some of these 'conflicts' are innocuous.

Can we attribute this epistemological reason for preferring hedonism over eudaemonism to Aristippus the Socratic, or does it belong to the later development of the Cyrenaic position? The discussions about the senses and the external world in the *Theaetetus* and about pleasure and the good in the *Philebus* do not introduce the precise epistemological view that we have ascribed to Aristippus. Xenophon refers to his indifference to long-term happiness,[23] but does not mention any defence of it. But the questions raised in the *Philebus* and *Theaetetus* show that an appeal to the affections on epistemological grounds is highly relevant to the arguments in these two dialogues. Hence it would not have been anachronistic or irrelevant for Aristippus the Socratic to have put forward this epistemological claim.

Aristippus has a further reason to argue in this way, in the light of Democritus' views. From the Cyrenaic point of view, Democritus expresses conflicting attitudes to the senses. He denies, as the Cyrenaics do, that the senses give us knowledge of external reality; he appeals to conflicting appearances to show that the senses cannot tell us whether anything external is really hot or cold. But in the area of practice he affirms both hedonism and eudaemonism.[24] He assumes that our sensory affections are misleading in failing to recognize the longer-term good, but he believes they are correct about the character of the good, in identifying the good with pleasure, whereas they are misleading about the character of the external world. But he does not explain why he draws a different conclusion in these two areas.[25]

It would be reasonable for Aristippus to believe that he has reached a more consistent position than Democritus reaches; whereas Democritus applies his sceptical arguments only to theoretical knowledge, Aristippus applies them to practical knowledge as well. Democritus sees no question, just as Socrates in the *Protagoras* sees none, about the consistency of hedonism with eudaemonism. But the *Gorgias* raises just this question. The position that our sources ascribe to the Cyrenaics suggests an argument that Aristippus might plausibly construct in defence of hedonism against the objections of the *Gorgias*. The appeal to our sensory affections exploits one aspect of Democritus' epistemology. Epicurus exploits a different aspect of Democritus, and reaches a different result about hedonism and eudaemonism. But Democritus and Plato show us why Aristippus the Socratic might reasonably have pursued his own defence of hedonism through an appeal to sensory affection.

33. Doubts about the Continuing Self

The argument from sensory affection supports a sceptical conclusion about happiness, showing that once we go beyond our immediate appearances of pleasure and good, we find ourselves unable to resolve conflicting beliefs about happiness. The Cyrenaics would have a further reason for rejecting happiness if they believed that the idea of happiness itself rests on an error. To speak of a person's happiness is to speak of a good that belongs to his life

---

[23] See *Mem.* ii 1.34 (n6 above).

[24] On Democritus see Socrates $21. Taylor, *ALD* 233, mentions 'a structural parallel between ethics and epistemology, in that each area of thought requires a contrast between immediately apprehended data (immediate pleasure in the practical sphere, perceptual data in the theoretical) and the truth revealed by reflexion, respectively the theses that the good is not immediate pleasure but long-term cheerfulness and that things are in reality not as they appear to the senses but as atomic theory shows them to be.'

[25] Taylor comments on the non-sceptical aspect of Democritus' eudaemonism, at 'Pleasure' 26.

as a whole; to believe in such a good we need to believe that one and the same person persists at all the times at which we consider his good. Do the Cyrenaics believe, on the epistemological basis they allow themselves, in this continuing self? The evidence is not clear, but the question is important enough to deserve some further discussion.

We may consider one argument that influenced some Greek philosophers, and then ask whether the premisses of the argument might be expected to appeal to the Cyrenaics. In an argument ascribed to Epicharmus, a debtor argues that he is not obliged to pay his debt because he has changed from how he was when he promised to pay it, and therefore is not the same person.[26] This argument begins from examples of quantitatively defined subjects—a length, a measure, a number, or a heap. For these subjects it is plausible to say that any 'growth' or 'shrinkage' implies going out of existence, since the subject has its quantitative properties essentially. The inference about the debtor presupposes that persons are also quantitatively defined subjects.[27]

In the *Theaetetus* Plato uses this argument to develop a Protagorean and Heracleitean theory of perception and its objects. According to this theory, all ostensible subjects with a number of qualities are really just heaps (*hathroismata*) of perceptible qualities (*Tht.* 157b8–c2). Since heaps are defined purely quantitatively, they are open to Epicharmus' argument; hence healthy Socrates is not the same person as sick Socrates, because of the change in the previously healthy Socrates (158e–159c).[28]

From the Cyrenaics' point of view, the continuing self is open to doubt. They may agree that I am aware of myself in my particular sensory affections; but the continuing self has to be a heap of these particular episodes of awareness extending into the past and future. Since it is a purely quantitative subject, undergoing change with every new affection, Epicharmus' argument applies, and it cannot be a continuing subject. Aristippus speaks of happiness as a collection (*sustêma*, DL ii 87), and speaks of the 'heaping' (*athroismos*, ii 90) of pleasures that produce happiness. If he thinks of happiness as a collection, not a genuine continuant, it would be reasonable for him to think of the self in the same way.

If Aristippus holds this view about a continuing self, he has a strong reason for claiming that any concern with an extended future for myself rests on illusion and unwarranted belief.[29] When Aristippus speaks of 'empty' belief,[30] he will not, if he sticks to his own epistemological

---

[26] See Plu. *CN* 1083ab = LS 28A. The reference to the debtor comes from the reports in Plu. *SN* 559a–b (in the course of an argument against a purely quantitative conception of the persistence of an individual human being or a city); *Tranq. An.* 473c–d (discussing the bad effects of forgetfulness).

[27] 'Suppose someone chooses to add a single pebble to a heap . . . or to take away one of those already there; do you think the number of pebbles would remain the same? . . . Now consider human beings in the same way: One person grows, and another shrinks; they are all in course of change the whole time. But a thing that naturally changes and never remains in the same state must always be different from what has changed. In the same way, you and I were one pair yesterday, are another today, and again will be another tomorrow, and will never remain the same people, according to this argument' (DL iii 11).

[28] Anon. *in Tht.* 70.5–26 = *CPF* iii 454–6 = LS 28B, wrongly ascribes this extreme view to Plato in *Symp.* 207d–208b. A connexion between the Heracleitean theory of change and Cyrenaic scepticism is noticed in Anon. *in Tht.* 65.18–39 = *CPF* iii 442, but it does not refer specifically to questions about continuing subjects. On whether the *Tht.* alludes to the Cyrenaic position see Giannantoni, *Cirenaici* 144–5; Mannebach, *ACF* 114. Tsouna-McKirahan, *ECS* 130-5, denies that the Cyrenaics accept the growing argument. See also Tsouna-McKirahan, 'Exception'.

[29] On pleasures of memory and anticipation see §154.

[30] 'The wise person will neither envy nor fall in love (*eran*) nor fear the gods superstitiously, since all these are a result of empty belief. He will, however, feel pain and fear, since these come about naturally' (DL ii 91).

principles, claim to know that the relevant beliefs are false; he will claim that they have no warrant, since they have no warrant from affections, which are the only source of immediate and irrefutable knowledge.

34. A Conflict between Hedonism and Eudaemonism?

We have found some reason to believe that Aristippus supports his doubts about eudaemonism by appeal to doubts about personal identity. To explain why he might be moved by these doubts, we have explored the implications of his scepticism about anything beyond immediate sensory affections. Our exploration has taken us beyond any direct evidence about the Cyrenaics. Speculations about personal identity, however, are not necessary for our main argument about the significance of Cyrenaic hedonism. Even if we reject all the reasons for believing that the Cyrenaics raise doubts about personal identity, we must admit that they are sceptics about anything beyond the affections, that they appeal to the affections to show that pleasure is good, and that they deny that happiness is the good. The link between their positive claim about pleasure and their negative claim about happiness is their reliance on the affections and senses.

Someone reflecting on Socrates' moral arguments might reasonably find the resort to the senses plausible. Socrates normally relies on what Aristotle calls the 'common beliefs' (*endoxa*). Though he criticizes his interlocutors, he takes some of their beliefs to be reliable, and uses these to modify others. But he does not explain why he takes some beliefs to be more reliable than others. It seems reasonable to ask for an explanation. For the conflicting appearances that support scepticism about external objects seem to raise even more serious questions in ethics. Different people, even within one society, disagree about good and evil; and when we take account of differences between different societies, it seems even more difficult to get beyond the conflicting appearances to any justifiable claims about what is really good or evil.

Both Socrates (in the *Protagoras*) and Aristippus follow the lead of Democritus in believing that an appeal to pleasure allows us to argue at an epistemologically more basic level that is free from the questions raised by conflicting appearances. In the *Protagoras* Socrates supposes that everyone acknowledges pleasure as the ultimate good, and that the anti-hedonist elements of common sense rest on a failure to distinguish short-term from long-term pleasure. He does not say why he takes everyone to agree about pleasure. Aristippus gives a reason that is similar to Democritus' reason; just as we must take the immediate appearances of our sensory affections to be evident, we must take our immediate affections of pleasure and pain to be evident. Socrates is right to suppose that, if we set aside superficial disagreements, we will find that we all treat pleasure as the good; we find this agreement when we focus on the affections that are beyond doubt.

But at this stage Aristippus departs from both Socrates and Democritus. In his view, they are right to turn to pleasure as the right epistemological foundation, but they inconsistently revert to unwarranted common sense by endorsing eudaemonism. Against them he argues that if we accept his argument for hedonism, we cannot be eudaemonists. For hedonism rests on the evident appearances of the affections, which do not recognize happiness as the end. We cannot, then, use Socrates' argument to show that everyone really accepts hedonism, once they distinguish short-term from long-term pleasure; that is an argument for hedonist eudaemonism, which we cannot defend from the affections.

This argument does not show that hedonism and eudaemonism are incompatible. But if it is cogent, it shows that the most plausible justification of hedonism undermines eudaemonism. Hedonism seems a plausible account of the good that rests on an uncontroversial epistemological basis. But this epistemological basis is too narrow to justify eudaemonism. If we take eudaemonism to be justified, we broaden our epistemological base so as to raise doubts about hedonism.

On this point Aristippus agrees with Plato (in the *Gorgias*, *Republic*, and *Philebus*) and Aristotle. But they draw a different conclusion, since they prefer eudaemonism over hedonism. Epicurus revives the combination of hedonism and eudaemonism that Socrates defends in the *Protagoras*; we will want to ask whether he has a way out of the Cyrenaic argument to show that one part of his position undermines the other.

4

THE CYNICS

35. Socrates and the Cynics

The Cynic school had a long life, extending well into the Roman Empire. It appears (from the patchy evidence provided by our sources) to have included sharply different attitudes on central moral questions. The early founders of Cynicism, Antisthenes and Diogenes, seem to have denied that pleasure is a good, and to have maintained that virtue is sufficient for happiness.[1] This side of Cynicism helps to explain why the Stoics trace their origins to Cynicism. Zeno the Stoic was a pupil of Crates the Cynic.[2] According to one Stoic, the sage will live like a Cynic; 'for the Cynic life is a short road to virtue'.[3] The Stoic Ariston of Chios shows the continuing appeal of Cynicism for Stoics; he deviates from other Stoics in a markedly Cynic direction.[4] But the aspect of Cynicism that appeals to Stoics is only one side of later Cynicism; other aspects are independent of Stoicism, and even opposed to it.[5]

The most helpful approach to the Cynics begins from their connexion with Socrates. Antisthenes appears in Xenophon's *Memorabilia* and *Symposium*, where he is one of Socrates' closest associates (*Mem.* iii 11.17). He wrote a number of works on different virtues, overlapping in content with Plato's Socratic dialogues.[6] Diogenes takes himself to put Antisthenes' principles into practice better than Antisthenes did.[7] Antisthenes accepts an austere interpretation of Socrates' principles.[8] Diogenes infers that conventional behaviour, ordinary comfort, courtesy, decency, sexual modesty, and so on, are insignificant. Hence we should not put any effort into them, but we should live without them as far as possible. That is why Diogenes is said to have lived in a barrel, masturbated in public, and so on. These

---

[1] The evidence (collected in *SR* VA 22–6) for treating Antisthenes as the founder of a Cynic 'school' is open to reasonable doubt. But for convenience I will treat both Antisthenes and Diogenes as Cynics. Cf. Tsouna-McKirahan, 'Origins' 369–77.

[2] See DL vi 91, vii 2–5; §161.

[3] DL vii 121. DL attributes this remark to the 2nd-century BC Stoic Apollodorus, not to one of the three major Stoics. But see n26 below and *SR* VA 136 for other references to the remark.

[4] Sx, *M* xi 64–7; DL vii 160 = LS 58 F–G.

[5] Seneca, *Ben.* vii 1.3–2.4 states the opinions of Demetrius the Cynic (cited by Stewart, 'Democritus' 181–4, as evidence of the currency of Democritus' sayings among Cynics). Demetrius agrees with the Stoics (2.2) in claiming that only the *honestum* is good. He rejects pleasure (with no qualification) as short-lived and beneath human nature. But he also recognizes a kind of pleasure that is free from disturbance and fit for human beings (2.3). Whether this concession to pleasure goes back to the original Cynics or not, it is easily introduced into a position that is generally opposed to pleasure.

[6] See *SR* VA 41–4.   [7] Dio Chrys. 8.1–2 = *SR* VB 584.   [8] See Xenophon, *Symp.* iv 61–4.

Cynic attitudes have Socratic sources. Socrates was also supposed to be quite indifferent to clothes, shoes, and washing, but he did not go to extremes in denying himself conventional goods and evils other than virtue.

The Cynics as well as the Cyrenaics dispute Plato's claim to uphold the most defensible form of an authentically Socratic position.[9] Our sources report some sharp comments by Plato and Diogenes on each other. Diogenes rejects Plato's theory of purely intelligible forms, and Plato describes Diogenes as 'Socrates gone mad'.[10] Plato may mean that Diogenes accepts some Socratic positions, but takes them to such extremes that the result is incredible, both theoretically and practically. This claim fits the Cynic attitude to Socrates' belief that virtue is sufficient for happiness. The Cynics take Socrates to imply that we have no reason to care about anything except virtue, and hence we have no reason to care about any of the non-moral goods that occupy most people in many aspects of their life.

Plato's attack on Diogenes raises a useful question about Socrates and the Cynics. We might take any of three possible attitudes: (1) Plato is right, because the Cynic outlook is a perversion of Socrates' views. (2) Diogenes is right, because Socrates' views really justify the Cynic outlook. (3) Neither of them is exactly right, but each has a legitimate objection to the other, because Socrates' views are consistent with a Cynic outlook, but do not require it.

If we pursue these questions about the Cynics, we may reasonably hope to understand the basis of the early Cynic position. But even if the questions were irrelevant to the historical understanding of Cynicism, they would still be highly relevant to the philosophical understanding of Socrates and Plato. For a clear statement of the relation between Socrates' views and the presumed views of Antisthenes and Diogenes will help us to see a possible development of Socratic principles that Plato tries hard to avoid. In separating the core of Socratic ethics from its Cynic expression, Plato tries to find an expression that rules out Cynic inferences.

36. Socratic Alternatives to Hedonism: Virtue or Self-Sufficiency?

Socrates' belief that virtue is necessary and sufficient for happiness is compatible both with hedonism and with the rejection of hedonism, and allows virtue to be either instrumentally or non-instrumentally good. The argument in the *Euthydemus* defends the necessity and sufficiency of virtue, but does not commit Socrates to a definite view on the other questions. The *Protagoras* combines the Socratic claim about virtue and happiness with hedonism. It argues that virtue is the measuring craft that allows us to maximize pleasure in our life as a whole, and is therefore necessary and sufficient for happiness. If we look beyond the present and the immediate future, we see that we increase our pleasure by observing the prescriptions of the cardinal virtues. The *Gorgias* raises reasonable doubt about this claim in the *Protagoras*, but what alternative does it offer?

---

[9] Aristippus on Plato: see §29n5.
[10] For Diogenes' comments on the forms see DL vi 53 = SR VB 62. Cf. VA 149, where the same story is attached to Antisthenes. For Antisthenes' comments on Plato see, e.g., DL vi 7. On Diogenes and Socrates see DL vi 54 = SR VB 59.

One answer relies on the conception of happiness that Socrates opposes to Callicles' conception. According to Socrates, those who lack nothing are happy, and the best way to achieve this condition is to adapt our desires to the means available for satisfying them; we have called this an 'adaptive' conception of happiness. Socrates implies that hedonism is plausible to the extent that it includes a conception of happiness as the satisfaction of one's desires and preferences, but Calliclean hedonism is mistaken to the extent that it requires the expansion of one's desires so as to maximize one's pleasure. Since happiness consists in satisfaction, not in maximization, and since our desires are plastic, we do not need to pursue the pleasures that involve previous pain, effort, and anxiety; we can achieve satisfaction better by fitting our desires to the available resources.

This reaction to the *Gorgias* recognizes that Socrates' argument raises a reasonable doubt about hedonist eudaemonism. If we favour an adaptive conception of happiness, we retain eudaemonism; for the adaptation of desires to circumstances protects us against the pain and frustration of future loss. The less susceptible we are to attractions that will cause us pain and disturbance if we lose them, the better we protect our future. This is the Cynic view that austerity makes us more adaptable.

These views may incline us to one of the positions discussed and rejected in the *Philebus* (43a–50e), identifying the most desirable state with the absence of both pain and pleasure.[11] Antisthenes denies that pleasure is either an instrumental or an intrinsic good, and claims he would rather go mad than feel pleasure.[12] According to this view, both the hedonism of Callicles and the hedonism of the *Protagoras* interfere with the adaptation of desires to circumstances. It is clear how this objection affects Calliclean hedonism, but Antisthenes might reasonably argue that it affects the *Protagoras* as well. Since pleasure essentially involves some psychic disturbance, and inevitably attracts us to external objects that we may or may not manage to acquire, it interferes with any rational strategy for the adaptation of desires to circumstances. If we adapt our desires to the available resources, we are free of many sources of pain, since pain results from unsatisfied desires; and once we see that happiness requires satisfaction rather than maximization, we will also free ourselves from the pleasure that results from the removal of pain, frustration, or anxiety. Since the pursuit of maximum pleasure is not the only source of pain and pleasure, our concentration on satisfaction may not free us entirely from pain and pleasure; Socrates does not guarantee that we will not suffer pain if someone sticks a knife in us. But pain and pleasure will no longer be the primary elements of good and evil.

This conception of happiness as adaptation and satisfaction still leaves virtue with a purely instrumental role. Instead of arguing that virtue is the science that measures pleasures and pains, Socrates argues that the cardinal virtues are means of restraining and ordering our desires so that we match them to the available resources. This is why he emphasizes temperance among the virtues (*Gorg.* 491d–e). Temperate people have learnt to modify their desires so that they do not exceed the reasonable limits; the adaptive conception fixes these reasonable limits according to the available resources. This conception of happiness gives us no reason for valuing temperance or any other cardinal virtue non-instrumentally.

---

[11] On anti-hedonism in the *Philebus* see Schofield, 'Dischereis' (who takes these people to hold Speusippus' views on pleasure, which are different from the Cynic views).

[12] See *SR* VA 119–22.

We may reach a different conclusion about virtue and happiness, however, if we consider Socrates' argument to show that Callicles' position is inconsistent. He does not move Callicles by simply contrasting the hedonist conception of happiness with the adaptive conception; Callicles remarks contemptuously that Socrates' conception implies that rocks and corpses are happy (492e). To show that Callicles cannot consistently be a hedonist and advocate bravery as a virtue, Socrates does not appeal to claims about satisfaction, but argues that Callicles' hedonism conflicts with the value that he attaches to rational agency. Bravery, according to Callicles, is valuable because it allows us to carry out our own plans and aims without the distraction of fear. Socrates argues that in valuing this aspect of bravery Callicles recognizes a non-hedonic good that may conflict with maximization of pleasure.

Socrates does not point out that his adaptive conception of happiness might well appear to be open to the objection that he urges against Callicles' hedonism. Callicles' derisive comment about rocks and corpses points out that we could have satisfied desires without rational agency. If we value rational agency for its own sake, we cannot agree that happiness consists simply in satisfaction of preferences.

If we attend to this aspect of the *Gorgias* we may be inclined to conclude that virtue is not simply a means to happiness, but identical to it. According to this view, we value rational agency not because it leads to satisfaction of desire, but for its own sake. This outlook on happiness may encourage us to accept the position that the *Philebus* opposes to hedonism—the identification of the good with rational intelligence. The *Republic* and the *Philebus* show that this is not the direction Plato takes; but it is an intelligible conclusion from the *Gorgias*.

The imprecise aspects of Socrates' alternative to hedonism may be relevant for understanding the Cynics. One might reasonably infer from the *Gorgias* both that Socrates endorses an adaptive conception of happiness and that he ascribes non-instrumental value to virtue. If we try to expound the outlook of the *Gorgias* and to put it into practice, we may find ourselves formulating an account of happiness that includes these inconsistent elements. This reflexion on Socrates may throw light on the Cynic position.

37. Happiness and Adaptation

In the *Euthydemus* Socrates concludes that alleged goods other than wisdom are not really good, but are 'greater goods' than their opposites if wisdom leads them. The Cynics try to explain the claims in the *Euthydemus* by appeal to the adaptive conception of happiness that Socrates defends in the *Gorgias*. Antisthenes claims to be proud of his 'wealth', even though he lacks what most people would recognize as wealth. He is wealthier than conventionally wealthy people because he has ample resources to satisfy his minimal desires (Xenophon, *Symp.* iv 34–45). Those who are rich in the conventional view are really needy, because they always want more and have too little to satisfy their needs.[13] Antisthenes, however, is used

---

[13] 'Need' or 'lack' (*endeia*) makes conventionally rich people commit crimes to get more. They are like people who eat and drink more and more and are never filled (iv 36–7). This picture of desire and filling recalls Plato's descriptions in the *Gorg.*, *R.* ix, and the *Phil.*

to the cold, and so does not need warm clothes; he satisfies his inevitable and minimal needs with whatever is available, and so he is not anxious for more.[14] His adaptation of desires to the circumstances is the basis of his virtues of temperance and justice; he lacks the urgent desires that would tempt him to intemperance and injustice.[15] This is why Antisthenes claims that virtue is sufficient for happiness.[16]

Antisthenes' description of the strategy suggested by an adaptive conception of happiness brings Socrates quite close to Diogenes. For it implies that the Cynic who lives in a barrel, wears no clothes, eats and drinks only what he needs to stay alive and active, and does not care what his more conventional neighbours think about him, achieves happiness, as long as he has formed only the desires that can be satisfied in this way of life.

If we identify virtue with the state of character that adapts desires to resources, we have a reason to affirm the Socratic claim that virtue is sufficient for happiness, and we can see why Socrates is right to infer that no supposed 'goods' other than virtue are really good. If we have a million dollars to spare, and we want to buy a house costing this amount, we will (to this extent) achieve satisfaction through adaptation by buying the house. But we have no reason to prefer having enough to buy this house over having enough to buy a tent in circumstances where we only want a tent. Provided that our desires match our resources, at either a high or a low level, we have no reason to prefer the high level of desires and resources over the low level.

Antisthenes' strategy seems reasonable if we accept Socrates' claim that wisdom is the only good (*Euthd.* 281e) and external goods (i.e., those external to wisdom)[17] are not good. But Socrates also says that when external goods are led by wisdom, they are 'greater goods' than their opposites (281d). How is this claim consistent with the claim that wisdom is the only good?

Socrates might answer that wealth (for instance) is a greater good than poverty, but still not a good; it is a greater good only in so far as it is closer to being a genuine good. Though it is preferable to poverty, Socrates may not agree that it is thereby good. What is good is the wise person's use of wealth; though we prefer to have wealth to use, we can still be virtuous by acting wisely in poverty.

This answer, however, raises further questions about Socrates' position. If wealth led by wisdom is a greater good than poverty led by wisdom, a wise person apparently ought to seek wealth rather than poverty. But if in some circumstances a wise person ought to seek wealth rather poverty, does it not follow that, in these circumstances, wealth is better than poverty? If it is better than poverty, is it not good in these circumstances? If it is good in these circumstances, does it not promote the agent's happiness in these circumstances?

One might defend Socrates by questioning some of the steps in this argument; that is how the Stoics maintain that virtue is the only good, while still avoiding the Cynic conclusion that we have no reason to prefer wealth to poverty.[18] Socrates does not make it clear how he

---

[14] 'If his body ever needs sexual intercourse, he can satisfy it with those women who are available; he tries those whom no one else wants' (iv 38).

[15] 'It is reasonable to expect those who aim at minimal use of resources (*euteleia*) to be more just than others; for those who are most satisfied with what is available (*hois . . . malista ta paronta arkei*) are the least prone to desire what belongs to others' (iv 42).

[16] See DL vi 11, discussed in §35 below.   [17] For convenience I use an Aristotelian term.

[18] See §§161–2.

intends to defend the consistency of his position. But at any rate he does not seem to agree with Diogenes' conclusion. Diogenes believes we have no reason to prefer more external goods to fewer. Socrates disagrees on this point, though he does not clarify the basis of his disagreement.

We might try a defence of Socrates that comes closer to the Cynic position. Perhaps it is easier to adapt our desires to circumstances if we have a reasonable supply of external goods. If we do not have to watch every penny to provide ourselves with a bare minimum of food and shelter, we need not eliminate as many desires as a poorer person would have to eliminate in order to match desires to resources. External goods, then, are preferable, not for those who have already achieved happiness, but for those who are looking for the best way to achieve it. According to this view, Diogenes has no reason to want more external goods than he has. If he has adapted his desires to his circumstances, the fact that adaptation might have been easier for him in less rigorous circumstances is irrelevant. If he has achieved the goal by a more difficult route, it does not matter that he might have taken an easier route.

38. Do the Cynics Improve on Socrates?

The argument so far suggests that Socrates' views on virtue and happiness give no reason to object to Diogenes' way of life as a possible route to happiness. If happiness requires adaptation, we might achieve it either with Diogenes' low level of external goods or with a higher level. We seem to have no reason to prefer one level to the other, if the supply of external goods is reliable. While Socrates, on this view, has no reason to object to the Cynic way of life, he has no more reason to reject a well-adapted life at a higher level of external goods.

These concessions to the Cynics do not make Socrates into a Cynic. For the Cynics do not simply claim to have found one route to happiness; they also defend the stronger conclusion that they have taken the best route. In particular, they claim they are better off than they would have been if they had got rid of fewer external goods and had adapted their desires to the higher level.

We might defend this Cynic claim by appeal to Socrates' assertion that if we are wise, we do not need good fortune in addition to wisdom. According to Socrates, wisdom guarantees us all the good fortune we need (*Euthd.* 280a–b). Diogenes might argue that this is true only if we plan for a minimal level of external goods. If Croesus adapts his desires to his enormous wealth, and lives temperately but without austerity, his adaptation of desires to circumstances is unstable. For (as we know from Herodotus) greater resources are exposed to circumstances that we cannot control, however wise we may be. If we are used to having more, it is harder for us to adapt our desires to having less than it would be if we were used to having less all along.

We might answer, on Socrates' behalf, that this argument for austerity fails to reckon with Socratic moral psychology. Socrates might argue that, contrary to Diogenes' suggestion, a higher level of external goods does not make it more difficult to adapt our desires to circumstances if we lose the external goods we had. A loss of external goods will make it more difficult to adapt ourselves to circumstances only if we remain stubbornly attached to aims and goals that we can no longer achieve, so that we regret our inability to achieve them. If that is our reaction to misfortune, our desires have not followed our beliefs about the good. But Socrates' argument in the *Protagoras* seeks to show that our desires necessarily follow our beliefs about the good. If this is correct, people who recognize that happiness consists in adaptation will not continue to desire the external goods they cannot have.

But this argument to show that we will not become too dependent on unreliable external goods proves too much for Socrates' purposes. If Socratic psychology is true, and enlightened people do not miss external goods that they lose, why should they bother keeping them in the first place? The most plausible argument for preferring a higher level of external goods claimed that they make adaptation easier; but for enlightened people who see that happiness consists in adaptation, they do not seem to make adaptation easier. If we know that happiness consists in adaptation, we will not regret the loss of external goods.

If, then, we combine strict Socratic psychology with an adaptive conception of happiness, we seem to have no reason to prefer Socrates' preference for a higher level of external goods or to prefer Diogenes' austerity. Neither outlook seems to contribute anything to the adaptation that is needed for happiness.

These implications of Socratic psychology may help to explain Antisthenes' apparent modification of Socrates' claims about virtue and happiness. He is reported as saying that virtue needs 'Socratic strength' added if it is to be sufficient for happiness.[19] He may intend to reject Socrates' assumption that our belief about what is better immediately determines our choice. Perhaps we need some further 'Socratic strength' to reconcile ourselves to a lower level of external goods even when we know it does not harm us.

If this is what Antisthenes means by his reference to Socratic strength, he might seem to support a preference for a higher level of external goods; for they seem to make adaptation easier for people whose desires will not automatically follow their beliefs about the good. But he might draw the opposite conclusion, that we should prefer a lower level of external goods. For even if more external goods make adaptation easier in favourable conditions, they also seem to make it less stable, because we cannot count on favourable conditions. If adaptation is more difficult in less favourable conditions, should we not get used to these conditions from the start, instead of waiting until it is more difficult for us to get used to them?

A similar argument explains why the Cynics are hostile to pleasure. If we think of happiness as adaptation, pleasure seems either dangerous or irrelevant. It is dangerous if we modify Socratic moral psychology enough to allow some degree of irrational attachment. Pleasure is an obvious source of such attachments; if we start to enjoy some unnecessary external good, we may find it more difficult to reconcile ourselves to the loss of it. This is why Antisthenes is not worried that the satisfaction of his minimal needs give him too little pleasure. On the contrary, he would prefer these satisfactions to give him less pleasure, since they seem to him to be 'pleasanter than is expedient' (*hediô tou sumpherontos*) (Xenophon, *Symp.* iv 39).

If pleasure does not cause us to form irrational attachments, it may none the less distract us from our real good. Things appear in a favourable light if we enjoy them, and this

---

[19] 'Virtue is self-sufficient for happiness, needing nothing added, except for Socratic strength' (DL vi 11).

appearance might mislead us into thinking they are good. But this appearance is no guide to our good, which consists in adaptation of desire. We are better off if we simply ignore pleasure, and get used to avoiding it; once we do that, we will find (following Diogenes' remarks about training) that pleasure and pain do not bother us. We will reach the state of freedom from affection (*apatheia*; cf. *Phil.* 21e2)[20] that makes it no longer necessary for us to concern ourselves about the potentially disruptive effects of pleasure.

Is this an unnecessarily austere attitude to pleasure? One might argue that the adaptation of our desires to circumstances and our awareness of our independence and self-sufficiency will itself be a source of pleasure. This sort of pleasure appears to be inseparable from the Cynic way of life, and might reasonably appear to be an advantage of being a Cynic. It is not surprising, then, that some sources take Diogenes to hold a favourable view of the pleasures that belong to the Cynic life.[21] But one may doubt whether this moderate interpretation of the Cynic attitude to pleasure takes proper account of Antisthenes' main point. Even if we take the right sort of pleasure in the right sorts of objects, it may appear, from Antisthenes' point of view, that this pleasure is still a non-rational attachment, and that it is still potentially dangerous. It may encourage us to prefer pleasure to pain, and so it may burden our lives with a concern that we could do without. The austere attitude ascribed to Antisthenes and Diogenes fits better with their aim of getting rid of all potentially disruptive and disturbing attachments and aims.

If, then, we prefer Cynic austerity over a less rigid attitude towards external goods, we have some reason to question Socrates' moral psychology. But it is not clear how far Diogenes advocates his austere way of life as a pattern for everyone to imitate in detail. He compares himself to a chorus-master who begins with too high a note so that the chorus will be able to hit the right note.[22] Cynic training produces appearances that give our souls 'free movement' for virtuous actions.[23] Perhaps Diogenes' ostentatious contempt for convention gives us the vivid appearance that observance of convention is not necessary for a reasonable and virtuous life. This appearance releases us from our unthinking attachment to convention and allows us to move freely towards the appropriately self-sufficient attitude. Diogenes may have hit too high a note, in so far as he has trampled on convention more than we need to once we have recognized its relative unimportance; but his exaggerations help us to see why external goods do not matter if we are trying to adapt our desires to circumstances. It

---

[20] See §55. On Aristotle's objections to *apatheia* see §85.

[21] Dio Chr. 8.20–6 represents Diogenes as claiming that we have to struggle against pleasure because it is deceptive, insinuating, and dangerous. Diogenes draws no distinction among pleasures here. On the contrary he suggests that 'it is not possible for anyone who keeps company with pleasure or even tries it out continuously to avoid being completely captured by it' (24). But 6.9–12 remarks that Diogenes got much more pleasure from his simple and inexpensive pursuits than others gain from more costly pursuits (he always enjoyed the change of seasons). Like Epicurus, he enjoyed simple food more than others enjoy costly food (6.12). The Persian king is worse off because of his fears and anxiety about poverty, illness, and death (6.35). But once the fear of death is removed, no further distress remains (6.42). Similarly, a remark ascribed to Diogenes describes *eudaimonia* as true enjoyment (*euphrainesthai*) and freedom from pain, so that reaches tranquillity (*hêsuchia*) and cheerfulness (*hilarotês*) (Stob. v 906.10–17). These passages make it easy to understand why some aspects of Cynicism appealed to Epicureans; see §143n4. Cynic attitudes to pleasure are fully discussed by Goulet-Cazé, *AC* (see, e.g., 45, 73).

[22] DL vi 35 = SR VB 266.

[23] In the *askêsis* of the soul the appropriate *phantasiai eulusian pros ta tês aretês erga parechontai* (DL vi 70 = SR VB 291). Cicero, *Fam.* xvi 18.1, uses *eulogia* for loose—i.e., not constipated—bowels; this metaphor is characteristic of Diogenes.

is helpful to practise austerity so that we do not get too attached to external goods that are unnecessary for happiness.

This attitude to external goods helps to explain why the traditional Greek heroes whom the Cynics praise are those who can cope with different circumstances, not those who set out to be ascetics. They praise Odysseus, whom Homer calls a 'man of many devices',[24] because he adapts himself to wealth and poverty, to war and peace, to prosperity and adversity, to Penelope, Circe, and Calypso. Another Cynic hero, Heracles, shows the same sort of adaptability in all the different circumstances required by his various labours.[25] Neither Odyssues nor Heracles tries to get rid of external goods. But each of them copes with sharp reversals of fortune, because (according to the Cynics) he can adapt his desires promptly to the circumstances. If we train ourselves to live Diogenes' life, we will be able to face reversals of fortune as resourcefully as Odysseus and Heracles did.

This understanding of Diogenes' advice makes his outlook seem a reasonable expression of the attitude to virtue and external goods that Socrates defends in the *Euthydemus*. It does not seem completely fair to describe Diogenes as Socrates gone mad. For it does not seem at all mad to defend Diogenes' attitude to external goods from Socratic premises. If the conclusion is mad, that is a reason for saying that the madness lies in the Socratic premises, not in Diogenes' inferences from them. If this defence of Diogenes rests on a mistaken account of Socrates' position, the mistake is at any rate not obvious. Though Socrates does not draw Diogenes' conclusions, we may fairly wonder how he could avoid them without giving up some of his claims in the *Euthydemus* and *Gorgias*.

39. Socrates and the Cynics: Is Virtue Identical to Happiness?

So far we have identified the Socratic aspects of the Cynic outlook by attending to Socrates' claims that virtue is sufficient for happiness and that happiness consists in the adaptation of one's desires to the circumstances. We might explain Socrates' views differently, however, by taking him to claim that virtue is identical to happiness, not simply an instrumental means to it. We have seen that Socrates' argument against Callicles seems to presuppose the non-instrumental value of rational agency, and therefore the non-instrumental value of virtue as the embodiment of practical reason. Does this conception of virtue and happiness fit the Cynic position? Diogenes Laertius attributes the view that virtue is the end to the Cynics, and in particular to Antisthenes.[26] But we do not know what remark by Antisthenes underlies this report.

If we believe that virtue is a non-instrumental good, that happiness includes all non-instrumental goods, and that virtue is necessary and sufficient for happiness, we must infer either that virtue is identical to happiness, or that the only components of happiness are

---

[24] See *Odyssey* i 1 (*andra . . . polutropon*).

[25] The Cynics' treatment of these Greek heroes is discussed by Hoisted, *CHCK*.

[26] This is part of DL's review of the doctrines that the Cynics held in common: 'They also hold that living in accord with virtue is the end, as Antisthenes says in the *Heracles*, similarly to the Stoics, since there is some common ground between these two schools. That is why they have said that Cynicism is a short road to virtue. And that was how Zeno of Citium lived' (DL vi 104).

virtue and whatever other goods virtue infallibly secures. If, for instance, virtue secures pleasure or peace of mind, these may be components of happiness that are in some way distinct from virtue, since non-virtuous people may also achieve them. But this view does not seem to be open to Socrates, since he affirms that wisdom is the only good; if pleasure and peace of mind are distinct from virtue, they cannot be goods, and hence they cannot be elements of happiness. Virtue seems to be the only element of happiness that Socrates can allow, if he takes virtue to be a non-instrumental good.

Though virtue may help us to adapt our desires to the circumstances, the adaptive conception of happiness does not agree completely with the view that virtue is identical to happiness. The cardinal virtues are only one means to secure adaptation of desires. I might have well-adapted desires by nature, because I happen to want very little, even though I do not see that adaptation is the most rational course of action; or my past experience may have reduced my desires to a minimal level. If happiness consists in adaptation, I am as happy if my desires are adapted to circumstances by these routes as I would be if they were adapted by practical reason. If, however, we believe that virtue is identical to happiness, only the adaptation that results from practical reason can belong to a happy life.

In Plato's early dialogues Socrates does not choose between these two accounts of the relation between virtue, happiness, and adaptation. These dialogues do not make it clear that he needs to choose between the two accounts. The *Gorgias* presents claims about adaptation and about virtue without saying how they affect each other. The Cynics do not seem to make the choices any clearer. We might take Diogenes to believe that nothing matters except virtue. From this point of view, he does not care whether his actions are offensive, shocking, bizarre, anti-social, unhealthy, or dangerous. These considerations do not matter to him once he has decided that only virtue matters; if he gave way to them he would be going back on his principles.

If we argue against him by suggesting that a conception of happiness with all these strange implications must have gone wrong somewhere, he might reply that our attempt to argue against his conception of the ultimate end is misguided. Choices (he might say) are reasonable in the light of our ends, but our ends must simply be chosen. Virtue and happiness consist in living with complete integrity in the light of our ultimate commitments.

Here we might find in Diogenes an expression of the 'existentialist' interpretation of Socrates' attitude to virtue. It denies that we can have any reason for pursuing virtue, as Socrates conceives it, rather than the vices opposed to the cardinal virtues. If the only virtue consists in integrity, it may not be very close to common views about the content of the virtues; in fact, it may have no specific content at all. This defence of Socratic integrity raises doubts about the first steps of Socratic moral inquiry. Socrates criticizes common moral beliefs, but he also relies on them to identify the outlines of the different virtues. But if we try Diogenes' defence of the view that virtue is all that matters, we may find ourselves moving away from the virtues as Socrates conceives them.

Cynicism, therefore, captures two distinct elements in Socrates' views about virtue and happiness. We might find Diogenes attractive either because of his adaptation or because of his integrity. From one point of view, he has achieved happiness because he is free from anxiety about unfulfilled desires. From another point of view, he is happy because he achieves what matters most, sticking firmly to his virtuous resolution without being distracted by unimportant external goods. Neither conception of happiness captures all that Socrates wants to say about the virtues, but each captures one element in Socrates' position.

40. An Objection to Cynicism

This account of Cynicism suggests that its attitude to external goods supports both an adaptive conception of happiness and the identification of virtue with happiness. But the conclusion is open to doubt. For we may reasonably doubt whether we can consistently regard virtue as the only non-instrumental good. The cardinal virtues try to achieve certain specific non-moral results that secure different ranges of external goods. Brave people do not simply try to act fearlessly; they face danger in order to protect themselves or their friends, or to secure safety and peace for their community. Just people do not simply try to restrain their acquisitive desires; they try to make sure that they do what they owe to other people, so that other people get what they deserve. What would be the point of trying to achieve these results if they were not good results? It is not clear why the virtuous person should be so concerned about them and make such efforts to secure them if they are not worth securing.

This argument also suggests that if we regard virtue as a non-instrumental good, we cannot accept an adapative conception of happiness. For the virtues do not infallibly secure the good results that they aim at; they are subject to fortune and to external circumstances. Hence virtuous people are liable to frustrated desires that they could avoid if they cared less about the virtues. Hence virtue is not the most effective way to achieve the adaptation of desires to circumstances.

According to this argument, Diogenes' view that external goods are worthless is incompatible with virtue. Virtuous people might choose to live in a barrel if any higher level of comfort would require, say, inappropriate compromises with unjust rulers. But they could not share his view that the external goods that they give up are worthless, so that he sacrifices nothing that is really worth having. The convictions about value that Diogenes offers to explain his way of life are inconsistent with the virtuous outlook. We should therefore conclude that his convictions express an adaptive conception of happiness that conflicts with belief in the non-instrumental goodness of virtue.

If this is a legitimate criticism of Diogenes, it is a legitimate criticism of Socrates as well. His claim that virtue is the only good is intended to show that he takes virtue seriously; it ought to explain why the Athenians ought to be concerned about virtue before external goods. What better reason could they have than the fact that virtue is the only good? On closer examination, however, the exclusive claim about the goodness of virtue turns out to be incompatible with a genuine commitment to virtue. A genuine commitment to virtue requires us to value the external ends that the virtuous person aims at; we do not seem to value them appropriately if we do not think they are goods and we do not aim at them as elements in happiness.

The existentialist interpretation avoids these objections by denying that the virtues require us to make any serious efforts to achieve specific external results. If virtue simply consists in the unwavering commitment to our ultimate values, whatever they may be, it does not require us to believe that any particular sort of external result is worth trying to achieve. Instead of believing that the point of virtue consists partly in aiming at these specific results, we might argue that specific types of action are significant only because they develop or display one's unwavering commitment and one's adaptability to circumstances. A labour of Heracles, for instance, might be praised not because it was worthwhile to have the Augean stables clean, but because Heracles' successful performance of this task displayed his strength and adaptability. But this purely athletic conception of virtue does not match the common view that a virtue involves real concern for a specific type of result.[27]

These questions about the goodness of virtue and of external goods are the starting point of Stoic arguments about virtue and the preferred indifferents. These arguments try to maintain and to defend the claim in the *Euthydemus* that virtue is the only good. But the same questions are also relevant to Plato's views on virtue and happiness. Though he does not argue that the belief that virtue is the only good is incompatible with the belief that it is a non-instrumental good, he may recognize the conflict between these beliefs. For in the *Republic* he does not maintain that virtue is purely instrumental to happiness, or that it is the only good, or that it is sufficient for happiness, or that happiness consists in adaptation. Whereas *Republic* i ends with the claim that justice is sufficient for happiness, the rest of the dialogue does not repeat this claim. In the *Philebus* Plato discusses both extreme hedonism and extreme anti-hedonism, and develops a composite conception of the good that rules out both hedonist and adaptive views. Here Plato makes it clear that the sense in which the good is 'sufficient' (*hikanon*) cannot be identified with the sense in which the Cynic claims to be self-sufficient and independent of external circumstances.

In all these cases, then, Plato abandons the Socratic claims that allow a Cynic to argue for Diogenes' attitude to external goods. *Republic* ii considers a situation that might invite a Cynic response; the just person suffers for being just and loses external goods. From the Cynic point of view, what he loses is worthless, and nothing to regret. But the *Republic* does not take this position. Plato argues at length to show that justice is preferable to injustice, even if the just person suffers for being just and the unjust person is well supplied with external goods; but he never suggests that the just person has lost nothing worth having, or that justice by itself makes him happy.

Plato may be aware of the Cynic use of Socrates' arguments. He does not argue that the Cynics have misunderstood Socrates. On the contrary, he implicitly agrees with the Cynics' understanding of him, or at least agrees that it legitimately develops a Socratic line of argument. To avoid the Cynic conclusions, he affirms that virtue is to be chosen for its own sake and refrains from affirming that virtue is sufficient for happiness, or that virtue is the only good. The Cynic arguments make Plato aware of the aspects of Socratic ethics that need to be reconsidered. Plato and Aristotle defend the ethical position that results from taking virtue as seriously as Socrates takes it, but does not offer the opening that Socrates offers to Cynic arguments.

---

[27] See Adam Smith on the Stoics, §182.

5

PLATO

41. Plato's Reflexions on Socrates

Aristotle takes some of the dialogues in which Socrates is the main speaker to express the views of Plato rather than Socrates. If we arrange the dialogues in accordance with his division, we can discern a reasonably plausible order of the dialogues, and a reasonably intelligible development in the views that 'Socrates' (the speaker) maintains in them. Though a detailed defence of these claims raises complicated questions about the Platonic corpus as a whole, we will form a reasonable view of Plato's views on Socratic ethics if we take the *Phaedo, Republic, Symposium, Phaedrus*, and *Philebus* as our main sources of Plato's views.

Plato may not have intended a sharp division between the dialogues that expound Socrates' views and those that develop his own views without any explicit Socratic precedent. The *Protagoras, Gorgias*, and *Meno* might plausibly be taken to mark a transition between exposition of the Socratic position and the introduction of a distinctively Platonic position. If we want to understand Plato's ethical views, we may usefully compare the *Republic* with the Socratic dialogues. The structure and style of the *Republic* encourages this comparison. For Book i is a short dialogue in the manner of the earlier dialogues, designed to introduce the main dialogue, which reflects at length on the themes introduced in Book i. Plato signals that he intends us to think about the issues raised in the Socratic dialogues, by providing us with a short dialogue that recalls some of these issues, but from his later point of view.[1]

We have seen that the one-sided Socratics develop Socrates' views in different directions. The Socratic positions that they consider are recognizable in Plato's early dialogues. If Cynic and Cyrenaic views go back to Plato's contemporaries, we should suppose that he writes the middle and late dialogues against a background of conflicting interpretations and evaluations of Socrates. According to the *Republic*, some identify the good with pleasure, others with intelligence (R. 505b). Plato mentions these two candidates again in the *Philebus* (11b–c). These descriptions capture the Cyrenaic and the Cynic attitudes to virtue, pleasure, and happiness. Plato disagrees with both of them. If we suppose that he has these opposed Socratic positions in mind, we may reasonably ask why he takes his views to be preferable to

---

[1] Some have argued, unconvincingly, that *Republic* i is an independent earlier dialogue, later added to the *Republic*. See Vlastos, *SIMP* 248–51. For further references see Irwin, *PE* 376.

those of Aristippus and Diogenes, and whether he can reasonably claim that they are more genuinely Socratic in spirit.

This debate about Socrates and about ethics in the Socratic spirit introduces later ethical debates. Aristotle agrees with Plato on the main points on which Plato disagrees with the one-sided Socratics. But Plato and Aristotle do not dominate later reflexion on Socrates or later ethical theory. On the contrary, the one-sided Socratics influence the main Hellenistic ethical theories; the Stoics seem to derive more from the Cynics, and the Epicureans from the Cyrenaics, than either school seems to derive from Plato or Aristotle. To see whether the Stoics or Epicureans are right, or both schools are wrong, we should ask why Plato rejects the one-sided positions, and why Aristotle agrees with him.

42. The Scope of Plato's Ethical Thought

Socrates is the first moral philosopher, but Plato is the first philosopher who places moral philosophy within a broader conception of philosophy. Aristotle notices that, whereas Socrates confines himself to ethics, Plato tries to connect Socratic concerns to more general issues in metaphysics and epistemology. These broader philosophical interests make it appropriate to discuss Plato's views in meta-ethics, especially the metaphysics and epistemology of morality, and in moral psychology.

Aristotle tells us that Plato treated the forms, the objects of Socrates' search for definitions, as non-sensible and separated from sensibles. He also makes it clear that Plato disagrees with Socrates in moral psychology; for though he criticizes Socrates for his denial of incontinence and for his general neglect of the role of the non-rational part of the soul in virtue, he never criticizes Plato on this point. We may reasonably follow Aristotle's lead, and explore the significance of these differences between Socrates and Plato.

On Socrates' views about virtue and happiness, we have less explicit guidance from Aristotle. But he offers an important implicit suggestion. In his view, the virtuous person correctly chooses virtue and virtuous action for their own sake, since they are non-instrumental goods. We have seen that Socrates does not express this view about virtue. Plato, however, expresses it clearly in *Republic* ii, where the interlocutors ask Socrates to prove that justice is worth choosing for itself, and not only for its consequences. If we compare Aristotle with the Socratic dialogues, on the one hand, and with the *Republic*, on the other hand, we see that on this point he agrees with Plato against Socrates.

With the help of these suggestions from Aristotle, we can now try to see why Plato departs from Socrates on these points. To understand his disagreements with Socrates, we have to assemble evidence from different dialogues, since Plato does not set it all out in a continuous treatment of ethical problems. His longest treatment of central ethical questions is contained in the *Republic*, but this treatment is not self-contained. We will understand it better if we consider passages from other dialogues that help to explain some of the important moves in the course of the *Republic*. After setting out Plato's main disagreements with Socrates, we will turn (in §57) to a more consecutive discussion of the *Republic*.[2]

---

[2] I do not intend to rely on any claims about the relative date of the dialogues I will discuss. Though I believe the *Phaedrus* and the *Philebus* are later than the *Republic*, I believe they may properly be used to clarify the *Republic*. They

43. Definitions and Disputes

According to Aristotle, Plato developed his theory of non-sensible, separated forms in response to Socrates' search for definitions in ethics, because he believed that Socratic definitions could not apply to sensible, and hence changeable, things (*Met.* 987a32–b10; 1078b12–1079a4; 1086a37–b11). What difference do these Platonic claims make to Socrates' inquiries into the virtues?

Though Socrates believes his inquiries are important, he also believes they fail. He never offers an account of a virtue that he announces as a correct answer to his question about what the virtue is. He reaches descriptions of the virtues that he apparently takes to be correct, so that, for instance, he regards all the virtues as the knowledge of good and evil; but he does not claim that any of them is a correct definition. Why is Socrates unsuccessful?

To estimate his prospects for success, we need to see what he expects from a definition. One of his conditions is epistemological. In the *Euthyphro* he asks for a 'pattern' or 'standard' (*paradeigma*) for judging that something is or is not an instance of piety. He seems to assume that such an account must eliminate 'disputed terms' (*Eu.* 7c10–d5). If we can describe a virtue only in terms that we cannot apply to particular cases without causing dispute, we have not found a paradigm.

This condition helps to explain why Socrates does not claim to have found definitions when he offers descriptions such as 'bravery is knowledge of what is to be feared and faced with confidence' (*La.* 199d1–2; *Pr.* 360d4–5), or the descriptions in the *Gorgias* of the virtues as types of psychic order (*Gorg.* 506e2–507b8). Further dispute might still arise about what is to be feared, or about what counts as the right order; these disputes would need to be settled by appeal to our judgments about fine, just, and good things, but those are the areas that are subject to dispute.

The *Euthyphro* points out that in some areas we can eliminate disputes about the application of a term by appealing to measurement. The *Protagoras* suggests that this method of eliminating disputes is open to us in ethics. Plato speaks of the 'measuring craft' that settles questions about goodness and badness by estimating present and future pleasures.

Socrates, therefore, seems to aim at reductive definitions of moral properties; they should reduce them to non-moral properties by eliminating the terms that cannot be applied without the use of moral judgments. Without these reductive accounts, proposed definitions offer only what Price later calls 'mere synonymies', defining one moral property only by reference to others, which have to be defined in turn by reference to it. Reductive definitions would reduce moral properties to those that Moore calls 'natural' properties, intending these to be non-evaluative and non-normative.[3]

These divisions of properties and terms (natural v. non-natural, moral v. non-moral, evaluative v. non-evaluative, normative v. non-normative) are not equivalent. But Socrates' remarks are too brief to make it reasonable for us to inquire more precisely into what he has in mind. It is enough for present purposes to notice that he assumes that we need

may express views that Plato has not explicitly formulated, but inarticulately takes for granted in the *Republic*. I have not said much about the ethical discussions in the *Laws*. For a brief discussion of Plato's later ethical views see Irwin, *PE*, chs. 19–20, and for a fuller discussion see Bobonich, *PUR*.

[3] See Price, *RPQM* 141; Moore, *PE* 93.

something more informative than a circle of definitions clarifying one moral property only by reference to others. Many who have sought definitions of moral properties have accepted this assumption. In saying that moral properties are an area of dispute, Socrates suggests that we can resolve moral disputes only by eliminating distinctively moral terms, and that we cannot find a suitable paradigm until we have done this.

44. Why Explanation Requires Non-sensible Forms

This epistemological demand on acceptable definitions already makes it difficult to find definitions of moral properties. But Socrates makes his task even more difficult by insisting that correct definitions must also meet his explanatory condition. In his view, an account of the property F must reveal the property that explains why F things are F. As the *Euthyphro* explains, we might find an account that is extensionally adequate but still fails to reveal the explanatory property; that is why 'the pious is what all the gods love' is not an adequate definition of the pious.

Plato notices that the explanatory demand makes the epistemological demand harder to satisfy. The explanatory demand involves a counterfactual test that appeals to change. If the gods were to love something different, and nothing else changed, it would not follow that what is pious also changes; for we assume that it is something about the pious itself that explains why the gods love it. Hence the account that Socrates rejects seems to meet the epistemological condition, but to fail the explanatory condition. Similarly, we might find an extensionally adequate account (let us suppose) of justice by identifying it with the provisions of Athenian law; such an account would also meet the epistemological condition. But it would not give us an explanatory account. Even if all and only the provisions of Athenian law were just, it would not follow that justice is to be defined as what Athenian law prescribes; for if Athenian law changed, and nothing else changed, it would not follow that what is just would change too. We assume, as we assumed about piety, that facts about just actions (etc.) themselves explain why just laws are just, and so we assume that changes in the law do not by themselves imply changes in what is just. The explanatory condition, therefore, requires us to reject proposed definitions that would be satisfactory if we required only extensional adequacy.

Reflexion on Socrates' explanatory condition, therefore, might reasonably lead us to doubt whether his epistemological condition is reasonable. The most plausible candidates for reductive definitions meeting the epistemological condition do not seem to satisfy the explanatory condition. Plato might reasonably conclude that we cannot expect a definition to satisfy both conditions and that we need to choose between them. Plato decides that the explanatory condition is more fundamental, and that we ought to give up the epistemological demand for a reductive definition that eliminates evaluative terms.

This is why Aristotle believes that Plato develops his account of non-sensible forms in response to Socrates' search for definitions of ethical properties. In the *Phaedo* Plato introduces the 'just itself' and all the other essences that concern Socrates, and claims that they are inaccessible to the senses (*Phd.* 65d4–5, 74a11, 75c10–d3, 76d7–9). A correct account of the forms must provide a satisfactory explanation of why things have the relevant properties. Being beautiful cannot be the same as being bright coloured, because being bright coloured is not the property that makes things beautiful (100c9–e3). Similarly, the fact that children bury their parents does not make this particular action of these children burying their parents fine; for that fact might equally be found in a shameful action (if, for instance, the children had murdered their parents first).

This explanatory demand helps us to understand Plato's repeated claim that whereas the form of F cannot be both F and not F, sensible Fs are both F and not-F, or (as he also expresses it) change from being F to being not-F. The many beautifuls (justs, equals, and so on) are both beautiful and ugly (R. 479a5–b10). In contrast to the F things that are both F and not F, the form of F must be free from this compresence of opposites (Symp. 210e5–211a5; cf. HMa. 291d1–3). Even if we believe that necessarily the gods love only what is pious, the god-beloved changes from being pious to being impious. If the gods were to love unjust action, and if unjust action is necessarily impious, god-beloved action would be impious; but the pious itself cannot undergo this change from being pious to being impious.

The explanatory role of the forms helps to explain why Plato claims that forms, in contrast to sensibles, are free of change and flux. The form of F must be free of flux, not liable to variation between being F and being not-F, whereas sensible Fs are liable to this variation (Phd. 78d–e). Sensible properties such as being what the gods love, or being prescribed by Athenian law, are liable to variation between being pious or just and being impious or unjust. Plato's explanatory demand suggests that the change he has in mind includes counterfactual change as well as actual change. If Athenian laws changed so that they rewarded murder rather than punishing it, and nothing else changed, Athenian laws would become unjust rather than just, but justice would not require us to reward murder. Even if actual Athenian law coincided with the demands of justice, we could not identify justice with the demands of Athenian law; for Athenian law is subject to change from being just to being unjust, whereas justice is not subject to these changes.

45. Appropriate Definitions

If Plato takes his claims about non-sensible and unchanging forms to follow from the acceptance of Socrates' explanatory condition and the rejection of Socrates' epistemological condition for definitions, we would expect him not to reject attempted definitions that fail to reduce moral properties to non-evaluative properties. Moreover, we might expect him to be readier than Socrates is to accept definitions that meet the explanatory but not the epistemological condition.

Our expectations are fulfilled by the progress of the argument in the Republic. At the outset Socrates rejects an account of justice as telling the truth and returning what we have received. This property of returning what we have received offers us a reductive definition, since no moral dispute enters into whether we have received something and whether we are returning it. But the property changes from being just to being unjust; it is unjust to return our friend's sword to him if he has gone mad and is threatening to kill himself (R. 331c7–9). Plato assumes that necessarily a just person does not inflict undeserved harm on others and that we would be doing this if we gave back our friend's sword in these circumstances.

Thrasymachus' intervention draws our attention to questions about the search for reductive definitions. For Thrasymachus wants 'perspicuous and accurate' (336c6–d4) accounts that eliminate such terms as 'due' or 'appropriate'. If we could satisfy Thrasymachus' demand, we would find accounts that would eliminate disputes by reducing moral to non-evaluative properties. The search for perspicuity and exactness seems to underlie Socrates' search for definitions of moral properties as well.

In *Republic* i Socrates does not comment directly on Thrasymachus' demand, and, since he offers no definition of justice, he does not make it clear whether or not he thinks he ought to satisfy it. But he certainly does not endorse the demand for a perspicuous and accurate account that would satisfy Thrasymachus. He seems to be sympathetic to Simonides' account of justice as 'rendering what is due to each person' (331e3–4). He does not say that this is an adequate account, but he does not rule it out on the ground that it contains a disputed evaluative term ('due').

We can reach a more positive conclusion, however, if we consider Book iv. This marks a sharp contrast with the inconclusive Socratic dialogues, which fail to reach accounts of the cardinal virtues. In Book iv Plato claims to define all of them as conditions of the well-ordered soul. He takes these definitions to satisfy the explanatory condition; he claims that virtuous acts are virtuous because they are appropriately related to good order in the soul. But if he still accepted the epistemological condition, he would not accept these definitions. For they do not eliminate disputed moral terms. Plato's account of justice has the same form as the Simonidean account. Justice involves 'doing one's own', one's proper function, and thereby 'having one's own', what is due to one (433e6–434a1). The explanations of 'doing one's own' and 'having one's own' imply that, like the Simonidean account, Plato's accounts contain moral terms, and so do not satisfy Thrasymachus' demand for perspicuous and accurate accounts.

The same is true of the other virtues that Plato discusses in *Republic* iv. Bravery is described as preservation of right belief under the control of the wisdom in the rational part; temperance is concord between the parts under the control of the wisdom in the rational part. Each of these accounts mentions the rational part and its wisdom, which is its knowledge of the good. Similarly, justice consists in each part doing its own work under the control of the wisdom in the rational part. These accounts would eliminate moral terms only if we could specify knowledge of the good in non-moral terms; and to do this we would need an account of the good in non-moral terms. Plato says nothing to suggest that he can provide such an account; nor does he suggest that he needs such an account in order to give an adequate account of the virtues.

It is not surprising, then, that Plato does not repeat Socrates' acknowledgment of failure in the search for definitions. He believes that he succeeds, not because he believes he can do just what Socrates was trying to do, but because he believes Socrates was trying to do what could not be done. Given that Socrates expected acceptable accounts to be both explanatory and reductive, he was right to think he failed to find accounts of the virtues. But Plato concludes that we should look for explanatory but non-reductive accounts, and he offers such accounts in the *Republic*.

On this point Plato agrees with Price and Moore in rejecting attempts to define moral properties as 'natural' properties (if natural properties are understood as non-normative properties). But he does not believe moral properties are simple or indefinable. Price and Moore reach this conclusion partly because they believe that a definition must analyse the definiendum into simpler elements. This demand for simplicity is not exactly the same as Socrates' demand for the elimination of disputed evaluative terms, but it has the same effect; for Price believes that if we use further evaluative terms in defining an evaluative property, we are offering a 'mere synonymy' rather than a proper definition. Plato implicitly answers this objection. In his view, an account that captures the appropriate explanatory role of the relevant property meets any reasonable condition on definitions. If we insist on the elimination of disputed terms, we cannot find accounts of moral properties.

With these arguments about non-sensible forms Plato formulates a meta-ethical position to support moral inquiry. Socrates' inquiries depend on meta-ethical presuppositions; Plato makes some of these presuppositions explicit, and tries to identify the metaphysical and epistemological commitments we undertake in looking for the moral properties that explain why things are good, just, fine, and so on. Aristotle correctly attributes this meta-ethical interest to Plato, taking it to be the source of the reflexions that result in the theory of non-sensible forms. While Plato's interest in the metaphysics and epistemology of the forms goes beyond its meta-ethical sources, his meta-ethical interests make him the founder of meta-ethical inquiry, and in particular of a distinctively realist, non-naturalist, non-reductive doctrine of the nature of moral properties.

46. Non-rational Desires

Aristotle mentions the theory of separated forms as a Platonic development of Socratic doctrine; Plato agrees with Socrates about the importance of forms in Socratic inquiry, but differs from Socrates in claiming that the forms are separate from sensibles. In moral psychology Aristotle claims that Plato disagrees more directly with Socrates. Aristotle criticizes Socrates for identifying the virtues with knowledge, and thereby eliminating the non-rational part of the soul, passion, and character (MM 1182a15–23); in rejecting a non-rational part of the soul, he makes the virtues 'pointless' (1183b8–18).[4] Aristotle praises Plato for recognizing a non-rational part of the soul (1182a23–6).

Aristotle sees that Socrates' cognitive account of the virtues depends on his rejection of the possibility of incontinence, and, more generally, on his rejection of non-rational human motives; if he did not reject them, he could not reasonably resist Protagoras' suggestion that virtue requires the training of non-rational desires, and so cannot be confined to knowledge (Pr. 352a4–c7). If, then, Plato recognizes a non-rational part of the soul, he should reject Socrates' views on incontinence, and should not hold a purely cognitive account of the virtues.

The main discussion of rational and non-rational desires appears in Republic iv. Though the Gorgias anticipates the discussion of parts, and the reference to these parts in the description of the different virtues (Gorg. 493b1–3; 505b), it does not argue as clearly for the partition of the soul. We may reasonably turn to the Republic, then, to see how and why Plato disagrees with Socrates.

---

4 On the MM see §66n3.

It is relatively easy to see how he disagrees with Socrates.[5] He remarks that sometimes we are thirsty, and yet refuse (or 'are unwilling', *ouk ethelein*, 439c2) to drink, because of some reason that inhibits us from drinking (439d1, *ek logismou*). He does not suggest that in such cases our belief that we ought not to drink or that it is better not to drink invariably controls our desire or determines our action. On the contrary, he suggests that our judgment about the good does not control us. He mentions the unfortunate Leontius, whose urge (*epithumia*) to look at corpses moved him to action even though he thought it was bad and shameful (439e6–440a3). Leontius does not provide a direct counter-example to Socrates, since the conflict he suffers involves two of his non-rational parts, the spirited and the appetitive parts. But Plato's comment on this example generalizes the point so that it also applies to a conflict between the rational part and the appetitive part (440a8–b7). He does not take it for granted that the desires of the rational part will always move us to action against the tendency of our non-rational desires.

Since Plato's description of these examples implies that it is possible for an agent to believe that one action is better than another, but to choose the one believed to be worse, he commits himself to rejecting Socrates' claim, defended in the *Protagoras*, that such choices are impossible. That is why he warns us not to assume that all our desires are for goods (438a1–5). The thesis that Plato questions is the Socratic thesis that all desire is for the good; Plato notices cases in which an agent acts on a desire that is not flexible in relation to beliefs about the good.

47. Why a Tripartite Soul?

While these points about the opposition between Plato and Socrates are relatively clear (though not wholly indisputable), it is more difficult to see why Plato disagrees with Socrates. Socrates recognizes cases that we intuitively describe as cases of incontinence; but he argues that this description embodies an error, and that there are no real cases of incontinence. Does Plato simply assert that there are such cases because they are intuitively obvious? That would not be much of an argument against Socrates' claim that the assumptions underlying our intuitive description are false.

If Plato were simply saying that incontinence is possible, despite Socrates' denial, it would be surprising that he takes so long to say it. For he embeds his remarks on incontinence in a division of the soul into three 'parts' or 'kinds'. We might reasonably expect Plato to use this tripartiton to explain how incontinence is possible, rather than simply to assert that it is possible. But to see how it might explain incontinence, we need to see what the tripartition means. Why should we assign different desires to three different parts?

Different mental activities do not require different parts of the soul (cf. 436a8–b3) unless they are contrary to each other; contrary activities require different explanatory principles (cf. *Phd.* 96c–97b, 100c–101c). To find the relevant kind of contrariety between desires Plato distinguishes those that rest on reasoning from those that are simply impulses towards certain satisfactions, and from those that display anger (R. 439c9–e4).

---

[5] Carone, 'Stoic', denies that Plato disagrees with Socrates on these points.

Many readers have been willing to accept Plato's two-way division between rational and non-rational desires, but unwilling to accept his three-way division into three parts, rational, spirited, and appetitive. The spirited (*thumoeides*) part has aroused most suspicion. It strikes many readers as being intrusive and ill-conceived; at first it seems to include only anger, but then it expands to love of honour. Neither of these descriptions seems to yield a class of desires parallel to the rational and non-rational. Some have suggested that Plato simply fabricates this part to provide an intra-psychic parallel to the three classes in the ideal state of the *Republic*.[6]

We may form a more favourable view of Plato's tripartition, however, if we attend more carefully to his description of the different parts. The mark of the rational part is not simply the fact that its desires depend on some sort of reasoning; for instrumental reasoning about how to satisfy hunger or thirst does not make the resulting desire for food or drink a rational desire. Though Plato does not make this point explicit in Book iv, he insists on it in Books viii–ix, in his description of the different kinds of unjust souls corresponding to the deviant constitutions. The oligarchic person engages in frequent and effective instrumental reasoning about how to make money; but in confining the rational part to this role, he subjects it to the desires of the appetitive part (553d1–8). The mere fact that he has engaged in instrumental reasoning does not make the resulting desires into desires of the rational part. The oligarchic person fails a condition for rational desire that Plato has already stated without explanation; we act on desires of the rational part only when the desires are based on a conception of what is good for the whole soul and for each part (442c6–8). This holistic, optimizing attitude belongs to desires that are flexible in relation to our conception of the ultimate good; hence, we may say that they involve eudaemonist rationality, as Socrates conceives it.

This description of the rational part helps us to understand the kind of 'contrariety' that is necessary for a division into parts. Plato does not believe that every sort of conflict between desires creates the relevant sort of contrariety; the desire for food and the desire for sleep may conflict if I am both very hungry and very sleepy, but Plato does not assign them to different parts. We come closer to Plato's idea of contrariety if we think of our forming desires that embody objections to other desires. To form an objection, we need something more than a mere aversion; we also need to have something against the desire we are averse to, so that we criticize it and reject it. We might, then, suggest that contrariety towards a desire requires an evaluative attitude towards it.

If this is what Plato has in mind, his tripartition is intelligible, and his description of the spirited part appears less arbitrary. For he notices that evaluative attitudes to desires are not confined to those that rest on the holistic outlook of optimizing practical reason. We can usefully distinguish criticisms based on some consideration of good and bad from those that are based on global practical reason. This distinction makes room for the distinctive outlook of the spirited part. To be angry and ashamed at our desires and at the actions they move us to, we need not evaluate them from the global perspective; we need only have some conception of good and bad beyond the satisfaction of this or that appetite.

---

[6] See, e.g., Penner, 'Thought'.

The suggestion that the spirited part embodies an evaluative, but incompletely evaluative, point of view, is illustrated by a remark of Aristotle's. He suggests that the spirited part hears the instructions of reason, but incompletely, like a hasty servant who rushes off to carry out an order before he has heard all of it. When he hears 'Bring me . . .', he does not wait to hear 'a pen', but, completing the instruction wrongly, goes to bring a book (*MM* 1202b12–21; *EN* 1149a25–b1).

We can grasp the same point by a comparison with one of Plato's bipartite divisions. In *Republic* x he discusses perceptual illusions in which (e.g.) the stick still appears bent to me, though I also believe, on the basis of relevant evidence, that it is really straight (*R.* 602c7–603a6). Here he contrasts the immediate visual impression, insensitive to evidence about the context, with the belief based on all the relevant evidence.[7] In this two-way contrast Plato does not mention any intermediate case. But reflexion on his principle of division suggests that he ought to allow the possibility of an intermediate case. For we might revise our initial impressions on the basis of some relevant evidence without considering everything relevant; hence we might form a belief that is sensitive to some evidence and insensitive to other evidence. The spirited part is partially sensitive in this way to evaluative considerations relevant to the acceptance and rejection of desires. Even though Plato sometimes uses a bipartite instead of a tripartite division, the underlying principle of division leaves room for a tripartition.

But even if a tripartition is intelligible, why is it relevant? Why not simply distinguish simple appetites (altogether insensitive to evaluation) from desires that respond (to whatever degree) to evaluation? Plato's tripartition is reasonable if he seeks to isolate a class of desires and motivational states that are partly responsive and partly non-responsive. This class includes many emotions that are relevant to morality. As Plato sees, anger, pride, self-esteem, and pity are not simple impulses. If I am hungry or cold, I feel the same way even if I reflect that I ought not to be hungry (I have just eaten quite enough) or cold. But anger is not quite the same; if I am angry at you for having kicked me, but I come to believe you did not kick me and so you are not an appropriate object of my anger, I will no longer be angry at you, though some other emotion may be left.[8] This does not mean my anger will respond to all the relevant considerations; even if I know this is not a good time to be angry, or that what you did is not important enough to be angry about, I may still be angry.

Recognition of incomplete evaluative outlooks is relevant for understanding both emotions and virtues. The desires of the appetitive part are similar to those in non-rational animals, in so far as they do not respond to considerations of better and worse. But Plato sees that considerations of better and worse are not confined to the global point of view of the rational part. Some of these considerations may be embodied in motives of the spirited part; this embodiment is comparatively rigid, in so far as the desires do not respond to all the relevant rational considerations.

---

[7] Plato describes them as two cases of belief (*doxazein*), 603a1–2.

[8] Butler explores this general point about emotions in his discussion of resentment in Sermon viii. In viii 5 he distinguishes purely instinctive and non-evaluative 'sudden anger' from anger, including some cases of 'hasty anger', that depends on some evaluation. As I understand Plato, Butler's 'sudden anger' does not belong to the spirited part, but some 'hasty anger' does. Bernard's note ad loc. mentions Hobbes as a source for Butler's distinction, but does not mention Plato. Against Bernard's suggestion that the NT use of '*thumos*' and '*orgē*' matches Butler's distinction see Kittel, *TDNT* iii 168.

The rigidity of spirited motives is relevant to the moral training of people who, in Plato's view, are not capable of guiding their life correctly by the outlook of the rational part. If their rational part is easily confused, and likely to reach the wrong conclusions, it may be better if they are controlled by the more rigid motives of the spirited part; for these motives may be trained to retain sounder views than the rational part would reach on its own account.

The spirited part has this role not only in people—such as the auxiliaries in Plato's state—whose rational part is incapable of guiding correctly, but also in people with an enlightened rational part. For we may recognize on some occasions that our reasoning is likely to be mistaken on other occasions—if, for instance, we have to decide what to do at very short notice in an emergency. In such cases it may be sensible to decide to allow our spirited emotions to guide us in the situation we foresee. If the rational part guides one's life as a whole, it may still decide not to impose its guidance on each particular occasion.

Plato may reasonably claim, therefore, that his tripartition of the soul allows a more complex and more plausible account of motivation than we can construct on the basis of Socrates' views, or on the basis of a simple division between rational and non-rational desires. The spirited part makes it especially clear why someone who shares Socrates' belief in the moral importance of practical reason need not be reluctant to allow desires that are not wholly responsive to practical reason. In the *Protagoras* Socrates suggested that if we recognize such desires, we allow knowledge to be dragged around like a slave. In the *Gorgias* Plato recognizes non-rational desires, but suggests only that they need to be restrained and controlled. In the *Republic* his view is more qualified. Some non-rational desires need to be restrained, but others help us to embody the control of practical reason. On this basis Plato might reasonably claim to be defending Socrates' claim that virtue requires the rule of practical reason, by giving up his over-simplified claims about the relation of reason to desire.

48. Why Parts of the Soul?

We have now seen why Plato has a reasonable argument against the Socratic rejection of non-rational desires, and why his tripartition of desires is not arbitrary, but an important element in his argument. But we have not yet explained why he represents his division as a partition. He does not simply classify desires into these three different types. He also ascribes to each part some of the features of a subject of desires; for some mental conflicts are described as disputes between the parts of the soul, as though these were somewhat similar to disputes between different people. How seriously should we take this aspect of the tripartition?

If Plato treated each part as an agent, he would apparently be duplicating a problem rather than solving it. If we are trying to understand the relations between desires that constitute an agent, we do not seem to make much progress by treating them as relations between agents; for we are presupposing the relations that we are trying to understand. This objection does not apply, however, if each part is a simplified agent that results from abstracting certain elements from an actual agent.[9]

---

[9] Bobonich, *PUR*, ch. 3, provides an illuminating treatment of the parts of the soul as agents, though he goes further in this direction than I would be inclined to go.

A non-rational part is similar to an agent in so far as it has some conception of itself. Each non-rational part can recognize the 'kinship' of reason to itself (402a3–4); hence it has some conception of itself that it can consider, to see what reason can do for it. In a well-governed soul the different parts agree about which part ought to rule (431d9–e1). Since the rational part rules in the interest of the whole soul and of each part (442c6–8), this is the basis on which each part consents to rule by the rational part. If the non-rational parts recognize that the rational part rules in their interest, they have a conception of themselves and of their interest. If we have a conception of ourselves, we refer to the past and future; we are capable of regret (in the minimal sense of displeasure at something we have done in the past, if, for instance, we have foolishly forgone some pleasure we could have had) and of fear and hope. If the non-rational parts have conceptions of themselves and some concern for themselves, they are capable of these attitudes.

If the appetitive part has desires that rest on this conception of itself, it is sometimes moved by the awareness that x is a more efficient instrumental means than y; considerations of efficiency tell me that one means fits better than another with my various appetitive aims. But we do not always act on these considerations; though we recognize that our future appetites will be satisfied if we do not satisfy this particular appetite now, we may choose to satisfy it none the less. This conflict of preferences, however, does not imply incontinence, since incontinence requires us to recognize the merits of a particular course of action apart from the strength of our desires. The appetitive part lacks a system of values that takes account of something more than the comparative strength of different desires. It lacks Butler's division between power and authority, which ascribes authority to the rational part.[10]

According to Plato, this outlook of the appetitive part is the outlook of a simplified agent who lacks the rational and holistic outlook of the ordinary rational agent. If we believe that the only function for practical reason is instrumental, revealing the means that causally contribute to satisfying non-rational desires for ends, we will believe that Plato's picture of appetitive agency is an accurate account of agency. The outlook that Plato ascribes to the appetitive part is very similar to the account of agency that we derive from the Greek Sceptics and from Hobbes and Hume. According to this account, virtue does not require practical reason to rule over non-rational passion; it simply requires the appropriate passions to be strong enough to dominate the others.

If each part of the soul has some aspects of agency, Plato's partition helps to explain some features of incontinence that provoke Socratic objections. Socrates sees that a single desire by itself does not explain an action; a particular desire makes an action intelligible because the desire itself is intelligible, fitting into some longer-term pattern of choices and actions. Socrates infers that desires make action intelligible because they ultimately aim at the agent's happiness. Plato, however, believes that happiness is not the only long-term aim that allows us to explain particular actions. The non-rational parts of the soul have some of the structure that Socrates attributes to the desires of the rational agent, but only the rational part has the structure that focusses on the agent's happiness. The tripartition of the soul suggests that incontinence is not only possible, but also—within certain limits, and from a restricted point of view—reasonable.

---

[10] See Butler, *S* ii 14.

It does not make clear, however, how incontinence happens. Does the non-rational part overcome because it is somehow too strong for the rational part? Or is the rational part somehow too lazy, so that it does not assert its position as forcefully as it should? These metaphors of strength, laziness, and forcefulness need further explanation before we can see whether Plato takes non-rational strength or rational deficiency to explain action against reason. Though he does not discuss incontinence fully, some of his remarks in the *Republic* allow us to grasp more clearly the sort of position he endorses.

49. The Tripartite Soul, Virtue, and Vice

So far we have seen how the doctrine of a tripartite soul contributes to the understanding of mental conflict, and hence to a sounder conception of moral education and the moral virtues. Plato has explained why virtue requires the co-operation of the different parts of the soul, under the control of the rational part. The control of the rational part ensures that the ends we choose on the basis of rational deliberation about the good will control our choices and actions.

This description of rational control is not yet a description of virtue. For the virtuous person makes the right choice of ends, but Plato acknowledges that some people's rational deliberation and choice of ends is mistaken. To explain the mistake, he appeals again to his account of the three parts of the soul. Since each of the non-rational parts includes a conception of itself and of its ultimate ends, the agent (the person whose soul includes all three parts) has a choice of different ways to think of himself; he may adopt a non-rational part's conception of itself as his conception of himself. Since each of the non-rational parts has a conception of itself that represents it (the part) as a sort of agent, the agent (the whole person) may think of himself as having only the sort of agency that a part recognizes.

Plato does not believe that people who accept the outlook of a non-rational part are virtuous, even though they are, in one respect, controlled by the rational part. The rational part chooses to accept the conception of one's ends that belongs to a non-rational part, and this choice is effective; to that extent the rational part controls. But since the ends that control the lives of these agents are the ends of a non-rational part, the non-rational part controls them.

Plato describes the different people who make these mistaken choices in his account of the different constitutions resulting from the collapse of the ideal state (R. viii–ix). The different individuals whose souls have the structure of the different imperfect constitutions are those who have made the wrong choices about the ends that are worth pursuing. As Plato puts it, each of the individuals has made a different decision about handing over power to one or another part (550b6, 553b–c). These decisions are made by the rational part, taking the point of view of the whole soul, but relying on a false conception of the interests of the whole soul, because it takes the outlook of a non-rational part too seriously. In handing over power to a non-rational part, the rational part abdicates responsibility and control.

This abdication is attractive to the rational part if it accepts the conception of practical reason that underlies the outlook of the non-rational parts. Their impoverished conception involves some degree of scepticism about the competence and scope of practical reason;

the only role they see for it is an instrumental role in finding ways to satisfy non-rational desires. If reason has no non-instrumental role, we cannot rely on it to answer questions about the ends we ought to pursue; we must rely on desires that are independent of reason. The non-rational parts present us with these desires. Hence someone whose rational part is unduly influenced by these views about the functions of the rational part will come to believe that his rational part ought not to be looking for any ends distinct from the ends of the non-rational parts, because it is not competent to find them. It convinces itself that Hume is right about the scope of practical reason.

Someone who sees only an instrumental role for practical reason implicitly denies that Butler's distinction between strength and authority applies to the choice of ends. In Butler's view, reasonable self-love is distinguished from the particular passions in so far as it acts on reasons for doing x that are recognized as distinct from the strength of my desire for doing x.[11] In deciding whether to do x or y, rational self-love does not simply try to register the comparative strength of my desire for x and for y, but considers the comparative merits of the actions themselves. If a strictly instrumental view of practical reason were right, there would be no comparative merits to be considered; hence there would be no basis apart from comparative strength of desires for deciding between one end and another.

We will doubt the strictly instrumental view, if we believe, contrary to Hume, that it is rational to plan for the efficient satisfaction of our desires. If we allow that this is rational, we seem to give practical reason a non-instrumental role. The efficient planner agrees that if I have desires of equal strength for A, B, and C, and if x will get me A and B, whereas y will get me only C at the cost of A and B, then I have reason to choose x over y. Hume denies that this concern for efficiency is rational; that is why he denies that it is contrary to reason to prefer the destruction of the world to the scratching of my finger. But his denial rests on his inadequately-defended view of the scope of practical reason.[12] If we believe, contrary to Hume, that concern for efficiency is rational because it rests on concern for my whole self, we have equally good reason for some discrimination among ends. If at the moment I care equally about A, B, and C, but I realize that any pursuit of C will prevent my getting A and B, whereas pursuit either of A or of B does not interfere with the pursuit of the other, why is it not rational for me to abandon C in favour of A and B? If comparative considerations can induce me to adjust my choice of means, they can also induce me to adjust my choice of ends.

The rational part finds appropriate ways to adjust desires because it has a conception of the interest of the whole soul that is distinct from the satisfaction of the desires of each part. In so far as it has a conception of a self that is independent of current desires and their strength, it has a point of view that allows it to criticize the aims of current desires. A non-rational part relies entirely on considerations that are independent of the considerations appealing to the other parts of the soul, and it gives no weight to the concerns of the other parts. The rational part, however, takes account of these concerns and their comparative merits. The fact that something satisfies our appetites is a point in its favour, whether or not it appeals to our sense of honour and shame; the fact that something appeals to our sense of honour is a point in its favour whether or not this fact is reflected in any of our appetites.

---

[11] See Butler, S ii 13.   [12] See Hume, T ii 3.3, §6, 416.

A non-rational part relies on considerations that are independent of the considerations appealing to the other parts of the soul, but the rational part takes proper account of these considerations and their comparative weight. The fact that something satisfies our appetites is a point in its favour, whether or not it appeals to our sense of honour and shame; the fact that something appeals to our sense of honour is a point in its favour whether or not this fact is reflected in any of our appetites. A non-rational part relies on considerations that are independent of the considerations appealing to the other parts of the soul, but the rational part takes proper account of these considerations and their comparative weight. The fact that something satisfies our appetites is a point in its favour, whether or not it appeals to our sense of honour and shame; the fact that something appeals to our sense of honour is a point in its favour whether or not this fact is reflected in any of our appetites. A non-rational part relies on considerations that are independent of the considerations appealing to the other parts of the soul, but the rational part takes proper account of these considerations and their comparative weight. The fact that something satisfies our appetites is a point in its favour, whether or not it appeals to our sense of honour and shame; the fact that something appeals to our sense of honour is a point in its favour whether or not this fact is reflected in any of our appetites.

The rational part, therefore, decides by considering the merits of different desires and their objects, from the point of view of the whole soul rather than a part. Once we recognize the one-sided outlook of the non-rational parts, we will see that we cannot adopt such an outlook if we are concerned with the good of the whole soul; even if we do not know what the good of the whole soul consists in, we can see that the non-rational parts are too one-sided to give us any reason for confidence in them. Plato develops these objections to the non-rational parts in order to show why we need to recognize non-instrumental practical reason. He argues that we are better off if we are guided by the rational part, since its outlook is impartial between the aims of the non-rational parts, and comprehensive in its concern for the whole soul.

This conclusion shows why Plato's partition of the soul does not simply reject Socrates' denial of incontinence. We might disagree with Socrates on the existence of non-rational desires and their potential conflict with rational desires, while still accepting his account of rational desires. Socrates says nothing to suggest that practical reason has anything more than an instrumental role in finding means to the satisfaction of a non-rational desire. In his view, the only ultimate end we pursue is happiness; for all he says, we might take our desire for happiness to be non-rational, and might take practical reason to be wholly concerned to find instrumental means to happiness. Plato's partition of the soul implies that the non-rational parts pursue distinct ultimate ends, and that the task of practical reason is to find the correct ultimate ends to pursue. Though neither Socrates nor Plato discusses these different views about practical reason formally and explicitly, it is convenient, and not too inaccurate, to summarize their differences by saying that Plato rejects Socrates' Humean conception in favour of a Butlerian conception.

Plato believes that this account of the rational part of the soul is important not only for moral psychology, but also for an account of the virtues. He believes that a well-ordered soul that is genuinely guided by practical reason will also possess the cardinal virtues, and in particular that it will be just. Contrary to Socrates, he does not affirm the unity of the virtues, since he does not identify all the cardinal virtues with wisdom. But he affirms their reciprocity. We cannot be genuinely brave unless we are guided by wisdom in the rational part of the soul, and similarly, we cannot have any of the other virtues unless our soul is guided by the rational part, with the other parts in harmony.[13] To see why Plato believes this, we need to look more closely at his conception of the virtues, and in particular at his conception of justice.

50. Why is Justice to be Chosen for Itself?

We found that in the earlier dialogues Socrates takes virtue to be sufficient for happiness, and that he affirms the unity of the virtues; hence he claims that the just person is happy. In *Republic* i he argues for this claim against Thrasymachus, but in Book ii Glaucon and Adeimantus persuade Socrates to re-open the question, because they find the answer to Thrasymachus unsatisfactory. Hence the Socrates of Book i appears to agree with the position of Socrates in the earlier dialogues, and the Socrates of *Republic* ii appears to regard that position as unsatisfactory. Is this appearance correct?

To see what is unsatisfactory about Socrates' previous answer, we need only consider Glaucon's demands on an adequate defence of justice. He expects a defence to show that justice is worth choosing both for its own sake and for its consequences, and he complains that Socrates has not shown that justice is worth choosing for its own sake (357b4–358a3). But even if Socrates answered this demand, he would not have satisfied Glaucon and Adeimantus. For they ask Socrates to prove not only that justice is some sort of non-instrumental good, but also that it is so great a non-instrumental good that the just person, simply by being just, is better off than anyone else, no matter how badly off the just person may be in other ways and no matter how well off anyone else may be in other ways (367a5–e5).

These demands have no parallel in the earlier dialogues or in *Republic* i. In these dialogues Socrates does not defend, and does not even formulate, the claim that justice is to be chosen for its own sake, apart from its consequences. All his claims about virtue are consistent with his believing that virtue is simply a causal means to the non-instrumental good of happiness, not a non-instrumental good in its own right. In describing virtue as the measuring craft that discovers what maximizes pleasure, Plato shows how virtue is instrumental to happiness. Similarly, if he accepts an adaptive conception of happiness, he treats virtue as a means to securing the appropriate match between desires and circumstances. We have found it difficult to decide whether Socrates always assumes this purely instrumental conception of virtue in relation to happiness, but we have found no reason to suppose that he explicitly rejects it. Plato, however, believes it is important to deny that justice is a purely instrumental good.

Glaucon and Adeimantus argue that this is important because it allows us to separate those who are really just from those who are only apparently just. In their view, if we value justice only for its consequences, we are not really just. If we value justice only for its

---

[13] On the unity and reciprocity of the virtues see §12.

consequences, and we find that we can secure these consequences by appearing just without the disadvantages that result from really being just, we will prefer apparent to real justice. Glaucon infers that if this is our preference we are not really just; for we do not expect a just person to be ready to abandon justice if he could gain equally good or better consequences by being unjust.

Glaucon illustrates his point by the example of Gyges' ring (359c6–360d7).[14] He considers a counterfactual situation in which someone can have all the advantages of appearing just, but also all the advantages of being actually unjust; Gyges gains all the benefits of aggression on other people, without being suspected of being unjust. Glaucon suggests that most people would prefer to be unjust, if they had Gyges' ring, and that therefore they are not really just, because they do not choose justice for its own sake.

Is this a reasonable condition for being just? Plato agrees with Kant in deciding someone's commitment to morality by considering circumstances in which the other motives that usually support one's commitment to morality do not support it; hence Kant considers cases in which honesty is not good for business, and cases in which we lack the sympathetic feelings that normally make us pleased to help other people.[15] Some of Plato's ancient critics agree with some of Kant's modern critics in rejecting this appeal to counterfactual circumstances as a test of genuine commitment to virtue. Carneades argues that in the reversal of fortune imagined by Glaucon it would be absurd to prefer the just person's situation (Cic. *Rep.* iii 27), but this does not show that we should not prefer justice in actual circumstances. As Cicero remarks, some philosophers (probably Epicureans[16]) reject the appeal to Gyges' ring since the example is fictitious, indeed impossible. Cicero replies that this objection is irrelevant,[17] but we might not agree. Why should the fact that we would choose injustice if we could have Gyges' ring show that, as things actually are, we really prefer the unjust person's life?

It is legitimate to object to counterfactual suppositions if the situations they describe are too remote from actual circumstances to allow us to see how our moral principles might apply to them, or if they differ from actual circumstances in exactly the respects that give our moral principles their point. If, for instance, Glaucon were to describe cases in which individuals are absolutely self-sufficient and invulnerable, needing no material goods for their own welfare, he might fairly be accused of removing the circumstances that give justice its point; the fact (if it is a fact) that we would not care about justice in these counterfactual circumstances would not at all show that we are not really just or that we care only about apparent justice.

Glaucon's counterfactual suppositions, however, simply make clearer, by abstraction and exaggeration, a consideration that is clearly relevant to our decisions in actual circumstances. If the only things that matter are the consequences of justice and injustice, then we have

---

[14] Cf. 612b. On what Plato says about Gyges in 359d1, and on the identity of Gyges, see Adam, *Rep.* i 126–7; Slings, *CNPP* 22–4.

[15] See Kant, *G* 397.   [16] See Holden on *Off.* iii 39.

[17] 'We put them on the rack, so that, if they reply that they would do what was expedient with the prospect of impunity, they admit that they are criminals' (Cic. *Off.* iii 39). See §158. Ambrose, *Off.* iii 30–2, repeats Cicero's story, but then adds (in 33–6) that he will not confine himself to fictions, but will offer actual Scriptural examples. He mentions David's decision to spare Saul's life (*1Kgs.* 16) and John the Baptist's decision to denounce Herod (*Mt.* 14:1–12) as two illustrations of the priority of the *honestum* over everything else (37; cf. §332).

reason to prefer injustice when it has better consequences. While the story of Gyges describes an unrealistic situation, the sort of opportunity that Gyges takes on a large scale is open to us on a smaller scale in realistic situations. For we all have the opportunity sometimes to commit injustice with impunity; and if we agree that Gyges had good reason to do what he did when the fear of punishment was removed, we must also agree that we have good reason to commit injustice when the fear of punishment is removed. The kinds of opportunities that Gyges exploits are precisely the kinds of opportunities that we expect a just person not to exploit; they are cases where we can commit injustice and get away with it. Hence anyone who thinks Gyges did the right thing in his situation shows an inadequate commitment to justice.

Is Glaucon right to suggest that most people endorse the choice that Gyges made? We might argue that he is wrong, by reminding ourselves of Glaucon's original explanation of justice by appeal to a social contract (R. 358b–359b). If we want the benefits of a peaceful and a stable society, it is reasonable for us all to agree to do what justice requires, for the sake of these consequences. But Gyges seems to neglect these benefits in his decision to act unjustly.

An account of justice that emphasizes the benefits of an agreement to observe rules of justice comes close to the views of Epicurus and Hobbes about the basis of morality in the pursuit of security. But Hobbes recognizes that Glaucon raises a reasonable question about this defence of justice. He considers the 'fool' who wonders why he should keep the agreements he has made if he can get away with violating them; though he admits the advantages to him of general observance of the rules of justice, he does not see why he should observe them.[18] The weakness of Hobbes's answer to the fool tends to support Glaucon's assumption that the benefits of agreeing to observe rules of justice do not answer his objections to people who choose justice for the sake of its consequences.

On this point justice seems to differ from the self-regarding virtues. In the case of temperance, we might argue that the 'natural' consequences of intemperate actions—the consequences that result apart from 'artificial' consequences coming from sanctions from other people or from divine rewards or punishments—show that we are better off by being temperate.[19] In the case of justice, however, the natural consequences seem to be good for other people, but not always good for the just agent. Hence an appeal to the consequences of justice seems to make injustice seem more reasonable. If we look at what actually happens, the artificial consequences of justice and injustice do not seem to change our minds; social sanctions can sometimes be avoided, and divine sanctions do not seem to operate uniformly in the present life.

Plato has made a reasonable case, therefore, to show that those who regard justice as a purely instrumental good imply that the life of the astute unjust person is better (358c5–6). The astute unjust person in actual circumstances does not take every opportunity to commit injustice; he takes the opportunities that promise him advantage with no danger of discovery. Most of us have some opportunities of this sort; in so far as we are willing to take them, we show (as Cicero says) that we really prefer to be unjust rather than just.

[18] On Epicurus see §158. On the fool see Hobbes, L 15.4.
[19] On natural v. artificial consequences see Foster, 'Mistake'; Mabbott, 'Utilitarian?'. Cf. §204.

51. How is Justice a Non-instrumental Good?

Kant uses a counterfactual argument somewhat similar to Plato's to argue that agents lack a good will and that their actions lack moral worth if they choose to do what duty requires for the sake of its good consequences. He concludes that we have a good will only if we choose 'duty for duty's sake', so that we choose what is morally required precisely because it is morally required and not because of some further aspect of it that is not essential to its being morally required.[20] Plato draws a similar conclusion to Kant's, in so far as he requires a just person to choose justice for the sake of justice. The fact that an action is just is a sufficient reason for the just person to choose it, irrespective of its other properties.

If we agree with Glaucon about what will happen if people choose justice only for the sake of its consequences, we may reasonably agree that it is better to persuade people to choose justice for itself, simply because it is just. A society of people who hold this belief might well be more stable and more cohesive than a society of people who choose justice only for its consequences. It is a further question, however, whether justice really is worth choosing for itself apart from its consequences. If we adapted the views of Critias or Mandeville, we might treat the belief that justice is to be chosen for itself as the outcome of artifice or convention.[21] Plato is sometimes ready to advocate the propagation of useful myths because of their social benefits, even if they are false.[22] If he took that view about justice, he would hold an 'opaque' two-level theory, in which the first-level reason for being just (as it appears to the just person) conflicts with the second-level justification for cultivating justice (from the point of view of the theorist). According to such a view, it is instrumentally beneficial to cultivate the just outlook that regards justice as worthwhile for itself; this is why we will take care to praise just people even though we do not believe they are right about the value of justice (cf. 360d2–7).

In the case of justice, however, Plato is not satisfied with an opaque two-level theory. Glaucon asks Socrates to show that a just person who chooses justice for itself is not deceived, and that therefore justice deserves to be chosen for its own sake. He assumes that if justice deserves to be chosen for itself, it must be a non-instrumental good. Hence Socrates is asked to show that it is a good to be chosen both for its own sake and for its consequences (357b4–358a9; 367c5–e1). Since it is agreed that it is worth choosing for its consequences, Socrates is asked to set these aside and to concentrate on showing that it is good in its own right, apart from its consequences.

What is needed to show that justice is good in its own right? We might expect Plato to claim that justice is good simply in so far as the predicate 'justice' attaches to it, and that no further reason can be given to show what makes it good. For any further reason, we might suppose, would have to introduce some other predicate besides 'justice'; hence it would not show that justice is good in so far as it is justice, and so would not show that it is good in its own right. The only sort of argument that could be given to show that justice is good in its own right, according to this conception, would consist in reminding us, by appeal to

---

[20] This is an over-simplified statement of Kant's requirement in *G* 400.
[21] This is Critias' explanation of the rise of belief in gods who punish injustice that society does not detect. See Sextus, *M* ix 54. On Mandeville see Kaye in Mandeville, *FB* i, lxiv–lxvi.
[22] Cf. 414b8–415d2 (the 'noble lie'); *Laws* 663d6–664a8.

different examples, that we implicitly treat justice as such a good, apart from predicating anything else of it.

But if this is what Plato meant by claiming that justice is good in its own right, the question that Glaucon and Adeimantus ask Socrates would be surprising. For they do not simply ask him to show that we treat justice as good in itself; they also say something about the property of justice that would make it good in itself. They ask him to show that a just person, by being just, is better off than an unjust person (361c3–d3), and to show that justice in the soul is the greatest good for the soul (366e5–367a4; 367b2–6, c5–e5). In claiming that something is good in itself, we claim that it is good for someone 'who is going to be happy' (358a1–3).

This statement of the question shows that Plato interprets the claim that justice is good in itself, and to be chosen for its own sake, as implying that (1) justice promotes happiness, by making a person happier than he would otherwise be, and that (2) we should prove this by showing that some other predicate than 'justice' belongs to justice. Glaucon and Adeimantus want Socrates to show what justice is; he was side-tracked from this question in his discussion with Thrasymachus (354a12–c3). They want him to answer this question by saying what justice 'does' in the soul (366e5–6; 367b4; e3). The answer to this question tells us what justice is; justice is a state of the soul, and we say what a state or 'power' is by saying what it does (477c1–d6). If we find a Socratic definition of a virtue, we do not simply repeat the predicate that we initially use to describe the definiendum; we find some other predicates that give us an account of the property we seek to define. If, then, a Socratic definition of justice shows that justice is good in its own right, Plato does not suppose that no other predicate can be substituted for 'justice' if we want to show that justice is good in its own right.

From these different remarks we can see what Plato believes is needed for a proof that justice is a non-instrumental good. He seeks to show that it is non-instrumentally good by showing that it benefits the just person and promotes his happiness. We find through a Socratic definition that justice essentially has some further aspect (some further predicate besides 'justice') that shows how it promotes happiness for the agent. The definition does not introduce a further property besides justice, but it introduces a further predicate of the same property.

We may wonder whether this explanation of Plato's position leaves him with a consistent view about what he wants to prove. We are supposed to show that justice is a non-instrumental good, and hence that it remains good even when we abstract from its consequences. But if we try to prove that justice promotes happiness, or that justice makes someone happier, are we not appealing to a consequence of justice? If so, Plato's account of what it is to be good in its own right seems to be an account of something different.

To resolve this apparent conflict in Plato's position, we need to explain how the claim that justice makes us happy does not introduce one of the consequences of justice that he has excluded from consideration. We can explain this if we suppose that 'Justice makes us happier' refers to a non-causal relation, not involving two distinct events or states.[23] If it

---

[23] More exactly, we might say that it is not an efficient-causal relation. It would be the relation that Aristotle calls 'formal causation'.

means that by being just we are happier, it says what justice is like in its own right, and does not refer to a causal consequence of justice.[24]

If happiness is not a consequence of justice, but justice makes the just person happy, justice must be a constituent of happiness, so that being happy is not separate from being just. By setting out to prove this about justice and happiness in the *Republic*, Plato goes beyond any of Socrates' arguments. We have seen that some of Socrates' remarks about virtue and happiness take the relation to be instrumental, and that his other remarks do not make it clear whether virtue is a means to happiness or identical to it. Plato's reflexions on the character of the just person convince him that we can show why it is worthwhile to be really just if and only if we can show that justice is a constituent of happiness.

52. Is Justice Sufficient for Happiness?

If justice is a non-instrumental good, it must be a constituent of happiness. But if Plato believes this, he does not commit himself to any view about how many constituents happiness has. If justice is the only constituent, justice is identical to happiness. According to this view, justice 'benefits' the just person by making him happy. If Plato takes this view, he remains close to Socrates. Even if, as we have argued, Socrates takes virtue to be instrumental to happiness, he always takes it to be necessary and sufficient for happiness. Plato agrees with him on this point if he takes justice to be identical to happiness.

Whether or not Plato takes justice to be the only constituent of happiness, he takes it to be necessary for happiness, and on this point he agrees with Socrates. To see how far he departs from Socrates, therefore, we need to ask whether he believes that justice is sufficient for happiness. What position does the *Republic* take on this question?

At first sight, the evidence is puzzling. In Book i Socrates states and defends the sufficiency of justice for happiness (353e10–354a9). The just person is better off than the unjust because justice is sufficient for happiness and injustice is sufficient for unhappiness. This was the position of the *Gorgias* (*Gorg.* 507a5–c7). The sufficiency thesis is never rejected in the *Republic*. But it is never repeated. In Books ii–ix Socrates sets out to prove only that the just person is in all circumstances happier than the unjust. This comparative thesis is consistent with the sufficiency thesis, but does not imply it. The comparative thesis is still true if happiness has other constituents besides justice, but justice is more important than the other constituents. We may say that if justice itself makes the just person happier than anyone else, it is the dominant component of happiness.

In Books ii–ix Plato defends the comparative thesis, but never the sufficiency thesis. Nor does he explicitly deny the sufficiency thesis. We might argue, then, that he takes the sufficiency thesis for granted, since it has been stated at the end of Book i, and is never rejected. But a retrospective comment in Book x casts doubt on this argument. Socrates recalls the fact that in Book ii they abstracted from the consequences of justice in order to show that justice itself is the best thing for the soul, and that one ought to act justly

---

[24] For further discussion of these questions about consequences of justice, and references to different views, see Irwin, *PE* §133.

(R. 612a8–b6). Having shown that, they can now legitimately consider what justice leads to if it is followed by its typical consequences in this life and its invariable consequences in the afterlife (612b7–c7). When we add these consequences to justice, we find that justice leads to happiness (621b8–d3).This conclusion does not imply the sufficiency thesis; for it does not imply that justice itself is sufficient for happiness, but only that justice, together with its consequences in this life and the afterlife, results in happiness.

This retrospective comment suggests that Plato does not take himself to have proved the sufficiency thesis in Books ii–ix. On this point the *Republic* differs from the *Gorgias*. The earlier dialogue also ends with a story about the afterlife, which reinforces the conclusion of the main argument of the dialogue, that justice is sufficient for happiness in this life, by showing that it leads to happiness in the afterlife as well. The *Republic*, however, introduces the afterlife to defend a claim that has not been defended in the main argument of the dialogue, that justice leads to happiness. Since Plato draws our attention in Book x to the restricted conclusion (the comparative thesis) that has been defended in the main argument, we may reasonably infer that he intends to defend only this restricted conclusion in the main argument (in Books ii–ix) and does not take himself to have defended the sufficiency thesis as well.

We can support this conclusion if we consider Plato's attitude to external goods in the *Republic*. In the *Euthydemus* Socrates supports the sufficiency thesis by claiming that nothing except wisdom is really good. In the *Gorgias* he supports it by assuming an adaptive conception of happiness.[25] But in the *Republic* he maintains neither of these views. He does not suggest that the external goods that the just person undeservedly loses are not genuine goods, or that they cannot deprive the just person of happiness. Though being just always makes us happier than we would be if we lacked justice and had all these external goods, Plato does not suggest that the loss of external goods is not a genuine harm.

It is unlikely that Plato's failure to say that external goods are not genuine goods is a mere oversight. The belief that they are not genuine goods is one source of the Cynic argument for austerity and rejection of external goods. Though Socrates in the early dialogues does not endorse Cynic austerity, we have seen that it is difficult for him to argue against it, given his claim about virtue and external goods. Plato's claims, however, do not offer any opening for a Cynic argument. If he believes that Socrates' position on external goods makes Cynicism seem too attractive, he has a good reason for sticking to a comparative claim about justice and happiness.

Why does Plato reject Cynic austerity? He might have either of two grounds for rejecting it: (1) He takes happiness to leave out some goods that are worth pursuing, and so he believes that, though justice is sufficient for happiness, external goods are worth pursuing apart from happiness. (2) He takes happiness to comprehend all goods that are worth pursuing, and so takes it to include external goods (as non-dominant components) as well as justice (the dominant component). It is unlikely, however, that he holds the first view. For when he claims that justice is a good that is worth choosing in its own right, he assumes that if it is such a good, it must benefit the just person by contributing to his happiness. This assumption is

---

[25] On *Euthd.* 281e see §15. On *Gorg.* 492e3–494a5 see §25.

reasonable only if Plato assumes that happiness is comprehensive. Probably, then, he holds the second view about the relation of external goods to happiness.

The *Republic* does not allow us to decide this question conclusively, because Plato does not tell us in any detail what he takes happiness to be, and hence does not tell us whether it is comprehensive. But he fills some of these gaps in the *Republic* with his discussion of the good in the *Philebus*. To understand his position, it will be useful to interrupt our discussion of the *Republic* to examine the relevant part of the *Philebus*. Even though the *Philebus* is a later dialogue than the *Republic*, it helps us to see why someone might reasonably say what Plato says in the *Republic*.

53. Inadequate Conceptions of Happiness

The *Philebus* begins with an instructive examination of two candidates for the ultimate good—pleasure and intelligence (*phronêsis; Phil.* 11b–c; cf. *R.* 505b). These candidates remind us of Cyrenaic and Cynic conceptions of the good, which we have traced to different directions of reflexion on the *Protagoras* and *Gorgias*. In the *Protagoras* Socrates endorses a hedonistic conception of the end. The *Gorgias* seems to reject hedonism, and the *Phaedo* (67–9) seems to speak with contempt about the balancing of pleasures and pains. Dialogues later than the *Phaedo* qualify this apparent hostility to pleasure. In *Republic* ix Plato implies that it is important to show that the just person gains more pleasure than the unjust (*R.* 580d–588a). The *Laws* explains why this is important, by affirming that it is pointless to expect us to act on the arguments for justice if we are not convinced that the just life is the pleasantest.[26]

The *Philebus* enters this debate about the relation of pleasure to the good. It is not clear whether Plato has the Cyrenaic and Cynic positions clearly in mind. He does not, for instance, take explicit notice of Aristippus' rejection of eudaemonism; the *Philebus* takes it for granted that defenders of both candidates for the good try to discover the state of one's soul that will make one's life happy (*Phil.* 11d5–6). But it is still worth asking whether Plato implicitly considers the questions that the one-sided Socratics raise about the good and happiness.

Plato rejects both of the one-sided candidates by appeal to general conditions on the good. These are 'formal' conditions, in so far as partisans of different candidates might fairly be expected to accept them as reasonable conditions for assessing their candidates. Plato does not explain why they are plausible formal conditions; he leaves that task for Aristotle.[27] In his view, the good must be complete (20d1), so that it lacks nothing and needs nothing added (20e5–21a2).[28] As in the *Euthydemus* and the *Gorgias*, Plato assumes that the goodness of actions, states of mind, and people depends on the human good, which is the goodness

---

[26] See *Laws* 662c5–d5; 733a1–734a8. For discussion of pleasure in the later dialogues see Bobonich, *PUR* 350–73.

[27] See §66.

[28] This abbreviates Plato's four conditions: (1) It is complete (*teleon*, 20d1). (2) It is adequate (*hikanon*, 20d4). (3) It is universally attractive; every agent who knows it pursues it, wants to get it, and cares nothing about anything else unless the agent can achieve this other thing together with goods (20d7–10; cf. *R.* 505d–e). (4) It lacks nothing, needs nothing added (*Phil.* 20e5–21a2). Probably (4) is intended to express, or to follow from, the previous conditions.

of a human life as a whole for the agent who lives it. Hence the discussion of pleasure and intelligence as candidates for being the good examines their claim to constitute the goodness of a good human life.

To show that pleasure is not the good, Socrates asks Protarchus whether the life of pleasure without intelligence is choiceworthy or not (21d3; cf. 22b6). We might be puzzled by this question. For Socrates takes 'intelligence' very broadly, so that it covers self-consciousness, memory, and anticipation, as well as rational reflexion. Surely no sensible hedonist will deny that intelligence, so understood, helps to increase one's pleasure. As Socrates argues in the *Protagoras*, we need rational calculation to find the life that gives us maximum pleasure on the whole; hence, we might suppose, hedonism cannot be supposed to advocate a life of pleasure without intelligence, since a life that maximizes pleasure must also include intelligence as a means to pleasure. We saw earlier that Socrates' assumptions in the *Protagoras* about prudence may go beyond what the Cyrenaic hedonist accepts.[29] But Plato seems to take account of the Cyrenaic view with his broad conception of intelligence. As he conceives it, even Cyrenaics believe that a life of maximum pleasure needs some intelligence. The supposition of a life of pleasure without intelligence does not seem to be relevant to any life that a hedonist would endorse. Perhaps, then, we might take this to be Plato's point: even a hedonist has to recognize some role for intelligence in the best life.[30]

But if this were Plato's point, it would not help him to show that pleasure alone cannot be the good. For if the place of intelligence in the best life were purely instrumental, its presence would not refute the claim that pleasure is the only non-instrumental good. To decide whether pleasure is the good, we ought not to consider a life that wholly lacks intelligence but maximizes pleasure; for we may be unable to conceive such a life. We ought instead to consider a life that maximizes pleasure in abstraction from the means to this pleasure. To make the point clear, we may imagine that the pleasure that actually results from intelligence results from some other process instead. Such an abstraction ought not to leave this life, regarded as pleasure without intelligence, deficient in any non-instrumental goodness. If, then, it lacks some non-instrumental goodness, pleasure is not the only non-instrumental good. Since this abstraction is relevant to the question about whether pleasure alone is the good, we may reasonably assume that this is what Plato intends, and see what we think of his argument on this assumption.

Plato argues that the life of pleasure without intelligence lacks the different forms of rational consciousness that involve the agent's thinking of himself as a rational agent persisting through his different experiences and pleasures. Being pleased is an aspect of a mental event or a state; it may be short-lived, and it has no particular internal structure (it does not consist, e.g., of first aiming at a goal and then achieving it). If we simply think of ourselves in short episodes that are long enough for pleasure and pain, we may overlook some desirable features of our state of mind that become clear only when we think of our whole life, and so think of ourselves as rational agents persisting through time. But if we think that pleasure is the only non-instrumental good, it should not matter whether we think of ourselves in episodes; we do not overlook any non-instrumental good if we think of ourselves that way.

---

[29] On the Cyrenaics see §29.   [30] See Gosling, *Phil.* 183.

If, then, we consider the form of consciousness that contains maximum pleasure, in abstraction from any means to it, we find that it remains at an elementary level. Since we lack memory, we do not remember that we had pleasure; in lacking belief, we lack the awareness that we are having the enjoyment we are having; in lacking rational calculation we lack the ability to calculate that we will enjoy ourselves in the future. In this condition we would not be living a properly human life, but the life of the most elementary sort of creature that is capable of feeling pleasure; and such a life would not be choiceworthy.[31]

If we have correctly understood Socrates' question, and the abstraction that it involves, we should understand his objection in the same way. He is not saying that a consistent hedonist would live the life of a non-rational animal. He means that the non-instrumental good contained in the hedonist's preferred life could equally be present in a non-rational animal; the fact that I am a rational agent makes no difference to the character of the non-instrumental goodness in my life.

The rational consciousness that concerns Plato is the sort involved in being aware of myself over time; memory, self-consciousness, and rational calculation are different ways I am aware of myself as the same agent in all these experiences. Plato does not speak simply of memory of pleasure in the past. He speaks in first-personal terms, of my remembering that I was previously enjoying myself (21c1). Part of what is good about a life, and part of what is missing in the unmixed life of pleasure, is the awareness of myself as a rational agent in my different experiences. Part of what makes memory and anticipation pleasant to me is my belief that they are mine. That belief is relevant to my enjoyment in so far as it connects these experiences with my concern for myself and my life as a whole.

Plato assumes that our self-concern as rational agents includes concern for ourselves as temporally extended rational consciousness. If hedonism attaches no intrinsic value to the relevant sort of rational consciousness of oneself, including memory and anticipation, it gives the wrong account of happiness. This argument in the *Philebus* develops a point in the *Gorgias* (in the argument with Callicles about bravery), arguing that hedonism conflicts with eudaemonism. If the good for us as rational agents must include rational concern for ourselves as rational agents, it cannot consist only in pleasure.

This is not a decisive argument against hedonism. A consistent hedonist may deny, as Sidgwick does,[32] that rational consciousness has any non-instrumental value. But it is difficult to accept this denial; if we suffer some loss of rational consciousness, we seem to be worse off, whether or not we happen to gain less pleasure as a result. If a hedonist claims that this belief about the non-instrumental value of rational consciousness is simply an intuitive common-sense assumption that does not deserve our confidence, we may reasonably ask

---

[31] 'But if you were without intellect, memory, knowledge, and true belief, you would necessarily, I imagine, in the first place be ignorant of this very thing, whether you were or were not enjoying yourself, given that you would be empty of all intelligence. . . . And . . . if you had no memory you would necessarily, I imagine, not even remember that you were once enjoying yourself, and no memory at all would remain of the pleasure striking you at the present moment. And again, if you had no true belief, you couldn't believe that you were enjoying yourself when you were; nor yet, if you were deprived of reasoning, could you reason that you would enjoy yourself later on. You would be living the life not of a human being, but of some sort of sea-lung or one of those living creatures of the ocean whose bodies are incased in shells' (21b6–c8).

[32] See Sidgwick, *ME* 395–6.

why the intuitive assumptions underlying hedonism deserve our confidence if they conflict with this other assumption.

This argument suggests a reasonable question about the hedonist eudaemonism of the *Protagoras*. If we ascribe only instrumental value to rational consciousness, we represent the ultimate end as available equally to non-rational agents. At the same time we represent it as an end for the whole of one's life. But why should we care about the whole of our lives unless we conceive ourselves as rational agents who plan, anticipate, and execute our plans? If we conceive ourselves in that way, how can the rational consciousness that belongs to our conception of ourselves have no non-instrumental value? If we are eudaemonists we seem to ascribe to rational consciousness the non-instrumental value that we deny to it in describing the good as simply pleasure.

Could a hedonist answer that the best life consists of pleasure, but only in some pleasures—those taken in forms of rational consciousness? On this view, not all pleasure is part of the good, but none the less the good is altogether constituted by some specific pleasures. But if pleasure taken in rational consciousness presupposes the intrinsic goodness of rational consciousness itself, an argument proving that the good consists in this specific sort of pleasure does not support hedonism. For if the pleasures are essentially tied to their objects, and if they involve the belief that the object is intrinsically good, we cannot be hedonists if we believe that the good life consists in these sorts of pleasures. If we understand the character of pleasures taken in rational consciousness, we have a reason not to be hedonists.

This question about the varieties of pleasure and their relations to their objects is discussed in the rather complicated later stages of the *Philebus*, and it is a central question in Aristotle's analysis of pleasure. Without going into all the complications, we may simply notice that Plato raises the question right at the beginning of the *Philebus*. For Socrates comments at the outset that pleasures vary because they are taken in different objects. He remarks that the temperate and the wise person take pleasure in being temperate and wise (12c8–d4), but he does not say that intemperate and foolish people take pleasure in their intemperance and foolishness. He suggests that the pleasures of the virtuous person depend on their object. We might try to explain this by saying that wise people take pleasure in wisdom because they regard it as non-instrumentally good.[33] If they are genuinely wise people, their belief about its goodness is true. And so, if the pleasure of wise people in their wisdom is part of the good, wisdom must be a non-instrumental good, so that pleasure itself cannot be the only non-instrumental good. A hedonist who restricts the pleasures to be included in the good does not refute Plato's objections to hedonism, but only confirms them.

54. Cyrenaic Hedonism v. Eudaemonism

When Plato argues against the identification of the good with pleasure, what versions of hedonism has he in mind? His argument is directly relevant to the unqualified hedonism of the *Protagoras*, the *Gorgias*, and the Cyrenaics, which refuses to distinguish good from

---

[33] Aristotle on pleasure; §95.

bad pleasures on any non-quantitative grounds. He recalls the position of the *Protagoras* in saying that Philebus takes 'pleasant' and 'good' to be two names for one thing (60a9–10). Does he also presuppose that the hedonist is a eudaemonist, as Socrates is in the *Protagoras*? In speaking of memory and anticipation, the *Philebus* may seem to presuppose that we are concerned with pleasure over the whole of one's life. This is how Socrates describes the hedonist at the beginning of the dialogue (11d4–12a1). Similarly, he asks Protarchus whether he would welcome living his whole life enjoying the greatest pleasures (21a8–9). And so we might suppose that Plato argues only against hedonist eudaemonism.

In that case, Cyrenaic hedonists may seem to avoid the force of Plato's argument by rejecting eudaemonism. They deny that they are trying to find a good to be achieved over the course of a whole extended life, and so they deny that they attach any value to planning for one's extended life. In their view there is nothing especially rational about thinking of one's life in such a way that one wants one's good to be appropriately spread over it. Since the good is pleasure, not happiness, it is achieved only in the pleasure of the moment, not in a sum of pleasure that is maximized over one's extended life. Hence Cyrenaics cannot be accused of explicitly ascribing purely instrumental value to rational consciousness while implicitly ascribing non-instrumental value to it. We might even say that the Cyrenaics use Plato's argument to show why hedonism has to reject eudaemonism. Socrates in the *Protagoras*, they might argue, relies on a eudaemonist assumption that cannot be defended on purely hedonist grounds; hence he introduces a non-hedonic value into an allegedly hedonist position. Plato's reasons for thinking that concern for temporally-extended agency recognizes a non-hedonic type of goodness show, according to the Cyrenaics, that hedonists ought not to be eudaemonists.

It does not follow, however, that Plato's argument is irrelevant to Cyrenaic non-eudaemonist hedonism. Even though he does not discuss it as a distinct position besides the hedonist eudaemonism he ascribes to Protarchus, some of his argument is relevant to attempts to defend hedonism by rejecting eudaemonism. Socrates tells Protarchus that the life he would lead without intelligence would not be the life of a human being, but the life of a shellfish with the most elementary form of life. As far as non-instrumental good is concerned, a rational conscious being would not differ from anything else capable of pleasure. This objection is not confined to the past and the future. Socrates also objects that the hedonist cannot attach non-instrumental value to our present recognition of our pleasure. Even if we restrict ourselves to the present, we can distinguish our being pleased from our second-order awareness that we are pleased. The hedonist cannot attach any value to consciousness of pleasure beyond the value of pleasure itself. But—Plato implies—we would surely believe we had lost some non-instrumental good if our enjoyment remained just as intense as it was, but we lost our consciousness that we were enjoying ourselves.

Cyrenaics might reply that it is unfair of Plato to exclude the value of consciousness of pleasure from their conception of the end. When they accept hedonism of the moment, they do not mean—they might argue—to exclude consciousness of pleasure. They are free to include this in the consciousness of the moment that they identify with the good.

This would not be a wholly satisfactory reply, for reasons we have already noticed. Plato is right to suggest that if we attach value to consciousness of pleasure, we are attaching value to consciousness and not just to pleasure. Even though pleasure itself is a mode of consciousness, the further consciousness of pleasure is something beyond pleasure, and introduces a new element of value.

But even if we do not insist on this Platonic rejoinder, Cyrenaics face a further difficult question. Plato suggests that the second-order consciousness includes self-consciousness; it is awareness of myself having a present pleasure. But what is required for awareness of myself? What, in other words, is the self that I am aware of when I attribute an experience of pleasure to it? Plato says something about this question when he suggests that if I lack memory, not only do I not recall my past pleasures, but I will also lack any memory of my pleasure in the present moment (21c2–4). But how can I be conscious of myself enjoying this pleasure if I retain no memory of it from one moment to another? Apparently I need enough memory to recognize this as an episode of pleasure in relation to other episodes of consciousness.

This minimal concession to memory requires further concessions. For the sort of memory that goes with self-consciousness is first-personal memory. I do not simply retain some past mode of consciousness; I ascribe some state of consciousness to one and the same self to whom I also ascribe a past and a future consciousness. It is reasonable of Plato, therefore, to introduce present self-consciousness in connexion with memory and anticipation; we cannot have any of these without the others. In all these cases we treat experiences as belonging to a single self that both unifies present experiences with each other and unifies experiences at different times. Plato discusses this unified self at some length in the *Theaetetus*; but there he just mentions past and future briefly (*Tht.* 186a9–b1). The *Philebus* makes clear some of the practical implications of recognizing the single self.

Once we see the place for the single temporally-extended self even in self-consciousness in the present, we see why it is reasonable for us to attribute non-instrumental value to rational consciousness. Since this rational consciousness in the present requires recognition of the single self present in memory, anticipation, and deliberation, it commits us to concern for the good of a temporally-extended self, and hence to eudaemonism.

Though Plato's argument is brief, it raises an appropriate question about the Cyrenaic attempt to avoid objections to hedonistic eudaemonism by abandoning eudaemonism. Plato's discussion of rational consciousness implies that the Cyrenaic attempt to confine non-instrumental goodness to the pleasure of the moment overlooks the self for whom the pleasure is valuable. When we try to understand the subject of the pleasure, we see that we cannot prevent the nature of the subject from affecting what is non-instrumentally good. For a rational conscious subject, pleasure without rational consciousness cannot be the only non-instrumental good.

55. Why Intelligence is Not the Good

Plato takes the completeness of the good to rule out not only hedonism but also the view that some state of rational consciousness alone is sufficient for happiness, whether or not it has any further effects. Protarchus the hedonist maintains, and Socrates does not deny, that a life of intelligence alone without pleasure would be unacceptable for a human being.[34]

---

[34] Plato's claim strictly applies to every being that is capable of intelligence (11b9–c2; 22b3–6).

Plato does not expect the agent making the choice between lives to regard herself as a purely rational agent, with none of the desires and feelings resulting from the non-rational aspects of human nature. The complete life for a human being cannot make her 'unaffected' (*apathês*) by the normal feelings and passions of human beings (*Phil.* 21e1–2).[35]

In denying that 'freedom from affection' (*apatheia*) is the human good, Plato rejects a conception that appeals, in different ways, to Socrates, the Cynics, and the Stoics. If we are free from the desires that lead us to look for pleasures that require bodily actions and external resources, we are free of the mental disturbance of desires waiting to be satisfied and from the pain resulting from failure and disappointment. But we also deny ourselves the possibility of successes and satisfactions that are appropriate for human nature. Happiness consists in rational direction and use of an appropriate range of desires and resources; it does not consist in the contraction of the task of rational direction to a point where we can guarantee success in our aims. In rejecting freedom from affection Plato anticipates Aristotle's view not only about virtue, but also about happiness.[36]

We might say that this argument against intelligence as the good emphasizes the non-rational side of human nature, whereas the argument against hedonism emphasized the rational side. This is part of the truth; for Plato agrees that if we had a purely rational nature, such as the gods have, intelligence would be the whole of our good (22c5–6). But Plato might also argue that the inclusion of pleasure is a further argument for the place of rational agency in the good. Attempts to eliminate pleasure contract the scope of rational action, so that practical reason no longer tries to secure the appropriate pleasures and external goods, but simply withdraws from aims and tasks whose outcome is not entirely up to us. Plato rejects this strategy of withdrawal.

His reasons for including pleasure, suitably directed by reason, in the good are relevant to his reasons for denying that virtue is sufficient for happiness. Part of what we value in practical reason is the fact that it is directed towards worthwhile ends beyond it. To give up the pursuit of some pleasures as worthwhile external ends is to remove part of the value that we reasonably ascribe to practical reason.

56. Responses to the *Philebus*

The conclusion of the *Philebus* endorses neither hedonism nor extreme opposition to pleasure. Intelligence is the supreme component of the good, but not the only component. The good also includes different types of pleasures. Pleasures that depend on rational activity and do not depend on bodily needs and disturbances are more important; but ordinary bodily pleasures are not excluded, though Plato does not welcome them with enthusiasm (65e–66a).

The *Philebus*, therefore, both contributes to a debate among Plato's contemporaries and suggests different strategies that might appeal to us if we are not satisfied with its contribution. The hedonist might argue that the position of Philebus has been dismissed too abruptly. The argument against hedonism rests on assumptions about the value of rational

---

[35] On *apatheia* see §38 and §85.   [36] Cf. *EN* 1104b24–6.

consciousness that a hedonist may have reason to question. Alternatively, a more moderate hedonist might fasten on Plato's selective acceptance of pleasure. Might we find a hedonist argument for choosing Plato's preferred pleasures over those that he rejects? He seems to suggest such an argument by remarking that some pleasures result from severe pain and cause still greater pain by increasing our appetite for them. These are the pleasures that Callicles takes to belong to happiness; but, we might suppose, a more careful hedonist can reject them because they cause us more trouble than they are worth.

But if the hedonist can find something to exploit in the *Philebus*, the extreme opponent of pleasure might also claim support from the dialogue. For even though Plato accepts some pleasures, he seems to suggest that he is conceding something to human weakness, and that for a god the life of intelligence would be the complete good (22c). Pleasure belongs to a life of changeable sensations, and we might suppose that the best form of existence would free us from dependence on the senses. If rational activity is valuable for itself, why should we also want some pleasant sensation added to it? The desire for added pleasure seems to reflect a human limitation that we might hope to escape. Perhaps, then, the lesson to learn from the *Philebus* is that we are best off when we are free of any concern about pleasure and pain because we are absorbed in the best activities. Plato's suggestion that we are even better off if we take pleasure in these activities may appear to be an ill-advised concession to the advocates of pleasure.

If we notice these different arguments about pleasure and the good that might be developed from suggestions in the *Philebus*, we do not imply that the argument of the dialogue is indeterminate or ambiguous. On the contrary, Plato considers both hedonism and extreme opposition to pleasure, and he rejects both positions in favour of the mixed life of intelligence and pleasure. But it would not be surprising if different readers found some parts of his argument more convincing than other parts. Plato defines his position both by reflexion on discussions among his contemporaries and by further thoughts on his own past engagement with pleasure and the good. He also presents a starting point for further defences of the different positions he examines.

57. Why Justice is Insufficient for Happiness

We turned to the *Philebus* in the hope of finding a conception of happiness that might fill a gap in the explicit argument of the *Republic*. Since Plato does not set out, in the main argument of the *Republic*, to prove that justice is sufficient for happiness, we may reasonably ask what conception of happiness he presupposes. The discussion of the good in the *Philebus* suggests an answer to this question, since it insists that the good must be complete; neither pleasure nor intelligence is the good, because we would reasonably prefer a life that contains both elements over a life that contains only one of them. Plato's argument implicitly raises questions about the interpretation of 'complete' and related notions. We will consider these questions more fully in discussing Aristotle's use and explanation of these conditions for the final good. For present purposes, it is enough to notice the relevance of the *Philebus* to the *Republic*. Though the *Philebus* does not directly discuss the role of external goods in happiness, the argument to show that pleasure needs to be added to intelligence might equally well be used to show that external goods need to be added to justice (and other virtues), if we are to achieve a complete good.

If, then, Plato assumes in the *Republic* that happiness is complete, he has a reason to reject the Socratic claim that justice is sufficient for happiness. For it seems reasonable for a just person to prefer a life that includes both justice and external goods (wealth, honour, safety, etc.) over a life that includes justice without these other goods. Indeed, it is difficult to see why justice should be concerned with keeping promises to pay debts, or making sure that people are not unfairly punished for crimes they did not commit, if money, imprisonment, and so on are not genuine goods and evils, and if they do not contribute to a person's happiness. If Plato denies that the just person is happy on this ground, he rejects Cynic austerity and its Socratic foundation. He sides with Aristotle and with the Peripatetic critics of Stoicism, who reject the Stoic identification of virtue with happiness.

Since Plato neither explicitly rejects the Socratic thesis nor explains why he rejects it, it is not surprising that his ancient readers hold different views about whether he accepts or rejects it. But we may support the anti-Socratic interpretation by noticing that those who are careful to distinguish Socrates from Plato also endorse the anti-Socratic interpretation. Chrysippus agrees with Socrates in accepting the sufficiency thesis, and criticizes Plato for rejecting it.[37] Some of the ancient readers who attribute the sufficiency thesis to the *Republic* fail to distinguish Socratic from Platonic views.[38] Some ancient Platonists, for instance, accept a 'unitarian' account of the Platonic dialogues, and take them all to express Plato's views.[39] If we follow the one-sided Socratics, Aristotle, and Chrysippus, in distinguishing Socratic from Platonic views, we ought also to agree with the ancient readers of the *Republic* who recognize that it does not maintain the sufficiency of justice for happiness. The *Philebus* suggests a good reason for the position of the *Republic*, though we would be unwise to assume that Plato must have had precisely this reason in mind.

If Plato holds a composite conception of happiness as a complete good, containing different parts, his whole position in *Republic* ii is intelligible. The composite conception shows why he believes that if justice is a non-instrumental good it must promote happiness; he believes this because he believes that happiness is complete, and that therefore any non-instrumental good is a component of happiness.[40] In his view, we have been given a good reason for being just if and only if we have been shown how justice promotes our happiness; he does not even consider the suggestion that we have overriding reason to be just even if justice does not promote our happiness. The same composite conception of happiness explains why justice is

---

[37] On Chrysippus see §161. On the Stoics' concern to distinguish Socratic from Platonic views see Long, 'Socrates' 16–18.

[38] Cicero tries to find the Socratic position in Plato, by appealing to the *Gorgias* and *Menexenus*. He takes it for granted that passages in these dialogues present Plato's views (*TD* v 35–6), even though he elsewhere recognizes a distinction between the Platonic and the historical Socrates (*Rep.* i 16).

[39] Atticus the Platonist takes Plato to hold a view close to the Stoic position, and so contrasts him sharply with Aristotle (Eusebius, *PE* 794c6–d13): he assumes that Plato's acceptance of the comparative thesis commits him to acceptance of the sufficiency thesis. Alcinous claims that in the *Euthydemus* Plato accepts the Stoic thesis that only the fine is good (*Did.* 27 = 180.33–7). He infers that this Stoic thesis expresses Plato's view in the *Republic* as well, and that Plato relies on this thesis to prove that the virtues are choiceworthy for their own sakes (181.5–9). See Dillon, *MP* 251–2, 299; Whittaker, *Alc.* 137n443. Lilla, *CA* 68–72, discusses Clement, *Strom.* iv 52.1–2, which appeals to R. 361e (cf. v 108.2). Annas, *PEON*, ch. 2, defends this Platonist view of the *Republic*.

[40] Contrast White, *CPR* 43–5, 80; *ICGE* 189–214.

insufficient for happiness; since justice by itself is not the complete good, happiness includes the external goods that are not infallibly secured by justice. In the light of his composite conception of happiness, Plato claims that justice is the dominant component in happiness. Since he does not explicitly develop a composite conception of happiness in the *Republic*, he does not explain why his formulation of the question about justice and happiness is the right one. But since the composite conception offers us the best way to understand his formulation, we may attribute it to him with reasonable confidence. His position is reasonable if he takes happiness to include a number of parts, including the various external goods whose presence makes just people happier than they would be with justice alone. At any rate, Aristotle sees that we need such a conception in order to defend Plato's claims about justice.[41]

58. Are Plato's Questions Reasonable?

In maintaining that the just person chooses justice for its own sake and demanding a proof that justice is worth choosing for its own sake, Plato begins a long tradition in moral philosophy. Many would agree that those who choose morally virtuous actions simply because of their consequences are missing the point of morality. Kant expresses this view strongly in claiming that only the person who does what is right because it is right has a genuinely good will. Though this demand on moral virtue is not universally accepted and is by no means beyond controversy, and though it demands further explication before we can see what the reasonable controversy is about, it seems to express one widely-shared conviction about morality. We may find it surprising that Socrates does not articulate Plato's demand. Though he expresses an unreserved commitment to morality, we have found that he does not explicitly insist that the moral virtues are non-instrumentally valuable. In insisting that they have this status, Plato goes beyond Socrates' claims. Perhaps he believes that Socrates' actual commitment to morality is better expressed through Plato's formula than through Socrates' apparently instrumental conception. As Adeimantus says, we would expect a non-instrumental defence of justice from someone who takes justice as seriously as Socrates takes it (R. 367d5–e1).

But though this aspect of Plato's demand on justice is widely accepted, his support for Socratic eudaemonism is often deplored. Some readers, indeed, assume that since he regards justice as non-instrumentally valuable, he cannot really mean that it is to be chosen only for the sake of one's own happiness. Schopenhauer praises Plato for insisting that virtue is to be praised for its own sake, and so he does not regard Plato as a eudaemonist; he takes him to be an exception to the eudaemonism of ancient ethics.[42] Reid expresses a more usual reaction. He complains that Plato, with the rest of the ancient moralists, reduce morality to self-love, and therefore cannot explain why virtue is to be chosen for its own sake.[43] Prichard states this objection to Plato most strongly, arguing that the *Republic* is not really about moral obligation. The concept of justice introduces morality, according to Prichard, but Plato's question about whether we 'ought' to be just is not about moral obligation, because Plato

---

[41] Aristotle and Plato on happiness; §66.

[42] 'For Plato, especially in the *Republic*, of which the main tendency is precisely this, expressly teaches that virtue is to be chosen for its own sake alone, even if unhappiness and ignominy should be inevitably associated with it' (WR i 524).

[43] See Reid, *EAP* iii 3–4, H 582b586a.

takes 'ought' to refer to one's own happiness.[44] According to the view of Plato's critics, moral requirements and principles ought not to be subordinate to any other principles, whether these other principles refer to the agent's good or to some other valued state of affairs.

Plato might reasonably reject these criticisms. Since he claims that justice is a dominant component of happiness, not merely an instrumental means to it, he might deny that he subordinates morality to other ends in any objectionable sense. One might go further and claim on his behalf that even if we think the moral point of view is independent and supreme, we should accept his version of eudaemonism. To say that morality is identical to, or dominant in, one's happiness is (on this view) simply to assert that the virtuous person values it above everything else.[45] We noticed earlier that this is one way to understand the Cynic conception of the supremacy of virtue.[46]

But if this is a reasonable defence against the charge that Plato subordinates morality to other ends, is eudaemonism still worth defending? For if our conception of happiness is not fixed and determinate independently of justice, we seem to lose one of the main reasons for accepting eudaemonism in the first place. An account of happiness seems to give us some basis both for the definition and for the justification of the moral virtues. We want our definitions to show how the virtues promote happiness, as previously understood, and once we have found the right definitions we will have shown why the virtues, so defined, are worth choosing for rational agents aiming at their happiness, as already defined. If we cannot say what happiness is apart from justice, we cannot appeal to concerns that are recognized as rational by just and non-just agents alike in order to show that the concerns of the just person are rational. But if we cannot use our conception of happiness for these purposes, what is the point of eudaemonism?[47]

It is useful to consider this question in trying to understand eudaemonist positions that try to preserve the justifying force of an appeal to happiness without making morality purely instrumental to non-moral aims. We need to see whether a description of happiness that does not yet incorporate the virtuous person's distinctive conception of its content can be definite enough to offer some reasonable basis for defending the virtuous person's conception. Aristotle and his successors try to set out an appropriate description of happiness; they try to fulfil a task that Plato sets in the *Republic* and the *Philebus*. Plato's raising of these questions supports Grote's judgment that *Republic* ii presents some of the basic questions for ethical theory.[48]

59. What is Psychic Justice?

Though Grote praises Plato for raising the right questions, he is far less impressed by Plato's answers. In his view, Plato entirely fails to show that the other-regarding virtue of justice

---

[44] See Prichard, *MO* 103–9, 118–19. He concludes that 'any teleological theory of duty can be rejected, even without considering its details, on the ground that it represents the moral "ought" as if it were the non-moral "ought", and so is not a theory of moral obligation at all' (119).

[45] See McDowell, 'Role' 16–20.   [46] On Socrates and the Cynics see §§20, 39.

[47] This is one way to express Sidgwick's criticism of non-hedonist versions of eudaemonism at *ME* 91–3.

[48] Grote, *HG* viii 539: 'Hardly anything in Plato's compositions is more powerful than those discourses. They present in a perspicuous and forcible manner, some of the most serious difficulties with which ethical theory is required to grapple.'

promotes one's happiness.[49] Plato's answer to his question relies on the tripartition of the soul that we have already discussed. His account of the soul allows him to introduce a virtue that he calls 'justice in the soul'. He argues that someone who has this virtue of psychic justice is happier than any who lack it, but, according to many critics, his argument, even if it is successful, is beside the point. For when Glaucon and Adeimantus were asking Socrates to prove that justice promotes happiness, the justice they had in mind was the other-regarding virtue that underlies our obeying the laws, paying debts, and so on. Why should we suppose that the psychic justice that Plato derives from his tripartition of the soul is this other-regarding virtue?

It is useful to approach these criticisms by discussing Plato's position in two stages. First, we may ask why psychic justice is a virtue, and how it is a dominant component of happiness. Secondly, we may turn to the connexion with other-regarding virtue. A clear understanding of what is non-instrumentally good about psychic justice may help us to see why Plato believes it is good for other people as well.

Plato conceives psychic justice as an intra-personal analogue of justice in the state. Justice in the state keeps the different classes performing their own functions, so that they do not cause disorder. Similarly, psychic justice keeps the different parts of the soul in order, so that they do not cause mental conflict and disorder (441d5–e2).

This simple description of psychic justice makes it misleadingly easy to show that it is good for the agent. For we may agree that the avoidance of mental conflict is good for us, no matter what our other values may be; and a simple way to describe psychic order is to say that it consists in the absence of disorder among the parts.[50]

This description, however, is too simple. If it were the whole truth about the role of the rational part, Plato would not have shown why psychic justice is non-instrumentally good. Some degree of psychic order seems to be instrumentally good; but it is not clear why we are better off the more psychic order we have, and it is not clear why we should take this to be a non-instrumental good, let alone a dominant non-instrumental good. We need a fuller description of the role of the rational part, as Plato conceives it.

Plato does not suggest that every soul dominated by a non-rational part is full of conflict and disorder; for we have seen that a non-rational part is capable of some kinds of concern for the future, and of forming future-oriented desires that are strong enough to prevent crippling mental conflict.[51] We do not need to be controlled by the rational part to keep order in the soul. Plato makes this point clear in his description of the deviant souls (Books viii–ix); some of these, at least, are free of crippling conflict, but none of them is controlled by the rational part.

---

[49] This objection is presented at length by Grote, POC iv 102–20. He contrasts other-regarding justice with self-regarding Platonic justice, claiming that the other-regarding sense 'is that which is in more common use; and it is that which Plato assumes provisionally when he puts forward the case of opponents in the speeches of Glaukon and Adeimantus' (103). According to Grote, Plato proves (at most) that self-regarding psychic justice promotes happiness. In commenting on the argument of Book ix Grote objects: 'But when this point is granted, nothing is proved about the just and the unjust man, except in a sense of these terms peculiar to Plato himself' (120). Some of the many further discussions are Prichard, MO 106; Sachs, 'Fallacy'; Vlastos, 'Justice'; Kraut, 'Reason'; Annas, IPR, ch. 6; Dahl, 'Defence'.

[50] Plato seems to distinguish psychic justice from mere continence (as Aristotle conceives it; see §84); just people do not have to struggle to restrain unruly impulses.

[51] See Hume on prudence and justice, T iii 2.7 §5.

In Plato's view, a just soul is controlled by its rational part if and only if the rational part has formed desires resting on wise deliberation about what is good for the whole soul and it uses these desires to guide the whole soul (442c5–d8). Even if someone's non-rational parts accept the instructions of the rational part, it does not follow that he also acts on wise deliberation about what is good for the whole soul. The oligarchic person, for instance, believes that the most important thing in life is making money, makes rational plans for this, and attaches his anger, shame, and pride exclusively to these plans. But Plato denies that such a person acts on a view about what is good for the whole soul; if the rational and the spirited part serve appetite, they do not perform their own functions (cf. 553d1–7).

The outlook of the rational part is wider than that of the other two parts, in so far as it has some conception of their good, and has some conception of them as forming parts of a whole. It incorporates, but also modifies, the outlooks of the two non-rational parts. If we can see all four sides of a building, we can understand the points of view of four observers each of whom can observe only one side; each point of view is misleading by itself, and even the sum of their four points of view is misleading, but we can see how far they are accurate if we understand the whole building of which they observe different parts.[52] The rational part takes this wider point of view on the desires and interests of the non-rational parts, so that it can satisfy their interests better than it would if it simply chose to be guided by their desires (586e7–587a2). This is why each of the virtues requires control by the rational part. Since the rational part takes the appropriate view of the good of the whole soul, it guides the impulses of the non-rational parts in the right direction. In this respect the different virtues might be regarded as aspects of psychic justice, so that we might expect Plato to affirm the unity of the virtues. He does not go as far as Socrates, however. Since distinct courses of training are needed for the different appetites and emotions that underlie bravery and temperance, he treats them as distinct virtues, even though they both consist in having a just and wise soul.

60. How Psychic Justice Fulfils the Human Function

This holistic practical reasoning and the resulting desires of the rational part are instrumentally beneficial, because they grasp the interests of the whole person impartially. But this instrumental function does not explain why it is also non-instrumentally good to be ruled by the rational part. Since Plato believes that any non-instrumental good is a part of happiness, we can see why psychic justice is a non-instrumental good only if we can see how it is a part of happiness. But to see this, we need some grasp of Plato's conception of happiness in the *Republic*.

In trying to answer this question, we have to face one of the gaps in the dialogue. It is unlikely that Socrates could prove to Thrasymachus that justice is a part of happiness if

---

[52] Murphy, *IPR* 32, comments: '. . . as Bosanquet said, "the rank of the intelligence comes primarily from its power to represent the whole", and its primary, or perhaps rather ultimate, task is to form a conception of the best life as what will most completely satisfy all the springs of desire in the agent . . .'. He refers to Bosanquet, *CPR* 365. The outlook of the rational part might also claim to be more objective; 'As in the theoretical case, we must take up a new, comprehensive viewpoint after stepping back and including our former perspective in what is to be understood. But here the new viewpoint will not be a new set of beliefs, but a new or extended set of values' (Nagel, *VN* 138).

Thrasymachus were right about the composition of happiness. Thrasymachus assumes that it consists in wealth, power, and all the other external goods that one might gain by being a tyrant (cf. 343e7–344c4). When Socrates argues in Book i that justice is sufficient for happiness, he does not mean that it is sufficient for gaining all the goods that Thrasymachus includes in happiness; but he does not offer any alternative conception. The arguments of Glaucon and Adeimantus make it even clearer that Socrates must disagree with Thrasymachus on this point; for it would be absurd to claim that the just person suffering extreme ill-fortune is happier than the unjust person if Thrasymachus had the right conception of happiness. Socrates needs to reform not only our initial conception of justice, but also our initial conception of happiness. But whereas the *Republic* expounds a revised conception of justice at some length, it offers very little to help us grasp Plato's conception of happiness.

He suggests some of his conception, however, in introducing the essential activity or 'function' (*ergon*) of a human being. Socrates appeals to functions in Book i, to clarify his claims about virtues. Given the human function, we can find the virtues; they are the states we need in order to perform our function well (352d8–353d2). The function of the soul is supervising, ruling, deliberating, and living (353d3–10); if justice is the virtue that allows the soul to perform this function well, the just person lives well and is happy. In this argument Socrates assumes that happiness consists in performing one's function well, but he does not explain why he believes this.

In Book iv Plato returns to the human function. He initially speaks of the 'work' or 'function' (*ergon* again) of different individuals and classes in the city. When individuals and classes perform their social function, that promotes the happiness of the whole city (421a8–c6), but it remains to be seen how their function is related to the function that was introduced in Book i. Plato explains the relation by saying that the social function provides an analogy or image of one's own function. Psychic justice is doing 'one's own' (443c–d) both in external actions and in the attitudes and relations of the parts of one's soul, which is truly oneself.[53] Justice is the psychic analogue to the health of the body; health maintains the natural order in the body, by ordering the different parts so that we can perform the normal activities of a human life. Justice maintains the natural order in the soul, so that we can engage in the human function. This is why someone who chooses psychic justice chooses the rule of the human being within him, rather than the rule of the lion (the spirited part) or the many-headed beast (the appetitive part; 589a6–b7).

Though he does not say explicitly that happiness consists in exercising the human function of rational agency, Plato's remarks about justice and the human function suggest that he assumes this conception of happiness. He seems to agree implicitly with Aristotle's claim that happiness consists in a life of rational activity because a human being is essentially a rational agent (*EN* i 7).[54] At the moment we need not try to explore questions about the legitimacy of appeals to the human function, or of arguments from the human function to the human good. It is enough to notice that Plato appeals to the human function to explain how justice is a non-instrumental good. If he is right about the nature of psychic justice, it is a part of happiness, because happiness consists in using practical reason to control the direction of one's life.

---

[53] On the interpretation of 'doing one's own work' see Irwin, *PE* §158.
[54] On Aristotle's function argument see §74.

We may support this claim about the *Republic* by recalling the argument in the *Philebus* about the character and composition of the good. Socrates advocates a life that includes intelligence for the creatures that are capable of it; he does not say that these creatures are essentially rational, but he does not suggest that his argument would work if rationality were an accidental or unimportant feature of them. In criticizing Protarchus, he suggests that a life of maximum pleasure without reason would not be a life for a human being, but might as well belong to some elementary form of animal existence (*Phil.* 21c6–d1). Those who reject a life guided by reason act against their nature (22b6–8). Plato insists that the good for a human being must be good for a creature with the nature of a human being; and hence it must be a good that consists in the exercise of rational agency. Here again the *Philebus* expresses more clearly a point about happiness that is presupposed, though not so clearly articulated, in the *Republic*.

61. The Philosopher as Ruler: A Conflict between Justice and Happiness?

Thrasymachus, Glaucon, and Adeimantus agree that it is difficult to see how my being just promotes my own good because justice is essentially 'another's good' (*R.* 344c; 367c2–5). Aristotle agrees with this description of justice (*EN* 1130a1–5); in his view, justice completes virtue by directing it to the good of others (*EN* 1129b25–1130a1). Plato and Aristotle disagree with Thrasymachus' assumption that justice is both another's good and a harm to the just agent; but they accept the first part of his assumption, and deny that it supports the second. If, then, Plato is recognizably talking about justice, he ought to show that psychic justice has this other-regarding aspect. But why is it reasonable to expect that someone who is rationally concerned with the good of the whole soul, and who deliberates about which ends to pursue, and values this practical reason as a part of happiness, will also be concerned for the good of others?

If we have grasped the connexion that Plato sees between psychic justice, the human function, and the human good, we can see why he takes psychic justice to be a non-instrumental good. We can also answer some of the reasons for believing that psychic justice is irrelevant to the other-regarding virtue of justice that ought to be Socrates' main concern. Plato mentions some 'commonplace' examples of unjust actions—theft, treachery, neglect of parents, etc.—and claims that the psychically just person would never do any of these (*R.* 442d–443b). We might object that someone without psychic conflict might have a careful premeditated plan to carry out any of these unjust acts and might execute his plan; why would this not be a case of psychic justice leading to an unjust act? Plato might reasonably answer that we have not shown that such a person is psychically just. If he steals because he covets what his neighbour has and wants it for his own gratification, or if he is angry at someone and assaults or kills them to get his own back, he is dominated by a non-rational part of the soul, and hence is not psychically just.

This reply on Plato's behalf is reasonable as far as it goes. Many unjust actions of the sort that concerned Thrasymachus and the others are undertaken because of aims of the non-rational parts, and someone who is really controlled by the rational part will not be tempted by such actions. The unjust actions considered in Books i–ii might all plausibly be traced to a non-rational motive that we would not endorse if we were controlled by the rational part and exercising the human function. It is not clear, however, that an appeal to an accurate account of psychic justice entirely disposes of objections relying on the other-regarding aspect of justice. Even if the psychically just people avoid most unjust actions, it does not seem obvious that they will have any positive concern for the good of others; but we might reasonably expect this positive concern in a virtue that can properly be called 'another's good'.

This is not simply a question that a critic might devise for Plato. Plato seems to agree that it is a legitimate question. The philosophers who rule the ideal city receive a prolonged and elaborate moral and intellectual training, until they eventually come to know the forms. They need this knowledge in order to find the appropriate goal in the light of which they can order social and individual life; the ideal city needs rulers who have grasped this single goal (519b8–c6). But though the philosophers are qualified to rule the city, a question arises about their desire to rule. Socrates suggests that after their intellectual enlightenment, they will suppose they are living in the Isles of the Blessed. Once they see the possibility of a better life spent in intellectual activity, they will not willingly undertake the task of ruling in the ideal city (519c). But it would be bad for the city if they were allowed to contemplate the forms without interruption; for they are the best qualified to rule, since their knowledge of the forms allows them to understand the shadows and likenesses in the cave (520c–d). If it is necessary, they will embody their conception of the forms in the institutions of the city and the characters of its citizens (500d); and since the interest of the city demands it, it becomes necessary for them to take their part in ruling.

Glaucon is surprised by these remarks of Socrates on the philosophers. He asks whether it is not unjust to demand this of the philosophers, since they are required to have a worse life when it is possible for them to have a better life (519d8–9). Socrates replies that the ideal city is designed for the happiness of all the citizens, not for the exclusive happiness of a single group (519e9–520a4); it is best for the whole city if it is ruled by people who do not regard ruling as a prize to be fought over, and so it is just to expect the philosophers to rule the city as a repayment for their upbringing (520a6–d8). We might suppose that if they are 'compelled' (520a8; e2) to return to government, and if they regard it as 'necessary' rather than 'fine' (540b2–5), they must be giving up happiness. If it promoted their happiness, why would they need to be compelled, and why would they not regard it as fine?[55]

---

[55] Foster, 'Implications', and White, *ICGE* 203–11, argue that the choice of the philosophers to rule involves a sacrifice of their own happiness. On the other side see Kraut, 'Return'. Foster regards it as the choice of duty over interest: 'It is remarkable because it contains the conception, expressed, to my knowledge, nowhere else in Greek philosophy, of Moral Obligation, or Duty.... In the *Republic* all the acts in the life of a Guardian up to the point at which he is bidden to return to the cave are ... determined as right or wrong according as they are or are not means to his highest good, which is the achievement of the best life. But the command to return to the cave both is and is clearly recognized to be a command to surrender a better life for a worse one. If this act therefore is right, it is right in a different sense from that of conducing to his highest good' (301–2). Foster emphasizes this passage as an exception to the general tendency of Greek ethics because he believes (partly under Hegelian influence; see Hegel, *PR* §184A) that the Greeks in general lack a clear enough conception of the difference between one's own good and the good of the community to formulate any general problem about duty and interest. Foster, however, does not uncritically accept all of Hegel's account of Plato; see *PPPH*, ch. 3. See also White, *ICGE*, ch. 4.

If we suppose that the obligations of justice conflict with the philosopher's happiness, we have to conclude that the initial question about justice and happiness has no simple answer. Philosophers develop their rational desires and aspirations, and by doing this they discover the ultimate good, which consists in the study of universal truths about the ultimate character of reality, revealed in the nature and structure of the forms. This change of focus from everyday concerns to the study of universal truths takes them beyond ordinary temptations to injustice; they will not be interested in the recognized goods that might lead them to want to get the better of their neighbours. In this way, they will avoid the commonplace manifestations of injustice (442e–443b). But they also renounce the normal sources of concern for the welfare of others. In the *Theaetetus* Socrates suggests that the philosopher will take no interest in what happens in the city or in what his neighbours are doing, because he is too absorbed in his study of the forms (*Tht.* 173c6–176a2). If this is Plato's view in the *Republic* too, ruling is a distraction from what is most worthwhile, and some necessity distinct from the rational necessity of pursuing one's ultimate good has to be imposed on the philosopher. Though the rational order of the just soul is non-instrumentally good for the philosopher, and though the philosopher will do actions required by justice and refrain from unjust actions, the other-regarding aspects of justice are not in themselves non-instrumentally good for him.

According to this view, the recognized moral virtues are useful partly for their 'purifying' or 'purgative' role (cf. *Phd.* 69a–e), in so far as they reduce the distracting effect of non-rational desires and so help us to concentrate on the development of the rational part that eventually leads to the grasp of the forms. They are also useful for their instrumental role in holding together the society that the philosophers need to maintain their daily life and to supply their needs. But the higher form of the virtues that belongs to the philosophers lacks any non-instrumental concern for the good of others.

This view of Plato's account of the virtues influences later Platonism in antiquity and beyond.[56] A complete history of moral philosophy might reasonably be expected to give this aspect of Platonism a prominent place. It marks a turn away from the Socratic tradition, in so far as it treats the moral virtues as preliminaries that can in due course be abandoned in favour of some higher way of life. Though they may have a legitimate instrumental role in the contingent circumstances of human life, they have no legitimate claim to capture any ultimate non-instrumental values.

62. The Philosopher as Ruler: No Sacrifice of Happiness?

But before we attribute this Platonist view on justice and happiness to Plato in the *Republic*, we should ask whether he commits himself to it. We may assume too readily that ruling requires the philosopher to give up a non-instrumentally valuable activity for something that is not worth choosing for its own sake as part of his happiness. It is not clear that Plato endorses this suggestion.

---

[56] Plotinus discusses civic and purifying virtues (referring to the *Phd.*) in *Enn.* i 2.1–3. See Annas, *PEON*, ch. 3; Gerson, P199; *AOP* 242–52; Sedley, 'Ideal'; Brittain, 'Attention'. Plotinus is also influenced by the intellectualist conception of happiness that he finds in Aristotle. On Aristotle see §82. On Christianity see §215. On Augustine see §234.

He intends this passage to throw light on his main question about whether it is worth our while to be just. For two aspects of this passage in Book vii recall some of the early moves in Book i: (1) In saying that the philosophers rule unwillingly, Socrates recalls his remark in Book i that in a city of good men rulers would take on their task reluctantly, in contrast to the eagerness of most people now for the spoils of office; they would be reluctant because they would realize that ruling is primarily for the benefit of the ruled (R. 347b5–d8). (2) In saying that the philosophers repay the city, Socrates recalls the very first attempted description of justice, as paying back what one has borrowed (331c). He implies that this first description, despite its inadequacy, captured something important about justice. These two recollections of Book i remind us of features of justice that might reasonably suggest that it is another's good.

Plato acknowledges that this is an important feature of justice, and that it seems to create a difficulty for his conception of the philosopher-rulers. They have just souls, in so far as they realize the human function in rational agency. But it seems that they would do this most fully if they continued their reflexions on the forms and did not have to turn back to the vexations of government and administration. Glaucon seems to be right to ask Socrates whether the philosophers are compelled to live a worse life than they would have led had they reflected without interruption on the forms.

But Socrates does not directly answer Glaucon's question about whether the philosophers have a worse life than they would have had if they had not been compelled to govern. He might give either of two answers to this question: (1) The city compels the philosophers to have a less happy life than they would otherwise have, but it does not treat them unjustly. (2) The city does not treat them unjustly and does not compel them to have a less happy life than they would otherwise have. Plato's position is difficult to settle, because it is difficult to see which of these two answers he gives.

In favour of the first answer, we must admit that Socrates directly answers only the question about justice. He argues that the city is asking the philosophers for a fair return for their philosophical upbringing (520a6–d5). He asks Glaucon whether, in the light of this consideration about justice, the philosophers will be unwilling (*ouk ethelêsousin*, 520d7) to take on the task of ruling. Glaucon answers that they will indeed be willing, since they are just people, and the city is requiring just action of them. Socrates reminds Glaucon that the ideal city is not constructed to secure the superior welfare of any one class in the city, but to secure the welfare of the whole city. We might infer that the philosophers have to sacrifice their welfare for the welfare of the whole city.

Socrates does not commit himself to the first answer, however. His comment on the organization of the ideal city shows that the philosopher is expected to care about other things besides her own good; it does not show that she is expected to care about these things for the sake of some ultimate end other than her own good. Moreover, the main strategy of the *Republic* might reasonably lead us to expect the second answer. Plato has set out to show that the just person is happier than anyone else, irrespective of any external advantages or disadvantages. He would raise a serious doubt about his strategy if he had to admit that the happiest person is the philosopher who evades his task of ruling and remains contemplating the forms. But we may suppose he has clearly conceded the most damaging point, when

Glaucon suggests that it is possible (*dunaton*) for the philosophers to lead a better life than the one they are required to lead.

We can perhaps see how to answer these questions if we reconsider Glaucon's remark. He asks 'Will we not treat them unjustly and make them live worse, it being possible (*dunaton*) for them to live better?' (519d8–9). But it is not clear whether 'it being possible . . .' is part of the question or an assertion of Glaucon's. Does he mean 'Given that they could live better, will we make them live worse?' Or does he mean 'Will we make them live worse in circumstances where they could live better?' If we understand him to ask the second question rather than the first, he does not assert that it is possible for the philosophers to live a better life than the life in which they share in ruling. In any case, Socrates does not concede that a better life really is possible for the philosophers, in the specific circumstances of the ideal city. If human beings were self-sufficient, or if government were not needed, perhaps the philosophers would have a better life open to them than the life that involves ruling. But in the actual circumstances—Plato may believe—no life better than the life of ruling is possible, because the life of ruling is the just life.

In that case, the references to compulsion and necessity do not show that the philosophers sacrifice happiness by taking part in government. Compulsion may include rational necessity, so that a course of action is 'necessary' or 'required' in so far as no other course is rationally acceptable; this sort of compulsion does not imply that I am not doing what I think best for the sake of my own happiness. Similarly, the fact that government in itself is necessary rather than fine does not show that the just action of taking part in government is not fine. In contrast to reflexion on the forms, government in itself is only instrumentally valuable; one would not choose it except for its results. But the just action that consists in taking part in government is fine, precisely in so far as it is required by justice. If we interpret Plato in this way, he does not concede that a sacrifice of theoretical study for the sake of a just person's obligations is a sacrifice of happiness.

63. Love, Self-Concern, and Concern for Others

But even if the *Republic* maintains consistently that the person with a just soul is concerned for others, and suffers no loss of happiness thereby, it does not explain why this is so. Plato assumes that the philosophers will recognize a necessity to express and to embody what they have learnt from their study of the forms, so that individuals, laws, and institutions manifest the same rational order (500b7–d9). He regards this as a rational necessity that the philosophers recognize as giving them a good reason to legislate. But he does not describe the basis of this rational necessity.

He suggests a possible basis, however, in saying that the philosophers act out of love (*erôs*) for wisdom and for the forms (485a10–d5; 490a–b; 499c1–2; 501c6). We might treat these brief references to eros simply as strong expressions of the philosophers' attachment to their philosophical activity. But it may be relevant that in other dialogues, especially in the *Symposium* and the *Phaedrus*, Plato explains how a desire that he calls 'eros' is an aspect of rational motivation. It is worth considering a few points from the discussion of eros in the *Symposium*, to see whether they throw any light on the questions that the *Republic* leaves without complete answers.

In the most relevant section of the *Symposium* Diotima, a woman of Mantinea, explains to Socrates that eros, initially understood as a desire for the 'beautiful' or 'fine' (*kalon*), really manifests the general desire for one's own happiness (*Symp.* 204e1–205d9). To explain the connexion between the desire for one's own happiness and the desire for the fine, she discusses rational concern for one's own future, which she compares to the propagation of one person by another. In self-concern for the future I seek to transmit my character and personality to someone who in some ways is different from myself. The persistence of a single person does not require any one component of the person to stay qualitatively the same through a person's lifetime; it requires the appropriate causal and qualitative connexions between different stages.[57] The future self that I have reason to be concerned about must carry on some of the traits that I value; hence, as Plato puts it, I aim at propagation in the 'beautiful' or 'fine' (*kalon*). Since enlightened self-concern belongs to the rational part, it rests on concerns based on our values, and not simply on the strength of our desires. That is why desire for one's own happiness leads to desire for the fine. I aim at my own preservation by aiming at the preservation of what I value in myself.

This analysis of self-concern is also relevant to concern for others because it helps to explain why I might reasonably value states of others besides myself. If I want to propagate states of myself that I value, I may do this by propagating them in others. I sometimes ought to prefer propagation of these traits in others, since I cannot always ensure my own continued existence, and this limitation may prevent me from fully realizing in myself everything that I might value in myself. In these cases the reasons that lead me to care about myself should lead me to prefer propagation of these valuable traits in another person. That is why Diotima mentions poets and legislators among those who have propagated themselves by propagation of the fine (208e5–209e4).[58]

The desire for propagation in the fine explains the philosopher's attachment to the forms as a manifestation of the general desire to propagate what one values. As we come to learn more about what is fine, we change our views about what is worth propagating. When we reach the form, we understand most fully what is really fine and beautiful, and that is what we want to propagate in ourselves and other people (210a4–212a7).[59]

Plato's explanation of the desire to propagate in the fine suggests that we would lack this desire if we were immortal, because we would not need to propagate valuable traits in others as a second-best to maintaining them in ourselves.[60] But this is not always his view. In the *Timaeus* he suggests that immortal agents also aim at propagation. The creator of the ordered world is a 'craftsman' (*dêmiourgos*), a good god who is free from spite; he does not take pleasure in making others worse off, and so he would not make anything worse than

---

[57] Plato's claims about persistence and self-concern are treated more elaborately in recent discussions of survival and identity, including Parfit, *RP*, ch. 12; Warner, 'Love'; Wolf, 'Self-interest'; Whiting, 'Friends'. See also §33.

[58] This issue is discussed by Price, *LFPA* 33–5.

[59] 212a2–7 is an especially important part of this passage, since it makes clear that the desire to propagate does not disappear once one has recognized the form of beauty. Insight into the form changes one's view about what to propagate.

[60] On questions about immortality see Price, *LFPA* 30–1.

he could make it. Since he wants everything to be as good as possible, he makes an ordered world out of the pre-cosmic disorder (*Tim.* 29d7–30c1).[61] Plato assumes that the god values his own goodness and wants to reproduce it in other things; hence the god aims at the existence of creatures who have something similar to his goodness. Even in an immortal agent, the desire for propagation rests on the desire to express and to extend the traits one values about oneself and to embody them in other things.

These few remarks of Plato's underlie Platonist and Christian doctrines of the overflowing love of God.[62] They also help to explain Plato's claims about the philosophers in the *Republic*. He claims that if some 'necessity' arises, the philosopher will be a good 'craftsman' (*dêmiourgos*) of justice and the other civic virtues (*R.* 500d4–9). We might have supposed, before taking account of the *Symposium*, that the necessity is externally imposed and results simply from the compulsion exercised by the rulers of the Platonic city. But we can now see that this is not the only source of the necessity that moves the philosophers. They are like the god of the *Timaeus* who wants to share his goodness with other things. Whereas the god creates other things to embody his goodness, the philosophers seek to reproduce in their fellow-citizens the states that they value in themselves. Since the states they value in themselves include psychic justice, they want to embody psychic justice in other people as far as possible.

64. Eudaemonism and Concern for Others

We can now say more about why the philosophers do not believe they sacrifice their happiness when they take their turn in ruling. Plato introduces the philosophers as paradigms of just people. If his claims about the philosophers are relevant to his claims about justice and happiness, his account of the motives of the philosopher should also clarify the outlook of a just person more generally. The account of eros in the *Symposium* shows why Plato does not think that the 'necessity' recognized by philosophers is confined to philosophers. The desire for reproduction in the fine is common to every rational agent, since we all care about our own preservation. Not all of us recognize that this rational concern for ourselves makes it reasonable to care about the good of others for their own sake; but we will recognize this if we reflect correctly on the nature of human happiness and the human soul.

Plato's argument in the *Symposium* supports his view about the relation between eudaemonism and morality, or—to express it in his terms—between the rational pursuit of one's own happiness and the aspects of justice that make it appear to be another's good and harmful to the just agent. He does not deny that the apparent facts about justice seem to raise a difficulty for his eudaemonism; in this respect it is quite appropriate, and not at all anachronistic, to say that he is concerned with an apparent conflict between duty and interest. We might suppose that eudaemonism makes it more difficult to explain concern for the good of others, and that we need to introduce some moral principle distinct from the pursuit of one's own happiness to justify the extension of non-instrumental concern beyond oneself. We will take Plato to agree with this view if we suppose that he believes the

---

[61] Taylor, *CPT* 78, suggests that in Plato's view, 'it is of the very nature of goodness and love to "overflow"'.
[62] See, e.g., Aquinas, *ST* 1a q20 a2 ad1.

philosophers sacrifice their happiness to their duty as rulers.[63] But we have found that this is not his view. He believes that the enlightened rational part of the soul has a holistic and comprehensive outlook that is also temporally comprehensive, and so looks forward to my future interests. An appropriately comprehensive concern for my present and future cannot allow my concerns to be confined to myself; for since I am concerned about the future embodiment of traits that I value in myself, I reasonably seek to propagate these traits in other people. As we learn more about which traits are valuable, we change our views about the traits that should be embodied in other people (*Symp.* 210a–211c).

But even if we agree with Plato's argument from concern for oneself to concern for others, we may doubt whether the concern for others that emerges from his argument is really concern for other people's interest, the sort of concern that is relevant to love and to morality. We recognize one important type of love for persons as non-instrumental concern for the good of others; this is how Aristotle describes the common conception of friendship.[64] But we might wonder whether the Platonic attitude to other persons is appropriately non-instrumental. Plato speaks of the effects of love as 'educating' or 'moulding' (*Phdr.* 252d5–e1) the beloved into the shape that the lover thinks appropriate. What has this to do with the interests of the beloved? If B is moulded into the shape in which B best satisfies A's desire for self-propagation, it seems to be A's interests rather than B's that guide the changes A tries to produce in B.

Plato's eudaemonism helps to explain why Platonic love includes concern for the interests of the other person. Since A is concerned for B as a way of propagating A, and since A cares about A's own interest for A's own sake, A will also care about B for B's own sake, not instrumentally to some further end. For in so far as B propagates A, B deserves the sort of concern that A applies to A. Though A certainly does it all for A's own sake, doing it for B's sake is doing it for A's sake, if B is A's way of propagating A. Just as A cares about the future stages of A as the results of intra-personal propagation, A has the same reason to care about B as the result of inter-personal propagation. For if B really carries on what A regards as valuable about A, then A has good reason to care about B in the same way as A cares about A.

We can make this point a little more concrete by reminding ourselves of the traits that an enlightened agent wants to propagate in others. These traits include the cardinal virtues, which embody the rational control that this agent values for its own sake. Hence we have reason to want to produce the cardinal virtues in other people too. But the cardinal virtues are the dominant element in everyone's good. Hence virtuous agents—those who value the cardinal virtues in themselves—also achieve the good of others.

This is simply an outline of Plato's argument from self-concern to concern for others. If he succeeds, he shows that agents with psychic justice also aim at the good of others, and so he defends his claim that they have the other-regarding virtue of justice that raised the main question of the *Republic*. Plato's claims raise reasonable doubts and questions at many points, but we need not pursue them in detail now, since the relevant issues arise again in later eudaemonist defences of morality.

The most important point in this argument is the strategy that other eudaemonists derive from Plato. He suggests that we find it difficult to connect self-interest with the good of

---

[63] See Foster, quoted above at n55.   [64] See *Rhet.* 1380b36–1381a1. On Aristotle see §122.

others because we have an incomplete conception of self-interest. Once we understand the scope of self-interest, correctly conceived, we see that it includes the morally appropriate concern for the interests of others. Whether or not Plato sees exactly how these two areas of concern are connected, his strategy is worth examining, because it conflicts with a common understanding of the major questions in ethics.

Philosophers who believe that morality is separate from self-interest and that it is not a simple matter to grasp the relation between the two principles are not raising a purely theoretical question. Nor is it purely a modern question. We can see from the questions of the interlocutors in the *Republic* that they do not find it obvious that a correct account of justice will demonstrate that it is part of the just agent's happiness. The position that Polus took in the *Gorgias*—that justice is finer than injustice though less beneficial to the agent (*Gorg.* 474c4–d2)—seems plausible to Plato's contemporaries and may well seem plausible to us.

Plato points out that the separation of morality from self-interest rests on a specific conception of self-interest. As we will see, Butler and Sidgwick, who sharply separate self-interest from morality, also conceive self-interest narrowly. It is worth asking whether this conception of self-interest is correct, and, if it is not correct, whether that matters for the question about self-interest and morality. Plato might be correct to question the common conception of self-interest, even if he is wrong to suppose that a correct conception resolves the questions about self-interest and morality. We can decide whether he is right or wrong only by further reflexion on the character and composition of happiness, and on the requirements of morality. Aristotle and the Stoics pursue this reflexion in some detail; if we examine their position, we can form some tentative view about the success of the eudaemonist approach to morality.

6

ARISTOTLE: HAPPINESS

65. Interpreting Aristotle

Aristotle's ethics will be prominent not only in these chapters that deal primarily with Aristotle, but also in many later chapters. Indeed, some of the discussion of his views will not be complete until the end of the book. The reasons that justify this constant return to Aristotle will give some idea of his significance.

On some points modern moralists disagree with Aristotle. His conception of an objective human good derived from a foundation in human nature is generally absent from modern moral theories; this is true of theories that in other respects differ as radically as those of Hobbes and Kant. Moreover, modern theories treat morality as the source of reasons and motives that are distinct from those of self-interest.[1] Despite their other disagreements, Butler, Hume, and Kant agree in rejecting the supremacy of reasons based on one's own good, whereas Aristotle seems to regard such reasons as supreme, both psychologically and rationally.

Aristotle provides not only a point of contrast, but also an aspect of continuity in the history of ethics. If we compare him with the modern moralists we have just mentioned, he represents the 'ancient' view. But he is a primary source and inspiration for mediaeval moral philosophy and its successors. Mediaeval philosophers, of whom Aquinas is the best known, interpret and develop Aristotle so as to form a position that justifiably regards itself as Aristotelian, but is no mere paraphrase of Aristotle.

If we neglect the continuity of the Aristotelian tradition, some contrasts between ancient and modern moral philosophy seem obvious. If we recognize the continuity of this tradition, the contrasts blur. This is especially true of some supposedly non-Aristotelian elements in modern moral philosophy. We might be inclined to believe that Aristotle lacks a conception of distinct moral reasons. But it is more difficult to believe this about Aquinas. And if Aquinas believes that his conception is based on Aristotle, we may be less confident that Aristotle differs from modern moral philosophy as sharply as we initially supposed. If we notice how later Aristotelians understand Aristotle, we may be persuaded to interpret him differently from how we would interpret him if we did not take account of these later versions of Aristotelian ethics.

---

[1] But see §368 on Scotus.

But should we allow these later versions to influence us in the interpretation of Aristotle? Even if Aquinas shows us how one might defend or exploit some aspects of Aristotle, should we not resist any attempt to explain Aristotle himself in the light of later reflexions? One might argue that a proper historical account of Aristotle ought to explain him without any reference to the ways in which later philosophers understand him, so that we have a neutral basis from which we can see who has understood him correctly. On this basis we might try to decide who has defended Aristotle, and who has defended some selected Aristotelian themes.

The task of separating the interpretation of Aristotle from the views of later expositors and defenders is less simple than it may appear. We understand the significance of Aristotle's claims only if we understand what they imply, and how they might be defended or attacked. These are questions for the philosophical critic, and later philosophical criticism may help us to grasp the point of what Aristotle says. Some later critics, therefore, may help us to understand Aristotle better than we would understand him if we ignored later philosophy. Some of Aquinas' main doctrines are not only inspired by Aristotle, but also make clear the implications of Aristotle's views. If this is true, we may reasonably rely on Aquinas in interpreting Aristotle. But he is not the only later critic who defends views about the significance and value of Aristotle; to reach a reasonable view of Aristotle we may need to compare Aquinas' views with the alternatives that other critics offer.[2]

Still, we cannot even argue convincingly that later critics have interpreted Aristotle correctly unless we have some idea of his position that does not already assume that they are correct. We need a preliminary account of Aristotle that helps us to see why his readers might reasonably be puzzled about how to understand and to develop his views. We need to see where Aristotle is inexplicit or silent, so that a critic needs to supply some argument or explanation. To reach a fair estimate of the views of different critics, we should exercise some restraint in our initial interpretation of Aristotle. We should make it clear why it might be reasonable to disagree about what Aristotle means, or about how to elaborate some of his claims to make them fit others.

We would be going too far in this direction, however, if we gave the impression that there is no right answer, that one interpretation cannot be defended as the best way of understanding and explaining Aristotle. To do justice to Aristotle in the history of ethics, we should recognize that answers to some questions of interpretation are not obvious, but can be found.

66. Aristotle's Main Contributions

Aristotle begins where Socrates and Plato left off. He recognizes that he continues the ethical inquiries they began. While he cites poets and sages as sources of moral views, he mentions only Socrates, Plato, Eudoxus, and Speusippus as sources of theoretical views that agree or disagree with his own—about the nature of the good, or pleasure, or virtue, or incontinence, for instance. Many of the topics of the *Ethics* are familiar to readers of the Platonic dialogues.[3]

---

[2] Other relevant discussions include those by Suarez, Butler, and Green.

[3] In speaking of the '*Ethics*' I refer to the *EN*, which I take to be the latest and best statement of Aristotle's ethical theory. This is the work that influences mediaeval and later moralists. (The role of the different ethical treatises in

In discussing happiness, the virtues, and pleasure Aristotle continues Plato's inquiries. In arguing that virtue promotes happiness, that the best life is also the pleasantest life, and that if we have one virtue we have all the virtues, he defends Plato's conclusions.

Aristotle often argues more fully than Plato argues for central Platonic claims, but this is not always true. Some significant exceptions are these: (1) Though Aristotle is as convinced as Plato is (see ix 4) that virtue always promotes happiness more than vice does, a defence of this claim is not a central element in the *Ethics* as it is in the *Republic*. (2) Though Aristotle relies on the Platonic division of the soul, he does not argue for it as fully as Plato does in *Republic* iv, but tends to take it for granted in, for instance, his doctrine of virtue as a mean and in his explanation of incontinence.⁴ (3) Though he mentions (in vi 13) that he accepts the reciprocity of the virtues, he discusses this topic less fully than Plato discusses it in the *Protagoras* and the *Statesman*; he confines himself to answering an objection to it.

We cannot explain Aristotle's comparative brevity on these points by supposing that he takes them to be unimportant; they are central elements of his moral theory. We might conjecture that he treats them briefly because he is relatively satisfied with Plato's treatment of them, and supposes that his audience will know what he means even if he does not expound his views at length.

This might lead us to a further conjecture; perhaps the topics that Aristotle treats at greater length are those on which he is not satisfied with Plato's discussion. If we identify the main features of the *Ethics* that are unfamiliar to a reader of Plato, how do they change or strengthen Plato's position?

In the *Republic* Plato does not explain or defend very fully the conception of happiness presupposed in his claim that justice promotes happiness. In the *Philebus* he has more to say about the nature of the human good; he sets out the general conditions of completeness, sufficiency, and universal attractiveness, and tries to show how these conditions support a life of pleasure combined with intelligence over either version of the unmixed life. He does not undertake the longer task of showing that these general conditions can be used to support a plausible account of the final good, or that this account justifies the virtues, as Plato conceives them.

Aristotle undertakes this task in the *Ethics*. He offers an account of the concept of the highest good, formal criteria⁵ for the good, and an argument from these formal criteria to a specific conception of happiness, identified with the highest good. He tries to show that he has found a true account of a human being's happiness, and a true account of the human virtues, and that these true accounts fit together in the right way. According to one reasonable interpretation, he argues that happiness is a composite good, and that the virtues are dominant parts of it.

In *Republic* iv Plato identifies the four major virtues with the well-ordered condition of the tripartite soul. But he does not say much about what actions can be expected from someone

---

Hellenistic philosophy is not so clear.) I refer only occasionally to the other two ethical works in the Aristotelian corpus, the *EE* and *MM*. Kenny, *APL*, chs. 1–3, Appendix 1, defends a different view of the relation between the ethical treatises. I follow most modern critics in supposing that the three books, *EN* v, vi, and vii, were originally written as part of the *EE*.

⁴ See 1102a18–32; 1104b24–6; 1110b10–19; 1149a24–b23. *DA* 432b3–7 also treats the partition of the soul as familiar. The controversy is about the nature of the parts and the relation between them, not about their reality.

⁵ On formal criteria see §53; §71 below.

with a well-ordered soul, or why these actions are virtuous actions. A treatise on ethics ought to include a fuller account of the virtues. If this fuller account fits Plato's eudaemonist starting point, it ought to argue that the different virtues can be understood in the light of a correct conception of happiness. Aristotle argues for this claim through his discussion of the virtues of character and intellect.

Aristotle follows Socrates and Plato in supposing that virtuous action is rational because it aims at an appropriate end. But this teleological assumption raises a difficulty. Socrates identifies teleological rationality with the productive rationality of a craft, so that virtues are choiceworthy because of some external end that they causally promote. Plato claims that justice is worth choosing for its own sake and not only for its causal results. He thereby implicitly denies that productive rationality is the only sort of rational goal-direction, but he does not offer a clear alternative. Aristotle, however, distinguishes two sorts of goal-directed actions: production (*poiêsis*) aims at some end other than the production itself, whereas in 'action' or 'activity' (*praxis*) 'good action itself is the end' (1140b7). He claims that some action can be understood teleologically though it is not simply a means to an end that is wholly external to it. His distinction shows how the virtues fit into happiness without having merely instrumental value, and why a virtuous person can both regard happiness as the ultimate end and choose virtuous action for its own sake.

A virtue of character is 'a state that decides' (*hexis prohairetikê*). Aristotle's account of 'decision' or 'election' (*prohairesis*)[6] expands Plato's remarks on the desires of the rational part of the soul. Decision is the product of wish (*boulêsis*) and deliberation. It is a central feature of responsible action and of virtue. In requiring the right decision, Aristotle seeks to describe the rational element in virtue. His description is, at first sight, paradoxical. For he claims that we decide on actions as promoting ends, not as ends themselves, but he also insists that the virtuous person decides on the virtuous action for its own sake. This paradox dissolves, and the coherence of Aristotle's position becomes clear, once we apply the distinction between production and activity to Aristotle's claims about decision. The virtuous person decides on virtuous actions as activities that in themselves, not simply through their consequences, partly achieve the end. A composite conception of happiness helps to explain the role of virtuous actions.

According to Aristotle, the mark of the virtuous person is the choice of virtuous action 'because it is fine (*kalon*)' or 'for the sake of the fine'. Plato often mentions the fine in connexion with virtue, but he does not appeal to it, as Aristotle does, in describing the motives of the virtuous person. Aristotle's contemporaries contrast acting for the sake of the fine with acting for the sake of one's own benefit; to say that virtuous people prefer the fine over the beneficial is to make it clear that they prefer the advantage of others over their own advantage. By insisting on an aspect of virtue that might seem to raise difficulties for his eudaemonism, Aristotle acknowledges that a eudaemonist must explain this aspect of virtue. He believes he can explain it by appeal to his composite conception of happiness.

---

[6] I have used both 'decision' (perhaps the least unsatisfactory English rendering) and 'election' (to prepare for Aquinas' use of 'electio') to render *prohairesis* and the cognate verb. In any case the rendering 'choice' should be avoided, since it conceals the fact that Aristotle often uses an ordinary Greek word for choice (*hairesis*), but does not suggest that *prohairesis* is identical to *hairesis*.

Justice and the rest of other-regarding morality seem difficult to justify by reference to one's own happiness. The difficulty convinced Thrasymachus that the other-regarding virtues cannot be rationally justified. To answer Thrasymachus, Aristotle does not concentrate on justice, as Plato does, but on friendship. One fifth of the whole *EN* is devoted to the description, analysis, and justification of friendship; the prominence of this virtue in Aristotle is one major point of difference from Plato's treatment of ethics. In showing how friendship is part of happiness, Aristotle explains how regard for others is not merely of instrumental value.

Some of these arguments show why we can consistently choose virtue for its own sake, because it is fine, and because it promotes our happiness. But it is not enough to show that we can take this attitude. We normally suppose, and Aristotle's readers suppose as well, that acceptance of morality is not simply one choice that we are free to make, but a choice that we must make. The 'must' here cannot be the 'must' of physical or psychological compulsion; virtue requires the free preference of morality over other options that are recognized as open. Aristotle relies on some suggestions of Plato's to argue that we must choose the moral virtues because they are uniquely appropriate for us as the kinds of beings that we are; he argues from the needs and characteristics of human nature to the appropriateness of choosing these specific virtues. The virtues constitute the good states of human beings; they make human beings good, and are good for human beings, as the kinds of things they are, just as healthy leaves, roots, and trunks make trees good trees and are good for trees. This goodness of human beings depends on the good of human beings, just as the goodness of trees depends on the good of trees.

The appeal to facts about human nature—whether we take them to be biological, psychological, or metaphysical—appears at crucial points in the argument, and plays a vital theoretical role in ethics, as Aristotle conceives it. This aspect of the *Ethics* has received severe criticism. If we agree with the criticism, then we may reasonably want to see how much of Aristotle's views on ethics can stand without the appeal to nature. If we reject the criticism, the task of eliminating the appeal to nature from Aristotle's position will appear less urgent.

These features of the *Ethics* suggest that Aristotle's argument is more systematic than we might initially suppose. The *Ethics* discusses happiness, virtue, friendship, pleasure, and contemplation in a loose framework that does not often advertise a cumulative argument. The prominence of relatively minor details (for instance, the different aspects of special justice, the minor intellectual virtues, the casuistical questions about friendship) may give the impression that Aristotle cares more about detailed description than about the broader questions of justification that occupy Plato in the *Republic*. This impression, however, is misleading. Aristotle believes that Plato has left him with the task of arguing that virtue and happiness fit together when each is properly understood. If we do not think of happiness as a composite end, and if we do not decide on virtue as a component of happiness, we cannot, in Aristotle's view, defend the eudaemonist position in the way that Plato sketches in the *Republic*. If, however, we understand happiness correctly, we can recognize the impartial and other-regarding aspects of the virtues within a eudaemonist argument.

Aristotle's treatment of virtue and happiness is controversial. The main Hellenistic schools—Cynics, Cyrenaics, Epicureans, and Stoics—accept this estimate of Aristotle's version of eudaemonism. The Cyrenaics reject eudaemonism altogether. The Stoics modify the Aristotelian conception of happiness to bring happiness closer to virtue; Epicurus rejects the assumption that virtue must be shown to be valuable for its own sake, not purely instrumentally.

The same sorts of doubts about Aristotelian eudaemonism underlie the still more radical criticisms by Christian moralists. Their objections seem to imply that Aristotle is basically misguided in taking one's own happiness and the cultivation of one's own virtue to be morally acceptable aims. These are the objections that Aquinas seeks to answer, by arguing that Aristotle's account of happiness and virtue supports a correct view of the human good and of the place of the moral virtues in it; this view, according to Aquinas, needs to be extended and transformed, but not rejected or abandoned, in the light of the Christian revelation.

67. Method

Near the beginning of the *Nicomachean Ethics* (i 3–4) and the *Eudemian Ethics* (i 6), Aristotle briefly discusses the proper method for moral philosophy. His remarks have influenced many of his successors, even including those who do not accept the rest of his ethical outlook, and they raise some questions about what moral philosophers should try to do and what they might hope to achieve.

He refers to common views about the ultimate good and happiness, and promises to proceed by examining the most widespread and plausible of common views (1095a28–30). By beginning from these views, we begin from what is 'known to us' (1095b2–4).[7] Aristotle sometimes cites common beliefs and the puzzles (*aproriai*) they raise,[8] and in one place he suggests that the aim of his ethical reflexion is to remove puzzles raised by common beliefs (1145b2–7).[9] This procedure is similar to the procedure of 'dialectic', as Aristotle describes it.

Dialectic is Aristotle's version of Socratic argument applied to common beliefs.[10] He tries to find the most plausible objections and puzzles that can be raised from common beliefs and against common beliefs, and looks for a resolution that resolves apparent contradictions and conflicts. By endorsing dialectical method in ethics Aristotle expresses the Socratic conviction that moral philosophy is accessible to those who are honest and persistent enough to inquire into their own basic convictions and the connexions between them. Moral theory, according to this Socratic view, does not require a whole philosophical system or a full understanding of reality as a whole. It is an autonomous discipline, in so far as its basic principles are independent of disputes in natural science and the rest of philosophy.

[7] 'Presumably, then, the starting point we should begin from is what is known to us. . . . the starting point is the that and if this is apparent enough to us, we will not need the why in addition; and if we have this good upbringing, we have the starting points, or can easily acquire them' (1095b3–8).

[8] See, e.g., i 8; 1143b36; 1144b32–4; viii 1; 1168a28–b13; 1169b3–8.

[9] The passage is quoted in §2n1. On puzzles (*aporiai*) cf. *Top.* 145b16–20. Aristotle says he will proceed in this way in the case of incontinence 'as in the other cases', implying that he offers a general statement on method. Since he does not say what 'the other cases' are, we cannot conclude for certain that the statement applies to all his ethical arguments, but such a conclusion is supported by the use of dialectical expressions throughout the *Ethics*. Contrast Annas, *MH* 142n3, claiming that this passage 'is sometimes wrongly elevated to a general strategy in ethics'.

[10] Dialectic is 'a method from which we will be able to syllogize from common beliefs (*endoxa*) about every topic proposed to us, and will say nothing conflicting when we give an account ourselves' (*Top.* 100a18–21).

We need to use a dialectical method in the *Ethics* because we are looking for the basic principles (*archai*) of a discipline.[11] We cannot rely on accepted principles in order to support ethical advice; for our inquiry looks for principles in the light of which we can decide the right basis for giving advice. Since we are 'on the road towards the principles' (1095a30–b1), we have to rely on some appropriate standard for acceptance of a theoretical principle. Aristotle suggests that the appropriate standard is success in finding the 'why' that explains the 'that'. The beliefs 'that' just people do not take bribes, 'that' one ought not to betray other people in danger just to save one's skin, and so on are the appropriate places to start.

What sort of 'why' explains the 'that'? We might think Aristotle's statement of his aim is ambiguous between explanation and justification. We might find an explanation that makes it clear why we hold the moral beliefs we hold. It might show that we are impressed by superficial analogies, that we remain attached to principles that once had socially desirable consequences but have outlived their usefulness, and that we fail to draw the logical implications of some of our beliefs that conflict with others that we also hold tenaciously. The explanation offered by this sort of 'why' would reasonably encourage us to question our moral outlook; the questions might either prompt us to look for something better or leave us in sceptical detachment.

Among ancient philosophers the Sceptics offer this potentially undermining 'why'. The modern philosophers who offer it include Mandeville, Sidgwick, and Mackie.[12] While these philosophers draw different conclusions from their undermining explanations, they agree in believing that a search for the 'why' exposes some error in the moral beliefs that we explain.

A different sort of 'why' might tell us not why we believe what we believe about morality, but why a brave person faces danger in some conditions but not in others, why we ought to keep our promises, and so on. The 'why' is understood as 'Why should we?' rather than 'Why do we?', and the answer we look for will justify the convictions that we began with. On this view, we have not found the 'why' we are looking for until we have found a justification for our initial beliefs.

These two approaches to the 'why' seem to require different treatments of the common beliefs we begin from. If we are looking for a justification, we apparently need to take a critical attitude to them; we will want to see where they seem inconsistent or irrational, and we will want to find some reasonable way of resolving inconsistencies. If we are looking for an explanation without a justification, we have no reason to try to resolve inconsistencies; on the contrary, exposure of them may help us to reveal the conflicting assumptions that underlie our beliefs.

Aristotle's treatment of common beliefs and the puzzles they raise suggests that he expects the 'why' to yield a justification, and not simply an explanation. He does not begin from all commonly-held beliefs indiscriminately, but tries to exclude those that seem simply to reflect particular people's bias in their specific circumstances. He tries to set out from those

---

[11] 'And it [sc. dialectic] is also useful for <finding> the first things in each science. For we cannot say anything about them from the proper principles of the science in question, since the principles are prior to everything else, but it is necessary to discuss them through the common beliefs on each subject. And this is proper to dialectic alone, or to it more than to anything else; for since it examines, it has a road towards the principles of all disciplines' (*Top.* 101a36–b4).

[12] See Mandeveille, *FB* i 56 (Kaye) = R 270; Sidgwick (n14 below); Mackie, *E*, chs. 1–2.

that are very widely held, or seem to have some argument in their favour.[13] Nor does he simply list the common beliefs; he seeks to 'examine' (*exetazein*) them, using Socrates' term for his cross-examinations of interlocutors. Like Socrates, he examines people's beliefs in order to expose the difficulties and puzzles that they raise. We look for a principle that allows us to resolve the puzzles, and to vindicate either all the common beliefs, or at least the 'most and most important' of them (1145b4–6). The principle that we ought to reach is 'known by nature', and not merely 'known to us'; it tells us how things are in their own right, apart from our beliefs and desires.

Though Aristotle describes his method as a search for justification, we may wonder whether he succeeds.[14] It is easy to suppose that he offers a systematic description of common moral beliefs. It is harder to see how he shows that some beliefs are more 'important' than others, and that these are the ones that should be preserved. We need to consider the standards he relies on in resolving the conflicts he finds in common beliefs, and why he believes these are reasonable standards.

He also gives a different account of his method in the *Ethics*. Instead of speaking of dialectic, he describes ethical inquiry as a sort of 'political science' (*politikê*, 1094b10–11).[15] Political science is a form of practical science, and its method is deliberative. It is the same cognitive state as prudence (*phronêsis*), which deliberates about what promotes happiness as a whole (1141b23–33). Deliberation assumes some end, and then considers what has to be done to secure it (1112b11–16). Once we have identified what we can do here and now to achieve our end, we make an election (*prohairesis*; 1113a9–12).

Aristotle suggests at the beginning of the *Ethics* that he will follow this deliberative method, but not in the usual way. In goal-directed crafts, such as medicine or building, we begin with a conception of the healthy condition we want to produce in the patient, or of the house we want to build; it is not our task to say what health is or a house is. In the *Ethics* Aristotle begins by introducing a final good as the ultimate end, but he does not begin by taking for granted the character and composition of this ultimate end. On the contrary, his first question asks what this final good is (1094a22–6). In this case the deliberative task includes the dialectical inquiry that is needed to find an account of the good; such an account will be the basic principle, and so (as the *Topics* remarks, 101a36–b4[16]) we have to discover it by dialectic.

Ethical inquiry differs from other forms of deliberative inquiry on this point because it lacks the usual basis for fixing a definite conception of the end that is to be realized in action. If we are trying to make bridles, our craft is controlled by the end set by the equestrian craft;

---

[13] 'Presumably, then, it is rather futile to examine all these beliefs, and it is enough to examine those that are most current or seem to have some argument for them' (1095a28–30). The appropriate common beliefs should be apparent (*phainomena*), 'but apparent not to just anyone, but to people of a certain sort; for it is an indefinitely long task to examine the things that make something apparent to just anyone' (*Top.* 170b6–8).

[14] Sidgwick understands Aristotle's account as a systematic description pointing the way to an undermining explanation of common sense: 'I had to read Aristotle again; and a light seemed to dawn upon me as to the meaning and drift of his procedure—especially in Books ii, iii, iv. of the *Ethics* . . . What he gave us there was the Common Sense Morality of Greece, reduced to consistency by careful comparison: given not as something external to him but as what "we"—he and others—think, ascertained by reflection. And was not this really the Socratic induction, elicited by interrogation?' (*ME* xxi). On Sidgwick's attitude to Aristotle see §115.

[15] The Greek has no noun here. 'Science' (*epistêmê*) or 'capacity' (*dunamis*) has to be supplied from 1094a26.

[16] Quoted in n11 above.

if we are trying to formulate a new pill to relieve headaches, our craft is controlled by the end set by pharmacy and medicine; but in political science we are trying to find the highest end, and so we cannot appeal to any higher end to give us a definite conception of our end. Since we are looking for a basic principle, we need dialectical inquiry.

Aristotle captures this difference between political science and most other sciences by saying that political science is practical rather than productive, because it is concerned with 'action' (*praxis*) and not simply with 'production' or 'making' (*poiêsis*). In Aristotle's strict sense of 'action', an action is itself the end that we aim at, not a mere means to some end external to it (1140b6–7). If we are trying to find the appropriate form of non-instrumental action, we cannot simply consider its causal consequences for the production of some external end; we need to see how it can non-instrumentally realize an end that it partly constitutes. Some of the central questions about Aristotle's ethics turn on our understanding of his claims about non-instrumental realization.

68. The Role of the Final Good

Aristotle takes his first step towards an account of the final good by explaining why it has to be the concern of political science. He begins: 'Every craft and every line of inquiry, and similarly action and decision, seems to aim at some good' (1094a1–2). Crafts and lines of inquiry are examples of productive reasoning, in which we seek some end that is external to the productive process itself. 'Action and decision' are to be contrasted with these productive processes, but Aristotle claims that non-instrumental action is included in his generalization.[17] Whenever one discipline is subordinate to another, the end of the superordinate discipline is more choiceworthy than the end of the subordinate discipline (1094a14–18), and this relation of subordination and superordination among ends applies to action no less than to production. Whenever a number of disciplines are under a single discipline, the single discipline is 'architectonic' in relation to the others.

These remarks introduce Aristotle's concept of an ultimate end to which every other end is subordinate; this is an end that we pursue for its own sake and for the sake of which we pursue everything else.[18] If there is such an end, it is the concern of the 'most controlling and most architectonic' science. If, then, we can conceive a supreme and most architectonic science, we can see that there is a final good, which must be its object.

Aristotle claims that the most architectonic science is political science. In some cases political science decides that a particular discipline is not worth learning at all; in other cases it prescribes the extent to which different disciplines ought to be practised. It regulates the disciplines that it allows to be practised, and this regulation extends even to the disciplines that are concerned with action rather than production (1094a28–b7). Since political science

---

[17] 'Some ends are activities, others are products beyond the activities' (1094a4–5) distinguishes *praxis* (the first case) from *poiêsis* (the second case).

[18] Some critics have argued that Aristotle commits a fallacy here, arguing from the fact that we do not pursue everything for the sake of some other end to the conclusion that there is just one end that we pursue for its own sake and for the sake of which we pursue everything else. This objection is clearly stated and defended by Ackrill, 'Eudaimonia'. Contrast Kraut, *AHG* 217–20. The objection fails to take seriously the 'if' in 1094a18.

has this regulative task, its end includes the ends of the other sciences, and so this end is the human good (1094a26–b7).

If the end of political science were not all-inclusive, it would be irrational, according to Aristotle, to allow political science ultimate authority in regulating all the other sciences. If there were some end superior to the end of political science, we ought to regulate all our other pursuits by reference to that end. And if there were an end co-ordinate with the end of political science, we could not allow political science the exclusive right to regulate other pursuits.

Aristotle assumes that it is rational to decide about the regulation of different pursuits only if we refer to some end that includes the value resulting from each of them.[19] Some regulative decisions need not refer to the absolutely final good, but should at least refer to a good that is final and all-embracing in relation to the pursuits being regulated. If, for instance, we tried to regulate both the production of leather and the production of swords by reference to purely military needs, we would reach the right level of production of swords, but we would underestimate the appropriate level of production of leather (since we need leather for shoes and for other non-military purposes, but we need swords only for military purposes). In that case we would not have chosen an appropriately inclusive end to regulate the two subordinate ends. The final good is appropriately inclusive in relation to all other ends that we might reasonably pursue.

Aristotle does not simply claim that political science has an all-inclusive end. He also claims that it studies fine and just things (1094b14–15) and that it studies virtue, and how to make citizens good and law-abiding (1102a7–10). This concern falls within the area of the comprehensive other-directed virtue that he calls 'general justice' (cf. 1129b11–27). Aristotle does not simply claim that the characters of citizens may affect the attainment of the final good pursued by politics. This fact about the virtues does not distinguish them from many other things that political science might consider; it seems to have the same reason for concern about the ends of many different subordinate sciences. When Aristotle marks virtue as a special concern of political science, he implies that virtue is especially closely linked to the final good; this link distinguishes virtue from the various other concerns of political science.

It is not trivial, then, to claim that ethics—the study of virtue and character—is a special or primary concern of political science—the science that regulates and organizes subordinate goods to produce the final good. Aristotle assumes the truth of some claim that he has not yet spelt out, about the link between virtue and the final good.

69. The Final Good and Happiness

Aristotle refers both to 'every craft and every line of inquiry' and to 'action and decision' (1094a1–2). He says that each of these seems to aim at some good, and he infers that there is some final good that we pursue for its own sake and for the sake of which we pursue

---

[19] A different view of subordination and inclusion is defended by Kraut, *AHG* 220–3. I doubt whether he takes sufficient account of the fact that political science embraces sciences concerned with *praxis*.

everything else. And so the argument that applies to crafts and similar disciplines should also apply to the actions and decisions of individuals.

To see why Aristotle believes an ultimate end can be discerned in the choices of individuals, we must understand what he means in claiming that 'action and decision seems to aim at some good'. The combination of action and decision suggests that the claim is not meant to apply to action on non-rational desires, but to pick out the distinctive character of action on a decision (*prohairesis*). If this is the point, then 'aim at some good' is to be taken de dicto, not de re;[20] it is a claim about the intentional object of these different forms of rational thought and action.[21]

Aristotle implies that every decision, expressing a desire for an object as good, thereby expresses a desire for an object as promoting the final good.[22] This feature of action on decision reflects the fact that decision is essentially rational desire, and is therefore subject to the rational teleological regulation that Aristotle describes in his account of political science. Since we accept this teleological regulation, we acknowledge our belief in the existence of a final good. Since—Aristotle assumes—we are correct in all this, there must be a final good; and this, being genuinely good, will be the ultimate end that fully satisfies our desires and aims (in the sense that it will satisfy the description 'good' that we apply to the ultimate end).

If Aristotle believes each of us actually pursues some final good as our ultimate end, he makes a psychological claim about the nature of rational agents, in so far as they act on decision. When he speaks of happiness, he says: 'we all do everything else for the sake of it' (1102a2). [23] He seems to accept three claims: (1) Each rational agent pursues some final good. (2) The final good that each agent pursues is happiness. (3) The happiness that each agent pursues is the agent's own happiness. The second of these claims states a form of eudaemonism, and the third states a form of egoism.

The first claim seems to rest on Aristotle's conception of rational regulation. In his view, each of us conforms to this pattern to some extent; we regulate the pursuit of some goals by referring to their impact on other goals and aims that we take to be more important. To the extent that we do this, we display deliberative rationality.[24]

This thesis about the final good is fairly minimal. What do we add when we add something about happiness?[25] Aristotle understands happiness as living well; it is a property of a life

---

[20] More exactly, it is a description of the agent's psychological state (perhaps not explicitly stated in the dictum) rather than of the actual object aimed at.

[21] 'The good is what everything aims at' is meant as a remark about rational agents (in Aristotle's case, though apparently not for Eudoxus; see 1172b9). Aristotle does not mean, then, that our wanting something necessarily makes it good.

[22] See §310.   [23] The antecedent of 'it' might be 'happiness' or 'the end'.

[24] This general view makes it easier to understand why, as has been noticed, Aristotle sometimes states his claim about the final good as a normative thesis. In EE 1214b6–14 (partly quoted in n31 below) he seems to say first that everyone sets (*thesthai*) some goal of living finely, and then explains that by saying that failure to have one's life ordered with reference to some end is a sign of great foolishness. In speaking of foolishness here, he does not seem to suggest that it is impossible to be so disorganized. But it is easy to see how Aristotle might claim both (i) each of us to some extent recognizes the value of rational regulation of ends; and (ii) many of us do very little of it; and hence (iii) we see the point of doing more of it than we do.

[25] Aristotle does not always sharply distinguish the claims about the final good from claims about happiness, and he takes it to be clear that the final good for human beings is happiness (1095a17–20). Still, he does not take the identity of the final good and happiness to be so trivial that it is not worth arguing for; indeed, he defends the identification at some length, by comparing features of the final good with features of happiness (EN i 7).

rather than of a moment in one's existence. In identifying the good with happiness, we introduce some temporal and structural dimensions. Aristotle agrees with Plato's *Philebus* in believing that we should think of the good as the good for a lifetime.[26] A mere reference to rational regulation does not say what we regulate in the light of what. The conception of a final good that I refer to might change from one moment to the next, and it might just reflect the whims that happen to strike me most strongly at the moment. In speaking of a good life, however, we conceive ourselves as having lifetimes, and try to organize their different stages in relation to each other. We also think of each activity as part of the life we live now, in so far as we think of how it affects our other current concerns. These two aspects of thinking about one's life are closely connected; the concerns that extend over one's lifetime explain why one has a reason to take account of aims and concerns that do not happen to be prominent in one's mind at a given moment.

Since an appeal to happiness adds this temporal and structural aspect to the rational regulation that is required by pursuit of a final good, Aristotle's claim that we pursue happiness is more informative than his claim that we pursue a final good. His further claim about happiness is quite plausible. One would have a rather slim basis for rational regulation of desires if one did not refer to one's life as a whole. If I just happen to desire one thing more strongly than another for a short time, why does that give me a reason to pay more attention to what I care more about, given that my preference may change quite soon? But if I regard one preference as especially belonging to me, and if I have some basis for that belief in a conception of myself as something relatively persistent, I have some reason for favouring one preference over another.

This way of explaining the appeal to happiness implies that Aristotle has in mind the happiness of the agent who deliberates with reference to the good and happiness; she is not simply considering someone's good and happiness, but her own.[27] Aristotle is a psychological egoist; he believes that every rational agent aims at his own happiness as the ultimate end. This is still not very clear, though. For we might still hold different views about the exact role that a reference to happiness is supposed to play in an agent's conscious deliberation on different occasions; if it does not play a large role in conscious deliberation, one might wonder exactly what the role of a conception of happiness is supposed to be. To answer this question, Aristotle relies on rational egoism; he thinks that each rational agent has overriding reason to do what best promotes his own happiness.[28]

---

[26] On the *Philebus* see §53.

[27] Does he mean only that we deliberate with a view to happiness, without saying whose happiness is involved? See Kraut, *AHG* 144–8. Admittedly, he often speaks of acting or choosing for the sake of happiness, without further specification (e.g. end of i 12). Still, some passages suggest that he means the egoist claim: (i) 1140a25. It seems to be characteristic of the wise person to be able to deliberate finely about the things good and beneficial to himself. Here the relevant sort of deliberation is referred to one's own happiness. (ii) ix 8. Aristotle defends the virtuous person against the charge of being a lover of self—not by arguing that he is not a lover of self, but by arguing that the way in which he loves himself does not make him indifferent to the interests of others. If Aristotle did not accept an egoist position here, he would surely reply that it is a misunderstanding to assume that the virtuous person is a lover of self. He argues instead that the proper degree of concern for others involves no sacrifice in one's own interest, once that is properly conceived. (iii) ix 4. In explaining why one has reason to be virtuous rather than vicious, Aristotle remarks that the condition of the vicious person is miserable, and therefore to be avoided, 1166b26. He assumes that the overriding reason for pursuing virtue and avoiding vice is their relation to one's own happiness and unhappiness.

[28] Psychological and rational egoism do not imply ethical egoism, which is often understood as the claim that one's own interests determine the sense of the moral 'ought'. This is the view that the happiness of the individual agent

If a final good plays the same role in individual deliberation as it plays in the deliberation of a political scientist, it should make a difference to our lives. Aristotle claims that it is worth our while to find out what the good is so that we will have a target to aim at (1094a22–6).[29] An account of the final good should distinguish the different parts of the end from the purely instrumental means to it, so that we can find what is worth pursuing for its own sake. [30]

70. The Final Good and the 'Three Lives'

By introducing happiness, Aristotle introduces a reference to a rational agent's life as a whole. To prepare for his own account of the appropriate criteria to be applied to a conception of a good life, he considers various conceptions that have been proposed. His objections to them help to clarify the criteria that he applies.

In reply to those who value the life of pleasure, Aristotle argues that they choose a way of life that is fit only for grazing animals (1095b19–20), not for rational agents. In a later comment on pleasure, he remarks that no one would choose to return to a child's level of thought and a child's pleasures, or accept pleasure from shameful actions (1174a1–4).[31]

We might think it unfair of Aristotle to identify the life of pleasure with the life of gross sensual pleasures (1095b21–2). But we can defend this move in the same way as we can defend Socrates' concentration on such pleasures in his argument with Callicles (*Gorg.* 494b3–495a4). Not every life of pleasure has to be confined to gross pleasures; but if we regard pleasure alone as the feature of a life that makes it desirable and happy, we cannot deny that 'the life of grazing animals' is a happy life. The features of such a life that make it unsuitable for rational agents do not matter if a purely hedonist account of the good is correct.

This brief dismissal of the life of pleasure is not Aristotle's last word on pleasure in the *Ethics*. Books vii and x discuss the nature of pleasure and the value of different types of pleasure. Aristotle believes that true judgments about pleasure imply that the virtuous person's life is also the pleasantest life. But these true judgments about pleasure imply that pleasure is not the only thing that makes a life happy; and so Aristotle's more complex view

---

determines the content of the moral virtues—or in specific cases the view that bravery, temperance, or justice, for instance, is a virtue, or is the particular virtue it is, because of its contribution to the virtuous agent's own happiness. In the second half of *EN* i 7, Aristotle insists on a very close connexion between happiness and virtue, but not on the sort of connexion that would follow from ethical egoism. He appeals to happiness to justify the moral virtues, but not directly to define their content.

[29] 'Then does not knowledge of this good also carry great weight for <our way of> life, and if we know it, are we not more likely, like archers who have a target to aim at, to hit the right mark? If so, we should try to grasp, in outline at any rate, what the good is, and which is its proper science or capacity.' (1094a22–6).

[30] '. . . we must first define in ourselves, neither rashly nor sluggishly, in which aspect of us living well is found and what things are necessary for it to belong to human beings; for health is not the same as the things needed for health, and so on in many other cases, so that neither is living finely the same as the things without which one cannot live finely. . . . For these are causes of the disputes about being happy, what it is and through what things it comes about; for things that are necessary for being happy are counted by some people as parts of happiness' (*EE* 1214b11–26).

[31] 'No one would choose to live with a child's level of thought throughout his life, even if he took as much pleasure as possible in the sorts of things that please children and enjoyed a child's pleasures, or to enjoy himself in doing one of the most shameful actions, even if he were never going to suffer pain' (1174a1–4) Cf. *EE* 1215b22–7. Aristotle relies here on Socrates' reply to Protarchus (he cites the *Philebus* at 1172b28) to show that pleasure cannot be the good.

about pleasure does not undermine his criticism of a life conducted on the assumption that pleasure alone makes a life happy.[32]

The life of honour depends on our being honoured by other people, and therefore makes us passive, not active, in relation to the most important aspect of our happiness. Against this we intuitively believe that the good is 'something of our own'; it expresses our rational agency, not an essentially passive aspect of us (1095b23–6; cf. 1159a12–33). Plato describes how the lover of honour suffers some misfortune that leads to his humiliation, and then turns to the love of gain (R. 553a–c). He illustrates Aristotle's objection that the life of honour leaves us too dependent on external fortunes. A correct account of the good should show that it is less dependent on external conditions than the life of honour turns out to be. We want to show that our own actions, rather than fortune, control our happiness (1100b7).

If we seek independence from external conditions, we may reasonably prefer the life of virtue over the life of honour. Being virtuous is minimally dependent on external conditions. If we follow Socrates in taking virtue to be sufficient for happiness, we can also claim, as Socrates does, that the virtuous person cannot be harmed, and therefore is independent of external conditions. The Cynics agree with Socrates, and may go beyond him. They may claim that virtue is not only sufficient for happiness, but also identical to it.[33]

Aristotle rejects the Socratic and Cynic position; he denies that virtue is identical to happiness by arguing that it is not sufficient for happiness. If we identify happiness with virtue, we must claim that someone can be happy when he is asleep or when he is suffering terrible misfortunes (1095b31–1096a2). Aristotle thinks we will agree that this is an absurd claim because both conditions prevent rational activity; when we are asleep we are inactive, and in terrible misfortunes we are victims of circumstances that 'impede many activities' (1100b29–30). Similarly, in Book vii he dismisses the view of those who think a virtuous person being tortured is happy; the pain we suffer in these conditions prevents the unimpeded activity that is essential to happiness (1153b14–25). Happiness is complete, but honour and virtue are not (1095b31–2), because each of them leaves out some good that belongs to the complete good. No one would call just people on the rack happy 'unless he were defending a philosophical thesis' (1096a1–2), and pursuing consistency without regard for the cost in plausibility.

The treatment of the three lives shows that Aristotle relies on three assumptions about the good: (1) It must involve a life suitable for human beings, as opposed to 'grazing animals'. (2) It must be 'our own', not too dependent on external conditions. (3) It must be complete, including all the major goods. A fuller statement of these assumptions should make clear their connexions. When, for instance, we assess completeness, we should take a complete good to involve suitable activities for a human being.[34] Some view about these activities will tell us how far happiness ought to be independent of external conditions, and how far it must depend on some external conditions. Hence it seems that some better grasp of the first assumption should help us to clarify the other two. Aristotle, therefore, discusses these three assumptions.[35] We ought to see how far his discussion clarifies the assumptions that we have identified in the argument of i 5.

---

[32] On pleasure see §72 below.   [33] On Socrates see §15. On the Cynics see §39.
[34] Cf. the reference to misfortune impeding activities at 1100b29–30, 1153b14–21.
[35] He examines completeness in the first part of EN i 7; he turns to independence of external conditions in i 9–11. In between these two discussions he examines the human function (second part of i 7).

71. A Comprehensive Conception of Happiness

Aristotle argues that the final good is to be identified with happiness, because happiness is the ultimate end, and therefore complete and self-sufficient (1097b20–1). He generalizes and explains his criticism of the three lives in i 5, by setting out some formal criteria for the final good, and showing that they are satisfied by happiness.

These criteria, adapted from those in the *Philebus*, are 'formal' in the sense that they do not presuppose conceptions of the good as definite as those embodied in the three lives. They are more general than the three lives, because they are intended to explain why a given life does or does not count as a happy life. If we grasp and examine the concept of a final good, we should be able to see whether his formal criteria are correct.

First (1097a22) Aristotle reverts to the connexion between the ultimate end and the final good. If there is one end of all actions, this will be the good, and if there are several ends, these will be the good. He seems to consider a plurality of equally ultimate ends. Next, he insists that the good must be complete (*teleion*).[36] He infers that if there is one complete thing, this will be the good, and if there are several, the most complete of these will be the good (1097a28).

We may be surprised at this reaction to the possibility of several ends. Instead of saying, as he previously said, that all these complete ends will be the good, he insists that just one of them, the most complete, is the good (1098a17–18, 1099a29–31). He takes happiness to be the unqualifiedly complete end; that is why it is the ultimate end, and therefore the one that we ought to pursue. It embraces all the goods that we have good reason to pursue for their own sakes. If two separate ends F and G both appeared to be unqualifiedly complete, we would (according to Aristotle) pursue both F and G for the sake of some third end H, including F and G; and then H would be the unqualifiedly complete end. The choice of the 'most complete' among several ends is not arbitrary, and does not require us to choose one as opposed to the others; for the most complete end includes the others.

This interpretation of unconditional completeness as implying comprehensiveness is supported by the further claim that happiness is self-sufficient, and is therefore not 'counted together' with other goods.[37] Self-sufficiency (1097b6) is what 'all by itself makes a life choiceworthy and lacking in nothing' (1097b14–15). Aristotle explains that he takes this to require a life that is sufficient not only for the person in question, but also for family, friends, and fellow-citizens. Aristotle does not simply argue that an individual's happiness requires the existence of family etc. as instrumental means. For he insists that what is sufficient for an individual's happiness must be sufficient for these other people's happiness too. The most plausible interpretation of self-sufficiency implies a comprehensive view of happiness. If there are a number of non-instrumental goods, happiness is not only comprehensive, but also composite, including these various goods as its parts (cf. 1129b18).[38]

---

[36] Ross generally translates '*teleion*' by 'final'. More recent translators (Irwin, Crisp, Broadie, and Rowe) prefer 'complete'. 'Perfect' might also be defended (see Kenny, *APL*, ch. 2, esp. 16–17). These translations might suggest different interpretations.

[37] For different interpretations of this important claim see Kenny, *AE* 204–5; Kraut, *AHG* 269–74; Aquinas at §280n52.

[38] The difference between a comprehensive and a composite conception is important in the discussion of happiness and contemplation. See §82 below.

If Aristotle accepts a comprehensive view of happiness, he can explain why happiness is the final good that is the basis of rational regulation of desires. In referring to happiness, we compare one possible course of action against another with reference to our conception of the appropriately-ordered whole that includes everything that we rightly value for its own sake. This comprehensive end is an appropriate basis for our decision to act in one way rather than another. Since Aristotle's claim that happiness is the final good, and that everyone pursues happiness, turns out to be reasonable if he accepts a comprehensive conception, we have good reason to attribute a comprehensive conception to him.

72. Happiness and Goodness

A comprehensive conception of happiness makes happiness include all non-instrumental goods. Aristotle clearly takes the goodness of non-ultimate goods to be connected to their contribution to their end. In each action and decision the good is the end; and the final good is the ultimate end (1097a16–24). We might attribute to Aristotle the view that the end of each action explains what is good about it, and therefore the ultimate end should explain what is good about all the actions and other goods that are subordinate to it.

The claim that the end of x explains the goodness of x is plausible in the case of instrumental goods. In this case x is good just in so far as x contributes to y, and the goodness of x is derivative from the goodness of y—if there were nothing good about y, x would be no use to us, and x would not be good. In this case we have to assume that the goodness of y is intelligible independently of the goodness of x. The fact that bridles fit on horses would not explain why bridles are good if we put bridles on horses only in order to increase the production of bridles.

If, then, we use this pattern to see how the final good explains the goodness of other things, we must say that its goodness is independently intelligible, and that the other things are good in so far as they are instrumental to it. According to this view, our reasons for wanting happiness are independent of our reasons for wanting other goods, and since they are independent, they provide reasons for wanting the goods that are instrumental to happiness.

If this is how happiness explains the goodness of subordinate goods, we will find what happiness is by finding what sort of thing plays this explanatory role, so that all other goods could be subordinate and instrumental to it. A hedonist theory readily meets this condition; for several reasons might persuade us that pleasure is an intrinsically intelligible end explaining what makes other things good. Aristotle certainly thinks happiness centrally involves pleasure, and he relies on the intuitive belief that a conception of the good leaving out pleasure would be seriously defective. But he does not accept a hedonist conception of happiness. Nor does he accept any other view that claims that all goods other than happiness are good only because of their instrumental contribution to happiness. He recognizes pleasure, honour, and virtue as non-instrumental goods (1097b2–4). If he accepts a comprehensive conception of happiness, he regards these goods as components of happiness.

He does not suppose, therefore, that the final good explains the goodness of other goods by reference to their instrumental contribution.[39] Indeed, the explanation seems to go the other way; the right account of happiness is right only if it includes the right non-instrumental goods. This feature of a comprehensive conception of happiness may provoke doubts about the role of happiness in deliberation and practical reason. If happiness is a compound of goods that are already recognized as non-instrumental goods, how can it be explanatory? This question raises the suspicion that some of Aristotle's basic principles promise us ethical insight, but simply provide unhelpful circles of definition.[40]

To answer this objection, we may consider the goodness we find in parts of organic wholes. A healthy body is healthy because it has the right number of healthy parts in the right relations to each other. One might say that the functioning of each part is good all by itself and non-instrumentally—it is better to have healthy toenails or a healthy heart. Still, it is better to have each of them in a healthy condition in the right relation to other healthy parts.

Hence the goodness of the goods that are non-instrumental but subordinate to happiness does not rest simply on their contribution to happiness, if that would require their goodness to be explained by the goodness of something whose goodness is independent of theirs. In another sense, however, their goodness consists solely in their contribution to happiness; once we see how they contribute to happiness, none of their goodness has been left out. Similarly, even if the good of having healthy toenails is entirely included in the good of having a healthy body, the relation need not be purely instrumental. Even if the goodness of happiness depends on the goodness of its components, reflexion on the nature of happiness may show us that some things are its components and are non-instrumentally good.[41]

We begin, then, with a schematic conception of happiness. As we see what satisfies that schema, we discover that various things are non-instrumentally good because they turn out to be parts of happiness. In particular, the various things that we recognize as virtues of character, and the associated activities, turn out to be parts of happiness. But we also begin with beliefs about non-instrumental goods, and we act on these beliefs, even without an explicit or detailed account of happiness. We learn about the content of happiness by comparing our view of happiness with our beliefs about which things are non-instrumental goods; equally, we justify, understand, and sometimes revise our beliefs about non-instrumental goods in the light of our conception of happiness.

Aristotle raises some of these issues when he contrasts happiness with honour, pleasure, understanding, and every virtue. He says that we choose these non-ultimate goods 'for their own sake—for if nothing came about from them we would choose them; but we also choose them for the sake of happiness, thinking that we will be happy through them' (1097b2–5).[42] He returns to the issue (discussed in i 1–2) about the relation of non-instrumental goods

---

[39] This claim needs to be reconsidered if we decide that Aristotle identifies happiness with contemplation. See below §82.

[40] Sidgwick objects to Plato and Aristotle on this ground, at ME 374–5.

[41] Some helpful developments of these distinctions: Moore, PE §§20–2.

[42] This might mean: (a) We choose each of them for its own sake—i.e., not for the sake of happiness—and also for the sake of happiness. I might, for instance, believe that honesty is the best policy (for the sake of happiness) and that I also have a moral reason for being honest (for its own sake, and not for the sake of happiness). (b) We choose each of them for its own sake, and that amounts to choosing them for the sake of happiness—since happiness is simply a

to the ultimate good. He argues that even disciplines concerned with action rather than production are subordinate to an architectonic discipline that co-ordinates and regulates them; in that case the end of the architectonic discipline includes the ends of the subordinate disciplines (1094b6–7). The non-instrumental goods pursued by the subordinate disciplines must, then, be parts of the ultimate good that includes them.

We can now see why choosing non-instrumental goods for the sake of happiness does not amount to choosing them for the sake of some result that comes about from them—some end that is wholly external to them. In choosing them as non-instrumental goods and for the sake of happiness, we choose them as parts of a whole. In this way, we can reconcile a commitment to eudaemonism with the recognition of non-instrumental goods that are related non-instrumentally to the final good.[43]

Aristotle seems to acknowledge here that to form the right conception of happiness we must have some conception of non-instrumental goods. This does not mean that our choice of them for their own sakes is unrelated to their relation to happiness. For I might choose pleasure, say, for its own sake, even if I could not get any of the other parts of happiness. Since I would recognize that pleasure is one component of happiness, I would recognize that one is better than none, and would still choose it. This might be what Aristotle means in saying that we would still choose it even if nothing came about from it; we would still choose it even if we could not get the other parts of happiness that it is related to and interacts with. But we also choose it for the sake of happiness in so far as we choose it as part of a whole, present in a context that makes it even more choiceworthy.

We therefore need some initial reason for choosing certain things for their own sake—a reason that is distinct from their relation to happiness. For if the comprehensive view of happiness is right, we cannot explain the goodness of all goods other than happiness simply by their instrumental relation to happiness. But we still have reason to connect them with happiness. For a general description of the good may give us reasons for thinking that this action rather than that is a part of the good, and therefore to be chosen for its own sake. We begin by choosing certain things for their own sake; and in the light of some more general

collection of things chosen for their own sake. (c) We choose each of them for its own sake, and therefore choose them for the sake of happiness, since happiness is expected to include everything chosen for its own sake.

Against (a) one may argue: (i) If Aristotle holds this view, then the rational person has to deliberate about two things: how to get the things that are goods in themselves, and how to make sure that they promote his happiness. But Aristotle recognizes only one thing to deliberate about; cf. 1140a25. (ii) If the two-part conception of intrinsic goods were correct, then happiness would not include all the goods we have reason to pursue. But Aristotle claims (in i 2) that it does include all of these. Interpretation (b) seeks to reduce choosing x for the sake of happiness to choosing x for its own sake. This reductive view makes it difficult to see why the discovery of what happiness is should be so important, if there is no difference between choosing something for itself and choosing it for the sake of happiness. Interpretation (c) agrees with (b) in denying that choosing these non-instrumental goods for their own sake amounts to choosing them for the sake of something other than happiness, so that happiness counts as something else coming about from them. But it disagrees with (b) in claiming that choosing for the sake of happiness is different from choosing for their own sakes. It suggests that when we choose these goods for their own sakes, we are choosing them as parts of happiness; they are still parts of happiness even if nothing further comes about from them. For discussion of (b) and (c) see Engberg-Pederson, *ATMI*, ch. 1.

[43] Though it is reasonable to speak of parts and whole in describing the relation of non-instrumental goods to happiness, this description (used in the *EE*) is not used in the *EN*. Aristotle might reasonably have thought it too simple to capture the centrality of virtue in happiness. This issue is relevant to a comparison between Aristotle and the Stoics. See §189. Cf. Ackrill, 'Eudaimonia' 195–6; Cooper, *RHGA* 122–7 (both of whom notice Aristotle's reserve in speaking of parts of happiness in the *EN*, though I do not completely agree with their explanations).

description of the good, we come to see that they are indeed choiceworthy for their own sakes.

This raises the question: how do we find the general description of the good that shows us what is choiceworthy about its components? Aristotle offers that in the function argument.

73. Implications of Eudaemonism

We claimed earlier that Aristotle is a psychological egoist, in so far as he claims that every rational agent pursues his own happiness as his ultimate end. We have postponed discussion of his claim until now, so that we can consider it in the light of his comprehensive conception of happiness. This comprehensive conception should make a difference to the content of his egoist thesis and to our views on its plausibility.

Many philosophers do not take psychological egoism seriously, because they are convinced by something like the argument Butler urges against Hobbes.[44] In Butler's view, the claim that we do everything as a means to our own satisfaction does not explain why we find our satisfaction where we do; contrary to the egoist view, our finding satisfaction in getting x presupposes a desire for x itself, which explains why we get the satisfaction in x rather than y.

Aristotle is not open to this objection. Butler's criticism assumes that egoism is being offered as an account of the first-order object of desire, so that my happiness is the only thing I desire for its own sake. But if one takes a comprehensive and composite view of happiness, eudaemonism is a claim about a second-order attitude—about how we think of the relation between first-order objects of desire that we desire for their own sakes. It says that we desire honour, pleasure, understanding etc. for their own sakes, but we also take account of their relation to each other and to the whole that they compose. Whether that is a plausible claim or not, it does not involve the sort of psychological egoism that is easily refutable.

Aristotle also maintains rational egoism; he claims that my own happiness is not only the ultimate object of my desire, but also the ultimate object for rational deliberation, the end that I ought to aim at above all. How far does this rational egoist claim constrain the sort of moral commitment that a rational person can take seriously? Some forms of egoism impose a tight constraint; if every moral virtue must ultimately promote some independently desirable state of myself alone, not every reasonable moral commitment seems to meet that condition.[45]

Nothing we have seen so far suggests that Aristotle takes the eudaemonist requirement to require subordination to states of myself alone. He says that my happiness, if it is self-sufficient, has to be sufficient for friends, family, and fellow-citizens (1097b8–13). He does not mean that the happiness of these other people affects my happiness only in so far as their welfare has some further effect on some state of me. If I have the appropriate sort of relation to them, their welfare is part of mine. In order to defend himself, Aristotle needs to show that my happiness requires me to be in the sort of relation to other people

---

[44] Butler, S i §6–7.

[45] By 'state of myself alone' I mean a state—my having a given height or weight, for instance—that is not essentially constituted in part by a state of something else. In Broad's terms, I am assuming that some moral commitments are neither self-confined nor self-centred. See Broad, 'Egoism', 249–50.

that makes their welfare a part of my own; nothing in his general conception of happiness rules this out. It is natural to treat these relations to others as 'parts' or 'constituents' of the agent's happiness.

If we say this much to show that Aristotle's eudaemonism does not exclude certain things, must we go to the other extreme by making it empty? Sidgwick dismisses the sort of view we have been describing, by saying that it is a form into which any ethical system can be cast without making any essential difference to its content.[46]

To answer Sidgwick, we need to show that some ethical outlooks have to reject Aristotle's eudaemonism, so that it cannot be compatible with every ethical outlook. It would be false if we had reason to reject any systematizing of our ends, along the lines implied by Aristotle's conception of eudaimonia. If our ends cannot be systematized, we cannot spell out the content of happiness in any way that makes it rational to think of our ends in the light of this ultimate end.

Alternatively, even if all our ends and commitments can be partly understood in the light of an ultimate end, Aristotle's eudaemonism might still be false; for perhaps not all our ends can be fully understood in the light of this ultimate end. This may be especially important in the case of moral reasons. Though a commitment to morality may well play a significant role in a life that conforms to a true conception of happiness, perhaps that role does not exhaust its rational force; for we may also have overriding reasons to act on moral considerations even on any possible occasions when they might conflict with eudaemonic considerations. (And this need not be true only of moral reasons.) If Aristotle is to answer this second line of objection, he must show that his eudaemonist constraint gives the appropriate degree of weight to each sort of consideration that it recognizes.

If Aristotle's eudaemonism is not empty, and these are objections that might refute it, we ought not to accept or reject his position before we examine his account of the virtues. His version of egoism is not open to immediate and crushing objections. We ought to see how far it illuminates the relevant questions.

---

[46] See Sidgwick, *ME* 95.

7

ARISTOTLE: NATURE

74. The Function Argument

So far we have examined the formal features of happiness as Aristotle conceives it. These features tell us the conditions that states and actions have to satisfy in order to provide a plausible conception of happiness. We have learned that happiness has to be comprehensive, because it is complete and self-sufficient, and we have seen why the recognized 'three lives' do not fit these conditions.

Aristotle recognizes that the formal conditions do not tell us what happiness is, and he offers to answer this question by beginning from the human function (or 'work' (*ergon*), 1097b22–5). Things of kind F fulfil their function by doing what is essential to their being Fs. They achieve their good as Fs if they fulfil their function in accordance with the virtue of Fs; for the virtue of Fs is the state that makes Fs good, and thereby causes them to fulfil their function well. A human being's function is activity of the rational soul; hence a human being's good is activity of the rational soul in accordance with complete virtue (1097b22–1098a20).

To see whether Aristotle is entitled to assert this connexion between the human function and the human good, we need to see what he means by 'function', whether he is right to claim that human beings have a function, and whether he correctly identifies the human function.

He asserts a connexion between the function of F and the good of F, in the case of craftsmen, organs, and organisms. He assumes that craftsmen and organs have functions, and he asks whether organisms have them as well (1097b30–3). His answer is Yes. He implies that the three different types of soul—nutritive, sensory, and rational—that he describes in the *De Anima* mark three different functions, which are the different lives of the creatures with different souls. Since human beings have rational souls, he denies that the human function could be the purely nutritive life that human beings share with plants, or the purely sensory life that they share with other animals. The different types of souls are the form and essence of plants, animals, and human beings; they are the actualization of the capacity of the different types of organic body (*DA* 412a27–8). In claiming that the goal-directed processes of nutrition and sense-perception are the essence and form of plants and animals, Aristotle identifies function with essence;[1] the function of these organisms is the type of activity that constitutes their soul. Since human beings have a soul, they have a function.

Here Aristotle explains what he means by attributing a function to human beings, and on what grounds he attributes it to them. His explanation suggests answers to some objections. Some critics allege that in attributing a function to something we imply that an intelligent designer has designed it for some purpose. In that case, the Function Argument illegitimately assumes a designer. Whether that assumption is true or false, Aristotle has not argued for it, so that (the objector maintains) his conclusion is unjustified. This objection fails because Aristotle's claims do not rely on an assumption about a designer. His claim about the human function relies on his conception of teleological explanation, which does not presuppose designing intelligence or cosmic roles. In his view, the function of an organism is its essence because it explains regularities and variations in its behaviour. We can find the relevant explanations whether or not we assume anything further about design or cosmic roles.[2]

Some have objected to Aristotle's argument from the functions of organs within an organism to the function of the whole organism. According to the objection, he commits a fallacy of composition, arguing that since each part of a human being has a function, referring to the whole, the whole human being must also have a function. This conclusion would be true (according to the objector) only if human beings were also parts of a larger system within which they had a role to play. But whatever Aristotle believes on this point, he does not commit a fallacy of composition. The examples of craftsmen and organs clarify his conception of function, but they are not intended to prove that a human being must have a function. He attributes a function to human beings on the same grounds that support his teleological account of living organisms.

Does he, however, exaggerate the importance of finding a unique function? Even if some specific activity were peculiar to human beings as opposed to other creatures, why would that matter from the ethical point of view? If we could show that combing hair or preparing for nuclear war is peculiar to human beings, we would not have shown that the human good consists in these activities. But such examples do not capture Aristotle's appeal to uniqueness. He has in mind the uniqueness of essence; the human function is unique only because the human kind and the human essence are distinct from other kinds and essences. This sort of unique function is a distinct kind of life, not a unique activity within a life.

This interpretation of uniqueness rests on the connexion between the three lives mentioned in the *Ethics* and the three souls mentioned in the *De Anima*. In Aristotle's account of the soul, the more complex souls include the functions of the simpler types of soul too. The sensory soul that belongs to animals includes the functions that belong to the nutritive soul in plants (*DA* 414b28–32). A dog has a sensory soul that includes nutritive functions; it does not have both a sensory soul and a nutritive soul. If we apply this conception of soul to the different lives identified with functions in the *Ethics*, we should infer that the sensory life ascribed to animals is not a life of sense as opposed to nutrition, but a life in which nutritive activities

---

[1] Function and essence; *PA* 648a15. Function and definition; *Pol.* 1253a23–5; Bonitz, *IA* 285a8–24.

[2] For some discussion of causation and final causation in Aristotle see Irwin, *AFP*, ch. 5; Meyer, 'Teleology'; Lear, *ADU* 25–42.

are guided and regulated by the senses for the sake of ends belonging to sensory creatures (including pleasure). Similarly, the rational soul includes nutritive and sensory activities; hence the rational life includes them; hence the function of a creature living a rational life includes them. The Function Argument does not show, and is not intended to show, that happiness consists in performing the activity that is most distinctive of human beings in relation to other organisms. It connects a human being's good with the characteristic and distinctive features of a rational agent's life as opposed to the life of other agents.[3]

Once we grasp what Aristotle means by speaking of a unique function, we can see what he means by speaking of a 'life according to reason'. We might suppose he means that the good of human beings consists in the activity of thinking, so that we achieve our good to the extent that we concentrate on thinking to the exclusion of other activities open to us. We might be more inclined to ascribe this conclusion to Aristotle if we look forward to Book x, where—according to one common interpretation—he identifies happiness with purely theoretical thought. But we ought not to derive this conclusion from the Function Argument. The life according to reason is a life, including nutritive and sensory activities, that is guided by reason, not a life that consists, as far as possible, in reasoning. The interpretation of Book x will concern us later. For the moment it is enough to say that the Function Argument does not argue that happiness consists exclusively in thought.

This judgment does not rest exclusively on the connexions between function, life, and soul. It is also confirmed by Aristotle's description of the life that embodies the human function. He says it is a life of the part of the soul that has reason, and that one part of this is the inherently rational part, while another is the part capable of obeying reason (1098a3–5).[4] The latter part is the non-rational part that we train by acquiring the virtues of character (cf. 1102b13–1103a10). Since the rational life includes the appropriate regulation of the potentially obedient part, Aristotle describes it as a life 'in accordance with reason or not without reason' (1098a7–8). In 'not without reason' he includes the non-rational states that listen to reason.

These clarifications of Aristotle's position remove the basis of some objections. But they still do not make it clear whether his claims about function and essence are plausible, or whether they support his claims about happiness. We need to look at these claims more closely.

75. Function, Essence, End, and Explanation

According to Aristotle, a function is a goal-directed motion or state. A motion or state is goal-directed when it has a final cause, or 'end'. A final cause is the real or apparent good whose presence explains the occurrence of the motion or state in question. This is explanatory, not because it is the cause, as we normally conceive it,[5] but because it is the

---

[3] On function and uniqueness contrast Kraut, *AHG* 312–19; Whiting, 'Function'.

[4] 'The remaining possibility, then, is some sort of life of action of the <part of the soul> that has reason. One <part> of it has reason as obeying reason; the other has it as itself having reason and thinking' (1098a3–5).

[5] The cause, as we normally conceive it, is approximately what Aristotle calls the 'moving' cause (*Phys.* 194b29–32), and what Aristotelian tradition (see Alexander, *Fat.* 166.22–6) calls the 'efficient' cause.

feature of the product that is causally relevant. The function of the hammer is the feature of the hammer that explains why the hammer came into existence as it did and why it has the other properties (shape, size, hardness, etc.) that it has.

This example suggests that an appeal to x's function may answer two questions: (1) A genetic question: Why was x made as it was? (2) A static question: Why is x as it is? The hammering function of a hammer answers both questions, but this does not seem to be true for all functions. In particular, it does not seem to be true of the functions of natural organs and organisms. We may not notice the difference between the two questions; for it is true both that the function of the eyes is to see and that this seeing function explains why the eyes have come into being (if we accept an evolutionary account). However, the seeing function that is genetically relevant (by explaining how the eyes came into being) is not the one that is statically relevant (by explaining what the eyes do); the genetically relevant function is the seeing that had survival value for the ancestors of this organism, whereas the statically relevant function is the seeing that contributes to the survival and flourishing of this organism.

Aristotle's position is most plausible if we take his claims about function to be statically explanatory, whether or not they are genetically explanatory. We may consider a parallel with artifacts. In some cases an artifact made to perform one function may perform another function in a different system. A heavy step from an old building may have fallen at just the place where it is a suitable part of a wall in a new building, and the new building may have been built around it. Alternatively, we might build a house (as Odysseus did) around an especially strong tree; the tree continues to grow and to support the house. In such cases, the genetically relevant function is not the statically explanatory function. The function that explains the current place of the tree trunk in the house is its function of supporting the roof. This is a genuinely explanatory function that implies various counterfactuals; if the trunk were to cease to support the roof, the house would be in danger of collapsing, and some other support would be needed to maintain the house.

These examples suggest how we might understand an organism by reference to its statically explanatory function. The frog's eyes have the function of seeing, because seeing deals with information from the environment in ways that help the frog's survival and maintenance. If the frog lost the use of its eyes, it would be severely harmed, or it would compensate in some way for the role previously performed by the eyes—perhaps it would rely more on its other senses to detect food. The eyes might perform this function, even if this function did not explain how they came into being; even if it is a coincidence (understood historically) that eyes perform this function, they might none the less perform it.[6]

If we understand functions statically, we need to recognize them in two distinct places: (1) We need to attribute some sort of function or activity to the whole organism or system. In attributing this function to the whole system, we describe the healthy or normal functioning that the system maintains. (2) In relation to this function of the whole system, we attribute functions to organs or sub-systems. In saying that the function of the eye is to see, we refer to two things: (i) A property of the system—its acquiring information through sensory

---

[6] Cummins, 'Functional', points out difficulties that arise for attempted functional explanations of how organs came into being.

contact with certain kinds of properties. (ii) A property of the organ—its behaving so that the organism acquires this information; certain ocular processes cause, or causally contribute to, the information-acquiring states that help to maintain the system as a whole.

If the function of an organ is different from the function of a system, claims about the human function need not commit a fallacy of composition, by inferring a function of the system from a function of an organ. Both functions are functions of something—the system or the organ. But only one function—the function of the organ—is its function within some system. To ascribe a function to the system as a whole is not to ascribe to it some function within a further system.

These claims about function are explanatory. The function we attribute to an organ causally explains how the organism performs one of its functions. This provides a genuine explanation to the extent that the two properties can be independently described and understood. 'The function of the hair is to make us hairy' provides no explanation, since the inference from having hair to being hairy, or from having fingers to being fingered, is too direct and purely logical. But 'the function of the eyes is to see' is more explanatory, if we distinguish the information-bearing aspects of seeing from the aspects of it that are ocular processes.

How many kinds of things are functional systems, if we apply these conditions? Functional systems are compounds that need to be distinguished from other compounds. We might say that a rock is a functional system, because it is hard and cubic and its different parts (physical and logical) maintain its hardness, cubic shape, and petrine nature. However, they do not maintain it through change; if we break off a bit, no part of it tends to restore its cubic shape. A rock that tended to repair itself so as to maintain its shape or size would be a functional system (we might regard it as a kind of plant). Functional systems are different from other compounds in so far as they tend to maintain, repair, and preserve themselves through change. The functions of a system are relatively stable and mutually-supporting features that preserve the system; the functions of the parts of the system explain how the system has these features.

These claims about stability and mutual support make explicit some of what we assume in speaking of the healthy or flourishing state of the organism. These conditions for functions make it clear why nothing has the function of producing cancers or tumours that are harmful to the system. Similarly, nothing has the function of producing a useless hump on someone's back, if this hump is not connected with other aspects of the functioning of the system.

The function of a whole organism is what Aristotle describes as a life. Since he contrasts the human function with nutritive and sensory lives, he claims that some things essentially have kinds of life that make them functional systems. Being alive involves self-maintenance, including the systematic replacement of parts and material for the maintenance of the whole system. Maintenance consists in different activities because it maintains different kinds of lives, and different lives involve different goals pursued by the system, not simply different ways of achieving the same goals. When Aristotle attributes a sensory life to animals, he does not simply refer to the fact that animals seek food and avoid danger by means of their senses; he also means that they seek sensory gratification and pleasure, so that they live a life for the senses, not only a life guided by the senses. If the sensory character of an animal life were not part of the goal, but simply a means to the goal pursued by a plant, it would not constitute a distinct kind of function for the whole organism.

76. Function and Practical Reason

If Aristotle's claims about functions and organisms are defensible, we must next consider his specific claims about the human function. After ruling out the lives of nutrition and sense, he concludes that the human function consists in life in accordance with reason, and, more precisely, in a life in which the rational part controls the non-rational part.[7]

What does he mean in saying that the good is a life of action (*praktikê*, 1098a3)? If 'action' (*praxis*) is to be given its technical sense here, he refers to actions chosen for their own sakes as ends in themselves (1140b6–7).[8] He has already alluded to this aspect of *praxis* in Book i (1094a3–5, 16–18, b4–7), and has already mentioned that some things are chosen both for their own sakes and for the sake of happiness (1097b2–5). These previous remarks make the point of the Function Argument clearer. Aristotle claims not only that the human function consists in some sort of behaviour guided by reason, but, more precisely, that it consists in the rational choice of actions valued for their own sakes. A life devoted to the pursuit of ends that do not result from rational choice of ends does not fulfil the human function, even if the agent exercises reason in deliberation about instrumental means to those ends.

This aspect of the Function Argument introduces an important aspect of the virtues and of their connexion with happiness. Since the virtuous person chooses certain kinds of actions for their own sakes (1105a28–33), an account of virtue should explain such choices, and an account that shows how virtue is rational should explain how such choice can be rational. From the beginning of the *Ethics* Aristotle takes non-instrumental *praxis* to be essential to happiness. In the Function Argument he claims that the sort of choice made by the virtuous person is a choice that is essential to rational agency; if we do not exercise rational choice in the choice of non-instrumental actions, we realize rational agency incompletely.

The Function Argument should clarify the account of virtue, since a virtue is a state in which one performs one's function well (1106a15–24). Doing the activities of F things well is connected with doing them in such a way as to promote one's good as F (1097b26). Hence a virtue is a state in which one makes the correct rational choice of ends, and chooses correctly the actions that are to be chosen for their own sakes. To say that the rational choice of ends is part of the human function is not to say that every human being does it to the same degree. Nor is it to say that the recognized virtues—bravery, justice, and so on—reflect the only possible, or the best, choice of ends. Aristotle still needs to explain why the recognized virtues of bravery, temperance, and so on, count as virtues according to the criterion imposed by the Function Argument. Still, his reference to a life of action already introduces a non-trivial constraint on an account of virtue; it ought to show how we fulfil the human function in states that express our rational choice of ends, not in those that

---

[7] 1098a3–5, quoted above n4.

[8] Grant's rendering 'a moral life of the rational part' (*EA* ad loc.) is an over-translation of *praktikê*, but it indicates part of Aristotle's point. On *praxis* v. *poiêsis* see §66.

neglect such choices. We must see whether this suggestion helps us to defend one specific conception of the virtues.

Though Aristotle's claims about the human function leave many ethical questions to be answered, they constitute a non-trivial starting point for an argument about the virtues. He claims that the distinctive function of a human being is the life 'of' the rational part, in the rather strong sense that practical reason is a part or element in the end, not simply a means to it. Moreover, the relevant sort of practical reason is the rational selection and choice of components of the human good.

Is Aristotle right to claim that non-instrumental practical reasoning and action constitute the essential function of a human being? We might be tempted to answer that they are essential from the ethical point of view, simply because they are an essential starting point for Aristotle's inquiry. Since the *Ethics* is about the rational choice of components of the human good, it concerns beings who raise that question. We ought not to be satisfied, however, with this answer. One might want to say that ethical inquiry is important precisely because, in addressing these beings, it addresses beings who are necessarily concerned with the questions that it raises. Hence we need to show that what is essential to human beings from the ethical point of view is also essential from some point of view that is not purely ethical, from which we can see that the concerns of ethics are correct.

Aristotle might reasonably argue that, given the role of practical reason in selecting the human good, it would be misguided to understand human beings as living the same kind of life, organized around the same goals, as other creatures. For the flexibility of a human being's goals in the light of convictions about their goodness transforms the role that they play in the explanation of a human being's actions. Moreover, the fact that human beings actually conceive goals as modifiable in the light of considerations about their lives—understood as temporally extended and capable of being shaped in particular ways—marks a different essence, and a different kind of creature that needs to be explained and understood differently.

The argument about happiness and virtue, therefore, will succeed if it moves in two directions and reaches the same result. Arguing in one direction, we begin from the claim that happiness requires the application of non-instrumental practical reasoning to our lives, and we try to find the virtues that attach the appropriate value to non-instrumental reason. Arguing in the other direction, we begin from the recognized moral virtues and look for the common features that make them moral virtues. If the argument succeeds, we find that the common features of the recognized virtues are exactly the features that we look for in the virtues that attach appropriate value to non-instrumental practical reason. To see whether these two directions of argument reach the same conclusion, we should see whether Aristotle shows that the virtues he recognizes are the sorts of virtues that his account of happiness demands.

77. Aristotelian Naturalism?

This account of the Function Argument attributes a naturalist position to Aristotle. He argues for his account of the human good from premises about the nature of human beings as rational animals. This naturalist position is the basis for the naturalism of, among others, the Stoics, Aquinas, and Suarez. It is the position of 'the ancient moralists' that Butler tries to defend in his Sermons.[9] Hume among others rejects it.[10]

Aristotle's claims about function do not simply say that we have natural tendencies. He also attributes to human beings a nature that is not simply the sum of all natural tendencies. To speak of a thing's nature and of what is in accord with its nature is to select among the natural tendencies, since they may not all accord with the nature of the whole.[11] Aristotle's conception of nature connects a thing's nature with its essence, and with the kind that it belongs to. Something's function and nature is connected with its essence; the essence of a natural organism is the whole system in which different parts, processes, and activities have functions that promote the maintenance of the whole. States and processes that are in accord with something's nature as a whole are suitable for the whole system. This holist conception of something's nature implies that not everything natural accords with a thing's nature. We have natural tendencies that need to be restrained because they do not accord with our nature as a whole; if we eat or drink too much, or tire too easily, or exert ourselves too much at the wrong times, we may be acting on natural tendencies, but we are acting against our nature as a whole. We may understand Aristotelian naturalism, therefore, as a holist doctrine, treating human nature as a whole and a system. Though this holist conception is most clearly articulated by Butler, it underlies Aristotle's views about nature and function.

Butler articulates a holist conception in order to contrast it with the view of (among others) Hobbes and Hume, who both accept claims about human nature, and rely on them in their account of the moral virtues. Though they believe many things are natural, they do not believe in a nature that is distinct from a collection of natural tendencies; in Butler's terms, they do not believe in nature as a system. Hence they are not naturalists, or (if we want to put it more precisely) they are not holistic naturalists. Butler's account of nature as a system helps us to grasp more precisely what Aristotle implies in his claims about function. Though he does not use 'nature' (phusis) in his statement of the Function Argument, the connexions he sees between function, soul, essence, and nature make it clear that he endorses holistic naturalism.[12]

Some aspects of naturalism are relatively easy to accept. If it simply claims that some judgments about human welfare can be justified by appeal to claims about human nature, it is fairly easy to accept. An appeal to nature might, for instance, support judgments about 'medical' aspects of welfare.[13] Such claims as 'Red wine is good for you' appeal to the facts about human nature that doctors and patients need to take account of. An appeal to these facts implicitly relies on a holist conception of nature. We do not mean that red wine strengthens some natural tendencies; we mean that it strengthens some and weakens others in ways that strengthen the natural system as a whole. From this point of view, even

---

[9] See Butler, S, P 13.

[10] See Hume, T iii 1.2 §10. Hume does not believe that all claims about human nature must be excluded from moral philosophy, but he rejects the naturalist position that we have outlined.

[11] On collections v. systems cf. Butler, S, P 24.

[12] Annas, 'Versions' and MH, ch. 4, discusses Aristotle's appeal to nature, and its development in later Peripatetics. A good example of this development is Alexander, Mant. 150.20–159.14, applying Aristotelian naturalism to the Stoic doctrine of conciliation and to justice (following EN v 7). Cf. §181.

[13] On 'medical goodness' see Von Wright, VG 50–62.

interventions that interfere with strong natural tendencies (such as transfusions of blood or transplantations of organs) may be in accord with nature, according to the holist conception.

Naturalism about the moral virtues goes beyond these relatively uncontroversial judgments about nature and welfare. It claims to derive conclusions about moral virtues from facts about human nature, because it claims that naturalist judgments about welfare go beyond medical aspects of human nature and include a sufficient basis for moral judgments.[14] The Function Argument is Aristotle's first move in an argument that explains the different moral virtues as different ways in which we fulfil our nature as rational agents in a life guided by non-instrumental practical reasoning.

78. A Non-Naturalist Account of the Function Argument

But though the Function Argument presents this naturalist thesis, we may still wonder how seriously to take it. It appears to rely on Aristotle's natural philosophy, including his views on essence, explanation, function, and soul. But we might wonder whether these philosophical views have any place in a dialectical approach to ethical argument. They might seem to go beyond common beliefs, since they rely on philosophical theories that we cannot expect to be familiar to the ordinary moral agent.[15]

These reflexions on Aristotle's method may encourage us to look for a non-naturalist interpretation of the Function Argument.[16] We can see room for such an interpretation if we notice different possible explications of the conclusion of the Function Argument, that we fulfil the human function through activity of the soul in accord with virtue.[17] The anti-naturalist claims that the reference to virtue in this conclusion undermines the naturalist view that we are to form a conception of human nature and to derive claims about the human good and virtue from it. On the contrary, according to the anti-naturalist, Aristotle is simply claiming that the activities belonging to virtue are those that we will count—if we are virtuous—as constituting our happiness. We do not need to show that virtue meets some further condition that makes it constitute happiness. The reference to the human function and to activity in accordance with reason simply shows that the virtuous person regards virtue as happiness.

This anti-naturalist view must assume that happiness is simply the object—whatever it turns out to be—to which we attach supreme value. Virtuous people attach supreme value

[14] A naturalist position may not constitute a complete moral theory. It may leave some moral questions unsettled; for an account of the genuine moral virtues might not settle all urgent and important questions about what these virtues might require in a particular situation. We might turn to casuistry to answer these further questions, as Aristotle does in ix 2–3.

[15] Aristotle himself might be taken to reject any appeal to non-ethical principles to support ethical common beliefs. He insists on the importance of arguing from 'proper principles' (oikeiai archai), those proper to each science (see Prior Analytics 46a17, and for other references see Irwin, AFP, ch. 2, n22; ch. 7, n15). He apologizes for intruding a discussion of the Platonic Form of the Good into the Ethics, saying that this metaphysical discussion is not really appropriate (1096b30–5; cf. 1155b8–10). This refusal to go into metaphysics is summarized rather dogmatically in MM 1182a27.

[16] See McDowell, 'Role' 16. Cf. Sidgwick's objection about tautology, ME 374.

[17] 'And so the human good proves to be activity of the soul in accord with virtue, and indeed with the best and most complete virtue, if there are more virtues than one. Moreover, it must be in a complete life. For one swallow does not make a spring, nor does one day; nor, similarly, does one day or a short time make us blessed and happy' (1098a15–20).

to virtue and so they will count virtue as happiness. That is why one appeals to the function of a human being; if virtuous people care most about a particular sort of activity, they say that this is the only completely fulfilling human life. They do not say this because they can show that virtue satisfied some distinct notion of a completely fulfilling human life. They say it because, given the fact that they care most about virtue, they will take it to constitute a completely fulfilling human life. In claiming that virtuous activity is happiness we do not claim to have proved something further about it beyond what we know already in attaching supreme value to virtue. We simply reaffirm that we attach supreme value to virtue.[18]

If this is the right account of claims about happiness, it is also the right account of claims about the connexion of happiness and human nature. These cannot, therefore, provide grounds for a particular conception of happiness; they simply affirm that attachment to virtue leads to the virtuous person's conception of human nature.[19] The people who care about the Aristotelian virtues identify themselves with their rational part; this identification is a result of, but not a ground for, accepting these virtues.

This anti-naturalist view needs to be considered and examined through a study of the *Ethics* as a whole. At the moment, we can only point out that it underestimates the content of the conclusion of the Function Argument. Aristotle introduces virtue into the conclusion only after he has identified happiness with an activity in accordance with reason, and especially with an activity in which practical reason controls the agent's non-rational desires in rational choice of ends for their own sake. The virtuous activity that constitutes happiness must meet this condition for rational activity. It is not a trivial truth that the virtuous activity normally recognized as such actually meets this condition. To show that it meets this condition we need to understand what sort of rational activity Aristotle has in mind, and then we need to see what sorts of virtues embody it.

For similar reasons, we underestimate the content of Aristotle's claims about happiness if we suppose that happiness is simply the object to which we attach supreme value. In Aristotle's view, virtuous people do not achieve happiness simply because they attach supreme value to virtuous action; they achieve it only in so far as virtuous action actually meets the appropriate conditions for happiness. These conditions include completeness, self-sufficiency, and realization of a human being's practical rationality. These conditions, as Aristotle has stated them so far, are not precise enough to allow an immediate decision about precisely which lives do or do not meet the conditions for happiness. But they are not entirely empty; Aristotle has already appealed to them to show that neither pleasure nor honour nor virtue can by itself constitute happiness.

79. Nature, Happiness, and External Goods

We can confirm this naturalist understanding of the Function Argument if we consider one part of the conclusion that is difficult for an anti-naturalist to explain. Aristotle believes that

---

[18] See McDowell, 'Role' 18–20.

[19] See Annas, *MH*, chs. 3–4. In her view, 'the appeal to nature is part of an ethical theory; it supports the other parts, but is not itself an appeal outside the theory altogether' (138).

his argument from the human function to an account of happiness implies that virtuous activity alone is not sufficient for happiness; for happiness requires both complete virtue and a complete life, and therefore cannot last for only a short time (1098a16–20). If he believed that there is nothing more to happiness than the supreme object of value for a virtuous person, he would have no reason for adding this condition. If a virtuous person attached supreme value to virtue or virtuous activity, he might achieve this for only a short time, and might not even care that he could not prolong it; but Aristotle believes that this attitude would reveal a basic error about happiness. Nor is the demand for a complete life a mere afterthought that can be easily detached from Aristotle's basic argument about happiness. On the contrary, it is meant to follow from the basic argument; happiness must be the complete good, and a complete good requires a complete life.

The next section of Book i (Chapters 9–11) clarifies the demand for a complete life, by saying more about how one ought to estimate the appropriate length of life. A complete length of time is one in which the agent can achieve 'great and fine things' (1101a13). This is shorter than a complete lifetime, since Aristotle thinks it is possible for people to be happy, to cease to be happy, and to become happy again (1101a8–13), but longer than a few minutes, days, or years. It must be long enough for someone to have carried out some significant plan of living a life according to virtue—to have formed some reasonably long-term projects and to have achieved them. Priam might have succeeded in this, even though things went badly for him after that.

Aristotle introduces this temporal dimension of a complete life because he recognizes a wider role for external conditions that are not in the agent's control. External conditions present the circumstances in which virtuous actions result in happiness. He believes that these circumstances are needed for happiness, and that some features of a life depending on external circumstances can make it better or worse. He already implied this when he rejected Socrates' position that virtue alone is sufficient for happiness (1095b31–1096a2). Hence, given his remarks about the complete life, he is entitled to claim that happiness requires external goods (1099a31).

Though external conditions may make it possible or impossible to achieve happiness, Aristotle does not believe that happiness consists, even in part, in the possession of external advantages. In arguing against the life of honour, he insists that happiness consists in our own activity, not in what other people think of us, or how the world treats us; happiness is 'something of our own, and hard to take away' (1095b25–6). Still, he wants to avoid the strongly counter-intuitive Socratic and Cynic view that virtue alone is sufficient for happiness, and that external goods do not matter at all. Eventually he claims that fortune does not control happiness, but is necessary for happiness, whereas virtuous activities control happiness (1100b8–11).[20] As Socrates claims in the *Euthydemus*, happiness consists not in the possession, but in the right use, of external goods.[21] But Aristotle adds, contrary to Socrates, that we achieve happiness only by the right use of an appropriate level of external goods; if we use external goods well, but have not got enough of them, we are virtuous, but not happy.

[20] '<Doing> well or badly is not in these <fortunes>, though human life needs them added, as we said; rather, activities in accordance with virtue control happiness, and the contrary activities control the contrary' (1100b8–11).
[21] Cf. §14.

We might object that if good fortune is necessary for happiness, it controls whether we are happy or not. If Aristotle's reason for denying that fortune controls happiness is simply that fortune is not sufficient for happiness, this does not distinguish fortune from virtue, since both are necessary but insufficient conditions. Why should virtuous activities control happiness, if they are only one of the necessary conditions for happiness?

Probably Aristotle means that if we assume a level of external goods that can reasonably be assumed, the most important condition—the one that in these conditions determines whether we are happy or not—is virtuous activity. If the roads are not in such a hazardous condition that a driver's skill and care make no difference, we can reasonably say that the driver's skill and care determine safety. Aristotle distinguishes the conditions that can more reasonably be assumed, and take relatively less attention from the individual, from those that demand special attention and planning. If happiness required an extraordinarily high level of external goods, the appropriate level of external goods could not normally be taken for granted; but an extraordinarily high level is not needed (1179a1–13).

The claim that happiness requires external circumstances is not difficult to understand, if Aristotle is a naturalist. According to naturalism, happiness requires the fulfilment of human nature, and therefore requires whatever conditions are necessary for the fulfilment of human nature, whether or not a particular person cares about these conditions or cares about the activities for which these conditions are necessary. The human function requires the exercise of practical reason in a creature who does not consist wholly in practical reason, but also has non-rational desires and bodily needs. Moreover, it requires the exercise of practical reason for a temporally extended being, and so it requires the external conditions that allow us to plan for the success of our aims over time. External circumstances that frustrate our non-rational desires and bodily needs, or that change in ways that make our rational planning futile or doomed to failure, do not allow the fulfilment of human nature, as Aristotle understands it. We ought not to be surprised that the rather abstract and general considerations developed in the Function Argument are closely followed by the detailed and concrete discussion of fortune and external goods. This concrete discussion fits quite intelligibly into the naturalism that we have found in the Function Argument.

80. Naturalism and 'Second Nature'

If we look forward into the rest of the *Ethics*, we can see some features of Aristotle's position that express a commitment to the naturalist doctrine we have described.[22] He does not think of practical reason simply as a means for the discovery of what nature requires.[23] A misleading way to conceive it would be to suppose that the relation of our practical reason to our nature is the same as its relation to the nature of some other species. We certainly use our practical reason instrumentally, to consider what would be good for dogs or horses, given their non-rational nature. But if a dog or a horse acquired the practical reason that we have, it would not use it in the same way as we use it on their behalf. For it would now be

[22] In this section I am describing and answering some points raised by McDowell in 'Naturalism'.
[23] See §76 above.

a rational creature, and practical rationality would be part of its nature. Its deliberative task would therefore be different from our task in deliberating about the needs of dogs or horses.

In the same way, we are not simply non-rational creatures who are also equipped with our own practical reason for finding out what we—in abstraction from our practical reason—need. As Aristotle himself insists, according to our account of the Function Argument, our nature consists partly in practical reasoning about ends. If we deliberate only about natural needs and goods that do not take account of practical reason, we do not deliberate for creatures with our nature.

We might wonder whether Aristotle's doctrine of nature and moral character raises a more serious objection to the sort of naturalism that we have described. In a consideration of moral education, it is reasonable to conceive 'nature' as our starting point, as the various traits, tendencies, and capacities that are formed into a virtuous character if moral education goes well. Aristotle sees that this formation is pervasive; he describes habit as 'like nature' (1152a30–3) that results from a thorough transformation of the nature that we began from.[24]

This observation about habit may seem to raise a difficulty for naturalism. Just as it seems unreasonable to seek a basis for morality in an account of nature that abstracts from practical reason, it seems unreasonable to seek it exclusively in the nature that is simply the starting point for moral development and education. For it is reasonable to suppose that our developed character gives us aims and needs that go beyond the natural tendencies that we began from; the mere fact that these aims and needs do not belong to our initial natural tendencies does not make them less important.[25] If naturalism attends exclusively to the initial natural tendencies, it seems to prefer, for no good reason, the demands of the immature over those of the mature creature. We might infer that if we are to take account of this point, we must stick to a strongly moralized version of naturalism that abandons any claim to seek a basis or justification for ethics outside the outlook of the morally virtuous person.

To see what these observations about development and character do and do not show, we need to separate two conceptions of nature. We may understand it temporally, as including just those traits that moral development begins from. If nature is understood in this way, as 'initial' nature, it is essentially immature. But one might also think of mature people, including the traits that belong to mature people with formed characters,[26] in abstraction from the particular way in which this or that person has matured. It is not essential to me that I have formed precisely the character I have formed. On the contrary, once I reach maturity, I have a certain kind of nature as a rational agent. I would still have this nature if I had a different character, and I share this nature with people who have formed their characters differently. Understood in this way, nature has not been left behind in the mature person with a fully-formed character. Let us call this 'mature nature'.

Mature nature is apparently relevant to ethics. For it seems appropriate to compare two mature agents, one with a virtuous character and one with a vicious character, and to ask

[24] For McDowell's views on second nature see 'Naturalism' 184.
[25] Mill insists on this point in 'Nature'.
[26] Here 'formed' characters should be taken to include those of vicious people and of people who are neither virtuous nor vicious.

146

which of these characters is appropriate to the agent's nature. We might answer 'Both', on the ground that each person has formed a character, so that both their characters trivially fulfil their natures. Aristotle, however, believes one ought to ask which character fulfils a person's nature, and that it is morally important that the virtuous person's character fulfils it, and the vicious person's does not. In becoming vicious, the vicious person does not transform his nature so that he is no longer harmed by being vicious; on the contrary, vice is bad for him precisely because it is bad for a creature who has the nature that he still has. The nature that is relevant here is his mature nature.[27]

If we understand mature nature in this way, we may still reasonably maintain a holistic version of naturalism that treats facts about nature as an external basis and justification for moral claims. We need not, therefore, retreat from our previous conclusion that Aristotle affirms a version of naturalism in the Function Argument. We can fairly rely on this conclusion in examining the rest of the *Ethics*.

81. The Extent of Naturalism in the *Ethics*

To see how significant naturalism is in the *Ethics* as a whole, we need to form some idea of what we would expect Aristotle to say if he develops a naturalist position, and then ask whether this is what he says. We might expect that the account of the virtues, for instance, would be systematically derived from the account of human nature. We would think about the human function, what it is to carry out the human function well, and therefore we would have a general formula for what a virtue is.

It is not easy to decide whether Aristotle says what a naturalist would expect him to say. He does not explicitly announce his descriptions of the virtues of character as applications or developments of the naturalist claims in the Function Argument. According to some interpreters, he takes for granted the heterogeneous list of virtues accepted by common sense. He offers sketches of these virtues, rather than complete specifications, because he does not tell us what to do in any detail. He does not seem to derive the accounts of the virtues from any theory, let alone a naturalist theory; he simply appears to remind us of the virtues that we already recognize.

A further objection to a naturalist interpretation turns on questions about deliberation and practical reason. Just as we might reasonably expect Aristotle's moral theory to rely on claims about nature, we might also expect such claims to be recognized in the deliberations of the moral agent. If Aristotle relies on substantive claims about human nature, we might expect them to appear somewhere in the deliberation of the political scientist or of the prudent person (the *phronimos*). But the non-naturalist sees no sign of this pattern of deliberation. Indeed, the prudent person does not seem to rely on any especially theoretical or complex basic principles in deliberation.[28]

The *Ethics* is not full of open appeals to principles embodying an account of human nature. If it were, there would be no dispute about whether Aristotle is a naturalist, or about whether naturalism has an important role in his moral theory. But this does not settle the

---

[27] On vice see §111.   [28] See Broadie, cited at §98n55.

question; we must still consider whether he appeals to claims about nature and whether these claims matter for the character of his theory.

In his discussion of self-sufficiency Aristotle explains that happiness must include the good not only of oneself but also of one's parents, children, wife, and in general of friends and fellow-citizens, since a human being is a political animal (1097b11). This is a brief but important remark; for it is used to support a non-obvious claim. Aristotle does not simply mean that we need other people to protect us, supply us with food, keep the streets clean, and so on. He makes the stronger claim that a person's good includes the good of these other people. That claim does not follow from the obvious empirical facts that show that other people are instrumentally necessary for one's good.

In the Function Argument Aristotle remarks that the part of the soul that 'has' reason is divided into the part that obeys reason and that part that has reason within it (1098a4). These two parts reappear later (i 13), and Aristotle assumes that virtue consists in the supremacy of the rational part (i.e., the inherently rational part) and the agreement of the non-rational part with it. This conclusion seems to emerge from the Function Argument, which claims that a human being's good will be found in living well in accordance with reason. This is one starting point for an account of the virtues; they are the different ways in which the non-rational part accepts the guidance of the rational part. Not surprisingly, then, Aristotle mentions function in his account of virtue (1106a15; 1139a15–17 (cf. *EE* 1219a33); 1144a6).[29]

In the account of friendship (1168b28), Aristotle argues that self-love is consistent with concern for others, because we are our rational part. The true lover of self loves this part, and therefore cares about the interests of others. Aristotle relies on a claim about what we essentially are, in order to support a controversial ethical conclusion.

In Book ix (ch. 9) he returns to the completeness and self-sufficiency of happiness. He argues that if happiness is to meet these conditions, it requires friends. He reasserts the political nature of human beings, and says that a human being is naturally suited to live with others (lit. 'of a nature to live together', 1169b16). His most elaborate defence of friendship begins by saying that this is what we find if we consider the question 'more with reference to nature' (1170a13). Facts about human nature also support the claim that justice is not purely a matter of convention and agreement; in Aristotle's view, some aspects of justice are natural, because they correspond to the needs of human nature (1134b30–1135a5). In these claims he makes it clear that the demands of nature are not confined to the satisfaction of basic natural needs; an appeal to nature gives us an account of the best condition because human nature constitutes a system whose tendencies are perfected in the best order. Virtue completes nature not by going beyond it, but by fully achieving it.[30]

Not all of these claims clearly rely on a theory of human nature, and no such theory is developed or defended in detail. But Aristotle seems to make some claims of a broadly psychological and metaphysical character about what human beings are like, and what they essentially are. In accepting this naturalist approach Plato and Aristotle begin a long tradition

---

[29] In the discussion of incontinence, Aristotle says that his last account is being given 'in accordance with nature' (*phusikôs*; 1147a24). This might just mean 'in accordance with the nature of the subject-matter', i.e., with reference to ethics in particular. But it might also refer specifically to claims about human nature.

[30] See Stobaeus, *Anth.* ii 123.21–124.14, from Arius Didymus' account of Aristotelian ethics. In particular Arius claims at 123.23–5 that moral virtue (*arête*) is more in accordance with nature than bodily excellences (*aretai*) are.

of ethical argument. Their approach has often been rejected and often been defended against objections. The objections and defences will concern us further in later chapters.[31] For the moment we may simply notice that Aristotle claims to derive some non-trivial ethical conclusions from his claims about human nature. We still need to ask how much these naturalist claims matter in the main argument of the *Ethics*.

82. Happiness, Function, and the Theoretical Life

An account of Aristotle's appeals to function and nature in the *Ethics* has to face the questions raised by his final remarks on happiness. In Book x he announces that after his discussion of the virtues and related questions, he will now say what happiness is (1176a30–2). After recalling some of the criteria he relied on in Book i, he declares that happiness consists in theoretical 'study' or 'contemplation' (*theôria*), grasping the ultimate universal truths about the universe (1177a12–18).

He argues for this conclusion by appeal to his earlier formal criteria, and especially by further appeal to the Function Argument. The exercise of theoretical reason in study is the best exercise of human reason; its activities are choiceworthy solely for their own sake, and in them a human being comes closest to the condition of a purely rational being, a god. Contemplation is the highest fulfilment of our nature as rational beings; it is the sort of rational activity that we share with the gods, who are rational beings with no need to apply reason to practice. Aristotle repeats his earlier claim that we are identical to our rational part, but now he uses it to connect our happiness with theoretical study (see esp. 1178a2). He infers that contemplation is the happiest life available to us, in so far as we have the rational intellects we share with gods (1177b26–1178a4).

Some aspects of Aristotle's attitude to theoretical study are not surprising in the light of the earlier books of the *Ethics*. In identifying happiness with the realization of our rational capacities, he leaves a special place for the way of life that realizes them constantly and for their own sake, without the distractions of purely instrumental action. It is intelligible that he represents the ideal as uninterrupted rational activity. In this life the demands of external circumstances do not take us away from the activity that we choose for its own sake.

But how large a role does Aristotle intend for the theoretical life? We might suppose that it constitutes the whole of happiness, and therefore gives Aristotle's answer to a central question in the *Republic*. According to one account of the *Republic*, the philosophers see the prospects of their greatest happiness in a life spent in the uninterrupted contemplation of the forms, and they suffer a loss of happiness by turning away from the life of uninterrupted study to take part in the government of the city (R. 519b7–d9).[32] We might take Aristotle to accept the option that Plato (we have argued) rejects, and to affirm that happiness is simply theoretical study. In that case, we suffer a loss of happiness to the extent that we turn away from this pursuit to providing for the necessities of life or even to practising the moral virtues.[33]

---

[31] On Aristotle's views on nature and justice see §136, 301.   [32] See §61.
[33] A full defence of a purely theoretical and non-comprehensive conception of happiness is offered by Kraut, *AHG*. Helpful later discussions include Kenny, *APL*; Lawrence, 'Ideal'; Charles, 'Well-being'; Scott, 'Well-being'.

If this is Aristotle's view, do we need to reconsider the interpretation of Book i that ascribes a comprehensive conception of happiness to Aristotle? Such a conception is consistent with a purely theoretical account of happiness; for the comprehensive conception says that happiness embraces all non-instrumental goods, and if contemplation is the only non-instrumental good, our comprehensive conception will say that contemplation is the only component of happiness. All other goods, including the virtues and virtuous action, will be instrumental goods that are good because of their causal contribution to contemplation.

This view, however, is difficult to reconcile with Aristotle's claim that virtues and virtuous actions are worth choosing for their own sakes (1097b2–5); the virtuous person decides on virtuous actions for their own sakes (1105a32), and because they are fine, and these attitudes do not treat virtue as a purely instrumental good. If, then, happiness is comprehensive, it must also be composite; for it cannot be comprehensive unless it includes virtuous action as well as theoretical study.

To reconcile these remarks about virtuous action with a comprehensive conception of happiness and a purely theoretical conception of happiness, we might argue that these remarks about virtuous action express the outlook of the morally virtuous person, which we abandon when we recognize that happiness is theoretical study. But Aristotle does not qualify his remarks about virtue by treating them as strictly provisional judgments from an inadequate point of view. Even in contexts where he mentions the importance of theoretical wisdom (1145a6–11), he does not retract his claim that the prudent person, who has the correct conception of the end (1142b31–3; 1144a20–b1), chooses virtuous action for its own sake (1144a13–20).

If, then, we still want to ascribe a purely theoretical conception of happiness to Aristotle, we might admit that he does not abandon his claims about the non-instrumental goodness of virtuous action, and argue instead that he does not regard happiness as comprehensive. In that case, virtues and the corresponding actions will be among the non-instrumental goods that we can choose independently of their contribution to happiness. Happiness is the best good, worth choosing over any possible combination of other non-instrumental goods, but not the whole good that we rationally aim at as our end; we can also aim at other goods on non-eudaemonic grounds, and thereby make our life better than it would be if we had happiness without them.[34]

But this view of happiness is difficult to reconcile with the role that Aristotle ascribes to it in Book i. How, for instance, could we suppose that a self-sufficient life must be sufficient for family, friends, and fellow-citizens, unless we suppose that happiness, by being a self-sufficient good, includes all goods worth choosing for their own sakes? The best single non-comprehensive good does not seem to meet this condition for self-sufficiency. Aristotle claims that we do everything for the sake of happiness (1102a2–3) and that we should decide all our actions with reference to our conception of happiness (*EE* 1214b9), but it is not clear how a non-comprehensive conception would make these claims reasonable. Aristotle does not forget this comprehensive conception in the later books of the *Ethics*; it underlies his account of why friendship is necessary for a happy life (1169b3–8, 1170b14–19).

---

[34] This general view might support a non-comprehensive interpretation of 1097b16–20. See §71.

For these reasons, it is difficult to reconcile Book i and Book x, if we take Book x to identify happiness with theoretical study. Neither a comprehensive nor a non-comprehensive conception of happiness allows us to fit a theoretical view with Aristotle's other remarks on happiness, virtue, and action. If, then, we are still convinced that Book x identifies happiness with contemplation, it is wiser to conclude that Aristotle's position is inconsistent. But, while this conclusion might be reasonable if we thought Aristotle did not intend to integrate Book x closely with the rest of the *Ethics*, it is unsatisfactory, in the light of his clear references back to earlier books in his statement of the features of happiness that are present in the theoretical life (x 6–7). He seems to have in mind the general theory that he has set out in the previous sections of the *Ethics* and to believe that his previous remarks allow, and even support, his claims about theoretical study.

Similar questions arise about whether we should take the conclusions in Book x to control our interpretation of Aristotle's claims about function and nature. A purely theoretical view of happiness fits a conception of the human function as consisting exclusively in the exercise of reason without any reference to the non-rational part of the soul. A proper understanding of the human essence, on this view, identifies our essence with the divine element in us, and therefore identifies our happiness with the independent and self-sufficient exercise of the activity proper to this divine element. It is difficult to reconcile this conception of the human essence and function with what we find in the rest of the *Ethics*, just as it is difficult to reconcile a purely theoretical conception of happiness with Aristotle's comments on happiness outside Book x. It seems better to attribute inconsistent lines of thought to Aristotle than to impose the purely theoretical view on the *Ethics* as a whole. But, for the reasons given above, it is difficult to explain how Aristotle could have failed to notice the inconsistency, given his obvious intention to integrate the argument of Book x with the earlier books.

Before we conclude that Aristotle is inconsistent, we have some reason to reconsider the claim that Book x holds a purely theoretical view. Some doubts about this claim arise if we examine some of Aristotle's reservations and qualifications about a purely theoretical view. He contrasts the happiest (*eudaimonestatos* 1178a7–8) life of the contemplator with the life of the rest of virtue, which is happiest to the second degree, because its activities are human (1178a9–10). To pursue the rest of virtue we need external resources, and we run the risk of failure in our efforts to change the external world. The contemplator does not depend on external resources in the same way. Still, Aristotle adds, he is a human being and lives together with others, and hence he chooses to realize the virtues, and for this human life he needs external resources.[35] Someone who chooses to realize the virtues also chooses virtuous actions for their own sakes; he does not choose them simply as instrumental means to theoretical study. We cannot choose to realize the virtues without the motivation of the virtuous person who chooses virtuous actions for their own sake. In connecting the choice to realize the virtues with recognition of our human nature Aristotle also connects it with happiness and with the Function Argument; for he argues from our nature to the composition of happiness.

---

[35] 'In so far as he is a human being, however, and lives together with a number of other human beings, he chooses to do the actions that accord with virtue. Hence he will need these sorts of things [sc. external resources] for living a human life' (1178b5–7).

These remarks about humanity and human nature suggest that Aristotle has not forgotten the interpretation of the human function that underlies the rest of the *Ethics*. He recognizes that as human beings we have non-rational as well as rational parts of our souls, have bodies as well as intellects, and are naturally social creatures. These aspects of our essence imply that theoretical study is not the complete good for human beings as they are, and therefore is not the whole of their happiness. Aristotle, therefore, still accepts a comprehensive and composite conception of happiness. He still affirms that virtues of character and the corresponding actions are elements of happiness for a rational agent. We need not, therefore, suppose that the *Ethics* holds inconsistent views about the character and composition of happiness.

But if this is true, we need not be too surprised that Aristotle makes the remarks about theoretical study that have tempted readers to attribute a purely theoretical conception to him. He praises theoretical study because it fulfils the most thoroughly rational part of our rational nature; it is therefore the best aspect of our happiness, and it would be the whole of our happiness if we were nothing more than our intellects.[36] But since we are something more than our intellects, our happiness consists in more than theoretical study. Aristotle's claims about the value of theoretical study raise further questions about the appropriate combination of study and moral virtue in the best life. He leaves these questions without detailed answers. But he does not suggest that the value of the theoretical aspects of the happy life casts doubt on the conclusions he has already reached about the connexion between human nature and the human good.[37]

---

[36] On Aquinas' treatment of the contemplative aspect of happiness see §§280–1.

[37] Aristotle's description of the theoretical aspects of happiness certainly encourages the development of a purely theoretical conception. Such a conception is present in Plotinus (see §61; Gerson, *AOP* 252–60) and in some versions of mediaeval Aristotelianism §280n47).

8

ARISTOTLE: VIRTUE

83. The Function Argument and the Virtues

We have noticed that Aristotle's references to the Function Argument mark some of the places in the *Ethics* where he relies on claims about human nature. These references determine the shape of his account of the virtues of character and intellect. The Function Argument concludes that virtue has a central place in happiness, since it identifies happiness with activity of the soul in accordance with virtue. Virtue, in turn, is the state in which something performs its function well, so as to achieve its good. This account of virtue is more informative than it may initially seem. Aristotle claims that the human function is realized in a life of action (*praxis*) of the rational part of the soul, and hence in the rational choice of actions to be valued for their own sakes. The realization of the human function requires harmony between the rational and the non-rational parts, under the control of the rational part.

These claims help to explain each other. For if the non-rational part dominates us, our non-rational desires give us our conception of worthwhile ends, so that we do not exercise our capacity for the rational choice of non-instrumental actions. Since a life in accordance with reason requires the rational choice of ends, control by reason cannot be simply adherence to a rational plan for the fulfilment of our non-rational desires. Control by the rational part must express our rational choice of ends. According to the Function Argument, the different virtues should be forms of control by the rational part in the choice of ends.

The introduction to the account of virtue (*EN* i 13) recalls the Function Argument, since it re-asserts the division of the soul into rational and non-rational parts (cf. 1098a3–5). Aristotle repeats his claim that the non-rational part is capable of agreeing with and obeying reason, and he now says a little more about what is needed for both these parts to live 'in accordance with reason'; the best condition of a person's soul is the one in which the two parts are in harmony, so that the rational part is in control and the non-rational part agrees with it. To distinguish harmony and agreement from mere control, he contrasts the virtuous and the vicious person with the continent and the incontinent person.

He returns again to the Function Argument in his general account of a virtue of character. Every virtue puts its possessor in a good state and causes the possessor to perform its function well (1106a16).[1] Similarly, we are to think of the intellectual virtues with reference to the agent's function (1139a15).[2] We fulfil our function by acting in accordance with both prudence and virtue of character (1144a6).

At these points in his account of virtue Aristotle recalls the Function Argument. But does he use or explain its conclusion? Does he show that the virtues are ways in which practical reason controls our desires and actions?

84. Virtue, Continence, Incontinence, and Vice

Aristotle uses the division between the rational and the non-rational parts of the soul to mark four conditions of the rational and non-rational parts of soul: (1) Vice: the rational and the non-rational parts agree in pursuing the wrong ends. (2) Incontinence: the rational and the non-rational parts disagree; the rational part pursues the right ends, but the non-rational part pursues the wrong ends, and overcomes the rational part. (3) Continence: the rational and the non-rational parts disagree; the non-rational part pursues the wrong ends, but the rational part pursues the right ends, and overcomes the non-rational part. (4) Virtue: the rational and the non-rational parts agree, under the control of the rational part, in pursuing the right ends.[3]

This fourfold division clarifies an issue that the *Republic* leaves obscure. We might gather from *Republic* iv that Plato identifies virtue with control by reason and vice with lack of control by reason. If vicious people, in Plato's view, suffer from conflict between the rational and the non-rational part, they must apparently be Aristotelian incontinents. But Aristotle answers that not every vicious person suffers conflict between the rational and non-rational parts. In some people the rational part may be so warped that it creates no conflict when they want to do the vicious action. We might suppose (though perhaps incorrectly) that Plato overlooks this possibility; at any rate, he does not draw attention to it explicitly.[4]

Similarly, control is not sufficient for virtue. The virtuous person does not simply control his non-rational part. We do not think someone is really a generous or kind person if he always has to control his stingy or spiteful impulses and always succeeds.[5] It is better to control such impulses than to leave them uncontrolled, but it is better not to have them, or at least not to have them to the degree where they need control. Someone who has to control the non-rational part because it tends to mislead him needs better training until it no longer misleads him.

But though Aristotle's fourfold division is better than the Platonic twofold division, it still needs to be clarified. First, we need to see what is wrong with a continent person. If we reject Socrates' denial of incontinence, we might be inclined to say that in the incontinent

---

[1] In *EE* 1218b37 this remark about virtue and function appears at the beginning of the Function Argument.

[2] Here Aristotle uses terms, e.g., *beltistê hexis*, reminiscent of the *EE* (to which, probably, this book of the *EN* originally belonged).

[3] In 1102b14–28 only the last three conditions are explicitly distinguished; but Aristotle must intend some description of vice similar to the one above, if he is to make disagreement between the parts a special mark of continence and incontinence.

[4] We have seen that this is an over-simplified account. See §§47–8, 105.

[5] We might suppose—mistakenly—that this claim about continence and virtue conflicts with Kant, G397.

person the non-rational desires are simply too strong for the rational desires. But in that case what does the continent person lack? Does he need to strengthen his rational desires, or weaken his non-rational desires? And how is he to do either? Does Aristotle believe that the appropriate training is a non-rational process of altering behaviour and attitudes? Or might the continent person acquire stronger, more effective, rational desires from fuller understanding? Or, if Aristotle has both of these in mind, how are they to be combined?

The description of the virtuous person raises further questions. Aristotle says that the other parts agree with reason (1102b28), not that it agrees with them (though this must also, in some way, be true), and that they obey it, not that it obeys them. He implies that the virtuous person's non-rational desires are not merely weaker than her rational desires, but also agree with them in some way that makes conflict and 'overcoming' unnecessary. How are the non-rational desires trained to reach this condition?

The vicious person also raises questions about agreement between the parts of the soul. He is parallel to the virtuous person in so far as his rational and non-rational parts are in agreement.[6] But other aspects of the vicious person are less clear. We might think of him either (1) as similar to the virtuous person in being controlled by reason, or (2) as contrary to the virtuous person in so far as his reason is controlled by his appetite.

The claim that both the virtuous and the vicious person act on their 'decision' or 'election' (*prohairesis*, e.g. 1150a20, 25; 1151a17) supports the first view. In that case, control by reason, even complete agreement with reason, is not sufficient for virtue. Virtuous and vicious people alike seem to be controlled by reason. If that is Aristotle's view, he cannot claim that a state is a virtue because it fully realizes practical reason; but the account of virtue that rests on the Function Argument seems to imply such a claim. Does Aristotle's conception of the vicious person conflict with the Function Argument?

If Aristotle tries to avoid this conclusion by maintaining that appetite dominates the rational part of the vicious person, can he still draw the right distinctions between vice, continence, and incontinence? The degree of rational control in the vicious person should separate him from the incontinent; and the degree of agreement between rational and non-rational desires should separate him from both the incontinent and the continent person. But how can this be true if appetite controls his rational part?

85. The Doctrine of the Mean

With these preliminary questions in mind, we may turn to Aristotle's explanation of his fourfold division and of his claims about acting in accordance with right reason (1103b31–4). He clarifies his conception of appropriate control by reason through his Doctrine of the Mean. For a normal and natural human emotion such as anger, four possibilities are open: (1) Indulgence, leaving it completely unchecked. (2) Suppression, as far as possible. (3) Control, as far as possible. (4) Harmony and agreement with the rational part. In treating

---

[6] Even if this is not clear in i 13, other remarks (e.g., 1150b29–1151a20) make it clear that the vicious person does not suffer the conflicts of desire characteristic of the incontinent person, and so is not overcome by strong wayward desires (1150a27–31).

virtue as a mean, Aristotle signals his adherence to the fourth solution, as opposed to any of the other three.

If we are to achieve virtue, we cannot, according to Aristotle, leave our non-rational tendencies without any deliberate intervention. Habituation—deliberate formation by practice—is necessary for reaching virtue (1104a11). Someone with unmodified natural tendencies would not even think about himself and his life as something distinct from momentary impulses.[7] Should we, then, try to eliminate them? Elimination is the aim of the 'insensible' person (cf. 1119a5–11), someone who rejects some or all of his non-rational impulses and desires. Theorists who defend this eliminative attitude define the virtues as kinds of freedom from passion (*apatheia*, 1104b24).[8]

The eliminative attitude might reasonably appeal to someone who generally sympathizes with Socrates' conception of virtue, but rejects the Socratic denial of non-rational desires. This may have been Antisthenes' reaction to Socrates.[9] If we take this attitude to Socrates, we might think the ideal condition for human nature is to get ourselves into the condition that Socrates thinks we are in naturally, where all our desires are responsive to reason. If our desires are not naturally in this state, we must eradicate all those that potentially conflict with reason. This modified Socratic view appeals to the Cynics. It underlies some of the criticism of pleasure in the *Philebus*. It influences the Stoics; they also use 'freedom from passion' as a complimentary description of the virtuous person's condition.[10]

Aristotle answers that virtuous people are free of the wrong kinds of feelings, but retain the right kinds, and hence are not free of passions altogether. His Peripatetic successors defend this position by advocating 'measured passion' (*metriopatheia*), in contrast to the Stoic doctrine of freedom from passion.[11] Why does he reject freedom from passion? Is it only because he thinks it unrealistic? Or does he think it would be undesirable even if it were realistic? Does he think that people without non-rational impulses would do the wrong actions? Or does he think there would be something wrong with such people even apart from their actions? The naturalism of the Function Argument suggests an answer. He regards the Cynic solution as a mistaken approach to the task of practical reason. He accepts the sort of constraint that a naturalist might be expected to accept. The prudent person should find the best life for human nature as it is, rather than trying to remove some aspects of human nature to make them easier to organize.

Aristotle also refuses to identify virtue with self-control. Since feelings and impulses themselves must reach the right degree and aim at the right objects, the virtuous person will not have to control impulses leading him in the wrong direction. His impulses themselves

---

[7] While this part of Aristotle's position is easy to grasp, a more complex question also arises. He concedes that some suitable tendencies to become virtuous are innate—he calls them 'natural virtue' (1144b3). But he denies that this could be genuine or full virtue. He believes we have to gain full virtue by habituation, practice, and rational understanding. Is this claim a merely empirical truth about virtue? Is Aristotle just saying that in fact we do not find people born with the right sort of feelings and rational understanding? Or is it more like an a priori claim, that the causal origin of the virtuous state of character is essential to it? On this view, a virtue of character must have been formed by the appropriate responses to certain kinds of situations. Such a constraint would be unreasonable if Aristotle were interested only in the behavioural output of a virtue. But it soon becomes fairly clear that this is not all he is concerned about; and so it is not so implausible to consider the claim about the necessity of a certain kind of causal origin.

[8] Aristotle may be referring to Speusippus, or to some Cynics. See §38; §55 on *Phil.*

[9] On Antisthenes see §38.   [10] See *Phil.* 44b–46a. On Stoic *apatheia* see §191.

[11] See Seneca, *Ep.* 116.1, quoted at §191n92.

lead him in the right direction. Does Aristotle object to mere self-control simply because the merely continent person will waste a lot of time, and wear himself out psychologically and perhaps morally? If that were his objection, it would apparently not apply to all continent people; continence would apparently be enough for virtue if it were easy. Perhaps some continent people are quite averse to doing what they do, but find it fairly easy to get themselves to do it. (Sometimes, for instance, we do tedious chores that we are averse to, but do not find very difficult.) Aristotle would have no reason to deny that they are virtuous if his objections are confined to the type of continence that is difficult to maintain.

He does not suggest, however, that continence would be virtue if it were easy to maintain. He identifies virtue with harmony between the rational and the non-rational part, and rejects the other three views of virtue, because of his initial claim that the virtues are not present by nature, but complete human nature (1103a23–6). They complete it because they actualize human capacities; to have a virtue is not simply to have a capacity, but to be determined to realize the capacity in a particular way. In contrast to the virtues, ordinary capacities are capacities for contraries (1106a6–11); to have a virtue is to realize only one of the contraries for which we have the capacity. We have completely realized it only if we have achieved harmony between the parts of the soul.

86. Virtue and Harmony

Aristotle's objections to the identification of virtue with freedom from passion or with self-control do not make it clear what sort of harmony marks the virtuous person. 'Extreme' harmony would be present in someone who, for instance, suffered some wounding insult, but realized that in these circumstances it would be better not to respond, and so had no inclination at all to respond.[12] A more 'moderate' harmony is present in someone who, in these conditions, has some inclination to respond to the insult, but not such a strong one that he needs to control it; once he sees that it would be best not to respond, his desire to respond does not threaten to upset his rational election, as it does in the merely continent person.

Should Aristotle advocate extreme or moderate harmony? Belief in extreme harmony suggests that if a virtuous person has to give up, e.g., some appetitive satisfaction, she does not regard herself as having any reason (even prima facie) to pursue the satisfaction; hence she suffers no loss by giving it up. To attribute such a view to Aristotle seems to assimilate him too closely to the insensible person's view.

Aristotle's account of 'mixed' actions (discussed in 1110a4–b9) supports moderate rather than extreme harmony. If x is a mixed action, and I am right to perform x rather than y, then (1) x is better than y, all things considered, but (2) x is still open to strong objections that cause me to regret doing x rather than y, and (3) the reasons for preferring x are so strong that I am compelled to do x, not because I had no choice, but because no other choice would have been tolerable.[13] In such a case (if, e.g., I have to break some non-trivial promise to

---

[12] This would be a form of what McDowell calls 'silencing'. At 'Hypothetical' 90–2 he argues that Aristotle needs a doctrine of silencing in order to explain how continence differs from virtue.

[13] I am ignoring some of the perplexing details of Aristotle's analysis. Clauses (2) and (3) seem to be needed to distinguish mixed actions from other actions that I choose only for their results.

A in order to meet B's needs in some grave emergency), I would not be more virtuous if I acted without regret; for the regret may be a sign that I owe apology or compensation. If I did not regret anything about my action, alleging that it was best all things considered, I would be missing some important feature of the situation.

The appropriate control of anger or appetite also seems to require moderate rather than extreme harmony. If the virtuous person had no inclination towards the retaliation that he has to forgo, perhaps he would be failing to recognize the gravity of the insult; his emotional reaction would be the same as if the insult did not matter at all. Surely he should sometimes recognize that the insult matters; even if he realizes it would be wrong to retaliate, he might well think differently about the person who insulted him, and this thought might make it reasonable for him to feel some justified resentment and some degree of desire to retaliate. If he did not feel it, his emotions would not accurately represent the different aspects of value in the situation; they would only represent the value all things considered.[14] But if the virtuous person's state is supposed to complete and fulfil human nature as a whole in its different aspects, his emotions should represent the different aspects of value, in so far as they are valuable for different aspects of a human being. Hence Aristotle seems to advocate moderate rather than extreme harmony.

87. Rationalist v. Anti-rationalist Accounts of Virtue

These features of virtue of character suggest that Aristotle develops the view that we would expect, in the light of the naturalism of the Function Argument; for he suggests that virtue consists in the fulfilment of the human function in rational activity guiding the other elements of human nature. The mark of virtue, on this view, is the full realization of one's capacity to be guided by practical reason.

The naturalist position requires a rationalist conception of virtue: if virtue fulfils the nature of a human being as a rational agent, it must consist essentially (though not exclusively) in practical reason. Hence Aristotle's conception of practical reason must be broad enough to show how the difference between the virtuous person and others is a difference in the development and realization of practical reason. More specifically, practical reason must be competent to select the aims and preferences of the virtuous person over those of the vicious person or the incontinent person or other non-virtuous people; virtuous people's choice of the right ends in their lives must be explained by the excellence of their practical reason. This rationalist view need not make practical reason the sole and sufficient determinant of virtue, independently of all other aspects of human nature; but it implies that practical reason makes the decisive difference—in some way to be explained—between virtue and other states.

Our discussion of 'a life of action (*praxis*) of the rational part' has already ascribed this broad conception of practical reason to Aristotle.[15] We have argued that he takes the distinctively human function to consist not merely in the use of reason, and not merely in the use of reason to select one action over another, but also in the use of reason in *praxis*, in action

---

[14] Cf. the Stoics on appearances and passions, §192.   [15] See §76.

chosen for its own sake. Reason would not have this use unless it were capable of justifying the choice of actions as ends in themselves. With this claim in mind, we expect Aristotle's account of virtue of character to identify a virtue with (perhaps among other things) the appropriate excellence of practical reason selecting ends in themselves. His account of virtue fits the naturalist claims in the Function Argument if and only if he explains how practical reason can fulfil this role.

We must, therefore, consider whether Aristotle has the broad conception of practical reason that we have described, and whether he incorporates it into his account of virtue. And so we must discuss any apparent evidence of an anti-rationalist view of virtue resting on a narrower conception of practical reason.

An anti-rationalist interpretation might begin from Aristotle's claims about the importance of non-rational moral education. He claims (in i 13 and ii 1) that virtue of character (êthikê aretê) is the virtue of the non-rational part of the soul, in contrast to the virtue of intellect, which belongs to the rational part. The proper training for the non-rational part is habituation (ethismos), which forms the right habits and traits in the well-trained person; and the most prominent aspect of habituation is training in the appropriate pleasures, pains, and other affective reactions.

Correct habituation is crucial for the formation of character (1103b22–5). It is difficult for reasoning and teaching to make any impact if we have not been well brought up in the right habits (1179b23–31);[16] otherwise we will not have the right starting points for formal instruction (1095b4–13). Simply understanding what is good or fine will not move us to do anything about it, because 'thought itself moves nothing' (1138b35). If we are to aim at the right end, we must have acquired virtue of character by habituation. Aristotle may appear to confirm this view in acknowledging that reason and prudence are confined to discovery of the means to this right end (1144a20–2; 1145a4–6; 1178a16–19).[17]

According to this anti-rationalist view, we are virtuous if and only if our feelings and impulses have been trained to take pleasure in the right actions, and we are moved primarily by these sorts of feelings. Our feelings are in harmony with reason in so far as they do not pursue inconsistent aims, or aims that cannot be achieved by any means at our disposal. Distinctively virtuous practical reason has no essential productive role in virtue of character, because we can acquire a virtue without any distinctively virtuous practical reason. Though we need to carry out instrumental reasoning, this is not distinctive of a virtuous person. Similarly, if the successful training of feelings and impulses is sufficient for virtue, a virtue does not even partly consist in any distinctively virtuous practical reason. We need instrumental reasoning to take us from the right aims to the right actions, but this instrumental reasoning is not distinctively virtuous.

Since an anti-rationalist interpretation of Aristotle has been influential,[18] it is worth developing in some detail, to see what sort of insight it may offer into Aristotle's position. It is especially useful to develop this view to contrast with Aquinas' view of Aristotle. Once

---

[16] Aristotle's remark that it is 'impossible or not easy' (1179b17) to overcome the effects of bad upbringing suggests some uncertainty about how strong a claim he wants to make (unless the 'or' is corrective, with the force of 'or rather').

[17] Similarly, one might offer an anti-rationalist interpretation of the claim that emotion rather than reason is the 'guide' or 'leader' of virtue; see MM 1206b17–29.

[18] One might take Aquinas at least to be influenced by an anti-rationalist interpretation, even if one denies (as I do) that he accepts it. See §316. Hutcheson, IMS 122, both ascribes it to Aristotle and accepts it on his own account.

we see why some features of Aristotle make an anti-rationalist view intelligible, even if they do not ultimately justify it, we must consider whether Aquinas is right to suppose that they fit into his rationalist conception of Aristotle's position.

88. Anti-rationalism: Virtue and Pleasure

Aristotle takes habituation to be important in moral education because habituation involves training in pleasure and pain; this is relevant to virtue of character, because the 'sign' of virtue is the appropriate pleasure.[19] It is easy to see why habituation matters if it includes our being rewarded for doing the right actions and punished for doing the wrong ones, so that we come to find the right actions pleasant and the wrong ones painful. It is more surprising that Aristotle actually takes the appropriate pleasure and pain to belong to the virtuous state of character, and not merely to the process of training that results in it.

Why should pleasure and pain be so prominent in the account of virtue? Aristotle's claims might surprise us, in the light of his earlier objections (in i 5) to the life of pleasure. If taking pleasure in virtuous actions is sufficient for virtue of character, devoting one's life to the pursuit of pleasure does not seem to be as bad as we might have thought when we read Aristotle's criticism of the life of pleasure.

We might argue that Aristotle's position is consistent because he rejects only the life of misdirected pleasure-seeking, not a life devoted to the appropriate pleasures. The virtuous person has been trained not to take mercenary pleasure in virtuous action; she does not choose just or temperate actions simply because she will be rewarded by other people, and so she would not be equally ready to choose unjust or intemperate actions if they received the same rewards. Her belief that the actions are just and temperate is necessary for her pleasure in them, and she would be ashamed and dismayed if she failed to choose them. If the 'life of pleasure' is the life of the mercenary pleasure-seeker who does not care what he does as long as it brings him the appropriate further rewards, it is not the outlook of the virtuous person.[20]

Still, Aristotle may appear to identify virtue of character with a non-rational condition. For we might come to be attached to virtuous action without forming any rational conception of what is good about it, or of why it deserves to be chosen over the contrary action. We may form a non-mercenary attachment to an activity we enjoy, or to a person whose company we enjoy, without any further rational conviction that this attachment is better than others that we might have formed. Sometimes, indeed, we might not see any reason to believe that this attachment is better than others; even if we come to enjoy Bach more than Beethoven, we may not believe that anyone can prove it is better to listen to Bach. If Aristotle identifies virtue with non-mercenary pleasure in virtuous action, he might conceive it as an attachment of the same kind.

---

[19] 'But we must take someone's pleasure or pain following on his actions to be a sign of his state. For if someone who abstains from bodily pleasures enjoys the abstinence itself, he is temperate; if he is grieved by it, he is intemperate. Again, if he stands firm against terrifying situations and enjoys it, or at least does not find it painful, he is brave; if he finds it painful, he is cowardly' (1104b3–8).

[20] The mercenary position that Aristotle rejects is similar to the one that Plato calls 'slavish' at *Phd.* 69a6–b3; cf. *R.* 365c1–7.

This emphasis on pleasure is intelligible if Aristotle is sympathetic to hedonism, and recommends virtue as the source of the greatest pleasure for virtuous people. Sometimes he might be taken to claim that they have been trained to find more pleasure in virtuous action than in any vicious action, so that, from their point of view, vicious action offers no pleasure as great as the pleasures they gain from acting virtuously (1153b9–19).[21] According to this view, the motive of the virtuous person is the same as that of the mercenary pleasure-seeker, to the extent that both aim at maximum pleasure; the virtuous person seems to differ only in pursuing virtuous objects of pleasure. Aristotle seems to recommend virtue to those who seek to maximize pleasure, not to condemn the hedonist outlook altogether. This is Epicurus' attitude to pleasure; the error of mercenary pleasure-seekers is their attempt to maximize pleasure by the wrong means.[22] If Aristotle agrees with Epicurus on this claim about pleasure, his view fits an anti-rationalist interpretation.

89. Anti-rationalism: Limits of Practical Reason

Aristotle describes a virtue as a state that elects (*hexis prohairetikê*, 1106b36), and his analysis of election clarifies the rational aspects of virtue. Election requires both a wish (*boulêsis*) for some end, and deliberation about the means to that end (*ta pros ta telê*, 1112b12), and hence election, like deliberation, is concerned with means to an end. When Aristotle says that thought moves nothing by itself, but contributes to action when it is combined with desire (1139a35–b1), it is reasonable to suppose that he has deliberation in mind. Similarly, we might suppose, the wish for the end is the desire that we acquire from habituation in pleasure and pain, rather than from rational reflexion.

The claim that deliberation is concerned with finding means to ends might be defended as a reasonable restriction on the proper extent of deliberation. Aristotle apparently asks us to identify our desires, and then to reflect on the courses of action that might help us to satisfy them. We rely on our self-knowledge about our desires and on our causal knowledge about the world. We can go wrong either because of errors about the world or because of errors in considering the effect of different states of the world on our desires, or because of errors in specifying the actual content of our desires. If we correct these errors, we improve our deliberation as a method of satisfying our desires.

This account of deliberation supports Aristotle's claim that it presupposes, and cannot produce, a conception of the end to be pursued. The activity that we have described begins from some desire that is clear and definite enough to allow us to look in one direction or another for the causal information that would be relevant to satisfying it. If our desire is not definite enough to allow us to ask the appropriate causal questions, we are not yet in a position to deliberate about satisfying it.

Consideration of these familiar facts may easily persuade us that Aristotle is not only right, but obviously right, to describe deliberation in the way he does. Since deliberation provides

---

[21] 'Indeed, presumably, if each state has its unimpeded activities, and happiness is the activity—if the activity is unimpeded—of all states or of some one of them, it follows that some unimpeded activity is most choiceworthy. But pleasure is this; and so some type of pleasure might be the best good even if most pleasures turn out to be bad without qualification' (1153b9–14).

[22] See §156.

the most readily understood model of practical reasoning, we may also be inclined to follow Aristotle in his conclusion that practical reason is confined to the discovery of means to ends that are pursued by desire.

Aristotle's description of deliberation also underlies his analysis of prudence. He says that virtue of character lies in the mean determined by the reason by which the prudent person would determine it (1106b36–1107a2). He takes prudence to be a deliberative virtue, and hence to be concerned with what promotes ends, not with the ends themselves. Virtue of character, therefore, makes the end right, and prudence makes the means right (1144a6–9). This restricted role assigned to prudence appears to support the anti-rationalist view of Aristotle's conception of virtue of character. If prudence is not competent to choose one end over another, and therefore does not make the end right, what could make the end right except some non-rational condition? The appropriate non-rational condition appears to be virtue of character, understood as the product of non-rational, non-deliberative habituation that precedes the growth of prudence.[23]

90. Anti-rationalism: Moral Virtue and Responsibility

This question about anti-rationalism leads us into a broader question about the connexion between moral virtue and responsibility. We often suppose that a moral virtue, as opposed to other types of excellence, is a state that we are free to acquire, and that we can be properly held responsible for not acquiring. This seems a plausible condition for moral virtue, even if it is easier to state than to satisfy. But if Aristotle believes that virtues of character are simply the result of a process of habituation in pleasure and pain, how could he suppose we are responsible for them?

Our answer to this question may either undermine or support an anti-rationalist view. Aristotle apparently ought not to hold such a view of virtue of character, if he holds that we are responsible for having or lacking virtues of character. But does he accept this view about virtue? Has he a conception of responsibility at all?

He has something to say about the *hekousion* and the *akousion*. These terms are often translated 'voluntary' and 'involuntary' (following the standard Latin renderings), and these translations suggest a concern with responsibility. But one might prefer the translation of '*hekousion*' and '*akousion*' by 'intentional' and 'unintentional' if one believed that these renderings have fewer anachronistic associations with responsibility.[24] Apart from this specific issue about Aristotle's discussion of the voluntary, some believe that Aristotle is not especially concerned to show that we are responsible for being virtuous or vicious.

If Aristotle has no conception of responsibility, or he is not concerned about our responsibility for being virtuous or vicious, his attitude to the virtues differs sharply from the attitude that we normally take to be characteristic of morality. We often suppose that if something is morally required of us, we are fairly blamed for failing to fulfil the requirement,

---

[23] Bradley, *ATHG* 239, presents an anti-rationalist account of Aristotle, and so draws a sharp contrast between Aristotle and Aquinas. On Aquinas' treatment of these issues in Aristotle see §316.

[24] Charles, *APA* 61, defends 'intentional' in preference to 'voluntary', but not on the basis of claims about anachronism.

and therefore it is in our power to fulfil it. Kant makes this assumption central in his conception of a moral imperative, but it is accepted in many views of morality, philosophical and non-philosophical, that are not purely Kantian. According to some critics, however, this assumption about responsibility is not part of the Aristotelian conception of virtue. This is one reason for saying that Aristotle's account of the virtues of character is not intended to be an account of the moral virtues.[25]

The issues about responsibility are relevant to the range of the virtues. For some of the virtues, such as magnificence, involve both a level of external assets and an instinctive good taste in dealing with them that do not seem to be things that an agent is responsible for. This is not surprising, if Aristotle is not especially concerned about responsibility.

Hume mentions this point about ancient and modern conceptions of virtue, in his discussion of some 'verbal disputes'.[26] He argues that ancient moralists count self-regarding as well as other-regarding traits, and excellences of intellect as well as of affection, as virtues.[27] He also claims that the distinction between voluntary and involuntary is unimportant. He seems to assume that Cicero's broad conception of the range of the virtues supports the claim that the ancient moralists are indifferent to the voluntary character of virtues. In Hume's view, Christian influence has made the issue about voluntariness seem important.[28]

Hume's claims make it especially important to compare the relevant parts of Aristotle with Aquinas. For Aquinas should be one of these people who warp reasoning from its natural course. He does what Hume accuses Christian moralists of doing, in so far as he connects virtue very closely with will, responsibility, and freedom. But Aquinas represents himself as drawing all the relevant distinctions in Aristotelian terms.

It is not surprising that Hume is an anti-rationalist about virtue; he draws attention to the views of the ancients (as he understands them) to support his own view that questions of responsibility are irrelevant to virtue and vice. Similarly, it is not surprising that Aquinas holds a rationalist view of virtue, and attributes such a view to Aristotle; such a view makes it easier, or apparently easier, to explain why we are responsible for being virtuous or vicious. Since Aquinas supposes that Aristotle wants to explain this connexion between virtue and responsibility, he also supposes that Aristotle has a conception of responsibility.

With the help of Hume, we might expect that if we set out from Aristotle, we can identify where Aquinas is wrong. If Aristotle is not concerned about responsibility, the alien elements added by Aquinas should be those that give a central place to responsibility in an account of the virtues. The most important of these alien elements is Aquinas' appeal to the will; for this is both a primary source of freedom and a primary source of the virtues; a moral virtue is partly constituted by an appropriate condition of one's will. It is easy to see how Aquinas connects virtue with responsibility, and hence with 'morality' as ordinarily conceived. To see whether Hume is right, we should ask whether this connexion is alien to Aristotle's way of understanding the virtues.[29]

---

[25] See Williams, ELP 174–7; 'Voluntary' 27; SN, ch. 3. On voluntariness and virtue cf. Butler, Diss. 2.

[26] Hume, IPM, App. iv.   [27] IPM, App. iv §10.   [28] IPM, App. iv §19.

[29] This view that takes Aristotle to be largely free of the characteristic elements of morality appears in Williams (see n25). It shows the influence of Nietzsche. Hume anticipates many of Nietzsche's alleged 'insights'; he attacks emphasis on 'morality' and responsibility without even knowing about Kant, who is a primary target of Nietzsche, MacIntyre, and Williams.

91. Anti-rationalism: The Voluntary

Between the general account of a virtue of character and the description of the particular virtues, the *Ethics* includes a discussion of the voluntary and the involuntary, of election, and of conditions for action and character being up to us. The connexion between virtue, virtuous action, and praise introduces the topic of praiseworthiness and hence—apparently—of responsibility. The objects of praise are the things that we ourselves, rather than necessity or fortune, are 'responsible for' (or 'causes of'; *aitioi*) (*EE* 1223a9–15).

We must decide the extent of praiseworthy action if we are to decide what aspects of happiness are in our power. Aristotle argues that it is important to show that happiness is not a product of fortune, just as in nature and in crafts the best outcome is not a product of fortune; it would conflict with our usual view of the connexion between non-coincidental causation and goodness if we believed that what we do is not the cause of our being happy (*EN* 1099b9–25). If what we do is the cause of our being happy, happiness should be identified with activity in accordance with virtue—and that is why children and animals incapable of the relevant sort of virtuous activity are also incapable of happiness (1099b25–1100a5). Virtue is in our power to an extent that is significant enough to make happiness in our power to a significant extent.[30]

Does this concern with what is in our power show that Aristotle is concerned with responsibility and freedom? We might answer No, on the ground that questions about responsibility involve questions about freedom, and freedom involves the will; for we might argue that we are responsible for our choice and free to choose only in so far as our will is able to choose between different desires, and we are not compelled to follow one or another desire. If we connect freedom with responsibility, we will say that agents are justly held responsible in so far as they have this freedom, depending on a capacity of their will. If, then, Aristotle has no concept of the will, he apparently cannot be concerned with freedom or responsibility, and his remarks about what is in our power or up to us do not express a concern with responsibility.

We might answer this argument by denying the connexion between responsibility, freedom, and will. Alternatively, we might accept this connexion, and consider whether Aristotle has a concept of the will. Since this question is worth considering in any case, we may take it for granted that a concern with responsibility requires a concept of the will, and see whether Aristotle meets this condition for being concerned with responsibility.

In *EN* iii 1, Aristotle suggests that voluntariness consists in acting not by force or because of ignorance, and that therefore an action is voluntary just in case 'the principle is in the agent, knowing the particulars in which the action consists' (1111a22–4). The claim about 'the principle in the agent' is apparently explained by the previous discussion of force, which specifies the only conditions under which Aristotle allows that the principle is outside the agent.

We can see the apparent distance between these conditions for voluntary action and any plausible conditions for responsibility, if we notice that Aristotle's conditions allow voluntary agents to include agents who do not seem to be responsible for their actions. Animals, children, and people acting under psychological compulsion or in conditions of

---

[30] I add the qualifications to recognize the fact that Aristotle does not conclude in i 9–10 that happiness is entirely in our control.

diminished responsibility, all meet Aristotle's conditions for voluntariness, since they can all act without being forced and in awareness of what they are doing. For the same reasons, the principle of their action seems to be within them.

Not only is this the implication of Aristotle's description of the voluntary; he also notices and insists on this implication. He objects to the suggestion that action on spirit and appetite is involuntary, because this suggestion implies that animals and children act involuntarily, and the implication is evidently false (1111a24–6). His conception of the voluntary here seems quite minimal. A mere proof that virtuous actions and states of character are voluntary, according to this minimal conception, gives us no reason for holding that we are responsible for being virtuous or for acting virtuously.

We might say that Aristotle makes a mistake, because he takes his conditions for voluntariness to be conditions for responsibility. But before we attribute this mistake to him, we ought to ask whether he is really concerned with responsibility. His relatively broad conception of the voluntary may puzzle us if we are thinking about responsibility, but it may puzzle us less if we recall that he identifies a virtue with the result of proper habituation in pleasures, pains, emotions, and other non-rational impulses. The relevant processes of habituation, and the actions resulting from habitual states, meet Aristotle's generous conditions for voluntary action. Whether or not they meet conditions for responsibility may be irrelevant to his specific concerns. Responsibility belongs to rational and free agents who are taken to have a certain kind of control over their impulses and inclinations; but these aspects of responsibility seem to have no place in Aristotle's conception of the voluntary, because they seem to have no place in his conception of virtue.

92. Anti-rationalism and the Weakness of Practical Reason: Incontinence

If Aristotle believes that virtue consists primarily in a condition of the non-rational part of the soul, produced by habituation of non-rational inclinations, he ought also to believe that failures to be virtuous are to be explained by some failure in the non-rational part, and, more specifically, by misdirected or incomplete habituation. If virtue does not consist primarily in the right condition of practical reason, failure of practical reason ought not to be the primary cause of failure to be virtuous. We can see whether Aristotle takes this anti-rationalist view if we examine his views of incontinence and vice.[31]

He takes both incontinence and continence to involve disagreement between the rational and non-rational parts (1102b12–28); incontinents are those who act on appetite rather than election (1111b13–14). On this point he follows the account of incontinence that Plato offers in *Republic* iv, and therefore disagrees with Socrates' denial of the possibility of incontinence. He rejects Socrates' view that only ignorance of what is better and worse underlies apparent incontinence; indeed, he asserts that the Socratic view conflicts with the appearances (1145b27–8).

---

[31] Aristotle's views on incontinence are puzzling, and the interpretation of them is controversial. Some useful discussions indicating the variety of possible interpretations are Wiggins, 'Weakness'; Charles, *APA*, chs. 3–4; Dahl, *PRAWW*, chs. 9–11; McDowell, 'Issues' 46–9.

Aristotle seems to support his disagreement with Socrates by arguing that the incontinent's practical reasoning is not defective. He has the right election (1152a17), and acts against it (1148a13–17; 1151a5–7 (cf. 1150b29–31); 1151a29–33). He has formed a 'good syllogism', a practical syllogism based on rational wish (*boulêsis*) and deliberation, reaching a conclusion that expresses his election (1147a25–8). This conclusion prohibits the very action that he later does because of incontinence (1147a34). He will act on this conclusion at once if he is able to act and is not hindered (1147a29–31). He can still say the words of the good conclusion when he is acting incontinently (1147a18–24; cf. b9–13).

The hindrance to action comes not from reasoning, but from appetite (1147a33–4; 1111b13–14). He is moved by the conclusion of a 'bad syllogism', based on appetite and perhaps on some deliberation (1142b18–20), focussed on the action prohibited by the conclusion of the good syllogism. Unlike the intemperate person, who 'thinks he ought' to do what he does (1146b22–4; 1151a23–4; 1152a4–6), the incontinent does not think he ought to do what he is doing. This difference results from the difference in their elections. When he is acting incontinently, the incontinent feels pain, because he is doing what he thinks is bad (*EE* 1224b19–21).

Aristotle seems to suggest, then, that the incontinent person makes the right election, but acts against it, because he is moved to act by a non-rational appetite that conflicts with the election he has made. He acts on the appetite because it is stronger than the rational wish that underlies the correct election. The Socratic appeal to ignorance is superfluous, since we can explain incontinence without it, and misguided, since it conflicts with obvious facts about the incontinent person's awareness of what he is doing.

These remarks may suggest that both continence and incontinence are possible for agents whose deliberation and election is entirely correct. Apparently, the incontinent agent has done all the appropriate reasoning and deliberation and come out with the right answer, but none the less prefers to do what he knows to be worse. It is a familiar fact that the rational desire is not always the strongest, because we are attracted by other things besides objects of rational desire. The agent's deliberative reflexion does not seem to explain incontinence.

These features of Aristotle's account of incontinence seem to express an anti-rationalist view of virtue. Aristotle falls short of a strongly and explicitly anti-rationalist view such as Hume's. For Hume insists that incontinent action is not really irrational after all; it is not acting against reason, since it is simply a preference for my foreseen lesser good over my foreseen greater good, and neither this preference nor the opposite preference is either rational or irrational.[32] Aristotle does not say this; he believes that incontinents act against correct reason. But in saying this he seems to mean that they act against reason that is subordinate to correctly habituated desire. The main tendency of his view of incontinence appears to be anti-rationalist.

93. Anti-rationalism: Vice

Aristotle's account of vice may also appear to be anti-rationalist, in so far as it treats vice as a sort of mirror-image of virtue. The vicious person, no less than the virtuous person, has the

---

[32] Hume, *T* ii 3.3 §6.

rational and the non-rational parts of the soul in agreement; for continent and incontinent people suffer conflict between the parts of the soul, and in this respect differ from both the virtuous and the vicious person (EN 1102b13–28). The vicious person is similar to the virtuous in so far as he acts on his election; that is how his attitude to his action differs from the incontinent person's.[33] The vicious person acts 'thinking it right' (oiomenos dein, 1152a5–6) to do what he does.

This picture suggests that the two parts of the vicious person's soul agree in accepting the guidance of the rational part. For if the rational part were purely subordinate to the non-rational part, the vicious person's deliberation would not result in elections; an election has to begin from a wish (boulêsis), which is a desire of the rational part. The incontinent person sometimes acts incontinently on deliberation, but he still acts on appetite rather than on wish (1111b13–15; 1142b17–20). This agreement within the vicious person's soul explains why he is not subject to the regret and changing of mind that is a mark of the incontinent (1150a21–2; 1150b29–36).

And so the vicious person seems to be exactly similar to the virtuous person in his relation to practical reason and non-rational desire. They equally follow reason. One has good ends and the other has bad ends; but this difference does not imply that one is guided by reason and the other is not. This picture of vice is anti-rationalist because it implies that we cannot identify virtue with control by reason. The vicious person differs from the incontinent in acting on his election. He is guided by practical reason and deliberation, but he rejects the virtuous person's conclusion. If two people are equally guided by practical reason, but come to opposite conclusions, practical reason itself cannot ensure the right conclusions.

Apparently, then, we reach the right conclusions only if we begin from the right starting points, acquired independently of practical reason. We might take this to be the point of Aristotle's remark that deliberation has to begin from some end given as a starting point. If practical reason, identified with deliberation, cannot supply the appropriate starting point, apparently it cannot be the crucial element in virtue. If the vicious person acts on his election, and hence on his rational choice, he must differ from the virtuous person in his non-rational impulses. This is just what we expect if virtue depends primarily on habituation. The vicious person has been habituated badly, and therefore does not grasp the right ends.

These different aspects of Aristotle's position present a case for an anti-rationalist interpretation. But the case rests on a selective treatment of the evidence. If we examine the different elements of the anti-rationalist position in the light of a fuller survey of the evidence, we will be able to see whether the anti-rationalist interpretation gives a satisfactory account of Aristotle's view.

94. Virtue, Election, and Reason

The first difficulty for an anti-rationalist account arises from Aristotle's description of virtue of character. Though he regards it as the product of habituation in pleasures and pains, he also takes it to have a rational component that does not fit an anti-rationalist interpretation.

---

[33] See 1146b19–24; 1148a4–11; 1150a16–22; 1151a5–10; 1152a5–6.

Someone who simply has well-trained non-rational desires does not satisfy the conditions of i 13, which implies that a person's function is fulfilled by agreement between the rational and the non-rational parts, under the control of the rational part (1102a5–7; b23–8). If Aristotle takes this condition seriously, we would not expect the rational part to be strictly subordinate to the non-rational as it would be if virtue were a state of the non-rational part.

Virtue is a state (hexis) rather than a feeling, because virtue is praiseworthy (1105b31), whereas simply having a certain kind of feeling is not praiseworthy. Aristotle seems to suggest that simply having a feeling concentrated on the right object is not sufficient for being praiseworthy. He does not yet tell us what is needed to make a praiseworthy state out of non-praiseworthy feelings.

Virtue of character is a state that elects, consisting in a mean determined by reason, and by the reason by which the prudent person would determine it (1106b36–1107a2). We might take these remarks about reason and the prudent person so that they do not require each virtuous person to have the reason and prudence that determine the mean. Do we perhaps have virtue of character if (like the non-ruling classes in the Republic) our emotions are guided by someone else's reason and prudence?

Aristotle's other remarks about the virtuous person rule out this possibility. The virtuous person must elect the virtuous action for its own sake (1105a32; 1144a19); but election rests on wish and deliberation, and correct deliberation is the task of the prudent person (1140a25–31); hence genuine virtue requires prudence, to order non-rational desires by correct reason (1144b21–5). In requiring prudence Aristotle requires the virtuous person to realize fully his capacity for rational determination of his actions and choices. Election of virtuous action for its own sake (1144a19) is necessary for 'full virtue' (kuria aretê, 1144b4), and we lack this unless we have prudence.

The fact that Aristotle makes reason and prudence prominent necessary conditions for virtue does not by itself refute an anti-rationalist interpretation. His remarks about prudence may make his position inconsistent, or they may be interpreted so as to fit an anti-rationalist view. But at least they present an anti-rationalist view with an objection that needs to be answered.

95. Pleasure and Reason

Aristotle takes virtue to result from habituation in pleasure and pain, and he regards appropriate pleasure and pain as a sign of having acquired the appropriate state of character. This emphasis on pleasure may appear to support an anti-rationalist interpretation, since it may seem to suggest that he identifies a virtue with a non-rational impulse or reaction. But to see whether this appearance is correct or misleading, we need to consider Aristotle's views on pleasure more closely; for the rational or non-rational character of virtue depends partly on the relation between pleasure and its object.

Aristotle agrees with Plato's suggestion in the Philebus that the virtuous person takes pleasure in being virtuous and acting virtuously, whereas the vicious person takes a different type of pleasure.[34] He develops this suggestion by claiming that pleasures differ in kind (or 'in

---

[34] See Plato, Phil. 12c8–d4, discussed in §53.

species', 1175a21–b1). In this claim he rejects the view that pleasure is a uniform sensation to which different kinds of pleasant action are connected only causally and instrumentally; this is the view that Protarchus defends in the *Philebus* (12b–13c). The instrumental conception of the relation between pleasure and its object supports a hedonist view of the good; for if one action is more valuable than another only because of the quantity of pleasure that results from it, the hedonist can plausibly claim that only a larger quantity of pleasure can be more valuable non-instrumentally.

Since Aristotle rejects Protarchus' claims about pleasure and its objects, it is not surprising that he rejects hedonism. He is sympathetic to some of the arguments that Aristippus and Eudoxus use to defend hedonism (*EN* 1172b9–25), but he does not believe that they support hedonism. He believes they are helpful in answering the extreme thesis that pleasure is not a good at all. He agrees with the hedonists in believing that pleasure is a good, but he rejects the stronger claim that pleasure is the good (1172b26–35).[35]

Aristotle objects to Protarchus' instrumental conception of pleasure and its object by pointing out that we do not believe one pleasure can be substituted for another in the ways that should be possible if the instrumental conception were right. According to the instrumental conception, it should not matter to us if we lost our capacity to enjoy athletic activity or playing music, as long as our loss of enjoyment were outweighed by a large enough quantity of pleasure in lying on the beach. But in fact we would think we had lost something valuable if we lost our capacity to enjoy these activities; the substitution of some different pleasures might compensate us to some degree, but it would not compensate us with more of the same thing that we had lost. It would be like compensating us with money for an accident in which we lost the use of our limbs; just as the money would not give us the use of our limbs back, the additional pleasure would not be more of the pleasure that we had lost. Aristotle recognizes this point by remarking that one kind of pleasure cannot be added to another to produce a greater pleasure; on the contrary, one kind tends to reduce the enjoyment we gain from the other kind (1175b1–24).

Our choice of pleasures and our views about compensation reflect the fact that the specific pleasure taken in a particular action essentially depends on our choosing that action for its own sake. Pleasure is a 'supervenient end' (1174b31–3) resulting from an activity that one pursues as an activity (*energeia*) rather than a mere process (*kinêsis*). It is an end because it is a distinct non-instrumental value beyond the activity that is its object; but it is only a supervenient end, because its non-instrumental value depends on the value of the activity on which the pleasure depends (1176a3–29). If someone pursues cruelty or self-indulgence for its own sake, his life is worse in so far as he enjoys those pursuits. If, however, someone values just and generous action for its own sake, his life is better in so far as he takes pleasure in these actions.

But if we take pleasure in just action in its own right, not simply as a means to some further result that yields pleasure, we need the appropriate beliefs about the non-instrumental value of just action. We have to regard just action as 'action' (*praxis*), in Aristotle's technical sense, rather than mere production; hence we have to regard it as containing its own end

---

[35] In *EN* vii Aristotle seems to argue primarily against extreme hostility to pleasure, such as one finds in the Cynics and in the dour people in Plato, *Phil.* 44b–d. Book x states the objections to hedonism more fully.

(1140b6–7). This rational conviction of the value of an action belongs to 'the life of action of the rational part' that realizes the human function. When we take pleasure on the basis of this conviction, and this conviction is correct, we are taking the virtuous person's pleasure in virtuous action.

Earlier we cited a passage in Book ii where Aristotle identifies a virtue with a state that takes pleasure in the right actions, and we took this passage to support an anti-rationalist account of his views on virtue. We can now see what is wrong with that treatment of the passage. Aristotle makes it clear that the special pleasure of a virtuous person must have a special object; the temperate person is the one who abstains from bodily pleasures and enjoys the abstention itself (1104b3–8). Aristotle means that he abstains from bodily pleasures that would be inappropriate (since the temperate person does not enjoy abstinence from appropriate pleasures). Virtuous people who enjoy this abstention do not enjoy it because it is abstention from bodily pleasures; they enjoy it because it is the right abstention, from the wrong pleasures. To form this enjoyment, they must have come to value rightness, and to reject wrongness, for their own sakes. Their judgment of value underlies the pleasure of the virtuous person. Such a rational appreciation of virtue requires more than feelings of pleasure and pain focussed on the right actions.

Aristotle's treatment of pleasure as a supervenient end helps to identify the pleasures that are results of a rational conviction, and so helps to explain how these pleasures conflict with hedonism. But we may wonder whether he does not go too far in connecting pleasures with evaluative beliefs.[36] How, on his account, are we to understand action simply 'for pleasure' (as we normally understand it)? We seem to do all sorts of things simply because they are enjoyable; our enjoyment does not seem to be a by-product of our convictions about the value of the actions. Aristotle apparently needs to give an account of acting simply for pleasure. He especially needs such an account to explain his description of the vicious person, who acts for the sake of pleasure (1146b22–4; 1150a19–21).[37]

His account of pleasure would be clearer if he distinguished two ways of pursuing something 'for its own sake': (1) We might pursue F for its own sake simply because we pursue it non-instrumentally, without regard for the consequences. (2) We might pursue F in its own right, because it is what it is. In the second case its being F gives us the reason for pursuing F non-instrumentally, but in the first case we might pursue the thing that is F without recognizing any property of it as a reason for pursuing F non-instrumentally. Aristotle does not explicitly distinguish these two ways of pursuing F for its own sake, but the difference between them helps us to clarify (or perhaps to revise) his account of pleasure. While not all pleasure requires a judgment about the value of its object, some pleasures—those we take in F qua F—require such a judgment. Non-instrumental pursuit without an evaluative judgment underlies pursuit of something simply for pleasure. Evaluative judgment underlies the pleasures of the virtuous person.

And so, even if Aristotle were to make the mistake of believing that all pleasure depends on an evaluative belief, the crucial part of his doctrine is secured if some pleasures depend on it. For that is all he needs to support his claim that pleasures differ in kind according to their

---

[36] A similar question arises about Butler's belief-dependent conception of pleasure in S xi 6.
[37] For further discussion of the vicious person see §109 below.

objects, and this is the claim that supports his objections to hedonism and his account of the distinctive pleasure that the virtuous person takes in being virtuous. He faces and answers a question that raises a persistent difficulty for the various hedonist theories of value that have been offered. Epicurus and Mill, in their different ways, try to remove the difficulty that Aristotle raises for hedonism, but they do not clearly succeed.[38]

Aristotle's references to virtue and pleasure, therefore, do not imply neglect of the rational component of virtue; they presuppose some rational evaluation of virtuous actions as good in themselves. We therefore expect Aristotle to describe the basis of this rational evaluation in virtuous people, to make clear the source of their special pleasure. Virtue involves the non-rational aspects of human nature, because we need our non-rational aspects to be brought into a virtuous condition; but virtue itself is primarily a rational condition. Pleasure has its proper place in happiness if it is part of a life that is guided by practical reason. Closer analysis of Aristotle's views on pleasure does not support an anti-rationalist interpretation, but counts against it.

96. Virtue, Election, and Deliberation

Since Aristotle identifies virtue with a state that elects (1106b36), a clearer understanding of his view requires some grasp of his conception of election. Until now, we have attended to his claim that election rests on deliberation about means to ends, and therefore is about means to ends (1111b26–30; 1113b3–4). According to this conception, a virtue must be a state that elects, because it aims at action, and election focusses our desires on specific actions.

But this is not all that Aristotle means in connecting virtue with election. The virtuous person must also elect the virtuous action for its own sake (1105a32; cf. 1144a19). This demand expresses the expectation that the just or generous person will act appropriately without the incentive of some further gain. Glaucon and Adeimantus express this expectation in *Republic* ii, in asking Socrates to show that the just person is happier by pursuing justice without regard to rewards and consequences.[39] Aristotle's demand for election of virtuous action for its own sake implies a rationalist interpretation of Glaucon and Adeimantus' expectation; for not just any choice of an action for its own sake, but only a rational, deliberative choice is the mark of a virtuous person.

Aristotle's demand is puzzling, in the light of his claim that election is only about means to ends. For if we elect something for its own sake, we elect it as an end; but, according to Aristotle, we elect only means. How, then, can the virtuous person elect the virtuous action for its own sake?

One answer leads us back to anti-rationalism. Perhaps Aristotle uses 'elect' loosely here. In that case, we might capture his intention better if we substituted 'choose' for 'elect'. This substitution removes the apparent conflict between the condition for virtue and the other claims about election.

---

[38] For Epicurus see §156. Mill deals with similar questions in his division between quantity and quality of pleasure in *U*, ch. 2.

[39] See §50.

This answer is unsatisfactory. For Aristotle's description of virtue carefully prepares for his reference to election (ii 4); moreover, this reference to election explains why we need a fuller examination of election (iii 2–3). Since the fuller examination professes to clarify the initial description of virtue, that description ought to refer to the sort of election that is described in the clarification. If we assume a loose use of 'election' in Book ii, we remove an apparent conflict only by introducing a real conflict; for the concept of election that is explained in Book iii will not be—contrary to Aristotle—the concept that was used in Book ii.

A different sort of answer is available, if we accept a comprehensive conception of happiness. For choosing x as a means to y may be a way of choosing x as an end in itself, not as purely instrumental to y. Plato's claims about justice in *Republic* ii suggest this treatment of means; they are coherent claims if and only if Plato conceives justice as a component of happiness, not a purely instrumental means to it.[40] According to this conception, justice is a component of happiness just in so far as it is a non-instrumental good that is a necessary part of the best life. In that case the claim that we choose justice for its own sake does not conflict with the claim that we choose it for the sake of happiness; on the contrary, each claim partly explains the other.

In examining *EN* i, and especially the completeness of happiness, we have seen that Aristotle needs to appeal to the same relation between non-instrumental goods and happiness. The composite conception of happiness explains how happiness can embrace the different forms of *praxis*, non-instrumental action chosen for its own sake. The same composite conception fits Aristotle's claims about election and deliberation, if we understand 'contributing to ends' or 'for the sake of ends' so that it includes components of the ends, and not only instrumental means to them.[41]

Hence the same understanding of ends and what promotes them explains both Aristotle's claims about happiness and his claims about election and virtue. The fact that it explains these two aspects of Aristotle's theory that would otherwise be perplexing is a reason for believing that it is the right interpretation of both aspects.[42]

Aristotle's claims about deliberation and election do not conflict, therefore, with his claim that the virtuous person elects virtuous action for its own sake. Deliberation is not about ends, in so far as it must begin with some end in view; the means that deliberation finds to promote that first end is an end in itself, if deliberation finds that it is a component of the first end. Moral deliberation begins with some conception of happiness, and deliberates until we find the states of character that are components of happiness. If we deliberate correctly, we find the moral virtues, and we elect these for their own sakes.

---

[40] See §52.

[41] These phrases give different ways of rendering Aristotle's phrase *pros to telos*, lit. 'towards the end', equivalent to 'for the sake of (*heneka*) the end'.

[42] This solution is developed by Aquinas. See, e.g., §251, 273. It is also widely accepted (without reference to Aquinas) in modern discussions of Aristotle, beginning (in English) from Greenwood, *EN VI* 46–9. See also Ackrill, 'Eudaimonia'; Wiggins, 'Deliberation'; Sorabji, 'Role'; Cooper, *RHGA*, ch. 1. Some problems and further issues are discussed by Charles, 'Ontology'. Some doubts about the conclusions I draw from this account of deliberation are expressed by McDowell, 'Issues' 30–6. This conception of means is also relevant to Mill's discussion of parts of happiness in *U*, ch. 4, and to Moore's criticism of Aristotle in *PE*, ch. 3.

97. Wish and Will

We must still clarify the aspect of an election that introduces a 'wish' (*boulêsis*). We might initially suppose that if we desire an end and we deliberate about the means to it, we elect the action that appears to be a means to the end. But this is not enough for an election, since Aristotle distinguishes wish from spirit and appetite, which are also desires for ends. We might, then, understand wish as desire that is not formed under the stimulus of some immediate pain, need, or provocation of the sort that produces the desires of appetite and spirit.[43] This sort of desire can be trained to conform to reason, in so far as it can more easily be trained to focus on more remote objects and is less tied to immediate satisfactions. Still, it belongs, as the other desires do, to the desiring part, which is inherently non-rational, though it is capable of following reason (cf. 1102b13–1103a2).

If this is the right account of Aristotle's view of wish, Aquinas is wrong to impose a rationalist interpretation, introducing a sort of desire that is peculiar to the rational part of the soul and distinct from non-rational desire.[44] An anti-rationalist view denies that the relation of different desires to reason constitutes an essential difference between them.

But the anti-rationalist view does not account for all of Aristotle's claims.[45] For wish is not simply a desire for an end; it is also a rational desire aiming at the good (*Rhet.* 1369a2–7). Aristotle assumes that to be moved in accordance with reason, we must be moved in accordance with wish (*DA* 433a22–5). He describes incontinence as the overcoming of wish by non-rational desire (434a11–14).[46] In a virtuous person, therefore, the desire for an end that underlies an election and the resulting virtuous action must be a rational desire. Aristotle suggests that the primary object of wish is happiness (*EN* 1111b26–30);[47] hence the virtuous person's election is based on a wish for one's own happiness, and deliberation about how to achieve it. This deliberation gives us the ends that are characteristic of the virtuous person.

This claim faces a difficulty in the role that Aristotle assigns to election. For he distinguishes election from wish, and he claims that when we act on a specific rational desire for some achievable object here and now we act on an election rather than a wish.[48] But if election fits into the threefold classification of desire, it must be wish, in the sense of 'wish' that makes wish co-ordinate with spirit and appetite. When Aristotle compares wish with election, he has already excluded the two non-rational forms of desire (1111b10–19), and so assumes that election is a form of wish. When he says that election is not to be identified with wish,

---

[43] Hence *boulêsis* is called a 'desire without pain' (*Top.* 146a36–b6). 'Velle' and 'voluntas' capture the non-urgent aspect of 'boulesthai' and 'boulêsis' quite well in Latin. See §240.

[44] 'For the scholastics, the will is precisely a rational desire, in the sense that it is an activity of the rational soul, which possesses in itself a desiring faculty distinct from the irrational desiring faculty—an idea totally foreign to Aristotle' (Gauthier, *EN* ii 194).

[45] This is clear, though not completely explicit in iii 2. Aristotle discusses *epithumia*, *thumos*, and then introduces *boulêsis* as the desire of rational part.

[46] In 434a12 I read *tên boulêsin*.

[47] He does not say this is the only possible ultimate object of wish, but he does not suggest anything else.

[48] Hence some are inclined to identify the will with *prohairesis* rather than *boulêsis*. See Ross, *Ar.* 199–200.

he adds that it none the less appears close to it (1111b19–20). The close connexion between election and wish suggests that they are both desires belonging to the rational part.[49]

Aristotle's remarks about election may help us to see whether wish is an essentially rational desire. If acting on wish is simply acting on a desire that has been affected by some sort of reasoning, any action resulting from deliberation should be action on wish. But Aristotle denies this. For we do not form an election simply by deliberating about how to satisfy a non-rational desire; the deliberation of an incontinent person about how to satisfy his appetites does not result in an election, and so does not arise from wish.[50] Action on wish is rational in some sense that goes beyond simply acting on deliberation about a non-rational desire; and so a wish must be rational in some sense that goes beyond simply being influenced by deliberation. Aristotle's claims about the connexion between election and wish tend to support Aquinas' view that Aristotle recognizes an essentially rational form of desire; and so Aquinas is justified in supposing that Aristotle recognizes the will.[51]

Aristotle's description of incontinence implies that the rational part of the soul has its own desires. As we have seen, he distinguishes a part of the soul that 'has reason fully and within itself' (1103a2) from a part that is 'non-rational, but shares in a way in reason' (1102b13–14). This second part does not include all desires.[52] For he takes incontinence to result from conflict between the rational and the non-rational parts. In the incontinent person something fights against and resists reason (1102b17–18), so that 'the impulses of incontinent people go in contrary directions' (1102b21). One of these contrary impulses belongs to the non-rational part that is capable of obeying reason but fails to obey reason in the incontinent person. The other impulse belongs to the part that is rational in its own right. In recognizing an impulse proper to the rational part, Aristotle seems to recognize essentially rational desire.

Similarly, he claims that election is contrary to appetite, whereas appetite is not contrary to appetite (1111b15–16), and that incontinent people act on appetite, but not on election (1111b13–14), even though they make the correct election (1151a5–7). In the incontinent person, then, appetite conflicts with election, which is a desire based on wish. Since the incontinent person suffers a conflict between the rational and the non-rational part, wish belongs to the rational part.

If Aristotle held an anti-rationalist view, he would raise far-reaching difficulties for his theory of virtue. An anti-rationalist view must apparently say that we form wishes by forming desires that are attached to objects that we believe to be good. First, (we might suppose) we pursue things that seem to offer pleasure or reward rather than pain or punishment,

---

[49] Aspasius emphasizes the connexion between *boulêsis* and *prohairesis*: 'Boulêsis appears close to *prohairesis*, since, first of all, it is in the rational part of the soul, where what most controls *prohairesis* (or "the most important part of *prohairesis*" (to *kuriôtaton tês prohaireseôs*)) is, and, second, because it is a part of *prohairesis*. For whenever intellect after having deliberated approves and chooses, *boulêsis*, being a desire, goes forward with it. And in fact we are in the habit of treating *boulesthai* and *prohaireisthai* as signifying the same thing. For instead of saying "I elect to farm my land" we say "I wish (volo) to farm my land", and we say "he has a good will (voluntas)", that is to say a good *prohairesis*' (68.27–32). The translation of the last sentence relies on Felicianus' Latin version (the Greek text has a lacuna).

[50] On the incontinent's deliberation see 1142b17–20. On his failure to act on *prohairesis* see 1111b13–14. On *prohairesis* and *boulêsis* see 1113a21 (where *kata tên boulêsin* should probably be read); 1113b3–5.

[51] Alexander argues that wish requires judgment and deliberation, because it is a rational desire. It is not itself an exercise of reason, but it follows on the appropriate exercise of reason, and specifically on deliberation (DA 74.6–13). Alexander is cited and unjustly criticized by Gauthier, 'St Maxime' 58.

[52] See Heliodorus, 24.40; Aspasius, 35.22; 36.2; Eustratius, 118.33–5. On *boulêsis* cf. Eustratius, 116.11–12.

but gradually we are habituated to pursue things that seem to be good rather than bad. Such a desire, however, may still be non-rational. If we have been correctly trained, we will be pleased with the thought that an action is good and fine; in fact this is how the temperate or brave person's non-rational desires react to the appropriate information. But these non-rational reactions do not count, in Aristotle's view, as expressions of wish and election. For while he agrees that we ought to form non-rational desires for things we believe to be good (1111a29–31), he does not suggest that every such desire is a wish. An anti-rationalist view seems to oversimplify Aristotle's conception of the different sorts of desires that are present in a well-trained person.

The anti-rationalist view might be defended by appeal to the last part of EN i 13, where Aristotle uses his division of parts of the soul to mark the division between virtues of character and virtues of intellect (1103a3–10). The virtues of intellect clearly belong to the rational part, and do not essentially consist in well-ordered desires; well-ordered desires belong to the virtues of character. Does this not imply that all well-ordered desires, including those belonging to the will, belong to the non-rational part?[53]

We ought not to draw this conclusion; for Aristotle neither says nor implies that the virtues of character belong exclusively to the non-rational part. He believes that none of them is exclusively a virtue of the rational part, since all of them essentially include some appropriate training of non-rational desires (those belonging to spirit and appetite). But to say this is consistent with saying that the virtues of character belong to the rational part in so far as they include the right election.

98. Prudence and Deliberation

Our explanation of wish and election rests on the assumption that we can deliberate about the components of happiness, and that the desire we reach as a result of this deliberation is a wish. In the light of this conception of happiness and deliberation, we can understand Aristotle's claim that the virtuous person elects virtuous action, but elects it for its own sake; his claim is intelligible in the light of his earlier claim that we choose virtues both for their own sake and for the sake of happiness. The same account of deliberation also helps to explain the role of deliberation in prudence. If we assume that every 'means' to an end (i.e., everything that 'promotes' or 'contributes to'[54] an end) is a purely instrumental means to it, Aristotle's views about prudence appear to be inconsistent; but if we avoid that assumption, they form a coherent conception of prudence.

Prudence has a wide scope. It deliberates about what contributes to living well as a whole (1140a28). It begins with nothing more specific than 'living well as a whole', and so it has to find the different things that promote living well. These include (according to Aristotle) the virtues that are components of happiness.[55] In so far as prudent people carry out this deliberation, they do the sort of thing that Aristotle announces as the task of political science (said to be the same state as prudence, 1141b23).[56]

---

[53] This seems to be the view of Aquinas, in EN §243, though it conflicts with his other views. See §257.
[54] See above n42.
[55] This is part of the 'grand end' interpretation criticized by Broadie at EA 198–202, and discussed by Kraut, 'Defence'.
[56] On the extent of deliberation see §322.

The task Aristotle sets himself in the *Ethics* is the task, at a very general level, that he assigns to prudence in Book vi. The *Ethics* begins with only some general views about *eudaimonia*, and without any definite or fixed specification of its components. The initial conception of happiness is not so vague that it allows just anything to count as a component of happiness. The formal conditions of i 7 rule out some mistaken accounts of the composition of happiness, including the accounts presupposed by the different ways of life rejected in i 5. But we cannot immediately derive the components of happiness from the formal conditions, even when they are supplemented by the Function Argument. To see the implications of Aristotle's conditions for happiness is to discover the components of happiness; and this discovery results from the deliberation that goes on in the treatise as a whole. These features of the *Ethics* clarify the role of deliberation and its capacity to discover intrinsic goods that are components of the end.

Aristotle's view of deliberation explains why deliberation is the characteristic function of prudence, and is concerned with what contributes to the end, but none the less prudence is a correct grasp of the end (1142b32–3).[57] Aristotle does not imply that some non-deliberative aspect of prudence is needed to grasp the end, or that we cannot grasp the end through deliberation. On the contrary, we would expect good deliberation about the components of happiness to reach a correct grasp of the end. Aristotle's remarks about deliberation and about the relation of prudence to the end support each other.

These remarks also help to explain why the role of virtue is to get the right end, and the role of prudence is to find the things contributing to the end (1145a5). Aristotle does not mean that prudence has no role in getting the right end; for the virtue that is said to grasp the right end is the 'complete' or 'full' (*kuria*) virtue that includes prudence. In saying that the function of prudence is to find what contributes to the end, Aristotle does not describe a task separate from the task of virtue. On the contrary, he means that the deliberative function of prudence reaches the right end that the virtuous person grasps.

If, then, we grasp Aristotle's views on deliberation and ends, we see that his position is consistent. It is also plausible, if we believe that he correctly describes his task in the *Ethics* as deliberation about the components of the end, and that his deliberative argument shows that the virtues he recognizes are components of happiness.

If practical reason and deliberation fulfil these tasks, they support one choice of ultimate ends rather than another. In claiming that the virtues of character include prudence, carrying out these deliberative functions, Aristotle shows how the virtues embody the subordination of non-rational desires to practical reason. To act in accordance with the virtues is to engage in 'a life of action of the rational part', since the virtues rest on the deliberation that identifies certain things as actions (*praxeis*) that have their ends within themselves.

Aristotle, therefore, presents the theory of virtue that his naturalism requires. His version of naturalism identifies the human function with a life of action of the rational part, and therefore requires a naturalist account of virtue to be a rationalist account. The Function Argument guides his account of the virtues and his claims about the relation of the virtues to prudence.

He does not take the non-rational components of the virtues to be irrelevant or unimportant. On the contrary, we have seen how his claims about the importance of non-rational

---

[57] A less probable translation makes prudence grasp the means to the end.

impulses, pleasures, and pains show how one might develop a strongly anti-rationalist account of the virtues of character and of the formation of ends. But Aristotle does not hold an anti-rationalist account; it would undermine the central role of the Function Argument in the *Ethics*. Non-rational elements are prominent in the account of virtue; for if virtue fulfils human nature, it fulfils the non-rational elements of human nature too.[58] But Aristotle's naturalism places the human function in a life guided by practical reason; hence the fulfilment of the non-rational elements of human nature includes their agreement with, and subordination to, practical reason.

It is not immediately evident that naturalism implies rationalism about virtue; it leaves open the possibility of a non-Aristotelian account of the human function that would not make virtue the excellence of practical reason. It is rather difficult, however, to make such a view convincing. For if we conceive human nature as a system rather than a collection, it is difficult to identify the relevant sort of system without saying that it is guided by practical reason; and if we seek to identify virtue with what is required by the system, it is most plausible to identify it with some sort of guidance by practical reason. This connexion between nature, reason, and virtue is characteristic not only of Aristotle, but of other naturalists as well—the Stoics, Aquinas, Suarez, and Butler. It is not accidental that Hume rejects both naturalism and rationalism. Though some philosophers try to maintain naturalism without rationalism, as Hutcheson does, or rationalism without naturalism, as (e.g.) Scotus, Clarke, and Price do, their attempts to defend one of the Aristotelian claims without the other result in a less defensible position.[59]

99. Virtue, Reason, and Responsibility

We have traced some of the details that fill in the outline sketched in the Function Argument. The different virtues of character are different ways in which the non-rational and rational parts of the soul agree, under the guidance of the rational part. Aristotle describes the guidance of the rational part further in identifying a virtue of character with a state that elects. Since election rests on deliberation about the composition of the ultimate end, not simply about instrumental means to it, the virtuous person's election results from a distinctive conception of what is non-instrumentally valuable. Control by the rational part, therefore, includes acceptance of a distinctive set of ends grasped by practical reason.

Even if the naturalism of the Function Argument requires this rationalist conception of virtue, is this conception at all plausible? Why should we prefer Aristotle's rationalist view over an anti-rationalist view that, as we have seen, we might construct from Aristotelian material? Even if Aristotle himself does not hold an anti-rationalist conception of virtue as primarily or exclusively a good condition of our emotions and other non-rational impulses, this anti-rationalist conception might be better than the conception he accepts.

Some of the further questions raised by this question may be explored by returning to the connexions between Aristotle's account of virtue and his views on responsibility. We have

---

[58] Hence Aquinas marks three aspects of natural law, corresponding to three elements of human nature. See *ST* 1–2 q94 a2, discussed at §311.

[59] See §368.

seen how certain aspects of these views seem to support an anti-rationalist view, and even suggest that he is not concerned with responsibility at all. We have also seen that Aristotle's views on the range of 'voluntary' or 'intentional' (hekousion) action do not suggest any connexion with the will or with freedom. For voluntary agents include non-rational animals and children, though we would normally attribute neither wills nor free action to them.

This broad scope of voluntary action, however, raises a further difficulty about the Ethics. It is not immediately clear why Aristotle thinks human beings are the only ethical agents. Ethics is about the virtues of character (êthos) that are acquired by habituation (ethismos); but non-rational animals can have their actions and desires modified by training that involves rewards and deprivations, and hence they seem capable of habituation and of forming a good or bad character.[60]

Aristotle suggests that non-rational agents are not ethical agents, because virtue and vice are objects of praise and blame; since only voluntary actions are open to praise or blame, only agents who act voluntarily are ethical agents. But this answer raises further puzzles. For, as he sees, the definition of voluntary action implies that non-rational animals act voluntarily (1111a24–6); and so they should apparently be open to praise and blame. It may seem plausible in any case to claim that we can praise or blame animals and children; for we train and habituate them, by communicating our pleasure and pain in their action. They still seem to be ethical agents.[61]

This conclusion presupposes that communication of pleasure and pain is praise and blame, and that an agent influenced by such communication is legitimately praised and blamed. We might reject the presuppositions. Perhaps such an agent does not really deserve praise and blame, and perhaps the positive and negative reinforcement we offer are not genuine praise and blame. Aristotle might reasonably argue that normal adult human beings are properly praised and blamed for their actions, and that animals are not; though we try to modify the behaviour of animals, we do not praise or blame them in the same way.

If Aristotle relies on this argument, he may believe that rational agents are morally responsible, and that genuine praise recognizes a responsible action. On this view, non-rational animals are incapable of responsibility, and so are not candidates for praise or blame, and hence are incapable of virtue or vice. But if Aristotle accepts this answer, he owes some account of responsibility that is distinct from his account of voluntariness; for mere voluntariness does not mark the right distinctions.

To see why non-rational agents are not responsible for their actions, we may consider cases where even rational agents acting on their desires seem not to be responsible for their actions. In cases of madness, or overpowering compulsive desires, we might argue that the agents are not responsible for what they do, and hence are not open to blame for it, because they cannot help acting on these desires. Even though they would act otherwise if they had different desires, or if they had the same desire with a different degree of strength, they are incapable (on this occasion) both of getting rid of this desire and of altering its strength. Hence, if the desire is strong enough to cause them to act on it, despite any rational desires and beliefs they have or might form, they are incapable of refraining from the action, and hence are not

---

[60] A similar question arises about the discussion of habituation, in the context of a general account of potentialities (Met. 1046a36–b13).
[61] Cf. Sorabji, AMHM 108–10.

responsible for it. If this is the condition of non-rational agents, and the condition of rational agents when they are not responsible for the actions caused by their desires, responsibility is not merely causation by desire; responsible agents must also somehow control their desires.

100. Voluntary Action in Rational Agents

To see whether Aristotle recognizes these points about responsibility, we should consider some initially puzzling features of his conditions for voluntariness. In forced action the principle (or origin; *archê*) of the movement is external, the agent himself contributes nothing (1110a2), and the 'action' is always painful; what we enjoy cannot be forced (1110b11–13). The cause is external in so far as the agent does not contribute; the agent's failure to feel pain is a contribution, in so far as she endorses, or acquiesces in, what she does (even though her choice or acquiescence is not causally necessary for it). If you push me into my enemy and I am pleased, the cause of my behaviour is not external and I contribute something, even if your push would have had the same result whatever I thought or felt; for if what I do with pleasure is unforced, it cannot have an external cause to which I contribute nothing. The behaviour has an internal cause, and I contribute to it, even though my contribution is unnecessary for the result; such behaviour is not involuntary.

Aristotle draws a related distinction in his discussion of ignorance. He argues that if I act because of ignorance, and do not regret my action, I have acted non-voluntarily, but not involuntarily; involuntary action requires regret as well as ignorance (1110b18–24; 1111a19–21). The causal process leading to the action is the same, but the attitude of the agent separates the genuinely involuntary actions from the others.

These features of Aristotle's description are intelligible if he is concerned with the relation of rational agency to the action. Though my pleasure and pain may make no actual difference to what happens, they indicate my attitude to the action, and so reveal my character (1104b3–11) and the election that has formed it. If I appear to be forced to break a promise, but am pleased by the result of this apparent force, I show that my character and election are defective. I show the same thing about myself if I act because of ignorance but without regret. Even if I would have avoided striking you so hard if I had known the blow would disable you, my pleasure at the result of the action I did because of ignorance shows a flaw in my character.

Why should Aristotle want our judgments about praiseworthiness and blameworthiness to focus on this aspect of the agent? He would be unjustified if my pleasure, pain, and regret were simply a further non-voluntary aspect of the action. But we have seen that he takes our pleasure and pain to follow our convictions about what is non-instrumentally valuable. Since our rational judgments of non-instrumental value determine the character of our wishes and elections, they form our character; hence our pleasure and pain reflects our character, and hence our elections, and hence the conception of the good that underlies our elections. This aspect of the agent is a distinctive feature of rational agency—the agent's conception of his good and the states of character he has formed to shape his whole life in a particular way. Distinctions that initially seem anomalous turn out to be reasonable in the light of Aristotle's view of pleasure, judgment, and rational agency.

The same concern with rational agency may underlie the claim that voluntary action is 'up to' the agent, and the principle must be 'in' the agent (1110a17–18; 1111a22–4; 1113b20–1). Aristotle takes these two conditions to be equivalent; the action is up to the agent, in so far as the principle of his doing it is in himself. The principle is strictly 'in us' only in so far as it is in our rational agency; otherwise it will only be incidentally in us, since one of our non-essential features will be the principle.[62]

Emphasis on rational agency goes too far, however, if it implies that we are responsible only for the actions that result from our election and deliberation. Since Aristotle accepts the Platonic division of desires, he recognizes that many actions result from passions that do not express an agent's deliberation and election about the good. The Doctrine of the Mean implies that such actions are part of the subject-matter of virtue and vice; the training that produces a virtue forms the tendency to have the right passions and to act correctly on them.

If actions on passion were voluntary simply because they are caused by states of the agent, as opposed to external forces, voluntariness would not explain praiseworthiness. For this causal origin is also present in non-rational animals; reference to it does not explain why non-rational animals are not praiseworthy and cannot develop virtues of character. Aristotle cannot simply cite the internal causal principle to justify his claim that we are responsible for action on passions.

Rational agency may influence one's action in different ways. Even if I act without deliberation and premeditation on a sudden impulse, the principle may still be in my character and election; for the presence or strength of my desire may result from the character and elections I have formed. I may have deliberately cultivated this sort of impulse, or I may have failed to do what I could reasonably be expected to do to prevent its growth. If my voluntary actions are related in this way to my election and character, their principle is in me in the relevant sense, and I am responsible for them (cf. 1113b30–1114a9).

If, then, we praise and blame agents for their actions in relation to their deliberation and election about the good, we reasonably confine praise and ascription of responsibility to rational agents. That sort of praise is not appropriate to non-rational agents, since they do not form a conception of their good; they do not conceive themselves as temporally extended agents with a possible good, and they do not modify their particular desires to fit that conception. Similarly, if virtue requires the formation of the right conception of one's good, Aristotle is right to believe that it requires the right election, and therefore is confined to agents capable of election.

This defence of Aristotle requires some reconsideration of the account of action that seemed to follow from his acceptance of the Platonic division of desires. The division seemed to imply that some of our actions are the product of passion without rational desire. Aristotle, however, seems to regard actions on passion, or many of them, as voluntary, and therefore praiseworthy or blameworthy. If that is so, they are connected to election and deliberation. Aristotle, however, does not explain exactly how this connexion is to be understood. If his account of action is to fit his views about the source and extent of responsibility, it needs to be expanded.[63]

---

[62] On Alexander's treatment of 'in us' and 'up to us' see §172.

[63] Aristotle's account of action on passion is obscure partly because he lacks anything that corresponds to the Stoic concept of assent, or to Aquinas' concept of consent. See §167, §§252–3.

101. Rational Agency and Character

Aristotle applies these claims about rational agency both to responsibility for action and to responsibility for character.[64] In iii 5 he appeals to the process of acquisition of the virtues to show that we are responsible for becoming virtuous or vicious. We might suppose that he traces responsibility back to some original condition of freedom. But this attempt to ground responsibility would raise a further difficulty. Why should we suppose that young children are the ones who are primarily responsible for their future character, given that they do not know about the effects of their present actions?

But Aristotle is not open to this objection, since he does not appeal to the choices made by young children. He suggests that someone who does not acknowledge the connexion between repeated actions and the formation of a state fails to pay attention to elementary and readily accessible facts about what happens to people (1114a9–13). This suggestion does not fit children, since these facts are not accessible to them. They are accessible, however, to adults, and we expect normal adults to pay attention to them, since 'they are in control of paying attention' (1114a3). Aristotle argues that it is foolish and irrational to go around committing injustice if we do not wish to be unjust, or to say (even truly) that we are committing injustice but do not wish to be unjust; for we know very well that repeated acts of injustice will tend to make us form the very outlook that we say we do not wish to have. Someone who none the less goes on recklessly committing injustice, or not thinking about whether his action is unjust, has only himself to blame. This remark is appropriate if and only if it is aimed at someone mature enough to understand these things, for whom it is not already too late to form his character to some degree in the right direction.

This argument allows us to correct an impression that we might have formed when we considered Aristotle's introduction to virtue of character. He claims that this virtue, in contrast to virtue of intellect, is acquired by habituation rather than teaching. We might infer that it is acquired by the non-rational training in pleasure and pain that children might receive; this is the sort of training that he seems to have in mind in Book ii. This view of habituation, however, is too narrow to be Aristotle's view. A virtue of character, the product of habituation, is a 'full virtue' (*kuria aretê*), including prudence and the election that elects the virtuous action for its own sake and for the sake of the fine (1144a13–20; b14–17). Since election results from deliberation, and the prudent person must deliberate about what promotes living well as a whole, the virtuous person's election must result from deliberation. These intellectual and deliberative processes must be included in habituation, since habituation is the process by which we acquire a virtue of character, and these intellectual and deliberative processes are needed for acquisition of such a virtue.[65]

Habituation, therefore, includes the acquisition and the exercise of the relevant deliberative capacities. Though Aristotle's description of the early stages of habituation emphasizes—not surprisingly—children's training in pleasure and pain, he does not take this training to be all

---

[64] On Alexander's discussion of responsibility for character see §172.
[65] On Aquinas' account of habituation see §285.

that is needed for virtue of character.[66] At the later stages of habituation, it is up to agents to elect different kinds of actions.

Our goals and values are up to us. For the ways in which we elect to habituate ourselves, and the sorts of situations we seek out, also tend to affect what we value; and, as Aristotle points out to the person who does injustice without wishing to be unjust, we can consciously set out to change our conception of the end by these methods. Our conception of the good is not fixed; we may have reasons for altering it when we see some of its consequences and compare them with other things we value. In any given situation where we deliberate and elect, we must take something for granted, because all deliberation starts from some conception of an end. But no specific conception of the end is always outside deliberation.

We can now understand Aristotle's reply to sceptics about responsibility for character. His opponent maintains that the ignorance and inattention normally regarded as culpable actually result from one's appearance of the good; since we cannot control this appearance, we cannot be held responsible for the results of acting on it (1114a31–1114b1). Aristotle replies that if we are in some way responsible for our state, then we are also in some way responsible for the appearance of the good (1114b1–3); our conception of the good is not fixed and uncontrollable.

This may seem a poor reply. For how, we might ask, can we be responsible for our state of character? The opponent argues that our conception of the good controls our state of character, but we are not responsible for our conception of our good. Aristotle does not seem to answer this argument by simply asserting that we are responsible for our state; for how could we be responsible for it except by forming it in accordance with our appearance of the good, which the opponent claims we are not responsible for?[67]

Aristotle's reply avoids this objection, however, because the conception of the good that forms our state of character is different from the one that results from the formation of the state. He argues that since we can alter the later conception in the light of the earlier one, the later one is in our control. Perhaps if we trace back later conceptions of the good to earlier ones, we eventually come to something that was not in our control; but this fact does not imply that none of the later conceptions is in our control. We cannot rely on deliberation to alter our whole conception of the good at one go; for unless we hold some elements of our conception of the good fixed, deliberation is impossible. Our whole conception of our good is not open to us to change all at once; but still our conception is under our control.[68]

---

[66] I do not mean to concede that being trained to take pleasure and pain in the right things is a non-rational process either. Quite the reverse is true, as we have seen, given Aristotle's conception of pleasure.

[67] For Epicurus' answer see §146. For the Stoic answer see §173.

[68] Aristotle now seems to offer two possibilities in competition with the opponent's position, not just one. The first is the one he has already endorsed; the character of the end is not given by nature, but something is also left to the agents themselves (1114b17). The other possibility is that the end is natural, but 'because the excellent person does the other things voluntarily, virtue is voluntary' (1114b18–19). In the second case as well as the first something comes about because of ourselves, and in the second case it comes about 'in the actions, even if not in the end' (1114b20–1). Aristotle accepts the first possibility (reasserted in 1114b22–4); but what is the second possibility, and why does it secure the result that virtue and vice are voluntary? The supposition he rejects says that we are not at all in control of our conception of what is good; this lack of control extends to our judgments about what is good in particular situations. A more moderate view claims that some conception of the end is fixed, but it is indeterminate enough to leave room for deliberation about what promotes it. If 'what promotes the end' includes constituents (see above n42), Aristotle is justified in claiming that virtuous and vicious people differ about the actions promoting their common end.

102. Moral Responsibility and Morality

Though Aristotle's remarks about the voluntary and its relation to action and character are brief and schematic, they express a conception of moral responsibility. He is concerned with the fair attribution of praise and blame for actions and states of character. He takes voluntariness to be the basis of praise and blame. He traces the voluntary character of actions and characters to the practical reason and election that form an agent's actions and reactions. Agents are responsible, and open to praise and blame, to the extent that they are rational agents.

Since the virtues of character are praiseworthy states, not simply states that we prefer to see present in ourselves and others, they express rational agency. A virtuous person acts on the right election; the right election results from the right wish and the right deliberation. The right wish—the rational desire for the end—may be the starting point of deliberation, but also (if it is for a more determinate end) the product of deliberation about the components of a less determinate end. This contribution of practical reason is the source of responsibility, and the basis for praise and blame.

It is not surprising that some readers deny that Aristotle is especially concerned with moral responsibility. For if we emphasize the role of habituation, pleasure, pain, and emotion in the virtues, and if we separate these from Aristotle's claims about practical reason, we will find it difficult to connect his account of the virtues with any reasonable view of moral responsibility. In that case, we may be more inclined to say that he identifies the voluntary simply with what is caused by some mental state of the agent, irrespective of how that state comes about. We have seen that such an account of the voluntary, as Aristotle conceives it, is not wholly implausible; if we attribute such an account to him, we will have some reason to deny that his claims about the voluntary are claims about moral responsibility.

This, however, is not the most plausible account of his claims about the voluntary; nor is the anti-rationalist account the most plausible account of his claims about virtue. When we lay the proper emphasis on the role of practical reason both in the account of the virtues and in the account of the voluntary, we can fairly speak of moral responsibility in Aristotle's moral theory.

103. Questions about Incontinence and Responsibility

Aristotle's conception of election, deliberation, and prudence helps to explain why he assigns a large role to practical reason in the formation and expression of a virtue of character. We have seen how the same features of practical reason explain his claims about responsibility for action and character. But does this rationalist account of virtue and of responsibility account for the difference between good and bad character? If the same practical reason is present not only in virtuous people, but also in the flawed characters of continent, incontinent, and vicious people, correct practical reason does not distinguish a good from a bad character. In that case, it is difficult to see how, on Aristotle's account, we can be responsible for these faulty states of character.

Aristotle denies, however, that the same condition of practical reason is present in virtuous and non-virtuous people. He claims that prudence is confined to virtuous people

(1144a36–b1), that prudence grasps the correct end (1142b33), and that the correct end appears only to the virtuous person (1144a34). The fulfilment of practical reason is distinctive of the virtuous person, so that the virtuous character differs from the others in the character of its practical reason.

This claim raises a question about incontinence. For Aristotle appears to accept a broadly Platonic account of incontinence, taking it to reflect disordered desires rather than false beliefs. In that case, his claim that prudence is confined to virtuous people might be an uninteresting verbal point, that we do not call it 'prudence' unless it is present in a virtuous person. More important, it will be difficult to see how he could regard us as responsible for acting incontinently. If he is concerned about responsibility, we need to see whether his views about incontinence allow him to claim that we are responsible for acting incontinently.

Aristotle appears to accept an anti-rationalist account of incontinence in so far as he rejects Socrates' explanation of incontinence by appeal to ignorance. To see that the appearance of anti-rationalism is misleading, we should consider the places where Aristotle shows some sympathy with some of Socrates' claims about incontinence. At the outset, he mentions Socrates' protest against the popular view that knowledge is liable to be dragged about like a slave (1145b23–4; Plato, *Pr.* 352b3–c2). Socrates probably means to challenge not only the view that knowledge can be overcome, but also the view that in these cases human agents are simply the victims of powerful psychological forces beyond their rational control. His rejection of incontinence is partly a protest against the view that it amounts to psychological compulsion.[69]

Aristotle distinguishes Socrates' protest—that it is shocking if knowledge is dragged about by non-rational desires (1145b23)—from Socrates' solution, which denies the possibility of incontinence (1145b25). In his own solution he claims to have removed Socrates' grounds for protest (1147b16). He implies that the Platonic account of incontinence does not adequately answer Socrates, but that his account shows how incontinence is different from psychological compulsion.

His answer emerges from his arguments to show that we are responsible for the actions that we do as a result of non-rational desires. He rejects the claim of those who say that pleasant and fine things force us to act because they are external and necessitate us.[70] Normal rational agents are responsible for voluntarily doing x rather than y, if they ought to do x rather than y and are justly praised for doing x (or blamed for doing y). Since praise or blame is also appropriate for action on non-rational desires, this action must be voluntary. Non-rational desires are human, and open to praise and blame, in so far as we affect their influence on us by making ourselves an easy prey to them.

Aristotle takes incontinent action to be voluntary (1152a15–16) and blameworthy (1148a2–4; b4–6). But he does not explain why it is different from the compulsive actions of insane people. Indeed, he actually claims that incontinents are similar to drunk and insane people (1147a10–18). The similarity cannot be too close, since madness implies that one is

---

[69] See §27.

[70] 'It is ludicrous to hold external things responsible rather than oneself, being an easy prey for such things, and ludicrous to hold oneself responsible for fine actions while holding pleasant things responsible for shameful actions' (1110b13–15).

not responsible for one's action. Even if incontinents are in some respect like insane people in not knowing what they are doing, their ignorance cannot make the action involuntary.

Aristotle suggests the relevant difference. In remarking that some desires are bestial rather than human, and hence are beyond virtue and vice, he observes that we do not ascribe temperance or intemperance to non-rational animals except metaphorically: 'For they have neither election nor rational calculation, but are outside <rational> nature, as insane human beings are' (1149b36–1150a1). The comparison with madness suggests that insane people are temporarily 'outside' the rational nature that includes rational calculation and election. If the incontinent's actions, as opposed to the insane person's, are open to assessment for virtue and vice, and open to praise and blame, he is not outside the influence of rational calculation and deliberation.

104. Incontinence, Ignorance, and Deliberation

The connexion between incontinence and deliberative error helps to explain why Aristotle claims that the incontinent person acts incontinently because of his ignorance, so that in a way Socrates is right. Socrates is wrong to deny that non-rational desires cause the relevant ignorance, but he is right, according to Aristotle, to claim that incontinence requires ignorance.

Some of Aristotle's comments on the cognitive effects of non-rational desires show why such desires may be a source of ignorance. Most people, he says, are deceived about the real good because pleasure appears good to them when it is not (1113a33–b2). The deception destroys a correct grasp of the good, so that someone loses his awareness of it, or never becomes aware of it at all (1140b11–20; 1144a31–6). Appetite—a desire for pleasure—differs from 'spirit' (thumos) because it creates this deceptive appearance by gradual insinuation (1149b4–18). The insinuations of appetite may master someone far enough to persuade him that he should pursue certain pleasures without limit; but incontinence precludes this total domination by appetite (1151a20–7).

If incontinents are partly persuaded by the claims of pleasure, we can understand Aristotle's answer to the claim that they are less open to rational persuasion than intemperate people are. The claim seems plausible, because intemperate people pursue pleasure on the basis of their election and rational preference, and hence seem to be open to the influence of reason, whereas incontinents illustrate the proverb 'If water chokes you, what will you wash it down with?' Since they are already persuaded that what they are doing is wrong, but they do it anyway, attempts to convince them otherwise may seem to be irrelevant to their condition (1146a31–b2).

Aristotle disagrees. Incontinents are more open to persuasion than intemperate people are, because incontinents retain the right principle, which intemperate people lack (1151a5–26). If the presence of the right principle is a basis for effective persuasion of incontinents, some change in their rational outlook on their action will change their action. In that case, some defect in their present rational outlook causes their incontinent action. Aristotle claims both that only the virtuous person has the right principle and that the incontinent has the right principle. If these claims are consistent, the incontinent has the right principle in some respects but lacks it in other respects. What are the relevant respects?

Since the principle that the virtuous person grasps refers to 'the end and the best' (1144a32–3), it rests on a true conception of happiness. I form this by considering myself and my life as a whole, since the final good has to be something whole and complete. Myself and my life as a whole include both the different stages of my life, and my different capacities, desires, and aims. For the prudent person deliberating about what contributes to 'living well as a whole' (1140a25–8), particular stages of life and temporary concerns or enthusiasms do not dominate practical reasoning. Other people, however, oscillate between different conceptions of the good according to what they feel most in need of at a particular time (1095a22–6). The virtuous person thinks about his life as a whole from the appropriate point of view, and so achieves a degree of unity and concord that both the incontinent and the vicious person lack (1166b6–26).

To reach the right election from a true conception of the good we rely on deliberation. Aristotle explains 'good deliberation' (*euboulia*), by describing the sort of correctness (*orthotês*) that it embodies. This correctness is not mere success in finding means to ends; it reaches a good result (1142b17–22), and proceeds by the appropriate steps (1142b22–7). Only the prudent person practises this good deliberation. An election, therefore, may be right or wrong in different ways. It may succeed or fail in identifying the right action to do in these specific circumstances. But even if it succeeds in this task, it may not choose the right action for the right reasons. To act for the right reasons is to know when it would be appropriate to act differently. I give a charitable gift, for instance, for the right reasons only if I still would give it even if it were not going to be widely known; I face this danger for the right reasons only if I would not face it if no appropriate cause were at stake. To know what election, and therefore what deliberation, people act on, we have to consider what influences their choice, not simply what they explicitly have in mind on this particular occasion. To understand their deliberation is to understand the Kantian 'maxim' of their action.[71]

The incontinent has a faulty conception of the good, because he is too influenced by desires that are especially strong at a particular time, and hence fails to think appropriately about his life as a whole. The primary and central type of incontinence involves the appetites that are characteristic of temperance and intemperance, because these appetites are especially urgent and especially liable to interfere with one's practical reason (1146b18–22).[72] The faults in his conception of the good infect his deliberation and his election, even though his election is in one respect correct.

His reasoning is partly false, even if he has not actually included any false steps in his explicit reflexion on this occasion. For he is wrong about what sorts of deviations from actual circumstances would require a different conclusion. In particular he does not see that even if his appetite for x were stronger, he ought to refrain from x; and so when his appetite is stronger, he changes his mind about whether to refrain from x. This change of mind betrays an error in his conception of happiness. In thinking about his final good, he does not steadily recognize the importance of thinking about his life as a whole, and so he does not admit that it would be a mistake to do what he feels like doing at the moment.

A correct account of incontinence, therefore, requires both the Socratic appeal to ignorance and the Platonic appeal to non-rational desires. Non-rational desires provide objects whose

---

[71] Cf. Kant, G421n.   [72] On the scope of incontinence and intemperance see §119.

attractions persuade the incontinent to form a mistaken conception of happiness and to deliberate incorrectly; these mistakes in practical reason are responsible for his incontinent action.

We can now understand where the continent person is similar to the incontinent. Though he chooses virtuous actions and performs them, he is reluctant to choose actions that the virtuous person chooses promptly and readily. We are reluctant to choose an action that we take to involve some major cost to us. The continent person mistakenly believes that virtuous actions are costly because he exaggerates the importance of the appetitive satisfaction that conflicts with virtuous action. He is right to believe that his action has some cost, but—like the incontinent person—he exaggerates the importance of this or that appetite because he does not focus steadily on its real importance in his life as a whole.

For this reason, Aristotle is justified in claiming that only the virtuous person has prudence and that the right end appears to no one else. These are not merely verbal points. Neither the incontinent nor the continent person has the specific grasp of the ultimate end that the prudent person has, and neither of them deliberates altogether correctly. Their defects result from an error in practical reason.

Continent and incontinent people, so understood, are responsible for their errors. A responsible agent differs from a non-responsible agent in having the capacity for rational desire, deliberation, and election; and he is responsible for his actions in so far as he affects them by election or failure to elect. If the incontinent fails to act on his election, but does not act compulsively, his condition must result from some culpable and corrigible lack of the right rational awareness. If he is responsible for his actions, the source of the incontinent action is not an overwhelming and compulsive desire, but some blameworthy error that is corrigible by rational deliberation.

The errors in the deliberation of the continent and the incontinent person explain why their deviation from virtue is blameworthy, in so far as it is derived from practical reason. The cognitive aspects of Aristotle's account of incontinence are initially surprising; but if we connect them both with his account of virtue and with his account of the voluntary, his position is coherent.

105. Vice, Reason, and Appetite

The naturalist and rationalist approach to virtue, practical reason, responsibility, and incontinence should also explain the difference between virtue and vice. Human nature is fulfiled, in Aristotle's view, by the complete development of practical reason about ends in the guidance of human life. But if the vicious person were guided by fully-developed practical reason about ends, he would live a 'life of action of the rational part' no less than the virtuous person does, and so he would fulfil the human function no less than the virtuous person does. A naturalist account of vice, therefore, ought to refute this claim about the equality of virtue and vice in relation to the human function.

Aristotle's conception of the vicious person treats intemperance as the paradigmatic vice.[73] His remarks about the difference between the incontinent and the vicious person in Book vii

---

[73] On intemperance see further §119.

are concerned with the special vice of intemperance. In Book ix he generalizes these claims to vicious people in general. In vicious people non-rational appetite dominates rational desire. They suffer from the internal conflict and self-hatred that is normally ascribed to incontinents (1166b6–13). They live in accordance with their passions, and gratify the non-rational part of the soul (1168b19–21; 1169a3–6). Only the virtuous person is free, or nearly free, of regret (1166a27–9; 1166b22–5). The vicious person seems to be similar to young people, who live in accordance with their passions, and so are not appropriate students of moral philosophy, and similar to the immature people who resemble the young on this point (1095a6–8). Virtue is rationally preferable to vice, because it is control by reason rather than by passion.[74]

The vicious person acts on his election, which expresses his wish, and hence his conception of happiness.[75] He acts, then, on his conception of happiness and his view about what is best overall. But he is not controlled by the rational part in the same way, or to the same degree, as the virtuous person. We may say that the non-rational part exercises local control if on a particular occasion its desires move us contrary to our rational aims, but it exercises global control to the extent that its desires are the basis of our aims. Incontinence involves local control by non-rational desires, and failure of local control by rational desires. But if we form our rational desires simply by considering ways to satisfy our non-rational desires, we display complete local control by a rational part that is subject to the global control of the non-rational part.[76] This is the condition of the vicious person. His rational outlook, not only his non-rational desire, is perverted.

To explain this perversion, we may appeal to Aristotle's demand for the virtuous person to elect the virtuous action for its own sake (1105a31–2). To satisfy this demand, the virtuous person must have found by deliberation that virtuous action is choiceworthy for its own sake. Aristotle emphasizes and amplifies this demand by insisting that the virtuous person must elect virtuous action 'because it is fine' (*kalon*). Good fighters who are moved by anger have not achieved the mean, because they do not fight 'because of the fine (*kalon*) or as reason <prescribes>, but because of passion' (1117a7–9). To achieve the mean in actions and passions is to act and to be affected 'as one ought' (*hôs dei*). To act as one ought is to act 'for the sake of the fine' (1120a23–9; 1121a1–4). Acting for the sake of the fine is a common feature of the virtues (1121b5–6).[77] Virtuous people have in mind the properties that make an action fine and virtuous, and they take these as a sufficient reason, apart from any further efficient-causal results, for choosing the action. In brief, the virtuous person elects virtuous action on principle.

The vicious person, however, does not elect vicious actions for their own sake and because they are fine. The fact that avoiding danger involves betraying a worthwhile cause because of unjustified fear is what makes it vicious, but this is not the feature that makes it appealing to a vicious person. He does not choose the vicious action on principle. Similarly, he does not avoid virtuous action because it violates his principles, but only because it interferes with his ends or does not promote them. This feature of the virtuous person's election distinguishes it from the vicious person's election, and is meant to justify Aristotle's claim that the vicious person is really controlled by non-rational desire, and not by practical reason. To understand

---

[74] I have discussed this further in *AFP* §203.
[75] In this claim about *prohairesis* and *boulêsis* I follow Anscombe, 'Thought'. Contrast Charles, *APA* 151.
[76] Plato distinguishes the two kinds of control in *R.* viii–ix. See §49.
[77] On the fine see §116.

this claim, we must look more closely at the connexion he sees between pursuit of the fine and control by reason.

106. Self-Love, Reason, and the Fine

In his discussion of self-love, Aristotle rejects one intuitive way of distinguishing virtue from vice. He notices that we might readily accuse the vicious person of loving himself too much, and praise the virtuous person for limiting self-love in favour of concern for others.[78] In his view, however, both virtuous and vicious people act out of self-love. The difference between them is that only the virtuous person loves himself as he really is. To love ourselves as we really are, we must gratify the most important or most controlling (*kuriôtaton*) part of ourselves. Aristotle compares this with the government of a city, which has the authority to act on behalf of the whole city and in that way represents the whole city. In claiming that this is what we really are, Aristotle denies that our choices constitute our identity. He claims that the virtuous person grasps a fact about our identity and the vicious person fails to grasp it.

To defend this claim, Aristotle argues that our essentially rational character is not manifested only in the choices of the virtuous person. We must presuppose it in understanding human action in general.[79] Continent action expresses 'our' plans and incontinent action frustrates them. Similarly, when we act on reason, our action is voluntary to a higher degree than when we act on non-rational desires. A plausible conception of the voluntary requires acknowledgment of the primacy of reason in the agent.[80] These distinctions between continence and incontinence and between voluntary and involuntary do not matter only to the virtuous person. We all seek to avoid incontinence and to be praised or blamed for our voluntary actions. Hence we all implicitly recognize ourselves as essentially rational.

These claims of Aristotle's embody a version of naturalism. They are 'ethical' claims in so far as they are concerned with human action and our understanding of it. But they do not seem to belong to ethics any more than to psychology or natural philosophy. They are not ethical claims specifically connected with goodness and badness in actions and characters. Since they are evaluative claims, we might reasonably take Aristotle to maintain a holistic version of naturalism.[81] He defends the claims of the Function Argument. The type of reason that he introduced there was the type that belongs to 'a life of action of the rational part'. Here, similarly, the reason with which he identifies a person must be practical reason, since that is the aspect of reason that is relevant to incontinence and to voluntary action.[82]

Aristotle repeats that those who love themselves in this way will also pursue the moral virtues. Vicious people pursue 'contested' goods, because they have the wrong conception of

---

[78] '... for those who like themselves most are criticized and denounced as self-lovers, as though this were something shameful. Indeed, the base person seems to go to every length for his own sake, and all the more the more vicious he is; hence he is accused, for instance, of doing nothing away from himself. The decent person, on the contrary, acts for what is fine, all the more the better he is, and for his friend's sake, disregarding what is his own' (1168a29–35).

[79] 'Similarly, someone is called continent or incontinent because his understanding is or is not the master, on the assumption that this is what each person is. Moreover, his own voluntary actions seem above all to be those involving reason. Clearly, then, this, or this above all, is what each person is, and the decent person likes this most of all' (1168b34–1169a2).

[80] Aquinas comments on this passage at *in EN* §1871, quoted at §244.   [81] See §80.

[82] See also 1166a16, and cf. with 1178a2.

themselves, and therefore have the wrong sort of self-love. Virtuous people have the correct conception of themselves as rational agents, so that they have the right sort of self-love, causing them to pursue the fine.[83] Concern for the fine results in the actions characteristic of the different moral virtues, because it systematically and non-coincidentally promotes the common good.[84]

Aristotle takes 'desiring the fine' to imply that what the virtuous person desires is in fact fine, not merely that the virtuous person's desire is guided by a conception of the fine. The vicious person is not guided even by a mistaken conception of the fine. He desires only what seems advantageous, not what is in fact advantageous for him. But he is not guided simply by a conception of advantage; the advantageous is instrumentally valuable for some external end (as Aristotle says about *poiêsis*), and so it must depend on some end that he desires for its own sake. Aristotle insists that the vicious person does not conceive this end as fine. We live in accordance with reason if and only if we aim at the fine.

107. How is the Fine Connected with Reason?

Aristotle's claims about the connexion between reason and the fine, and between passion and advantage, may well puzzle us. We might, indeed, expect the reverse connexion. A brave action, for instance, often seems to require a fearless and self-sacrificing outlook indifferent to rational calculation. In the *Rhetoric* Aristotle acknowledges that this view of fine action is part of the common conception of the virtues.[85] We might suppose that he has the same aspect of the fine in mind when he connects it especially with bravery and with a sense of shame (1116a27–9). But this is not how he explains pursuit of the fine. In his view, it rests on the belief that there is something valuable about this action (for instance) apart from the fact that it appeals to us, or appears to be a means to something that appeals to us.[86]

This claim about desire for the fine exploits a familiar feature of desire for the good. Both Plato and Aristotle distinguish desires of the rational part from desires of the appetitive part by claiming that a rational desire is 'good-dependent', because it attaches itself to this or that specific object only on the assumption that the object is good all things considered. But desires may depend on beliefs about the good even if they depend on a conception of the good that simply identifies the good with the satisfaction of good-independent desires. This is not what Aristotle has in mind. He imposes a stronger condition by insisting that the relevant desires are thoroughly good-dependent; even the ultimate ends that form our conception of the good are based on a conviction about value that is prior to desire. At no

[83] 'That is why he most of all is a self-lover, but a different kind from the self-lover who is reproached. He differs from him as much as the life guided by reason differs from the life guided by feelings, and as much as the desire for what is fine differs from the desire for what seems advantageous' (1169a3–6).

[84] 'Those who are unusually eager to do fine actions are welcomed and praised by everyone. And when everyone strains to achieve what is fine and concentrates on the finest actions, everything that is right will be done for the common good, and each person individually will receive the greatest of goods, since that is the character of virtue' (1169a6–11).

[85] Cf. *Rhet.* 1390a15–17; 1358b38–1359a5; Plato, *Phdr.* 238b7–c4; Irwin, *PE* §208. On the connexion between the fine and spirited desire see Cooper, 'Reason' 276–9.

[86] Aristotle appears to say that what is fine is the primary object of rational desire (*boulêsis*), and that the conviction that something is fine is logically prior to our having a desire (*orexis*) for it; we have a desire for it because it seems fine, but it is false that it seems fine because we have a desire for it (*Met.* 1072a25–30).

point in forming our conception of the good do we take for granted some object of desire that simply appeals to us independently of any prior conviction of its value.

Aristotle suggests that rational desire for the fine is thoroughly good-dependent in this way. The demand to choose virtuous action because it is fine is more stringent than the demand to pursue it non-instrumentally. For we might have an attachment to virtuous action that is both non-instrumental and non-rational; we stick to it even when we gain no further instrumental benefit from it, but we do not stick to it because we have some rational conviction about what makes it worth sticking to in these circumstances. The virtuous person's choices rest on convictions about the good that have formed her views about the goals that are worth choosing. She attaches intrinsic value to the rational choice of ends, and to the pursuit of those ends that she pursues as a result of rational choice.

A simple way to express this attitude is to say that we believe that our basic practical principles and values have something to be said for them beyond the fact that we happen to have them.[87] On this basis we might distinguish values from mere preferences. My preference for F is a mere preference if I have no objection to having my preference for F replaced by a preference for G, provided that I could satisfy my preference for G at least as much as I satisfy my current preference for F. But my preference for F expresses my values (principles) if it is false that equal satisfaction of my preference for G would by itself make the replacement unobjectionable to me.

In Aristotle's view, the vicious person pursues 'contested' goods, trying to benefit himself at other people's expense by 'over-reaching' them, simply because these goods satisfy his preferences.[88] He fails, therefore, to act on the kind of self-love that Aristotle has described. He denies or overlooks the possibility of the full application of practical reason to his choice of ends, and in this way fails to value himself as a rational agent. The vicious person regards advantage as the only concern of practical reason, since he believes that his inclinations are beyond rational criticism, so that practical reason can only serve his inclinations. The virtuous person, by contrast, believes that discovery of the fine is a proper function of practical reason. Aristotle contrasts those who form an end on the basis of inclination from those who form an end on the basis of judgments about its value.

This difference between virtuous and vicious people does not imply that the vicious person lacks a conception of virtues or of fine action. He can see, for instance, that it is good for him, given his inclinations, to cultivate some aspects of bravery and temperance (as Aristotle understands them) so that he can execute his longer-term aims. He can also regard some actions and traits of personality as fine, because they are admirable in their own right apart from their effects; perhaps, for instance, he takes this view of someone who displays his power and wealth in magnificent actions (as the vicious person conceives them). But even if he recognizes fine actions, he does not take the virtuous person's attitude to them, because he does not elect actions because they are fine. To elect is to choose on the basis of one's conception of happiness; to elect something because it is fine is to choose it for itself because of its value apart from one's own inclinations. The virtuous person conceives

---

[87] Taylor's conception of 'strong evaluation' suggests this distinction. See 'Agency'.

[88] On contested (lit. 'fought-over') goods see 1168b21; Plato, *R.* 586a1–b5; Cic. *Off.* i 51–2; iii 42; §182n42; §404. On over-reaching (*pleonexia*) see 1129b8–10; Plato, *R.* 349b–350c; 586b1. On Green's conception of a non-competitive good see *PE* §245.

happiness as constituted by actions chosen for their value apart from inclination, but this is not the vicious person's conception of happiness.[89]

108. Vice and Pleasure

If we have grasped Aristotle's basic division between virtuous and vicious people, we ought to be able to explain remarks about vice that would otherwise be difficult to explain. Some of these remarks attribute a special preoccupation with pleasure to the vicious person. He believes it is always right to pursue the available pleasure (1146b22–4),[90] and he pursues excesses of pleasure 'because of election, because of themselves and because of nothing else resulting from them' (1150a19–21).

These descriptions of the vicious election recall the first of the three lives that are presented as unsuccessful candidates for happiness. Aristotle suggests that those who devote themselves to pleasure choose the life of grazing animals, because they devote themselves to unrestrained physical gratification (1095b19–20). He has often been criticized for maintaining this connexion between the pursuit of pleasure, a purely animal existence, and gross physical gratification; some believe that in maintaining this connexion he contradicts his own more careful discussion of pleasure in Books vii and x. The same questions arise about his comments on vice. Even the vice of intemperance does not seem the same as a tendency to unrestrained gratification. This tendency seems an even less plausible mark of vice in general.

Aristotle's claim rests on the contrast between guidance by reason and guidance by the passions. The vicious person prefers one action over another simply because it appeals to him, not because of some further conviction about its value. One way to express this attitude to our actions is to say that we do them simply for the pleasure of it. Aristotle expresses this fact by saying that the vicious person thinks he should always pursue the pleasant thing that is available. He probably does not mean that the vicious person is in principle less likely than other people to forgo immediate pleasure for some strategic reason. On the contrary, we might expect a vicious person to think more strategically, in some ways, than a virtuous person, since he is free of the moral constraints that limit the virtuous person's strategic efficiency. Aristotle probably means that the vicious person settles his ends by consulting his preferences and inclinations, and does not try to educate his preferences and inclinations by consideration of what is worth pursuing.

109. The Vicious Person's Regret

The way in which vicious people form their elections on the basis of inclination may also help to explain Aristotle's surprising claim that they are especially prone to psychic conflict, and in particular to regret (1166a29).[91]

---

[89] Cf. Sherman, FC 113–17.

[90] Aristotle's phrase 'the pleasant thing at hand' (*to paron hêdu*, 1146b23) might refer to what is temporally present, but more probably it means 'available' or 'open'. On vice and pleasure see §95 above.

[91] I will use 'regret' simply to represent *metameleia*, without implying that this is always the most appropriate English rendering.

This feature is meant to show that because vicious people are controlled by the non-rational part, they lack the appropriate sort of self-love. But Aristotle's claim is difficult to accept. He distinguishes the harmony in the vicious person from the conflict in the incontinent person. Why, then, does he claim that the vicious person suffers conflict and regret after all?

Virtuous people suffer the regret that simply involves wishing that something different had happened. Since they care about external goods, they sometimes have reason to wish that things had turned out better than they actually did. Similarly, they have reason to regret their actions, to the extent of wishing that they had, for instance, known enough to do something different. Indeed, we might say that in so far as they care more than vicious people care about the good of other people, they must have more potential occasions for regret.

A different sort of regret often results from blaming oneself for what one did or decided to do. This is the regret that results from believing I ought to have known something I did not know, or that I ought to have decided differently in the light of what I did know; it is often called 'remorse', as opposed to mere regret.[92] In Aristotle's view, virtuous people are free of remorse. They have nothing to blame or to reproach themselves for, and they are not prone to blame themselves falsely (cf. 1128b16–31). Any genuine occasion for blame would also be a mark of incomplete virtue.

Does the vicious person differ on this point? If he is really vicious, he does not care that what he did was vicious. Why, then, would he blame himself, or feel ashamed of himself, for having done it? Why does Aristotle expect that vicious people will hate themselves, and, in extreme cases, hate and flee life (1166b12–13)?

Perhaps Aristotle notices that vicious people do not do their best to follow a particular standard, whereas virtuous people do their best to identify and to carry out the brave or just course of action. Since they cannot be just while also being grossly lazy or negligent in the pursuit of justice, virtuous people have no occasion to blame themselves for negligence or laziness in the pursuit of justice. Vice, by contrast, does not involve doing one's best to avoid being virtuous, or doing one's best to pursue the vicious course of action; hence vice is consistent with being careless or inattentive or lazy in choosing one's actions in the light of one's conception of the good, and a vicious person might well blame himself for this. But since not all vicious people need be like this, they do not all seem to be subject to the regret that includes remorse and self-reproach.

Aristotle has a better case if he relies on the fact that the vicious person cares about his ends only in so far as they fulfil his inclinations. He has a basis for regret that the virtuous person lacks, because the virtuous person has a distinctive reason for not regretting his past choice. The virtuous person attaches value to acting on a non-strategic conviction about what is fine and good, apart from its usefulness in fulfilling his inclinations; and so he will not regret having acted on that conviction. On the contrary, he will be satisfied with himself, since he has done what he rationally cares most about doing. The vicious person lacks this reason for self-satisfaction; for he does not care about acting on any non-strategic conviction. The fact that he has acted on such a conviction is not a source of satisfaction; hence he has no retrospective satisfaction opposing his dissatisfaction at how things turned out. The frustration of his inclinations is an unopposed reason for regret about his past actions. The

---

[92] See Williams, 'Luck' 30–2. His view about the relevant distinctions is more sceptical than mine.

vicious person, then, lacks a particular basis for self-satisfaction[93] (or, as Aristotle puts it, self-love) that is available to the virtuous person. Aristotle is right to say that the vicious person is subject to regret that the virtuous person avoids.

This is not a sufficient reason for preferring to be a virtuous person, if the basis of his self-satisfaction is not appropriate. When we say that someone is 'self-satisfied' in a bad sense, we mean that they are more satisfied than they have any reason to be. If I am wrongly self-satisfied with being F, I may be wrong either because I am not F, or because being F is not good enough to justify my satisfaction in it. If the virtuous person is wrong to be satisfied with having acted on his non-strategic conviction, he deludes himself in taking this satisfaction to outweigh the failures he has suffered from a strategic point of view. Aristotle needs to explain why the virtuous person is right to attach such importance to acting on his non-strategic convictions.

110. The Instability of the Vicious Person

The character of the vicious person's regret suggests that his attitude to himself and to his future differs from the attitude of the virtuous person. He conceives himself as nothing more than a sequence of appetites and satisfactions, and he takes his good to depend on what he happens to want at a particular time. He exercises practical reason by finding measures that seem to secure his future satisfaction, but this concern for his future depends on the persistence of the same desires and appetites. He has no further reason to be concerned about a future self that (for all he knows) may have changed quite significantly.

The virtuous person, by contrast, forms his state of character on principle. He asks what sort of person he ought to be, and how he should conceive himself as a rational agent with an extended life. The recognition of an extended life is necessary for having a conception of one's happiness; and so it is not peculiar to the virtuous person. But the view that one ought to be a certain sort of person, or that some aspects of oneself deserve to be developed more than others, is an evaluative judgment that the vicious person does not make. Such a judgment implies that the actual desires and aims that strike us are not beyond criticism or evaluation.

This difference between the vicious and the virtuous person results from different forms of reflexion about the self. We may attend either to the aims it actually has or to the ways it is capable of forming and organizing its aims. The vicious person attends more to the first aspect of the self (the actual aims), and regards the second as primarily a way to satisfy the first. The virtuous person attends more to the second aspect of the self (the way it forms aims), and regards the first as raw material to be organized by the second. Aristotle recognizes these different forms of reflexion in claiming that the vicious person prefers the animal, non-human, non-rational outlook to the outlook of practical reason. This claim would be false if it denied that the vicious person can have a perfectly rational, coherent plan for his life; but it is true if it refers to the sort of self whose aims are to be satisfied.

[93] My non-pejorative use of 'self-satisfaction' is partly derived from Green, *PE* §154.

These different attitudes to the self and to self-concern imply a different basis for the sort of self-concern that protects the present self against future circumstances, and the future self against present circumstances. Sometimes I ensure now that I will carry out my present plan even though I will be averse to it in the future; I do this when I 'burn my bridges' and prevent myself now from acting later on my later fears, or when I now throw away the key to the cupboard containing the whisky I will want later on. Sometimes, however, I ensure now that I will be able to carry out my future aim, even though I do not feel like it at present. I do this when I get a tooth filled, or I reluctantly try to re-learn French before visiting France. Both a virtuous person and a vicious person may display these forms of self-concern, but not for the same reasons.

The virtuous person tries to satisfy her present and her future desires because they pursue goals that embody non-strategic convictions. She has a reason to make it easier to satisfy these desires and more difficult to satisfy any impulses that might conflict with these non-strategic convictions. The vicious person, however, is not moved by non-strategic convictions; she regards her future desires as the results of future impulses, just as her present desires result from past and present impulses. A vicious person has no reason to protect the present self against the future self, or the future self against the present. Hence she cannot justify the forms of self-concern that the virtuous person can justify. She may happen to prefer the future without decaying teeth over the nearer future without a painful filling, or the future that includes the frustration of a future desire for the whisky over the future that includes the satisfaction of that desire. But she has no reason for this self-concern.[94]

This point about self-concern corresponds to our earlier point about regret. The virtuous person has a basis for self-satisfaction in looking back at past choices. The same basis for self-satisfaction guides her attitude to her future self, since she regards the future self as the product of rational non-strategic convictions. The vicious person has no reason for satisfaction in either her past elections or in the future self that will be formed by present elections, or in the present self that both looks back on the past and decides about the future.

Vicious people, therefore, lack an important aspect of self-love, and are liable to self-hatred. Since they form rational plans, they are capable of disapproving of themselves when they violate them, but, since the rational plans are themselves unstable devices for satisfying changing inclinations, they are liable to frustration. If A and B have some friendly attitudes to each other, A may find it useful to borrow money from B without repaying it, even driving B to destitution. Once A sees what has happened to B, A may be angry at himself for what he has done to B. Since A's rational plans simply follow the comparative strength of A's inclinations at different times, nothing about A's character protects A from choosing actions that he will later hate himself for having chosen. A's self-hatred is the sort of hatred that we direct at an opponent who has frustrated our current aims.

These features of vicious people result from their refusal to form their rational elections by consideration of what is fine; hence, Aristotle is entitled to treat these features as essential to vice. He need not rely on the assumption (true or false) that vicious people always have some residual respect for morality that is the source of their disapproval of themselves. On

---

[94] Cf. Hume's discussion of prudence, T iii 2.7 §5.

the contrary, the less their respect for the outlook guided by considerations of the fine, the more liable they are to self-hatred.

111. Vice, Reason, and Nature

Has Aristotle found sufficient conditions for vice? Could not someone have the attitude to non-strategic convictions that Aristotle attributes to the vicious person, while still doing the actions expected of a virtuous person? Aristotle assumes that if we confine ourselves to purely strategic aims, we will tend to violate the demands of the virtues; but need this be so? Might we not find, because of temperament or upbringing, that we care about prudence, altruism, and justice, so that we face dangers, keep our promises, control our appetites, do one good turn in return for another, perform spontaneous acts of beneficence, and so on? If we have the appropriate sentiments, we will also want to be free from the regret that would result from violating the standards embodied in these sentiments. Hence, if we have the appropriate sentiments, we will be able to 'bear our own survey', as Hume puts it.[95]

This objection to Aristotle expresses the sentimentalist view of virtue that we find in Hobbes, Hutcheson, and Hume. In their view, no judgments about the non-strategic value of our ends are needed for virtue. If virtuous and vicious people have the same sort of commitment to their ends, our rational convictions do not make us virtuous rather than vicious. If our impulses and inclinations had been different, then we would have turned out vicious rather than virtuous. But why, we may ask, should this sort of contingency be found unwelcome?

In support of Aristotle, we may reply that we do not take a sentimentalist attitude to our basic values. We suppose that something can be said in their favour beyond the fact that we have them; and we do not take our aversion to losing them as a mere fact about our aversion, but as a fact about the actual badness of losing them. These attitudes to our values may be mistaken. But to the extent that a Hobbesian or Humean outlook implies that we are wrong, it challenges an important element in our conception of ourselves and our ends; if that is so, then we may fairly ask whether the arguments supporting such an outlook are cogent enough to discredit this element in our conception of ourselves.

Aristotle's account of vice, therefore, supports his account of virtue and incontinence. Virtue expresses the correct election that embodies the harmony of the rational and non-rational parts under the local and global control of the rational part. Vice expresses the incorrect election that embodies the agreement of the rational and non-rational parts under the local control of the rational part, but the global control of the non-rational part. Aristotle has defended his claim that virtue differs from vice in its degree of connexion to practical reason. By doing so, he has shown that the Function Argument gives the right account of virtue of character. We might have supposed that a plausible conception of virtue, continence, incontinence, and vice conflicts with Aristotle's initial claim that the virtues of character are different ways of guiding our action in accordance with practical reason; we might even have supposed that Aristotle's views about these different conditions support an

[95] See Hume, T iii 3.6 §6.

anti-rationalist view that would conflict with the Function Argument, as we have understood it. But the more closely we examine those aspects of Aristotle's theory that seem to require an anti-rationalist account, the more clearly we can see that he defends a rationalist account. On this point he follows the lead that he gives in the Function Argument. In claiming that the virtues complete human nature, he claims that they complete the nature of human beings as rational agents.

9

ARISTOTLE: VIRTUE AND MORALITY

112. Why Virtues?

Aristotle formulates an account of the virtues, conceived as states of character; he does not seek primarily to find an account of the different types of actions that a virtuous person chooses. Why does he speak of virtues rather than actions? His preference for virtues indicates that he is in some sense a 'virtue theorist'; but in what sense is this true? Different claims about the priority of virtues over actions need to be considered.

To assert ontological priority for virtue over right action is to claim that the rightness of actions depends on their being produced by virtues, so that (1) an action is right only if it is done by a virtuous agent, and (2) the agent's being virtuous explains the act's being right, and the reverse is not true.

Aristotle rejects the first claim; for he recognizes that an action can be temperate, just, brave, etc., without being done by a person with the relevant virtues. But does he accept the second claim? The most plausible support for it is his remark that actions are just (etc.) when they are such as the just person would do (1105b5). It is not clear, however, that this remark is meant to say what an action's being just consists in. In the case of many virtues, Aristotle seems to avoid any such constitutive or explanatory claim; he often describes the sort of action that is virtuous without reference to the state of the virtuous agent. Perhaps different things need to be said about different virtues; the same account of virtues and actions may not be appropriate for bravery, temperance, justice, generosity, magnificence, and wit. But it is difficult to attribute the claim about ontological priority to Aristotle; to this extent, he does not seem to be a virtue theorist.

If we deny that virtues are ontologically prior to right actions, we might still maintain that they are epistemically prior, because no one but a virtuous person can tell what sort of action is virtuous, and therefore we cannot say what sorts of actions are virtuous except by saying what a virtuous person is like and adding that virtuous actions are those a virtuous person will choose. Some of Aristotle's remarks might suggest a belief in this epistemic priority of virtue. He holds that things are good if they seem so to a virtuous person, so that the virtuous person is the measure of what is good and bad (1176a15; 1113a29).[1] Moreover, he insists that we cannot lay down fixed and exceptionless rules that always allow us to identify virtuous actions in particular situations; we have to be content with things that are usually true (1094b19; 1103b34; 1164b27). Sometimes we cannot give a general definition that will tell us what to do in particular situations; and the discrimination has to depend on perception (1109b20; 1126a31). This is why the prudent person needs perception (1142a23). We might rely on these remarks to support the conclusion that, according to Aristotle, we cannot identify right actions apart from the judgment of the prudent person.

This interpretation, however, raises further questions about the virtuous person's judgments. How does she judge that an action is virtuous, if she has no antecedent conception of what makes an action brave, just, generous, and so on, but must simply rely on her own judgment that this or that action is brave (etc.)? The doctrine of the prudent person as measure does not imply the strong epistemic thesis. It simply says that the virtuous person's judgments are reliably right, not that we cannot find out what is right without asking a virtuous person. Moreover, the extent of indeterminacy that Aristotle allows is consistent with being able to say quite a lot, without reference to virtuous people, about which actions are virtuous.[2] We have no good reason to believe that Aristotle maintains the epistemic priority of virtue.[3]

One might instead assert practical priority, claiming that we are more likely to do the right actions if we cultivate the virtues than if we attempt directly to do the right actions. This sort of argument is familiar from discussions of indirect utilitarianism.[4] According to this view, we will conform best to our ultimate criterion of the right if we act without explicit consideration of utility, but we rely on rules whose justification refers to utility. We might say something similar about the virtues. Instead of asking ourselves, for instance, what the right way to face danger is, we are better off if we try to cultivate in ourselves an appropriate mixture of fear, confidence, and appreciation of the relative values involved. If we have formed this state, we will be better able to act well than we would be if we had to deliberate de novo on each occasion about what would promote the common good. Aristotle gives an example of this line of argument, in his treatment of sudden dangers (1117a17); it applies more generally to the deliberation of the virtuous person.

He probably accepts practical priority for the virtues. Not every action by a virtuous person exercising a virtue needs to result immediately from the thought 'This is a fine thing to do' or 'This will promote the common good'. The appropriate thought may be 'This gift will benefit this person' or 'This pleasure is all right, but that one is bad'. These more specific descriptions will often trigger actions; Aristotle's accounts of the particular virtues

---

[1] These passages might also be used in support of an ontological claim (depending on how we understand 'measure'). One might (but need not) take Cooper to maintain such a claim at 'Reason' 276n.

[2] See further Irwin, 'Inexact'.

[3] Hursthouse, *OVE*, contains a careful discussion of the specific commitments of a virtue theory. She rejects (80) one claim about epistemic priority (see Hudson, *HCM* 42–3)—the claim that we can tell what action is just only by knowing what the just person is like. But she affirms explanatory priority of virtuous states to virtuous to action: 'The theoretical distinction between the two [sc. virtue ethics and deontology] is that the familiar rules, and their applications in particular cases, are given entirely different backings. According to deontology, I must not tell this lie because, applying the (correct) rule 'Do not lie' to this case, I find that lying is prohibited. According to virtue ethics, I must not tell this lie because it would be dishonest to do so, and dishonesty is a vice' (39). I doubt whether Aristotle is committed to this claim about explanatory priority.

[4] See esp. Berkeley, 'Obedience'.

suggest some of the specific descriptions. Virtuous people do not recite all the features of a given action that make it the right one for promoting the common good.[5] They are moved by the appropriate descriptions in some systematic way that they recognize and value as promoting the common good.

We will accept some priority in justification if we take virtuous actions to be justified primarily as the product of virtues, and do not take virtues to be justified primarily as the source of virtuous actions. But this claim about priority seems to be open to objection. If we have no independent reason to care about the actions resulting from the virtues, but we claim that the virtues are organized for the production of these actions, what reason have we to value the virtues? Critics of the Stoics often raise this objection.[6]

Aristotle does not accept the claim about priority in justification in its unqualified form, but he accepts a qualified version. He believes that the value of achieving the common good contributes to explaining why the virtuous person wants to promote it, but the value of trying to achieve it is not exhausted by the instrumental value of the tendency of virtue to achieve it.

To support this claim, Aristotle argues: (1) The appropriate form of rational activity fulfils the agent's function and so promotes the agent's own happiness. (2) Active concern for the common good is this appropriate form of rational activity. (3) Having this active concern for the common good is having the virtues of character. (4) Hence having the virtues of character promotes the agent's happiness.

This argument refers to active concern for the common good—trying to promote it. It does not refer simply to success in promoting the common good. If Aristotle can establish the premisses of this argument, he can defend concern for the common good on eudaemonist grounds. This is not simply an instrumental justification of virtue and virtuous action for their results.

113. The Content of the Virtues

Aristotle's theory of the virtues answers some questions in moral psychology, explaining the connexions between virtue, reason, desire, pleasure, and responsibility. An answer to these questions, however, is only a part of what we might reasonably expect. We also expect an answer to normative questions, about what a virtuous person will do in different types of situations. But readers have disagreed sharply about Aristotle's success in answering these normative questions. Some of these disagreements are better discussed in later chapters, when we come to consider the ways in which different theorists either develop his position (as they understand it) or turn in a different direction. But it will be helpful if we introduce some of the disagreements in this chapter, so that we can identify the features of Aristotle's account that have raised controversies of interpretation and of philosophical assessment.

Some critics have suggested that the Doctrine of the Mean is Aristotle's attempt to take us from general claims about virtue of character to specific claims about how many virtues there are, and about the types of actions they require. This suggestion about the mean has

---

[5] Some relevant questions are discussed by Williams, 'Acting', and Hursthouse, 'Reasons'.
[6] See esp. Cic. F iv 68–9; cf. §187.

some support in Aristotle; for he presents the different virtues as different mean states, to be contrasted with the extreme states that are the different vices. Since the mean is understood in quantitative terms, we might try to make it a practical guide by understanding it as a counsel of moderation: when we can define extremes, we should aim at somewhere in the middle.

This interpretation of the mean partly explains why early modern moralists, in the course of questioning the broadly Aristotelian outlook of mediaeval moral philosophy, attack the Doctrine of the Mean, and seek to offer a better answer to the questions to which they think the Aristotelian doctrine gives false answers. Hobbes, Grotius, and Pufendorf, for instance,[7] offer their own views as rivals to an Aristotelian account that identifies the different virtues with different forms of moderation. It is easy for them to show that the Aristotelian doctrine, as they understand it, fails in its task. It does not seem to fit every virtue (since not every virtue seems to be a form of moderation), and it does not seem to give the right practical advice (since the moderate reaction does not always seem to be the right one).

What we have already said about the mean shows that such objections rest on misinterpretation. Aristotle introduces the mean to show that virtue requires neither the complete indulgence nor the complete suppression of the non-rational part of the soul, and that it requires more than control by the rational part (which is continence, not virtue). But he does not suggest that a moderate display of emotion is always the right answer, or that, in considering what to do in specific situations, it is normally helpful to look for the moderate solution.

But if we reject this attempt to derive specific practical advice from the Doctrine of the Mean, and we offer no alternative, we leave a large gap in Aristotle's position. He offers fairly detailed descriptions of specific virtues and of the actions that can be expected from them. How are these descriptions to be defended, and does Aristotle's general theory of virtue make them easier to defend? If we cannot answer these questions, we make it difficult to see any connexion between the specific virtues and the views on happiness and virtue that we have considered so far.

Our discussion of Aristotle so far leads us to expect two things from his account of the virtues: (1) It ought to develop naturalism into a systematic theory of the virtues. Given Aristotle's account of human nature and the human function, we ought to see that certain specific states of character rather than others turn out to be virtues appropriate to human nature. Such an account will show that naturalist claims are not empty or trivial. (2) It ought to develop naturalism into a systematic theory of morality. Naturalist claims ought to vindicate the moral virtues as appropriate for human nature.

If naturalism met the first expectation but not the second, it would answer the accusation of emptiness and triviality, but it would be a theory of the human good that raises doubts about the rational claims of morality on us. This is not Aristotle's intention. Hence he needs to satisfy both expectations. Moreover, he must satisfy them systematically. If it were simply a coincidence that the virtues recognized by naturalism include the moral virtues, but naturalism gives us no good reason to expect this, it would fall short of a rational explanation and defence of morality. The systematic theory of the virtues should show that the virtues are moral virtues.[8]

---

[7] See Hobbes, *L* 15.40; Grotius, *JBP* Pref. §43–5; Pufendorf, *JNG* i 2.

[8] Among those who have incorporated Aristotle, as they understand him, into their own position, we will consider especially Aquinas and T. H. Green, and so we will not say much about their positions here.

114. Are the Virtues of Character Moral Virtues?

This may appear to be an unreasonable expectation to impose on Aristotle. Should we assume that the virtues of character, as he conceives them, are moral virtues, or that he has any explicit or implicit conception of morality? Some critics have argued that Aristotle has no concept of morality, and that it is a mistake to attribute any beliefs about moral virtues to him. Some have argued that it is also hopeless to look for anything like moral virtues in the Aristotelian virtues of character.

To see whether or not it is worth our while to look for moral beliefs or moral virtues in Aristotle, we should consider what we ought to be looking for. What should convince us that Aristotle has some conception of morality, or that the virtues he recognizes are moral virtues? Among the marks of morality many would include these features:[9]

1. Impartiality—morality does not look at actions from the point of view of the agent, but from the point of view of the interests of everyone affected.

2. Concern for others—it gives some non-derivative weight to acting for the interests of others besides the agent. Someone who is moved only by concern for his own welfare, or by a purely aesthetic concern (to preserve all the works of art in the world, for instance) is probably not moved by moral considerations. If I think of other people without regard to their welfare, I probably do not think of them as objects of moral concern.[10]

3. Responsibility—morally right actions and moral goodness are a source of legitimate praise, and failure to do them is a source of legitimate blame; people are legitimately held responsible for acting or failing to act morally.

4. Importance—morality matters. We perhaps ought not to insist that any recognizable moral view must treat moral principles as the ones that matter most; but unless a set of principles counts for quite a lot with someone, we might be reluctant to say that they are moral principles for that agent.[11]

Some critics doubt whether these conditions are sufficient for a conception of morality; some argue that we should also include a belief in distinctively moral obligations.[12]

---

[9] Frankena, 'Concept' 156, suggests that a moral outlook includes 'judgments, rules, principles, ideals, etc., which . . . concern the relations of one individual . . . to others, . . . involve or call for a consideration of the effects of his actions on others (not necessarily all others), not from the point of view of his own interests or aesthetic enjoyments, but from their own point of view'. Warnock, *OM* 26, explains the scope of morality through its object: ' . . . the "general object" of morality, appreciation of which may enable us to *understand* the basis of moral evaluation, is to contribute to betterment—or non-deterioration—of the human predicament, primarily and essentially by seeking to countervail "limited sympathies" and their potentially most damaging effects. It is the proper business of morality, and the generic object of moral evaluation . . . to expand our sympathies, or, better, to reduce the liability to damage inherent in their natural tendency to be narrowly restricted'.

[10] On questions about the scope of 'moral' see Foot, 'Beliefs'.   [11] Cf. Hare, *FR* 169.

[12] On moral obligation see Anscombe, 'Modern'. Williams also suggests that morality essentially includes moral obligation. He describes morality as 'a peculiar development of the ethical . . . It peculiarly emphasizes certain ethical notions rather than others, developing in particular a special notion of obligation, and it has some peculiar presuppositions' (*ELP* 6). It is not easy, however, to list the features of morality, as Williams understands them, or to distinguish them from the special features of the Kantian view, which he says is only one 'representation' of morality (174). But he seems to recognize these conditions: (1) Characteristically moral obligation is concerned with action that 'must be in the agent's power' (175). (2) Moral obligations 'cannot conflict, ultimately, really, or at the end of the line' (176). (3) They are inescapable in the sense that 'the fact that a given agent would prefer not to be in this system or bound by its rules will not

Alternatively we might object that these conditions are too stringent; they may not seem necessary for an intuitive conception of morality that can be used to determine whether Aristotle recognizes moral virtues. If we insist on all these conditions, we may appear to presuppose the truth of a Kantian conception of morality; but it does not seem very surprising to discover that Aristotle has no conception of morality, if that means only that he is not a Kantian. One might also doubt whether Hume has a conception of the moral, if we apply Kantian criteria; for his idea of 'personal merit' includes both voluntary and non-voluntary traits, provided that they are useful or agreeable to the agent or to others. He argues that we should not make voluntariness a test for moral virtues.[13]

But even if the conception of morality that we have sketched includes some Kantian elements, this may not matter. For if we show that Aristotle has a conception of morality, measured by this standard, we will also have done something to show that it is not a specifically Kantian, or specifically modern, or specifically Christian, conception. We can remove the suspicion that we are introducing an irrelevant standard by showing that it is also Aristotle's standard.[14]

Even if an intuitive conception of morality has these components, they may not co-exist easily; in fact they may sometimes appear to conflict. We might wonder, then, why we ought to recognize one set of virtues (and so on) that meet all these conditions, rather than distinct sets of virtues meeting one or another condition. But we ought at least to try to understand the presence of these components in our intuitive concept. Whether or not these are exactly the right conditions to impose, it is worth asking whether a theorist recognizes such principles or virtues; for it makes a difference whether or not a person or a society recognizes that such principles have a special status. We will understand Aristotle's position on these aspects of the virtues if we examine the relevant aspects of his views on responsibility and on the good of others, and see how these views affect his claims about the virtues.

We have already examined Aristotle's views on responsibility, and seen why we ought to ascribe to him a conception of moral responsibility. On this point, his concern with virtues of character is a concern with morality. But Aristotle's eudaemonism suggests to some critics that he is not concerned with morality.[15] Since the virtues are to be understood by reference to the agent's happiness, an account of the virtues focusses on the agent, not on other people or on people impartially.

Is this a reasonable criticism of Aristotle? We ought to recall that his appeal to happiness does not offer a wholly non-evaluative starting point from which evaluative conclusions are to be inferred; his naturalism does not try to derive the normative from the non-normative.

---

excuse him; nor will blaming him be based on a misunderstanding. Blame is the characteristic reaction of the morality system' (177). Though Williams warns that 'morality is not one determinate set of ethical thoughts' (174), these three conditions give some idea of what he means when he claims that the Greeks 'had certainly not arrived at the distinctive preoccupations of the system *morality*, with its emphasis on a very special notion of obligation. (In this . . . they were very fortunate)' (32). Just as the Greeks were fortunate to have avoided morality, 'we would be better off without it' (174). Everson discusses Anscombe and Williams helpfully in 'Introduction'.

[13] On Hume see §90 above.

[14] Annas also speaks of an 'intuitive' understanding of morality (*MH* 452), which she describes in some detail (120–31). Her description is less Kantian than mine. She argues plausibly that ancient theories of the virtues do some of the work that we might expect an account of morality to do.

[15] Prichard, *MO* 13, finds Aristotle's *Ethics* disappointing because it discusses happiness rather than morality. See §80.

Nor does it necessarily claim to derive the whole content of morality from a purely non-moral foundation. Aristotle claims to connect three sorts of judgments that are not obviously connected: judgments about human nature, judgments about welfare, and judgments about morality. In Aristotle's view, these three types of judgments should constitute a systematic theory that connects morality and happiness to the fulfilment of natural capacities. We may legitimately use moral judgments and judgments about welfare to expand or to clarify our conception of human nature. But since judgments about nature and about welfare do not simply reflect our moral judgments, but also include content that does not depend on moral judgments, it is a non-trivial and worthwhile task to show that the three types of judgments support one another.[16]

115. Is Aristotle an Unsystematic Theorist?

Before we consider whether Aristotle offers any account of morality, we ought to consider some reasons for doubting whether he even intends to offer the naturalist theory we have outlined. Sidgwick argues that Aristotle's treatment of the virtues is theoretically unambitious, because it is simply a detailed and impartial description of common sense. Aristotle does not argue systematically from features of happiness to a theoretical account of the virtues, but simply consults the accepted views of his contemporaries, without trying to reconstruct, revise, or justify them.[17] Aristotle's general attitude to the virtues is a form of 'aesthetic intuitionism'; it does not take the virtues to exemplify some general principle that vindicates the relevant actions and traits of character, but it presents them simply as objects of immediate quasi-aesthetic admiration.[18] The appeal to the fine manifests this aesthetic intuitionism; the virtuous person is expected to see the beauty and appropriateness in this sort of action, without relying on any further reason. Ethical theory, as Aristotle conceives it, has no further argument to show that the virtuous person sees the right things.[19]

---

[16] On the ambitions of a naturalist and eudaemonist theory see §§77, 81.

[17] The attitude that Sidgwick attributes to Aristotle is similar to the attitude that he attributes to the common sense of his own time: 'Liberality appears to require an external abundance in the gift even more than a self-sacrificing disposition. It seems therefore to be possible only to the rich: and, as I have hinted, in the admiration commonly accorded it there seems to be mingled an element rather aesthetic than moral. For we are all apt to admire power, and we recognize the latent power of wealth gracefully exhibited in a certain degree of careless profusion when the object is to give happiness to others. Indeed the vulgar admire the same carelessness as manifested even in selfish luxury' (ME 324–5). ' ... the restriction of the sphere of courage to danger in war, and of that of temperance to certain bodily pleasures, as well as the want of distinction between selfish and benevolent expenditure in describing liberality, illustrate the fragmentariness and superficiality of treatment to which mere analysis of the common usage of ethical terms is always liable to lead' (OHE 64).

[18] According to Sidgwick's view of aesthetic intuitionism, 'We can give only a general account of the virtue—a description, not a definition—and leave it to trained insight to find in any particular circumstances the act that will best realize it' (ME 228). In describing bravery Aristotle 'is merely following closely and impartially the lines of Common Sense, of the ethico-aesthetic sentiment of his society' (GSM 91), and 'simply conceives the brave man as realizing moral beauty in his act' (92).

[19] Sidgwick recognizes that a historian might suggest utilitarian features of bravery that would explain its tendency to excite this sort of quasi-aesthetic admiration; but he insists that the historian's explanation is no part of the outlook that is being explained. 'Aristotle sees that the sphere of the virtue of courage (andreia), as recognized by the common sense of Greece, is restricted to dangers in war: and we can now explain this limitation by a reference to the utilitarian importance of this kind of courage, at a period of history when the individual's happiness was bound up more completely than it now

Sidgwick claims to find this attitude to the virtues in Aristotle's character-sketches, and especially in his sketches of those traits of character that do not strike us as obvious candidates for being moral virtues. These Aristotelian virtues include generosity and magnificence, the virtues concerned with money and other material resources.[20] Aristotle does not distinguish self-regarding from benevolent expenditures, but simply admires the wealth and power that are displayed in conspicuous consumption, regulated by conventional good taste, but without any necessary reference to a common good.[21] He fails to penetrate below the surface of common beliefs to their ethical basis, and he fails to see that the appropriate critical principles may lead both to a more systematic account of common sense and to criticism and revision of it.

But if we agree that Aristotle records common sense from the standpoint of aesthetic intuitionism, we might conclude that (contrary to Sidgwick) there is nothing wrong with this; for we may believe that aesthetic intuitionism gives the best account of our grasp of ultimate moral principles. Later intuitionists argue that it is misguided to look for any more basic principles underlying the different judgments that define the different virtues.[22]

Alternatively, we might endorse Aristotle's approach (as Sidgwick describes it) on the ground that we ought not to look for ultimate principles at all. A particularist holds that particular judgments are not to be justified by appeal to more general principles, even to those that are grasped intuitively, because particular judgments are basic. Aristotle's non-theoretical sketches of the virtues remind us of the sort of person who makes the correct particular judgments that belong to the different virtues.[23]

We would have a related, but distinct, reason for agreeing with Sidgwick's version of Aristotle, if we accepted some degree of cultural and historical relativism about the virtues. When we try to specify general principles about the virtues, we try to give precise guidance for the specific situations that a specific agent meets in a specific set of cultural, historical, and social circumstances; perhaps it is simply an illusion to suppose that a general theory of virtue

is with the welfare of his state, while the very existence of the latter was more frequently imperilled by hostile invasions: but this explanation lies quite beyond the range of Aristotle's own reflection . . . The admiration felt by early man for beauties or excellences of character seems to have been as direct and unreflective as his admiration of any other beauty' (*ME* 456). Common sense, in Sidgwick's description, displays some degree of 'unconscious utilitarianism' (*GSM* 90; *ME* 453–7), and utilitarian considerations might explain some of Aristotle's judgments, but these considerations are no part of Aristotle's own view.

[20] 'And an examination of these would show very clearly how simply Aristotle is following the ethico-aesthetic—or even purely aesthetic—sentiment of admiration for certain qualities in the conduct of a Greek gentleman, and how far he is from conceiving self-devotion to a social end as essential to the notion of virtue. For example, his account of liberality is startling to a modern reader from its want of distinction between self-regarding and benevolent expenditure. Compare also his account of *megalopsuchia*' (*GSM* 96–7).

[21] Sidgwick sums up his commendation and criticism of Aristotle in this general verdict: 'There is enough just and close analytical observation contained in this famous account of virtues and vices to give it a permanent interest over and above its historical value; but it does not seem to be based on any serious attempt to consider human conduct exhaustively, and exhibit the patterns of goodness appropriate to the different parts, functions, and relations . . .' (*OHE* 63–4; quotation continued in n17 above). From Sidgwick's point of view, this is a defect in Aristotle's position. Sidgwick seeks to show that his own theory passes the test that Aristotle fails.

[22] Hence Price speaks of 'heads of virtue', *RPQM* 165. Ross, *RG* 34–5, agrees with him.

[23] This point is derived from McDowell, 'Rational aspects', 93 and n7: 'Aristotle's scepticism about universal truths in ethics implies that the content of this general conception [sc. of what doing well is] cannot be definitively written down, in a shape suitable for deduction of particular practical conclusions. No doubt it can be gestured at, perhaps by way of reminder to people who share it (cf. 1095b4–6), by listing virtues and giving character sketches of their possessors, as Aristotle of course does in Books III–V.' See also McDowell, 'Issues' 29; Irwin, 'Inexact'.

could both provide detailed enough instructions to be a useful practical guide and be derived simply from very general principles about human nature and rational agency. To supply the necessary content for his theory of the virtues, Aristotle introduces the recognized virtues that are historically familiar to him; and similarly, we might argue, other philosophers are equally justified in introducing the virtues that are familiar to them.[24]

Perhaps, then, all we can reasonably expect of moral philosophy is the articulation of the views of a particular society or culture. The philosopher may introduce general principles, but these principles lack the sort of non-historical content that would make them a basis for criticizing one or another historical embodiment of the virtues. On this view, Aristotle's treatment of the virtues will remind us that moral theories are historically conditioned, and that it is foolish to look for a non-historical point of view from which we can try to criticize the Aristotelian conception of the virtues in contrast to some other conception.[25]

These different claims about the virtues offer different defences of Aristotle on the assumption that Sidgwick describes his account of the virtues correctly. But does Sidgwick's description fit Aristotle's account?

116. Virtue and the Fine[26]

To see whether Aristotle has a systematic naturalist theory of the virtues, we should ask what his different virtues have in common. In his view, their common aim is the fine (*kalon*), since it is characteristic of the virtuous person to choose virtuous action 'because it is fine' or 'for the sake of the fine'.[27] '*Kalon*' might also be translated by 'beautiful'; and so this claim about the virtuous person might be taken, as Sidgwick suggests, to show that Aristotle is an aesthetic intuitionist. According to this view, acting for the sake of the fine is achieved in an immediate, non-deliberative, disinterested response to the perceived appropriateness of an action.

We have good reason, however, to deny that when Aristotle connects the virtues with the fine, he primarily has aesthetic beauty in mind. We have already noticed that he connects pursuit of the fine with living in accordance with reason rather than passion (1169a5–6).[28] We treat our actions and aims as fine when we regard them as having some value independent of our inclination towards them.

This rational concern for the fine goes beyond any narrow and exclusive concern for one's own interest (*Rhet.* 1358b38; 1389a32–5; 1389b35; *EN* 1104b31; 1169a6); when everyone concentrates on fine action, their action promotes the common good (1169a6–11). This fine

---

[24] See MacIntyre, *AV*, ch. 12.

[25] One might draw this conclusion (perhaps with some over-simplification) from MacIntyre, *AV*, ch. 5. His position in *WJWR* is more complex.

[26] On the fine cf. Rogers, '*Kalon*'; Cooper, 'Reason'; Lear, *HLHG*, ch. 6. 116.

[27] See 1116b3; 1116b31; 1117a8; 1117b9; 1119a18 (the fine is connected with acting 'as one ought' and 'as correct reason says', two aspects of the Doctrine of the Mean); 1120a11 (connected with benefiting another); 1120a23 (actions are fine and for the sake of the fine); 1122b6 (the virtuous person spends for the sake of the fine; for this is a common feature of the virtues); 1123a25 (acting for the sake of the fine contrasted with acting to display one's wealth); 1126b29 (the fine is the standard for social interaction); 1127a28 (telling the truth about oneself is fine and praiseworthy).

[28] See §106 above.

action expresses the virtues, because actions display great virtue in so far as they especially benefit others (*Rhet.* 1366b3–4;[29] *EN* 1120a11; 1121a27–30; 1123a31–2). Fine action is both intrinsically good and praiseworthy (*EE* 1248b17–25; cf. *EN* 1101b31–2; 1155a28–31; *Rhet.* 1366a33–6), and actions displaying great virtue especially deserve praise (*Rhet.* 1367b28). Since these actions are praiseworthy, they are voluntary (*EN* 1109b31; *EE* 1223a9–15).

Aristotle does not say as much about the fine as we might expect him to, given its importance in his account of the virtues; some of his successors see its importance, and try to describe it more fully.[30] But he says enough to show that fine actions are not simply beautiful or admirable from just any point of view. As Sidgwick remarks, we (or Aristotle's readers) might admire grand gestures and pointless extravagance as signs of great wealth or power; or we might be impressed by great physical strength or endurance. But this sort of admiration is not a ground for counting something as fine. A fine action must be praiseworthy, not simply admirable, and so it must be voluntary; and it must aim at the common good, not simply the benefit of the agent.

Aristotle intends, therefore, some systematic connexion between virtue, the fine, and the common good of a particular community. Fineness may be an appropriate object of some sort of aesthetic admiration in moral contexts; but if the aesthetic admiration is essentially a response to the promotion of the common good, the promotion of the common good must be an essential characteristic of fine actions (states of character, etc.) in moral contexts.

These features of fine actions do not show that by 'fine' Aristotle means 'promoting the common good'. It is difficult to show that he thinks 'fine' has different senses in aesthetic and in moral contexts. The most plausible account of the sense of the term would probably be 'admirable', in the sense of 'deserving admiration'. Promotion of the common good is what constitutes fineness in moral contexts. It would therefore have a claim to supply a Socratic definition of what the fine is, or (to use Ross's terms) it would be the fine-making characteristic, but not an account of the concept of the fine.[31]

In claiming that the rational pursuit of the fine involves concern for a common good, Aristotle implies that if we live in accordance with reason, we are concerned for a common good. This is why the connexion between virtue and the fine answers the objection that self-love always conflicts with concern for the good of others. For virtuous people's self-love is directed to themselves as lovers of the fine, and when everyone competes to do what is finest, that is beneficial to the common interest (*EN* 1169a6).

These claims suggest that Aristotle intends—whether or not he carries out his intention—to give a systematic account of the virtues of character, and that the system in the account refers essentially to their concern for the fine.[32] For this aspect of the virtues makes it true that the virtuous person fulfils the human function of living a life of action guided by reason.

[29] Green calls attention to this passage, at *PE* §248.   [30] See §§180, 332.

[31] On Socratic definition see §11. For Ross's distinction see *RG* 9–10.

[32] Moore, *PE* §106, criticizes Aristotle on the ground that he does not consistently take action for the sake of the fine to be necessary for virtue. Moore does not offer convincing evidence. Part of his case relies on the questionable rendering of '*hexis*' as 'habit'.

117. Justice, the Common Good, and Concern for the Fine

Aristotle's claims about the fine are not the only ground for connecting the virtues of character in general with the good of others besides the agent. For he also claims that virtue as a whole is the same as general justice (1129b25). General justice is not co-ordinate with each of the specific virtues. Rather, it is in some way identical to virtue as a whole; special justice is an expression of general justice, but so is each of the other virtues. General justice is the complete exercise of complete virtue (1129b30–1), and complete virtue in relation to another person (1129b27). General justice and complete virtue are the same state of character, but 'their being is not the same' (1130a12). General justice prescribes the actions that are prescribed by the right laws, and these are the actions that promote and maintain happiness and its parts for the political community (1129b17–19). Hence those who believe that virtue conflicts with one's own happiness point to general justice. Thrasymachus' claim that justice is another's good (Plato, R. 343c3) seems to be true for a virtue that is defined by its reference to the benefit of another (EN 1130a3–5; 1134b2–6); the question raised in the Republic should arise especially about general justice, as Aristotle conceives it.

Aristotle believes that Thrasymachus' question arises not only about general justice, but also about bravery, temperance, and the other virtues. For in claiming that general justice is the same state of character as complete virtue, he implies that if we have the other virtues, we also have the concern for the common good that is characteristic of justice. General justice is not a further state of character that a person with the other virtues needs in order to be completely virtuous; if it were, it would be a part of virtue, which Aristotle denies (1130a8–10). It is already present in the other virtues. Hence it is not a distinct virtue in the way in which temperance and bravery are distinct virtues; it is a characteristic of the person who has all the other virtues. He explains this point in arguing that general justice completes virtue because we show that we have virtue by using it in our relations to others; many people can manage to behave virtuously in what concerns themselves, but fail in their relations to others (1129b31–1130a1). Concern for the common good and the happiness of the community follows from the other virtues of character.

General justice does not simply follow from the other virtues as a whole. It also follows from each of the other virtues. This implication rests on Aristotle's belief in the reciprocity of the virtues. Though he rejects the Socratic belief in the unity of the virtues, he agrees with Plato's view in the Republic that the virtues are inseparable.[33] He argues: each virtue requires prudence; if we have prudence, we have all the virtues; and hence if we have one virtue we have all the virtues (1144b32–1145a2). Each virtue requires prudence to grasp the right end as a result of deliberation about what promotes happiness; hence none of the virtues is separable from prudence. But the right end is apparent only to the virtuous person, because anyone else is liable to be warped by misguided pleasure (1144a29–36). Temperance preserves prudence because it prevents our judgment from being warped by the attraction of pleasures that we tend to value more than we would if we considered their value without inappropriate bias (1140b11–20). Each of the virtues, therefore, requires each of the others.

---

[33] On the unity and reciprocity of the virtues see §12 (Socrates); §§49 and §59 (Plato); §185 (Stoics); §325 (Aquinas); §375 (Scotus).

We might be dissatisfied with this argument. Why should we not say instead that each virtue requires only the element of prudence that grasps the end proper to this virtue? And why not say that this element of prudence needs only the sort of virtue that prevents a misguided judgment about this proper end? Aristotle rejects this division of prudence into specific elements of prudence concerned with the specific ends proper to the different virtues. If prudence were divided in this way, we might find that the different specific prudences corresponding to the different virtues gave us contradictory advice, so that the requirements of bravery and justice, for instance, might conflict. But Aristotle rejects the possibility of such conflict (MM 1199b36–1200a11). Similarly, he denies that we can go too far in cultivating any one of the virtues, in the same way as we can go too far in the pursuit of wealth or honour or some other external good. All goods are liable to misuse, except for virtue (Rhet. 1355b4–5). Each of the virtues aims at the right use of other goods, and aims at the mean; but the right use and the mean preclude any excess in relation to the demands of prudence (MM 1200a12–34).

These replies to the suggestion that virtues might conflict reveal an assumption implicit in Aristotle's claims about the mean. He does not suppose that the mean is fixed by reference to the demands of just one virtue, isolated from the others. We cannot find the mean appropriate to temperance by reflexion on a limited area of concerns that are somehow proprietary to temperance in contrast to the other virtues. He believes that each virtue has to respond to the concerns of the other virtues; that is why each virtue requires the whole of the unified body of knowledge that belongs to prudence. Since prudence grasps the contents of happiness, it prescribes the actions for each virtue in the light of the demands of happiness as a whole.

The doctrine of the reciprocity of the virtues helps to explain why each virtue has to respond to the demands of justice. If we have any of the virtues of character, we have general justice; and so whatever is responsible for the presence of general justice in a virtuous person must be present in each of the virtues. But this would still be true even if general justice were a part of virtue as a whole, as temperance is. Since Aristotle denies that general justice is a part of virtue, he intends a closer connexion between the demands of bravery and general justice than between the demands of bravery and temperance. How does his account of the virtues of character make it reasonable to expect this especially close connexion between a specific virtue and general justice?

Aristotle can answer this question if he appeals to the virtuous person's concern with the fine. This motive is necessary for each of the virtues; and if pursuit of the fine promotes the common good, this motive ensures that general justice is already present in virtue of character. The virtuous person finds the mean for each virtue by finding what is fine, and so by finding what promotes the common good; the action meeting these conditions is also just. Being fine and being just are still two distinct properties of an action. To claim that an action is just is to claim that it promotes happiness for the political community. To claim that it is fine is to claim that it is intrinsically good and praiseworthy. The basis for both these claims is the claim that the action promotes the common good. When Aristotle says that fine and just things are the subject-matter of political science (EN 1094b14), he assumes a connexion that he explains in his other remarks about fineness and justice.

118. The Fine and the Virtues of Character: Bravery

Even if Aristotle accepts this connexion between the virtues, the fine, the common good, and general justice, does the connexion guide his account of the virtues of character? Though he is relatively inexplicit about this aspect of these virtues, he is not totally silent. His general claims about the fine help to explain claims that would otherwise be puzzling.

Aristotle insists that bravery is displayed primarily in the danger of death in war (1115a25–9), because this danger is both the greatest danger (because it is the danger of death) and the finest danger (since it concerns death in war). This restriction of the scope of the virtue departs significantly from common sense. For common sense (both our own and the Greeks') might assume that people can be brave if they face danger fearlessly in a private feud or a daring crime. The bank robber may face dangers as great as those that soldiers face in war. But Aristotle denies that bank robbers are brave, because the danger they face is not fine. They do not face the danger for the sake of a common good, and therefore they do not act virtuously.

Aristotle does not interpret the common good in strictly utilitarian terms. It may be useful for a state if some citizens cheerfully sacrifice themselves for the good of others; but Aristotle does not think this sort of self-sacrifice is necessarily appropriate for the brave person. For he notices that some people may face death because of foolish optimism (1115b28), others because of foolish fearlessness (1115b24), others because of shame (1116a18), others because of indifference to their lives. He remarks that the last people will often make the best professional soldiers (1117b17–20).

None of these motives, useful though they may be, is characteristic of bravery. Brave people are less tractable and less useful in some cases, because they need to be convinced that they are sacrificing themselves for some worthwhile cause; but once they are convinced, they are ready in some circumstances to face hopeless odds that would daunt the professional soldier (1116b15–23). The brave person's discriminating attitude marks the difference between concern for the common good and a tendency to be useful to a community.

Even among people who have roughly the right sort of motive Aristotle's discriminations conflict with common sense. He does not even agree that the average citizen-soldier fighting for his city is necessarily brave; if citizens are moved exclusively by thoughts of honour, shame, and punishment, they are not brave (1116a17–20). These restrictions show that Aristotle insists on the right sort of rational concern for the common good for its own sake in a genuinely virtuous person. If we understand concern for the fine in this way, we can explain why he distinguishes genuine bravery from the different attitudes that might be confused with it. If we do not connect concern for the fine with concern for the common good, we will find it difficult to discern the principle behind his distinctions.

119. The Fine and the Virtues: Temperance

Temperance raises more difficult questions for an account of the fine that emphasizes the common good. While it is fairly plausible to suggest that bravery involves some concern with the good of others, temperance seems more obviously self-regarding. Indeed temperance may well seem to be so clearly self-regarding that it is not a genuinely moral virtue at all.[34] But Aristotle claims that temperate people, no less than people with the other virtues, are guided by their view of the fine when they restrain or indulge particular appetites (1119a11–20). If our account of the fine is right, we ought to find that temperate people regulate their pursuit of bodily pleasures by reference to the common good. Do Aristotle's remarks on temperance suggest that he has this sort of regulation in mind?

Though he takes temperance to be concerned with the pleasures of touch and taste, he does not include all these pleasures (cf. 1118b4–8). He picks out the pleasures associated with appetites for food, drink, and sex, because he assumes that the people who pursue them without restraint are especially bestial and slavish (1118b1–4, 10–11). The intemperate person is slavish in so far as he is wholly occupied with the pursuit of these particular satisfactions and thinks of everything else as simply a means to promoting these satisfactions. This feature of intemperance matches Aristotle's general conception of vice.[35] The slavish person is not wholly irrational, since he conforms to some instrumental conditions for rationality, but this is the only kind of guidance by reason that he accepts.[36] He takes a purely mercenary attitude to rational deliberation and attaches no intrinsic value to the exercise of his capacities as a rational agent; that is why he has no concern for the fine.

Does Aristotle believe that the intemperate person's indifference to the fine includes indifference to the common good? He displays indifference to the common good because his efforts to satisfy his appetites lead him to ignore the good of others. That is why the intemperate person is prone to wanton aggression (hubris, 1129b21). Wantonly aggressive people pursue their ends by physical assaults, including sexual assaults (1148b30). More generally, they try to humiliate other people for their own pleasure or gain (1115a22; 1124a26–b6; 1149b20–2). Intemperance makes someone especially prone to extravagance, and susceptible to flatterers (1121a30–b10). Its characteristic desires tend to dominate a person and to make him indifferent to his distinctively rational characteristics, and therefore tend to make him indifferent to the claims of other people.

These features of the intemperate person fit Aristotle's description of the vicious person who is indifferent to the common good. The intemperate person will be aggressive in the pursuit of the 'contested' goods that people normally fight over (1168b15–19). He is dominated by the sort of self-love that is directed to the non-rational part of the soul (1168b19–21); this is the type of self-love that conflicts with pursuit of the virtues and the common good. The more intemperate we are, the more likely we are to have desires that conflict with other people's desires, and the less likely we are to co-operate with others (1167b9–16).

Temperance, therefore, as Aristotle conceives it, is not a purely self-regarding virtue, and its concern for the fine is not a purely self-regarding concern. When he claims that temperate

---

[34] On self-regarding virtues see §313. For Butler's view see *Diss.* 6: 'It should seem, that a due concern about our own interest or happiness, and a reasonable endeavour to secure and promote it, which is, I think, very much the meaning of the word prudence in our language; it should seem that this is virtue, and the contrary behaviour faulty and blameable; since, in the calmest way of reflection, we approve of the first, and condemn the other conduct, both in ourselves and others'.

[35] On intemperance as the paradigmatic vice see §105.

[36] It is not easy to state conditions for instrumental rationality. It raise some difficulties for Hume in *T* ii 3.3 and for Kant in *G*, ch. 2.

people are concerned for the fine, he means that they regulate the appetites that especially encourage disregard for the interests of others because they encourage concern for one's own gratification without regard to oneself or to others. The appropriate regulation of these appetites does not consist simply in preventing them from harming oneself. Aristotle believes that we have reached the mean that constitutes temperance only if we have adjusted our own appetites and pleasures to the interests of others as well as ourselves. In this virtue as well as in bravery, aiming at the fine includes concern for the common good.

We may miss this aspect of Aristotle's view of temperance if we disagree with his psychological claim that the particular appetites he mentions are the ones that particularly tend to dominate an agent and to make him indifferent to his rational capacities. In that case we might be less inclined to believe that intemperance is a paradigmatic vice. But a disagreement on this point should not conceal the point of his concern with these appetites. He believes that their special urgency, and their tendency to encourage indifference to one's rational capacities, also explain the particular importance of incontinence, as he understands it. In his view, incontinence, properly speaking, is confined to the appetites that are the concern of temperance. Because temperance restrains these appetites that corrupt one's practical reason (1144a29–b1), it has a special role in preserving prudence (1140b11–20). It preserves the rational concern for the fine, and thereby preserves concern for the common good.

120. The Fine and the Virtues: Generosity and Magnificence

If we were trying to show that Aristotle is not primarily concerned with virtues that we normally regard as moral, and that his attitude to the fine reflects aesthetic appreciation rather than moral evaluation, we might plausibly cite the virtues of generosity, magnificence, and magnanimity. These may well appear to reflect cultural ideals of good taste and good form, rather than any specifically moral concern. None the less, Aristotle maintains that generous and magnificent people act for the sake of the fine, as all virtuous people do (1122b6–7). If concern for the fine in these virtues is confined to these aesthetic and cultural ideals, we need to modify our claim that concern for the fine includes concern for the common good. We need to look more closely, therefore, to see whether the details of Aristotle's account support the claims about the fine that we have defended in considering bravery and temperance. For these purposes, we may confine ourselves to magnificence, since it seems more plausible in this case that the virtue consists mainly in good taste, apart from any moral aims or concerns.

Closer study shows that magnificent people regulate their expenditure by reference to the common good. They avoid ostentation even in private expenses, such as building themselves houses (1123a6–10); for they do not want private houses to be more imposing than public buildings, for instance. They avoid the errors of the ostentatious person who performs his public services in ways that display his wealth but do not benefit the common good (1123a20–7). They are moved by consideration of the common good, and they take account of it even in private expenses, if these affect the common good. (1122b19–23; 1123a1–5).[37]

---

[37] This sort of excellence is found in 'the sorts of expenses called honourable, . . .—and in expenses that provoke a good competition for honour, for the common good . . . .' (1122b19–22). ' . . . in expenses that concern the whole city, or

It would be exaggerated to claim that all the actions characteristic of the magnificent person result from a desire to promote the common good. The Aristotelian virtue includes expenditures on oneself and on one's friends that do not affect the common good; promotion of the common good is not necessary for them to be fine and admirable. But even these actions that do not aim at a common good are regulated by the virtuous person's concern for a common good. A gift to his friend, for instance, will be attractive because it is a source of gratitude and honour; but he will also give it for the friend's own sake, and he cares especially about the gratitude and honour coming from his friend because he cares about his friend for the friend's own sake. If the generous person really cares about the common good of himself and his friend, it is reasonable for him to be unconcerned about any sharp distinction between his own good and the good of the other.[38] Similarly, concern for the common good of the larger community restrains him from ostentatious expenditure that would provoke a pointless competition in displays of wealth. This, then, is another virtue that guides an agent's choices and actions in just the way that we ought to expect if we are right about Aristotle's conception of the fine.

121. The Fine and the Virtues: Magnanimity

Interpreters often cite Aristotle's account of magnanimity to show that his conception of virtue is difficult to reconcile with our conception of a moral virtue.[39] Sometimes his attitude seems to be more aesthetic than moral, in so far as he seems to admire the grand scale of magnanimous action (1123b6–8), and refers to morally insignificant details of how the magnanimous person walks and speaks (1125a12–16). Moreover, the magnanimous person seems rather devoted to himself; his self-assertive and disdainful pride seems to mark a sharp contrast with Christian virtue and, more generally, with a conception of morality that emphasizes concern for others.

But exclusive attention to these features of Aristotle's picture is misleading; it ignores the fact that the magnanimous person is concerned with the fine and the common good. He recognizes the priority of virtue and the fine in his attitude to external goods. He cares about honour, but only for virtuous actions; and since he cares most about acting virtuously, he does not think honour, or any other external good, is very important (1124a12–17). The greatest reward that other people can give him is the greatest honour, but he knows that he deserves this only if he knows that virtue deserves the greatest honour. He knows this only if he also knows that virtue is the greatest of the goods that compose happiness, greater

---

the people in it with a reputation for worth—the receiving of foreign guests and sending them off, gifts and exchanges of gifts. For the magnificent person spends on the common good, not on himself...' (1123a1–5).

[38] Sidgwick acknowledges the relevance of friendship in these contexts: 'One defect in Aristotle's account of virtue which strikes a modern reader is that benevolence is not recognized, except obscurely in the imperfect form of liberality. This deficiency, however, is to some extent supplied by a separate discussion on the relations of kind affection which bind men together' (OHE 66). The imperfection of liberality is presumably the lack of distinction between types of expenditure that Sidgwick has commented on; and friendship is what supplies the deficiency to some extent.

[39] 'The traits by which Aristotle characterizes in detail this flower of noble life are all the more interesting from their discrepancy with the Christian ideal' (OHE 63). In speaking of the Christian ideal Sidgwick no doubt includes humility, which he describes with something less than enthusiasm (ME 334–6). See also Aquinas on magnanimity and humility, §331.

than honour or any other external good. If virtue were not the greatest good, it would not deserve the greatest honour. He believes that he deserves honour because he believes in the supreme value of virtue; hence he does not believe that the rewards of vice are great enough to justify vicious action. For the same reasons he cares more about the honours he receives from the right people and for the right reasons. Magnanimity requires the right outlook on external goods, and on 'every sort of good and ill fortune' (1124a14), and hence on honour. It is guided by belief in the supremacy of virtue over honour and therefore over all other external goods (1124a16–20).

We reveal our view of the relative value of virtue and other goods by our reaction to dangers that threaten us with the loss of these other goods. Aristotle argues that virtue is dominant over all external goods; though happiness is vulnerable to fortune, virtue is not.[40] Happy people can lose their happiness, but retain their virtue, and therefore will remain happier than they would be if they had retained the other goods without virtue. The virtue we need for facing these vicissitudes of fortune is magnanimity (1100b32–3), because it relies on a correct estimate of the supreme value of virtue. The magnanimous person takes a 'moderate' (*metrios*) attitude to all external goods, so that he is neither overjoyed by good fortune nor excessively grieved by misfortune (1124a15–16); he is therefore calm in the face of misfortune (1100b31–2, *eukolôs*).

On this point Aristotle endorses Socrates' firmness in the face of the danger of death. But he rejects Socrates' view that virtue is the only real good. Hence he also rejects the Stoic treatment of magnanimity that assumes the Stoic identification of virtue with happiness.[41] A magnanimous person believes that if extra goods of fortune are added to a happy person's life, they make it happier, both because they themselves adorn it and because his use of them is fine and virtuous (1100b26–8). He recognizes that the external goods are desirable adornments, and he uses them properly to become more virtuous. He does not compromise the supremacy of virtue; Aristotle insists that 'in reality only the good person is honourable' (1124a25). Though the magnanimous person sees no reason to sacrifice or compromise his virtue for the sake of external goods, he welcomes them none the less.

In deciding whether to risk his life and fortune, he is guided by the common good. He values his life and does not throw it away cheaply; but he is ready to sacrifice it for the common good, in some worthwhile cause (1124b6–9, 23–6). He does not guide his life by reference to another person, with the crucial exception of a friend (1124b31–1125a2). His concern for the fine is regulated, as the magnificent person's is, by consideration of the common good.

In these and other ways, the characteristics of magnanimity should dispel the initial impression that Aristotle is not really describing a moral virtue. Study of his sketch of magnanimity in the context of his other remarks about virtue and external goods should lead us to quite the opposite conclusion. The magnanimous person embodies the attitude to external goods that affirms the primacy of virtue and concern for the fine. He rejects the common view that the virtuous person's concern for the fine and the common good involves some sacrifice of happiness; though he recognizes that this concern may involve the loss of some significant components of happiness, he maintains that it always secures the dominant component of happiness.

---

[40] See §79.   [41] See DL vii 92–3, quoted at §185n67.

122. How can Friendship Justify Morality?

This discussion of some of the individual virtues of character has confirmed our account of Aristotle's conception of the fine and of the characteristics that make actions fine. His general claims about the fine and about the connexion between general justice and virtue of character should lead us to expect that his discussion of individual virtues will explain how they express concern for a common good. We have considered some of the virtues that might seem to falsify such an expectation, either because they seem purely self-regarding or because they do not seem to be concerned with moral questions at all. Examination of Aristotle's account shows that he recognizes the importance of the common good not only in his general remarks about the fine, but also in his more detailed remarks about the actions that manifest the different virtues. These detailed remarks make it easier to understand why he believes that general justice is included in the other virtues of character; for each of them includes the concern for the fine and the common good that is required by general justice.

If we have understood how Aristotle's account of the virtues fits into his account of happiness, and carries out the line of argument anticipated in the Function Argument, we can see how he fits some states of character into his eudaemonist framework. He offers a systematic naturalist theory that is also a systematic moral theory. Each virtue of character represents 'the life of action of the rational part'. It includes agreement between the rational and the non-rational part under the guidance of the rational part; it aims at the fine and the common good; and it co-ordinates this aim with the appropriate sort of interest in external goods. The virtuous person decides on the virtuous action for its own sake.[42] The feature of the action that makes it virtuous also makes it choiceworthy for its own sake to the virtuous person. The relevant feature is the fineness of the action. Since actions are fine in so far as they promote the common good, the virtuous person aims at the promotion of the common good, and chooses actions for that reason.

Aristotle's conception of the virtues of character, therefore, matches a reasonable conception of morality. Not only do his virtues cover the area of morality, given their concern with the fine, but they also reflect Aristotle's concept of morality. His views about the fine, and about its connexion with praise and responsibility, show that he does not simply describe virtues that we might classify as moral, but also regards them as essentially moral virtues.

Since Aristotle regards the virtues of character as moral virtues, he faces a question that arises for Plato in the *Republic*: why should someone who is rationally concerned with his own interest concern himself with the interests of others in the ways required by the moral virtues? His answer to this question will determine how much he thinks morality matters, and therefore will determine how far his views on morality overlap with the intuitive views we began with.

This question would not arise if Aristotle had no conception of distinctively moral virtues; we can readily see how his conception of happiness might justify such virtues as bravery

---

[42] By this he does not simply mean that there is some description of the virtuous action under which it is choiceworthy for its own sake. The action of wearing part of the tread off my shoe might be choiceworthy for its own sake in so far as it coincides with going for a walk; but in that case it would not be true that I choose wearing down my shoe, as such, for its own sake.

and temperance, if they were purely self-regarding. We find it more difficult to see how he can justify other-regarding virtues. Since the virtues of character are defined with reference to the common good, not the agent's good, he is not entitled to assume without argument that they will promote the agent's own good.

The references to a common good, to general justice, and to a community suggest that we should attend to Aristotle's account of friendship, since this is the virtue appropriate to communities, and itself includes the perfection of justice (1155a22–8; 1159b25–1160a8). Aristotle certainly agrees that the happy life must include friendship; and we might expect his defence of friendship to supply a defence of justice and of the moral component of the virtues.

To justify a moral virtue and its associated actions we must show that they are choiceworthy for their own sake, and not as a mere instrumental means. For Aristotle insists quite reasonably that the virtuous person chooses virtue and virtuous action for their own sake and because they are fine; their fineness is not a sign of instrumental benefit, but itself a sufficient reason for choosing them. If virtue is to be justified by reference to happiness, it must be itself a component of happiness, not merely advantageous as a means to it.

Justice raises a difficulty for this demand, since it is the virtue appropriate to a political community aiming at mutual advantage (1160a8–14). Political friendship (i.e., the friendship of fellow-citizens), therefore, is friendship for advantage, not the sort of friendship that includes concern for the other person for his own sake. It is advantageous to cultivate friendship for advantage, and to do what benefits the political community is to our mutual advantage. To this extent Aristotle might defend the practice of general justice and the other moral virtues. But such a defence does not show that they are to be chosen for their own sakes; it is not clear why I should value for its own sake an action or a state of character maintaining a community that rests on advantage.

This problem exposes a general problem about the relation between justice and friendship for advantage. If I have made a bargain with you, and the time comes to keep it, the claims of friendship for advantage justify me in considering my own advantage, and in choosing my action for its advantageous consequences to me. But if I am also a just person, I keep the bargain because it is a just action to be chosen for its own sake. The appeal to friendship for advantage seems to offer no support for the just person's attitude. Our attempt to find a defence of justice by appeal to the common good of a political community maintained by political friendship seems to have led us only to an instrumental concern with justice.

123. Friendship and Concern for Others

Aristotle, however, recognizes three main types of friendship. One aims at pleasure, one at advantage. The third involves goodwill to the other in his own right, and concern for the other for the other's own sake. His views about the best type of friendship may help to justify the sort of concern that Aristotle needs to justify in his defence of justice. He agrees with Thrasymachus' view that justice is 'another's good' (1130a3–5), but he does not agree that it is harmful to the just person. He believes that Thrasymachus is wrong, because concern for the good of others for their own sake is appropriate for human nature. He defends this claim by arguing that such concern belongs to the best kind of friendship. The fact that the friend is 'another self' (*allos autos*) explains this concern for her good, by showing how I have reason to regard her good as part of my own. If we can understand the basis for concern in this case, we can perhaps see how it can be extended to other cases.

To see what kind of concern Aristotle has in mind, we may distinguish some different possibilities: (1) In unselfish concern A wants to do x for B, simply because B wants x done or because it would be better for B, not because A gains any further benefit from doing x. A shows this concern for B if A moves to one side to avoid walking over B's gouty toes, when A has nothing else to gain by doing this. This is the unselfish sentiment whose reality Butler and Hume (e.g.) defend against the psychological egoism of Hobbes.[43] (2) In other-directed concern, A wants to do x for B for B's own sake, not for A's sake. Aristotle describes this attitude as 'goodwill' (*eunoia*). (3) In intrinsic concern, A wants to do x for B because of B in B's own right, because of who B is.

Aristotle's account of friendship does not discuss unselfish concern, but considers other-directed and intrinsic concern. In his view, other-directed concern requires intrinsic concern, and is therefore confined to the best type of friendship. Other-directed concern for a person is concern for him because he is the person he is. Aristotle explains 'the person he is' as 'the sort of person he is' and 'the sort of character he has'. He infers that love of the other person for his own sake is love of him for the character he has. But only the virtuous person loves another person for his character; and the only person he loves for his character is another virtuous person. Hence the friendship between virtuous people embodies other-directed concern (1156b7–12). Such concern is absent from other friendships; for non-virtuous people care about a friend not for himself (i.e., what he essentially is), but for some coincidental property of him, and therefore do not care about him for his own sake.[44]

We might reasonably doubt some of Aristotle's claims. First, why should 'for his own sake' be understood with the emphasis on 'his own' so that it means 'for the sake of his essence'? Could we not have properly other-directed concern if we simply counted the other person's own desire for some good as providing a reason in itself, apart from any self-confined concern of mine, for trying to get that good for him?

This sort of concern, however, does not imply concern for the interests and welfare of the other. For our interests are determined, according to Aristotle, by our nature, and not simply by actual or counterfactual desires. No one could reasonably choose, in one's own interest, to revert to the mentality of a child, even if all one's childish desires were satisfied (1174a1–4); hence the satisfaction of my desires may not achieve my welfare.[45] If, then,

---

[43] See, e.g., Hume, *IPM* v. 39: 'Let us suppose such a person ever so selfish; let private interest have ingrossed ever so much his attention; yet in instances, where that is not concerned, he must unavoidably feel *some* propensity to the good of mankind, and make it an object of choice, if every thing else be equal. Would any man, who is walking along, tread as willingly on another's gouty toes, whom he has no quarrel with, as on the hard flint and pavement?'

[44] '<Friends for advantage love the other> not in accordance with himself, but in so far as they will get some good from him. Similarly also for those who love because of pleasure; for they like a witty person not because he is the sort of person he is, but because he is pleasant to themselves' (1156a10–16). At first, Aristotle appears to accept the common belief (*phasi*) that friendship involves other-direction and active goodwill (1155b31–4). If this common belief applied to all three types of friendship, they should all involve active goodwill (1156a3–5). But Aristotle insists that goodwill is not found in the lower friendships (1167a10–14). Cooper, 'Forms', argues that all three types involve goodwill and other-directed concern.

[45] A similar argument is offered by Mill in *U*, ch. 2.

concern for the other for her own sake requires concern for her welfare, it cannot consist wholly in my willingness to do something for her because she wants it.

Aristotle now has a reason to deny that non-virtuous people can be concerned about a friend for his own sake. These people are friends for advantage and pleasure. They may be willing to do what a friend wants, simply because she wants it, and not because of any further benefit to themselves; but they do this only because they look on the friend as a source of pleasure or advantage. They do not rely on any conception of the friend herself and of her welfare, as distinct from her desires; hence their concern for her is not guided by any concern for her welfare.

If, then, we are concerned for the other as the person he is, we must try to satisfy or develop the desires that promote his good; we will count some desires for less because they are transitory, or express relatively superficial aspects of himself, or rest on mistaken views about his good. Concern for the other for his own sake must be concern for the other as the particular rational agent that she is.

124. The Friend as Another Self

If this claim about friendship is to help us identify the attitudes and actions proper to friends, we need to find some more content for 'concern for the other as the particular rational agent that she is'. Aristotle seeks to clarify this sort of concern by saying that in the best type of friendship the friend is 'another self' (or 'another oneself'). Aristotle argues in *EN* ix 4 that the features of complete friendship correspond to the good person's attitude to himself. We cannot see what is really good for others if we lack the right conception of the others as they are; we lack this conception unless we have the right conception of ourselves, and value ourselves appropriately. Hence the appropriate form of self-love is needed for the appropriate form of love for others.[46]

Aristotle needs to show that the conditions for the friend's being another self are uniquely satisfied by the best type of friendship. Treatment of a person as another self includes two apparently contradictory aspects: (1) Treating the person as someone else. (2) Treating the person as myself. To show that the two aspects are consistent, Aristotle needs to explain what each of them involves.

His claim that the friend is 'another self' might be better expressed by saying that the friend is another 'oneself'. Aristotle does not mean simply that the friend is a self, in the sense of 'self' in which we take 'a self' to be roughly equivalent to 'a person'. Both friends and non-friends are other selves in this minimal sense. Aristotle intends the more controversial claim that for Heracles his friend is another Heracles.[47] To treat a friend as another myself, I have to treat him as somehow being another me, not simply as another person. How are we to do this?

According to Aristotle, friendship consists in 'living together' or 'sharing one's life' (*suzên*), since this is rational activity, and therefore suitable for rational agents.[48] But simply to

---

[46] For Aquinas' view see §336.   [47] See *MM* 1213a10–13; *EE* 1245a29–35.

[48] 'The excellent person is related to his friend in the same way as he is related to himself, since a friend is another self; and therefore, just as his own being is choiceworthy for him, the friend's being is choiceworthy for him in the same

say that friends share rational activity is still too imprecise; for apparently people who are friends simply for pleasure or advantage might pursue mathematics, or crosswords, together without treating each other as other selves. The thought, reasoning, and conversation characteristic of friends must include practical reasoning, since this defines the distinctively human form of living together.[49]

But not all forms of co-operation in practical reasoning and thinking involve friendship, let alone the friendship that treats the friend as another self. I might consult another person for advice without being at all concerned about her for her own sake. When I consult another, I decide what weight to give his advice, according to my views of his competence and goodwill and the relation of his views to my own ends. I can treat my own practical reasoning in this way, to some degree; for I might distrust my competence in some areas. But I cannot take this attitude to all my ends; at some point I must rely on some of my own ends in order to evaluate other ends and other aspects of my outlook. Hence there must be some ends that belong to me, and not simply to some agent, or part of an agent, whom I consult.

In treating my ends as my own, I treat them as significant for me in their own right, not simply as a source of advice that I consider in so far as it fits my own ends. This does not mean that I seek to satisfy all my desires and aims equally; for I have to frustrate some if they conflict too severely with others. But I do not reject any aim simply on the ground that it is not instrumental to my other ends. If I took that attitude to some of my aims and desires, I would be treating them as though they were someone else's ends. In treating them as my own ends, as opposed to someone else's ends, I think of them as worthy of consideration in their own right.

We can now see how one person can regard another person as 'another self', in Aristotle's special sense, and we can distinguish this relation from relations that might be confused with it. I do not regard you as another self if I do not distinguish you from myself; for in that case I would not regard you as another. Moreover, I cannot regard you as another self if I regard you as nothing more than a part of myself; for in that case, I would not regard you as a self. To treat you as another self, I must regard your ends as I regard my own, and hence as worthy of consideration in their own right. I do not simply consult you for advice about

---

or a similar way. We agreed that someone's own being is choiceworthy because he perceives that he is good, and this sort of perception is pleasant in itself. He must, then, perceive his friend's being <together with his own>, and he will do this if they live together and share rational discourse (*logos*) and thought. For in the case of human beings, living together seems to consist in this sharing of rational discourse and thought, and not, as in the case of grazing animals, in sharing the same pasture' (1170b5–14). '. . . what friends find most choiceworthy is living together. For friendship is community, and we are related to our friend as we are related to ourselves. Hence, since the perception of our own being is choiceworthy, so is the perception of our friend's being. Perception is active when we live with him; hence, not surprisingly, this is what we seek. Whatever someone <regards as> his being, or the end for which he chooses to be alive, that is the activity he wishes to pursue in his friend's company. Hence some friends drink together, others play dice, while others do gymnastics and go hunting, or do philosophy. They spend their days together on whichever pursuit in life they like most; for since they want to live with their friends, they share the actions in which they find their common life' (1171b32–1172a8).

[49] 'It is evident why a human being is more of a political animal than is any bee or any gregarious animal; for nature, we say, does nothing pointlessly, and a human being is the only animal with rational discourse. . . . rational discourse is for making clear what is expedient or harmful, and hence what is just or unjust. For this is distinctive of human beings in contrast to the other animals, that they are the only ones with a perception of good and evil, and of just and unjust, and so on; and it is community in these that produces a household and a city' (*Pol.* 1253a8–18).

what I should do. Your ends belong to you, but since you are another self, I value them non-instrumentally, whether or not they promote my other ends. If I take this view of your ends in relation to mine, I act for your sake as well as for my own sake.

A person's thought and deliberation belong to him in so far as they are connected through wish, deliberation, and election, expressing his conception of his ultimate good. His actions belong to him in so far as they result from his wish, deliberation, and election. If one treats another as one treats oneself, the other person's reasoning and thinking have the same role as one's own in producing one's action. The two selves share the same goals and the same conception of the ultimate good, in so far as each wants the other person's good as part of his own good. They co-operate in deliberation, decision, and action; and the thoughts and actions of each provide reasons for the future thoughts and actions of the other.

If friends are other selves, each must care about the good of the other for the other's own sake, just as he cares about his own good for his own sake. Hence Aristotle's claims about the other self are true of the best type of friendship. Since the distinctive feature of my concern for myself is its non-instrumental character, I treat another as another self only by expressing the same non-instrumental concern for the other. I treat the other's ends as mine, but not simply as a subset of my ends. Subsets of my ends do not necessarily deserve consideration as constituting all the ends of a whole self, but the ends of the other person constitute the ends of the other whole self as well as being my ends.

125. Why Other Selves?

Now that we have understood what is implied by treating the friend as another self, we can consider why one's own happiness requires friends whom one treats in this way. Why should we prefer a life including such friends over a life that does not include them?

Admittedly, if I already have friends of this sort, my happiness includes theirs; for since my happiness requires the fulfilment of my ends, and their ends are among my ends, my happiness requires the fulfilment of their ends among my ends. But once we recognize this, we may doubt whether it is better to have such friends than to lack them. Having friends seems to make it more difficult to secure my happiness, since it now becomes hostage to the happiness of other people whose aims, actions, and welfare I control even less than I control my own. Would I not be better off if I could conceive my happiness as including only my own self-centred ends that do not ascribe non-instrumental value to the good of others? This question expresses a preference for a certain kind of 'self-sufficiency' that reduces my dependence on conditions that I do not control.[50]

Aristotle's naturalist conception of one's good rejects this appeal to self-sufficiency. One's good is not measured by the fulfilment of one's desires. In claiming that happiness requires the fulfilment of one's nature, he does not mean that one naturally has certain desires that are fulfiled by friendship, or that one naturally has needs that cannot be satisfied without the instrumental contribution of friendship. If this were his view, friendship would no longer

[50] See Socrates on the adaptive conception of happiness at §25. For Epicurus' view see §§151–4. This conception of self-sufficiency (as a property of a person) has to be distinguished from the conception of self-sufficiency (as a property of a good) that Aristotle imposes on an account of happiness. See §71.

be good for us if we could get rid of the specific desires that it satisfies, or if we could find something else to make the same instrumental contribution to the satisfaction of our needs.

But this is not his view. He denies that we achieve our happiness by fitting our desires to the opportunities available for fulfilment; such an attitude is incompatible with his treatment of the virtues concerned with external goods. Happiness requires the fulfilment of an agent's capacities, some of which require external goods; that is why virtue is not sufficient for happiness. Even though friends make us more dependent—in one respect—on external conditions, we need them for our happiness.

To appreciate the role that Aristotle attributes to friends who are other selves, we should compare the activity characteristic of this type of friendship with the activity that fulfils the human function. His account of 'living together' tries to establish the relevant connexion. He relies on his claim that the human function consists in a life of action guided by the rational part of the soul. His discussion of self-love and of the virtues of character (in ix 8) shows that such a life includes the pursuit of the fine, not merely of the pleasant and the expedient. If our practical reasoning did not include reasoning about the fine, it would be confined to instrumental reasoning about means to satisfy the ends presented to us by non-rational desires; and so one distinctive capacity of rational agents would not be realized. Since the central activity of friendship is practical reasoning about what is good and fine non-instrumentally, it fulfils the human function; for this is the type of activity that Aristotle takes to be characteristic of human nature.

Virtuous people enjoy the awareness of their own activity, and find the same enjoyment in a friend's activity, which requires the sharing of life and activity.[51] A friend is a further source of the sorts of actions that we enjoy and value when they are our own actions. What we find pleasant and valuable in our own actions is the causal relation of our deliberation and choice to them. We enjoy our friend's actions in the same way, because we have the same sort of causal relation to them. The other self extends our characteristically rational activities.

This conclusion, however, does not yet justify Aristotle's claims about friendship. For pursuit of the fine does not require friendship. Admittedly, it is extended by friendship, since we can deliberate more about the fine if we share the deliberation with friends. But a mere increase in quantity of deliberation does not show that shared deliberation fulfils the human function more than solitary deliberation would. Nor need 'solitary' deliberation be completely cut off from other people; it could still use other people as advisers or critics, without giving non-instrumental status to their ends. What is distinctively valuable about the rational activity made possible by friendship?

Different aspects of friendship suggest that its distinctive extension of practical reason is not merely quantitative, but actually helps to create a life that is guided by practical reason. Co-operation with a friend who is another self allows us to undertake projects of greater complexity than we could undertake otherwise; and so it develops and exercises practical reason more fully. We are not confined to projects that we could carry out from our own resources, or to those that will be mutually advantageous to oneself and to one's friend for

---

[51] Arguments for friendship based on self-knowledge are offered at *MM* 1213a10–27; *EE* 1245a29–37; *EN* 1169b30–1170a4. Cooper, 'Friendship and good', gives them a central place in Aristotle's argument. I do not believe they are as important as arguments from shared deliberation.

advantage. In extending co-operation, friendship makes more aspects of our lives subject to practical reason, and so makes our lives more completely controlled by practical reason.

This reference to completeness helps to explain why the contribution of friendship is not merely quantitative. We might have thought that I could have my life guided by practical reason to the highest possible degree without friendship, and that friendship would simply add more activities that I could guide by practical reason. In that case friendship would be simply one of the 'adornments' of a happy life that, in Aristotle's view, may make a person happier, but are not needed for happiness itself (1100b26).[52] This is not the role that Aristotle has in mind for friendship. It does not simply add areas of rational control, but it is necessary if my life is to be fully guided by practical reason.

The argument relies on the role of external goods in happiness. In Aristotle's view, many aspects of my welfare are subject to fortune and external conditions, because some genuine goods cannot be controlled by my unaided practical reason. Co-operation makes some of these goods subject to our joint practical reason and action. If, for instance, I have friends who care about me for my own sake, I need not rely entirely on chance or on mutual advantage to find financial aid if I have bad luck. The service provided by a friend is good for me not simply because it provides me with something I want, but also because it allows me to count on having the material resources I need, and therefore allows me to make rational plans for aspects of my life that would otherwise be more subject to chance.

This contribution of friendship is not merely additive. If we form moderately complex aims to satisfy the normal needs of human beings, we expose our welfare to external circumstances. We all have reason, therefore, to seek ways of foreseeing and controlling external circumstances so that they do not frustrate our aims. For this purpose we need the help of other people anyhow. But if we have the help of friends whom we treat as other selves, many aspects of our lives become reliable and stable in circumstances that would otherwise expose us to the effects of changes in the balance of mutual advantage. As Aristotle remarks, concern for friends for their own sake is more stable than concern for them on the basis of advantage or pleasure (1156b11–12).

This benefit that we gain from the best type of friendship is not altogether absent in the inferior friendships. Each type of friendship involves some degree of co-operation and makes some aspects of our lives less subject to chance. The outlook of the best type of friendship, however, affects more of our lives and transforms our aims in ways that promote the realization of our rational capacities.

The role of friendship in transforming our aims results from co-operation in thought and reasoning, and specifically in practical reasoning and deliberation. I identify the appropriate ends to pursue by reflexion on the ends that seem worth choosing for their own sakes, and on my ability to achieve them. If we treat friends as other selves, we give their ends and their reflexion the same status as we give our own.

To see why this makes a significant difference to our deliberation, we need to make explicit a point that Aristotle does not emphasize. If the good for a human being consists in the fulfilment of one's capacities as a rational agent, any realistic plan for achieving this good must demand some specialization and limitation. Human capacities, and even the capacities

---

[52] See above §121.

of a particular human being, include many more than a single individual can fulfil; if we are to fulfil some to a reasonably high level, we have to forgo others. Not everyone can be a great poet, a great athlete, a great musician, and so on; and even an individual who could be any one of these may not be capable of being all at once. Different people may have different views about the extent to which it is reasonable to achieve some of these aims at the expense of others.

If we know that other people achieve aspects of the human good that we do not achieve, we may admire their achievements and find pleasure in them. But their achievements do not affect us as our own achievements do. The actions of friends, however, give us the sort of pleasure that we gain from those actions of ours that we value for their own sakes as parts of our good. For the actions of our friends result from aims and deliberation to which we give the status that we give to our own aims and deliberation, since we treat friends as other selves.

To understand the particular value of the actions of our friends, we need to recall that they are not simply parts of ourselves. If Arthur is a dedicated poet, and Bill is a dedicated athlete, and Arthur and Bill are friends, it does not follow that Arthur combines within himself the outlook and aims of a poet and an athlete as parts of a single self. These two outlooks may not be capable of co-existing within a single self. Part of the value of a friendship lies in the fact that we can care about the activities of another as our own activities, even though we recognize that they cannot be combined with our own activities as parts of a single life.

The sharing of aims and deliberation in friendship does not simply affect the sorts of achievements in which I take the pleasure that I take in my own; it also affects the aims that I seek to fulfil. If I recognize A, B, and C as my ends, I pursue each of them differently from the way I would pursue it if it were my only end. If, for instance, some restraint in pursuing A makes it easier to pursue B, or if pursuing first C and then A is easier and more efficient than pursuing first A and then C, I will modify my pursuit of A. If my friend has further aims that I consider in their own right, they should also modify my deliberation about the extent to which, and the circumstances in which, I should pursue my own ends. The total end I will pursue will be different from the one I would pursue if I were just considering my own ends.

This effect of friendship would not matter very much if friends pursued exactly the same goals, in the same proportion; in that case, they would simply have to make room for each other.[53] But it matters more if friends have good reason to pursue different goals. Their different goals alter each one's deliberation about her own good and the ways to achieve it. If we can rely on friendship of this sort, valuable pursuits that we cannot adopt as our own individual pursuits none-the-less matter to us in the same way as our individual pursuits matter to us. Friends achieve this result more readily if they are different in some ways; recognition of this familiar feature of friendships would be a welcome addition to Aristotle's theory.[54]

---

[53] As Aristotle points out in discussing fine action at 1169a32–4.

[54] Marx and Engels, *GI* 53 (Part 1, section on 'Private property and communism') argue that the limitation of one's pursuits to only a part of what human nature is capable of is a severe harm to a person. In their view, this is a feature of pre-communist modes of production and social life, but in full communist society each person will be able to realize all the forms of human achievement to a level that is currently unimaginable. They do not try to make this plausible in any

Differences between friends are not prominent in Aristotle's theory, because he emphasizes the fact that, in the best type of friendship, each of the friends is virtuous, so that in this respect the friends must be similar. This degree of similarity is necessary for each of them to count the aims of the other as worth considering on the same terms as his own aims. If a virtuous person cannot trust the aims and deliberation of a friend to be virtuous, she cannot have a friendship of the best type, and cannot treat the other person as another self. Since this degree of mutual trust about aims and deliberation is necessary for the best kind of friendship and for the relevant sort of common deliberation, it is reasonable for Aristotle to emphasize this respect of similarity between the aims of virtuous people. But this emphasis does not require him to overlook the aspects of difference between friends.

Sometimes Aristotle recognizes the significance of differences between virtuous people. In the *Ethics* he mentions the different contributions of husband and wife to common aims (1162a19–27). In the *Politics* his account of the composition of a city insists that the essential features of a city presuppose differences between citizens. While citizens have to be, in the appropriate respects, equal and similar in virtue, they must also be different, if they are to achieve the appropriate sorts of common aims. Plato makes the citizens of his ideal city so similar that he is in danger of destroying the distinctive structure and aims of a city altogether.[55] Contrary to Plato's view, a complete and self-sufficient life requires a community including fellow-citizens who contribute different elements to a common good. Since an individual citizen develops only some of the capacities whose development promotes his good, he cannot have a complete and self-sufficient life if everyone else develops exactly the same capacities (*Pol.* 1261b10–15; 1263b29–35). We lack self-sufficiency if we lack a complete and self-sufficient good that needs nothing added (*EN* 1169b3–8; 1170b17–19).[56]

Friendship contributes to this complete good, because it allows us to achieve goods for ourselves that we cannot achieve without the co-operation that belongs to other selves in the best kind of friendship. Other people have different opportunities, different ends, and different points of view in deliberation. When we treat these as belonging to other selves whom we count in our deliberation as we count ourselves, we more completely fulfil our own capacities as rational agents living a life of action of the rational part. Attention to these aspects of friendship and to their connexion with the Function Argument shows how Aristotle's description and defence of friendship supports the naturalist position that underlies the *Ethics*.

126. The Extension of Friendship

This defence of friendship answers one question about the role of morality in Aristotle's account of the virtues, but leaves us with other questions. For it refers to the best type

detail. If they are right, the argument for Aristotelian friendship from individual limitations does not apply to all possible forms of society.

[55] See the objections to the *Republic* in *Pol.* 1261a10–b9; 1264b15–25; 1329a21–6. For present purposes we need not consider the accuracy or fairness of Aristotle's criticisms. Plato recognizes part of Aristotle's main point at *R.* 369b5–7, but applies it only to lack of self-sufficiency in instrumental means.

[56] See n50 above on self-sufficiency.

of friendship, involving a few completely virtuous people who know each other well and share the central activities of their lives. Such a relation is too restricted to defend the non-instrumental concern for justice that Aristotle requires. Since he insists that the best type of friendship must be restricted to a few rather unusual people (*EN* ix 10), he cannot treat it as the basis for relations between fellow-citizens following principles of justice.

Still, complete friendship is relevant to the question about justice. For some features of complete friendship are present in other relations to a sufficient degree to justify the sort of intrinsic concern that Aristotle assumes. The crucial features are those that make a friend another self. The non-instrumental concern that results from regarding someone as another self is capable of extension beyond complete friendship.

We can already see the possibility of such extension in Aristotle's discussion of friendship within families. The child counts as his parent's 'other self' because of their family connexion (*EN* 1161b27–9). Hence, the parent is intrinsically concerned with the child's welfare, not simply with the parent's own pleasure or advantage (1159a28–33; 1166a2–6). Parents and children who are bound by such ties are not always virtuous people. The child is the parent's other self because he is scarcely separate from the parent, and for this reason the parent finds the child's actions very closely related to the parent's thoughts and deliberations. He is crucially different from a virtuous friend; for he does not co-operate in deliberation and practical reason. He has goals in common with the parent only because at this stage, he has no developed aims and goals that are independent of the parent's. He is perhaps more like an extension of the parent than a genuinely other self.

Still, some of the reasons that justify complete friendship between rational agents who are capable of independent and co-operative deliberation will also justify familial friendship. A parent extends himself and the scope of his practical reason in a fairly clear and intelligible way through his relation to his child; and for this reason his natural attachment to the child provides an element of his own good. Though this friendship does not provide a model for complete friendship, it shares the other-directed concern that extends the agent's goals.

Some of the features of complete friendship are also present in the nameless virtue of character that is similar to friendship except in so far as it lacks the affective elements of friendship (1126b20–5)—we may call it 'friendliness'. The friendship that this virtue resembles is the best kind; for the friendly person does what is expected of a virtuous friend. His attitude to others does not rest on consideration of his own pleasure or advantage; hence it seems to involve concern for the other person for the other person's own sake.

Though Aristotle does not explain why the friendly person takes his characteristic attitude, we can perhaps explain it by reference to complete friendship. A fellow-citizen may not be virtuous, and therefore cannot be expected to be another self as much as one virtuous person is for another. Nor does the virtuous person share his life with every fellow-citizen to the extent he shares it with a virtuous friend. But the fellow-citizen may still have some aims with which a virtuous person can reasonably identify his own. If the extent that the other is virtuous enough to share similar aims with a virtuous person, the virtuous person can extend his practical reason in the same way as with a virtuous friend.

Here we can see some grounds for the sort of concern that might underlie the virtue of justice, as Aristotle conceives it. A rational person has good reason to form a community with others whose good concerns him for the sake of the others themselves. The shared life of rational thought in such a community consists in deliberation about aspects of the common good. If we are concerned about other people in this way, we regard them to some extent as other selves, and so we identify our aims and interests with theirs in co-operative deliberation and action. To the extent that we care about the interests of the community and of its members for their own sakes, we also have reason to value justice and just action for their own sake, since these express our concern for the community and its members.

127. Different Aspects of Friendship in the Political Community

Does Aristotle's account of friendship between citizens recognize the points we have noticed? We might think it does not. When he discusses the friendship of citizens, he treats it as a type of friendship for advantage.[57] He contrasts the friendship of fellow-citizens with the best kind of friendship, by remarking that we can have the first kind of friendship, but not the second, with many people (1171a17–20).

If the point of political friendship is instrumental benefit, it does not concern itself with any non-instrumental goods achieved by the city. Aristotle, however, believes that the city achieves some non-instrumental good, and that political theorists who overlook this misunderstand the essential features of the city.[58] No doubt political activity promotes the common advantage of the citizens; but this is not all the goodness that Aristotle attaches to it. The value of political friendship does not explain the non-instrumental goodness of political activity.

Human beings show that they are naturally political in so far as they form communities apart from the pursuit of mutual aid. These communities display friendship.[59] But not all kinds of friendship are relevant to the special end of the city; we can live together, and form friendships, by forming families, societies, and other groups smaller than a city (*Pol.* 1280b36–9). The ends achieved by these smaller groups cannot be the end characteristic of a city.[60] The end of the city is the life that includes sharing in deliberation and choice about the beneficial and the just.

---

[57] 'The friendship of citizens is constituted according to the useful most of all. For they seem to come together because the individual is not self-sufficient, since they would have come together anyhow for the sake of living together' (*EE* 1242a6–9) '<The city> seems to have come together originally and to remain in being for the sake of advantage; for legislators also aim at this, and say that what is for the common advantage is just' (*EN* 1160a11–14). On political friendship see Cooper, 'Political animals'.

[58] '... a human being is a naturally political animal. That is why, even when they have no need of mutual help, they desire none the less to live together; at the same time common advantage draws them together, to the extent that it contributes something to living finely for each person. Living finely, then, more than anything else, is the goal of a city, both for all the citizens in common and for each separately.' (*Pol.* 1278b19–26).

[59] 'Evidently, then, a city is not a community for living in the same place, for preventing the unjust treatment of one member by another, and for exchange; all these are necessary conditions for a city, but their presence does not make a city. Rather, the city is a community for living well for both households and families, aiming at a complete and self-sufficient life, but this requires them to live in the same place, and to intermarry. That is why kinship-groups, brotherhoods, cult-communities, and pastimes in a shared life have developed in cities; that is the product of friendship, since the election to spend our lives together is friendship' (*Pol.* 1280b29–39).

[60] '... a city is a community of families and villages in a complete and self-sufficient life; and this, as we say, is living happily and finely. Hence we must take the political community to be for the sake of fine actions, and not for the sake of living together' (*Pol.* 1281a1–4).

These claims about the city help to explain how it achieves the ends of complete friendship, even though the friendship of the citizens is not complete friendship. Cooperative ruling is part of a citizen's good, because it includes deliberation about the fine and good, and hence about the ends worth pursuing. If we regard another person's views about the fine and good as worth considering in their own right, we regard that other person as being—to that extent—another self, and we are concerned about him for his own sake. Once we see the point of complete friendship, we also see why the distinctive activities of the city are non-instrumentally good. Aristotle claims that political activity is a non-instrumental good; he does not explicitly mark the connexion with complete friendship. But if we recognize the connexion, we can see that the attitudes characteristic of complete friendship also explain why political activity is a non-instrumental good.

Here also Aristotle's position is more plausible if we insist more strongly than he does on the incompleteness of individuals and the importance of difference between friends. Once we see that other selves—those whom we care about for their own sakes—promote our happiness partly by being different from us and in allowing us to achieve elements of our welfare that we could not otherwise achieve, we can also see why the extension of this concern to others who are not virtuous friends is also reasonable. The provisions of justice suit human nature because they rest on the concern for others that also underlies friendship; they secure a complete life for rational agents. This is why Aristotle claims that justice is based on nature, and not purely on law and convention. Though he does not appeal explicitly to 'natural law', as principles that can be derived from the understanding of human nature, his argument depends on the appeal to nature that also supports a doctrine of natural law.[61]

Aristotle's naturalism makes an important difference to his argument. In claiming that friendship fulfils human nature, he claims that its goodness is non-instrumental, and is not wholly dependent on our desires or on our natural weakness or vulnerability. It is required by our rational agency, and especially by the rational agency that deliberates about non-instrumental goodness and chooses actions for their non-instrumental goodness. The rational appropriateness of friendship does not depend on its providing goods that we might acquire without friendship. It is because we are naturally social creatures that friendship is good for us (*EN* 1169b16–19).

128. Friendship and Morality

Friendship, as Aristotle conceives it, is difficult for us to classify. It is less subjective—less dependent on private preference and taste—than the friendship that most of us recognize. But it is also less impartial—less separated from the aims of the particular agent—than the morality that most of us recognize. This is probably not a difference between Aristotle's views and modern views of morality. For he does not suggest that concern for others should be confined to friends (even the extended group in a city), or that most people think it should be confined. He remarks that in some circumstances we recognize that all human

---

[61] On natural law and natural justice see §§135, 197, 199, 312.

beings have something in common and have some degree of friendship for one another (1155a21–2[62]), but this remark makes no noticeable difference to his theory of friendship. The ethical relation that he describes seems too 'moralistic' (as we might say) for friendship, as many people conceive it, and too restrictive for morality.

To support the objection that Aristotle's conception of friendship is insufficiently subjective and too moralistic, we might argue that he does not explain the aspects of friendship that involve choice, individuality, and even chance. If we are friends with another person, we are friends with that particular person, and not simply with an instance of virtuous character who happens to live near us or work in the same place. We do not suppose we have equal reason to become friends with anyone else of equal or superior virtue who happens to turn up. Even if we acknowledge that other people might equally deserve our friendship, we do not infer that we ought to form friendships with all the deserving people we encounter. Aristotle himself seems to allow this; he does not seem to think that all equally deserving people ought to be friends. Can he account for the important way in which friendship seems to concentrate on particular people?

To defend Aristotle, we need to see why loving the other person for his character as a virtuous person is not the same as loving him simply as one virtuous person among many. If a particular virtuous person has a particular way of being a virtuous person, a friend who loves that aspect of him does not simply love him as some virtuous person or other. Moreover, an Aristotelian theory must acknowledge that different virtuous people have different ways of being virtuous. For a virtuous person's life is demanding enough to prescribe many actions that a single person cannot do if he chooses to do other virtuous actions. We have already emphasized—partly to correct Aristotle—the importance of differences between virtuous people. This correction helps to make other aspects of his position more intelligible.

A virtuous person therefore chooses for himself a particular way of being a virtuous person, and will recognize that other people will choose different ways. If love for a particular way of being a virtuous person is part of friendship for another virtuous person, it is clear why time and familiarity are required, and why the same friendship is not necessarily demanded for another equally virtuous person. It takes far more time to know the way in which this particular person is virtuous than it takes to recognize him as a virtuous person. If friendship requires this more difficult knowledge, a virtuous person has reason to limit it to a rather small subset of the virtuous people he knows.

But if we are convinced by this argument, and agree that Aristotle can explain why complete friendship, as he understands it, is limited to relatively few virtuous people, we might still object that his view is excessively moralized, and also moralized in the wrong way. For not only familiar views about friendship, but also familiar views about morality seem to conflict with Aristotle's assumption that if I am a virtuous person and you are to be a friend about whom I care for your own sake, you must yourself be a virtuous person. His assumption seems to conflict with the common view that we both can and should care about non-virtuous people for their own sakes. But it also seems to conflict with his own argument (as we have understood it) for the extension of non-instrumental concern to non-virtuous people through the extension of friendship.

---

[62] Barbeyrac notices this passage in his comment on Grotius, *JBP*, Pref. §6.

To see how much room Aristotle allows for the extension of friendship, we should distinguish three things that the virtuous person has reason to care about for their own sake: (1) the particular way this other virtuous person is virtuous; (2) the other person's virtuous character; (3) the aspects of the other person's character that allow me to esteem him and to see how his aims match mine in a way that allows co-operation.

In the virtuous friend we recognize all three features; that is what makes the friendship complete. In other people we do not recognize all three features, but we may still recognize features that make some aspects of complete friendship appropriate: (a) In another virtuous person whom we do not know well enough to count as a friend, we cannot recognize the first feature, but we still recognize the second, and, therefore, the third. (b) In a non-virtuous person we cannot recognize the first and second features, but we can still recognize the third feature, and therefore recognize a basis for non-instrumental concern and co-operation. For recognition of this person as another self may, in the right circumstances, allow the extension of my own concerns that allows me to achieve a self-sufficient good. Hence, some elements of Aristotelian non-instrumental friendship are reasonably extended to non-virtuous people.[63]

Still, an Aristotelian explanation of this extended friendship must assume that such friendship depends on some degree of admiration, esteem, and liking for the other person, not simply on the recognition of a moral claim he has on me. We may suppose that Aristotle has missed an essential element of morality, and that the concern characteristic of friendship cannot possibly be the basis for the sort of concern that is characteristic of morality. For, we may argue, moral concern is concern for others for their own sake that is based simply on what we owe to others; from this point of view, it does not matter whether we have any of these 'Aristotelian' attitudes.

On closer inspection, however, it is more difficult to maintain that morality requires only the sort of respect or concern for others that consists in recognizing that we owe them something, without any of the Aristotelian attitudes. To believe that no features of another person deserve admiration or esteem in their own right, we would have to believe that he displays no trace of the Aristotelian virtues in his thoughts or actions. But is difficult to see how such an agent could be an ordinary rational agent to whom we could recognize moral obligations. We might argue that failure to accord some appropriate admiration and esteem to other people in general is unfair and insulting.

If such complaints are justified, Aristotelian attitudes may be necessary for the proper sort of concern for others, not an optional extra to be added to the basic moral requirement of respect. Though his conception of friendship may seem to sit awkwardly between our views on friendship and on generalized concern for others, it may in fact show us something inadequate in our own conceptions. Mere subjective liking for another may not lead us to a concern for the real good of the other; mere generalized respect for another person may not embody the proper sort of concern for him.

But even if the extension of co-operative concern to a wide range of other people is morally desirable, we might suspect that it is self-defeating. If Aristotelian other-directed concern, involving co-operation, is extended to all the cases of concern for others that we might think important, the relevant notion of co-operation may seem useless. We can perhaps see

---

[63] Brink, 'Rational egoism', explores some relevant questions.

how a friend or a fellow-citizen co-operates with me so that we share a common good; but how could such an argument apply to everyone about whom I am morally obliged to be concerned for his own sake?

The Aristotelian argument requires us to believe that the other selves for whom I am concerned for their own sake also extend myself, so that I can take, to some degree, the same sort of interest in their aims that I take in my own. It is comparatively easy to suppose this for people with whom I have some relation of friendship or co-operation apart from my benefiting them; it is harder to suppose it about someone else who simply has a claim on my concern. But Aristotle's explanation applies even here. To regard another as deserving concern for his own sake is to regard him as being to some degree another self; and I have reason to do this in so far as I have reason to want to achieve my good through the actions of others as well as through my own. By taking the appropriate attitude and acting for the other person's benefit, I allow my good to be achieved by my rational deliberation and decision, in another's actions as well as in my own.

The conclusion we have drawn from Aristotle's views on friendship is paradoxical, but perhaps useful. It is natural to assume that the attitudes underlying Aristotelian friendship are suitable for the special and exclusive relations that Aristotle describes, but unsuitable for understanding any more general moral concern for others. This assumption, however, is not justified. Once we distinguish the different attitudes that underlie Aristotelian friendship, we find that some of them are appropriately extended to other people in general, not simply to the restricted range of people that Aristotle has in mind.

129. Aristotelian and other Conceptions of Morality

We have now seen why it is reasonable to ascribe to Aristotle some conception of moral virtues, and why he regards them as components of a rational agent's good. A rational agent has reason to value virtuous action for its own sake, because it is fine, and as an expression of general justice; in all these ways it contributes to his own happiness, which includes the happiness of family, friends, and fellow-citizens. Having seen this we can see what is surprising or controversial in Aristotle's conception of morality, and what we might learn about morality from examining his conception of it.

The course of the argument may revive some of the initial doubts about whether Aristotle is talking about morality at all. For even extended friendship and concern for others is still self-referential;[64] it depends on the relation of other people and their aims to my own. Morality, however, may seem to require concern for other people just because they are other people, irrespective of their relation to me. For moral principles as often understood, prescribe the proper treatment of a person as a person, not because he stands in some particular relation to me. If we take morality to imply a detached, impartial view of the interests of the people involved, we may separate its demands from those of family, friends, or community. We may even think that confining it to persons is still too narrow, and that the proper focus of moral concern is interests, desires, and possibilities of pleasure and

[64] Cf. Broad, 'Egoism', cited at §73n46.

pain, whether these happen to belong to a person or to some other sentient subject, and irrespective of how the interests are distributed between different subjects.

The more we are inclined to associate morality with impartiality, impersonality, and detachment, the more surprised we will be by Aristotle's treatment of it. For while he takes seriously the requirements of justice and fairness, he tries to derive them from self-regarding and self-centred concerns; the close connexion between friendship, the common good, and justice shows his preferred direction of argument and justification.

This is not merely a theoretical difference from other ways of thinking about morality; it also affects the moral principles that Aristotle accepts and emphasizes. Duties are owed to other people as friends and fellow-citizens sharing goals and interests with the agent, not simply other people. Non-members of a community have no clear moral claims on me. The human beings or nearly-human beings who cannot be fellow-members of a community are legitimately treated as natural slaves and used as instruments for my benefit rather than theirs.

Seeing these apparent implications, we may infer that Aristotle must have approached the understanding of morality from the wrong direction. If his efforts to understand it from the self-regarding direction fail, should we examine it from the strictly impartial and detached point of view?

Such a response may be an unwise concession to Bentham or Kant against Aristotle. We are entitled to reject Aristotle's approach only if we are convinced that appeals to friendship, community, and co-operation fail to justify moral principles with a wider scope than Aristotle recognizes. We should not assume that the conclusions that he draws are the conclusions that his principles justify. On the contrary, our discussion of his claims about other selves has shown how he gives a reason for the extension of non-instrumental concern far beyond the complete friendship in which he primarily recognizes such concern. If the appropriate recognition of other selves eventually allows concern for non-virtuous people for whom some degree of esteem and admiration is appropriate, Aristotelian non-instrumental concern extends to the people who seem appropriate from the moral point of view.

But even if Aristotle extends other-directed concern so that it has the right range, it will not be the same degree of concern. As we pass from the best type of friendship to a lesser degree of identification with the goals and aims of the other person, the extent of our concern for the other decreases. The most general form of concern will still be concern for the other for his own sake, but it will involve a less complete identification of my interest with the interest of the other. Hence other sorts of attachment impose differential concern for others. This approach to the interests of others is not egoistic, in the sense of placing one's self-confined interests above the interests of others. But it is egocentric, since one decides what one owes to others partly by their degree of connexion with oneself. Such an approach rejects the completely impartial outlook of both Kantian and utilitarian principles.

This egocentric aspect of Aristotle's view does not necessarily indicate an error in it; indeed, it may be a theoretical advantage.[65] For it explains why we might recognize a more stringent requirement corresponding to our closer connexion with some people than with

---

[65] See Broad's comments on common-sense morality, 'Features' 43–57, against Moore.

others. Direct utilitarians have to reject any such requirement.[66] Indirect utilitarians may try to justify it up to a point; but we may doubt whether the indirect utilitarian reasons that can be found are the reasons that actually seem to us to justify such differential moral weight. Aristotle's account allows us to predict the differential weight and to explain it simply, and to follow it without apology or excuse.

Aristotle's approach works outwards from the agent's self-regarding concerns, in contrast to a Kantian concentration on persons and a utilitarian concentration on interests. But these approaches do not exclude each other, unless each one is taken to be the basis of morality, to which other points of view are subordinate. If we regard the three approaches as genuine aspects of morality, we must face possible conflicts between their requirements. But the fact that different moral principles require incompatible actions should not necessarily persuade us of the falsity of any of the principles.

Aristotle, therefore, may not have found the whole truth about morality; some aspects of morality may be better defended from an impartial standpoint, as opposed to his egocentric standpoint, beginning from the aims and goals of a particular person. Morality may be the product of two distinct but partly convergent outlooks. Both an Aristotelian and an impartial line of argument may explain some things about morality and conflict with some other things we believe about it. Morality might be less rationally compelling if we could not look on most of it from these two points of view—just as it might be less compelling if both deontological and teleological accounts of it could not plausibly explain the moral phenomena. Even if some moral beliefs leave us strongly disinclined to believe the consequences of Aristotle's view, that is not in itself a sufficient reason for rejecting his view.

We probably cannot decide unequivocally that Aristotle's conception of morality does or does not match ours; for we probably lack any pre-theoretical conception of morality that is definite enough either to agree or to disagree with Aristotle, or with Bentham or Kant. Rather, our beliefs about morality include some that Aristotle may plausibly claim to explain, as well as others that do not fit his account. Aristotle's conception of morality is not inaccessibly remote from ours. His explanation of morality may advance our understanding of it.

---

[66] Cf. Godwin's discussion in *EPJ* ii. 2.

10

THE SCEPTICS

130. Scepticism in the History of Greek Ethics

Our most extensive evidence on Sceptical argument about ethics comes from Sextus Empiricus, writing in the second century AD.[1] Sextus describes his outlook as 'Pyrrhonian', referring to Pyrrhon, who lived around 360 to 270 BC, and hence was a contemporary of Aristotle, Zeno, and Epicurus. The Pyrrhonian outlook was revived by Aenesidemus in the first century BC, who is cited by Sextus. It is difficult, therefore, to say how much of Sextus' 'Pyrrhonian' position is derived from Pyrrhon himself, how much from Aenesidemus, and how much from elsewhere.

Despite these historical difficulties, it is reasonable to discuss Scepticism between Aristotle and the Epicureans and Stoics. Even if the specific Sceptical arguments in Sextus were formulated long after the lifetime of Aristotle, it is useful to see how they emerge naturally from arguments and claims in Plato and Aristotle. Moreover, both the Epicureans and the Stoics regard their views as offering replies to Sceptical objections. Though we do not know which Sceptical objections might be earlier or later than particular Epicurean or Stoic doctrines, it is helpful (and probably often accurate historically) to survey some Sceptical doubts before examining attempts to answer them.

Sextus' ethical arguments often apply to ethics some of the argumentative techniques that rest on his general epistemological assumptions. A discussion of these assumptions and their status within the Sceptical outlook would take us too far away from moral philosophy. But a sketch will give some idea of influential Sceptical ideas that raise questions about the prospects of constructive moral philosophy and about the outlook that replaces it for a Sceptic.

These aspects of Scepticism are relevant not only to ancient moral philosophy, but also to modern moral philosophy after the rediscovery of Sextus in the 16th century. Hobbes and Hume show the influence of the Sceptical outlook, and Hume's scepticism deserves comparison with Sextus. Some of Sextus' arguments also anticipate arguments in modern philosophy against moral objectivity.[2]

---

[1] I use 'Sceptical' with the initial capital to refer to the school (or movement) in ancient philosophy, and 'sceptical' to refer more broadly to a philosophical position that embraces (e.g.) the scepticism of Hume.

[2] See Mackie, *E*, chs. 1–2; Annas, 'Values'; n35 below.

131. The Sceptic as an Investigator

Sextus says that the origin of Scepticism is the hope of tranquillity; able people were disturbed by the variation in things and were puzzled about what they should assent to, and so they inquired into what is true in things and what is false, on the assumption that a decision on this point would lead them to tranquillity (P i 12). This variation in 'things' is variation in what people say about them and in how they appear; this is the variation that leads us to be puzzled about what we should assent to.

Sceptics are 'investigators' (*skeptikoi*) because they investigate this variation in things. The Sceptical method systematically opposes the appearances, and the result of its investigation is the tranquillity that 'able people' are looking for when they are trying to decide between opposing appearances. But the Sceptics do not reach tranquillity by deciding. They discover that they cannot decide, because opposing appearances seem equally credible; and so they suspend judgment, believing none of the opposing appearances that puzzled them. Their suspension of judgment leads to tranquillity.[3]

Sextus suggests that the ultimate ends of the Sceptic and the non-Sceptical investigator[4] are the same, since they both want to achieve tranquillity. But their more intermediate ends are different. The Sceptic was once a non-Sceptical investigator. His intermediate end used to be a decision about the truth and falsity of the opposing appearances, because he assumed that this decision would secure tranquillity. But he did not get what he expected. He could not reach any decision, and so could not achieve the intermediate end that was to lead him to tranquillity. But he none the less achieved tranquillity; it was an unexpected result of the suspension of judgment that followed his failure to reach a decision (P i 26–7).

Does the Sceptic who has achieved tranquillity on one question and proceeds to investigate other questions do this with the aim of achieving tranquillity? We might answer No. Since he did not achieve tranquillity by aiming at it, but only as an incidental result of his failure to achieve the supposed means to it, we might suppose that he no longer takes it as his end. But it is difficult to see how he can avoid it. If he still wants tranquillity and sees that it results from the suspension of judgment, he will form a desire to achieve suspension of judgment. The non-Sceptical inquirer feared this result, but the Sceptic aims at it.

But is Sextus right to claim that the non-Sceptical inquirer seeks tranquillity (*ataraxia*, P i 25)? He might say that without some disturbance (*tarachê*) we cannot begin an inquiry, since we have no motive to start. In that case it is true that we want to end the particular disturbance that raises the question for this inquiry. But we do not simply want to end it; we want to end it appropriately, by answering our question. Sextus seems to suggest that we will equally have achieved our end if we answer our question and if we no longer want

---

[3] 'The Sceptical ability is the ability to oppose things appearing to things thought in any way at all. From this ability we proceed through the equipollence in the opposed objects and arguments, and arrive, first, at suspension of judgment, and, after that, at freedom from disturbance . . . . By "things appearing" we now understand those things that appear to the senses . . . . By "equipollence" we mean equality in credibility and the lack of it, so that neither of the conflicting arguments stands out as more credible than the other. "Suspension of judgment" is the repose of thought, because of which we neither deny nor affirm something' (P i 8–10).

[4] I will also call the non-Sceptic a 'dogmatist', following Sextus' use of '*dogmatikos*' for one who holds beliefs (*doxai*, *dogmata*). In saying this, I pass over some controversy about the relation between *dogma*, *doxa*, and belief. See esp. Barnes, 'Beliefs'.

to ask it, since in either case we will have removed the original disturbance. Whereas we want absence of disturbance achieved by a particular route (by answering our question), he supposes we want absence of disturbance, whatever the route.[5]

Sextus is mistaken, then, if he means to suggest that the non-Sceptical inquirer and the Sceptical inquirer have the same ultimate aim, or that the Sceptic has coincidentally achieved the very end that the non-Sceptical inquirer failed to achieve. Sextus conveys the mistaken suggestion by comparing the inquirer with Apelles the painter, who despaired of achieving a particular effect in his painting, and then accidentally achieved it when he threw the sponge at the canvas in frustration (P i 28–9). According to Sextus, the inquirer achieves tranquillity in the same way, by giving up his original search for the truth.

The comparison with Apelles is misleading. Apelles (we may grant) achieved exactly what he was aiming at, though without trying to (at this last stage). But the inquirer who gives up seeking the truth does not achieve his original aim, which was to remove disturbance by the route of answering his initial question; since the route was part of his aim, he achieves his aim if and only if he removes his disturbance by that route. If we set out to travel by the coastal route from Sorrento to Amalfi, we do not achieve our aim if we fall asleep in Sorrento and are taken by helicopter to Amalfi, even though we reach Amalfi.

Sextus' assumption deserves attention because it seems to insinuate an unwarranted claim about tranquillity. If he were right to say that the non-sceptical inquirer aims at mere tranquillity (i.e., tranquillity irrespective of the route to it), he would not have to convince people who are not yet Sceptics that they have a reason to take an interest in Scepticism; for they would recognize such a reason as soon as they learned that Sceptics promise tranquillity. But if non-Sceptics do not aim at mere tranquillity, why should they care if the Sceptic achieves it?

The ultimate end the Sceptic achieves, therefore, does not seem to be an end that everyone else already aims at. On the contrary; we might reasonably find the Sceptics' position unattractive, if they achieve mere tranquillity with no further concern for finding the truth. But perhaps this does not matter to Sextus' argument. Perhaps he is not recommending his way of life by mentioning its ultimate end of tranquillity. He may simply point out that if we follow the stages of inquiry, we will find ourselves in the Sceptics' tranquil state, whether or not we would have thought it the most desirable state before we became Sceptics.[6]

The description of inquiry raises a further question. Does Sextus describe a procedure that we—Sceptics or non-sceptics—might pursue with the hope of achieving tranquillity? Or does he describe a procedure that all committed inquirers must pursue if they want to find out the truth? In the first case, non-sceptics who are not interested in mere tranquillity might reasonably ask why they should pursue this procedure. In the second case, however, their attitude to mere tranquillity does not matter; whatever they think about it, the systematic pursuit of inquiry leads them to suspension of judgment, and, fortunately, suspension leads to tranquillity.

---

[5] Cf. Striker, 'Ataraxia' 185–6 (on the Stoics).

[6] Timon suggested that Pyrrhon's Sceptical position was the way to tranquillity, and therefore to happiness. See Eusebius, PE xiv 18.2–4 = LS 1F; Striker, 'Ataraxia' 189; Bett, PAL 106–10.

A decision between these two views of inquiry depends on how far Sceptical inquiry is similar to or different from ordinary inquiry, as practised by someone who is not yet a Sceptic. Sometimes Sextus speaks as though any fair-minded inquirer who consistently follows appropriate standards of proof and argument, measured by a non-sceptical standard of appropriateness, will find that an equally strong case can be made for contradictory positions, and that therefore suspension of judgment is the only rational response. Sometimes, however, he speaks as though he presents any arguments, however good or bad they may appear to a non-sceptic, that will tend to shake our initial convictions and incline us towards suspension of judgment (P iii 280–1). The Sceptic does this out of 'love of humanity' (280), to help other people towards tranquillity. We reach tranquillity more easily, in his view, if we simply accumulate as many arguments as we need to induce us to form the appearance that contradictory positions are equipollent, and so to suspend judgment.

This attitude is different from the non-sceptic's; for the non-sceptic is concerned with the strength of the arguments that lead to the appearance of equipollence. Even if I find myself confronted with arguments that I cannot decide between, they may not appear equipollent; I may decide that some of them are probably misleading, and that I should examine them again. And even if they appear equipollent, I will not necessarily suspend judgment; for I may question some of the premisses of the arguments that have brought me to my present state.

This non-sceptical approach will not save us from suspension of judgment, however, if we find no rational alternative to the admission of equipollence. The difference between Sextus' approach and the non-sceptical approach does not matter, if Sextus has enough arguments that will seem plausible to the non-sceptic, and if the principles on which we might re-examine the arguments leading to the appearance of equipollence are themselves open to challenges leading to the appearance of equipollence. Though Sextus does not consider a possible way out for the non-sceptic who re-examines the premisses leading to equipollence, this possible way out may itself be closed by Sceptical argument. We need to consider Sextus' arguments and possible replies to them, to see whether the non-sceptic has any way out.

132. Socrates as a Source of Scepticism

Sextus discusses arguments and strategies that he derives from earlier philosophers. It is worth mentioning some of these earlier sources, to show that the questions that concern the Sceptic arise in non-sceptical Greek moralists.

Sextus attributes the use of conflicting appearances to support a sceptical or nihilist position to Democritus, who argues that if honey appears sweet to some and bitter to others, it is neither sweet nor bitter (P ii 63; i 213). Moral beliefs seem to allow a similar argument from conflicting appearances. Socrates' contemporaries were well aware of apparent conflicts in moral beliefs between different societies.[7] But conflict could scarcely be confined to conflict between societies; even within one society individuals seemed to hold conflicting beliefs.

---

[7] See, e.g., Herodotus iii 38. Herodotus does not draw a nihilist or sceptical or relativist conclusion.

This argument from conflicting appearances to scepticism or nihilism might appear to gain powerful support from Socrates. Even in areas of apparent consensus Socrates points out that people do not agree as much as they might suppose they do. Not only do Socrates' interlocutors disagree with him, but they also find that they disagree with each other. Polus and Callicles might not have noticed that they disagree about the fine and the good, and about the relation between justice and self-interest; discussion with Socrates reveals their disagreement. Similarly, Nicias and Laches discover that they disagree about bravery in ways that they might not previously have noticed.

Socrates' practice of examining others by asking them questions that he does not answer himself helps to explain why one tradition in ancient Scepticism traced its origins to him. In the third century BC Arcesilaus took the Academy in a Sceptical direction that it retained until the first century.[8] The character of Socratic argument helps to explain why the Academy founded by Plato turned towards Scepticism. One might claim to be faithful to Socrates, and therefore to the Socratic spirit in Plato, by pursuing cross-examination and refutation, exposing conflicts but claiming no knowledge of one's own.

Plato notices that these aspects of Socrates might be exploited for sceptical purposes. Someone who has absorbed conventional beliefs but then undergoes Socratic cross-examination may find that his initial beliefs waver in the face of apparently plausible objections that he cannot immediately answer.[9] Plato believes that this is an unwelcome result of Socratic examination in many people. He does not consider the possibility that our loss of confidence in our initial beliefs may be confined to the theoretical level, with no practical effect. On the contrary, he assumes that if we believe nothing is really just or fine any more than its opposite, we will not be concerned to do what we previously thought just or fine. He believes that if we listen to this side of Socratic argument, we will both become sceptics and cease to care about justice.

If this is the result of scepticism, what are we to say about Socrates himself? If he has no answer to the questions he asks, but differs from his interlocutors only in recognizing the extent of his ignorance, might we not also expect him to be less concerned about the conventional moral beliefs that he has undermined? Socrates professes unwavering concern for justice and the rest of the virtues. But might we not decide that he is being inconsistent, or at least irresolute in failing to pursue his arguments to their logical conclusion? Someone who took this view of Socrates might admire his praise of virtue, but regret his failure to give a positive account of what it is or why it is worth our while.[10]

According to Plato, the view of Socrates that leads us to scepticism is one-sided, just as the Cynic and Cyrenaic views are. It does not reflect a true estimate of philosophical argument; it is a slander on philosophy. In his view, Socratic argument, properly understood, leads us to the conclusion of the *Republic*, that some actions are really just, and that it is always better

---

[8] On Arcesilaus as a Socratic and Sceptic see Cic. *F* ii 2 = LS 68J; Sx. *P* i 232–4 = LS 68I.

[9] '. . . You know that some beliefs about just and fine things were taught us in childhood, and we've been brought up under them as parents, obeying and honouring them . . . . Now suppose . . . some questioner comes and asks what the fine is, and in answer he says what he has heard from the legislator, and then the argument refutes him in many and various ways, until it drives him into believing that nothing is fine any more than it is shameful, or just and good any more than the reverse, and so on for all the things he most honoured. Do you think he will still honour and obey them as before?' (Plato, *R*. 538c–e).

[10] This reaction is similar to the one described at Plato[?], *Clitopho* 410b–d.

for us to be just than to be unjust. But the elaborate structure of the *Republic* shows that Plato does not think it is an easy matter to establish the positive side of Socratic doctrine. The relatively simple arguments of Book i do not convince Glaucon and Adeimantus that Socrates has answered Thrasymachus (R. 357a; 358b). Plato needs the account of the individual soul and the ideal state before he thinks he has an adequate answer.

133. Protagoras and Plato

The destructive effect of scepticism on ordinary moral beliefs also concerns Protagoras, whose answer is worth comparing with Plato's.[11] He solves the problem of conflicting appearances by answering that both the conflicting views are true. For the person who feels hot the wind is hot, and for the one who feels cold the wind is cold.[12] Similarly, for those to whom murder appears unjust it is unjust and for those to whom it appears just it is just.[13]

It is difficult to decide what Protagoras means by this claim. Some possible views are these: (1) Justice (say) is relational; nothing is just non-relationally, but what is just is just for particular people in particular circumstances, and what is just for some people in their circumstances may be unjust for different people in different circumstances. (2) Justice is simply a product of different people's opinions. Just as I am in pain if I feel pain, so also (on this view) it is just for Athenians to avoid murder and incest if they think it is just. (3) It is not absolutely true that murder is unjust; it is only relatively true, relatively to those who think it is unjust. (4) It is not true that murder is unjust; it is only true in the view of those who think it is unjust.

These different views might all be called 'relativist', but the use of this term may encourage us to confuse them. The first view does not support Protagoras' view about appearances; the mere fact that different medicines are good for people in different conditions does make it true that what each person thinks is healthy is healthy for him. Both Plato and Aristotle argue against the inference from variation to the rejection of objective goodness and rightness (*Tht.* 177d; *EN* 1094b14–19). The other three views, however, all reject objective facts about justice, and offer ways of understanding moral claims that avoid Sceptical suspension of judgment.

If any of these is the right way to understand moral claims, facts about conflicting appearances may lead us to accept equipollence; to this extent Sextus is right to suggest that Protagoras' introduction of relativity is similar to Sceptical argument (P i 216–17; M vii 60, 64). But Protagoras implies that acceptance of equipollence need not lead us to suspension of judgment. For even though we recognize that there is nothing to choose, objectively

---

[11] I will suppose for present purposes that the positions I attribute to Protagoras on the basis of Plato's *Theaetetus* belong to the historical Protagoras.

[12] 'He [sc. Protagoras] says, doesn't he, that a human being is the measure of all things—of things that are, how they are, and of things that are not, how they are not? I suppose you've read that? . . . Sometimes, when the same wind is blowing, one of us shivers, the other does not, or one shivers a bit, the other a lot . . . . Are we to say that the wind in itself is cold or not cold? Or are we to agree with Protagoras that it is cold for the one who shivers, and not for the other?' (Plato, *Tht.* 152a–b).

[13] ' . . . the things that have seemed good to a city and that it has laid down, are just for the city that has laid them down, for as long as they remain laid down' (*Tht.* 177d).

speaking, between Athenian and Persian judgments about justice, we may none the less continue to affirm Athenian or Persian judgments, if we are Athenians or Persians.

Protagoras' view (understood in one of these three ways) anticipates later attempts to pre-empt an argument for scepticism by rejecting objectivity and restricting our epistemological claims so that they are not threatened by sceptical argument. If Protagoras is right, Sextus is wrong to suppose that objectivism and Scepticism are the only options worth considering. We need not suspend judgment simply because objectivism is refuted.

Whereas Plato suggests that one-sided Socratic criticism leads to the practical rejection of just actions, he does not raise this objection to the Protagorean position. He distinguishes Protagoras' position from the view of those who agree with him in saying that ordinary morality is simply a matter of convention (*nomos*) and therefore not to be taken seriously (cf. *Laws* 889e–890a). Protagoras does not suggest that if moral properties do not belong to nature (*phusis; Laws* 889d7), we should reject morality. He denies that we are committed to the objectivist conception of moral properties that is refuted by the discovery that they are not natural.

Still, Plato argues that Protagoras' position does not allow us to engage in our ordinary moral practices. In Protagoras' view, as long as we continue to make ordinary judgments about justice, without believing that they are true of any objective reality, we will continue to uphold ordinary morality; hence he rejects the criticisms of those who allege that the Protagorean position supports immorality in practice. Plato answers that upholding ordinary morality consists in more than simply repeating conventional moral judgments. We also suppose it is possible to improve moral judgments by reflexion and argument, and we suppose that some people are better than others at advising us. We try to improve our judgments, not simply to seem to ourselves to improve them. Therefore we must assume that some things are really better than others, whether or not they appear to be, and that we can discover enough about them to modify our initial moral judgments (*Tht.* 177d–179b).

Just as Protagoras' argument anticipates later attempts to avoid scepticism, so also Plato's reply anticipates later objections to these attempts. He argues that Protagoras needs to explain not only how he can affirm ordinary moral judgments, but also how he can treat them in the way we treat them when we claim to discover reasons for changing our mind for the better. Plato's argument assumes that we accept objective judgments about goodness as a basis for reforming our judgments about justice.

134. Aristotle and Conflicting Appearances

Aristotle's approach to common beliefs shows how parts of his method might be used to support Scepticism and how he intends to avoid any sceptical conclusion. In his view, we ought to set out the appearances, and go through the puzzles; this is the only way to look for an adequate solution (*Met.* 995a24–b4). We reach a puzzle (*aporia*) when we seem to have equally cogent arguments for two incompatible conclusions; Aristotle compares this condition to being bound and being unable to make further progress. He seeks a solution that will allow us to make progress.

The condition that Aristotle describes as puzzlement is similar to the condition that Sextus describes as the recognition of equipollence. If we find equally cogent arguments for two incompatible conclusions, we have to regard them as equipollent, so that we have no reason to go for one rather than the other. Sextus suggests that the next step is suspension of judgment, on which tranquillity follows coincidentally. We might indeed be tempted to react sceptically to the elaborate list of puzzles about being that Aristotle presents in *Metaphysics* iii. But Aristotle argues that this is the wrong reaction. We should suspend judgment only if our appearance of equipollence is supported by further inquiry. We need to re-examine the conclusions to see if they are really incompatible; we need to re-examine the premises to see if they remain plausible once we see that they seem to lead to the puzzle; and we need to re-examine the arguments, to see whether they really lead us cogently from plausible premises to unacceptable conclusions. Aristotle believes that a re-examination leads us to a resolution of the puzzles and a re-affirmation of the appearances, or at least of 'most and the most important' of them (*EN* 1145b4–6).

We might reply that Aristotle's belief is merely groundless optimism. The further premises that we might rely on in re-examining the routes to each side of our puzzle may themselves be open to the doubts arising from conflicting appearances. If the Sceptics repeat their questions at each stage, how can we ever start the constructive re-examination that Aristotle recommends?

In Aristotle's view, however, the fact that we have reached a conclusion that seems absurd, in the light of the beliefs that seem most plausible, is a good reason for supposing that our argument has gone wrong. If we conclude that virtue is identical to happiness, despite our firm conviction that virtue does not secure all the goods we need for happiness, we have reason to reject our conclusion and to look for the mistake in our argument (cf. 1095b30–1096a2). Similarly, if we conclude that pleasure is not a good at all, we cast doubt on the credibility of our whole argument (cf. 1172b35–1173a2).

By defending an anti-sceptical position on these grounds, Aristotle invites a further Sceptical objection. Why should we give a special status to these convictions that we use to cast doubt on conclusions that grossly violate the appearances? The later Sceptic Agrippa presents this objection as a trilemma: either our privileged convictions rest on no argument, or they rest on further argument, which is either infinitely regressive or circular, and in any of these cases they do not deserve their privileged position (Sx *P* i 164–9, 178–9; DL ix 88–9).

This Sceptical argument raises basic questions in epistemology that bear on moral epistemology. The trilemma is pertinent to Aristotle, since he rejects infinite regress and circular argument as means of demonstration (*APo* i 3), so that he seems to be left only with an appeal to some sort of non-inferential justification for the premises of demonstration.[14] If he argued in the same way about dialectical argument in ethics, he would demand rather a lot for the premises of cogent ethical arguments.

If we do not suppose that Aristotle is always a foundationalist, relying on non-inferentially justified basic principles, we may suppose that he appeals to some considerations of coherence. Perhaps he holds that we may legitimately appeal to convictions that have a central role in our ethical convictions as a whole, and that we may rely on them to decide

[14] Cf. Irwin, *AFP*, ch. 6; Barnes, *TS*, ch. 4.

which of our other convictions are most plausible, and therefore rely on them to resolve the puzzles that we can generate from the appearances. This defence fits the argument Aristotle offers in the *Ethics*, where he avoids any foundationalist appeal to principles that are non-inferentially justified.

This defence against Agrippa raises a question about the legitimacy of resorting to coherence. If we are already convinced that circular argument is illegitimate, we will disallow Aristotle's defence that appeals to coherence. But should we have already made up our mind against all circular argument? If we do, we will rule out some apparently reasonable arguments that rely on considerations of coherence. This is a holist argument for holism; it argues from coherence that we ought to allow arguments from coherence and therefore ought to take a non-Sceptical attitude.[15]

If Sextus (or Agrippa) were himself a foundationalist, or could presume that all his opponents are foundationalists, he might reasonably reject the holist argument for holism. But his opponents are not all foundationalists; even if we are wrong about Aristotle, the Stoics appeal to the coherence of their whole system as a reason for believing it. And if the Sceptic is a foundationalist himself, does he not take a dogmatic position that is inconsistent with his Scepticism? If he refrains from affirming it, but simply says it is how things appear to him, his opponents have no reason to share his appearance.

These points take us beyond anything that Aristotle says in the *Ethics*. But they suggest that his approach to ethics both invites Sceptical treatment, and at the same time suggests answers to some Sceptical arguments. Aristotle's approach to puzzles about common beliefs shows that the process leading from recognition of conflict to suspension of judgment is not inevitable. He has good reason to deny that a non-sceptic is rationally committed to the steps that lead a Sceptic to suspension of judgment. We have a good reason, therefore, to treat the Sceptical description of inquiry as a description of an activity that we will pursue only if we have already accepted some of the most questionable aspects of Scepticism. We have no reason to share the Sceptic's aim of achieving mere tranquillity.

135. Aristotle on Nature and Convention

One of Aristotle's replies to a Sceptical objection is similar to Plato's reply to Protagoras. Plato argues that Protagoras' rejection of objective justice cannot plausibly be extended to objective goodness, since we need objective goodness to explain our efforts to improve our views on justice. Aristotle also appeals to goodness to cast doubt on claims about justice. He notices that variations in fine and just things lead people to believe that nothing is fine and just by nature. He answers that good things also vary; in some circumstances goods such as bravery and wealth can cause some harm (*EN* 1094b14–19). Aristotle assumes that this sort of variation gives us no reason to conclude that nothing is good by nature and that all goods are merely matters of convention.

This brief reply to a Protagorean argument relies on a strategy that Aristotle often relies on in his claims about goods. Whatever is really good for us is good for us as having the

---

[15] For present purposes I am not distinguishing holism from appeals to coherence. Nor am I giving a precise account of the relevant sort of coherence.

nature we have; that is why we need to find the function of human beings in order to find the human good. All genuine goods are good 'by nature'; their nature makes them good for us given our nature.[16]

We might reply to this claim about natural goods by arguing that the goods recognized by Aristotle are not good for everyone in all circumstances. Medicines are good for some and bad for others; even virtue benefits some and harms others. How, then, can their nature and ours make them good? Aristotle replies by denying that natural goods are always good or good for everyone. They are good only for the right sort of person in the right circumstances. Hence we do not show that wealth is not a good if we find that it harms some people in some circumstances; these are the people who do not know how to use it. Similarly, a good diet for a healthy person is not good for sick people (cf. 1129b1–6; 1173b22–5).[17] To be good is not to be good irrespective of the person or the circumstances, or in every respect. Virtue is the most unrestricted good, because it is good for everyone in all circumstances. But it is not good in every respect; if unjust people persecute the just person, justice causes some harm to the just person, though it is still good for him on the whole.

Aristotle's treatment of variation in goods helps him to explain natural justice. He recognizes that some requirements of justice are based on law or convention (*nomos, sunthêkê*, 1134b18–24). If particular states pass different laws about weights or measures, or about the prescribed form of sacrifice, justice requires the keeping of these different laws, and hence requires different things in different places. But Aristotle denies that all requirements of justice depend on laws in this way (1134b24–1135a5). There is one naturally just constitution, which suits the right sort of people in the right circumstances, though it would not suit every society in all circumstances. In the *Politics* Aristotle describes the types of society and the types of situations that would make it unwise and unjust, in those circumstances, to adopt the constitution he thinks is naturally just. This variation in justice does not threaten the belief in natural justice.

But if Aristotle admits all this, does he make the idea of natural justice practically irrelevant for most people in most circumstances? This conclusion does not follow. Even if we cannot adopt a just constitution overnight, we should prefer changes that bring us closer to suitable conditions for the just constitution over changes that take us further away from these conditions. Similarly, an unhealthy or unjust person should prefer changes that bring him closer to being healthy or just, so that he can benefit from things that are naturally good for human beings.

One might still dispute Aristotle's claim to be able to identify natural goods, if one doubts his claim to be able to give an account of the relevant aspects of human nature. But his claims are reasonable. We can see why health is closer to our natural condition than illness, and we can see why we fulfil human nature by rational activity more than we do by being forced into mindless and exhausting labour. The relevant conception of nature and the natural needs to be explained further; Butler tries to explain it by distinguishing the respect in which illness and health are equally natural from the respect in which health is more natural than illness.[18]

---

[16] On Aristotle's appeals to nature see §81. On later appeals to natural law see §§197, 199, 301.
[17] Some of these questions about unqualified and natural goods are discussed at *Top.* 115b11–35.
[18] See Butler, *S* P24.

Aristotle's claims about nature, therefore, do not collapse in the face of arguments about variation. He not only suggests some points on which Sceptical arguments might fasten, but also indicates how one might answer these arguments.

136. Arguments against Objective Goodness

The views of Plato and Aristotle on natural goodness help us to evaluate the arguments that Sextus offers against objectivity in ethics. He tries to induce the appearance of equipollence by pointing out conflicting appearances about questions of conduct (*P* i 145). If he succeeds, we cannot say what property a given subject has in its nature, but only what property it appears to have in relation to a given way of life, or practice, or law (163). This is one of the 'tropes' (or 'modes') of argument that lead us to suspend judgment about 'the nature of external subjects' (163).

The oppositions that Sextus mentions are too various to show that we can say nothing about the nature of external subjects. In some of the cases he mentions, we might say that one of the opposing views is mistaken; for instance, the Taurians might be wrong to sacrifice strangers to Artemis (149). In some cases each of two 'conflicting' practices might be equally acceptable because it is sanctioned by custom; perhaps it would be reasonable for Ethiopians to tattoo their children, but unreasonable for Greek parents to tattoo their children in violation of Greek customs (148). In some cases different circumstances might make different actions reasonable; perhaps Heracles should not normally have occupied himself in spinning wool, but was right to do it in the house of Omphale (157). If any of these explanations works for any of Sextus' examples, that example does not serve its purpose. Hence, before we are convinced by his overall argument, we need to be confident that enough of his examples resist any of these explanations.

Not every case of variation shows that we cannot say anything about the real nature of a thing, as opposed to its appearances. If (as Heracleitus remarks) sea-water is good for fishes but bad for human beings, we learn something about the nature of sea-water, because we learn something about its real effects on different kinds of creatures; we do not learn only about how sea-water appears. The fact that we learn about a relational rather than a non-relational property of something does not show that we learn about an apparent rather than a real property. We might suspect that Sextus confuses (or is confused by) the use of 'in its own right' (*kath'hauto*) to refer to non-relational ('intrinsic') properties versus relational properties, and its use to refer to objective ('as it is in itself') versus non-objective properties. If we take goodness to be relational, we do not thereby accept relativism or deny objective goodness.

Sextus might protest that some of the attempted explanations of variety beg the question. Can we fairly dismiss the opposition between Taurian approval of human sacrifice and Greek disapproval of it by saying that the Taurians are wrong? If we agree with the Greeks, no doubt we will think the Taurians are wrong, but the Taurians are equally convinced that they are right. If we appeal to the more general principle that innocent human beings who do not threaten anyone's life ought not to be deliberately killed, not everyone accepts that principle. If we say that the right people, or the people who ought to be trusted, accept it,

Sextus will ask how we are to identify these people. At some point we must refuse to answer the further question, or go on to infinity, or argue in a circle. In other words, we are forced into Agrippa's trilemma.

But if this is the right way to continue the conversation between Sceptics and their opponents after the point where Sextus stops, conflicting appearances do not give him a decisive argument for equipollence. We have to accept equipollence only if we reject the other explanations of the conflicts or apparent conflicts between appearances. We will reject the other explanations only if we subject them to Agrippa's trilemma. But the trilemma defeats the explanations only if all the options it offers are unacceptable. We have seen that Sextus does not give dogmatists a good reason, from their point of view, to reject all the options offered by the trilemma. If Sextus does not appeal to the trilemma, but to his more specific claims about conflicting appearances of goodness, his arguments do not defeat competing explanations of variation. Hence his arguments seem to fail, whether we take them to be specifically about ethics or to rely on the resort to Agrippa's trilemma.

137. Natural Goodness

This conclusion on Sextus' arguments from conflicting appearances helps us to evaluate his arguments to show that nothing is by nature good or bad (P iii 179; M xi 69).[19] It is easy to see why these arguments are so prominent in his case for Scepticism, given the importance of natural goodness in Plato and Aristotle (not to mention their successors). The reply to Protagoras in the *Theaetetus* and the defence of natural justice in the *Ethics* answer doubts about the objectivity of justice by arguing from the objectivity of goodness, relying on claims about natural suitability and appropriateness. A defence of Scepticism should show, therefore, that the assumptions about nature and goodness are subject to doubts that lead to the appearance of equipollence.

Sextus' objections assume that if something is good by nature it ought to be good for everyone (M xi 69). Fire is by nature hot, and therefore heats everything, whereas snow is cold by nature and therefore cools everything; similarly, then (he argues), natural goods should be good for everyone. This argument rests on too few examples. A certain kind of poison may be lethal, even if it is possible to prevent its being lethal in a particular case by taking small amounts of it in advance. Even if we need to qualify the claim that this poison is lethal, we need not concede that it only appears lethal.

Not only do Sextus' examples fail to prove his general point, but the general point is controversial in any case, since some of his opponents reject it. Aristotle insists that not all natural goods are good for everyone; bad people are better off without some natural goods, until they become better, and so become able to benefit from the natural goods. In Aristotle's view, many natural goods only benefit people in the right state and in the right circumstances.

One might wonder why Sextus overlooks this Aristotelian reply to his generalization about natural goods. His attitude is intelligible, however, if we recall his treatment of

---

[19] These arguments, and possible differences between P and M, are discussed by Bett, *AE*, e.g. at 97–105.

conflicting appearances. If we defend Aristotle by saying that natural goods are good only for well-disposed people in favourable conditions, the Sceptic might reasonably ask us how we tell which people are well-disposed or what conditions are favourable. Any principle we offer will be subject to further Sceptical questions, forcing us into Agrippa's trilemma.

A similar point explains another surprising feature of Sextus' treatment. He assumes not only that natural goods must be good for everyone, but also that they must appear good to everyone. First he says that a natural good must move everyone alike who is in a natural state, but then he repeats the demand without the mention of a natural state.[20] A natural good would move everyone only if everyone desired it; hence Sextus assumes that if something is a natural good, everyone desires it. But the believer in natural goods can apparently reply that even if natural goods were to benefit everyone, some people would be blind to this fact because they do not understand enough about goods.

The Sceptic's next move asks who is to distinguish the people who do not recognize their own good from those who recognize it (cf. Ar. *Met.* 1009b2–11; 1011a3–11). Aristotle does not take this sort of doubt seriously; he answers that we have to recognize some things without a demonstration (1011a11–13). To disallow the Aristotelian answer, the Sceptic needs to claim—or rather, to take the dogmatist to believe—that all the horns of Agrippa's trilemma are unacceptable.

The Sceptical discussion of natural goods, therefore, does not seem to deploy powerful arguments against dogmatists. Believers in natural goods can reasonably point out that the Sceptic misinterprets them in claiming that natural goods must be good for everyone and that everyone must desire them and believe them to be good. The Sceptical reply to this charge of misinterpretation takes us from particular questions about ethics to the more general epistemological issues raised by Agrippa's trilemma. Though Agrippa's trilemma appears to the Sceptic to provide a powerful argument against the dogmatists, we have no reason to agree.

138. Sceptical Tranquillity

But even if we reject Sextus' particular arguments against dogmatism in ethics, we might still be attracted to the Sceptical position by the claim that tranquillity results from suspension of judgment. This may appear to be a welcome result, because the dogmatist also wants to be rid of disturbance. Sextus argues at length that the Sceptic will be more tranquil than the dogmatist, because he will be free of the anxieties that result from the conviction that some things are really good and bad (*M* xi 141–61; *P* iii 235–8). If dogmatists are aiming at tranquillity, and they find that the Sceptics have got there first, they seem to have an ethical reason to favour the Sceptical strategy for achieving tranquillity; hence they seem to have a reason to suspend judgment, and hence to focus on the considerations that induce the appearance of equipollence.

Sextus does not claim that Sceptics are completely free of disturbance. They are liable to desires and passions that do not depend on the belief that something is good or bad.

---

[20] At *P* iii 179 Sextus first has *homoiôs pantas kinei tous kata phusin, hôs phasin, echontas*, but then simply has *pantas kinei hôs agathon*.

Whatever we think about pain, and whether or not we claim (as Cynics and Stoics claim) that it is not bad, we will want to be rid of the sensation that arises if a knife is stuck into our leg. Similarly, we will want the continuation of the pleasant sensation that arises, whether we want it to or not, when we satisfy our hunger (M xi 149).

Dogmatists are subject to these passions no less than Sceptics are, but they are also subject to the further disturbances that result from the conviction that things are really good or bad. These convictions about value make us concerned about things that we have no natural and inevitable desire for; any such concern involves a deliberate effort to get the relevant good, and deliberate effort involves some initial disturbance when we recognize that we have not yet got this good. Moreover, convictions about good and bad involve us in further disturbance even about inevitable pains and pleasures. If we believe that it is bad to be cut, we make an effort to avoid it, and our effort involves disturbance beyond what we suffer if we are cut; similarly, if it happens to us, we think we ought to have avoided it and ought to avoid it in future, and so we suffer a further disturbance beyond our inevitable suffering (M xi 158–60).

In contrast to the dogmatist, the Sceptic is tranquil because he has freed himself from beliefs by suspending judgment. He does not try to remove his disturbances by finding out the truth. He still suffers the natural and inevitable passions that do not depend on beliefs about value. Hence the end he achieves is 'tranquillity in things that accord with belief and moderate passion in things that are compelled' (P i 25). He achieves complete freedom from the disturbance that results from belief, since he gives up belief. He cannot achieve complete freedom from the disturbance that results from passions, because some of this disturbance is inevitable and independent of belief; but since he achieves freedom from the dogmatists' disturbance and adds no new disturbance of his own, his passions are less disturbing than the dogmatist's passions (P i 29–30). He thereby achieves 'the most complete (teleiotatên) happiness' (M xi 160–1).

Is Sextus right to claim that the Sceptic's suspension of judgment will result in tranquillity? Might we not wonder whether we have done the right thing in suspending judgment and so be anxious to find out? If Sextus' claim is an empirical prediction, it seems to be open to question. If we found ourselves unable to make up our minds between apparently equipollent positions, and we felt ourselves becoming indifferent to the question, as Sextus suggests we will, might we not resist this tendency?

Some answers to these questions depend on the questions we originally asked about Sextus' conception of inquiry. If we agree with him that tranquillity is the ultimate end, because tranquillity is happiness, and we take our inquiry into the truth to be a means to tranquillity, perhaps we will become tranquil and remain in our tranquil state once we have suspended judgment, if we still believe that tranquillity is the ultimate end.

This conception of the Sceptic's method rests on the dogmatic conviction that tranquillity is the ultimate end. Sextus, however, claims that the principles that the Sceptic relies on to reach his conclusion do not remain with him as settled beliefs; they are like the laxative that eliminates itself with everything else (P i 206; cf. ii 188). If we eliminate the conviction that tranquillity is happiness, why should we not be anxious about whether we have done the right thing by becoming tranquil? The Sceptic seems to achieve tranquillity only if he maintains a dogmatic conviction about happiness; but that conviction seems to be a source of anxiety.

Sextus might deny that this is a serious difficulty. In putting forward tranquillity as the ultimate end, he might claim to be agreeing with other philosophers.[21] If he is right, and no one will question the assumption that tranquillity is happiness, it will not occur to anyone to be anxious about whether it is correct. To show that others agree with him, Sextus might cite passages in which some Stoics identify happiness with a 'good flow of life' (*eurhoia biou*).[22] This good flow might be identified with tranquillity. Similarly, the conception of happiness as tranquillity seems to agree with Epicurus' conception of happiness, and in general with an adaptive conception.

But these similarities with the views of dogmatic philosophers do not justify Sextus in taking it to be beyond controversy that tranquillity is the ultimate end. While the Stoics believe that the virtuous person achieves the ultimate end, and is thereby tranquil, they do not infer that tranquillity simpliciter is the ultimate end. The tranquillity that they value is not mere tranquillity, but the tranquillity of the virtuous person. Sextus' mistake in separating tranquillity from the preferred route to it is similar to his mistake in representing tranquillity as the goal of inquiry into the truth.

It is more difficult to distinguish the Epicurean conception of happiness from Sextus' view of tranquillity as the end. Sextus and Epicurus agree that we have basic bodily needs that need to be met and that a tolerable life has to include satisfaction of these needs. Epicurus, however, has a more positive attitude to this satisfaction. He regards the pleasure that results from it as a contribution to happiness, whereas Sextus speaks of it simply as 'relief' (M xi 149). Sextus can hardly go as far as Epicurus on this point; for if he were to regard pleasure as a part or the whole of happiness, he would apparently have to regard pleasure as a good, contrary to his argument for suspending judgment about goods (xi 73–4). Epicurus' non-sceptical position also helps him to accumulate greater pleasures; memory and anticipation of conversations with friends (for instance) increases his present pleasure because he believes that these were and will be good aspects of his life. Since Sextus denies himself these pleasures by abandoning belief in goods, he cannot claim Epicurus' support for his assumptions about happiness.

Epicurus also suggests a counter-example to Sextus' view that abandonment of belief will reduce anxiety. The Sceptic suspends judgment on the question of whether death is an evil, but Epicurus suggests (according to Lucretius) that this suspension does not ensure freedom from anxiety. The underlying fear of being dead, even in someone who denies that we survive death, causes us to pursue honour, wealth, power, and other unsatisfying goals, to distract us from our fear of death. Though we may not find this example plausible, it suggests that Sextus is wrong to suppose that fears that are not based on beliefs or on bodily needs cannot cause us severe anxiety and disturbance. If irrational fears persist, we need to find some way to deal with them. Epicurus suggests that we have to take deliberate steps to strengthen our conviction that the fears are irrational and to train ourselves to take pleasures based on rational beliefs. If he is right on this point, Sextus is wrong to suggest that abandonment of belief reduces anxiety and that the formation of belief increases it.

---

[21] See Bett, *AE* 144–5.   [22] See §182; Striker, 'Tranquillity' 185–6.

This comparison with Epicurus suggests that the Epicurean and the Sceptical claims about tranquillity are only superficially similar. Sextus cannot appeal to the agreement of philosophers to support his belief (or assumption, or appearance) that tranquillity is happiness. Hence he gives us no reason to agree that the Sceptic who achieves tranquillity and moderate passion thereby achieves the most complete happiness (M xi 160–1).

Apart from these questions about the disputed character of Sextus' conception of happiness, we might wonder whether he can consistently claim both that he suspends judgment and that he puts forward tranquillity and moderate passion as the end. His position is inconsistent only if he puts forward a belief that tranquillity is good. If it simply appears to him to be good, or to be the end, he can consistently put forward the appearance without committing himself to any belief. On this view, he does not offer a dogmatist a reason for taking tranquillity to be the end; he simply records how things appear to him after he has suspended judgment about goods and abandoned any belief about them.

But why should we predict that the same thing will happen to us as happened to Sextus, so that if we suspend judgment and thereby achieve tranquillity, tranquillity will appear to us to be the end? Perhaps he means that if we lack any conviction about goods, we will have no reason-based desire to change our tranquil state for any other, and hence no motive for forming a negative view of it; therefore we will have a favourable appearance of it. A state we do not want to change for anything else, he might argue, is the one that appears to us as the ultimate end.

In this way, then, we might understand Sextus' remarks about the end so that they do not conflict with his rejection of beliefs about the nature of happiness, along with other beliefs. Aenesidemus is reported to have argued against any dogmatic account of the ultimate end.[23] Sextus can consistently endorse such arguments while recording the appearance that a Sceptic will acquire about happiness and the ultimate end.

But though this position is consistent, it might reasonably turn a dogmatist against Scepticism. If tranquillity appears to the Sceptic to be the whole of happiness, but we believe that happiness is more than tranquillity, we have a reason for wanting to avoid the Sceptic's predicament. If we find the arguments for equipollence irresistible, we may find that we have to suspend judgment, and share the Sceptic's appearance about the end; but if we reject the appearance about the end, we have a reason to avoid the appearance of equipollence if we can. No doubt it is better to be undisturbed than to suffer from painful and pointless anxiety; but the dogmatist has no reason to agree that these are the only possibilities to be considered.

139. Actions without Beliefs?

Sextus has an answer to some of these dogmatic objections if he can show that the Sceptic's life is more attractive than the dogmatist allows. If he is right about this, the Sceptic may not miss much by holding the false—as the dogmatist supposes—appearance that tranquillity is the whole of happiness. Dogmatists argue that the Sceptic who lives by his appearances

---

[23] See Photius, *Bibl.* 170b31–5 = LS 72L(7).

will be both inactive and inconsistent. (1) He will be inactive (they claim) because he will neither choose nor avoid anything. (2) He will be inconsistent, because if a tyrant orders him to do something wrong, he will either refuse to do it and suffer death or agree to do it to avoid torture; in either case he will choose and avoid, contrary to his lacking any belief that something is to be chosen or avoided (M xi 162–4).

These two criticisms may appear inconsistent. Do the dogmatists not admit that (contrary to their first criticism) the Sceptic is active, if they believe that he will do something in response to the tyrant? But they are more consistent than they initially appear. They suggest that the Sceptic will do nothing unless external circumstances force him to; when they force him to act, they reveal that he has some convictions, despite his normal lethargy and lack of commitment. Sometimes he cannot be simply inactive and like a vegetable, because circumstances require him to choose; and then he shows that he has some convictions after all.

These criticisms rely on the 'inaction' (apraxia) argument that both Stoics and Epicureans use to show that the Sceptic is incapable of action if he has no beliefs. The Stoics argue that since the Sceptic refuses to assent to any appearances, and since action is impossible without assent, the Sceptic makes action impossible; they assume, therefore, that every action presupposes assent.[24]

In Sextus' view, the Stoics misunderstand the Sceptic's point in saying that he refuses assent and therefore refuses to form beliefs. He does not refuse assent altogether; for he assents to the passions that are necessitated by appearance (P i 13). But what does Sextus mean by this? The Stoics believe that assent matters because it is up to us; it is our own contribution, not simply an automatic result of the appearances, and it makes our actions voluntary in so far as they depend on our assent. Sextus, however, does not think of assent as being up to us; it is simply a reaction to appearances (i 19), not dependent on our will or on our other beliefs or reasoning. All we assent to, or more precisely 'concede' (sunchôrein, i 20), or 'yield' to (i 193), is that things appear a certain way to us.[25] We yield or concede only in a negative sense, so that if we have an appearance of being warmed we do not say that we believe we are not being warmed or that we are being cooled (i 13). The Sceptic argues that this sort of concession to appearances is sufficient for action. If we adhere to the appearances, we can live a life without belief, following nature, the passions, the customary laws and practices, and the various crafts (i 23–4).

When Sextus claims that he acts on appearances, but not on beliefs, does he draw a tenable distinction? We can see what he means if we recall that the Stoics take assent to be rational in so far as it responds to our conception of the evidence. It is directed to the truth,

---

[24] See Plu. Col. 1122a–d: 'Suspension of judgment about everything was not shaken even by those who worked hard and drew out their treatises and arguments against it. Finally these people brought out the 'inaction' argument like a Gorgon from the Stoa against it, and then stopped .... For action needs two things, the appearance of the suitable, and impulse towards what has appeared suitable, neither of which conflicts with suspension; for the argument for suspension removes us from belief, not from impulse or from appearance. And so whenever something suitable appears, we have no need of belief to be moved and carried off towards it; impulse comes at once, being a movement and carrying off of the soul ....' Cf. Cic. Ac. ii 37–9: '... since this is the greatest difference between an animal and something inanimate, that an animal does something—for an animal doing nothing cannot even be thought of—either we must deny sense to it or we must attribute the assent that is in our power to it .... Therefore, whoever removes either appearance or assent removes all action from life.'

[25] On Stoic views about yielding to appearances see §167.

in so far as we recognize that further evidence bearing on the truth of the appearance would be a ground for changing our assent. If we assent rashly (without having stopped to think) or we yield weakly (to a strongly suggestive appearance), we do not consider the evidence as we should, but we recognize that it is relevant. The Sceptics are right to claim that some appearances are non-doxastic in so far as they are not responsive to consideration of the evidence. Plausible examples are easiest to find among sensory appearances. The stick still looks bent in water even when I firmly believe it is straight. In a less purely sensory case, a snake may look dangerous even when I know it is harmless. If these are the appearances that the Sceptic yields to, Sextus is right to claim that they do not require belief in their truth.[26]

Our contrast between the Stoics and the Sceptics on assent might suggest that the Stoics think action is impossible without the sort of rational assent and reason-based belief that the Sceptic avoids. But this suggestion would not be quite correct. For the Stoic also believes that action is possible without assent. The Sceptic's account of appearance and action fits the Stoic account of the action of non-rational animals and pre-rational children.[27]

Then do the Stoics simply misunderstand the Sceptic when they object that he cannot act without assent and belief? Their objection may be clearer if we distinguish 'action' as goal-directed movement, such as non-rational agents are capable of, from 'action' understood as a peculiar feature of rational agents. Aristotle understands 'action' (*praxis*) in this narrower sense, and the Stoics agree with him.[28] When they say that the Sceptic will be inactive, they do not mean that he will be immobile, or that he will lack goal-directed behaviour. They mean that his goal-directed behaviour will not be rational action.

We might wonder whether this way of understanding the Stoics' point about inaction does not make it uninteresting. It simply seems to repeat the point that the Sceptic abandons rational belief; for rational action differs from other goal-directed behaviour in being based on rational belief. If the Sceptics are told they abandon rational action, they might agree, but answer that this is no objection to them; for rational action depends on the sort of belief that they have found to be groundless.

The Stoics' objection may have more force, however. If some part of the Sceptic's life turns out to depend on the rational beliefs that he says he gives up, his lack of belief excludes even the kind of life that he professes to lead. If, however, he revises his account of the life he leads to match his abandonment of belief, that life may seem less attractive than it seemed when he included elements that have turned out to presuppose rational belief. In that case, we may find that his appearance of tranquillity being the ultimate end results in

[26] This is a controversial claim about the Sceptic's lack of belief. See the papers in Burnyeat and Frede, *OS*; Fine, 'Dogmata'.

[27] See §§166–7. Plutarch attacks the Stoics for pretending in their controversy with the Academic Sceptics that action requires assent, while acknowledging elsewhere that we can act without assent. See, *SR* 1057a: 'And indeed in the contests with the Academics most of the argument of Chrysippus himself and of Antipater is about what? It is about their claim that someone does not act or have impulse without assent and that those are talking fiction and empty assumptions who claim that when the right appearance has occurred we at once are impelled without having yielded or assented. But again Chrysippus says that both the god and the sage produce false appearances, wanting us not to assent or yield, but only to act and be impelled towards what appears, but we, being base, assent to such appearances because of weakness.'

[28] See *EN* 1139a18–20. Alexander, *Fat.* 34, 205.28, represents the Stoics as distinguishing *energein* from *prattein*, which is confined to rational animals (*ta men tôn zô(i)ôn energêsei monon, ta de praxei ta logika*; cf. 206.5, *tois praktikois te kai logikois zô(i)ois*). According to Seneca, *Ep.* 113.18, no rational animal acts except on the basis of assent.

an unattractive life. To see whether this criticism from the Stoic point of view is plausible, we need to look more closely at the sort of life the Sceptic professes to lead.

140. What kind of Life can we live without Beliefs?

The critics object that the Sceptic cannot really live without beliefs, because he must act on a belief when someone compels him to act in a dangerous situation. If the tyrant threatens him with death unless he gives false evidence against an innocent person, will he not act on his belief about which course of action seems better (*M* xi 164)?[29] This case is relevant to the Sceptic's account of his way of life, because it does not seem plausible to explain his action as simply a natural or involuntary response to his natural passions. Aristotle insists that some actions that people choose to do are so bad that no plea of compulsion could excuse us; we might concede that fear compelled someone to hand over his money to a thief, but we would not allow that fear compelled him to kill his mother (*EN* 1110a26–9). In such cases we believe the agent has a choice and that he is responsible for how he chooses.

If we treat Sextus' example as one of these cases, we can see why the dogmatists find his account unsatisfactory. Even if (the objector argues) we concede that the Sceptic can sometimes act on how things appear to him without belief, he cannot explain his action in these critical cases by mere appearance. Since we suppose he is responsible for an important choice that he makes, we also suppose that he acts on some conviction about which action is better. If Scepticism were correct about responding to natural needs, we might suppose that the Sceptic would simply be moved by his natural fear of death, rather than by the purely conventional badness of causing the death of an innocent person. Hence we might expect that the Sceptic would explain his choice by the unconvincing plea of compulsion. But the objector protests that (following Aristotle) we would never accept such a plea in these cases.

Sextus answers this objection (xi 166) by considering the suggestion that a Sceptic always chooses the 'easier' option, which in this case would be the betrayal of an innocent person. We might infer this from the immediate context, in which Sextus suggests that the Sceptic is bothered only by the pains that arise inevitably from nature, and not by any additional belief that he undergoes anything that is really bad (xi 155–9). The natural aversion to death makes the threat of immediate death painful to him, and we might doubt whether the alleged badness of betraying an innocent person could affect him as strongly.

To show that the Sceptic's attitude is more complex than this, Sextus reminds us that his outlook indicates to him a life in accordance with law and custom as well as his natural needs (*P* i 17). The Sceptics' fourfold way of life without belief (*adoxastôs*) includes not only (1) nature and (2) passion, but also (3) law and custom, and (4) the crafts (*P* i 23–4; cf. *M* ix 49). Sextus is right to expand the Sceptic's life in this way; for he mentions natural needs not because he thinks they are really more important than others simply by being natural, but only because he thinks they make a strong impression on us. Hence anything that creates a strong impression makes some difference to the Sceptic's way of life.

---

[29] On the historical basis of Sextus' example see Bett, *AE* 175–6.

Sextus is right to argue that laws, customs, and the practice of a craft can create strong impressions that move us to action. Once I have put my hand on a hot stove, I do not need to be taught not to do it again; the appearance of a hot stove near my hand results in a further appearance of painfulness that causes me to move it away. I need more teaching or habituation to train me not to steal, but if the teaching is successful it will create an aversion to stealing. When I grow up, become a Sceptic, and abandon my beliefs, I abandon my belief that it is wrong to steal; but if my training has succeeded, I retain the appearance of its being wrong and the resulting aversion to stealing. Similarly, if I have been well trained in a craft, I will not even think of using a saw or a drill in the wrong way. Even if I cease to believe there are right and wrong ways to use these tools, it will still appear right to use them one way and I will keep on using them in this way.

This is a plausible case for the Sceptic's claim that we can act on moral principles without believing them. We are familiar with people who feel so guilty about doing something that they have been taught is wrong that, even if they think there is nothing wrong with it, they (as we say) 'cannot bring themselves' to do it; and even if they do it, they still have some of the feelings of disapproval that they would have had if they had believed it was wrong. The Sceptic suggests that this strong appearance of right and wrong underlies his moral outlook and practices, without any belief about right and wrong.

How seriously should we take Sextus' claim that in living by appearances without belief, the Sceptic follows everyday life (P i 23)?[30] If we consider the account of upbringing and training that results in the Sceptic's adherence without belief to accepted norms, we might suppose that this would also be a plausible account of ordinary people's outlook. Most of us (one might argue) do not stop to think about whether we ought to use a knife to spread butter on our bread rather than wipe the bread across the butter, or whether to brake when we come to a red light, or whether to pay for the newspaper we have bought rather than run out of the shop. We do these things because we have been trained to do them; whether the training was difficult or easy, once we have been trained to do them we do not give them a second thought. In this respect, as Aristotle pointed out, habit is like nature (EN 1152a30–3). The dogmatist's suggestion that before we choose to pay for the newspaper we need rational assent to the proposition that it is good to pay for it seems extravagant; it sounds more like a description of a philosopher deciding whether to pay for his newspaper. Deliberation and assent seem unnecessary, and even dangerous. If we really stopped to think about whether to pay for the newspaper, some people might decide, correctly or incorrectly, that it is better to go out without paying. If we tried to conform to the dogmatist's description of us, the results would be unwelcome.

This defence of the Sceptic's conception of ordinary life goes beyond the claim that it is empirically possible for there to be some strange people who act without belief. It defends the Sceptics by saying that acting without belief is perfectly familiar to us, because we do it all the time. The strange people are not the ones who live without beliefs, but the ones whose thoughts and actions fit the dogmatists' description.

---

[30] Cf. ii 102, 246. Bett, AE 175, adds further references and discussions. He probably takes Sextus' claim less seriously than it deserves to be taken (in 'it is not clear to me that he loses anything significant by giving it up').

141. Scepticism, Belief, and Deliberation: Sextus, Hobbes, and Hume

Our defence of Sextus' claim that the Sceptic lives an ordinary life introduces us to an important adaptation of Scepticism for a non-sceptical purpose. If Sextus' description of a life without belief describes the life of ordinary people, we may wonder whether the Sceptic has not conceded too much to the dogmatist. Verbally, the Sceptic differs from ordinary people, because ordinary people say 'I think it's going to rain', and explain their action by saying 'I thought it would be wrong'. Sextus concedes that the dogmatists are right in taking these remarks to express belief and assent, as the dogmatists understand them. That is why he says the Sceptic lives without belief. But why should he not disagree with the dogmatists at an earlier stage, and deny that belief involves rational assent? Why not simply say that belief is nothing more than the Sceptic allows himself—a strong appearance resulting from the senses, passions, upbringing, or training?

This is approximately Hume's account of belief.[31] In his view, the difference between simply entertaining a proposition and believing it consists in the degree of vividness with which you entertain it; it is an introspectible property of the idea itself. Contrary to Stoic claims about assent, belief does not involve responsiveness to evidence or reasons. It is very similar, therefore, to the sort of appearance that the Sceptic yields to when he has given up belief. Hume follows Hobbes in using Sceptical attempts to replace dogmatic notions of belief, desire, and choice as the basis for an analysis of these mental states. Whereas Sextus rejects belief, Hobbes and Hume accept it, but they analyse it in terms that fit Sextus' substitute for it. Though their account of mental states connected with belief and action appears to be non-Sceptical, it really agrees with the Sceptics' main point.[32]

Once we grasp the similarity between Hume's account of belief and Sextus' account of appearance, we can estimate how far Hume disagrees with Sextus about the effects of Sceptical argument. According to Sextus, Sceptical argument causes us to give up our beliefs and to live without belief. According to Hume, however, sceptical argument refutes our beliefs by showing that they are false,[33] but it cannot permanently cause us to give them up. Since we cannot live without belief, we have to discard our sceptical doubts when we have to live, though we admit that sceptical argument has shown that our beliefs are unjustified.[34]

---

[31] 'We may here take this occasion to observe a very remarkable error, which being frequently inculcated in the schools, has become a kind of established maxim... This error consists in the vulgar division of the acts of the understanding, into conception, judgment, and reasoning... This act of the mind [sc. judgment] has never yet been explained by any philosopher; and therefore I am at liberty to propose my hypothesis concerning it; which is that it is only a strong and steady conception of any idea, and such as approaches in some measure to an immediate impression' (Hume, *T* i 3.7 §5n).

[32] For Hobbes's view see *L* 6.53.

[33] 'Accordingly we find that all the conclusions which the vulgar form on this head are directly contrary to those which are confirmed by philosophy. For philosophy informs us that every thing which appears to the mind is nothing but a perception and is interrupted, and dependent on the mind; whereas the vulgar confound perceptions and objects, and attribute a distinct continued existence to the very things they feel or see' (*T* i 4.2 §14).

[34] 'But a Pyrrhonian cannot expect, that his philosophy will have any constant influence on the mind: or if it had, that its influence would be beneficial to society. On the contrary, he must acknowledge, if he will acknowledge anything, that all human life must perish were his principles universally and steadily to prevail.... It is true; so fatal an event is very little to be dreaded. Nature is always too strong for principle' (*IHU* 12 §23). 'Most fortunately it happens, that since

These reactions to scepticism might lead us to suppose that Hume believes that scepticism leads to inaction. He accepts the dogmatists' view that, contrary to Sextus, we cannot live without belief. But the difference from Sextus is smaller than it seems. For the belief that Hume takes to be necessary for action is belief as he understands it, which is simply the Sceptic's vivid appearance. Hume supposes that in living by appearances we live as ordinary people live. He argues that the attempt to find a rational basis for moral beliefs is a philosophical undertaking whose failure makes no difference to the ordinary way we hold our beliefs. Just as our belief that the sun will rise tomorrow is undisturbed even when we see that it lacks rational justification, our moral sentiments are unaffected even when we see that they lack rational foundation.

Once we see this basic agreement in substance between Sextus and Hume on appearance, belief, and action, we may reasonably question an initially attractive and apparently significant contrast that some critics have drawn between ancient Scepticism and modern scepticism, in Humean and other varieties. Ancient Scepticism seems to have a practical aim, since it expects that we will live without belief, abandoning any moral beliefs (as well as other beliefs) that we might have previously formed. Modern scepticism, however, seems to be purely theoretical, and insulated from any practical effects on 'first-order' moral beliefs and practices.[35]

The formulation of this contrast is itself obscure, since the notion of the 'first-order' is often taken for granted without adequate explanation.[36] But even if we grant that we roughly understand the contrast, it does not seem completely appropriate. Sextus claims to live an everyday life because he lives by appearances; hence he does not behave differently from ordinary people. Hume claims not to disturb moral practice because he believes it involves living by appearances rather than rational convictions. If we believe Sextus undermines practice because ordinary people live by rational conviction, we must say the same about Humean scepticism. If, however, we accept Hume's reasons for saying he does not disturb moral practice, we must grant that Sextus does not disturb it either. The practical implications of each form of scepticism seem equally large or small. Hume argues that Sextus ought not to have agreed with the dogmatists about the nature of belief; hence he defends Sextus' claim that the Sceptic does not disturb ordinary life, and so he defends the substance of the Sceptical position without the appearance of paradox.

142. Do we Need Beliefs?

Now that we have tried to give a sympathetic defence and expansion of Sextus' claim that the Sceptic lives an everyday life, we may return to the question that was raised about

reason is incapable of dispelling these clouds, nature herself suffices to that purpose, and cures me of this philosophical melancholy and delirium . . .' (T i 4.7 §9).

[35] See Burnyeat, 'Can the sceptic?' (on living without belief); 'Time and place' 111–23 (attributing the origin of 'insulation' of theoretical questions from ordinary life to Kant); Annas, 'Values' 216–19; LS i 460. For a more plausible comparison between ancient and modern scepticism see Price, RPQM 53–6.

[36] Mackie, E 19, mentions 'the well-known and generally recognized difference between first and second order questions'. Both Burnyeat and Annas refer to him. But it is difficult to explain this distinction satisfactorily, and even more difficult to align it with the distinction between views that do, and views that do not, have practical effects.

the tyrant threatening us with death unless we do something wrong. Sextus answers that the Sceptic may well (*tuchon*) refuse to do the wrong action even if he pays with his life.[37] Nothing about the Sceptic's way of life excludes the possibility that his aversion from acting wrongly will be strong enough to move him to accept death in order to avoid the wrong action. If Aristotle is right about habituation, ordinary moral training and social pressure may result in its appearing 'unthinkable' to the Sceptic to act wrongly in such a case.

Sextus does not say that the Sceptic will make the morally right choice in this situation, but only that he may make it. He may equally choose to preserve his life at the price of acting wrongly, if his aversion to death is stronger than his aversion to wrong action. What he will choose depends especially on his own history and social environment. From Hume's point of view, this is simply a fact that has to be faced; we cannot form moral convictions that are immune to these sorts of influences, but we can try to make sure that they result from the sorts of influences that we approve of.

Does this show that Sextus' description of stronger and weaker appearances captures the moral outlook of everyday life? To see what he might be missing, we may refer to Kant's treatment of a rather similar example (*KpV* 30).[38] Kant contrasts a case where the cost of satisfying our lust is death with a case where the cost of doing what we believe to be right is death. In the first case our choice depends on which desire is stronger, but in the second it depends on what choice we think is better. In the second case (as Butler puts it), we act on the basis of authority, on the merits of different courses of action, and not simply on the basis of strength. Butler believes that 'nothing can be reduced to a greater absurdity' than the denial of any difference between strength and authority.[39]

Sextus accepts the view that Butler criticizes as absurd. What is absurd about it? To see Butler's point, we may ask what determines the strength of one or the other of the Sceptic's appearances. It is fairly easy to see the differences between the two situations that Kant describes. In one of them we simply recognize desires of different strength. In the other the strength of our desire depends on our view of the merits of the proposed course of action; reflexion on these merits changes the strength of our desire. If further reflexion convinced us that there is nothing wrong with what the tyrant is pressing us to do, we might decide to do it, even if we still found it repugnant. Our view about the merits of the action affects both how strongly we want to do it, and what it would take to change our mind about doing it. While there may be cases in which we cannot bring ourselves to do something even after we have convinced ourselves that nothing is wrong with it, most cases in which we refuse to do something wrong are not like this.

Ordinary life, therefore, contains rational resources for altering the strength of our appearances and impulses. If Sextus is right about how the Sceptic lives, he lacks these resources. Therefore the Sceptic does not live an ordinary life. The Stoics are entitled to object that the Sceptic rules out action, if action is understood as the type of goal-directed

---

[37] 'When he is being compelled by a tyrant to do something forbidden, it may happen that because of a preconception in accordance with ancestral laws and with customs he will choose the one and avoid the other; and he will certainly bear the discomfort more easily in comparison with the dogmatist, because he holds no belief in addition to this <discomfort>, as the dogmatist does' (M xi 166).

[38] See Kant, *KpV* 30.   [39] See Butler, *S* ii 17.

movement that is characteristic of a rational agent. A life without these resources for determining the strength of our impulses and desires would not be a human life. The fact that the Sceptic lacks these resources is a reason for thinking that something has gone wrong for us if we find ourselves living a life without belief, and hence it is a reason for thinking that something must have gone wrong with the arguments that lead to suspension of judgment.

11

EPICURUS

143. Epicurus' Aims

Epicurus' theoretical and practical aims seem impressively unified. He defends the atomism of Democritus, and argues that Democritean hedonism fits this general view of the world. On the one hand, the empiricist epistemology that supports atomism also supports hedonism. On the other hand, the atomist view of the world, with its denial of life after death, secures peace of mind and freedom from anxiety, and so ought to be adopted on hedonist grounds.

Closer inspection, however, shows that some of Epicurus' leading aims are not derived from Democritus, and that some questions can be raised about whether they fit his defence of atomism. Democritus defends atomism by taking a sceptical attitude to the capacity of the senses to tell us about an external world. The Cyrenaics agree with this scepticism about the senses, but deny that rational argument independent of the senses can justify a non-sceptical conclusion; hence they remain sceptics. Epicurus believes that reliance on the senses justifies a non-sceptical conclusion about the external world and acceptance of the atomic theory; we do not need to abandon empiricism for rationalism in order to accept atomism.

Equally he believes that hedonism supports eudaemonism and the recognized virtues. He defends the hedonism of Democritus, and rejects the anti-hedonist arguments of two lines in the Socratic tradition—the Platonic-Aristotelian and the Cynic. In accepting hedonism he agrees with Aristippus. But he departs from the Cyrenaic solution in rejecting the aspects of Aristippean hedonism that lead to a way of life far different from the recognized moral virtues.[1] He denies the Cyrenaic view that a defence of hedonism conflicts with ordinary beliefs about the value of happiness and the rationality of the moral virtues.

His position is closer, therefore, to the hedonism of Socrates in the *Protagoras* than to Cyrenaic hedonism. Aristippus could be said to take Socratic hedonism seriously and to reject Socrates' defence of common morality. Both Plato and the Cynics agree with Aristippus, in so far as they think hedonism and the moral virtues are incompatible. Epicurus challenges this point on which his opponents all agree; here he may be a more authentic Socratic than

---

[1] On Epicurus and the Cyrenaics see U 450–3, Arr. 127–9 (referring to a work of Aristippus on Plato).

the others.[2] Both in epistemology and in ethics, therefore, he rejects the conclusions that the Cyrenaics draw from their initial reliance on the senses.

This defence of the senses and of hedonism suggests a possible line of criticism. Plutarch attacks Colotes the Epicurean for attacking Cyrenaic doctrines to which the Epicureans are also committed.[3] Though Epicurus thinks he can accept the veracity of the senses without having to fall into Cyrenaic sceptical extremes, he concedes the crucial points (according to Plutarch) to the Cyrenaics. Though Plutarch is not on the whole a fair or discerning critic, this particular criticism raises worthwhile questions about Epicurean epistemology, and about the basis of Epicurean moral theory.

Though Epicurus is primarily a hedonist, some of his ethical principles try to absorb plausible views that some people take to conflict with hedonism. Both the Cyrenaics and the Cynics reject the hedonism of the *Protagoras*, on grounds that emerge from the criticisms in the *Gorgias*. Whereas the Cyrenaics formulate a more extreme version of hedonism, the Cynics reject hedonism in favour of an adaptive conception of happiness. Epicurus attacks the Cynics as 'enemies of Greece'.[4] In contrast to Stoic sympathy towards Cynicism, he insists that the sage will not act like a Cynic (DL × 119). None the less his ethical position agrees on some central points with the Cynics against the Cyrenaics. He agrees with their view that happiness depends on adapting one's desires to circumstances rather than in the accumulation of the most intense sensations of pleasure. Epicurean sages, no less than Cynic sages, are independent of external conditions and can find their happiness in conditions that are in their power.

Epicurus was not the only one to try to combine Cynic self-sufficiency with hedonism. Though Antisthenes rejected pleasure altogether, one might deny that Cynicism requires such hostility to pleasure. It would not be unreasonable to interpret the Cynic as enjoying a way of life that leaves him content with what he has and free of disturbance and anxiety about external goods. This combination of Cynicism and hedonism appealed to later Cynics, and may have influenced their interpretation of Democritus. Epicurus' partial sympathy with Cynicism, therefore, is not as surprising as it might seem if we considered only the opposition between the Cyrenaics and Cynics.[5]

Epicurus' sympathy with Cynic freedom and self-sufficiency helps to explain the urgency of his concern with freedom and determinism. This concern is connected to, though not the same as, the Cynic attitude. Epicurus puts forward his ethical views to show that it is in our power to do something about the direction of our lives. We do not have to live with all the anxieties that (in his view) result from our basic anxiety about death, but it is up to us to change our direction and our attitude by accepting the Epicurean outlook. For this reason it is important to show that our actions are really in our power, and that arguments for the version of determinism that excludes freedom ('hard' determinism)[6] are unsound.

---

[2] The only explicit reference to Socrates in Epicurus is Arr. 10.2 (p. 164). Other evidence: Plu. *Col.* 1086e = U 237; 1118cd = U 314; Cic. *Br.* 292 = U 231. On Epicurean attitudes to Socrates cf. Cic. *ND* i 93; Obbink, *PP* i 379–80.

[3] 'The arguments that Colotes finds welcome and agreeable in the writings of Epicurus he neither understands nor recognizes when he finds them put forward by other people' (*Col.* 1121a).

[4] DL × 8. The reference to the Cynics, however, depends on an emendation.

[5] On Cynicism and pleasure see §36. On the Cynic interpretation of Democritus see Stewart, 'Cynics', esp. 185. He traces the absorption of hedonism into Cynicism to Bion of Borysthenes, on whom see Kindstrand, *BB* 58–70 (who argues that the early Cynics are not opponents of pleasure).

[6] See §147 below.

This outline of Epicurus' aims suggests a question. The Cyrenaics raise some serious diffi-culties for the hedonist eudaemonism that both Democritus and Socrates (in the *Protagoras*) accept. Epicurus' revival of hedonist eudaemonism has been historically influential; later hedonists have defended something closer to his version of hedonism than to the Cyrenaic version. But does he give good reasons for a hedonist to reject the Cyrenaic doubts about eudaemonism?[7]

144. Hedonism

Epicurus defends his hedonism in two ways: (1) He thinks his empiricist epistemology guarantees that pleasure is the end.[8] (2) But he also claims to prove his point by dialectical argument from ordinary beliefs.[9] First, Epicurus appeals to the evidence of the senses, to show that the pursuit of pleasure as the end is natural and inevitable. Then he recognizes that not everyone is a hedonist, and he offers to explain how the errors of non-hedonists might arise, 'so that you may see clearly the origin of this mistake of people who reject pleasure and praise pain' (Cic. *F* i 32). Rather than relying simply on the senses, Epicurus claims that a 'preconception' about pleasure underlies our beliefs about the good.[10]

Our view on the plausibility of Epicurus' hedonist position depends on what we think of these two lines of argument. Even if they are both reasonable, it is a further question whether they are arguments for the same conclusion.

The epistemological argument for hedonism expresses Epicurus' view that our sensations of pleasure are the analogue to sensory perceptions, which he takes to be invariably true (DL × 146–7). While Epicurus agrees with Aristotle in pursuing ethical inquiry, and other sorts of inquiry, from 'appearances', he has a different view of what the relevant appearances are. Those that Aristotle appeals to include common beliefs and reflective judgments, not simply the immediate impressions of the senses. But Epicurus believes, for anti-sceptical epistemological reasons (DL × 146), that immediate impressions are the only appropriate source of evidence.

Hence he agrees with Aristippus' view that sensations (or 'affections', *pathê*) are immediate and irrefutable. But he thinks he can maintain this while avoiding Cyrenaic scepticism about the existence of external objects. According to the Cyrenaics, the senses give us conflicting appearances about, for instance, the shape of a stick, since they make it look bent when we see it under water and straight when we see it out of water. We might suppose that we have to reject one of these appearances as false; if the stick is straight, the appearance of its being bent seems to be false. Epicurus disagrees. He argues that the stick sometimes emits atoms that make a bent shape (when it is in water) and sometimes emits atoms that make a straight shape. We need not reject the appearance of the bent stick, if we avoid the rash

---

[7] Long, 'Legacy' 633 , comments on Cyrenaic and Epicurean hedonism: '. . . Epicurus' version won out, as it deserved to do. By the middle of the third century BC Cyrenaic philosophy was obsolete.'

[8] On the sensory basis of Epicurus' claims about pleasure see Gosling and Taylor, *GP* 347–8.

[9] The difference between the two lines of argument appears in Cic. *F* i 30–42.

[10] Cic. *F* i 31 'quasi naturalem atque insitam . . . notionem' refers to a preconception (*prolêpsis*). Cf. DL × 33; LS i 88–9. On Stoic appeals to preconceptions see §165.

prediction that the stick will usually appear bent. Both the bent and the straight appearances are correct; but we need to distinguish the relatively permanent features of external objects from those that they take on in particular situations (Sx. *M* vii 208–9).[11]

Just as we follow the senses as guides to reality, so also we should follow our sensory affections as guides to the good.[12] Animals and children show us the natural tendency of our affections, before they are overlaid by misguided conventional beliefs about good and evil.[13] If we attend to our affections, we recognize pleasure as the primary good, since it is the basis of all our natural conceptions of goodness, and as the ultimate good, since we aim at it in all our actions.[14]

In beliefs about the external world Epicurus argues that we do not reject our appearance of the bent stick, but we rely on our appearance of the straight stick in our predictions about how the stick will appear in the future; we do not reject the senses, but avoid rash inferences from sensory appearances. Similarly, we do not reject our sensory appearance that every pleasure is good, but neither do we rashly infer that every pleasure is to be chosen. Nor do we choose on the basis of something other than pleasure. We choose those actions that reliably offer pleasure over time, just as we rely on the sensory appearances that reliably inform us about the appearance of the stick over time. Our selective attitude towards pleasures does not conflict with hedonism; on the contrary, it follows from our initial appearance that pleasure is the good.[15] If we look for what is reliably pleasant over time, we see that we need the 'measuring science' of the *Protagoras*.[16]

145. Epicurean Eudaemonism v. Cyrenaic Hedonism

In these claims about pleasure and the good Epicurus both accepts the Cyrenaic starting point in sensory affections and argues that, without going beyond these affections, we can justify a selective attitude to pains and pleasures. This selective attitude aims at achieving greater pleasure than pain over time; it puts forward happiness over one's life, rather than immediate pleasure, as the ultimate good. Does Epicurus give a good reason for disagreeing with the Cyrenaics on this point?

It is helpful to consider his parallel argument about the senses and external objects, which claims to overcome Cyrenaic scepticism about objects. According to Epicurus, we can justify complete confidence in the senses if we accept the atomic theory and its account

---

[11] On Epicurus' views on the criterion, and on pleasure as a criterion see Gosling and Taylor, *GP* 397–407.

[12] For Stoic criticism of this conception of desire and pleasure see §166.

[13] 'He employs as proof of pleasure's being the end the fact that animals as soon as they are born delight in pleasure but repel (or 'collide with') trouble, naturally and apart from reason. Hence we avoid pain purely affectively (*autopathôs*)' (DL × 137). On appeals to pre-rational experience by Epicureans and others see Brunschwig, 'Cradle'.

[14] 'Hence we call pleasure the origin and goal (*archên kai telos*) of living blessedly. For we know this as our first and congenital good; from this all our choice and aversion has its origin, and we refer to this, discriminating every good by using affection as the standard' (DL × 128–9).

[15] 'And since this [sc. pleasure] is the first and connatural good, because of this we also do not choose every pleasure, but sometimes we pass over many pleasures, whenever the discomfort that follows from them is more; and we take many pains to be greater than pleasures, whenever greater pleasure follows for us after we have withstood the pains for a long time' (DL × 129).

[16] 'But by commensuration and by looking at things advantageous and disadvantageous it is appropriate to discriminate all these things' (DL × 130). Cf. Eusebius, *PE* xiv 21 (769a); Seneca, *De otio* 7.3 (both at U 442).

of perception; for the theory tells us that the stick produces a bent atomic configuration when it is in water and a straight one when it is out of water. Since it is usually out of water, we think it is straight, because it usually produces a straight atomic configuration. This atomic explanation helps us to see why our appearance of the stick as bent is true, as far as it goes.

This explanation does not answer Cyrenaic scepticism. For the Cyrenaics argue that, on the basis of sensory affection alone, we cannot justifiably believe in external objects. Epicurus does not show how his atomic theory could be accepted on the evidential basis that the Cyrenaics accept. To believe in objects composed of atoms emitting atomic configurations from their surfaces, we cannot appeal simply to the evidence of our sensory affections.

Epicurus' hedonist eudaemonism vindicates our sensory appearance of every pleasure being good. This appearance is correct, since every pleasure in its own right is good. Contrary to Plato and Aristotle, no pleasure is bad in its own right by being taken in an inappropriate object.[17] In deciding to forgo some pleasures, we do not rely on some end other than pleasure; we consider only what will produce most pleasure on the whole.

This eudaemonism does not answer the Cyrenaic appeal to sensory affections. For Epicurus does not explain why the fact that our affections endorse pleasure justifies us in treating maximum long-term pleasure as the end. The eudaemonist outlook does not seem to rest on affections.

Epicurus exposes this difficulty by appealing, as the Cyrenaics do, to the affections of non-rational animals and of children. These are appropriate witnesses because they give us access to our affections before reasoning and conventional beliefs are superimposed on them. We may grant, for present purposes, that these creatures pursue pleasure as good.[18] But they do not agree with Epicurus in postponing pleasure and accepting pain for the sake of greater long-term pleasure. The capacity to look ahead and to measure pleasures against pains seems to result from some degree of maturity and rationality that non-rational animals and children do not display.

Should Epicurus abandon the appeal to animals and children and the claim that he rests his account of the ultimate good on an appeal to sensory affections? Perhaps the appeal to the senses is a survival of Cyrenaic doctrine that he ought to have abandoned together with the Cyrenaic conception of the end. Would he not be better off if he frankly claimed to rely on reason rather than simply on primitive sensory affections? He might claim that the belief that pleasure is happiness is a basic preconception in our ethical outlook. No doubt it is based on experiences of pleasure as good, but it explains and supports these experiences in the light of a rational eudaemonist principle that goes beyond sensory affections.

This further departure from the Cyrenaics would have several benefits for Epicurus, but it would also have a severe cost. Since he relies on sensory affections to show that pleasure is the only good, he accepts Cyrenaic epistemological assumptions. But if we once agree that rational reflexion on our affections in the light of our life as a whole is needed to support hedonist eudaemonism, why not argue that the same rational reflexion reveals further goods besides pleasure? If Epicurus goes beyond the Cyrenaic epistemological basis, he leaves himself open to this Platonic and Aristotelian argument. Cicero has a good reason,

---

[17] Cf. Plato, *Phil.* 12c6–13b5; Aristotle, *EN* 1173b20–31.   [18] For Stoic views on animals and children see §166.

therefore, to conclude that the Cyrenaics draw out the consequences of hedonism more consistently than Epicurus does.[19]

But even if we reject Epicurus' attempt to defend hedonist eudaemonism by appeal to sensory affections, we may still believe his position is defensible on a different epistemological basis. He might argue for hedonism as an account of happiness by appeal to ordinary convictions—Aristotelian common beliefs—about good and evil. Platonic and Aristotelian arguments convince the Cyrenaics that common ethical beliefs rule out hedonism; that is why they look for an epistemological basis independent of common beliefs. Epicurus might try to show that the Cyrenaics concede a point too easily to Plato and Aristotle, and that enlightened hedonist principles explain common beliefs. This is Mill's, as opposed to Bentham's, defence of hedonism.[20]

This approach to Epicurus deserves discussion. It certainly captures some of his arguments about pleasure and good. Moreover, even if it does not wholly capture Epicurus' position, it may be a plausible defence of some of his ethical views, freed from the epistemological basis on which he rests them.

146. Why Freedom Matters

Epicurus' emphasis on happiness, in opposition to the Cyrenaic emphasis on immediate pleasure, expresses a broader aim of his ethical theory. It is intended to give us a prescription for intervening in our lives and modifying them by deliberate action so that we do not drift along with conventional views about goods, and so deprive ourselves of happiness. Epicurus agrees with the Cynics in claiming that it is up to us to live as we choose and that we can affect our lives by deliberate decision and action.

As far as we know, the Cynics do not concern themselves with the metaphysical implications of these claims, since they do not concern themselves with the non-ethical aspects of philosophy. But Aristotle points out some of the implications of our assumptions about agency and freedom; they presuppose that, as he puts it, it is up to us whether we have vicious or virtuous characters. In *EN* iii 5 Aristotle defends this claim.[21] But his defence may seem unsatisfactory. He may be taken to argue that we are responsible for our state of character because we are responsible for the actions that form it. But our actions depend on our appearance of the good; and does that not depend on our character? If we say that it does not depend on our character, but on how we were before we had formed a state of character, we seem to go back to our childhood, when we seem to be less, rather than more, in control of our lives than when we are adults.

If, then, we can trace our actions and characters back to our childhood, we can surely trace them back further to the external influences of heredity and environment, and so to

---

[19] 'He [sc. Epicurus] supports most strongly what nature itself, as he says, lays down and approves, namely pleasure and pain. To these he refers everything we pursue and everything we avoid. But though Aristippus and the Cyrenaics defend this better and more openly (liberius), still I judge them to be such that nothing appears more unworthy of a human being' (Cic. *F* i 23). 'For who is worthy of the name of human being who would want to spend one whole day in this sort of pleasure? The Cyrenaics, indeed, do not shrink from this; your friends [sc. the Epicureans] act more respectably, but perhaps the Cyrenaics act more consistently' (Cic. *F* ii 114).

[20] See Mill, *U*, ch. 2.   [21] See §91.

causes external to ourselves and our choices. If these external influences determine all our later states and actions, how can our actions be in our control?

This helps to explain why Epicurus believes that determinism excludes freedom and responsibility for our character and action; he says it would be better to believe in the gods of popular mythology than to believe in the 'fate' accepted by philosophers (DL × 134), since determinism leaves us without hope of free action to shape our lives. In speaking of the philosophers who hold a doctrine of fate Epicurus probably has Stoic determinism in mind. But his opponents are not confined to the Stoics. The early atomists accept a determinist version of atomism, holding that everything happens by necessity.[22] Just as Epicurus tries to answer Democritus' sceptical attitude to the senses without rejecting atomism, he tries to show that atomism does not require determinism.

147. Why we should Reject Compatibilism

These objections to the doctrine of fate assume that determinism is necessarily hard determinism, because the incompatibilist is right to claim that determinism excludes responsibility. Aristotle does not discuss incompatibilism. Nor does Epicurus explain why he believes it. But we can gather his reasons from his emphasis on necessity and on the past. Aristotle believes that an action is up to us in so far as the origin (or 'principle', *archê*) is in us, or we ourselves are the origin. But if determinism is true, how can the origin be in us?

To show that determinism excludes an origin in us, Epicurus assumes that the origin of my action is the earliest event whose occurrence is sufficient for my action. If we express this kind of sufficiency as a Philonic truth-functional conditional, so that if the origin happens, my action happens, the relation of sufficiency is transitive; if an earlier event is sufficient for a later event, it is also sufficient for all the events for which the later event is sufficient.[23] Now if determinism is true, we can trace a series of sufficient conditions back in time from my action to the event sufficient for it, to the event sufficient for that event, and so on, until we reach the distant past. In one of the Stoics' examples, the action of felling the oak on Mount Pelion is sufficient, in a deterministic universe, for Medea's killing of her children.[24] But if a sufficient condition for my action occurs in the distant past, that is also where we must find the origin of my action. Hence the origin of my action is outside me, and Aristotle is wrong to claim that the origin of my action is in me.

The same reasoning from determinism helps to explain why Aristotle is wrong, in a deterministic universe, to claim that what I do is up to me and in my power. Epicurus assumes that if an action is up to me to do, it is possible for me to do it and not to do it. But if external causes are sufficient for my action, they necessitate the action. Hence it is necessary, given the past external causes, that I do what I do, and hence it is not possible for me not to do it. Since it is not up to me, I am not responsible for it.

---

[22] 'Leucippus says that everything happens by necessity, and that necessity is the same as fate. For he says in *On Mind*: 'Nothing happens at random, but everything happens for a reason and by necessity'. (Stob. i 72.11–14 = DK 67 B 2).

[23] On conditionals see, e.g., Sx. *M* viii 112–17; Mates, *SL* 42–51.   [24] See §169.

148. Why we should Reject Determinism

Epicurus believes that this argument refutes the 'soft determinist' position of the Stoics (the combination of determinism and compatibilism). But it does not refute hard determinism (determinism plus incompatiblism, implying the denial of freedom). He is convinced, however, that we should abandon determinism, in order to maintain freedom.

He rejects determinism not only because it conflicts with his ethical views, but also because he believes that it is self-undermining even apart from ethics. He considers an opponent who says we do nothing by our own agency, because the causes of our actions are in the distant past. Epicurus now applies this thesis to our beliefs. If we ourselves are not the causes of our beliefs, but the causes are in the distant past, we do not hold our beliefs for any reasons; for to hold beliefs for reasons is to be caused to hold them by these reasons. Nor can we ever even have good reasons for believing anything; for good reasons are considerations that could cause us to believe, but there are no such things if the causes of our actions are in the distant past. If, then, someone's belief that all our actions have causes in the distant past is true, he does not hold it for a good reason and there is no good reason to hold it.[25]

If the causal claim about reasons is true, this argument shows that if we denied that our mental states and our recognition of reasons really cause our actions, our denial would undermine its own credibility (though not necessarily its truth). Moreover, Epicurus is right to suppose that our beliefs about responsibility rely on the belief that we ourselves, through our recognition of reasons guiding our choices, cause our actions. If we denied that, we would imply not only that we are never responsible, but also that we never believe things for a reason. Epicurus may be right to suggest that Democritus had denied, on the basis of determinism, that we cause our actions and beliefs, and had thereby undermined his argument.[26]

Epicurus supposes that all determinists deny, whether they recognize it or not, that we cause our own actions, because they claim that actions have sufficient conditions in the distant past. Hence he believes that his argument about self-undermining applies to determinism.

The doctrine of causation that he relies on is open to question. His assumption that the origin of an action is its earliest sufficient condition supports both his argument for incompatibilism and his argument to show that determinism undermines itself. But a compatibilist has no reason to accept this assumption. Aristotle does not accept it; his

---

[25] 'We rebuke, oppose, and reform one another on the assumption that we have the cause in ourselves also, not merely in our initial constitution and in the random necessity of things that surround and enter us. For suppose that someone were to claim that rebuking and being rebuked themselves have the very same random necessity of whatever happens to be present to oneself at a time. . . . still, he would be leaving intact this very behaviour that, in our own case, produces the preconception of the cause. . . . And even if he goes on to infinity saying that this action of his is in turn necessitated, always appealing to arguments, he does not draw the further conclusion [??] that he still leaves in himself the cause of having argued correctly, and in his opponent the cause of having argued incorrectly. . . .' (*On nature* = Arr. 34.27 − 30 = LS 20 C.2–12) This argument is preserved in a fragmentary condition, and the text depends on conjecture (it is especially uncertain at ?? above).

[26] 'The first men to give a satisfactory account of causes were not only much greater than their predecessors, but also many times greater than their successors. And yet—even though in many things they had relieved us from great evils—they overlooked themselves <in looking for causes>, so as to make necessity and the random the causes of everything. Indeed, the account expounding this view collapsed, when the great man [sc. Democritus] overlooked the conflict between his actions and his belief' (*On Nature* = Arr. 34.30 = LS 20 C.13–14)

claim that each of his 'four causes' is an origin would be false if he accepted it.[27] Nor do the Stoics accept it; they argue against it by presenting a fuller account of causes and their mutual relations.[28] If we reject Epicurus' assumption, we should reject both his argument for incompatibilism and his argument to show that determinism undermines itself.

149. Epicurus' Indeterminism

Since Epicurus has argued against compatibilism and determinism, and accepts freedom and responsibility, he endorses indeterminism.[29] He secures the falsity of determinism by arguing that our atoms swerve indeterministically, and that therefore our choice and action are undetermined. Since the swerve breaks the deterministic sequence, the origin of my action is in me and nowhere else. The process of thought and deliberation leading to choice is indeterministic; previous events, including my previous choices, are not sufficient conditions for my choices.[30]

We might well wonder whether Epicurus' cure is worse than the disease. The introduction of uncaused changes seems to imply that my character and my previous choices have no regular and reliable casual connexions to my current deliberation and choice. But we seem to appeal to such connexions in any plausible claims about responsibility and the appropriateness of praise or blame.[31]

This is a reasonable objection to Epicurus' solution, but it does not answer the main point of his argument. Even if the atomic swerve is not the best way to secure indeterminism, we have to accept some version of indeterminism if we both believe in freedom and agree with his arguments against compatibilism and determinism.[32] Alexander defends an indeterminist account of Aristotle without appeal to any swerve; he accepts Epicurean arguments against determinism, believing that Aristotle's arguments against the compatibility of universal necessity and responsibility also demonstrate the incompatibility of determinism with

---

[27] See *Physics* ii 3.   [28] See §169.

[29] This combination of indeterminism and belief in freedom is often called 'libertarianism'—misleadingly, since compatibilists may also believe in liberty.

[30] The atomic swerve is not mentioned in the extant works of Epicurus. The clearest evidence comes from Lucretius and Cicero: '. . . what is the source of this free will for living things all over the earth? What is the source, I ask, of this will wrested from fate, this will through which we move forward wherever our pleasure leads each one of us, and, similarly, through which we swerve in our motions, neither at a fixed time nor at a fixed place, but just where our mind has carried us? For certainly a person's own will gives him a start for this movement, . . . But that the mind itself has no internal necessity in all it does, and is not forced, like a passive victim, to bear and undergo—this results from the tiny swerve of the elements, at no fixed place and at no fixed time' (Lucr. ii 256–93) 'Epicurus thinks that the necessity of fate is avoided by the swerve of an atom . . . He is forced to concede, by the facts themselves if not by his words, that this swerve happens without a cause. . . . Epicurus introduced this line of reasoning because he was afraid that if an atom always moved by natural and necessary weight, nothing would be free for us, since the mind would be moved in such a way that it would be compelled by the motion of atoms' (Cic. *Fat.* 22–3). The sources do not make it clear how often in a person's lifetime a swerve is supposed to happen, or exactly when it happens in the sequence of events that results in a voluntary action. See LS i 110–12; Furley, *TSGA* 232–6.

[31] See Hume, *IHU* 8 §§26–8.

[32] 'Carneades spoke more acutely, in teaching that the Epicureans could defend their view without this imaginary swerve. For since Epicurus taught that there could be some voluntary movement of the mind, it would have been better to defend that than to introduce the swerve, especially given that they cannot find a cause for it' (Cic. *Fat.* 23).

responsibility. This is the point of contention between the Stoic defence of compatibilism and Alexander's indeterminist defence of Aristotle.[33]

150. Indeterminism and Epicurus' Ethical Theory

If Epicurus' version of indeterminism is reasonable, he has removed an objection to his conviction that our choices and actions are up to us, and that we can change our character and outlook by deliberate action. But the truth of indeterminism does not vindicate his conviction. If indeterminism is true, it does not follow that we are free; freedom requires not only the absence of determination, but also the right kind of relation to our actions. What is the source of Epicurus' conviction that we are free?

He might argue that the senses guarantee our freedom, so that it has the same support as our conviction that pleasure is the good. Perhaps Lucretius appeals to our experience of not being compelled when we make up our minds and act.[34] But this is a frail support for a doctrine of freedom; since a determinist has no difficulty in accounting for this experience, it could be present in a world that, according to Epicurus, allows no freedom.

Epicurus would be on stronger ground if he treated our conviction about freedom as a preconception that does not simply report sensory experience.[35] It is a presupposition of our ethical outlook, both on ourselves and on others, for reasons that Aristotle points out in his discussion of the voluntary. But if Epicurus rests his conviction about freedom on our ethical outlook, his argument seems to be dialectical, appealing to basic common beliefs and trying to vindicate them. If this is his method of argument about freedom, why should it not be his method of argument about the good? In his claims about freedom, as in his claims about pleasure and happiness, he seems to argue from a more Aristotelian basis than he acknowledges.

151. Types of Pleasure

This general point about Epicurus' method prepares us for his dispute with the Cyrenaics about the type of pleasure that is the ultimate good. Aristippus understands pleasure as a psychic change and movement. Epicurus recognizes this 'kinetic' pleasure, but he also recognizes 'static' (or 'katastematic') as well as 'kinetic' pleasures; he includes tranquillity and freedom from pain under static pleasures (DL X 136). If I have a kinetic pleasure at a particular time, something must have changed from my previous condition, but I can have a static pleasure for a long period without any changes or distinguishable episodes of pleasure.[36]

Epicurus distinguishes these two types of pleasure in order to assert the value of static pleasures. He does not deny that kinetic pleasures are goods, but he believes that other hedonists exaggerate their goodness, and ignore or underestimate the goodness of static pleasures.

---

[33] On Alexander see §172.   [34] See Lucr. ii 251–83.   [35] See the reference to a preconception in n10 above.
[36] On the appropriate rendering of 'katastēmatikē' see Gosling and Taylor, GP 373–4; Cooper, 'Pleasure' 512 (who argue that katastematic pleasures are pleasures of the organism in its proper condition (katastēma)). For discussion of the difference between kinetic and katastematic pleasures see Gosling and Taylor, GP, ch. 19; LS i 123–4.

Since we have natural and necessary appetites (*epithumiai*) (DL × 127), and failure to satisfy them with kinetic pleasure causes pain and disturbance, the pleasure that removes this pain is a good. A prudent person recognizes that these necessary desires can be satisfied without great effort and anxiety, because we can train ourselves to form modest demands (DL × 130, 145).

We also have natural desires that are unnecessary—e.g., for variation in food and drink beyond what we need to remove hunger and thirst.[37] Epicurus recognizes that some of this variation in pleasure is desirable in a life that fulfils necessary appetites (× 144). If we go beyond moderate variation, and put great effort into satisfying unnecessary but natural desires, we follow 'empty belief' (× 149). Desires that are neither natural nor necessary are entirely the product of empty belief; we believe we need something that corresponds not at all to our natural needs, but is simply the product of conventional and mistaken views about goods. These desires include the desire for honour and reputation.[38]

Epicurus believes it is useful to distinguish these types of desires and the corresponding pleasures, in order to show that a hedonist need not pursue Calliclean pleasures, which result in ever-expanding appetites and demand ever-expanding resources (Lucr. vi 9–34). With appropriate training we can make our natural and necessary desires moderate and easy to satisfy.[39] Since we need not suffer pain from restraint of non-necessary natural desires, we will keep them to a moderate level. Since we recognize that we can achieve freedom from pain and an appropriate level of kinetic pleasure without non-necessary non-natural desires, we will suppress these desires altogether.

Is this a good reply to Callicles? In response to Socrates' adaptive conception of happiness, Callicles says it is the condition of a corpse or a rock (Plato, *Gorg.* 492e3–6). The Cyrenaics complain in similar terms of Epicurus' conception of happiness.[40] Epicurus believes that this reaction is a mistake, but how can he show that is a mistake, or explain why we make it?

152. Fear of Death as the Source of Excessive Desires

Epicurus suggests that if we accept a more demanding conception of happiness than the one he defends, we are victims of anxiety about death and our post-mortem existence. In his view, the most impious belief we can hold about the gods is the belief that they punish the wicked and reward the good (DL × 123–4). This belief makes us fear death, and the fear of death disturbs us so that we are unreasonably attached to demanding desires and pleasures. We have to learn 'the limits of life' in order to see that it is easy to achieve happiness (× 146). Unless we know that we do not exist after death, we cannot enjoy pleasures unmixed with pain,[41] since they will always be mixed with anxiety about death.

---

[37] 'Epicurus has assigned a common limit to pleasures, namely the removal of everything painful. In his view, nature has increased the pleasant to the point where it removes the painful, but nature allows pleasure no further increase in size; pleasure simply admits of some non-necessary variations once it reaches a point of no distress' (Plu. *NP* 1088c). Cf. DL × 149 + scholion.

[38] Cf. Cic. *F* i 45.

[39] 'The one who well knows the limits of life knows that what removes the pain resulting from need (*endeia*) and makes the whole of life complete is easily provided, so that he does not need in addition things acquired in competition' (× 146). Cf. 130–1.

[40] Clement, *Strom.* ii 21, 130.7–8. See §36. On Callicles cf. §25.

[41] × 143 *akeraious*. Bailey ad loc. appositely cites Lucr. iii 39–40.

We might wonder why the fear of death should make any difference. Even if we fear it, can we not agree with Epicurus' defence of an adaptive conception of happiness, and train ourselves to have moderate desires that are easily satisfied without bringing severe pains to follow? This advice seems to be unaffected by fear or fearlessness towards death.

Perhaps Epicurus means that if we took his advice about adaptation, but still feared death, we would achieve only partial tranquillity. For even if our non-necessary appetites did not bother us, the fear of death would still bother us. To distract ourselves from the fear of death, we occupy ourselves with non-necessary appetites and aims.

Lucretius develops this argument at greater length. He mentions three cases where we can see that the fear of death is the basic motive of our actions: (1) Some people say that they do not believe in life after death, and that they fear illness and disgrace more than death. But even if they are exiled in disgrace for terrible crimes, they stay alive, and even sacrifice to the gods (Lucr. iii 41–58). (2) We fear a bad reputation and a life of poverty because they seem to threaten us with death (iii 65–7); fear of death causes us to go to all lengths to avoid these alleged evils, so that we compete for honours and power, and shrink from no crimes to achieve our ends (59–86). (3) We try to distract ourselves from a weight that lies on our minds by frantic activity, as though that would relieve our minds (1053–75).

The third of these cases is especially relevant because, as Lucretius remarks, the pursuits that result from our fear of death are not directly related to life and death. Lucretius' claim is intelligible in the first and second cases, where the actions he considers might be understood as ways of protecting ourselves against premature death (in the second case) or against whatever awaits us after death (in the first case). But in the third case Lucretius suggests that because we do not know the cause of the weight on our minds (pondus inesse animo, 1054), we try to relieve it with ineffective remedies. We try to escape ourselves and we hate ourselves,[42] because we do not know what is the matter with us. Even though we form and act on unnecessary appetites, they do not remove the weight on our minds, because they cannot remove our underlying fear of death (DL × 142).

Though Lucretius' suggestions about our hidden motives and lack of self-understanding are intriguing, they do not seem wholly convincing. Even if we did not fear death in itself, we might still fear having our lives made worse; if we fear that, we may take the defensive measures that Epicurus regards as unnecessary. Conversely, even if we cannot wholly remove the fear of death, it is not clear why it should obsess us to the degree that Lucretius assumes. Why should we not be able to control this fear, just as we control other fears? Epicurus believes that if we have moderate desires, we can face fortune without excessive fear; why should we not also face death in this spirit?

153. Does Epicurus Show that Death is Not an Evil?

But if, despite these doubts, we agree with Epicurus' claims about the far-reaching effects of the fear of death, we may reasonably ask how he proposes to remove it. He believes that we fear death because we fear the possibility of pain after death. We cannot suffer pain,

---

[42] 'hoc se quisque modo fugit ... ingratis haeret et odit', 1068–9.

however, if we do not exist. Hence Epicurus suggests that the remedy for fear of death is the conviction that we do not exist after death.[43]

We might argue that this belief will not always remove the irrational fear of death. Lucretius admits that we are sometimes moved by fear of death to hate our present condition, and that this hatred sometimes causes us to kill ourselves, even though we bring on ourselves the condition that we originally feared (Lucr. iii 79–82). But he believes that if we attend constantly to the proofs of the Epicurean position, we can accustom ourselves to dismissing our fear of death, so that we eventually get rid of it.

Epicurus' cure for our fear of death succeeds only if he is right about what we fear in death. In his view, we fear death because of the evils that may follow it, so that if we do not exist after death, we have nothing to fear about death. But why should we agree that this is the only thing we fear about death? Why should we not believe that it is bad for us (in some cases at least) to have our life ended, and so fear the cessation of our life? Lucretius answers that we do not think it is bad for us that we did not exist in the past before we were born, and that therefore we ought not to think it is bad for us that we will not exist in the future after our death (Lucr. iii 972–7). Something can be bad for us only at a time when we exist to suffer the badness (iii 861–3).

These Epicurean arguments do not seem cogent if we are not already hedonists. The past and the future will seem different to us if we care about our plans and intentions; for since these are directed to the future and are frustrated if our future life is cut short, our future non-existence seems worse than our past non-existence. Similarly, if we care about fulfilling our plans and intentions, and not only about the pleasant experience that results from fulfilling them, we will believe we are harmed by whatever prevents their fulfilment, whether or not we will be conscious of the prevention.

If Epicurus relieves us from the fear of death only if we accept his hedonism, what does that show about his ethical theory? On the one hand, we might say that this counts in favour of his ethical theory, if it relieves us from the fear of death; we ought, therefore, to become hedonists. On the other hand, we might regard this as an objection to his theory, if it implies that death is not bad; for surely (we might reply) death is manifestly bad, and a theory that denies this has gone wrong somewhere. This objection suggests that Epicurean hedonism cannot be defended on dialectical grounds; it seems not to capture some fairly clear common beliefs about good and evil, in the special case of death.

Perhaps Epicurus' argument would seem more plausible if we agreed with him about the pervasive and crippling character of the fear of death, and we agreed that the only way to get rid of this fear is to believe that death is not an evil. But he seems to exaggerate the disease in order to promote his cure. It is not obvious that the fear of death has all the effects he ascribes to it. Nor is it clear that we can get rid of the pervasive fear only by coming to believe that death is not an evil. Could we not regard it as evil, and therefore fear it to some degree, but keep our fear in proper proportion, so that it does not ruin our lives?

This alternative to Epicurean denial of the badness of death might seem rather complacent if our beliefs about life after death conflicted sharply with our moral convictions about how to live our present life. If we had good reason to believe that unjust, cruel, and selfish people

---

[43] On Epicurus' arguments on death see Furley, 'Nothing to us?'; Mitsis, 'Duration'.

will be rewarded in the afterlife and that virtuous people will be punished, we would face a conflict between morality and self-interest. Mill claims that in the face of such a conflict, he would choose morality and face eternal punishment for it.[44] But Epicurus does not believe that we face this conflict if we believe in an afterlife. Though Lucretius argues that religion can encourage us to act badly (Lucr. i 80–101), he does not claim that if we believed in life after death, we would have reason to prefer vice to virtue in general. On the contrary, he suggests that, if we thought about it, we would see that the gods could not really command the evil actions that people do in the name of religion (such actions as Agamemnon's sacrifice of Iphigeneia). Reflexion of this sort will tend to reduce any appearance of conflict between our moral views and our beliefs about what the gods reward and punish.

154. Kinetic Pleasure v. Freedom from Pain

Let us now put aside Epicurus' particular concern about the fear of death, and return to his argument against Calliclean pleasures. Even if the fear of death does not move us to distract ourselves with kinetic pleasures, we might none the less suppose that the Cyrenaics are right to reject the sacrifice of kinetic pleasure that results from Epicurus' moderate attitude. How can he show that they are wrong on hedonistic grounds?

To understand his answer, we have to see why he takes static pleasure to be preferable to kinetic pleasure. He argues that if we satisfy our natural and necessary appetites, and limit our natural and unnecessary ones, we will achieve tranquillity, which is our ultimate end.[45] The true principle that pleasure is the ultimate end does not imply that Calliclean pleasure is the ultimate end; it implies that tranquillity is the end.[46]

Why should we agree that tranquillity is our ultimate end? Epicurus seems to argue that we pursue kinetic pleasure as a result of the appetite and pain that we remove by the pleasure, and in order to remove that appetite and pain. If, then, we could be free of the appetite and pain, and were conscious of this freedom, we would already have reached the state that we try to reach through our pursuit of kinetic pleasure. Moreover, we are better off if we are free of appetite and pain in the first place than if we remove them through kinetic pleasure; for in the first case we never suffer the pain that we suffer in the second case; we have the positive state of freedom from pain without having to go through pain and appetite to reach it.

In this argument Epicurus introduces an adaptive conception of happiness that he shares with Socrates (in the *Gorgias*). Unlike some Cynics, he does not advocate deliberate austerity;

---

[44] See Mill, *ESWHP*, ch. 7 = *CW* ix 103.

[45] 'For the unwavering study of these things [sc. the types of appetites] knows how to refer all choice and avoidance to the health of the soul and to the tranquillity of the soul, since this is the end of living blessedly. For this is what we do everything for the sake of—so that we will suffer neither pain nor disturbance. And once we reach this, all the soul's buffeting is over, since the animal has nowhere to go, as though it still lacked anything, and nothing further that it seeks to fill up the good of the soul and the body. For the time we have need of pleasure is when we are in pain through the absence of pleasure; but when we are no longer in pain we no longer lack [or 'need', *deometha*] pleasure' (DL x 128).

[46] 'Whenever we say, therefore, that pleasure is the end, we do not mean the pleasures of the prodigal or the pleasures of gratification, as some suppose through ignorance and because they disagree with us or misunderstand us, but <we mean> the absence of pain in the body and of disturbance in the soul' (DL x 131).

he does not suggest that we ought to reject the pleasures that result from greater material resources. On the contrary, he argues that if we fit our desires to the circumstances, we can enjoy greater resources and still avoid disappointment if we find ourselves with smaller resources.[47] In all circumstances we have desires that are adapted so as to ensure their satisfaction.

How are we to explain this use of an adaptive claim about happiness? How, in particular, is it related to Epicurus' hedonism? According to one view, the adaptive conception is subordinate to hedonism; Epicurus recommends the adaptive strategy because it is the best way to secure maximum pleasure. In that case the measuring science that compares quantities of pleasure tells us that we secure more pleasure through the adaptive strategy and the static pleasures that we gain from it. The quantity of kinetic pleasures we gain is comparatively small, since we avoid getting attached to any pleasures that are expensive in external resources; but (on this view) the quantity of static pleasure is great enough to make our life pleasanter than it would be if we pursued kinetic pleasures more vigorously.

An alternative view makes hedonism subordinate to an adaptive conception. Pleasure is worth pursuing because we have natural appetites that are satisfied by pleasures that remove our pains. The goodness of the pleasure, however, consists not in the fact that it is pleasure, but in the fact that it satisfies our desires. The satisfaction of desire is the ultimate good, and the adaptive strategy secures that. It also secures a moderate quantity of pleasure, but that reflects the fact that our desires aim at pleasure, not an essential element of the good.

The first view, making adaptation and satisfaction subordinate to hedonism, is closer to Epicurus' doctrine. He introduces his claims about self-sufficiency in order to show why pleasure is the ultimate good, on the assumption that the Epicurean's self-sufficient life can be defended on hedonist grounds. But this view runs into some difficulties that make it reasonable to consider the second view.

How can Epicurus show that static pleasures, combined with moderate kinetic pleasures, yield greater pleasure than we would gain from greater attention to kinetic pleasures? A defender of Callicles might reply that though 'expensive' kinetic pleasures involve more pain, anxiety, and possible frustration, they are worth it. Epicurus might claim that this defence overlooks the fact that the pleasure of eating, say, is valuable only because it removes the pain of hunger. If we are simply trying to get rid of the pain, we would be better off if we had no pain to begin with. But the Calliclean might reject this view, arguing that the pleasant sensation is valuable in its own right, apart from the fact that it replaces the pain of hunger. That is why we have good reason to pursue greater pleasures even at the cost of more pains. Eating salted nuts to get more pleasure from drinking beer is the pattern of rational choice, according to this Calliclean view.

Cicero's discussion of Epicurus on these questions is rather unsympathetic and sometimes obtuse, but it points to a reasonable objection. Cicero suggests that Epicurus believes that

---

[47] 'And we count self-sufficiency (*autarkeia*) a great good, not so that, whatever happens, we may use only a few things, but so that if we do not have many, we may use few, being genuinely persuaded that those who need luxury least have the pleasantest gratification from it, and that whatever is natural is easily provided and only whatever is empty is hard to provide' (DL × 130; cf. parallels in U 490).

the absence of pain is a kind of pleasure, in the strong sense that the state of being free of pain is, in its own right, a state of pleasure (Cic. *F* ii 13–20). Probably Cicero is wrong about this. Epicurus does not mean that the state of tranquillity and freedom from pain is, as such, a state of feeling pleasure. In speaking of static pleasure he refers to the pleasure we take in being free of pain and anxiety. He is right to claim that this state is a distinct sort of pleasure beside kinetic pleasure. But if we reject Cicero's criticism, and we recognize that this is the sort of pleasure Epicurus has in mind, it is still not clear why we should prefer it, on hedonist grounds, to kinetic pleasure.

Might we say that some people are simply more like Callicles and others are more like Epicurus, and that the decision depends on whether we enjoy thrills more than we are averse to risk? Epicurus does not seem to discuss the Callicleans fairly. He attacks them on the ground that their expensive pleasures cannot free us from the fear of death (DL × 142). But if we grant that, and we take care to convince ourselves that we have no life after death, why should we not pursue Calliclean pleasures without anxiety about life after death? Perhaps Epicurus believes that he need not bother about this case, because people indulge in such pleasures only to distract themselves from the fear of death (as Lucretius suggests). But it is not clear why this should be the only reason for pursuing Calliclean pleasures. It would not be reasonable for him to tell the Callicleans that they will shorten their lives; for he has argued that we have no reason to regard death as bad, and hence no reason to wish our lives could be prolonged.

Epicurus describes the life of tranquillity in more detail to show that it does not require us to abandon kinetic pleasure altogether and does not leave us in the condition of a corpse. He insists that he can form no conception of the good without the kinetic pleasures of the senses (DL × 6; Cic. *TD* iii 41–2; U 67–8). He assumes, then, that the demands of nature in normal conditions will be enough to ensure that we have more than minimal natural appetites and that we will have the resources to satisfy them. In this condition we will not increase our pleasure, since we have already achieved tranquillity, but we will maintain it by varying our kinetic pleasures (DL × 144; Plu. *NP* 1088c).

To show that this life increases our quantity of pleasure, Epicurus appeals to his eudaemonism. We have to count not only the pleasures and pains that arise from our immediate bodily condition, but also those that arise from memory and anticipation.[48] On this point he differs from the Cyrenaics, who regard the belief that I suffered in the past and will suffer in the future as the product of empty belief.[49] Since Epicurus counts the pleasures and pains that result from the clear sense of my continuity in the past and the future, he argues that the tranquil life increases their quantity. If I remember myself having fairly uninterrupted past pleasures, and, because of my tranquil and undemanding attitude, can look forward to similar pleasures, I increase my present pleasure. Since I aim at pleasure in my life as a whole, my moderate accumulation of pleasure at different times makes a large total that I can increase by pleasures of memory and anticipation.

Epicurus' reflexions on his final illness rely on this tendency of pleasures to multiply through memory. In his letter to Idomeneus, he calls the last day of his life a 'blessed' day, because, despite the severity of his present pain, his recollection of past conversations with

---

[48] '. . . only the present buffets the flesh, but past, present, and future buffet the soul' (DL × 137).   [49] See §33.

Idomeneus produces pleasure to outweigh the pain.[50] The pleasures of the mind recollecting or anticipating are capable of altering the hedonic balance produced by ordinary bodily pleasures (Cic. F i 55). According to his opponents, he compiled lists of past kinetic pleasures to keep in his memory.[51]

On this point the Epicureans are better off than the Cyrenaics. If any pleasures of memory and anticipation depend on my thinking of myself as the subject of the past and future pleasures, the Cyrenaics do not attach any value to them, since they depend on an empty belief in my identity through time.[52] Since they are doubtful about the continuing self, they will forgo the pleasures that depend on a firm conviction such as Epicurus' conviction that he is the same person who had the pleasant conversations with Idomeneus.

But the pleasures that the Epicureans gain from their conviction about the continuing self come with a cost. For Epicureans seem to be worse off than the Cyrenaics are in suffering pains of memory and anticipation (Cic. F i 57). The Cyrenaics believe that the anticipation of future evils makes them less severe when they actually come, whereas Epicurus believes that anticipation makes them worse (Cic. TD iii 29–33). This is why Epicureans need moderate desires that create no anxiety about their future satisfaction. Cyrenaics, however, believe that if they are unconcerned about their (supposed) future states, they can enjoy their more extravagant present pleasures without unwelcome anxiety.

This comparison of the Epicurean and Cyrenaic outlook makes it difficult to see how a Cyrenaic or a Calliclean is mistaken in calculation of quantity of pleasure. Perhaps some people simply prefer the ups and downs of Calliclean pleasures to the more even tenor of the Epicurean life. If Epicurus had to concede that the choice between his outlook and the Calliclean outlook depends on different people's basic preferences, he would still be free to prescribe Epicurean discipline for himself and like-minded people. But he would be wrong to suppose that the Calliclean outlook must rest on a mistake. If the choice between ways of life depends on one's basic preferences, the good turns out to be satisfaction of one's ultimate preferences, whatever they might be.

155. Is Epicurus a Hedonist?

If these are reasonable objections to a hedonist defence of Epicurus' preference for static pleasure and a moderate degree of kinetic pleasure, it is worth considering the non-hedonist alternative. Epicurus sometimes seems to support this alternative; for he claims that the ultimate end is bodily health and psychic tranquillity, and that we do everything for the sake of these (DL × 128). When we are free of pain, we no longer need pleasure.[53] By this Epicurus might mean either (i) that when we are free of pain, this is itself a source of pleasure and we need no more pleasure in addition, or (ii) that when we are free of pain, pleasure no

---

[50] The pains of his present state could not be exceeded (*huperbolēn ouk apoleiponta tou en heautois megethous*). But the enjoyment in his soul of past discussions with friends outweighed (lit., 'was set up against', *antiparetatteto*) these, so as to make this a blessed (*makarian*) day (DL × 22 = LS 24D).

[51] Plu. *NP* 1089a-c = U 431, 436; Cic. F ii 106.   [52] See §33.

[53] 'For the time when we need (*chreian echomen*) pleasure is whenever we suffer pain from pleasure not being present; but whenever we do not suffer pain, we no longer need (*deometha*) pleasure' (× 128). Cf. Seneca, *Ep.* 66.45 = U 434.

longer matters to us. The second claim suggests that tranquillity rather than pleasure is the ultimate end.

This is a perplexing point in Epicurus' argument, because immediately after he has said that when we are free of pain we no longer enjoy pleasure, he affirms that this is why (*dia touto*, × 128–9) we say that pleasure is the origin and goal. This connexion of thought supports a hedonist interpretation of his remark about freedom from pain, but leaves us puzzled about why he has just said that tranquillity, rather than pleasure, is the ultimate end. It is reasonable, even if incorrect, of Cicero to suggest that Epicurus fails to distinguish absence of pain from pleasure. We may want to distinguish tranquillity from the pleasure taken in tranquillity, but it is not clear that Epicurus always distinguishes them.

The juxtaposition of Epicurus' claims about tranquillity with his claims about pleasure raises a further question about the epistemological basis of these claims. Since he appeals to our pre-rational experience of pleasure to show that pleasure is the end, and since he takes concern for pleasure to underlie concern for tranquillity, he implies that pre-rational experience of pleasure supports the pursuit of tranquillity. Cicero justly criticizes this claim (F ii 31–2). Just as eudaemonism goes beyond any hedonist doctrine that could be supported by appeal to sensory affection, the preference for static pleasure and for tranquillity seems to go beyond Epicurus' professed epistemological basis.

But if we consider adaptation and tranquillity as accounts of the ultimate end, independent of any hedonist basis, how plausible does Epicurus make them seem? The Calliclean and Cyrenaic criticism that he has described the condition of a corpse is inaccurate, since Epicurean happiness requires consciousness; but it suggests a criticism that a non-hedonist might offer. Epicurus' conception does not discriminate among the satisfied desires of different people. Those whose desires are minimal, or childish, or cruel, are all equally happy as long as their desires are equally satisfied. We might adapt one of Aristotle's objections to hedonism, and say that we would not reasonably want to return to the condition of a child on condition that our childish desires would all be fulfilled (*EN* 1174a1–4).

Epicurus, therefore, does not seem to hold a stable position between Cyrenaic hedonism and non-hedonist eudaemonism. His hedonist defence of tranquillity as the highest good does not show how tranquillity offers a larger quantity of pleasure. If he defends tranquillity on non-hedonist grounds, by appeal to an adaptive conception of happiness, he leaves room for the consideration of further non-hedonic values. If we go beyond hedonism to adaptation, why not go further and accept the Platonic and Aristotelian identification of happiness with a non-hedonic good?

156. Hedonism and Good Pleasures

Epicurus has an answer to this question if he defends his version of hedonism or his adaptive conception of happiness by dialectical argument in comparison with common beliefs. Plato and Aristotle believe that (i) if virtue is non-instrumentally valuable, hedonism is false; and since they affirm that (ii) virtue is non-instrumentally good, they conclude that (iii) hedonism is false. Epicurus agrees with their first claim, but rejects their conclusion; hence he rejects their second claim, and denies that virtues are non-instrumentally good.[54] Hence he denies that the fine is a good distinct from the pleasant.[55] He suggests that what is fine is what receives praise, that the praise is a source of pleasure and that this resulting pleasure is what makes fine things good.[56]

Epicurus attacks those, including Aristotle, who claim that the virtues and the fine are goods in themselves independently of whether or not they are sources of pleasure (cf. *EN* 1174a3–7). Aristotle's claim about the virtues is counterfactual; he agrees with Epicurus in believing that virtue and virtuous action are sources of pleasure, but he also believes they are good apart from their hedonic value. He therefore disagrees with Epicurus about how virtue and virtuous action are 'sources' of pleasure. Since, in Aristotle's view, they are non-instrumental goods in their own right apart from the pleasure they produce, they are 'sources' of pleasure by being objects of their special pleasure in their own right. To find this special pleasure in the virtues, we have to believe they are good apart from their pleasure. Since Epicurus does not believe they are good apart from their pleasure, he cannot regard them as objects of pleasure in their own right; they are sources of pleasure in a purely causal sense, by producing results that are pleasant in themselves or instrumental to such results.

Epicurus seeks to explain the Aristotelian belief about virtue as an 'empty' belief, based on a mistaken inference from a true premiss. Common sense and the Peripatetics are right to believe that the pleasures of profligate and self-indulgent people are not the good, and that other things besides these pleasures are valuable. From this true premiss we may mistakenly infer that we must recognize non-hedonic non-instrumental value, and that we must attribute such value to the virtues. Epicurus agrees with common sense in rejecting the Cyrenaic and Calliclean conceptions of pleasure and the good, but he gives a hedonist defence of his agreement. In his view the static pleasures of contentment are more important than the kinetic pleasures that simply provide variation.

Epicurus' view of the end shows (in his view) that ordinary virtuous actions and virtues are effective strategies for gaining Epicurean pleasures. To estimate the balance of pleasure and pains that produces contentment, we need wisdom; and this wisdom prescribes the other virtues (DL × 132; Cic. *F* i 46–54). Epicurus accepts a hedonist argument to reconcile the hedonism of Plato's *Protagoras* with the critique of Calliclean hedonism in the *Gorgias*.[57]

Hence he agrees with Socrates' criticism of Callicles, but he believes that it affects only Cyrenaic hedonism. Similarly, he agrees with the criticism of Calliclean pleasures in the *Philebus*, provided it is also restricted to Cyrenaic hedonism.

He therefore develops Aristotle's defence of pleasure. In Aristotle's view, people think pleasure is bad because of the inferior kinds of pleasures that they are used to (*EN*

---

[54] '. . . and this is the nature of the good, if you apply your mind to it correctly, and then stand firm, and do not walk around idly (*kenôs peripatê(i)*) chattering about the good' (Plu. *NP* 1091b = U 423). It is a plausible guess that (as the Loeb edition suggests) *peripatê(i)* refers to the Peripatetics. '. . . they <the Epicureans> shout that the good is found in the belly, that would not buy the virtues all in a lump at the price of a penny with a hole in it, if all pleasure was entirely expelled from them' (Plu. *Col.* 1108c = U 512). See further Cic. *TD* iii 41–3; Seneca, *Ep.* 85.18 = U 508; LS 21 O, P.

[55] 'I spit on the fine and on those who idly (*kenôs*) admire it, whenever it produces no pleasure' (Athen. *Deipn.* 547a = U 512).

[56] Cic. *F* ii 48–50; *Acad.* ii 140; Epict. ii 22.21.

[57] This reconciling strategy is defended, e.g., by Gosling and Taylor, *GP* 70–5. See §24.

1153b33–1154a1). But since not all pleasures have the effects of Calliclean pleasures, the best life, as Aristotle affirms, is the pleasantest life (1153b9–14).[58] This defence of pleasure supports Epicurus' view that opponents of hedonism have attacked it unfairly with arguments that apply only to Calliclean hedonism. Once we identify the sort of pleasure that constitutes the end, we see that Epicurean hedonism can freely accept Socrates' criticisms of Callicles, and can agree with Socrates' choice of pleasures on strictly hedonistic grounds (referring to the static pleasure of contentment and tranquillity).

The same argument explains how hedonism can accommodate the conception of the good that Socrates in the *Gorgias* puts forward as an alternative to hedonism—the adaptive conception of happiness. In saying that the happy person is self-sufficient and lacks nothing, Epicurus recalls Socrates' suggestion to Callicles (492e). Whereas Socrates seemed to reject hedonism by appeal to an adaptive conception of happiness, Epicurus suggests that Epicurean hedonism—emphasizing the static above the kinetic pleasures—fits an adaptive conception.

To say that hedonism 'fits' an adaptive conception is not to say which claim about happiness is prior to which. In Epicurus' official view hedonism should come first; we should be able to see that nature and immediate sensations support Epicurean over Cyrenaic hedonism. Once we find that, the fit between Epicurean hedonism and the adaptive conception of happiness should be part of Epicurus' dialectical argument showing how his view of happiness explains some common beliefs, but not a necessary part of his argument to show that pleasure is the good. In fact it is hard to accept Epicurus' official view; we seem to have no reason to prefer Epicurean over Cyrenaic views of what natural impulses show us (indeed, as we suggested, the Cyrenaics seem to have a strong case here) unless we independently accept some claim about self-sufficiency as a plausible constraint on any account of the good. But if Epicurus uses that sort of argument, he relies more on dialectical argument than he officially claims to; and if he relies on this common belief about self-sufficiency, he is open to dialectical challenge that might question his interpretation of this common belief or adduce other common beliefs. His attempt to justify the virtues by appeal to Epicurean hedonism raises quite difficult questions about the form of his ethical argument.

We have already seen why it is difficult to defend Epicurus' discriminations among pleasures on hedonist grounds. Aristotle believes that we need some independent non-hedonist conception of goodness to identify the good pleasures, and that therefore his defence of good pleasures is not a defence of hedonism. Epicurus' case against Aristotle depends on the success of his argument to show that Calliclean hedonists are wrong about the quantity of pleasure they can expect; but that argument is open to question.

157. A Defence of Virtue?

If we agree with Epicurus in accepting the form of hedonism that fits into an adaptive conception of happiness, does he make a case for the recognized cardinal virtues? If pleasure

---

[58] Epicurus may have noticed that much of the discussion of pleasure in *EN* vii could be used in defence of Epicurean hedonism. See §88; Rist, *Ep.* 101. *EN* x is much less suitable for this purpose, either because Aristotle has changed his mind or because he is showing his hand more clearly.

is a good, it is reasonable to expect that a hedonist case for the virtues will succeed to some degree; for, as Plato and Aristotle believe, part of the point of the virtues is to protect and to secure other goods. It is plausible, therefore, to claim, as Epicurus does, that temperate people secure pleasures and reduce their anxiety by their temperate actions. It is more difficult to believe, however, that brave actions reflect the most sensible strategy for maximizing one's own pleasure. Even if some of them can be defended as means to securing longer-term pleasure, this explanation does not seem to cover brave action as a whole.

Epicurus would also be right to claim that we value the virtues partly for their instrumental benefit in securing pleasures, and that we would think less of them if they did not secure benefits that we already value apart from our concern with virtue (Cic. *F* i 42). But it is more difficult to see how this is the whole of the value that we attach to the virtues. Virtuous people do fine actions just because they are fine; they attach value to this sort of action without reference to its further instrumental benefits. We might follow Aristotle in accepting this conviction, without saying that virtue is the only non-instrumental good.

Epicurus does not even try to accommodate this feature of common beliefs about virtue. He tries to explain away this belief as the product of a reasonable desire for stable commitment to virtuous action, together with the empty belief that we cannot secure such a commitment if we attach only instrumental value to virtue and virtuous action. Epicurean hedonism seeks to show how we can secure a stable commitment without recognizing any non-hedonic non-instrumental value. But it simply ignores the aspects of common belief that reject a purely instrumental status for virtue. Cicero quite reasonably endorses the Stoics' criticism of Epicurus on this point.[59]

Is it reasonable for Epicurus simply to dismiss all aspects of common sense that attach non-instrumental value to virtue? The answer depends partly on his method. If he argues dialectically, as Aristotle does, his failure to capture this element of common sense raises a reasonable doubt about his account of virtue. If, however, he relies on sensory affections to give a non-dialectical basis for hedonism, he has a reason to discount non-hedonist aspects of common sense. Dialectical argument, on this view, tends to confirm conclusions reached by appeal to Epicurean epistemology, and to remove objections that might be derived from common sense, but he does not need it to prove his basic principles. Hence he gives a reason for accepting the hedonist aspects of common sense and using them in dialectical argument, while discarding non-hedonist errors.

This defence of Epicurus, however, reminds us of the weakness of his argument from sensory affections to his version of hedonism. If we stick to his ostensible epistemological

---

[59] 'You will be ashamed of the picture that Cleanthes used to draw so aptly in his lectures. He would instruct his audience to imagine a painting representing pleasure decked as a queen ... The virtues would attend her, as servants who would do nothing, and recognize no duty, except to serve pleasure. They would simply warn her in a whisper ... to avoid any thoughtless action that might offend public opinion, or anything that might lead to pain.... But Epicurus, you will tell me, ... says that anyone who does not live finely cannot live pleasantly. As if I cared what Epicurus says or denies! I ask this: What is it consistent for someone who places the highest good in pleasure to say? ... Epicurus himself says that the life of gratification is not to be criticized, if these people are not complete fools—that is to say, if they have neither longings nor fears.... And so, once you Epicureans direct everything by reference to pleasure, you cannot uphold or retain virtue. For a man must not be thought good and just if he refrains from doing injustice for fear of anything bad <for himself>.... As long as he <avoids injustice because he> is afraid, he is not just, and assuredly, as soon as he ceases to be afraid, he will not be just ... In this way you Epicureans undoubtedly teach the pretence of justice instead of true and stable justice' (Cic. *F* ii 69–71). Cf. §180.

starting point, it is difficult to see why we should prefer Epicurean over Cyrenaic hedonism. We have dialectical reasons for preferring Epicurean hedonism; but we seem to have equally strong dialectical reasons for preferring a non-hedonist account of goodness to a hedonist account. If, then, Epicurus needs to go beyond his epistemological basis in order to defend his version of hedonism, he seems to leave himself open to dialectical arguments against his position on the virtues. His total position will seem plausible to us only if we waver inconsistently between the epistemology that supports Cyrenaic hedonism and the dialectical method that answers the Cyrenaics through arguments that cast doubt on Epicurean hedonism as well.

158. Justice and its Consequences: Epicurus v. Plato

The difficulties in the Epicurean account of the virtues are conspicuous in the virtues to which Plato and Aristotle, respectively, devote most attention—justice and friendship. These create a special difficulty for Epicurus, since both Plato and Aristotle attach some importance to the motives and aims of the person who has each of these virtues. Plato contrasts the genuinely just person with the person who has a mere 'façade' of justice; the genuinely just person values justice for its own sake, even when the consequences are dangerous. Aristotle attributes the same attitude to the just person, and to the virtuous person generally, since such a person does the virtuous action for its own sake and because it is fine. The best type of friendship, in Aristotle's view, involves concern for the friend for the friend's own sake, not purely for the sake of pleasure or advantage. These other-directed virtues therefore present a special challenge to Epicurus.

In his view, Plato's attitude to justice reflects an 'empty belief' that can safely be rejected on Epicurean grounds. Epicurus endorses the account of justice that Glaucon and Adeimantus propose. Justice is simply the result of an agreement to avoid mutual aggression, 'to prevent people harming each other or being harmed by each other' (DL x 150).[60] Lucretius suggests that these agreements developed gradually when people wanted the assurance of non-aggression (Lucr. v 1019–20). Such agreements are reasonable for Epicurean hedonists, since they want to remove the anxiety and disturbance that might result if they cannot be assured of non-aggression. Since they value security more than they value the extra kinetic pleasures that they might gain by aggression, they will prefer a stable agreement over an unstable situation in which they have more opportunities for aggression. On this point Epicurus is better off than Hobbes, who does not accept the Epicurean aim of self-sufficiency and adaptation.[61]

An Epicurean who joins such an agreement has good reasons to observe rules of justice when observance is necessary for the stability of society; for Epicurean prudence looks ahead to the longer term, and it cares less for short-term opportunities for kinetic pleasure than for longer-term assurance of tranquillity. Hence Lucretius suggests that most people willingly stick to their agreements about non-aggression (v 1024–5), and some Epicureans claim that

---

[60] Cf. Cic. F i 50–3, 59–61; LS 22.
[61] For one source of failure to adapt ourselves to circumstances see, e.g., Hobbes, L18.20.

if everyone were always aware of the utility of different actions, no one would need to be compelled by laws and sanctions.[62]

This defence of justice, however, does not seem to answer free riders. Some unjust actions that are open to me would apparently benefit me without any threat to the stability of the whole system that depends on general observance of rules of justice; why should I not choose these actions, on Epicurus' principles? He answers that if I consider my good from an Epicurean point of view, I will see that these unjust actions do not really benefit me. If I attach the appropriate weight to tranquillity, I will be relatively indifferent to the increased kinetic pleasure I might gain by injustice, and I will try to avoid the loss of tranquillity that I will suffer from the fear of punishment (DL x 151).[63] Epicurean hedonism suggests that the fears and anxieties suffered by the unjust person make injustice unappealing from the hedonic point of view. To be moved by this argument we must accept Epicurus' view that the pains and pleasures of anticipation are more important than they will seem if we take a Cyrenaic attitude to them.

The Epicurean attitude to kinetic pleasure and tranquillity helps to answer an objection to this defence of justice. We might argue that Epicurus is too pessimistic. Often we can be reasonably confident of escaping punishment for unjust action; why should we not prefer it in such cases? Epicurus might reasonably answer that, since tranquillity is much more important than a gain in kinetic pleasure, any increase of anxiety resulting from fear of punishment is so much worse than the loss of a prospect of kinetic pleasure that we are justified in insuring ourselves even against an improbable catastrophic loss. People who commit injustice to secure power or wealth for themselves are doubly mistaken; they suffer anxiety about being caught, and if they succeed their wealth and power causes them further anxiety (Lucr. v 1113–35).

These arguments against injustice do not wholly remove the case for selective unjust action. Epicureans do not reduce their desires to the absolute minimum that makes more than minimal kinetic pleasure uninteresting to them. As Epicurus says, self-sufficiency and adaptation do not require us to make do with little if we can have more without danger. If a reasonable estimate of probabilities makes it very improbable that we will suffer for our unjust action, an Epicurean who is not subject to unreasonable fears has a reason to act unjustly on some occasions.

Epicurus' view provokes the question that Plato raises with Gyges' ring. Plato removes the fear of punishment, and maintains that this is the situation in which we should ask whether someone is genuinely just. Epicurus agrees with the ancient critics who believe Plato applies an inappropriate standard in looking for the just person.[64] Plato's demand appeals to an absurdly unrealistic case; he would not be interested in such a case unless he held the empty belief that justice is worth choosing for its own sake apart from its consequences. Since this is an empty belief, it is not surprising that when we remove the reasons for being just that are derived from its consequences, we have no reason left.

---

[62] Porphyry, *Abst.* i 8.4 = LS 22M (4).

[63] Epicurus might argue that, even if discovery of our injustice is not very probable, the cost is so severe that we ought to be especially averse to this risk. This may be one aspect of Hobbes's reply to the 'fool' at §15.5.

[64] Cic. *Off.* iii 39, quoted at §50.

The Epicurean reply to Plato brings us back to the question we raised earlier about Epicurus' treatment of the belief that virtue is to be valued for itself. Justice is the hardest virtue for him to deal with, since it seems easiest in this case to see that someone who does not value virtue for itself will not act as we expect a virtuous person to act. If Epicurus admits that he would commit injustice if he had Gyges' ring, he admits that he would commit injustice in any case where he had reasonable assurance that he could avoid punishment for advantageous unjust action. If there are more of these cases than Epicurus allows, the Epicurean violates the standards that common sense imposes on a just person, even if common sense does not explicitly require a just person to choose justice for its own sake. Since Epicurus' assessment of the comparative benefits of just and unjust action may reasonably appear to exaggerate the disadvantages of unjust action for an Epicurean, he does not show that the Epicurean acts as a just person acts.

If this is a fair objection, Cicero has some reason to assert that those who exclude virtue from the final good cannot give an acceptable account of the virtues, and cannot themselves consistently acquire or practise the virtues (Cic. *Off.* i 5).[65] The charge that those who would choose injustice if they had Gyges' ring really have only a 'façade' of justice (Plato, *R.* 365c4) is a reasonable objection to Epicurus.

159. The Value of Friendship: Epicurus and Aristotle

Epicurus is more conciliatory towards common beliefs on friendship than on justice. According to Aristotle, the best kind of friend seeks the good of the other for the other's own sake, and in this way differs from friends for pleasure or advantage. We might expect Epicurus to reject the best type of Aristotelian friendship as the product of empty belief that something other than one's own pleasure is non-instrumentally good. This is his view of Plato's belief in the non-instrumental goodness of justice. A parallel view of friendship might try to show that the behaviour that Aristotle takes to be peculiar to the best kind of friendship can be found in friendships for advantage and pleasure, as long as we have an Epicurean conception of advantage and pleasure. But Epicurus' view does not seem to be quite so simple.

The difference between friendship and justice is intelligible if we consider the different character of actions in the two virtues. Plato argues that most people do not believe that just actions are worth choosing for their own sakes. Epicurus believes that this view is correct; justice is desirable only because of the instrumental benefits of the system that just behaviour supports. Something similar might be true of Aristotle's friendships for advantage, which might be treated as forms of alliance.[66] But in the case of friendships for pleasure we seem to enjoy the company of our friends apart from any further advantage. Epicurus reasonably wants to capture this difference within his theory.

He gives a high place to friendship, placing it first among the provisions made by wisdom for a happy life (DL x 148; Cic. *F* i 65). Friendship gives us some greater security in life, and so frees us from anxiety more effectively than we free ourselves by securing wealth and

---

[65] Quoted at §162. [66] Lucretius speaks of 'amicities', v 1019.

power (Cic. *F* ii 82). But it is also a source of pleasure in itself; indeed, it is pleasanter to benefit others than to receive benefits oneself (Plu. *NP* 1097a = U 544), and for the sake of one's friend one will even undergo severe pains (Plu. *Col.* 1111b = U 546). Since acts of friendship give us pleasure by themselves, apart from their further benefits, Epicurus regards friendship as a virtue because of itself rather than its consequences.[67]

These claims about friendship combine some features of Aristotelian friendship for advantage and friendship for pleasure. Epicurus suggests that like-minded friends who share the Epicurean outlook are both sources of mutual support and sources of pleasure, since they have formed the sort of outlook that we find congenial. Hence Epicurus recalls with pleasure the conversations with his friend (DL × 22).

Apparently, Epicurus' views were criticized for failing to allow the best kind of Aristotelian friendship, which requires us to love the other for the other's own sake. Since different Epicureans answered this criticism in different ways, Epicurus' views were probably not completely clear, since none of the defenders is accused of contradicting any of his explicit remarks. Cicero mentions three Epicurean accounts of friendship (*F* i 65–70; ii 78–84); each of them shows a possible defence of Epicurus' views.

The first view denies that in Epicurean friendship we come to care about the good of the other for the other's own sake. To form this concern we would have to believe that the good of the other is non-instrumentally good. But since that would be a non-instrumental good other than pleasure, it is not open to a consistent Epicurean. The Epicurean enjoys the company of his friend because it yields pleasures that he values independently of caring about the interests of the friend. This view, then, admits that Epicurus cannot accept the best kind of Aristotelian friendship, but argues that this is no loss. In valuing concern for the other for the other's own sake, we are victims of empty belief, because we do not recognize the essential aspects of friendship on a hedonist basis (*F* i 66). To gain the security that we value in friendship, we must love our friends equally with ourselves.[68] That is why we are pleased by the pleasures of our friends, just as we are by our own, and suffer in their sufferings. But this equality does not imply that we are concerned non-instrumentally for our friends.[69]

The second defence of Epicurean friendship seems to differ from the first by arguing that we initially care about friends for the sake of the instrumental benefits we gain from them, but then we come to care about them for their own sakes.[70] These Epicureans mention other examples where we initially care about something instrumentally, but then come to care about it for its own sake, even when it yields no further pleasure; we come to enjoy being in places where we have previously found pleasure or benefit, after we become attached to them in their own right (*F* i 69).[71]

---

[67] 'All friendship is a virtue (*aretê*) because of itself, and it has its origin from benefit' (*Sent. Vat.* 23 = Arr. 6.23). Some editors emend *aretê* to *hairetê*, 'choiceworthy' (see Arr. pp. 558–9, appealing to Stob. *Ecl.* ii 120.15–20); if we emend, we will prefer 'but' over 'and' in the second clause. The emended text gives Epicurus the second Epicurean view (Cic. *F* i 69; see below). But the emendation is unnecessary (see LS ii on 22 F).

[68] '...nisi aeque amicos et nosmet ipsos diligamus' (*F* i 67).

[69] One might argue against this conclusion by maintaining that (i) if we love ourselves non-instrumentally and our friends only instrumentally, we love our friends less than we love ourselves, and (ii) we love ourselves non-instrumentally. But both of these premises are open to doubt on Epicurean grounds. Epicurus on friendship is discussed by Mitsis, *EET*, ch. 3.

[70] '...ipsi amici propter se ipsos amentur' (*F* i 69).

[71] For wider doubts about whether Epicurus is a psychological hedonist see Cooper, 'Pleasure' 485–94.

The third defence traces friendship to an agreement between wise people to love their friends as much as they love themselves.[72] This defence agrees with the first against the second in taking equal love to be sufficient for friendship without non-instrumental concern. But it disagrees with the first defence in taking this equal love to be the result of an agreement, rather than the result of interactions that initially have no such aim. Both the other defences stress the difference between the initial aims of a friendship and the further aims that grow as a result of mutual interaction. Whereas the third defence treats friendship as similar to justice, in resting on agreement, the other two argue, more plausibly, that the motives characteristic of friendship grow from different motives. These defences use the resources available to an Epicurean to construct a more credible account of friendship.

The second defence differs from the other two in so far as it accepts the Aristotelian demand for non-instrumental concern. The examples that Cicero mentions show why non-instrumental concern is compatible with hedonism. The previous association between a place or an activity or a person and instrumental benefit leading to pleasure causes us to form a non-instrumental preference. This is how Mill explains the outlook of a miser who comes to care about money for its own sake, or the music-lover who comes to care about music for its own sake after having cared about it only for the sake of instrumental benefits.[73]

But if this is what the Epicureans mean, the non-instrumental concern seems to rest on 'empty belief'. We might explain the conviction that virtue is a non-instrumental good in the same way, as a product of our habitual association of the virtues with the production of pleasure. But Epicurus does not infer that virtue is a non-instrumental good; on the contrary, he rejects that view on hedonist grounds. Should an Epicurean not take the same view about friendship? It is not clear why non-instrumental concern is any more rational in the case of friendship than it would be in the case of virtue.

We might answer this objection by denying that Epicurean friendship (according to the second defence) treats non-instrumental concern as simply the product of mental association between friendship and the means to pleasure. We might say that the early stages of friendship allow us to recognize that friends and their interests are non-instrumental goods. The pleasure that we take in friendship, on this view, rests partly on the non-instrumental value that we attach to the interests of our friends and to the activities characteristic of the best kind of friendship.

This explanation shows why non-instrumental concern need not result from empty belief. It is rather similar to the Stoic explanation of the growth of non-instrumental concern for practical reason as a result of the instrumental use of practical reason.[74] But the result recognizes a type of value that does not fit a hedonist theory of value. In that case Epicurus cannot consistently maintain hedonism and accept the second defence of friendship as including non-instrumental concern for the other.

On the whole, the first defence of friendship is probably the best way to explain Epicurus' position. In contrast to the third defence, it marks the difference between justice and friendship. Just actions do not lead directly to pleasure, but are only instrumental to further results that lead to pleasure, whereas friendship is pleasant because of the activities of

---

[72] 'foedus esse quoddam . . . ut ne minus amicos quam se ipsos diligant' (F i 70). [73] Mill, U, ch. 4.
[74] See §179.

friendship themselves. In contrast to the second defence, the first does not expose Epicurus to the charge of endorsing empty beliefs about friendship while rejecting them about the cardinal virtues.

None of these Epicurean defences of friendship shows that Epicurus can meet reasonable Aristotelian standards for friendship. As Cicero points out, Epicurus assumes that friends contribute more to our security, tranquillity, and pleasure than we could gain through pursuing external resources without much regard for friendship (F ii 84–5). We might dispute his assumption by remarking that friendships involve us in efforts on behalf of our friends, and expose us to pains, dangers, and disappointments when things go wrong for our friends. Epicurus and Lucretius mock those who seek political power to gain security; they argue that the increase in anxiety makes the pursuit of security futile. But can we not say the same about friendship? If we want to avoid anxiety and disappointment, we might modify our desires in accordance with Epicurus' advice about self-sufficiency; we will enjoy the company of others when we can have it at no serious cost to ourselves, but avoid the attachments that threaten us with disappointment. This would be the outlook of fair-weather friendship.

We might well agree with Epicurus if he were to reply that the pleasures resulting from friendship outweigh the security that we gain from the fair-weather friendship that avoids the normal commitments of friendship. But our agreement with this reply rests on a non-hedonist conviction that friendship is worthwhile, and that therefore its pleasures make up for the resulting insecurity. Epicurean hedonism seems to reverse the appropriate relation between the value of friendship and the pleasures resulting from it.

160. Difficulties in Epicureanism

The discussion of Epicurean defences of friendship illustrates and reinforces a point that we have noticed at other points in Epicurus' position. His convictions about goods seem to outrun the theory of goodness that ought to support them. In so far as he is a hedonist, and supports hedonism by appeal to immediate experience, he does not give good reasons for preferring Epicurean over Cyrenaic hedonism. His defence of the Socratic hedonist eudaemonism of the *Protagoras*, relies on his version of hedonism, which is difficult to defend on purely hedonistic grounds. His defence of an adaptive conception of happiness does not answer Aristotelian objections; to show that he is right to ignore those objections, he should show more convincingly than he does that they rest on empty belief. Though he wants to defend the recognized virtues, he does not show that Epicurean hedonism justifies the common belief that they involve choosing virtuous and fine action for its own sake. To be justified in rejecting that common belief, he needs to have convinced us of a hedonist position; but then he has to rely on those arguments from immediate experience that we have found to be a weak link in his general theory.

Aristotle's arguments against a hedonistic theory of the good suggest that hedonism conflicts with two aspects of his outlook: (1) his conception of human nature, and of the connexion between human nature and the human good; (2) his conception of reasonable methods of ethical argument, appealing to reflective common beliefs. Epicurus tries to answer these Aristotelian objections. He seeks a firm epistemological basis for hedonism, in order to overcome common beliefs that count against hedonism. But his epistemological basis is not convincing in its own right; and even if it were convincing, it would not support the version of hedonism that is needed for Epicurus' ethical argument.

Not everything worth considering in his ethical outlook depends on his theory of the good. His views about pleasure, freedom, virtue, and friendship include reasonable elements that do not depend on his hedonism. But without his hedonism they do not constitute a coherent ethical theory.

12

STOICISM: ACTION, PASSION, AND REASON

161. The Stoics and their Predecessors

Stoicism is the most ambitious and comprehensive of the philosophical outlooks normally described as 'Hellenistic' (also including Epicureans, Cyrenaics, and Pyrrhonian and Academic Sceptics). 'Hellenistic' has been used by modern historians to refer to the Greek world (the areas influenced by Greek language and culture) between the death of Alexander (323 BC) and the principate of Augustus (from 31 BC). Some modern writers have held that Greek philosophy in this period reflects the characteristics of the Hellenistic 'age', in contrast to the classical 'age' of Plato and Aristotle. This attempt to link philosophers closely with the outlook of an 'age' is especially characteristic of Hegel's approach to the history of moral and political philosophy.[1]

Characteristics of the Hellenistic age have sometimes appeared to explain some of the distinctive features of Stoic ethics. The (supposed) decline of the Greek city, and the growth of larger units of government, tended (according to this view) to turn an individual's effort away from political and social life to the cultivation of inner freedom and virtue that depends on ourselves, not on unstable external conditions. In this respect Hellenistic ethics appears to be more individualistic and less social than the ethics of Plato and Aristotle.

The historical claims underlying this story about the interaction of politics, society, culture, and philosophy are worth discussing.[2] We need not discuss them here, however, since they do not contribute much to the understanding of Stoic moral philosophy. The Stoic doctrines that might be taken as responses to remote government, individual insecurity, and other aspects of the Hellenistic age, are all intelligible responses to the views of Socrates, Plato, and Aristotle. Indeed, the most 'individualistic' of the Stoic views are intelligible developments of Socratic ethics, and are therefore perfectly intelligible against the background of the classical Greek states. Hegel deals with this aspect of Socrates by declaring (absurdly) that

---

[1] See Hegel's comment on Plato's *Republic* at *Hist.* ii 96 Haldane & Simson = Suhrkamp ed xix 111.

[2] For a concise statement of historical reasons for doubting that the 'Hellenistic age' marks any radical discontinuity in social and political outlooks see Jones, 'Age'.

Athenian democracy was in decline in Socrates' time.[3] We are better advised to try to see where the Stoics enter the arguments that their predecessors have begun. They respond quite reasonably to some of the difficulties that arise for Plato and Aristotle.

This generalization might need some modification to fit the development of Stoicism in the five centuries from Zeno (born in 334 BC, twelve years before the death of Aristotle) to Marcus Aurelius (died in AD 180). The three major Stoics, Zeno, Cleanthes, and Chrysippus, lived during the Hellenistic period. No complete work by any of them has survived; we have to gather their views from fragments and paraphrases (often found in hostile critics, such as Galen and Plutarch). The fullest discussions of Stoic ethics come from Cicero, Seneca, and Epictetus, who lived under the later Roman Republic and earlier Empire. A complete study of Stoic ethics would need to discuss possible differences between the major Stoic sources, but for our purposes we can set aside such questions. Even if the position we are describing was not completely worked out in the three major Stoics, it is impressively coherent, and deserves study as a whole.

The Stoics agree with the Epicureans in defending some aspects of Socrates' position against Plato and Aristotle. In doing so, they follow the one-sided Socratic schools. The Cyrenaics defend Socratic hedonism. Since they agree with Plato and Aristotle that hedonism conflicts with eudaemonism, they abandon eudaemonism. This defence of Socratic hedonism raises doubts about whether the Socratic virtues are worth cultivating. Epicurus tries to support the virtues by defending the eudaemonist hedonism of the *Protagoras* against Platonic and Aristotelian criticisms. The Stoics agree with the position of the Cynics, who defend the sufficiency of virtue for happiness. Following the Cynics, they advocate inflexible integrity in complete indifference to any gain or loss of external goods. In their view, the Peripatetics fail to meet these standards for an adequate defence of virtue.[4]

This Cynic influence on Stoicism begins with Zeno, who was a pupil of Crates the Cynic, and is still present in Seneca, who sometimes presents Cynic doctrines sympathetically.[5] But the Stoics differ from the Cynics about why virtue is sufficient for happiness. The one-sided Socratics, following Socrates, generally combine the sufficiency thesis with instrumentalism; they regard virtue as a purely instrumental means to happiness, and take happiness to be wholly external to virtue.[6] Plato and Aristotle criticize this instrumentalist doctrine, arguing that virtue is to be chosen for its own sake, as a part of happiness. The Stoics accept the objections to instrumentalism, but they do not draw Plato's and Aristotle's conclusion. They notice that Socrates' claim that virtue is sufficient for happiness need not be defended, as Socrates and the Cynics defend it, by treating virtue as an infallible instrumental means to happiness. They prefer to defend it by arguing that virtue is identical to happiness, and hence its sole component. In their view, all the recognized non-moral, external goods and evils are neither good nor bad, but simply indifferent, since they neither promote nor impede happiness.

---

[3] See Hegel, *PR* §138.   [4] See Sen. *Ep.* 92.19–20.   [5] See Sen. *Ben.* vii 1–2, discussed at §35n5.
[6] We have seen, however, that it is not always clear whether Socrates and the Cynics maintain this purely instrumental conception of virtue. It may be more accurate to say that they do not clearly reject instrumentalism than to say that they affirm it. See §39.

This revision—or, as the Stoics may suppose, interpretation—of Socrates retains a central Socratic paradox.[7] According to Aristotle, the claim that virtue is sufficient for happiness is so implausible that no one would maintain it except as a philosophical exercise.[8] Plato and Aristotle regard external, non-moral goods (health, physical safety, freedom from pain, etc.) as components of happiness that are not infallibly secured by virtue. Hence they believe virtue is insufficient for happiness. The Stoics recognize that they disagree with Plato and Aristotle on this point.[9]

Though the Stoics reject the Platonic and Aristotelian view, they try to explain why it might seem plausible. All external 'goods' and 'evils' are really indifferent, and hence virtue is the whole of happiness. Still, even though health is not good and illness is not bad, we have good reason to try to be healthy rather than ill. That is why health is a 'preferred' indifferent, and illness is a 'non-preferred' indifferent.

162. Eudaemonism

However paradoxical the Stoics' position may appear, it avoids the extreme paradox (in the view of most Greek moralists) of rejecting eudaemonism. The Cyrenaics agree with Plato and Aristotle that hedonism is inconsistent with eudaemonism; to defend hedonism against Plato and Aristotle they abandon eudaemonism. An extreme position opposite to Cyrenaic non-eudaemonist hedonism would be an 'extreme moralist' claim that virtue is the only thing that matters, without reference to happiness. Cynic opponents of the Cyrenaics, however, do not seem to adopt extreme moralism. Their defence of virtue as the only thing that matters depends on an adaptive conception of happiness and on their claim that virtue secures the appropriate adaptation. This asymmetry between the Cyrenaic treatment of pleasure and the Cynic treatment of virtue suggests that it is more plausible to regard pleasure as an independently intelligible object of desire than to regard virtue this way; the Cynics do not take virtue to matter independently of happiness. Hence extreme moralism,

---

[7] Cicero comments: 'Since these <Stoic views> are amazing, and contrary to the opinions of everyone (and the Stoics themselves call them *paradoxa*), I wanted to try to see whether they could be brought into the light ... And I wrote all the more readily in so far as these views that they call *paradoxa* seem to me to be Socratic to the highest degree and by a long way the truest' (Cic. *Parad*. 4). On the Socratic paradoxes see §9. On the Stoics and Socrates cf. Cic. *Ac*. ii 136; *TD* iii 10; Long, 'Socrates'; Striker, 'Socrates'.

[8] See *EN* 1095b30–1096a2; 1153b14–25; §70.

[9] In Chrysippus' view, Plato does away with justice and any other genuine virtue because he recognizes such things as health as goods (Plu. *SR* 1040d). Chrysippus probably has the *Republic* in mind (cf. 1040a–b). Plutarch is a Platonist, and often criticizes the Stoics for misunderstanding the philosophers they discuss. But in this case, he raises no objection to Chrysippus' interpretation of Plato; he criticizes him not for misinterpreting Plato, but for disagreeing with the Platonic and Aristotelian doctrine. We have no evidence to suggest that Chrysippus attacks Socrates for the mistake that he attributes to Plato. On the contrary, the Stoics recognize, as Cicero does (*Parad*. 4), the Socratic origin of their views on virtue and happiness. In contrast to Chrysippus, however, some other Stoics try to identify the Platonic view with the Stoic view, and therefore with the Socratic view. Antipater the Stoic wrote a work in three books asserting that according to Plato only the fine is good, and that therefore virtue is self-sufficient for happiness (Clement, *Strom*. v 97.6 = *SVF* iii, Antip. 56). If he thought it necessary to write a whole treatise on this question, other Stoics probably disagreed with his interpretation of Plato.

opposite to non-eudaemonist hedonism, is only a logical possibility within Hellenistic ethics; no one actually tries it.[10]

The Stoics recognize an ultimate end for rational action, and they follow Aristotle in identifying the end with happiness.[11] They also agree with Aristotle in taking happiness to include all and only genuine goods; for they take their claim that 'only the fine is good' to be equivalent to the claim that virtue is self-sufficient for happiness (Cic. F. iii 26–9). If happiness included other things besides goods, the proof that virtue is the only good would not show that it is sufficient by itself for happiness.

Later moral philosophy disagrees with the Stoics on this point, and offers different options. On the one hand, Scotus affirms non-eudaemonist moralism against the eudaemonism (as he understands it) of Aristotle and Aquinas. On the other hand, Hobbes and his successors follow the Cyrenaics in rejecting eudaemonism (though without drawing all the Cyrenaic conclusions). Most of Hobbes's opponents defend extreme moralism rather than eudaemonism. These modern moralists, such as Price and Reid, who defend the non-instrumental and overriding value of morality are often explicitly sympathetic to Stoicism, but they separate their defence of morality from Stoic eudaemonism.[12]

This difference between the Stoics and their modern defenders may provoke us to ask how much eudaemonism matters in the Stoics' position. Is their acceptance of eudaemonism merely a verbal concession to their predecessors, or to common ways of speaking? Or does it make a difference to the substance of their moral theory, and especially to their conception of the value of the moral virtues? An answer to these questions will help us to decide whether later moralists depart significantly from their predecessors in trying to defend virtue without reference to happiness.

The Stoics affirm that their eudaemonism is necessary for a correct appreciation of the non-instrumental value of the virtues, and therefore necessary for having the virtues. We have the virtues only if we see the connexion between virtue and happiness; for if we take happiness not to include virtue, and so measure it by our own advantage, we cannot consistently cultivate the virtues.[13] Individual Epicureans, for instance, may be virtuous people, but, if they are, their outlook is inconsistent with the implications of their theory (Cic. F. ii 80). Since their conception of the final good leaves out the right (*expers honestatis*, Cic. F. ii 35), it demotes the virtues to a purely instrumental status that the virtuous person rejects.[14]

---

[10] On the Cynics see §39.

[11] They define the end as 'that for the sake of which all things are done appropriately, while it is done for the sake of nothing' (Stob. ii 46.5–7 = SVF iii 2; cf. ii 76.21–3). 'They say that the end is being happy, for the sake of which all things are done, while it is done, but for the sake of nothing' (Stob. ii 77.16–17 = LS 63A). They distinguish happiness (*eudaimonia*), which is the 'goal' (*skopos*), from 'being happy' (*eudaimonein*), which is the act of achieving the goal (ii 77.23–7 = LS 63A).

[12] See Price, *RPQM* 257; Reid, *EAP* 586a H.

[13] 'But some schools distort every duty (officium) by the ends of goods and evils that they present. For anyone who introduces the supreme good in such a way that it has no connexion with virtue, and measures it by his own advantages, and not by the right (honestum), this person, if he is consistent with himself and is not sometimes overcome by goodness of nature, could not cultivate either friendship or justice or generosity; and certainly he cannot possibly be brave if he judges pain the highest evil, or temperate if he takes pleasure to be the highest good' (*Off.* i 5).

[14] I will normally use 'right' to render *honestum* and 'fine' (as before) to render *kalon*. This is awkward, since Cicero uses the Latin term to render the Greek. But it is not wholly misleading, since the Latin terms lack the aesthetic character of the Greek. Latin allows a distinction between the beautiful (pulchrum) and the right (honestum) that marks two

The Stoics assert that we have reason to value virtue and virtuous action as non-instrumentally good if and only if we regard them as a part of happiness. They do not endorse the extreme moralist view that the requirements of moral virtue and of rightness require agents to act against their happiness or to act without regard to their happiness. They believe that we have reason to value virtue and virtuous action appropriately if and only if we have reason to regard them as non-instrumentally good. But (from the eudaemonist point of view) we have reason to value virtue and virtuous action as non-instrumentally good if and only if we regard them as a part of happiness. Hence (the Stoics conclude) we have reason to value them appropriately if and only if we regard them as a part of happiness.

This eudaemonist argument conflicts with different moralist claims. A non-eudaemonist argues that we have sufficient reason to pursue virtue above all other goods or advantages even if it conflicts with our happiness or it does not affect it either way. This non-eudaemonist view is defended by, for instance, Scotus, Butler, and Kant; it claims only that happiness is not needed for a sufficient justification of virtue. It does not claim that happiness is irrelevant, or that it cannot provide any reason; on the contrary, both Butler and Kant believe that an appeal to happiness provides an important further defence of morality.

In contrast to this non-eudaemonist view, a rigorist form of moralism is anti-eudaemonist, claiming that we value virtue appropriately only if we do not regard it as a part of, or a means to, our happiness. This rigorism may be traced back to Augustine's objections to self-love. It is explicit and prominent in the French Quietists and in Mandeville. Schopenhauer and Prichard are later defenders of rigorism.[15] These strongly anti-eudaemonist moralists defend the position that the Stoics denounce as incompatible with the morally virtuous outlook.

Both the Stoics and their opponents defend their position as the only one that allows the correct estimate of the value of the moral virtues. To see whether this is a significant dispute, and what can be said on either side of it, we ought to try to understand the Stoic position, and especially its eudaemonist elements.

163. Reactions to Stoic Ethics

The different aspects of Stoicism that we have surveyed help to explain why estimates of it have been so various. Its influence has been continuous from the Church Fathers, to Aquinas (who knows it from Patristic sources), and to modern moralists. But different people have attended to different elements of the Stoic view. Some of the disagreements about Stoicism already appear in Cicero's comments, and they have affected interpretation and criticism of the Stoic position ever since.

Some critics attack the apparently extravagant character of the Stoic conclusions. Since all reputed goods and evils except virtue and vice are indifferents, the Stoic sage apparently

---

aspects of the Greek term. A translation that might cover all the uses of *honestum* and *pulchrum* would be 'admirable'. See further §332.

[15] See Mandeville, *FB* i 56 (Kaye) = R 270; Schopenhauer, *WR* i 524; Prichard, *MO* 13.

sees no reason to be strongly concerned about anything other than virtue and vice.[16] This reaction results from one-sided attention to the points on which the Stoics seem to agree with the Cynic interpretation of Socrates. To show that this reaction is misguided, the Stoics need to show that they depart far enough from Cynics to avoid the least credible aspects of the Cynic position.[17]

Other critics, however, argue that the Stoics agree with Aristotle on the substantive issues. Cicero suggests that when we see the Stoic 'paradoxes' from close range, they no longer seem so paradoxical (Cic. F iv 74). The Academic Carneades claims that the Stoics' disagreements with Aristotle are merely verbal.[18] These critics attend to the Stoic doctrine of preferred indifferents, claiming that it concedes the substance of what Aristotle claims about the importance of external goods.

The choice facing the Stoics is parallel, in some ways, to the choice facing Epicurus. When Epicurus follows the Cyrenaics in accepting the hedonist aspects of Socratic ethics, he seems to be open to the objections that Plato and Aristotle raise against hedonism. In answering these objections, he seems to be in danger of abandoning the features of his position that distinguish it from Aristotle's position. Similarly, when the Stoics follow the Cynics in accepting the side of Socratic ethics that treats virtue as the only good, they seem to be open to the objections that Plato and Aristotle raise against this Socratic thesis. Their answers to these objections may seem to concede to Aristotle the essential points on which the Stoics claim to disagree with him, and hence may seem to make the Stoic position only verbally different from the Aristotelian.

To fix this question more precisely, we should notice that the claim about 'verbal difference' is ambiguous, and may refer to either of two quite different claims about the Stoics: (1) The difference between Aristotle and the Stoics would be purely verbal in a sense that would make it trivial, if for every Stoic claim about (say) preferred indifferents we could substitute an Aristotelian claim about external goods, and reach a theoretically equivalent conclusion. (2) But if the Stoics agree with the Aristotelians about 'substance' in the sense of agreeing about what a virtuous person ought to do on every particular occasion, it does not follow that any further differences between the two positions are trivial or unimportant. We need moral theory to explain and to justify virtuous action, and not only to tell us what to do. If the Stoics give better reasons for the same actions, their effort is worth while.

It is relatively easy to argue that the Stoics agree with Peripatetics about actions, and that in this sense they agree in 'substance'. But it would be a mistake to infer, as some ancient critics perhaps infer, that the disagreement with Aristotelians is unimportant; for the difference in theory may be important. We need to keep these different possibilities in mind when we compare the Stoic with the Peripatetic position.

---

[16] Cicero contrasts this inhuman and absurd obsession with moral virtue with the warmer and more appealing attitude of the Peripatetics (*Pro Murena* 61–3).

[17] This interpretation of Stoic indifference to non-moral considerations underlies the criticisms in Sorabji, *AMHM* 140; Nussbaum, *TD* 360–3, 416–17; Adam Smith, §182 below.

[18] 'Carneades never ceased to contend that in all of this inquiry under the head of goods and evils, the Stoics' dispute with the Peripatetics was about names, not about facts' (*Cic. F.* iii 41). For other remarks about the purely verbal character of Stoic disagreements with Aristotle see *F.* iv 20, 72; v 22.

164. Stoic Strategies

The Stoics' reasons for preferring their revision of the Socratic position over the Platonic and Aristotelian revisions will be clearer if we understand their methods of ethical argument and their views about the place of ethics within their philosophical system. They emphasize the coherence and connexion in their philosophy as a whole (Cic. *F.* iii 73–4). Different Stoics teach ethics in different ways that express different aspects of the system. Chrysippus believes that the three parts of philosophy should be taught in the order: logic, ethics, physics (i.e., natural philosophy), culminating in theology.[19] Zeno, by contrast, is reported to have favoured the order: logic, physics, ethics.[20]

This suggestion of disagreement or inconsistency may be misleading. Chrysippus intends the study of physics and theology to be relevant to ethics; Zeus and the 'common nature' of the universe are the starting point for ethical doctrines.[21] Hence Chrysippus seems to agree with Zeno in deriving ethics from natural philosophy. But different orders of exposition reflect different types of priority. As Aristotle recognizes, what is prior 'to us', in our learning, may be posterior 'by nature', in the structure of a completed science. Aristotle relies on this division to mark out the distinct roles of dialectical argument (relying on common beliefs) and demonstrative argument (relying on scientific principles already established). The Stoics might reasonably rely on a similar distinction.[22]

Moreover, some ethical claims might be prior to physics and theology and some might be derived from physical or theological premises. The Stoics believe that the universe is governed by a divine providential intelligence, aiming at the good of the whole and of each part. To find some reason for believing this, we need some account of the good of each part of the universe, including ourselves. If we assumed that the good is sensual pleasure or freedom from pain, we would expect a providential order of the universe to maximize our pleasure or to minimize our pain. Before we know what to expect from a providential order, we need some conception of our good.

Some part of ethics, then, seems to precede arguments to show that a providential intelligence governs the world. This does not mean that our initial ethical convictions cannot be revised in the light of our understanding of the world and of our place in it. The Stoics believe that in promoting the good of the whole we promote our own good;[23]

---

[19] 'Chrysippus: "... I believe there are three parts of the philosopher's subject of study ... One part is logical, one ethical, one physical. Of these logic must be put first, then ethics, then physics. And the last part of physics is the account of the gods; hence the transmission of that is called "initiation".""' (Plu. *SR* 1035a = *SVF* ii 42 = LS 26C).

[20] For different orders cf. DL vii 40 = *SVF* ii 41; Sx. *M* vii 22–3; *PH* ii 13.

[21] 'For hear what he says about these things in the third book *On the Gods*: "For we can find no other origin (*archê*) or genesis of justice than the one proceeding from Zeus and common nature. For from here everything of this kind must have its origin if we are going to say anything about goods and evils." And again he says in his *Natural Postulates*: "For there is no other and no more appropriate approach to the account of goods and evils, or to the virtues, or to happiness, than the one that proceeds from common nature and the government of the world order." The account of nature, then, turns out to be at the same time before and behind ethics, according to Chrysippus' (Plu. *SR* 1035c–d).

[22] See Aristotle, *EN* 1095b2–4: see §67. This division in Stoic arguments is suggested by the title of a work by Chrysippus, 'On the fact that the ancients accepted dialectic together with demonstrations' (DL vii 201, one of three ethical works by Chrysippus on dialectic). See Brunschwig, 'Title'; Cooper, 'Moral duty' 440.

[23] 'Always remember what is your own, and what belongs to another; and you will not be disturbed. Chrysippus therefore said well, "So long as future things are uncertain, I always cling to whatever is more adapted to gaining the things in accord with nature; for God himself has made me disposed to elect (*eklektikon*) such things. But if I knew that it

perhaps we have to take the point of view of cosmic providence before we can see that the good of the whole is our good.

It is reasonable, then, for the Stoics to argue in both directions between natural philosophy and ethics. It is worth our while to see what conclusions they defend apart from theology. This is useful both because it allows us to grasp the ethical basis of Stoic theology and because it allows us to see how they argue with their predecessors, apart from any appeal to specifically Stoic doctrines in natural philosophy and theology.

165. Preconceptions

The Stoics recognize that they need some non-theological ethical principles, and some form of ethical argument to support these principles. Just after quoting Chrysippus' remarks about the derivation of ethics from Zeus and universal nature, Plutarch quotes his claim that he relies on human life and on ethical 'preconceptions'. These are basic in our ethical thinking because they are the principles and standards[24] in the light of which we assess our other ethical beliefs.[25] Plutarch believes that this appeal to human life and to preconceptions conflicts with the paradoxical aspects of the Stoic view. But the Stoics disagree; they believe that the apparent paradoxes of their position result from their adherence to preconceptions.

Sometimes, then, Stoic views seem to violate common sense, and the contrary view may seem persuasive because it avoids the apparent paradoxes of Stoicism.[26] But the Stoics answer that their views are really closer to common sense, properly understood, than rival theories are. If some other beliefs conflict with preconceptions, we ought, in the Stoic view, to give up the other beliefs rather than the preconceptions.

In Epictetus' view, we must both understand the preconceptions and align our other views with them.[27] Different people's assent to the same preconceptions does not prevent

---

was fated for me to be sick, I would even move toward it; for the foot also, if it had intelligence, would move to go into the mud." ' (Epict. ii 6.9–10 = LS 58J. It is not clear where the quotation from Chrysippus ends). Epictetus denies that acting for the good of the whole involves self-sacrifice. See ii 5.24–6.

[24] Preconceptions are *kanones*. See Epict. i 28.28, quoted in n26. They are the equivalent of standard weights that we use to settle how heavy things are, instead of relying haphazardly on our appearances (i 28.28–30).

[25] 'Chrysippus says that the account of goods and evils that he introduces and approves keeps closest to life, and especially to the inborn preconceptions (*prolêpseis*). For he has said this in the third book of his *Protreptics*. But in the first book he says that this account draws a human being away from all other things <apart from virtue>, as being nothing to us and contributing nothing to happiness' (Plu. *SR* 1041e). The *prolêpsis* of a craft or a profession is its fundamental assumption or conception; see Epict. iv 8.6, 10.

[26] 'If the persuasiveness of things makes some things appear to be good, when they are not good, let us seek to bring reinforcements at that point. If habit oppresses us, we should try to assemble reinforcements against that. . . . You hear uninstructed people (*idiôtai*) say: "That poor man! He is dead. His father or mother perished. He was cut off by an untimely death and in a foreign land." Listen to the contrary arguments. Drag yourself away from the common ways of speaking. Oppose to one habit the contrary habit. . . . Against the persuasiveness of things we ought to have evident preconceptions, cleaned and polished, and ready to hand' (Epict. i 27.2–6). ' "And so when women are carried off, when children are made captives, and when the men are killed, are these not evils?" . . . Let us come to the standards (*kanones*); bring forward the preconceptions' (i 28.26–8). Continued in n31.

[27] 'Preconceptions are common to all human beings; and preconception does not conflict with preconception. For which of us does not assume that the good is beneficial and choiceworthy, and that we must seek and pursue it in every circumstance? Which of us does not assume that the just is fine and fitting? Whence then comes the conflict? In the application of preconceptions to particular realities when one says "He has acted finely, he is brave", while another

disagreement; but with careful attention to our agreed preconceptions we will eventually reach agreement.[28] We assume at the outset that the preconceptions are consistent. If we do not assume this about our preconceptions as a whole, or at least (as Aristotle says) about 'the most and most important' of them, we have no further basis for deciding which ethical beliefs we should accept or reject, and hence we implicitly challenge all our ethical beliefs.[29]

These are insufficient reasons for asserting that our preconceptions are consistent. For the Sceptics argue that we should acknowledge conflicts among our most basic ethical beliefs, and should therefore draw a Sceptical conclusion.[30] The Stoics cannot reasonably ignore or dismiss this Sceptical alternative by assuming that preconceptions must be consistent. But they may fairly assume at the outset that they are consistent, so that we can see whether this assumption allows us to understand our ethical beliefs as a coherent and plausible position. If they can be aligned with our preconceptions so that the result is coherent and plausible, we have answered the Sceptical claims about conflicts.

Epictetus warns us that our preconceptions will seem to us to conflict, if we confuse the real content of preconceptions with the hasty conventional assumptions that we rely on in applying preconceptions to particular situations. But if we do not follow hasty conventional assumptions, and we apply preconceptions systematically, we find, in Epictetus' view, that their application to specific types of situations undermines our thoughtless conventional assumptions.

We may hastily suppose, for instance, that it would be cowardly to refrain from retaliating against criticism by another person, even if we know we have deserved it. A traditional Greek view holds that a real man retaliates for injury, whether or not it is deserved. But we will reject this view, once we recall that cowardice involves acting out of inappropriate fear, that honesty requires us to accept justified criticism, and that acting out of honesty is not acting out of inappropriate fear. Similarly, we ought not to believe that only a coward refuses a challenge to a duel. If a duel is a foolish way of settling a quarrel, refusal of a challenge does not betray cowardice, since it rests on appropriate moral considerations.

Many Platonic and Aristotelian ethical arguments rely on beliefs that the Stoics call preconceptions. In the Socratic dialogues, the preconceptions are our general assumptions about the virtues. Since Laches agrees with Socrates that bravery is always fine, he reconsiders

says "Not at all; he's crazy". Hence people's conflict with one other arises' (i 22.1–4 = LS 40S). 'What, then, is it to be educated? It consists in learning to apply the natural preconceptions to the particular beings conformably to nature' (i 22.9 = LS 40S). 'Let him not be a fool. Let him learn, as Socrates would say, "what is each of the things that are"; and let him not apply his preconceptions at random to each of the particular beings. For this is the cause of all evils to men—not to be able to apply the common preconceptions to the particular things' (iv 1.41–2).

[28] 'What misleads most people is what misleads Theopompus the rhetorician, who actually attacks Plato for wanting to define each thing. What does he say? "Did none of us speak of good or just before you [sc. Plato]? Or when we did not grasp what each of these is, did we utter the sounds insignificantly and emptily?" Who tells you, Theopompus, that we did not have natural conceptions and preconceptions of each of these? But we cannot fit our preconceptions to the corresponding beings if we have not articulated them and examined this very thing—what sort of being is to be assigned to each of them. . . . Which of us does not talk about good and evil and beneficial and harmful? For which of us does not have a preconception of each of these? Then you have an articulated and complete preconception? Prove it. . . . Apply it well to particular beings . . . ' (ii 17.5–11).

[29] See Aristotle, EN 1145b2–7 (quoted at §67); 1172b35–1173a2. Sidgwick considers this sort of challenge in the concluding chapter of ME.

[30] See §136.

his view that senseless endurance is brave; he recognizes that it is shameful and not fine, and so he infers that it is not after all brave (Plato, *La.* 193d1–8).

More controversial appeals to preconceptions introduce distinctively Stoic doctrines. We suppose that a just person who is suddenly impoverished because of his just action has suffered some genuine harm, and is really worse off. The Stoics argue, however, that we will no longer suppose this, once we apply all our preconceptions to the situation, and once we interpret each of them so that it is consistent with all the others. In this case we must recognize that (1) we always ought to be just, no matter what it costs us; (2) just actions sometimes lead to impoverishment; (3) we never lose any genuine good by doing what we ought to do. The third step in this argument is the most difficult to accept.[31]

The Stoic doctrine of preconceptions suggests the standards that are relevant for evaluating ethical arguments. In the Stoic view, non-Stoic views have to violate principles that we can recognize as basic in our ethical reflexion. If the Stoic view is the only one that avoids conflict with these principles, we ought to accept it, however paradoxical it may initially appear. We have to apply our preconceptions to reject or to modify the appearance that previously invited thoughtless assent. To avoid this thoughtless assent, we have to 'exercise' by reminding ourselves of the relevant preconceptions, so that appearances do not drag us off or sweep us away by their immediate appeal (their 'sharpness').[32] Agamemnon and Achilles and other tragic characters made mistakes because they simply 'followed their appearances' by assenting without proper reflection (i 28.31). We can avoid their mistakes if we are ready for the misleading suggestions that we may receive from appearances; we must remind ourselves that the situations that appear bad are not really bad.[33]

To understand how we can criticize appearances in the light of our preconceptions, we need to look more closely at Stoic accounts of mind and action. Socrates does not try to explain why his elenctic approach to common-sense moral views is difficult to accept, or why his resolution of the puzzles in common sense is the right one. Even Plato and Aristotle do not make it completely clear why common beliefs, on the one hand, are wrong enough to need dialectical examination, but, on the other hand, are near enough to the truth to provide reasonable starting points for this examination. The Stoics try to explain these points.

Their explanation begins from facts about nature. In their view, an examination of human nature and mental development should lead us to expect that our moral beliefs will be subject to error and distortion; that is why we do not immediately believe Stoic claims about

---

[31] An example of this form of argument appears in Epictetus' remarks on death: 'When death appears an evil, we ought to have at hand the argument that it is appropriate to avoid evil things, and death is a necessary thing <and therefore cannot be avoided>. For what am I do to? Where I am to go to escape it?' (Epict. i 27.7–8, continuing quotation in n26 above).

[32] 'As we exercise against sophistical questions, so we should exercise ourselves daily against appearances; for they also propose questions to us. "So-and-so's son is dead." Answer: Not chosen (*aprohaireton*); not evil. "He was in pain at this." A matter for choice (*prohairetikon*); evil. "He has endured it nobly." A matter for choice; good. And if we habituate ourselves this way, we will progress. For we will never assent to anything unless we have a grasping (*kataleptikê*) appearance of it' (Epict. iii 8.1–4). We learn to say 'Wait for me a minute, appearance; let me see what you are, and about what; let me put you to the test' (ii 18.24).

[33] (Continued from n31 above.) 'Where we intend to judge of weights, we do not judge at random... But in things that depend on the primary and sole cause of success (*katorthoun*; see §184) or failure, of good flow or bad flow, of being unfortunate or fortunate, there only we act randomly and rashly. Nowhere is there anything like scales, nowhere anything like a standard, but something has appeared and at once I act on it.... What are people who follow every appearance called? "They are called madmen."' (i 28.28–33).

virtue and happiness. But they also try to show that the development of practical reason makes it possible for us to form rational preconceptions and to use them for the constructive criticism of our moral beliefs.

166. Nature, Conciliation, and Appearances

The Stoics argue that the pursuit of natural advantages[34] (health, physical security, social relations, family life, and so on) is a reasonable result of our natural development. On the other hand, this same natural development also shows us why these objectives[35] are not genuine goods, and why virtue is really the only good. This argument from natural development relies on the Stoic account of 'conciliation' (oikeiôsis).[36]

The Stoics begin with a creature's initial impulse towards its own preservation and its own good.[37] The creature is conciliated to its environment, and so detects things that are good for it. But this conciliation would not benefit creatures unless they were also conciliated to themselves, and so loved themselves and their preservation.[38] Their systematically goal-directed activities manifest self-love.[39] An animal does not occasionally adopt means to particular ends; it displays some broad overall system and consistency in attitudes to the environment.[40] Self-love regulates and co-ordinates a creature's desires as a whole.[41]

This gives us a preliminary idea of the good. A creature's welfare consists in the co-ordinated achievement of the primary impulses that are directed towards the fulfilment of our natural needs.[42] Animals and human beings act for their own good through their cognitive access to the world. This access comes through the senses and the resulting

---

[34] I translate ta prôta kata phusin (lit. the 'primary things in accordance with nature') by 'natural advantages'.

[35] 'Objective' is the Stoic term; see §178.

[36] See DL vii 85 = LS 56A, Cic. F. iii 16–20; Striker, 'Role'; Engberg-Pederson, 'Discovering'. We might also render oikeiôsis by 'appropriation', 'endearment', or 'adaptation'.

[37] 'The nature of all things has generated us, and has placed in us, and planted at once in those very first principles by which we were born, a love and endearment to ourselves, so much that nothing at all would be dearer and weightier to us than ourselves. And she thought that this would be the foundation for maintaining the perpetuity of human beings, if each one of us, as soon as he is delivered into the light, first of all acquired a sense and affection of those things which by the earlier philosophers were called "the first things according to nature" [Gellius quotes in Greek], so that of course he would delight in all the things suitable for his body and would avoid all the unsuitable things' (Aulus Gellius, NA xii 5.7, continued in §180n28).

[38] 'As soon as a creature is born it is conciliated to itself and commended towards conserving itself and towards loving its state and those things that conserve its state' (Cic. F iii 16).

[39] 'It is not surprising that they are born with that without which they would be born pointlessly. This is the first piece of equipment that nature placed in them for their preservation—their conciliation and attachment to themselves. They could not have been preserved unless they wanted it' (Sen. Ep. 121.24).

[40] 'There must be something to which other things are to be referred. I seek pleasure. For whom? For myself. So I take care for myself. I avoid pain. On whose behalf? On my own. Hence I take care for myself. If I do everything because of my care for myself, my care for myself comes before everything' (Sen. Ep. 121.17).

[41] 'We were asking whether all animals had some sense (sensus) of their constitution. It is clearest of all that they have from the way they move their limbs suitably and nimbly just as though they had been trained for it. . . . Nature is more easily understood (intelligitur) than explained (enarratur); and so the child does not know (novit) what a constitution is, but knows his own constitution. What an animal is he does not know (nescit); but he senses that he is an animal' (Sen. Ep. 121.5–11).

[42] 'For nature which has given us the soul has also given us the body, and has conciliated us to the completion (teleiotês) and the sorts of provisions needful for each of them. And so someone deprived of the completion according to nature of the one of these would not live according to nature either . . .' (Alex. Mant. 163.14–17)

'appearances' (*phantasiai*); through them things appear a certain way to us, and when we have a suitable appearance, it results in an impulse (*hormê*) to get something. The Stoics do not claim that a young animal has an explicit conception of itself and a desire directed on the self defined by that conception. Seneca insists that some sort of non-explicit knowledge is all that is ascribed. The creature's behaviour justifies us in ascribing mental states to it with the content 'This is good for me' or something like that; for it acts in ways we would expect creatures with such a belief to act.

The Stoics believe they have said enough to undermine a hedonist conception of the final good. To explain action and the development of rational choice we must assume, in the Stoic view, that we desire natural goods for ourselves for their own sake. Pleasure is only a supervenient end, resulting from the experience following our achievement of the natural goods (Cic. *F.* iii 17). We must assume a desire for our self-preservation if the process is to begin.

A hedonist might answer that a creature acquires a desire for pleasure after some early experience of it. We might find that a creature is inert, needs to be moved by others, or moves at random until its first experience of pleasure, after which it concentrates on pleasure as its end. But the Stoics could fairly reply that this is not what we find. From the start we find fairly organized and consistent behaviour, best explained on the assumption that the creature desires its own good and acts on its beliefs about it; and its own good will consist in the satisfaction of its natural impulses. As Cicero remarks, no one would be indifferent between being sound in limb and being maimed, even if it made no difference to efficiency (*F.* iii 17). Apparently, pleasure is not all we care about; our behaviour would be inexplicable if we did not care about the natural goods for their own sake.

Epicurus is wrong, therefore, in the Stoic view, to suppose that the study of natural development supports a hedonist account of the good. His position reflects the influence of Cyrenaic anti-eudaemonism. If we focus narrowly on our experience in a particular situation, we may reasonably argue that in achieving the satisfaction of our natural desires we achieve pleasure, and that we find this pleasure attractive to us on future occasions also. If, then, we thought of our desires and satisfactions as a sequence of episodes linked only by memory and anticipation, we might be attracted by the hedonist position.[43] If the Cyrenaics are right in their objections to a continuing self, an agent is simply a sequence of episodes of pleasure or pain, linked by memory and anticipation. In the Stoic view, however, the Cyrenaic and Epicurean description of pleasure and desire leaves out the aspects of agency that are captured by the doctrine of conciliation.

Stoic claims about conciliation attend to the system and pattern in desires. Even before agents are guided by explicit preconceptions, their desires are more than a collection of impulses aimed at unconnected satisfactions. They are linked by a common concern for the agent as a whole, conceived as a continuing self. Though the Stoics agree that agents without explicit reason have no explicit conception of themselves as continuing agents, a non-explicit conception of themselves explains the system and co-ordination in their desires. Once we see this system, we cannot suppose that the pleasure of satisfying particular desires is all that they care about for its own sake.

---

[43] See §154; Brunschwig, 'Cradle'.

At an early stage, human beings are like other animals; their appearances include an attractive element, so that if something appears pleasant (etc.), it thereby excites impulse and produces action. Later, however, we acquire the capacity to assent to our appearances and to dissent from them. Our appearances do not change their character; the things that appeared pleasant still appear pleasant, and are therefore still attractive, but we no longer follow them without question. We do not follow them until we assent.

Assent is not simply a further appearance directed to the initial appearance. If we formed a tendency to accept or to welcome some appearances and to reject others, we would have what Hume calls a 'lively idea'.[44] But this is not what the Stoics identify with assent. They argue that whereas appearance is passive, and depends on the environment, assent is active (Sx. *M* vii 237).[45] Appearance is involuntary, and assent is voluntary and depends on our judgment (*krisis*) (viii 397).[46] Assent implies 'conviction' or 'persuasion' (*peisma*), which the Sceptic avoids (viii 159).[47]

Since assent is rational, it applies the distinctive rationality of human agents to action. Epictetus claims that human beings fulfil their nature by exercising their rationality,[48] and they exercise this rationality in their assents and dissents.

167. Passions as Assents

Though our capacity to assent includes the capacity to reflect on our appearances and to criticize them, its first exercises do not lead us far from our appearances. When we begin to assent, we are used to having appearances that have moved us to action by themselves. These same appearances are still strongly suggestive, and we tend to assent to them.[49] This sort of assent 'yields' to appearances (Plu. *SR* 1056f = LS 41E; 1057a = LS 53S), and results in an 'affection' or 'passion' (*pathos*). A passion is an 'immediate' or 'fresh' assent that consists in yielding to an appearance that some natural advantage or disadvantage is good or evil.[50] In immediate assents we yield to our first appearances of how things are. Sometimes we yield immediately because the appearance comes on us suddenly and without preparation.[51]

---

[44] See Hume's account of belief, *T* i 3.7 §5.

[45] Hence proof is the product of thought (*dianoia*) and assent, which are rational (*logika*) (Sx. *M* viii 301).

[46] Cicero draws the same contrast: Zeno contrasts the receptivity of appearance with the assent of the mind 'which he wants to be up to us and voluntary' (*in nobis positam et voluntariam*) (*Ac.* i 40 = LS 40B). Assent is 'in our power' (*in nostra potestate sita*) (ii 37 = LS 40O).

[47] On Sceptical assent see §139.

[48] 'God needed other animals using their appearances, but needed us understanding our use of them. And so for other animals it is enough to eat, drink, rest, copulate and the other things that fulfil what belongs to them. But for us, to whom God has also given the power of understanding, these things are no longer enough; if we do not act the right way, the orderly way, in the way that follows the nature and constitution of each, we will not achieve our end' (Epict. i 6.13–15 = LS 63E).

[49] On suggestive appearances see Long, 'Psychology', 579.

[50] 'All impulses are assents, but some are practical and include the moving part (of the soul). . . . They say that a passion is an impulse that is excessive and disobedient to choosing reason, or a non-rational movement of the soul contrary to nature. All passions belong to the leading part of the soul' (Stob. ii 88.1–10 = LS 33I and 65A). On Sceptical claims about yielding to appearances see §139.

[51] Hence Poseidonius advises preparation. See Galen, *PHP* iv 7.6–8 = 282.1–14; we should imagine the situations in advance (*proanaplattein, protupoun*).

At other times we may yield immediately because we have not questioned the truth of the suggestion made by the appearance.[52]

In saying that we yield to appearances, the Stoics seek to explain and to correct the common assumption that the passions are ways of being affected rather than ways of acting. They do not accept this assumption, since they identify a passion with an immediate assent, and all assent is active. Neither animals nor young children have passions,[53] because they act on appearance alone, whereas rational agents act on appearance only after assenting to it. When we act on passion, we act on minimal assent, since we fail to interfere with or to question the suggestion that the appearance makes.

By insisting that passion involves assent, the Stoics implicitly deny that we can act on our passions against all our beliefs.[54] If we seem to act against our beliefs, we really have wavering or oscillating beliefs; though we act against some of our beliefs, we act on other beliefs.[55] Similarly, passions cannot persist without the relevant beliefs about good and bad.[56] The passions that the Stoics identify with immediate assents include anger, fear, lust, and all the others that Plato and Aristotle ascribe to the non-rational parts of the soul.

When the Stoics say that a passion is a mistaken belief that a natural advantage is good, they mean that we assent to the appearance as offering us a real good. But they do not simply mean that we regard the apparent good as good some things considered. When we act on assent to an appearance, we act on the outlook that Plato and Aristotle ascribe to the rational part of the soul; we take the apparent good to be good all things considered. Plato is right to see some non-rational element in the passions, but wrong about where he puts it. The non-rational element lies in the appearance, but not in the belief and desire on which we act; for between the appearance and the action comes assent to the contemplated action as best overall. Plato distinguishes the rational part from the other two parts of the soul by attributing desires and beliefs about the overall good to the rational part, but not to the other two parts. The Stoics argue that passions belong to the rational part because they all assent to the action as good overall.

None the less, the Stoics recognize a way in which passions conflict with reason[57] even though they depend essentially on false evaluative (and therefore, in one sense, rational) beliefs. We may form a belief irrationally, on insufficient evidence, or without adding up the evidence correctly. And once we have formed it, we may stick to it irrationally, because we are wrongly unimpressed by counter-evidence. The fact that a passion is unreasonable in this way does not mean that the underlying belief is wholly non-rational, or that it is immune

---

[52] At Galen, *PHP* iv 7.12–17 = 284.3–17 = LS 65O, an immediate opinion seems to be formed as a result of some immediate stimulus or occasion. This seems to be what Poseidonius assumes when he asks Chrysippus to explain why the temporal closeness of the occasion for the belief should matter (Galen, *PHP* iv 7.6 = 282.5). Cicero, however, argues that the passion goes away as a result of further reflexion on the situation (*TD* iii 74). If we retain the impressions, thoughts, and attitudes that led to the passion, the relevant belief remains immediate.

[53] See Cic. *TD* iv 31; Galen, *PHP* iv 5.3–4 = 260.8–13; v 1.10 = 294.17–20; Origen, *in Matt.* iii 92 = SVF iii 477.

[54] I use 'belief' broadly, to cover both true and false assents (and so more broadly than the Stoics use '*doxa*').

[55] '. . . passion is not something other than reason, nor is there dispute and conflict between the two; rather the single reason turns in both directions, escaping our notice by the suddenness and speed of the change. . . . In fact appetites, anger, fear and all such things are inferior beliefs and judgments, not coming to be in some one part of the soul, but inclinations, yieldings, assents and impulses of the whole leading part . . .' (Plu. *VM* 446f–447a = LS 65G) Cf. Galen, *PHP* iv 4.6–7 = 252.1–5 = SVF iii 462.

[56] Cf. Epict. i 28.6–9 (on Medea); ii 26.4.

[57] Cic. *Off.* i 136; *TD* iv 31; Galen, *PHP* iv 2.19–27 = 242.12–244.9 = SVF iii 462.

to rational persuasion. For we may still change the belief when we come to realize that our reason for holding it is less good than our reason for accepting the counter-evidence. We think we follow our passions against our rational assent, because we do not realize that our belief that (say) we ought always to avenge insults is very tenacious. It is so tenacious that even when we think we have persuaded ourselves out of it, we are not really persuaded, but still revert to our old view if we are insulted. Where common sense thinks it sees a conflict between rational assent and passion, the Stoics see wavering and vacillation between two conflicting rational assents resting on conflicting beliefs about what is best.

In his discussion of the passions Chrysippus examines the features of the passions that have led some people to recognize a non-rational part, and he tries to show how the Stoic position accounts for these features. Some sources quote passages in which he seems to recognize the non-rational character of (for instance) anger, and our tendency to persist in it even when we recognize that we ought not to.[58] Galen even claims that another Stoic, Poseidonius, returned to the Platonic position, and criticized the other Stoics for ignoring the non-rational part.[59]

Critics find the Stoic position puzzling and inconsistent because it is not purely Socratic. Chrysippus believes that he can both recognize the apparently non-rational character of passions and still maintain his analysis of them as assents. In his view, the non-rational aspect of the passion is present in the appearance that underlies it. The suggestiveness of the appearance—the feature of it that makes it easy for us to yield to it in our assent—is a product of our experience, and (in many cases) of our upbringing and our interaction with other people. Plato and Aristotle are right, therefore, to say that passions are sometimes difficult to resist, but they are wrong about what resistance involves, and about what happens when we fail to resist them. We have to resist, and we sometimes fail to resist, the powerful suggestiveness of the underlying appearance; in failing to resist it, we are too

[58] 'Chrysippus himself agrees not once or twice but very often that some other power than the rational power in the souls of men is responsible for passions. . . . Whatever things men do wrongly, he refers some to depraved judgment, others to slackness and weakness of soul; similarly, in the things they do correctly, correct judgment leads the way, with good tension in the soul. But in such cases judgment is the work of the rational power of the soul; similarly, good tension is vigour and virtue of another power besides the rational, a power which Chrysippus himself names tension. . . . In these remarks he is showing clearly what sort of thing a passion is' (Galen, *PHP* iv 6.1–3 = 270.10–24). 'That is why these people say, when the actual things force them, that not every judgment is a passion, but only the one that arouses a violent and excessive impulse—they are conceding that what judges and what is affected in us are different things, just as the mover and the moved are. And when Chrysippus himself in many places defines endurance and continence as states that follow choosing reason, he is clearly being compelled by the actual things to concede that the thing following in us is different from the thing which it follows when it obeys and fights when it does not obey' (Plu. *VM* 449c). '. . . Chrysippus evidently contradicts himself . . . when he is writing about the definition of the things to do with affection. He says it is a non-rational movement contrary to nature, and an excessive impulse. Then he explains "non-rational" by saying that it is what has been said without reason and judgment. And for an example of excessive impulse he cites people running hard. Now both these points conflict with the view that affections are judgments. We will recognize this more clearly by transcribing his own statements: "We must first of all be aware that the rational animal is by nature a follower of reason, an agent according to reason as its leader. Often, however, it is moved in a different way too from some things to some things, when it is pushed further in disobedience to reason. . . . For this irrational (part) must be taken to be disobedient to reason and turned away from reason."' (Galen, *PHP* iv 2.8–12 = 240.11–24).

[59] 'But in the places where [Chrysippus] refutes himself and at the same time conflicts with the things appearing clearly, in these I think someone would be ashamed and would turn in a better direction. This is what Poseidonius did, since he was ashamed to agree with the clearly false doctrine of the other Stoics' (Galen, *PHP* v 1.10 = 294.13–17). In 'at the same time . . .' Galen alludes to Aristotle, *EN* 1145b28. See also *PHP* v 6.33 = 332.18–22. Probably Galen is wrong about Poseidonius. See Kidd, 'Poseidonius'; Cooper, 'Poseidonius'.

easily persuaded that things are as they appear to be. Passion affects us not by overriding our assent, but by forming it on the wrong basis.

In the light of this view of the passions, the Stoics explain the apparent phenomena of incontinence. In their view, the allegedly incontinent action in these cases is action on assent, since it is a voluntary action; and if it is an action on assent, the agent judges that the action is best, all things considered. Rational assent wavers and vacillates, but it is not overcome by non-rational desires. This description of incontinence seems to differ sharply from Aristotle's conception of incontinence as failure to follow my rational judgment of what is better on the whole. But Aristotle concedes a point to the Stoics; for he does not think it is possible to know that x is rationally preferable to y and, at the same time as one knows this, to choose and to do y rather than x. Incontinent people, in his view, lose their grasp of the true principles whenever they act incontinently. (EN 1147b9–17). In admitting that ignorance must be part of any explanation of incontinence, Aristotle seems to accept the central Stoic claim.

168. How can we Correct our Assents?

This outline of the Stoic account of the passions helps to clarify the ethical task we face when we become capable of practical reasoning. The task is parallel to the task that faces us in assenting to or dissenting from our perceptual appearances. Assent to the appearance of my hand in front of me in ordinary circumstances rests on the belief that all the evidence available to me favours the truth of the appearance. If I assent unwisely to an appearance, I am hasty or careless in assuming that the weight of evidence favours its truth.

In these cases, my assent to the appearance rests on a judgment about its relation to my other beliefs about available evidence. The same is true in assents to appearances about good and evil. Even impulsive people assent when they yield to their appearances; their outlook and values influence the sorts of appearances that they will give way to, even though they do not usually attend explicitly or reflectively to the relevant considerations. The mere fact that the appearance suggests that revenge (for instance) is good does not explain why we seek revenge; for not all agents who have appearances suggesting this also yield to the appearance. Whether or not we yield to the appearance also depends on our more general and reflective values; if they permit us to yield to this sort of appearance, then we yield to it, and otherwise we do not yield to it.

Since we have strongly suggestive appearances, we need to take deliberate steps to resist their suggestions; even if the suggestions are sometimes correct, we should not simply take it for granted that the balance of rational considerations favours assenting to them.

169. Questions about Responsibility

The Stoics' doctrine of the passions helps to explain why they claim that assent is the distinctive element in human action. We can understand their claim still better if we grasp the role of assent in their account of responsibility. They agree with Aristotle in believing that it is up to us to be virtuous or vicious, and in believing that virtuous actions 'control' (kuriai) happiness. Indeed they go further than Aristotle goes in claiming that happiness is in our power. Their views are coherent only if the state or activity that they identify with virtue and with happiness is one that, according to their theory of responsibility, we are responsible for.

The Stoics believe that they can satisfy this demand for coherence in their theory of action and moral theory. For they believe that, once we understand the role of assent in relation to appearance, we grasp the distinctive feature of rational agency that underlies both responsibility and virtue. Once we see what makes us rational agents, we can see what makes us responsible agents, and how we can become virtuous and happy. This attempt to explain virtue and happiness by appeal to a conception of agency is implicit in Aristotle. The Stoics offer a more explicit and systematic argument from reason to responsibility and to virtue. Their clarification and modification of Aristotle's position suggest some of the further clarifications and developments that result in Aquinas' defence of an Aristotelian position.[60]

The Stoics differ from Aristotle in presenting an elaborate theory of moral responsibility that fits into the rest of their philosophical system. Their theory embraces compatibilism and soft determinism.[61] They accept causal determinism for reasons connected with their natural philosophy and natural theology; determinism is part of their doctrine of fate (or 'destiny', *heimarmenê*).[62]

Stoic determinism convinces some ancient critics that the Stoics are committed to the rejection of human freedom, since they affirm that all events, including all human actions, are made inevitable by events in the distant past. The Stoics, however, deny that they are committed to a hard determinist conclusion that rejects freedom. To show that freedom is compatible with Stoic determinism, they defend a division between different types of causes, and then argue that the causal role they assign to assent is exactly the role that is needed for freedom and responsibility.

Their division of causes rests on broader claims about causation and explanation, not simply on claims about responsibility. Stoic determinism does not imply that the real cause of an event is found in the distant past.[63] The distant past includes an 'antecedent' cause of every effect, but it does not include the principal cause. Similarly, it provides necessary conditions for an event. But neither the antecedent cause nor the necessary conditions are the 'principal' cause.[64] Oedipus would not have killed Laius unless Laius had fathered

---

[60] On Aquinas see §270.   [61] See §148.

[62] 'They say that this world-order is one. It includes in it all the things that are. It is governed by living, rational and understanding nature, so that it has the eternal organization of things that are proceeding in a certain series and order. . . . And so nothing comes to be in the universe in such a way that something else does not in any case follow on it, bound to it as to its cause. Nor again can any of the things following be separated from the things preceding so as not to follow one of them as being bound to it. Rather, on everything that comes to be something else follows, depending on it as on its cause by necessity; and everything that happens has something before it, on which it depends as on its cause. For nothing in the universe either is or comes to be without a cause, because nothing in it is loosed and separated from all the things that have come before. . . . They say that something's coming to be without a cause is similar to something's coming to be from nothing, and similarly impossible' (Alex. *Fat.* 2, 191.30–192.15 = LS 55N) For detailed discussion see Bobzien, *DFSP*, ch. 1.

[63] '. . . the cause should not be understood so that whatever is antecedent to anything is the cause of it, but only what precedes something productively. My going down into the Campus was not the cause of my playing tennis, nor was Hecuba the cause of death for the Trojans because she bore Alexander, nor Tyndareus for Agamemnon because he begot Clytaemnestra. For by these standards a well-dressed traveller will also be said to be the cause for the robber of being robbed by him' (Cic. *Fat.* 34). On the Stoics' 'swarm' of causes cf. Alex. *Fat.* 192.17–28 = LS 55N. Cf. LS 55 J–M.

[64] 'Among causes some are originative, some containing, some cooperative, some sine qua non. The originative are those that first provide a starting-point, for something to come to be, as beauty provides a starting-point for desire in

Oedipus, and he would not have killed him with a brick unless the brick had been hard enough to crush Laius' skull. Neither of these, however, is the cause of Oedipus' killing Laius; Laius' fathering Oedipus is an antecedent cause, and the facts about the brick and Laius' skull are necessary conditions.[65]

The Stoic conception of the principal cause relies on an intuitive sense of the difference between 'the cause' and the various causal 'factors' or 'determinants' of an event. The Stoics take it for granted that 'the' cause is appropriately explanatory, so that even if F causally determines G, it does not follow that F is the cause of G. Events in the distant past are not the cause of my present intentional action, since its causes in the distant past are antecedent but not principal causes. Though an antecedent cause may make an event inevitable, it does not explain why it happens. To explain an event, we must connect the antecedent causes with the cause that more directly explains the event; this cause is the principal cause. Being a principal cause is a non-transitive relation, whereas being an antecedent cause is transitive.

The Stoics assume that we need to explain an event's having a specific property in specific circumstances. Different people might reach different conclusions about 'the' cause of an accident, if they try to explain different things. If we drive inattentively on an unusually bad patch of road, and we have an accident, it might be true both that we would not have had an accident if we had been more careful, and that we would not have had it if the road had been in better condition. We may identify the relevant properties by contrast with the circumstances that are being taken for granted. Our inattention can be blamed for our accident, given that we ought to notice bad patches on a road. The bad condition of the road can be blamed, given that roads ought to be good enough to accommodate occasional inattentiveness in drivers. Two different explananda correspond to the different conditions that we might reasonably take for granted, and so we may find two different principal causes for the different properties to be explained.

170. Assent as Principal Cause

The Stoics connect these claims about causation with their claims about assent by claiming that the principal cause of a rational agent's action is the agent's assent. The existence of an external object is a necessary condition, and the appearance caused by the object is an antecedent cause; but neither of these is the principal cause. Without assuming any break

---

intemperate people. For when it is seen it produces a desiring condition, but not necessarily. Containing causes are those that are synonymously called self-complete, since they are productive of the effect self-sufficiently through themselves. All the causes in order are to be shown in the case of a learner. For the father is the originative cause of the learning, the teacher the containing, the nature of the learner the cooperative, and time has the account of the things sine qua non. A cause so called primarily is what is productive, of something actively' (Clement, *Strom.* viii 9.25.1–5 = SVF ii 345).

[65] 'Chrysippus...both rejected necessity and wanted nothing to happen without previous causes; and so he distinguishes kinds of causes, so that he can both escape necessity and hold on to fate. "For", he says, "among causes some are perfect and principal, others auxiliary and proximate. Hence we say that all things happen by fate by antecedent causes, but do not want this to be understood as perfect and principal causes, but auxiliary and proximate causes." ... He says: "Someone who has pushed a roller gives it an origin of motion, but he has not given it the capacity to roll. So also something seen when it confronts us will indeed imprint and, so to speak, seal its character in the mind; but our assent will be in our power, and, as we said about the roller, once it is struck from outside for the rest it will be moved by its own force and nature." ' (Cic. *Fat.* 41–3 = LS 62C). See Bobzien, *DFSP*, ch. 6.

in causal determination, we can identify the principal cause of an action with the agent's assent, not with the antecedent conditions of the assent.[66]

We might object that sometimes the appearance rather than the assent may be the principal cause. Iago, for instance, plots against Othello on the mere suspicion that Othello has slept with Iago's wife.[67] He expects correctly that Othello will turn against Desdemona on the mere accusation of infidelity, without further reflexion, if the accuser is someone he trusts.[68] Iago has only to create the appearance of honesty in himself and unfaithfulness in Desdemona. Since Othello's assent can be taken for granted, what explains his action is the appearance.

The Stoics disagree. Iago and Othello are similar to Agamemnon and Achilles, whom Epictetus cites as examples of people who give way too easily to their appearances.[69] In both cases, the Stoics argue that the principal cause, the one that makes the crucial difference in the relevant circumstances, is the agent's assent. Iago begins with the assumption that Othello is of a free and open nature; he is not like Iago in being especially prone to jealousy on the basis of the slightest suspicion. Since Iago is especially prone to jealousy, he knows how to create the circumstances that will arouse jealousy; but what arouses jealousy in Othello is his readiness to trust Iago. Iago's reference to Othello's 'free and open nature' refers, in the Stoic view, to Othello's tendency to assent to some things rather than others. Iago's schemes work on Othello and would not work on someone less naive and trusting (towards Iago) than Othello.

The Stoic claim that assent is the principal cause is defensible, if we are careful to say what it is the principal cause of. To say simply that it is the principal cause of 'the action' is not precise enough. It is the principal cause of Othello's action because Othello's assent explains why he acts on an appearance that someone else might have had without acting on it. Othello has made what the Stoics call a weak and rash assent to the appearance; he has failed to resist the suggestion made by the appearance in cases where someone else would have resisted it.

171. Fate v. Necessity

The Stoics argue that, since the agent's assent is the principal cause, not everything happens by fate in such a way as to remove responsibility. Antecedent causes do not make my action necessary, and hence the doctrine of fate does not import the type of necessity that is inconsistent with responsibility.[70]

Chrysippus is not entitled to say this, if 'making necessary' means something like 'leaving no alternative causally possible'. For if determinism is true, then an earlier event on a causal

---

[66] '. . . every animal qua animal when it is moved is moved with the movement according to impulse, the movement coming to be from fate through the animal. . . . But these movements come to be through impulse and assent, while the movements of other things come to be some because of heaviness, some because of heat, and some according to some other <cause>. . . ; hence we say that this movement is up to animals' (Alex. *Fat.* 13, 182.6–18 = *SVF* ii 979).

[67] 'I hate the Moor; | and it is thought abroad that 'twixt my sheets | h'as done my office. I know not if 't be true; | but I, for mere suspicion in that kind, | will do as if for surety' (*Othello* i 3.380).

[68] 'The Moor is of a free and open nature | that thinks men honest that but seem to be so; and will as tenderly be led by th' nose | as asses are' (i 3.393).

[69] Epict. i 28.31. See §165 above.

[70] Some of Cicero's remarks in *Fat.* 43 = LS 62C might mislead us into supposing that the Stoics introduce an element of indeterminism here.

chain, however long, guarantees the later event and leaves no alternative possible, given the past and the laws of nature. Chrysippus understands 'making necessary' differently; he believes that the necessity that excludes freedom is the sort of necessity that is independent of our rational choices. In his view, the Stoics are not committed to this kind of necessity.[71]

Origen discusses this question in order to answer Celsus' charge that Judas was not responsible for betraying Jesus. Since the fact that it was true in the distant past that Judas would betray Jesus implies that Judas would betray Jesus, did this fact about the distant past make it inevitable that Judas would betray Jesus, in such a way that Judas could do nothing about it? Celsus answers Yes, and infers that Judas is not responsible for betraying Jesus.[72]

The Stoics, however, argue that it is a mistake to argue from 'this event in the distant past implied that Judas would betray Jesus' to the conclusion 'this event in the distant past all by itself resulted in Judas' betrayal of Jesus'. The betrayal of Jesus results only if many other things, including Judas' decision to betray Jesus, intervene. Since Judas' decision is a necessary part of the sequence resulting in the betrayal of Jesus, Judas cannot plead that the betrayal was inevitable no matter what he decided, and hence he cannot escape responsibility.[73] His decision to betray Jesus was 'confatal' with the betrayal of Jesus.[74]

This is a good answer to a fatalist argument that relies simply on past truth. The Stoics believe that an incompatibilist makes a mistake similar to the one that a fatalist makes. In their view, the incompatibilist is right to argue that we cannot be responsible for our actions if the past and the laws of nature determine our actions irrespective of what we choose. The incompatibilist overlooks the fact, however, that the past events determine my actions only because they lead to the assent and choice that is the principal cause of my action. Since my assent plays a crucial causal role in the production of my action, it is reasonable to hold me responsible for the action.

[71] Augustine says the Stoics distinguished types of causes in order to avoid allowing the necessitation that excludes responsibility: 'For if in our case we mean by "necessity" the sort that is not in our power but achieves what it is capable of even if we will it not to happen (etiam si nolimus), such as the necessity of dying, then it is clear that our wills, by which we live either rightly or wrongly, are not subject to that sort of necessity. For we do many things which we would not do if we did not will to do them. Among these belongs first of will willing itself. For it happens if we will it to happen, and if we do not will it, it does not happen; for we would not will if we did not will to will. If on the other hand we mean by 'necessity' the sort according to which we say it is necessary for something to be or to come to be a certain way, I see no reason why we should be afraid that that sort will take away the freedom of our will from us' (CD v 10a). Augustine argues that we need to reject only the first kind of necessity, the sort that is independent of our wills, if we are to be free of the necessity that threatens responsibility.

[72] This argument is derived from the argument for fatalism that Aristotle rejects in his discussion of the 'sea battle'. See De Int. 19a22–b1.

[73] [Celsus on Jesus' prophecy that Judas would betray him.] 'If he foretold these things, being a god, then in any case what he foretold had to come to be. A god, then, so perverted his own disciples and prophets, with whom he ate and drank, that they became unholy and impious . . . [Origen replies] Celsus thinks that something predicted by some sort of foreknowledge happens because of this—because it was predicted. We do not concede this. . . . We deny that the one foreknowing removes what is capable of coming to be and of not coming to be . . . From Jesus' having foretold correctly the things about his future betrayer or his denier <Peter> it does not follow that he came to be the cause of impious and unholy actions' (Origen, Cels. ii 20). Cf. Augustine §10.

[74] 'These philosophers . . . argue: "If it is fate for you to recover from this illness, you will recover whether you bring a doctor or you do not. Similarly, if it is fate for you not to recover from this illness, you will not recover, whether you bring a doctor or you do not. But one or the other is fate; hence there is no point in bringing a doctor." This sort of argument is rightly called lazy and inactive, because by the same principle all action is removed from life. . . . Chrysippus attacks this argument: . . . If it is fated "Oedipus will be born to Laius", it cannot be said "whether Laius has been with a woman or not". Here the thing is complex and confatal—for that is what he calls it because it is fated thus both that Laius will lie with a woman and that by her he will beget Oedipus. . . .' (Cic. Fat. 28–30 = LS 55S, 70G).

172. Incompatibilist Objections

We may find this a superficial answer to the incompatibilist's objections.[75] The Stoics seem to suggest that if the causal chain has to pass through our choices and assents, we are responsible for the actions. But Alexander argues that this suggestion does not satisfy plausible Aristotelian conditions for responsibility, because no determinist position satisfies these conditions. In defending incompatibilism and indeterminism, Alexander agrees with Epicurus.[76]

Alexander appeals to two Aristotelian conditions for responsibility: (1) When we deliberate, we believe we can do either of two possible actions, and if we are responsible for our action, our belief must be true. Responsibility presupposes, then, that it is 'up to us' to do what we do as opposed to something else. (2) When we are responsible for our action, we ourselves are the 'principles' or 'origins' (*archai*), the origins are in us, and we are in control (*kurioi*) of the actions.[77]

In Alexander's view, these claims must be understood in an indeterminist sense.[78] The Stoics violate Aristotle's first condition, which requires alternatives that are up to us; for, in their view, an unbroken chain of sufficient conditions leads from events that happened thousands of years ago all the way to my action. Hence past events make my action inevitable; hence it cannot be up to me to act differently. The Stoics also violate Aristotle's second condition, which requires the origin to be in us. For the Stoic doctrine of causes and fate implies that our reasoning, deliberation, and rational assent have external causes, so that (Alexander infers) we ourselves are not the origins of our actions, and so nothing is up to us (Alex. *Fat.* 14, 185.7–21; *Mant.* 173.10–21).

The Stoics accept the Aristotelian conditions, but reject Alexander's interpretation. They accept the demand for alternatives and for internal origins within Stoic determinism. They believe that actions in accordance with our impulses have our assents as their principal causes. Hence they come about 'by fate through the animal' (Alex. *Fat.* 13, 182.12 = LS 62G), and this makes them up to us.

This Stoic claim, according to Alexander, overlooks a difference between human agents and other principal causes. Something does not become responsible for its motions simply because it is their principal cause; fire is not responsible for moving upwards. Other subjects besides human agents are only causally responsible, whereas we are also morally responsible,

---

[75] Cf. §225.　　[76] See §149.　　[77] On these conditions in Aristotle see §100.

[78] '. . . the voluntary and the up to us are not the same. For what comes to be from an unforced assent is voluntary; but up to us is what comes to be with assent that is according to reason and judgment. Hence if something is up to us it is voluntary, but not everything voluntary is up to us. For non-rational animals too do voluntarily what they do according to the impulse and assent in them; but it is peculiar to a human being that some of the things coming to be from him are up to him. For his being rational is this—his having in him reason that is judge and discoverer of the appearances that fall on him and in general of things to be done and not to be done. Hence the other animals, which yield to appearances alone have in these the causes of their assents and impulses to action. But a human being has reason as a judge of appearances falling on him from outside about things to be done. He uses this reason to examine each appearance, to see not only whether it appears to be such as it appears, but also whether it is. If he finds by investigation according to reason that its being is different from its appearance, he does not give way to it simply because it appears such, but because it is not also such, he objects to it. . . . Being rational is nothing else than this, being an origin of actions. . . . And if we have from nature the freedom to do something after deliberation, it is clear we would have the freedom also to do something else through deliberation, and do not in any case (i.e. necessarily) do what we do after deliberation if we do deliberate' (Alex. *Fat.* 14, 183.26–185.7). See also §101 (Aristotle); §265 (Aquinas); §§369–70 (Scotus).

being open to praise and blame. Since principal causation implies nothing more than causal responsibility, it cannot justify praise and blame. And so even if an action results from assent and impulse, it does not follow that it is up to us. The Stoics may have given an adequate account of the voluntary (183.24–6); but voluntary action is not necessarily up to us.[79] What is up to us is 'what comes about with the assent in accordance with reason and judgment' (183.28–9), and this is peculiar to human beings (cf. *Mant.* 172.25–173.3).

Alexander claims that the Stoics eliminate real responsibility. Critics of the Stoics do not simply want to find some use for the phrase 'up to us', but also want to prove the reality of what the name signifies, namely sovereignty (*to autexousion*) over our actions (*Fat.* 14 = 182.22–4). The earliest attested uses of this term '*autexousion*' are political, referring to a ruler who is not subject to any other ruler. Hence Philo sometimes combines it with 'having full powers' (*autokratôr*), and often applies it to the absolute sovereignty of God.[80] The corresponding abstract noun '*autexousiotês*' is rendered in later Latin sources by 'liberum arbitrium'.[81] In using the term to refer to what he thinks the Stoics cannot allow, Alexander makes it clear that he wants to safeguard the agent's independence of external circumstances; hence he combines 'sovereign' with 'free' (*eleutheron*), another term whose political use is attested earlier than its metaphysical use (*Fat.* 18 = 188.20–1).[82] In using these two political terms Alexander does not take himself to be introducing a different concept from Aristotle's concept of what is up to us; he takes himself to identify more precisely the property of human actions that this concept introduces.

Alexander assumes that I am free and sovereign over my action only if my reason is also in my control. But any determinist history of the formation of my desires seems to assign control to something other than my reason, and hence to something other than me. He assumes that I control my actions only if my reasons and rational deliberation control them. But this control, in his view, also implies that I control whatever controls my reasons and deliberation. If we are determinists, and we look for the origins that have determined our current desires and assents, we must go back to our upbringing, early training, and other things that are all out of our control. If an unbroken causal history leads back to causes that never were in our control and are not in our control, we do not seem to control our actions now. Our assents and desires have causes that are in our control only if the causal sequence is broken at the right place.

---

[79] Alexander implies that the Stoics attribute assent to all animals. For justified doubts about whether he represents them accurately see Sharples, *Fat.*, in Alex. pp. 144–6.

[80] At Philo, *Leg. Alleg.* iii 73., *autexousios dunasteia* is ascribed to God. Hence Moses addresses the *autexousion tou theou kratos*—appropriately rendered by the Loeb translation as 'absolute sovereignty' (*Plant.* 46). God governs the world by an *autexousios* and *autokratôr basileia* (*Heres* 301). In comparison with God, the real being (*to on*), none of the other gods is *autexousios* (*Ebr.* 43). In contrast to God, the sun and moon are not *autexousia*, but passively moved (*Cherub.* 88). Among human beings, the delusion of being more than human arises from the possession of wealth followed by *autexousios hegemonia* (*Cain* 115). If we are enlightened and led away from the body and the senses, we no longer imagine we gain knowledge through a mind (*gnômê*) that is *autokratôr* and *autexousios* (*Heres* 85). The connexion between 'being in one's own power' and freedom is marked in Diodorus Siculus xiv 105.4, where prisoners of war are released *autexousioi*.

[81] 'Liberum arbitrium' is used with a sense similar to that of '*autexousios*' and '*autokratôr*', meaning 'with full powers'. For its political and legal uses see *OLD* s.v. arbitrium, 4d.

[82] Epictetus uses 'sovereign' and 'free' together at ii 2.3 (things that are *epi* you are *autexousia kai phusei eleuthera*); iv 1.56 (Do you think *eleutheria* is *autexousion* and *autonomon*?); 62; 68; 100 (what God has given me of my own and *autexousion* is *ta prohairetika*). On liberum arbitrium see §265. Bobzien, *DFSP*, ch. 7, discusses Epictetus and earlier Stoics on freedom (with a brief remark on *autexousiotês*, 335–6).

Hence Alexander thinks a satisfactory account of responsibility, involving the claim that our actions are up to us and in our control, must be indeterminist. He follows Aristotle in believing that if something is up to us, the origin must be in us, and that in so far as we are rational we are origins of actions (*Fat.* 184.15–16; *Mant.* 173.6–10). Then he infers that if there is any external cause of our reasoning, deliberation, and rational assent, we ourselves are not the origins of our actions, and hence nothing is up to us (*Fat.* 185.7–21; *Mant.* 173.10–21). But if the result of deliberation is not causally determined, something of which we ourselves are the origin is the cause of our action. Alexander rejects the assumption that if we prefer x over y in one situation and y over x in another, there must have been some causally significant difference in the two cases; the fact is just that we faced the same choice in the same circumstances on two occasions, chose one way on one occasion and the other way on another, and there is no further causal explanation of our choice (*Fat.* 185.21–186.3).

Alexander's objections to the Stoics rest on the assumption that my freedom depends on my capacity to choose between alternatives; that is why he infers both that freedom is peculiar to rational agents, and that it requires indeterminism. But we need not accept both inferences. Perhaps freedom consists in acting in the light of recognition of reasons for doing x rather than y. Hence it requires rational choice, based on the recognition of reasons for alternative courses of action, and hence it is not open to non-rational agents. This appeal to rational choice between alternatives allows a compatibilist account of responsibility.[83] The Stoics can reasonably argue that they have shown how human choices are free.

173. Assent as the Basis for Responsibility

The Stoics reject Alexander's charge that in accepting determinism they preclude responsibility. They rest their case against him on the claim that our assent is the principal cause of our actions. Why does this causal role matter so much for responsibility?

The mere fact that we are the principal causes of something does not make us morally responsible for it, since, as Alexander remarks, plants, animals, and other non-responsible agents can also be principal causes. The Stoics, however, argue that since assent is the principal cause, we are morally responsible. Since the general evaluative outlook that causes assent is itself open to alteration by deliberation and reflexion, it is appropriate to praise and blame agents who act on assent.

This link between assent and responsibility depends on the rational character of assent and of praise and blame. The Stoics believe that our assent is open to influence by rational evaluation, and that praise and blame are forms of rational evaluation, pointing out reasons for and against an action that are appropriately taken into account by an agent who considers whether to assent to an appearance that suggests doing the action.

If praise and blame were not concerned with reasons, but were simply expressions of favourable and aversive reactions, or if assent were not influenced by reasons, but only by causal processes immune to reasons, the Stoics would lose the basis for their claim that actions caused by assents are proper objects of praise and blame. Since, however, they are

---

[83] See Meyer, 'Responsibility' 234–40.

right to believe that praise, blame, reasons, and assent are connected in the ways they claim, they have a good case for believing we are justly held responsible for the actions we assent to. Hence they also have a good reason for claiming that the conditions that Alexander interprets in an indeterminist sense—'up to us', 'in our power', and so on—are properly interpreted so as to refer to the controlling role of assent and reason.

Aristotle's account of responsibility is closer to the Stoic position than to Alexander's.[84] While he affirms the conditions that Alexander interprets in an indeterminist sense, he does not interpret them in this sense. He argues that rational agents are rightly held responsible for their voluntary actions because these are actions of agents who are capable of rational deliberation and election. The Stoics go further, and insist that we are responsible for those actions that actually express—either by reflexion on appearances or by simply going along with them—the outlook that is embodied in the agent's elections (as Aristotle understands them).[85] This further element in the Stoic position modifies and develops Aristotle, but it does not depart sharply from his position.

Later expositors of Aristotle's position are right, therefore, to mention assent. When Aspasius explains Aristotle's remark that belief precedes election, he takes him to mean that reason must assent to something as choiceworthy, and after that desire follows, so that an election results (Asp. *in EN* 70.14–20). Alexander places what is up to us in rational assent that comes about through deliberation (*Fat.* 184.10–15); this is a sufficient basis for responsibility because the agent is responsible (*aitios*) for his assent (186.10–12). Deliberation is relevant to election and to something's being up to us, because it is the basis for rational assent, which does not simply give way to the initial appearance (Alex. *Quaest.* iii 13, 107.6–19); hence deliberation and the resultant rational assent justify us in claiming that an action is up to us (*DA* 73.7–13).[86] When Alexander introduces this element of the Stoic position into his account of Aristotle, he supports the conclusion that rationality, rather than (as he supposes) indeterminism, is essential to free and responsible agency.

174. Passions, Assent, and Responsibility

Once we grasp the connexion between assent and responsibility, we may look more sympathetically on an initially surprising feature of the Stoic doctrine of the passions. We might be surprised that the Stoics insist that passions are assents. But they defend their position by pointing out that we can be praised and blamed for having particular passions and for acting on them (Cic. *TD* iv 31). We could not fairly be praised and blamed if our passions were outside our rational control, and so not determined by our rational assent (which the Stoics take to be crucial for control and responsibility).[87] But if we accept a non-Stoic view of the passions, we must (in the Stoic view) regard passions as compulsive states; and then we cannot explain why they are not outside the area of responsible action (as bodily diseases often are).

---

[84] See §100.   [85] In emphasizing actual influence the Stoics come close to Aquinas' position (§255).

[86] This introduction of the Stoic doctrine of assent into an Aristotelian account of what is up to us is discussed by Gauthier, 'St Maxime' 69.

[87] See Cic. *TD* iv 14: passions come about 'iudicio et opinione' and are 'in nostra potestate'. Cf. Epict. i 11.33.

The Stoics' argument is this: (1) Action on passions is voluntary; that is why we are responsible for it. (2) If it is voluntary, it requires assent. (3) We assent to an action as being best all things considered. (4) But passions do not rest on a true judgment that an action is best all things considered. (5) Hence acting on passion is acting on a false assent to an action as best all things considered. In the fourth claim the Stoics acknowledge the intuitive division between passions and correct rational judgment, and so acknowledge that there is something non-rational or irrational about the passions. In (2) and (3) they state conditions for responsibility, and in (1) claim that these conditions must apply to action on passions. In the light of (1)–(3), we cannot claim that the passions belong to a non-rational part of the soul that moves us to action independently of rational assent; for if we claimed this, we would thereby be claiming that we are not responsible for action on passions. We cannot claim, therefore, that non-rational movements and appearances are themselves sufficient for passions. That is why the Stoics conclude that the passions, strictly speaking, consist in assents; since they cannot consist in true and reflective assents, they must consist in false and hasty assents.

This part of the Stoic argument raises a question for Aristotle. He apparently accepts the first two premises. His attitude to the third is less clear. The Stoics suppose that the assent must be assent to the appearance that a course of action is good. In Aristotle's account of action, this assent is a constituent of rational desire and election, in contrast to action on non-rational desire. If he believes that we are responsible for action on passions, and not only for action on rational desire, then he has a reason to reject (3). In that case, however, he needs some alternative explanation of our responsibility for such actions; we have found that it is difficult to find any explanation that does not appeal to the connexion between responsibility and rational desire and election. If we affirm such a connexion, it is difficult to resist (3), and then it is difficult to resist the rest of the Stoic argument.

The Stoics have good reasons, then, for taking the Aristotelian view to be inadequate, since it fails to explain a crucial aspect of our responsibility for acting on passions. We should not assume, however, that the Stoic solution is the best. For the Stoics must not only explain why we are responsible for acting on passions; they must also explain why passions influence in the ways they do. These two demands on the Stoic theory seem to lead in opposite directions. For we tend to assume that the influence of the passions is incompatible with their simply resting on beliefs about the good. When we focus on this feature of the passions, the Aristotelian view becomes more attractive. The Stoics seek to show that they can incorporate the attractive aspects of their opponents' view while still maintaining our responsibility for acting on passions.

175. Action and Practical Reason

We have now seen why the Stoics' doctrine of assent affects their account of passion and action, and their defence of human freedom. Their treatment of assent is relevant to our initial questions about their method in moral inquiry, because assent is the result of rational reflexion on appearances, and this rational reflexion is the basis of the moral inquiry that leads to moral virtue. We may express this point briefly by saying that the practical reason underlying moral responsibility is the practical reason underlying virtue.

This brief statement, however, may appear to be unhelpful. If the Stoics are right about passions, some degree of rational reflexion on appearances is necessary for passions and for responsible human action; but why should we believe that this reflexion is at all similar to the reflexion that underlies virtue? And why does the fact that morally responsible agents engage in some rational reflexion give them reason to become virtuous?

These questions help us to see why the Stoics believe that their account of responsibility supports their account of virtue. In their view, if we engage in the minimal practical reason that is necessary for responsibility, we have a good reason (whether or not we see it) to engage in the further practical reason that is sufficient for virtue. To see whether this claim is correct, we need a fuller description of both kinds of practical reason, to see whether they are connected in ways that support the Stoic case.

What sort of reasoning underlies the assents needed for action and responsibility? The Stoic account of the passions suggests that a limited form of reasoning might be sufficient. If I assent to or dissent from one appearance, I may be guided by beliefs that are dominated by other appearances. I may, for instance, be angry at you, and so believe that I ought to retaliate for your insult, because of the further appearance that one ought always to retaliate against insults, or that you are a dangerous enemy. My capacity for reasoned assent, then, allows me to bring other appearances to bear on my attitude to this appearance.

But if this is the only way I can evaluate my appearances, the Stoics seem to face a question about responsibility. For, in their view, appearances are passive and not (in general) up to me, whereas assent is active; the active character of assent explains why it is voluntary and why I am responsible for actions on assent. If, however, assents all depend on further appearances, it is difficult to see how they could be the basis of responsibility. If my assent is determined by the strongest and most vivid appearance, an appeal to assent does not show that I am anything other than a passive subject of appearances. Even Sceptics can manage the sort of assent that is determined by the most vivid appearance, since it simply involves yielding to appearances.

The Stoics have a reasonable answer to this objection if they do not believe that assent is determined by the strongest or most vivid appearance. Their arguments against the Sceptics show that they believe assent is not determined by appearances.[88] In assenting to a perceptual appearance, we are capable of some rational response to evidence and reasons, whether or not they correspond to our most vivid appearance. Similarly, in assenting to an appearance that something is good, we are capable of considering the merits of the appearance and of other appearances apart from their strength and vividness.

This part of the Stoic conception of rational assent reaffirms the Platonic and Aristotelian conception of rational desire that is based on reasoning about the good and not simply about the satisfaction of non-rational desires. This is the rational desire that justifies the claim that we are responsible agents and that our actions are up to us; 'us' refers especially to us as capable of assent based on practical reasoning and not just on appearances. Given this conception of assent, Sceptics who put their Scepticism into practice would be incapable of assent, and therefore of rational action.

[88] On the 'inaction' argument see §139.

In the light of this understanding of the Stoics' views on assent, we can avoid a mistaken interpretation of some of their claims about passions. They claim that a passion is a 'yielding' or a 'weak' assent to an appearance, as though we simply gave way to a stronger force. If this were a correct account of the relevant sort of yielding, the difference between the Stoics and the Sceptics on assent would disappear. But it is not what the Stoics mean by 'yielding'. When we yield, we go along with a suggestion made by an appearance, because we judge, without adequate reflexion, that it is best to go along with it. We go wrong by failing to reflect appropriately; but we retain the capacity for such reflexion.

How, then, can we engage in the sort of practical reflexion that allows us to reach the right estimate of our appearances? Is it even appropriate to speak of a right or wrong estimate of them? To find a Stoic answer to these questions, we need to return to the doctrine of preconceptions. For in the Stoics' view, we all apply these imperfectly to the evaluation of appearances; if we applied them thoroughly, we would reach the virtues.

13

STOICISM: VIRTUE
AND HAPPINESS

176. Practical Reason and Preconceptions

According to the Stoics, human beings are first guided by appearance and impulse, but later by assent. Though this assent includes some capacity to evaluate and to criticize appearances, the capacity is actualized only by degrees. At first we accept or reject appearances without systematic reflexion, but later we acquire reason as a 'craftsman of impulse', so that we modify and shape our impulses and actions more systematically and do not go along with appearances so readily.[1]

Once we start to examine our appearances, we introduce preconceptions. For in considering whether or not to accept an appearance, we evaluate it by some standard, and preconceptions supply the most general standards (*kanones*) by which we evaluate claims about goodness and badness.[2] They do not begin from nothing. We are already well stocked with appearances of good and bad, and disposed to accept them. But we also rely on standards that justify us in sometimes rejecting our appearances. What are these standards?

According to the Stoics, practical reason gives us a different view of ourselves. Our earliest interactions with the world manifest conciliation and self-love. But when we acquire practical reason, we change our conception of the self to be loved. For we now recognize ourselves as extending through different desires at a time and over time.[3] Seneca compares

---

[1] 'Since reason has been given to rational creatures as a more complete form of leadership, living in accordance with reason turns out correctly to be in accordance with nature for them; for reason is added later <to the initial impulses> as a craftsman of impulse' (DL vii 86 = LS 57A). On the translation see LS ii 344; Striker, 'Role' 288n11 (whom I follow).

[2] See Epict. i 28.28, quoted in §165.

[3] 'The most important difference between human beings and beasts is this: Beasts, in so far as they are moved by sense, conciliate themselves only to what is at hand and present, since they are aware of very little of the past and future. A human being, on the other hand, shares in reason, through which he traces consequences, sees the causes of things, notices the mutual relations of effects and causes, compares similarities, and combines and connects future with present things; and so he easily sees the course of his whole life, and prepares the things necessary for living that life' (Cic. *Off.* i 11). 'For human beings, though they differ from beasts in many other ways, yet they differ most in this one thing—that they have reason given them by nature, and a sharp and active mind, carrying on many things at the same time; . . . for it sees the causes and consequences of things, transfers similarities, combines separated things, combines future things with present, and embraces the whole condition of the life that follows' (Cic. *F.* ii 45). Reid quotes the first passage in *EAP* ii 2, H581a.

a human life to a series of concentric circles—the largest extending from birth to death and smaller ones covering youth and childhood.[4]

This picture of a life as a series of circles suggests that we recognize ourselves as temporally extended both forwards and backwards. If we draw a circle with the present as its centre, the conception that includes the projected later stages of our life must also include the earlier stages. We gradually come to conceive of ourselves as having a wider temporal extent, and we include the earlier stages that had a narrower horizon. Two stages belong to the same person in so far as at least one of them has a conception of a life that includes the conception of the other stage as a part of it.[5]

We need not understand this idea of a total life in purely temporal terms. Practical reason may also be applied not only to different times in my life but also to different aspects of myself. I may unwisely focus on the short term, or unwisely postpone shorter-term benefit for the sake of assuring my future; the first error is wastefulness, and the second is timidity or miserliness. Equally, I may unwisely focus on some aspects of my welfare, or the development of some of my capacities, that are especially vivid to me. If I am so absorbed in a particular pursuit that I forget about other things that deserve my attention at least as much, I fail to consider myself as a whole. If I reflect rationally on my life, I extend my circle of concern to everything that deserves my concern, beyond the things that happen to catch my attention now. A rational agent with an appropriately articulated conception of herself thinks of her different concerns as belonging to a circle that includes all of them in systematic connexion.

Practical reason gives us a wider view not only of different times in our lives, but also of different aspects of ourselves. A rational agent forms an extended conception of herself in so far as she thinks of different concerns as belonging to a circle that includes all of them in a systematic connexion to each other.

177. Practical Reason, Consistency, and Agreement

This extended conception of ourselves and our lives changes our estimate of appearances. Since I now care about myself as a single person in the extended past, present, and extended future, I take a new attitude to the natural advantages that are the objects of my impulses and passions; I consider their impact on my life and goals as a whole, not just on the parts of my life that are vivid to me now. Reason becomes a craftsman of impulse by helping me to organize my desires and plans so that I secure as many of the natural advantages as I can. The Stoics express this point in describing the ultimate end as 'living in agreement' (*homologoumenôs*). Their description suggests a minimal demand of practical reason for consistency.

---

[4] 'Our whole life is composed of parts and has larger circles enclosing smaller. There is one that embraces and bounds all; this extends from our day of birth to our last day. There is another that marks off the years of youth. There is another that includes the whole of childhood in its scope. Then there is a year in itself including all the times that are multiplied to compose our life' (Sen. *Ep.* 12.6).

[5] For further development of this appeal to concentric circles see Hierocles in Stob. iv 671.4–673.18 = LS 57G. See Inwood, 'Hierocles'; §194 below.

If the Stoics have mere consistency in mind, they do not seem to have given an account of the good. One might suppose that there could be many different consistent and incompatible plans. But the Stoics do not refer to mere consistency; for they do not agree that all consistent plans equally achieve an agent's good. In their view, the good is not just living consistently, but living in agreement with nature. Our initial impulses give us a natural preference for health over sickness, for relief of hunger over starvation, and so on. The task of practical reason is not simply to devise some internally consistent plan that prevents these impulses from undermining each other. When the Stoics speak of agreement 'with nature', they seem to intend the addition simply to explain what they mean by 'agreement', rather than to impose a further condition.[6]

Agreement with nature is not simply agreement with the different impulses that a particular person has acquired with a particular degree of strength. In forming a conception of myself, I also think of myself as having a nature. In destroying my health because of some short-term impulse, I harm myself, even if I do not care much about this harm at the moment. One of the preconceptions that I use in evaluating particular impulses is my conception of the various needs and capacities that constitute my nature. If I were to confine my practical reasoning to the satisfaction of my actual desires, I would have failed to bring within my circle of concern those parts of me that are not currently vivid to me. When the Stoics introduce agreement with nature, they reject a subjective conception of one's good.

178. The Use and the Value of Practical Reason

This sketch of our preconceptions about ourselves, our nature, and our good suggests the outline of an account of virtue. We might expect the Stoics to claim that virtues are those capacities or states of character and intellect that contribute to the achievement of the natural goods. Virtuous people seem to be those who are skilled in co-ordinating their desires so as to achieve consistency with nature.

This account of virtue is not completely wrong about the Stoic position. Virtue is, among other things, the 'craft of the whole of life'.[7] The Stoics take the end to be 'living with understanding of the things that come about by nature, choosing those that are in accord with nature and rejecting the contrary things'.[8] Virtue is the craft that allows us to live with this understanding. If this formula is understood as the Stoics understand it, it captures their position. But in order to grasp their distinctive understanding of it, we may usefully begin with an initially plausible view that falls short of what they intend. According to this initially plausible view, happiness consists in achieving the natural advantages, and virtue is to be valued as a means to achieving happiness.

Natural growth and the complexity of the natural goods stimulate practical reason. Creatures who wanted very few things or lived in an odd world might never face a choice between getting more of A at the cost of sacrificing B and getting more of B at the cost of C.

---

[6] For different Stoic formulae explaining the kind of 'agreement' that is intended see Stob. ii 75.11–76.15 = LS 63B (cf. SVF iii 12); DL vii 87–9.

[7] See Philo, Leg. Alleg. i 57–8 = SVF iii 202. Cf. Sx. M xi 170; Striker, 'Antipater'.

[8] Cic. F. ii 34. Cf. iii 31 = LS 64A; iv 14.

But since we face these choices, we both exercise and recognize the capacity to decide these questions by practical reason; and so we recognize its instrumental value.

In learning the best way to pursue natural advantages, we learn to perform 'appropriate' action (*kathêkon*, officium).[9] The action is appropriate for the situation, for the nature of the agent, and for the epistemic situation in which the agent decides what to do. Hence appropriate action is 'consequentiality (*to akolouthon*) in life, which, having been done,[10] has a reasonable defence' (Stob. ii 85.13–15 = LS 59B; cf. DL vii 107 = LS 59C). Cicero says it is 'approvable' (probabile), 'in such a way that an account (ratio) can be given of it' (Cic. *F.* iii 58 = LS 59E). 'Consequentiality' refers to what follows from, and is suitable to, the nature of the subject. The definition of appropriate action applies to plants as well as animals and human beings; but in rational creatures it is 'consequentiality in way of life'.[11] A rational creature's way of life, as opposed to a plant's or animal's life, involves rational choice; and so appropriate action finds what is suitable for one choice in the light of the other choices that the agent makes if he chooses in accordance with his nature.

The appeal to a 'reasonable defence' suggests that the standard of appropriateness we should apply depends on the agent's epistemic situation. We can give a reasonable defence of an action even if it turned out to have bad results, as long as we could not reasonably be expected to foresee them, and the action was reasonable in the light of what we could reasonably have been expected to foresee. We need not show that we were certain, or in a position to be certain, about the results of our action, but only that we had good reason to act as we did, in the light of what we knew and reasonably believed at the time.

In saying that an appropriate action 'has' a reasonable defence, the Stoics do not mean that an action is appropriate only if the agent herself gives a reasonable defence of it; they mean that a reasonable defence is available. Though a plant cannot give a reasonable defence of turning towards the sun, its turning is appropriate. Similarly, appropriate human actions may be done for all sorts of reasons, or purely by accident; appropriateness implies only that the right sort of defence is available.

To capture the relation between virtue and the result it seeks to achieve, the Stoics distinguish 'stochastic' (i.e., 'aiming') from non-stochastic crafts.[12] Their distinction rests on a division between the end (*finis*, *telos*) and the objective (*propositum*, *prokeimenon*) of an action or craft. The end is the faultless exercise of the craft, whereas the objective is the external result that this faultless exercise tries to achieve. In a non-stochastic craft, such as arithmetic, the achievement of the end of the craft, which is the faultless exercise of the craft, is sufficient for achieving the objective. If we add or subtract, but get the wrong answer, we must have made a mistake in the exercise of the craft and failed to achieve its end. But in a stochastic craft faultless exercise does not necessarily secure the objective. The end of the

---

[9] On Zeno's explanation of the term *kathêkon* see DL vii 108 = LS 59C; Cooper, 'Moral duty' 436n. 'Incumbent' might capture Zeno's explanation; it justifies the later translation of 'officium' by 'duty'.

[10] This participial clause probably means 'if it were done'. The Stoics do not suggest that it has to have been done before we can consider whether it has a reasonable defence.

[11] When the formula is applied to human beings, *bios* (Stob. ii 85.18) is substituted for *zôê*, used in the general formula that applies also to plants and animals (ii 85.14).

[12] This is not a purely Stoic division; Alexander endorses it at *in Top.* 32.20–34.5 (cf. n82 below); *Quaest.* 61.1–28 = *SVF* iii 19. He uses 'function', *ergon*, where the Stoics use 'end', and 'end', where the Stoics use 'objective'. Here he follows Aristotle's usage. Aristotle agrees with the Stoics that external success should not be the aim of someone practising the stochastic crafts of rhetoric, dialectic, and medicine (*Rhet.* 1355b10–14; *Top.* 101b5–10).

archer is doing all he can to shoot straight at the target; the objective is hitting the target. The craft is stochastic because we can achieve the end without achieving the objective. Even if our exercise of the craft is faultless, we may still miss the target; perhaps the wind blew it over or someone moved it (Cic. *F.* iii 22 = LS 64F).[13]

This difference between end and objective is reflected in the deliberations of an expert in a craft. Though we might at first suppose that the expert ought to be guided simply by beliefs about how to achieve the objective of the craft, this is not straightforwardly true. It is not the doctor's task to think about everything that might go wrong between his competent treatment and the external success; the patient might not be receptive to treatment, or might be hit by a falling tree on the way home from the hospital. Nor should the dialectician think about how to persuade someone who will not listen to rational argument. If craftsmen tried to adapt their practice to fit all possible external hazards, they would guess wrongly and come out worse than they would have if they had just aimed at the appropriate exercise of skill in the craft.[14]

A virtue is similar to a stochastic craft, in so far as it has an objective (achieving the natural advantages) and an end (doing all we can to achieve the natural advantages), and achieving the end is not sufficient for achieving the objective. Virtuous action, therefore, is not sufficient for achieving the life according to nature, which includes the natural advantages.

The Stoics are right to compare virtue with a stochastic craft to this extent. Justice in a state requires laws that protect people against arbitrary arrest, because freedom from arbitrary arrest is valuable for agents with the aims and natural limitations of human beings. Normally we do not undertake a craft unless we value the product; the features of the product determine what counts as skill in the craft (Cic. *F.* v 16 = LS 64E). The expert's deliberation requires thought about the objective of the craft; this thought about the objective forms our conception of the end, which is the action that constitutes the best exercise of the craft.

This account suggests four conclusions: (1) The content of the virtues is determined by the natural advantages that they try to secure. (2) Happiness consists in securing the natural advantages. (3) Virtue is not identical to happiness. (4) Virtue is to be valued for the sake of happiness, but not for its own sake. The Stoics accept the first of these conclusions, but reject the other three. Many ancient critics believe that the resulting position is inconsistent. To see why the Stoics believe it is both consistent and reasonable, we must return to their views about practical reason and the natural advantages.

179. The Non-instrumental Value of Practical Reason

The Stoics reject a purely instrumental conception of virtue on the ground that it conflicts with our preconception that virtue is to be valued for its own sake. But how do we know that we have this preconception, and how do we know it is consistent with the preconceptions that seem to underlie our views about virtue and the natural advantages?

---

[13] On ends and objectives see Striker 'Antipater'; Irwin, 'Conceptions' 228–34; Taylor, 'Hellenistic' 237–9; Inwood, 'Goal' 550–2; Annas, *MH* 400–5.

[14] These examples are derived from Aristotle (cited in n12 above).

The Stoics appeal to their account of conciliation and the growth of practical reason, to show that the description we have given so far is incomplete. Since we need practical reason to discover the appropriate actions in different situations, we recognize the instrumental value of practical reason by using it to find appropriate actions. But when we are acquainted with practical reason, and we recognize its role in guiding our choices, we see that it is also non-instrumentally valuable. According to Cicero's comparison, our friend Smith introduces us to Jones, but, once we know Jones better, we admire and value Jones more than Smith (Cic. *F.* iii 23). Natural impulses introduce us and 'commend' us to reason; but once we have recognized it, we value it more than we value the natural goods. At first we value it as an instrumental means to the natural goods, but once we attend to it, we see that it is to be valued for itself.[15]

In this case as in others, I discover that I value x for itself by finding that I prefer x and y together over y without x. If I valued x only as a means to y, I would be satisfied if I got y by means of z rather than x (if z is an equally efficient means to y). But we do not treat all means as purely instrumental. Even if I walk in order to get to work (not simply for the sake of walking), I still might not be equally satisfied if I could get to work in some other equally efficient way. If I would not prefer this equally efficient alternative, I value walking for itself. The Stoics suggest that something analogous is true about practical reason.[16] Even if practical reasoning must always be partly instrumental, its value is not purely instrumental. I prefer to achieve my objectives by rational planning, rather than to achieve them by some other equally efficient means; hence I do not value practical reason simply as an instrumental means; hence I attach non-instrumental value to it.

Once we have discovered practical reason, we discover that the value we attach to it is not purely instrumental. Even if some method other than practical reason were equally efficient in securing our other objectives, we would not give up practical reasoning; for we take our practical reasoning to be essential to ourselves.[17] It would be irrational for me to give up the exercise of reason for the sake of some specific objective. For the value of the objective is its value for me, and as I become self-conscious I become aware of myself as an essentially rational agent. If I ceased to be a rational agent, I would cease to exist, and any objective I would have gained by doing so would no longer be valuable for me, but only for the non-rational agent who would replace me.[18]

Discovery of the non-instrumental value of practical reason is part of self-discovery through conciliation. After the piecemeal exercise of practical reason, I remember my past plans, how they succeeded and failed, and I plan for the future. I become aware of myself as something more than a collection of impulses; I regard myself as a temporally extended rational planner. When I notice this I come to value my preservation as a rational planner more than I value the satisfaction of the particular impulses. I come to prefer 'order and

---

[15] This passage is discussed by Striker, 'Following' 8–10; Annas, 'Prudence'; Frede, 'Good'.

[16] The analogy with walking is not complete. For while we might go for a walk with no further purpose, practical reason seems to depend on our having some further purpose that we want to achieve; as the Stoics say, practical reason needs some material to work on.

[17] Kant argues that reason is less efficient than other means for achieving satisfaction of our other desires would be. See *G* 395. Hence he thinks the supposition I have mentioned is not merely counterfactual. His main argument is not weakened, however, if the supposition is false, as long as the counterfactual claim is true.

[18] For similar ideas in Butler see *S* ii 17.

concord' (Cic. *F.* iii 21 = LS 59D) in action over the natural goods that are the result of successful action.

We can now understand better the Stoic description of the end as 'living with understanding of the things that come about by nature, choosing those that are in accord with nature and rejecting the contrary things'.[19] We might have understood this as a description of how to achieve the end, so that the end, strictly speaking, would be the possession or enjoyment of the natural advantages rather than the activity of choosing them. But now we see that the Stoics intend to refer precisely to the activity of rational choosing. They see non-instrumental value in the practical reason that is exercised in choosing the appropriate natural advantages, not only in the successful results of our choice.

180. The Non-instrumental Value of Virtue

The Stoics believe that once we recognize the non-instrumental value of practical reason, we can also understand why and how virtue is a non-instrumental good. They reject Epicurus' view that virtue is purely instrumental to an external end; and so their explanation of the way in which virtue is a craft takes account of this Aristotelian objection to Epicurus. [20] If one treats virtue as a generalized craft directed at the natural goods, one grasps part of the character of virtue. But, according to the Stoics, this parallel leaves out the crucial feature of virtue. Unlike productive crafts, such as medicine and carpentry, it has a non-instrumentally good end that is not outside its own exercise, but is internal to it (Cic. *F.* iii 24 = LS 64H).

If we recognize an internal end for the craft of virtue, we can see that virtuous action is worth choosing for its own sake. In recognizing this feature of virtuous action, the Stoics appeal to widespread agreement on the non-instrumental value of actions that are taken to be virtuous (iii 37–8). They do not take this to be a controversial feature of their position; hence they do not suppose that one has to accept the whole Stoic outlook before one can attribute non-instrumental goodness to virtue. Human beings and animals alike sacrifice themselves even at enormous cost to themselves; and we admire these actions as virtuous and fine (*kala*, *honesta*).[21]

Since the Stoics are eudaemonists, they believe that if virtue has non-instrumental value, the final good includes virtue as a component. If we take the final good to be unconnected with virtue, and so measure it by our own advantage, and not by fineness, we cannot

---

[19] Cic. *F.* ii 34. See above §178.

[20] See Cic. *F.* ii 69–71, quoted at §157. Cf. Augustine's use of this criterion for virtue, §229.

[21] See Sx. *M* xi 99; Bett, *AE* ad loc. Cic. *F.* ii 109–10 suggests that the Stoics do not take the behaviour of animals to imply that animals pursue the fine; they take it to indicate the animal origins of human pursuit of the fine. Cf. DL vii 127 = LS 61I: 'And they say that virtue is choiceworthy for itself. For we are ashamed at what we do badly, as if knowing that only the fine is good'. Cic. *Leg.* i 40: 'If a penalty, and not nature, were needed to keep people from injustice, what anxiety would disturb the wicked if the fear of punishment were removed? But in fact none of them has ever been so brazen that he has not either denied that he committed the crime or else fabricated some ground of just grievance, seeking a defence for his crime in some right (*ius*) of nature.' Cic. *Leg.* i 48: 'Right (*ius*) and everything fine (*honestum*) are to be sought for themselves. Indeed all good men love fairness (*aequitas*) itself and right itself, and it does not belong to a good man to go astray in loving what is not to be loved for its own sake. Hence right is to be sought and cultivated for itself. If right, then justice too; if this, then all the rest of the virtues too are to be cultivated for themselves.'

consistently cultivate friendship, justice, generosity, or bravery.[22] Any conception of the final good that leaves out fineness demotes the virtues to a purely instrumental status that conflicts with the outlook of the virtuous person (Cic. *F.* ii 35).

This objection presupposes that each of the virtues includes some conviction about the value of the actions it prescribes. The just person, for instance, not only does just actions, but does them for their own sake, in the conviction that they are worth doing simply because they are just, and not because of some further causal result. This is why Cyrenaic and Epicurean conceptions of the end leave out fineness (expertes honestatis, ii 35). If the fine is 'something that is itself to be desired, by its own character (sua vi) and for itself', the Epicureans are wrong (ii 44).

These Stoic claims about virtue have Platonic and Aristotelian sources. Latin sources use *honestum* to render the Greek *kalon*, often rendered 'noble' or 'fine'.[23] Much of what the Stoics say about the right has parallels in Aristotle's claims about the virtues and the fine. We have seen that Aristotle offers no systematic account of the fine, but says enough to show that he takes it to be the central and distinctive concern of the virtuous person. In later Peripatetic writers the fine is more prominent, though they do not offer the detailed account that Aristotle lacks.

Only one passage in the Aristotelian Corpus describes the fine as the end (*telos*) of virtue (*MM* 1190a28), though one might reasonably claim that other passages imply that it has this status. But Aspasius (*in EN* 81.23; 82.34; 117.30) and Alexander (*Mant.* 155.12–13) treat this as a standard formula for the relation of the fine to virtue. They introduce remarks on the fine into contexts where they are perfectly appropriate, but have no precise precedent in Aristotle. The fine is prominent, for instance, in Alexander's argument for the reciprocity of the virtues (*Mant.* 154.30–155.13). He takes the best kind of friendship to be friendship for the fine, whereas Aristotle calls it friendship for virtue (*in Top.* 271.25–6).[24] He argues that one ought to choose pleasure for the sake of the fine, not the other way round (*Dub. et Sol.* 151.19–152.33).[25] Aspasius emphasizes the connexion between the fineness and the praiseworthiness of virtue (*in EN* 32.11; cf. *EN* 1101b31–2). In explaining how vice corrupts ethical principles, he suggests that it prevents us from recognizing that happiness consists in fine actions (*in EN* 136.19–23). Aristotle does not mention this particular effect of corruption (*EN* 1151a15); Aspasius probably mentions it because of his conviction that the fine is the goal of virtue. Similarly, when he considers how pain impedes the virtuous person's actions, he emphasizes that it impedes fine actions (*in En* 150.15), though Aristotle does not say this in so many words (*EN* 1153b9–12).

Whether or not these remarks on the fine reflect Stoic influence, they suggest correctly that Stoics and Peripatetics agree about the place of the fine in an account of virtue. Latin writers are right to choose 'honestum' (honourable) to translate 'kalon'. They recognize that the fine is a proper object of praise, as opposed to liking, pleasure, or admiration, and it makes people praiseworthy (DL vii 100; Cic. *F.* iii 27 = LS 60N). Latin writers as

---

[22] See Cic. *Off.* i 5, quoted at §162. The reference to hedonism suggests that Cicero has Epicureans especially in mind. He distinguishes questions about their personal character from questions about the implications of their theory (*F.* ii 80).

[23] Frede, 'Good', discusses the Stoic concept of the honestum, denying that it is a concept of moral goodness.

[24] See also *in Top.* 95.3–5; 148.25–149.2 (on *to deon* and *to kalon*).

[25] Some of the works cited may not be genuine works of Alexander.

well as Greek see a connexion between the fine and the beautiful. We recognize the fine through our conception of beauty, loveliness, fittingness or appropriateness (*convenientia*), constancy, and order (Cic. *Off.* i 14).[26] We grasp the fine by analogy with beauty, recognizing due proportion (*summetria*) of parts and whole in both cases (Stob. ii 63.1–5). But we do not appreciate the fine in exactly the way we appreciate the beautiful; Latin writers mark the difference by using 'honestum' rather than 'pulchrum' (beautiful) to render '*kalon*'.

The honestum is an object of praise because it deserves praise in its own right, whether or not it is actually praised (Cic. *Off.* i 14).[27] It draws us by its own character, not by its satisfaction of some prior desire of ours (Stob. ii 100.21–2). It involves acting for reasons that are not confined to oneself and one's own benefit; this is why concern for the honestum is contrasted with concern for one's own advantage (*commodum*: Cic. *Off.* i 5). Honestum action is appropriate for a human being because human beings are rational and because they are social, finding their good in the good of the smaller and larger communities they belong to; hence action is honestum in so far as it is the sort of action that results from rational concern for the common good.

The honestum is recognized by reason, the special capacity of human beings that makes one capable of surveying the whole of one's life.[28] This same reason encourages us to cultivate the intellectual and social virtues, so that the four cardinal virtues can be recognized as the different forms of rightness (Cic. *F.* ii 45–8). They are different forms of rightness because all the virtues and the corresponding actions are praiseworthy in their own right, whether or not they are actually praised (ii 49).

For these reasons it is appropriate to translate 'honestum' and '*kalon*' by 'right'. The Stoics agree with Aristotle, and with even more emphasis, in using these terms for the area of morality. The different virtues correspond to different aspects of the right, because they involve recognizing actions as worthwhile for their own sakes, and not simply because their causal consequences satisfy some previous desire. The virtuous person acknowledges

---

[26] 'And it is no small force of nature and reason that only this animal [sc. the human being] is aware of what order is, what is suitable, what is appropriate in actions and words. Hence no other animal is aware of beauty, loveliness, and suitability (*convenientia*) of parts, in the things we are aware of by sight. Nature and reason, extending this similarity from the eyes to the mind find that beauty, constancy, and order are far more to be maintained in deliberations and actions. They are careful to do nothing in an improper or unmanly way, and in all thoughts and actions to do and think nothing to gratify appetite (*libidinose*). The rightness that we are inquiring about is made and achieved from these things; even if it is not admired, it is none the less right, and, as we truly assert, it is praiseworthy by its nature even if no one praises it' (Cic. *Off.* i 14).

[27] Cf. Cic. *F.* ii 45: 'By honestum, then, I understand whatever is such that, with all advantage removed, without any rewards or fruits, can be rightly praised through itself.... <The best people> do very many things for this one reason—because it is appropriate, correct, and honestum—even though they see no reward following from it.' Holden ad *Off.* i 14 quotes from Berkeley, *Alciphron* 3.3: 'Doubtless there is a beauty of the mind, a charm in virtue, a symmetry and proportion in the moral world. This moral beauty was known to the ancients by the name of honestum or *to kalon*.' In this dialogue Berkeley expresses doubts about appeals to the honestum.

[28] 'Afterwards through the stages of growth with age reason was born from its seeds, and also consideration in employing deliberation, the awareness of genuine fineness (honestas) and usefulness, and a more subtle and considered discrimination between suitable and unsuitable things. And in this way the worthiness of what is fine and fitting glistened and shone above everything else ... And nothing else was counted really and without qualification good except the fine, and nothing bad except what was shameful. All the other things—the things which were in the middle and were neither fine nor shameful—it was decided that these were neither good nor bad. But productions and relations were distinguished each by its aspects—these are what the philosophers call the preferred and non-preferred things. Therefore pleasure and pain too, as far as concerns the end itself of living well and blessedly, were left in the things in the middle, and judged to be neither among the goods nor among the evils' (Aulus Gellius, *NA* xii 5.7 (continues §166n37)).

reasons that rest on the value of the actions themselves, not simply on the fact that these actions match his previous desires.

The Stoics believe that the common belief that virtue is non-instrumentally good supports their account of virtue and practical reason. This common belief is an apparent preconception. We will justifiably regard it as a genuine preconception if a reasonable interpretation of it and of other apparent preconceptions produces a consistent result. The Stoics argue for consistency by claiming that our preconception about practical reason supports our preconception about virtue. Hence they connect practical reason, recognition of the right, and the pursuit of the cardinal virtues (Cic. *F.* ii 45–7; *Off.* i 11–17). We recognize that the exercise of practical reason is to be valued for its own sake, not purely instrumentally. But we also believe that the virtues and their exercise are to be valued for their own sake. This belief about the virtues is reasonable because the virtues are manifestations of practical reason.

181. Virtue as the Only Good

The Stoic position so far might seem attractive to a Platonist or an Aristotelian. Indeed, some Peripatetics see that the Stoic claims about conciliation help to explain the Aristotelian views about nature that underlie the function argument.[29] These considerations might persuade us that virtue is a non-instrumental good and a necessary condition for happiness. The Stoic account of the fine makes it clear what Aristotle commits himself to in claiming that the virtuous person acts for the sake of the fine.

We can now try to understand the more surprising and less Aristotelian claim that the good is 'living with understanding of the things that come about by nature, choosing those that are in accord with nature . . .'.[30] The Stoics also describe the end as 'acting reasonably in the selection of things according to nature', and 'living one's life completing all the appropriate actions' (DL vii 88 = LS 59J).[31] These are plausible descriptions of the virtuous life, and the Stoics have good grounds for saying that this is a non-instrumental good. The references to reasonable selection and to appropriate action indicate that virtuous choice is an exercise of practical reason, and choiceworthy for its own sake on that ground. But it is surprising that the Stoics treat these as descriptions not only of virtue, but also of happiness, because they identify virtue with happiness.

According to the Stoics, however, the identity of virtue with happiness does not depend on some new argument distinct from the arguments from conciliation and from preconceptions. They believe that these arguments, correctly understood, prove that virtue is the only good, the only thing worth choosing (*haireton, expetendum,* Cic. *F.* iii 21 = LS 59D) for its own sake, and that the other supposed goods—the natural advantages—are neither good nor bad, but indifferent (iii 22 = LS 59D).[32] The Stoics express the same doctrine about virtue and

---

[29] On non-Stoic appeals to conciliation see Annas, 'Hellenistic'; §77n12.
[30] Cic. *F.* ii 34. See above §178.
[31] These accounts of the end are offered by Diogenes and Archedemus. Antipater holds a similar view. See Stob. ii 76.9–15; Clement, *Strom.* ii 129.1–3; Plu. *CN* 1072d = *SVF* iii (Antip.) 58–9.
[32] Cf. Stob. ii 46.5–10 = *SVF* iii 2; 16–19 = *SVF* iii 16 (quoted below n45).

happiness by claiming that 'only the fine is good'. Since they believe that happiness includes all goods, their claim that virtue is the only good implies that virtue is identical to happiness. Hence they believe that virtue is sufficient for happiness, and so endorse the Socratic and Cynic thesis that Aristotle takes to be indefensible.

They insist that the different recognized virtues are possible only for someone who thinks virtue sufficient for happiness. If we care about any other goods as parts of happiness, we will be tempted to sacrifice virtuous action to these other goods, and so we will not be committed unreservedly to virtuous action as virtuous people are. The good requires living in agreement with nature; virtuous people do this because they live in agreement with reason, which they have naturally come to value most. They are happy and fortunate; nothing impedes or prevents them; they need nothing (iii 25 = LS 64H).

The Stoics argue that everything good must be praiseworthy, and that only the fine is praiseworthy.[33] Critics object that the argument simply begs the question against those who recognize honour, wealth, and so on as goods (iv 48–9). The Stoics might answer that for someone who takes virtue seriously not every sort of wealth or honour will be part of his good; he will reject what he might gain by theft or fraud, and stick to praiseworthy and honestly earned wealth and honour. But all we can infer from these considerations is that only virtue and the goods that it produces are praiseworthy. This is less restrictive than the Stoics' conclusion.

A second argument maintains that our life is happy if and only if we can be proud of it, and that this is true only if we live finely (iii 28). In the Stoics' view, if we have been virtuous, we can be proud of our lives, because we will not have failed to do anything we ought to have done that it was fully in our power to do. The argument is persuasive if we agree that pride is properly directed to our own achievements, and that only what is in our control is our own achievement.

A further argument relies on the same attitude to events that are not our own achievements. According to the Stoics, the brave person despises all the accidents that can happen to human beings, so that only what is shameful is bad.[34] They assume, questionably, that if we are

---

[33] The arguments mentioned in this paragraph and the next two are taken from the series of syllogistic arguments for the sufficiency of virtue that are reported in Cic. *F.* iii 27 = LS 60N; iv 50; Plu. *SR* 1039c = *SVF* iii 29: 'In his book On The Fine Chrysippus tries to demonstrate that only the fine is good, and uses arguments such as these: "The good is chosen, the chosen is approved, the approved is praised; the praised is fine." Again: "The good is gratifying, the gratifying is impressive, the impressive is fine." ' Cf. also Cic. *TD* v 43; 45 = *SVF* iii 37. On the intended force of these arguments see Schofield, 'Syllogisms'.

[34] See Aulus Gellius, *NA* xviii 1.4–8 = *SVF* iii 56: [A discussion between a Stoic and a Peripatetic.] 'And there the Stoic thought that a man could gain a happy life by virtue of mind alone, and the deepest wretchedness by vice alone, even though virtue lacked and vice had all the other goods, which they called bodily and external. Against this the Peripatetic agreed that the wretched life comes about by vices of the mind and by evildoing alone. Still he insisted that virtue alone was not at all sufficient to complete all the elements of a happy life; for bodily non-deformity and health, attractive appearance, personal wealth, good reputation and all the other goods of the body and of fortune seemed necessary to achieve a happy life fully. The Stoic protested here, and was surprised that the Peripatetic treated these two things, virtue and vice, differently. For virtue and vice are two contraries; the wretched and the happy life are also equally contraries. Why does he [sc. the opponent] not retain in both the force and nature of a contrary, when he regards vice alone as sufficient to produce wretchedness of life, but does not regard virtue alone as sufficient to produce a happy life? The Stoic said that this above all was conflicting and inconsistent for someone who acknowledged that a happy life could by no means be produced if virtue alone was missing, but then denied that when virtue alone is present a happy life comes to be. He granted and accorded honour to virtue when it was missing, but withheld the same honour when virtue was present and seeking it.' Cf. Sen. *Ep.* 85.2 = *SVF* iii 58.

rightly proud and pleased with our achievements in our life, we are happy, and the fact that other things might go badly is irrelevant to our happiness.

Similarly, we may question the Stoics' use of arguments from the *Euthydemus*. They contrast virtue with external goods by pointing out that external goods can be misused, whereas virtue cannot, and that external goods are sometimes harmful, whereas virtue always benefits us (DL vii 103 = LS 58A).[35] These differences between virtue and other goods justify us in giving virtue a different place in relation to happiness, so that, as Aristotle claims, it is a dominant good. But the Stoics do not seem justified in inferring that alleged goods other than virtue are not goods at all because they sometimes harm us. If they simply mean that these other goods are not goods 'without reservation' or 'unconditionally' (as Kant puts it),[36] they seem to repeat Peripatetic doctrine in paradoxical terms. But if they agree with Socrates' argument in the *Euthydemus*, they seem to accept a purely adaptive conception of happiness, as he does. Such a conception seems to conflict with their arguments to show that the natural advantages and the life according to nature are legitimate objects of pursuit.

This objection brings us to the main difficulty in the Stoic position. For while it appeals to preconceptions, it seems to violate preconceptions that are at least as clear. As the Stoics agree, we begin by treating natural advantages as goods. When we discover practical reason, we discover that they are not the only goods, and that practical reason is an overriding good. But we seem to have no good reason to abandon our previous belief that the natural advantages are also goods. If our belief in the goodness of some natural advantages is a firm preconception, the Stoics violate their own method.

In reply to this objection, they argue that the preconceptions really support their apparently counter-intuitive claim. They rely on the preconception that happiness is the ultimate end; then they argue that natural advantages are not part of the ultimate end, and so they infer that natural advantages cannot be part of happiness.

But why should we agree that these natural advantages are not parts of the ultimate good? The Stoics admit that we pursue some of them for their own sakes, and they recognize that this pursuit is the natural and reasonable result of conciliation. It is difficult to see, then, why we should exclude them from the ultimate end.[37]

182. Indifferents

The Stoics believe that this objection rests on a misunderstanding of their estimate of natural advantages, and in particular on a misunderstanding of their claim that these natural advantages are neither good nor bad, but indifferent. Some critics allege that this Stoic claim supports extreme moralism, and agrees with the Cynics that moral virtue is the only thing deserving rational concern.

This extreme moralism has been one of the attractive features of Stoicism to some later readers. It expresses a 'stoical' indifference to anything that happens to us that is not within

---

[35] On the *Euthydemus* cf. §14.   [36] See Kant, *G* 393.
[37] This is the gist of the criticism that Cicero presents in *F.* iv.

our control. If we can convince ourselves that none of these things matters, we can train ourselves not to be concerned about them, and to face them with resolution. We might easily believe that we find this attitude expressed in the *Meditations* of Marcus Aurelius.[38] The same attitude appeals to Justus Lipsius in the turbulent conditions of Northern Europe in the sixteenth century. His book *On Constancy* offers Stoic indifference as a cure for the anxiety and turmoil that he suffers from his involvement in the wars in the Netherlands. If he can convince himself that these external events do not matter, he will no longer be disturbed by them.[39] This is why the Stoic doctrine of indifferents leads to Stoic 'freedom from passion' (*apatheia*); once we see that externals do not matter, they no longer arouse disturbing emotions in us. Once we recognize that non-moral 'goods' and 'evils' are not really good and evil, but indifferent, we also lose our concern about them.

We will need to consider this interpretation of Stoic freedom from passion later.[40] First, we need to see whether this 'stoical' attitude rests on a correct understanding of the doctrine of indifferents. What we have already said about the Stoics' view of natural advantages should make it seem surprising if they claim that such things do not matter; for virtuous people seem to occupy themselves in trying to get them. It seems unreasonable to deny that we have reason to be concerned about non-moral goods; would we not be foolish to choose fewer of them, other things being equal, if we could have had more?[41]

We can reconcile the virtuous person's efforts to secure indifferents with lack of concern for them if we suppose that the virtuous person regards the pursuit of indifferents as a sort of game. In other crafts and skills the productive process does not always aim primarily at the existence of the product. Sometimes it is simply the occasion for a display of skill; an accomplished cook might cook an absurdly elaborate and inedible dish simply to display cooking skill. In games of skill, the moves are simply a means to the exercise of skill; the point is to devise a game that requires the display of certain kinds of skill (e.g., by making it artificially difficult to do some things). Perhaps the Stoics take this attitude to life. If so, natural advantages are unimportant in themselves, but virtuous people take an interest in them because they provide an opportunity for the display of practical reasoning. Adam Smith ascribes this attitude to the Stoics.[42]

---

[38] See Marcus Aurelius, *Meditations* ii 11.2–4 (see Farquharson ad loc.); v 20.

[39] Lipsius sets out his generally careful and sympathetic exposition of Stoicism in *MSP*. He discusses the passions in iii 7. After setting out the Stoic doctrine, he cites the objections of Lactantius and Augustine, and endorses the position that he takes to be favoured by Scripture and the Fathers, defending the moderation rather than the elimination of passions (159–60). In *De Constantia* Lipsius relies on Stoic views most explicitly in i 7, where he speaks of 'false goods and evils' as 'those which are not in us but around us, and which do not properly benefit or harm this inner human being, that is to say the mind. And so I will not call them good or bad in fact and in their character (re et ratione); I will admit that they are goods by opinion, and by a sort of common sense of the masses.' Lipsius' views are discussed by Kraye in Schmitt and Skinner, *CHRP* 370–2; Cooper, 'Lipsius'.

[40] See §191.   [41] Cf. Alex. *in Top.* 211.9–14, quoted below in n51.

[42] 'Human life the Stoics appear to have considered as a game of great skill; in which, however, there was a mixture of chance, or of what is vulgarly considered to be chance. In such games the stake is commonly a trifle, and the whole pleasure of the game arises from playing well, from playing fairly, and playing skillfully. If notwithstanding all his skill, however, the good player should, by the influence of chance, happen to lose, the loss ought to be a matter, rather of merriment, than of serious sorrow. . . . Human life, with all the advantages which can possibly attend it, ought, according to the Stoics, to be regarded but as a mere two-penny stake; a matter by far too insignificant to merit any anxious concern. Our only anxious concern ought to be, not about the stake, but about the proper method of playing' (Smith, *TMS* vii 2.1.24, 278–9). For the Stoic use of a comparison with games see Cic. *Off.* iii 42; §404. Striker, 'Antipater', develops the comparison. Cf. §40 on the athletic conception of virtue.

This interpretation of the Stoics might lead us to suppose that they basically conceive happiness as a kind of feeling of self-satisfaction and contentment, and that they care about virtue primarily as a means to this sort of contentment. According to this view, they would agree with the Epicureans about the character of the end, and disagree about the means to achieving it. We might support such an interpretation by appealing to their description of the end as 'good flow'.[43] On this basis Adam Smith ascribes an adaptive conception of happiness to the Stoics.[44]

While this view of happiness and the indifferents might allow us to ascribe a consistent view to the Stoics, the resulting view would not be very attractive. If virtue is happiness, and therefore is the only end of our appropriate actions,[45] virtuous people make an appropriate attempt to protect a child from danger for the sake of their own virtue. They do not aim at the child's safety, but at the exercise of their virtue in the attempt. This view may well seem both repellent and self-defeating. It seems repellent if Stoic sages are supposed to care only about their own character rather than the needs of other people. It seems self-defeating if we cannot explain why it is a virtuous action to protect someone from danger and a vicious action to expose them to needless danger; why should we discriminate between the two actions unless safety is something we ought to aim at and danger is something we ought to avoid?

In a game of skill this question does not arise; for it is to some extent arbitrary what moves are allowed, and we might change the rules if we think the game is too easy, or too difficult, or too dull for the spectators. But if we think of appropriate actions as arbitrarily chosen means for the display of virtue, we seem to violate our preconceptions. It does not seem arbitrary that virtuous people display their practical reason and their fearlessness in defending their community rather than in a daring bank robbery. Whatever we might display in actions that do not aim at the appropriate natural advantages for the appropriate people, it does not seem to be a virtue.

183. Preferred Indifferents

The Stoics believe that if we take them to advocate inappropriate detachment from natural advantages, we misunderstand their doctrine of indifferents. They recognize different sorts of indifferents (Cic. *F.* iii 50 = LS 58I; DL vii 104–6).[46] Pure indifferents give us no reason from any point of view to prefer them. But the natural advantages that are the initial objects of a creature's desire are not pure indifferents. Both they and their contraries are indifferent in relation to happiness, since they are neither parts of happiness nor instrumental means

---

[43] See Stob. ii 77.20–1 = LS 63A: 'Zeno defined happiness in this way: "Happiness is good flow (*eurhoia*) of life."' See also Epict. i 4, 1, 3; Sen. *Ep.* 85.2; Irwin, 'Conceptions' 225; Striker, 'Tranquillity', 185–6.

[44] See Smith, *TMS* iii 3.26–31.

[45] See Stob. ii 46.5–10 = *SVF* iii 2: 'The Stoics say, by way of a definition: "The end is that for the sake of which everything is done appropriately, while it itself is done for the sake of nothing." They also define it this way: "That for the sake of which other things are, while it itself is for the sake of nothing." And again: "That towards which all the things done appropriately in our life have their reference, while it itself has reference to nothing."' Stob. ii 77.16–19 = *SVF* iii 16 = LS 63A: 'They say that the end is being happy, (*eudaimonein*), for the sake of which everything is done, while it itself is done, but for the sake of nothing. This is found in living according to virtue; in living consistently; and further, this being the same thing, in living according to nature.'

[46] I do not discuss Ariston's views on indifferents (see Cic. *F.* iii 50 = LS 58I; DL vii 160 = LS 31N).

to it. Hence none of them is 'chosen' (*haireton*); for only goods—and hence only virtue and what promotes it—are properly 'chosen'.[47] But they are not indifferent in every respect.

The natural advantages are 'preferred' (or 'promoted', *proêgmena*) indifferents, and their contraries are non-preferred (Cic. *F.* iii 51–2), because we have reason to prefer the first and to reject the second.[48] We have reason to prefer the natural advantages because they promote a life in accord with nature; though they are indifferent towards happiness, they are not indifferent towards life in accord with nature.[49]

Since natural advantages are to be preferred, they also have value. Though they are not objects of choice (in the strict sense that applies only to goods), they are objects of appropriate selection; hence they have either non-instrumental or instrumental selective value. We have reason to select health rather than illness, when these are the options we face, and this is a complete description of the practically relevant features of the situation.[50] They are not choiceworthy, because we are not justified in choosing them without qualification; this unqualified choice, in all situations and irrespective of the price to be paid in natural disadvantages, is reasonable only for virtue.

This clarification of the Stoic claims about indifferents suggests that the Stoics believe preferred and non-preferred indifferents matter, and that the virtuous person has good reason to be concerned about them. Whatever the point of the doctrine of indifferents may be, it is not intended to detach us from concern for indifferents; if the Stoics had intended to do that, they would not have attributed non-instrumental value to some preferred indifferents, and they would not have said that they contribute to the life in accord with nature.

But if this is all true, what is the point of calling these natural advantages indifferents? If some indifferents are to be preferred, and have selective value, a life that includes these indifferents together with virtue seems to be preferable to a life that includes virtue without these indifferents. If such a life is preferable, it seems to be a happier life. How, then, can the Stoics claim that virtue is the whole of happiness?[51]

---

[47] On choiceworthiness and other types of value see Stob. ii 83.10–84.3 = *SVF* iii 124 = LS 58D; DL vii 105 = *SVF* iii 126 = LS 58B.

[48] 'Of things that are they say some are goods, some evils, some neither. Goods are the virtues—prudence, justice, bravery, temperance and the rest. Evils are the opposites—folly, injustice and the rest. Neither goods nor evils are those things which neither benefit nor harm—such as life, health, pleasure, beauty, strength, wealth, good reputation, good birth—and the opposites of these—death, sickness, trouble, ugliness, weakness, poverty, bad reputation, low birth and things like them, . . . Of indifferents some are called preferred, others non-preferred. Preferred are those that have value, non-preferred those that have disvalue. They call value, first, a contribution to the consistent life—every good is such a contribution; second, some capacity or use which is an intermediary contributor towards the life according to nature, which is like speaking of the contribution to the life according to nature made by wealth or health . . . Of preferred things some are preferred because of themselves, some because of other things, others both because of themselves and because of other things. Because of themselves, natural gifts, progress [sc. towards virtue] and the like. Because of other things, wealth, good birth and the like; both because of themselves and because of other things, strength, keen senses, bodily soundness—because of themselves because they are according to nature, and because of other things because they provide many useful results. . . . Further, of appropriate things some are always appropriate, others not always. Living according to nature is always appropriate; questioning and answering and walking and the like are not always' (DL vii 101–9 = *SVF* iii 117 = LS 58A–C. Cf. Sx. *M* xi 59–63).

[49] Stob. ii 79.18–80.13; 83.10–84.2 = LS 58C–D.

[50] For different views on whether any indifferents have non-instrumental value see LS i, 357–9 (whom I agree with); Lesses, 'Virtue' 110–17; Frede, 'Good' 92 ('. . . the desire for them in a rational person can only be the desire for them as mere means to the good').

[51] Alex. *in Top.* 211.9–14 = *SVF* iii 62, states an Aristotelian objection: 'Thus it would be shown that each of the things called preferred indifferents by the later philosophers is choiceworthy and good. For when each of them is added to virtue

184. Crafts, Ends, and Objectives

These difficulties arise from the Stoics' claim that happiness does not embrace all objects of rational preference. In refusing to extend happiness this far, they reject Aristotle's belief that happiness is comprehensive. To see why they reject it, we need to return to their division between stochastic and non-stochastic crafts.[52] In all stochastic crafts the proper concern of the expert in a stochastic craft is the internal end rather than the external objective, but the character of the end differs from one stochastic craft to another. In many crafts the end is not valued for its own sake; though we can distinguish the end of medicine from the objective, we have no reason to care about the proper exercise of the craft except in so far as we take it to be the best means towards the objective of curing people. In the case of virtue, however, the Stoics believe that the end has non-instrumental value. We have already seen the grounds for this belief, in the Stoic account of development and conciliation. When we are introduced to practical reason through its instrumental use, we come to recognize that it is valuable for itself, so that the end, as well as the objective, of appropriate rational action has non-instrumental value (Cic. F. iii 23–4 = LS 64H).

The Stoic view of virtue as a stochastic craft might appear to disagree with Aristotle. In treating virtue as a craft the Stoics seem to return to a Socratic position, and to reject Aristotle's separation of craft from virtue. According to Aristotle, craft involves productive reason aiming at 'production' (poiêsis) that has an end distinct from it; prudence, on the contrary, involves purely practical reason, aiming at 'action' (praxis) that has an internal end. For prudence 'acting well' (eupraxia) is the end; the wise person sees that the value of the activity does not depend on any end beyond the activity itself (EN 1140b6). Since the Stoics seem to treat virtue as a stochastic craft, they seem to treat it as productive.

But the Stoics agree with Aristotle in believing that virtuous action is its own end. Though virtue is a stochastic craft, the objective that it pursues is not its end; the end, as Aristotle believes, is virtuous action itself. Virtuous action is the realization of practical reason, and it consists in doing what we reasonably can to secure the natural advantages. Aristotle believes that virtue has these two features. The Stoics signal their agreement with him by interpreting the analogy between virtue and craft so as to allow for these features.

Their conception of the internal end is clear in their description of the distinctive features of the virtuous person's action. Since they call this action a 'success' (katorthôma),[53] we might suppose that virtuous people succeed more often than other people do in, say, relieving suffering, or defending their community from danger. But this is not the sort of success that the Stoics have in mind. Chrysippus contrasts the sage with a non-sage who does all the appropriate actions that the sage does, but not for the sage's reasons. He insists that this non-sage is not yet virtuous. Someone progressing towards virtue might perform all

---

it makes the whole more choiceworthy for the virtuous person. For a life in accordance with virtue is more choiceworthy if it comes with health and affluence and good reputation. For choiceworthy things and things to be avoided are judged by the choice and avoidance of the virtuous person.'

[52] See §178 above.

[53] A *katorthôma* is 'an appropriate action (*kathêkon*) having all the measures, or . . . a complete appropriate action' (Stob. ii 93.14–16 = LS 59K; cf. 85.18–86.4 = LS 59B).

the appropriate actions, but would not be virtuous without having done them for the right reason.[54]

Virtuous people do the appropriate action for the right reason, because of its appropriateness. Their action is successful, and not merely appropriate, because the relevant success consists in acting for the right reason.[55] Virtuous people do the appropriate actions for the right reason, not simply on some particular occasions, but from a fixed and firm state of character.[56] They act reasonably, exercising right reason in choosing appropriate actions because they are appropriate and suitable for human nature.[57]

On these points the Stoics agree with Aristotle's claim that the virtuous person acts justly, temperately, and so on, by choosing the virtuous action for its own sake. In requiring virtuous people to act 'in accordance with correct reason' (Stob. ii 96.22 = LS 59M) the Stoics recall an Aristotelian formula for virtue (EN 1103b31–4; 1144b21–30). They also recall Aristotle's use of adverbs (acting justly, temperately, etc.) to mark the distinctive feature of the virtuous character. Aristotle contrasts acting justly with simply doing just actions (1105a28–b9). Similarly, the Stoics contrast a complete appropriate action with an incomplete one by saying that the complete appropriate action is performed in the right way; if, for instance, returning a deposit is an appropriate action, returning it justly is a successful action (Cic. F. iii 59 = LS 59F).

If appropriate action implied success in getting a preferred indifferent (its objective), sages would not take it as their end; for we cannot expect that our efforts to gain preferred indifferents will always succeed, and we ought not even to think directly about external success when we make our choices.[58] But in saying that, the Stoics make it clear why sages take appropriate action as their end. We can give a reasonable defence of an action even if it turned out to have bad results, as long as we can show that we could not reasonably be expected to foresee them, and that the action was reasonable in the light of what we could reasonably be expected to foresee. Since virtuous people value practical reason for its own sake, and regard the exercise of practical reason in acting reasonably (eulogistein)[59] as the end of virtuous action, their distinctive success consists in their achievement of the relevant end, not in achievement of the objective that determines the character of the end.

185. The Connexion of the Virtues

These views about the end of virtuous action help to explain the Stoics' careful treatment of questions about the unity and reciprocity of the virtues. We might have expected their

---

[54] 'Chrysippus: "The one who is progressing to the limit performs all appropriate things and omits none." But he says that this man's life is not yet happy; happiness supervenes on it when these intermediate actions acquire firmness and tenacity and get some peculiar fixity' (Stob. v 906.19–907.5 = LS 59I).

[55] 'The Stoics think that all the works (of a craft) are common, and belong to all; they are distinguished by coming to be from a craftsman's disposition or a non-craftsman's. For the work of a virtuous person is not to care for parents and to honour them in other ways; his work is to do this from prudence. . . . Hence the one who has a craft of living is the one whose peculiar work is to act from the best disposition in each of his actions' (Sx. M xi 200).

[56] Cf. Plu. VM 3, 441c = SVF i 202 = LS 61B; Sen. Ep. 95.57.

[57] See the accounts of the good offered by Diogenes and Archedemus (DL vii 88 = LS 59J, quoted at §181 above). These equally apply to virtue.

[58] See the references to Aristotle in n12 above (on stochastic crafts).   [59] See §178 above.

return to Socratic moral psychology and their rejection of non-rational parts of the soul to result in Socrates' belief in the unity of the virtues. Plato and Aristotle reject the Socratic view because they take different conditions of the non-rational parts of the soul to differentiate the virtues.[60] Some ancient critics believe that the Stoics ought to take the same position if they are consistent. According to Plutarch, Ariston holds a view close to Socrates' belief in the unity of the virtues, since he suggests that the virtues differ merely in their subject-matter, and therefore in a purely relational property; if x is to the left of y, it does not follow that x and y differ in any other respect than this, and Ariston suggests that the fact that we use different names for virtue in different fields of operation does not indicate anything more than a purely relational difference between the supposed 'virtues'.[61]

Chrysippus disagrees with Ariston; he intends the difference between the virtues to be more than purely relational. He suggests that the difference is one of those differences in relational properties that reflect an internal difference between the subjects of the relational properties.[62] It is less clear, however, what he thinks the difference is; his opponents suggest that he attributes so much unity to the virtues that he has no basis for recognizing the right sort of difference.[63] He insists that they all have the same objects of study.[64] In each virtuous action the virtuous person will apply the same knowledge, and her action will have all the virtues properly predicated of it; by paying her debt because this is the right thing to do she will have performed a successful action (*katorthôma*) in which she acts bravely, temperately, justly and wisely, and will herself be brave and so on.[65]

According to Chrysippus, the virtues differ in their different subject-matters (*kephalaia*).[66] Each includes a distinct function in relation to a distinct range of passions. The definitions of the different virtues suggest that each has a different natural passion to deal with, and hence a different type of appearance to which the virtuous person must refuse her assent.[67] In the

---

[60] See §12 (Socrates); §49 (Plato); §117 (Aristotle).

[61] 'Ariston of Chios ... made virtue one in essence, and called it health, but in relations many different virtues. It is as though we wanted to call sight lightvision when it grasps light things, darkvision when it grasps dark things, or something else of this sort. For virtue too when it examines what is to be done and not done is called prudence; when it orders appetite and defines the moderate and the opportune in pleasures it is called temperance; when it is engaged in associations and agreements with others it is called justice' (Plu. *VM* 440e–441a).

[62] On the Stoic doctrine of relations and qualities see Simp. *in Catg.* 165.32–166.29, partly in LS 29C.

[63] Galen, *PHP* vii.1.9–10 = 430.11–12 = SVF iii 259: 'We have also recalled the works of Poseidonius in which he praises the old account, while he refutes the mistakes of Chrysippus about the affections of the soul and the difference of the virtues. For just as the affections of the soul are removed, if it has only the rational part and there is no emotional and no appetitive part, so also all the virtues are removed except prudence. But if we were to give a full account here of Chrysippus' four books On The Difference of The Virtues and were to examine them and the things he has said in one other book That The Virtues are Qualifications, rebutting the argument of Ariston—that would take not one or two books, but three or four.'

[64] 'They say that the virtues mutually follow each other, and whoever has one has all; for their objects of study (*theôrêmata*) are common, as Chrysippus says in On The Virtues i' (DL vii 125).

[65] Plu. *SR* 1041a–b: 'In the Demonstrations on Justice Chrysippus says explicitly that every right action is a lawful action and a just action; an action done in accordance with continence or endurance or prudence or bravery is a right action; hence it is also a just action. How then does he not allow justice to those to whom he allows prudence and bravery and continence, when all their right actions in the virtues just mentioned are thereby just actions too?'

[66] DL vii 126: 'Each of the virtues is concentrated (*kephalaiousthai*) on some peculiar subject (*kephalaion*) of its own—bravery about what is to be withstood, prudence about what is to be done and avoided and neither; similarly the others too are concerned with their proper subjects' Cf. Stob. ii 63.6–11 = LS 63D.

[67] DL vii 92–3 gives accounts of the different virtues: 'Prudence is the knowledge of good things and evil and neither. Bravery is the knowledge of what is to be chosen and avoided and neither. ... Magnanimity is the knowledge or state making someone superior to the things that happen to good and bad people alike. Continence is a disposition never

Stoic view, an action in accordance with one virtue is also in accordance with all the other virtues, but the virtuous person is not always exercising his bravery or temperance. If I pay a debt I do a brave action and act bravely, since bravery, if it is a genuine virtue, requires me to do all the right actions; but I do not exercise bravery in this action, since I do not rely on my special ability to resist dangerous situations by withholding assent to appearances that might lead me to believe I face some genuine evil.[68]

To show that a virtuous person's action must always accord with all the virtues, the Stoics distinguish primary and secondary subject-matters.[69] While each virtue has its own primary subject-matter, its secondary subject-matter extends to all the other virtues. That is why sages act justly every time they act temperately. To see what the Stoics mean by taking every virtue to be somehow present in every virtuous action, we may return to their claim that virtuous people's action is 'complete' appropriate action that achieves 'all the measures', and that they choose the reasonable action because it is reasonable. The Stoics follow Aristotle in believing that a bank robber who carries out a dangerous raid without fear or hesitation is not really doing a brave action, whereas a soldier who did the same (from one point of view) type of action in a just war would be doing a brave action. The brave person faces the danger because it is required by a just cause; if the cause were not just, the brave person would recognize this and would not face the danger. Similarly, virtuous people perform other virtuous actions on the assumption that they are required or permitted by the other virtues. Their performance of a virtuous and successful action is marked by the counterfactuals that are true of them, so that they would act differently if their allegedly brave action were prohibited by justice, and so on.

If this is what the Stoics mean, their opponents are mistaken in claiming that they have an inconsistent view of the difference and connexion of the virtues. The differences explain why different aspects of a virtuous person's training are immediately relevant on different occasions, so that different thoughts, plans, and temptations belong to brave action and to temperate action. The connexion is justified by the role of all the virtues in fixing the considerations that require or permit the actions that correspond to the individual virtues. Though the underlying moral psychology of the Stoic doctrine of virtues differs sharply from Aristotle's doctrine of rational and non-rational desires, the Stoic explanation of difference and connexion is close to Aristotle's implicit view. The degree of agreement with Aristotle reflects a broader agreement in concern with the virtuous person's reasons. The Stoics

---

overcome in what is according to correct reason, or a state invincible by pleasures. Endurance is the knowledge or the state of what is to be persevered in, not persevered in, or neither.' On passion and assent see Aulus Gellius, *NA* xix 1.18, quoted at n102 below.

[68] I use 'exercise' rather unnaturally to represent Chrysippus' technical use of *chrêsthai*, corresponding to *andrizesthai*, *deilainein* etc. See Plu. *SR* 1046e: '. . . in Ethical Inquiries vi Chrysippus says that the decent man is not always acting bravely (*andrizesthai*) nor the base always acting in a cowardly way . . . And he says it is plausible that the base man is not always acting intemperately either. If, then, acting bravely is such as exercising bravery and acting cowardly is such as exercising cowardice, the Stoics say conflicting things, when they say both that whoever has virtues or vices acts according to them all at once, and that the decent man is not always acting bravely, and the base man not always acting cowardly.'

[69] 'For the subject matters of prudence are, primarily, to study and do what is to be done, but according to the secondary account, to study also what should be assigned, and what should be chosen and what should be endured, in order to do unwaveringly what is to be done' (Stob. ii 63.11–15 = LS 61D). The passage continues with parallel accounts of the primary and secondary subject-matters of the other cardinal virtues.

agree with Aristotle in believing that the virtuous person essentially acts for the appropriate reasons; they express this doctrine in claiming that virtuous action, as such, is the end of virtue.

186. Concern for Preferred Indifferents

Now that we have traced these points of agreement with Aristotle's conception of the virtuous person's outlook, we can consider whether the Stoics' doctrine of indifferents marks a crucial disagreement with Aristotle. Once we understand how virtuous action is the internal end of virtue and how preferred indifferents are its external objective, should we take the Stoics to mean that indifferents do not matter? Do they, as Adam Smith suggests, regard life as simply an opportunity to display virtue in actions that do not matter in their own right? If they held this view, their conception of the virtuous person's outlook would differ sharply from Aristotle's conception.

But Smith's view does not fit Stoic explanations of our reasons for trying to achieve preferred indifferents. According to Seneca, some Aristotelian external goods provide a wide field for several virtues, whereas poverty leaves room only for endurance; others add enjoyment to life. Sages prefer both sorts of advantages as non-instrumentally valuable.[70] Preferred indifferents that do not hinder virtue deserve our concern because they are in accord with nature, not because they are good.[71] The only genuine good in the pursuit of preferred indifferents is the exercise of good judgment in selecting them, but this is not the only reason for trying to get them.

For these reasons, the fact that Stoic sages regard external goods and evils as indifferent does not mean that they regard them as unimportant. If Smith's view were correct, sages would not care whether they had achieved preferred indifferents or not, as long as they had sufficient scope for practical reasoning; hence they would have no reason to try to improve their level of preferred indifferents, or to try to resist any reduction in preferred indifferents. This, however, is not the attitude of the sage. A sage tries to raise the level of preferred indifferents, as long as this is consistent with the demands of virtue, and tries to avoid a major loss of preferred indifferents, within the constraints imposed by virtue.

This is the attitude we ought to expect, given that the preferred indifferents contribute to the life in accord with nature. Virtue does not require us to abandon the pursuit of this life; nor does it insist that being virtuous is all there is to living in accord with nature. The Stoics do not dismiss as unimportant the aspects of human nature that require preferred indifferents for their fulfilment. To criticize them for dismissing these aspects of human nature is to misunderstand the significance of their doctrine that virtue is the ultimate end and the only good.[72]

---

[70] 'Indeed, which of our sages—I mean, of our school, for whom the only good is virtue—will deny that these things we call indifferents also have some value in themselves and that some are preferable to others?' (Sen. *VB* 22.4) Seneca marks Aristotle's division between external goods that provide resources (*chorêgia*) for virtuous actions and those that 'adorn' (*sunepikosmein*) a virtuous life (*EN* 1099a31–3; 1100b8–11; 26–8).

[71] ' "Won't you seek them?" Of course I'll seek them. Not because they are good, but because they are in accord with nature, and because they will be taken by me with good judgment. "Then what will be good in them?" Only this, that they are chosen well' (Sen. *Ep.* 92.11 = LS 64J).

[72] This misunderstanding underlies the criticism of Stoicism in Cic. *F.* iv 28.

The Stoics' doctrine of suicide illustrates their view of the importance of preferred indifferents. They believe that external conditions can deteriorate far enough to justify a sage in committing suicide.[73] Since sages remain virtuous, they remain happy. Their reason for committing suicide cannot be that they have lost, or are about to lose, necessary conditions for being happy. Their decision to commit suicide is influenced by the actual or threatened loss of preferred indifferents for themselves or for people they care about.

This doctrine that happy people will commit suicide because of external conditions that present no threat to their happiness strikes opponents of Stoicism as bizarre. Plutarch finds it strange that Chrysippus believes we ought to decide whether to remain alive not by considering goods and evils, but by considering the indifferents that are in accord with or contrary to nature.[74] But Chrysippus' view is not so strange, once we understand the status that the Stoics assign to indifferents. For the fact that sages are happy does not mean that they have everything that they have good reason to try to achieve; it does not even mean that they have a life that a rational person ought to continue. The Stoics' doctrine of suicide is an extreme example of the importance that they attach to preferred indifferents. This aspect of the doctrine ought not to surprise us, if we have understood the difference between the end and the objective, and the value that they ascribe to the objective.

187. The Selective Value of Virtue and the Preferred Indifferents

If this is what the Stoics mean, they should agree that though virtuous action is the end of virtue, the achievement of the end plus the objective has greater value than the achievement of the end without the objective. But do they believe this? The views that they maintain might well appear to be inconsistent. They claim: (1) Virtue has selective value. (2) Preferred indifferents have selective value. (3) Virtue is not sufficient for getting the preferred indifferents, since the 'success' of a virtuous action consists in its complete appropriateness (perfectum officium), not in the external success of achieving the objective of getting preferred indifferents (Cic. F. iii 59 = LS 59F). (4) Virtue together with preferred indifferents has no greater selective value than virtue alone (iii 45; cf. iv 29 = LS 64K; v 71; 90). (5) Virtue with preferred indifferents is preferable to virtue alone (iii 44).

It is not clear how the fourth of these claims is consistent with the first three. The first three seem to follow from the Stoic conception of the indifferents, but then the fourth seems to revert to a more extreme view. According to the Stoics, the value of preferred indifferents 'must be obscured and destroyed and must perish because of the brilliance and greatness of virtue'. That is why virtue plus health has no more selective value than virtue alone.

It is difficult to understand the Stoic view. Some examples suggest that the value of preferred indifferents is trivial in comparison with that of virtue. But this assessment is open

---

[73] 'A sage will make his own reasonable departure from life, for the sake of his country or his friends, or if he falls into excessively severe pain or suffers mutilation or contracts an incurable disease' (DL vii 130 = LS 66H).

[74] Plu. SR 1042d–e = SVF iii 759. Cf. CN 1063c–f; Alex. Mant. 168.1–20 = SVF iii 764; Annas, MH 408–9; Cooper, 'Suicide'.

to objection. Even if health and freedom from pain are less important than virtue, they still seem to be important; the Stoic view that they are natural advantages needed for a life in accord with nature seems to imply that they are important (cf. iv 31–3). The Stoics acknowledge this in their fifth claim. Hence it is difficult to see how the fourth claim is consistent with the fifth.

The Stoic position seems contradictory because it seems rational to select the condition that we agree is preferable, and hence this condition seems to have greater selective value. But the Stoics have an answer, if they rely on their conception of successful action as complete appropriate action. Since virtuous people act successfully, they always make appropriate and reasonable attempts to secure preferred indifferents. We can never face a choice, therefore, between a fully virtuous action (i.e., an action done virtuously, as the virtuous person does it) and an action that tries to secure the appropriate preferred indifferents; for the virtuous course of action necessarily tries to secure appropriate preferred indifferents. Any considerations that might favour our securing these specific preferred indifferents must already be properly counted in the virtuous choice; for this virtuous choice already incorporates the rational selection of preferred indifferents.

We can now understand why the Stoics claim that virtue alone has the same selective value as virtue plus preferred indifferents. For purposes of selection the two states of affairs are equivalent; for in selecting the fully virtuous action we necessarily select the appropriate preferred indifferents, and hence we could never select virtuous action that does not aim at preferred indifferents. Hence, from the forward-looking point of view of the agent selecting, any selection of virtuous action is necessarily a selection of appropriate preferred indifferents, and so includes the selective value of this latter selection.

But though this is true from the forward-looking, deliberative point of view of the selector, it does not follow that the virtuous action secures the preferred indifferents it selects. From the retrospective point of view, the successful outcome of the reasonable effort to secure preferred indifferents is preferable to the reasonable but unsuccessful effort. But this difference between the outcomes is not a difference in selection; the virtuous person always selects the successful outcome, though he cannot guarantee it.

Stoic claims about the selective value of virtue alone and virtue plus preferred indifferents are reasonable in the light of the Stoic account of virtue. The key to understanding is the account of virtue as reasonable selection of preferred indifferents. Properly understood, this account implies that virtuous people are rationally concerned to achieve preferred indifferents, not that they take them to be unimportant.

188. Why Virtue is Praiseworthy

The Stoics intend their division between the end and the objective of virtue to distinguish what virtuous people think about from what they hope to achieve; this is the parallel between virtues and stochastic crafts. They also intend it to distinguish the aspect of virtuous action that is up to us and praiseworthy from the aspect that is not wholly up to us and is a matter for congratulation rather than praise. Since they believe that virtue and virtuous action are up to us, they need to show that they consist in our assents, rather than in conditions that do not depend on our assent and therefore are not up to us.[75]

Their position faces objections drawn from different types of external conditions. Sometimes virtuous action seems so easy, because of favourable external conditions, that it is trivial, and therefore reflects no credit on us. According to the Stoics, virtuous action is admirable, praiseworthy, and impressive.[76] But not all the actions of a virtuous person are impressive or praiseworthy; temperate abstention from seducing an unattractive woman is unimpressive, but the Stoics must regard it as no less praiseworthy than an act of heroic virtue. Chrysippus admits that we ought not to praise trivial examples of virtuous action.[77]

A Stoic can answer this difficulty by distinguishing the virtuous action as such from its objective results. There is nothing praiseworthy in resisting something that no one would find tempting, and nothing brave in resisting a pain that needs no resisting. The mere fact that someone had done these trivial things would not make her praiseworthy. But a virtuous person does these things because she is virtuous; as Chrysippus says, they are coincidental results of virtue.[78] Even when no effort is required to achieve the appropriate objective, the virtuous person assents to resisting pain, or danger, or sensual pleasure, on all the appropriate occasions; this assent explains the trivially easy virtuous actions. Since she is not being praised for the trivially easy action, but for the assent that extends to all appropriate occasions, she is to be praised no less for the right assent when she does trivially easy actions than when the appropriate action is more difficult.

It does not follow that no important distinctions can be drawn between different virtuous and vicious actions. If one is virtuous, it is preferable to exercise virtue in actions that promote the objective of living in accord with nature; and if one is vicious, it is preferable if one's vicious actions do not seriously impede this objective. Hence we have good reason to encourage some virtuous actions more vigorously than others; but that does not make them more praiseworthy.

This difference between the assent and the preferable results explains what the Stoics mean in claiming that all successes and all errors are equal (DL vii 120).[79] he virtuous person assents to the appropriate, rationally defensible action, because it is rationally defensible. Since successful action (*katorthôma*) consists in this sort of assent based on these sorts of reasons, all such actions are equally successful actions; and since error is failure to assent correctly, it is displayed equally in all actions that result from such failure. In so far as human beings act on the reasons characteristic of virtue, their virtuous actions are no less

---

[75] 'The fine is up to us. What is up to us we get through ourselves. What we get through ourselves comes about by the agency of nothing else. Hence the fine comes about for us by the agency of nothing else; and if by the agency of nothing else, then not by the agency of the gods either' (Alex. *Quaest.* 26.22–5 = *SVF* iii 32).

[76] See Plu. *SR* 1039c, quoted in n77.

[77] 'These latter statements conflict with the first. For either every good is praiseworthy, and then temperately abstaining from the old woman would be praiseworthy; or this is not praiseworthy, and then it will not be true that every good is impressive or gratifying, but the statement is undermined' (Plu. *SR* 1039c). 'Chrysippus says, in the treatise on Zeus: "While actions according to the virtues are proper (*oikeia*) to us, the preferred things are among such things as bravely stretching out one's finger, temperately abstaining from an ugly and moribund old woman, and hearing without rash assent that three is exactly four. One who sets out to praise and eulogize people through such examples displays a kind of frigidity . . . And further we are repelled by praise of such examples of the coincidental results of virtue, such as abstaining from a moribund old woman, and undergoing a fleabite with endurance." Who else is needed, then, as the accuser of Chrysippus' own doctrines?' (1038f–1039a; cf. *CN* 1061a).

[78] For 'coincidental results', *sumbainonta*, see Plu. *SR* 1039a, quoted in n77.   [79] Cf. *SVF* iii 524–32.

impressive than those of gods (Plu. *SR* 1038c; *CN* 1076a–b); a virtuous human being is no less completely virtuous than a god (Stob. ii 98.14–15).

These Stoic claims about assent also offer an answer to another sort of objection derived from external conditions. Sometimes these conditions seem not too easy, but too difficult. As Aristotle says, it is impossible or difficult to do fine actions without external resources (*EN* 1099a31–b6). Alexander uses Aristotle's claim to attack the Stoic claim that happiness is up to us. He argues that if virtue is concerned with the selection of things according to nature, as the Stoics think, then such things (wealth, health etc.) are necessary to provide virtue with its material (Alex. *Mant.* 160.1–8). But a craft, say flute-playing, cannot control the supply of flutes, but depends on their supply for its proper activities. Now virtue is a craft; and since external goods[80] are needed as its material for virtuous action, virtue cannot supply them for itself, and virtuous action depends on them. Indeed the sage sometimes takes himself to be justified in committing suicide when the supply of external goods is too small (160.27–9).

In Alexander's view, each craft has two sorts of exercise—its exercise in preferable and in non-preferable conditions (160.31–161.1); a craft, for instance, exercises itself both in playing good flutes and in playing bad flutes. In that case, 'just as in the other crafts the end is in the exercises about wished-for things and in preferable conditions,[81] the same will be true in the case of virtue, if it is a craft' (161.1–3). While recognizing that virtue is exercised in bad external conditions, Alexander suggests that this is not really the proper exercise of virtue, because it achieves its end only in preferable conditions. Since the end of virtuous action is happiness, as the Stoics agree, virtue turns out to be insufficient for happiness, by being insufficient for the achievement of its end.

The Stoics believe they can answer this sort of objection by attending to the virtuous person's assent, since this determines the praiseworthy aspect of a virtuous action. Admittedly, we have good reason to prefer the virtuous action that takes advantage of favourable circumstances and ample resources to achieve the preferable results. Sages take all reasonable steps to find the preferable circumstances for their actions, since the results of virtuous actions in these circumstances are themselves preferable. But, in the Stoic view, these preferable aspects of virtuous action do not make it more or less fine and praiseworthy.

Alexander is right to claim that since virtue is the craft of selecting correctly among externals, external goods and evils provide its material. But the Stoics argue that virtue is not the craft of selecting among a reasonably plentiful supply of external goods; it is the craft of selecting among any external goods and evils that may be present. Since we can rely on the presence of some external goods and evils while we are alive, there is no reason to suppose that the virtuous person will go short of material. The end that virtuous people aim at is acting reasonably in the pursuit of preferred indifferents. They achieve this aim even in less preferable conditions. They certainly prefer to exercise virtue in favourable conditions, but that makes no difference to whether they achieve their end. Alexander overlooks the grounds for the Stoic division between the end and the objective of virtuous action.

---

[80] I use Aristotle's term. The Stoics do not accept this description of them, but that does not matter for present purposes.

[81] Read *prohêgoumenois* for *prohêgoumenais*, 161.2.

The Stoics might reasonably claim that their division between end and objective removes a difficulty that faces Aristotle. For Aristotle agrees with them in believing that acting virtuously is praiseworthy, fine, and up to us. If, as Alexander suggests, our action is less fine in adverse circumstances, it seems to be less praiseworthy, and hence acting virtuously does not seem to be up to us. Aristotle rejects this conclusion; he maintains that virtuous people remain virtuous in misfortune, because they make the finest use of the materials available to them, as skilled craftsmen do (EN 1100b35–1101a6). We might argue that the praiseworthy and fine aspect of virtuous action is unaffected by external conditions. The Stoics, therefore, might claim to defend Aristotle's basic position.

189. Why should Virtue be Identified with Happiness?

We have explored the Stoics' division between goods and indifferents, and the related division between ends and objectives, in order to explain their claim that virtue is identical to happiness. We have found that the two Stoic divisions are reasonable, and that they help the Stoics to defend their view that virtuous action is the end of virtue, and that virtue is praiseworthy. But we may still not be convinced that these divisions make it any more plausible to claim that happiness consists only of virtue. Indeed, we might argue, as Alexander does, that the division between ends and objectives makes it clear that the Stoics are wrong to identify virtue with happiness. We should regard virtue as a stochastic craft of which virtuous action is the end, and happiness is the objective.[82]

The Stoics, however, maintain that happiness is the end, not the objective, of virtue. In saying that happiness is the end of virtue, they agree verbally with Aristotle; but once they distinguish the end from the objective, they are not entitled to assume without argument that Aristotle treats happiness as the end rather than the objective of virtue. Alexander suggests that Aristotle's position, expressed in Stoic terms, makes happiness the objective, because it includes preferred indifferents that are not in our control. Can the Stoics fairly claim that Aristotle, despite what he sometimes says, really ought to agree with them?

We might try to express Aristotle's view by saying, as he sometimes says, that happiness has parts, and that virtue is one of these parts or components.[83] He believes that virtue is an especially important component of happiness, to be preferred, as Plato believes, over any collection of external goods. Hence we must apparently be able to assess the comparative value of virtue and the other components of happiness. Such an assessment requires the point of view of an assessor.

But how do we capture the point of view of the assessor? If a rational agent assesses truly, the relevant point of view must be that of the self for whom these different goods are supposed to be good. In the Stoic view, however, virtue is not simply one of the goods to be weighed by the self. It also defines the point of view from which we should weigh,

---

[82] 'But in the case of stochastic crafts, it is no longer true that the end is up to the craftsman, just as neither is being happy up to virtuous people, if it is not true that only the fine is good' (in Top. 34.3–5). In the last sentence I read to kalon agathon, following Striker, 'Antipater' 314n. I use Stoic terms (and hence use 'objective' rather than 'end') to express the distinction that Alexander draws; see n12 above.

[83] See EE 1214b24–7. Cf. §72n44.

because it is essential to the self that weighs correctly. We ought not, then, to think of virtue as though something other than it assigned it its place in the compound that is happiness. Plato notices this point in the *Philebus*. He begins by treating intelligence (*phronêsis*) as an element in the mixture; we try to decide how much it should count in comparison with pleasure. But then he points out that this picture is misleading. Intelligence is 'the cause of the mixture' (23d7–8), because intelligence decides how much intelligence and how much pleasure should go in the mixture.

This claim may be implicit in the Stoics' description of the growth of virtue (Cic. *F.* iii 21 = LS 59D). Virtue is the rational planning that assigns different things a place in our life; hence it is 'the cause of the mixture', and not simply one of the elements that are assigned a place in the mixture. To treat it as simply a component of the good is to assume that something else assigns it its place. When we speak of different things as good or bad for me, we presuppose a conception of me as the being for whom the different things are good or bad. Aristotle himself expresses this point in claiming that the human good must be good for something with the nature of a human being, as explained by the Function Argument. If my being virtuous somehow defines me, other things cannot be good for me unless I am virtuous; if I were to cease to be virtuous, these other things would not still be good for me.

How could my being virtuous and my being myself be so closely connected? The Stoics rely on their claim that virtue is the exercise of practical reason, and on the connexion between one's conception of oneself and one's conception of oneself as a rational agent. In explaining why I care about my interests over time, and exactly what I care about in being concerned about myself over time, we have to include the fact that I care about carrying out my plans because they are my rational plans.[84] Though we may initially value rational planning for the sake of the results we achieve by it, we also come to value for its own sake the achieving of these results by rational planning (Cic. *F.* iii 23); we are not indifferent to the means by which these results come about. The fact that we actually care about the execution of our plans makes it intelligible that we care about our future in the way we do. Hence concern for rational agency for its own sake is essential to the self for whom other things are preferable. Hence we cannot compare virtue with other goods to see how good each of them is: virtue carries out the comparison, since it is essential to the self for whom these other goods are good.

The Stoics might reasonably be dissatisfied, therefore, with a conception of virtue and happiness that treats virtue simply as a component of happiness. In thinking about components, we think about things that have different weights or degrees of importance in happiness. But we must weigh or assess degrees by reference to some standard. Virtue itself is the standard by which other things have to be weighed, because it is essential to the self for whom different things must be good, and is not one of the goods to be weighed. Its status in happiness cannot be the status of a mere component.

This argument about the special status of virtue is not alien to Aristotle. Perhaps it is implicit in Aristotle's account of self-love; virtuous people love themselves as virtuous because they recognize their rational agency as themselves. Doubts about whether virtue is a component of happiness may also be Aristotelian; for the *EN* does not speak as explicitly of

---

[84] Cf. Epicurus in §154.

parts of happiness as the other ethical works do.[85] From the Stoic point of view, the reasons for denying that virtue is a part of happiness are also reasons for affirming that virtue is identical to happiness.

We might reject this Stoic conclusion. However inappropriate it may be to regard virtue as simply a part of happiness, we must apparently recognize that some external goods (as Aristotle describes them) or preferred indifferents (as the Stoics describe them) are worth selecting for themselves, and have more than merely instrumental value. Must we not, then, allow that they are parts of happiness, given the comprehensive character of happiness?

190. Two Roles of Aristotelian Happiness

The Stoics believe that they can answer this defence of Aristotle by appealing to their division between ends and objectives, and by showing how it clarifies some of Aristotle's own claims about happiness.

Aristotle regards happiness as an end that we aim at; part of the point of thinking about it is to change our aims. He believes that the discovery of what the good is should strongly influence our way of life, so that we will be like archers with a target to aim at (EN 1094a22–4). An explicit and correct conception of happiness will improve our practical reasoning, by giving it the appropriate principle (1144a32). Happiness is the ultimate object of wish that provides the starting point for deliberation (1111b28). Practical reasoning begins from a desire for doing well, and doing well is the end (1139b3–4); hence prudence is the correct apprehension of this end (1142b32). Aristotle believes that happiness is an end that we can explicitly conceive, and that our explicit conception of it guides our deliberation and decision.

Our conception of happiness also gives us a measure of success, since it shows us whether someone has had the sort of life that it is reasonable to hope for. This role of happiness is most obvious in Aristotle's remarks on good fortune. One's initial circumstances constrain the possible results of rational deliberation, and further external circumstances affect the actual results of our particular deliberation. If I do not inherit wealth, I cannot deliberate about how I am to use my inherited wealth wisely; and if I invest money wisely to raise further funds for famine relief, but the stock market unexpectedly crashes, my wise project fails. To see whether we have achieved happiness, we consider the actual results of our deliberations and actions. Aristotle therefore denies that virtuous action is sufficient for happiness, on the ground that it does not infallibly achieve the valuable external results that are sought in virtuous action. That is why Alexander takes him to reject the Stoic thesis that virtue is self-sufficient for happiness.[86]

From the Stoic point of view, the different roles of happiness in Aristotle, as an end to aim at and as a measure of success, betray some confusion. For Aristotle also recognizes the legitimacy of marking the Stoic division between end and objective. We saw that he recognizes it in the case of crafts.[87] He does not mention an analogous division in the case of virtue and happiness, but he relies implicitly on such a division when he considers the

---

[85] See n71 above.   [86] See §188 above.   [87] See n12 above.

relation of virtue to its external results. He often claims that virtuous people act 'because an action is fine', or 'for the sake of the fine',[88] but he also believes that they act for the sake of their happiness.

These two uses of 'for the sake of' correspond to the end and the objective. Reflexion about happiness tells us that the good of others plays an essential role in it, and that therefore we have sufficient reason to act for the benefit of others who are suitably related to us, without any further thought about our own good. Brave or just people, for instance, do not stop to think about whether facing this danger now or keeping this promise now is part of their happiness. It would be a bad thing—just as it is in the stochastic crafts—if they did stop to think about this. Aristotle sees that an objective—happiness, as Aristotle understands it—regulates our aims, but is not itself an aim in particular actions. Our conception of the external advantages achieved by bravery helps to explain why we regard bravery, rather than cowardice, as a virtue to be chosen for its own sake; but we do not focus on these external advantages in deciding to act bravely.

The Stoics use this point to support their view of happiness. The sort of life that Aristotle regards as happy is subject to misfortunes; and so when we deliberate about what to do, we ought not to be thinking about all the ways in which things might go wrong, since we may not be able to take any systematic or beneficial account of these factors anyhow. It is better to follow the conception of the practical aim—virtuous action—that has been formed in the light of the various elements of the preferable way of life (which Aristotle identifies with happiness), and in the light of a reasonable strategy for getting them. Aristotle seems to admit that the conception of the end that actually guides virtuous people is their conception of fine action. Since our conception of happiness is our conception of the end that guides our action, he ought to identify happiness with fine action. Aristotle, therefore, ought to conclude that virtuous action is the ultimate end, and is therefore to be identified with happiness.

The Stoic conception of action and explanation clarifies Aristotle's claims about the end of action, and thereby suggests that his position is inconsistent. He believes that our conception of the end of an action is the proximate efficient cause of that action. Since happiness is the end of action, and the proximate efficient cause of virtuous people's actions is their conception of fine and virtuous action, happiness should be fine and virtuous action. But Aristotle rejects this conclusion, since he maintains that happiness includes external goods. According to the Stoics, Aristotle's conception of happiness conflicts with the role of happiness as an end. Since Aristotle agrees with the Stoic conception of happiness as an end, he needs to reconsider his overall view of happiness.[89]

If this is the right way to connect Aristotelian with Stoic views, the Stoics are right to claim that Aristotle ought to endorse their distinction between end and objective, and that he ought to agree that the virtuous person's end is the fine. It is a further question whether happiness ought to be counted as the end or as the objective. The Stoics can give an Aristotelian quite a good reason for deciding to reform Aristotle's own usage, and to confine the use of 'happiness' to the end. Aristotle agrees that an explicit conception of happiness should be the starting point for our deliberation and choice; to assign this role to happiness

---

[88] See §116.   [89] On the different roles of Aristotle's conception of happiness see also Aquinas, §281.

is to treat it as the internal end, rather than the external objective. But Aristotle also seems to admit that the conception of the end that actually guides virtuous people is their conception of fine action; and so he ought to identify happiness with fine action. Aristotle, therefore, ought to conclude that virtuous action is identical to happiness.

According to the Stoics, it would be a mistake to reject this conclusion on the assumption that it gives too little weight to the preferred indifferents. In setting out the Stoic and the Aristotelian positions, it is difficult to avoid giving the impression that virtuous action for the sake of the fine is different from virtuous action for the sake of preferred indifferents (when one has a correct conception of them). But any such impression is misleading, for the reasons we have seen in discussing the definition of successful action and its implications for the doctrine of selective value.[90] For the Stoics argue that in taking virtue as my end, I am not neglecting preferred indifferents; my end is doing all I reasonably can to secure them. Virtuous people do not, in the Stoic view, give up some reasonable opportunity that Aristotle advises them to take for pursuing preferred indifferents.

Our comparison of Stoic and Aristotle claims about the role of happiness supports the Stoics' claim to argue from preconceptions about virtue and goods. This claim may seem absurd, since the Stoics' doctrine seems to fly in the face of firm convictions that natural advantages are goods and that they contribute to our happiness. This is why Aristotle dismisses the identification of virtue with happiness as a paradox that only a philosopher would maintain in order to avoid refutation. The Stoics reply to this Aristotelian objection. They argue that our preconceptions support the claims that are needed for their position: the division between ends and objectives, the view that the virtuous person's end is fine action, and the treatment of happiness as the virtuous person's end, not his objective. Each of these claims is Aristotelian, but their combination supports the Stoic view that virtue and virtuous action are the virtuous person's end, and that therefore virtue is identical to happiness.

We might reject this conclusion, if we took it to imply that nothing except virtue matters; for we might argue that such an implication reveals the conflict between Stoicism and our firm preconceptions. But the Stoics argue that their doctrine of indifferents does not imply that indifferents do not matter. They accept the ordinary view that practical reason has the task of finding the best way to secure preferred indifferents, and that a rational person ought to try hard to secure them. Once we understand how the Stoics distinguish goods (components of happiness, the end of virtue) from preferred indifferents (components of the life in accord with nature, the objective of virtue), we will not be surprised that the Stoics tell us to try hard to secure indifferents that are not parts of happiness. The conflict between this doctrine and our preconceptions is merely apparent and superficial; on closer inspection, we see that the Stoic doctrines take account of the substance of our preconceptions.

In some ways, therefore, the Stoic doctrine that virtue is identical to happiness is, as some ancient critics suggest, less radical and important than it may initially seem. For it does not imply the restriction of one's rational concerns to one's own state of character, or complete indifference to the outcome of one's actions in the world. Aristotle rejects

---

[90] See §187 above.

the identification of virtue with happiness because it overlooks the rational significance of external goods for a virtuous person. The Stoics may reasonably reply that their doctrine is not open to this objection. Their division between end and objective, together with their definition of successful action, shows that virtuous people take every reasonable step to secure preferred indifferents and attribute the appropriate selective value to them. Everything that Aristotle wants to claim about the importance of rational concern for external goods is captured within the Stoic doctrine of virtue, happiness, and preferred indifferents.

Should we then infer that the Stoic doctrine is only verbally different from the Aristotelian doctrine? The Stoics have good reason to reject this inference. Their doctrine seeks to mark a clear division between the end that I ought to have in mind as a guide to my deliberation, and the objective that I ought to have in mind in forming my end, but not as a guide to deliberation. The virtues are states of character formed by reflexion on suitable objectives, but the virtuous person is not moved primarily by direct reflexion on the objectives of virtuous action.

But though it is unfair to describe the Stoic doctrine as only verbally different from Aristotle, this description reminds us that the Stoics believe their main point can be conveyed without claiming that natural advantages are only indifferents and not goods.[91] Chrysippus believes that if one recognizes the different role of virtue and of preferred indifferents, one grasps the essential point of Stoic doctrine even if one follows Aristotle in treating preferred indifferents as external goods. If we follow Aristotle here, we reduce even further the appearance of conflict between Stoic doctrine and our preconceptions about goods. In conceding this point to Aristotle and to common sense, Chrysippus shows that he wants us to draw the Stoic distinctions whether or not we express them in Stoic terms.

This clarification suggests a similar clarification of Chrysippus' claims about virtue and happiness. If we speak of preferred indifferents as goods, we can also say that happiness includes more than virtue (since the Stoics agree that happiness includes all goods). But we can avoid anti-Stoic interpretations of this remark if we agree with the Stoic view that virtuous actions and praiseworthy goods are the internal end of virtue, and we treat happiness as the external objective. Chrysippus' clarification suggests that the main points the Stoics want to convey are the difference between praiseworthy and preferred objects of rational concern, and the virtuous person's immediate preoccupation with the praiseworthy rather than the preferred objects. On these points the Stoics do not repeat Aristotle; they take themselves to clarify and correct his position. But their conclusions are not alien to Aristotle's main doctrines about virtue and happiness.

---

[91] 'And in On Goods i he in a way concedes and allows anyone who wants to call the preferred things goods and the opposites of them evils, in these words: "If someone wants in accordance with such distinctions to call one of them good and the other evil, being directed to these things [sc. the significates of 'preferred things' and 'non-preferred things'], and does not go astray at random, it is to be accepted. For he will not be astray about the significates, and for the rest he aims at common practice in use of names." And so here he combines and unites the preferred with the good. But elsewhere on the contrary he says that none of these at all is anything to us, but reason pulls us back and turns us away from all these sorts of things' (Plu. *SR* 1048a = LS 58H). Chrysippus envisages someone who grants the distinction that the Stoics draw between goods and preferred indifferents, but still chooses to call preferred indifferents goods. I follow the interpretation of Cherniss, ad loc., rather than that of LS 58H (defended in vol. ii ad loc.).

191. Freedom from Passion

This account of the Stoic doctrine of happiness and virtue removes some possible sources of misunderstanding. The Stoics speak of natural advantages as indifferents, but they believe that these indifferents are proper objects of rational concern and effort. The point of Stoic doctrine is not to advise detachment from the concerns that occupy other people. While the Stoics agree with Plato and Aristotle in believing that we have good reason to prefer the virtues over the accumulation of external goods without the virtues, they do not imply that external goods are unimportant.

This conclusion, however, seems to conflict with yet another apparently paradoxical Stoic doctrine, that the sage has no passions, but is 'unaffected' or 'passionless' (apathês). The Stoics defend this doctrine in opposition to the Peripatetic doctrine of 'moderate affection' (metriopatheia), arguing that the Peripatetic position rests on a confused analysis of passions. Since a passion is an immediate assent to an indifferent as good or evil, the sage who knows that no indifferent is good or evil, gets rid of passions and does not merely control or temper them.[92]

This explanation of the sage's freedom from passion seems to revive an earlier objection. If sages regard natural advantages and disadvantages as indifferent, how can they take them seriously? For if they do not fear the prospect of losing them, are not grieved by having lost them, are not angry about the deliberate infliction of pain on innocent victims, and so on, are they not detached from the concerns that occupy people who regard these indifferents as good and evil?[93]

Some readers have praised the Stoics for this detachment from indifferents. Stoics detach themselves from ordinary concerns by deciding that they do not matter. They assure us that how the world affects us depends on how we choose to think about it; in this sense all good and evil depends on our conception, or, as one might interpret Hamlet, 'there's nothing good or bad but thinking makes it so'.[94] If we decide to detach ourselves from the supposed goods and evils that are not in our power, we save ourselves from effort that is exposed to failure. We also save ourselves from the emotional effects of engagement and failure. This

---

[92] 'It has often been asked whether it is better to have moderate passions or no passions. We Stoics expel them, whereas the Peripatetics temper them. I do not see how any moderate condition of a disease could be healthy or useful. Don't be afraid; I am not depriving you of anything that you do not want to be denied to you' (Sen. Ep. 116.1; cf. 85.3). Simpl. in Epict. Ench. 23.54–24.2, suggests that one ought to regard metriopatheia as simply a step on the way to apatheia.

[93] 'In this area there are no precepts of philosophers. For they were deceived by a false appearance of virtue and removed kindness (or "pity", pietas) from human beings. In trying to cure vices they increased them. And while these same people often agree that participation in human society is to be continued, they altogether separate themselves from society by the rigour of their inhuman virtue' (Lactantius, Div. Inst. vi 10.11–12 = SVF iii 450; for the context of this passage see §228.) 'The Stoics, therefore, are mad; they do not moderate <passions>, but cut them off, and in a way want to castrate a human being of things that are implanted by nature' (Div. Inst. vi 15.3). This charge against the Stoics is discussed further by Knuuttila, EAMP 68–71.

[94] pan hupolêpsis, Marc. Aur. ii 15; xii 8, 22, 26; Farquharson, i 294 (on ii 15) cites 'Hamlet' ii 2.247–8. According to Jenkins, H 467–8, 'This common reflexion was probably given currency by Montaigne's essay "That the taste of goods or evils doth greatly depend on the opinion we have of them"'. See Montaigne, i 14, which begins with a reference to Epict. Ench. 5: 'Les hommes (dit une sentence Grecque ancienne) sont tourmentez par les opinions qu'ils ont des choses, non par les choses mesmes'. The following discussion does not entirely endorse this sentiment; see esp. §16–17 on Poseidonius' gout. Montaigne suggests that in this case the Stoic solution is merely verbal and that our senses assure us that pain is a genuine evil.

neo-Stoic conclusion casts freedom from passion in a good light.[95] If, however, we think that society and community with others depends on shared concern for results, and on shared emotions evoked by success and failure, we may well believe that the doctrine of freedom from passion is a Stoic error.

But before we accept either the neo-Stoic or the anti-Stoic conclusion, we should ask what the Stoics mean by claiming that the sage is free of passion. We should take account of the Stoic claim that the sage not only is free of affections but also has 'good affections' (*eupatheiai*). The Stoics apply the names of some apparent passions to the sage who is free from passion. They deny him pleasure, fear, and appetite, but allow him joy, caution, and wish.[96] The sage entirely lacks the uncompromising tendency, based on anger, to insist that a criminal should be punished more than he deserves. He assents to nothing that conflicts with a rationally-justified judgment about preferred indifferents, and so he has no anger. The good affective states are the reasonable reactions to situations that provoke passions in other people.

In what ways are these reasonable reactions in the sage similar to or different from passions in other people? Seneca argues that freedom from passion (*apatheia*) does not make sages indifferent to the losses that provoke passions in other people. If they were completely indifferent and unconcerned, seeing no reason to prefer being healthy over being ill, they would be Cynics. But since they prefer to have some of the things that they sometimes lose, they are not unconcerned, even though they are free from passions (Sen. *Ep.* 9.2–5).[97]

Does this defence answer the charge that the sage is detached? If sages make the appropriate rational judgments about preferred indifferents, and act on these judgments, they can reasonably claim to be concerned. But is their concern not wholly unemotional? We are inclined to say that there is more to a passion than a mistaken judgment about good and evil. But since (we may believe) the Stoics do not recognize this in their cognitive account of passions, the sort of concern that they ascribe to the sage fails to capture the normal human emotions that characteristically go with concern and effort.

To see what exactly the Stoics lack, we should recall their account of passions. They identify passions with assents, but not with every sort of assent; passions also require the immediate ('fresh') assent that consists in yielding to a suggestive appearance. Sages lack passions, because a passion has several elements and anyone who lacks any of these elements lacks a passion, just as anyone who lacks any of the elements of wisdom is a fool.[98] But, just as some fools may have some important elements of wisdom, someone who is free of passion may have some important elements of a passion.

The element of a passion that may persist in someone who has eliminated the mistaken assent is the suggestive appearance that encourages the assent. The Stoics do not expect to

---

[95] See Lipsius, n39 above.

[96] 'And they say that there are three ways of being well affected—joy, caution, and wish. Joy is opposed to pleasure, being reasonable elation. Caution is opposed to fear, being reasonable avoidance; for the sage will not fear at all, but will be cautious. And wish is opposed to appetite, being reasonable desire. . . . And they say that the sage is also unaffected, because he is not carried away. But another sort of unaffected person is the bad person, where "unaffected" is equivalent to "insensitive" and "relentless" ' (DL vii 17).

[97] 'The sage is self-sufficient, not in the sense that he wants (vult) to be without a friend, but in the sense that he can do without him. And when I say "can", I mean that he bears it with his mind undisturbed (aequo animo)' (Sen. *Ep.* 9.5).

[98] On this 'all or nothing' attitude see Brunschwig, 'Conjunctive'.

eliminate the appearances that, if we assented to them, would result in passions.[99] They do not suggest that appearances are totally plastic,[100] or that we can expect them to conform completely to correct assents. Though we eliminate passions, because we can eliminate the weak and rash assents, we do not eliminate the appearances that make the suggestions that we tend to assent to.[101]

Epictetus acknowledges the persistence of suggestive and potentially misleading appearances in the sage. These appearances explain why sages go pale if they are in danger of shipwreck; at first they affect sages in the way that appearances affect non-rational animals.[102] Sages, however, do not react to these appearances as fools react; fools assent thoughtlessly to the appearance of good or evil, whereas sages do not assent without the appropriate examination of the appearance. Poseidonius' gout made him groan; but still he insisted that it was not bad. Though sages may be moved to tears by an affecting scene in a play, they do not believe that impoverishment and bereavement, however affecting, are bad.[103]

In Epictetus' view, we need to bring reason to bear to stop the outbreak of misguided desire. If we do not do this, then the next time we get the corresponding appearance, we will be aroused more quickly to the desire (Epict. ii 18.8–9). How well we have brought reason to bear will be clear the next time a disturbing appearance arises (ii 16.20).[104] Sages react to some preferred indifferents with a suggestive appearance that may urge them towards

[99] 'But since the newly born human being is provided with these first types of awareness (sensus) of pain and pleasure, before the growth of judgment and reason, and indeed is conciliated to pleasure by nature, but separated and alienated from pain as though from some dangerous enemy—this is why reason, added later, can hardly pluck up by the roots and extinguish these affections, that are thoroughly implanted in him from the first. He is always struggling with them, represses them when they leap up, tramples on them, and forces them to submit to him and obey him. And so you have seen the philosopher, relying on the reason of his decision, struggling with the violence of desires and the leaping of pain, giving way not at all, conceding nothing, nor, as many people in pain do, screaming, lamenting, calling himself wretched and unhappy—but allowing only sharp gasping and deep groans, signs and indications of someone who is not overcome or conquered by pain, but is struggling to overcome and conquer it' (Aulus Gellius, NA xii 5.7).

[100] They are plastic to some degree. Increased understanding modifies the character of our appearances, not simply our tendency to assent to them; the expert's appearances are different from the ordinary person's. See DL vii 51 = LS 39A: 'Moreover some appearances are rational, some non-rational. The rational are those of rational animals, the non-rational those of non-rational animals. The rational ones are thoughts; the non-rational have no name [i.e. no special name of their own]. And some are expert (technikai), some non-expert. For we must admit that a picture is looked at in one way by an expert, and in another way by a non-expert' Cf. Cic. Ac. ii 20; Epict. ii 18.23–4.

[101] Sen. Ep. 71.27: 'I do not remove the sage from among human beings, nor do I exclude feelings of distress (dolores) from him as from some rock that is incapable of any awareness (sensus)'. The sage differs from other people because he has unshaken opinions. 'The sage will tremble and be distressed and grow pale; for these are all modes of awareness belonging to the body (corporis sensus). Then where is the calamity, where is the genuine evil? Clearly it happens if these things pervert his mind (animus)' (29). This aspect of Seneca's view is discussed by Inwood, 'Dualism' 177.

[102] '. . . not because any belief in any evil has been accepted, but because of some rapid and unpremeditated movements that outrun ("praevertentibus"; perhaps "anticipate" or "forestall") the function of mind and reason. Soon, however, that sage does not endorse—that is to say, does not assent to, and does not add his belief to, such appearances (phantasias), namely these frightening impressions (visa), but he rejects and repudiates them, and nothing in these appearances seems (videtur) to him to be something to be feared (metuendum)' (Aulus Gellius, NA xix 1.17–18 = Epict. fr. 9).

[103] '. . . the fool supposes things to be really as harsh and severe as they appeared to him to be when his mind was first struck, and once he has received them, also endorses them with his assent and adds his belief to them, as though they were rightly to be feared. . . . The sage, however, while he is changed in complexion and facial expression for a short time and to a limited degree, does not assent, but at once holds on to the strength of his opinion' (Aulus Gellius, NA xix 1.19–20 = Epict. fr. 9). Cf. Sen. De Ira i 3.3–8; ii 3.1 = LS 65X; 4.1; Cic. TD ii 61 (Poseidonius' gout); iii 61, 72.

[104] Epictetus asks: 'When you meet an attractive woman, do you resist the appearance? If your neighbour comes into money, aren't you bitten by envy?' (Epict. iii 2.8). We have some control over the character of our appearances; if we realize it would be bad to pursue the pleasure suggested by a particular appearance, then we can avoid imagining (anazōgraphein) the actual enjoyment of the pleasure (ii 18.16, 25).

assent. They do not have to struggle against passions (since they have eliminated them), but they have to make some effort to avoid the mental disturbance that may result from suggestive appearances.

192. Appearances without Passions

If the sage's appearances include so many elements of passions, and if the sage attends selectively to their suggestions, how might we expect the sage to react to ordinary human concerns? The Stoics seem to take an austere attitude to most people's emotions. Epictetus advises us to think of the death of a child or friend as though it were the breaking of a pot or a jug. We might take him to be advising us to cultivate a careless attitude, treating the death of a child or friend as a trivial matter, not worth taking seriously. Stoics do not seem to value the immediate and suggestive appearance that, in ordinary people, precedes grief.

This conclusion, however, may rest on a misunderstanding of Epictetus' advice. He does not imply that the death of a child or friend really matters no more than the breaking of a pot. He advises us to use this thought to dislodge us from our previous attachment to external goods.[105] He assumes that we need to counter a tendency in our appearances to go too far, and that we can do this by taking account of features of the situation that a particular appearance tends to neglect. The appearances that underlie passions tend to draw our attention to only one of the practically relevant aspects of a situation. Sometimes they draw our attention to the most relevant feature, but sometimes they mislead us by diverting attention from equally relevant or more relevant features. Epictetus wants us to recall features that we tend to overlook because of the appearance that underlies the passion. The comparison between the loss of a child and the loss of a cup reminds us of our conviction that good and ill fortune are no part of happiness, since they are no part of virtue. If we keep this in mind, we will not confuse cases in which we lose a preferred indifferent with cases in which life is not worth living because we are really deprived of happiness.

But if we counteract our appearances in this way, we do not claim that no preferred indifferent matters at all. We are right to have the appearance of having lost something highly preferable if a child or a friend dies, and we are right to have a more strongly suggestive and disturbing appearance in this case than if we had lost a cup. Sages have appearances that make them vividly aware of preferred and non-preferred indifferents. But this aspect of passions is separable from mistaken assent to the appearance suggesting that something good or evil is involved; that is why sages have no passions, even though they have suggestive appearances.

If the Stoics believed that the appearances appropriate to the loss of a friend or child are the same as those appropriate to the loss of a cup, critics might reasonably claim that they violate our preconceptions. But they do not believe this. They lack emotions only in so far as they do not assent to any appearance that natural advantages are good.[106] Since they

---

[105] Epictetus recommends the training (*askêsis*, iii 24.84) that can be used to prevent the attachment to external goods from becoming misguided.

[106] Contrast Striker, 'Following' 68–71.

maintain that natural advantages contribute to the life in accordance with nature, they care about acquiring them. They share the responses of other people, in so far as they focus sharply and vividly on the preferred and non-preferred aspects of indifferents.

Does the sage's lack of passion prevent sympathy with other people? If you are a Stoic sage and you see me suffering, you will not suppose that anything bad is happening to me, and so you will see no reason for the sympathy or compassion that would follow the belief that I have suffered a real harm. Moreover, since you are not subject to passions yourself, my suffering will not move you to any passion in response. In this respect, therefore, the sage is incapable of sympathy. But Stoics might reasonably argue that passion is not essential to the ethically significant aspects of sympathy, and that sages recognize these aspects through their vivid appearances of preferred and non-preferred indifferents. They recognize that we are liable to suffer significant non-preferred indifferents, and they have vivid and insistent appearances of these sufferings in other people. These appearances give them a good reason for doing something to relieve the sufferings of others.[107]

Does a Stoic sage lack some essential element of virtue by lacking passions? It is difficult to defend this charge on an Aristotelian basis. For Aristotle agrees that a virtuous person should have been trained to realize that the loss of external goods is not an occasion for despair, and that a blow to one's reputation does not threaten the most important aspects of one's happiness. Virtuous people should not retain other people's irrational and excessive reactions to external successes and failures. Their reactions should be proportionate to the value of the situations they react to, and these reactions should never threaten our recognition of the supreme value of virtue. These are the proportionate reactions that the Stoics try to describe more clearly; though sages have no passions, they might claim to react in the ways that Aristotle recommends.

193. Is the Sage really Free of Passion?

We might wonder whether this defence of the Stoics proves too much. Once we see that their views about virtue, happiness, and the indifferents do not imply that natural advantages are unimportant, or that virtue is the only thing we should be concerned about, we may be inclined to sympathize with critics who believe that Stoics and Peripatetics differ only verbally. Similarly, once we see that their views about freedom from passion do not eliminate suggestive appearances about value, we may be inclined to conclude that Stoic sages really have passions and that their freedom from passion differs only verbally from Peripatetic moderated passion.[108]

The Stoics admit that suggestive appearances can move us to some reaction even without any intervening assent. But, in their view, these appearances are not emotions, but preliminaries to them; a passion requires something further than a momentary inclination towards the action suggested by an appearance, and anything more than a momentary inclination requires assent. The sage lacks the crucial assent.

[107] The sage should not be passionless (*apathês*) like a rock, but should 'observe natural and acquired relations' in acknowledging duties (*kathêkonta*) (Epict. iii 2.4 = LS 56C).

[108] This view that the Stoics attribute emotions to the sage is Augustine's view in *CD* ix 4. See §220.

The Stoics do not suggest that we ought to try to remove all the suggestive elements in our appearances. The appearance that it is bad for us to be impoverished is not completely wrong, because impoverishment is in fact a non-preferred indifferent, and it is normally reasonable for us to try to avoid it.[109] Perhaps our best method for detecting preferred and non-preferred indifferents essentially involves selective and critical reliance on suggestive appearances. It would be a mistake to suppress the suggestion that it is bad to be tortured or impoverished, if this is the best way to turn our attention to these non-preferred indifferents.

We may be doubtful about this defence of the Stoic position because it relies on the claim that assent is essential for passion, and this claim is one of the most controversial elements of the Stoic doctrine of passions. If we doubt whether passions include assent, we may believe that the other features of passions, as the Stoics conceive them, are sufficient by themselves for passions. Even if we agree with the Stoics' separation of goods from preferred indifferents, we may still doubt their claims about the passions.

The Stoics' account of passions rests partly on the plausible claim that action on passion is responsible action. They assume, reasonably, that an account of passions ought to make it clear how we can be responsible for acting on our passions. They make this clear by taking assent to be necessary for a passion, so that our responsibility for acting on passion follows from the Stoic doctrine of responsibility. If we want to reject the Stoic account of passions, we need to show either that we are not responsible for acting on passion, or that the Stoics are wrong to connect responsibility with assent, or that we can connect passions with assent and responsibility without making assent part of a passion. Since Augustine and Aquinas contribute to this debate by modifying the Stoic position in different places, we can postpone further discussion until we come to their accounts of the passions.

194. The Extent of Friendship

Now that we have surveyed some aspects of the Stoics' doctrine of happiness, virtue, and the preferred indifferents, we may consider some of their views on the other-regarding virtues. These views are original and important in their own right; they also show how the Stoics try to distinguish those elements of human life that constitute the aim of rational action from those that constitute its preferred objective. Some of the apparently conflicting aspects of Stoic social and political morality are intelligible in the light of their doctrines about virtue and happiness.

The Stoics identify two lives: (1) The life in which the appropriate intrinsic value is attached to the exercise of practical reason in relation to the rest of human nature. (2) The life in which the moral virtues are given the appropriate place. The Stoics think these apparently distinct lives are united by the concept of the fine (honestum). In examining the growth of reason, we find that we come to value it for its own sake. Virtuous people value virtuous action for its own sake, as something fine. The Stoics suggest that each of these

---

[109] This argument for the cognitive usefulness of appearances is still easier to defend if the sage simply has the appearance that he is suffering a non-preferred indifferent. For this appearance is true, and he would be quite mistaken if he did not take it into account in his deliberation.

outlooks commits us to the other; the virtues are to be valued for their own sake because they are exercises or expressions of practical reason.

This claim is relatively plausible for self-regarding virtues. But an obvious question arises about the virtues that essentially require concern for others. Aristotelian friendship seems to justify only limited concern for others. Do the Stoics go further?

Aristotle does not argue that the extent of concern for others ought to be limited. He recognizes natural friendship and conciliation between all human beings (EN 1155a16–21).[110] He makes a similar remark in discussing the ways in which friendship with a slave is and is not possible.[111] He claims that in so far as we share humanity with other human beings, we actually are friends to them; common humanity is not simply the basis for possible friendship, but implies some form of actual friendship.

How does Aristotle explain this friendship, and what does he think it involves? He compares it with the relation of justice that actually holds between all human beings in so far as they are capable of sharing in law and agreement. The capacity for sharing in law and agreement means that relations of justice are actual, not merely possible. Perhaps Aristotle means that since it is possible to make a just or an unjust law and agreement between human beings, facts about justice are antecedent to any law; for if justice were the product of law and agreement, the law and agreement themselves could not be assessed as just and unjust.

Perhaps one might explain friendship in the same way. As we have seen, Aristotle allows some elements of complete friendship between virtuous people to be extended beyond one's complete friends to fellow-citizens whom one recognizes as sufficiently virtuous to share in common deliberation in which each person counts as 'another self' whose interests matter for their own sake. If he can show that we recognize some degree of virtue in every other person, because each person is a rational agent, he can reasonably argue that we must already have some relation of friendship to every other person, and that every other person counts as 'another self' for us.

But even if this is a legitimate inference from some of Aristotle's remarks about friendship, Aristotle gives us no help with it. He does not try to show that his quite careful and detailed account of the different types of friendship and of the moral basis of friendship makes it reasonable to recognize friendship for humanity.

The Stoics differ from Aristotle on this point. For they claim that all human beings form a community that gives them obligations to one another. We might assume that this cosmopolitan outlook rests on a moral foundation that emphasizes impartial concern for human welfare, as opposed to the egocentric (in the sense we have explained) Aristotelian outlook.[112]

---

[110] See §128.

[111] 'In so far as he is a slave, then, there is no friendship with him. But there is friendship with him in so far as he is a human being. For every human being seems to have some relation of justice with everyone who is capable of community in law and agreement; hence <every human being seems> also <to have> friendship <with every human being>, to the extent that <every human being> is a human being' (EN 1161b5–8).

[112] Barbeyrac, 'Morality' 66, believes that Aristotle misses the central elements of morality: 'Thus this vast genius of nature, this philosopher, for whom such numbers have so great a veneration; proves to be grossly ignorant of, and without any scruple treads under foot, one of the most evident principles of the law of nature'. Cf. Tuck, NRT 174–7. To illustrate his charge, Barbeyrac especially condemns Aristotle's willingness to permit abortion in some circumstances (Politics 1335b19–26). Among recent writers Donagan, TM 4, argues that Aristotle has no clear conception of morality: 'The Stoics, rather than Aristotle or Plato, are to be credited with forming the first reasonably clear conception of

Closer examination of the Stoics, however, casts doubt on this assumption. Their starting-point is no less egocentric than Aristotle's, and at several points they rely on Aristotle's conception of friendship. The fact that they can use Aristotelian principles to support concern for the interests of humanity in general shows that the Aristotelian principles are more flexible than we might have supposed. In our attempts to see how far Aristotelian concern for other selves can reasonably be extended, we have begun the line of argument that the Stoics pursue in some detail.[113]

The main Stoic argument relies on a parallel between two roles of practical reason: (i) concern for my own life as a whole, and (ii) concern for the good of others as well as myself. This parallel is introduced by Plato in the *Symposium*,[114] and is present also in Aristotle. The two roles are parallel, because both exercises of practical reason extend its scope beyond my immediate concerns and interests. In one case, I see that my good belongs to different stages of myself. In the other case, it see that it also belongs to people other than myself. In both cases I extend my conception of my good, and in doing so I adapt more of my life to practical reason.

The Stoics express this idea of the extension of practical reason through their suggestive metaphor of expanding circles. We have seen how they use this metaphor to capture our conception of our own life as a series of circles of expanding concern. They use the same picture of expanding circles to explain our relation to other people. Hence Hierocles introduces the circles into his account of conciliation (*oikeiôsis*).[115] He describes an agent's relation to other people by assuming several 'circles'. The first of these circles includes one's body; others include one's immediate and extended family, one's fellow-citizens, and eventually the whole human race. Hierocles suggests that we belong to these circles whether we are virtuous or vicious, but that if we are virtuous we draw people in the more remote circles into closer circles (Stob. iv 671.7–673.11 = LS 57G).

This metaphor of expanding circles has a different significance in relation to other people from its significance in relation to a single person. In recognizing expanding circles in my own life, I recognize that different actions and experiences at different times are all states of one and the same person—myself; the common centre of all the circles expresses the fact that the owner of all the experiences and the agent of all the actions is one and the same person. But when the circles include different people, rather than different states of the same person, their common centre does not indicate that they are really all states of the same person.

The significance of the metaphor is clear, however, when Hierocles says it is a mark of virtue to draw people into closer circles. Incorporation of a person in a circle is similar to incorporation of one person's states in the circles of that person, in so far as it marks a type of concern. When only one person is involved, that person cares for a future state as his own, because he recognizes that it is his own. When a second person is involved, A's inclusion of

---

morality.... Obviously there is a strong moral element in Aristotle's theory of ethical virtue; but he did not succeed in distinguishing moral virtue as such, the virtue of a man as a man, from political virtue, the virtue of a citizen of a good city.' Donagan's claim is not easily reconciled with Aristotle, *Politics* iii 4; since Aristotle argues that a good person must be a citizen of a good city, he must distinguish the two concepts.

[113] Stoic arguments for extension of concern are discussed, and taken to be inconsistent, by McCabe, 'Extend'.

[114] See §§63–4.   [115] On conciliation see above §179.

B in a circle around A marks the fact that A has some of the concern for B that A has for A. Whatever I incorporate in a circle is something that I care about in the way I care about myself.

In their description of circles, therefore, the Stoics adapt Aristotle's idea of the friend as another self, another person whom I care about in the way I care about myself. The Stoics pursue this idea further than Aristotle does. Eventually, the virtuous person's circles of concern include the whole human race. Just as longer-term self-concern expands the scope of my practical reason, so does concern for others, and for a larger number of others in different relations to me.

195. Expanding Circles of Friendship

The Stoics treat these concentric circles dynamically, not just statically. The mark of a virtuous person is to move people from more distant circles into closer circles, so that a virtuous person shows the sort of concern for more distant people that other people show for people closer to them. But how is this inward movement to be understood?

Two different interpretations, with different moral implications, might be defended: (1) If I am a virtuous person, I eventually fit the whole human race into the inmost circle, the one that initially contains only myself. The metaphor of circles expresses claims about the moral equality of everyone, and about the universal 'point of view of the cosmos' that Stoic sages take on their actions.[116] (2) If I am virtuous, I bring people closer to me than a non-virtuous person brings them to himself, but I still maintain a distinction between circles; I do not put everyone into the same circle. The plurality of circles recognizes the differences between moral concern for different people.

The second interpretation is more plausible. The point of the expanding circles is probably not that we eventually treat everyone the same way. The point is that people who would be outside our circles of concern move into them, so that we recognize some community with them. The Stoic sources do not suggest that the virtuous person recognizes just the same obligations to everyone. They suggest that the people who are more distant for non-virtuous people become closer for the virtuous person.

This second interpretation, recognizing different degrees of closeness corresponding to different circles, fits Cicero's claim that we have different obligations to people in different sorts of relations with us. Our duties (officia) to human beings in general do not involve self-sacrifice; they involve benefits to others without harm to ourselves. Cicero illustrates these benefits by the example of one person lighting another person's lamp without losing any of his own light.[117] He mentions ties of race, city, family, ties with other virtuous people,

---

[116] See Annas, MH 268–70.

[117] 'Now the things that belong to all human beings in common seem to be of the sort laid down by Ennius . . . : "A human being who kindly shows the way to someone who is lost is as one who lights another's lamp by his own, so that his own shines no less for him when he has lit the light for the other." This example suffices for him to teach us that, if there is some help we can give without loss to ourselves, we ought to give it even to a stranger' (Cic. Off. i 51).

and so on, as sources of different duties. He does not say that all have to be objects of equal concern.[118]

196. The Characteristics of Friendship

We have suggested that Stoic claims about expanding circles of concern exploit Aristotle's view that friendship involves the recognition of people as 'other selves', and that the Stoics go beyond Aristotle in claiming that everyone else ought to be recognized as another self. But their attempt to expand Aristotelian friendship may appear misguided, once we consider the sorts of relations that Aristotle takes to be characteristic of friendship. His argument seems to presuppose continuing interaction between friends. He describes their characteristic activity as the sharing of 'reasoning and thought'. They engage in shared deliberation, argument, reflexion, and so on. Friendship is an element of one's good partly because one can engage in this co-operative practical reasoning.

The interactive aspects of friendship help to explain why Aristotle does not normally extend it to all humanity. Fellow-citizens (in the sort of state that Aristotle has in mind) interact in ways that make friendship intelligible. Moreover, we interact with other people whom we happen to encounter; Aristotle mentions meetings between travellers (*EN* 1155a21). But if friendship involves interaction and co-operation, we cannot be friends of people with whom we do not interact.

We can better understand the issues that these aspects of friendship raise for the Stoic position if we consider a related Aristotelian objection. The importance that the Stoics attach to community and to extended concern appears to conflict with the Stoic view that happiness and virtue are identical. From Aristotle's point of view, we might argue as follows: (1) Happiness requires virtue, because happiness is the fulfilment of rational nature. (2) The fulfilment of rational nature requires the extension of practical reason to concern for others. (3) This extension of practical reason requires community with others. (4) Hence happiness requires community with others. (5) Community with others requires interaction. (6) The relevant interaction is not entirely up to me. (7) Hence happiness is not entirely up to me.

The Stoics accept the first four steps of this argument; that is why they argue for expanding circles of concern. But they seem to overlook (5) and (6). If happiness requires interaction, and not simply an action of the virtuous person, it does not depend wholly on the virtuous person; hence it does not seem to consist wholly in virtue and virtuous activities. But the claim that the relevant sort of community requires interaction appears plausible; for practical

---

[118] 'But perhaps we should examine more thoroughly what are the natural principles of human fellowship and community (societatis). First is something that is seen in the fellowship of the entire human race. For the bonding consists of reason and speech, which conciliate human beings to one another through teaching, learning, communicating, discussing, and judging, and unite them in a kind of natural community.... Now there are a great many degrees of community (societas) among human beings. To proceed beyond the limitless (infinita) community, there is the closer one of belonging to the same people, tribe, and tongue, by which human beings are very closely tied together. A closer tie still binds citizens of the same city (civitas)...But there is an even closer tie within a family. Starting from that boundless (immensa) community of the human race, we end with something small and narrow...But of all the bonds of fellowship, there is none nobler, none more powerful than when good men of congenial character are joined in intimate friendship; for really, if we discover in another that moral goodness (honestum) on which I dwell so much, it attracts us and makes us friends to the one in whose character it seems to dwell.' (Cic. *Off*. i 50–5).

reason is expanded and developed further when other people contribute to my practical reasoning than when I reason without the co-operative contribution of others. Hence step (2) seems to support step (5). Since the Stoics agree that happiness requires the fulfilment of rational nature, they must apparently recognize the value of interaction. Hence the reasons that justify their claim that happiness includes virtue also seem to justify the Aristotelian claim that happiness includes more than virtue, and in particular that it includes more than what is up to me.

197. Stoic Political Theory

To see how the Stoics deal with these Aristotelian objections about virtue, happiness, and friendship, it is useful to take a wider view of the Stoic position. In particular, some features of the Stoics' political theory reveal some of their distinctive arguments about community. Some peculiarities of the Stoics' doctrine of friendship are connected to their apparently conflicting claims about the state. The sources seem to present inconsistent fragments of political views; but closer inspection suggests the consistent moral claims that underlie them.[119]

We can distinguish these different attitudes to states and political institutions in Stoic sources: (1) Some Stoics criticize existing states, and propose radical alternatives. Zeno advocates an ideal state that goes even further than Plato's in abandoning the institutions of existing societies.[120] (2) Some Stoics suggest that existing states are not only flawed, but are not even genuine states at all, because the only genuine state would have to consist of virtuous people.[121] (3) Sometimes the Stoics do not seem to be concerned with the institutions of a state, as ordinarily understood, but only with the community that already exists among all virtuous people, in so far as they accept a common law by following common rational principles. (4) Sometimes the Stoics appear to be less interested in ideal states than in understanding existing states as part of a single worldwide community of rational agents, not only of virtuous agents.[122] These different claims seem to suggest that

---

[119] Schofield, *SIC* and 'Social', contain helpful discussions of questions in Stoic political theory.

[120] '...[Zeno] declares at the beginning of his *Republic* that ordinary education is useless. Secondly, he says that all those who are not virtuous are one another's opponents, at war, slaves, foreigners, to one another...Again, in the *Republic* he sets up virtuous people alone as citizens, friends, kin, and free, so that, in the Stoic view, parents and children are adversaries, since they are not wise. He is said to lay down in the *Republic* that women are to be held in common, and (at line 200) that people should build neither temples nor courthouses nor gymnasia in the cities' (DL vii 32–3 = LS 67B). Schofield *SIC*, ch. 1, discusses Chrysippus' objections to Zeno's radical proposals.

[121] 'They say a city is a mass of human beings who dwell in the same place, that is governed by law. It is clear thereby that this predicate is proper to none of the so-called cities that are foolish and lawless . . . For just as the one who lacks the rational part is not a human being either, so also what is not law-abiding is not a city; and if it is foolish and disorderly, it could not be law-abiding' (Dio Chrys. 36.20).

[122] 'Let us grasp in our minds two commonwealths. One is great and truly common, including both gods and human beings, in which we do not look at this or that corner of the earth, but we measure the boundaries of our city together with the path of the sun. The other is the one we have been enrolled in by the circumstances of our birth. This is the commonwealth of the Athenians or the Carthaginians, or of some other city that belongs to some specific human beings, but not to all human beings' (Sen. *De Otio* 4.1 = LS 67K, discussed in Schofield, *SIC*, ch. 4.) 'What is there—never mind in human beings, but in all of heaven and earth—more divine than reason? And when this has grown and been perfected, it is rightly called prudence. Since, then, nothing is better than reason, and since it is in human beings and in gods, the first community of human beings and gods is in reason. Now those who share reason also have right reason in common;

Stoic political theory is about different subjects, and indeed that it is not a single body of theory at all, but a series of different observations that lead in different directions.

Zeno's *Republic* disagrees with Plato, and with existing societies, and proposes an alternative ideal state with unconventional institutions. Probably Zeno argues that many of the institutions that people take for granted as essential for a just city and a decent way of life are really indifferent, and need to be examined to see whether they are preferred indifferents that achieve the appropriate results in specific circumstances. He and Chrysippus perhaps suggest that a city of virtuous people would not need the institutions found in actual states. Here, then, they understand 'a community of virtuous people' as a specific group of people forming something like a Greek *polis*.

But the Stoics also seem to think of a different sort of community of virtuous people. They believe that virtuous people everywhere form a community, whether or not they are gathered together in a political community that actually shares the sorts of causal interactions that belong to the ordinary institutions of government. In this sense, we can live in the community of virtuous people even if we are in Norway and all the other virtuous people are in New Zealand, and we do not know of their existence. From the Stoic point of view, one might argue that the community of virtuous people is a more significant community than the one constituted by the particular political community we are born into; and so virtuous people will treat one another as fellow-citizens, however distant (in ordinary terms) they may be from one another.[123]

However, the Stoics also recognize a world community, a cosmopolis that is not restricted to virtuous people. It is similar to the community of the virtuous in so far as it does not include any institutions of government that produce the normal sort of causal interactions and influences among citizens. In the Stoics' view, this sort of community has one law. The rational principles followed by human beings and God constitute the natural law, a universally valid guide for individual and social life. This universal community is not (or not simply) an ideal for a worldwide community that might replace existing states. The Stoics speak of it as already existing in the present world.

Does the claim that a universal community already exists depend on Stoic theological assumptions? We might take the Stoics to mean that a single community must have a single ruler, and that the Stoic God is the ruler. If the world were exactly as it is, but the Stoics were wrong to say that it is ruled by a single divine intelligence, would they have to abandon their claim about its being a single community of rational agents?

This question takes us back to the issues about Aristotelian friendship. When we see how the Stoics interpret and develop some Aristotelian claims, we can see what they mean in recognizing a community of the wise, and a community of rational agents.

---

and since right reason is law, we must suppose that we human beings and the gods are made a community by law' (Cic. *Leg.* i 23). 'True law is correct reason agreeing with nature, diffused through everyone, constant, everlasting. It calls to duty by commanding, and deters from wrongdoing by forbidding. It neither commands good people in vain nor moves bad people either by commanding or by forbidding. . . . And God will be the one common master and commander of all—God, who has found and promulgated the law and is its judge. Anyone who does not obey it flees from himself and shuns the nature of a human being, and by this very fact pays the greatest penalties, even if he escapes the other things commonly accounted punishments' (Lactantius, *Div. Inst.* vi 8.6–9 = Cic. *Rep.* iii 33 = LS 67S). See §206 (Christianity); §284 (Aquinas).

[123] On the community of reason see Schofield, *SIC* 72.

198. The Community of Sages

The Stoics' view of the relevant types of community is intelligible in the light of Aristotle's views on friendship between virtuous people. Aristotle says virtuous people share reason and thought (*logos* and *dianoia*); and these are the connexions that the Stoics describe in explaining friendship among sages. In their view, Aristotle picks the right features of friendship, but unduly restricts the types of friendship in which these features can be found.

One relation that the Stoics exploit appears in Aristotle's discussion of goodwill (*eunoia*). According to Aristotle, goodwill involves concern for the other person for the other's own sake, but it does not involve the interaction that is characteristic of friendship (*EN* ix 5). Aristotle suggests that this goodwill is the starting point of friendship, but it is 'inactive friendship' (1167a10–14). Goodwill for another virtuous person expresses a common point of view. In recognizing another virtuous person, we recognize another person who cares about virtuous action for its own sake, and wants his actions and life to be subject to practical reason. And so we recognize such people as ones with whom we already share a common point of view, and therefore as ones with whom we can share common deliberation, if the appropriate interaction becomes possible.

According to the Stoics, Aristotle's claims about goodwill explain how the Stoic sage has friendship with all other sages. If Zeno is a sage, friendship with other sages is open to him, even if he does not know whether there are any other sages, where they exist, or who any individual sage is. Zeno is a friend to any other sages there might be, whether or not he knows that there are any. When Zeno recognizes the possibility of another sage, he treats this other sage as another self; he regards the interests of the other as mattering in the way in which Zeno's own interests matter to him.

From Aristotle's point of view, we might reply that Zeno's attempt to include all other sages in his circle of concern is an idle exercise unless he interacts appropriately with a specific sage. Let us suppose there is a sage in China whom Zeno has never heard of—call him Confucius. We might say that though Zeno and Confucius would be concerned about each other if they met, they have merely potential concern if they do not meet. That is the point of saying that they have inactive friendship, until they know they have mutual goodwill and can do something about it.

The Stoics might reply, however, that the appropriate sort of interaction does not require the mutual knowledge that Zeno and Confucius lack. If Jane bequeaths all her money to her fourth grandson, even though at her death she has only three grandsons, she does something for her fourth grandson, even though she does not know who he is. Similarly, the mere fact that Zeno and Confucius do not know each other does not mean that their outlooks do not affect each other. Each may be influenced by the point of view of the other, without knowing who the other is.

To see how this might be true, we need to consider what is involved in being a sage. In the Stoics' view, the sage is perfectly free of any distortion of the rational outlook by the influence of appearances. Though the sage has got rid of passions, he still has the appearances that distort our judgment unless we are vigilant, as Epictetus says, in examining them.[124] But how do we avoid this distorting influence?

In some cases, Zeno's judgment may be in danger of being distorted because he is forming his views in Athens, or among the people he knows best, or because he is thinking about his particular situation as a slave or a slave-owner. To find the point of view of a sage, he needs to separate himself from the distorting influences of these specific features of his own situation. He might do this if he takes the point of view of a sage like Confucius, who lacks the appearances that encourage Zeno to draw one conclusion rather than another. But Confucius' point of view is a source of good advice for Zeno only if Zeno thinks of Confucius without the particular biases of Confucius' environment.

Would it be an idle ceremony for Zeno to think of Confucius in this way, without knowing whether there is any such person? The mere fact that he cannot ask Confucius what he thinks does not mean that it is a waste of time to ask himself what Confucius would think. He can still helpfully try to take Confucius' point of view. Unless we think of someone who does not face the distorting influences of our local situation, we will find it difficult to avoid these influences.

We might consider some Stoic reflexions on political institutions in this light. Zeno and Chrysippus reach apparently bizarre conclusions because they consider the point and use of different institutions and practices without reference to the fact that these are familiar. From the point of view of a sage who is not immersed in the customs and traditions of the Greek world, the current institutions may well seem unnecessary or harmful. It does not follow that the fact that we are used to these institutions is irrelevant in making actual political recommendations. But clarity about the value of the institutions requires us to grasp the point of view of the sage who reflects on them in abstraction from what we happen to be used to.[125]

This appeal to the point of view of another sage is relevant to the Aristotelian objection that Stoic friendship between sages is inactive because it does not involve interaction. From the Stoic point of view, this friendship involves a certain sort of mutual influence. Each one of Zeno and Confucius is influenced, in forming his own views, by the views of another sage who is removed from his own particular environment. Hence each of them attends to the point of view of the other in trying to form his own point of view. The outlooks of two virtuous people influence each other even if neither is aware of the existence of the other.

It is too simple, therefore, to object that Stoic friendship does not include interaction, and therefore falls short of genuine friendship. Since the Stoic sage relies on points of view other than his own in forming his own point of view, it would be a mistake to argue that reference to the other sage's point of view is idle. Hence the reason that an Aristotelian might give for believing that friendship between sages is mere goodwill is not a good reason. Even though the mutual influence of two points of view is not the same as causal interaction between two people, it is not the same as mutual goodwill. The point of view that each sage recognizes in the other also makes a difference to thought and deliberation.

---

[124] See §165.   [125] Cicero comments on Cynic and Stoic attitudes to social conventions at *Off.* i 128–9, 148.

199. The Community of Human Beings

If we have some ground for believing that Stoic sages have friendship with one another, can we extend the same sort of argument to explain why the Stoics recognize not only a community of sages, but also a community of all rational agents? In their view, the sage regards himself as part of this community. That is why he is *philanthrôpos*, a lover of humanity.[126] He is a friend to all human beings, not only to sages. But it is not only the sage who has this friendship towards other people in general. The Stoics also claim that all rational agents have it towards one another; that is what makes them a community bound by friendship.

To see how such friendship is possible, we need to rely on the feature that all rational agents share with sages. Sages take the point of view of practical reason, freed from the distorting influence of appearances. Other people do not manage this with the same degree of success, but, if they are rational agents, they do some of it. To recognize the common law of reason is to recognize a community of interest with other rational agents to the extent that they are reliable contributors to common rational deliberation. To be a sage is to be open to the point of view of another sage, in the sense we have explained. To be a rational agent is to be, to some degree, responsive to the views of other rational agents, as such.

If this is a correct account of the Stoic position, the friendship of all rational agents for one another is not only consistent with the mutual friendship of sages, but required by it. Sages are friends because they are complete rational agents, steadily moved by the outlook of reason rather than the distorting influences of appearance and passion. They differ from other human beings in fully achieving what other people partly achieve. Other people agree with the sage in taking the point of view of reason; they therefore listen to the views of other rational agents as participants in their deliberation. This is why a sage loves humanity and takes pleasure in the sight of many other human beings.[127]

In this case also, the Stoics can satisfy Aristotle's demand for mutual influence even among people who do not know of each other's existence. If I try to deliberate from the point of view of a rational agent who is free of the distorting influences of my environment, I have to take that person's point of view, and I have to be influenced by it. Even if I do not actually encounter any such person, I learn about that person's views and respond to them.

The Stoics speak of a common natural law that everyone recognizes and that no one can violate without 'fleeing from himself and shunning the nature of a human being' (Cic. *Rep.* iii 33 = LS 67S).[128] They assume that rational agents are capable of engaging in common deliberation with other rational agents so that they reach a common point of view. From this common point of view they find the principles that ought to guide their individual and collective behaviour.

---

[126] On *philanthrôpia* cf. Epict. iii 24.64–6 (Diogenes showed his *philanthrôpia* by treating the whole earth as his native country (*patris*)); iv 8.30–2 (Cynic *philanthrôpia* shown by willingness to share the Cynic attitude to virtue and happiness); iv 4.27; Clem. *Strom.* ii 41.6. On the wider use of this term see *TDNT* ix 108–12.

[127] 'For what is a pleasanter sight to a lover of humanity than many human beings? . . . "But their noise is too much for me." No doubt your hearing is impeded. Then what is that to you? Is your ability to make use of appearances impeded?' (Epict. iv 4.27–8).

[128] Quoted in full at n122 above.

This assumption of a common point of view, however, faces some difficulties. Suppose that Zeno and Confucius are deliberating as sages do, and are both responsive to the other's point of view. They agree that one virtue is bravery and that a brave person fights for his city. This is how it seems to Zeno when he recognizes that Confucius also thinks it right to fight for one's city. But this agreement implies that it may be right for one brave person to fight for Athens against Sparta, and for another to fight for Sparta against Athens. Given this mutual antagonism, how can they have a common point of view?

One might say that the only possible common point of view among brave people would be respect for the other person's bravery. One might respect the other person in this way, while still making strenuous efforts to kill him; that seems to be the attitude of Greeks and Trojans in the *Iliad*.

We might reach this conclusion for various reasons: (1) We might believe that competition is the right way to settle this dispute between states, so that on this point the two brave people take a common point of view. This would be similar to the view that it is all right for us to compete for the same job, or to play on two opposed teams. Hence this example would not constitute an objection to the view that in recognizing other virtuous people we recognize common purposes that we share with them. (2) Instead we might argue that considerations of what is fair or right do not apply to such cases, so that there is no answer to a question about how the disputes that lead to conflict ought to be settled.

This second answer is similar to the Hobbesian view, and would be an objection to the suggestion that recognition of virtue in another person marks a possibility for common deliberation. Hence the Stoics need to argue that the first answer is correct—that virtuous people can find a rationally acceptable answer by common deliberation about how to deal with dispute or conflict.

200. Limitations of Stoic Friendship

We have examined these Stoic views of friendship in order to see how Stoics might answer the Aristotelian objection that the recognition of friendship as a good compromises the Stoic position that virtue is sufficient for happiness. According to this objection, friendship and community require the existence of suitable other people; and since their existence is not up to me, not all the elements of the good are in my control, and not all are guaranteed by virtue. Without these other people I can have only goodwill, but no proper friendship.

We now see that this Aristotelian objection is too simple. Stoic sages are capable of a certain kind of friendship, going beyond mere goodwill and involving mutual influence, with other sages, whether or not these sages exist or are known to one another. Moreover, all rational beings have this friendship, to some degree, with other rational beings. This sort of friendship gives the Stoics an answer to the Aristotelian objection.

Still, the very fact that this sort of friendship is worthwhile gives a reason for thinking it is even better to have actual friends whose point of view we can learn about from what they tell us and not simply from our own reasoning. If Zeno tries to take the point of view of Confucius, free from the distorting influences of Zeno's own environment, he may not succeed completely. If he knows an actual Chinese sage, he may do better, since he no longer relies entirely on his own reason to find the point of view of the sage. Even if a sage is not subject to this error, he may appropriately welcome the agreement of another actual sage, to confirm the correctness of his judgment. If anyone is prone to error in trying to discover the views of the sage, he has reason to welcome the help of other people who are willing to make the same effort to discover these views. The Stoic explanation of friendship suggests an Aristotelian comment: even if other actual people are not needed for friendship, they seem to be needed for the best operation of friendship. Hence they seem to be needed for human beings to achieve their complete good.

If this is true of friendship, it is also relevant to arguments between Stoics and Aristotelians on virtuous action 'in preferable conditions'. Alexander argues that each craft has two sorts of exercise—its exercise in preferable and in non-preferable conditions (*Mant.* 160.31–161.1); a craft, for instance, exercises itself both in playing good flutes and in playing bad flutes. While recognizing Aristotle's point that virtue is exercised in bad external conditions, Alexander suggests that this is not really the proper exercise of virtue, and that the proper exercise requires preferable conditions.[129]

If Alexander's remark about the end of the virtues takes the end to be fully virtuous action (i.e., the Stoic use of 'end'), neither the Stoics or Aristotle ought to agree with him. On the contrary; in so far as the virtuous person acts in accordance with right reason for its own sake, he does this just as well in bad conditions. If Alexander means 'end' in a broader sense, corresponding to the Stoic 'objective', he is right to say that the virtuous person prefers virtuous action in good conditions. The Stoics agree with this, but their agreement does not threaten their claim about virtue. They need not agree that it is less properly virtuous action even in bad conditions.

But perhaps more can be said on Alexander's behalf. The Stoics claim that 'action' is an appropriate aim for the virtuous person, because action is up to us; since we can get that completely right, the best actions are up to us and do not depend on external circumstances; hence the complete fulfilment of human nature in action is up to us. This argument, however, neglects the ways in which the best kind of action is not up to us. If we find the best action by learning from experience, and this experience requires favourable circumstances, the best actions are not entirely up to us.

This conclusion bears on the previous discussion about the fulfilment and extension of practical reason, in friendship and expanding circles. If the best rational action requires interaction, the Stoics may be wrong to claim that rational agency is wholly up to me. They may still be right to claim that some aspect of rational agency is up to me and is more valuable than anything else.

We might, therefore, sympathize with the criticism that is developed in *De Finibus* iv (esp. 34–48) against the Stoics.[130] The critic argues that the Stoics assume that happiness is the fulfilment of rational human nature; that is why they identify happiness with rational agency and virtue. But since the fulfilment of rational nature requires more than virtue, the Stoics should admit that if happiness includes virtue, it includes more than virtue. In particular, community with others seems to be necessary for the full development of practical reason;

---

[129] 'Just as in the other crafts the end is in the exercises about wished-for things and in preferable conditions (*en prohêgoumenois*), the same will be true in the case of virtue, if it is a craft' (*Mant.* 161.1–3).

[130] Augustine endorses this criticism; see §227.

and if the Stoics believe that practical reason is at least part of happiness, they should agree that its full development is necessary for happiness.

To agree with this criticism is not to reject the Stoic claim that virtue matters more than any combination of external goods. Aristotle also accepts that claim. The Stoics have made it clearer why virtue matters more than external goods; they argue that it completes the practical reason that is essential to the agent for whom external goods are good. But this point about virtue does not justify the conclusion that virtue is the whole of happiness. If we are at all sympathetic to Aristotle's function argument, apparently we must take happiness to include more than virtue.

201. Estimate of the Stoic Position

To see what is especially significant and especially difficult to believe in the Stoic view of friendship, we may contrast it with a sentimentalist and a Kantian account of the proper extent of concern for other people.

According to a sentimentalist outlook (accepted by Hutcheson, Hume, and Adam Smith), the extent to which we are capable of sympathy defines the extent of concern. Hence we do not need community (societas), as the Stoics conceive it. But sympathy has the disadvantage that it seems to be variable in ways that seem rationally irrelevant. Some people find sympathy easier than others do, and we find it easier to direct to some people than to others. But the proper extent of concern for others does not seem to vary along these dimensions. One might believe that sympathy ought to be formed in appropriate ways by principles that are independent of it. Hence sympathy does not seem a sufficient basis of concern for others.

Against this position, Kant argues that rational agents deserve respect from others, irrespective of anyone's sympathies. This view has an advantage over the sentimentalist appeal to sympathy, since it helps to explain why a certain sort of sympathy is appropriate, instead of inverting the order. But it also has a possible disadvantage, since it might not appear to explain why concern for others might require positive action. Can we not show respect for someone or something by leaving them alone and refraining from harming them in certain ways?

The Stoics agree with neither of these views. They treat the other not as simply an object of sympathy or of respect, but as a certain kind of participant; that is why they lay such emphasis on community. This view may seem implausible if we assume that concern for others simply involves duties of aid. For we might say that we have this duty whether or not we have had or are going to have any co-operative relations with this person, or we even think of them as suitable for co-operative relations. However, attention to duties of aid may give us an inadequate conception of the character of obligations to others. Obligations to others often involve the recognition of someone as worth taking account of, and as worth listening to. Simply regarding the other as someone without opinions or convictions would be failing in some basic obligation. The Stoic emphasis on community clarifies the relevant aspect of concern for others. The claim that human beings form a societas is neither a commonplace nor a mere aspiration; it involves a disputable but reasonable ethical claim about the status of other people.

14

CHRISTIAN THEOLOGY
AND MORAL PHILOSOPHY

202. Christian Influences

From the beginning Christian theologians have explored some of the connexions, contrasts, and oppositions between their Christian outlook and the principles of moral philosophy. Though Christianity is not primarily a system of morality, and though its moral principles are not all peculiarly Christian, it expresses a distinct point of view about morality.[1] Conversely, moral philosophers have tried to examine the moral claims of Christianity from the standpoint of a moral theory that does not set out from specifically Christian premisses. Sometimes philosophers have used moral philosophy as a source of arguments against Christian belief. An early opponent who uses moral philosophy for this purpose is Origen's Platonist opponent Celsus; he claims that Christians have misunderstood and corrupted the doctrine of the Greek philosophers in this area as in others.[2] But in some cases—including Clement, Origen, and Augustine—the Christian theologian and the moral philosopher have been the same person arguing in two different directions from different premisses. This attempt to use moral philosophy and Christian theology to support each other is pursued in most detail by Aquinas.

Since these interactions and mutual influences begin with comparisons between Christianity and Greek moral systems, it will be useful to begin with some apparent implications of Christian belief, to see where we might expect to see points of conflict or influence. The influence of Christian belief is neither uniform nor straightforward; nor does it always lead a moral philosopher in one definite direction. On the contrary; Christian belief is not a source of uniformity, but a source of new directions and options in moral philosophy.

Different reasons can be given for the variety of Christian influences on moral philosophy: (1) First of all, the different Greek moral systems were not formulated in detailed and

---

[1] 'But the mere ethical teaching, however important, is the least important, because the least distinctive part of Christianity' (Lightfoot, SPEP 328).

[2] See Origen, Cels. vi 15–16. Celsus also claims that the Christians are unoriginal in their moral doctrine (i 4; they have nothing kainon or semnon to offer). Origen replies that divine justice presupposes the common awareness of morality (alluding to Rm. 2:15 in hin'anapologêtos pas anthrôpos eiê).

authoritative prescriptions; they left room for developments and interpretations leading in different directions. This is true even of Stoicism; though later Stoics worked out the moral implications of Stoicism in some detail, they did not formulate an authoritative body of orthodox Stoic teaching that would have resisted further external influence. (2) The same is true of Christian belief. When Christians came to acknowledge the authority of the Law, the Prophets, and some of the Wisdom literature of the Jews, together with the Gospels, Epistles, and other books of the New Testament, they accepted the widely different attitudes to moral questions expressed in these different parts of the Scriptures (not to mention further differences within these different parts). (3) Christian belief is connected to ethics in several different ways, both in its fundamental principles and in its more detailed applications. On the one hand, Christian doctrines of the nature of God, human nature, sin, grace, salvation, and the Incarnation, all rest on ethical assumptions that might be supported or contested on the basis of philosophical views on goodness, justice, virtue, freedom, and responsibility. On the other hand, the rather specific moral precepts of the Jewish law, the Gospels, the letters of Paul, and other early Christian pastoral writings, make relatively precise moral demands that interact with a different side of Greek moral systems.

It is not to be assumed, then, that the various aspects of Christian influence are even consistent, let alone uniform; for one ought not to assume without argument that the various moral implications of different aspects of Christianity are consistent. An examination of the relations between Christian belief and moral philosophy might show whether the total Christian position on moral questions is consistent, and how far it is defensible from the point of view of moral philosophy.

Even Christians do not always affirm the consistency of the views that can be derived from the canonical Christian Scriptures.[3] Marcion, for instance, rejected the Jewish element in Christian ethics as mere legalism, antagonistic to an essentially Christian outlook, and he treated St Paul's opposition between law and gospel as the basic Christian insight. Though Marcion was declared a heretic, his attitude was simply an extreme version of the view that the Christian outlook is basically incompatible with the acceptance of morality as a body of laws or rules that we can reasonably be expected to observe.[4] Those who have rejected this opposition between Jewish law and Christian gospel have none the less disagreed about the attitude that a Christian ought to take to Greek moral systems.

Three different approaches may be distinguished: (1) Against Celsus' critique of Christianity, Origen argues that Christian morality is not only consistent with moral philosophy, as understood by the Greek philosophers, but actually brings out the best in it. He argues that we can see, from the point of view of Greek moral philosophy itself, the moral excellence of the Christian moral outlook, so that this is actually a point in favour of Christianity,

---

[3] I use 'canonical' so as to include both the NT, as accepted by all Christian confessions and the OT as accepted by Roman and Orthodox authorities. This OT includes the 'Deuterocanonical' books contained in LXX and Vulg., but eventually rejected from the Jewish canon (which was fixed in the late first cent. AD). The Christian OT, as set out in 382 (Denz. §179), and affirmed in 397 (Denz. §186), included the Deuterocanonical books. Protestant sources refer to them as the 'Apocrypha'. According to the English Articles, the Church reads them 'for example of life and instruction of manners' (Art. 6). Some of these books are important sources for moral philosophy. On the formation of the Jewish canon see Anderson, 'Canonical' 132–59. On Christian views of the OT canon see Sparks, 'Jerome' 532–4.

[4] Tertullian attacks Marcion at length in *Marc*. See n105 below.

judged from a philosophical point of view.[5] This approach is developed most fully and convincingly by Aquinas. (2) Some argue that Christianity presents a moral outlook that conflicts fundamentally with the Greek outlook. From this point of view, the Greek outlook rests on assumptions about the world and about human beings that are shown to be clearly false in the light of the Christian revelation. Christian believers must replace the Greek systems with a quite different system resting on the authority of revelation and divine commands. To the Greeks the Christian system is bound to be foolishness,[6] and Christians are mistaken if they try to argue the Greeks out of their belief. Since Christianity reveals the truth about God and about human beings, it reveals the truth about morality; and just as God is different from what natural reason takes him to be, morality is different from what natural reason takes it to be. (3) Some argue that Christianity neither fulfils nor destroys Greek morality, because it does not take a moral position. Christianity displays the pointlessness of trying to satisfy God with our moral goodness; we can never succeed, and Christianity tells us we can achieve salvation without moral virtue. On this view, Christianity tells us about our relations with God, not about how to get on with other people. It is still important to get on with other people, and we need moral reflexion to tell us how to do it; but this is a separate area from religion. Theology does not prescribe the principles of medicine or agriculture, and we have no more reason to expect it to prescribe the principles of ethics. From this point of view, both of the previous approaches to Christianity and ethics rest on the same false assumption, that Christianity has ethical implications that make it either a fulfilment of Greek ethics or a challenge to it.

Our choice among these positions does not depend on whether we are Christian believers or not. We might take the first, harmonizing, position without inferring that Christianity is true, and we might take one of the other positions without inferring that Christianity is false. The second position is accepted, to some degree, by Scotus and Ockham, and by Calvin; it strongly influences post-Reformation Christian moral thinking.[7] It also influences Nietzsche, who uses it to contrast 'Greek' with 'Jewish' attitudes.[8] The third position is at least a powerful tendency in Luther's thinking. None of the three positions should be treated, without further argument, as the position that is clearly demanded by Christian belief.

We have stated each of these positions in rather extreme terms. Several more moderate positions are available if we believe that one of the extreme positions is true about some aspects of Christianity and one of the others is true about other aspects of it. We might, for instance, claim that some Christian precepts (including, say, the Decalogue) are part of ordinary rational morality, other precepts are specifically Christian moral demands, and still others are part of the Christian way of life, but no part of morality. A moderate position of this sort faces its own difficulties about consistency. We may wonder, for instance, what the relation between these different areas is supposed to be; how are we to avoid conflict between them?

Our discussion of these questions will not focus primarily on 'Christian morality', if that is taken to consist of a set of moral principles or precepts that are either distinctively or characteristically Christian. We will primarily consider Christian views about morality.

---

[5] See Origen, n2 above.
[6] See *1 Cor.* 1:23. Justin, *Ap.* 1.13, alluding to this passage, denies that Christian belief is irrational or foolish.
[7] See §312nn64–5 (Leo xiii).   [8] See Nietzsche, *GM* 17.

We will see that NT writers express or assume controversial and challenging views about the basic principles and aims of morality, and about the extent to which they can be treated as guides to action.[9]

203. Questions for Moral Theory

The Jewish and Christian Scriptures are not treatises on moral philosophy; moreover, most of them are not informed by any systematic theoretical position.[10] But they raise questions for moral philosophy. A survey of these questions should clarify one major influence on the reflexions of moral philosophers, whether or not they consciously reflect on Jewish or Christian doctrines. This chapter is not an essay in Biblical scholarship, or on moral theology or Christian ethics.[11] It does not try to describe questions that the Biblical writers intend to ask, but only tries to sketch some questions that arise for philosophical reflexion on the Biblical doctrines.

In the eighteenth year of Josiah king of Judah, the high priest Hilkiah said to Shaphan the secretary, 'I have found the book of the law in the house of the Lord' (*2Kg.* 22:8).[12] Shaphan read the book to the king, and 'when the king heard the words of the book of the law, he tore his clothes . . . "for great is the wrath of the Lord that is kindled against us, because our ancestors did not obey the words of this book, to do according to all that is written concerning us"' (22:11, 13). The book is generally supposed to have been *Deuteronomy*, which contains the code of law delivered by Moses.[13]

Moses claims that this code is in some way complete and comprehensive.[14] The laws apply to all aspects of life, both to the service of God and to social life. They carry the promise of rewards for disobedience and of punishment for disobedience. But the Hebrews are not to observe these laws simply because of their sanctions, or out of fear or loyalty towards God. They ought also to see that the laws deserve to be kept for their inherent wisdom; even non-Israelites are expected to recognize the excellence of the laws of Israel.[15]

But it is difficult to see how the code meets these expectations. It is not arranged in any explicit order. It does not represent any of its provisions as any more important than any others. Nor does it explicitly divide them into religious, moral, ceremonial, social, or economic, though we might recognize provisions dealing with these different areas of life. Nor does it suggest that some provisions are more general, and others are more

---

[9] For this purpose I will not consider possible differences between different NT writers. I will also treat all the NT letters ostensibly by Paul as authentic.

[10] A possible exception is *Wisdom*. The non-canonical *4 Maccabees* (included in LXX, but not in Vulg.; see Charlesworth, *OTP* ii 531–2) is based on a Stoic conception of the cardinal virtues. See also §328n18.

[11] The scope of moral theology and Christian ethics is discussed by Kirk, *SPMT*, ch. 1.

[12] Biblical quotations are usually taken from NRSV, sometimes slightly modified. The Greek text of the NT may be found in *GNT*.

[13] On the date of *Deuteronomy* and its relation to the reforms of Josiah see Weinfeld, *Deut. 1–11*, 65, 81.

[14] 'You must neither add anything to what I command you nor take away anything from it, but keep the commandments of the Lord your God with which I am charging you' (*Dt.* 4:2).

[15] 'Keep them and do them; for that will be your wisdom and your understanding in the sight of the peoples, who, when they hear all these statutes, will say, "Surely this great nation is a wise and discerning people." For what other great nation has a god so near to it as the Lord our God is whenever we call to him? And what other great nation has statutes and ordinances as just as this entire law that I am setting before you today?' (*Dt.* 4:6–8).

specific applications of them that might be more appropriate for some times and places than for others. Nor does it distinguish the absolutely compulsory from the desirable but non-compulsory. It has the outward form of a list of instructions, all of which are equally obligatory. Unlike the 'prefaces' in Plato's code of law in the *Laws*, the Deuteronomic code contains no full explanations or justifications of its different provisions. It does not defend the initial claim that a fair-minded outsider can recognize the wisdom and justice of these laws.

The code begins with the Decalogue (*Dt.* 5:6–21), a set of somewhat more general instructions. These instructions differ from specific laws in that they carry no stated penalty. In some cases (for instance, the prohibition on murder) they need interpretation before they could be the subject-matter of laws; something more needs to be said before we know what sort of killing is prohibited.[16] Hence we might suppose that the Decalogue contains the principles that underlie the more detailed instructions that follow.[17] After the Decalogue Moses gives a still more general command: 'The Lord is our God, the Lord alone. You shall love the Lord your God with all your heart, and with all your soul, and with all your might' (6: 4). Perhaps this is a general principle that is expressed in what follows.

The Decalogue, however, does not seem to be designed as the complete moral basis for the Deuteronomic code. Moses does not argue that all his detailed instructions fall under the provisions of the Decalogue, and it would be difficult to argue for this claim. On the one hand, many laws seem to be mere instructions, for which a reason is neither given nor easily found: these include the prohibition on eating anything in the water that lacks fins and scales (14:10), on ploughing with an ox and an ass (22:10), and on wearing clothes made of a mixture of linen and wool (22:11). On the other hand, some laws seem to rely on a moral basis distinct from the Decalogue. Neither the provisions for humane treatment of slaves and servants nor the requirement to leave some of one's crop to be gleaned by the alien, the orphan, and the widow (24:19–21) seem to be explained by the Decalogue, since nothing in the Decalogue explicitly prohibits cruelty or ungenerosity.[18] Other parts of the Decalogue do not seem suitable for a code of laws carrying sanctions; it is difficult to see how the prohibition of coveting could be made a matter for legal prohibition and punishment at all.[19]

But though the Deuteronomic code is not explicitly derived from any moral principles, Moses suggests what some of the relevant principles might be. He appeals to past experience: 'You shall also love the stranger, for you were strangers in the land of Egypt' (10:19). Slave-owners are to provide generously for freed slaves because the Hebrews were once slaves and were freed.[20] Moses does not say why the Hebrews should remember their condition in Egypt, but he seems to rely on some appeal to sympathy. When the Hebrews recall that they have been slaves, they are not moved by self-interest in their treatment of their own

---

[16] On the commandment against murder see Aquinas, *ST* 1-2 q100 a8 ad 3; §314n77.

[17] References to the Decalogue elsewhere in the OT; *Hos.* 4:2; *Ps.* 50:7,18–19; 81:10–11. Philo, *Dec.* i 154, claims that the Ten Commandments are summaries (*kephalaia*) of the provisions of the various special laws. Josephus' account of the Decalogue does not suggest that it has this role; see *Ant. Jud.* iii 91–2.

[18] Weinfeld, *Dt. 1–11* 250, argues that 'there is no justification for the claim that the Decalogue constitutes the epitome of Israelite morality'. He points, in particular, to the omission of the requirements of love for one's neighbour and for the stranger.

[19] On the tenth commandment see Weinfeld, *Dt. 1–11* 317. Philo, *Dec.* i 142–53, treats it as applying to excessive *epithumia* in general.

[20] 'Remember that you were a slave in the land of Egypt, and the Lord your God redeemed you; for this reason I lay this command upon you today' (15:15; cf. 5:15; *Ex.* 22:21–7; *Lv.* 19:33–4).

slaves, but they recall what it is like to be a slave. This recollection is intended to result in a more generous attitude to their own slaves. The formulation of the commandment to keep the sabbath requires this generous attitude.[21]

Even the command to acknowledge and love God is not left without a reason. Before giving the first commandment, God says: 'I am the Lord your God, who brought you out of the land of Egypt, out of the house of slavery' (5:6; cf. 6:21; 26:5–10). God appeals to a principle of reciprocity. Gratitude for past benefits, and not merely hope of future rewards and fear of future punishments, seems to be the primary motive for obeying God.

Are the provisions of the code the right ones to follow simply because God prescribes them, or can any other reason be given to show why any of them is better than another possible provision? Though Moses suggests that other nations will recognize the justice and wisdom of these laws, he does not say how they are to identify the features of a law that make it just and wise. Hence it is not clear how we are to show that other nations ought to admire these laws.

The lack of explicit justification in the Deuteronomic code, in contrast with Plato's *Laws,* helps to explain some elements of Jewish and Christian moral reflexion. If we try to understand why some actions are allowed and others prohibited by the code, or we wonder whether something should be added to or taken away from the code, we recognize that an unordered list of undifferentiated commands is inadequate, and we look for some rational order in them. We see, for instance, that not all the laws are equally important and not all have the same purpose; hence we might distinguish the moral from the ceremonial, or the more important from the less important, or the compulsory from the desirable. To mark these distinctions, we need to rely on principles that the code does not explicitly contain.

204. The Difference between the Moral and the Ceremonial Law

These distinctions between different elements of the law appear especially in the prophetic books. Different writers try to separate the principal from the subordinate requirements of the law. Sometimes they distinguish outward observance from the appropriate spirit of reverence towards God, and they insist that the observance is worthless without the spirit.[22] The Psalmist claims not only to observe the law, but also to love it, to admire its wisdom, and to delight in it whole-heartedly.[23] His attitude is discriminating, in so far as he takes reverence and delight in the law to matter more than simple observance in one's behaviour. But this attitude is directed equally towards all the laws, and he gives no reason for believing that any of them are wise and just. Perhaps he alludes to a reason when he mentions that

---

[21] Driver, *Dt.* 85, comments: 'The philanthropic motive assigned for the observance of the sabbath is in accordance with the spirit which prevails elsewhere in *Dt.*'. On the 'humanitarian' aspects of Deuteronomy see also Weinfeld, *Dt. 1–11* 21. Driver and Weinfeld cite 10:19; 12:12; 14:20–1, 29; 15:12–18 (contrast *Ex.* 21:1–11); 16:11,14; 24:17–20.

[22] 'For you have no delight in sacrifice; if I were to give a burnt offering, you would not be pleased. The sacrifice acceptable to God is a broken spirit; a broken and a contrite heart, O God, you will not despise' (*Ps.* 51:16–17).

[23] See esp. the whole of *Ps.* 119 (e.g., vv. 14–16: 'I delight in the way of your decrees as much as in all riches.... I will delight in your statutes; I will not forget your word'). Cf. *Ps.* 19:9–11, quoted in n114 below.

God the lawgiver is also God the creator, but he does not say how these two aspects of God give a reason for finding justice in the law.[24]

Elsewhere, however, the appropriate attitude to the law includes some capacity to discriminate. God condemns those who commit theft and adultery while they recite the words of the law.[25] The Psalmist implies that the violation of these commands is more serious than the violation of commands about animal sacrifices would be. Prophets and Psalmists often suggest that the appropriate spirit for the faithful observer of the law is also the spirit that puts the moral requirements above the ceremonial require-ments.[26] This discriminating attitude to the Mosaic law has no justification in the explicit provisions of the law itself. *Deuteronomy* does not distinguish moral from cere-monial commands, and therefore does not suggest that the moral commands are more important, still less that the ceremonial commands are unimportant. What explains the discrimination?

It would not be enough to say that the breach of the moral requirements results in harm to society. For, from the point of view of *Deuteronomy*, the same is true of any breach of the ceremonial requirements. God threatens to punish Israel for idolatry, sabbath-breaking, and eating unclean foods, no less than for oppression of the poor or slaves, or for toleration of theft or murder. To distinguish the moral from the ceremonial, we need to say that the harm resulting from violations of the moral parts of the law results even apart from divine punishments. These laws that benefit individuals and society by their observance (and not simply because of divine favour resulting from their observance) are especially prominent in prayers for the welfare of society. Hence the Psalmist asks God to give the king justice.[27]

The moral law is not always sharply distinguished from other aspects of the law. When the historical books mention the different kings who did not do 'what was right in the sight of the Lord', they refer equally to religious, ceremonial, and moral observances and violations. The successors of Solomon both perform the wrong sorts of sacrifices and oppress the people.[28] Ahab and Jezebel, for instance, both encourage the priests of Baal and have Naboth murdered for refusing to sell his ancestral vineyard.[29]

Still, some division between the moral and the ceremonial is fairly clear, though not completely sharp. Injustice, fraud, and theft appear regularly in the list of grave offences

[24] 'Your hands have made me and fashioned me; give me understanding that I may learn your commandments' (*Ps.* 119:73). *Ps.* 19 suggests the same connexion between God as creator and God as wise legislator: 'The heavens are telling the glory of God (v.1) ... The law of the Lord is perfect ...' (v.7). Cf. *Is.* 45:19: 'I did not say to the offspring of Jacob, "Seek me in chaos". I the Lord speak the truth. I declare what is right.'

[25] 'But to the wicked God says: "What right have you to recite my statutes, or take my covenant on your lips? For you hate discipline, and cast my words behind you. You make friends with a thief when you see one, and you keep company with adulterers."' (*Ps.* 50:16–18).

[26] 'With what shall I come before the Lord ...? Shall I come before him with burnt offerings ...? He has told you, O mortal, what is good; and what does the Lord require of you but to do justice, and to love kindness, and to walk humbly with your God?' (*Mic.* 6:6–8).

[27] 'May he judge your people with righteousness, and your poor with justice. May the mountains yield prosperity for the people, and the hills in righteousness. May he defend the cause of the poor of the people, give deliverance to the needy, and crush the oppressor' (*Ps.* 72:2–4; cf. vv. 12–14).

[28] Sacrifices: see *1 Kgs.* 13:1–3. Oppression: 'Now, whereas my father laid on you a heavy yoke, I will add to your yoke. My father disciplined you with whips, but I will discipline you with scorpions' (*1 Kgs.* 12:11).

[29] Naboth: *1 Kg.* 21.

that are contrasted with failure to fulfil the laws about sacrifice.[30] But it is not clear what these grave offences have in common, or why they are grave. Ezekiel's summary account of a righteous person requires generosity and justice, and abstention from idolatry, from adultery, and from approaching a woman during her menstrual period (*Ezk.* 18:6).[31] The insertion of this one ritual offence suggests that the distinction between the moral and the ceremonial is implicitly recognized, but not completely clear.

No OT book appeals explicitly to a principle of reciprocity in order to explain a law. But we have found an implicit appeal to such a principle in the defence of laws about freeing slaves. The story of Uriah the Hittite appeals to reciprocity as a more general principle (*2Sam.* 11:2–12:23). After David has seduced Bathsheba, and arranged for Uriah to be killed in battle, the prophet Nathan tells David the story of the poor man with his one ewe lamb that the rich man took away from him. When David condemns the rich man, Nathan tells him that his condemnation of the rich man applies to himself as well.[32] David can now see how what he has done is similar in the relevant ways to the action of the rich man who 'had no pity', because he did not consider the situation of the poor man who had only the one ewe lamb. David recognizes, when his own interests and desires are not involved, that the rich man acted unjustly, because he did not consider what he would reasonably have wanted if he had been in the situation of the poor man. He admits that this parallel applies to himself, since he did not consider what he would reasonably have wanted in the situation of Uriah.

In this case the appeal to the point of view of the victim does not involve past experience, as the appeal to slavery in Egypt did. It involves an appeal to an impartial judgment between the benefits and harms of the agent and the victim, and what it would be reasonable to want if the circumstances were reversed. From this point of view, David admits that he violated the command against murder by killing Uriah.[33] He might have answered that he did not actually kill Uriah, but simply arranged to have him placed in a dangerous position where he might have been placed anyhow; in this way he might claim to have avoided any violation of the commandment prohibiting murder. But when he thinks about his action from an impartial point of view, and so recognizes what he was really trying to do, he sees that this defence fails.

Reflexion on these breaches of the law suggests that they are wrong because, apart from any command, they inflict a harm on another person that one would reasonably want not to suffer oneself if one were in the position of the other. We are required to do for others what we would reasonably want for ourselves in their position. In considering what we owe to another, we are required to consider the other's interests and our own impartially, by considering what we would reasonably want, and using that as a guide to action that may benefit the other at our own expense.

---

[30] See *Am.* 5:10–11: 'They hate the one who reproves in the gate, and they abhor the one who speaks the truth. Therefore, because you trample on the poor . . . you have built houses of hewn stone, but you shall not live in them . . .'. Cf. 2:6–8; 4:1; 5:21–4; 8:4–6. Cf. the description of the just person in *Ps.* 15.

[31] This prohibition is not repeated in the similar summaries in 18:10–17.

[32] 'Then David's anger was greatly kindled against the man. He said to Nathan, "As the Lord lives, the man who has done this deserves to die; he shall restore the lamb fourfold, because he did this thing, and because he had no pity." Nathan said to David, "You are the man!" ' (*2Sam.* 12:5–7).

[33] 'You have struck down Uriah the Hittite with the sword, and have taken his wife to be your wife, and have killed him with the sword of the Ammonites' (12:9).

This reasoning helps to distinguish the moral from the ceremonial law. The command to offer sacrifices does not allow a similar justification by appeal to what one can defend from an impartial point of view. The moral demand for an impartial point of view is summed up in one commandment, not included in the Decalogue. In Leviticus, a series of moral prohibitions is followed by the requirement to love one's neighbour as oneself, which is immediately followed by a prohibition on allowing different species of animals to inter-breed.[34]

This juxtaposition of a moral with a ritual command might be taken to show that the code does not distinguish commands of these two types.[35] The command to love our neighbour is not explained; nor is it given any special status in the code. It appears neither in *Deuteronomy* nor in *Exodus*, and even *Leviticus* does not say that it underlies any of the other laws. Still, its position at the end of a series of moral commands and before a series of ceremonial commands may be significant. The author may indicate some recognition of the appropriateness of this command as a summary of the moral commands, and of its inappropriateness as a summary of the ceremonial commands about mixing animals, crops, or fields. Love of one's neighbour as oneself does not seem to explain, apart from a divine command, why one should not weave linen with wool.

Even this brief consideration of OT attitudes to the law should warn us against unqualified acceptance of a tempting generalization. It is tempting to say that the OT attitude to morality is legal and theocentric, covering morality only as a part, not sharply distinguished from other parts, of a way of life that consists essentially in the observance of divine commands and prohibitions with no further rational basis. This generalization fits the outward form of the Deuteronomic code accurately enough; it gives us reason not to find in the code any clear division between the moral and the ceremonial. But if we restrict ourselves to this generalization based on the Deuteronomic code, we overlook the implicit distinction that is drawn both in the code itself and in the comments of other OT writers. The view that principles for right relations between people are accessible to natural reason and can be justified by appeal to an impartial consideration of interests is certainly not the OT view of morality, but it is a theme in the OT; without it, the ways in which the different obligations of the law are distinguished become unintelligible. An attempt to understand morality on the basis of natural reason, apart from divine revelation, is not alien to the OT; on the contrary, some features of the OT require us to make this attempt.[36]

OT views on morality are not exhausted by the comments on the divine law and its different provisions. A large part of the OT consists of the 'sapiential' books, in particular *Proverbs*, *Ecclesiastes*, *Wisdom*, and *Sirach*.[37] These books advocate wisdom in the conduct of one's individual life; many passages make no essential reference to God or to the divine law. Advice

[34] 'You shall not hate in your heart anyone of your kin; you shall reprove your neighbour, or you will incur guilt yourself. You shall not take vengeance or bear a grudge against any of your people, but you shall love your neighbour as yourself: I am the Lord. You shall keep my statutes. You shall not let your animals breed with a different kind; you shall not sow your fields with two kinds of seed; nor shall you put on a garment made of two different materials' (*Lv.* 19:17–19).

[35] Sanderson comments on this. See *Obl.* 4.16.

[36] See Barr, *BFNT* 100: 'The law itself, then, in its content has numerous suggestions that point towards operations akin to those of natural law or natural theology'. Cf. Barton, *EOT*, esp. ch. 4. Philo, *Dec.* i 132, explains how the violation of the commandment forbidding murder is also a violation of the laws of nature.

[37] On the sapiential books see Scott, *PE* Intro., esp. xix–xxv.

to avoid laziness, dissipation, flattery, indebtedness, difficult wives, false friends, prostitutes, compromising situations, risky loans, and so on, is justified by the prospect of bad future consequences in the present life. The consequences can be seen if we consider the actions and their effects on us and on other people, without any assumptions about God's disapproval.

Advice to avoid immorality that does not seem directly harmful, from this narrow prudential point of view, is sometimes justified by the threat of divine punishment inflicted on the wrongdoer in this life. The predominant tone of the sapiential books implies that the wise person will be just, merciful, and God-fearing because that will be a more effective means of securing the very same benefits that the grasping, avaricious, treacherous, and cruel person tries to gain by his actions. In the case of the self-regarding virtues, the effects of actions themselves bring desirable 'natural consequences'. But in the case of other-regarding virtues, it is not so clear that our actions have the natural consequences we would like; they are bad for us only because God attaches unwelcome 'artificial consequences' through the sanctions of rewards and punishments. These assumptions are as prominent in the sapiential books as in many of the Psalms. They are the assumptions that Glaucon and Adeimantus in *Republic* ii condemn as the common, but mistaken, conception of why it is worth our while to be just.[38] Plato could easily have found numerous passages in the OT to illustrate the attitude he condemns.

This attitude raises a question: If justice and mercy do not seem to pay, and if the God-fearing suffer misfortunes, what point is there in being just? It is not only Plato who raises this question. The author of *Job* raises it at length and does not explicitly answer it. The author of *Ecclesiastes* raises the same question. He does not always assume that wickedness will meet divine punishment; he recognizes that the wicked flourish and the just suffer in this life, and he does not believe in an afterlife to redress the balance. He concludes that there is no answer (*Eccl.* 8:10–9:2), that the whole course of the world is 'vanity', and the best thing is to enjoy our brief life.[39]

The sapiential books usually do not express this degree of doubt about divine justice; they assume that God rewards some actions and punishes others. They do not usually say why God rewards and punishes this or that particular action. Lazy workers and those who give short weight are condemned, but the reason for the condemnation is not clear.[40] Sometimes, however, the writers suggest that the wise person's actions benefit others as well.[41] They

---

[38] See Plato, §50.

[39] 'Everything that confronts them is vanity, since the same fate comes to all, to the righteous and the wicked, to the good and the evil, to the clean and the unclean, to those who sacrifice and those who do not sacrifice . . . The living know that they will die, but the dead know nothing; they have no more reward, and even the memory of them is lost . . . Go, eat your bread with enjoyment, and drink your wine with a merry heart, for God has long ago approved what you do' (*Eccl.* 9:1–7). Clement, *Strom.* v 14, 90.2, suggests that Epicurus derived his belief that the universe is without purpose (*automaton*) from a misunderstanding of the remark in *Eccl.* that all is vanity (*mataiotês*). Though some connexion between *Eccl.* and Greek thought has sometimes been suggested, the suggestion has no firm basis. See Rankin, *IB* v 14–15; Scott, *PE* 196–7.

[40] 'Like vinegar to the teeth, and smoke to the eyes, so are the lazy to their employers' (*Pr.* 10:26). 'A false balance is an abomination to the Lord, but an accurate weight is his delight' (11:1). *Lv.* 19.35–6 and *Dt.* 25.13–16 also appeal directly to God to explain the prohibition on false weights. Perhaps a social ground is given for the prohibition on bribes at *Dt.* 16:19–20: 'You must not pervert justice; you must not show partiality; and you must not take bribes, for a bribe blinds the eyes of the wise and subverts the cause of those who are in the right. Justice, and only justice, you shall follow, that you may live and occupy the land that the Lord your God is giving you.'

[41] 'When it goes well with the righteous, the city rejoices, and when the wicked perish there is jubilation. By the blessing of the upright a city is exalted, but it is overthrown by the mouth of the wicked' (*Pr.* 11:10–11).

take it for granted that God does not reward and punish arbitrarily, but rewards those actions that would benefit the community whether or not he rewarded them. But the fact that certain actions benefit the community is not offered as a reason for pursuing them. The rather narrow range of consequences normally taken to constitute reasons for acting one way or another is an obvious weakness, from the moral point of view, in the outlook that underlies this prudential advice.

But the authors of the sapiential books have more to say about the basis of their instructions. Some aspects of wisdom consist in self-confined calculating prudence about one's own life, but the wise person also shares to some degree in the wisdom that guides God in the creation of the universe, the course of history, and the ordering of human society. God's justice is equally shown in the natural universe and in divine provisions for relations between human beings.[42] Wise people do not simply plan for their own lives with a view to their own wealth, reputation, and security; they also do their part in the wise and just ordering of relations between human beings, and thereby share in God's justice and mercy.

Sometimes the authors suggest that participation in this wisdom is not simply a means to further material benefits but a good to be chosen for its own sake.[43] *Job* concludes with an affirmation of God's wisdom in creation, implying that there is more to human wisdom than the narrow prudence by which Job's interlocutors have measured both divine and human morality (*Job* 42:1–6). Earlier, the book praises wisdom; it suggests that human wisdom consists in acceptance of the divine wisdom that is concerned with the good of creation and of human society (28:25–38).

In these places the sapiential books offer more than practical advice to secure material benefits. Someone who argues that observance of the moral requirements of the law is good for an individual apart from material consequences for the individual's self-confined interest argues against the usual tendency of the sapiential books, and of the OT as a whole. But such an argument can also legitimately claim support in the OT. If we are concerned to discover the significance of the OT for later moral theory, we need to recognize the different conclusions that can intelligibly be derived from it. It is not unreasonable for Clement to find a parallel in the OT for the Stoic view that virtue is to be chosen for its own sake and is sufficient for happiness.[44]

205. Law and Gospel

These different features of the moral outlook of the OT help to explain some of the assumptions that the NT does not question, and some of the questions that NT writers take to be worth raising.

---

[42] Solomon prays: 'O God of my ancestors and Lord of mercy, who have made all things by your word, and by your wisdom have formed humankind to have dominion over the creatures you have made, and rule the world in holiness and righteousness, and pronounce judgment in uprightness of soul . . .' (*Wis.* 9:1–3).

[43] 'If riches are a desirable possession in life, what is richer than wisdom, the active cause of all things? . . . And if anyone loves righteousness, her labours are virtues; for she teaches self-control and prudence, justice and courage; nothing in life is more profitable for mortals than these' (*Wis.* 8:5–7).

[44] See Clement, *Strom.* v 14, 96.5: 'The barbarian [sc. Jewish] philosophy knows that only the fine is good and that virtue is self-sufficient for happiness . . .'. Clement quotes *Dt.* 30:20, which is not the best passage to support his point.

No NT writer challenges the view that the requirements of morality are divine laws, attended with rewards and punishments, and that the hope of reward is an appropriate reason for observing them. On the contrary, emphasis on reward becomes all the more confident. Job's doubts about the advice of the sapiential writers rest on the assumption that the present life is the only one that need be considered. The doctrine of immortality gives an answer to Job's worries; Dives and Lazarus face the reversal of their fortunes in the next life (*Lk.* 6:20–5; 16:25). Paul insists that if the doctrine of immortality is false, Christians 'are of all people most to be pitied' (*1Cor.* 15:19).

Different NT writers suggest, however, that this is not a sufficient account of the reasons to keep the moral law. Jesus suggests that the goodness and perfection of God should be a model for a human moral outlook, just because of its goodness and perfection.[45] He rejects the attitude of those who turn to him in the hope of divine rewards, and reminds them that they have already learned what is good through the moral law.[46] The moral law has a special status among the commandments. When Jesus is asked which of the commandments is greatest, he picks out the requirement to love God and to love one's neighbour as oneself. His interlocutors recognize that his choice of these two commandments distinguishes the moral from the ceremonial law.[47]

These aspects of the teaching of Jesus might suggest that he simply distinguishes the moral from the ceremonial law and urges more constant observance of the moral law; that is why he criticizes those who make a parade of their ritual observances and neglect the moral aspects of the law.[48] He claims he has not come to abolish the law and the prophets, but to fulfil them (*Mt.* 5:17–20), and he includes the ceremonial commands among the binding commands of the law. But he agrees with the prophets who give priority to the moral over the ceremonial commands. Hence, when he tells the disciples that their justice has to exceed that of the scribes and Pharisees, we might take him to enjoin observance of the moral law.[49]

206. Natural Law

How do we identify the moral law and distinguish it from other aspects of the Mosaic law? Some passages in the OT suggest that at least some parts of the law are not the exclusive

---

[45] 'You have heard that it was said, "You shall love your neighbour and hate your enemy". But I say to you, Love your enemies and pray for those who persecute you, so that you may be children of your Father in heaven; for he makes his sun rise on the evil and on the good, and sends rain on the righteous and on the unrighteous.... Be perfect, therefore, as your heavenly Father is perfect' (*Mt.* 5:43–8).

[46] '... a man ran up and knelt before him, and asked him, "Good teacher, what must I do to inherit eternal life?" Jesus said to him, "Why do you call me good? No one is good but God alone. You know the commandments: 'You shall not murder...'"' (*Mk.* 10:17–19).

[47] 'Then the scribe said to him, "You are right, Teacher; ... this is much more important than all whole burnt offerings and sacrifice." When Jesus saw that he answered wisely, he said to him, "You are not far from the kingdom of God."' (*Mk.* 12:32–4).

[48] See *Mt.* 23:23: 'Woe to you, scribes and Pharisees, hypocrites! For you tithe mint, dill, and cumin, and have neglected the weightier matters of the law: justice and mercy and faith'. Davies and Allison, *Mt.* ad loc, quote Jewish sources that distinguish more and less important elements in the law. Cf. *Mt.* 15:1–20.

[49] See *Mt.* 5:20. 'Justice', *dikaiosunê*, corresponds to 'righteousness' in most English versions. I have preferred 'justice', partly because it appropriately recalls Plato's and Aristotle's broad use of '*dikaiosunê*' (see §§59, 117), and partly to display the connexion with 'justify' (*dikaioun* and cognates); see n87 below.

possession of the Jews; foreigners are supposed to be able to recognize the wisdom of the Jewish laws. Philo finds support for this universal access to the law in the story of Abraham, who was faithful and just without the guidance of a written law. Abraham fulfilled the requirements of the law 'not having been taught by written words, but by unwritten nature, having been eager to follow them by healthy and uncorrupted impulses' (*Abr.* 275). Philo concludes: 'According to some, he was law-abiding (*nomimos*). But in fact, as our account showed, he was [a] law himself, and an unwritten statute' (276).

Philo's use of this phrase 'a law himself' for the virtuous person recalls similar phrases in Aristotle. The *Politics* mentions the 'god among human beings' who has to be allowed to rule monarchically because he cannot reasonably be restrained by laws that are meant to regulate equals; these superior people 'are themselves [a] law' (*Pol.* 1284a23). A more helpful parallel appears in the discussion of the virtue connected with wit. The appropriately cultivated person knows where to draw the line between innocent jokes and the sort of abuse (*loidorein*) that is prohibited by the law; and so he is 'a sort of law to himself' (*EN* 1128a32).

In speaking of Abraham as being his own law and as relying on nature, Philo implies that the moral law is accessible to everyone by nature. Though he does not use the phrase 'natural law', the phrase captures his claim about Abraham. St Paul uses similar terms to describe the capacity of the Gentiles to grasp the moral law. He says they are 'law to themselves' without the guidance of the Mosaic law.[50] They grasp the requirements of morality without external legislation because their conscience guides them.[51] Their own judgment of their actions either endorses or condemns the actions, and Paul implies that it reaches the right conclusion often enough for some of them to observe the moral law.

Paul goes beyond both Aristotle's and Philo's use of the conception of a law to oneself. They both use it to refer to virtuous people, in contrast to people who are not laws to themselves; virtuous people differ from the rest in not needing external law. St Paul, by contrast, seems to take Gentiles indiscriminately, and not only those who regularly observe the law, to be a law to themselves. Their self-condemnation as well as their self-approval indicates the operation of their internal law.[52]

Paul's references to nature and to law encourage Christian writers to incorporate the Stoic conception of natural law. Lactantius uses Cicero to summarize the Stoic view.[53] He affirms that the natural law described by the Stoics is also the moral law set out in the Scriptures.[54]

---

[50] 'For whenever Gentiles, those who have not law, by nature do the things belonging to the law, these, not having law, are law to themselves, <since> they show the work of the law written in their hearts, their conscience co-witnessing, and their reasonings among one another accusing or else excusing' (*Rm.* 2:14–15). On the distinction between 'law' and 'the law' see Sanday and Headlam, *R*58. They paraphrase part of the passage: 'For whenever any of them instinctively put in practice the precepts of the Law, their own moral sense supplies them with the law they need' (54).

[51] This passage from Romans is used in the account of conscience in *Gaudium et Spes* (in Alberigo et al., *Decreta*), §16: 'In the depths of conscience a human being discovers a law that he does not give to himself, but that he is required to obey, and whose voice, always calling him to love and to do the good and to avoid the evil, sounds in the ears of his heart where it is needed: Do this, avoid that. For a human being has a law written in his heart by God, obedience to which is his dignity and according to which he will be judged (cf. *Rm.* 2:14–16). Conscience is the most secret core and sanctuary of a human being, in which he is alone with God, whose voice echoes in his depths. . . . In a wonderful manner conscience reveals the law that is fulfilled by love of God and of one's neighbour.'

[52] On different interpretations of this passage see §232.

[53] Lactantius, *Div. Inst.* vi 8.6–9 = Cic. *Rep.* iii 33, quoted at §178n12.

[54] 'Who that is acquainted with the mystery of God could so significantly expound the law of God, as a man far removed from the knowledge of the truth has set forth that law? But I consider that they who speak true things

Through the Scriptures we can discern the content of the natural law more fully than pagan philosophers could ever discern it, but the philosophers and the Scriptures rely on the same basic principles.

Though the NT writers never try to show in detail how the moral law of the OT expresses the basic principles of the natural law, as the Stoics conceive it, they assume that their views about the vices to be condemned and the virtues to be praised correspond with enlightened pagan views. When Paul lists the vices found in the contemporary world and tells Christians to avoid them, the vices are familiar.[55] If Christians replace these vices with the appropriate virtues, they will both deserve and receive the praise and commendation of their non-Christian neighbours.[56] That is why the Roman authorities will generally (though not invariably) recognize that they are good citizens.[57]

And so when Paul follows Jesus in taking the command to love one's neighbour as a summary of the law in relation to other people, he also takes it to sum up the requirements of the natural law.[58] The Christian gospel sets out clearly the moral principles that Christians share with Jews and pagans, and (in Paul's view) traces their practical consequences.

207. Perfectionism

This description of the moral doctrine of the NT is not false, but it is incomplete. While it is legitimate to emphasize the connexions that the NT writers see between Christian morality and the principles of pagan morality, it would be one-sided to overlook the aspects of Christian moral doctrine that do not fit so easily into an account of Christian morality as a forceful presentation of the requirements of natural law. That 'purely rational' account of Christian morality (as we may describe it) is popular among 18th-century rationalists.[59]

We have already noticed some elements of Christian morality that do not seem to fit the purely rational account. Though Jesus appeals to moral principles that his hearers already accept, he seems to go beyond them to some rather questionable extremes. He commends those who do not simply do what most people would regard as fulfilling their moral obligations, but also 'hunger and thirst for justice' (*Mt.* 5:6). When he contrasts the provisions of the old law with his instructions ('You have heard that it was said . . . But I say to you . . .'), he urges people to go beyond the standard interpretation of the moral law.

---

unconsciously are to be so regarded as though they divined under the influence of some spirit. But if he had also known or explained what precepts constituted the law itself as well as he saw the force and purport of the divine law, he would not have discharged the office of a philosopher, but of a prophet. And because he was unable to do this, we must do it, to whom the law itself has been delivered by the one great master and ruler of all, God' (*Div. Inst.* vi 8.10–12). On the sequel see §228 below.

[55] See, e.g., *Rm.* 1:29–32; *Gal.* 5:19–21.

[56] See, e.g., *Phil.* 4:5: 'Let your *epieikes* be known to everyone'. This term is rendered by 'gentleness', 'forbearance', and 'moderation' in different English versions. (Vulg. has 'modestia'.) Cf. *2Cor.* 10:1; *1Pet.* 2:18. The contrast between *epieikeia* and misguidedly rigid concern for justice in *EN* v 10 suggests a suitable sense for the NT passages. Sometimes *epieikeia* is connected with *philanthrôpia* (see *TDNT* ii 589–90).

[57] *1Pet.* 3:13–14: 'Now who will harm you if you are eager to do what is good? But even if you do suffer for your justice (*dia dikaiosunên*), you are blessed.' Cf. *Rm.* 13:3–4.

[58] See *Rm.* 13:8–10, quoted below at n73.

[59] The rationalist position is defended by Clarke and Balguy; see, e.g., Clarke, *Disc.* Prop. x, 675 H. Waterland attacks their view in 'Remarks'.

Whereas most people take the command to love one's neighbour to allow limited concern, confined to those who are close to us or connected to us in some way, he demands love of one's enemies and persecutors.[60]

We might take Jesus to be asserting that the command to love one's neighbour is an adequate summary of the law, but inadequate to express the moral ideal that he recommends. When he demands justice that 'exceeds the justice of the scribes and Pharisees' (Mt. 5:20), he might be taken to expose the ethical inadequacy of the old moral law. But this does not seem to be his view. When he is asked for an interpretation of the command to love one's neighbour, he tells the parable of the Good Samaritan.[61] Though this does not say directly how 'neighbour' is to be understood in the command, it suggests that the command requires us to treat everyone we encounter who needs our help as a 'neighbour'. When Jesus claims to describe a more complete form of justice than that of the Scribes and Pharisees, he does not take himself to be criticizing the moral law, but to be criticizing them for not grasping its full implications.

But how is this criticism to be justified? If we take Christians to be advocating a more complete observance of the moral law and recognized virtues, we can fairly ask whether the outlook they advocate really expresses the aims of a genuinely virtuous person. We might be inclined to answer that Christian moral precepts seem to display unreasonable extremism, even fanaticism; the contrast between Christian and Aristotelian precepts seems rather sharp, and does not seem to tell in favour of the Christian precepts. Jesus forbids not only murder, but even insulting words; not only adultery, but even looking lustfully on a woman. He tells us to give to whoever asks us, and not to withhold our cloak if someone takes our coat.[62] When the rich young man who claims to have kept the commandments asks Jesus where he still falls short, Jesus tells him that he needs to sell all he has and give it to the poor.[63] In the face of such advice one might not blame the young man for going away grieving. The instructions do not seem to give a plausible interpretation of the demands of the virtues.

We might object that Christian precepts seem to insist on the demands of one virtue in isolation, and thereby seem to forget that the demands of each virtue are partly regulated by the demands of other virtues and of the goods promoted by the virtues. Selling all we have and giving it to the poor may fulfil the demands of benevolence to these particular people, but it may evidently leave us less well equipped to fulfil the demands of other virtues that require the good use of our material resources.

[60] See Mt. 5:43–8, quoted at n45 above.
[61] See Lk. 10:25 : 'Just then a lawyer stood up to test Jesus. "Teacher", he said, "what must I do to inherit eternal life?" He said to him, "What is written in the law? What do you read there?" He answered, "You shall love the Lord your God with all your heart, and with all your soul, and with all your strength, and with all your mind; and your neighbour as yourself." And he said to him, "You have given the right answer; do this, and you will live." But wanting to justify himself, he asked Jesus, "And who is my neighbour?" '
[62] Mt. 5:21–42.
[63] Mt. 19:16–22: 'Then someone came to him and said, "Teacher, what good deed must I do, to have eternal life?" And he said to him, "Why do you ask me about what is good? There is only one who is good. If you wish to enter into life, keep the commandments." He said to him, "Which ones?" And Jesus said, "You shall not murder; You shall not commit adultery; You shall not steal; You shall not bear false witness, Honour your father and mother: also, You shall love your neighbor as yourself." The young man said to him, "I have kept all these; what do I still lack?" Jesus said to him, "If you wish to be perfect, go, sell your possessions, and give the money to the poor, and you will have treasure in heaven; then come, follow me." When the young man heard this word, he went away grieving, for he had many possessions.'

Christian moralists who consider these precepts of Christian ethics soon recognize that they cannot be treated as practical instructions that might be expected to replace the Decalogue.[64] But if that is not their point, what is their point?

208. The Moral Law and the Consciousness of Sin

The apparently extreme demands of Christian moral precepts help to explain another way in which Jesus goes beyond a simple emphasis on the observance of the moral law. In his view, a clear awareness of the requirements of the law ought to result in an equally clear awareness of our failure to keep the law. He contrasts the Pharisee who regards himself as a scrupulous observer of the moral and the ceremonial law with the tax-collector who admits that he is a sinner, and he commends the attitude of the self-confessed sinner over the self-righteous keeper of the law.[65]

When Jesus says that the tax-collector rather than the Pharisee went home 'justified' (*dedikaiômenos*), he anticipates a central theme in St Paul's account of the Christian moral outlook. According to Paul, Gentiles and Jews alike have violated the demands of the moral law. The Gentiles have turned away from their natural knowledge of God and the moral law, and have turned to lust, greed, and conflict (*Rm.* 1:18–32). The Jews have an advantage, since the details of the moral law have been revealed to them.[66] But they have not used this advantage properly; they have turned away from God through sin, no less than the Gentiles have.[67]

The role of the moral law—either the less specific natural law known to everyone or the more specific instructions of the Mosaic Law—is to make us aware of our failure to meet its moral demands. The explicit divine commands in the Mosaic law make it possible to count up sins in detail, and they transform sins into transgressions.[68] The more clearly we grasp the demands of the law, the more clearly we recognize our failure to satisfy them.

How can Paul defend this apparently pessimistic view of the effects of our awareness of the moral law? His pessimism might be easier to understand if he were referring to all the details of the Mosaic law, which, according to one count, amounted to 613 distinct commands. But though the Pharisee may have these commands in mind (since he mentions his regular

---

[64] Clement, *Quis* 11–19, explains Jesus' advice to the rich man to sell all he has as advice to get rid of disruptive passions and desires.

[65] 'He also told this parable to some who trusted in themselves that they were just and regarded others with contempt: "Two men went up into the temple to pray, one a Pharisee and the other a tax collector. The Pharisee, standing by himself, was praying thus: 'God, I thank you that I am not like other people: thieves, rogues, adulterers, or even like this tax collector. I fast twice a week; I give a tenth of all my income.' But the tax collector, standing far off, would not even look up to heaven, but was beating his breast and saying, 'God, be merciful to me a sinner!' I tell you, this man went down to his house justified rather than the other; for all who exalt themselves will be humbled, but all who humble themselves will be exalted."' (*Lk.* 18:9–14).

[66] 'Then what advantage has the Jew? Or what is the value of circumcision? Much in every way. To begin with, the Jews are entrusted with the oracles of God' (*Rm.* 3:1–2).

[67] 'Are we Jews any better off? No, not at all; for we have already charged that all, both Jews and Greeks, are under the power of sin . . . For "no human being will be justified in his [sc. God's] sight" by deeds prescribed by the law, for through the law comes the knowledge [or 'recognition', *epignôsis*] of sin' (*Rm.* 3:9–20).

[68] '. . . sin was indeed in the world before the law was given, but sin is not reckoned [or 'counted up', *ellogeitai*] when there is no law' (*Rm.* 5:13). 'For the law brings wrath; but where there is no law, neither is there violation (*parabasis*)' (4:15).

fasting), Paul is not referring to them. Once we distinguish the moral from the ceremonial law, we can subtract quite a few from the 613 commands. Paul has in mind our failure to observe the moral commands. But if this is what he refers to, we might think his verdict is prejudiced. The Decalogue is not easy to observe for everyone all the time, but one might doubt whether it is so difficult that we should all be constantly oppressed by our failure to observe it.

Paul's pessimism is easier to understand if we take the demands of the law to include not only the provisions of the Decalogue, but also the various perfectionist demands that Jesus imposes on his disciples and on some who incautiously consult him on moral questions. If the law demands the perfection of those who love their enemies, turn the other cheek, comply with every request, and give all they have to the poor, we might well agree that we sin by falling short of these demands of the law. In the light of these demands, we should endorse the response of the tax-collector rather than the Pharisee.

But if Paul relies on Jesus' perfectionist interpretation of the law, has he not weakened his case? We will identify ourselves with the tax-collector only if we accept the perfectionist demands; but we might regard these as a fanatical exaggeration of morality, and if we reject the exaggeration, we may look sceptically at Paul's claim that sin is inescapable for all of us all the time. He seems to exaggerate the disease in order to commend his cure, but we might think a more moderate cure is more appropriate for a more realistic assessment of the disease.

If we are to understand Jesus' apparent perfectionism better, we need to pay less attention to his specific precepts. Though he tells the rich young man to sell all he has and give it to the poor, he does not give this advice or instruction to everyone. The tax-collector Zacchaeus does not even give up his occupation, but he promises to make generous restitution for previous dishonesty and to give half of his possessions to the poor.[69] If he defrauded taxpayers, he violated the command against stealing, but in the scale of his restitution and in the promise to give away half of his possessions, he went beyond any requirement that could plausibly be derived from the Mosaic law.

The extreme and exaggerated elements in Jesus' moral teaching seem to convey the same point that Zacchaeus conveys in his promise. Jesus warns against the understanding of the moral law as a set of instructions specifying duties that can be fulfilled by particular actions. A civil code of law that threatens punishment ought to be confined to such instructions; for we reasonably want to be in a position to know whether we are liable to punishment, and we want to know what to do in order to avoid it. If the instructions were too imprecise for us to know what to do to fulfil them, or if they were infinitely demanding, so that we could never know whether we had done enough, they would be interfering and oppressive. Jesus implies that the moral law is different from a civil code in this respect. He fulfils the law (Mt. 5:17) by insisting that it requires a degree of perfection that goes beyond behavioural conformity. A code that requires behavioural conformity is a reasonable concession to human limitations, but it does not capture the point of the moral law.[70]

---

[69] 'Zacchaeus stood there and said to the Lord, "Look, half of my possessions, Lord, I will give to the poor; and if I have defrauded any one of anything, I pay back four times as much." Then Jesus said to him, "Today salvation has come to this house, because he too is a son of Abraham. For the Son of Man came to seek out and to save the lost." ' (Lk. 19:8–10).

[70] 'He said to them, "It was because you were so hard-hearted that Moses allowed you to divorce your wives, but from the beginning it was not so. And I say to you: whoever divorces his wife, except for unchastity, and marries another,

As Jesus understands the moral law, its point is to prescribe the love of one's neighbour as oneself, without the restrictions that human limitations impose on this attitude. The normal understanding of the love of one's neighbour includes some allowance for ordinary attitudes that restrict the degree of concern that can reasonably be expected. We are allowed to hate our enemies provided that we show some consideration for those who are more closely connected with us. We are allowed to take an eye for an eye and a tooth for a tooth, provided that we go no further than this in taking revenge. But the point of these commands, as Jesus understands it, is not the positive command both to love one's neighbour and to hate one's enemy, but the positive command to love one's neighbour on the assumption that we inevitably hate our enemies. We would be better off if we lacked the motives that—as things are—make it reasonable to restrict the scope of the command to love one's neighbour to those who are not our enemies.

St Paul accepts the same perfectionist understanding of the point of the moral law. The tenth commandment of the Decalogue is different from the others in so far as it prohibits desires rather than actions.[71] In explaining his inability to keep the law, Paul takes this commandment rather than the other nine for his example, suggesting that the commandment itself gives an opportunity to sin.[72] To support his case, he interprets the commandment quite broadly. The commandment prohibits inappropriate desire for anything that belongs to one's neighbour, understanding this as a desire to harm one's neighbour. I covet my neighbour's car by wanting to steal his battered Ford, but I do not—apparently—violate the commandment if I want a battered Ford, or if I want a new Lexus in order to humiliate him when I park it next to his battered Ford. A moderate and realistic interpretation of the commandment might say: Given that you desire honour, wealth, status, and superiority, don't take this desire so far that you try to steal from your neighbour. Paul, however, assumes a more extreme and perfectionist understanding of the commandment, taking it to prohibit all 'coveting', and hence all inappropriate desire.

The contrast between the moderate and the extreme interpretation of the commandment makes it easier to see why Paul supposes that the law gives sin its opportunity. The moderate interpretation takes it for granted that we have inappropriate desires for wealth and domination, and simply tells us not to go as far as attempts to dispossess our neighbour. But if this is all the commandment says, it permits the inappropriate desires that might encourage us to steal from our neighbour. But if the point of the commandment is to prescribe proper consideration for our neighbour, ought it not to prohibit the more general desire (say) to get the better of my neighbour, and to prohibit the inappropriate desires that make his possessions seem attractive to us? This argument supports the extreme interpretation that takes the commandment to prohibit all coveting.

---

commits adultery." The disciples said to him, "If such is the case of a man with his wife, it is better not to marry." ' (Mt. 19:8–10).

[71] 'Neither shall you covet your neighbour's wife. Neither shall you desire your neighbour's house . . . or anything that belongs to your neighbour' (Dt. 5:21).

[72] 'What then should we say? That the law is sin? By no means! Yet, if it had not been for the law, I would not have known sin. I would not have known what it is to covet if the law had not said, "You shall not covet." But sin, seizing an opportunity in the commandment, produced in me all kinds of covetousness' (Rm. 7:7–8).

Paul accepts the extreme interpretation when he introduces the command to love one's neighbour. He follows Jesus in treating this command as a summary of the law.[73] But he agrees with Jesus (on the Good Samaritan) in taking love of one's neighbour to extend to everyone. We fulfil law by loving 'another' (*ton heteron*), not simply by loving our neighbour and hating our enemy. If we claim that the commandments are summed up in the commandment to love one's neighbour, we might mean (1) that all it takes to love our neighbour, in the relevant sense, is to avoid murder, adultery, etc., or (2) that the fulfilment of the commandments involves nothing less than the universal love of other people. Paul clearly intends the second claim. Love does no evil to another; it does not simply refrain from the different types of action prohibited by the Decalogue (on the moderate interpretation), but avoids all the evils that are not explicitly prohibited. And so when Paul says that love fulfils the law, he does not mean that it simply observes the law by avoiding explicitly prohibited behaviour. He means that it achieves the real aim of the law, according to the perfectionist interpretation.

If Paul is right in his claims about the point of the law, it is more reasonable for him to claim that no one keeps the law, and that the law brings the consciousness of sin. If we see that the law aims at mitigating the bad effects of misguided desires, but leaves the desires unmodified, anyone who agrees with the aim of the law should also agree that it would be better to modify the desires that make the prohibitions of the law necessary. Hence it is reasonable to claim, as Jesus and Paul both claim, that the right interpretation of the demands of the law is the perfectionist interpretation.

At this point, however, one might protest that different parts of Paul's perfectionism are in conflict. For he admits that if we take seriously the perfectionist aspect of the moral law, we have to recognize our incapacity to keep the law, and our incapacity to deal with our tendencies to rebel against the law. This recognition creates an acute sense of sin. Might we not argue that if perfectionism has this result, it cannot after all be the right way to look at the moral law? One might suppose it would be better to keep one's aspirations realistic than to be a perfectionist who is oppressed, and perhaps paralysed, by a sense of one's imperfection? If the sense of sin is self-inflicted, would we not be better off without it?

Jesus answers this objection by commending the tax-collector who asked God to be merciful to him as a sinner. According to Jesus, this man went home 'justified' (or 'vindicated').[74] This claim states briefly what Paul argues at length. If we recognize the demands of the moral law, and our inability to keep them, our conclusion need not be a paralysing and hopeless sense of sin; God through Christ provides the remedy for the condition that we recognize through reflexion on the law.[75]

---

[73] 'Owe no one anything, except to love one another; for the one who loves another has fulfilled law. For the commandments, "You shall not commit adultery, You shall not murder, You shall not steal, You shall not covet," and any other commandment, are summed up in this word, "You shall love your neighbour as yourself." Love does not do evil (*kakon*) to a neighbour; therefore love is the fulfilling of law' (*Rm.* 13:8–10).

[74] See n65 above.

[75] 'Wretched man that I am! Who will rescue me from this body of death? Thanks be to God through Jesus Christ our Lord!' (*Rm.* 7:24–5). Interpreters dispute about whether this passage refers to experience before or after justification and regeneration. Sanday and Headlam, *R*186, suggest that it might refer to either: '. . . whether the moment described is before or after the embracing of Christianity, in any case abstraction is made of all that is Christian. Law and the soul are brought face to face with each other, and there is nothing between them.' Cf. §222.

209. Justification

To explain how Paul understands the solution to the problem that he raises in his discussion of the demands of the law, we need to confront one of the most difficult and controversial areas of his theology. He takes up Jesus' claim that the tax-collector who prayed for God's mercy on him went home 'justified'. According to Paul, we are saved by the grace of God through faith in Christ for good works, so that we can fulfil the aims of morality that we would otherwise be unable to fulfil.[76] In 'by grace' Paul refers to God as the primary agent; God does not respond to our success in keeping the moral law. In 'through faith' he refers to the means; faith is the response elicited by God's unearned favour.

The understanding of God's unearned favour relies on our understanding of the point of the moral law. Morality aims at love of God and one's neighbour, free from the limits imposed by human aims and impulses that conflict with appropriate concern for oneself and one's neighbour. God has taken the lead in showing such love towards us without restriction or limitation.[77] The particular manifestation of divine love that is meant to elicit the response of faith and moral goodness is the life and death of Christ. He is mentioned as an 'atoning sacrifice' (or 'expiation', *hilasmos*) for human sin. The death and resurrection of Jesus are the means of securing justification by faith, because they express God's grace towards sinners.[78]

In speaking of Christ as a sacrifice, Paul represents him as a victim of human sin who also takes on himself the punishment that would otherwise fall on human beings for their sins. This conception of the atonement makes it a process of substitution and propitiation; God is angry at sin, but when an innocent person takes on the punishment that is due to the guilty, God's anger is removed because someone has suffered, and so he allows the guilty to go unpunished. If this is the moral basis of atonement for sin, it may reflect credit on Jesus for accepting the role of a substitute to be sacrificed, but it may appear to raise questions about the God who is willing to allow the suffering of an innocent person as a necessary but acceptable substitute for the suffering of the guilty. If God is willing not to punish the guilty, why should he insist on the suffering of an innocent person as a substitute?

These questions about the atonement have provided ample material both for critics of Christianity and for Christian theologians trying to explain and to defend the doctrine. Without going into these controversies, we may notice some aspects of the atonement that suggest something different from the propitiation of an angry God through innocent suffering. Jesus manifests the unrestricted love of one's neighbour that is the aim of the moral law. Since he was completely human, he had the motives that in other people create conflicts with the aims of morality; that was why the devil tested him by appealing to his

---

[76] 'For by grace you have been saved through faith, and this is not your own doing; it is the gift of God—not the result of works, so that no one may boast. For we are what he has made us, created in Christ Jesus for good works, which God prepared beforehand, for us to walk in them' (*Eph.* 2:8–10).

[77] 'In this is love, not that we loved God but that he loved us and sent his Son to be the atoning sacrifice for our sins. Beloved, if God loved us so much, we also ought to love one another' (*1Jn.* 4:10–11).

[78] '. . . they are justified by his grace as a gift, through the redemption that is in Christ Jesus, whom God put forward as a sacrifice of atonement, through faith' (*Rm.* 3:24–5). 'Through faith' should probably be construed with 'justified'. NRSV renders 'effective through faith', RSV 'to be received by faith'.

hunger, his desire to show his divine power, and his desire to rule human societies.[79] The various inducements offered by the devil do not turn Jesus away from the love and service of God. Nor should we suppose that he suffers severe conflict, as a continent person would.[80] Facing the necessity of having to suffer, he finds it painful, but he does not want to avoid it if it is appropriate.[81] He was tested in the way human beings are, but without sinning.[82]

The writer of *Hebrews* implies that the exemplary aspects of Christ are closely connected with his sacrificial aspects.[83] He was able to do what a human being ought to do, but other human beings fail to do, since he kept his will and action firmly directed towards the love of his neighbour. For this reason he was even willing to be put to death for crimes of which he was innocent, rather than withdraw from his primary purpose. In these respects he serves as an example, in so far as we can focus on the life of Jesus to assure us that the perfection demanded by the moral law is possible for human beings.

This exemplary role of Christ's human nature and human life captures one element of the Christian claim that he is a suitable sacrifice to take away the sins of the people (*Jn.* 1:29; *Heb.* 2:17). But the suggestion that he is simply an ideal who might inspire imitation falls short of NT views about the effectiveness of his life. John claims that Christ does not simply give an example, but also gives us the power to imitate the example.[84] Divine grace gives us the desire and the ability to follow Christ, by freeing us from domination by the motives that interfere with the will to love our neighbour as ourselves. That is why Paul calls on Christians to share in Christ's resurrection by living appropriately.[85] This is a realistic demand because we do not rely on our own abilities to carry it out, but we can rely on divine help through the presence of God in the Holy Spirit.[86] The life and death of Christ are effective because God does not leave us to our own efforts in putting them into practice.

Paul speaks of this process of release from sin as 'justification'. The tax-collector who confessed his failure to keep the law was 'justified', and Paul claims that God justifies us by his grace. But what exactly Paul means by 'justify' is not completely clear. He claims that Abraham was justified by his faith, because his faith 'was counted for him as justice'

---

[79] See *Lk.* 4:1–13. The fact that Jesus is said to be hungry (v.2) makes it clear that he has the different desires that the devil appeals to. After these three tests, the devil departs only temporarily (v.13), showing that Jesus still has desires that would make different sins attractive to him.

[80] On continence v. virtue see Aristotle, §84. The English versions that render '*peirazesthai*' by 'tempted' rather than 'tested' may give the misleading impression that Jesus displays continence (if we take 'tempted' in the modern sense). The testing of (e.g.) *Mk.* 8:11 does not refer to anything that Jesus found 'tempting'.

[81] ' "Father, if you are willing, remove this cup from me; yet, not my will, but yours, be done" ' (*Lk.* 22:42). Cf. *Jn.* 12:27–8: ' "Now my soul is troubled. And what should I say? 'Father, save me from this hour'? No, it is for this reason that I have come to this hour. Father, glorify your name." '

[82] 'Therefore he had to become like his brothers and sisters in every respect, so that he might be a merciful and faithful high priest in the service of God, to make a sacrifice of atonement for the sins of the people. For because he himself was tested by what he suffered, he is able to help those who are being tested' (*Heb.* 2:17–18). 'For we do not have a high priest who is unable to sympathize with our weaknesses, but we have one who in every respect has been tested as we are, yet without sin' (4:15).

[83] For these two aspects see *BCP* Easter 2: 'Almighty God, who hast given thine only Son to be unto us both a sacrifice for sin, and also an example of godly life . . .'.

[84] 'But to all who received him, who believed in his name, he gave power to become children of God . . .' (*Jn.* 1:12).

[85] 'If then you have been raised with Christ, seek the things that are above, where Christ is, seated at the right hand of God. Set your minds on things that are above, not on things that are on earth' (*Col.* 3:1–2). 'So you also must consider yourselves dead to sin and alive to God in Christ Jesus' (*Rm.* 6:11).

[86] '. . . if by the Spirit you put to death the deeds of the body you will live. For all who are led by the Spirit of God are sons of God' (*Rm.* 8:13–14).

(*Rm.* 4:3). 'Count as' might be understood to mean that if F is counted as G, F is G, or to mean that F is not G, but is being treated as a substitute for G. If a piece of paper with the appropriate design and signature and issued by the proper authority counts as a 50 euro note, it is a 50 euro note. But if a pound note counts as a pound weight of gold, it is not a pound of gold, but is being used as a substitute. In the case of Abraham, Paul seems to have the first use of 'counted as' in mind, since he also refers to Abraham's 'justice of faith' (*Rm.* 4:11); his faith in God was justice in itself and the source of his further justice.

Similarly, then, when Paul speaks of us as being justified by faith, he does not seem to mean simply that if we have the relevant faith, we are treated as just when we are not just. Admittedly, we are in one respect treated as just when we are not; if God forgives us our sins, God allows us to proceed as though we had not sinned, and in this respect treats us as if we were just. But Paul also claims that the death of Christ secures 'justification (*dikaiôsis*) of life' (5:18) and that it will make many people just (5:19). Justification and justice 'of life' can hardly refer simply to being forgiven; they seem to refer to a way of life that manifests justice.[87] He does not seem to restrict justification to a declaration of forgiveness or acquittal.

210. Moral Implications

These few aspects of the Christian account of sin and release from sin help to explain why the NT attitude to morality seems both highly pessimistic and unrealistically optimistic. On the one hand, it emphasizes the inescapable presence of sin and the universal failure to satisfy the demands of the moral law. On the other hand, it argues that divine grace and the resulting faith produce justice; once we are no longer under law but under grace, sin has lost its domination over us (*Rm.* 6:14). Belief in the life, work, and person of Jesus is supposed to produce a reform of character and action, leading us away from the outlook of the flesh towards the outlook of the spirit (*Rm.* 8:1–11).

We have found some reason to accept the perfectionist interpretation of the moral law, as Jesus and Paul understand it. They are justified in claiming that the explicit provisions of the law fall short of its spirit; the spirit aims at the removal of the barriers to love of one's neighbour that are assumed in the behavioural precepts of the law. But if Paul believes that grace and faith release us from the domination of sin, should he not claim that Christians will be able to fulfil the moral law perfectly?

The NT writers do not expose themselves to easy refutation by predicting that believing Christians are entirely free of the sin that prevents us from achieving the aims of morality. Different writers recognize in different ways the inescapable fact that Christians are still subject to sin.[88] And so they need to explain what difference it makes that Christians have been regenerated by divine grace through faith in Christ.

---

[87] '... those who receive the abundance of grace and the free gift of justice <will> reign in life through the one man Jesus Christ. ... one man's act of justice (*dikaiôma*) leads to justification (*dikaiôsis*) and life for all. ... by one man's obedience many will be made just ... so that ... grace also might reign through justice to eternal life through Jesus Christ our Lord' (*Rm.* 5:17–21). English versions may introduce confusion by using both 'righteousness' and 'justification' for '*dikaiosunê*'. Some contentious questions about the sense of 'justification' are discussed briefly by Sanday and Headlam, *R* 28–31, 147–53. See also §351–2, 419.

[88] See, e.g., *Heb.* 10:19–31; *1Jn.* 2:1–2; 5:16–21.

A simple answer would be that, for the justified, sin no longer matters, since it has already been forgiven and they are no longer under law, but under grace. According to this view, we have no reason to be concerned about avoiding sin. Paul sees that this antinomian answer may seem attractive, and so he argues vigorously against it.[89] In his view, justification matters not because sin no longer matters, but because we can avoid sin more than we could have avoided it otherwise. Christians have been freed from sin and enslaved to justice (Rm. 6:18); they are dead to sin (6:11); and they are no longer under law, but under grace (6:14). Even if we have been freed from sin, it is still open to us to sin, but because we have been freed from sin, we ought not to subject ourselves to it (6:12). Contrary to the antinomian answer, justifying grace and faith open a new opportunity, by making it open to us to avoid sin in some way in which it was not previously open.

In Paul's view, we have this new opportunity because faith in Christ allows us to share in the love of Christ.[90] Without his example and his inspiration, we would have no basis for believing that we can fulfil the spirit of the moral law; but the life of Jesus shows us how a human being can be guided by love of one's neighbour without being subject to the restrictions that separate the explicit provisions of the moral law from its spirit. We can therefore rely on hope, which does not let us down, because it has a firm basis in the example of Christ. The example 'inspires' us not only in the ordinary sense in which an admirable person serves as an inspiration, but also in so far as God the Holy Spirit actually moves us to act on the example of Christ.[91] Someone else might wish it were possible to act in the spirit of appropriate love for one's neighbour, but without reference to Christ this remains a mere wish; that is why those who are without God are also without hope.[92] If we have the realistic hope that rests on belief in the example of Christ, we can reject the persistent tendencies that have caused us to act against the spirit of the moral law.[93]

Paul argues, therefore, that recognition and acceptance of the love of God make it realistic to aim at goals that might otherwise be dismissed as products of merely wishful thinking. He describes these goals by repeating the familiar commandment to love one's neighbour as oneself, which is simply a summary of the moral law (Rm. 13:8–10; Gal. 5:13–14). In this respect Christian freedom does not release Christians from the demands of the old law, but reasserts them in their demanding perfectionist form. The perfectionist version of the law is the one that leads us to acute awareness of sin, and therefore would lead us to despair if we had no Christian faith and hope. But because we have Christian faith and hope, the demands of the moral law are realistic. Though we do not always satisfy them, we can reasonably

[89] 'What then shall we say? Are we to continue in sin in order that grace may abound? By no means! How can we who died to sin go on living in it?' (Rm. 6:1) Cf. §420n112.

[90] 'Therefore be imitators of God, as beloved children. And walk in love, as Christ loved us and gave himself up for us, a fragrant offering and sacrifice to God' (Eph. 5:1–2).

[91] '. . . hope does not disappoint us, because God's love has been poured into our hearts through the Holy Spirit that has been given to us . . . . God proves his love for us in that while we were still sinners Christ died for us' (Rm. 5:5–8).

[92] '. . . you were at that time without Christ, being aliens from the commonwealth of Israel, and strangers to the covenants of promise, having no hope and without God in the world. . . . He has abolished the law with its commandments and ordinances, that he might create in himself one new humanity in place of the two, so making peace . . .' (Eph. 2:12–15).

[93] 'Put off the old man (anthrôpon) who belongs to your former manner of life and is corrupt through deceitful lusts, and be renewed in the spirit of your minds, and put on the new man, created after the likeness of God in true justice and holiness' (Eph. 4:22–4).

be guided by them and try to approach them, instead of regarding them as a distant ideal. Paul urges the Colossians to seek the things that are above; he does not say they will grasp them at once, but he argues that they can reasonably aim at them.[94] Christians can form the outlook of the 'spirit', guided by the Holy Spirit, so that they take a new attitude towards the provisions of the law. They can now grasp the demand for perfection embodied in the moral law, and they can do something about fulfilling it.[95]

Paul's ethical instructions try to identify some of the practical implications of the realistic pursuit of Christian perfection. One might suppose that they would require him to take literally the extreme demands that Jesus contrasts with the demands of the old law. But he does not draw this conclusion. He does not urge Christians to refrain from anger or lustful thoughts, or to give away all their possessions. He recommends marriage as a remedy for lust, on the assumption that people will feel lust (*1Cor.* 7:8–9). He tells us to be angry without sinning, and not to let the sun go down on our anger, on the assumption that we are sometimes right to be angry.[96] He instructs us to give generously for the relief of people in need, on the assumption that we will still have something left to give to others and to maintain ourselves (*1Cor.* 16:1–2). He does not approve of reliance on other people's generosity if we can avoid it; those unwilling to work should not be allowed to take advantage of other people's work (*2Th.* 3:10).

In arguing that the Christian has new resources for discerning moral ideals and for acting on them, Paul commits himself to claims that can be assessed from the point of view of moral theory. It is not up to him to decide what counts as justice, greed, dishonesty, or generosity. In claiming that the Christian avoids sin and practises righteousness, Paul places the Christian in a comparison with the moral practices and outlooks of non-Christians, and claims that Christians more completely fulfil the aims that non-Christians themselves recognize as morally admirable.

211.   The Christian Conception of Morality

From these few elements of the NT we can extract some claims about morality that underlie Christian doctrines about sin and justification. In one way Christians add nothing to the moral law; for they recognize the love of God and one's neighbour as an adequate summary of the demands of the moral law as a whole, and they take these two great commandments to indicate the relative importance of different provisions of the law. The law that is summarized in these two great commandments is the Mosaic law, but not only the Mosaic law; for the natural law that is also accessible to the Gentiles can also be summed up in the two great commandments. The Gentiles do not know as much as the Jews know by divine revelation about what the moral law requires; but they can recognize enough moral requirements to be open to judgment for their just or unjust actions (*Rm.* 2:6–13). In this

---

[94] *Col.* 3:1–2, quoted above n85.

[95] 'Do not be assimilated to this world but be transformed by the renewal of your mind, that you may discern what is the will of God—what is good and acceptable and perfect' (*Rm.* 12:2).

[96] 'Be angry (*orgizesthe*) and do not sin; do not let the sun go down on your angry mood (*parorgismos*), and do not make room for the devil' (*Eph.* 4:26–7). The point may be obscured if we do not distinguish *orgê* from *parorgismos*.

respect Christians have nothing to add; they try to follow the same moral law that Jews and Gentiles also follow, and therefore their actions and outlook are open to evaluation by the moral outlook that is common to Jews and Gentiles, Christians and non-Christians.

In another respect, however, Christians have something to add. For they argue that neither Jews nor Gentiles recognize what the moral law requires. Though they agree that the commandment to love one's neighbour summarizes the social aspects of the law (as opposed to those that directly concern one's relation to God), they do not see what this commandment commits them to. If they did, they would agree that it involves the appropriate direction of our aims and motives to the love of our neighbour, and the removal of the aims and motives that interfere with the spirit of the moral law. But our clear awareness of these perfectionist demands of the moral law makes us aware of our incapacity to meet them.

At this point no specifically Christian theological claims have been introduced. We do not have to be Christians in order to accept the demand for perfection; we simply need to think seriously and systematically about the spirit underlying the moral law. Nor do we need to be Christians in order to recognize our incapacity to fulfil the demand for perfection; we simply need to notice the aims and tendencies in us that make it unrealistic to expect full compliance with the law. Jesus takes the actual character of contemporary formulations of the law to support his case. Recognizing our 'hardness of heart', we do not expect compliance with the spirit of the law, but we frame particular regulations so that they do not demand more than people can be realistically expected to manage. This realistic policy is not necessarily mistaken, but if we take it to express the aim of the law, we are mistaken. Since we admit that these human limitations are regrettable from a moral point of view, we acknowledge that the spirit of the moral law demands more than the realistic formulations of it.

We might agree with the Christian distinction between the explicit formulations of the law and the demands that express the spirit of the law, but should we also agree in acknowledging our inability to fulfil the spirit of the law? Greek moral philosophers agree that the spirit of morality cannot be captured in the sorts of behavioural regulations that Jesus attributes to the old law (in what 'you have heard said').[97] That is why they take the good person to have virtues of character, not simply to behave in the ways expected. The virtuous person does the right actions because they are right; that motive is central both to the Aristotelian and to the Stoic account of the virtues. Might we not say that the Greek moralists recognize the demand to conform to the spirit of the moral law but avoid the pessimistic Christian conclusion about our incapacity to fulfil it?

In defence of Christian perfectionism one might notice that the Greek moralists do not give a very clear account of the relation between the demands of morality and human limitations. Aristotle perhaps approaches the question in his separation of human from divine and heroic virtue (EN 1145a18–30), and in his remark that human virtues have to take account of human nature and its limitations (1115b7–11). But it is not clear how he fixes the limits of human nature. Perhaps we would no longer be human beings if we lost certain kinds of imperfections, and we would not need to acquire virtues of character. But other limitations may simply reflect what can be realistically expected of people as they are.

---

[97] See Mt. 5:21, 27, 31, 33, 38, 43. See above §207.

The Stoics have more to say than Aristotle about our tendency to fall short of the ideal presented to us by the virtues; for they admit that the sage who completely embodies the virtues is difficult to find. Chrysippus did not think he was a sage, and different Stoics claimed that there had been none, one, or two sages.[98] But the Stoics do not explain why most of us fail to be sages. Is it because most of us do not learn quickly enough to learn everything that a sage has to learn, or because what the sage knows is too difficult for most of us to grasp, or because we do not want to do what a sage has to do?

The Stoics do not discuss this question in detail, but if they discussed it, they would give some possible support to Christian pessimism about our capacity to follow the moral law from our own resources. Though the Stoics hold a cognitive conception of the passions, this does not commit them to the over-simple claim that as soon as we accept the outlook of morality, we will follow it. For they recognize that acceptance of the virtuous outlook may be insecure; we are still subject to the influence of the passions, and they still produce appearances that encourage us to violate the principles we have accepted. If we are not sages, we are still liable to oscillate in our beliefs, and hence to act inconsistently. The Stoics do not draw the pessimistic Christian conclusion from their recognition of this oscillation; Epictetus urges us to train ourselves to avoid the misleading influence of appearances, but does not suggest that we will fail in this task.[99] St Paul might reasonably agree with Epictetus' account of the temptations that we face from misleading appearances; he simply adds that we are misled if we think that we simply need to learn more or to try harder in order to free ourselves from their influence. Whereas Epictetus simply warns us not to underestimate the difficulty of the task, NT writers warn us that we deceive ourselves if we hold out the prospect of complete success as a result of our unaided efforts.[100]

The point of Christian pessimism, however, is not to reject the perfectionist aspects of Greek moral systems. On the contrary, the perfectionist aspects support the Christian doctrines of justification and sanctification. The moral law presents us with an ideal that we recognize, and so it encourages us to wish we could achieve it. This is an unrealistic wish, however, unless we accept the Christian account of how we can fulfil it. Though we cannot fulfil it without the help of God, we can fulfil it with the help of divine grace, moving us to believe in the sinless life of Christ, and to accept the inspiration of the Holy Spirit in following the example of Christ.

It would be a mistake to infer that the Christian outlook is simply a means to keeping the moral law. If we tried to accept it for that reason, we would defeat our own ends; for it has the appropriate moral effects only if we accept it as true in its own right. But if the Christians are right, they can claim some support in the moral outlook that enlightened moral philosophy endorses. For Greek moral philosophy claims to identify the ideal of perfection that is incompletely grasped in ordinary moral agency. According to the Christian critic, this ideal confronts us with our incapacity to realize it from our own resources; hence

---

[98] See Sx M ix 133; Plu. SR 1048e; CN 1076b; Eusebius, PE vi 8.12–16.   [99] On Epictetus see §191.

[100] 'If we say we have no sin, we deceive ourselves, and the truth is not in us. If we confess our sins, he is faithful and just, and will forgive our sins and cleanse us from all injustice. If we say we have not sinned, we make him a liar, and his word is not in us' (1Jn 1:8–10; cf. §223n57). 'For I delight in the law of God, in my inmost self, but I see in my members another law at war with the law of my mind and making me captive to the law of sin which dwells in my members. Wretched man that I am! Who will deliver me from this body of death?' (Rm. 7:22–4).

we have to acknowledge, from the moral point of view, that the Christian outlook rests on a reasonable diagnosis of our condition. Moreover, Christians claim that divine grace and justifying faith result in a degree of progress towards the moral ideal that we could not otherwise achieve; hence we have to acknowledge that this Christian goal is morally legitimate.

According to the Christian analysis, therefore, the moral law points beyond itself. Though some elements of morality are useful for regulating human interactions in mutually beneficial ways, the perfectionist elements prescribe a way of life that transforms our goals and aspirations for individual and social life. Instead of simply wanting to prevent various offences against our neighbour, we seek to love our neighbour as ourselves. Once we aim at this end, we look for the resources to fulfil it. Once we recognize that our natural resources cannot fulfil it, we cannot reasonably refuse a hearing to Christian views about how to achieve the aims of morality.

The Christian analysis of morality invites three possible replies: (1) Christians are right to assert that the perfectionist elements in Greek and Jewish moral systems support the Christian analysis. We should therefore reject these perfectionist elements in favour of a more modest and realistic conception of morality. (2) We should retain the perfectionist elements of morality, but reject Christian pessimism about our capacity to achieve them from our own resources; we should prefer the Stoic over the Christian treatment of perfection. (3) We should accept perfectionism and Christian pessimism, but reject Christian optimism, since it rests on unacceptable theological views. We should simply learn to live with our limited ability to realize the ideals that morality presents to us. We may find it easier to do this if we notice that Christians have to do it as well, since they do not claim (if they have any sense) that grace and faith ensure moral perfection.

Since each of these replies to the Christian analysis is worth considering, and since all of them face some objections, the Christian analysis raises some difficult and persistent questions about central elements in the moral outlook. On these points Christian theory about morality—its claims about the nature and implications of moral ideals—are even more important than claims about the specific requirements of morality.

212. Moral Psychology

We have argued that the Christian conception of morality and its relation to human imperfection does not rest on claims about the moral law or about the moral virtues that would appear alien to Greek moral philosophy. We can either confirm or undermine this argument if we compare Christian views, explicit or implicit, with some of the basic claims and assumptions of Greek theorists, as we have described them so far.

We may find it most difficult to find any place in Christianity for the moral psychology that underlies Greek moral systems. We have found that Socrates' successors do not wholly reject Socrates' claim that happiness and virtue depend on knowledge, and that failure to achieve either happiness or virtue is to be explained by ignorance of one's own good. While Platonic and Peripatetic moralists insist on the reality of a non-rational part of the soul, they do not reject the basic Socratic presuppositions. Aristotle's' account of incontinence shows how the Socratic appeal to ignorance of the good co-exists with the Platonic tripartition. That is why the modified Socratic position of the Stoics can answer the objections that Plato and Aristotle raised against the initial Socratic position.

We might suppose that Christians reject this Socratic presupposition, since they recognize a basic human tendency to sin that remains in us whatever we know about the good. St Paul affirms that even if I know the good, I still find myself choosing the evil. To suppose that the source of error is simply ignorance of the good is to underestimate the pervasive character of sin in human choice. Augustine enthusiastically insists on the pervasiveness and inevitability of sin, and so he might reasonably be expected to reject the assumptions that underlie Socratic moral psychology.

In fact, a strongly non-Socratic approach to moral error can be found in the Greek tradition, even though it does not become part of one of the dominant moral systems. We might interpret Plato's belief in a non-rational part of the soul as the recognition of a source of motivation that is not only independent of beliefs about the good, but also unresponsive to them. Such a doctrine of non-rational desire is easy to connect with the claim in the *Timaeus* that matter is the source of a 'wandering cause' that is the source of evil.[101] In the *Timaeus* Plato does not make the non-rational part wholly unresponsive to the rational part; on both the psychological and the cosmological level reason persuades necessity. It would be easy, however, to suppose that the *Timaeus* supports a more radical dualism than Plato affirms, between the material, bodily, and non-rational on the one side and the immaterial, psychic, and rational on the other side. This radical dualism is more strongly affirmed in later Platonism.[102]

We might well expect such a doctrine to be a suitable way to express Christian convictions about the inevitability of sin. And we might suppose that St Paul's frequent contrast between 'flesh' and 'spirit' expresses a radical dualist doctrine. Such a doctrine treats a human being as a combination of two distinct quasi-personal agents that are moved by sharply distinct motives, and have no basis for agreement on shared principles to guide their action. Some passages in Plato's *Republic* might be taken to support such a view. Though we have found reasons to doubt this interpretation of the *Republic*, it might appear to express a version of Platonic dualism that fits Pauline dualism. When Paul claims that the flesh and the spirit have conflicting desires, we might take him to maintain a basically anti-Socratic psychological and metaphysical dualism.[103]

The Christian theologian cannot go too far in this direction, however. If the inevitable urge to sin were inherent in matter and in the body, then it would be part of God's creation, and its presence would conflict with the claim that what God created was good. Since Platonism does not accept a doctrine of creation from nothing, it does not face this difficulty. But

---

[101] On the wandering cause see *Tim.* 47e3–48b3. Some disputes about Plato's views on this question are discussed by Cherniss, 'Sources'. Plotinus' view is discussed by Gerson, *P* 191–8.

[102] The anti-Socratic elements of Plato's doctrine of the non-rational soul are especially emphasized in Galen's *PHP*, where Galen uses Poseidonius' criticisms of Chrysippus to maintain the antagonism of the non-rational part to the influence of reason. See esp. *PHP* v 316.21–322.26 (De L) = F169 EK, with Kidd's comment ad loc in EK ii 615. Alcinous, *Did.* 32.1–4, also highlights the opposition between a Platonic and a Stoic view of the passions.

[103] 'For the flesh lusts (*epithmei*) against the spirit—and the spirit is against the flesh, since these are opposed to each other—in order that you not do the things you will (*thelête*)' (*Gal.* 5:17). The translation is difficult because of ambiguous syntax. On Augustine's use of this passage see §227n76. On Melanchthon's use see §418.

since it treats the world as the work of a good and benevolent Demiurge, who has imposed reason and goodness on unordered matter, it does not accept an account of flesh and matter that that would trace it to the influence of a cosmic force competing with the benevolent Demiurge. That is why Plotinus rejects the cosmological dualism of the Gnostics.[104]

From the Christian point of view, radical Platonic dualism about non-rational desire makes it too easy to sympathize with a version of cosmological dualism that gained considerable support among Christians. Marcionite, Gnostic, and Manichean doctrines used the opposition between flesh and spirit to support the view that some elements in the cosmos are independent of and hostile to the benevolent God. Marcion claimed Paul's support for his claims.[105] But if Paul does not treat the opposition of flesh to spirit as a conflict between two antagonistic agents, he does not accept a dualist conception of motivation. His claims provide no basis for a strongly dualist conception. Flesh and spirit are not two distinct agents. The outlook of the flesh is our outlook when we reject the spirit of the moral law in favour of the various aims that seem to us (rightly or wrongly) to conflict with it. The outlook of the spirit is our outlook when we are guided by the Holy Spirit so that we guide our action in accordance with the aims of the moral law. Paul does not prescribe an ascetic outlook for Christian believers in general. He does not treat the motives that sometimes oppose the moral law as being fundamentally opposed to it. We can harmonize them with the demands of love for our neighbour if we interpret those demands appropriately and form the realistic hope of fulfilling them.

The Christian doctrine of sin, therefore, does not rely on a conception of motivation and mental conflict that is sharply separated from the outlook of the Greek philosophers. While Paul certainly does not endorse the modified Socratic attitude of the Stoics, his views can readily be expressed within their conception of will and passion. If we use the resources that the Stoics allow themselves in their discussion of the attractive and potentially deceptive character of appearances, we can explain what Paul means by speaking of the persistent influence of the flesh.

This conclusion is a subject of dispute in later Christian reflexion. Augustine explains Pauline moral psychology by reference to Stoic doctrine, as he understands it. Aquinas explains Paul through his Aristotelian moral psychology. But Augustine and Aquinas do not differ as much as this contrast might suggest, since Augustine's interpretation of the Stoic view tends to assimilate it to an Aristotelian view, and Aquinas' interpretation of Aristotle is in turn influenced by Augustine's version of Stoicism. Some of the Reformers reject Aquinas' explanations as un-Biblical and as serious distortions of the doctrine of the NT.[106] We will need to discuss some of these disputes later; but for the moment we have found no reason to suppose that the ancient moralists lack the means to express Christian doctrine within their moral psychology.

---

[104] See Plotinus, *Enn.* ii 9. In ii 9.6.24–8 he accuses the Gnostics of misunderstanding Plato, and in ii 9.16 he argues that the genuine Platonist will admire, rather than denigrate, the created world. On Augustine's view see §228.

[105] According to Tertullian, *Marc.* i 19, 'Marcion's distinctive and principal work is the separation of the law and the gospel'. In iii 14–17 Tertullian argues against Marcion's view by urging that the ethical doctrine of Jesus does not contradict the OT. Origen defends the same position in *Princ.* ii 5, on the just and the good (where he rejects any opposition between the justice and the goodness (benevolence) of God).

[106] See Melanchthon, discussed in §418.

213. Free Will

Our discussion of NT views on motivation has so far left aside questions about freedom and responsibility. Christian views on these questions have provoked some dispute. On the one hand, we might suppose that the Christian doctrines of predestination and divine grace either deny free will or make it irrelevant to the relations of God and humanity. On the other hand, we might take Christian views on reward and punishment to require a more definite conception of the will and its freedom than we can find in the Greek moralists.

Our discussion of the Greek moralists has found that the Stoic conception of freedom and responsibility captures the Aristotelian conception as well, and that Alexander is mistaken in arguing that Aristotle either affirms or is committed to an indeterminist account of freedom. Alexander agrees with Epicurus in holding an indeterminist account. If we are considering whether Christian doctrines either allow or require belief in human freedom, we may well be disposed to give different answers if we hold compatibilist or incompatibilist views. Epicurus rejects determinism on the ground that it commits us to a doctrine of predetermination and fate that rules out human freedom. If Christians believe in divine predestination, they clearly violate Epicurus' conditions for freedom; but if we believe a compatibilist account of freedom is viable, we will not take it to be obvious that a belief in predestination excludes freedom; we will want to know more about the implications of the doctrine of predestination.

Some of the apparently conflicting elements in the Christian position are already present in the OT. Many passages insist on the power of God over human societies and human history and on the incapacity of human beings to resist the divine will; this seems to be the doctrine that Epicurus rejects. This conception of divine power is briefly expressed in the description of God as the potter and human beings as the clay formed according to the divine design; human beings seem to have no more power to resist God's will than the power that clay has to resist the potter.[107] While it would be inappropriate to treat such remarks as precise statements of an articulated doctrine of predestination, they show that such a doctrine might reasonably claim to express central aspects in the outlook of the OT.

On the other side, however, Sirach seems to affirm human freedom, by claiming that God left us in the power of our own choice.[108] This claim about freedom is intended to answer those who claim that God's power leaves us no choice about what we do, and in particular gives us no choice about whether we observe or violate the requirements of the law. The judicial side of the OT rejects any attempt to throw responsibility for sin on to God. Admittedly, some passages assert that God visits the merits and the sins of the fathers on the children (e.g., *Ex.* 20:5); they might be taken to assert that the fate of the children is fixed by the behaviour of their fathers, however good or bad the children might be. This

---

[107] 'Woe to those . . . who say, "Who sees us? Who knows us?" . . . Shall the potter be regarded as the clay; that the thing made should say of its maker, "He did not make me"; or the thing formed say of him who formed it, "He has no understanding"?' (*Is.* 29:15–16). 'Woe to him who strives with his Maker, an earthen vessel with the potter! Does the clay say to him who fashions it, "What are you making"? or "Your work has no handles"?' (*Is.* 45:9)

[108] 'The Lord . . . created humankind in the beginning, and left them in the power of their own free choice (*diabouliou*; Vulg. consilii). If you choose (*theléis*), you can keep the commandments, and to act faithfully is a matter of your own choice. . . . He has not commanded anyone to be wicked, and he has not given anyone permission to sin' (*Sir.* 15:13–21). Aquinas cites parts of this passage several times (e.g. *ST* 1a q22 a2 obj4; ad4; q83 a1 sc).

would be the counterpart to the hereditary curse lying on Orestes or Oedipus. But Ezekiel rejects any conception of divine punishment that would remove individual responsibility; he insists that each one will be punished for his own sin, and that if anyone turns away from sin, he will not be punished.[109]

The OT writers do not explain how this affirmation of individual responsibility is to be reconciled with divine power exercised in divine predestination. They do not seem to regard it as a restriction of divine power, as though God's designs did not include any provision for particular human beings to act one way or another. Nor do they suggest (or deny) that human beings are individually responsible only if their actions are undetermined and are not the result of God's predestination. But at any rate they make it clear that human beings are held individually responsible for their actions, and that this is the basis of praise and blame.

A prominent element in Pauline Christianity reaffirms the sovereignty of God as the potter moulding his clay, and so it might reasonably raise doubts about the reality or importance of free will.[110] God's predestination chooses some people for condemnation and others for salvation irrespective of their merits. All of us are incapable of avoiding sin, because of the sin of Adam (*Rm.* 5:12–19). Nor can we avoid sin through our own choice, independently of divine grace; for only the grace of God enables some people to turn to God in faith. This exercise of God's grace is not a response to our success in keeping the moral law; it is God's free gift, and not a response to human merits.[111] Even if believers have a different moral outlook from that of unbelievers, and even if they do better than unbelievers in following the demands of morality, this is itself the effect of divine grace; it is not their unaided achievement.

We might respond to these Pauline doctrines by concluding that Paul affirms the unreality or the irrelevance of free will. The role that he assigns to divine grace may appear to eliminate responsibility for goodness and badness altogether. Even if we do not go this far, and we claim that some things are, in some intelligible sense, in our power, this seems not to matter for what ultimately happens to us; for the ultimate cause is God's grace and predestination, not our own merits or demerits.[112]

Paul recognizes that this is a natural and initially plausible reaction to his views about sin and salvation. But he insists that it is a mistaken reaction. He believes, as Jewish writers believe, that God demands moral goodness, and that God will reward the just and punish the wicked in accordance with their choice. This judicial role for God is pointless, as Paul recognizes, if we do not hold that individuals are responsible for acting well or badly and that this responsibility makes it fair to reward or punish them. The fact that Gentiles have some natural knowledge of God is important from this judicial point of view; it explains why they are without excuse in behaving immorally (*Rm.* 1:20). Since the Gentiles can grasp the

---

[109] 'What do you mean by repeating this proverb concerning the land of Israel, "The fathers have eaten sour grapes, and the children's teeth are set on edge"? As I live, says the Lord God, this proverb shall no more be used by you in Israel. Behold, all souls are mine; the soul of the father as well as the soul of the son is mine: the soul that sins shall die. If a man is righteous and does what is lawful and right . . . he shall surely live, says the Lord God' (*Ezk.* 18:2–9).

[110] 'You will say to me then, "Why does he [sc. God] still find fault? For who can resist his will?" But who are you, a man, to answer back to God? Will what is moulded say to its moulder, "Why have you made me thus?" Has the potter no right over the clay, to make out of the same lump one vessel for beauty and another for menial use?' (*Rm.* 9:19–21).

[111] 'For no human being will be justified in his sight by works of the law, since through the law comes knowledge of sin' (*Rm.* 3:20).

[112] Cf. §225.

moral law without the revelation of the Mosaic law, they can also be fairly rewarded and punished for their observance or violation of the moral law, in so far as they are aware of it (*Rm.* 2:6–13). These retributive attitudes do not apply only outside the Christian gospel, as though grace, faith, and justification made them irrelevant. On the contrary, Paul tells Christians that God punishes violations of the moral law, no matter who is guilty of them (*Eph.* 5:6). Whatever it means for Christians to be free of subjection to the law, it does not mean that the moral law no longer applies to them or that they are not responsible for observing it.

These judicial aspects of Christianity recall Ezekiel's and Sirach's insistence on individual responsibility. If we take them seriously, we may be inclined to criticize Greek ethics not for giving too large a role to human effort and responsibility, but for giving it too small a role. If we explain error by ignorance, we may seem to provide too weak a basis for claims about responsibility, since ignorance normally removes responsibility for the action done on the basis of the ignorance. The sort of responsibility that could affect salvation or condemnation must apparently be responsibility of the clearest and most robust type; and this seems to be the deliberate and free choice of evil in full knowledge of its evil character. This seems to be the sort of freedom that Eve and Adam had when they deliberately disobeyed God's instructions. The indeterminist position developed by Alexander seems more suitable than Stoic compatibilism for capturing the sort of freedom that could support theological claims about Adam's sin or about the basis of rewards and punishments.

These different possible attitudes to questions about responsibility may themselves point to a basic contradiction within the Christian position. If it turns out that predestination and grace undermine any robust type of fundamental human responsibility, whereas claims about sin, reward, and punishment require this fundamental responsibility, then different aspects of the Christian position undermine each other. But we will not draw this conclusion if we take a compatibilist position seriously. Though compatibilism alone does not ensure that the Christian position is coherent or plausible, it at least suggests a possible argument for coherence. If we can identify the connexion between our mental states and our actions that make us responsible for our actions, and we can show that the Pauline doctrine of predestination and election allows this connexion, we can show how Paul's view is coherent. Moreover, once we have found the relevant connexion, we may be able to show that an indeterminist doctrine of responsibility also fits the doctrine of predestination.[113]

These Christian views on predestination and responsibility make it difficult to accept Epicurus' claim that divine providence, as the Stoics conceive it, does not allow responsibility. But Epicurus' view is by no means typical of Greek philosophers' views on these questions. We have seen that other views are either sympathetic to compatibilism (Aristotle) or explicitly compatibilist (the Stoics). These views suggest ways of understanding the Christian doctrine. Since NT writers assume, but do not argue in any detail, that divine predestination and election allow, and even ensure, human freedom, they seem to need the theories of the Greek moralists to explain how their position might be interpreted and defended.

---

[113] This topic is treated by Scotus, Ockham, Molina, and Suarez.

214. Eudaemonism

Aristotelian and Stoic doctrines of will and responsibility are closely connected with eudaemonism; for both Aristotle and the Stoics suppose that will and rational desire essentially aim at happiness, and that we act freely to the extent that we are guided or regulated by this overriding aim. Similarly, they accept eudaemonism as a basic principle for the understanding and justification of the virtues. Even though virtues are directly connected to the fine rather than to the good of the agent, they deserve the attention of a rational agent in so far as they can be shown to promote her good. Both Aristotle and the Stoics defend the virtues from a eudaemonist point of view, by explaining the virtues by reference to the common good and by arguing that sharing in the common good is essential to one's own good.

One aspect of Christianity fits naturally into Greek eudaemonism, since it claims to describe the way to salvation. Christian moral principles are partly derived from the Mosaic law, which often appeals to the effects of observance or violation on one's own happiness. 'Do this, and you will live' is a frequent comment on different commandments, and Jesus echoes it (*Lk.* 10:28). He agrees with the Psalmist that there is great reward in the keeping of the law (*Ps.* 19:11).

What is the nature of the reward? In so far as a general reason is given for observing the demands of the Law, they are represented as commands of God, on the assumption that this is a sufficient reason for obedience. But it is not clear why it should be a sufficient reason. Different reasons for obeying divine commands might be given: (1) We might say that morality prescribes what is good for individuals and communities, and that God, being good and wise, knows what promotes these goods and commands us to do what promotes them, so that we have good reason to observe his commands. (2) We might claim that God's commandments constitute moral rightness and that we ought to do what he commands just because he commands it. (3) We might claim that God's commandments come with punishments and rewards and that these sanctions give us our reason for obeying them. Since these sanctions are more powerful than anything we could lose by obeying God's commands, we have an overriding reason to obey.

Among these reasons the third is the least complicated; it makes the observance of moral requirements purely instrumental to some goal desired for non-moral reasons. This way of explaining the status of morality provokes the objection that Christian attitudes to morality are purely instrumental in the way condemned by Plato in *Republic* ii, and that they do not allow us to care about morality for its own sake. Neither the first nor the second reason is open to this objection. The first reason allows an appeal to divine commands to be integrated smoothly into a eudaemonist account of the basis of morality. The second rejects the eudaemonist framework, since it claims that we have a sufficient reason for obeying divine commands quite apart from any connexion with our own good or with the good of others. This is the sort of reason that Scotus has in mind in speaking of the love of God as the basis of morality.

The sorts of reasons that are available depend to some extent on the scope of the law. In the OT the moral law is only sometimes distinguished from the ceremonial; and if we think

392

of ritual and ceremony as part of the law, we can hardly give the first reason for observing it. But to the extent that the OT writers distinguish the moral law, they also recognize to some degree that it is worth keeping for its own sake; hence the Psalmist distinguishes its inherent desirability from the reward that it promises.[114] For reasons we have already seen, the Christian outlook endorses this attitude to the moral law. While no NT writer ever rejects concern for eternal happiness as a suitable reason for keeping the moral law, the NT does not suggest that this is the only reason for keeping it.

Do we find the second attitude among Biblical writers? Do they treat the fact that God has commanded an action as constituting its rightness? They certainly praise obedience to divine commands, but it is not clear that any of them gives this account of the rightness of commands. In a way, this conclusion is unhelpful, since they do not raise the philosophical question at all. But it is more helpful to notice that such an account of rightness does not even seem to be strongly suggested by Biblical views, and does not seem to be what Biblical writers have in mind. In saying that what God commands is right, they do not seem to mean that the right is whatever an authoritative ruler says it is, and that God is the most authoritative ruler. They also imply, and sometimes assert, that God has a claim on our obedience because of God's moral characteristics, which are recognizable apart from the acceptance of God's commands. Hence the Decalogue begins with the reminder that God has brought Israel out of Egypt, and deserves Israel's obedience for that reason (Dt. 5:6–7). This is partly an appeal to gratitude, but partly also an appeal to God's demonstrated goodness; the Israelites are expected to believe not only that they owe God something for past services, but also that God has proved the sort of goodness that provides some distinct reason for accepting a moral authority. Abraham argues that since God must always do right, God could not possibly allow the innocent to be destroyed with the guilty (Gn. 18:23–32).

Neither OT nor NT writers, then, give us any reason to suppose that Jewish or Christian conceptions of morality as divine law introduce some account of the basis of morality that stands outside Greek eudaemonism. The outlook of Plato, Aristotle, and the Stoics allows us to explain the role of divine law in morality and practical reason. This is not to say that Greek eudaemonism is the only outlook on morality that fits Christian claims; emphasis on God's unconditional demands might be taken to support rejection of eudaemonism, for the reasons given by Scotus. Christian claims about morality are open to different theoretical analyses, including the analysis offered by the Greek moralists. We have no grounds for claiming that the moral outlook of Christianity introduces elements that cannot be understood within the theories of the Greek moralists.[115]

215. The Virtues

The major Greek moral systems recognize, broadly speaking, the same virtues and agree to a considerable extent about their content. Even the Stoics, who hold a sharply different

---

[114] '. . . the judgments of the Lord are true and righteous altogether. More to be desired are they than gold, . . . sweeter far than honey . . . . By them also is your servant enlightened, and in keeping them there is great reward' (Ps. 19:9–11).

[115] Here I am trying to cast doubt on (e.g.) Sidgwick's over-emphasis on the juridical aspects of Christian morality, in OHE 110–11. This over-emphasis leads Sidgwick to treat Christianity as the primary historical source of what he calls a 'jural' conception of ethics (ME 2).

conception of the ultimate end from Aristotle's, defend the traditional virtues; what they require of the temperate person is recognizably connected with what Plato requires of the temperate person. Though the Stoics do not agree with the Aristotelian doctrine of the mean that allows the virtuous person to retain anger, sexual desire, hatred, and fear to an appropriate degree, they recognize an appropriate analogue to the moderated passions of the Aristotelian virtues; we reasonably expect the Stoic sage to be moved by the virtues to act in the ways in which Aristotle's virtuous person acts.

This broad agreement about the nature and content of the virtues implies some respect for the ordinary concerns of social life. The virtues are not intended to withdraw us from society; they are intended to develop traits that will seem useful and attractive (with qualifications) to ordinary people who have not accepted an Aristotelian or a Stoic conception of the final good. Admittedly, this general correspondence with ordinary aims and aspirations does not extend to every detail; an important part of ethical theory is the criticism of some ordinary aims and the conception of goodness and badness that underlies them. Still, it remains true that theorists expect ordinary people to admire an adherent of a moral theory, once they understand what he is really aiming at. Even Plato supposes that when ordinary people understand the philosopher, and are free of popular prejudices about him, they will admire rather than despise him.

This is not the only strand in Greek theories about the virtues, however. A different strand, with its origins in the *Phaedo* and the *Republic*, is more strongly other-worldly, regarding true virtues as ways of eliminating our concern for ordinary goods and aims. These virtues belong to the philosopher who tries to escape from the world, and ultimately from imprisonment in the body. If he succeeds in his aims, he does not even know the way to the market-place or to the civic centre (Plato, *Tht.* 173c6–e1). Though Aristotle does not connect this ideal of escape with psycho-physical dualism, he certainly seems to accept the ideal itself to a considerable degree; his approval of theoretical contemplation may easily seem to threaten his approval of the recognized moral virtues as aspects of the good. Whatever Plato and Aristotle themselves believe on this question, the anti-social and other-worldly tendency in their position is developed to an extreme degree in later Platonism; according to Plotinus, true virtue frees us from concerns that attach us to the body and to the material world, and turns us to the proper concerns of the soul.[116]

This 'extremist' side of Greek ethics seems to be close to the Christian position. Christians are told not to be disturbed if the world hates them, since they live by different standards and are guided by different aims. Since they are devoted to the life in Christ, they are unconcerned with the normal aims of social life. As Paul says, 'While we are at home in the body, we are absent from the Lord' (*2Cor.* 5:6). Our good cannot be achieved until after the resurrection; 'for the things that are seen are temporal, but the things that are not seen are eternal' (*2Cor.* 4:18). Since the citizenship of Christians is in heaven (*Phil.* 3:20),[117] they may well be expected to withdraw from the concerns of ordinary life in society. From this point of view, the ascetic and monastic tendencies in early Christianity are not surprising.[118]

---

[116] For Plato's views see §61n57.

[117] The *politeuma* of Christians is the state in which they have their citizenship; cf. Philo, *Conf.* 78 (the wise are temporary dwellers on earth, whose *patris* is heaven).

[118] Kirk, *VG* 85–94, 174–234, discusses the growth of rigorist and monastic outlooks in Christianity.

Attitudes to marriage and slavery are designed to minimize disturbance and distraction so that the Christian can focus on what really matters.

If we concentrate on this side of the Christian ideal, Christianity seems to be hostile to morality. Even if Christians are not prone to injustice, intemperance, and cowardice, because they do not care about the temporal goods to be gained by these vices, they do not seem to have the contrasting virtues; for these seem to require some favourable attitude to the temporal goods that they safeguard. Naturally, Christians claim to have eliminated the vices that result from excessive attention to temporal goods; but apparently they ought to recognize that they advocate the elimination of the virtues as well.

This attitude to the recognized virtues suggests that the Christian way of life does not embody a moral outlook, but transcends the moral point of view altogether. It leaves behind the moral concern for other people's welfare in the present life. Ordinary moral rules and practices turn out either to depend on a misguided attachment to worldly goods or to serve as first steps on the path to detachment from the world. We might understand some of Jesus' injunctions in this light. When he tells us to give to those who ask and to turn the other cheek, we might understand these instructions as intended to convey the spirit of love for our neighbour as ourselves; in that case we might want to interpret them so that we do not give everything away thoughtlessly, and so that we do not encourage people to put up with injuries that ought to be prevented or punished. But if we understand these as instructions for detaching ourselves from worldly concerns, we might interpret them more literally; if giving to those who ask leaves us with nothing more to use for other people's material benefit, that does not matter if we are simply trying to get rid of such concerns.

This strongly ascetic attitude to ordinary morality may lead us to the life of the Desert Fathers. But since that is hardly a life to suit everyone, a more moderate version of the same detached attitude to ordinary morality might contrast the attitude of the Christian qua Christian with the attitude of the Christian qua human being and citizen. Perhaps the Christian is not concerned, qua Christian, with morality except for its purifying function in detaching us from worldly concerns. But since many Christians cannot pursue complete detachment, they can detach their Christian concerns from their concerns as citizens and members of society. This moderately other-worldly attitude distinguishes the Christian from the 'secular' aspects of life and does not reject the morality needed to maintain secular society, though it does not take it very seriously either. Christian detachment, according to the moderate view, does not drive us into the desert, but allows us to pursue spiritual detachment while we still retain the ordinary moral concerns of citizens to the right degree. This outlook might claim to render to Caesar what belongs to Caesar and to God what belongs to God (*Lk.* 20:20–6).

Either the extreme or the moderate version of Christian detachment implies some reserve towards the moral virtues; they cannot themselves be elements in the human good, even though they may help us towards it. This attitude of reserve agrees with the Platonist conception of the moral virtues as 'purgative', as first steps towards a way of life that no longer treats them as major parts of the good. Such reserve, however, does not fit the moralistic side of Christianity any more than it fits the moralistic side of Greek moral theories. Since the NT writers insist on love of one's neighbour as a necessary result of, and even an essential element in, love of God, they do not endorse Christian detachment.[119]

Since love of one's neighbour as oneself includes the whole law, it also includes the different moral virtues; for these incorporate the requirements of properly-directed love of oneself and others.[120] Both OT and NT writers agree with Greek moralists in taking virtues to require the appropriate aims and motives, and not just the appropriate behaviour. While Christian faith and hope give a distinct reason for trying to act on the moral virtues, and a distinct basis for considering one's prospect of success, the virtues that they approve of include the cardinal virtues recognized by the Greek moralists.

This conclusion also serves to sum up our survey of Christian views about morality. We have found that, while Christian writers express controversial views about morality, these views do not require a moral theory outside the range of theories defended by the Greek moralists. We have therefore found some reason to believe that any moral philosophers who try to express Christian views within a Platonic, Aristotelian, or Stoic theory are not evidently wasting their time. Only closer examination will show whether this apparently reasonable aim of expressing Christian views within Greek moral theory is really reasonable. Definite views on each side of this question are defended by Aquinas, who describes the Christian virtues within an explicitly Aristotelian framework, and by Scotus, Ockham, and Luther, who take Christian doctrine to require the decisive rejection of an Aristotelian framework. All of these Christian moralists claim support for their incompatible views from Augustine. This is not wholly surprising, since we have noticed elements in Christianity that might be developed into a more radical critique of the moral outlook. We will see how Augustine develops some of these elements, but also maintains the moralistic side of Christianity.

[119] 'We love, because he first loved us. Those who say, "I love God", and hate their brothers or sisters, are liars; for those who do not love a brother or sister whom they have seen cannot love God whom they have not seen' (*1Jn.* 4:19–20).

[120] On the relation between self-love and love of others see §416.

15

AUGUSTINE

216. The Rejection of Greek Ethics?

In the *City of God* Augustine claims that Christians and pagans form two societies identified by their different shared objects of love. As St Paul says, the citizenship of Christians is in heaven and not on earth.[1] In the city of God the love of God prevails, and in the earthly city the love of self prevails (*CD* xiv 13f, 28a).[2] The Christian community distinguishes itself from the pagan world by its different aims and goals. Since the difference of aims is sharp enough to constitute two distinct societies, the ethical outlook of one society might appear to be sharply opposed to the ethical outlook of the other.

Augustine shows both why we might take the two outlooks to be radically opposed and why we might reasonably suppose they can be reconciled. One clear and important strand in his thought presents a sharp antagonism between the Christian and the Greek outlook. But it would be one-sided to attend only to this strand and to ignore the views that place Augustine firmly in the Greek tradition.

Augustine's work influences mediaeval ethics in complex ways. One might divide mediaeval philosophers into 'Augustinians' and 'Aristotelians' and ascribe Platonism in metaphysics and epistemology and voluntarism in ethics to the Augustinians.[3] But this is not how all the mediaeval philosophers look at it. Aquinas, for instance, denies any conflict between Augustinian and Aristotelian views; he often argues that Augustine's views agree with Aquinas' Aristotelian position.[4] On the other side, Scotus quotes Augustine at crucial places to defend departures from Aquinas' Aristotelian position.[5]

Questions about the real or alleged opposition between Augustine and Aristotelian Scholasticism are not confined to mediaeval philosophy. They also affect disputes about the conflict between Christianity and Aristotelianism. The Reformers appeal freely to Augustine, to show that Aristotelian Scholasticism distorts the Christian position. The Jansenists appeal to Augustine for a similar purpose.[6] Some of the conflicts between the 'Augustinians' and

---

[1] *Phil.* 3:20. See §215.

[2] Quoted and discussed at §226 below. References to book and chapter alone refer to *CD* (including the letters that Welldon uses for sections within chapters).

[3] Some disputes about mediaeval 'Aristotelian' and 'Augustinian' views are summarized by Kent, *VW* 10–18.

[4] On Aquinas see §240.   [5] On Scotus see §§365–6.   [6] See §417.

the 'Aristotelians' involve theological issues outside moral philosophy; but some of them involve issues in moral philosophy and moral psychology as well. If these later Augustinian views are right, Aquinas distorts Augustine by selective exposition.

It is not surprising that Augustine can be quoted, quite fairly, on both sides of the issues in dispute between Aquinas and his contemporaries and successors; for his own position on these issues is not straightforward. It is easy to discover tensions, even apparent conflicts, in Augustine's position. Do they simply reflect his haste, or his carelessness, or his tendency to conduct controversy in rather extreme and unqualified terms? Or do they reflect a deeper conflict in his position? If they reflect a deeper conflict, is this a conflict in Augustine's attempt to explain the Christian position, or a conflict in the position itself?

217. The Importance of the Will: Rejection of Psychological Dualism

An apparently distinctive feature of Augustine's moral psychology, in comparison with the moral psychology underlying Greek ethics, is his conception of the will and its role in mental activity. The general tendency of Greek moral philosophy is rationalist and eudaemonist; the Greek moralists understand action as the product of rational desire aiming at one's own happiness, and influenced in various ways by non-rational passions. Though Platonic, Aristotelian, and Stoic theories differ about the nature of the passions and their relation to reason, they broadly agree about the character of rational desire and its relation to action. Aristotle expresses this point of agreement in saying that my rational part, pursuing my happiness, is myself (EN 1168b34–1169a3). Augustine's emphasis on the primacy of the will may appear to mark a point of disagreement with this aspect of Greek rationalist moral psychology.

Augustine's conception of the will, like many of his philosophical views, is influenced by theological controversy and by his understanding of the Scriptures. He agrees with Sirach's claim that God left human beings 'in the power of their own choice'.[7] But the paradigm of human free choice does not seem to fit Greek rationalism. For apparently God clearly offered the greater good to Adam and Eve, and they deliberately rejected it for a known lesser good. It seems, then, that they must have freely chosen to reject the greater good. We might give the same account of sin in ordinary people under the law or (sometimes) under grace. St Paul suggests that we recognize what the law requires of us and recognize that it is good, but reject it none the less. Since rejection belongs to the will, the will seems to reject the apparently greater good.

Adam and Eve, therefore, seem to suggest a strongly voluntarist conception of the will, so that it is free to act against the greater good presented by reason. But a different conception seems to underlie some of St Paul's views about the sources of sin. He appeals to the opposition between flesh and spirit; and part of Augustine's conception of the will results from his efforts to understand this opposition. St Paul seems to say that the flesh is the source of sin, and that it coerces us into sinful behaviour despite the reluctance of our spiritual side.

---

[7] *Sir.* 15:13. See §213n108.

The flesh seems to be connected with the body and with non-rational desires and passions, whereas the spirit seems to be the source of rational choice.

This dualistic view seems especially clear in Paul's description of the impotence of human efforts to follow the moral law; though we want (in some way) to follow the law, we cannot.[8] Here our will seems to belong to the spirit and our inability to follow it seems to come from the flesh. A quasi-Platonic account of Paul's division takes the flesh and the spirit to correspond to the rational and the non-rational parts of the soul, and explains the conflict between flesh and spirit as a trial of strength between the two parts. The side that is overcome is compelled, not persuaded, so that we do not act freely and responsibly.[9] According to this view, the voluntarist account of Adam and Eve gives us the wrong account of sin; the struggle between flesh and spirit leaves no room for free choice by the will.

This interpretation of St Paul relies on a quasi-Platonic account of choice. But Augustine is wary of any such account, since it may appear to support Manichean dualism.[10] As part of their general view of the universe as the scene of a struggle between good and evil, the Manicheans treat will and motivation as a trial of strength between opposing forces. They treat the conflict between rational and irrational motives as a conflict between forces that recognize no common considerations and that are not themselves subject to the choice of the will. Augustine acknowledges that Platonists reject Manichean cosmic dualism, but, in his view, they do not entirely free themselves from Manichean error; for they believe that the body is the source of sin by being the source of non-rational desire (*CD* xiv 5b). Augustine believes that the Platonist view, like the Manichean view, makes us subject to mental influences and tendencies that move us to action independently of our will.

Augustine rejects the quasi-Platonic and Manichean view, because it introduces two antagonistic wills.[11] This view eliminates the single deliberating agent, and substitutes a conflict whose outcome is independent of our choice. Though Augustine also sometimes recognizes two 'wills', he does not have two Manichean wills in mind. He simply refers to two tendencies of the will; he refuses to take the extra step of allowing that these are the expressions of two opposed minds or (we might say) personalities that simply conflict, without having anything to say to each other. He insists that 'it was I who was willing and I who was unwilling; I was I' (*Conf.* viii 22).[12]

Augustine has a good reason to attack the quasi-Platonic and Manichean view, since it is not an implausible interpretation of St Paul's view of the nature of sin. If such an interpretation of Paul were correct, then, Augustine believes, the Pauline view would

---

[8] 'I do not do what I will to do (non enim quod volo, hoc ago), but what I do is what I hate. If, however, what I do is what I do not will to do, I consent (consentio) to the law, since it is good. As it is, however, it is not I who do that action, but the sin that lives in me. For I know that nothing good lives in me—that is to say in my flesh. For willing (velle) is available (adiacet) to me, but I do not find a way to carry out the good. [In the previous sentence Vulg. departs a little from the best Greek text.] For what I do is not the good that I will, but what I do is the evil that I will not to do. But if I do what I will not to do, it is not I who carry it out, but the sin that lives in me' (*Rm.* 7:15–20 Vulg.). Paul presents the same picture in *Gal.* 5:17, quoted below at n76.

[9] This is not a genuinely Platonic account, for reasons discussed in §49.

[10] On dualism and Christianity see §212.

[11] 'Let them perish from before your face, O God, just as all empty talkers and misleaders of the mind perish, those who, when they notice two wills in deliberation, have asserted that they are two natures of two minds, one good and the other bad' (*Conf.* viii 22).

[12] . . . ego eram qui volebam, ego qui nolebam. Ego ego eram.

completely undermine unified agency, rational control, and responsibility for sin. He needs to show that the Pauline view does not force these Manichean conclusions on us.

He seeks, therefore, an account of will, passion, and action that avoids both the radical voluntarist account of Adam and Eve and the radical dualism that exploits the Pauline division between flesh and spirit. Radical voluntarism does not seem to explain the influence of non-rational motivation creating the conflict between flesh and spirit. But recognition of that conflict should not, in his view, dissolve the will into conflicting forces that make free choice and responsibility unintelligible. His discussions of the will try to satisfy these criteria for an adequate account.

218. The Will and Other Mental States

As the attack on Manichean dualism suggests, Augustine believes that a unified agent needs a single will. He takes a single will to be necessary not only for unified agency, but also for a unified self, as cognitive subject as well as agent. The will orders and directs not only our desires, but also our perceptions, memories, and beliefs, in the direction it has chosen. Since the will has this dominant role, its primary affection or 'love' directs the agent's desire.[13]

Augustine's conception of will is derived from Aristotle's conception of *boulêsis*, taken over by the Stoics; the Greek term is rendered in Cicero and Seneca by 'voluntas'.[14] According to the Aristotelian and Stoic conception, *boulêsis* is essentially rational desire, focussed on the final good. But we might suppose that this rationalist conception of *boulêsis* conflicts with Augustine's conception of the will as the source of the unity of agency.

To overcome Manichean psychological dualism, we might claim on Augustine's behalf that the same will is involved in the choices of the flesh and of the spirit, in so far as we 'identify' ourselves with each sort of choice.[15] I identify myself with a choice in so far as I acknowledge it as my own, and not simply as the result of some force distinct from me. Drug addicts who struggle against their addiction are unwilling addicts who do not identify themselves with their desires for the drugs, whereas 'willing addicts' identify themselves with the desires, whether or not they can do anything about them. The mark of identification, we might suppose, is the second-order desire that endorses the first-order desire; if I want to want the drug, I identify myself with the want, and my want to want it constitutes my will. But if I am to identify myself with a choice I must have some distinct conception of the self. This conception cannot necessarily include the choice I identify myself with; if it did, no act of identification would be possible. Nor can it necessarily exclude that choice, for the same reason. But, according to Augustine, I can identify myself either with the aims of rational

---

[13] 'Just as the will connects the sense to the body <being perceived>, so also it connects the memory to the sense, and the eye of the thinker's mind to the memory. But what combines and connects these things itself also disconnects and separates them—and this is the will' (*Trin.* xi 15; cf. ix 12). 'On the Holy Spirit, I have shown nothing that appears similar to it in this likeness [aenigmate; cf. *1Cor.* 13:12] except for our will, or love or liking, which is a stronger form of will, since our will, which is present in us by nature, has different affections corresponding to how different things are present to it or confront it to which we are attracted or from which we are repelled' (*Trin.* xv 41).

[14] On Cicero's and Seneca's treatment of voluntas see Gauthier, *EN* i.1, 256–8. He rather unjustly accuses them of confusion, but correctly remarks that they do not depart from the Stoic analysis of action. Cf. §240n20 (on Aquinas).

[15] This line of argument is explored by Frankfurt, 'Freedom', 16–19; Taylor, 'Agency' 15–18; Nagel, *VN* 118, 122–3.

desire or with those of non-rational desire; hence my conception of myself as what chooses and identifies itself with something cannot be a conception of myself either as necessarily guided by rational desire or as necessarily guided by non-rational desire.

If, then, my conception of myself is a conception of something other than rational and non-rational desire, my freedom to choose does not appear to be a property either of rational or of non-rational desire. If we grant that we can identify ourselves with either rational or non-rational desire, we must have some capacity to choose between them, and this capacity cannot be either inherently rational or inherently non-rational. If we did not allow that we have this capacity to choose, we would have to say that the predominance of reason or passion depends simply on whether reason or passion is stronger. In that case I would be entirely passive, and would not be making a choice that identifies myself with one choice or the other. I seem to choose how to act and what sort of person to be, by my acts of identification and endorsement, and this 'I' who chooses is not simply the intersection of psychic forces.

These reflexions on Augustine's claims about the will suggest a conception of will (voluntas) and of freewill (liberum arbitrium) that fits neither the Aristotelian nor the Stoic view of choice.[16] Aristotle does not recognize the self and its power of choice (arbitrium) as a further thing besides the rational and the non-rational parts. The Stoics give assent a more central role than Aristotle gives it, but in doing this they do not abandon rationalism; on the contrary, they assume that we assent in the light of our conception of the good, and so they reaffirm Socratic rationalism even more strongly. Augustine, however, appears to recognize the self that chooses as something apart from rational desire and passion, and therefore identifies the self especially with the will. We might take him to deny that we all desire the good and that we go in the right or the wrong direction by having true or false beliefs about what promotes our good. Simply recognizing the greater good is insufficient (he may suppose) for acting on it; we must also choose it, and this choice depends on an act of the will that is not bound to choose the apparently greater good. Our consciousness of our will is inseparable from consciousness of ourselves, and we attribute an action to ourselves precisely in so far as we attribute it to our will.[17]

On these grounds, we might plausibly attribute to Augustine a belief in the will as expressed in acts of identification through second-order desire and endorsement. We act freely in so far as we guide our actions by these acts of identification and are not moved by

---

[16] I use 'freewill' (one word) to render 'liberum arbitrium'. On arbitrium see §235n3.

[17] 'For there is nothing that I am aware of so securely and intimately as that I have a will and that by it I am moved towards enjoying something. For I cannot at all find anything to call my own if the will, by which I want and do not want, is not mine. And so to whom must it be attributed, if I do something evil through the will, if not to myself? For since the good God made me, and I do nothing good except through the will, it is clear enough that it was given to me for this purpose rather <than for doing evil>. For unless the movement by which the will is turned in this or that direction were voluntary and placed in our power, a human being would neither be praiseworthy when he turns the hinge of the will towards higher things, nor blameworthy when he turns it towards lower things' (*Lib. Arb.* iii 3). 'And I was making an effort to grasp what I was being told, that the free judgment of the will is the cause of our bad actions.... What was raising me towards your light was the fact that I knew that I had a will as well as I knew that I was alive. And so, when I wanted or did not want something, I was most certain that it was no one other than myself who wanted or did not want, and I was recognizing more and more that that was where the cause of my sin lay. On the other hand, I saw that what I did against my will was something that happened to me rather than something I did...' (*Conf.* vii 5).

desires that we refuse to endorse. If the second-order acts of identification are at a higher order than rational and non-rational desires and do not necessarily endorse either sort of desire, they seem to be neither rational nor non-rational. This aspect of Augustine inspires mediaeval voluntarists. They believe they have Augustinian grounds for denying that we are necessarily moved by our beliefs about the greater good and by the rational desire that aims at this greater good.

If Augustine holds a voluntarist conception of the will, he faces further questions. How are we to understand the acts of self-identification? If they are simply second-order desires, we might wonder why the mere fact of being second-order should ensure identification of oneself with the action. If I am simply aware of a first-order desire, without any further desire, I am aware that I have this desire, and in this sense I identify the desire as mine. Why should we need anything more than self-awareness and self-ascription of desire?

We might protest that self-identification requires more than the mere awareness of a desire as mine. I identify myself with a desire—we might say—if I acknowledge it as authentically mine, so that it proceeds from my basic values and aims rather than from coercion by some alien force. If I repudiate a desire that I am aware of, I treat it as alien to myself. Second-order desire marks endorsement, and second-order aversion marks repudiation.

But if this is our reason for invoking second-order attitudes, they do not seem to do the work they are intended for. If I can regard some of my first-order desires as alien and unwelcome, why can I not take the same view of some of my desires of a higher order? It is not clear how a desire avoids being perverse and alien simply by being higher-order. One might answer that the mere fact of being higher-order is not the crucial fact about the desire that expresses my identification of myself with an action. Perhaps I identify myself with an action or a desire in so far as I recognize it as expressing my basic values; for this purpose my basic values reflect my rational choices about my life as a whole rather than urges—either transitory or persistent—that conflict with these choices. According to this view, the will that expresses my identification of myself with a desire is an essentially rational will that results from rational reflexion on my particular aims and desires in relation to my other concerns.

But this conclusion about the essentially rational character of the will seems to bring us back to the Aristotelian or Stoic view that Augustine appears to reject. Since we seem to be capable of endorsing either rational or non-rational desires, and therefore capable of identifying ourselves with either type of desire, the will that endorses them apparently cannot be either rational or non-rational. Our inquiry into the conditions for identification of oneself with one's desires seems to have led us to inconsistent results, since it seems to imply that the will is both essentially rational and not essentially rational.

We can resolve this inconsistency if we can show either (1) that the relevant sort of identification is possible even if the will is neither rational nor non-rational, or (2) that an essentially rational will can endorse non-rational desires. The first is the voluntarist solution, and the second the intellectualist. If we look a little more closely at Augustine, we may be able to see whether he favours one or the other of these solutions, or he remains undecided between them, or the texts do not allow us to settle the question.[18]

---

[18] On the use of 'voluntarism' and 'intellectualism' see §269.

219. Will and Passion: Stoics v. Peripatetics

To see whether Augustine accepts a voluntarist or an intellectualist conception of the will, it may be useful to consider his views about the relation between the will and the passions. Since he defends his claims about the will by comparison and contrast with Peripatetic and Stoic views, we can perhaps see where he thinks he improves on these views by relying on his conception of the will. In particular we may hope to see how he understands the relation between the will and practical reason aiming at the good. For Aristotle claims that the passions, in contrast to the will, are not focussed on the overall good. The Stoics disagree with him, in so far as they deny the existence of any desires in rational agents that are not focussed on overall good; the passions are misguided rational desires. If Augustine chooses the Aristotelian or the Stoic side in this dispute, he agrees that the will is focussed on the overall good. But if he rejects both sides, he may also reject the point they agree on, about the necessary connexion between the will and the good.

He distinguishes the Platonic and Aristotelian view, recognizing the passions as a distinct source of non-rational motivation still present in a virtuous person, from the Stoic view, which denies that the sage is subject to passions.[19] He neither completely endorses nor completely rejects either of these views, as he understands them.[20] But he rejects the Stoics' formulation of their position; for they represent it as an alternative to the Peripatetic position, whereas in fact, according to Augustine, it is simply the Peripatetic position expressed in different words.

The Stoics recognize that there are non-rational, involuntary appearances, but insist that it is up to us to be moved or unmoved by them.[21] In their view, the involuntary appearance is not the passion itself; for a genuine passion requires assent. They agree with Aristotle in believing that a passion is sufficient for action; but since, in their view, action requires assent, a passion must include assent. Since assent to an action treats it as being best all things considered, passions must include the belief that their object is best all things considered, and so, contrary to Aristotle, they cannot be independent of such a belief.

According to Augustine, this is a purely verbal difference between the Stoics and the Aristotelians. The Stoics recognize that we are subject to non-rational appearances and movements that we cannot control on a particular occasion; but these are precisely the sorts of movements that the Peripatetics identify with passions; and so the Stoics agree

---

[19] 'There are two views held by philosophers about these movements of the mind that the Greeks call *pathê*. Some Latin writers call them "disturbances", as Cicero does; some call them "affections" or "affects"; others call them "passions", as Apuleius does, following the Greek more closely. Some philosophers say that these disturbances or affections or passions come upon even the sage, but are controlled and subjected to reason, so that the supremacy of the mind imposes laws on them in some way, by which they are kept to the necessary limit. This is the opinion of the Platonists and Aristotelians . . . But others, such as the Stoics, do not agree that passions of this sort come upon the sage at all' (*CD* ix 4a). See also viii 17a.

[20] On Augustine's treatment of the passions see Kent, *VW* 206–12; Sorabji, *EPM* 378–84; Colish, *ST* ii 207–37; Knuuttila, *EAMP* 152–72.

[21] 'The Stoics' view was that as far as appearances of the mind, which they call phantasiai, are concerned, it is not in our power whether or when they will occur to the mind . . . but it does not follow that a belief that there is something bad will arise in the mind, or that the mind will accept (adprobare) them and consent (consentiri) to them' (*CD* ix 4f). Augustine uses 'adprobare' and 'consentiri' to represent the Stoic 'assent', *sunkatathesis*. Cf. *Acad.* i 11; iii 26; iii 30–6; Gauthier, *EN* i 259–60 (who alleges that Cicero and Augustine misunderstand the Stoics).

with the Peripatetics in recognizing the existence of such states.[22] Augustine illustrates his point by quoting a passage from Epictetus, with alterations that convey his evaluation of the Stoic position. According to Epictetus, the appearances 'run ahead' of reason and assent; the fool consents to the passions and the sage refuses assent.[23] But in Augustine's version of the passage, the passions run ahead of reason by declaring that some state of affairs is good or bad. By making the Stoics recognize passions prior to assent, Augustine makes it clear that he takes Stoic appearances to be only verbally different from Aristotelian passions.[24]

This account of the Stoic position is disputable. The Stoics believe that an appearance without assent is not a genuine passion, because we are responsible—in their view, as in Aristotle's—for acting on passion and we can be responsible—in the Stoic view—only for what depends on assent. They might fairly point out that Aristotle has no clear account of why we are responsible for acting on passions, and they argue that he cannot give a clear account without endorsing the Stoic view of the passions.[25] This dispute about the nature of the passions is apparently not a verbal dispute. It is a dispute about the states that are sufficient for voluntary and responsible action.

220. Augustine's Objections to the Stoics on Passions

If Augustine claims that the Stoic position differs only verbally from the Peripatetic, he should not say that the Peripatetics are right in their attitude to the passions and that the Stoics are wrong; if the difference is purely verbal, each position is substantively either right or wrong on all the same issues. Surprisingly, however, he criticizes the Stoics for errors that he does not attribute to the Peripatetics.

Augustine argues that a Christian should not simply condemn someone for being angry or distressed or afraid, but should first ask why they have these passions, recognizing that it may be right to have them (CD ix 5a). The Stoics are wrong to reject 'pity' or 'compassion'

---

[22] 'It seems to me, therefore, that in this question also, about whether the passions of the mind come to the sage, or he is wholly removed from them, the Stoics raise a controversy about words rather than things' (CD ix 4c).

[23] The passage from Epictetus is a passage preserved by Aulus Gellius. 'Aulus Gellius says that he read in this book that the Stoics' view was that as far as appearances of the mind, which they call phantasiai, are concerned, it is not in our power whether or when they will occur to the mind. When they come from alarming and formidable things, they necessarily move the mind even of the sage, so that for a little he trembles with fear, or is depressed by sadness, these passions running ahead of the work of reason and self-control; but it does not follow that a belief that there is something bad will arise in the mind, or that the mind will accept (adprobare) them and consent (consentiri) to them. For this consent is, they believe, in our power, and there is this difference between the mind of the sage and that of the fool, that the fool's mind yields to these same passions and fits the consent of the intellect to them, whereas the mind of the sage, though it necessarily undergoes them, yet retains with unshaken intellect a true and steady belief (sententia) about the things that it ought rationally to seek or avoid' (CD ix 4f–g). The passage from Gellius is quoted at §191n102.

[24] 'If this is true, there is no difference, or next to none, between the opinion of the Stoics and that of the other philosophers regarding passions and disturbances of the mind; for both sides defend the mind and reason of the sage from mastery by passions. And perhaps the Stoics say that they do not come upon the sage because the passions in no way cloud by any error or undermine by any lapse the wisdom that makes him a sage. But they occur in the mind of the sage, without damage to his wisdom; they occur because of those things that they call advantages or disadvantages, though they refuse to call them goods or evils. For certainly if that philosopher had thought nothing of those things which he thought he was about to lose by shipwreck—life and bodily safety—he would not have been so terrified by his danger as to be betrayed by the witness of his pallor' (ix 4h–i).

[25] On passion and responsibility cf. §100 (Aristotle), §169 (Stoics).

(misericordia) as a vice.[26] Seneca recognizes 'clemency' as a virtue (*Clem.* i 3), but wrongly separates it from pity, taking pity to include the wrong sort of assent. Since Augustine rejects the Stoic criticism of pity, he believes that clemency, as Seneca understands it, falls short of the affective attitude that is morally required and praiseworthy in some circumstances.

But this criticism does not seem to affect the Stoics' real view, as Augustine understands it. For he also claims that, according to Epictetus, a passion such as pity is acceptable, provided that it does not interfere with the agent's virtue (*CD* ix 5c). In the Stoic view, this state that Augustine calls a passion is really just an appearance preliminary to a passion. When Seneca praises clemency and rejects the passion of pity, he means that our appearance ought not to move us to thoughtless assent, which is included in the passion of pity. When Augustine claims to disagree with Seneca, he does not really disagree with Seneca's claim; for he does not claim that a passion moves us to action without assent.[27]

It is puzzling, then, that he criticizes the Stoics' attempt to eliminate passions. According to Augustine, the evils of human life are proper matters for sorrow, and someone who professes to consider them without sorrow (dolor) is all the more miserable to the extent that he has even lost human feeling when he thinks he has reached happiness (xix 7e). Augustine seems to have the Stoics in mind when he criticizes those who forbid sorrow at the death of a friend; since this sorrow is the natural result of genuine friendship, people who forbid this sorrow to us implicitly forbid friendship to us as well (xix 8c).

These objections are puzzling because they do not seem to affect the Stoic position, as Augustine expounds it. The Stoics recognize non-rational appearances preliminary to passions; a sage has such states, which Augustine identifies with passions. In that case, the Stoics do not eliminate the states that Augustine describes as sorrow at the evils of life or the death of a friend. Augustine could fairly object to the Stoics' view if he could show that we ought not only to have these appearances but also to act on them without assent; but he makes no such claim.

We might suppose that Augustine rejects the Stoic belief in the sage's freedom from passion, because he claims that passions are inevitable in our present life. Passions did not belong to human life before the Fall (xiv 10), and will not belong to the blessed in the afterlife (xiv 9l), but they are a permanent feature of our present condition. But he implies that he does not disagree substantively with the Stoics on this point; for he repeats that when they advocate the elimination of passions, they are not disagreeing substantively with those who take the elimination of passions to be impossible or undesirable (xiv 8a–b). Freedom from passion, as the Stoics conceive it, does not imply freedom from the appearances that are preliminary to passions; but since these appearances count, for Augustine, as passions, the Stoics agree in substance with his belief in the inevitability of passions.

Augustine clarifies his dispute with the Stoics by distinguishing two ways of being without passions. He explains that 'freedom from passion' might refer (a) to a life without passions 'that occur contrary to reason and disturb the mind', or (b) to a life in which passions cannot occur to the mind at all (xiv 9l–m). Though the first sort of freedom from passions would

---

[26] See Seneca, *Clem.* ii 5; Cicero, *TD* iii 20–1.
[27] See also Aquinas, *ST* 1–2 q59 a1 obj3, ad3, discussing this chapter.

be desirable, we cannot realistically expect it in our present sinful condition. The second sort would be undesirable; to live without fear and sorrow would be to lack the appropriate reactions to the circumstances of human life.

In rejecting the second sort of freedom from passion Augustine does not disagree in principle with the Stoics. For he does not argue that we should act on the sort of state that the Stoics call a passion—a rash and foolish assent based on a non-rational appearance. Instead he points out that the non-rational appearance is appropriate and useful if it is directed to the right objects and we use it to guide us in the right direction. Since the Stoics agree that appearances can point out preferred and non-preferred indifferents to us, they have no reason to reject Augustine's claim about the value of appearances.

221. Will and Passions

This defence of Augustine's claim that the Stoics disagree only verbally with him depends on his identifying a passion with a non-rational state that precedes any assent. But he does not always seem to take this view of the passions. Sometimes he seems to see a much closer connexion between the passions and the will, suggesting that the character of the will determines whether our passions are good or bad; when the will is good, the passions themselves are expressions of the good will.[28]

Augustine believes that virtues include rightly-ordered passions; here he agrees with the Peripatetics, as Aquinas sees.[29] If we identify the passion with the non-rational appearance, the Stoics have no reason to disagree with this claim. But Augustine goes further, and claims that the passions are not only subject to the will, but actually are different expressions of the will;[30] the various tendencies of the will constitute our different affections.[31]

His argument seems to require an unexpected point of agreement with the Stoics; he seems to assume that we have a genuine passion only if we have assented to an appearance. Earlier, however, he tries to reconcile the Stoic with the Peripatetic view and his own view by claiming that 'pre-passions' (as the Stoics understand them) are really passions;[32] this claim is true only if passions precede assent.

---

[28] 'The character of a human being's will makes a difference. For if the will is misdirected, then because of this someone will have misdirected movements [i.e. passions]; if, on the other hand, the will is correct, these movements will be not only not blameworthy, but actually praiseworthy. For the will is in all of them; indeed all of them are nothing other than forms of will (voluntates). For what are appetite and joy except the will in consenting to the things we want? And what are fear and sadness except the will dissenting from the things we do not want? . . . And in general, as a human being's will is attracted or repelled, in accordance with the variety of things that are pursued or avoided, it is changed and turned into one or another sort of affection' (CD xiv 6a). [The citizens of the city of God still have affections.] 'And because their love is correct, they have all these affections correctly directed' (xiv 9a).

[29] ST 1–2 q59 a2 sc, citing CD xiv 6a.

[30] He cannot say that every tendency of the will in every rational agent is an affection; for he recognizes that God (ix 5d), Adam and Eve before the Fall (xiv 10), and the blessed in the afterlife (xiv 9) have wills without passions. The suggestion that different states of the will invariably involve different passions is an over-statement.

[31] Augustine uses 'adfectio' here for 'passion', not 'passio' or 'perturbatio'; he would surely not defend his claim if either of these other two terms were substituted. Scotus cites this passage in support of his claim that virtues are in the will as opposed to the passions, contrary to Aquinas' view that the passions are the subject of the moral virtues (3Sent. d33 q1 sch. = OO vii 2, 698 §4 = W 324). Cf. §372. The unclarity in Augustine's position explains how he can be cited in support of these two opposed positions about virtue and passion.

[32] On appearances and 'pre-passions' cf. §167.

In claiming that the will is present in all the passions Augustine seems to agree that passions require assent. This is the Stoic view. Augustine, then, seems to accept the Stoic view, as the Stoics themselves formulate it; he seems to reject the Peripatetic view, maintained by him elsewhere, that passion precedes assent.

How important is this conflict in Augustine's presentation of his view of the passions in relation to the Stoic view? We might suppose that his acceptance of the Stoic position is an over-statement. Perhaps he fails to distinguish two claims about the role of passions in action: (1) Passions move us to action because they include assent. (2) They move us to action in so far as we assent to them. The first claim connects passion and motivation by making assent internal to a passion; the second explains it by making assent a further condition for action. 'Move us to action' has to be understood differently in the two claims. The first claim explains how a passion can be (in Stoic terms) a principal cause, in so far as it includes assent. The second claim makes it only a contributing or 'antecedent' cause, in so far as it still requires a further act of consent by the will.

Does it matter which of these two views we take? We might, as Augustine suggests, make many of the same claims within either view; but it is important to be clear about which view we prefer, if we are to say what is good or bad about the passions. Most of what Augustine has to say, especially in his account of the inevitability and appropriateness of passions in this life, fits better with the second view. The attitudes that he takes to be inevitable and appropriate seem to be more like appearances than like assents (as the Stoics understand them). And so we probably ought to take the second view of the passions to be his considered view. Aquinas decides that this is the right way to understand the relation of will to passion; he reaches this conclusion by attention to Aristotle rather than to Augustine, but he might reasonably defend it by appeal to Augustine.[33]

222. Platonists and Peripatetics on Passions

These remarks about the Stoics suggest that Augustine agrees with the Stoic view that motivation by passion requires assent. He generally seems to identify passions with the appearances that the Stoics regard as preliminary to passions; and this is why he believes that the Stoics really believe in passions, as Plato and Aristotle understand them. This description of the issues implies that Augustine takes the Platonic and Peripatetic view to identify passions with something prior to assent (as the Stoics understand it).

He now faces a question: does the Platonic and Aristotelian view hold that passions can move us to action without assent?[34] Though it is reasonable to attribute this view to both Plato and Aristotle, it seems to raise serious difficulties about responsibility for acting on passions. For if passions can move us without assent, they can apparently compel us to act irrespective of our rational judgment about whether or not we ought to act in this way. If they can compel us, how can we be responsible for acting on them? If we are not responsible for acting on them, it seems to be a purely natural fact, not subject to our will, that we act on passions. This conclusion agrees with the quasi-Platonist interpretation of St Paul on flesh and spirit.[35]

---

[33] See §246.   [34] See §100.   [35] See n9 above; §212.

Augustine rejects this interpretation of Paul. He believes it supports a Manichean conception of sin as compulsion by an alien force. In reply to the Manicheans he insists that sin presupposes will and freedom.[36] The Manicheans misunderstand Paul's claims about flesh and spirit. They are wrong because Paul's remarks about flesh do not mean that the body is the source of all sin; 'it is not corruptible flesh that made the soul sinful, but the sinful soul that made the flesh corruptible' (CD xiv 3d).[37] We are guided by the 'flesh' in so far as we are guided by a merely human outlook in which our will is turned in the wrong direction. Hence Paul even says that he is carnal despite having received the grace of God, because he partly takes the point of view of the flesh, not the point of view of the Spirit.[38] But when we are guided by the flesh, we do not lose our freedom to reject its guidance.[39]

The source of our freedom is the will, which determines our action by its judgment about what promotes our happiness. Augustine assumes that we always seek happiness. Sin consists in falsehood (mendacium) because it results from the false belief that something that really will not contribute to happiness will contribute to it.[40] We sin not because we are compelled independently of our rational judgment and assent, but because we assent mistakenly to a course of action that does not contribute to our happiness.

Though Augustine's account of the place of the passions in sin relies on a Peripatetic rather than a Stoic conception of the passions, it does not abandon the Stoic view that we act on passions only by assenting. It differs from the Stoic view only in making the assent external to the passion. Augustine rejects the Stoic view of the passions, but retains the Stoic view that we act freely and responsibly in so far as we assent. Our assent depends on our belief about what promotes our happiness, and hence it presupposes the basic desire for happiness. Though Augustine insists on the potentially misleading influence of the passions, he does not suggest that they mislead us by moving us independently of the will. When we examine his critique of Stoic views on the passions, and the alternative that he offers, we find that he departs from the Stoics far less than we might have supposed from his initial objections.

[36] 'Therefore sin is the will to retain or to acquire what justice forbids, and from which one is free to abstain. But if one is not free, it is not will' (De duab. anim. 15; cf. Retrac. i 15.4). 'And therefore whatever these souls do, if they do it by nature and not by will, that is to say, if they lack the free movement of the mind both towards doing and towards not doing; if, finally no capacity of abstaining from their action is allowed them, we cannot accept sin in them' (De duab. anim. 17). Augustine's views are discussed by Wetzel, ALV 90–5.

[37] This passage refers in the first instance to original sin, but more generally to the relation of the will to non-rational appetites.

[38] Ep. Pel. i 17. Cf. Retrac. i 23.1; Iul. iii 62.

[39] 'But one must take care not to suppose that in these words the free arbitration of the will (liberum voluntatis arbitrium) is taken away from us ... For then he is overcome by sin, while he tries to live justly by his own power, without the help of the liberating grace of God. But he has it in his freewill to believe in the liberator and to accept grace' (Prop. Rm. 44). As Augustine explains in Retrac. i 23.1, he changes his view about the exegesis of this passage in Rm. 7 (cf. §208n75). In Prop. (and in Lib. Arb. ii 51) he takes it to apply to someone who is not yet under grace. In his later work he takes it to apply also to someone under grace; see Iul. ii 13; iii 62. But he does not abandon his view about the presence of freewill at both stages. In Lib. Arb. iii 53 Augustine argues that even if we cannot avoid particular actions that are prompted by passion despite our better judgment, we are none the less responsible for failure to seek the help of God to overcome these passions. See §233 below.

[40] 'Sin does not come about except by that will by which we will that it may go well for us or will that it may not go badly for us. Hence there is falsehood in the fact that, when we act so that it may go well for us, this results in it going badly for us, or when we act so that it may be better for us, this results in its going worse for us' (CD xiv 4c).

223. The Primacy of the Will

These claims introduce Augustine's eudaemonism, and apply it to the understanding of sin. In his view, the will is not free to pursue something other than happiness, and the source of error and sin is a false belief about the sources of happiness. These claims are Stoic and Socratic. In rejecting the unwelcome form of dualism that he attributes to the Platonists, Augustine accepts the intellectualist side of the Stoic account of motivation. Hence he concludes that the will, rather than any external influence or internal force, is the cause of the mind's being subject to sin.[41]

This role of the will explains our susceptibility to sin in the different conditions of our passions. Augustine distinguishes four conditions of humanity: before the law, under the law, under grace, and in peace (*Prop. Rm.* 13–18). Adam was not influenced by his passions, since he had no passions. He was free not to sin, and his sin resulted simply from his will, because he chose to exercise his freedom badly.[42] His nature as a created being did not make his fall inevitable. We are worse off than Adam was, because we have perverse passions and we often give way to them. We therefore have less freewill than Adam had.[43] Still, we are not compelled to sin independently of our will and our rational judgment. In our condition after the fall of Adam and under the law, we are not free from sin, but we are capable of refusing consent to sinful passions, even though we do not always resist them successfully.[44] When we are under grace, we are no longer subject to sin in the same way; we have not yet lost the desires that lead us towards sin, but grace helps us not to be overcome by them.[45]

What does Augustine mean in suggesting that when we are under law, and before we are under grace, we are overcome by sin? He refers, as he often does, to St Paul's remark that sin causes me to do the evil that I do not want to do.[46] Does he claim, then, on Paul's behalf, that our sin is not the product of our freewill, but simply the inevitable result of our corrupt desires? He makes it clear that this is not what he means. Sin consists in the consent by the will; if we were compelled by misguided passions independent of our will, the result of this compulsion would not be sin. Even under law, therefore, only erroneous consent,

---

[41] 'Nothing else makes the mind a companion of appetite than its own will and freewill' (*Lib. Arb.* i 21). '[It is agreed that] nothing makes the mind a slave to lust except the mind's own will' (iii 2).

[42] 'A good will, then, is the work of God, since man was made by God with a good will. On the other hand, the first bad <act of> will, since it preceded all evil works in man, was a declining towards his own works from the work of God, rather than any <positive> work. And that is why someone's works are bad: it is because they are according to oneself, and not according to God' (*CD* xiv 11c). Cf. xiii 14b; xii 8a.

[43] 'Freewill was perfectly present in the first man, but in us before grace there is no freewill so that we do not sin, but only so that we are unwilling to sin' (*Prop. Rm.* 13–18). '[God does this] so that the heavenly city, in exile on earth, may learn not to be confident in the freedom of its own judgment, but may hope to call on the name of the Lord God. For the will in <its> nature was made good by the good God, but it was made changeable by the unchangeable God, since it was made from nothing. And so the will can turn from good to do evil, which comes about by free judgment, and can turn from evil to do good, which does not come about without divine help. By this free judgment of the will, then, as the human race advanced and grew, a mixture and a sort of combination of the two cities came about as a result of association in wickedness' (*CD* xv 21f–22a).

[44] 'Under the law, we fight, but we are overcome; for we admit that the things we do are bad, and in admitting that they are bad, we certainly are unwilling to do them, but because grace has not yet come, we are overcome' (*Prop. Rm.* 13–18).

[45] 'Though some desires of the flesh, as long as we are in this life, fight against our spirit and lead it towards sin, still the spirit, not consenting to these desires, since it is fixed in grace and the charity of God, ceases to sin. For we sin not in the depraved desire itself, but in our consent' (*Prop. Rm.* 13–18).

[46] See above n39.

not corrupt desire, is responsible for sin; Paul does not deny the free judgment of the will (*Prop. Rm.* 60). We are capable of correcting our consent so that we turn to faith in God. For God does not choose one person rather than another on the basis of good works, but on the basis of faith, which rests on consent, and therefore is up to us.[47] The will consents or refuses, and is not coerced by non-rational desires.

In ascribing this role to consent, Augustine affirms that an incontinent agent must acknowledge his incontinent action as his own; that is why he is responsible for it.[48] We may hate our actions, but if we consent to the misguided desire to do them, they are still our actions, and we cannot claim that we are not the ones who do them. Incontinence consists in wrong consent, just as continence consists in withholding it.[49]

How does Augustine reconcile the primacy of the will with the inevitability of sin?[50] Sin is inevitable because we inherit the nature corrupted by the Fall, and so we have desires and passions against our will (*CD* xiv 15e). The corruption of our non-rational nature, however, does not corrupt the will so far that we become unable to refuse consent to these non-rational desires.[51] Still, sin is inevitable, and it is mere arrogance to pretend that we can avoid it in this life.[52] But how can this be inevitable, if consent by the will is necessary for sin, and the will is not coerced?

Augustine assumes that our wills are limited by our limited insight and understanding. The Fall of Adam and Eve makes us more susceptible to the influence of our passions; for whether we choose it or not, some things appear in an especially vivid favourable light. In this sense they may be irresistibly attractive to us—not because they compel us irrespective of what appears good and bad to us, but because they appear good to us as long as we do not reflect appropriately on their degrees of goodness and badness in specific circumstances.

---

[47] 'That we believe, comes from us. That we do good works, comes from him who gives the Holy Spirit to those who believe in him' (*Prop. Rm.* 60). In *Retrac.* i 23.2 Augustine corrects himself: '. . . I would certainly not have said that if I had then known that faith itself is found among the gifts of God that are given 'in the same Spirit'. Both, therefore, are our own because of the judgment of the will, and yet both are given through 'the Spirit of faith' and charity . . . Both belong to God, because he himself prepares our will; and both belong to us, because they do not come about unless we are willing.' The effect of this correction is not to diminish the place of freewill, but to extend it; for Augustine affirms that something can be both the gift of God and the effect of freewill.

[48] 'Someone is much deceived, however, who while consenting to the lust of his flesh, and deciding to do what it desires and determining to do it, supposes he ought still to say 'It is not I that do it', even if he hates <himself> because he consents. For two things are true of him at once: he himself hates, because he has recognized that it is bad, and he himself does it, because he determines to do it. . . . The one, therefore, who says 'It is now not I who do it, but the sin that dwells in me', if he simply has the lust, he speaks the truth; but he does not speak the truth if he decides by the consent of his heart and also carries it through by the service provided by his body' (*De nupt. et concup.* i 31). 'What is the 'turning aside of the heart' but consent? For whoever in his heart has not consented with any turning aside of the heart to the suggestions that strike him from whatever appearances there may be, has not yet spoken. But if he has consented, he has already spoken in his heart, even if he has not made the sound with his mouth. Even if he has not done the action with his hand or any part whatever of his body, he has done what he has already determined by his thought that he ought to do' (*Cont.* 3). The first passage just quoted shows that Augustine does not interpret *Rm.* 7 as a description of incontinent action. On Aquinas' discussion see §254.

[49] See *Ep.* 98.1: 'One is not held liable to punishment by the sin of another without one's consent'. The context is a discussion of original sin. Cf. *Secund. Man.* 13.

[50] The development of a doctrine of original sin is traced by Williams, *IFOS*, chs. 4–5. See esp. 307–10 (on misinterpretation of *Rm.* 5:11); 368–72 (an unsympathetic judgment on Augustine's views about the freedom of fallen humanity).

[51] This claim needs qualification in the light of *Lib. Arb.* iii 52, discussed in n40 above.

[52] 'If we say we have no sin, we deceive ourselves and the truth is not in us' (*CD* xiv 9l, from *1Jn* 1:8). Cf. xxii 23d.; §211n100.

Our will is freer when it is not subject to the misleading attraction of the goods presented by the passions.[53] Still, it is free to refuse to consent to them even in our present condition. Augustine's acceptance of Stoic claims about the necessity of consent for voluntary and responsible action makes his attitude to freedom and sin consistent and defensible.[54]

224. The Will and the Good: Eudaemonism and Intellectualism

We have found that Augustine agrees with the Stoics in affirming the necessity of consent for freedom and responsibility. This affirmation is part of his reason for asserting the primacy of the will. The Stoics also assert that consent is consent to something's being good; they still maintain the Socratic claim that we are not free to reject the apparently greater good. Augustine also seems to agree with the Stoics in affirming this intellectualist view of choice and action. We suggested earlier that voluntarists might be correct in claiming Augustine's support for a conception of the will that is distinct from rational and non-rational desire, as Aristotle conceives them. But we have now found reasons for questioning this suggestion; if Augustine's claims about the will really agree with Stoic claims about consent, he does not seem to depart from Stoic intellectualism at all. His position sounds different from the Stoics' position, in so far as he attributes assent to the will rather than to reason, both in ordinary cognition and in action (*Acad.* i 11; iii 26, 30–6). But he apparently intends no significant doctrinal difference. Sometimes he speaks of the mind consenting to appearances (*CD* ix 4f-g (mens, animus), 5c), as though this is just the same thing as the will consenting (xiv 6a). He does not commit himself to any claims about the will that are inconsistent with the Stoic view of assent.[55]

Stoic intellectualism includes eudaemonism, claiming that the good we pursue is our own final good, happiness. Augustine accepts eudaemonism as well. He assumes that we always seek happiness; 'For everyone wills to be happy even by living in such a way that one cannot achieve happiness' (xiv 4c). We turn towards God because we recognize him as the source of our own highest good, not because we turn from our own happiness to some other good (xix 4a). The basic question about our lives is the question about how to achieve happiness.[56] Christians do not disagree with others on this point;[57] they disagree only in claiming that happiness depends on God.[58] This eudaemonist assumption seems to underlie Augustine's

---

[53] See xiv 11f; xxii 30f–h.

[54] Different elements in Augustine's doctrine of freedom are discussed by Burnaby, *AD* 226–34; Te Selle, *AT* 290–3; Wetzel, *ALV* 198–206.

[55] Greek Stoic sources do not speak of *boulêsis* being involved in assent. But it is natural to speak this way in Latin. For the Stoics believe that assent is *hekousion*, which is rendered into Latin as 'voluntarium', and hence easily associated with voluntas.

[56] 'Should you hesitate to say that you are ignorant of these things, given that if someone asks you what you know, you can answer that you know how a human being can be blessed even without these things? . . . For the one who asks how he is to achieve a blessed life, certainly asks nothing else than where the ultimate good is, that is to say, where the highest human good is placed, not by worthless or rash opinion, but by certain and unshaken truth' (*Ep.* 118.13). Cf. Burnaby, *AD* 45.

[57] 'For to desire a blessed life, to will it, to yearn for it, long for it, pursue it—I think this is common to all human beings. . . . For the good person is good for this very reason, to become blessed. And the bad person would not be bad unless he hoped that he could be blessed from being bad' (*Serm.* 150.4).

[58] See *Serm.* 150, just quoted; *Ep.* 118.15 (quoted below n131); *BV* 11 (on the importance of stability, leading to the identification of the highest good with God); *En. in Ps.* 32.2.18; *Mor. Eccl.* 9–10; *83 Qq.* 35; *Trin.* xiii 7: 'But it is remarkable

account of sin.[59] We do not fall into sin because we pursue our own happiness as opposed to some other ultimate end that we ought to pursue instead.

Augustine uses his eudaemonist conception of the will even to explain the apparently unpromising case of the sin of Adam and Eve. We might be inclined to suppose that Satan induced them to reject the obviously greater apparent good, but this is not how Augustine understands the Fall. It results from the bad use of free will (xiii 14b), but not from deliberate rejection of the greater apparent good. Adam and Eve wanted to exercise the freedom of their wills by rejecting subordination to God; that is why the punishment of their sin is our lack of freedom in relation to our own non-rational desires (xiii 13b). We show the same misguided love of freedom in our refusal to be equal with others and subordinate to God; we struggle against others and against God so that we can dominate others and free ourselves of domination by God (xix 121).[60]

This attempt to trace sin, both Adam and Eve's sin and our sin, to arrogance and self-assertion does not conflict with eudaemonism. If we value our freedom, we aim to increase it. We may easily suppose that we increase our freedom by reducing our subordination, and that we reduce our subordination by refusing to obey any superior. That is why disobedience was especially appealing to Adam and Eve. They were mistaken; but their particular mistake would not have appealed to them if they had not been rational agents pursuing their overall good.

We have no reason, therefore, to attribute voluntarism to Augustine. He emphasizes the role of the will in free and responsible action because he believes that non-rational desires can move us to free action only with our consent; he does not claim that the will moves us independently of the greater apparent good. He accepts Stoic intellectualism and avoids voluntarism.

225. Freewill and Determination

These claims about the will in relation to passions and to desire for the good clarify some of Augustine's views about conditions for freedom and responsibility. He places freedom in the consent of the will, and identifies the will with an unforced movement of the mind.[61] The will is free in relation to the passions in so far as it is capable of consenting or not consenting to the actions suggested by the passions. The will is not similarly free in relation to the apparent good, but Augustine does not suggest that this lack of freedom involves any lack of the freedom relevant to responsibility.

---

when all share one will to achieve and to retain blessedness, whence arises such a great difference and variation of wills about blessedness itself; it is not because anyone does not want blessedness, but it is because not all know it'. Cf. Burnaby, *AD* 47.

[59] See xiv 4c, quoted above, n44.   [60] Quoted at §233 below.

[61] 'For our will is best known to us; for I would not even know that I willed if I did not know what the will itself is. Hence it is defined in this way: the will is the movement of the soul, with nothing forcing it, towards not losing something or towards getting something' (*Duab. Anim.* 14). Augustine continues by arguing against the Manichean view that we have two wills. In *Retrac.* i 15.3, he comments on this remark about forcing: 'For if one would not have done a thing if one had refused to do it, one was not forced to do it. And whoever sins in knowledge, if he can without sin resist the one who is <trying to> force him to sin, but does not resist, he sins of his own will, since the one who can resist is not forced to give way.'

These arguments for freedom, however, may seem not to recognize the most serious difficulty. Alexander and Epicurus argue that freedom is incompatible with determinism, because complete causal determination implies the absence of the type of possibility that is necessary for freedom. The question about determinism arises in an especially acute form for Augustine, since some strong form of determinism seems not only to be compatible with Christian theology, but actually to be required by it. Even if we show that the Fall and sin can be explained without the assumption of psychological compulsion coming from outside the will, we have not yet taken account of the Christian view that all of this is part of God's predestination. Critics of Christianity believe that belief in predestination undermines freedom. Celsus presents this charge clearly and effectively. Origen answers it by appeal to Stoic doctrines, especially the Stoic refutation of the 'Lazy Argument' (Origen, *Cels.* ii 20).[62]

The question about freewill and determination is especially acute for Augustine, because the role he attributes to God rules out some of the easier answers to the question. He does not believe that God simply foreknows how we will act on the basis of our own undetermined choices; that is the error he attributes to Pelagius. God chooses to create us as descendants of Adam prone to sin, and God chooses to save us from sin by the intervention of divine grace. The primary and decisive causal agent in what happens to us seems to be God; how, then, can we claim that what we do is really up to us in a way that makes us, rather than God, responsible for it? St Paul recognizes that people will ask this question about his position.[63] Since Augustine agrees with Paul's position, he has to defend it against questions about responsibility.

Augustine offers a compatibilist defence (*CD* v 9). He argues that divine foreknowledge does not take away acting on our will. God's foreknowledge still allows us 'to do by our will whatever we recognize and know not to be done by us except by our willing' (v 9g).[64] Since God creates and foreknows the whole order of causes, he creates and foreknows our actions resulting from will, just as he creates and foreknows the actions of animals that result from their impulses (v 9g, l, o).

Against this defence of compatibilism Alexander argues that we do not ensure responsibility by proving that our decisions and choices have some causal role parallel to the causal role of desires and impulses in non-rational animals; for responsibility (so Alexander claims) requires the special causal role that makes us the origins of our actions, in such a way that nothing external to us makes them necessary and inevitable.[65] Augustine's claim that our wills are part of the created order does not seem to show that they have the appropriate sort of causal role.

To answer this objection, Augustine distinguishes different types of necessity and asks which type excludes freedom.[66] In one case an event is necessary because it will happen

---

[62] On the Lazy Argument cf. §171.

[63] 'So it depends not upon man's will or exertion, but upon God's mercy' (*Rm.* 9:16). For the following verses see §213n110.

[64] In 'except by our willing' Augustine relies (as he does in *Retrac.*, as quoted above, n47) on the principle that if we do x and would have not done x unless we had willed to do x, we are not forced to do x, and we do x freely.

[65] See §172.

[66] In v 9–10 Augustine seems to attribute freedom to the will and to its judgment (arbitrium) indifferently. Hence he speaks of 'liberam voluntatem' (9c), 'libertas voluntatis' (10b), 'arbitrium voluntatis' (9d, e, i), 'liberum arbitrium' (10c), and 'liberum voluntatis arbitrium' (9e).

whether we will it to happen or not to happen. Our will, however, is not wholly subject to such necessity, since we do many things that we would not do if we did not will to do them; a clear example of this is willing itself, which we cannot do without willing (v 10a-b). If, however, necessity is simply taken to be the fact that something must happen one way or another, this is no threat to the freedom of our will (v 10b). God is also subject to some necessity of this sort, since God cannot die and cannot err; but this sort of necessity does not cancel God's freedom.

In Augustine's view, therefore, the vital question about freedom is the one that he has already answered in his account of the will and the passions. Once he shows that the will has a causal role independent of, though not uninfluenced by, the suggestions made by the passions, he takes himself to have shown all that is needed in order to vindicate claims about responsibility. The fact that this causal role of the will is itself the product of antecedent causes is irrelevant, in his view, to the claims about freedom that matter for responsibility.

Since Augustine holds this compatibilist view about freedom, it is not surprising that he takes his views about grace and predestination to be consistent with freedom and responsibility for sin. He claims that while we are able to sin from our own resources, we are unable to achieve virtue without the grace of God (xv 21e; xv 6e). But since we achieve virtue through our will, we do it freely with the help of divine grace.

226. Pagan Morality and Natural Law

Augustine's treatment of the will and its freedom follows the eudaemonist outlook of Greek ethics, in so far as he takes a rational agent's will to aim at the agent's own happiness as the ultimate end. The ultimate end determines the direction of our love, which marks the overriding tendency of our will (*Trin.* xv 41); virtue is the proper direction or 'order' of love (*CD* xv 22d). The direction of love determines not only the character of an individual, but also the character of a society. Augustine defines a people (populus) as 'an association of rational beings united by a common agreement on the things it loves' (diligit) (xix 24a); and the character of a particular society is to be assessed by examining its objects of love.

Does Augustine's agreement with Greek ethics go any further than this general claim about happiness? Does he believe that Greek ethics is anywhere near the truth in its account of the constitution of happiness? We might suppose he does not believe this, if we attend to his description of the two 'cities' or societies that are separated by their different beliefs about the good. These two cities are opposed, because in the earthly city the love of self prevails (praecessit), whereas in the heavenly city the love of God prevails (xiv 13f).[67] Christians ought to abandon the outlook of the earthly city and form the outlook of the heavenly city. Since one's conception of happiness determines the direction of one's love, we can direct our love rightly only if we form the right conception of happiness. The outlook of the heavenly city, therefore, exposes the errors in the conception of happiness that underlies the earthly city.

---

[67] '... two loves have made two cities; the earthly city is the product of love of self going as far as contempt for God, and the heavenly city is the product of the love of God going as far as contempt for self' (xiv 28a). In 'going as far as' (usque ad) Augustine does not reject the love of self, and he does not urge contempt for self. He makes a claim about what is primary and secondary. Cf. Scotus on sin and self-love, §365.

To see what Augustine means in advising Christians to abandon the outlook of the earthly city, we need to consider his attitude to pagan morality and pagan moral theory. His contrast between the two societies with their different objects of love suggests that he turns away from the pagan outlook to a distinctively Christian point of view that rests on principles sharply opposed to pagan principles. But closer examination of his position suggests a less sharp opposition between the pagan and the Christian outlook.

Augustine has to explain the remarks by St Paul that some readers take to imply acceptance of a Stoic conception of natural law. Paul argues that Gentiles who lack the Mosaic law are nevertheless a law to themselves. We might take this to mean that they are aware of basic moral principles, and that their conscientious recognition of them guides their evaluation of their actions. Some Christian writers, however, do not believe that Paul could be allowing the Gentiles to fulfil any of the demands of the law without revelation. In their view, such a suggestion would conflict with Paul's doctrine of our absolute dependence on divine grace to free us from sin. To forestall any suggestion that Paul refers to the natural law, Ambrosiaster claims that the 'Gentiles' Paul refers to are only Gentile Christians.[68]

This interpretation of Paul sometimes attracts Augustine.[69] In his fullest discussion of this passage in *Romans* (*S et L* 43–9) he mentions Ambrosiaster's view. But he also mentions the interpretation that takes Paul to ascribe awareness of a natural law to the Gentiles; 'what was imprinted on their hearts through the image of God when they were created has not been entirely destroyed' (*S et L* 48).[70] He does not endorse either interpretation in preference to the other.[71] Elsewhere he accepts a natural law that allows everyone access to some natural understanding of morality.[72] On this point he does not entirely separate the Christian moral outlook from the pagan. We should not interpret the division between the two cities so as to ignore the common moral outlook that Christians share with pagans.

To see how much this common moral outlook contains, we may ask how far Augustine disagrees with pagan conceptions of happiness. In particular, what conception of happiness is embodied in the earthly city in which self-love prevails? Augustine might intend different answers: (1) It is the 'ordinary' pagan conception of happiness as consisting primarily in external goods; Plato, Aristotle, and the Stoics all reject this conception, and attribute a primary place in happiness to virtue. (2) It is the 'philosophical' pagan conception of happiness, as presented by the philosophers who attribute a primary place to virtue. (3) It is

---

[68] On Ambrosiaster (i.e., pseudo-Ambrose) see Quasten, *P* iv 180–9. On *Rm*. 2 see *CSEL* 81.1, pp. 75–6. At 76.5 he says that, according to Paul, the 'work of the law' is faith. But he still recognizes the natural law, taking it to be the source of the Golden Rule (note on 5:12 = 166.6–10). He mentions examples in *Genesis* and *Exodus* of moral attitudes that did not rest on any written law. Some other Patristic references to natural law are cited by Crowe, *CPNL* 57–62 (including parallels for the connexion with the Golden Rule).

[69] At *Iul.* iv 25 Augustine mentions only Ambrosiaster's view. But the second view would also fit Augustine's objection to Julian's claim that the pagans have genuine virtues.

[70] For further quotation see n127 below.

[71] On *Romans* and natural law see Chrysostom, *Rm*. 5 (on 2:14): 'When he says "by nature", he means 'by the reasonings from nature'"'; (on 2:16): 'For conscience and reason suffice in place of the law. By this he showed . . . that God made human beings self-sufficient (*autarkês*), so as to be able to choose virtue and to avoid vice'. Cf. §301 (Aquinas); §412 (Reformers). Among commentaries on *Rm*. Cranfield ad loc. follows Ambrosiaster (and Augustine's first interpretation), whereas Moo and Byrne follow Augustine's second interpretation. The relation of Paul's views to Stoicism is explored inconclusively by Martens, 'Stoic'. Cf. Crowe, *CPNL* 52–7.

[72] See *Ep.* 106.15; *Ps.* 57.1; 118.4.

both the ordinary and the philosophical conception. Which of these conceptions defines the aim of the earthly city?

227. The Character of Happiness

Augustine agrees with the general view that happiness must be complete (cf. xi 13a). He takes this to imply, however, that happiness must also be permanent; contrary to Aristotle, he does not allow that we have achieved happiness if we are in a state that we are in danger of losing (BV 11). This demand for permanence leads Augustine to favour the Stoics against the Peripatetics; for the Stoics place happiness in a good that we can retain throughout our lives, by identifying it with virtue (BV 25).[73]

Augustine, however, rejects the Stoics' explanation of the permanence of happiness; for he rejects their view that external, non-moral goods and evils are indifferent, and so not parts of happiness. Since the Stoics would prefer to live in favourable rather than adverse conditions, even if they would tolerate adverse conditions, they should allow that happiness includes favourable conditions (Trin. xiii 10). Hence their rejection of external goods must be only verbal; on this topic, as on questions about the passions, they agree with other people more than their terminology would suggest. Varro is right to argue that a human being consists of both soul and body, and not of soul without body, and that therefore the primary natural advantages (prima naturae) must be included in the human good (CD xix 3a–d).[74] Still, the Stoics are right to insist on the primacy of virtue, since this is needed for the right use of all other goods.[75]

Given these characteristics of happiness, it is not open to us in this life. If virtue is insufficient for happiness, and happiness includes goods that are vulnerable to external circumstances, our life lacks the stability and permanent goodness that, as the Stoics agree, is necessary for happiness (xix 4a–g). The Stoics themselves implicitly recognize the instability of human life, since they recognize that things can go badly enough to make it reasonable to put an end to our lives by suicide (xix 4n–p).

The Stoics are more seriously wrong about the place of virtue in happiness. Virtue would secure happiness only if it eliminated vice, but the virtues we are capable of in this life do not eliminate vice. To have impulses or inclinations that we do not consent to is still to have a vice (xix 4i).[76] Even though prudence teaches us not to consent to bad inclinations, and even though temperance causes us not to consent to them, these virtues cannot remove the evil of having these bad inclinations.[77] Since Augustine believes, contrary to the Stoics, that

---

[73] Cf. Wetzel, ALV 57.

[74] For this argument against the Stoics see Cic. F. iv 36–9; §183.

[75] xix 3e: 'For among all goods of body or soul, virtue puts none ahead of itself. For it makes good use both of itself and of the other goods that make a human being happy.'

[76] Augustine appeals to Gal. 5:17 Vulg: 'For the flesh has appetites against the spirit, and the spirit against the flesh, for these oppose each other, so that you do not do what you will'. For a different rendering see §212n103. Augustine supplies 'has appetites' (concupiscit) with 'the spirit' (Vulg., like the Greek, has no verb). He interprets Rm. 7 in the same way; see n8 above.

[77] 'For <prudence> itself teaches that it is bad to consent to sinning and good not to consent to lust for sinning. But that bad thing that prudence teaches us not to consent to and that temperance makes us not consent to, neither prudence nor temperance removes from this life' (xix 4l).

the presence of all the virtues we are capable of reaching in this life still leaves us with vice, he does not agree that virtue is sufficient for happiness.

Augustine does not mean that the goods in which moralists have placed happiness are not worth having. He simply argues that we cannot reasonably expect to attain them in this life. Indeed, he argues that the pursuit of them exposes us to further evils. Concern for the good of others leads to social life; this is part of the human good, but it brings further evils with it. Societies need laws, and therefore need magistrates to apply laws, but these magistrates have to decide in ignorance of people's real motives. Societies conflict, and wars break out; whether just or unjust, these are sources of further misery, and the Stoics who refuse to lament the conditions of human life lack appropriate sympathy for our situation (xix 5–8).[78]

The Christian attitude avoids these errors of pagan philosophy. Christians do not deny the evils of the present life, and do not affirm that they have achieved happiness simply by accepting Christianity. They recognize that the degree of happiness obtainable in the present life is imperfect; they achieve happiness only in hope, by recognizing that they can attain it fully only in the afterlife (xix 4y–z).

Though Augustine criticizes pagan conceptions of happiness, he also relies on criteria for happiness defended by pagan philosophers. On the one hand, the Stoics show that happiness must be stable and permanent. On the other hand, the Peripatetics show that happiness must include more than virtue. These philosophical arguments show that we cannot be happy in this life. Pagan philosophers, unwilling to conclude that happiness is unattainable, modify some of the initial assumptions about happiness, so that happiness is less permanent than we might have hoped, or else includes only virtue and excludes much of what we value.

From Augustine's point of view, the pagan philosophers are correct in believing that happiness is attainable, but their belief is vindicated only if we recognize that the present life is not the only one to be considered. Christian belief not only criticizes pagan views, but also justifies them better than the pagan conception of the world can justify them. An examination of Greek ethics shows that some of the distinctive claims of Stoic ethics (that happiness is stable and permanent) and Peripatetic ethics (that it includes more than virtue) are reasonable and difficult to abandon. But since these claims appear to conflict, Greek moralists abandon one or the other. We find that the claims are consistent if we do not confine ourselves to the present life. Greek ethics as a whole appears reasonable and consistent only in the light of a Christian view of this life and the afterlife. The Christian view that in this life we can achieve happiness only in hope conflicts with the views of Greek moralists about the conditions in which we can achieve happiness; but it reconciles all the plausible claims about happiness that they cannot reconcile.

Even if Augustine were wrong to claim that we can hope for complete happiness in an after-life, he might still be right to claim that happiness is unattainable in this life. But if he is right in this latter claim, we still need not abandon the pursuit of happiness as a compound of external goods appropriately directed by virtue; for even if happiness is not completely attainable, our position is not so hopeless (for all Augustine has shown) that we have no reason to try to come closer to happiness. Still, Augustine suggests that in some circumstances despair would turn out to be justified from a purely pagan perspective, but

---

[78] This criticism of the Stoics revives the questions discussed in §220 above.

unjustified from a Christian perspective.[79] If the Christian perspective is correct, it gives us some reason for confidence in pursuing the aims that we would otherwise have to pursue in an attitude of doubt about the prospects of success.[80]

Pagan moral philosophy does not seem to be the outlook of the earthly city, as Augustine understands it. For the moralists agree with many of his objections to the earthly city; they also believe that the pursuit of the ordinary pagan conception of happiness leads to conflict, competition, unstable and intermittent peace, and the other evils that Augustine mentions in the earthly city. It would be more difficult for him to show that an earthly city guided by philosophical pagan views of happiness would be subject to the same evils to the same extent.

Perhaps, however, Augustine takes the difference between the two conceptions of the good to be relatively unimportant for his critique of the earthly city. Even if the philosophical conception is superior, and even if it would remove some or most of the evils of the earthly city if it were practised, he has reasons for saying that it cannot be practised.[81] Even if everyone were to accept the philosophical pagan conception, it would not secure their happiness, and so they would suffer the evils that result from adverse external conditions. More important, they could not even attain virtue, as they conceive it; since they would still be subject to sin, they would be subject to the results of sin that disturb the peace of the earthly city. This part of his argument rests on objections to the pagan conception of virtue. We should now consider these objections.

228. Pagan Virtue

We have found that Augustine's attitude to pagan philosophical views of happiness is critical, but also constructive. This may not appear to be his attitude towards pagan conceptions of virtue. He has become notorious for his claim that the so-called virtues of pagans are not genuine virtues at all, but just 'glittering sins' (splendida peccata).[82] This phrase does not appear in Augustine; it may be an invention of Bayle's Dictionary.[83] Leibniz rejects Bayle's view, which he also takes to be Augustine's.[84] But even if Bayle's phrase is not Augustine's, does it none the less capture Augustine's view? He believes that without faith

---

[79] Cf. Kant's discussion of the possibility of realizing the highest good, KpV 130.

[80] Self-love and eudaemonism: see Burnaby, AD 116–26, 255–6; O'Donovan, PSLSA, ch. 6.

[81] This criticism reflects the distinction between compliance utility and acceptance utility. Cf. Brandt's discussion of viability at TGR 212–14.

[82] Mausbach, EHA ii 259, suggests that the tag was constructed from Iul. iv 20 and Retr. i 3.2.

[83] 'Please notice carefully that in speaking of the good morals of some atheists, I have not attributed any real virtues to them. Their sobriety, their chastity, their probity, their contempt for riches, their zeal for the public good, their inclination to be helpful to their neighbour were not the effect of the love of God and tended neither to honour nor to glorify him. They themselves were the source and end of all this. Self-love was the basis, the boundaries, and the cause of it. These were only glittering sins, splendida peccata, as St Augustine has said of all the fine actions of the pagans' (Bayle, Dict. 401 (Clarification I)).

[84] '. . . our vices doubtless exceed our virtues, and this is the effect of original sin. It is nevertheless true that also on that point men in general exaggerate things, and that even some theologians disparage man so much that they wrong the providence of the Author of mankind. That is why I am not in favour of those who thought to do great honour to our religion by saying that the virtues of the pagans were only splendida peccata, splendid vices (vices éclatantes). It is a sally of St Augustine's which has no foundation in holy Scripture, and which offends reason' (Leibniz, Theod. §259).

and true religion there can be no true virtues, and so he infers that all alleged virtues without true religion are really vices.[85] He therefore seems to repudiate all pagan conceptions of virtue.[86]

Lactantius anticipates some aspects of Augustine's criticism of the pagan outlook. In his view, the pagans' awareness of the natural law did not make them completely virtuous.[87] He gives two reasons: (1) They did not know the content of the natural law, but simply identified their local laws and customs with the requirements of justice (*Div. Inst.* vi 9.2–7). (2) Even if they did know the content of the law, all their good actions were futile (supervacua et inania, 9.8). Hence all their justice was like a body without a head (9.9). These empty virtues leave pagans with nothing to congratulate themselves on (9.17). In this passage Lactantius does not go as far as to deny that the pagans could acquire virtues; he says only that they are futile, not that they are not virtues. But he also argues that without the hope of immortality they are irrational; if we have only this life to consider, we are foolish to bear the burdens imposed by the virtues and to forgo the pleasures that they forbid (9.18–23). It is not clear that this attitude to the moral outlook is consistent with Lactantius' description of the natural sociability of human beings (vi 10).[88]

Augustine's criticism of pagan virtue elaborates some of Lactantius' objections, but also qualifies them. His views remain a topic of discussion and controversy, both in moral philosophy and in the theology of sin and justification. Peter Lombard's reference to Augustine's views about the sinfulness of pagans makes them a recurrent topic of discussion.[89] Aquinas argues against the 'Augustinian' position, arguing that Augustine does not hold it and that Christian moral philosophy and theology do not require it.[90] But in the Reformation and Counter-Reformation, and in later disputes between the Jansenists and the Jesuits, some theologians argue both that Augustine accepts the 'Augustinian' attacks on pagan virtues and that the attack is correct.[91]

His position on pagan virtue should show us whether he repudiates the main tradition of Greek moral philosophy by rejecting its conception of virtue, and, more generally, whether he allows the possibility of a common conception of morality that pagans and Christians can share. The 'Augustinian' attitude to pagan virtue supports the Christian tendency to maintain that non-Christian morality is so irredeemably entangled with the errors of non-Christians that it must be rejected with all the rest of these errors. According to this view, non-Christian morality rests on pagan errors; it is a point of division between Christians and pagans, not a point of agreement.

---

[85] 'For though some people regard virtues as genuine and right (verae atque honestae) when they are directed towards themselves and are not sought for the sake of anything else, even then they are swollen (inflatae) and arrogant (superbae), and therefore are not to be judged virtues, but vices. For just as what makes the flesh live is not from the flesh but above the flesh, so also what makes a human being live happily is not from a human being but above him' (*CD* xix 25b). Augustine relies on St Paul's remark that 'everything that is not from faith is sin' (*Rm.* 14:23).

[86] See Kent, *VW* 25–8. She endorses Bayle's account: 'Hence the famous claim that all the virtues of pagan Rome, because they were not directed to the Christian God, were merely "splendid vices"—an expression Augustine himself never used but that does capture his viewpoint with reasonable accuracy' (25–6).

[87] Lactantius on natural law; see §§197, 206.

[88] Here he condemns the Stoics for their lack of human feeling; see §191n93.

[89] Lombard, *2Sent.* d41 c1–2, asks 'whether every aim and action of unbelievers is bad'. For discussion see Lottin, *EM*, ch. 2.

[90] See §356.   [91] See §417.

This general attitude to the idea of a common morality is not specifically Christian. One might compare the Marxian or Marxist analysis of morality as the product of presuppositions peculiar to pre-communist society. According to this analysis, capitalism might be perfectly just, and the revolutionary will reject justice along with the rest of capitalism; the revolutionary ideal is a non-moral ideal.[92] This attitude to morality agrees with the 'Augustinian' attack on pagan virtue in its rejection of a common, neutral morality.

We might draw a less extreme conclusion from 'Augustinian' rejection of a common morality. Perhaps we should reject the idea of a common conception of moral virtue, but accept common moral behaviour. Even if Augustine shows that one's conception of moral virtue cannot be separated from one's views about God and the world, people with these different conceptions of virtue still need to live with one another, and need to agree on ways to avoid mutual destruction. Even if we have different conceptions of the virtue of justice, we can agree that we all benefit from certain just actions. The common core of morality is not a set of virtues, but a set of patterns of behaviour, whatever their underlying motives may be.[93]

Augustine offers some support for this idea of a purely behavioural core of morality. After he denounces pagan virtues (xix 25b), he reminds the members of the city of God that they have to deal with the members of the earthly city (xix 26). The earthly city aims at earthly peace, and Christians have an interest in the maintenance of earthly peace, even though they are simply resident aliens in the earthly city. Hence they have an interest in maintaining good order and generally useful behaviour, without any concern for the motives of the people who conform to the appropriate patterns of behaviour. Plato suggests in some places that we have reason to cultivate popular or civic virtues in order to regulate everyday life, but the most important virtues are those that purify us from concern with the body and concentrate our attention on more important things.[94] Augustine knows of this Platonic doctrine from Plotinus' elaboration of it, and we might suppose that his claims about earthly peace express a similar view about the purely instrumental role of ordinary moral virtues. His claims about earthly peace might suggest an application of his views about virtue to questions about the social function of morality. We should ask whether such an application embodies his most considered views about pagan virtue.

229. The Direction of the Will

To understand Augustine's objections to pagan virtue, we must understand two claims: (1) S has a virtue only if S has the right aims and motives. (2) Pagans necessarily lack real virtues, in so far as they lack the right aims and motives.[95]

---

[92] This account of Marx's attitude to morality is defended by Wood, *KM*, chs. 9–10. It may be a one-sided account of Marx, just as the analogous account would be, at best, a one-sided account of Augustine.

[93] One might take these reflexions to underlie Strawson's 'Social morality' and Rawls's view in *PL* 12–13. Perhaps Christian and pagan moral philosophy are two different forms of 'comprehensive moral philosophy' (as Rawls calls it), but they have no moral philosophy, and hence no conception of moral virtue in common, even if they agree on some points about how we should encourage people to behave.

[94] On Plato and Plotinus see §61.

[95] Augustine applies his objections to 'pagan virtue' not only to atheists, or polytheists, or deists, but also to Manicheans and Pelagians, who reject Catholic doctrines about (for instance) creation, sin, grace, good works, and the Incarnation. For many purposes finer distinctions must be drawn. See Wang, *SAVP*, ch. 3.

The first claim reflects Augustine's view that a virtue is primarily a condition of the will, and especially an expression of the direction of one's love.⁹⁶ If the will correctly aims at the right ultimate end, and the expressions of will towards the means are rightly connected with it, the agent is virtuous.⁹⁷ Virtue is precisely the good use of freewill.⁹⁸ This demand on virtue agrees with Platonists, Aristotelians, and Stoics. Moralists of these schools, in contrast to the Epicureans, all believe that virtuous people differ from other people in their conception of the ultimate end, not simply in their views about how to get it. If we are merely disposed to do the appropriate actions for the sake of some genuine good, we have not yet acquired a virtue.

We might reasonably agree with Augustine and with the other ancient moralists who believe that correct behaviour is insufficient for a virtue. We might even agree that virtue requires the choice of the right action for the right reason, looking to the very fact that makes the action right. This demand might be understood, as Kant understands it, non-teleologically, so that it does not refer to any connexion between virtuous action and one's ultimate end. But since Augustine is a eudaemonist, he believes that the right choice of virtue and virtuous action requires direction towards the right ultimate end. This teleological criterion supports his argument to show that pagan virtues cannot be genuine virtues.

Augustine follows Greek moralists in connecting the teleological criterion with the doctrine of the reciprocity of the virtues. He treats this as a philosophers' doctrine, without Scriptural authority, but he takes it to impose a reasonable demand on an account of the virtues.⁹⁹ Since genuine bravery is regulated by prudence, we cannot say that Bill and Ben are equally brave, but Ben is more prudent than Bill.¹⁰⁰ Agreeing with Aristotle, Augustine argues that prudence has a special role in making each virtue respect the requirements of the other virtues.¹⁰¹ Bravery itself must be prudent and just because the demands of prudence

---

⁹⁶ 'And so it seems to me that a short and true definition of virtue is: the [correct] direction of love' (*CD* xv 22d) 'And so a correct will is good love, and a misdirected will is bad love' (xiv 7e).

⁹⁷ 'For the acts of will are correct and all connected to each other if that <act of> will to which they are all referred is good. If, however, it is bad, they are all bad. And so the connected series of correct acts of will is a road taken by those rising to blessedness, proceeding, one might say, by firm steps; but the entanglement of bad and misdirected acts of will is a bond that will bind whoever acts in this way, so that he will be thrown out into outer darkness' (*Trin.* xi 10).

⁹⁸ 'Among intermediate goods is found the free judgment of the will, because we can make a bad as well [as a good] use of it. However, its character is such that we cannot live correctly without it. For its good use is virtue, which is to be placed among the great goods, those which no one can use badly' (*Retrac.* i 9.6). At *ST* 1–2 q55 a1 obj2, Aquinas attributes Augustine's description of virtue as the good use of freewill to *Lib. Arb.* ii. The words do not actually appear there, but they summarize ii 51. See §284.

⁹⁹ *Ep.* 167 separates RV from the Stoic doctrine of the equality of sins and the alleged consequence that there are no degrees of virtue.

¹⁰⁰ 'For if you say that these people are equal in bravery, but that one excels in prudence, it follows that this one's bravery is less prudent; but thereby they are not equal in bravery either, since that one's bravery is more prudent' (*Trin.* vi 6). Cf. *Ep.* 167.5, 7. Aquinas discusses Augustine in *Virt. Card.* ad12, quoting the passage from *Trin.*

¹⁰¹ 'But has he who has one virtue all virtues? And has he no virtues who lacks one? ... As to the inseparable co-existence of the virtues, this is a doctrine as to which, if indeed I remember rightly what, indeed, I have almost forgotten (though perhaps I am mistaken), all philosophers who affirm that virtues are essential to the right conduct of life are agreed. ... Those who maintain that whoever has one virtue has all, and that whoever lacks one lacks all, reason correctly from the fact that prudence cannot be cowardly, nor unjust, nor intemperate; for if it were any of these, it would no longer be prudence. Moreover, if it is prudence only when it is brave, and just, and temperate, then certainly wherever it exists it must have the other virtues along with it. Similarly, bravery cannot be imprudent or intemperate or unjust; temperance must necessarily be prudent, brave, and just; and justice does not exist unless it is prudent, brave, and temperate' (*Ep.* 167.4–5).

and of the other virtues are demands of bravery itself, not external demands that inhibit or reject the demands of bravery.[102]

If every virtue is subject to the demands of prudence, and prudence aims at the right end for all the virtues, acceptance of RV commits us to acceptance of the teleological criterion. Augustine affirms the criterion in his own version of RV, which unifies the four cardinal virtues in the love of God.[103] His reliance on this criterion is amply justified by central doctrines of the Greek moralists.

230. Pagan Virtues and Misdirected Will

The teleological criterion is especially prominent in Augustine's reply to a Pelagian critic, Julian of Eclanum.[104] Julian cites the virtues of the pagans as an objection to Augustine's doctrines about the effects of original sin and the role of grace, faith, and good works. He speaks as though the right actions were sufficient for virtue, and hence he neglects the teleological criterion.[105] Once we apply it, we see that virtuous actions (i.e., the actions proper to a virtue, those that a virtuous person would do) proceed from a virtue only if they are directed to the right end.[106]

In Augustine's view, pagans cannot act from appropriate motives. To attribute the correct motives to a pagan is to ignore Christ's teaching that a bad tree cannot bring forth good fruit. Julian might reply (as Augustine notices) that someone might be a good tree in so far as he is a human being and a bad tree in so far as he is an unbeliever. Augustine counters that, since pagans must clearly be bad trees, Julian is forced to say that they are bad trees bearing good fruit, contrary to the Gospel.[107]

---

[102] Walsh, 'Buridan' 455, argues that Augustine doubts RV. But in *Ep*. 167 Augustine agrees with the unanimous view of the philosophers (as he describes it) about RV. He does not dispute RV, but disputes the claim that all vices are equal. In the passage omitted from the previous quotation he says: 'If this [sc. RV] is true, the view of the apostles is confirmed. But what I want is to have the view explained, not confirmed, since of itself it stands firmer in our esteem than all the authority of philosophers could make it. And even if what has just been said concerning virtues and vices were true, it would not follow that all sins are thereby equal.' In §10 he repeats that RV lacks divine authority, and therefore should not be cited to confirm Scripture. In §14 he accepts RV, rejects the equality of sins, and argues that different people have virtues in them to different degrees. See Lottin, *PM* iii, ch. 13.

[103] 'If virtue leads us towards a happy life, I would hold virtue to be nothing else than the highest love of God. For what is called virtue in four parts is so called, as far as I understand it, from the varied effect of love itself' (*Mor. Eccl.* i 25; cf. *Retrac.* i 7.3).

[104] Augustine worked on *CD* from 413 to 426. He wrote *Iul.* c.421. See Quasten, *P* iv 363, 389. To simplify matters, I assume that Julian held the views that Augustine attributes to him.

[105] 'You know, therefore, that virtues are to be distinguished from vices not by the duties, but by the ends. Now a duty is what is to be done, but the end is that because of which the duty is to be done. When, therefore, a person does something in which he does not seem to sin, if he does not do it because of what he ought, he is convicted of sin' (*Iul.* iv 21).

[106] '...the prudence of misers, by which they work out various sorts of gain, is no true virtue; nor the justice of misers, by which they scorn what belongs to other people, from fear of severe punishment; nor the temperance of misers, by which they restrain desire for excess pleasures, whenever they are expensive; nor the bravery of misers, by which, as Horace says, "they travel over seas, over mountains, through fire, to escape poverty"' (*Iul.* iv 19). Quoted by Aquinas, *ST* 2-2 q23 a7. See §356n72.

[107] 'I ask you whether he does these good works well or evilly. If he does them in an evil way, though they are good, you cannot deny that he who does anything in an evil way sins, regardless of what he does. But since you do not wish him to sin when he does these things, you will surely say that he does good and he does it well. Therefore, a bad tree brings forth good fruit, and, according to the truth, this cannot happen . . . Will you answer that he is a good tree, not in

Julian might suggest that a pagan may have a good will if (for instance) he has a merciful will. Augustine answers that it is not always a good thing to be merciful, so that being merciful is not itself sufficient for virtue. Even if it is a good work to act out of natural compassion in itself, it is still a good that the pagan misuses because he acts unbelievingly.[108] If, therefore, we apply the teleological criterion, understood as Augustine seems to understand it here, pagans seem to lack genuine virtue.[109]

The reply to Julian and its attack on pagan virtue have often been cited in support of an extreme view, that any alleged virtue in a pagan is really not virtuous, but sinful, because it is directed to a bad end.[110] To see whether Augustine is really committed to this extreme view, we should examine the teleological criterion more closely. It assumes that the presence or absence of the right conception of the end of a virtuous action (in someone who does the actions of a virtuous person) determines the presence or absence of the relevant virtue. That is why someone who applies virtuous actions to a bad end must, to that extent, lack a virtue. In that case, someone who applies virtuous actions to a good end must, to that extent, have a virtue.

This way of expressing the teleological criterion shows that it would be too simple to conclude that S lacks virtue altogether if S directs virtuous action to a bad end. For perhaps S directs virtuous action both to a good end and to a bad end, so that S has both a virtue and a vice. The question 'Does S act for a good or a bad end?' is too simple, since more than one end may be relevant to whether S is virtuous, or vicious, or both.

If the teleological criterion simply requires us to aim at some genuine good, it is neither plausible nor Augustinian. For (to go back to his examples) misers may aim at genuine goods, and to that extent aim at good ends, in so far as they aim at harmony with their neighbours, or control of their own appetites; none the less they lack virtue because they subordinate these good ends to their own miserliness.

To see what is wrong with the miser and with the end of his alleged prudence and temperance, we need to recognize that he has the wrong conception of the relation of these virtues and their characteristic actions to the ultimate end. He takes these virtues and virtuous actions to be merely instrumental to his own material security and independence (let us say), which are 'external goods', not necessarily secured by virtuous action. If he were a virtuous person, he would recognize that virtue dominates external goods in the ultimate end; for the sake of one's happiness one ought always to prefer the virtues over all combinations of external goods. The miser does not see that the virtues dominate. Let us say that he fails to grasp the morally correct end, or that he lacks the morally correct conception of the ultimate end.

---

so far as he is unbelieving, but in so far as he is a human being? . . . Therefore, there would be no bad tree of which it is said that it cannot bear good fruits. . . . It is not, therefore, in so far as he is a human being, which is the work of God, but as being of bad will, that he is a bad tree and cannot produce good fruits. Consider, then, whether you have the nerve to say that an unbelieving will is a good will' (*Iul.* iv 30).

[108] 'And he does this good thing badly, if he does it unfaithfully; now whoever does something badly, thereby sins' (*Iul.* iv 31).

[109] A pseudo-Augustinian gloss on St Paul seems to sum up his view: 'A gloss of Augustine commenting on *Rm.* 14:23, "All that is not from faith is sin", says: "The whole life of an unbeliever is sin: and nothing is good without the highest good." ' (Aquinas, *ST* 1–2 q63 a2 obj1; *De Virt.* a9 obj2). Cf. *Ioann.* 45.2–3.

[110] For comments by the Reformers see §417. McGrath, *ID* 33, attributes this extreme view to Augustine: 'The *virtutes impiorum* are *iustae* in terms of their *officium*, but have no value in obtaining felicity'.

The morally correct conception of the ultimate end is not the same as the unqualifiedly correct conception. For conceptions of the ultimate end may be correct and incorrect to different degrees. We can see this easily if we begin from a rather crude idea of the structure of the ultimate end. If happiness consists of just three components, A, B, and C, S may do a brave action for the sake of A, which S correctly regards as a component of the ultimate end. However, S may still have a defective conception of the ultimate end; for S may suppose that it consists only of A, or that it includes D as well as the three genuine components, and so on. S is not like Augustine's miser, who chooses virtuous action for a mistaken end, but S is still open to criticism for an erroneous conception of the ultimate end.

A teleological criterion for virtue, therefore, might be made more precise in either of two ways: (1) A moderately strict criterion: S has a virtue if and only if S acts on the morally correct conception of the ultimate end. (2) An extremely strict criterion: S has a virtue if and only if S's virtuous action is guided by a wholly correct conception of the ultimate end.

Augustine needs to show that his demands on virtue are reasonable. He does not suppose that he simply stipulates necessary conditions for a virtue; he believes his favoured necessary conditions are independently plausible. In appealing to some teleological criterion, he relies on an independently plausible condition for a virtue (at least, within the assumptions shared by most ancient moralists). Does he intend the extremely strict interpretation of the plausible teleological criterion?

The extremely strict criterion gives a clear reason for denying that pagans have any virtues; for their conception of the ultimate end is seriously mistaken. But this criterion does not express a reasonable demand on a virtue; we do not seem to rely on it in our normal judgments about virtues. If S's just actions are regulated by the appropriate non-instrumental concern for justice and for the other aspects of morality, we might reasonably regard S as a just person, even if S erroneously believes that some parts of happiness consist in foolish amusements, or S has bad taste in music or painting or architecture.[111] These errors apparently need not affect the correctness of S's estimate of the nature and value of justice, and hence they need not affect S's being just.

The possibility of a morally correct, but not wholly correct, conception of the ultimate end emerges from Aristotle's contrast between the virtues of character and of intellect.[112] Virtues of character require some virtue of intellect, since they require prudence; but they do not require all the virtues of intellect. Aristotle does not suggest that someone with all the moral virtues must also have a true conception of the contemplative, non-moral component of happiness. He contrasts the life that includes contemplation with the 'life in accordance with the other <sort of> virtue' which is happiest only to a secondary degree (EN 1178a9).

Aristotle accepts Augustine's teleological criterion, since he agrees that a virtuous person must not only do the right action but also do it for the right end. He expresses this criterion by saying that the virtuous person must decide on the virtuous action for its own sake

---

[111] This example might not seem so plausible to Aristotle. For, in his view, magnificence (megaloprepeia) is a moral virtue, and a magnificent person is expected to show good taste both in commissioning new buildings for the city and in commissioning a new house for himself (EN 1123a6–10). I believe it would still be possible to find examples (apart from the one I develop about moral virtue and theôria below) that would make the relevant point for Aristotle.

[112] This possibility does not emerge clearly from the Stoic position, which identifies moral virtue with happiness.

(1105a32), and because it is fine (1120a23–4; 1122b6–7). Since virtuous people (like everyone else) act for the sake of their own happiness, they satisfy Aristotle's demand because they regard virtue and virtuous action as dominant components of happiness. Their conception of the ultimate end is correct to this extent, and Aristotle takes this degree of correctness to imply virtue of character.

The difference between the moderately strict and the extremely strict criterion matters, if the ultimate end is a compound of logically distinct components. But an Augustinian might reject this conception of the end. Perhaps the only correct conception of the ultimate end is the conception derived from true piety, and we either grasp this conception or entirely lack it.[113] No room will be left, therefore, for any partially correct conception of the ultimate end; nothing could satisfy the moderately strict criterion without satisfying the extremely strict one. Is Augustine committed to this answer?

231. The Aim of Pagan Virtue

To explore his understanding of the teleological criterion, we should consider how it applies to Greek conceptions of virtue and happiness. Different philosophical schools agree that the virtues are to be chosen for their own sake and for the sake of happiness; hence they attribute non-instrumental value to the virtues. Moreover, they do not regard the virtues as minor non-instrumental goods, and hence as relatively trivial aspects of happiness. On the contrary, they agree that the virtues dominate external goods. Beyond these points of agreement, different schools disagree.[114] The Stoics believe that virtue and happiness are identical, so that they take virtue to be the sole component of happiness. The Peripatetics believe that virtue is only one aspect of happiness, and that happiness includes other states and activities too.

Augustine attacks all these pagan views (*CD* xix 4), but he does not attack all their claims about virtue and happiness. He denies that virtue, as the Stoics conceive it, is possible in this life, and he argues that, even if it were possible, it would not ensure our happiness.[115] He also rejects the Peripatetic view that we can be happy in this life. Truly virtuous people need true piety, in order to recognize that they cannot achieve happiness in this life (4x). Still, he does not deny that virtue is superior to all external goods, and deserves to be chosen for its own sake. He recognizes that virtue claims (vindicet, 4h) this status, and he seems to agree with this claim; for he affirms that nothing is better or more useful in a human being.[116] He approves not only of the specific virtues that the philosophers recognize (as opposed to the philosophers' views about what the virtues are like and how we can achieve them in this life), but also of their view that the virtues should express themselves in social life that seeks co-operation with others rather than domination over them.[117] Though the

---

[113] One might derive this conclusion from the disjunction 'aut cupiditate aut caritate' in *Trin.* ix 13. See §417n62.

[114] I will not discuss Augustine's comments on Plato and Platonism in ethics, since I do not want an argument for the partial correctness of pagan conceptions of the ultimate end to rest on the theistic character of a given view.

[115] 'Therefore, those who admit that these things are bad, such as the Peripatetics, and the Old Academy, whose sect Varro defends, speak more acceptably' (xix 4q).

[116] '...the virtues themselves, than which certainly nothing better and more useful is found in a human being <in our life> here...' (xix 4u).

[117] xix 5 begins: '<These pagan philosophers> want the life of the sage to be social, and on this point we approve of their position more fully'.

earthly peace that is the aim of philosophical virtue is inferior to heavenly peace, it is worth pursuing.[118]

Does Augustine believe that the philosophers are partly right in their views about non-instrumental goods, especially in their belief that virtue is a non-instrumental good that deserves to be chosen for its own sake? If he agrees with them on these points, he must also agree that their conception of the ultimate end is partly correct, since they take these goods to be parts of it. If, then, they act on this moral outlook, they act for the sake of a morally correct, and hence partly correct, conception of the ultimate end.

Augustine discusses the Stoic attack on the Epicurean view that the virtues are instruments of pleasure. He argues that we still hold an instrumental view of virtue if we simply modify the Epicurean position by making virtue instrumental to the praise of other people or to one's own self-satisfaction.[119] His argument appeals to the conviction that virtue is to be valued for its own sake, and not simply as a means to some further end, whether pleasure or self-approval. If this is his own conviction, he agrees with the Peripatetic and Stoic moralists.

Augustine's denunciation of pagan virtue, however, raises difficulties. He mentions people who take a virtue to be genuine and right if it is directed towards itself and is not sought for the sake of anything else (xix 25b).[120] Their alleged virtues are swollen and arrogant, and so must be judged vices rather than virtues. Does he mean that virtues are not to be chosen for their own sake at all, but only for God's sake?

He rejects the view that we ought to love the virtues entirely for their own sake, and hence not at all for the sake of happiness. If we did that, we would—contrary to our intention—cease to love the virtues, since we would no longer love that for the sake of which we love them.[121] But Augustine does not suggest that this self-defeating attitude to the virtues results from loving them for their own sake. Pagans are right to believe that the virtues are to be chosen for their own sake. They violate their own standards, if they turn out to value virtuous action simply for the sake of human approval.[122]

If this is Augustine's view about the non-instrumental value of virtue, he agrees that the pagan moral philosophers have a partly correct conception of the ultimate end. It matters, therefore, whether we accept the moderately strict or the extremely strict teleological criterion for virtue. If the pagan moralists act on their conception of virtue and are judged by the moderately strict criterion, they have both virtues and vices. But on the extremely strict criterion they have vices and no virtues.

---

[118] 'However, even this people <alienated from God> loves a kind of peace of its own that is not to be disapproved of' (xix 26a).

[119] v 20. Cf. Cic. F. ii 69.   [120] Quoted in §228 above.

[121] See Trin. xiii 11: 'Unless perhaps the virtues, which we love in this way for the sake of happiness alone, dare to persuade us in such a way that we do not love happiness itself. If they do this, we even cease to love them, whenever we do not love that because of which alone we loved them.' Cf. Aquinas, ST 2-2 q123 a7 obj2. (Aquinas has a slightly different text.)

[122] This claim about loving virtue for its own sake raises some difficult questions about Augustine's various views. If (i) we look at it in the light of the distinction between enjoyment (fruitio) and use (usus) that Augustine explores in Doctr. Chr. i, (ii) we suppose (relying on, e.g., i 40) that human beings are to be used not enjoyed, and (iii) we suppose that use is a purely instrumental attitude, then Augustine is committed to a purely instrumental attitude to the virtues. But these suppositions about fruitio and usus are questionable, and it is not clear, in any case, that Augustine adheres to this distinction in other works. See O'Donovan, PSLSA 24–9; 'Usus'; Burnaby, AD 104–10.

The moderately strict criterion is preferable to the extremely strict criterion. If Augustine relies on it, he does not appeal directly to his own theological and moral outlook, but examines pagan moral philosophy by a standard that pagan philosophers accept; hence his critique deserves their attention for philosophical reasons. If he accepts the moderate criterion, he ought to agree that pagans who act on the moral outlook of the Greek moralists have virtues, even though they also have vices, in so far as they are arrogant.

232. Are Pagan Virtues Genuine Virtues?

Does Augustine recognize that he is committed to this conclusion about pagan virtue? He does not explore the implications of the fact that pagan moralists take the virtues to be non-instrumental goods. But some of his remarks are more favourable than we might expect from his sweeping attacks on pagan virtue.

In a letter written a few years earlier than the *City of God* and *Against Julian*, he argues that the Christian faith encourages the growth of virtues that turn us towards the city of God; then he considers the attitude of the Christian towards the earthly city. He argues that the Romans displayed 'civil virtues' that maintained their community.[123] Faith adds to these civil virtues, but does not reject them.

In writing against Julian, Augustine suggests that the Romans who displayed these civil virtues really served demons or human glory.[124] This suggestion does not contradict Augustine's favourable judgment in the letter. In answering Julian, Augustine emphasizes the pagan and sinful attitude of the Romans with civic virtues. But this does not require him to deny that the virtuous Romans had a morally correct conception of the end of virtue. This morally correct conception of the end does not disappear when it is combined with incorrect views of the supernatural ultimate end.

We might try to explain these passages through a simple application of Augustine's distinction between action (officium) and end (finis). Perhaps Augustine means that the Romans did the right actions, but for the wrong end, so that their virtue is purely behavioural. This is the conception of 'civil' or 'political' virtue that some later moralists have in mind when they allow pagans nothing more than civil virtue.[125]

This simple division between action and end does not capture the complexity of the pagan conception of virtue, as Augustine understands it. The Stoic and Peripatetic attitude to virtue manifests a morally correct conception of the ultimate end, as well as the right

---

[123] '. . . so that, as long as we are exiled from there [sc. the heavenly city], we may bear with those, if we cannot correct them, who, with vices unpunished, want the preservation of the commonwealth that the first Romans established and increased by their virtues; though they did not have true piety towards the true God, which was able to lead them to the eternal city by saving religion, even so they maintained an uprightness proper to them, which was able to suffice for the establishing, increasing, and maintaining of the earthly city. For in this way God showed, in the Roman empire of such great wealth and fame, the power of civil virtues, even without the true religion, so that it might be understood that, with this true religion added, human beings are made citizens of another city, whose ruler is true, whose light is charity, and whose measure is eternity' (*Ep.* 138.17, written in 412).

[124] '. . . these people, who showed Babylonian love for the earthly homeland, and by civic virtue, not true <virtue> but similar to true <virtue>, served demons or human glory—Fabricii, Reguli, Fabii, Scipiones, Camilli, and the others of the same sort' (*Iul.* iv 26).

[125] Lottin, *EM* 77, 83–8. The *Augsburg Confession* (Art. 18) speaks of 'civilis iustitia', citing pseudo-Augustine. See §418.

action. Hence the virtue that can be ascribed to these pagans cannot be purely behavioural. Epicureans can behave correctly, but Augustine believes that they differ from Stoics and Peripatetics in their capacity for virtues. Since virtues are marked by the morally correct conception of the ultimate end, as well as the correct action, pagans who follow Stoic or Peripatetic views have virtues.

Augustine's views about the moral condition of pagans take account of St Paul's claim that Gentiles fulfil the demands of the law (*Rm.* 2:14–16; *S et L* 43–8).[126] He allows that 'Gentiles' may refer to pagans whom we praise for their actions, even though they act for the wrong end.[127] 'Praising them for their actions' does not seem to imply the mere recognition that they behave correctly; Augustine also seems to suggest that pagans also have some grasp of morality that goes beyond mere behavioural conformity. He confirms this suggestion in his approval of the love that human beings can manifest to one another in the relations of families, friends, and fellow-citizens. He approves not only of correct behaviour to others, but also of its underlying motive.[128]

These points on which Augustine agrees with pagan virtue make it reasonable for him to allow it a partially correct conception of the ultimate end. We are closer to happiness if we have the right aims and find them frustrated than if we have the wrong aims and fulfil them. Someone who aims at living according to the virtues for their own sake has one important element in happiness, since having the right aims is itself a part of happiness.[129] A pagan who has the moral virtues aims to live in accord with them, and has the morally correct conception of the ultimate end. To this extent, therefore, someone with the pagan virtues has genuine virtues.[130]

This discussion of Augustine's views on the pagan moralists suggests that a simple division between the right action and the right end is too simple. He needs to say that the pagan virtues embody a conception of the end that is morally correct—since the elements of happiness that it recognizes are genuine elements of it—but also incorrect—since it fails to recognize other genuine elements of happiness.

---

[126] See §226 above.

[127] '. . . some of <their> actions—though they are those of impious people who do not truly and justly worship the true God—we not only cannot blame, but even deservedly and correctly praise, since they have been done, so far as we read or know or hear, according to the rule of justice; though if we discuss with what end these actions are done, we scarcely find any that deserve the praise and defence appropriate to justice. Still, since God's image has not been so completely erased in the human soul by the stain of earthly affections, as to have left remaining there not even the merest outlines, from which it can justly be said that even in this very impiety of life it certainly does or understands some things belonging to the law (facere aliqua legis vel sapere) . . .' (*S et L* 48).

[128] 'Have lawful charity therefore. It is human, but, as I said, lawful. Moreover, it is not lawful only in such a way that it is allowed, but lawful in such a way that if it is lacking, <the lack> is blamed. Let it be lawful for you to love your spouses, love your sons, to love your friends, to love your fellow citizens with human charity' (*Serm.* 349.2). This passage is discussed by Wang, *SAVP* 47. Pius VI quotes this passage and *S et L* 48, in his condemnation of the Synod of Pistoia; Denz. §2624, also discussed by Wang. See §417n62.

[129] 'And someone already has one good, and a considerable good, namely that very good will itself, if he desires to rejoice in the goods that human nature is capable of, and not in any bad action or acquisition, and pursues such goods as can be present even in this wretched life with a prudent, temperate, brave, and just mind, and achieves them as far as he is able . . .' (*Trin.* xiii 9).

[130] My discussion of pagan virtues is indebted to Wang's discussion (*SAVP* 45–57) of the 'vertus décevantes'. I doubt, however, whether he is right to explain them as belonging to a will that aims at particular good ends, without directing them to any ultimate end. This explanation does not seem to fit Augustine's eudaemonism; nor does Wang cite any specific evidence to show that Augustine recognizes the possibility of aiming at particular goods without an ultimate good. (The passage I cited from *Trin.* xiii 11 (in n121 above) suggests that he denies any such possibility).

If Augustine should recognize these virtuous aspects of the pagan virtues as well as the sinful aspects that result from pagan ignorance of the true character of the good, he should also explain, qualify, or supplement his claim that pagan virtues are really vices. It is consistent to claim that pagan virtues are virtues and that they are vices; some features of them make them virtues and other features make them vices. The two claims are consistent because virtues are good states or conditions or actualizations of some capacity or tendency; pagan virtues are good states of one capacity, but bad states of another.

233. Pagan Arrogance

One might, however, argue that this solution works only if the pagan conception makes an error of omission rather than commission. But Augustine has in mind an error of commission as well as omission. He charges that pagan virtue not only lacks the right conception of the end, but also includes a mistaken conception of the end, because it expresses arrogance (superbia).

In Augustine's view, 'no one without true piety, that is, without the true worship of God, can have true virtue, and it is not true virtue when it serves human glory' (CD v 19f). Those who advocate the choice of virtue for its own sake without reference to God really choose it for the sake of human glory, because they choose it for the sake of their own self-approval. In doing this they display arrogance. Two mistakes are characteristic of the arrogant person: (1) He attributes to himself what in fact he achieves only in dependence on God. (2) He fails to recognize the shortcomings in his own achievements (v 19g). This is why Augustine believes we would be arrogant if we were to claim to be free of passions in this life (xiv 9l, r).

The same arrogance that produced the sin of Adam and Eve against God encourages us to believe in our own unaided success; that is why arrogance is the beginning of all sin (xiv 13a). Lifting up one's heart to oneself rather than to God is the sort of arrogance that eventually abases us, since it turns us away from God (xiv 13d–e). In turning towards God, we recognize that we are subject to sin and conflict in this present life, but that we can call on the help of God to reduce the power of misguided desires and aims (xxii 23a).[131]

It is useful, though over-simplified, to distinguish arrogance towards God from arrogance towards other human beings. Arrogance towards God causes us to deny our dependence on God, and so to exaggerate our own importance and our own achievements in relation to God. Arrogance towards other people causes us to compete with them, to care more about our own interests than about theirs, and to compare ourselves favourably with them without justification. Neither Romulus nor Remus could tolerate anything less than domination over the other. Cain envied Abel's goodness, but Abel did not envy Cain, and did not seek domination over Cain (xv 5a–d). Arrogance '. . . perversely imitates God. For it

---

[131] 'Give me someone who sees quickly that the mind is not happy by its own good, when it is happy—otherwise it would never be unhappy. . . . For when the mind takes pleasure in itself as if in its own good, it is arrogant. But when it recognizes that it is changeable, . . . and notices that wisdom is unchangeable, it must at the same time notice that wisdom is above its own [sc. the mind's] nature . . . Thus ceasing and subsiding from boasting and from conceit in itself, it tries to adhere to God' (Ep. 118.15).

hates equality with one's fellows under God, but it wants to impose on one's fellows one's own domination in place of God' (xix 12l).

In this passage Augustine argues that arrogance towards God results in arrogance towards other human beings. Arrogance towards God, as he conceives it, is not a purely theological error; it has moral consequences for one's relations with other people. None the less, the two aspects of arrogance need to be distinguished. For, even if all those who refuse to acknowledge their dependence on God are arrogant, they may be arrogant to different degrees, and some moral outlooks may encourage arrogance towards other people more than other outlooks encourage it. If our moral outlook encourages us to compete against other people, and to pursue our own interests at their expense, and if it also encourages us to praise and esteem the winners in such competitions, Augustine is right to charge that the (alleged) virtues recognized by such a moral outlook are themselves both effects and causes of arrogance.

Some pagan conceptions of virtue might well be open to such objections. One might plausibly argue that, for instance, the Homeric conception of the virtues encourages the attitudes that Augustine attributes to Romulus, Remus, and Cain. But these objections do not apply to the Aristotelian and Stoic conceptions of virtue. If those who accept these conceptions of virtue are arrogant, that is not the fault of these conceptions of virtue. Augustine observes that virtuous people are pleased, and not disappointed, by the presence of goodness in others as well as in themselves.[132] Aristotle also expects this outlook in virtuous people; they do not regard virtue as a good to fight over, but give their friend the opportunity to do a fine action instead of trying to do it themselves (EN 1169a6–11, 31–4). Augustine has no quarrel with Aristotle on this point.

If, then, pagans actually acquire the states of character that Aristotle and the Stoics count as virtues, they will not be more arrogant towards other people than they would otherwise have been. On the contrary, they will have acquired the non-competitive attitude that Augustine opposes to the arrogant person's desire for domination over others. The virtuous person pursues virtue and virtuous action for their own sake; he does not subordinate them to his own desire for recognition by others or by himself. Augustine, therefore, has no good reason to maintain that the pagan virtues, as opposed to other aspects of the pagan outlook, are a special source or manifestation of arrogance. No arrogance is inherent in the pursuit of the virtues recognized by pagan moralists, or in action from the motives that they teach us to value. These virtues do not teach us to treat human glory as a dominant, or even prominent, part of the ultimate end of our actions.

To say this is not to reject Augustine's charge that pagans manifest arrogance in their virtuous actions. That charge is justified, if we manifest arrogance by failure to acknowledge the specific forms of dependence on God that Augustine describes. As we have seen, Christian moralists do not disagree with Stoic moralists (for instance) about the demands of the moral law; they accept, and indeed insist on, the perfectionist aspects of Stoicism. They criticize the pagan moralists for not explaining our failure to achieve the perfection demanded by morality. The Stoics implicitly acknowledge this failure, by admitting the rarity of the sage,

---

[132] 'Indeed, someone who refuses to have this possession in common will not have it at all, and he will find that he possesses a fuller measure of it the more fully he is able to love the one who shares it with him' (xv 5d).

but they still speak as though we could achieve the virtues if we attended to Stoic advice. Hence they still regard virtue as our own unaided achievement; and if they think they have achieved it, they deceive themselves (as St John puts it).[133] This sort of arrogance is pervasive in the life of pagans, because they do not admit their incapacity to achieve their own moral ideals; they think of their virtuous actions and states of character in the arrogant way in which they think of all their achievements.

These arguments do not show that pagan virtues are really vices. Though virtues that belong to pagans are necessarily virtues of arrogant people, they do not aim at the distinctive ends of arrogant people; they aim at praiseworthy ends that are equally appropriate ends for anyone who lacks arrogance. The connexion between arrogance and pagan virtues does not imply that pagan virtues themselves are special manifestations of arrogance.

From Augustine's theological point of view, pagans are indeed open to objection for being pagan, since they lack the relevant beliefs about grace and sin. But they are not open to objection for their realization or partial realization of the pagan conceptions of the virtues. We can therefore recognize and accept his views about the nature and extent of arrogance in the pagan outlook without retracting our previous account of pagan virtue. When we take proper account of the effects of arrogance in the pagan outlook, we must still agree that the pagan virtues embody a partly correct conception of the ultimate end of human life.

234. Self-Love, Arrogance, and the Earthly City

Augustine's objections to arrogance explain how virtue involves the right direction of the will. Our will is wrongly directed if it is directed towards ourselves, and rightly directed if it is directed towards God; this is why self-love underlies the earthly city and the love of God underlies the heavenly city. The self-love of the earthly city is the source of its conflicts, because our arrogance refuses to accept others as our equals (*CD* xv 5b; xix 12l). We are free of these conflicts only when we abandon self-love for the love of God.

In drawing this contrast, however, we may easily exaggerate the extent of Augustine's opposition to pagan virtue. He does not suggest that self-love is to be rejected altogether; he only rejects the self-love that goes as far as contempt of God. This form of self-love asserts the agent's own independence and self-sufficiency in relation to virtue. The love of God involves contempt of self only to the extent that it is required by the love of God; it does not require the contempt of self altogether. We would show complete contempt of self, for instance, if we became indifferent to our own happiness, or if we did not care about achieving the degree of virtue that is possible for us. The love of God requires only the contempt of self that recognizes our own inability to achieve virtue completely, and recognizes our need of the help of God to achieve the degree of virtue that we achieve.[134]

---

[133] See *1Jn.* 1:8–10, quoted at §211n100.

[134] 'For it is not possible for one who loves God not to love himself; on the contrary, the only one who knows how to love himself is the one who loves God. If the one who loves himself adequately is the one who acts diligently to enjoy the highest and true good, and if this is nothing other than God, who can delay in loving himself if he is a lover of God? And should there be no bond of love between human beings themselves? On the contrary, there should be such a bond

Augustine does not want us to dismiss his moral claims as Christian dogma that is irrelevant to pagan moral philosophy. He claims that his critique of pagan virtue appeals to standards that pagan moralists themselves must accept. A pagan moralist has to explain why people seem to fail in their attempts to live up to the standards set by pagan virtues. Augustine suggests that this pervasive failure is best understood by reference to an unavoidable tendency to sin, and that the more anxious we are about observing the standards of pagan virtues, the more we encourage the tendency to sin that undermines the virtues; this is Paul's analysis of the effects of acknowledging the moral law.

If we were to agree with Augustine on these psychological facts, without accepting his theological explanation, we would be in a similar position to the one we would be in if we accepted his claims about the prevalence of evil in the world without accepting his views about the prospects of happiness in an afterlife. In both cases we would have to follow the way of life that seems rationally preferable to us, but in the face of severe doubts about our prospects of success. These doubts are removed in the light of Augustine's claim that God co-operating with us can do for us what we cannot do for ourselves. If Augustine is right, it is realistic for us to hope for a higher degree of conformity to the virtues than we could expect if we trusted in our own resources and neglected the help of God. Though his claims about the prevalence of sin might initially appear pessimistic, he actually avoids the pessimism that, in his view, results from recognizing the psychological facts without their theological explanation.

Augustine does not believe, then, that he undermines the practice of the virtues, as pagan moralists understand them; he seeks to remove the obstacles imposed by human sin, and especially by human arrogance, to the practice of the virtues. The cardinal virtues recognized by pagan moralists require the regulation of passions by rational desire focussed on one's own good and the good of others, especially the good of the society whose good is part of one's own good. Augustine agrees with this conception of the virtues, and claims that we are in a better position to practise them if we recognize our dependence on God for our growth in virtue, and the insufficiency of the goods of this world for our complete happiness.

The good of a human society, judged from a purely human point of view, is 'earthly peace'. Compared with the 'heavenly peace' sought by the city of God, it is incomplete and unstable. But a Christian does not lose interest in earthly peace in the light of heavenly peace. When Paul claims that the sufferings of the present do not match future glory (Rm. 8:18), he might be taken to advocate indifference to the worldly goods that make sense of ordinary human virtues. Augustine, however, does not take Paul this way; he claims, against the Stoics, that external goods are really part of the human good, and that they are worth pursuing, though they are secondary to the complete happiness of the afterlife.

This is why Augustine agrees with Jeremiah's call to pray for the peace of Babylon, 'because in her peace is your peace' (CD xix 26b). The heavenly city uses the peace of the earthly city because it is necessary for this mortal life (xix 17d), and because it is a way towards heavenly peace (xix 17f). Earthly peace is a solace for the misery of our present condition, in contrast to the joy of happiness that we receive only through heavenly peace

of love that no more certain path to the love of God should be believed possible than charity of a human being towards a human being' (Mor. Eccl. 48). 'You love yourself appropriately (salubriter) if you love God more than yourself' (49). See Burnaby, AD 90.

(xix 27a). But it is a necessary consolation, because it helps to achieve the human good, so far as it can be achieved in present conditions.

Why does Augustine not take the more radical line that might seem attractive from a Christian point of view, of declaring the good of earthly societies to be irrelevant for those who have their eyes firmly fixed on preparation for the afterlife? This radical attitude is one source of the Christian monasticism that abandons the struggles of ordinary human communities for a more direct pursuit of a supernatural end.[135] Augustine does not take this line, because he does not regard pagan moral philosophy as completely misguided from a Christian point of view. He believes that pagan moral philosophy has identified genuine elements of the human good; since Christianity does not abandon the pursuit of the human good, it retains the appropriate goals of a virtuous life.

When we first confront Augustine's apparently sharp contrasts between the false happiness pursued by pagans and the true happiness pursued by Christians, between the false virtues of pagans and the true virtues that depend on true piety, and between the earthly city and the heavenly city, we may well infer that he intends the Christian outlook to replace pagan morality with a different morality, or to abandon morality altogether for a non-moral goal. The fact that this inference is easy and natural explains why Augustine has been used by Christian writers who have gone in one of these directions, and why a non-Christian reader might find in him a damaging attack on the foundations of Greek pagan moral theory. These inferences, however, do not do justice to Augustine's argument as a whole. If we do not focus exclusively on the sharp contrasts he draws, but attend to the details of his criticism of the pagan outlook, we find that his attack is less radical than it initially appears. He belongs to the tradition in Christian moral thinking that seeks to strengthen and to complete, not to destroy, the outlook of non-theological moral theory.

---

[135] The relation of Augustine to world-renouncing Christian monasticism is explored by Kirk, *VG*, chs. 5–6, esp. 242–57, 330–46.

16

AQUINAS: WILL

235. Aims

Aquinas has at least three aims in his moral philosophy: (1) He tries to say what Aristotle means, and what an Aristotelian conception of morality commits us to. (2) He tries to show that this conception of morality is defensible on philosophical grounds. (3) He seeks to show that it also satisfies the theological and moral demands of Christian doctrine.[1]

The third aim explains why his fullest treatment of ethics appears in the *Summa Theologiae*. Aquinas also expounds Aristotle's *Ethics* in his commentary, but there he mainly restricts himself to exposition of Aristotle's theory.[2] In the *Summa*, however, he raises wider questions about Aristotelian ethics, and so he discusses many issues that Aristotle does not discuss, and does not even formulate. Questions about, for instance, the relation of the virtues to divine grace and original sin arise only within a specific theological framework. But Aquinas discusses them with reference to an Aristotelian moral theory. He begins his discussion of the infused moral virtues from his Aristotelian conception of a moral virtue. His discussion of divine grace and human freewill relies on an Aristotelian conception of freedom and of the will.[3]

Aquinas' success or failure in his third aim is historically important, since his successors also try to connect moral philosophy with Christian theology. Some object to Aquinas' position by claiming that it is not adequate for the expression of Christian doctrines about human agency, the human good, and their relation to the will of God. Others believe that Christian faith conflicts with and supersedes the outlook of non-theological moral philosophy; a defence of this belief also requires some account of the outlook of moral philosophy.

---

[1] On these aims cf. §357.

[2] The commentary on the *Ethics* is discussed by Jaffa, *TA*; Gauthier, in Aquinas, *SLE* 235–57; Bourke, '*Ethics*'; and most fully by Doig, *APCE*, who argues for its philosophical (as opposed to theological) character.

[3] 'Freewill' renders 'liberum arbitrium'. This rendering may be misleading, since the Latin does not immediately suggest, as the English does, that the problem primarily concerns the freedom of the will (voluntas). I will render 'arbitrium' by 'choice'. 'Judgment' would perhaps come closest to Aquinas' conception of arbitrium (hence he associates arbitrium with iudicium, and appeals to the use of 'arbitrium' for a verdict (cf. English 'arbitrate'). But his conception rests on his theory of liberum arbitrium, not simply on the ordinary concept of arbitrium; hence a less precise translation is preferable. See §§218, §267.

Aquinas' third aim is also philosophically important. If Christian doctrines rested on conceptions of freedom, responsibility, or merit that are unintelligible or repugnant from the point of view of moral theory, that would be a serious objection to them. If they are both intelligible and morally plausible, they are not open to this objection. The task of showing that Aquinas succeeds in his third aim is too complex for us to attempt in this account of his moral philosophy; but we will find some reasons for believing that his strategy is more plausible than it has sometimes seemed to critics.[4]

Even if Aquinas fails in his third aim, he may succeed in either or both of his first two aims. He does not explicitly separate the different parts of his theory that seek to carry out these different aims. But it is reasonable for us to try to separate them, if we want to see which parts of his position we might accept or reject, and on what grounds.

Aquinas' aims assume some distinction between moral philosophy and moral theology. He does not devote a specific section of the *Summa* to moral philosophy; the work as a whole belongs to moral theology. But he distinguishes arguments and considerations that are proper to moral philosophy; they appeal to human reason and argument, not to the authorities cited by the Christian theologian. Moral philosophy deals with human beings as having freewill and control over their actions; hence a denial that human beings are free would be 'destructive of all moral philosophy and political activity' (*SG* ii 60 §1374; *in Periherm.* i 14 = P xviii 33b), not only of the Christian faith (*Mal.* q6 a1). Considerations about what is excessive or defective, useful or right are the concern of moral philosophy, as distinct from theology (*2Sent.* d24 q2 a2 = P vi 599a).[5] The moral philosopher studies sin as a violation of reason, whereas the theologian studies it as a violation of the divine law.[6]

In looking for moral philosophy in the *Summa*, we are looking for arguments and claims that are defended or defensible without reference to the distinctive sources of Christian dogma. These arguments and claims in Aquinas present us with a system of moral philosophy.

236. Interpretations of Aristotle

Aquinas tries to present an account of ethics that is also the best interpretation of Aristotle. But what sort of interpretation does he offer?

Two familiar ways of conceiving someone's relation to a historical predecessor do not fit Aquinas' aims in the *Summa*: (1) The expositor or commentator, in a narrow sense, is engaged in Aristotelian exegesis. This is Aquinas' aim in his commentaries on Aristotle;

---

[4] For some discussion of Aquinas' third aim see §343. Sidgwick presents a negative view: '[Aquinas'] effort was, indeed, foredoomed to failure, since it attempted the impossible task of framing a coherent system out of the heterogeneous data furnished by Scripture, the Fathers, the Church, and "the Philosopher"; and whatever philosophic quality is to be found in the work of Thomas belongs to it in spite of, not in consequence of, its method' (*OHE* 148).

[5] On the difference between moral philosophy and theology cf. *2Sent.* d40 q1 a5 = P vi 750a; *3Sent.* d23 q2 a4 qla 2 obj3, ad3 = P vii 251b, 252b. Some critics deny that Aquinas is really engaged in moral philosophy in the *Summa*. See Bradley, *ATHG*, ch. 1; Jordan, 'Ideals'.

[6] See 1-2 q71 a6 ad5: 'The theologian considers sin chiefly in so far as it is an offence against God. But the moral philosopher considers it chiefly in so far as it is contrary to reason'. Aquinas' position is discussed by Vasquez, *Disp.* 97 c.3, p. 658; Suarez, *Leg.* ii 6.17.

he seeks, as other commentators do, to explain particular passages by reference to other passages, and especially by spelling out compressed or inexplicit arguments and claims with the help of resources that Aristotle provides.[7] (2) 'Neo-Aristotelian' theorists incorporate Aristotelian insights in a theory that examines different questions from those that concern Aristotle. If, for instance, we try to show how an Aristotelian account of the virtues offers a reasonable option distinct from Kantian and utilitarian conceptions of morality, we approach Aristotle with a different philosophical agenda. Different 'neo-' theories may incorporate more or less Aristotle. Though the earlier model may be a genuine and deep source of inspiration for the later work, the aims and spirit of the later work are different.[8]

To understand and to evaluate Aquinas' use of Aristotle, it is useful to introduce a further option: (3) One might be a 'defender' of Aristotle without being either simply an expositor or simply a neo-Aristotelian theorist. To defend Aristotle without embedding one's defence in a neo-Aristotelian theory is to notice a difficulty or question that Aristotle raises, and to answer it with something that is available to Aristotle, but not actually formulated or used by him.

This conception of a defender rests on assumptions about what is 'available' to Aristotle. Perhaps a defence is available to Aristotle if he might reasonably be expected to think of it had he persistently pursued questions that a contemporary might have asked him. An expositor may find that Aristotle does not take up a particular question or that he leaves a loose end. Here a defender may point out that Aristotle could have taken up this question and answered it, though perhaps not without some modification of other things he says. We may then come to see that his position is more defensible, given what Aristotle himself takes to be important, if he goes in one direction than if he goes in another.

This division between expositors, defenders, and neo-theorists does not exclude the possibility of one person's pursuing all three approaches. But it may suggest some of the right questions to ask about Aquinas. While he sometimes speaks as an expositor of Aristotle, and sometimes as a neo-Aristotelian theorist, some important questions concern his success or failure as a defender of Aristotle.[9] A defence does not fail simply because it relies on claims or arguments that Aristotle does not make. But it fails if it clearly relies on claims or arguments that basically change the character of Aristotle's theory for reasons that he could not reasonably be expected to accept, given his basic outlook. To decide whether a defence succeeds or fails requires some philosophical judgment on whether a particular claim is 'basic' in Aristotle's position. Hence we cannot decide on purely historical grounds whether Aquinas' theory is basically Aristotelian or distorts Aristotle, if 'purely historical' grounds exclude philosophical evaluation.[10]

---

[7] On Aquinas' approach to Aristotle see Chenu, UST 153n57. On Aquinas' concern with the intention of the author being discussed he cites ST 1a q79 a7 ad1; 1-2 q50 a1 (where Aquinas argues about the intention of Aristotle by appealing both to the immediate context and to what he says in another work). On the purpose of philosophy see *in DC* i, lect. 22: 'The study of philosophy does not aim at knowledge of what people have thought, but at knowledge of how the truth of things is'. See also Doig, APCE xii–xiv. Cf. Scotus' comment on Aristotle, §357n2.

[8] Contrasting examples of neo-Aristotelian views may be found in McDowell, MVR and Foot, NG.

[9] On approaches to authorities see Chenu, UST 144–55.

[10] Contrast Kent's remarks on a 'historical reading of the *Ethics*', VW 74, and on 'distortions' of Aristotle, 93.

237. The Form of Aquinas' Argument

To defend Aristotle, Aquinas derives his ethical theory from conditions on rational agency. His theory seems to be reductive, because of two claims: (1) The facts that vindicate Aquinas' account of freedom, happiness, and the virtues are facts that, in his view, we must already recognize if we are to understand rational agents and their actions. (2) But the facts that we recognize in understanding rational agents do not seem to be facts that we must already recognize as facts about freedom, happiness, and the virtues.

Only the second claim affirms the priority that we need for a reduction. If we affirm the first and deny the second, we claim that knowledge of morality and knowledge of rational agency are inter-dependent, but not that the knowledge of rational agency is prior. But Aquinas does not affirm the second claim as clearly as he affirms the first. Does acceptance of his claims about rational agency depend on any of his moral theory? Must we, for instance, already agree that rational agents are free, or that they pursue happiness, if we are to accept his account of rational agency?

To see whether Aquinas either intends to offer a reductive argument or actually offers one, we should try to set out his position in the order that a reductive argument would demand. We should not rely on any claims about freedom or morality in explaining or defending his claims about rational agency. If these constraints prevent us from attributing an intelligible or coherent position to Aquinas, we will have some reason to suppose that he does not intend to present a reductive argument, but intends simply to demonstrate the coherence of claims about rational agents and about freedom and morality.

If we accept a cogent reductive argument, we can defend a true account of morality without appeal to any further facts than those facts about rational agency that we must already recognize independently of morality. This reductive claim is both ontological and epistemological. It says that if the facts about rational agency are fixed, then the facts about morality are fixed too. It also says that once we recognize the facts about rational agency, we have sufficient reason for accepting a particular moral theory too. It does not follow, however, that once we recognize the facts about rational agency, we also recognize that we have sufficient reason for accepting the moral theory. Aquinas tries to show us that we have this sufficient reason.

Aquinas seeks an account that unifies the aspects of moral theory that concern prudence, universal conscience (synderesis), natural law, and the ultimate good. We might resist this unifying tendency; these aspects of moral theory might be derived from more than one source of moral principles. It is not obvious, for instance, that the moral requirements imposed by natural law are just the ones that can be reached by reflexion on what one needs for one's own happiness. We might even suppose that if we attempt to reduce the one set of requirements to the other, we lose some essential moral content; the impersonal, objective requirements of natural law may appear to be different from the advice that self-interested agents might give themselves. Similarly, it is not obvious that the principles grasped by conscience are just the ones that the prudent person relies on in deliberation about happiness.

Aquinas, however, argues that all these apparently different sources of moral principles are really the same, and that they all rely on just the same basic facts about rational agency.[11] His claims about agency affect the details as well as the general aims of his moral theory.

238. Aquinas and Naturalism

The claim that moral principles express truths about rational agency may appear to fit a Kantian theory better than it fits an Aristotelian theory. Kant (according to some readers) appeals to a priori truths about the abstract form of practical reason and rational agency, in abstraction from facts about actual human beings, whereas Aristotle recognizes the relevance of psychological and social facts of the sort that Kant rejects as 'mere' anthropology. Aristotle (on this view) is a naturalist and Kant rejects naturalism. If our description of Aquinas is right, he seems more Kantian than Aristotelian.

This contrast, however, between Kant and Aristotle is misleading. For it suggests that appeals to human nature must rely on contingent and empirical facts about human nature (since they do not apply to all possible rational agents, but rest on empirical information about particular human beings).[12] Our account of Aristotle's naturalism should have cast some doubt on any such understanding of naturalism.[13] Aristotle does not rely only on contingent empirical facts about human beings; his account of the human function and of the division of the soul is not a generalization about human beings, but an account of the essence of a human being as a rational animal. Aquinas' position, therefore, might be Aristotelian and naturalist even if it describes facts that Kant believes are known a priori.

But if Aquinas' argument is reductive in the sense that we suggested, it opposes Kant's view that, apart from our moral beliefs, we have no reason to attribute freedom to human beings. Sometimes Kant recognizes a self-sufficient point of view of 'nature', which leaves us no room for the recognition of freedom, responsibility, or good and bad wills. Since freedom rests on morality, which is outside nature, the point of view of nature cannot be the only point of view that grasps reality.[14]

This Kantian position conflicts not only with a reductive version of Aquinas' position, but also with the version that asserts coherence and mutual support between truths about rational agency and truths about morality. We might say that, for Aquinas, the moral point of view stays within the point of view of nature, because it introduces no non-natural claims about causation and freedom. Alternatively, we might say that he denies the possibility of a point of view of nature that excludes freedom. From one point of view, Aquinas demands less for morality than Kant demands. From another point of view, he demands more for nature than Kant demands.

The main disagreement concerns the non-moral understanding of human beings. In Kant's view, we can achieve this understanding from the point of view of nature, which does not require us to understand human beings as free agents. But in Aquinas' view, the understanding of human action as part of nature requires the recognition of human freedom.

---

[11] See §309.

[12] This way of stating the issue reflects a Kantian (and controversial) view about the connexion between the empirical and the contingent.

[13] See §§75–6.   [14] On the opposition of freedom and nature see, e.g., Kant, *KrV* A547/B575.

He believes that reasons, action, and freedom have a place in our understanding of the natural world, and therefore have a place in morality.

Claims about agency are especially important in this dispute. Aquinas does not seem to believe that we must already take the point of view of morality, as distinct from the causal and explanatory attitude, in order to see that human beings are free agents. He believes that a complete account of human beings as natural objects requires us to recognize that they are free, and that they pursue a good that consists in their perfection. Even if he is right, he may not yet have found a sufficient basis for an account of morality; but he has a more plausible basis than he would have if he confined himself to the natural point of view, as Kant understands it.

This dispute about the division between nature and freedom is one major point of contrast between the Aristotelian and the Kantian approach to morality. Some believe it is not a dispute mainly about morality; perhaps the Aristotelian approach rests on a view of the world that may have been tenable for Aristotle and Aquinas, but is no longer tenable in the light of modern science. If, for instance, the Aristotelian approach rests on aspects of Aristotelian teleology that later science has refuted, anyone who rejects the Aristotelian world view must accept Kant's view about what is included in nature.[15]

This account of part of the dispute between an Aristotelian and a Kantian position raises a question about Aquinas: do his claims about rational agency rest on assumptions that are scientifically incredible? If they do not, then either the incredible claims enter with the transition from rational agency to morality, or else his position cannot be dismissed as scientifically incredible. If we cannot dismiss it on this ground, we should compare it with the Kantian position on philosophical grounds.

239. The Structure of Aquinas' Ethical Theory

In the Prima Secundae, Aquinas begins his discussion of ethics with the ultimate end. Unlike Aristotle, he gives a reason for beginning here. His treatment of ethics examines human beings in so far as they are made in the image of God, and thereby are the source of their own actions, because they have freewill and power over their actions.[16] The ultimate end comes first because it is the goal of free action, and the basis for understanding it. The next two sections of the Prima Secundae depart from Aristotle's order of exposition, to examine human actions and passions. Since happiness is about distinctively human actions, as opposed to other sorts of actions done by human beings, we need an account of human actions in order to understand the actions that achieve happiness. The moral virtues are primarily concerned with human actions. Since happiness, being the good proper to a human being, involves properly human actions, the actions characteristic of the virtues are especially relevant to happiness.[17] But the virtues are concerned not only with the distinctively human

---

[15] See Darwall, *BMIO* 7–8; Korsgaard, *SN* 3–5, 21–3.

[16] 'Since, as Damascene says, a human being is said to be made in the image of God, in so far as by 'image' is meant something with understanding, free by its judgment (arbitrium) and with power in itself', . . . it remains for us to consider God's image, i.e. a human being, in so far as he also is the source (principium) of his actions, as having freewill and power over his own actions' (*ST* 1–2 Prol.). On Damascene cf. 1a q93 a9; *Ver.* q24 a2 sc1.

[17] 'And since happiness is the good proper to a human being, those acts that are properly human are more closely connected to happiness than those that are common to a human being and other animals. First, then, we must consider

and rational actions, but also with actions on passion, which human beings share with other animals; hence a discussion of passions introduces the account of the virtues. Aquinas treats the passions after the will because the will affects the passions; though we share passions with non-rational animals (1-2 q6 intr.), the passions do not move us to action in the same way as they move non-rational animals.

Aquinas' claims about virtue and happiness imply that the virtues result from the exercise of freewill (1-2 q55 a1 ad2). Happiness is the ultimate end for free rational agents who are self-movers and who control their actions; and so if the moral virtues promote happiness, they exercise the freewill of rational agents. Since the moral virtues require the right relation between the rational and the non-rational desires of a rational agent, we can exercise our freewill so as to reach the right relation between rational and non-rational desires; for if the virtues were not in our control, they would not be primary elements of happiness, which primarily consists in actions that are in our control.

Aquinas' claims about virtue assume that rational desires can control and modify non-rational desires. If it were not up to us, to some significant degree, to have non-rational desires of the right intensity for the right objects, it would not be up to us to have the virtues, and the virtues would not be primary elements of happiness. Hence the right account of the relation between the passions and the will is a pre-condition for the right account of the virtues, and for the right account of the sources of sin.

This discussion of action and passion comes between the treatment of the ultimate end (Book i of Aristotle's *Ethics*) and the treatment of states and virtues (Book ii of the *Ethics*). Aquinas' predecessors do not follow exactly this order, but reflexion on Aristotle supports it. Aristotle introduces a discussion of the voluntary between the general account of the virtues and the description of the particular virtues (*EN* iii 1–5), and in the account of the virtues, he refers briefly to the division between passion and rational desire, and to the distinctive features of states of character (ii 5). Aquinas clarifies Aristotle's position by setting out these aspects of his theory of action before the account of the virtues.[18]

The central element in this argument is Aquinas' account of the will. Once we understand the nature of the will and its relation to intellect and to passion, we also understand the source of freedom, the basis of ethics, and the foundation of virtue. For a rational agent essentially has a will that necessarily pursues an ultimate end and acts on deliberation about what promotes that end. Deliberation influences action both directly, by causing action on rational desire, and indirectly, by interacting with the passions. The nature of will and of deliberation explain why rational agents are free and responsible, why they necessarily pursue their own happiness, and why they need virtues, both moral and intellectual, to

those acts that are proper to a human being, and secondly, those that are common to a human being and the other animals and are called passions' (1-2 q6 intr.).

[18] Jordan, 'Ideals', discusses the structure and organization of *ST*, including 1–2. He remarks that the order Aquinas chooses is not Aristotle's, but he does not discuss reasons that might persuade a reader of Aristotle that Aristotle might have chosen a better order. At 87–9 he discusses the treatment of the ultimate end and of theory of action.

achieve this happiness. The relation of the will to passions explains why we act freely even when we do not act directly on will and deliberation, and why virtues require the perfection of the passions as well as the will.

240. Augustine and Aristotle

This focus on the will has no explicit precedent in Aristotle. It seems to reflect the influence of Christian moralists, and especially Augustine. Aquinas begins from Augustine's claim that the will is that by which we sin and live rightly, and so cannot be attached unchangeably either to good or to evil (1a q82 a2 sc; *Ver.* q22 a6 sc1, quoting Augustine, *Retract.* i 9).[19] He proceeds to defend Augustine's philosophical and theological claims about the will and its relation to freedom, virtue, sin, and grace.

To defend Augustine, however, Aquinas has to interpret him carefully. He often cites Augustine in the questions on the ultimate end and on human action, so that he can fix the right interpretation through a discussion of the different philosophical issues. In many of the objections that begin his questions, Aquinas cites Augustine in order to examine the apparent difficulties that arise from an Augustinian point of view. He also cites him as the authority in the 'sed contra' that follows the objections; sometimes cites him both in the objections and in the 'sed contra'. A simple comparison of citations might lead us to the hasty conclusion that Augustine contradicts himself. To refute this hasty conclusion, Aquinas' replies often return to the passages from Augustine that were quoted in the objections, to show that a reasonable interpretation makes Augustine consistent both with himself and with Aquinas.[20]

But though Aquinas constantly keeps Augustine in mind, and though he agrees with Augustine's emphasis on the will, he does not begin from a distinctively Augustinian account of the will. In speaking of 'will' (voluntas) he simply uses the standard Latin translation of '*boulêsis*', Aristotle's term for rational desire,[21] and in speaking of the 'voluntary' (voluntarium) he refers to Aristotle's division between the voluntary (*hekousion*) and the involuntary (*akousion*). He does not force Aristotle into an Augustinian framework. On the

---

[19] Cf. *Mal.* q3 a3 sc1–2. He also agrees with Augustine's claim that unless something is voluntary it cannot be a sin (*Ver.* q22 a6 sc2, quoting Augustine, *VR* 14; *Retract.* i 13). He begins his discussion of virtue with Augustine's claim that virtue is the good use of freewill (1-2 q55 a1 ad2); the rest of his discussion seeks to clarify Augustine's claim, and so to fix the sense in which it is true.

[20] In the treatises on the last end and on human action Augustine is cited in the initial objections: q4 a3; a7; q6 a8; q9a1; a2; a5; a6; q10 a4; q12 a4. He is cited in the 'sed contra' at q1 a3; a6; a7; q2 a7; a8; q3 a1; a5; q6 a4; q11 a1. He is cited in the objections and the 'sed contra' at q1 a8; q4 a1; q15 a4; q16 a1; a2. He is cited in the objections, 'sed contra', and replies at q5 a8; q11 a2; a3 (also corpus); a4; q12 a1; q16 a3; q17 a9. He is cited both in the objections and in the replies at q9 a5; q12 a3; a4; q15 a1; q17 a5; a9. He is cited in the corpus of the article at q4 a8; q5 a3, and in both objections and corpus at q1 a5; q3 a4 (also in replies).

[21] The translation is justified by the correspondence of the non-technical uses of 'velle' and 'voluntas' in Ciceronian Latin with '*boulesthai*' and '*boulêsis*' in Greek. (In *TD* iv 12 Cicero translates the Stoic term found in (e.g.) DL vii 116.) Cf. §218n14. *Boulêsis* is prominent in Damascene's account of thought and action (under the influence of Maximus the Confessor; see Gauthier, *EN* i 262–5; 'Maxime' 52–7). Aquinas uses Damascene's remarks on *thelêsis* and *boulêsis* to clarify the relation of will to freewill. See 1a q83 a4 obj1, sc; 3a q18 a3 obj1; Damasc. *EF* 36.55.

contrary, he sets out from an Aristotelian position, as he conceives it, and seeks to show that Augustine's claims are all defensible within an Aristotelian framework.[22]

Following Aristotle, he distinguishes will, as rational desire (*boulêsis*), from non-rational desire (*epithumia* and *thumos*). Since will is essentially rational desire, it realizes a capacity distinct from non-rational sensory desire (*Ver.* q22 a4); the different ways in which we grasp the objects of rational and non-rational desires mark two capacities (1a q80 a2).[23] This rationalist conception of *boulêsis* rests on solid Aristotelian support.[24]

241. Rational Agency, Voluntary Action, and Freedom

Aquinas believes that if we recognize the will, as Aristotle conceives it, we can grasp the connexions between some basic claims in Aristotelian ethics. We believe that we are rational agents with the capacity for practical reasoning and deliberation, that we act voluntarily, and that we have freewill. Aquinas recognizes that the questions 'Do we act voluntarily?' (1-2 q6 a1) and 'Do we have freewill?' (1a q83 a1) may appear to be separate;[25] he sees that his conditions for rational agency, Aristotle's conditions for voluntary agency, and the conditions for freewill may appear to mark three different features of rational agents. But he believes that we act voluntarily and we have freewill just in so far as we have wills and are capable of practical reasoning and deliberation. A correct account of the will and the passions justifies us (in his view) in claiming that we act voluntarily and have freewill. Rational agents with wills control their actions, whereas non-rational agents are moved by their desires without the intervention of will, and therefore do not control their actions. Hence rational agents act voluntarily, according to Aristotle's criteria, and have freewill. Aquinas, therefore, defends a reduction of the voluntary and of freewill to the exercise of will in rational choice.[26]

His reductive argument might be questioned. On the one hand, his conditions seem too strict to cover all voluntary action, as Aristotle conceives it; for Aristotle seems to recognize voluntary actions that do not express rational agency. On the other hand, they seem too broad to pick out free actions; for it seems possible for rational agents to lack freewill. Aquinas can answer these objections if he can appeal to criteria for voluntariness and freedom that he and his opponents accept, and can show that his conditions satisfy these criteria. Freewill presents him with the more difficult task; for it is more difficult to find mutually acceptable criteria. Many of Aquinas' contemporaries and successors argue that his Aristotelian principles do not support an appropriately robust conception of freedom. To decide whether these critics are right or wrong, we need to examine his account of the will.

---

[22] Some of Aquinas' reflexions on Augustine can be found in the various passages cited in Augustine; see, e.g., §221.

[23] He recognizes that in Aristotle's list of the different types of capacities of the soul, desire is mentioned without distinction (*Ver.* q22 a4 obj 4), but he appeals to Aristotle's division in *DA* 432b5 between *boulêsis* and the other desires (*in DA* iii 14 §§802–3; 1a q82 a5 sc; q87 a4; *Ver.* q22 a4 sc1).

[24] On the suggestion that Aquinas' interpretation is anachronistic see §97.   [25] See §260n1.

[26] Reduction: see §237.

242. Will and Properly Human Actions

Will is essentially rational desire,[27] because it is determined by free judgment,[28] in contrast to sensory desire, which operates without free judgment.[29] Since human beings have essentially rational desires, they have reflective control over their choices, and so they are not purely passive in relation to their desires. We exercise free judgment and reflective control because rational desire conceives its object 'in accordance with some universal character (ratio), as when it desires something because it is good' (1a 80 a2 ad2).

To have a will and to act on it is not only to pursue some end, but also to move or guide oneself towards an end, rather than simply tending towards an end.[30] Human beings do this in so far as they perform 'human actions', properly so called. These belong to human beings as such, who differ from irrational creatures by controlling their own actions (suorum actuum dominus, 1-2 q1 a1) through will and reason; actions proceeding 'from deliberated will' are properly human actions. 'Actions of a human being' that are not properly human actions include unconscious movements and reflexes (tapping one's feet, stroking one's beard).[31]

This division between properly human actions and actions of human beings does not mention human actions on passion. Non-rational animals act, as Aquinas agrees, on their sensory desires, their passions; in doing so, they seem to act for the sake of an end (q1 a2). Human beings also seem to act on passions, not always on deliberated will; and when we act on passions, we act for the sake of an end. But Aquinas seems to exclude these from properly human actions; his treatment of the nature of human action distinguishes properly human actions from the actions common to human and other animals, which are actions on passion.[32]

---

[27] Voluntas nominat rationalem appetitum, 1-2 q6 a2 ad1. Cf. 1a q81 a1; q87 a4; 1-2, q6 introd.; q8 a1.

[28] Will is 'a desire following the apprehension by the one who desires in accordance with free judgment. And of this sort is rational or intellectual desire, which is called the will' (1-2 q26 a1). Cf. 1a q82 a5; q87 a4; 1-2, q6 introd.; q8 a1. I use 'desire' for 'appetitus', which Aquinas uses to translate 'orexis'. This may cause confusion, since some philosophers distinguish will from desire. Moreover, Aquinas also ascribes appetitus to non-conscious beings; cf. 1a q80 a1 on natural appetitus. But it is difficult to find a rendering that will convey this wide scope of appetitus. 'Appetite' seems even less suitable than 'desire', except on etymological grounds. I use 'appetite' to translate 'epithumia' (for which Aquinas uses 'concupiscentia').

[29] '[Sensory appetite] follows apprehension by the one who desires, but from necessity, not from free judgment. And of this sort is sensory desire in beasts; in human beings, however, it has some share in freedom, to the extent that it obeys reason' (1-2 q26 a1).

[30] 'Nevertheless it must be observed that a thing tends to an end, by its action or movement, in two ways: in one way, as moving itself towards the end, as a human being does; in another way, as moved by another towards the end, ... Therefore those things that have reason, move themselves to an end, because they control their actions through freewill, which is a capacity of will and reason' (1-2 q1 a2). The relevant conception of control (dominium) is helpfully discussed, with special reference to Ver. q24 a2, by Gallagher, 'Will' 564–9.

[31] 'Actions of this sort are not properly human actions; since they do not proceed from deliberation of reason, which is the proper principle of human acts. Therefore they have indeed an imagined end, but not one presented through reason' (1-2 q1 a1 ad3). Reflex actions are done 'without the attention of the intellect' (SG iii 2 §1876). On human actions cf. 2Sent. d25 q1 a3 sol = P vi 615b.

[32] 'Now among human acts some are proper to human beings, while others are common to human beings and other animals. And since happiness is the proper good of human beings, the acts that are properly human are more closely related to happiness than the acts that are common to human beings and other animals . . . which <acts> are called passions of the soul' (1-2 q6 intr.).

He does not really intend, however, to exclude actions on passion from properly human actions. Properly human actions are voluntary, since they proceed from the will (voluntas);[33] but actions on passion are voluntary if they are appropriately related to the will (1-2 q6 a6–7; q10 a3). Hence actions on passion are included, through their relation to the will, among the properly human actions, and therefore among those that are directed towards an ultimate end. The discussion of voluntary action shows how this is possible.

A grasp of properly human actions, therefore, requires some grasp of Aquinas' views on the passions. Though the Prima Secundae discusses human action before the passions, the account of action presupposes a conception of the passions; the order of discussion in the First Part, where the passions come before the will, is in some ways more helpful. It will be useful, therefore, to introduce Aquinas' views about non-rational agency and about the passions before we go further with his account of properly human action; for he intends his view of human action to be flexible enough to include both deliberately willed action and action on passion that is suitably related to the will.

243. Rational v. Non-rational Agents

Aquinas' description of the will and action explains his claim that rational agents are self-directing in some way that distinguishes them from non-rational agents. The relevant features of rational agents are easier to grasp if we compare rational agents with non-rational agents who lack these features.

Non-rational agents lack the concept of an end, and 'therefore they cannot direct anything towards an end' (1-2 q1 a2). They cannot aim at an end, because they do not 'consider that through their movement they can achieve an end, which is proper to one who aims' (q12 a5 ad3). They lack the perfect knowledge of an end, which consists not only in apprehending the thing that is an end, but also in a grasp (cognitio) of the character (ratio) of the end and of the relation of the means to the end (q6 a2).

Non-rational animals do not reach satisfaction (fruitio) in the achievement of an end, because satisfaction demands a perfect cognitive grasp of the end, and such a grasp requires a grasp of the 'universal character of end and good' (q11 a2), including a grasp of the relation between a particular good and the final good (cf. q11 a2 ad2). This cognitive grasp distinguishes will from sensory desire. Rational agents 'are inclined to good with the cognition by which they grasp the character itself of good' (1a q59 a1).[34] This is why they do not have their inclination determined for them from outside, but determine it for themselves (*Ver.* q22 a4).

Why is this not true of a non-rational agent? A dog may stop eating or drinking if its attention is distracted; is it not capable, then, of being inclined towards something

---

[33] 'And since the acts properly called human are the voluntary acts, from the fact that will is rational desire, which is proper to human beings, we must consider acts in so far as they are voluntary' (1-2 q6 intr.).

[34] Non-rational agents 'are inclined towards good with some sort of cognition (cognitio)—not in such a way that they grasp (cognoscere) the character itself of the good, but they grasp some sort of particular good, as the sense does that grasps sweet, white, and so on' (1a q59 a1).

different? Rational agents may also stop what they are doing if they imagine something unappealing; if I am eating oysters and they suddenly seem slimy and disgusting, I may stop eating them. But surely non-rational agents can change their preferences in this way too.

Aquinas might reply that, in the case just described, I do not direct my action towards the object of desire. In directing my action towards an end, I endorse the action as a means to an end that I value in relation to my other ends. But if I find oysters slimy and disgusting, I may not believe they are bad to eat; despite my aversion, I might decide that they are good to eat, and direct my action towards eating them (if, for instance, I believe there is nothing wrong with them and there is no other suitable food available). An aversion does not necessarily change the evaluation that directs our action towards an object.

Aquinas marks this contrast between rational and non-rational agency by distinguishing determination to a particular good from determination to a universal good. Since the object of the will is the universal good, creatures that lack reason cannot have a will because they cannot grasp a universal good, but are determined to some particular good (1-2 q1 a2 ad3).[35] This is why they lack election.

For similar reasons rational agents pursue a universal good, and are not necessarily determined to any particular good: 'because the good is of many sorts (multiplex), the will is not necessarily determined to one thing' (1a q82 a2 ad1; 1-2 q10 a2). The will tends towards the universal good grasped by reason, whereas sensory desire tends only towards a particular good grasped by the sensory power (1a q80 a2 ad2; 1-2 q19 a3).[36]

Aquinas claims that since rational agents conceive and pursue a universal good, they differ from non-rational agents in so far as they grasp the concept of an end, and they direct and move themselves towards an end instead of being directed and moved towards it. The contrast between activity and passivity helps to explain how the will differs from a passion in rational agents, and how rational agents are agents to a higher degree than non-rational agents are. But what is the connexion between pursuit of an ultimate end and active agency?

We can see some connexion if we consider how recognition of an end as an end might differ from simply being moved towards an end. Perhaps I could recognize bread as bread, and notice that sometimes I find myself wanting to eat bread. This might still, in Aquinas' view, fall short of recognizing eating bread as an end of mine; to recognize it as an end (we might argue) I have to recognize it as something desirable, something I find worth pursuing. In saying that I find it worth pursuing, I might also remark that I do not find it desirable to eat bread in all circumstances; to say when I find it desirable, I have to relate it to the other things I find worth pursuing. To relate it to these other things, I have to have a conception of some more universal good—something that makes eating bread desirable on the occasions when it is desirable.

---

[35] ' . . . sensory desire is determined to some one particular thing in accordance with the direction of nature, whereas the will is determined to some one common thing, the good in accordance with the direction of nature, but is in an undetermined condition in relation to particular goods' (1-2 q13 a2).

[36] It is possible for a non-rational passion to be directed against something universal, but not possible for it to be directed against something qua universal (1-2 q29 a6). A sheep, for instance, may hate wolves universally, in so far as everything that looks like a wolf will excite the same reaction; but it does not follow that the sheep has picked out the class of wolves and formed a view about it.

If Aquinas accepts some argument such as this, he can explain why 'grasping the concept of an end' in the intended sense requires grasp of a universal good, and why it implies self-direction. I direct my own action, instead of simply being moved by features of external objects, in so far as I assess my initial value judgments about external objects in the light of my other value judgments. My action is determined not simply by whether I find this or that object attractive, but also by the broader evaluative judgments that constitute myself. Since rational agents guide their actions by a conception of the end that recognizes what is worthwhile in one or another action and end, Aquinas believes that directing one's own action, knowing the end, and presenting the end to oneself, all involve one another and all involve a grasp of some universal good.

Non-rational agents, therefore, lack control over their actions, and so are not self-movers. Though they act for an end,[37] they do not act for an ultimate end, since they do not move themselves, but are moved by something else. Human beings are self-movers because they have control (dominium)[38] over their actions, by having freewill, which is a 'capacity of will and reason' (q1 a2).[39]

Non-rational agents lack control of their actions because they are naturally determined to follow the desire that naturally arises in them from sense-perception and their natural constitution. Hence they are moved by a natural instinct, but they do not direct their movement towards an end (q12 a5).[40] Their inclination is not in their own power.[41] They lack consent because they lack the capacity of a rational creature to apply or not to apply its desire to one or another object (q15 a2); consent is an active rather than a passive determination of desire (q15 a2 ad1). They lack election because they are not in a position to elect one thing among a number of possible objects of election.

Sensory desire, therefore, 'is determined to some one particular thing in accordance with the direction of nature', whereas the rational will is determined to the ultimate end, but not to the particular goods that it elects.[42] Non-rational agents act on their judgment (iudicium)

---

[37] Even non-conscious natural objects (ea quae omnino cognitione carent, q1 a2), act for an end.

[38] Cf. 1a q29 a1.

[39] Quoted from Lombard, 2Sent. d24 c3: 'And it is called "free" with reference to the will, which can be turned in either direction. But it is called "arbitrium" with reference to reason, to which that capacity or ability belongs, and to which it also belongs to discriminate between good and evil.'

[40] 'For an animal on the sight of something pleasant is unable not to have an appetite (concupiscere) for it, because those animals do not have mastery over their inclination, so that they do not act, but rather are acted on (non agunt, sed aguntur), as Damascene says' (Ver. q22 a4). See Damasc. EF 36 Kotter (= ii 22): 'In non-rational animals impulse (hormê) towards action immediately follows orexis, because their orexis is non-rational. That is why the desire of non-rational things is neither called thelêsis nor boulêsis; for thelêsis is a rational and free (autexousios) natural desire. But in the case of human beings, since they are rational, the natural desire is led rather than leading; for a human being is moved freely (autexousiôs) and with reason, since the cognitive and the vital capacities are joined together in him. And so he desires freely, wills (bouletai) freely, freely inquires and examines, freely deliberates, freely judges, freely is disposed (diatithetai), freely decides, freely has an impulse, and freely acts, in the case of things that are according to nature' (lines 86–94 Kotter). In c.41 (= ii 27) Damascene argues that the difference between being led by nature and leading it lies in whether or not we can oppose (antilegein) a natural desire. Our capacity to oppose it is the basis of our being subject to praise and blame.

[41] '[A rational nature] has the inclination itself in its power, so that it is not necessary for it to be inclined towards an apprehended object of desire (appetibile), but it is able to be inclined or not to be inclined. And so the inclination itself is not determined for him by something else, but by [the rational nature] itself' (Ver. q22 a4). Cf. Ver. q24 a2 sc 2; Damasc. EF 41 Kotter (= ii 27), lines 15–22 (which uses agousin and agontai; 'lead' and 'are led' are the right renderings, so that the Latin is inexact). This passage is widely used, for different purposes. Ockham, OT i 501 (quoted in §388), uses it in support of indeterminism.

[42] 'Now the difference between sensory desire and will is that . . . sensory desire is determined to some one particular thing, in accordance with the direction of nature, whereas will, while being determined to one common thing, namely

about what is to be done, but their judgment is determined to one thing. They do not 'judge from their own judgment',[43] and so they do not have complete freedom, but only a conditioned freedom (*Ver.* q24 a2 = M 438b). Hence we can say that they act 'of their own accord',[44] but not from free election (*Ver.* q24 a2 ad1).

244. The Passivity of the Passions

This contrast between rational agents, moved to action by will and reason, and non-rational agents who have no will, but are moved simply by their sensory desires, reflects the nature of the passions; for they explain the goal-directed movements of animals, without reference to reason and universal goodness. By understanding how passions explain actions, we can understand the difference from explanations that introduce will.[45]

An account of the passions is also relevant to human agency because human beings are rational, but not purely rational. They are moved by other impulses that do not belong to the will. Since we act on passions, we act as non-rational animals do. But since we are rational agents, passions in us are open to influences that non-rational agents lack.[46]

Passions include the states of the soul that Plato and Aristotle attribute to its two non-rational parts. Aquinas takes both of these parts to belong to sensory desire, in contrast to intellectual desire, which he identifies with the will.[47] The difference between sensory desire and will corresponds to the difference between sensory and intellectual cognition.[48] Both types of desire tend towards particular external things, but intellectual desire 'is moved towards them in accordance with some universal character' (1a q80 a2 ad2). Sensory desires are based simply on sensory cognition of an object as apparently attractive, not on the further recognition of it as embodying some universal character, which would (in Aquinas' view) require the pursuit of an ultimate good.[49]

We might doubt whether the passions are in themselves non-rational, by pointing out that we regularly attribute states that seem like passions, such as love and joy, to the will or to purely rational beings (God and the angels; cf. 1a q20 a1 ad1).[50] Aquinas answers that in these beings love, joy, and so on are not passions. The names of some passions also refer to purely rational states that resemble specific passions. 'Love', for instance, refers not

the good, in accordance with the direction of nature, is undetermined in relation to particular goods. And for that reason it belongs properly to the will to elect, not to sensory desire, which is the only desire in non-rational animals. And that is why election does not fit non-rational animals' (1-2 q13 a2).

[43] One might translate this phrase 'about their own judgment' (iudicare de suo iudicio). See MacDonald, 'Libertarian'.

[44] Or 'on their own initiative' (sua sponte); cf. *in EN* §435.

[45] Jordan, 'Ideals' 89, discusses the prominence of the passions in *ST* 1–2, in comparison with Aquinas' predecessors. At 88n32 he appeals to *in EN* iv 17 (§882) to support the claim that Aquinas thinks Aristotle relegated a treatment of passions to the *Rhetoric*; in fact Aquinas makes this claim only about some passions.

[46] Knuuttila, *EAMP*, ch. 3, discusses Aquinas and his predecessors on emotions. See also Ockham, *OT* ix 186–8.

[47] On sensory v. intellectual desire see 1a q80 a2; q81 a2; 1-2 q22 a3.

[48] 1a q80 a2: 'Because what is grasped through intellect is of another kind than what is grasped through sense, it follows that intellectual desire is of another kind than sensory desire'.

[49] The passions are non-rational by involving passivity and suffering. A subject does not have a passion, in the proper sense, simply by being receptive; if it is to be passive, it must also be changed by what it receives (1-2 q22 a1). Passions, therefore, do not belong to the rational part of the soul, or to the will in its own right (q22 a3). King, 'Passions', esp. 102–10, discusses the passivity of the passions.

[50] For Augustine's view on these apparent passions see §221.

only to the passion of love, but also to intellectual love. This rational state differs from a passion because it is not necessarily attracted by its object, but pursues it in accordance with the 'free judgment' (liberum iudicium) of the will.[51] Similarly, the will's pursuit of the final good is necessary, but not a passion; the will has an 'inclination' (1a q82 a1), and inclination belongs to all desire (1a q81 a1), not only to passions. A subject moved by passions is not merely inclined, but also 'drawn' or 'attracted' towards the object (q22 a1–2).

How is this distinction between inclination and passive attraction to be marked?[52] In some cases, if a subject is attracted to a given object, it withdraws from what is suitable to itself in order to pursue the object; that is why illness seems to be more of a 'passion' (i.e., suffering, undergoing) than health is (q22 a1). If something interacts with external objects in the normal way appropriate for a healthy organism, we are less inclined to say it is passive or that things are happening to it; but if it has to be restored to health by external intervention, we are more inclined to treat this as a passion. We suppose that x is passive in relation to y to the extent that x's interaction with y is determined by features of x and y that are largely independent of the other features of x that constitute the tendency of x itself.[53]

This basis for distinguishing x's passivity from x's activity depends on how much we attribute to x itself.[54] In some cases, no doubt, the distinction is arbitrary, or depends on the context. We speak of plants turning towards the sun, but perhaps we might equally speak of them being drawn towards the sun. But if something has a relatively definite nature and characteristics, and especially if these are teleologically understood, the distinction between activity and passivity is fairly clear and useful. We say that an aeroplane's speed is 500 knots if it travels at 500 knots in normal winds. If it meets very strong headwinds or tailwinds, we might say it is being held back or pushed along. In saying this we do not mean that in normal conditions the wind does not contribute to the aeroplane's speed; we mean that the normal contribution is the one that makes relatively little difference to what the aeroplane itself does as a result of its design.[55]

This notion of passivity clarifies the character of the passions. Their operation is not necessarily harmful to their subject, but they operate relatively independently of the nature and tendencies of the whole subject. The passions of hunger and thirst, for instance, are natural, and are often good for the creatures that have them, but they operate relatively independently of a creature's whole nature. Whether a horse drinks or not depends on whether it is thirsty; sometimes one has to drag it to the water when it needs a drink, and

---

[51] 1-2 q26 a1–2; cf. q27 a1; q30 a1; q31 a3.

[52] Aquinas' specific reason depends on the claim that passion and passivity require a material subject, and hence require a change in the body; this cannot apply to the rational will, since its action does not involve a bodily change (q22 a3). This is not a good reason. Aquinas seems to be committed to the claim that if we discover that intellectual operations involve bodily changes, we thereby discover that they are also passions, and hence that the will is also a passion. It soon becomes clear, however, that Aquinas' reasons for distinguishing the will from passions do not depend on physiological speculations.

[53] Aquinas discusses different types of passivity at ST 1a q79 a2. Cf. Reid's discussion of active power and its connexion to will at EAP, H 523a.

[54] Cf. Luther's claims about activity and passivity; see §418.

[55] On the passivity of emotions see D'Arcy in BF xix, pp. xxii–xxiii; Peters, 'Passivity' 120–2; Mace, 'Passivity' 140–1; De Sousa, RE 10–12, 41–3, 318–19.

sometimes one has to stop it drinking when it needs to stop. In each case the operation of thirst depends primarily on facts about the horse at the time and about how the water looks to it. Since the operation of thirst depends on these relatively 'local' facts about the horse and the environment at a particular time, it seems more like something happening to the horse than like something it does.[56]

This account of the passivity of the passions supports Aquinas' claims that the passions are different from the will and that we are not passive in acting on the will. The will does not operate against, or independently of, ourselves; it pursues the ultimate end, and our conception of the end expresses ourselves. In being moved by our wills, and hence by our conception of the final good, we ourselves are in control of our actions.[57]

Aquinas believes, therefore, that the passions are passive and non-rational because they are independent of the agent's conception of the good, and therefore operate relatively independently of the agent herself. He takes pursuit of a final good to be characteristic of properly human actions.

245. The Passions and Sensory Desire

This contrast with pursuit of the good explains a further feature of the passions. Aquinas connects them with sensory desire, which responds to particulars, in contrast to intellectual desire, which seeks things 'in accordance with some universal character' (1a q80 a2 ad2). This claim may puzzle us, since the passions clearly seem to respond to a universal character. We are angry about a particular action not simply as this particular action, but as an insult or a slight; we are afraid of a noise not as the particular noise it is, but as a sign of danger. Since Aquinas recognizes these intentional aspects of the different passions, he should acknowledge that in one sense they respond to a 'universal character'. When he denies that they respond to a universal character, he means that they respond to 'particular goods' in contrast to the universal good pursued by the will (1a q82 a5; 1-2 q1 a2 ad3).[58]

The relation of passions to particular goods supports Aquinas' claim that the primary passion is love, because it is the impulse towards good (q26 a1; q27 a1). A partial love, directed towards particular objects regarded as good, is the basis of the passions of the appetitive (concupiscent) part, and these in turn are the basis of the passions of the spirited (irascible) part. Moreover the primary object of love (as a passion of the appetitive part) is one's own good, so that the desire for the good that is the object of one's love is a manifestation of self-love (q27 a3, amans proprie amat seipsum).

---

[56] On aspects of passivity cf. Spinoza, *Ethics* 4p33.

[57] On the will and the self cf. *in EN*, §1871: 'He [sc. Aristotle] observes that what human beings do through reason they seem to have done themselves most of all, and these seem <most of all> to have been done voluntarily. But as for the things a human being does through concupiscence or anger, he almost does not [L; M reads 'because he does not'] seem to have done them himself by his own will, but because he is led by an external motion. And thus it is evident that a human being is especially what accords with intellect and reason. Hence he especially loves himself when he loves intellect and reason.'

[58] Cf. 1a q82 a5; 59 a4 (the object of will is bonum secundum communem rationem boni). The object of a passion is '... a sensible good ... taken without qualification' (1-2 q23 a1, a2). The object of the will is what is good without qualification (*Ver.* q25 a1 = M 469b; a3 = M 473b), in contrast to particular goods. Cf. *in DA* iii 14 (§804).

The two non-rational parts agree with the rational part, therefore, in so far as they have some good as their object; for sensory desire as a whole is concerned with good 'in so far as it is pleasant from the point of view of sense and suitable to nature' (1a q82 a5).[59] To this extent the aims of the sensory desire seem to be commensurable with, and responsive to, the aims of the will. But they differ from the aims of the will, since sensory desires rest only on an apprehension of good 'under a determinate character of good' (in DA iii 14 (§804)).[60]

Sensory desire is moved by the estimative capacity (aestimativa virtus), so that when a sheep takes a wolf to be an enemy, it is afraid (1a q78 a4).[61] This capacity requires imagination and memory; for the information it conveys (that the wolf is an enemy) is not immediately available to the senses.[62] In a human being the estimative capacity is the cognitive capacity, or 'particular reason', which in turn is moved by universal reason (1a q81 a3; Ver. q18 a7 ad7).

Each passion attends exclusively to its proper goods; it is indifferent to good all things considered. The choices made by the will, however, rest on some comparison between the goodness of different objects. Non-rational animals do not judge freely, because they do not judge from comparison (collatio), whereas rational agents rely on comparison (1a q83 a1).[63] Similarly, since our passions follow our sensory judgment, they do not rely on comparison or inquiry, but follow an immediate (subitum) judgment (1-2 q45 a4; q17 a7c, ad1).[64] If a passion could generalize from the apparent goodness of its proper object to goodness in general, it would have to grasp the feature of its object that makes it worth pursuing, apart from any antecedent desire. But to grasp this feature, we need to recognize the merits of the object in its own right. Since intellect recognizes this feature, the will rather than the passions responds to it.

Will and passion are distinguished by the contrast between particular and universal concern; Aquinas identifies this contrast both with the contrast between local and global concern and with the contrast between passive attraction and active inclination. To understand the common element in these contrasts, we must examine more closely the relation that Aquinas sees between the passions and the intellectual desire for the good. Since human agents have both wills and passions, they have some of the features of rational and of non-rational agents. But these two types of agency do not simply co-exist in human beings. They also influence each other, and their mutual influence determines the character of human agency.

---

[59] This description of the passions and their objects may indicate some difference between Aquinas' conception and the Platonic and Aristotelian conception of the non-rational parts of the soul. Aquinas accepts the Platonic and Aristotelian division (1a q81 a2), but he does not seem to distinguish the objects of the non-rational parts as sharply as Plato and Aristotle do. In his view, the irascible part is concerned with the gratification of appetite (concupiscentia); its distinctive feature is its concern with this gratification in so far as it involves some difficulty (arduum) that has to be overcome (1a q81 a2).

[60] Aquinas implies that the sensory desire itself conceives its object as good. For in saying that the will 'looks at' (respicere) the good 'under the common character of good' (sub communi ratione boni, 1a q82 a5), he contrasts this with the way that the sensory desire 'looks at' its object. The 'common character of good' gives an intentional description of the will (as 'looks at' would itself suggest), and Aquinas must also intend an intentional description of sensory desire.

[61] See 1a q78 a4; q81 a3. Cf. 3a Supp. q92 a2. Price, P 139–42, speaks of 'perceptual acceptance'.

[62] See 2Sent d24 q2 a1 sol. = P vi 597b; Ver. q25 a2. Presumably a perception is associated with some awareness of the wolf inflicting pain or of the nest providing security—though Aquinas does not say that this has to come from actual experience of this association.

[63] See §245 above on comparison.   [64] Cf. in DA iii 16 (§§842–3).

246. Criticism of the Stoics on the Passions

The differences between the passions and the will show why the passions do not simply express one's will. According to Aquinas, the Stoics claim that every passion is bad, because they do not distinguish rational from non-rational desires. They recognize that the passions conflict with correct rational judgments, but they do not see that this is true because passions rest on non-rational desires. Instead, they claim that the passions are mistaken rational judgments that rest on incorrect reasoning and false belief about the good (1-2 q24 a2). The Stoics therefore believe that all passions are bad, and that the presence of any passion makes an action worse (q24 a3; cf. 2-2 q123 a10). Aquinas rejects each part of the Stoic position, and defends the Peripatetic position against Cicero's criticism.[65]

Aquinas agrees with Augustine's judgment that the dispute between Stoics and Peripatetics is largely verbal.[66] This judgment is partly correct. When the Stoics claim that passions are all bad, and the Peripatetics claim that some passions are good, the two sides do not directly contradict each other; they have different conceptions of a passion, and if the Peripatetics had accepted the Stoic conception, they would have agreed that the passions are all bad. In this respect the disagreement is verbal. However, the whole dispute between Peripatetics and Stoics is not merely verbal. In particular, their disagreement about the nature of a passion is not merely verbal, since it introduces some large questions about the relation of passions to will and reason.

Aquinas is right to say that the Stoics do not believe in non-rational desires; they believe that sensory cognition results in desire only when rational cognition intervenes. But this Stoic claim is not the crucial point of difference between the Stoic position and his own. The Stoics recognize non-rational motions resulting in appearances; Augustine argues that these appearances are really passions, and Aquinas agrees with him.[67] The Stoics, however, do not regard these as passions; even if they conceded that they are non-rational desires belonging to a non-rational part of the soul, they would still deny that they are genuine passions.

In answer to the Stoics, Aquinas claims that the passions cannot be reduced to erroneous rational assent. Though he endorses Augustine's claim that 'One's passions are bad if one's love is bad; good, if it is good', he does not endorse Augustine's identification of the passions with the different expressions of will that embody a person's love.[68] Moral goodness belongs to passions that are subject to reason and rightly formed or guided or permitted by it (q24 a1 ad3). When we are moved to action by the passions, the will also contributes to our action;

---

[65] See also 2-2 q158 a1 ad1; *Mal.* q12 a1.   [66] See §219.

[67] See *Ver.* q26 a8 ad2; Aug. *CD* ix 4f; §221. Aquinas is sometimes sympathetic to the Stoic conception of a 'pre-passion' (propassio). See 3a q15 a4; a6 ad1; a7 ad1. He distinguishes sadness 'in accordance with a complete passion' (secundum passionem perfectam) from sadness 'in accordance with a pre-passion', and attributes only the latter to Christ. By 'complete passion' he seems to mean the sort of passion that is capable of carrying away reason by securing consent: 'sometimes in us <ordinary human beings> movements of this sort do not stop in sensory desire, but draw reason <with them>'. Christ did not have this sort of passion. In using 'pre-passion', Aquinas gives the misleading impression that he agrees with the Stoics in regarding such a state as only a precursor of a genuine passion; but his explanation counteracts this impression.

[68] 1-2 q24 a1 sc; q59 a2 sc; *Mal.* q10 a1 ad10; Aug., *CD* xiv 6a. See §220.

they do not move us to action by themselves, but are 'subject to the command of reason and the will' (1-2 q24 a1).

Aquinas, therefore, retains the Platonic-Aristotelian view that passions are non-rational in their own right (secundum se consideratae, q24 a1). Here his position is intuitively more plausible than the Stoic position. But it includes a counter-intuitive element that is absent from the Stoic position. Passions sometimes seem to be sufficient by themselves to move us to action. If we are afraid of a barking dog, we may avoid it without further reflexion, but we may still regard ourselves as responsible for acting as we do. It is initially plausible to attribute this view of the passions to Aristotle. [69] The Stoics also believe, but for non-Aristotelian reasons, that passions move us by themselves, since they take passions to include assent.

Aquinas believes, however, that the passions do not characteristically move us to action by themselves; they require the co-operation of will, which essentially pursues the final good. He has to explain, then, why the will, aiming at the final good, sometimes endorses the passions, which do not aim at the final good. We will understand his view better if we first consider more fully the implications of his claim that the will pursues the universal good.

247. Will and the Ultimate Good

Rational agents have wills, essentially rational desires, in so far as they desire something because it is good, and hence desire in accord with some universal character.[70] They pursue particular goods not simply because they are attracted to a specific sort of object, but also because they take the object to have some valued property that gives a reason for pursuing it.[71] Aquinas captures this aspect of a rational desire in 'because it is good'; in acting on rational desire we assume that an object is good. This desire is rational because it proceeds by free judgment, not natural judgment, and by rational comparison, not natural instinct.[72] Comparison is connected with free judgment, because free agents are capable of choosing different things in a particular situation, and so they need some means of comparing the different possibilities.

This comparison is the task of deliberative inquiry (1-2 q13 a1 ad1). If we form the desire for x as a result of deliberation, we form a desire for x as better than y, as a result of deliberation that shows why x rather than y deserves to be chosen. Deliberative and

---

[69] See §167.

[70] 'Intellectual desire, though it tends towards individual things outside the soul, tends towards them in accordance with some universal character (ratio), as when it desires something because it is good' (1a q80 a2 ad2). Aristotle takes rational desire to be directed to the good, and he denies such a desire to non-rational agents because they lack the apprehension of the universal (EN 1147b3–5). See Irwin, AFP §169.

[71] See Aristotle, EN 1111b16–18, with Aquinas, in EN §441.

[72] 'But a human being acts from judgment, because by his apprehensive power he judges that something should be avoided or sought. But because this judgment, in the case of some particular act, is not from a natural instinct, but from some act of comparison in the reason, therefore he acts from free judgment and retains the power of being inclined to various things' (1a q83 a1).

non-deliberative desires are different kinds of desire because a deliberative desire is liable to change in circumstances that would not necessarily affect a non-deliberative desire. This is one difference between the will and the passions.[73]

This deliberation guiding the choice of a rational agent refers different options to an ultimate end. This ultimate end is the 'universal good', contrasted with the particular non-ultimate goods that we decide to pursue as a result of deliberation, for the sake of the ultimate good (1a q82 a2). The ultimate good is universal or 'common'—the one good that we aim at in pursuing the different goods we choose.[74] The common good that guides deliberation is a final good that provides a basis for selecting what seems best overall (all things considered).

248. The Influence of the Ultimate End

These features of the ultimate end are relevant to actions that result from explicit comparison and deliberation. But since not all of our actions come about in this way, we may suppose that we do not pursue the final good in all our actions. Aquinas answers this doubt by arguing that the influence of the ultimate end extends to actions that do not rest directly on deliberation.

Our conception of an end directs us and limits our commitment to means. It exercises this influence even on actions that do not explicitly refer to it. Even if we do not think about the ultimate end (q1 a6 obj3), we may act for its sake. Travellers on a journey from London to Glasgow try to go from Preston to Carlisle because of their decision to go to Glasgow. They may only be thinking now about how to get from Preston to Carlisle, not about how to get to Glasgow; but they would not be thinking now about getting to Carlisle if they had not decided to go to Glasgow. Their aim is directed ultimately towards the ultimate end, but immediately towards some more proximate end.[75] The reference to the ultimate end

---

[73] See §245 above.

[74] '. . . since voluntary actions receive their species from the end, . . . they must receive their genus from the ultimate end, which is common, just as natural things are placed in a genus in accordance with a common formal character. Since, then, all things that can be desired by the will, in so far as they are such, belong to one genus, it is necessary for the ultimate end to be one. And this is especially so because in every genus there is one first principle, and the ultimate end has the character of a first principle . . .' (1-2 q1 a5).

The Marietti edn. comments on the claim that the ultimate end is common: 'Sive universalis non quidem in sensu stricto seu *in praedicando*, sed large *in causando* (causalitate finali)'. The argument from pursuit of a common good to pursuit of a final good is not completely clear. Aquinas suggests that since (a) acts of will get their character (species) from the end they aim at, and (b) all acts of will constitute a single genus, it follows that (c) they must have a single ultimate end to give them their common character. His conclusion, however, does not follow. The common character of all acts of will is simply the fact that they aim at some good or other—as Aquinas puts it, that they aim at the good in general. This does not show that they have to aim at a single final good.

[75] 'One need not always be thinking of the ultimate end, whenever one desires or does something: for the power (virtus) of the first aim (intentio), which has a view to the ultimate end, remains in any desire at all of anything, even if one is not actually thinking of the ultimate end. In this way it is not necessary for anyone who is walking along a road to be thinking of the end at every step' (1-2 q1 a6 ad3).' . . . though aiming always aims at an end, it need not always aim at the ultimate end' (q12 a2). Cf. *SG* iii 138, §3126: 'The preceding will remains in power (virtute) in the whole execution of the action, and makes the action praiseworthy, even when the agent will not be thinking, while he carries out the action, about the purpose of the will because of which be began the action'. Cf. §361

explains why they are in Preston, why they are trying to reach Carlisle, and why they would in some circumstances not try to reach Carlisle (if, for instance, they learned that they could not reach Glasgow from Carlisle).

Since the ultimate end directs and limits our actions even when we are not reflecting on it, Aquinas is right to say that we act for the sake of it. We select a proximate end in the light of reflexion on an ultimate end, and continue to pursue the proximate end without further reflexion on the ultimate end. Hence the power (virtus) of the first aim remains in our pursuit of more proximate ends.

This 'virtual' aiming also fits cases in which we have not reflected on an ultimate end in order to select this proximate end, but none the less our conception of an ultimate end guides our pursuit of this proximate end. Sometimes my conception of an ultimate end permits (say) my walking, so that if it had explicitly prohibited my walking, I would not have walked without hesitation. Alternatively, it may regulate my walking, so that if I reflect on my ultimate end, and come to believe that it rules out my walking, I will recognize that as a reason not to walk.

If my ultimate end permits or regulates, the claim that I will my particular actions for the sake of a single ultimate end becomes more plausible. A desire or action is subordinate to my desire for the final good—whether or not it originates in my conception of the final good—if my conception of the final good permits it or regulates it.

If the will controls action permissively or regulatively, and if it controls in the light of an ultimate good, Aquinas is justified in claiming that an account of rational agency leads us into a discussion of the ultimate good. He follows Aristotle in beginning his systematic treatment of ethics with an account of the ultimate end of human action, which he identifies with happiness. If he is right so far, he vindicates one aspect of Aristotle's eudaemonist attitude to practical reason and morality.

Aristotle believes that the pursuit of happiness as ultimate end is the basis of morality for all rational agents, but he does not say much about why he believes that all rational agents pursue an ultimate end and that this end is happiness. He leaves unsettled some questions about the status of happiness. Even if we agreed with Aristotle that we all pursue happiness, we might take this to be a contingent and alterable psychological fact; it might be parallel to a natural tendency to selfishness or short-sightedness that we seek to correct through morality. This interpretation of Aristotle should be rejected, but he does not argue fully against it. Aquinas believes that the pursuit of an ultimate end is neither a baseless assumption of Aristotle's nor a merely contingent feature of human beings, but a necessary feature of rational agency and of the will. If he is right, an ethical theory suitable for rational and free agents must begin from the ultimate end.

The *Summa* places the discussion of the ultimate end at the beginning of the Prima Secundae, after the discussion of will and freewill in the First Part, and before the treatment of the voluntary, action, and passion, in the Prima Secundae. In Aquinas' view, it is essential to rational desire, and hence essential to will, that it pursues an ultimate end. Reference to an ultimate end is necessary for the deliberation and rational comparison of options that Aquinas takes to be necessary for the will.[76]

---

[76] Cf. Reid on rational principles, *EAP* H 545a.

These claims about the ultimate end help to explain how human beings are free and responsible. Freedom depends on deliberation and rational comparison, and these require deliberation in the light of an ultimate end. Our pursuit of an ultimate end is necessary for freedom, not a restriction on freedom. It is distinctive of rational agents that they pursue an ultimate end, because this pursuit embodies their capacity for moving and directing themselves.

17

AQUINAS: ACTION

249. Will and Action

Now that we have discussed the differences between will and passion, we can see how they help to explain properly human action. In so far as we are rational agents with wills, we pursue an ultimate end. But we are not purely rational agents, since we also have passions that do not wholly depend on our rational wills. Hence, any plausible account of will and action must explain how will and passion are related in moving us to action. Aquinas has assumed that passions are not the source of our ultimate ends. This assumption is controversial, since it seems reasonable to believe that the ends we pursue are influenced by our specific passions and their relative strength. How can Aquinas take account of this apparently reasonable belief within his general views about the will and the ultimate end?

If Aquinas describes the relation of will and passion to action, he commits himself to a position on questions about freedom and responsibility. At first sight, he seems likely to commit himself to the denial of freedom. His account of rational agency suggests that rational agents necessarily execute their conception of the ultimate end in their actions. But many suppose that free agents cannot be necessitated in this way. In opposition to such doubts, Aquinas argues that his views about the will and the ultimate end vindicate belief in human freedom. We will be able to appreciate his argument most easily if we discuss his account of will and action before turning to his views about freedom. His account of action does not presuppose (in Aquinas' view) any specific conception about freedom, but it allows us to derive a plausible account of freedom.

250. Aiming at Ends

If we act on will, we form a conception of a universal good and an ultimate end, and we are guided by it in acting as we do. Other capacities besides will are involved in being guided by the ultimate end; Aquinas discusses them in his analysis of human action (ST 1-2 q6–17). Will requires the capacity for rational comparison with reference to a universal good, and the capacity for deliberation that investigates ways of achieving the ultimate good. Through these capacities we act on 'deliberated will' (1-2 q1 a1 ad3),[1] so as to perform properly human acts. Aquinas describes the relation between these different capacities in the causation of action. Whether or not they are all exercised in temporally distinct stages on the way to a given action, they mark different features of rational agency.[2]

But since actions on passion also seem to be properly human acts, in contrast to the thoughtless scratching of one's beard, we may wonder how they are related to Aquinas' account of properly human acts. At first sight, his account is too elaborate to cover actions on passion. But they do not require an entirely different account; his account of rational action explains how they are properly human actions.

Rational agency, in contrast to animal agency, requires rational comparison. If we necessarily willed the ultimate end as having some highly determinate content specifying a particular action, we would not be rational agents, since we would not act on rational comparison of different possible objects of pursuit. Rational agents guide themselves towards an end by acting on rational comparison that leads to election of appropriate subordinate ends.[3] On this basis Aquinas distinguishes 'natural' from 'elective' love; elective love results from deliberation about goods chosen for the sake of the ultimate end.[4]

This deliberation begins from our aiming at (intendere) an end, not simply from wishing it. To wish for an end is only to recognize that we would prefer getting something over failing to get it, or that we would be pleased if we could get it; this sort of wish is simply a 'velleity'.[5] We might have several such preferences, but to begin deliberation we must set out to satisfy one rather than another of them. We direct ourselves towards getting an end; 'for we are said to aim at health not simply because we will it, but because we will to reach it through something else' (q12 a1 ad4). 'Through something else' refers to means, but not to any particular means; we can aim at an end without having determined the means, which are the concern of election (q12 a4 ad3). By 'directing' (ordinare) ourselves towards trying to attain the end (q12 a1 ad1), we differ from non-rational agents.[6]

Aiming and self-direction involve rational selection, which presupposes a relatively specific conception of the end to be achieved. If I am to do anything towards achieving the ultimate end I aim at, I have to form some view about its composition, so that I can find the means to the components.[7] This conception equips me to aim at one or another non-ultimate end (q12 a2).

---

[1] See §242.

[2] They are different features making up a complete exercise of the will in action. But the earlier ones can exist without the later on a particular occasion. See Donagan, 'Action', esp. 654; Finnis, *Aq.* 62–71; Bradley, *ATHG* 342.

[3] See *Ver.* q22 a7, quoted in §273.

[4] '...the will tends naturally to its ultimate end; for every human being naturally wills happiness. And from this natural will all other wills are caused, since whatever a human being wills he wills because of the end. Therefore the love (dilectio) of the good that a human being naturally wills as an end is natural love; but the love derived from this, which is of a good that is loved because of the end, is elective love' (1a q60 a2).

[5] aliquis vellet illud, si esset possibile, q13 a5 ad1.

[6] '...to aim (intendere) is to tend (tendere) towards something; and this belongs to the mover and to the moved. ...non-rational animals also aim at an end, to the extent that they are moved to something by natural instinct. But in another way aiming at an end belongs to the mover, in so far as he directs the movement of himself or another towards an end. This belongs only to reason. That is why non-rational animals do not aim at an end in this way, which is aiming properly and principally ...' (1-2 q12 a5).

[7] '...the acquiring of wine and clothing is included in wealth, as in something common to both, so that nothing prevents someone who aims at wealth from aiming at both the other things at the same time' (1-2 q12 a3 ad2).

In contrast to rational agents, non-rational animals lack 'consideration' of their action and their end.[8] Consideration is part of directing myself towards an end through some specific means, and it limits my commitment to a given means. If I pursue y as a means to x, that attitude controls my pursuit of y, in different ways: (1) I will no longer pursue y if I do not believe it promotes x. (2) I will no longer pursue y if, even though I see that y promotes x, I also see that it would be bad to keep on pursuing x in this situation. (3) If, however, I also pursue y for the sake of z, which is more important than x, I will keep on pursuing y as long as it achieves z, provided that it does not interfere with anything more important than z.

Hence Aquinas believes that if we direct our action towards an end, we are also in control of our actions. Rational agents aim at an end in directing themselves actively, not in being directed passively.[9] I direct my action towards an end in so far as I limit my inclination towards this action by my estimate of the end that it is directed to. To do this, I must also be able to estimate the value of this end;[10] hence I must have some idea of what makes it an end for me and of what is good about it. This is why rational agents must present the end to themselves.[11]

251. Deliberation

Since the mental states leading from will to action include aiming, they also include deliberation. Aiming, as opposed to merely wishing, requires us to look for means to our end. Election presupposes our having found means, and deliberation connects aiming with electing by finding means. Rational agents are active rather than passive in so far as they have wills rather than simply passions. Their having wills makes them active by giving them control of their actions through deliberation.[12] Since rational agents can choose between opposites through this deliberation, their doing one of the opposites rather than the other is in their control.

The extent of our control, therefore, depends on how many questions are open to deliberation and election. Aquinas agrees with Aristotle in believing that deliberation is confined to means to ends, but some 'means' are also ends reached by deliberation (q14 a2). An end aimed at on one occasion may be an object of deliberation with reference to a further

---

[8] 'Non-rational animals are moved towards an end, not as though they considered that they can reach the end by their movement, which is proper to one who aims, but by their appetite for an end they are moved towards the end by natural instinct, as though moved by something else, as are the other things that are moved naturally' (1-2 q12 a5 ad3).

[9] '. . . it is proper to a rational nature to tend towards an end as leading or guiding itself towards the end; it is proper, on the other hand, to a non-rational nature to tend towards an end as led or guided by another' (1-2 q1 a2). '. . . directing towards an end is characteristic of what leads itself towards an end. Being directed towards an end, on the other hand, is characteristic of what is led by another towards an end' (1–2 a1 a2 ad2).

[10] '. . . for the will, which is desire for a previously-grasped end tends towards something only under the character of the good, which is its object' (SG iii 16 §1988).

[11] Rational agents move themselves 'by reference to the end, which they present (praestituunt) to themselves. And this does not happen without reason and intellect, whose function it is to grasp the proportion of the end and of what is towards the end, and to direct the one towards the other' (1a q18 a3).

[12] 'A human being is master of his action as a result of the fact that he has deliberation (deliberationem) about his actions. For from the fact that deliberating reason is related to opposites it results that the will is capable <of going> in both directions' (1-2 q6 a2 ad2).

end on another occasion (q14 a2).[13] Deliberation in the light of an end includes questions about what an end consists in.[14] If we control our actions and our ends, we are capable of effective deliberation about the ends that we take to constitute the ultimate end.

This description might suggest that control of one's ends and actions requires deliberation. But this is not exactly Aquinas' view. We need deliberation when there is some room for doubt, and therefore some need for inquiry, about the options open to us; and so we do not deliberate if there is no room for doubt or inquiry (q14 a4). But the angels elect without doubt and deliberation.[15] Election requires reasoned judgment that is based on, and responsive to, our conception of the universal good. Deliberation is necessary if we need it to form a reasoned judgment; but election requires only the reasoned judgment.[16] This judgment in non-deliberative rational agents is counterfactually deliberative; if there were doubt about the desirability of the option chosen, they would settle the question by deliberation. This capacity for deliberation is needed to ensure that agents do not choose this option simply because they are incapable of considering any grounds for doubt about it. Responsiveness of rational judgments to considerations of the good often, but not always, requires deliberation.

252. Consent and Election

Between deliberation and election Aquinas introduces consent. If we form a conception of something as desirable, we still may not be moved to act on our conception. Before we can act, we have to engage our capacities to move ourselves; and this 'engaging' or 'application' of our motive capacities is what Aquinas calls consent.[17] Non-rational animals cannot apply their motive capacities, and therefore cannot consent. A stick can move a stone, but only the agent who has it in his power to move the stick can actually apply the stick to moving the stone. Since non-rational animals do not have their desiderative motion in their power, they cannot apply their desire to action (q15 a2). They do not have their desiderative motion in their power, because they do not control it. Control involves application and consent.

By introducing consent into his account of action Aquinas draws on the Stoic view that rational human action depends on assent rather than simple appearance. Augustine takes over this Stoic analysis. Nemesius and Damascene combine it with the Aristotelian analysis, and Aquinas follows.[18] Stoic assent, however, seems to lack two features of Aristotelian

---

[13] Moreover, if there is doubt about an end, it is not sufficiently determined to be taken as an end for deliberation; 'hence as long as it is taken to be doubtful, it is not taken to be an end' (1-2 q14 a2 ad1). Something that might be proposed as an end is open to deliberation in the light of some further end (see q14 a2 ad2).

[14] For constituents cf. q12 a3 ad2 (continentur sub); *Ver.* q22 a7 on merit (quoted in §273).

[15] 'As a human being's estimation in speculative matters differs from an angel's in this, that the latter is without inquiry, whereas the former proceeds through inquiry, so it is in practical matters. Hence in the angels there is election, but not with the inquiring deliberation of counsel, but by the instant (subitam) acceptance of truth' (1a q59 a3 ad1).

[16] 'Election presupposes deliberation on account of its judgment or decision (iudicii vel sententiae). And so when the judgment or decision is evident without inquiry, the inquiry of deliberation is not needed' (1-2 q14 a4 ad1). See also 3a q18 a4, esp. ad2 (on the will of Christ and of the blessed): 'And so if something is judged as to be done without previous doubt and inquiry, this is enough for election'. On freewill and uncertainty see §266.

[17] ipsa applicatio appetitivae virtutis, 1-2 q15 a1. On consent and sin see q74 a8.

[18] See Lottin, *PM* i 422f–3; Wittmann, *ETA* 153. Aquinas distinguishes consent from assent, claiming that assent is to a proposition, whereas consent is to an action (1-2 q15 a1 ad3). In q15 a3 obj3, sc, Aquinas takes Damascene's use of

election: (1) Aristotle believes that election essentially involves preference for one alternative over another.[19] He does not simply mean that in choosing one thing we forgo other things; he means that when we elect we act on a view about the merits of one course of action as opposed to another. (2) Hence election rests on examination of the comparative merits of different courses of action, and so rests on deliberation.

According to the Stoics, assent need not result from rational reflexion and consideration of alternatives. A clear and striking apprehensive appearance 'all but grabs us by the hair and draws us into assent' (Sx M vii 257). If we are uncritical and too easily impressed by appearances, we may 'yield' to them without proper reflexion. Assent seems to be present in many situations where we do not consider alternatives. But Aquinas treats consent as the result of deliberation, and he agrees with Aristotle's view that deliberation guides our action in accordance with our will by resulting in an election. Hence he treats consent as a preliminary to election. Consent recognizes something as satisfactory; from this preliminary recognition election picks out one of the satisfactory things as better than another. If we recognize only one thing as satisfactory, the same action is both consent and election; in this case they differ only in definition (ratione tantum). If we recognize several things as satisfactory, we elect one over the others.[20]

In the case where only one option seems satisfactory, Aquinas suggests that we elect this option through deliberation that shows it is better than unsatisfactory courses of action. Perhaps he means that the unsatisfactory options would not secure our end at all or would be such costly means of securing our end that it would be more reasonable to give up our end than to secure it by these means; the satisfactory options, then, make it reasonable to keep pursuing our current end in our current circumstances. If this is what Aquinas means, he is justified in saying that we elect the course of action that we find satisfactory.

But is this the only case he needs to consider? Might we not find one means satisfactory and consent to it without having compared it either with unsatisfactory options or with other satisfactory options? Can we not consent and act with less consideration than Aquinas has in mind? And can we not pick x over y without any conviction that x is better, once we have consented to both x and y as satisfactory? It does not seem obvious that whenever we consent to or endorse a course of action and act on our consent, we must have deliberated about it and judged that it is best all things considered. The separation of consent from election seems reasonable and helpful precisely because it leaves open such possibilities; if we allow them, not every action requires a comparative judgment. If Aquinas takes action to require both consent and election, he does not exploit the degree of flexibility that his

'sententia' (i.e., gnômê) to refer to consent. See Damasc. EF 36, 77–80. Augustine speaks of 'assent' or 'consent' as the mark of free action; CD ix 4f; Nupt. i 31. Cf. §223. On the Stoics see §170.

[19] See EN 1112a15–17; EE 1226b5–9. Cf. Nemesius, NH 101.8–14.

[20] 'Election includes something that consent has not, namely, a certain relation to something to which something else is preferred: and therefore after consent there still remains an election. For it may happen that by aid of deliberation several means have been found conducive to the end, and through each of these being approved, consent has been given to each: but after approving of many, we have given our preference to one by choosing it. But if we approve of only one, consent and election do not differ in reality, but only in definition (ratione tantum). And so we call it consent in so far as we approve of doing that thing, but election in so far as we prefer it to those that we do not approve of' (1-2 q15 a3 ad3).

notion of consent would allow. But some of his discussion of different types of action is more plausible if consent and action sometimes happen without election.[21]

253. The Influence of the Passions on the Will

So far Aquinas has analysed human actions that proceed from will to deliberation and election; these are the actions that make human beings rational agents. But they are not the only actions that need to be analysed. He treats rational desire as the basis of some, but not all, properly human actions, since he believes that actions on passion are properly human actions if they are appropriately related to the will. Passions differ from will in so far as they attend to particular goods, and not to the universal good that is the object of rational desire. If we act out of fear, for instance, the analysis of action on will cannot be applied without modification to our action. The analysis needs to be modified in order to include actions on passion among properly human actions.

The passions affect our action because they include appearances of particular goods, and thereby influence us to form judgments about the goodness of a situation. If I am angry, I judge that there is something good about getting my own back on you. Since this judgment may be completely thoughtless, and may not rest on any consideration of other features of the situation beyond the offence and the opportunity of revenge, it is an immediate (as Aquinas says, 'sudden') reaction; since it does not rest on any thought of overall goodness, it does not engage the will.[22] Hence Aquinas often speaks of 'sudden motions' that are contrary to someone's will.[23]

Sometimes one of these sudden motions moves us to action 'beyond the command of reason, even though it could have (potuisset) been impeded by reason if reason had foreseen' (q17 a7). In such cases the passions move us contrary to reason (1a q81 a3 ad2). Even when the motions of passion are not sudden, passion sometimes compels us in such a way that reason is impotent to resist and is 'totally bound', as in cases of drunkenness and madness. In these cases we necessarily follow the tendency of the passion and act involuntarily.[24]

Not all binding, however, takes away voluntariness. Sometimes passion influences the will by appealing to it, and not by coercing it so as to make it incapable of resisting. Our will follows our conception of the overall good, which rests on our comparative estimate of various specific goods. Passions influence this comparative estimate by bringing particular goods to our attention and presenting them in a favourable light that alters our estimate of how good they are.

---

[21] See below §255.

[22] In these cases the sensory faculty '... does not compare or inquire into the particular circumstances of the situation, but has a sudden judgment' (1-2 q45 a4). Cf. 1-2 q77 a6; cf. 2-2 q125 a4; 143 a1.

[23] Sudden motions: cf. *2Sent* d24 q3 a5 = P vi 607b; *ST* 1-2 q74 a10 (a motion of infidelity preceding deliberation constitutes only a venial sin); *2Sent* d28 q1 a2 = P vi 643b; *ST* 1-2 q17 a7c; ad1; q88 a2 (sudden motion without deliberation makes only a venial sin); a5; q89 a3; 2-2 q13 a2 ad3 (blasphemy by sudden motion, if one does not consider the blasphemous meaning of the words); q55 a8 ad3 (sudden motion of anger); q156 a4. See Seneca in §166; Knuuttila, *EAMP* 178–95; Sorabji, *EPM*, chs. 22–4. On comparison as characteristic of will see 1a q83 a1.

[24] Binding: 1-2 q10 a3; q77 a7; q80 a3; 2–2 q150 a4 ad3. *Mal.* q3 a3 ad9 (Ligato autem usu rationis, nihil imputatur homini ad peccatum, sicut nec bestiae); q3 a4; *in Ioan.* xi 7 = P x 503a.

Appetite, therefore, 'inclines' the will towards the object of the appetite (1-2 q6 a7; cf. 1a q81 a1 ad3). The will no longer wills what it previously willed, but now wills what it previously rejected (1-2 q6 a7 ad2).[25] In such cases the passions attract our attention to particular goods, and so 'cloud' reason.[26] But reason is not completely submerged by passion; the free judgment of reason remains to some extent, so that the will does not necessarily follow the tendency of the passion.[27]

In these cases of clouding without complete binding, the passions affect the will in either of two ways: (1) They distract us, in so far as a passion strengthens the motion of the sensory appetite, and diverts our attention to it, so that 'the proper motion of rational desire, which is the will, slackens or entirely gives out' (q77 a1). (2) The appearance presented by the passion tends to affect our imagination and judgment, so that we judge the object of the passion more favourably than we otherwise would. But these cases of clouded reason do not prevent the proper use of reason (q77 a7); we are still capable of closing out (excludere) the passion, by turning to other thoughts, or of preventing it from achieving its aim.[28]

According to this analysis, passion does not interrupt the normal sequence of aiming, deliberation, consent, and election. Its role is indirect, since it may incline or warp our judgment at different stages so as to influence our aiming or our deliberation; different ends or means may seem more plausible candidates for our attention because passions put them in a different light.

254. The Influence of the Will on the Passions

This description of the influence of the passions may suggest that they are 'subject to the command of reason and the will' (1-2 q24 a1) only in so far as we can avoid or resist their distorting influence on our deliberation and choice. But this is not all that Aquinas has in mind; he believes that the will not only can avoid following the passions, but also can influence them. In describing the different kinds of influence that the will exercises he clarifies his conception of the passions.

If the passions were not interested in the objects that interest the will, or if they never recognized the authority of the will,[29] the will could effectively change, inhibit, or order the course of the passions only by force. It might exercise force in restraint, as when someone locks the whisky in the cupboard and gives someone else the key; in this case, he does not lose his desire for the whisky, but simply finds he cannot satisfy it. It might also exercise force by arousing stronger passions to overcome the deviant passion; the fear of pain from punishment or the hope of pleasure from reward might overcome anger or fear of immediate danger.

---

[25] Aquinas accepts this analysis of incontinence (cf. q77 a2). See §§289–90.

[26] Clouding reason: 1-2 q10 a3 ad2; cf. q24 a3 ad3; *Mal.* q3 a11 = M 514b; q16 a2 obj5; *in Iob* xii 2 = P xiv 53b. On 'submerging' (absorbere) cf. 2-2 q46 a3; q53 a6; q123 a8.

[27] '... but sometimes, though reason is clouded by passion, still some of reason remains free. And in accordance with this someone is able to drive back the passion totally or at any rate to keep himself from following the passion' (q10 a3 ad2).

[28] Resisting passion: q10 a3; q77 a7–8; q80 a3; 2-2 q155 a3 ad3; q156 a1; q175 a2 ad2.

[29] On authority see Butler, *S* ii 14.

But this is not the only sort of influence that Aquinas allows the will. He often endorses Aristotle's claim that the rational part exercises political, not despotic, rule over the non-rational parts (1a q81 a3 ad2).[30] In political rule the subjects have their own will in some matters (1-2 q56 a4 ad3). The political metaphor suggests that in human beings passions arise independently of the will, but do not normally dominate it; 'human beings who act from passion are capable of not following the passion' (q15 a2 ad3; q26 a1; q42 a4). Aquinas appeals to a remark of St Paul's: 'For it is not the good that I will that I do, but it is the evil that I hate that I do' (*Rm.* 7.19; q10 a3). Aquinas suggests that St Paul uses 'do' to refer to appetite (concupiscere). Though we cannot avoid the appetite, we can still avoid consenting to it.[31] The appetitive part is not wholly subject to reason, but it is still under our control, through the consent or refusal of reason and will, in contrast to the situation of mad people, in whom reason is wholly submerged by passion. Unless the passions wholly bind reason, they are subject to reason and obey it (1-2 q24 a1; q42 a4).

The political metaphor suggests that the passions recognize the authority of reason. Aquinas implies that the passions respond to the considerations that guide the will. Anger, for instance, may make it difficult to form and to attend to the judgment of reason, but its end is not wholly unresponsive to reason. In so far as the passion pursues a particular good, it pursues it as being good for the agent. If we discover that a particular good is not good on the whole for the agent, the passion changes. Similarly, the will can excite a passion by concentrating our attention on a particular good to which we are especially responsive.[32]

This connexion between the passions and the pursuit of the good still leaves a basic difference between Aquinas' position and the Socratic and Stoic position. The Socratic view asserts that the value judgment belonging to a particular passion is the judgment that this or that is better on the whole; fear of a particular danger is the judgment that it is better on the whole to avoid the danger. If, then, we avoid the danger when it is better on the whole to face it, we must have made a false judgment about what is better on the whole. Plato and Aristotle reject his view, and Aquinas agrees with them. If we act on the judgment that x is good, we may not judge that x is best on the whole. If we notice that there is something to be said for x, that may move us to try to get x; we may not stop to think about what might be said against x. Our pursuit of the universal good lies in the background, explaining why we would prefer y over x if we stopped to think that y is on the whole better than x; but we do not refer every judgment about a particular good to our conception of the universal

---

[30] Cf. 1-2 q17 a7; q56 a4 ad3; q58 a2.

[31] ' Although the will cannot prevent the movement of appetite from rising up, about which the Apostle says "The evil that I hate, I do"—in other words, "I desire", none the less the will is capable of not willing to have the appetite, or of not consenting to the appetite. And in this way it does not necessarily follow the movement of appetite' (1-2 q10 a3 ad1). For this exegesis cf. q17 a7 obj1 (Glossa); 1a q83 a1 ad1. Aquinas defends it at length, *in Rom.* vii 3 = P xiii 70b–71a. He considers two interpretations, one applying to a person under sin, and one applying to a person under grace. The explanation of 'agere' as 'concupiscere' belongs to the second interpretation: 'when he [sc. Paul] says "I do", we should understand incomplete action, which consists only in sensory desire, not reaching as far as consent of reason'. Augustine accepts this interpretation at *Nupt.* 31; *in Ioann.* 41.12. For Augustine's various views Luther, *Rom.* ad loc., cites, *Ep. Pel.* i 17; *Iul.* ii 13–14; iii 62: *Prop. Rom.* 44; *Retr.* i 23.1.

[32] ... universal reason commands sensory desire, which is divided into appetitive and spirited, and this desire obeys it. ... for by applying certain universal considerations, anger or fear or the like may be moderated or aggravated' (1a q81 a3).

good.[33] In this case we may say that the content of our value judgment about the particular good does not include any judgment about the universal good, but we are sensitive to the universal good.

According to this pattern, a passion inclines us to value judgments that we would not otherwise have formed (1-2 q9 a2). Under its influence we form particular value judgments ('it would be good to retaliate for this insult') whose generalizations ('it is good to retaliate for insults') we would not accept if we considered them (q9 a2 ad2). When we are influenced by passions, we do not judge on the basis that we would normally endorse. A passion makes some particular course of action appear more attractive than it would appear otherwise.

This description does justice to the common view that something about the passions is non-rational. The Stoics suppose that we can do justice to this common view only to a limited extent, by treating passions as false rational judgments about overall good. Aquinas argues that passions neither are nor contain judgments about overall good; they contain value judgments that are not based on judgments about overall good, and hence they may conflict with our view of overall good. Passions are neither completely independent of, nor contrary to, the all-things-considered judgment of reason. If a known alcoholic asks me urgently for a bottle of whisky, I may give it to him, out of a generous or compassionate impulse. I do not form the judgment that it is best, all things considered, to give it to him; and to this extent the Stoics are wrong to say that acting on passions is acting on a false belief about the good. If, however, I could make it clear to myself that I am really harming him by doing what he wants, I would (in Aquinas' view) change my mind about giving it to him; to that extent my generous impulse is not independent of my views about what is best all things considered.

This view may seem to underestimate the independence of the passions from rational considerations. Since passions seem to persist even if we are sure we ought not to follow them, they cannot be altogether responsive to the will. Aquinas could concede this point in some cases without damage to his overall view that they express judgments about goodness. For a passion may respond to some significant good that still matters, even when we discover that it is not the overriding good in this situation. It is often reasonable to regret what has happened, to be afraid about what one knows is the best thing to do, and so on. The passions are consistent with our judgments of overall good, because they are directed towards the particular goods that we still take seriously.[34]

Aquinas, therefore, neither reduces the passions to erroneous judgments about the universal good nor makes them so independent of the universal good that they are outside the control of the will. He admits that sometimes the passions move us in a direction that the will is powerless to prevent; but he denies that this is normally the effect of the passions. Since they present their objects as particular goods, they are sensitive to considerations of goodness presented by reason and will.

---

[33] Similarly, Ross, *RG* 19, describes a prima-facie duty as a characteristic that would make an action a 'duty proper' if it were the only morally significant character of the action.

[34] This reply covers some cases of stubborn passions that persist despite our rational convictions. But it does not seem to cover all of them. The most difficult cases for Aquinas to explain seem to be cases of incontinence; see §295.

255. Action without Deliberation?

We might agree with Aquinas' account of the role of the passions as far as it goes, but still criticize it for being incomplete. No doubt passions may be relevant to deliberation and election in the ways he describes. But they also seem to be sources of human actions without deliberation and election. Non-rational animals act on their passions without deliberation and election. Some of our actions seem to be similar to theirs; fear, anger, and pleasure, seem to move us without our stopping to think. But these actions are properly human actions (q1 a1);[35] they are self-conscious, and above the level of mere reflexes, but without deliberation and will. The 'immediacy' of passions cannot be confined to 'sudden judgments' that reason and will respond to; they seem to move us to action without reason. Do they not therefore move us without will?

Aquinas agrees that passions sometimes move us in this way, when they entirely submerge reason, as in madness. But this concession does not deal with all apparent cases of acting on passion without deliberation. If we eat when we are hungry, or speak sharply because we are angry, we do not seem to be overcome by passion or incapable of deliberating; we simply have not deliberated. Aquinas believes that in such cases the passions are subject to the will because they depend on our consent (q10 a3 ad1).

To see what he means by this, we have to return to our earlier questions about consent. If we cannot act on consent without also having deliberated and elected, Aquinas seems to have too rigid a conception of action that is subject to the will. To require deliberation on each occasion is to ignore the contrast between impulsive, non-reflective actions and actions that result from reflexion and deliberation. Can he, then, consistently allow consent without deliberation?

We may answer this question by going back to his discussion of the ultimate end.[36] He argues that our conception of an end may permit or regulate our actions even if we do not think of it on each occasion. If the will permits and regulates, we can act on passions without deliberation.[37] If the action was wrong, the will made an error by omission; the error depends on a cause or occasion of omission that is subject to the will.[38] What I do now without an election on this occasion results from previous election, if I have elected to allow myself to be affected by certain sorts of desires, or if I have declined the opportunity to avoid them.[39]

If we can consent by our failure to dissent, we can consent to an action that we recognize as conflicting with our conception of our ultimate end. We may consent to a sinful action

---

[35] On reflexes see §242.   [36] See §248.

[37] '... Something is said to be voluntary directly or indirectly; directly, if the will tends towards it; indirectly, if the will was able (potuit) to prohibit it, but does not prohibit (prohibet) it' (q77 a7). In 'was able ... does not prohibit' Aquinas implies that it need not be true at the time (as in the case of drunkenness) that the will can any longer prohibit it. Cf. the pilot who might cause an accident by steering badly or by leaving the steering to someone incompetent; q6 a3; q71 a5. On negative consent cf. q15 a4 ad3: 'The higher reason is said to consent not only because it always moves to act, according to the eternal reasons; but also because it fails to dissent according to those same reasons'.

[38] See q71 a5. On ignorance as a cause of sin cf. q76.

[39] Odysseus tied to the mast has elected to be affected by passions that he could have avoided. He has also elected to prevent himself from acting on them.

even if our ultimate moral principles do not approve it; for we consent if they fail to prevent the sinful action (q74 a7 ad2). Hence my will, through my conception of my ultimate end, influences actions that conflict with my conception of the ultimate end. In such cases, our consent reveals an implicit conflict in my conception of the ultimate end. Even though I may have a correct positive account of its elements, I do not recognize that this positive account requires me to rule out certain actions that I consent to. My failure to recognize all the implications of my conception of the ultimate end makes it intelligible that I allow actions that, if I thought about them more carefully, I would not allow.[40]

Aquinas' views on regulation and permission also suggest that we act on passion if we simply consent to the passion by non-intervention. Non-intervention need not result from a deliberate choice not to intervene; we may simply be too hasty or too lazy to think about whether we ought to intervene. Such haste or laziness partly depends on our will, just as the later stages of a journey are dependent on the elections that we made at earlier stages; for our previous deliberation and choice affect our later tendency to stop and think or to proceed without thinking.

These features of Aquinas' account show that it is more flexible in its treatment of action on passion than we might at first suppose. We would be wrong to confine the role of passions to their influence on our judgments in a standard action on deliberation and election. They can also move us without deliberation, through consent that consists in failure to dissent when we could dissent. Even in such actions they depend on the will.

Aquinas sticks to his initial description of the will as essentially rational desire aiming at a universal good. This description underlies his argument that the will necessarily aims at an ultimate good, which it pursues as a result of deliberative inquiry. The role of the ultimate good and deliberation separates the will from the passions, which are not directed towards the final good in the same way. Since the will has a regulative and permissive role in relation to passions, its influence extends beyond the actions that directly involve it.

The claim that we have a will, so understood, is reasonable. Aquinas' claims about the universal good, the final good, aiming, and deliberation, emphasize the structural and holistic character of rational desire. He points out that our rational desire for one object depends on the connexion of this desire with other desires that fit together in some fairly systematic structure. It is also reasonable to argue that passions differ from rational desires in lacking this systematic connexion with the rest of one's aims.

Aquinas argues that these features of rational agency also allow us to understand issues about freedom and about morality that might initially appear quite distinct from the questions about agency. In seeing how he applies his claims about agency to these other issues, we will also understand these claims better.

256. The Inter-dependence of Will and Practical Reason

This analysis of action is intended to explain how will moves us to action and how our action is essentially rational. Aquinas believes that he has found the right role for reason, will, and

---

[40] This conflict is the basis of Aquinas' account of incontinence. See §296.

desire, in contrast to more extreme views that fail to do justice to these different aspects of action. It is sometimes difficult, however, to see what is at stake in the decision between Aquinas' view and the extreme views, and hence it is sometimes difficult to see whether his different formulations of his own position amount to a consistent or plausible position.

It may be useful to distinguish two questions, and to introduce some terms to express them: (1) Is the will determined by the greater good as presented by reason? To answer Yes is to be an intellectualist. To answer No is to be a voluntarist.[41] (2) Is the will determined by the strongest passion, as an animal's choice is determined? To answer No is to be a rationalist. To answer Yes is to be an anti-rationalist.[42]

Aquinas rejects the extreme intellectualist view that reason is the primary cause of rational action, so that will is simply an intermediary cause that is ultimately explained by reference to reason. He also rejects the extreme voluntarist view that will is the primary cause of rational action and reason is only a secondary cause, so that the role of reason is subordinate to the role of will. Against these two extreme views Aquinas argues that action proceeds primarily from the will, but the will is rational desire, and is therefore essentially guided by our intellectual conception of the greatest good. A voluntarist rejects this account of action, but still agrees with Aquinas in accepting rationalism about the relation of will to passion. We will eventually need to ask whether this combination of voluntarism and rationalism is coherent or plausible; but if we do not recognize the difference between intellectualism and rationalism, we cannot even see the questions that need to be asked.

One dispute between intellectualists and voluntarists depends on claims about logical and explanatory priority. An extreme intellectualist view claims that we can explain action through a conception of practical reason that is logically independent of will; will and rational desire enter only as intermediate causes that are wholly explained by practical reason. According to this view, the basic explanation refers to our cognitive grasp of facts about the good, independently of any desire directed towards them. An extreme voluntarist view, by contrast, claims that we begin from an account of will that is not essentially formed by practical reason; facts about the good and practical reason become relevant only because of some prior and independent facts about will. If this is the right way to describe the two extreme positions, we may try to understand Aquinas' position as a denial of the claims about priority that define the two extremes.

Aquinas emphasizes the distinction between the cognitive and the motive aspects of a rational agent (1a q20 a1 ad1; q76 a1; *in DA* §824). These two aspects display different 'directions of fit' (to use a later term); the intellect tries to conform itself to reality, whereas the will goes outside itself to make reality conform to it.[43] The will moves the body because it is a form of desire, but the intellect does not move the body except through desire, 'whose motion presupposes the action of the intellect' (1a q76 a1). Reason is not the primary cause,

---

[41] On the use of 'voluntarism' by historians see Bonansea, 'Voluntarism' 95n.

[42] For further discussion of these positions see §§389–91.

[43] ' . . . cognition comes about through the fact that the thing cognized is in the cognizer. Hence his intellect extends itself to what is outside it, in accordance with the fact that what is essentially outside it is suitable (natum) for being in some way in it. Will, by contrast, extends itself to what is outside it in accordance with the fact that by a certain sort of tendency (inclinatio) it aims (tendit) in some way at an external thing. Now it belongs to one capacity to have something external within itself, and to another capacity to aim itself at an external thing' (1a q59 a2). On direction of fit see Anscombe, *Intention* 56–7; Smith, *MP* 111–25.

because intellect and will are two distinct capacities (*Ver.* q22 a10; *ST* 1a q80 a1; q82 a3) and both are needed to explain action. Knowledge by itself simply gives us a capacity to act as we choose (1-2 q56 a3), whereas willing causes us to do a particular sort of action. Knowing our good and how to achieve it would not be connected with our action if our desire did not fix on our good. Aquinas agrees with Aristotle's claim that thought by itself moves nothing, and that in order to initiate motion it must be 'thought for the sake of some end' (*EN* 1139a35–6). Aristotle believes that this goal-directed thought initiating action requires the presence of desire. Similarly, Aquinas asserts that our cognitive capacity does not move us without desire as intermediary.[44]

257. How is the Will Rational?

To show that he does not simply identify the will with practical reason, Aquinas argues that the desiring capacity—both sensory desire and will—participates in reason, but is not rational through its essence (1-2 q58 a2).[45] We might naturally take him to mean that it is not essential to an act of will to follow reason. This is the sense in which the passions participate in reason but are not essentially rational; they sometimes agree with reason, and sometimes do not, so that it is not essential to them to be guided by reason.

But this is not what Aquinas means in saying that the will is rational only by participation. If he meant that the will is not essentially rational, but may (like the passions) follow or not follow reason, he would embrace the extreme voluntarist position that will is definable independently of reason. But he rejects extreme voluntarism. He does not believe the will can be non-rational; while there are non-rational forms of desire, there are no non-rational

---

[44] Vis cognitiva non movet nisi mediante appetitiva, 1a q20 a1 ad1.

[45] Aquinas believes that his view of the will as rational by participation agrees with Aristotle's view in *EN* i 13; see *in EN* §§240–1. In Aristotle, the parts that are 'obedient' to reason seem to be the non-rational desires, whereas *boulêsis* seems to belong to the rational part—as Aquinas himself notices elsewhere (1a q82 a1 obj2). Aquinas assumes, however, that all desire belongs to the non-rational part that 'participates in a way in reason' (*EN* 1102b13–14). Aquinas often appeals to this passage in support of his claim that the will is rational by participation (*ST* 1-2 q56 a6 ad2; q59 a4 ad2; a61 a2c, ad2; 2-2 q58 a4 ad3). In *EN* i 7 Aristotle marks a similar division between the two parts of the soul that 'have reason'. One of these actually has reason within it, while the other is 'obedient to' or 'persuadable by' (*epipeithes*, persuasibile) reason (*EN* 1098a4–5). Here also Aquinas supposes that the 'persuadable' part is meant to include the will as well as sensory desire. Indeed Aquinas concludes from this passage that happiness is taken to consist more principally in the contemplative than in the active life (*in EN* §126).

This explanation, however, does not work. First Aquinas claims that 'the appetitive (concupiscibilis) power, and every desiring power, including the irascible power and the will, participate in some way in reason' (§240). But at once he seems to contradict this claim. After remarking that the intellect is not subject to the actions of any bodily power, he says that the same is true of the will, 'which is in reason, as is said in *De Anima* iii' (§241). Having said this, however, he reverts to his first view, saying that one part of the soul, including both sensory desire and the will, is non-rational in its own right, but rational by participation (§242). It is difficult to see how the will can both be in the rational part and be non-rational in its own right.

Aquinas' attempt to understand the non-rational part as including the will is especially difficult to reconcile with his account of Aristotle's remarks on incontinence. For he sees that Aristotle means to attribute a correct decision to the rational part of both the continent and the incontinent person, and that the non-rational part 'obstructs reason, that is to say, impedes it in carrying out its election' (§237); the obstructing element is sensory desire. Now Aquinas recognizes that election is an act of the will (§486; 1a q83 a3; 1-2 q13 a1), and so he must agree that the incontinent person's sensory desire obstructs his will. If this is true, then one of the conflicting parts of the soul must include the will and the other must include sensory desire; hence Aristotle must take the rational part to include the will, and therefore to include rational desires. Aquinas should have concluded that i 13 includes the will in the rational part.

forms of will. Since the will depends on intellect, there is no will independent of reason. If we have a will, the intellect moves the will by presenting the object of will, and thereby 'directing' (ordinare) the will.[46]

'Rational by participation', therefore, does not mean 'not essentially rational'. It would be better expressed by 'derivatively rational'. The will is derivatively rational, because its rationality depends on something else that is non-derivatively rational; it presupposes the operation of intellect and reason, and is not identical to it.[47] It depends on rational beliefs and judgments, which are themselves rational 'through their essence' ('per essentiam', 1-2 q61 a2). Though Aquinas' terms might mislead the unwary reader into inferring that the will is not essentially rational, his explanation of the terms rejects this inference.

In treating the will as derivatively rational because of its relation to reason, Aquinas takes intellect to be prior to will and independent of it in one respect; it does not need to be moved by the will, whereas the will needs to be moved by the apprehensive capacity (1a q82 a4 ad3). If each capacity had to be moved by the other, the claim that either of them explains action would result in an infinite regress. To avoid a regress, Aquinas claims that the intellect initiates the motions of the will through 'command', which is an act of reason presupposing an act of will.[48] Commanding is essentially an act of reason because it involves directing someone towards something to be done, by 'intimating or declaring'. Reason intimates or declares either (1) 'absolutely' through a verb in the indicative mood (as in the gerundive 'This is to be done by you') or (2) 'by moving' B to do x, through a verb in the imperative mood (as in 'Do this').[49]

An indicative intimation intimates 'absolutely' because it simply intimates. Imperative intimation goes beyond simple intimation, since it intimates by moving. 'By moving', cannot mean 'by actually setting in motion', since not all imperative intimations are obeyed, and those that are not obeyed do not set anyone in motion. An imperative intimation is a 'setting in motion' in the conative sense, an explicit attempt by A to move B to do x. In this sense, pushing against a rock that (as I discover) I cannot actually move is also a 'setting in motion'. This all belongs to reason, because it is a function of reason to reach and to formulate the

---

[46] 'Now it is evident that, in a sense, reason precedes the will and directs its act: that is to say, in so far as the will aims at its object in accordance with the directing of reason, by the fact that the power of apprehending presents the power of desiring with its object. And so the act by which the will aims at something proposed to it as good, through being directed towards the end by reason, is materially an act of will, but formally an act of reason' (1-2 q13 a1).

[47] See discussion of Scotus' use of Aquinas' formula, §359.

[48] In SG iii 10 §1945 Aquinas first speaks of the power of moving one's limbs 'to execute the command of the will (imperium voluntatis)', and then of this same motive power as executing the command of reason (imperium rationis).

[49] 'Command is an act of reason, but with an act of will presupposed. . . . Now command is essentially indeed an act of reason: for the commander directs (ordinare) the one commanded to do something, by intimating or declaring; and to direct thus by intimating or declaring is an act of reason. But reason can intimate or declare something in two ways. First, absolutely: and this intimation is expressed by a verb in the indicative mood, as when one person says to another: "This is to be done (faciendum) by you." Sometimes, however, the reason intimates something to someone by moving him to it; and this intimation is expressed by a verb in the imperative mood, as when it is said to someone: "Do this". Now the first mover, among the powers of the soul, to the doing of an act is the will . . . Since therefore the second mover does not move, except in the power of the first mover, it follows that this very fact that reason moves by commanding belongs to it from the power of the will. Hence the remaining possibility is that command is an act of reason, with an act of the will presupposed, in the power of which <act of will> reason, by its command, moves <us> to the execution of the act' (1-2 q17 a1). The role of will in command is explained more fully in 4Sent. d15 q4 a1 sol. 1 ad3 = P vii 736b–737a; Quodl. ix q5 a2 = P ix 596b. Both passages maintain that command and prayer are none the less properly acts of reason. Cf. Bradley, ATHG 352–3. Cajetan ad 1-2 q17 a1 = L vi 119 defends the intellectualist view of imperium, arguing that it follows from acceptance of the claim that prudence is 'prescriptive' (praeceptiva). He attacks Scotus for ascribing imperium to will.

conclusion that is the content of the command. Aquinas does not suggest that deliberation simply causes our desire to pass from the end through the prediction that this action will promote the end.[50] We recognize that the action deserves to be done, and our recognition moves our will. In this respect, intellect commands acts of the will (q17 a5).

But intellect does not command all acts of the will, since it presupposes an act of will. We would not deliberate, and hence we would not reach a conclusion that could be the content of a command, unless we had wills that aimed at the good. The simple recognition that something deserves to be done would make no systematic difference to our action unless we had wills—forms of desire that respond to what deserves to be done. If we could recognize what is worth doing, but we had no wills, our recognition that it is worthwhile to learn to play the violin would not affect us in itself; it would affect us only if we already had some non-rational preference for playing the violin or for some end to which it seems to be a means. In commanding ourselves to learn to play the violin because it is worthwhile, we presuppose that this is a consideration that matters to us. Hence intellect moves the will as final cause, whereas the will moves the intellect as efficient cause (1a q82 a4). What intellect commands as worthwhile becomes an end for us to pursue, because we have wills that respond to what seems worthwhile. Intellect 'by itself' moves nothing, since it has no mechanism for moving the body independently of the will. Any role that we can attribute to the intellect in initiating action is a role that requires the operation of the will.

This account avoids an infinite regress because the presupposed act of will does not require a further act of intellect. Nothing further commands us to attend to what seems to deserve our attention, since commands presuppose an initial disposition to attend to it. This initial disposition is a state of will. It does not require a prior command; indeed such a prior command would be futile without the appropriate state of will. But it does not make Aquinas a voluntarist; for the initial disposition is not logically independent of reason. We cannot define will without reference to practical intellect.

258. The Influence of Will on Intellect

This relation between will and intellect affects the ways in which the will may influence the results of the operation of intellect. The 'active' function of the will is prominent in interpretations that minimize the extent of Aquinas' intellectualism.[51] He points out that our deliberation is influenced not only by the end that we want to achieve, but also by whether we choose to deliberate, how much we choose to deliberate, and what we choose to consider in our deliberation.[52] Since these choices depend on the will, some operations of intellect depend on will. Though the exercise of will in election depends on intellect, the will does not depend wholly on intellect. It also depends on the initial contribution of will in controlling the focus and the character of our deliberation.

---

[50] This predictive view is developed by Hobbes and Hume.

[51] See Lottin, *PM* i 276–80; iii 2, 652–7. His interpretation underlies Hisette's claim, *Enquête* 245, accepted by Wippel, '1277' 256–7. See §358.

[52] Cf. Aquinas' comments on the exercise of other capacities: 'One can not-will on this occasion to think about happiness, because the acts themselves of intellect and will as well [as exercises of other capacities] are particular' (*Mal.* q6 = M 560a).

These considerations exclude a version of intellectualism that claims that the intellect, operating wholly independently of the will, determines the will. But they do not imply that the will ever operates wholly independently of the intellect. Let us consider the operations of will that influence our deliberation when we choose what to deliberate about, whether to reconsider the results of our deliberation, and so on. Aquinas would take these operations of will to support a voluntarist account of the will if he believed that they proceed independently of our conception of the good. But we have no reason to attribute this belief to him. If I decide it would be a waste of my time to deliberate elaborately about whether to wear a grey shirt or a blue shirt, and so conclude my deliberation quickly, that may be because I think it does not matter much which shirt I wear, or because I notice that I need to go out in two minutes. My will influences my deliberation, but it is itself influenced by my views about what would be better; and so even the influencing will depends on the intellect.

Sometimes these operations of the will explain why we do not act on our initial conception of what is better. Our preferences and interests may cause us to reason badly, so that we do not always discover what contributes best to the ultimate good, even when this discovery is open to us. Moreover, we are sometimes so hasty or biased that we do not stop to think about the ultimate good. We even reject particular goods that initially appear to promote the ultimate good; for we may attend to the aspects that make them undesirable rather than to those that make them desirable (1-2 q13 a6). Since only the ultimate good has no such aspects, every subordinate good can be rejected by an agent who focuses on its undesirable aspects. If we attend to the bad aspects of something that initially appeared to promote the ultimate good, we may not desire or choose this object. We may attend unreasonably to the good aspects of a bad object or to the bad aspects of a good one, and so we do not act on the best reasons that we initially recognize. Hence the will fails, in one respect, to follow reason, so that it is not necessarily determined by reason.

But the role of the will in focussing our attention and controlling our deliberation does not always distort the operations of intellect. It is often legitimate, and even indispensable. Since subordinate goods and evils have many good and bad aspects corresponding to different elements of the ultimate good and the means to them, we could not deliberate efficiently or effectively at all if we did not focus on some questions rather than others, and we did not form some views about how long it is worth our while to deliberate on different questions. These views cannot all be subject to deliberation on each occasion; if they were, we could never get started.[53] But they are not immune to deliberation on all occasions; I may discover, when I think about it, that sometimes I miss opportunities by fussing for too long on minor questions, and that at other times I make mistakes because I take the wrong things for granted in deliberation.

These examples suggest what Aquinas means in saying that will influences intellect. He does not hold a voluntarist conception of this role of will; for he does not claim that in this role the will is free to choose independently of the apparent good. Hence he does not suggest that I might will not to deliberate now even if it seems good to deliberate and nothing seems

---

[53] On the threat of a regress see *Mal.* q6 = M 559b. Aquinas argues that to explain the first movement of the will, we need to appeal to an external mover, God; he does not say that the will initiates the movement itself.

to me to count against taking time to deliberate.[54] In his view, 'human beings determine themselves through reason to will this or that, which is really good or apparently good' (1-2 q9 a6 ad3).[55] If the acts of will that determine the operations of intellect did not themselves depend on the apparent good, how could Aquinas claim that they are acts of will? Why would they belong to the will rather than to some other desire? If he recognized acts of will that are independent of the apparent good, his position would be inconsistent; but he does not recognize them. On the contrary, he claims that, whereas the will moves the intellect to its exercise, it moves other things in this or that way because of how the good appears to it.[56]

The will moves the intellect as efficient cause whereas the intellect moves the will as formal and final cause.[57] The intellect has a causal role because it presents to the will the end that explains the will's willing a particular action (bodily or mental) for the sake of the end; and in presenting this end it also gives the will the relevant form (being the will to achieve this end). These different causal roles express the fact that our will moves us in a particular direction only because it aims at a particular end as good, and depends on the intellect to present it to us as good.

Aquinas' position, therefore, is moderate rather than extreme intellectualism, but it is a form of intellectualism rather than a combination of intellectualism and voluntarism. It avoids the extreme intellectualist claim that intellect independent of will determines will and action, but it also avoids the voluntarist claim that will independent of intellect determines intellect and action. We necessarily desire what we apprehend as promoting the ultimate good; if we fail to choose something that at first seemed to promote the ultimate good, we have changed our mind about whether it really promotes the ultimate good.[58] We act rationally in so far as intellect constrains the operation of the will. In Aquinas' view, we cannot firmly believe that x rather than y promotes the good, and then—while still clearly understanding and firmly believing this—will y rather than x. This intellectual constraint on the will applies no less to the acts of will that influence deliberation than to those that result from deliberation.

---

[54] This claim needs to be restricted to willing. We are also influenced by passions, but their influence is not relevant to deciding whether Aquinas concedes something to voluntarism.

[55] Lottin, *PM* iii 2, 65, Hisette, *Enquête* 244, and Wippel, '1277', 256n66–7, all try to restrict this remark to the final practical judgment, which depends on the influence of the will. But it is arbitrary to suppose that it does not also apply to the acts of will that influence deliberation.

[56] 'The motion of the subject itself is from some agent. And since every agent acts for an end, . . . the principle (or origin; principium) of this motion is from the end. . . . Now good in common, which has the character of an end, is the object of the will. Consequently, in this respect, the will moves the other capacities of the soul to their acts . . . On the other hand, the object moves by determining the act, in the way a formal principle does . . . Now the first formal principle is the universal being and truth, which is the object of the intellect. And therefore by this kind of motion the intellect moves the will, as presenting its object to it' (1-2 q9 a1).

[57] 1-2 q9 a1 ad3; *Ver.* q22 a12 = M (1b).

[58] ' . . . if some object that is universally good and good in accordance with every consideration is put forward for the will, the will necessarily aims at it, if it wills anything. But if some object that is not good in accordance with every consideration is put forward for the will, it will not necessarily be carried towards it. And since a lack of any good whatever has the character of not-good, it follows that only the good that is perfect and lacking in nothing is the sort of good that the will cannot fail to will; and this good is happiness. But the other goods, namely particular goods, in so far as they lack some good, can be taken as not good, and in accordance with this consideration they can be rejected or approved by the will . . . ' (*ST* 1-2 q10 a2). ' . . . It is quite possible that, if any two things are put forward as equal in accordance with one consideration, still a condition about one of them may be considered through which it is superior, so that the will is turned more towards it than towards the other' (q13 a6 ad3). On changing attention and voluntarism see §362.

259. Will, Reason, and Desire

The significance of Aquinas' view about the roles of will, intellect, and desire may be clearer if we consider later disputes between rationalism and anti-rationalism (or 'sentimentalism') about whether 'reason' or 'passion' moves us to action.[59] These disputes are clearer if we recall our earlier division between intellectualism and rationalism, since modern disputes tends to run the two positions together.

Aquinas agrees with Aristotle in rejecting the extreme intellectualist position, later maintained by Clarke, that thought without desire motivates.[60] That is why Hutcheson claims that Aristotle and the Scholastics support his anti-rationalism.[61] He assumes that their rejection of extreme intellectualism about intellect and will implies the rejection of rationalism about will and passion. In his view, reason moves us only in so far as it presents means to some independently-desired end; the fact that we desire a certain sort of object explains why other objects are worth choosing.

Aquinas, however, implicitly rejects this argument from the rejection of extreme intellectualism to the rejection of rationalism, because he rejects the anti-rationalist view of reasons. Contrary to Hutcheson and Hume, he believes in external reasons—reasons whose goodness or badness does not consist simply in their relation to other desires of the agent.[62] Internal reasons are internal to, because they depend on, the actual desires of the agent; agents have the relevant reasons ultimately because they have the relevant desires. If I want to go to a film, I have an internal reason to buy a ticket, but I have no reason to buy a ticket apart from my desire to go to the film, and I have no reason (we may assume) to want to go to the film rather than to amuse myself in some other way that is equally available to me. External reasons consist in facts that are not connected to agents' desires in this way. To have an external reason is to have a good reason for choosing x over y whose goodness does not consist simply in the fact that x will do more than y will do for some further end. Aquinas takes these external reasons to be the basis of 'intellectual love' (1-2 q26 a1–2) that is not based simply on the prior desires of the agent. He believes that will is essentially rational, because it is essentially moved by intellectual love and by external reasons; the relevant reasons are derived from the independent merits of a proposed action, apart from one's antecedent preferences.

Belief in external reasons constrains one's account of the ultimate good. Aquinas claims that rational agents choose by 'rational comparison' of particular goods. One might suppose that we rationally compare particular goods if we consider the strength of our preference for each of them, and choose among them in accordance with the strength of our preference. But if we choose among ends in accordance with external reasons, the rational comparison of ends considers more than the comparative strength of our desire for them. We consider the merits of our various preferences, and we correct our preferences as a result of reflexion on their merits.

If, then, Aquinas' belief in external reasons supports rationalism against anti-rationalism, and if his claims about will and intellect support intellectualism against voluntarism, is it

---

[59] See §391.   [60] See Aristotle, *DA* 433a22–3; *EN* 1139a35–6; Aquinas, *in DA* §824–5; *in EN* §1135.

[61] See Hutcheson, *IMS* 122.

[62] On internal v. external reasons see §§336–7; Williams, 'Internal'; McDowell, 'External'; Taylor, 'Agency'.

misleading of him to reject extreme intellectualism? Though he says that desire as well as intellect is needed for action, does he empty this claim of content when he adds his views about intellectual love and external reasons? He might answer that he differs from extreme intellectualism in insisting that external reasons move us only in so far as they tell us about goods. To say that things are good is not simply to say that there are external reasons for pursuing them; it also implies that the external reasons fit together in the teleological structure that embodies the ultimate good.

This teleological structure implies that a given external reason is not a reason that we can immediately see in its own right; it must also fit into an appropriate structure of ends. In this respect Clarke's extreme intellectualism fits his foundationalist and intuitionist epistemology. In rejecting this position and insisting on a basic desire for the ultimate good, Aquinas implies that we can grasp external reasons only in relation to each other and to their common end. He is therefore a rationalist about will and passion, since he does not believe that the rational merits of a given action are determined by an antecedent desire with some determinate content. He believes that our desires are directed towards action on the recognition of the rational merits of a course of action.

18

AQUINAS: FREEDOM

---

260. Voluntary Action and the Will

Aquinas believes that his conception of the will and the passions and of their relations allows us to understand the distinction (i) between voluntary and involuntary actions, and (ii) between free and unfree actions. According to Aquinas, these are really one distinction that depends on the presence or absence of the appropriate relation between will and action. It is not obvious, however, that they are really one distinction. We may begin with Aquinas' treatment of the voluntary, and then consider why he believes that this also provides an adequate treatment of questions about freewill.[1]

Aquinas regards the will as the source of the actions that Aristotle counts as voluntary (*hekousion*).[2] According to Aquinas, Aristotle attributes to *boulêsis* the properties that belong to the will (voluntas). If Aquinas is right about this, 'voluntas' is a good translation of 'boulêsis', and 'voluntarium' is a good translation of 'hekousion'. If a voluntary action is a product of the will, it is also a product of deliberation and election. Voluntary actions are the proper objects of praise and blame (*ST* 1-2 q6 a2 obj3), because the complete form of voluntariness makes praise and blame appropriate.[3] Our capacity to deliberate gives us control over our actions, and so allows us to modify our actions in response to praise and blame.

Non-rational agents lack the complete form of voluntary action, since they are not open to praise and blame (q6 a2).[4] The complete form of the voluntary requires the complete knowledge of the end and the relation of means to end.[5] If we have this grasp of the end and

---

[1] In some of his discussions of will and freewill, the voluntary has no distinct place in the argument. In *2Sent* d24–5 he discusses questions about the will in the course of a discussion of freewill. The discussions in *Ver.* qq22–4 and in *ST* 1a begin with a discussion of the will and proceed to discuss freewill, but they do not discuss the voluntary separately. *ST* 1a treats the will in q82; a2 touches on questions about the voluntary, without actually using 'voluntarium'. *ST* 1–2, however, treats many of the same questions by discussing issues about the voluntary.

[2] I use 'voluntary' to translate 'hekousion', without meaning to beg any question in favour of Aquinas' view. For Aristotle's views on the voluntary see §100.

[3] '<Praise and blame> follow on a voluntary action that is in accordance with the complete form (perfecta ratio) of the voluntary, the sort that is not found in non-rational animals' (q6 a2 ad3).

[4] These agents act 'of their own accord' without being capable of the sort of voluntary action that depends on the will (1-2 q6 a2; *in EN* §427; *Ver.* q24 a2 ad1). See §243.

[5] '... not only does one grasp the thing that is the end, but one also grasps the character (ratio) of the end and how the thing directed to the end is related to the end' (q6 a2).

the means, we can deliberate about the means, and as a result of deliberation we can pursue or refrain from pursuing the end.⁶

These conditions for voluntary action may appear to be too restrictive to capture Aristotle's view. Aristotle allows voluntary action in two cases where Aquinas apparently cannot allow it: (1) Aristotle allows that non-rational agents, including non-human animals and young children, act voluntarily. Aquinas, however, argues that since they lack deliberation, election, and will, they do not act voluntarily; they act voluntarily only to a lower degree (q6 a2).⁷ (2) Aristotle believes that actions on non-rational desire are normally voluntary, and therefore open to praise and blame. Aquinas' conditions for voluntary action appear to make it more difficult to treat such actions as voluntary, since they do not appear to result from will and deliberation.

These two cases may seem to stand or fall together. If we must recognize voluntary action without deliberation in human beings, must we recognize it in non-rational agents? If the inability of animals to deliberate does not disqualify them, are they voluntary agents? Aquinas cannot reasonably deny that actions on non-rational desires are voluntary; for he agrees with Aristotle that they are open to praise and blame. How can they be voluntary, according to Aquinas' criterion?

261. How Action on Passions is Voluntary

Aquinas' answer relies on his analysis of the passions, and especially on his views about the relation of will to passion. In formulating these views, he confronts a Stoic objection to a Peripatetic account of the passions. According to the Stoics, the Peripatetics take passions to be independent of a judgment that an action is best all things considered, and so cannot explain why action on passion is voluntary and responsible.⁸

If the Stoics are right on this point, Augustine cannot be right in claiming that the non-rational motion itself is the passion. If he were right, we would not be responsible for acting on our passions, because they would be entirely separate from rational assent. Augustine's account of our responsibility for acting on passions suggests that, contrary to his criticism of the Stoics, they require assent.⁹

Augustine's answer to the Stoics raises a question for Aquinas. If voluntary action depends on the will, it seems to depend on rational assent. But if passions are independent of rational assent, they apparently cannot be sources of voluntary action. If they are sources of voluntary action, must he agree with the Stoics that they are forms of rational assent?

He appeals to Aristotle's remark that we are not praised or blamed for simply having passions, but only for being in a good or bad state in relation to passions.¹⁰ If we are

---

⁶ 'for from the fact that deliberating reason is related to contraries, the will is capable of going in both directions' (q6 a2 ad2).

⁷ This claim about a lower degree of voluntariness also applies to children. But it needs to be modified, as Aquinas realizes, to account for the gradual acquisition of reason, and hence of free choice, in children. See 1a q99 a1; q101 a2; 3a q80 a9 ad3.

⁸ Their argument is set out at §167.   ⁹ See §221.

¹⁰ EN 1105b31–1106a2; 1-2 q24 a1 ad3; q59 a1 sc; in EN §§300–1. The Latin version oddly translates aprohairetôs, EN 1106a3, by 'non sponte'. Aquinas reasonably understands this as meaning '<non> ex arbitrio rationis', in EN §301.

responsible for what we do, we cannot be acting on the passion alone, but the passion must be appropriately controlled by reason. The relevant form of control by reason is consent given by the will (q10 a3 ad1), which makes action on a passion voluntary.

If consent requires deliberation and election on each occasion when we act, the resulting picture of voluntary action on passions is implausible, since we often act on passion without deliberation, and we seem to act voluntarily in some of these cases. We have seen, however, that Aquinas does not commit himself to the implausible picture; he does not require actual deliberation on every occasion of consent. He allows a permissive and regulative role for our conception of the end, and therefore for the will, in actions that are not the direct result of deliberation and election.[11]

The indirect role for the will allows consent to permitted actions, not only to those that we elect as a direct result of deliberation. Actions are voluntary in so far as we consent to them (1-2 q15 a4 ad2), and reason consents either by actually initiating the movement or by not dissenting (q15 a4 ad3).[12] The permitted actions from which reason does not dissent are indirectly rather than directly voluntary (q77 a7). This role of the will shows how action on passions is voluntary, and therefore how passion can be a cause of sin. Since all sins are voluntary, they must proceed in some way from the will, and so must be suitably connected with election; but they need not all be directly elected.

The permissive operation of will and election supports Aquinas' account of how we are responsible for acting on passions, as Aristotle claims (*EN* 1111a29–31).[13] Aristotle remarks that instead of holding pleasant or fine things responsible for our actions, we should regard ourselves as the causes, as being 'an easy prey' to such things (1110b13–14). Aquinas explains Aristotle by appealing to the capacity of the will to accept or reject the suggestions of passion.[14] According to Aristotle, we may be responsible for falling ill, by 'living incontinently and not following the advice of the doctors'; in that case he is voluntarily ill (1114a15–16). Similarly, as Aquinas puts it, the agent's will is engaged in becoming vicious.[15] Aquinas' appeal to consent clarifies Aristotle's position. We are open to praise and blame for actions that are direct or indirect products of will and deliberation. If the error results from a deliberative failure of the agent, and if the agent can correct this failure, praise and blame are appropriate.

If Aquinas is right about the relations between the passions and the will, action on passion is normally voluntary. If he supposed that when we act on passion, we form a judgment about what is good overall and see that this agrees with the prompting of the passion, his position would be difficult to defend. But since he has a more flexible view about the different

---

[11] See §§248 and §255.　　[12] Quoted at §255.

[13] 'For no matter how much anger or appetite grows, a human being does not rush into action, unless the consent of rational desire is added. Further, the first claim seems inappropriate in the same way, namely someone's saying that goods that one ought to desire in accordance with passion as well <as rational desire> are not voluntary. For reason leads us through will to desire those things that we ought to' (*in EN* §428).

[14] '. . . it is ridiculous . . . not to accuse oneself on the ground that one makes oneself an easy prey, that is to say, permits oneself to be overcome by pleasant objects of this sort. For our will is not moved of necessity by such objects of desire, but it is capable of attaching itself to them and of not attaching itself to them' (*in EN* §403).

[15] Aristotle adds that a person for whom vice has become habitual cannot immediately become virtuous simply by willing to. Aquinas does not take him to mean that vice becomes altogether beyond the agent's control: '. . . after they have become such [sc. unjust and incontinent], it is no longer in their power, that is to say, to cease immediately from being unjust or incontinent, but for this a great deal of effort and practice is needed' (*in EN* §513).

ways in which the will endorses or permits, voluntary action on passion does not require an unrealistic degree of rational intervention. He has a reasonable defence, therefore, of his claim that voluntary action proceeds from the will.[16]

262. The Will as the Source of Virtue and Vice

Aquinas' conception of the voluntary implies that if we regard an action as voluntary, and hence as open to praise and blame, we must trace it to the will. Among the sources of rational action—the object apprehended, the apprehension of it, the will, and the motive power that executes the commands of reason—only the will is the proper source of virtue and vice. If the other sources were present without will, we would have no reason to praise or to blame (SG iii 10 §§1945–6).

This conclusion, however, raises a difficulty. If a morally bad and vicious action results from the will, it results from some defect of the will. This defect cannot be natural or merely accidental, since such defects cannot be the source of moral badness. But if the defect is itself a voluntary defect, it appears to be a moral error (peccatum); and then we must ask what makes it a moral error; if we must cite some further voluntary defect that is a moral error, we face an infinite regress.

The solution, in Aquinas' view, is to identify a defect in the will that is voluntary, but not a moral error (SG iii 10 §1947b). To identify the relevant defect Aquinas describes the proper and 'perfect', non-defective operation of the will. Just as the proper function of sensory desire is to be moved by sensory apprehension, the proper function of will is to be moved by reason itself (10 §1948). Since reason moves by presenting an end as good, and since it can present many goods and ends, the proper function of will is to be moved by the good that is proper to the agent; in that case, a morally good action follows. A morally bad action results when the will breaks out towards action (in actionem prorumpit) either (i) on an apprehension belonging to sense, or (ii) on an apprehension of reason presenting some good different from one's proper good (10 §1949).

The first of these two errors involves a misdirected attitude towards reason.[17] As a result of a 'sudden' apprehension of sense,[18] the will turns towards some good that is pleasing to sense. As a result of reasoning that arrives at some good that is not good now, or not good in the relevant way, the will turns towards it as though towards its proper good. Here we have the sort of error by the will that explains morally bad action.[19] Aquinas distinguishes (a) the 'turning' that consists in the will's looking favourably on a good that is pleasing to sense, from (b) the sort of 'turning' that consists in the willing that produces command and

---

[16] The defence is not complete. On incontinence see §§295–6.

[17] Cf. 1-2 q75 a1: 'a will lacking the direction of correct reason and divine law, aiming at some changeable good, causes the act of sin in its own right, but causes the misdirection of the act coincidentally and apart from its aim'. See §289.

[18] On suddenness see §253 above.

[19] 'Now this defect of direction is voluntary; for it is in the power of the will to will and not to will. It is likewise in its power for reason actually to consider or to cease from considering, or to consider this or that. Still this defect is not a moral evil: for, if reason considers nothing, or considers a good of any sort, that is not yet a sin (peccatum) until the will turns (tendat) towards some wrong (indebitum) end, which is then an act of will' (SG iii 10 §1950). This passage is discussed further at §297.

action. Only the second sort of turning is a moral error. Since we explain the second sort of turning by reference to the first, we avoid an infinite regress of explanation.

The first sort of turning consists in considering x to the exclusion of y.[20] There is nothing wrong with considering a particular sensory pleasure, if we also notice that we have decisive reasons to avoid it here and now. Similarly, it is legitimate to notice that our deliberation has identified x as having something to be said for it, if we also notice that further deliberation reveals decisive reasons for avoiding it. Since neither of these sorts of consideration involves error, the erroneous consideration that Aquinas intends is one-sided consideration of something other than one's proper good as revealed by practical reason. The consideration may be one-sided either by ignoring deliberation altogether, in favour of the 'sudden' apprehension of sense, or by unreasonably halting one's recognition of the results of deliberation.

This one-sided consideration is an act of the will. According to Aquinas, it does not lead us into an infinite regress, because it is not a moral error, though it is a mistake. It is necessary for a moral error, because we cannot choose the wrong option without prior consideration of the option.[21] But it is not the moral error. We have made no moral error until we come to an act of will directed towards action. Hence our appeal to one-sided consideration does not invoke a moral error to explain moral error; but since we appeal to an act of will, we explain how moral error is voluntary.

Aquinas clarifies his point with an analogy. If a piece of wood ought to be cut straight by using a ruler, but a carpenter fails to use the ruler, the faulty cutting is caused by the non-use of the appropriate standard. Similarly, if we choose an action without reference to the appropriate standard, the rule of reason and the divine law, this non-use 'is presupposed in the will before the misdirected election' (*Mal.* q1 a3 = M 455b). For this non-use of the rule 'we need not seek any cause, because for this the freedom of the will itself is sufficient, the freedom through which it is capable of acting and not acting' (q1 a3 = M 455b). In saying that we need not seek any cause, Aquinas does not mean that the non-use of the rule has no cause; for he goes on to say that the capacity of the will to act and not to act is sufficient. He means that we need not seek any further cause beyond the freedom of the will.

The will's failure to consider the right things is not yet a moral error. The moral error enters when we proceed to will and to act on the basis of one-sided consideration.[22] But it is not clear that this distinction helps Aquinas to avoid an infinite regress. Even if the error of one-sided consideration is not a moral error, it needs to be explained. Any attempted explanation seems to face the difficulties he has previously mentioned (*SG* iii 10 §1946). Neither the object apprehended nor the apprehensive capacity is the source of moral error;

---

[20] Hence he says that when we sin from passion, passion diverts reason from the actual consideration of the correct end (*2Sent* d7 q1 a2 = P vi 447a, referring to Aristotle, *EN* vii).

[21] '. . . no one is bound to do something except through the fact that he considers that this is to be done; that is why people, in common speech, seem to understand conscience as some actual consideration by reason' (*2Sent* d24 q2 a4 = P vi 601b).

[22] 'And this fact itself of not attending actually to such a rule considered in itself is not evil, either fault (culpa) or penalty (poena), because the mind is not required to, and is not able to, attend actually to this sort of rule always; but it receives the character of fault first of all from this, that without actual consideration of the rule it proceeds to an election of this sort, just as a craftsman does not err (peccat) in the fact that he does not always hold the measure, but from the fact that he proceeds to cut without holding the measure; and similarly the fault (culpa) of the will is not in the fact that it does not attend actually to the rule of reason or divine law, but from the fact that it proceeds to elect without holding the rule or measure of this sort' (*Mal.* q1 a3 = M 455b).

but if either of them is the source of one-sided consideration, then one-sided consideration does not seem to be voluntary, and so seems not to be the source of moral error. But if the source of one-sided consideration is a further act of will, the same questions can apparently be raised about the cause of this further act of will, and then we seem to be forced into an infinite regress.

Aquinas answers that one-sided consideration is a defect of will and that it is voluntary, not because it was caused by a previous act of will, but because it is in the power of the will whether reason considers it or not (iii 10 §1950). This claim about power distinguishes the voluntariness of one-sided consideration from the voluntariness of moral error. Moral error is voluntary because it is caused by one-sided consideration, which is an act of the will; but this act of the will is voluntary because it is within the power of the will.

To see why something's being in the power of the will is relevant to voluntariness, we should recall that the will is essentially rational desire aiming at the ultimate good as conceived by reason. It is sensitive to the results of rational reflection about what promotes this ultimate good, and hence sensitive to beliefs about the comparative value of different actions. If one-sided consideration is within the power of the will, it is not simply an unavoidable psychological fact that we pursue the goods presented by sensory apprehension or by incomplete deliberation; if it were unavoidable, we would not be open to praise and blame because of it.[23] One-sided consideration is in the power of the will because such consideration is affected by rational reflection; for if we see that we are wrong to exclude considerations that deserve to be considered, we will change our minds about what should be considered, and we will make our consideration less one-sided.

Why does this flexibility of our will to rational reflection ensure that the error of one-sided consideration is voluntary? Aquinas relies on the connexion of voluntariness with the appropriateness of praise and blame. Praise and blame involve the presentation of considerations that deserve to be considered; the agents have considered them (in the case of praise) or failed to consider them (in the case of blame). Since the will is sensitive to these considerations, actions that are in the power of the will are proper objects of praise and blame, and therefore are voluntary.

Aquinas does not represent one-sided consideration as an act of the will that is independent of reason. If it were independent of reason, it would not be an act of the will; for will is desire that is essentially guided by reason. The condition of our will that makes us prone to one-sided attention results from our beliefs about the good and our reasoning about what promotes it. The voluntariness of the acts of a will in this condition does not depend on whether these acts have come about through voluntary acts of will. It depends on their being acts of a will that is responsive to praise and blame. Aquinas' claims about voluntary action and voluntary states of will do not rely ultimately on an appeal to a series of voluntary acts; he sees that such a series threatens him with an infinite regress. His claims rely ultimately on the rational character of the will.

---

[23] 'If, then, it were true that the will would of necessity accept the impression of some pleasing thing attracting it, just as a natural body of necessity accepts the impression of the thing acting on it, then it would be altogether the same in the will as it is in natural things. It is not so, however, because, however much the external sensible thing attracts, it is still in the power of the will to receive or not to accept it. Hence the cause of the evil that occurs from what accepts it is not the pleasant thing that initiates motion, but more the will itself' (*Mal.* q1 a3 = M 455a).

263. The Connexion between Voluntariness and Freewill

Aquinas' account of the will and of voluntary action is Aristotelian in so far as it develops and elaborates Aristotle's views about the ultimate end, deliberation, and election. It might appear to ignore the most important questions about freewill. Even if we were persuaded of the truth of hard determinism, and so believed that no one is free, we might believe that actions caused by mental states of agents must be distinguished from other events that happen to these agents. We might, then, have some use for Aristotle's conception of the voluntary, even if we denied freewill. Hence a proof that agents act voluntarily does not show that they have genuine freewill.

This attempt to separate the voluntary from freewill overlooks one important claim that Aristotle and Aquinas accept—that voluntariness justifies praise and blame. An adequate account of freewill ought to justify praise and blame. If, for instance, we affirmed hard determinism, but conceded that our lack of freewill does not prevent us from being open to justified praise and blame, we would not really deny the reality of freewill. In deciding what counts as the presence or absence of freewill, we should rely on our views about conditions that would or would not support justified praise and blame.

Does this approach make it too easy to prove that we have freewill? One might object that even a hard determinist can find room for praise and blame. Since our favourable and unfavourable reactions to people may influence their future behaviour, can we not justify praise and blame whatever we conclude about the metaphysical facts? But attempts to influence them need not treat them as responsible for their actions. Hence we cannot decide questions about conditions for responsibility simply by looking at conditions for praise and blame.

This objection fails, because the practices that are held to be consistent with hard determinism are not sufficient to justify praise and blame. Reactions or manipulations that try to alter future behaviour do not constitute praise and blame; we may recognize that someone is not justly open to praise or blame for what they have done, even though it would be useful to react favourably or unfavourably. In regarding someone as deserving praise and blame, we make a retrospective judgment relying on what they have done and the mental states in which they have done it. If I accidentally prevent a robbery by driving past a lonely house just as the robbers are about to begin work, it might be useful to reward me for what I did, since that might encourage me or others to do the same sort of thing; but I would not deserve any praise if the good result of my action was entirely accidental. Similarly, if I take every reasonable precaution to keep my bull fenced in, but he gets out, it may be reasonable to fine me, since the fine may encourage me or others to be even more careful about keeping bulls; but I would not deserve any blame if the bad result was entirely accidental. The conditions in which it is useful to impose rewards or sanctions are different from those in which we deserve praise or blame. The conditions for deserving praise and blame—not simply conditions in which rewards or sanctions may be useful—are relevant to finding an adequate account of responsibility.

In assuming that we can reasonably make judgments about when, and on what basis, people deserve praise and blame, we rely on specific moral judgments. If these judgments are mistaken, the pursuit of conditions for freewill is misguided. If retrospective praise and blame, focussing on what people have done and the mental states in which they have done it, is morally misguided, nothing justifies them; hence we cannot be free and responsible.

This does not mean, however, that judgments about responsibility rest on an insecure basis. For many retrospective moral judgments about desert, praise, and blame are not particularly insecure. Indeed, it is difficult to imagine giving them up; those who have questioned them have usually been moved by the apparent difficulty of finding any metaphysical basis for them, not by their inherent implausibility. It is reasonable, then, to rely, as Aristotle does, on judgments about praise and blame. If, for instance, we want to know whether a capacity for opposites is necessary for freewill, we should ask whether it would be fair to praise or blame agents for their actions if they lacked such a capacity. Since Aquinas presents his account of the voluntary as an account of the basis of justified praise and blame, he believes that if we are voluntary agents, we also have freewill. Hence he argues that voluntary agency, as he understands it, meets the reasonable conditions that people have in mind when they raise questions about freewill.

264. Objections to an Aristotelian Account of Freewill

To see why the Aristotelian account of the voluntary, as we have understood it, apparently cannot give sufficient conditions for freewill, we may begin with an aspect of freewill that Aristotle implicitly recognizes. In his view, if we are responsible for an action, it is up to us to do and not to do that action.[24] But an account of voluntary actions that relies simply, as Aquinas does, on their relation to will and deliberation, does not seem to incorporate this requirement. Alexander believes that if an action is up to us, or in our power, we must act freely (*autoexousiôs*); he infers that not all voluntary action is free action.[25] Freewill should remove necessity from our choices and actions.[26]

Freewill involves some sort of alternative possibilities. The will desires the ultimate end from necessity, but it does not pursue other objects of desire from necessity (1a q82 a1–2); if we did pursue everything from necessity, in the relevant sense, we would not have freewill. We are in control of our doing x or not-x in so far as we are not determined to either one of x or not-x; if we were determined to one outcome, we would not have freewill.[27]

Aquinas supposes that the question about freewill is about whether I freely choose to do this or that particular action. My freedom in making the choice depends on whether I freely make the judgment underlying the choice (1a q83 a2 obj1). If freewill is a potentiality, it must be identified with the potentiality that ensures freedom in our judgments (ad1).[28]

This aspect of freewill appears to support an incompatibilist claim about freedom and causal determinism. The truth of causal determinism seems to imply that we are necessitated

---

[24] See §§100, 172.

[25] In the Latin versions of Nemesius and Damascene, 'liberum arbitrium' is used to translate *autexousiotês* and cognates. On the Greek term see §172.

[26] Freedom to go wrong: voluntary agents, in quorum potestate est subducere se ab ordinatione divini intellectus; in quo malum culpae consistit (1a q17 a1).

[27] See 1-2 q10 a1 ad3; *Pot.* q3 a13; *Mal.* q3 a3 ad5.

[28] In 1a q83 a4 obj1 Aquinas infers from Damasc. *EF* 36.124–31 that Damascene identifies *boulêsis* with liberum arbitrium.

to do whatever we do. But (the incompatibilist argues) if we are necessitated, it is not up to us to do otherwise, and hence we do not act freely. If Aquinas agrees, he cannot say that free action consists simply in action suitably connected to will and deliberation; he must also claim that such action is causally undetermined.

265. Will as the Source of Freewill

To show that freewill is the same as will, Aquinas considers reasons for believing they are different.[29] He recognizes that some people have taken Damascene's distinction between *thelêsis* and *boulêsis* to divide will from free choice (1a q83 a4 obj1).[30] If, as Aquinas believes, will is determined by one's conception of the ultimate end, one might infer that, for this very reason, will cannot be identified with freewill, which must include some undetermined element distinct from the will. Freewill, therefore, stands (on this view) above other intellectual and motive capacities, and must be distinct from them all (*2Sent* d24 q1 a3 obj5 = P vi 595a).

Aquinas argues that, on the contrary, freewill is found in the will. His account of the will meets two reasonable conditions for an account of freewill: (1) It shows how freewill is, as we normally suppose, essentially connected with the basis for responsibility; for Aquinas believes that justified claims about responsibility and about praise and blame must appeal to control, direct or indirect, by the will. (2) It shows why freewill requires the capacity for opposites; for will gives us the capacity for rational choice between different courses of action. As Aquinas explains the nature of will, it frees us from determination to some particular course of action, and therefore gives us the sort of choice between opposites that is required for freedom.

He therefore defends a reductive account of freewill.[31] In his view, questions about freewill can be reduced to questions about will, and his account of the will shows that we

---

[29] See 1a q83 a4; 3a q18 a3–4; *2Sent* d24 q1 a3 = P vi 595b (on whether freewill is a different capacity from will and reason); *Ver.* q24 a6.

[30] Lottin, *PM* i 403, attributes this interpretation of Damascene to Alexander of Hales. For Damascene's views on *thelêsis* see *EF* 36.51–3: '*Thelêsis* is an innate capacity in the soul, desiring what is according to [its] nature, and containing all the things that belong essentially to [its] nature'. The substance aims at its own full being (ontotês). Hence natural *thelêma* is defined: '. . .*thelêma* is a rational and vital orexis directed only towards natural things and so *thelêsis* is this very natural and rational desire, a simple capacity. For the desire of non-rational things, since it is not rational, is not called *thelêsis*. *Boulêsis* is a particular sort of (*poia*) natural *thelêsis*, in other words a rational and vital *orexis* for some thing (*pragma*). For there is present in the human soul a capacity for desiring rationally. And so when this natural desire is naturally moved towards some thing (*pragma*), it is called *boulêsis*; for *boulêsis* is rational desiring and aiming at (*ephesis*) some thing' (56–64). The difference between *boulêsis* and *thelêsis* seems to be that *boulêsis* fixes on some determinate object (*pragma*; 'un objet determiné', Lottin, *PM* i 396). In 36.65–70 Damascene mentions various determinate objects that we might have a *boulêsis* for—e.g. to fornicate or to act temperately or to fall asleep. The same distinction is drawn more fully in 124–31, where *thelêsis* is said to be the simple capacity for *thelein*, and *boulêsis* is *thelêsis* about something (*peri ti*). The division between *boulêsis* and *bouleusis*, 71–7, mostly follows Aristotle. Aquinas discusses Damascene on *boulêsis* and *thelêsis* at 3a q18 a3.

[31] Damasc. *EF* 38.38–40 implies that *hekousion* is wider than *prohairesis*, because children and non-rational animals act *hekousiôs*. In 40.1–8 he argues that *to autexousion* and *to eph'hêmin* (which are identified) involve deliberation, and at 41.1 he claims that *to autexousion* requires *to logikon*. But he also believes that everything *hekousion* is up to us, 40.3–5. In 41.15 he argues that non-rational animals are not *autexousia*, because they are non-rational and cannot oppose their natural impulses. It is not clear how this is to be reconciled with the initial claim that non-rational animals act *hekousiôs*. Damascene seems to need Aquinas' distinction between two grades of voluntariness. In 36.86–94, Damascene closely connects being rational and being *autexousios*. Here he follows Maximus Confessor, PG 91.17d–20a, except that he introduces *autexousios* where Maximus has *kat'exousian*. On Maximus see Gauthier, 'Maxime' 56–7.

have freewill.[32] Will incorporates the essential conditions of freedom, because it includes free judgment. The relevant freedom in judgment consists in rationality, because we are free of the domination of passions in so far as we can act on our judgment of the merits of an action, in contrast to the strength of our desire to do it.[33] Since human beings have essentially rational desires, they are not simply passive in relation to their desires; rational desire gives us the reflective control that is missing in accounts of choice that omit the will.

Reflective control introduces freedom because it allows the consideration of alternatives that is characteristic of rational agents. Inanimate things are 'inclined' to various results (or, we might say, have tendencies for different things), but nothing within them initiates the motion towards those things. Non-rational animals have something within them that inclines them towards an object, but they do not control this inclination. Rational animals control it, so that they are not necessarily inclined to the object of desire, but are capable of being inclined or not inclined towards the object of desire.

At this point Aquinas recognizes the connexion between freewill and judgment (iudicium); in fact he explains 'freewill' or 'free arbitration' (liberum arbitrium) as consisting in 'free judgment' (liberum iudicium) (1a q59 a3). Both rational and non-rational agents act on the basis of judgment, but animals do not act on the basis of free judgment.[34] In a human being the relevant judgment results 'from some comparison of reason', and so is free. Rational comparison gives us freedom because it allows us to decide between different options; 'a human being has freewill from the very fact that a human being is rational' (1a q83 a1). Since human beings can deliberate about their actions, they are in control of their actions. Since deliberating reason is capable of going in both directions, the will is capable of going in both directions (1-2 q6 a2 ad2).

This capacity of a rational agent is connected with rational apprehension of the end and the means.[35] Because reason can form different conceptions of the good through its apprehension of end and means, the will can be moved freely towards different things. Hence the 'root' of freedom is the will, in so far as the will is the subject of the relevant type of freedom. But since the will is the subject of freedom in so far as it is rational, reason is the cause of freedom.[36] Philosophers concerned about freewill have been concerned, in Aquinas' view, with just those features of rational agency that he captures in his account of the will.

---

[32] *Ver.* q24 a6 sc1, refers to Damasc. *EF* 58.61: *autoexousiotês de ouden heteron estin ei mê hê thelêsis.* Cf. 41.11–22 on *autoexousiotês* and reason. Damascene agrees with Nemesius, *NH* 40 §317, who says that the things that are *kuriôs eph'hêmin* are 'all the things belonging to the soul and the things we deliberate about' (where the second conjunct seems to specify the range of things up to us, judging by the examples that Nemesius gives in §318).

[33] '[Will is] a desire following the apprehension by the one who desires in accordance with free judgment. And of this sort is rational or intellectual desire, which is called the will' (1-2 q26 a1). '[Sensory desire] follows apprehension by the one who desires, but from necessity, not from free judgment. And of this sort is sensory desire in beasts; in human beings, however, it has some share in freedom, to the extent that it obeys reason' (1-2 q26 a1).

[34] Quaedam vero agunt quodam arbitrio, sed non libero, sicut animalia irrationalia; . . . sed hoc iudicium non est sibi liberum (1a q59 a3). On arbitrium and iudicium in Aquinas' predecessors see Lottin, *PM* i 116–23.

[35] 'But the fact that something determines for itself its inclination towards an end cannot come about unless it knows the end and the relation of the end to things that are towards the end; and this is confined to reason. And so this sort of desire that is not determined by necessity from something else follows the apprehension of reason; hence rational desire, which is called will, is a different capacity from sensory desire' (*Ver.* q22 a4).

[36] 'The root of freedom is the will, as subject; but the root as cause is reason. For the reason why the will can freely be moved towards different things is that reason can have different conceptions of good. And that is why philosophers define freewill as free judgment from reason, taking reason to be the cause of freedom' (1-2 q17 a1 ad2).

Previous writers on freewill agree that it is connected with free choice. Aquinas claims to have found a place for free choice within his account of the will, through his description of election as the outcome of will and deliberation. Therefore he identifies the exercise of freewill with election, which he takes to be an exercise of will. Electing is different from merely willing, but it does not require any further capacity beyond willing and deliberating (*2Sent* d24 q1 a3 sol. = P 595b). Willing and electing are different states of the same capacity (d24 q1 a3 ad4 = P 596a).

Our having freewill, therefore, does not follow immediately from the fact that reason moves us in so far as it grasps an ultimate end;[37] for our pursuit of the ultimate end is not open to freewill, since we have no alternative to it. The intellectual activity that implies freewill is deliberation about different options, resulting in the election of one of the options.[38] Freewill is 'that by which <rational creatures> deliberate and elect' (consiliantur et eligunt, 1a q22 a2 ad4); it is the will in so far as it is exercised in election.[39] Different conceptions of the good express human freedom to the extent that they rest on deliberation and election. Hence free will belongs to will because of a specific feature of will—its capacity to choose on the basis of deliberation and election.[40]

266. Freewill as Absence of Necessitation

This claim about election shows how Aquinas acknowledges the generally-recognized connexion between freewill and choice between alternatives. But has he shown that this choice is free choice? When we speak of freewill, we normally contrast freedom with necessity, and so we assume that an exercise of freewill cannot have been necessitated. Aquinas seeks to incorporate this aspect of freedom in his position. Though we necessarily will the indeterminate ultimate end, it is still left to us to deliberate about what we think it consists in, and therefore we are not necessitated to choose the particular action that we eventually elect.

This absence of necessitation does not consist simply in the absence of external compulsion. Non-rational animals are not externally compelled, but still lack freewill. Rational agents consider and compare different options; hence we control which one we choose.[41] A non-rational agent may be determined by some state of itself to do x rather than not-x as a means to y, but it does not control whether to do x or not-x. It is in our control only in so far as we have some capacity for comparing x with not-x; this capacity belongs to a deliberating agent.[42]

---

[37] On the ultimate end see 1-2 q3 a4 ad3; 2–2 q4 a7.

[38] See 1-2 q6 a2 ad2, quoted above §260. On election, free choice, means, and ends see also 1a q60 a2; q62 a8 ad2; 1-2 q109 a2 ad1.

[39] Unde etiam eiusdem potentiae est velle et eligere. Et propter hoc voluntas et liberum arbitrium non sunt duae potentiae, sed una (1a q83 a4). See also 1a q83 a3 sed c: Liberum autem arbitrium est secundum quod eligimus.

[40] *Ver.* q24 a6: Unde liberum arbitrium est ipsa voluntas. Nominat autem eam non absolute, sed in ordine ad aliquem actum eius, qui est eligere. Cf. *ST* 1a q59 a3; 2–2 q24 a1 ad 3; *SG* iii 155 §3282.

[41] Cf. 1a q83 a4 obj1 on Damascene: voluntas quae est circa aliquid quasi unius per comparationem ad alterum. See also q83 a1: a sheep judges by natural judgment, but not free judgment, quia non ex collatione, sed ex naturali instinctu hoc iudicat.

[42] Cf. *in Met.* ix 4 §820. See Scotus §369 on his use of this capacity for opposites.

Hence Aquinas often distinguishes the respect in which the will is moved necessarily from the respect in which it is not. It is moved naturally and necessarily towards the ultimate end, but is not moved necessarily towards the particular goods it pursues (1a q82 a1–2; 1-2 q10 a1–2; *Ver.* q22 a5–6). We necessarily pursue whatever appears good from every point of view, so that there is no aspect of it that we could focus on to conclude that it is not worth pursuing. Only the ultimate end, correctly understood, is of this sort; and this is part of what Aquinas means in calling it the 'universal' and 'perfect' good. Other things can be regarded as not being good from some point of view, and so we do not pursue them necessarily (*Mal.* q6 = M 559b).[43]

These remarks might suggest that the uncertainty of the goodness of non-final goods gives us freewill in relation to them. If there were no room for reasonable doubt about their goodness, would we lose our freedom in the choice of them? Aquinas confronts a related question about uncertainty in his discussion of deliberation and election. He argues that uncertainty, inquiry, and deliberation are not necessary for election.[44] Since he allows election without uncertainty, and since he takes election to imply freewill, he also allows freewill without uncertainty.

He therefore claims that God and the angels have freedom, even though they do not need to inquire and they do not face uncertainty. God does not will necessarily everything that he wills. God wills his goodness necessarily, and he wills some other things because of his goodness, but these things are not necessary for his goodness, and he does not will them necessarily.[45] This is why God has freewill.[46] Angels do not choose what they do through deliberation, since their mode of knowledge does not need inquiry; and so their freedom does not rest on deliberation (1a q59 a3 ad1). In these cases where there is no uncertainty and no inquiry, Aquinas argues that nonetheless 'wherever there is intellect, there is freewill'.[47] Freedom rests on the fact that our choice of one good over another is determined by our judgment about its greater goodness; in human agents this judgment about goodness results from deliberation.

267. Freewill as Rational Agency

Aquinas claims to have shown that our choice is not necessitated, given his account of choice. He intends his analysis of rational agency to explain his account of freedom. His view is not that we have freewill despite our lacking freedom in relation to the ultimate end. On the contrary, we have freewill precisely because we are not free not to pursue an ultimate

---

[43] Cf. §276.   [44] See §251.

[45] 'God wills things other than from himself in so far as they are directed towards his own goodness as their end. Now we do not necessarily will things that are towards an end in willing an end, unless they are such that without them the end cannot be . . . Hence, since the goodness of God is perfect, and can be without other things, . . . his willing things other than himself is not absolutely necessary' (1a q19 a3). Ockham is not satisfied by Aquinas' explanation of how God acts freely in so far as he acts through intellect; see §396.

[46] 'We have freewill in respect of those things that we do not will necessarily, or by natural instinct. For our willing to be happy does not belong to freewill, but to natural instinct. Hence other animals also that are moved towards something by natural instinct are not said to be moved by freewill. Since, therefore, God of necessity wills his own goodness, but other things not of necessity, . . . he has freewill in respect of those things that he does not will of necessity' (1a q19 a10).

[47] '. . . only the agent that has intellect is capable of acting by free judgment, in so far as it recognizes the universal character of the good, from which it is capable of judging that this or that is good' (1a q59 a3).

end. The free judgment of rational agents belongs to deliberation about what promotes the overall good; without that there would be no genuine election.

Free choice requires election because non-rational desire is 'determined to one object', whereas rational desire is not. Hence creatures with only non-rational desire lack election (1-2 q13 a2) and freewill (*Ver.* q24 a2). They are free in relation to external circumstances, but not in relation to their desires, since the relative strength of their desires determines their action. Rational agents are free in relation to their desires, since they can alter the relative strength of their desires.[48]

If we did not pursue a final good, we would have no basis for evaluating one object of desire in comparison to another; when we compare one object of desire in the light of what matters most to us, we rely on our conception of our final good, as Aquinas understands it. If we did not choose between different desires on this basis, nothing more than strength of desires would be involved, and so we would not be free in relation to our desires.

It is essential, therefore, to the rationality and freedom of rational agents that the will necessarily pursues an ultimate end and freely chooses the means to it.[49] In so far as the will necessarily pursues an ultimate end, it is not free; its freedom consists in our capacity for deliberation and election directed to means towards this ultimate end. We act rationally in so far as we regulate our actions and choices by some deliberate and reflective view of their connexion with the ultimate end; this feature of rational action distinguishes it from the action of non-rational animals, who lack the conception of an ultimate end and so cannot regulate their actions by it. Since we choose in the light of reflexion and deliberation, our will is free and we are in control (*domini*) of our own actions; for our practical reason, rather than the influence of external stimuli or some natural disposition, determines what we choose.

268. Freedom and External Reasons

Aquinas' argument about freedom and non-necessitation concludes that freewill consists in practical reason. Will differs from mere inclination, or appetite, or impulse, or caprice, because we do not just find ourselves desiring things and acting on our desires; we also consider whether we have some good reason for acting on this desire rather than that one, and we stop to think about the merits of the case before going in one or another direction. Our will differs from the impulses of non-rational animals, because they cannot do anything about their desires, whereas it is up to us to choose whether or not to act on this or that desire.

These aspects of the will identify the feature of us that supports claims about freedom. We are free to do something about our actions and desires because we can examine possible courses of action on their merits, and guide our action by the results of this examination. We are free because we are determined by the comparative merits of different courses of action, and are not dominated by one or another impulse.

---

[48] The human intellect directs itself to some things, and in doing so, presents ends to itself; still, pursuit of the ultimate end is presented to us by nature, so that we cannot not will the ultimate end. The ultimate end corresponds to the first principles that our intellect cannot reject. We have a lower grade of life than God has, in so far as we receive our ultimate end from something external to us (1a q18 a3).

[49] 1a q60 a2; 1a q82 a1–2; 1-2 q10 a1–2.

This intellectualist view of freedom and the will goes naturally with a belief in external reasons. While the two beliefs are logically independent, acceptance of one makes it easier to accept the other. If rational and free agents are determined by consideration of the merits of the case, and not simply by their desires, there must be some merits for them to consider. If there were nothing for us to be right about, what we had the best reason to do would just depend on what we happened to want. Our acting on reasons would ultimately rest on the sort of motivation (determination by desires that are independent of the merits of the case) that we want to contrast with acting on reason (acting on the merits of the case). The scope for action that responds to the merits of the case would be strictly limited, so that our freedom would also be strictly limited.

If, then, an intellectualist view of freedom is correct, but there are no external reasons, we are free only in the choice of means to ends. In the light of our degree of preference for certain ends, we can be objectively right or wrong about the courses of action that will achieve them most effectively; but we cannot be right or wrong about the merits of the ends we pursue, and so our freedom cannot extend to the choice of them. If, however, we are free in the choice of ends, we must recognize external reasons; we must be able to appeal to some reason, apart from the strength of our desire, for pursuing one end over another. A free agent acts on consideration of the merits of pursuing different ends.

Aquinas believes we are free in the choice of ends, and so he believes that our choice rests on external reasons. Though we are not free to refrain from pursuing some conception or another of an ultimate end, we are free to criticize and revise the preferences that form our determinate conception of an ultimate end. We are free in relation to ends because we can choose them in accordance with standards of goodness that are external to our desiring and valuing.

Aquinas needs to show, then, that we have the relevant capacity for rational choice about conceptions of the final good. If he is to show that freedom, as he understands it, extends to ultimate ends, he has to defend a belief in external reasons. We still need to see what he has to say on this point. We may appropriately return to this question when we discuss his views on the nature of the ultimate end and its role in the practical reasoning that leads to the formation of the moral virtues.[50]

269. The Place of Will and Intellect in Freedom

Aquinas' account of the source of freewill supports an intellectualist account of freedom.[51] He believes that the capacity of reason to move the will explains how the will is free.[52] Freedom is the capacity to be moved by the merits of a course of action, not simply by one's desires. If our assessment of the comparative merits of two courses of action did not move us, but some further preference or desire were needed, we would not be free. For unless that further desire were open to determination by comparative merits, we would act simply on inclination and not on rational assessment, and so we would not be free after all. Hence

[50] See §320.
[51] 'S. Thomas, ut omnes norunt, defendit quemdam Intellectualismum moderatum', Marietti ed. ad 1-2 q15 (p. 592).
[52] The 'root' of freedom is the will, but reason is the cause of this freedom, q17 a1 ad3.

determination of the will by the intellect is not only compatible with freedom, but necessary for it.

This conclusion may appear to be a threat to freewill. We may suppose that if the will is determined by intellect, we must lack freewill; for though the choice of our will is not necessitated by any cause external to ourselves, it is none the less necessitated by a cause external to the will. If the intellect is a necessitating cause external to the will, do we not lack the sort of freedom that is an appropriate basis for praise and blame? The intellectualist doctrine seems to support Socrates and the Stoics, because it reduces virtue to knowledge and vice to ignorance. If this reductive view were correct, then, apparently, vicious people would appropriately be pitied for their ignorance, not blamed for their errors. Aquinas rejects Socratic intellectualism, and hence rejects the reduction of vice to ignorance. His voluntarist opponents, however, argue that he has not really escaped from the basic Socratic error.[53]

Sometimes Aquinas denies that he holds the intellectualist position that his opponents attribute to him; he implies that their objections would in some way be reasonable if they really applied to his position. Sometimes, however, he argues that these objections apply to his position, but are not reasonable, since they misconceive the sort of freedom that is needed for freewill.

He answers critics by arguing that his version of intellectualism distinguishes blameworthy error from non-blameworthy ignorance. It is open to us to distort our conception of what is best all things considered; sometimes we focus on a few aspects of a situation, under the influence of a passion, and sometimes we refrain from thinking seriously about what is best overall.[54] But it is not open to us to act against our conception of what is best once we have it steadily in mind. We are free not because we can act against our conception of the good, but because we are capable of rational choice based on deliberation about the good.

Aquinas therefore rejects the voluntarist defence that makes the will free to choose contrary to the conclusions reached by intellect. In his view, our ascribing rationality to the will (in the sense just explained) maintains the freedom that is necessary for freewill. To see whether he is right, we should compare his view with voluntarist objections. Comparison will be easier after we have considered Scotus' and Ockham's objections to Aquinas' view of freewill.

270. Freedom, Necessity, and Determination

Aquinas believes that by connecting freedom with the rational comparison of alternatives he has resolved disputes about freewill. If the rational comparison of alternatives is the source of freewill, we have an intelligible basis for praise and blame. Praise and blame are reasonable in so far as they respond to our basis for choosing the action we actually did over others that we considered or could reasonably be expected to have considered. Aquinas argues that agents who meet his conditions for having wills are appropriately praised and blamed, since they have the appropriate basis for the consideration of alternatives; and so he concludes that they have freewill.

---

[53] On the use of 'voluntarism' by historians see Bonansea, 'Voluntarism' 83n. See §365.   [54] See n19 above.

This reference to consideration of alternatives applies also to those agents who elect without needing to consider alternatives. As we have seen, Aquinas does not take actual uncertainty or doubt to be necessary for election or for freewill.[55] God and the angels do not consider alternatives when they act freely. Still, their choice is not limited by inability to consider any alternatives that ought to be considered. They choose the action they choose as a result of thought that appropriately weighs any different options that they need to weigh; the fact that no weighing is necessary does not make it any less true that their thought is capable of weighing. Since no inability to weigh causes them to act as they do without deliberation, they act freely.[56] This is Aquinas' answer to voluntarist critics who claim that we cannot have freewill unless the will is free to reject the conclusions of the intellect.

This dispute between Aquinas and the opponents of his intellectualism may suggest a more basic objection.[57] His treatment of freewill may appear to be superficial because he does not ask whether or not our actions are causally determined. Incompatibilists suppose that if causation is necessitation, and unbroken chains of causally sufficient conditions underlie all our choices and actions, we lack freewill. But Aquinas' conditions for freewill could be satisfied even if all our choices and actions were causally necessitated. Does he therefore overlook the most serious objection to the reality of freewill?

Aquinas agrees with some of the intuitions underlying incompatibilism. He believes that some sort of necessity is a threat to freewill. When he affirms that human beings have freewill, he implies that we are not determined to a choice of one of the alternatives in front of us; he implies that if we were determined in the relevant way we would not have freewill (1-2 q83 a1). Similarly, his discussion of the will in 1–2 includes an argument to show that external movers do not move the will by necessity (q10 a4).[58] He believes that his account of the will secures the kind of freedom that belongs to freewill; the will is not determined to one choice, except in the case of the ultimate end. Its choice of non-ultimate goods is 'not determined', in the respect that it is not determined independently of our reasoning; it rests on the consideration of alternatives.

Aquinas does not suggest that choice is undetermined in the relevant respect only if it is not deterministically caused.[59] He does not argue that if our choice between alternatives were deterministically caused, we would not have freewill. His treatment of the issues about determination and necessitation suggests that he does not take causal determinism by itself to exclude freewill.[60]

Similarly, he does not believe that external causation excludes freewill; for the control implied by freewill does not require the agent to be the ultimate first cause (1a q83 a1 ad3; 1-2 q9 a6). The fact that God is the ultimate first cause does not exclude human freewill. God is the first cause of voluntary actions, but they would not be voluntary if the will were merely an instrument of God's causality (cf. 1a q19 a8). When the Holy Spirit moves the

---

[55] See §266 above.

[56] Similarly, the blessed have become incapable of sinning, but have not lost any freedom or goodness in their action; *SG* iii 138 §3120; iv 92.

[57] On the relation between voluntarism and incompatibilism see §371.

[58] Further treatments of necessity: *Ver.* q24 a1–2; *Mal.* q6 = M 559b; *SG* iii 85. See also §344.

[59] He believes that the will of rational agents is immaterial, and so cannot be determined by external physical causes (1-2 q9 a5); but his immaterialism is not necessary for his defence of freewill.

[60] For further discussion of rationalism and compatibilism see §367.

will to voluntary action, it moves us in such a way that the will freely chooses its actions; otherwise the Holy Spirit would be moving us as merely passive subjects (2-2 q23 a2). If external causes do not remove the operation of the appropriate causal sequence that includes rational comparison leading to election, they do not remove freewill.[61]

Though the discussion of God's causal influence on our actions does not affirm determinism, it does not rest on incompatibilist assumptions either. Aquinas' claim that our wills are the causes of our actions, and that we are responsible for our actions in so far as our wills produce them, requires us to distinguish causes from other causal influences and from standing or normal conditions. It does not require us to recognize an indeterminist sequence.

Aquinas' position is not explicitly compatibilist, since it does not directly address the issue about determinism and freedom. The questions about what he calls 'determination to one thing' are not about causal determinism, as it is understood in debates between Stoics and Epicureans and in later debates about determinism and necessitation. But though he does not explicitly formulate the issue, his position is implicitly compatibilist, because he presents sufficient conditions for freedom that do not require the falsity of causal determinism.[62]

Aquinas is an implicit compatibilist rather than a soft determinist. He does not affirm causal determinism, and the aspects of his position that commit him to implicit compatibilism do not commit him to implicit determinism. Reasons that he might offer for rejecting determinism do not affect his compatibilism about freedom, if they do not affect his account of the sufficient conditions for freedom.

In the passages we have discussed, Aquinas does not directly answer questions about determinism. But his treatment of the first cause and secondary causes shows that his defence of freewill does not rely on the rejection of determinism. His defence supports his attempted reconciliation of human freewill with the Christian doctrines of original sin and divine grace. Further discussion will be appropriate when we come to his views on these questions.[63]

Our discussion of Aquinas on freewill has included considerable repetition of questions discussed earlier, in our account of his views on the will, happiness, the passions, deliberation, and election. This repetition has tried to make clear the main point of his account of freewill. In his view, we can understand the nature of freewill, and why we have it, once we have a correct account of the will and rational agency; we simply need to see how those features bear on the questions about freewill. Freewill raises no further questions besides those that we have already answered in understanding rational agency. On this point Aquinas develops and applies the reductive strategy that we have attributed to him.[64]

---

[61] On external determination cf. §371n84.

[62] Some believe his account of free judgment involves indeterminism. See Kretzmann, 'Goodness'; MacDonald, 'Libertarian'; Stump, *Aq.*, ch. 9. Contrast Pasnau, *TAHN* 214–33. Cf. §371.

[63] See §§347–9. [64] See §265 above on Aquinas' reductive strategy.

19

AQUINAS: THE ULTIMATE END

271. Why Must the Will Pursue the Ultimate Good?

The claim that a rational will must pursue an ultimate good supports Aquinas' whole argument about action and ethics. Will differs from passion because it is guided by rational comparison of goods, which compares them with reference to an ultimate end. This rational comparison is also the basis of freedom, since it gives us control over our desires and actions. But we might doubt whether the appropriate rational comparison of goods requires reference to an ultimate end. If we compare the merits of different options by considering the features that make each option worth choosing, do we introduce a final good?

To desire something as good, as opposed to simply finding it attractive, is to desire it for reasons that respond to our beliefs about other goods. In bringing these beliefs to bear on our present situation, we compare possible objects of choice by reference to our general views about goods. These general views express a conception of the relative importance of different goods. In the light of this conception we make the relatively systematic comparative estimates and practical judgments about the overall good that are characteristic of rational agents.

Rational agents normally follow some fairly stable pattern in making comparative judgments. Normally they do not prefer A+B to C+D and then immediately prefer C+D over A+B, if nothing is relevantly different on the two occasions. But do they pursue just one ultimate end? Apparently we can evaluate some of our actions by seeing how they affect our end A, and other actions by seeing how they affect our end B, without any comparison of A with B. Perhaps we have no view about the relative importance of A and B, and hence no view about what to do if we think one action will promote A, but impede B, and the alternative will impede A, but promote B.[1] In such a case both A and B are ultimate ends, but neither A nor B is the ultimate end. If our choices and values display this pattern, should we not reject Aquinas' claim that we pursue just one ultimate end?

---

[1] This situation would be like a chart showing the chain of command for an army in which different instructions tell us to do whatever two different commanders say, but their instructions may conflict. Perhaps, for instance, the chart says 'When you have to decide whether to use nuclear weapons, follow the orders of A', but it also says 'When you are considering an attack that will cause many civilian casualties, follow the orders of B'. Since some situations will meet both descriptions, we may get conflicting instructions, with no way to resolve them.

He might fairly reply that we find it rationally unsatisfactory to pursue two ultimate ends that offer us no answers to important practical questions. If we must choose between pursuing A and pursuing B, but we have no idea of the comparative value of A and B, we are dissatisfied with our conception of comparative values. Our dissatisfaction supports Aquinas' claim about the one ultimate end; for we would not be dissatisfied if we did not want some rational estimate of the comparative value of our ends. Our dissatisfaction presupposes that all our ends ought to be co-ordinated, and that none ought to be insulated from comparison with others; hence we already value the co-ordination of all our ends, and we pursue a single co-ordinated system. This is the system that Aquinas describes as a single ultimate end.

Aquinas' claim that the will necessarily takes the ultimate end as its object is not simply a statement of psychological necessity; it is not comparable, for instance, to the claim that we tend to prefer the interests of people we know well, or tend to prefer what will happen in a month over what will happen in ten years. Nor, on the other hand, is it logically necessary that every conceivable agent with desires, or even every conceivable agent capable of deliberation about the satisfaction of its desires, pursues an ultimate end. Aquinas' description of an ultimate end offers a partial definition of a will. If we could show that an agent's desires were not arranged and modified in the light of some conception of an ultimate end, we would thereby have shown that the agent is not rational and has no will. Aquinas' claim that human beings have wills, therefore, does not follow from the mere fact that we have desires, or even from the fact that we are capable of influencing them in some ways by deliberation. In claiming that we have wills, he claims that our desire and deliberation have the structure that relies on a comprehensive ultimate end.

272. The Final Good and the Natural Law

Aquinas follows Aristotle by introducing the ultimate end at the beginning of his discussion of ethics in the Prima Secundae (*ST* 1-2 qq1–5). He makes its significance clearer by returning to it in his treatise on law (beginning at q90). In his treatment of natural law he claims that the first precept is the principle that good is to be done and pursued and evil avoided (q94 a2). This is the practical parallel to the Principle of Non-Contradiction, which is the ultimate principle underlying all theoretical reasoning.[2] Both ultimate principles are present by nature in rational agents. Just as the intellect cannot fail to accept PNC, we cannot fail to will the ultimate end.[3] The principle of voluntary movements is the 'good in common' and the ultimate end, which corresponds to the first principles of demonstration in theoretical cases.[4] All rational action, therefore, depends on the desire for the ultimate end, which is

[2] 'Just as being is the first thing that falls under apprehension without qualification, so good is the first thing that falls under the apprehension of practical reason, which is directed towards action; for every agent acts for the sake of an end, which has the character of good' (1-2 q94 a2).

[3] 'But although our intellect activates itself towards some things, nonetheless others are presented to it by nature, as first principles are, about which it cannot be in any other state, and the ultimate end, which it cannot not will' (1a q18 a3).

[4] '...it is necessary that the principle in whatever things are appropriate (conveniunt) to a thing is natural. This appears evidently in the case of intellect: for the principles of intellectual cognition are naturally grasped (nota). And similarly the principle of voluntary movements must be something naturally willed. Now this is the good in common, at which the will aims naturally, as each power aims at its object; and again it is the last end, which has the position among objects of desire that first principles of demonstration have among objects of understanding...' (1-2 q10 a1).

the basic principle that belongs to us through natural law (q91 a2 ad2). Since the natural law is a rational principle, it is guided by the first principle of practical reason, which directs us towards the ultimate end.[5] Necessary acceptance of PNC makes someone a rational subject of belief and knowledge; necessary pursuit of the ultimate good makes someone a rational agent.

The reference to the ultimate end explains why natural law prescribes that good is to be done.[6] Aquinas does not intend a definitional equivalence, saying that 'good' is to be defined as 'what is to be done'.[7] In saying that what is to be done is good, he means that whatever is to be done must be related to the ultimate good. In rational agents, acting for the sake of good involves acting for the sake of an ultimate good that embodies the rational structure in one's aims. Aquinas' account of happiness articulates this structure.

Since the pursuit of this good is the first principle of natural law, subordinate principles should describe a system of ends that embodies the rational structure of the ultimate good.[8] Aquinas does not intend merely the very weak claim that whatever is prescribed by the natural law is good in some respect. He means that natural law prescribes actions that promote the final good of human beings. If the final good is the basis for all the laws of nature, it must extend over all practical concerns that could be questions for practical reason.

273. Subordinate Ends

These claims about the natural law and subordinate ends introduce a further element in Aquinas' view of the status of the ultimate end. We have seen so far why he thinks we pursue only one ultimate end. But we might agree with him on this point without yet agreeing that the ultimate end must be comprehensive, applying to all areas of life and choice. His remarks on the natural law imply that the ultimate end is comprehensive; why does he believe this?

We will deny that the ultimate end is comprehensive if we deny that all our practical principles are subordinate to it. Aquinas' argument, as we have considered it so far, shows us that we recognize an ultimate end to the extent that we think one aim should be adjusted in the light of our other aims. It is reasonable to take this attitude to some aims; but might we not reasonably hold some aims or principles to be exempt from adjustment in the light of our other aims? If there are such aims or principles, apparently they are not covered by Aquinas' argument to show that our aims are subordinate to the ultimate end. Even if whatever we

[5] '. . . law belongs to whatever is a principle of human acts, because it is a rule and measure. Now just as reason is a principle of human acts, so also in reason itself there is something that is a principle in relation to all the other things. Hence it is necessary that law belongs principally and most of all to this principle. Now the first principle in matters of action, which practical reason is about, is the ultimate end. Now the ultimate end of human life is happiness or blessedness, as stated above. Hence it is necessary that the law regards most of all the direction (ordo) that leads towards happiness' (1-2 q90 a2).

[6] 'And thus the first principle in practical reason is the one founded on the character of good, which [sc. character] is that good is what all things desire (appetunt). This, then, is the first precept of the law, that good is to be done and pursued, and evil is to be avoided' (1-2 q94 a2).

[7] Contrast Grisez, 'Principle' 353–8.

[8] 'And on this precept all the other precepts of natural law are founded, so that all those things to be done (or avoided) that practical reason naturally apprehends to be goods for human beings belong to the precepts of natural law' (1-2 q94 a2).

will for the sake of an ultimate end is willed for the sake of one and the same ultimate end, we might still insist that many of our aims stand outside this framework of aims directed towards an ultimate end, so that they do not fit into a teleological structure at all.

Aquinas considers this objection when he argues that we aim at a single ultimate end in everything that we will (q1 a6). He allows that amusements, for instance, do not appear to be directed towards any further end; we choose them simply for their own sake, and we recognize that we gain nothing from them beyond the amusing activity itself (q1 a6 obj1). But these are not the only activities that seem to be outside a teleological structure. Other things that we value for their own sakes, apart from any further benefit that we gain from them, seem to raise the same difficulty. One might take this view of moral principles.[9]

To answer this objection, Aquinas clarifies his claim that we will ends for the sake of an ultimate end. We might falsely suppose that if there is an ultimate end, and we pursue all other things for its sake, then we do not pursue these other things for their own sakes.[10] Aquinas, however, recognizes deliberation resulting in election of constituent ends. If we aim at wealth, we may also aim at the acquisition of wine and clothes, because 'they are contained under wealth, as under some one common thing' (q12 a3 ad2). 'Contained' indicates the relation of constituent to constituted. It is reasonable to elect one such end over another in so far as it is a more significant element in the ultimate end that contains it.[11] Goods pursued for their own sakes may be pursued for the sake of some more ultimate good that includes them.[12]

People who allegedly pursue several ultimate ends, therefore, really pursue one ultimate end.[13] In choosing something for the sake of an end, we need not be ordering it towards some external end (q1 a6 ad1); we may include it in a complete good (q1 a6 ad2).[14] In saying that these constituent goods are 'directed towards' (ordinare ad) the end, Aquinas implies that the relation of means to end need not be a purely causal relation in which the end is external to the means, but may also be the relation between a whole and a part or between an indeterminate end and a determinate end that specifies it.[15]

This explanation makes it plausible to claim that we pursue non-instrumental goods for the sake of an ultimate good. The claim would not be plausible if the final good were wholly external to these non-instrumental goods. Since, however, direction towards an ultimate end includes the relation of parts to a whole as well as the relation of instrumental means to an external end, subordination to an ultimate end does not make the subordinate good purely instrumental. If amusements, for instance, are directed towards the ultimate end,

---

[9] For Scotus' view see §363.

[10] Aristotle answers this objection by arguing that we pursue some goods both for their own sakes and for the sake of happiness. See §72.

[11] '. . . wherever there are found a number of ends, there can be election between these, in so far as they are directed to a more ultimate end' (q13 a3 ad2).

[12] See also §320.

[13] '. . . all those many things were being taken to have the character of one perfect good composed of them (ex his constituti), by those who were placing (ponebant) the ultimate end in them' (q1 a5 ad1).

[14] The 'et similiter' beginning ad2 suggests that 'comprehenditur' is meant to indicate the same relation that was suggested (in ad1) in saying that the ultimate end is not an external end.

[15] See also *Mal.* q6 = M 559a: under the highest good 'comprehenduntur omnes fines'. Cf. *Ver.* q22 a7: We do not gain merit from aiming at happiness in general—for that is a necessary desire for 'se esse completum in bonitate'. But we gain merit from aiming at a conception of happiness: 'Sed in quo ista completio consistit . . . non est ei determinatum a natura'.

they need not be directed to some end that is wholly external to them; they are directed to the good of the agent himself, just in so far as they are amusements or recreations (1-2 q1 a6 ad1; 2-2 q168 a2 ad3). These subordinate goods are included (comprehenditur, a6 ad2) within the ultimate good, and the ultimate good is composed (constitutum, a5 ad1) of them. The subordination of goods pursued for their own sakes to the ultimate good is not subordination to an external end, but the subordination of part to whole.[16] Aquinas' eudaemonism, therefore, does not make subordinate goods purely instrumental to the final good.

This conclusion shows only that a reference to the final good is harmless, not that it is reasonable. To show why it is also reasonable, Aquinas appeals to the general principle that whatever we desire we desire as being good (sub ratione boni). He argues that we must regard any good as either the perfect good or as tending towards the perfect good; 'for a beginning of everything is invariably directed towards its completion (consummatio)' (a6).

This claim is trivial if it means simply that in willing to do x, we will to complete our doing of x, to carry out x completely. But it is not trivial, if it implies direction towards a complete end. To defend the non-trivial claim, Aquinas assumes that our direction of an action towards a specific end is conditional. If, for instance, we recognize that an amusement interferes with something more important, we see a reason for restricting the amusement. We must have already recognized that the value of the amusement is connected with the value of other things that we pursue for their own sake. We try to adjust the pursuit of these different ends to each other because we take them all to contribute to some ultimate and comprehensive good.

Rational agents accept an ordered plurality of ends, and want the satisfaction of their desires to correspond to the comparative value they attach to each end. If, then, they pursue x for its own sake, they do not pursue x unconditionally, irrespective of its relation to anything else; they want their pursuit of x to be suitably adjusted to the pursuit of other things they value for their own sake. To adjust one end to others is to recognize the structure of an ultimate end embracing them all; hence the rational pursuit of any one particular end for its own sake requires its subordination to an ultimate end.[17]

It is easiest to agree with Aquinas in cases where the non-ultimate good has finite value, so that on some occasions we are better off not pursuing it; reference to the ultimate end prevents excessive pursuit of any one subordinate good. But he does not confine himself to these cases. Even if we cannot pursue a specific good to excess (if, e.g., moral virtue or contemplation or the knowledge of God is of this sort), the ultimate end is relevant. For rational agents think of each good they pursue in the light of other goods with different roles in their overall conception of what is worth choosing and pursuing. This overall conception may show that some component has unrestricted or infinite value in relation to the others. In that case the point of referring to the ultimate end is not to restrict one's pursuit of a particular good, but to explain and justify one's pursuit of it, by showing how it fits one's total conception.[18]

---

[16] This point is also relevant to prudence and deliberation; see §320.

[17] Aquinas discusses the all-embracing character of happiness further in *4Sent* d49 q1 a3 sol. 4 = P vii 1193ab, and briefly in *SG* i 101 §839 (unusquisque in beatitudinem suam ordinat quicquid vult). On Scotus and Cajetan see §361.

[18] Kant opposes this teleological assumption; see, e.g., *KpV* 74.

We can now see the possible place of the moral virtues in a person's good, and the relation of Aquinas' view of the ultimate end to his general schema. His claim about the relation of morality to the ultimate end does not reduce morality to a merely instrumental or external role. We can choose virtue for its own sake as the object of our more immediate aim, even though we aim at the ultimate good (2-2 q123 a7; in EN §§549–50).

The example of amusements suggests another objection to the eudaemonist position. We might say that actions done for the sake of amusement are not done for any ulterior end. Though we might choose them as parts of happiness if we stopped to think about them, we do not actually stop to think about their relation to other actions and aims, but we simply do them on the spur of the moment, without rational deliberation. To answer this objection, we must appeal to Aquinas' description of the influence of the will; he attributes a permissive role to the will, so that the will often remains in the background, until an occasion for deliberation arises.[19] If our conception of the final good has this permissive role, and if it influences our views about amusements when we deliberate about them, the claim that the final good is pervasive avoids an unrealistic conception of impulsive actions.

274. Aiming at Perfection

So far we have spoken without distinction of the ultimate good and of happiness. Does Aquinas intend any distinction? In the EN Aristotle takes it to be clear and generally agreed, but not trivial, that happiness is the final good. Aquinas' position is similar. Though sometimes he speaks indifferently of the ultimate good and of happiness,[20] he normally suggests that we add something in speaking of happiness. When he introduces happiness in Part I, he identifies it with 'the ultimate perfection of a rational or intellectual nature' (1a q62 a1). Since happiness is the perfection of a rational nature, it must itself be a perfect, complete, and comprehensive good, a 'state perfected by the collection of all goods' (q26 a1 ad1).[21] Perfection is the only thing that meets the conditions for being the ultimate end, and all rational agents desire their perfection as the ultimate end.[22]

He maintains that our aiming at perfection is the basis of (1) our willing only one ultimate end, and of (2) our willing everything we will for the sake of the one ultimate end (1-2 q1 a5–6). Both claims depend on Aquinas' views about the completeness of the final good; he sees that this is the crucial feature of the final good described by Aristotle.

He maintains that we have only one ultimate end because everything seeks its perfection, and therefore seeks an end that fulfils its desire.[23] Perfection clarifies completeness and

---

[19] On this permissive role for the ultimate end see §248.

[20] At 1-2 q1 intro, happiness is introduced simply with 'ponitur'. At q1 a7 sc, Aquinas cites Augustine, who says everyone agrees in seeking 'ultimum finem, qui est beatitudo'. At q2 intro, Aquinas takes it for granted that the discussion has been about beatitudo.

[21] Cf. 1-2 q3 a2 ad2; a3 ad2; q4 a7 ad2; Mal. q6 = M 559b.

[22] 'Hence both an angel and a human being naturally desire their good and their perfection. And this is loving oneself' (1a q60 a3).

[23] 'Since everything seeks (appetit) its perfection, what someone seeks as ultimate end is what he seeks as a good that is perfect and that completes himself. . . . It is necessary, therefore, that the ultimate end should so fulfil the whole of a human being's desire (appetitus) that nothing is left to be desired outside it. And this would not be possible if anything external to it were needed for his perfection' (1-2 q1 a5).

finality, and explains why these are rationally desirable features of one's end. The desire[24] for perfection is the desire for one's actualization.[25] This is common to all living creatures, since they are organized for the specific vital activities that constitute their actuality and end, specified by their form.[26] The life that constitutes the healthy state of a creature is the one that actualizes its natural capacities. This connexion between the good, completeness, and perfection commits Aquinas to a naturalist account of the good, resting on an essentialist claim about human beings. He identifies the good not simply with the systematic satisfaction of one's desires, but with the systematic application of rational activity to one's life, because this activity is the essential activity of a human being.[27]

The general claim about seeking perfection is intelligible and reasonable, if it is taken to apply to the natural organization of creatures. But we might be more doubtful, if it is also meant as a claim about the desires of rational creatures. Is it plausible to claim that, whatever we actually desire, the ultimate end for the sake of which we desire it is our self-actualization?

One aspect of perfection is familiar. When Aquinas says that the ultimate end must 'so fulfill the whole of a human being's desire that nothing is left to be desired outside it' (q1 a5), he implies that perfection includes comprehensiveness.[28] Since rational comparison of different specific ends refers to an ultimate end, this ultimate end has to include all the specific ends that can be rationally compared; for if it neglected any of these ends, we could not rationally compare the neglected ends with other ends, and so we could not will them. If, then, comprehensiveness simply includes all our specific ends, it follows from the concept of an ultimate end.

The reference to one's own perfection, however, appears to make the ultimate end self-referential. This is not an obvious feature of mere comprehensiveness. My desire to have some co-ordinated compound of the various ends I pursue does not seem to be a desire for some state of myself, whereas the desire for my own perfection seems to be a desire directed to a state of myself. What entitles Aquinas to this further claim about the ultimate end?

275. Intellectual Love

Why is a comprehensive end not necessarily a suitable ultimate end? We have seen that Aquinas denies that all reasons are 'internal' to preferences by being derived from what I

---

[24] This 'desire' might more accurately be called a 'tendency', appetitus. On the difference between appetitus and desire see §242n28.

[25] 'The character of good consists in this, that something is desirable. Hence the Philosopher says 'Good is what all things desire'. Now it is clear that a thing is desirable only in so far as it is perfect; for all desire their own perfection. But everything is perfect so far as it is actual. Therefore it is clear that a thing is good in so far as it is a being; for being is the actuality of each thing' (1a q5 a1; cf. q6 a1). On the connexions between goodness, perfection, and being see MacDonald, 'Relation'; Kretzmann and Stump, 'Being'.

[26] See 1-2 q55 a1: 'The perfection of each thing is considered especially in the direction (ordo) towards its end. But the end of a capacity is the actuality.' Cf. 1a q4 a1; q5 a5; q19 a3 obj 2; ad2; 1-2 q3 a2; 2-2 q184 a1; SG i 39 §840; ii 41 §1171; iii 64 §2394; 4Sent d7 q1 a1 sol.1 = P vii 583a.

[27] '. . . Some activities are naturally appropriate (convenientes) to a human being, which are correct in themselves, and not merely as being laid down by law' (SG iii 129 §3011). This chapter is quoted more fully in §307n39.

[28] Cf. Aristotle, Met. 1021b12; Aquinas, in Met. §1034. Cajetan ad a5 (L vi 13–14) explains Aquinas' argument in ad1 and ad2.

need to fulfil these preferences.[29] If we act on preference-based reasons, and we prefer an end that systematically arranges and orders all our preferences according to their strength, we have a reason for pursuing a comprehensive end. Perhaps I want a comprehensive plan that directs all my desires and actions towards collecting Rembrandts, which is the only thing I care about for itself. More realistically, we might have a number of ends that we pursue for their own sakes, and we might give reasons, based on the strength of our preferences for each end, for sacrificing one for the sake of another. But we may not be able to give any further reason for caring about these ends, or for caring about them in this order. In that case, we can give a reason for pursuing A rather than B, because A results in C and B results in D, and we prefer C over D; but we can give no further reason for preferring C over D.

If all our reasons are based on preferences, we may have a comprehensive ultimate end, but we cannot have a reason for having this comprehensive end resting on these preferences. For if all our reasons are based on preferences, we have exhausted our reasons in stating the ultimate preferences that determine our comprehensive end. When we confront alternatives to our total preferences, we must agree that we have no reason to prefer our preferences over the alternatives, or vice versa. This attitude to our ultimate preferences and alternatives to them fits our view of some of our ends. In some cases we regard our particular ends as a brute fact, a matter of taste, temperament, environment, and so on, and we recognize that we would not be worse off if we exchanged these ends for others, provided that our taste, temperament, and so on were adjusted to suit. Though I may prefer playing a violin to playing a trumpet, I need not think I would have suffered some major loss if I came to prefer the trumpet.

But this does not seem to be our view of all our ultimate ends. We normally assume that they cannot all be replaced without loss. I might be content to have my preference for one instrument replaced by my preference for another, but I would think myself worse off if my preference for music were replaced by a preference for gambling, even if I could afford to gamble, and even if I did not miss playing music; indeed, I might believe I would be even worse off if I did not regret the change. Similarly, though I might find that my concern for other people—family, colleagues, friends—imposes some irksome demands on me, I believe I would lose something significant if I no longer cared about these other people, and that I would lose even more if I did not regret my failure to care about them. If we treat our ends in this way, so that we believe we can assess them on their merits, not simply by their relation to our other desires and preferences, we assume that not all our reasons are based on preferences. We treat some of them as 'external' to our preferences, because they depend on the merits of different ends, and these merits are not exhausted by the relations of these ends to our desires and preferences.

Aquinas recognizes this feature of ends and reasons, in his treatment of intellectual love. He distinguishes sensory love, belonging to the non-rational parts of the soul, from intellectual love, belonging to the will.[30] Following Plato and Aristotle, he believes that a distinct type of desire belongs to each part of the tripartite soul. Following Augustine—also influenced by Plato—he treats love as the primary source of one's pursuit of different ends,

---

[29] For more explanation of internal and external reasons see §259.   [30] On intellectual love see §§259, 336.

and hence as the primary passion.[31] But he does not infer that a non-rational passion underlies all our pursuit of ends; for intellectual love is not a passion, but belongs to intellectual desire.[32] This sort of love belongs to God and the angels, who have no passions.[33] It rests on a prior grasp by intellect,[34] which grasps its object 'under the common character of good', not simply as an object of some prior inclination.[35]

This intellectual love gives us the freedom that non-rational creatures lack.[36] If we are guided by intellectual love in the pursuit of ends that we take to constitute the ultimate end, we recognize something good about them apart from our having some prior inclination towards them. Prior inclination belongs to the non-rational forms of love, but intellectual love is guided by the features of the object itself, not by their relation to some desire of ours.

The difference between intellectual and sensory love clarifies Aquinas' claim that we have a natural desire for the good. This may sound similar to the claim that we have a natural desire for sensory gratification or for revenge (objects of the non-rational parts). But this is not what he means. The desires of the non-rational parts aim at things that we recognize as actual objects of our desires (or means to achieving these objects). The desire of the rational part is directed to things whose properties merit their being desired, not to things that are already desired.

If we act on intellectual love, we recognize the merits of our end; we 'present' the end to ourselves, and thereby see the end as good (1a q18 a3).[37] Regarding an end as good involves some explicit belief or implicit assumption about its relation to other ends, and about their importance. If I thought that this action would achieve some less important end but impede some more important end, I would change my mind about whether I ought to do it or not; and so the end I present to myself on particular occasions is open to being influenced by my views about the relative importance of my different ends. If I were not open to this influence, there would be something lacking in my rational agency. But my conception of the importance of different ends cannot simply represent their contribution to the fulfilment of my preferences. If my reasons for choosing my ends were simply based on preferences, my ends would not be objects of intellectual love.

The doctrine of intellectual love shows, therefore, that Aquinas recognizes external reasons for preferring one set of ends to another. When we bring them under an ultimate end, we are not just guided by our preferences, and we do not treat the ultimate end as

[31] On Augustine see §218.

[32] See 1-2 q4 a3 obj3, ad3; q26 a1; a2; q28 a6 ad1. Cf. *3Sent* d26 q2 a1 ad1 = P vii 284b.

[33] '... in an intellectual nature we find a natural inclination in accordance with the will; in the sensory nature, in accordance with sensory desire... Therefore, since an angel is an intellectual nature, there must be a natural love in his will' (1a q60 a1). Cf. q20 a1; *Div. Nom.* 4.12 = P xv 320.

[34] '... although in God the will and the intellect are the same, still, since it belongs to the character of love that it proceeds only from a conception in the intellect, the procession of love is different in direction (ordo) from the procession of the Word in God' (1a q27 a3 ad3).

[35] 'But the will regards good under the common character of good, and therefore in the will, which is intellectual desire, no <further> desiring powers are distinguished...' (1a q82 a5).

[36] 'In this way it is clear, therefore, that on this point natural and voluntary desire differ: Natural inclination is a desire from an external principle, and for that reason lacks freedom, because what is free is what is cause of itself; but the inclination of the voluntary is a desire by the will of the agent himself, and that is why the will has freedom.... And hence it is that all the other powers of the soul, apart from will, are forced by their objects; for all the other powers have a natural desire only in respect of their object, whereas the will has, in addition to natural inclination, a further inclination of which the willing agent himself is the cause. And the same is to be said about love...' (*3Sent* d27 q1 a2 = P vii 294b).

[37] Quoted in §267.

simply an ordered collection of objects of our basic preferences. We also treat it as including external reasons in support of our basic preferences.

276. Reasons and Perfection

We introduced Aquinas' views on intellectual love in order to explain why he describes the ultimate end as perfection. But we may wonder whether these views do not cast doubt on his position. When he says we aim at our own perfection, he suggests that we are guided by a concern for states of ourselves rather than for the value of the ends we pursue. Is this a misleading account of ends that are objects of intellectual love? If intellectual love forms my aim of curing cancer, I believe that cancer being cured is good in its own right, apart from my preferring or pursuing it. Hence my primary aim is that cancer be cured. I regard my achievement of this particular aim as a perfection of myself; but it does not follow that my primary concern is with my own perfection. On the contrary, my concern for my perfection seems to be subordinate to my aim of curing cancer.

This description of the aims guided by intellectual love leaves out a self-referential aspect. My concern is guided by convictions about the value of outcomes—e.g., cancer being eliminated; but it may not be solely guided by them. I have external reasons not only for preferring specific results, but also for trying to contribute to them in the right way. In that case, I do not aim simply at the cure for cancer being discovered; I aim to discover the cure for cancer through my scientific investigation, not simply to be somewhere on the causal chain that results in the cure for cancer.

We can see the significance of my causal contribution by contrast with causal chains that include me, but do not make the discovery of the cure for cancer my achievement: (1) I might know (by reading in an infallible Book of Life) that some trivial error of mine (e.g., forgetting to wash my hands before conducting an experiment) will result in discovery of the cure for cancer. In that case I will be pleased that I am going to make this trivial error, but I will not treat the result as an achievement of mine. (2) I might know that if I ruthlessly torture innocent people, the cure for cancer will be discovered. In that case I will not want to undertake this course of action; my aim of my discovering (or taking part with others in discovering) the cure for cancer does not require willingness to pursue the discovery by these immoral means. I need not always be attending to my role in what I bring about; such constant attention might be justly criticized as inappropriate self-absorption, even self-indulgence. But complete indifference to my role would be indifference to myself as an agent.[38]

Since it is reasonable for me to aim at my achieving, or partly achieving, the cure for cancer in the right way, the objects of intellectual love are sometimes self-referential. In the second case just described, my choice of means reveals a reasonable preference for one state of myself over another. If I reasonably prefer one state of myself over another, Aquinas is right to say that I care about my own perfection. We can now see that the introduction

---

[38] One might say that such indifference would involve 'one thought too few', in contrast to Williams' cases of (allegedly) 'one thought too many'. See Williams's, 'Persons' 18, and (at more length) 'Acting'.

of perfection adds two further features to the final good beyond mere comprehensiveness: (i) Intellectual love and external reasons, and (ii) rational concern for one's role in securing rationally preferable results.

Aquinas' claims about perfection do not, therefore, make us unreasonably self-absorbed. Concern for our own perfection does not make us indifferent to the value of external conditions, actions, and states of affairs in their own right. It implies that we are also concerned about our own relation to, and causal influence on, these external states of affairs. The self-referential aspects of Aquinas' claims about perfection make clear our concern with actions as well as results.

When we are guided by external reasons and by intellectual love, our attitude to our ends is partly, though not entirely, self-referential. We sometimes say that we would be impoverished, or diminished, if we lacked certain aims. In saying this we imply that we lose something that is valuable apart from satisfying our desires. If its value depended on our desire, we would not have lost anything if we changed our desires and satisfied our new ones as much as we satisfied our old ones. We recognize value in ourselves as rational agents distinct from particular desires and aims. As Kant puts it, we regard ourselves as objective ends imposing a limit on the pursuit of subjective ends.[39]

Aquinas, is right, then, to speak of perfection. Rational agents prefer the more complete to the less complete satisfaction of their desires, as long as the degree of satisfaction is proportionate to the value they attribute to the fulfilment of each desire. If they thought their plan for fulfilling their desires left out a rationally significant aspect of themselves, they would not accept their plan. This pursuit of perfection goes beyond mere comprehensiveness. The pursuit of mere comprehensiveness involves planning in the light of my aims as they are; even though it involves adjusting one aim to another, it does not require any further criticism. The pursuit of perfection, however, requires the further evaluation of my ultimate aims to see whether they match a correct conception of myself and what is rationally most significant about me. Agents who pursue comprehensiveness because they pursue their perfection must raise questions that agents who pursue mere comprehensiveness do not raise.[40]

277. Is the Pursuit of Perfection Necessary?

According to Aquinas, therefore, the ultimate end is happiness, understood as the perfection of the agent rather than simply the satisfaction of the agent's desires. This understanding of happiness raises a difficulty for his claim that a rational agent with a will necessarily pursues happiness. We have explained this claim by considering Aquinas' arguments to show that a rational agent necessarily pursues an ultimate end. We initially explained his conception of an ultimate end by treating it as a comprehensive end, but we saw that mere comprehensiveness falls short of his claims about perfection. Once we add the claims about perfection to Aquinas' conception of the ultimate end, does it remain plausible to claim that every rational agent necessarily pursues this sort of ultimate end?[41]

---

[39] See Kant, G 430–1.   [40] See §333.
[41] On the importance of perfection see Cajetan's defence of Aquinas against Scotus, §361.

To show that the pursuit of perfection is not an optional extra to be added to rational agency, Aquinas must appeal to the connexion between pursuing perfection and seeing one's end as good. To see the end as good is to see it as an object of intellectual love. To regard one's ends as beyond criticism is to deny that any rational grounds might influence one in favour of them or against them. But to regard one's ends as objects of the will is to regard them as rationally desirable in their own right. If, then, we think of ourselves as agents regarding our ends as objects of the will, we must regard them as rationally desirable, and hence as objects of intellectual love, defensible on some ground apart from the fact that we happen to desire them.[42] Since the pursuit of perfection involves the appraisal of ends to see whether they are defensible on grounds apart from being desired, Aquinas has a reason for taking it to be essential to agents whose choice of ends expresses their will.

A demand for the pursuit of perfection may appear to exaggerate the conditions for being a rational agent. It is easy to agree with the assumption that we are rational agents with wills, if that simply means that we are 'minimal' rational agents: some of our desires express our will, by being based on reason. Aquinas' claim about perfection, however, applies to us only if we are 'maximal' rational agents, expressing our will in our desires for ends. Even if we agree that we are minimal rational agents, it is less clear that we are maximal rational agents. In fact—we might object—we are not maximal rational agents, if maximal rational agency requires us to apply some standard of perfection to criticize and evaluate our ends.

Aquinas might reply that we regard ourselves as maximal rational agents not because we apply a standard of perfection, but because we recognize it as applicable. When we look for reasons for our desires, we acknowledge the relevance of external reasons and intellectual love. We do not suppose that our own or other people's ends are beyond criticism and evaluation; indeed we care about them because we suppose there is something more to be said for them than that we merely desire them. In applying critical standards to ourselves and to others, and in accepting or rejecting the criticisms of others, we acknowledge standards of perfection. The demand for perfection, therefore, is derived from the basic fact that the will aims at the good as such. If this feature of the will implies that we desire goods that are good independently of our desiring them, so that our desiring them does not constitute their goodness, our conception of the ultimate end appeals to a standard of perfection beyond mere comprehensiveness.

278. The Place of Happiness in Aquinas' Argument

Aquinas tries to show that his account of the will illuminates our views on happiness. We might have supposed that it is an open question whether rational agents pursue happiness, or some other end, so that questions about happiness are left open by answers to questions about rational agency. Aquinas argues that, despite appearances, his answer to questions about rational agency settles questions about happiness too.

To show this, he appeals to the finality and comprehensiveness of happiness, as it is normally understood. We normally take it to be an end not pursued for the sake of any

---

[42] Some of Aquinas' claims about intellectual love are captured in Taylor's conception of 'strong evaluation', in 'Agency'.

further end, and to include all non-instrumental goods that are worth pursuing. But these features must be features of the ultimate good that is the primary object of rational will; for if the will did not aim at such an end, we could not deliberate appropriately about action. A rational agent must choose an action in the light of some view about how the good to be achieved by the action interacts with the other goods that are worth pursuing. If our view were less comprehensive than this, we would be leaving out some consideration that might matter in deciding what to do, and so we would not be exercising practical reason appropriately.

This argument explains how the pursuit of happiness follows from rational willing, as Aquinas understands it, provided we confine ourselves to the comprehensive character of happiness. It is not so obvious why happiness, understood as perfection, is the uniquely suitable object of a will. To connect perfection with willing, he must rely on his claim that rational agency includes intellectual love, which rests on reasons that are distinct from the satisfaction of desires.

If Aquinas is right on these points, happiness fits into the reductive task of the *Summa*. We do not need some further reason for pursuing happiness, once we understand that happiness is simply the ultimate end that we have reason to pursue as the ultimate object of the will.

279. Criteria for Happiness

We have now examined Aquinas' derivation of eudaemonism from basic features of rational action. He argues that agents who have wills necessarily act on external reasons and intellectual love, and therefore pursue an ultimate end that achieves their perfection. This argument brings him to the starting point of Aristotle's *Ethics*, the pursuit of happiness as the ultimate end. Aquinas defends Aristotle by showing that this is a legitimate starting-point for ethics. He also corrects Aristotle, or removes a possible misunderstanding, by showing that the pursuit of happiness is not a mere assumption, or a more or less plausible empirical claim, but a necessary feature of rational agency.

Aristotle acknowledges that if we agree that we all pursue a final good, we still have not settled the content of the good. But he does not think that the admission of a final good is completely empty. He sets out some formal criteria for the good, arguing that any acceptable conception must show that the good is complete and self-sufficient. This is the point at which he argues that happiness is to be identified with the final good. These formal criteria underlie his argument to show that happiness requires the fulfilment of the human function.

Aquinas relies on his views about perfection to interpret Aristotle's function argument.[43] A thing's good consists in its perfection; its form is the first perfection, and the actualization

---

[43] Aquinas recognizes Aristotle's different questions about the ultimate good. (The stages of his argument are discussed by MacDonald, 'Ultimate'.) He begins 1-2 q1 with goal-directed action, and then considers the concept of a final good. In a4 he introduces the ultimate end, and in a5–7 he clarifies some of the formal conditions. These formal conditions are used in q2 to eliminate various candidates for happiness; Aquinas perhaps sees that Aristotle implicitly does this in *EN* i 4. Having shown that different candidates fail the formal criteria, Aquinas now answers the question 'What is happiness?', and in q3 he sets out his own candidates that meet the formal criteria to the appropriate degree. He supports Aristotle's claim that happiness belongs to human lives, not to the lives of non-rational animals or of children (*EN* 1099b32–1100a4). Since happiness is the perfection of a rational or intellectual nature (1a q62 a1), it has the properties that belong to an end of rational willing.

(operatio) is the second perfection. Hence Aquinas understands Aristotle's claims about the 'function' or 'work' (*ergon*, opus) of human beings as claims about their proper actualization (operatio; *in EN* §119–21).[44] Something's happiness consists in the perfection of its own proper activity (operatio).[45] In a rational agent, the proper activity is the use of practical reason in the specific way that Aquinas has described. Since rational agency involves action based on intellectual love and external reasons, this is the kind of action in which the fulfilment of the human function consists.

If his arguments succeed, Aquinas shows that Aristotle's formal criteria restrict the sort of end that can be the object of a rational will. Our conception of the end is the basis for claims about the moral virtues, their relation to the good of others, the place of pleasure in the good life, and so on. Aquinas does not appeal to these claims in arguing for his conception of the end; he relies on more general claims about reasons and rational wills. Hence the formal criteria for happiness do not rest on specifically moral beliefs about the sorts of states and activities that are plausible candidates for happiness. If we can defend the formal criteria without reference to the specific moral disputes that we might expect them to resolve, we can legitimately appeal to them in resolving these disputes. This does not mean that the content of morality is to be derived entirely from a non-moral starting point. We may need to rely on some moral considerations and assumptions to defend the formal criteria; but, if Aquinas is right, these are not the specific moral beliefs that are in dispute when we discuss candidates for happiness.

280. How is Happiness Self-Sufficient?

Aquinas' treatment of the criteria for happiness suggests some answers to apparent difficulties in Aristotle. The most serious question arises from the two apparently incompatible conceptions of happiness that Aristotle seems to endorse. In *EN* i he seems to imply that the moral virtues and the actions expressing them constitute happiness (at least partly), but in Book x he argues—according to one interpretation—that happiness consists exclusively in theoretical contemplation.[46]

This question about Aristotle raises further questions for Christian readers. Some might be tempted to suppose that Aristotle identifies happiness straightforwardly with contemplation.

---

[44] Aquinas recognizes a virtue 'in all things, in so far as they have proper activities (operationes) in which they are perfected for acting well from their proper virtue' (*3Sent* d34 q1 a1 = P vii 381a). Other passages recalling Aristotle's claims about function: *3Sent* d33 q2 a4 = P vii 364a; d35 q1 a2 = P vii 403a; *4Sent* d49 q1 a2 sol.2 = P vii 1188b; *SG* iii 44 §2216; iii 129 §3011.

[45] '. . . happiness is the highest perfection of a human being. Now each thing is perfect in so far as it is in actuality; for potentiality without actuality is imperfect. Happiness, therefore, must consist in a human being's ultimate actuality. But it is evident that activity (operatio) is the ultimate actuality of the agent (operans). . . And hence it is that in other things also a given thing is said to be "for the sake of its activity". It is necessary, therefore, for human happiness to be activity' (1-2 q3 a2). The quotation is from Aristotle, *De Caelo* 286a7–8; cf. *Virt. Comm* q1 a1 = M 708b. Aquinas explains this passage through his own views about perfection: 'Everything that has a proper activity is because of the activity. For any given thing seeks (appetit) its own perfection as its own end, and the activity is the ultimate perfection of the thing' (*in De Caelo* ii 4 = P xix 87b).

[46] See §82: The theses condemned by the Bishop of Paris in 1277 (see §358) included allegedly Aristotelian views endorsing strict intellectualism. See Prop. 144 in Piché, *CP* 122): quod omne bonum. quod homini possibile est, consistit in virtutibus intellectualibus. See Wieland, 'Reception' 663; 'Happiness' 682. On Averroism see Bradley, *ATHG* 404–23; Gauthier, *EN* i 132; 'Commentaires' 230–93.

A Christian reader might understand contemplation as contemplation of God, and so might infer that Aristotle's account of happiness endorses the monastic life. But this would be too easy; whereas Aristotle's account of contemplation excludes the moral virtues, a Christian conception of the knowledge of God includes the love of God, and the love of God requires concern for the moral virtues; hence a strictly intellectualist Aristotelian conception of happiness seems to conflict with Christianity.[47]

Further examination of Aristotelian contemplation seems to raise a more serious conflict with Christian views on the good. In Aristotle's view, contemplation brings us as close to divinity as we can come, but is not especially theological; the proper objects of contemplation are laws about planets or mathematical figures, not about a transcendent God. One might infer that we can achieve our good by our own efforts, without reference to the transcendent God known through the Christian revelation. Anyone who drew this conclusion from Aristotle would be in conflict with Christian theology and ethics. Hence orthodox Christians might take this conflict to justify the rejection of Aristotelian eudaemonism.

Alternatively, if we suppose that Aristotle identifies happiness, wholly or partly, with the exercise of the moral virtues, we introduce another possible conflict with Christian doctrine. For these moral virtues are purely human virtues that can be achieved in this life, in activities that are in the power of any rational person, without any knowledge of God or of God's action on us. Aristotelian ethics seems to offer a purely natural route to the human good, in opposition to the Christian view that divine grace is needed for the grade of moral virtue that achieves happiness.

These objections to Aristotle are consistent with the acceptance of Aristotelian eudaemonism; but a Christian moralist might also doubt whether eudaemonism fits the Christian understanding of morality. If the moral virtues embody requirements of the divine law, we might suppose that they require our obedience unconditionally, whether or not they promote our happiness. Eudaemonism, on this view, appears to imply an inappropriate conception of the Christian virtues and of the outlook they prescribe.

At first sight, Aquinas' claims about happiness do not seem to resolve these questions. On the contrary, they seem to result in the conflict that readers have alleged in Aristotle. On the one hand, he argues, by appeal to the formal criteria and their relation to his account of the will, that the ultimate end is comprehensive, including all the goods that a rational agent pursues for their own sakes. On the other hand, he describes an ultimate good that has only one component. The vision of God is a simple and uniform state of infinite value. Has Aquinas therefore abandoned his comprehensive conception?

His answer to this objection depends on a qualification in his claim that complete happiness is the vision of God. He believes that this complete happiness can be achieved only in the afterlife, when we gain all the features of happiness that we cannot achieve in this life. In this life we can achieve only incomplete happiness, which includes the moral virtues; their

---

[47] See §373: Anselm argues that a genuine concern for moral rightness in itself requires us to transcend our natural desire for happiness (*De Casu Diaboli* 12–14; see §363).

goodness is not completely absorbed in the imperfect vision of God that we achieve in this life. Hence Aristotle is right, in Aquinas' view, to make the moral virtues parts of the happiness we can achieve in this life.

Complete happiness differs from incomplete in its stability. If happiness is a suitable end for the whole life of a rational agent, it should be stable; if it were liable to be destroyed by circumstances entirely outside our control, it would not be a reasonable aim for all our actions. On these grounds (cf. 1-2 q2 a3 ad3) Aquinas argues that the ultimate good cannot consist in wealth or honour or other external goods. But he also infers that happiness cannot be achieved in this life (q5 a3), because the vicissitudes of human life make its goods transitory rather than stable, and human imperfections make even the best activities imperfect.[48]

But even if the goods that we can achieve were stable, they would not constitute the complete good. The will is directed to the universal good, not at any particular good (q2 a7). Hence no good of the soul can be the ultimate good, and no created good can fully satisfy the human will (q2 a8). These are particular and 'participated' goods.[49] Every good other than the final good itself lacks some good from some point of view; this is why deliberation is needed for us to choose it.[50]

In these claims about particular goods, Aquinas does not mean that everyone who chooses them will in fact be dissatisfied with the result in some way. He believes that even the best combination of goods that we can select in this life leaves us with some rational basis for dissatisfaction. Even the goods that we choose as a result of correct deliberation require, in the circumstances of human life, the renunciation of other genuine goods. Hence none of these particular goods can completely satisfy the will. Only the vision of God himself can fully satisfy us (q3 a1, 8).

Hence, neither the life of contemplation nor the life of moral virtue, nor the mixed life of contemplation and moral virtue, meets Aristotle's formal criteria, if we restrict ourselves to this life. Aristotle (according to Aquinas) draws this conclusion from his formal criteria; he recognizes perfect and imperfect types of happiness, and believes that perfect happiness cannot be achieved in this life. The degree of happiness we achieve in this life does not satisfy the formal criteria, and therefore it falls short of perfect happiness. The formal criteria, therefore, answer two different questions: (1) Sometimes they help to specify general principles that perfect happiness must satisfy; this is what is meant if we claim that happiness is complete and stable and fully satisfies desire. The happiness we achieve in this life fails these conditions. (2) Sometimes they help to specify the happiness attainable in this life, which is the closest we can come to satisfying them.

Is Aquinas right to claim that Aristotle recognizes that the happiness of this life is incomplete? To support his view of Aristotle, he discusses the claim that happiness is complete because it is self-sufficient, and therefore 'lacking in nothing'. He believes Aristotle accepts two interpretations of this claim about happiness: (1) A maximal interpretation: What is complete cannot have anything added, because it is already incapable of improvement.

---

[48] See *SG* iii 48 §2248: 'Everything that is moved towards an end desires naturally to be stable and at rest in it. . . . But in this life there is no assured (certa) stability.' In his support Aquinas cites Aristotle, *EN* 1100b4–7. Cf. Aug. *CD* ix 15a ('all human beings, as long as they are mortal, are necessarily also miserable'), cited by Wieland, 'Happiness' 673.

[49] 1a q103 a2; q105 a4; q106 a2; 1-2 q9 a6.   [50] On deliberation see §267.

(2) A moderate interpretation: It needs nothing added (though it could have things added), because it is good enough already, though it is capable of improvement. The maximal interpretation, taking the good to include every good, applies to God as the 'total good' (in *EN* §115). The moderate interpretation applies to the happiness that can be acquired in this life.[51]

The happiness that Aristotle describes in the *Ethics* satisfies the moderate interpretation of 'lacks nothing'. It needs nothing added because it includes all that we can reasonably ask for in our circumstances. Since it includes both contemplation and moral virtue, it fulfils human nature as a whole, as far as this is possible in present circumstances, and it achieves the degree of stability that we can reasonably ask for. Hence we ought not to be disturbed that it does not include more, even though we recognize that it does not satisfy the maximal condition for lacking nothing.

281. Two Grades of Happiness

In proposing these two interpretations of self-sufficiency Aquinas raises a difficult question about Aristotle's position. Sometimes Aristotle seems to intend the maximal interpretation. He argues, for instance, that virtue is insufficient for happiness because a virtuous person's life could be made better (*EN* 1095b31–1096a2). One might suppose that if something can be added to a given candidate for happiness, that candidate fails (1170b17–19).

Sometimes, however, Aristotle seems to reject a maximal interpretation. For he believes that happiness can be achieved in the ordinary course of human life, and that it is both capable of being made better by addition of external goods and capable of being lost because of misfortune (1100b22–30). If the maximal interpretation were right, the fact that some candidate for happiness can be either improved or lost would disqualify the candidate, as Aquinas also recognizes (*in EN* i 16 §194). Since Aristotle does not take the very strict view about who can be called happy, he seems not to accept the maximal interpretation of 'complete'.

Aquinas also believes a moderate interpretation is needed to justify Aristotle's claim that in this life happiness is an activity (operatio, *energeia*) (1-2 q3 a2).[52] One might object (obj4) that in a happy person's life activities often get interrupted; since the person can be called happy even during the interruption, how can happiness be activity? Aquinas replies (ad4) that interruption does not show that happiness is not an activity; it simply shows that the happiness we can get in this life is imperfect.

Both the maximal and the moderate interpretation are needed (according to Aquinas) to explain Aristotle's remarks on happiness and stability. Aristotle acknowledges that a person's

---

[51] '...in itself it contains everything that is necessary in itself, but not everything that can come to a human being. Hence it can be made better by something else being added. But the desire of a human being does not remain agitated (inquietum), because desire regulated by reason, as the desire of a happy person must be, has no disturbance about the things that are not necessary, even though they are possible to obtain. This then is what he says is appropriate to happiness most of all, that even not counted together with other things it is choiceworthy' (*in EN* i 9 §116). 'Even' in the last clause renders the translatio recens (P xxi 19b, not in L). Kenny, ' Aristotelian happiness', esp. 18, discusses Aquinas' account of self-sufficiency.

[52] On operatio see §279 above.

happiness is not completely stable, but can be lost through misfortune. And so he says that since the future is unclear to us, but we think of happiness as an end that is altogether complete in every way, we should count such people as happy 'as human beings'—happy to the extent that human beings can be happy (*EN* 1101a19). In 'altogether complete in every way' Aristotle refers to a maximal condition for lacking nothing. If we apply this condition, we cannot regard human beings as happy. Hence his qualification 'as human beings' indicates some restriction of the claim that we can be happy, once we insist that happiness must be 'altogether complete in every way'. Aquinas infers that Aristotle is speaking of human, and therefore imperfect, happiness, not of perfect happiness.[53] Aristotle recognizes that the happiness he thinks is possible has the imperfections that belong to this life.

Aquinas agrees, therefore, that the life Aristotle has described is complete in so far as it has all that can reasonably be expected, within the changeable circumstances of human life. But something can be added to make such happiness better; for Aristotle admits that the instability of such happiness is a defect in it. And so Aquinas infers that Aristotle thinks the happiness obtainable in this life does not meet the maximal conditions for happiness, and therefore is not perfect happiness (see *in EN* §§201–2).[54]

The division between imperfect and perfect happiness not only clarifies Aristotle, but also makes a practical difference. Aquinas helps us to separate what it is reasonable to aim at from what it is reasonable to prefer. The sort of happiness that Aristotle calls human is the sort that is reasonable to aim at in the ordinary circumstances of human life. In the light of this end we can reasonably decide what to do, what virtues to cultivate, and so on. Given the conditions of human life, we ought not to expect the perfect happiness that is altogether untouched by external circumstances, altogether permanent, and so on.[55] We ought not to try to escape the ups and downs of human life by denying that external goods are needed for happiness (1-2 q4 a7; cf. 2–2 q186 a3 ad4). In this context the moderate conditions for happiness are the appropriate guide to action. The maximal conditions might mislead us; if we were to insist on the maximum possible stability and intellectual activity, we might prefer a life of contemplation, which would not fulfil human nature in the circumstances of this life.

Once we understand that we ought to plan for the circumstances of this life, we see why we ought to agree with Aristotle's view that happiness includes the exercise of the moral

---

[53] 'We do not deny, . . . that some participation in blessedness can be present in this life, in so far as a human being is perfected in the goods of theoretical reason principally, and of practical reason secondarily. And this is the happiness that the Philosopher decides about in the book of the Ethics, while neither asserting nor denying another happiness that is after this life' (*4Sent.* d49 q1 a1 sol.4 = P vii 1186). Similarly, *SG* iii 48 §2254, distinguishes the 'ratio perfecta' of happiness from the participation that is possible in this life. On strictly human happiness see Bradley, *ATHG* 400.

[54] The Latin version of *EN* 1101a7–8 takes 'He will not be happy if he falls into the fortunes of Priam' to mean 'Since he is happy, he will not fall into the fortunes of Priam' ('Neque utique beatus Priami in fortunis incidet', *in EN* §122). The correct interpretation is probably 'If he remains happy, he will not fall into the fortunes of Priam', allowing—contrary to Aquinas—that someone who is happy now can cease to be happy and fall into the fortunes of Priam. Aquinas therefore assumes that external ill-fortune does not take away happiness. All that can take away happiness is the sort of misfortune that would impede the operation of virtue totally, by causing insanity; and that would be the end of a life of virtue (§197), so that it would not really violate the principle that happiness cannot be lost in one's life. This sort of happiness that can be taken away by insanity is imperfect happiness. If Aquinas had interpreted Aristotle correctly here, he would have had an even stronger case for his view that we must take Aristotle to be speaking of imperfect happiness. See also 1-2 q5 a4 on loss of virtue.

[55] Reflexion on the Stoics' distinction between *telos* and *prokeimenon* also suggests a division between the end that it is reasonable to aim at and the one that it is reasonable to hope for. See §178. Aquinas' two grades of happiness recognize these different roles for a conception of happiness.

virtues, even though they may make some aspects of life more unstable than they would otherwise be. Happiness, therefore, requires external goods (1-2 q4 a7) and the activities that express a human being's social nature (q4 a8). Imperfect happiness fulfils a human being's natural tendency to live in society, just as perfect happiness fulfils our tendency to find out the truth about God (q94 a2). The happiness attainable in this life can be lost, though it is not totally removed as long as virtue remains intact.[56]

282. The Complete Good

But though we should rely on the moderate conditions for happiness in thinking about this life, we should not ignore the maximal conditions. Aristotle and Aquinas agree that these conditions for happiness describe a life that would be preferable for us if we could achieve it without ceasing to be the people we are; but Aquinas takes a different view about their practical significance. From Aristotle's point of view, this sort of life is an unattainable ideal, since it presupposes the absence of unalterable features of human life; but it gives us some idea of what we might try to approach in certain respects.[57] But according to Aquinas, we can satisfy the maximal conditions for happiness in the next life (q3 a8). The vision of the divine essence can be completely achieved, not in this life, but in the next.

This complete happiness is supernatural. Aquinas claims that it is both good for a human being and beyond what a human being is naturally capable of and suited for.[58] But are these two features compatible? We might think they are not compatible within Aquinas' position, since he follows Aristotle in identifying the human good with the realization of human capacities. To defend himself, he needs to distinguish (i) an idealized conception of human nature that we could use to find what is good for a human being, and (ii) a conception in the light of which we can see what a human being is now capable of.

To clarify this distinction, we might consider the relation of physical health to human capacities and the human good. It would probably be better for us, being the sorts of creatures we are, to be free of illness, but this human good is beyond our current human capacity. A completely healthy existence would affect the relative importance of some goods, but it would fulfil human nature rather than changing it into the nature of some other creature. This idealized human being would still be a human being. Moreover, historical changes in human limitations suggest that some idealizations of this sort are reasonable. In certain ways, many human beings are less exposed to such external misfortunes as starvation, enslavement, physical violence, and illness than most human beings once were. The needs of human beings have therefore changed in some respects; we may not need the resources for protecting ourselves individually from physical violence that individuals once needed. But in some important ways these changes have not changed the human good; it was always good for human beings to be free of the threat of physical violence, even though it was once not realistic for them to expect lives that would normally be free of the threat. The

---

[56] 'Still, external changes cannot take such happiness away altogether, because the activity of virtue still remains, as long as a human being bears the adversities themselves in a praiseworthy way' (1-2 q5 a4).

[57] See §82.   [58] See 2-2 q2 a3.

removal of this significant limitation of the human condition does not make us into some other creature, nor change the basic character of our good.

It is difficult, therefore, to maintain that mortality or physical vulnerability, for instance, are necessary conditions for any recognizably human good. Hence it is reasonable of Aquinas to describe a good that is still the human good even though it presupposes the absence of unavoidable limitations in our present existence. The vision of God is the complete good for a human being, even though it lacks those aspects of the imperfect good that reflect some of the contingent, and in his view temporary, limits of embodied human beings.

In arguing that the vision of God is the complete good, Aquinas accepts a part of Aristotle's argument to show that the final good includes contemplation. The vision of God is the final good because it uniquely satisfies our desire for a universal good (q2 a7). A rational will that pursues the universal good must also pursue a complete and final good.[59] But when the goods available in a human life are measured against the standard of universality and completeness, they all fail. None of them can completely satisfy the will, because even the largest practically available set of them excludes some other genuine goods. The vision of God, however, once we completely attain it, leaves no attainable good outside it. This is why Aquinas thinks the vision of God is the ultimate end for human beings; the desire for happiness includes in a way the desire for the knowledge of God.[60]

This account of complete happiness does not conflict with the view that happiness should fulfil human nature as a whole; for the vision of God completely fulfils our nature in the afterlife. The formal criteria for happiness support a comprehensive conception that makes happiness include all non-instrumental goods; but they do not tell us how many non-instrumental goods there are. Hence the formal criteria leave open the identification of happiness with a single good.

We might identify happiness with a single good if we claimed that there is only one non-instrumental good. But it is difficult to see how Aquinas could claim this about the vision of God, any more than Aristotle could claim it about theoretical study. Following Aristotle, Aquinas also recognizes moral virtues and virtuous actions as non-instrumental goods. Since we can achieve these goods without achieving the vision of God, they are distinct non-instrumental goods.

But he has a more plausible way to reconcile the comprehensive conception of happiness with the view that happiness has only one component. If some one activity realizes the different aspects of goodness that we pursue in many different kinds of activities, we can realize the same aspects of goodness either by pursuing many activities or by pursuing this one activity. We do not identify this one good with happiness simply because it is the single best good; we must also show that it realizes the aspects of goodness in other non-instrumental goods. In this case we can say that the final good is comprehensive, not because it includes all the non-instrumentally good activities, but because it includes

---

[59] See 1-2 q1 a5, discussed at §247.

[60] 'God is the happiness of a human being. For a human being naturally desires happiness; and what a human being naturally desires, he naturally cognizes (cognoscitur ab eodem). But this is not cognizing God without qualification, just as cognizing the one who is coming is not cognizing Peter, even though Peter is the one who is coming. For many suppose that the perfect good of a human being, which is happiness, is wealth, some that it is pleasures, and others that it is something else' (1a q2 a1 ad1). We all desire God implicitly, not explicitly; *Ver.* q22 a2.

511

all the aspects of goodness found in these activities. We do not necessarily abandon a comprehensive conception of happiness if we argue that in some circumstances only one activity is necessary for us to achieve happiness.

Aristotle goes some way in this direction, by arguing that the different features we seek in happiness belong most of all to theoretical study (EN x 7). He does not, however, take this line of argument to show that theoretical study is the whole of happiness. He argues that it is the one activity that best exemplifies the various features of happiness, but he does not argue that it completely exemplifies them; he does not argue, therefore, that theoretical study completely satisfies the conditions for the complete good. But Aquinas uses this argument to show that the vision of God is the complete good, and therefore the only component of happiness.

But if he relies on this argument, he seems to invite an objection that arises for Aristotle if he identifies happiness with contemplation. Aristotle also claims that his conception of happiness gives us a sufficient reason for practising the moral virtues for their own sakes. If this claim is justified, it is not enough to show that the moral virtues are non-instrumentally good, if the respects in which they are good are completely absorbed in contemplation; he should also show that in human life we have a good reason to pursue their goodness through the practice of the virtues themselves. If Aquinas believes that the vision of God absorbs all the goodness that is found in the various non-instrumental goods, does he not make the practice of the moral virtues superfluous from the point of view of happiness?

Aquinas is open to this objection if he argues that the vision of God, like Aristotelian contemplation, is so much better than any other single good that in our present life we should devote ourselves to it, even to the exclusion of everything else. But he does not argue this way. He believes that contemplative activity is the best activity (1-2 q3 a5), but he does not infer that contemplation of God constitutes complete happiness in this life. The vision of God in the next life differs from contemplation in this life in not requiring the renunciation of other forms of goodness. Aristotle sees that greater devotion to contemplation in the circumstances of human life requires renunciation of other goods and their goodness; moral action, which is the good of practical intellect, is not derivative from, or included in, the good of contemplation. Aquinas agrees with him on this point, and therefore he does not advocate the maximum pursuit of contemplation in this life.

The vision of God in the next life, however, is not simply one among a number of goods; it includes the goodness of other goods. One need not renounce other sorts of goodness, therefore, in order to devote oneself more fully to the vision of God in the next life, since one achieves all these other forms of goodness in the vision of their source (q4 a7 ad2). The completeness and stability of perfect happiness makes it unattainable for us in this life; but the vision of God in the next life satisfies the conditions that cannot be satisfied in this life. If the vision of the divine essence is possible and it has the properties that Aquinas says it has, it meets Aristotle's conditions for happiness. Aristotle's conditions for the most desirable end are only imperfectly satisfied by the most desirable practical end for human life under present human circumstances; but the vision of the divine essence fulfils Aristotle's demands on the final good.[61]

---

[61] On the place of contemplation in Aquinas' view of the ultimate end see Grisez, 'Natural law' 27–36; MacDonald, 'Reply'.

Hence Aquinas concludes that the perfect happiness of the next life will consist wholly in contemplation, whereas the imperfect happiness of this life consists 'primarily and principally' in contemplation, but secondarily in the actions of the practical intellect directing human actions and passions (q3 a5).[62] A purely contemplative conception of happiness in this life would violate the demand for completeness, since contemplation in this life, as opposed to the vision of God in the next life, is not our complete good.

283. The Pursuit of the Two Grades of Happiness

Aquinas explores these different claims of the contemplative life and the life including moral virtue, in his discussion of the religious orders and other conditions within the Church. To understand his comparative judgments, we must see what options he compares. If the only options are (1) a contemplative life that does not include the moral virtues as components, but only needs them as necessary conditions, and (2) an active life that has no primary role for contemplation, then the contemplative life wins (2-2 q180 a2–3; q182 a1). But if the options include (3) a contemplative life that also includes the activity of moral virtue as a component, this third life wins. Hence the condition of a bishop is more perfect than the condition of a member of a religious order, because a bishop contemplates both for his own sake and for the sake of others (q184 a7 ad1–3). A life that includes both contemplation and the transmission of its results to others is better than the one that consists in contemplation alone (q188 a6).

Aquinas relies on two features of his interpretation of Aristotle: (1) Contemplation is the supreme element in human happiness, and so a purely contemplative life is better than a life of moral virtue without contemplation. (2) Neither of these lives constitutes human happiness, and the life that combines both elements is superior to each of these lives. In following these two threads from Aristotle, Aquinas tries to reconcile the legitimate claims of each type of life, without granting that either of them by itself is sufficient for human happiness.[63]

These views about happiness confirm that the moral virtues are parts of happiness. If Aquinas simply identified happiness with contemplation of God, he would face the problem

---

[62] 'Therefore ultimate and perfect blessedness, which we look for in the future life, all principally [Leonine omits 'principally'] consists in contemplation. But imperfect happiness, such as can be had here, consists first and principally in contemplation, but secondarily in an operation of the practical intellect directing human actions and passions, as stated in the Ethics' (1-2 q3 a5). Aquinas' reference to Aristotle shows that he interprets *EN* 1178a9; b3–7, as referring to two aspects of a single life rather than to two different lives. This is not so clear, however, at *in EN* x 11 §2097, 'felicitas maxime consistit in operatione contemplativa' or at x 12 §2110, [the contemplator is] 'maxime felix, quantum homo in hac vita felix esse potest'. Aquinas' use of 'maxime' in these passages might suggest that contemplation is the best part of happiness in this life, not all of it. §2111 represents Aristotle as having said that perfect happiness is 'primarily and principally' in accordance with the theoretical intellect, but also introduces a 'secondary happiness' that consists in the activity of the moral virtues. Neither of these seems to correspond exactly to the imperfect happiness of this life consisting in both contemplation and the moral virtues. At i 10, §126, Aquinas argues (by appeal to the function argument) that happiness consists 'more principally' in the contemplative than in the active life. Perhaps he recognizes that Aristotle does not actually mention a mixed life; still, he thinks a mixed life is the sort of life that Aristotle has in mind for happiness in this life. On this point the *ST* seems to interpret Aristotle more freely than *in EN* does. Further discussion of Aquinas on Aristotle on happiness: see Bradley, *ATHG* 394–5.

[63] A different assessment of Aquinas' treatment of Aristotle in relation to Aquinas' own views about the two lives is offered by Kenny, 'Aristotelian happiness' 25–7.

that Aristotle would face if he accepted a purely contemplative conception of happiness. But he does not claim that renunciation of the practical for the purely contemplative life achieves happiness in this life. For in this life we act through an animal body, and attend to the needs that arise for ourselves and others because we have animal bodies. In the next life the vision of God will belong to the soul alone or to the soul united with a spiritual rather than an animal body.[64] In the circumstances of our present life we ought not to ignore the needs and interests that arise from an animal body.[65]

Aquinas therefore has a systematic reason to regard the moral virtues as more than mere instruments to happiness, even though they are no part of the perfect happiness that is available to us in the next life. To reject the moral virtues would be to deny that our happiness is connected with our nature as human beings who have bodies and passions; to deny this would be to claim that reflexion on our human nature misleads us about the sources of our happiness and of the virtues that achieve it.

Such a negative conclusion about reflexion on our nature would conflict with Aquinas' belief in the agreement of the natural law with the eternal, divine law. In his view, our knowledge of our nature in our present life makes us aware of our capacities and needs, and of the sources of our welfare. Our welfare consists in the development and expression of the rational aspect of our nature directing the other aspects. Since the moral virtues embody that direction by reason, they help us to achieve happiness. The connexion between the divine law, the natural law, and knowledge of our nature gives Aquinas, no less than a non-theological moralist, a legitimate concern with the moral virtues and with their role in the happiness that is attainable in this life.

Aristotle believes that happiness is up to us to a significant degree. The Stoics find his answer on this point unsatisfactory.[66] The same question arises for Aquinas. For if he takes Aristotle's account of happiness to describe the imperfect happiness attainable in human life, and if he identifies complete happiness with the vision of God in the afterlife, he needs to say how far each grade of happiness is up to us.

Aquinas recognizes that happiness must be something that a human being can achieve; but he denies that it must be possible to achieve it entirely through one's own action. He draws a parallel with other necessary goods; though human beings are not naturally equipped with clothing and shelter, they have the means to make up this deficiency. Similarly, though they are not equipped to reach the vision of God by themselves,[67] they have freewill, allowing them to be turned to God; and so to this extent perfect happiness is open to a human being (1-2 q5 a5 ad1).

The division between perfect and imperfect happiness makes it clearer how far happiness is up to us. Imperfect happiness does not require complete stability of fortune. Virtue is the most stable element in imperfect happiness; we cannot wholly lose this type of happiness unless we decline from virtue to vice (q5 a4). This type of happiness, therefore, is up to us.

---

[64] vel erit in anima sine corpore; vel erit in anima corpori unita non iam animali, sed spirituali (1-2 q4 a7). 'Vel . . . vel' indicates alternative possibilities about what the subject of the vision of God is, not about whether we do or do not have spiritual bodies. Cf Suppl. q79 a1.

[65] Aquinas rejects the Stoic view that the only good is the honestum and the only evil the inhonestum. In his view, the honestum is the principal human good and the inhonestum the principal evil, because they belong to reason (3a q15 a6 ad 2).

[66] See §189.   [67] See 1a q12 a4; q62 a1; q62 a2 ad3 on turning to God.

Perfect happiness, on the other hand, must be completely stable; and this is open to us only by a further operation of God's grace. This further operation of grace has to be examined carefully to see how far it allows our turning to God to be up to us. Here, then, Aquinas relies on the coherence of his doctrine of free choice and its consistency with the role he ascribes to divine grace.

Aquinas' view of happiness combines three prominent aspects of his moral theory: (1) his reflexions on Aristotle; (2) his aim of presenting ethics as part of a systematic theory of rational agency; (3) his Christian theology. He argues that Aristotle's conception of happiness as a complete good identifies the necessary ultimate end for a rational and free will. Moreover, this demand for completeness supports the distinctively Christian claim that happiness consists in the vision of God in the afterlife. Aquinas identifies perfect happiness with the vision of God, but he also treats the happiness of this life as a worthwhile aim, while acknowledging its instability. He presents moral virtue, not as a rival to contemplation, but as a necessary partner. He therefore claims to vindicate the Aristotelian moral virtues.

20

AQUINAS: MORAL VIRTUE

284. Virtue and Freewill

According to Aquinas' account of the will, rational agents necessarily pursue happiness as their ultimate end. If a correct account of the will vindicates the role that eudaemonist ethical theory attributes to happiness, it should explain why happiness requires the cultivation of the virtues. Virtuous and vicious agents differ in so far as they make different choices about how to pursue the ultimate end.

The virtues are important because we have freewill. Aquinas claims that the pursuit of an ultimate end is essential for human freedom; he is right only if this ultimate end has the right characteristics. If our awareness of it included an exhaustive grasp of its contents and of the means to it, and if this grasp were independent of rational reflexion and deliberation, our actions would not express freedom of choice and we would not be in control of our actions (*ST* 1a q82 a2). We are in control of our actions by pursuing means to an ultimate end, because both our grasp of the content of the end and the choice of instrumental means to it are open to practical reason, and (in human beings) to deliberation.[1] We necessarily pursue happiness in so far as we necessarily pursue some end that we think is complete and achieves our own completion, leaving no good outside it. But we do not thereby have a clear conception of what constitutes this end or of how to achieve it. To form the correct conception of happiness, and to execute this conception, we need the moral virtues; for 'the proper ends of the virtues are directed towards happiness as towards the ultimate end' (1-2 q13 a3 ad1).

The will necessarily pursues happiness because happiness (the complete and comprehensive end) necessarily seems good to any rational agent, from whatever point of view it is considered. This is not true of the components of happiness, however. We pursue virtue, or wealth, or honour, only because we look at them in a certain way that is not necessary; our view of these constituents is alterable by rational reflexion and deliberation.

---

[1] The claim about freedom does not mean that the content of the final good must be uncertain to every sort of free agent. See §§251 and 267 on God and the angels. Their certainty about the content of the final good does not threaten their freedom, because their grasp is not independent of their awareness of the rational merits of what they grasp. According to Scotus, Aquinas' attribution of necessity to willing the ultimate end is a threat to freedom. See §362 and Cajetan's discussion in §361.

Both virtuous and vicious agents act on freewill. Aquinas agrees with Augustine that an act of virtue is the 'good use of freewill' (q55 a1 ad2); he infers that virtue is the state that is directed towards this good use of freewill. Both our rational pursuit of the ultimate end and our natural non-rational inclinations are beyond our control, but we still have free choice in being virtuous or vicious. Our non-rational inclinations do not incline us irresistibly, but are subject to the will, since we can still elect one of a number of options (1a q83 a1 ad5; 1-2 q13 a6). Hence our character is up to our free choice.

The distinctive features of virtuous or vicious people must, therefore, be accessible to free choice, and so to deliberation. A state of the non-rational parts that is independent of the will cannot determine the end for deliberation. If it did, correct aiming at the end would not be a matter for deliberation, and so could not express freewill. Aquinas' account of the will, freedom, and happiness, as we have traced it so far, makes room for virtues as expressions of freewill. Rational agents share a schematic conception of the end. Deliberation must consider the different ends that constitute the ultimate end. These are questions to which virtuous and vicious people give different answers that explain their different choices.

These features of the will and of freedom explain why the virtues involve practical reason and deliberation. Aquinas also appeals to his conception of the will to explain why the virtues involve more than rational desire. Once we understand the nature of the passions and the will, we can see how the passions may agree or disagree with the will, and how the will may guide or neglect the passions. The right form of agreement and guidance depends on the moral virtues.

285. Will and the Formation of Character

If Aquinas' conception of the moral virtues fits his claims about the will and freedom, the will, rather than some non-rational condition independent of us, must make us virtuous or vicious. We have rational capacities for contraries, as Aristotle describes them, because we can choose between contrary courses of action that are equally within our power.[2] Aristotle says that desire or election 'controls' (*kurion*) the particular way in which a rational capacity is exercised (*Met.* 1048a9–11). This controlling election is the function of the will, as Aquinas conceives it. The will itself is not a capacity for contraries, but our having a will gives us this capacity. It would not be open to us to do a given action or its contrary unless we could deliberate on the merits of these contraries and could choose the one that appears better.[3]

To form states of character that exercise rational capacities in one particular direction, we need habituation (*ethismos*; assuetudo, 1-2 q63 a2; *in EN* ii 1, §247). Sometimes one might suppose that Aristotle identifies habituation with the sort of habit-forming training that a child might undergo, so that it precedes the sort of instruction that presupposes

---

[2] 'The rational capacities, which are proper to a human being, are not fixed (determinatae) on one <actualization>, but are related in no fixed way to many <actualizations>; but they are fixed on particular actualizations through states (habitus)' (q55 a1; cf. q49 a4). If we render 'habitus' by 'habit', we suggest misleadingly that a habitus is a mere tendency or custom (I may be in the habit of taking a particular route home, but this is not my habitus). See Kenny in BF xxii, pp. xxi–xxii (who favours 'disposition').

[3] For Scotus' interpretation of the claim about our capacity for contraries, see §369.

will, deliberation, and election. It is easy to suppose this, if one notices that Aristotle takes habituation to begin with the training of children (*EN* 1104b11–13; *in EN* ii 3, §268). But Aristotle does not intend purely non-rational training. For he believes that a virtue of character acquired by habituation includes the correct election, which requires prudence. If correct habituation did not ensure correct election, the virtue acquired by habituation would not include correct election. Hence habituation must be partly a rational process that, at some stages, presupposes will and election.[4]

Aquinas grasps the rational aspects of Aristotelian habituation; that is why he maintains that a state is formed by will rather than passion. Though it begins with non-rational training, the formative activities that he discusses are rational. They mould our non-rational tendencies, and form the sensory parts of the soul into a state, in so far as they 'operate at the command of reason', and so 'can be directed towards different <ends>' (1-2 q50 a3). The will can form a state, because a state is a capacity of reason and so can be directed in different ways towards action (q50 a5). It must be directed to some determinate goal, since our natural tendency towards the ultimate end is not directed to a sufficiently determinate end for us to achieve our ultimate end (q50 a5 ad1).

The actions that form states of character are rational actions proceeding from the will: '. . . the states of the moral virtues are caused in the desiring capacities, in so far as they are moved by reason' (q51 a2). A state is formed in so far as reason succeeds in 'overcoming' (*supervincere*) the desiring capacity. But it cannot do this in just one action, since a particular action is concerned with determinate circumstances and features of a situation (q51 a3). To 'overcome' desire by forming the right state, we need to generalize correctly, 'so that desire moves towards the same thing in most cases, in the way that nature does' (q51 a3).

'Overcoming' desire takes time because one's desires already have specific tendencies derived from passions; we modify, but we do not abolish, these tendencies, and this process takes time. We learn to recognize brave or generous actions in different conditions, so that we gradually learn which tendencies should be encouraged or restrained. In general, 'the states of the desiring part are caused by the fact that reason naturally moves the desiring part' (q53 a1). In the case of the virtues, the relevant state 'can be caused from human actions, in so far as such actions proceed from reason' (q63 a2).

Since habituation results from reason operating on desire, non-rational animals cannot form states. They can be trained, and to this extent they can be said to have states. But they lack the sort of state that is relevant to the virtues, because they do not control their actions, either in forming or in actualizing a state.[5] Control over one's actions is the mark of a rational agent, since such an agent can deliberate about what to do in the light of a conception of the ultimate end.

Since the appropriate state of character requires the proper exercise of the will in action, it requires the right aiming (*intentio*) and deliberation, leading to the right election. Hence Aristotle defines a moral virtue as a 'state that elects' (*hexis prohairetikē*). This definition may appear too narrow for the range of actions that he recognizes as characteristic of virtue. Though actions on the right election are an important subset of the virtuous actions

---

[4] See §101.

[5] 'They lack the characteristic of a state as far as concerns the exercise of the will, because they do not have control over exercising or not exercising, which seems to belong to what is characteristic of a state' (q50 a3 ad2).

characteristic of the virtuous person, they are not the only ones. Aristotle assumes that many voluntary actions are produced by the non-rational parts of the soul apart from election, and that the virtuous person performs these actions, and not only actions on election, in a characteristic and distinctive way. The feelings and immediate reactions that the virtuous person has without election are, as Aristotle insists, important signs of the virtuous character.

According to Aquinas, election belongs to all fully voluntary actions. We act virtuously in so far as we act on election, through the proper direction of the will by reason in the use of one's natural capacities. But he seems to allow voluntary actions that do not meet his strictest conditions, if they result from consent without election.[6] His claims about directly and indirectly voluntary actions allow the actions characteristic of virtues to include actions that are not the direct result of deliberation. His views about the sources of voluntary action influence his analysis of virtue and vice and of conditions related to them.

286. Reason, Passion, and Virtue

These features of Aquinas' position prepare us for an account of the virtues as expressions of the will that also include an important role for the passions as the source of indirectly voluntary actions that depend on the consent of the will. By introducing the virtues after the discussion of passions and states (1-2 q55), he follows Aristotle, who describes the virtues of character as states that regulate the passions in the ways that achieve the appropriate mean conditions. This emphasis on the passions distinguishes Aristotle's account from the Socratic and Stoic conception of the virtues as purely cognitive states. If Aquinas' account of the relations between the passions and the will is correct, it should explain how the passions are relevant to virtues that are elective states.

Aristotle's emphasis on the passions might seem to lead towards a strongly anti-Socratic view that makes non-rational desire the dominant element in virtue. According to this view, virtue is primarily a good condition of the passions; these form the right desires, and these desires are the basis for correct practical reasoning. Practical reason can be used well or badly, but it cannot regulate itself or turn itself in the right direction. It is turned in the right direction in so far as it agrees with well-trained desires.[7]

Aquinas is sympathetic to one aspect of this view. He believes that freedom is a property of the will, which is rational 'by participation'.[8] Since the virtues exercise our freedom, they belong to will, and not simply to intellect. But though he rejects an extreme intellectualist view, he does not make passions prior to the will in moral virtue.[9] If the direction of the will depended on the direction of the passions, and the direction of the passions did not depend on the will, we would not be free to direct either our passions or our will correctly, and so we would not be free to be virtuous or vicious.

Aquinas places freewill in the ability of the will to pursue one or another end through rational comparison resulting from deliberation. The virtues, then, include will, rational comparison, and deliberation, which belong to freewill. An extreme anti-rationalist picture

---

[6] See §252.   [7] This anti-rationalist account of Aristotle is discussed in §89.

[8] See §257.   [9] On intellectualism, voluntarism, rationalism, and sentimentalism see §259.

of virtue, subordinating will and deliberation to passions, would destroy his cumulative argument about ethics. An extreme intellectualist picture, implying that virtue is simply a matter of knowledge and that vice is simply the product of non-culpable ignorance, would be equally damaging. He needs an account of virtue that fits his broader theoretical claims about freedom, reason, and the will.

287. The Passions as Subjects of Virtues

Since the passions both influence the will and are influenced by it, correct deliberation and choice requires the co-operation of the passions. Aquinas claims that some moral virtues are virtues of the non-rational parts, and not simply virtues that involve them; this is what he means by saying that the non-rational parts are the 'subjects' of these virtues (1-2 q56 a4 sc).[10] He does not simply mean that a virtue requires passions to be trained or modified in some way. Bravery and temperance, for instance, involve bodily training, but they are not bodily virtues in the way that health and strength are, nor is the body the subject of these virtues. If the passions are subjects of moral virtues, they cannot merely provide suitable material or support.[11]

The passions are important because the actions characteristic of the virtues include the whole range of 'human acts'. These include not only actions that are the direct product of election, but also the actions that we control (domini).[12] These include actions resulting from passions, since passion does not prevent consent and election.[13] But since passions impede the use of reason in particular actions, purely intellectual virtues do not ensure right action.[14] A passion may make something appear so attractive that it is difficult to refuse one's consent to it; in such cases reason is 'clouded', though not made ineffective.

This feature of the passions helps to explain why they are subjects, and not simply necessary conditions, of moral virtues. Parts of the body have no distinct principle of action that is capable of opposing reason, and so moral virtue does not belong to them; but since the passions have their own principles, they need their distinct perfections to prevent these

[10] 'Temperance, however, in so far as it is a human virtue, is about appetites for sensory pleasures, which belong to the appetitive power. . . . And for that reason temperance, in so far as it is a human virtue, is in the appetitive part . . . But temperance is spoken of in <the angels> in so far as they display their will under control (moderate) in accordance with the standard (regula) of the divine will' (1a q59 a4 ad3).

[11] Aquinas' doctrine is examined by Graff, SPGV esp. ii 64–73.

[12] See Virt. a4 = M 717b: 'Whatever action, therefore, is in a human being's control is a proper action of virtue; not, however, those actions that are not in a human being's control. . . . Therefore, in whatever is the source (principium) of action of the sort that is in a human being's control, there we can place human virtue.'

[13] To explain how these actions are in our control, he often quotes Aristotle's remark that reason exercises a political rather than a despotic rule over the non-rational parts of the soul (1a q81 a3 ad2). Cf. Virt. a4 = M 717b: 'just as kings and rulers of states are in control of free people who have the right and ability of rebellion in relation to some precepts of the king or ruler'. On the political metaphor see §254.

[14] '. . . the desiring capacity obeys reason, not altogether at its nod, but with some contradiction. That is why the Philosopher says that "reason commands the desiring capacity by a political power", the sort by which someone is set over free subjects who have a certain right (ius) of contradiction. . . . And so for a human being to act well it is necessary not only for reason to be well disposed through a state of intellectual virtue, but also for the desiring capacity to be well disposed through a state of moral virtue' (1-2 q58 a2). I omit the cases in which a passion entirely takes away the use of reason. See §253.

principles from opposing reason.[15] Even if my arm or my leg does not move when I want it to, it does not impede me by presenting the attractions of not moving it. But if I am lazy, it appears pleasant to stay where I am, or irksome to move. These are principles that can oppose reason, and so I need to secure the co-operation of my passions. This is part of Aquinas' reason for treating the passions as subjects of virtue.

He recognizes, however, that his claim about the passions is open to question. One might argue that since sin does not consist in the having of a passion, virtue cannot consist in this either (*Virt.* a4 obj1). Aquinas grants the claim about sin, but maintains that the non-rational parts are subjects of virtues.[16] Both sin and virtue essentially consist in reason's 'moving or consenting'[17] in right or wrong action, but the passions are relevant in so far as they influence the will towards right or wrong action. Virtue belongs to them only in so far as they obey reason (1-2 q55 a4 ad3).[18] They do not have 'the character of good or bad' in themselves, but belong to virtue only in so far as they conform to reason, and hence to election.[19] This is why Aristotle defines a virtue as a state concerned with election.[20]

288. Means, Ends, and the Virtues

To support his claim that the passions are subjects of moral virtues, Aquinas points out, following Aristotle, that moral virtue makes the end correct and prudence makes the means correct. He considers the argument that since the principal expression of moral virtue is election, which does not belong to the non-rational parts, moral virtue does not belong to them either (1-2 q56 a4 obj4). He rejects this argument, on the ground that correct election requires both correct aiming at the end and correct grasp of the means to it. Since correct aiming in relation to the passions belongs to the good arrangement of the non-rational parts, correct election partly proceeds from them too; hence moral virtue belongs to them, while prudence, concerned with the means to ends, belongs to reason.[21]

As Aquinas understands Aristotle, the practical intellect operates through the intellectual virtue of prudence. Since prudence is concerned with means to ends, it does not prescribe the ends for moral virtue.[22] It presupposes the moral virtues, which turn us towards the

---

[15] *Virt.* a4: '. . . but in the lower desire, which is capable of rebelling against reason, something is necessary by which it follows without rebellion the action that reason commands'.

[16] At 2-2 q155 a4 Aquinas argues that the passions, rather than the will, are the subject of temperance, because they have been improved so as to be subject to reason (ipse appetitus sensitivus est subiectus rationi). If we treated the will as the subject of temperance, we would be assimilating temperance to continence.

[17] *Virt.* a4 ad1: ratione movente vel consentiente.

[18] For Scotus' criticism of Aquinas see §372.

[19] '. . . the movement of virtue has its principle in reason and its terminus in desire, in so far as it is moved by reason' (1-2 q59 a1).

[20] When Augustine appears to identify some passions, such as pity, with virtues, Aquinas argues that he must be taken to mean that the tendency to pity in accordance with reason is virtuous (q59 a1 ad3), Cf. §289.

[21] 'In election there are two things, namely, aiming at the end, which belongs to moral virtue, and the preferential choice (praeacceptio) of what is towards the end, which belongs to prudence. Now the fact that people have the right aim towards the end with reference to the passions of the soul results from the good disposition of the spirited and appetitive parts. And for that reason the moral virtues that are about the passions are in the spirited and appetitive parts, but prudence is in reason' (q56 a4 ad4).

[22] See 1a q22 a1 ad3; q23 a4; q113 a1 ad2; 1-2 q57 a5; 2–2 q47 a6; q56 a1.

right ends (q58 a5); hence there can be no prudence without the moral virtues. If a purely intellectual virtue could provide a first principle for moral virtue, apparently the practical intellect itself would be a source of motivation, contrary to Aquinas' assertion that the will is irreducible to practical intellect. Just as the correct use of intellect requires the will directed to the right end, so also prudence requires the moral virtues directed to the right end, if the deliberation of the prudent person is to guide virtuous actions.

In the light of this assumption that practical reason depends on will, Aquinas defends Aristotle's claim that moral virtue is concerned with ends, and prudence with means to ends (EN 1144a6–9, 20–2; 1145a5–6; 1178a16–19).[23] Since Aquinas resists the assimilation of will to reason, he might appear to make the passions dominant in directing the will. If he were to accept this view, it would be reasonable for him to take the moral virtues to belong primarily to the non-rational parts.

He cannot, however, consistently accept this argument for treating the passions as the subject of moral virtues; it conflicts with his rationalist position about will and reason, and takes him too far in the direction of sentimentalism, making desire prior to reason.[24] Though he rejects the extreme intellectualist view that reason moves us without will, Aquinas does not agree that the will gets the right aim from passions that are independent of will; for if the passions were the source of the right aim, we would not be free to choose one or another end. Since we are free to choose ends, deliberation cannot have the narrow scope that we would assume if we thought that passions direct the will. Aquinas' claims about happiness and subordinate ends imply that we can deliberate about how to specify a schematic conception of an end; deliberation is not confined to cases in which we already have a definite conception of the end given to us through desires independent of will.

It is puzzling, then, that Aquinas argues from the role of moral virtue in setting ends to the claim that the passions are the subject of the moral virtues. If his claims about passion and virtue are consistent with his general view of the will and deliberation, he cannot claim that the passions are the subjects of moral virtue because they give us the correct ends.[25]

289. The Positive Contribution of the Passions

Since the passions tend to move us on the basis of considerations that also appeal to the will, Aquinas infers that they must have a distinct positive role in the virtues. He rejects the Stoic view that the passions are always bad, and that moral virtue requires their elimination (1-2 q24 a2–3; q59 a2–3). Passions are constituents of a virtue in so far as they are subject to reason and moved by reason (q56 a4).[26]

These relations to reason do not simply require the passions to be regulated by reason. Aquinas also believes that virtuous human beings are better off with well-trained passions

---

[23] Aquinas quotes EN 1144a6–9 at 2–2 q47 a6 sc. In Aquinas' terms, virtue has the correct intentio towards the end. See in EN vi 10 §1273 (cf. §1269). On intentio as aiming at the end rather than the means see 1-2 q12 a4.

[24] See §259.   [25] Cf. Bradley, ATHG 239.   [26] See esp. Ver. q26 a7; Mal. q3 a11; q12 a1.

than they would be if they were guided simply by practical reason and had no passions to interfere with it. Augustine is right, therefore, to argue that in a person with a good will it is better to have the right passions than to have no passions (*CD* xiv 6a).

Aquinas discusses two contributions of the passions (1-2 q24 a3). First, reason is capable of regulating passions, and it produces a better good the more things it regulates. If the passions guide reason, they 'cloud' it, and to that extent make actions worse by obscuring the appropriate grounds for action.[27] Secondly, passions improve actions when they are guided by reason.[28] They give greater intensity to our motives to act virtuously (cf. q30 a1 ad1), and we may reasonably elect to have a certain kind of passion in order to act more eagerly, with the co-operation of the sensory appetite.[29]

The passions contribute most directly to virtue through this second function. A passion absorbs some of one's attention, and turns it away from other things that may appear to be as good as or better than the object of the passion; and it encourages a more favourable view of the object of the passion than one would otherwise take. This absorption of attention may sometimes distract us inappropriately, but it may also sometimes improve us. We need to form a state that predisposes us to react in a specific way to specific circumstances, instead of relying on our deliberative capacities to work out the right answer on each occasion by 'radical' deliberation, setting out from the ultimate end.[30]

We can avoid any need for radical deliberation on each occasion if we have formed passions that are constituents or results of virtuous states, in so far as they are subject to the will.[31] This is why mercy (*misericordia*) may be a virtue; the passion of mercy is not a virtue, but if mercy proceeds from an elective state it acquires the character of a virtue (2-2 q30 a3 ad4). Similarly, we may regard repentance (*poenitentia*) either as an elective state that produces the right regret on the right occasions, or as the regret that results from such a state; in the first case it is a virtue, and in the second it is the actualization of a virtue (3a q85 a1; cf. q84 a9). But if we regard shame (*verecundia*) simply as a passion, and not as the result of an elective state, we do not count it as a virtue (2-2 q144 a1 ad1).

This connexion between will and passion explains why we can act virtuously even when we act 'suddenly', without deliberation. Aquinas mentions two sorts of sudden action: (1) One sort results from the immediate response of a passion without the intervention of the will; this is a 'sudden motion' that falls short of consent. (2) A second sort of sudden action results from the antecedent tendency of our state (ex inclinatione habitus). Aquinas illustrates this from Aristotle's example of people acting bravely in sudden emergencies, because such action proceeds from their state of character. The state has been formed by previous deliberation, so that new deliberation is not needed in an emergency when one

---

[27] '. . . for it is more praiseworthy if one does an act of charity from a judgment of reason than if one does it solely from the passion of pity' (q24 a3 ad1). Aquinas' use of 'ex *sola* passione' makes his point clear. His position is similar to Kant's in *G* 398–400.

[28] '. . . by way of election, namely when someone by a judgment of reason elects to be affected by a passion in order to act more promptly, having sensory desire co-operating. And in this way a passion of the soul adds to the goodness of an action' (1-2 q24 a3 ad1).

[29] For this function cf. 1-2 q77 a6 ad2; 2–2 q2 a10; *Ver.* q24 a12; *Virt.* a1 sc2.

[30] The formation of such a state is relevant to Herman's discussion of a 'deliberative field', in *PMJ* 193–5 (e.g.), and to Wiggins' remarks on 'salience', 'Deliberation' 230–4.

[31] '. . . virtue cannot be present except in those acts that proceed out of the command of will, even though they are also acts of the sensory parts' (*2Sent* d24 q3 a2 ad3 = P vi 604b).

needs to act at once.[32] A state has been completely formed only when it includes this capacity for immediate action.[33]

In the second case of sudden action, Aquinas agrees that, as in the first case, no deliberation immediately precedes the action, but he still regards the action as being elected, because previous deliberation has determined the end to be pursued in such situations. Hence, when something apparently suitable to the end appears in such situations, we choose it without further deliberation; but our choice is still an election, because it is the result of our having formed an end by previous deliberation.

Radical deliberation on each occasion is foolish, not only because it takes too long and is so complicated that we may easily make mistakes, but also because fear, inclination, self-interest, and so on sometimes distort our view. When we form a state of character, we cultivate passions that tend to counteract the distorting effects of other passions and lead us to attend to the right features of different situations. We need correct attention to generalize correctly. According to the parable of the Good Samaritan, the requirement to love one's neighbour applies to cases where another person is alien to us in obvious ways; we need to attend to the fact that this is another person needing help, not to his being alien.

Well-trained passions not only help us to avoid distortion, but also turn us in the right direction. When we reflect at leisure, outside a situation where we need to make an immediate decision, we may notice that in some situations this or that feature deserves our attention. But if we leave it to our rational judgment to work this out by a scrutiny of the situation whenever we need to make an immediate decision, we may be, at the least, inefficient, since we may take an unreasonably long time to survey all the conceivably relevant aspects of the situation. Even if we take all the time we need, we may still act badly, since it is not always easy to see, when we are in a situation, the features that become clearer to us from a more detached point of view. We are better off with a passion trained to focus on the right features.

The passions do not merely remind us of what we have previously recognized as relevant. They may also bring to our attention an aspect of the situation that we had not thought was relevant, or had even dismissed as irrelevant. We might, for instance, have decided that we ought to punish a child for some misdeed, and that her distress at being punished is irrelevant. But once we actually see how distressed she is, we may wonder whether the punishment that we thought was fair is unnecessarily severe. A soldier might have no doubt that the war he is fighting is just even if it harms innocent civilians, but when he sees the

---

[32] 'For the activity is more from the state to the extent that it is less from premeditation. For things evident in advance, i.e., known in advance, someone will elect in advance from reason and thought without <the appropriate> state, but sudden actions are in accordance with one's state. But this is not to be understood as saying that the activity in accordance with a state of virtue can be altogether without deliberation, since virtue is an elective state, but that the one who has the state has the end in his election determined; so that whenever something arises as suitable to that end, it is at once elected, unless it is hindered by some attention and further deliberation' (*Ver.* q24 a12 = M 461a). Aquinas alludes to Aristotle on emergencies, *EN* 1117a17–22; see §86.

[33] 'For unless a rational capacity tends through a state in some way to one <actualization>, it will always be required, whenever it is necessary to act, for some inquiry about the action to precede; this is clear about someone who wants to consider, not yet having the state of scientific knowledge, and about someone who wants to act in accordance with virtue, lacking the state of virtue. Hence the Philosopher says ... that sudden actions are from one's state' (*Virt.* a1 = M 709a). In the last sentence Aquinas cites *EN* v 3, which (in his capitulation) begins at 1129b11. I do not know what he has in mind, unless he is taking some of the actions listed in this chapter to be 'sudden'.

extent of the suffering it causes, he may wonder whether it is really worth it. In some such cases, our passions may cause us to reconsider the ends we aim at, and in this respect may form our conception of the end.

We should not always have second thoughts whenever our passions revolt against the action that we have elected. If I decide I was wrong in a dispute with you, and ought to apologize to you, perhaps I still ought to do it even if I still dislike you and your reaction to the apology is ungracious. To explain the difference between this case and the cases where passions ought to change our mind, we need to estimate how reliable passions are in various situations. Our tendency to sympathize with other people's suffering is—in some people—a desirable tendency that has been formed in the right ways. Our tendency to find our enemies and opponents disagreeable may not be as desirable. The passions that we justifiably rely on in forming second thoughts about our elections are passions that have been formed by our states of character, and hence by our elections.

We sometimes benefit, then, from passions that cause us to attend to some aspects of a situation and to ignore others. Though these passions are not infallible, we may be better off if we sometimes follow them than if we always ignore them. The virtues turn the passions in a beneficial direction. The right passions prepare us to avoid evils and to pursue goods (q59 a3), and so prepare us for virtuous actions (2-2 q123 a9–10). If we have the appropriate passion, the situation appears good or bad in a particular way, in advance of rational reflexion about it, since the passions make us aware of different particular goods. It is often unwise to wait for rational reflexion to examine all the relevant features of a situation. If a well-trained passion helps us to focus on the right features without reflexion, we are better off.

If passions are directed towards certain particular goods, and are normally subject to the will, it is sometimes reasonable to develop a tendency to focus on certain particular goods. An account of the virtues, therefore, should identify both the rational desires we should develop, and the tendencies to selective attention that we should form in the light of our rational desires. In Aquinas' view, the non-rational tendency to focus on some features of situations is often the best way for practical reason to apply itself to particular situations (cf. 2-2 q123 a9–10).

The positive role of well-trained passions helps to explain why our having the right aim towards the end results from (contingit ex) the good state of the non-rational parts (q56 a4 ad4).[34] We saw earlier that this claim might be taken to express a strongly anti-rationalist account of our choice of ends, implying that the passions, as opposed to will and deliberation, form our conception of ends. Such an account would raise grave difficulties for Aquinas, given his other views about the role of will and deliberation.

His remarks about the benefits of well-trained passions, however, do not conflict with his rationalist views on reason and will. Deliberation and practical reason discover the right

---

[34] '... In order to be in a correct state about particular principles of things that can be done, which are ends, it is necessary for a human being to be perfected through certain states in accordance with which it comes to be in a certain way connatural to a human being to judge correctly about an end. And this comes about through moral virtue; for the virtuous person judges correctly about the end of virtue, because "such as a person is, so the end appears to him", as it is said in Ethics iii. And thereby, in order to have correct reason about things that can be done, which is prudence, it is necessary for a human being to have moral virtue' (1-2 q58 a5). Cajetan comments (L vi 377b, quoted by M 257b): 'Prudence is not in reason without qualification, but as directed towards desire, and it depends essentially on desire, from which depends the precept, its actualization, and from which varies the appearance of the end, its principle'.

conception of the end by finding the constituents of happiness. This role of deliberation allows an important role to the passions in maintaining and expressing our grasp of the right end. Since the passions absorb our attention, and so turn it in a good or bad direction, they make it easier or harder to attend to the right ends. If we are to attend to the right ends, we need well-trained passions to help us and to remove potential hindrances. None the less, practical reason discovers the right ends. The passions do not discover ends, but they help us to retain our grasp of the ends we have discovered. To make sure that passions do this on the right occasions, we should form them in the light of our rational conception of the good. Hence they must be subject to reason.

If we look back at the passage where Aquinas says that the passions determine the right ends (q56 a4 ad4),[35] we might say that Aquinas overstates the role of the passions, and that we can see the overstatement if we compare this passage with his other remarks about prudence and the role of the passions. Alternatively, we might try to interpret this passage so that it fits his other remarks. We ought not to treat the passage, straightforwardly interpreted, as an accurate statement of his general position about the role of passions in fixing the right ends.

290. Will, Passion, and Virtue

Aquinas has a good case, therefore, for his claim that passions are not merely instrumental to the virtues. Since they have their own awareness of good and evil that constitutes a distinct source of goal-directed action, they need to be perfected in their own right, and not simply subjected to rational desire. They belong to virtues only in so far as they accord with reason (1-2 q56 a4 ad1). They must, therefore, be subject to a good will; for we need a good will if any other tendency or ability or state is to be correctly formed and guided.[36] The non-rational parts are perfected by moral virtue, which consists in the right relation to the rational part. The rational part itself is perfected not by moral virtue, but by prudence, which is distinct, though inseparable, from the moral virtues (q56 a2 ad3).

Aquinas claims that the passions are the only subjects of some moral virtues, assuming that if passions are the subject of a given virtue, the will cannot also be a subject of it. But why should he not say instead that both will and passions are subjects of each virtue? Just as the passions are perfected by being brought into agreement with a rightly-ordered will, so also the will is rightly ordered by deliberating correctly about what promotes happiness. The will and the passions together seem to constitute the state of character that disposes us to the right election.

Aquinas, however, does not allow the will to be either the subject or a subject of all the moral virtues. It is the subject only of some moral virtues—those that turn us to concern

---

[35] Quoted in n21.

[36] 'The subject of a state that is called a virtue without qualification cannot be anything other than the will or another capacity to the extent that it is moved by the will. The reason for this is that the will moves all the other capacities that are in any way rational, to their actualizations, as has been said above [i.e., q9 a1; q17 a1, 5; 1a q82 a4]; and for this reason whatever a human being does well in actualization comes about from the fact that the human being has a good will' (1-2 q56 a3).

for other people or to the love of God (1-2 q56 a6; *Virt.* a5). The will is necessary for the self-regarding virtues, but it does not need to be perfected, since it already seeks one's own good; we simply need to make the non-rational desires agree with what the will already seeks. We do not need to perfect the will, since the object of the will is a good that is proportionate to the will. The other-regarding virtues, however, require the will to be trained, so that it seeks an object that is not proportionate to it. Aquinas seems to mean that the will is the subject of other-regarding virtue because we need to be trained to see why we should benefit others besides ourselves; presumably he thinks such training should proceed through deliberation that results in the recognition of the good in benefiting others.

But this training in good deliberation seems to be needed for all virtues, not only for other-regarding virtue. If we are not trained to deliberate correctly, we may falsely believe that we should not restrain or modify our sensory appetites. To correct false belief resting on bad deliberation or failure to deliberate, we must learn to deliberate correctly, so that we turn our will in the direction that makes us brave or temperate. Aquinas does not give a good reason for making the will the subject of the other-regarding virtues alone. His claims about the role of the will suggest that both the will and the passions are subjects of moral virtue, because the virtues express both a good will and well-directed passions. He is justified in saying that the non-rational parts themselves have the moral virtues, and are not simply instruments of the will. But he regularly claims that the non-rational parts are subjects of virtue in so far as they follow reason. We do justice to this claim if we insist that the virtues include a good will. The place of the will in Aquinas' account of freedom demands an equally prominent place for it in his account of moral virtue; he does not emphasize the prominence of the will as much as he should.[37]

This puzzling feature of his discussion of the moral virtues is all the more puzzling in the light of his treatment of sin. He insists that the will is the subject of mortal sin, because mortal sin requires us to aim at the wrong end. Though passions may contribute to the formation of the wrong aim, the wrong aim requires the engagement of the will.[38] This is an equally good reason for insisting that the will is a subject of moral virtue.

291. Moral and Intellectual Virtues

Aquinas' doctrine of the directive role of the will in the moral virtues influences his discussion of the intellectual virtues, and especially his departures from Aristotle. If intellectual virtues belong purely to the understanding, and if their objects are higher than those of the moral virtues, they threaten the directive role of the will. Aquinas believes that we achieve happiness in so far as correct reason forms the will and the will directs our passions and actions so as to form and to act on virtuous states of character. But if the goods achieved by the intellectual virtues are superior, why not pursue them even when they conflict with the moral virtues? Aristotle implicitly raises this problem, since he claims that theoretical reason is superior to practical reason. Aquinas believes that the truth in this claim does not threaten the directive role of the moral virtues, and therefore of the will.

---

[37] For Scotus' criticism see §372.   [38] See §298.

His initial description of a virtue implies that the intellectual virtues do not meet all the necessary conditions for being virtues. Virtue involves the right use of the free will directing the agent's rational capacities in the right direction. We may, however, have and exercise the intellectual virtues without using them correctly. How, then, can the Aristotelian intellectual virtues really be virtues?

Aquinas distinguishes unqualified (simpliciter) from qualified (secundum quid) virtues, and argues that the intellectual virtues are only qualified virtues (1-2 q56 a3; cf. Virt. a7). The primary subject of virtue is the will, in so far as the will is necessary for the rational capacities to be correctly used in every respect. If we have an intellectual virtue, we have a well-developed state of intellect, and so we have used our rational capacities well. But if we have a misguided will, we do not use our intellectual virtues correctly. They are mere rational capacities in relation to the will that is free to use them one way or the other (Virt. a7).

Moral virtue, therefore, regulates intellectual virtue. If an intellectual virtue itself is no more than a capacity, and if the use of the capacity requires the will, the right use of the intellectual virtues requires the rightly-ordered will. Since the right ordering of the will requires moral virtue, the right use of the intellectual virtues requires the moral virtues. This right use of the intellectual virtues confers merit on their exercise (1-2 q57 a1).

Aquinas has no Aristotelian authority for his claim; he cites only Gregory the Great. Aristotle maintains that prudence has some supervisory role in relation to theoretical wisdom, but it is not superior; it simply seeks to facilitate theoretical wisdom (EN 1145a6–11), as a steward would.[39] This comparison does not acknowledge that we have to decide whether and in what circumstances to exercise theoretical wisdom, if other pursuits also claim our attention. Apparently we need some supervisory virtue, just as we need a supervisory discipline to regulate the occasions and circumstances for the worship of the gods (as Aristotle remarks, 1145a10–11). Aquinas seems to have this supervisory function in mind. His suggestion that charity is an appropriate directing principle introduces a Christian element, but the directive role of moral virtue is Aristotelian.

Aristotle ought to accept Aquinas' observation that the intellectual virtues would leave open the possibility of misuse, if they could (contrary to fact) be present without the moral virtues.[40] Even if we plan our lives entirely for the exercise of the intellectual virtues, we need something more if we are to exercise them in the right way. Someone with a totally disordered will could not focus on the most worthwhile intellectual pursuits, but would be distracted by entertaining but worthless diversions, and so on. If we could somehow automatically focus on the best exercise of the intellectual virtues—the contemplation of necessary truths—we would not need the moral virtues to prevent our being diverted into trivial intellectual pursuits. But we would still need the directive functions of the moral virtues. For someone who has the ability and the overriding desire to contemplate may still fail to turn his attention and his efforts in the right direction; he may be easily distracted

---

[39] See Aristotle, MM 1198b9–20. Aquinas' comment on EN 1145a6–11 recognizes the superiority of theoretical wisdom in a way that allows a supervisory role for prudence. He says that prudence does not prescribe to wisdom 'the way in which it ought to judge about divine things' (in EN vi 11 §1290).

[40] This is a counterfactual supposition, since prudence is one of the intellectual virtues, and it cannot be present without the moral virtues.

by the more ordinary needs of daily life. Alternatively, he may be so careless about them that they eventually demand too much of his attention. For all these reasons we need a well-directed will besides the intellectual virtues (2-2 q180 a2).

Aquinas seems to recognize a further role for the moral virtues in turning contemplative activity in a morally acceptable direction. The choice of occasions for contemplation should be regulated by charity, which includes love of our neighbour as well as love of God (q184 a7 ad3).[41] Aristotle has a reason to agree with this if he attaches some independent value to the moral virtues and their exercise. Since we have good reason to believe that Aristotle attaches independent value to the moral virtues, Aquinas argues for an Aristotelian conclusion.

And so, while the doctrine of the regulative role of the moral virtues is not Aristotle's doctrine, it is not un-Aristotelian either. The regulative role of the moral virtues is derived from the regulative role of the good will. This role has different but related effects on the passions and on the intellectual virtues. In the case of the passions, guidance by the good will turns our passions towards the right objects. In the case of the intellectual virtues, the good will does not alter the objects, but it modifies the occasions for the exercise of the virtues. The directive and regulative aspects of the free will control Aquinas' account of the virtues.[42]

292. Vice and Sin

If Aquinas has given an adequate account of the relation between will and passion in virtue, it should help him to explain deviations from virtue. The deviations recognized by Aristotle are incontinence and vice. Aquinas recognizes these too; the most prominent deviation that he discusses, however, is sin, which does not receive a distinct treatment in Aristotle.

Sin is not essentially an offence against God. From the theological point of view, Aquinas endorses Augustine's account of sin as a violation of the eternal law. From the point of view of moral philosophy, however, a sin is an error contrary to reason.[43] Whereas vice is the state contrary to virtue, a sin is simply the bad act that is contrary to the act of virtue. It is a 'misdirected act' (actus inordinatus), in contrast to the 'act of virtue', which is 'a directed and required (debitus) act'. Sin 'is opposed to virtue in respect of that <end> towards which virtue is directed' (q71 a1).

The task of explaining error, and especially sin, is a test for Aquinas' account of the will, and in particular for its rationalist elements. If virtue depends on grasping the right principles through deliberation, sinful and vicious people do not grasp the right principles,

---

[41] 'As Gregory says, "Let a leader be foremost in action, and more uplifted than others by contemplation," because it belongs to them to contemplate, not only for their own sakes, but also for the purpose of instructing others. Hence he says . . . that the words "They will declare the memory . . . of your sweetness" apply to perfect men returning after their contemplation' (2-2 q184 a7 ad3). See also §§282–3.

[42] Aquinas' claims about acquired and infused virtues seem to give him a further reason for recognizing some possibility of the 'misuse' of virtue. See §354.

[43] 'The theologian considers sin especially in so far as it is an offence against God, but the moral philosopher considers it in so far as it is contrary to reason. Hence Augustine defines sin with reference to its being "contrary to the eternal law," more fittingly than with reference to its being contrary to reason, especially since we are ruled through the eternal law in many things that surpass human reason, as we are in things that belong to faith.' (1-2 q71 a6 ad5).

or do not see their application to a particular case. The role of the passions in sin should not compromise the connexion between deliberation, will, freedom, and responsibility. Hence Aquinas should not explain sin through the sentimentalist claim that the bad passions are simply too strong (or the good ones too weak).

But if we reject sentimentalism, we still might not be convinced by a rationalist explanation of sin and vice. Why (we might ask) is sin so bad if it is nothing more than ignorance? If virtuous and vicious people pursue the same end, and the vicious are simply mistaken about the means to it, do they not deserve pity rather than blame? Their choice of vice rather than virtue seems to be the result of ignorance, not an exercise of freewill. To make vice voluntary, on this view, we must suppose that a free agent can have a conception of the ultimate good and the means to it, and still knowingly refuse to take these means. This is a voluntarist conception of the source of vice.[44]

To answer this objection to his doctrine of the will, Aquinas might argue that he does not reduce sin to ignorance. Alternatively, he might agree that he reduces it to ignorance, but argue that sin is culpable ignorance, and therefore is the grave evil that we intuitively take it to be.

293. Virtue v. Continence

In trying to explain sin and vice, Aquinas has less help from Aristotle than he has in his account of the virtues. Aristotle's description of deviations from virtue is brief and incomplete. Some of the gaps that he leaves raise questions that Aquinas tries to answer.

Actions may embody virtue or fall short of it to different degrees, but Aristotle mentions only some of the differences. Not every virtuous (just, temperate, etc.) action is an 'act of virtue' that is produced by virtue. Aristotle claims that only an agent who acts from a virtuous state acts justly, as opposed to simply doing a just action. Among the actions that are virtuous without being done virtuously, some are done because of ignorance or coercion (as when people are threatened with death if they run from the enemy; cf. EN 1116a29–b3); these deserve no praise. Others, however, are done for a reason that does not express virtue in the agent, but is still a ground for praise. Those who do brave actions out of love of honour deserve praise, though they have citizen bravery rather than genuine bravery (1116a17–29). We might explain this by saying that they care about being honoured for bravery. They will not do just anything for the sake of being honoured, and they are not indifferent about whether bravery or cowardice is honoured; they act on the true conviction that bravery is honourable, and so their actions deserve praise. But since they lack the virtuous person's conviction that brave actions are worth doing even without honour, they do not act bravely.

What ought we to say, then, about the person who, unlike the previous people, acts from the virtuous person's motive, but only intermittently, and who therefore lacks the constancy of virtue? Aristotle suggests that electing the virtuous action for its own sake and electing from a firm and stable state are two conditions for being a virtuous person (1105a31–3). Could someone satisfy only the first condition? Does Aristotle believe that the incontinent

---

[44] Cf. Scotus' view, §361.

is such a person? One might infer this from his remark that incontinents have the right election.

But if stability is the only difference between the incontinent and the virtuous person, apparently the continent person ought to be virtuous. For it seems quite possible (for all Aristotle says) for some people to be continent and stable. Do they not have a firm and stable state that causes them to elect the virtuous action for its own sake? The same question can be raised about Aquinas' explanation of Aristotle's conditions. In his view, firmness requires constancy within oneself, and stability requires immunity to external hazards.[45]

Perhaps Aristotle believes that continence is not a firm and stable state. Even if some people manage to act correctly despite their wayward appetites, they are always, he might suppose, in danger of lapsing into incontinence, and so they do not reliably produce the right actions even if they have a good record. Perhaps Aristotle assumes that if we act continently often enough, we will turn into virtuous people because the appetites that we overcome will gradually weaken. This seems a rather arbitrary assumption, however. Even if our wayward desires weaken because they are repeatedly denied satisfaction, we might have a persistent feeling of regret and reluctance about having to forgo their satisfaction, even in cases where we ought not to regret forgoing it. Surely someone who always managed to restrain his greedy or cruel or angry impulses, but always resented having to do it, would not have an appetitive part in harmony with the rational part? Aristotle, then, ought to deny that repeated acts of continence manifest virtue.

Stable continence falls short of virtue because continent and incontinent people lack the right election. Aristotle insists that the right election requires a virtuous state of character (1139a33–5; 1144a20–2), and that the right end appears only to the virtuous person (1144a29–b1; 1145a4–6). The virtuous person differs from the continent and the incontinent not simply in stability, but also in the election each of them makes at a particular time; neither the continent nor the incontinent person is capable of the virtuous person's election.[46] This election comes from 'good deliberation' (*euboulia*), which requires the correct grasp of the end and true deliberation from it. The identity of a particular election is determined not only by the particular action (paying a debt, helping the victim of an accident) but also by the deliberation that produces it, which includes the reason for which one elects it now, and would or would not elect it in different circumstances.

This conception of the identity of an election allows Aristotle to notice differences between elections that may from some points of view appear the same. Both the brave person and the imperfectly brave person may elect to face this particular moderate danger because bravery requires them to face it. The imperfectly brave person, however, is not convinced that it

---

[45] 'The third condition is in accordance with the character of a state—namely, that someone acts firmly, i.e. constantly as far as he himself is concerned, and immovably, i.e., disturbed by nothing external on a particular occasion, because he has the virtuous election and acts in accordance with it' (*in EN* ii 4 §283).

[46] We might take this claim to embody a non-standard use of 'election'. In some cases (we might say) Aristotle uses it to refer to something that happens on a particular occasion, but in other cases he identifies an agent's election with his general and fixed outlook or attitude. In the first sense of 'election', the incontinent, the continent, and the virtuous person all make the same election, and Aristotle is right to say that the incontinent has the right election. In the second sense, only the virtuous person has the right election, since the other agents lack the appropriately fixed attitude. More probably, Aristotle has the same sense of 'election' in mind throughout, and he always refers to a choice made at a particular time.

would be best to stand firm even in greater danger; his reasoning is different from the brave person's because the counterfactuals he accepts are different. The virtuous person accepts the right conclusion for all and only the right reasons, whereas the imperfectly virtuous people accept it for some of the right and some of the wrong reasons.

These features of deliberation suggest how the virtuous differ from imperfect people. Aquinas examines degrees of imperfection at some length, especially in his distinctions between sin and vice.

294. The Sources of Sin

Since a sin is a blameworthy action, Aquinas looks for the causes of actions that warrant blame without proceeding from vice. In each case he wants to show that when ignorance plays a causal role in sin, it is not the ignorance itself that is the source of the sinfulness of the action; the sinfulness results from some mistaken choice or failure to choose, and so belongs to the will.

Since Aquinas supposes that normal people have the resources to reach the right conclusions about action, he has to show why they fail to use these resources. The three different causes he mentions are ignorance, passion, and 'deliberate fault' (certa malitia).[47] In each case he affirms the primacy of the will as the source of responsibility, and therefore the crucial contributor to the sin.

In his discussion of ignorance Aquinas seeks to separate the excusing ignorance of particular facts from the ignorance that results from negligence or deliberate error. Sin does not result if the agent cannot overcome the ignorance, or it concerns something that he cannot reasonably be expected (tenetur) to know (1-2 q76 a2). Ignorance is a source of sin if we can reasonably be expected to know the specific thing we are ignorant of, and we have failed to acquire the relevant knowledge either by deliberate refusal or by negligence (q74 a5; q76 a3).

These comments about ignorance suggest that an appeal to ignorance cannot be the complete explanation of sin. For Aquinas suggests that blameworthy ignorance must be traced back to a cause that is distinct from ignorance—either to deliberate failure or to negligence.[48] To understand the cause of these failures we must consider the condition of the will or the passions that underlies them.

This analysis connects sin with virtue and vice, and, still more fundamentally, with the will and rational agency. Aquinas would face a serious difficulty if reasonable views about the nature and sources of moral errors could not be shown to fit his views about the will and its relation to reason and passion. His rationalist and eudaemonist conception of the will invites objections from two different directions: (1) We suppose that passions can be the source both of errors and of right actions. Aquinas has to explain how this can be so, given that he regards the passions as subject to the will, and takes the consent of the will

---

[47] Fearon in BF xxv renders 'certa malitia' by 'resolute malice'. q78 a1 obj1 explains 'ex certa malitia' by 'ex industria' = 'on purpose'. Mal. q3 a12 identifies 'ex malitia' with 'ex certa scientia'.
[48] See §262.

to be necessary for voluntary action. (2) We do not suppose, however, that error can be attributed exclusively to the passions, or that the difference between right and wrong action can be simply identified with the difference between guidance by passion and guidance by will and reason. For we suppose that we can make a deliberate and knowing choice of the wrong action, not under the influence of any passion.

Aquinas answers the first objection through his account of sin resulting from passion. He answers the second through his account of sin resulting from deliberate fault. In both cases he argues that the source of the error lies in a mistake by the will. Either the temporary influence of a passion attracts the will to an object that we would normally reject, or we make a mistake about the constituents of the good, even when we are not under the immediate influence of passion. Aquinas' view of the will explains not only what a virtue is and how we acquire virtue, but also how we fail to acquire it and how we lapse from it.

295. Passion and Sin: The Problem of Incontinence[49]

Sometimes the condition of the will that underlies blameworthy ignorance is the result of passion. Aquinas needs to explain this claim so that it fits his views about will and responsibility. He does not argue, for instance, that the passions cause sin by compelling us to follow them. Since sins are voluntary, the will is their primary subject; the other subjects of sin are powers that can be moved or restrained by the will (q74 a2–3). This claim about the will suggests that (as we have noticed) a parallel account of the subject of virtue would be more plausible than the account Aquinas actually offers.[50]

The will can be moved by the passions indirectly (q77 a1 ad2). Sometimes they distract us. Sometimes they attract us by presenting something that looks good, even though further examination would show that it is not good on the whole (q77 a1). If our will were entirely overcome by the passions, so that we could not use reason at all to guide our actions, we would not be responsible for our actions and there would be no sin (unless we were responsible for allowing the passions to overcome us) (q77 a7; 2–2 q150 a4). Though passion may diminish the sin (q77 a6), it does not remove it, as long as the will has the appropriate causal role. The passions cannot be the subject of mortal sin; for mortal sin requires us to aim at the wrong end, which is proper to the will (1-2 q74 a4).[51] The passions contribute to sin by presenting something attractive that invites the will to consent.

We might suppose, however, that incontinence is voluntary and blameworthy action in which we act on passion against a settled judgment of practical reason. Aquinas can accept this description only if it is suitably qualified. If the incontinent action is, as he believes, voluntary, it must depend on the consent of the will. But how can the will consent to something other than the apparently greater good? Aquinas answers these questions by defending a modified Socratic account of incontinence (1-2 q77 a2; 2–2 q155 a3; 156 a1). Misdirected passion misleads our reason and will, so that we do not recognize the

---

[49] Saarinen, *WWMT* 118–31, examines Aquinas' views in their historical context.
[50] On the subject of virtue see §287.   [51] On mortal sin see §299n80.

overall badness of what we are doing. Incontinents, therefore, elect badly, because appetite influences them to change their election.[52]

Both the continent and the incontinent person lack the correct desire for the end (1-2 q58 a3 ad2; a5). Continent people grasp the end correctly, since their rational part works correctly.[53] But (as we saw in discussing Aristotle) not every sort of correct grasp of the end ensures the right sort of desire for the end. Continent people lack the right desire for the end, because their sensory desire is defective.[54] They face the demands of reason reluctantly, because their reason is somewhat clouded by the attractiveness of the goals presented by non-rational desires. Since they value the objects of their non-rational desires more than they should, they lack the right desire for the end, even though they desire (in one way) the right end. Similarly, incontinent people lack the right principles because of disordered non-rational desires (q58 a5).

This account might lead us to attribute to Aquinas a more sentimentalist view than he intends. He does not mean that in order to grasp ends correctly, we must add non-rational desire to rational desire. Nor does he suppose that non-rational desire forces us to abandon our plans; if it did, incontinent actions would not be voluntary. He suggests that the incontinent person knows the right universal principle, but the principle is corrupted in a particular case by some passion.

When the principle is corrupted, incontinents still do what they believe to be good, but sensory appetite (concupiscentia) affects beliefs about what is good; the object of appetite 'seems to be good, even though it is contrary to the universal judgment of reason' (q58 a5). Their appetite hinders them from considering the facts that would lead them to draw the appropriate conclusion in the particular case.[55] Since the resulting incontinent action is voluntary, the hindrance caused by passion does not make reason entirely ineffective. The

---

[52] 'In the one who does something through appetite, as the incontinent does, the previous will by which he was repudiating what he has the appetite for does not remain, but it [or 'he'?] is changed towards willing what he was previously repudiating. Accordingly, ... what is done through appetite is in no way involuntary. For the incontinent in relation to appetite acts counter to what he was previously proposing, but not counter to what he now wills . . . . (1-2 q6 a7 ad2). 'If appetite were to destroy knowledge altogether, as happens with those who become mad because of appetite, it would follow that appetite would take away the voluntary. . . . But sometimes in actions done through appetite knowledge is not completely destroyed, because the capacity to know is not destroyed entirely, but only the actual consideration in some particular possible act. Nevertheless, this itself is voluntary, in as much as what is in the capacity of the will is said to be voluntary, such as not acting, and not willing, and similarly not considering; for the will can resist the passion . . .' (ad3). 'Again, similarly, reason has the same state in both, since both the continent and the incontinent have correct reason, and each of them, while outside passion, elects on purpose not to follow his illicit appetites. But the first difference between them is found in their election, because the continent person, though he undergoes strong pleasures and appetites, elects not to follow them, because of reason, whereas the incontinent person elects to follow them, the contradiction of reason not hindering (non obstante contradictione rationis). Hence continence must reside in that power of the soul, whose act is election, and that power is the will . . .' (2-2 q155 a3). '. . . these passions, however strong they may be, are not the sufficient cause of incontinence, but only the occasion, since, so long as the use of reason remains, a human being can always resist his passions. . . . The cause of incontinence in itself belongs to the soul, which does not resist a passion by reason' (2-2 q156 a1). At in EN §439 (quia non immanet propriae [L; proprie, M] electioni propter concupiscentiam) Aquinas adds his own gloss to what Aristotle says, to show that Aristotle need not be denying that the incontinent acts on election.

[53] He attributes 'perfectio rationalis partis' to the continent; cf. 'quantumcumque rationalis pars sit perfecta' (q58 a3 ad2).

[54] . . . si appetitus sensitivus, quem movet rationalis pars, non sit perfectus (q58 a3 ad2).

[55] Cf. q77 a2: non considerat in particulari id quod scit in universali, inquantum passio impedit talem considerationem. See §250 on consideration.

incontinent's passion 'binds' reason (q77 a2 ad4), but this type of binding does not exclude consent and election.[56]

Aquinas is committed, therefore, to some elements of a Socratic account of incontinence. Incontinents, as he conceives them, do not know perfectly well that what they do is worse, all things considered, than some other available action. Many critics have argued that Socrates' denial of this knowledge to the incontinent person 'conflicts with the appearances'.[57] Many of these critics have added that the Aristotelian version of the Socratic position—knowledge in general, but ignorance in the particular case—retains the least credible aspect of the Socratic position. The same question arises about Aquinas' solution. If, however, he had agreed that incontinent people know that what they do is the worse option, he would have to concede either that they act contrary to the consent of the will, or that their will consents to what they know to be worse. The first concession implies that incontinents are not responsible for incontinent actions. The second concession undermines Aquinas' conception of the will and of the basis of human freedom.[58]

296. How Incontinence is Based on Consent

He defends his view of incontinence by arguing that since incontinent action is voluntary, it results from mistaken election.[59] But he does not mean that (for instance) the incontinent person temporarily believes that it is best, all things considered, to seduce his neighbour's wife, or to get himself drunk. If someone sins as a result of passion, '<his> purpose tends towards a good end, even though this purpose is interrupted for the moment because of passion' (q78 a4). He retains the correct end, but temporarily fails to pursue it, without electing the incontinent action as the best overall. His reason is 'bound', but this is the kind of binding that does not take away the use of reason, and therefore does not make our action involuntary.[60] Since incontinents act voluntarily, their action is explained by their

---

[56] On the two kinds of binding see §253.

[57] In commenting on this passage (*EN* 1145b27–31) Aquinas says: 'For we see clearly that some people do what they know to be bad. And if it is true that they sin because of ignorance that arises in them while they are in a passion—appetite or anger, say—it is best to inquire what sort of ignorance this is.' By adding to Aristotle, Aquinas alludes to his own view of Aristotle's solution.

[58] On this point about freedom Scotus rejects Aquinas' view; see §§360–1.

[59] Since vicious people also act on mistaken election, we might suppose that incontinents are temporarily vicious, differing from vicious people only because the mistaken election does not last as long. This supposition is explored by Kent, 'Transitory'.

[60] See *2Sent* d39 q3 a2 ad5 = P vi 741b: A defect in the conclusion of a practical syllogism arises 'from the force of passions that submerge and (as it were) bind the judgment of reason in a particular case, so that it does not actually consider this nor its opposite, but the will follows the pleasant thing that sense proposes'. Passion absorbs reason in considering some particular, so that the incontinent 'when he comes to this particular, since the state of correct reason has been bound through appetite, the person cannot advance to actual correct consideration about particulars' (*3Sent* d31 q1 a1 = P vii 333a, punctuation altered). Cf. *3Sent* d17 q1 a4 sc2. This is a temporary binding by passion (cf. *Iob* vii 4 = P xiv 33a) that does not take away voluntariness and sin (*Iob* xii 2 = P xiv 54a). Cf. *SG* iii 108 §2834. Extreme pleasure binds reason in a way or impedes it, just as in drunk people who have the use of reason bound or impeded (1-2 q33 a3; cf. q34 a1 ad1; *Mal.* q3 a8 = M 509a). People who are partly drunk get angry, *tamquam habentes iudicium rationis, sed impeditum* (1-2 q46 a4 ad3). Aquinas seems to distinguish the binding of people who are asleep or insane or drunk from the binding that is present in incontinents (though he is not completely clear about this; cf. *Mal.* q3 a9 = M 511b). In cases of voluntary error, it is up to us to prevent the binding of reason by passion (*Mal.* q3 a10, ad1, 2). Sometimes the

will and election, but not in the ordinary way. When we sin from passion, we sin 'electing (eligens), but not from election'. We elect to follow the mistaken suggestion of the passion in a direction that we would not take if the passion had not suggested it to us.[61]

Aquinas perhaps means to contrast two judgments: (1) It is best all things considered to do what my passion tells me (and it tells me to do x). (2) Doing x is best all things considered here and now (and my passion tells me to do x). When we sin from passion, we make the first sort of judgment, but not the second. The passion—my desire for revenge, for instance—does not alter my conception of the good so that I really think it better to take revenge even at the cost of all the resulting evils. But revenge is attractive enough to make me think it is all right to listen to my passion on this occasion rather than to follow my conception of the good. If I choose to ignore the content of my conception of the good, my choice reflects my views about my ultimate end and about when it is necessary or desirable to act on deliberation about the good. Such choices confirm Aquinas' distinction between actions that we do 'electing' and those we do 'from election'. What the incontinent elects as best is not seducing the wife of one's neighbour, but following the suggestion of the passion. He allows himself to be persuaded that it is best to follow his passion here and now, because he attends more to the attractiveness of the object of the passion than to the demands of his conception of the good.

Incontinents are not to be blamed simply for listening to a current passion; for that may sometimes be a sensible thing to do. It is wise to attend to our passions if they help us to identify what matters when we try to deliberate.[62] They may do this even when they conflict with our initial rational judgment; if, for instance, we are vividly aware of the suffering inflicted by our (as we supposed) just punishment, we may have a good reason to follow our current reaction, and to think again about whether the punishment is really just.

Incontinents are mistaken because they listen to the wrong sort of passion. We attend to our reluctance to inflict severe suffering because we assume that such reluctance is generally appropriate; but we would be wrong to attend to our dislike of the person to whom we think we owe an apology. The incontinent person is at fault for his willingness to follow a passion

---

passion binds the reason in such a way that it causes an election; here it cannot be the source of involuntary action (*Mal.* q3 a12 ad12 = M 516b). Aquinas introduces binding in his account of Aristotle on incontinence. See *in EN* vii 3 §1347; 6 §1394; 10 §1460.

[61] In these cases 'the election is the first principle of sinning, given that it is caused from passion; and for that reason such a person is not said to sin from election, though he sins electing' (*Mal.* q3 a12 ad11). The passion 'causes the election in so far as it binds reason for the moment' (*Mal.* q3 a12 ad12). 'It is one thing to sin electing and another to sin from election. For one who sins from passion, sins electing but not from election, because election is not in him the first principle of his sin, but he is induced from passion to elect what he would not elect if he were outside the passion' (1-2 q78 a4 ad3). 'Now in the intemperate person the will turns towards sin from its own election, which proceeds from a state acquired through habituation, whereas in the incontinent the will turns towards sin from some passion' (2-2 q156 a3). 'Now in both the incontinent and the intemperate person, ignorance arises from desire being turned towards something, either through passion, as in the incontinent, or through a state [of character], as in the intemperate person. Nevertheless greater ignorance is caused in this way in the intemperate than in the incontinent. In one respect as regards duration, since in the incontinent this ignorance lasts only while the passion lasts . . . In another respect the ignorance of the intemperate person is greater as regards what he does not know. For the ignorance of the incontinent person concerns some particular object of election, in so far as he thinks that this is now to be elected; but the intemperate person is ignorant about the end itself, inasmuch as he judges this thing good, to follow his appetites without restraint. Hence the Philosopher says that "the incontinent is better than the intemperate person, because the best principle is preserved in him", namely the right estimate of the end' (2-2 q156 a3 ad1). See also §255 on indirectly voluntary actions.

[62] See above §289.

without examination; he complacently assumes that it is all right to follow this passion, even though it inclines him to do what he thinks is worse on the basis of his deliberation. His assumption is made easier by the immediate attractiveness of an action suggested by a passion.[63]

We can now see how the incontinent's judgment is temporarily warped by passion, even though he has also formed a judgment that opposes the suggestion of his passions. We can see something similar in other cases where we elect a procedure rather than an action. If I decide to do whatever you decide on, I may still think it best to follow this procedure, even if I also deliberate directly about the action on my own account and think it would be better not to do it. This apparent conflict of judgments corresponds, in Aquinas' view, to the condition of the incontinent.

His account of action suggests an alternative or supplement to this claim that the incontinent acts 'electing but not from election'. The passions are sources of voluntary action in so far as the will consents to them.[64] Since Aquinas thinks consent differs from election in requiring only the judgment that a proposed action is satisfactory (placet) rather than the judgment that it is best, we might suggest that the incontinent judges only that it is all right to do what passion suggests, even though he also judges that it would be best all things considered not to get drunk now.

We can also understand this attitude by considering inter-personal cases. If a child asks a parent for another sweet, the parent may judge that it is better overall not to give the sweet, but none the less suppose it is all right to give way to the child's demand, if the child is being a nuisance. Further reflexion might convince the parent that it would be better not to give way, but to put up with the nuisance, and she may even be aware of this, but at the moment she may be so fed up with the child's complaints that she thinks it is all right to give way to them.[65]

We might take this role of consent to show that we need not assume an election whenever we choose one action over another. Alternatively, we might say that it gives the minimal conditions in which we elect one action over another; we elect x over y provided that we consent to x when our passions suggest doing x. This role for consent explains how the will of the incontinent person is engaged, even if he does not view his action as the best available in the circumstances.

Aquinas' account of consent suggests yet a further possible role for the will. We have taken consent to require the judgment that the action consented to is satisfactory or acceptable. But he does not always require consent to include this positive judgment. Sometimes he suggests that we can consent to x simply by failing to dissent from x when we have the opportunity. This 'tacit' or 'negative' consent may fit the role of the will in incontinent action. Even if the incontinent person does not judge it to be best, or even satisfactory, to follow his appetite, perhaps his will is capable of intervening to prevent the incontinent action, but consents negatively by non-intervention.

---

[63] On the relation between this distinction and Green's claims about the will see Green, PE §147.

[64] 'Sometimes, however, the passion is not great enough to take away the use of reason altogether; and then reason can shut out the passion, by turning to other thoughts, or it can prevent it from having its effect, because one's limbs are not applied to action except by the consent of reason, as stated above. And so such a passion does not excuse from sin altogether' (1-2 q77 a7).

[65] On prematurely ceasing deliberation see §262.

Negative consent should not include every failure to intervene in a choice. Failure to intervene might be explained in various ways—inattention, psychological compulsion, indifference to overall good. None of these explanations fits Aquinas' view of negative consent. In the incontinent's negative consent, non-intervention results from some deliberative failure. Incontinents (in Aquinas' view) have failed to make clear to themselves why it is bad to follow the policy of acquiescence in the suggestions made by appetites in these circumstances. He still appeals to ignorance; incontinents would not act as they do if they had clearly seen what is wrong with the policy that they follow.

This account explains why common sense is right to believe that incontinents know that what they are doing is wrong; for Aquinas agrees that they can act against an explicit judgment that what they are doing is worse all things considered. This judgment comes from their deliberation focussed directly on the action. Common sense, however, does not distinguish this judgment from a judgment on whether it is all right to go along with the passions on this occasion. In Aquinas' view, incontinents consent to going along with the passions; their consent comes from deliberation about the procedure rather than the action. The difference between these two questions for deliberation shows why common sense might be right about the incontinent's attitude to one question, without considering the other question. Aquinas alters and expands Aristotle's account to allow a more credible analysis of the incontinent person's choice.

297. Deliberate Fault

Sin through deliberate fault seems to be similar to sin through passion in so far as it results from 'disorder' or 'misdirection' (inordinatio, 1-2 q78 a1) that leads to the choice of a lesser good over a greater. If one's consent leads to sin, the good that the will consents to is the lesser good, so that the will is disordered. Aquinas' description of sin through deliberate fault suggests that the passions play some role in presenting the lesser good that the disordered will pursues. But if we sin through deliberate fault, our pursuit of a lesser good is not simply the result of an occurrent passion that diverts us from our normal way of comparing different goods; the movement towards sin is proper to the will.[66] In this case we cannot plead the excuse of a misdirected passion misleading us on a particular occasion (ad horam). We have a mistaken conception of the composition of the end, and we follow this conception even when we are not being influenced by a passion. Sinners from deliberate fault may still value the higher goods, but they value lower goods more than they should, and they are prepared to risk a loss of higher goods to keep the lower goods (q78 a1).[67]

Intellectual error is part of this sin, but not its cause. Our intellectual error would be the cause if we reflected on the components of happiness and reached the wrong answer—if, for instance, we concluded that fornication is not a sin (Mal. q2 a3 ad9). Deliberate fault,

---

[66] 'A sin from deliberate fault is more serious than a sin from passion, for three reasons. First, because, as sin consists chiefly in will, to the extent that the movement of sin is more proper to the will, to that extent, other things being equal, a sin is more serious. Now when one sins from deliberate fault, the movement of sin is more proper to the will, which is moved towards evil from itself . . .' (1-2 q78 a4).

[67] See §319.

however, results from a misdirected affection for something that warps our conception of the good.[68] The judgment of intellect is warped by our antecedent and unquestioned preferences.[69] We deliberate on the right occasions, but we stop when we have reached a good that ought not to stop our deliberation; we ought to look for reasons that might tell against pursuing this immediately attractive good, but we do not bother to look for them. We stop when our misguided affection makes it sufficiently attractive to us to persuade us that no further deliberation is needed (*SG* iii 10 §1950).[70]

Different roles of passion and consent divide venial (i.e., pardonable) from mortal sins.[71] Sudden motions of the passions may be undesirable, but they are simply venial sins, because they include no consent.[72] Consent to the object of a passion makes a sin mortal (1-2 q77 a8). Deliberation and consent determine whether we have turned away from the right conception of the ultimate end.[73] Some sins are mortal in their genus, because no one could undertake them without having a warped conception of the ultimate good; still, simply thinking of them is not a mortal sin. If we also elect them, we sin mortally.[74] In suggesting that the choice of immoral action involves a false conception of the end, Aquinas implies that the right conception of the ultimate end requires recognition of the non-instrumental value of morally virtuous action; that is why the virtuous person and the sinner do not disagree simply about the choice of means to an end.

The division between venial and mortal sin, as Aquinas conceives it, does not imply that all mortal sins are sins from deliberate fault. Sins resulting from passion may also be mortal, since they result in voluntary action when the will consents to them. In sins from passion and in sins from deliberate fault, deliberation is prematurely halted and diverted. In sins from passion this is because of the suddenness of the passion. In sins from deliberate fault, deliberation stops too soon because it is warped even when we are not subject to a sudden passion. In both cases, we do not complete deliberation as we should.

298. Sin and Vice

Aquinas believes that sin from deliberate fault is compatible with the absence of vice. The misdirection of the will involved in deliberate fault may be intermittent or partial, so that it does not turn the will completely in the wrong direction (q78 a3). In the vicious person 'the will is inclined towards sinning from its own election, which proceeds from a state acquired through habituation' (2-2 q156 a3). The first clause does not distinguish vice from deliberate fault; the distinction lies in the second clause, mentioning a state acquired through repetition and habituation.

Is the difference between deliberate fault and vice just a matter of frequency? Could a non-vicious person's sin from deliberate fault be just as bad as a vicious person's, and involve

---

[68] 'When someone has a misdirected affection for something, the judgment of intellect is impeded in a particular object of election because of misdirected affection. And thus the defect (*vitium*) is not in cognition but in affection. And that is why one who sins in this way is not said to sin out of ignorance, but in ignorance, as is said in *Ethics* III' (*Mal.* q2 a3 ad9).

[69] Cf. Aristotle on vice, §84. On intemperance see Bradley, *ATHG* 279–81.   [70] See §248.

[71] See 1-2 q72 a5–6; q74 a9; q77 a8; q87 a5; q88 a1.   [72] See 1-2 q74 a10; q77 a8; q89 a3.

[73] See q88 a2; q89 a4 (angels do not deliberate); 2-2 q33 a2 ad3; q44 a4.

[74] See 2-2 q35 a3; q36 a3, ad1; q37 a1; q38 a1.

an equally corrupt will, so that it would fail to be vicious simply because it was not habitual? Or must the non-vicious person's election be less corrupt than the vicious person's?

Mere frequency does not mark the right division.[75] If someone's election at a particular time is so bad that it is committed to all the actual and counterfactual choices of a vicious person, for the vicious person's reasons, then the agent has turned so far in the vicious direction that he seems to have become vicious. If he is capable of returning to the virtuous person's outlook, virtue and vice are not as permanent as Aristotle takes them to be. Even if the agent does not change his state of character in these cases, the distinction between a sinful condition and a vicious state is not very important, since they may both include the same misdirection of the will.

It is more plausible to claim that sin from deliberate fault involves a misdirected election that is different from the incontinent person's election, but still not as bad as the vicious person's. The relevant differences may not be obvious if we think of an election too narrowly as a choice of a single action. From this point of view, someone who sins from deliberate fault seems quite similar to the vicious person. Suppose, for instance, that a public official takes a bribe to allow a firm to pollute the water supply. He recognizes that he violates the responsibilities of his office and damages the health of his fellow-citizens, but definitely decides that he is willing to take the bribe under these conditions. Someone who is willing to do this shows himself to be different from an incontinent person (who gives way to a sudden temptation), and different from a person with misguided affections (who turns a blind eye to the pollution to protect the reputation of his daughter, who has stolen from the firm).

Still, his election is different from the vicious person's. For an election is the product of deliberation, and different sequences of deliberation result in different elections, even if the elections settle on the same action.[76] An agent's deliberation represents the reasons that weigh with him, and the value he attaches to the pursuit of different ends. Someone could form the wrong election about this particular action, by mistakenly thinking that in these circumstances the gain from taking the bribe is great enough to justify an unjust action; but he need not believe, as the vicious person does, that considerations of justice count for little or nothing in comparison with the rewards of injustice. His threshold for preferring the gains of an unjust action is lower than it should be, but not as low as it would be in a genuinely unjust person.

This description of the non-vicious person who sins from deliberate fault helps to explain why this sort of sin does not completely destroy the virtue that is opposed to it. Even if someone reaches the wrong conclusion on a particular occasion, he may not act for all the wrong reasons that move a vicious person, and may not share the vicious person's indifference to the right reasons. The error that leads the official to think it is all right to take a bribe on this occasion does not by itself show that he would, say, be indifferent if his subordinates failed to do their jobs properly; he need not have lost all the attitudes characteristic of a just person. He is inconsistent in defending his own wrongdoing while trying to prevent wrongdoing by others; this inconsistency distinguishes him from the thoroughly unjust person. Sinning from deliberate fault does not require the whole state

---

[75] Arpaly, UV 93–8, discusses relevant questions about frequency and stability.

[76] On deliberation and election see Aristotle's discussion of good deliberation in EN vi 9, and the next note.

and outlook of the vicious person; if we deliberate wrongly on a particular occasion, or on a specific type of occasion, we still may not reject all the patterns of deliberation that are characteristic of the virtuous person.

299. Sin and Virtue

For these reasons, we might agree with Aquinas in suggesting that sin, even beyond continence and incontinence, is consistent with the absence of vice. This is a plausible addition to Aristotle, suggesting how we ought to conceive some of the conditions intermediate between virtue and vice. It is more surprising that Aquinas takes all the types of sins he distinguishes, including sin from deliberate fault, to be compatible with the presence of virtue. If he is right about this, not everyone who commits sin is in a condition between virtue and vice; some may be virtuous.

Aquinas argues that sin is compatible with acquired virtues because virtues are states that do not necessarily produce their appropriate effects in the appropriate circumstances. Instead 'a man uses it [sc. the state] when he wills' (1-2 q71 a4). Aquinas, agreeing with a comment by Averroes, seems to be treating virtues as though they conformed to the principle that Aristotle lays down for rational capacities, that they can be used in opposite ways. A vicious person who sins need not always sin from deliberate fault, but sometimes may simply be swayed by passion, and sometimes may even do a virtuous action, 'because his reason is not completely corrupted through the bad state, but some of it remains undamaged' (1-2 q78 a2). Similarly, we may suppose, our will may be correctly directed far enough to form a virtuous state, but still be imperfect enough to elect not to exercise that state on a particular occasion.

This parallel between virtue and vice is difficult to reconcile with Aristotle's and Aquinas' conception of the moral virtues. Aristotle does not treat the virtues as a mere set of capacities that are so detached from one's will that one can still decide whether to exercise them or not. On the contrary, the virtues constitute a determinate way of using one's rational capacities. Aquinas brings out this feature of the virtues even more clearly than Aristotle does, in so far as he approves the description of virtuous action as 'the good use of freewill' (q55 a1 ad2) and of the virtues as the states that produce this good use. In describing virtues as states, Aquinas says correctly that they direct our rational capacities to the right actualizations (q55 a1); this is why we need states as well as capacities (cf. q49 a4). Aquinas' claim about virtue and sin seems to reduce virtue to one of the rational capacities that it was supposed to direct towards the right actualization, as though some further virtue were needed to ensure the right use of the virtue.

We might be especially doubtful about his suggestion that we decide whether or not to exercise our virtue. We can understand the claim that we decide whether or not to exercise our medical knowledge or our knowledge of French. We consider whether this is the right occasion, and we might be right or wrong in our estimate of the occasion. We might also decide to use our knowledge well or badly. But these are the points on which Aristotle contrasts a craft with a virtue. Aquinas seems to revert to the view that virtues can be used well or badly.

Against these objections, we might defend Aquinas' position as a realistic conception of virtue. If a virtue is a relatively permanent condition, it may persist despite a relatively isolated error; for a single error does not necessarily destroy the accumulated tendencies and dispositions that have been built up in a virtuous person's character. Perhaps the virtuous person ought to be allowed to lapse occasionally without being demoted to an intermediate position between virtue and vice.

This claim seems defensible independently of Aquinas' suggestion that we can decide whether or not to exercise our virtue. The most plausible way to explain occasional lapses is to say not that we decide not to exercise our virtue in this case, but that we fail to think about this case in the way a virtuous person would, and in the way in which we normally think about such cases. In thinking this way, we do not show our decision about how to use the virtue we have; we betray the fact that we lack the complete virtue, though we have enough of the virtue to make us brave (for instance), rather than vicious or intermediate between virtue and vice.

This way of understanding virtue is not Aristotle's way, but we might defend it by appeal to Aristotle. The virtuous person's election requires good deliberation, which requires not only the correct conclusion, but the conclusion resulting from the right reasoning (EN 1142b22–4).[77] Correct reasoning requires a grasp of the right reasons for the action, and hence of the changes in circumstances that would or would not require a different action. Someone who faces danger for the right reasons knows that she still ought to face it if she were offered a bribe to avoid it, but ought not to face it out of mere bravado if nothing worthwhile would be gained by facing it. In this respect, the demand for acting on the right reasons captures the sort of commitment that Kant captures in his account of the good will.[78]

Most people do not completely meet these demands. Many of us are willing to face a moderate degree of danger, enough to keep us from cowardice in ordinary circumstances, but we would not necessarily be willing to face the special dangers that many Germans during the Third Reich might have had to face in order to protect their Jewish neighbours from harm. Still, even though we lack the degree of commitment that the complete virtue demands, we might not agree that we all entirely lack the virtue of bravery.

This reflexion on ordinary human limitations supports Aquinas' view that a specific virtue does not prevent some of the sins contrary to the virtue. To be free of these limitations is to have a 'heroic' virtue.[79] Such a virtue is a gift of the Holy Spirit, not an achievement of our unaided effort. In denying that acquired virtues exclude the sins opposed to them, Aquinas fits his treatment of the Aristotelian virtues into his theological outlook. But his claims are independently plausible. If we recognize the 'normal' circumstances in which we expect someone's commitment to a virtue to be firm and stable, we can allow a virtue to someone who has this sort of stable commitment, without ruling out the possibility of lapses.

---

[77] Aquinas, in EN vi 8 §1230, takes Aristotle to be speaking of finding the right end but pursuing it through the wrong means (malam viam: L text); this is a misunderstanding of ho men dei (quod oportet) and di'hou (per quod) in the text. Hence he illustrates the point with an example of someone who steals to help a poor man. §1231 tries to explain away the oddity of treating the end as the conclusion and the means as the middle term. Contrast the explanation offered in Irwin, EN, on vi 9.5. Aquinas agrees with Albert, SE vi 14 §560.

[78] See Kant, G 398–400.

[79] See 1-2 q54 a3; q68 a2; 2–2 q159 a2 ad1; 3a q7 a2 ad2.

Though Aquinas allows virtue to co-exist with sin, he does not allow virtues to exist without one another. On this point he accepts the reciprocity of the virtues.[80] Since the loss of any one virtue expels prudence, and prudence is required for any of the virtues, the loss of any one virtue expels all the others 'as far as concerns the complete and formal being of virtue'. All that remains in that case is 'tendencies (inclinationes) towards acts of the virtues, acts which do not have the character (ratio) of virtue' (1-2 q73 a1 ad2).[81]

Perhaps Aquinas' belief in the fallibility of virtue would be more plausible if he did not connect it so closely with his claim that frequency of failure separates sin from vice. An 'isolated' error does not convict an agent of vice, but 'isolation' may not be simply a matter of frequency. If someone has acted fairly and justly in cases where he has had little temptation to act unfairly, but he sins from deliberate fault on the few occasions on which he gains something by unfairness, we might reasonably conclude that he is unjust. Even though he has lapsed on only a few occasions, these are occasions that normally face a just person and are of the sort that the virtue is designed to cope with.

By contrast, if someone acts justly in the situations that normally provide a test of someone's commitment to justice, but lapses when he faces some unusual temptation, or he is unprepared, has his attention distracted, or is in some other condition making it more than normally difficult to act justly, we might conclude that he is still just, though he has the bad luck to be in one of these conditions more often than most people are. The second person's lapses are more isolated from his character than the first person's lapses are, even though they may be more frequent.

Aquinas may be wrong, then, to focus on frequency and rarity of lapses as the basis for distinguishing sin from vice. He ought to focus on actions that do or do not tend to destroy the state of character that a virtuous agent has built up. Frequency is often a rough guide to such actions, but, as we can see if we consider some cases, it is not the right basis for drawing the relevant distinctions.

300. The General Tendency of Aquinas' View of Virtue

Aquinas' discussion of sin and vice is a test case for his claims about the will and virtue. This is one of the most obscure areas of Aristotle's discussion; Aquinas tries to clarify Aristotle by appeal to aspects of the will that he emphasizes more strongly than Aristotle does. In particular he relies on his account of the relations between the passions and the will. He does not remove all the obscurities in Aristotle, partly because his conception of consent and election is obscure on some points. Still, a reasonable interpretation of his remarks on consent explains sin and vice also. In examining vice as well as virtue, Aquinas demonstrates the explanatory power of his account of agency.

---

[80] 'One act even of mortal sin does not remove the state of acquired virtue. But if the acts are multiplied so much that the contrary state is produced, then the state of <the> acquired virtue is expelled. And when this <one> virtue has been expelled, prudence is expelled; for when a human being acts against any one of the virtues, he acts against prudence' (q73 a1 ad2).

[81] On the reciprocity of the virtues see §325.

His account of moral virtue emphasizes the aspect of Aristotle's account that connects virtue with correct election.[82] Aquinas has not only Aristotle's reasons, but also some reasons of his own, for emphasizing this feature of the virtues. The virtues are states that express freewill, and human beings have freewill in so far as they deliberate and elect; hence the virtues embody a distinct form of deliberation and election. Aquinas' claims about action and freedom agree with Aristotle's claim that correct election is the mark of moral virtue.

Aquinas, no less than Aristotle, has to explain why the moral virtues are essentially forms of correct deliberation and election, if they are so closely connected with the passions. The passions do not move us to free action without the consent of the will; they are elements of moral virtues in so far as they are subject to the consent of the will. To decide whether Aquinas makes Aristotle's position better or worse, we need to decide whether his views about consent capture the ways in which passions contribute to the goodness or badness of actions and characters.

While these views on the will and on election determine Aquinas' general theory of the moral virtues, he does not always seem to follow them. We have seen why it is difficult to reconcile his views on the importance of the will and correct election with his claim that the passions, as opposed to the will, are the subjects of some moral virtues. He would follow his general theory more consistently if he allowed both will and passion to be the subject of each virtue that involves the regulation of passion. This view that allows two subjects seems to fit better than Aquinas' actual view fits with the specific remarks he makes about the virtues and passions.

The claim that virtue consists in correct deliberation and election requires a credible account of the relevant sort of deliberation. Aquinas seeks this account through his discussion of prudence, which opens further questions about his view of practical reason.

---

[82] See §111.

21

AQUINAS: NATURAL LAW

---

301. Questions Raised by Natural Law

Our discussion of the moral virtues has led us to some questions about Aquinas' conception of practical reason. But before we can examine these questions, we need to consider an aspect of his moral theory that may appear to lead him in a different direction.

So far we have presented his approach to morality as a teleological theory; it begins from an account of the rational will aiming at the ultimate end and deliberating about the actions that achieve it. This deliberation results in the formation of the will and the passions in specific states of character aiming at the ultimate end.

But Aquinas also treats morality as a set of principles specifying the requirements of natural law.[1] He finds an Aristotelian source for his doctrine of natural law. Aristotle divides natural from legal justice; according to Aquinas, natural justice is embodied in the principles of natural law.[2] Jurists tend to speak of natural right (ius) only when they refer to the nature common to human beings and other animals. When they refer to a human being's nature as human 'in so far as he discerns wrong (turpe) and right (honestum) in accordance with reason', they speak of the right (ius) of nations; but Aquinas insists that both aspects of a human being's nature are included under natural justice (in EN v 12 §1019). The principles that he mentions here are those he normally includes under natural law; they are universally valid and (in a way to be further explained) universally known (ST 1-2 q94 a4).

Mediaeval discussion of natural law is derived from Stoic sources. Christian writers use Stoic claims to interpret St Paul's remarks on the Gentiles who are a 'law to themselves'.[3] Their discussion of natural law develops independently of any reference to Aristotle. Aquinas, however, combines it with his exposition of Aristotelian ethics. He implies that questions

---

[1] 'Just as the human soul has a natural state by which it comes to know the principles of theoretical sciences, a state we call understanding of principles, so also it has a natural state that possesses the first principles of matters of action, principles which are natural principles of natural right (ius). And this state belongs to universal conscience (synderesim)' (Ver. q16 a1). On the relation of ius and lex see 2-2 q57 a1 ad2. Cf. Suarez, Leg. i 2.4.

[2] '... in practical matters there are some principles naturally known, indemonstrable principles of a sort and <principles> close (propinqua) to these, such as that evil is to be avoided, no one is to be unjustly injured, theft is not to be committed, and so on' (in EN v 12 §1018).

[3] On Rm. 2:14 and earlier discussions see §§206 and §232. On discussions of natural law before Aquinas see Lottin, PM ii, ch. 3.

about natural law belong to an inquiry into natural justice. He connects St Paul's claims with his own doctrine of conscience and practical reason.[4] On the strength of St Paul's description of the Gentiles, Aquinas argues that conscience makes us aware of a natural law.[5]

This conception of morality as consisting in principles of a universal natural law may seem to conflict with the self-centred eudaemonism of a teleological conception of the virtues. Prescription independent of our desires seems to conflict with the dependence of the virtues on our desire for happiness. If this is Aquinas' view of natural law, his moral theory includes important non-teleological elements. If natural law is independent of eudaemonist practical reason, Aquinas recognizes an independent source of moral principles, and so raises questions about conflict and priority.

We will see, however, that Aquinas does not intend his doctrine of natural law to introduce any conflict with the eudaemonist aspects of his claims about the virtues. On the contrary, it both relies on and supports his general account of the will and of rational action. It will be useful to discuss his view of natural law before turning to his account of practical reason and of the morally right.

302. Questions about Law

Aquinas' claims about natural law depend on his general treatment of law. The Treatise on Law follows the Treatise on Vices and Sins, because law is one of God's means for leading us back from sin to God. Aquinas describes how sin obscures and distorts our grasp of moral

---

[4] 'He commends in them [sc. the Gentiles] the observance of the law, when he says "they do naturally the things contained in the law", that is to say, the things that the law commands, namely as far as concerns moral precepts, which are from the dictate of natural reason, just as it is also said about Job that he was just, upright and God-fearing, and avoiding evil. . . . "naturally" can be taken to mean "through the natural law showing them what is to be done", according to that passage "Many say: 'Who will show us good things?'. Imprinted [upon us is the light of your countenance, O Lord]", which is the light of natural reason, in which is the image of God. . . . He shows their worthiness, namely in the fact that, while not having a law of this particular sort, they are a law to themselves, namely to the extent that they carry out the duty of the law bearing on themselves, by instructing themselves and leading themselves towards good, because, as the Philosopher says, "law is discourse that has compulsion, proceeding from a certain sort of prudence and understanding". [*EN* 1180a21; contrast the translation at *in EN* x 14 §1505.] And that is why it is said that "law is not laid down for a just person" [*1Tim*. 1:9]—that is to say, he is not compelled by external law—"but" it is laid down "for unjust people", who need to be compelled externally. And this is the highest degree of worthiness (dignitas) in human beings, namely that they are led not by others but by themselves towards good' (*in Rom.* ii 3). On *1Tim*. 1:9 cf. *SG* iii 128 §3008.

In the passage omitted here Aquinas discusses Augustine's first interpretation (Ambrosiaster's) of the passage in *Romans*. See §226. He says: 'But as to his saying "naturally", a question arises. For it seems to support the Pelagians, who said that a human being by his natural [abilities] can observe all the precepts of the law. Hence "naturally" should be explained as meaning "through nature reformed by grace". For he is speaking of Gentiles converted to faith, who by the help of the grace of Christ had begun to observe the moral [precepts] of the law.' Augustine's first interpretation does not commit Paul to claims about natural law. But most of Aquinas' exposition relies on the second interpretation he offers (a development of Augustine's second interpretation), which takes Paul to attribute some awareness of morality to everyone.

At 'Imprinted . . .' Aquinas quotes the first word of *Psalms* 4:7. His Vulg. Psalter, reading 'imprinted' (signatum), follows LXX (*esêmeiôthê*). The same verse is quoted by Augustine in *S et L*. Sanderson, *DOC* 4.12, notes that he will avoid reliance on this verse, since other people's use of it rests on a defective translation.

[5] He quotes the Gloss on the passage in *Romans*: 'Though they [sc. the Gentiles] have not got the written law, still they have the natural law, by which anyone understands and is conscious to himself (sibi conscius est) what is good and what is evil' (1-2 q91 a2 sc). He also quotes the passage at 1-2 q109 a4 obj1; *Virt*. a8 obj3; *Ver*. q11 a2 obj5; q17 a1 sc2. He alludes to it at 1a q79 a13; *Quodl*. q3 a26 = P ix 504b. On the highest degree of dignitas, which consists in following the law without coercion, see *SG* iii 128 §3008: '[They] are a law to themselves, since they have charity, which inclines them in place of a law and makes them act generously (liberaliter)'.

principles, especially when we face particular situations and choices to which the principles are relevant.[6] To overcome these effects of sin, God instructs us through law and helps us through grace,[7] and among the laws that God has given to instruct us is the natural law.

Aquinas discusses the necessary conditions for a law and the way in which natural law satisfies them. His discussion is cautious, and not entirely unambiguous. It results in considerable dispute among later Scholastics who discuss the relation of morality to natural law and the way in which natural law is law.

At this point in the *Summa*, we have learnt about moral virtues and the principles of practical reason. When Aquinas tells us that these are the content of a natural law, we might take him in either of two ways: (a) An inflationary view: These are not only principles of practical reason, but also precepts of a natural law; because they are precepts of a law, they have some practical significance that they would not have otherwise. (b) A deflationary view: By being principles of practical reason they count as precepts of a natural law; on the correct understanding of law, that is all it takes for them to be a sort of law. Their being a law adds nothing to the practical significance they already have as principles of practical reason.

These two views of natural law correspond to two ways of connecting morality and law. (1) We might regard law as a social institution, involving a recognized legislator issuing orders demanding compliance, and we might try to understand morality as consisting of the orders issued by some legislator. In that case we assimilate moral principles to our prior understanding of law and legal principles. (2) We might begin from our understanding of moral principles, and try to form a conception of law that allows us to understand moral principles as a sort of law. In that case, we assimilate some laws to our prior understanding of moral principles.

If Aquinas uses the first direction of argument, he takes morality to consist essentially and fundamentally in the requirements of some law, and therefore may reasonably be called a 'natural law moralist'. Some 17th-century moralists, and especially Cumberland, Locke, and Pufendorf, are natural law moralists in this sense. We might suppose that Aquinas agrees with them in making legal obligations and demands fundamental in morality. If that is his view, he departs from an Aristotelian view of morality.[8]

If, however, Aquinas uses the second direction of argument, he does not conclude that morality is fundamentally law. His identification of morality with one kind of law clarifies the nature of one kind of law by reference to morality; it does not explain morality by reference to law.

His initial remarks might reasonably suggest that he holds an inflationary view, and that his account of morality as law rests on an antecedent understanding of law. In his view, law is a rule[9] that involves commands, moves agents to action, imposes obligation, and requires publication.[10] If these features of law essentially involve legislation and a legislator, natural

---

[6] See §313 below.

[7] 'For the external principle moving us towards the good is God, who both instructs us through law and helps us through grace' (1-2 q90 pref.) Jordan, 'Scientia' 90, discusses the position of the Treatise on Law in *ST* 1–2. See also Westberg, *RPR* 229–30.

[8] This is the conclusion of Anscombe, 'Modern'.

[9] 1-2 q90 a1: 'Law is some sort of (quaedam) rule and measure of acts, in accordance with which someone is led towards acting or is restrained from acting; for law (lex) is spoken of from binding (ligare), because it binds (obligat) one to acting'.

[10] q90 a4: 'A law is imposed on others by way of a rule and measure. Now a rule or measure is imposed by being applied to those who ought to be regulated and measured by it. Hence, in order for a law to acquire the power of obliging that is proper to a law, it is necessary that it be applied to the human beings who ought (debent) to be regulated by it.

law essentially involves legislation and a legislator. To see whether he takes these features to imply legislation, we need to consider the components of his account of a law.

303. Law and Obligation

The specific way in which law moves to action is 'obliging' or 'binding' to action (q90 a1).[11] When Aquinas speaks of our being 'bound' or 'obliged' he often seems to have in mind some specific act of binding. In this sense he speaks of an obligation resulting from a promise (2-2 q88 a1), including the vows made at one's baptism or in entering into some specific condition of life.[12] In all these cases obligation seems to presuppose an act of obliging. If, then, natural law necessarily obliges, it should involve some specific act of obliging by God and our awareness of it as coming from this source.[13]

In contrast to this narrow use of 'oblige', Aquinas uses 'ought' (debere) and 'duty' (debitum) in cases where they do not seem to rest on any act of obliging. A duty or something due (debitum) implies a 'need' or 'exigence' (1a q21 a1 ad3). Aquinas distinguishes what is due morally from what is due legally. When something is due legally, it involves constraint by a law; this is what he normally calls 'obligation'. What is due morally is demanded by moral rightness; it does not result from anyone's act of imposing an obligation.[14] A moral duty results from 'the appropriateness of the thing' (convenientia rei) (1-2 q60 a3).[15]

Aquinas does not identify a duty of justice with a duty that we are obliged (obligari) to perform; he identifies it with a duty that we can reasonably be compelled by law to perform, so that when we are compelled by law, we are obliged. Hence he tends to use 'due' or

---

Such application is made by its being brought to their notice by the publication itself. Therefore publication is necessary for the law to obtain its power.'

[11] Something that is moved by natural necessity cannot be bound; fire, for instance, is not bound to move upwards (*Ver.* q17 a3 c). Conscience binds us only in so far as it gives us knowledge of a law made by a superior, and specifically of a divine law (*Ver.* q17 a3 c = M 332b). 'A human being does not make a law for himself, but through the act of his cognition, by which he recognizes (cognoscit) a law made by another, he is bound to fulfilling the law' (q17 a3 ad1). Similarly, the discussion of the question whether a mistaken conscience obliges (1-2 q19 a5) seems to assume that conscience presents its demand as a command of God (esp. ad2). See also *2Sent.* d39 q3 a3 ad3; *Ver.* q17 a4, esp. ad2.

[12] See 2-2 q185 a5; Supp. q43 a2; q61 a3.

[13] Suarez relies on this inference in order to suggest that Aquinas agrees with him in taking natural law to involve a divine command. See, e.g., *Leg.* ii 6.10.

[14] 'The legal due is that which one is constrained by law (lege adstringitur) to render; and this due is chiefly the concern of justice, which is the principal virtue. On the other hand, the moral due is what someone owes (debet) out of the rightness (honestas) of virtue: and since a due implies necessity, this kind of due has two degrees. For one due is so necessary that without it rightness in morality (honestas morum) cannot be maintained; and this has more of the character of due. . . . There is another due that is necessary in the sense that it conduces to greater rightness, although without it rightness may be maintained. This due is the concern of generosity, affability or friendship, or the like, all of which . . . have little of the character of the due' (2-2 q80 a1).

[15] Sometimes Aquinas distinguishes legal from moral justice, in accordance with (respectively) 'a rule of a determining law' and 'a rule of reason' that involves something due (2-2 q58 a11). Within the morally due, we must also distinguish what is strictly required (tamquam necessarium) and 'prescribed' (praeceptum) from what is better and 'mandated' (mandatum) (1-2 q99 a5; cf. 2-2 q23 a3 ad1). In the second case of the morally due, what is due is due 'not out of a necessity of justice, but because of a certain moral equity, as in the case of benefits received in return for nothing' (2-2 q31 a3 ad3). In the case of what is due by justice, 'someone may be bound (obligari potest) by a fixed contract', but in the second case something is due out of friendship, 'and to this due civil obligation does not apply' (q78 a2 ad2). In the case of the legally due, someone can be compelled by law, whereas the morally due is due 'out of some sort of moral goodness (honestate)' (q102 a2; cf. q117 a5 ad1; q118 a3 ad2). Moral goodness is relevant even when nothing is due as a matter of justice (q106 a1 ad2; a4 ad1; q114 a2).

'ought' (debere) to cover the broad area of moral requirements in general, and to use 'oblige' when he is thinking of a duty as imposed by law. This, however, is a tendency rather than an absolute rule; for the broad scope of 'law' allows a broad scope to 'obligation' as well.[16]

The distinction between duty and obligation clarifies the sort of moral requirement that applies to God. God is not under any obligations, because no one imposes them on God. Still, something is due to God's creatures, if it is needed to fulfil their nature (q111 a1 ad2). God has duties, and these have an important role in Aquinas' account of justification and salvation. God does not owe us existence; he gives it to us out of 'pure generosity'.[17] God does not owe grace or glory to us, except on the assumption that he has ordered things this way; but he owes it to himself to fulfill his own ordering (q114 a1).[18]

Aquinas believes that these duties hold because of facts distinct from any act of imposition by a legislator. The natural law rests on these sorts of duties, rather than any imposed obligation. The special relation of rational creatures to the eternal law does not consist in our recognition of the eternal law as a command of a superior. We share in divine providence by exercising foresight for ourselves and for others (q91 a2). We share in the divine reason in so far as our own reason is naturally illuminated so that we distinguish good from bad.[19] This participation in the eternal law, in discriminating good from bad and having foresight for oneself and others, constitutes natural law.[20]

Aquinas, therefore, does not take all law to involve an obligation that requires an act of will by an imposer. The necessary connexion between law and obligation is fulfilled by a principle that presents requirements (debita).

304. Law, Reason, and Ends

But even if obligation does not require imposition, Aquinas also agrees that law prescribes and prohibits. Does this feature of law imply acts of prescription and prohibition by a commander expressing will?

Aquinas argues that, since commanding belongs to reason, law must belong to reason. Since a law involves a 'rule' (or 'standard', regula) and a 'measure' (mensura), and a rule

---

[16] Contrast Suarez, *Leg.* i 11.2.

[17] *SG* ii 44 §1217: 'God . . . from no debt, but from sheer generosity, brought things into being'. In the proper sense, creation does not involve justice, because justice requires the existence of someone to whom something is due; 'but if justice is understood broadly, we can say that there is justice in the creation of things, to the extent that it fits divine goodness' (ii 28) Cf. 1a q21 a3.

[18] 'To each is due what is his own. Now what is directed to someone is what is said to be his own. Thus the servant is of <i.e., belongs to> the master, and not conversely; for what is free is whatever is its own cause. In the word "debt", therefore, is implied some direction of requirement or necessity of something in relation to the thing to which it is directed. . . . in the divine operations debt may be regarded in two ways, either in so far as something is owed to God, or in so far as something is owed to a created thing. And in both ways God renders what is owed. . . . God exercises justice, when he gives to each thing what is owed to it according to the character (ratio) of its nature and condition. . . . And although God in this way gives what is owed to each thing, still God himself is not also a debtor, since he is not directed to other things, but rather other things are directed to him.' (1a q21 a1 ad3).

[19] 'the light of natural reason, by which light we distinguish what is good and bad, which belongs to natural law . . .' (q91 a2).

[20] Cajetan's commentary supports this general view. He maintains that the relevant standard (regula) of action comes from the intellect (ad 1–2 q90 = L vii 150). He treats God's providence as a measure and a binding standard (regula obligatoria; ad q91 a1 = 153), expressed in the divine law, which is given to human beings to govern themselves (ad q93 a3 = 165). He does not suggest that any divine command is needed for natural law to be a binding standard.

and measure involves reason, law involves reason.[21] 'Rule' might suggest a standard that is created by a legislative act of making a rule; such a standard might be expressed in the imperative mood. But Aquinas has a different sort of 'rule' or 'standard' in mind. A legislated rule addressed to tenants in a building might say: 'Tenants must respect the right of other tenants to peace and quiet at night'. The standard underlying this legislated rule is the right of tenants to peace and quiet. This is the sort of standard that Aquinas has in mind; it may be the basis of a legislative act, but it is not itself the result of a legislative act.[22]

In his view, reason is the rule and measure of human actions. This rule distinguishes genuinely human actions from those acts of a human being that are not properly human actions.[23] Reason is the measure of human actions because human actions differ from other movements in so far as reason 'fixes' or 'presents' (praestituere) the end. It fixes the end by directing us towards (ordinare ad) the end.[24] The standard grasped by reason is the one that practical reason relies on in directing one's action to an end. The standard that is distinctive of law is a rational standard. Hence law, in contrast to an arbitrary act of will, is the product of reason.[25]

Similarly, Aquinas rejects the apparently plausible inference from the fact that law commands to the conclusion that it requires the expression of the will of a commander; for he claims, as he claimed earlier, that commanding belongs to reason rather than will (1-2 q17 a1).[26] The commanding function of law is fulfilled by directing our action (cf. *Ver.* q22 a12 ad4), through either an indicative or an imperative declaration (intimare). It does not require an explicit attempt to move anyone to action, since indicative declarations do not include this explicit attempt. A command by reason presupposes an act of the will, because it succeeds in moving us to action only if we will an end to which the command is relevant; but the command itself need not contain any attempt to move us to action.[27]

This broad conception of commands explains why Aquinas, following Aristotle, says that prudence is 'prescriptive' (praeceptiva), but belongs to practical reason (1-2 q57 a6). Similarly, he agrees that a law is a command, but he does not understand a command as a

---

[21] 'Law is some sort of (quaedam) rule and measure of acts, in accordance with which someone is led towards acting or is restrained from acting; for law (lex) is spoken of from binding (ligare), because it binds (obligat) one to acting. Now the rule and measure of human acts is reason, which is the first principle of human acts, as is clear from what has been said above. For it belongs to reason to direct towards an end, which is the first principle in things to be done, according to the Philosopher. Now in any given genus whatever is the principle is the rule and measure of that genus: for instance, unity in the genus of numbers, and the first motion in the genus of motions. Hence the remaining possibility is that law is something that belongs to reason' (1-2 q90 a1).

[22] On Aquinas' use of 'regula' see Suarez, *Leg.* ii 5.6. He comments on the broad use of 'mensura' and 'regula' in 2-2 q141 a6 and ad1, and he argues that this use is too broad to be the sense intended in speaking of a law.

[23] See 1-2 q6 intro, quoted at §239n17.

[24] praestituere: 1-2 q66 a3 ad3; 2-2 q47 a6 ad3. Aquinas claims that the end is the first principle in things to be done (in agendis). To see how this claim is consistent with the claim that reason is the first principle of human acts (actuum), we need to distinguish two claims: (i) The starting point in deciding what I am to do (in agendis) is the end, since practical reason has to deliberate towards the end. (ii) But the starting point of distinctively human action is reason, because the rational presentation of a more proximate end directed towards the ultimate end is the source of distinctively human action.

[25] 'Reason has its power of moving from the will . . .; for from the fact that one wills the end, reason commands about the things towards the end. But in order that the will about the things commanded may have the character of law, it needs to be regulated by some sort of reason. And in this way it is to be understood that the will of the sovereign has the force of law; otherwise the sovereign's will would be iniquity rather than law' (q90 a1 ad3).

[26] Cf. *4Sent* d15 q4 a1 sol.1 = P vii 756b–757a. See §246.

[27] On the significance of Aquinas' broad conception of command cf. Suarez, *Leg.* i 4.14; ii 6.3.

simple expression of will. He understands it as the rational direction (ordinare)[28] of oneself towards an end and towards one's conclusion about what needs to be done to achieve the end.

Aquinas, therefore, agrees that a law binds and obliges. But he does not infer that law involves the will either of the commander or of the commanded. A law consists in its being true that one ought to do x, on the assumption that one wills y. This law moves us only if we will y, but the law exists whether or not the commander or the commanded wills y, and whether or not the commander wills the commanded to pursue y.

So far Aquinas has argued that a law exists if reason presents an end and the means to it. He has not suggested that it requires a command in addition to the rational presentation of an end and the means. His discussion of law and a common good confirms this connexion between law and goal-directed reasoning. Since practical reason directs us towards the ultimate end, this is also the concern of law (q90 a2). Law involves practical thought, and hence deliberation aimed at one's own happiness. It is directed to a common good rather than to one's individual good, because a common good is a more 'perfect' or 'complete' good.[29] In turning to the end pursued by law, we do not turn away from individual happiness, but we complete it.

Aquinas' remarks, therefore, distinguish law from any legislative act proceeding from the will of a legislator. If the existence of rational agents who guide their actions by rational presentation of ends and deliberation about means to these ends constitutes the existence of a natural law, the existence of a legislator issuing commands is not necessary.

305. Law and Publication

The last condition that apparently connects law with acts of legislation is the demand for publication. Aquinas argues that publication (promulgatio) is necessary for law, and that natural law is published because God has placed it in human minds (q90 a4 ad1).[30] Does he imply that God's action is necessary for the existence of a natural law? How else could it have been published to all human minds?

We have reason to doubt whether he implies this, if we examine his conditions for publication. He claims that publication requires a law to be applied to those who ought (debent) to be regulated by it. But one might take this in either of two ways: (1) Unless someone has performed an act of publishing to us, no law applies to us. (2) Unless we are in the cognitive situation of having had a law published to us, no law applies to us.

---

[28] On ordinare cf. 2-2 q81 a5.

[29] See 1-2 q9 a1; q19 a10; q83 a1 ad5; SG iii 17 §1994; 39 §2168; 146 §3196.

[30] 1-2 q90 a4: '. . . a law is imposed on others by way of a rule and measure. Now a rule or measure is imposed by being applied to those who are regulated and measured. Hence, in order for a law to acquire the power of obliging that is proper to a law, it is necessary that it be applied to the human beings who ought (debent) to be regulated in accordance with it. Such application is made by its being brought to their notice from the publication itself. Hence publication is necessary for the law to have its power. Thus from the four preceding articles, the definition of law may be gathered: and it is nothing else than a directing of reason to a common good, by the one who has care of the community, which has been published.' ad1: 'The publication of the natural law is from the very fact that God placed it in the minds of human beings to be recognized (cognoscendam) naturally'.

Aquinas intends the second claim. A law is brought to our notice (deducitur in notitiam), and God has done this by placing the natural law in us 'to be recognized' (cognoscendam) naturally. Publication does not require that we actually know it, but only that it is available for us to know. We would be bound by the law if we were in the right cognitive condition to come to know the law, even if no one had put us in this condition. Aquinas does not suggest that I am obliged to do x only if someone tells me that he wants me to do x, or that I am obliged to do x only if I recognize that someone is telling me that he wants me to do x. His conditions allow publication without a publisher. In that case we have a further reason to suppose that natural law exists if there are rational beings who are capable of grasping rational principles to direct their actions towards ends.

306. Eternal Law and Natural Law

But even if the natural law does not essentially include any act of commanding or promulgation, it is essentially connected to the eternal law that is grasped by the mind of God. Must it not, therefore, include some divine mental act, even if it is not an act of commanding or publishing?

Aquinas argues that there is an eternal law in God's reason (q91 a1), and that there is a natural law in human beings, in so far as they share in the eternal law in a special way, by exercising foresight for themselves and others (q91 a2).[31] If rational creatures simply conformed to the eternal law, it would not thereby be present in them. It is present in them because they have foresight for themselves and others. This foresight is a law because it is a rule of reason directing them towards the appropriate end. Rational beings are conscious of the natural law, and so are a law to themselves. The specific natural inclination that manifests our share of divine providence is our concern for the welfare of ourselves and others. God has this sort of foresight for us and for every part of creation; we share in it in so far as we have some foresight for ourselves and others.[32]

The natural law in us, therefore, is our disposition to deliberate with reference to our own ultimate end. We direct our actions towards the ultimate end through natural law, because that is how we exercise providence for ourselves.[33] We are a law to ourselves, and we have the natural law in ourselves, because we direct our actions towards our happiness.[34]

---

[31] Quoted in next note.

[32] '. . . it is obvious that all things share in some way in the eternal law, namely to the extent that from its impression on them they have a tendency towards the acts and ends proper to them. Among other things, however, a rational creature is subject to divine providence in a more excellent way, to the extent that it itself acquires a share in providence, by exercising foresight (providens) for itself and others. Thus it shares in eternal reason, through which it has a natural inclination to the required (debitum) action and end. And in a rational creature this participation in the eternal law is called the natural law' (1-2 q91 a2). On providence and prudence cf. Ver. q5 a1 ad6: 'For the eternal law should be considered to be in God in the way in which naturally recognized principles of action are understood to be in us, from which we advance in deliberating and electing; and this is prudence or forethought (providentia). And so the law of our intellect is related to prudence as a principle <is related to a conclusion> in a demonstration.'

[33] 'For all reasoning is derived from principles that are naturally known, and all desire of means to an end is derived from natural desire for the ultimate end. And so it is also necessary that the first directing of our acts towards the end comes about through natural law' (q91 a2 ad2).

[34] Cf. 4Sent. d33 q1 a1 = P vii 967a, quoted in n56.

Attention to natural law, therefore, does not turn us away from the eudaemonist outlook that has been characteristic of the *Summa* so far. It leads us back to the analysis of will, reason, and action that underlies Aquinas' claims about rational aiming and happiness.

Aquinas' conception of natural law is therefore reductive and deflationary in one respect. He does not take our awareness of the natural law to be a new source of moral insight distinct from our reflexion on our happiness; nor does he take it to provide distinct grounds for virtuous action, apart from those that have already appeared to practical reason. He has argued that, on a reasonable understanding of law, his discussion of the virtues and practical reason shows that we are aware of a natural law within us. To recognize this natural law, we need not recognize God as a legislator. Aquinas certainly believes in God as a legislator, but he does not take the truth of this belief to be essential to the existence of natural law.

It is less clear whether Aquinas believes that natural law is wholly external to the reason and will of rational agents. If natural law essentially includes precepts, and precepts essentially include an exercise of command (imperium), natural law essentially includes the act of reason that is required for command. Though precepts need not be in imperative form (in the narrow sense in which we normally understand it), they must apparently consist in something more than the existence of the facts that are grasped by rational agents.

Aquinas' position therefore seems to distinguish—though only implicitly—the facts grasped by rational agents from the rational agents' grasping of them, and seems to require both of these for the existence of natural law. But the facts themselves, independently of any command of God, provide rational agents with reasons for acting. Hence, when Aquinas discusses the precepts of the natural law, he mentions the natural facts that provide reasons for us to grasp. Though these facts do not seem to be sufficient for natural law, they are sufficient to make it true that we ought (debere) to act in certain ways.[35]

307. The Natural Law and the Will of God

This explanation of natural law separates the existence of natural law in human beings from the instructions of any legislator. None the less, Aquinas believes that the natural law is also divine law. It comes from God in two ways: (1) God has created us with this nature, these natural inclinations, and this natural grasp of the principles of natural law. (2) God wills that we obey the natural law, and commands us to obey it; moreover, we are required (teneri) by the natural law to conform our will to the will of God (1-2 q19 a9-10; *Ver.* q23 a7).

These two aspects of natural law are necessarily connected with Aquinas' conception of the nature and will of God. It is impossible, within Aquinas' conception of God, for God to create us as we are without commanding us to obey the principles that we grasp naturally and are naturally inclined to follow. For the natural law prescribes what is right and good for us, and God, being good, necessarily wills what is right and good for the creatures he has created.[36] Given that we have been created with the nature we have, we benefit from

---

[35] See further Suarez, *Leg.* ii 9.4.

[36] '. . . since a debt paid out of divine justice is either owed to God or owed to some creature, neither sort of debt can be omitted in any work of God. For God cannot do anything that is not appropriate to his wisdom and goodness; and this is the way in which . . . anything is owed to God. And similarly, whatever he does in created things he does in

being commanded to obey the natural law, and so, given God's nature, God cannot fail to will that we obey the natural law, and cannot fail to command us to obey it. The apparent possibility of God's creating us and not commanding us to obey the natural law is merely apparent; it appears possible only if we do not know enough about the nature of God.

Aquinas, therefore, emphasizes that God does not make it right to observe natural law by willing it, but prescribes actions that are already right in themselves, not right simply as a result of God's prescription.[37] Actions are right in themselves because they promote the end of human life; that is why God commands them.[38] God's will to prescribe the observance of the natural law rests on God's understanding of the fact that the natural law expresses what is good and bad for human beings because of their nature.[39]

The necessary connexion between God's will and God's understanding of what is naturally good for human beings does not limit God's freedom. If God creates the world because God sees it is good to do so, and if God commands us to follow the natural law because God sees it is good to command creatures to do what suits their nature, God's freedom is not thereby restricted.

accordance with appropriate direction and proportion, in which the character of justice consists. Thus justice must be in all God's works' (1a q21 a4).

[37] 'For the precept is of two sorts—i.e., of natural and of positive right (ius). The things prohibited by a precept of natural right are those that are bad in their own right (secundum se). But those prohibited by precepts of positive right are those that can be occasions of bad things; or else the things prescribed (praecipiuntur) are things that direct towards virtue, which the legislator aims to bring about' (4Sent d15 q3 a1 sol 4 = P vii 729a).

[38] 'An action is said to be bad in its own right. And this is true in so far as the action disagrees with correctness of reason. For each nature has in it a natural tendency towards its end; and thereby there is in reason a natural correctness through which it tends towards the end; and thereby whatever leads away from that end disagrees with reason. And because the natural law is the <law> in accordance with which reason is correct, that is why Augustine says . . . that something is called a sin in so far as it disagrees with the eternal law, whose expression is this very natural law. And so, the more an action leads away from the end of human life, the more serious is a sin in its own right' (2Sent d42 q2 a5). Aquinas cites Augustine, Faust. xxii 27 (also discussed in 1-2 q71 a6; see §292), which explicitly refers only to eternal law (factum vel dictum vel concupitum aliquid contra legem aeternam), but warrants Aquinas' reference to the natural law, by introducing the connexion between eternal law and natural order: 'The eternal law is divine reason or the will of God, commanding the conservation of natural order, and forbidding its disturbance. We must, then, ask what the natural order is in a human being.'

[39] '. . . the things prescribed by divine law have correctness not only because they are laid down by law, but also in accord with nature. (1) For by the precepts of the divine law the human mind is subordinated to God, and all the other things in a human being are subordinated to reason. But this is just what natural direction (ordo) requires, that the inferior be subject to the superior. Therefore the things commanded by the divine law are in themselves naturally correct. (2) Human beings by divine providence are allotted a natural criterion of reason (naturale iudicatorium rationis) as the principle of their proper activities. Now natural principles are directed to things that are naturally. Therefore there are activities naturally appropriate (convenientes) to a human being that are correct in their own right, and not merely as being laid down by law. (3) Whatever things have a definite nature, these things must have definite activities appropriate to that nature: for the proper activity of each thing follows its nature. Now it is settled that the nature of human beings is definite. There must therefore be certain activities that in themselves are appropriate to a human being. (4) Wherever something is natural to a given subject, any other thing without which the first thing cannot be had must also be natural; for nature does not fail in necessities. Now it is natural to a human being to be a social animal; this is shown from the fact that one human being alone is not sufficient for all the things that are necessary for human life. Therefore the things without which human society cannot be preserved are naturally appropriate to a human being. Such things are securing to every person what is his own, and refraining from acts of injustice (iniuriis). Some things, therefore, among human actions are naturally correct. . . . It is clear, therefore, that good and bad in human actions are not only in accord with the laying down of law, but in accord with natural direction (ordinem). That is why it is said in a Psalm "The judgments of the Lord are righteous, justified in themselves" [Ps. 18:10]. But this rules out the position of those who say that things are just and correct only by the laying down of a law' (SG iii 129 §§3009–13, 3017–19). 'Iudicatorium' is also translated by 'judgment', 'code', 'tribunal'. M ad §3011 cites ST 1-2 q71 a6 ad4; Ver. q17 a1 obj5 ad5; ST 1a q79 a13. On this chapter see also §274.

Human beings act freely in so far as they follow their ultimate end; but their ultimate end is external to them, since they receive it from God. Moreover, facts about goodness and badness are external to any particular human agent, in so far as they exist independently of any individual. The good that God aims at is not external to God in this way, and so God is not determined by the good in the way that human beings are. The relevant good is God's own goodness, and it is not external to God in the way that the human good is external to human beings.[40]

God is omnipotent in so far as God's rational will is not restrained by anything external.[41] But this does not mean that God is free to change himself. In particular God is not free not to have the sort of will that prefers the good; for if God lacked such a will, God would be less perfect than he is. God does not will of necessity everything that he wills (1a q19 a3); he could have created a better world than the one he chose to create (q25 a6).[42] Still, God is not free not to choose what seems to him better all things considered. On this point Aquinas is an intellectualist about God's freedom.[43]

The will of God is not subject to the eternal law; for it is itself the eternal law.[44] Particular aspects of creation result from God's willing to carry out some plan that God's reason grasps as part of the eternal law. But God's will, God's reason, and the eternal law are not three independent things. Given God's simplicity and eternity, they are three ways of referring to the same thing. God's will is not compelled by something external to and independent of it. Divine freedom, therefore, does not require God's will to be capable of changing the eternal law. The eternal law expresses God's free will.

These facts about God imply that the rightness and goodness of the principles of natural law are not independent of God; since it is necessary that God wills what is right and good, the principles of natural law would not be right and good if God did not will them. Still, they are not constituted or created by God's will. For God's will necessarily recognizes right and good that are not created by his will.

The relation between the first principle and the subordinate principles of natural law presupposes that natural rightness is distinct from the will of God. It is not always obvious how the higher principles of natural law justify one or another specific subordinate principle. But the task of reaching subordinate principles is not simply a task for legislation, human or divine. It is a task for rational inquiry and discovery. Neither a human nor a divine legislator

---

[40] 'And so as concerns things divinely willed, we should recognize that there is something that it is absolutely necessary for God to will, but this is not true of all the things God wills. For the divine will has a necessary relation to its own goodness, which is its proper object. Hence God of necessity wills the being of his goodness, just as our will of necessity wills happiness . . . But God wills things apart from himself in so far as they are directed to his goodness as towards their end' (1a q19 a3).

[41] '. . . anything that can have the character of being is included among the absolutely possible things, in respect of which God is said to be omnipotent. Now nothing is opposed to the character of being, except non-being. Therefore, whatever implies being and non-being at the same time is inconsistent with the character of the absolutely possible thing that is subject to the divine omnipotence' (1a q25 a3).

[42] Difficulties in Aquinas' position are explored by Kretzmann, *MT* 217–25; *MC* 130–41; 'General'; 'Particular'. Cf. §§347, 396.

[43] On intellectualism see §268.

[44] '. . . since the will of God is his very essence, it is subject neither to the divine government, nor to the eternal law, but is the same thing as the eternal law. In another way we can speak of the divine will, as concerns the things themselves that God wills about creatures; these things are subject to the eternal law, in so far as their concept [ratio] is in divine wisdom' (1-2 q93 a4 ad1). Cf. q91 a1c, ad1.

is free to legislate as he pleases about rightness and goodness, because the relevant facts are independent of legislative acts. The scope for pure legislation is limited to the area of the civil law, where the general requirements of human nature and human society do not give us a reason to prefer one option over another. At the higher levels of natural law, God is not sovereign over it in the sense of being free to change it at will.

Though God is not free to violate the natural law or to refrain from commanding its observance, God's legislative role is not confined to endorsing the provisions of natural law. God also commands actions that are not commanded by natural law, which it would not be wrong to omit if they had not been commanded. Violation of such a command is 'bad because it is prohibited' (malum quia prohibitum) rather than 'prohibited because it is bad' (prohibitum quia malum), whereas violations of natural law are prohibited because they are bad.[45]

In allowing that God's legislation can make some actions wrong that would not otherwise be wrong, Aquinas does not retract his view that right and wrong are prior to God's legislative will. God's right to legislate and our obligation to obey God's legislation presuppose a principle, independent of God's legislative will, that prescribes obedience to the legitimate commands of a legislator. The wrongness—prior to God's legislation—of disobeying God is presupposed by the possibility of God's legislation making specific actions right or wrong.

308. What is Natural about Natural Law?

We have now seen what Aquinas does and does not mean by speaking of natural law as a kind of law. We have considered the different reasons that might be given for attributing to him the view that it consists essentially in acts of divine legislation, and we have found that none of these reasons is cogent. He discusses the features of law that seem to refer to acts of legislation (obligation, rule, command, publication), and argues that they do not imply any acts of legislation, but belong to the natural law in so far as it belongs to the nature of rational agents. In this respect, Aquinas reduces facts about natural law to facts about rational agents.

---

[45] Violations of natural law are bad without prohibition, and therefore are prohibited because they are bad. Violations of divine positive law, however, are bad only because they are prohibited. See 1-2 q71 a6 ad4 (we can speak of every sin being bad because it is forbidden by natural law from the very fact that it is misdirected (inordinatum)); 2-2 q57 a2 ad3 (both divine and human law include things that are naturaliter iusta, whose violation is prohibited because it is bad, and things that are bad because prohibited); in 1Tim. 1.3 = P x 588b (what conflicts with natural law is bad in its own right, whereas what conflicts with positive law is bad because prohibited). Some sins are sinful only because they are prohibited, and would not otherwise be sinful. The most significant of these sins is the sin of Eve and Adam in eating the apple. See 2Sent d21 q2 a2 sc1 = P vi 575b (Adam sinned by doing what was bad only because it was prohibited). Many, however, sin by doing what is bad in both ways, both in its own right and because it is prohibited. On Adam's sin see §412; Mal. q2 a6 = M 480b (some actions are sins only because prohibited); q2 a9 ad4 = M 487a (in things that are bad in their own right, not only because they are prohibited, disobedience is not the whole evil; hence sins can differ in degree in accordance with the good that one loses); CT 188 (eating from the tree of knowledge of good and evil was not prohibited because it was antecedently bad, but God commanded human beings to observe this moderate prohibition simply on the ground that God prohibited the eating). Similarly, some ways to salvation are required only because they are commanded. See in Ioann. 13.2 §6 = P x 529b (Jesus' washing of Peter's feet was necessary for salvation only because it was prescribed).

What, then, makes natural law natural? It is different, as the Stoics argue, from any positive law. It is also different, as the Christian Fathers insist, from the revealed law that we know from the Scriptures.[46] It is not separate from the divine law, since it is part of the eternal law; but it is not the whole of the divine law. Aquinas begins with the aspects of divine law that we know naturally, before he proceeds to explain why we also need the revealed law of the Pentateuch and the Gospel.

In calling natural law natural, he makes at least three claims about its status: (1) He refers to our way of knowing the law. To know the precepts of positive law, we need specific information about a particular community, but to know the precepts of the natural law we need no special education or information. We have the relevant knowledge by nature, without education or training, and no matter how bad our education and training may be. Our natural knowledge of the natural law is the basis for acquiring knowledge of further practical principles (1-2 q91 a3). Different people are aware of these first principles of practical reason to different extents, and with different degrees of explicitness; but since we all grasp them in some way, we naturally participate in the eternal law (q91 a2).[47] Our awareness of the first principles of natural law is meant to explain how it is possible for us to guide our action correctly by reason and will. (2) The natural law is natural not only because of how we know it, but also because of its content. It applies to us in virtue of our nature. The principles of natural law are the correct principles for us to follow as the sorts of creatures we are with the natures we have. In so far as we know the principles of the natural law, we learn something about our nature and about what is suitable for us.[48] (3) This law is natural for us in so far as we naturally follow it. We naturally participate in the eternal law not only by knowing what is suitable for our nature, but also by naturally behaving in accordance with it. This is why Aquinas claims that the precepts of the natural law are revealed in our natural inclinations (q91 a2).

It is not logically necessary for one and the same law to have all these features. Natural knowledge (or some degree of cognition) of a truth does not make it a truth about our nature. We might, for instance, have been born with some innate cognition of arithmetic or some innate awareness of a quality-space of colours, but our innate cognition would not necessarily be about our nature; we would not necessarily understand arithmetic or colours better by reflexion on our nature. It seems logically possible for God to give us natural knowledge of practical principles that are similarly unrelated to our nature. In such an apparently possible world, the principles that prescribe what is suitable for our nature might be unknown to us; or else we might be able to learn about them without knowing them naturally, and we might discover that they are quite different from the principles that we know naturally. Again, knowledge—whether natural or not—of the principles that suit our nature seems to be consistent with the absence of any inclination to act on them. Apparently, we might be aware of what suits our nature, but—because of some perversity in our will—be disinclined to act on it.

---

[46] See Lactantius, quoted in §197. Cf. §206.

[47] This claim about natural awareness of the law does not undermine the claim that rational agents differ from non-rational in being guided by reason and will, as opposed to natural desire (q91 a2 obj2; ad2; ad 2 quoted above n33).

[48] See *SG* iii 129, quoted above n39.

Aquinas believes our world is a bit like these worlds, in so far as our knowledge and our inclination are imperfect. Original sin leaves us with misdirected desires that tend to obscure our knowledge and to pervert our inclinations and actions. This imperfection in our nature means that we cannot simply discover what is naturally suitable for us by an indiscriminate survey of our natural beliefs and inclinations. If we took these as our guides, we would treat the impulses of our misdirected desires as impulses towards what is naturally suitable. To avoid the distorting effects of misdirected desires, we must rely on our knowledge of human nature and the ultimate human end, and use this to identify the natural beliefs and inclinations that tell us what is suitable for our nature. In the *Summa* Aquinas discusses sin immediately before law, so that we recognize some of the tendencies of misdirected desires, and do not identify them with the requirements of our nature.

With these qualifications and reservations, Aquinas takes the three aspects of the naturalness of the natural law to be connected. He appeals to natural beliefs and inclinations in order to support his claims about what is naturally suitable, though these appeals are not left to stand on their own without support from the rest of his ethical theory. To justify his claims about the coincidence of these three features in natural law, he has to show that some set of principles meets all his three conditions; they must be naturally known, they must be about what suits our nature, and we must have a natural inclination to follow them.

309. The Relevance of Natural Law

The precepts of natural law ought to specify the content of the natural inclinations that make us aware of what is suitable for our nature. But they seem quite heterogeneous. Some of them seem to be nearly tautologies, or at least conceptual or analytic truths. We might say this about 'Good is to be done and evil is to be avoided'. Others, such as 'Theft must not be committed' (*in EN* v 12 §1018) seem to have more moral content; they seem to be moral rules corresponding to parts of the Decalogue (1-2 q100 a1, 3). Aquinas recognizes this variety in precepts of natural law, and arranges them in order, claiming that the more specific are derived from the higher principles. We must understand both the character of the higher principles and the sort of derivation he has in mind.

The very first precept of natural law is the principle that good is to be done; the other precepts are founded on this one.[49] This principle is not a mere tautology. It connects the discussion of natural law with Aquinas' exposition of the good as the ultimate end. For rational agents, good is what is to be done, in so far as they have wills that aim at their objects as good, not as merely attractive. We will something as good in so far as we choose it for some reason beyond the mere fact that we desire it. We choose for reasons independent of desire in so far as we assess particular goods with reference to one another in our conception of the ultimate good.[50] In claiming that his principle about the good is the very first principle of natural law, Aquinas implies that all the prescriptions of the natural law must fit the teleological structure that he has described in his discussion of the ultimate end.

The claim that moral principles are provisions of natural law does not require us to cast our moral reasoning in quasi-legal form. If Aquinas had intended this, it would have been

---

[49] See §272; Bradley, *ATHG* 282–8, 312–13. [50] See §275.

appropriate to mention natural law at the beginning of his ethical argument, rather than waiting until he has presented an account of the virtues. He seems to introduce natural law so that we can understand something about what we have already discovered without reference to natural law.

The point of referring to natural law is most easily seen if we consider the difference between rational and non-rational creatures (q91 a2).[51] The specific natural inclination that manifests our share of divine providence is our own concern for the welfare of ourselves and others. God has this sort of foresight for us and for every part of creation; we share in it through our own foresight for ourselves and others. The sort of foresight that gives us a share in the natural law is not simply concern for the future; it is concern for ourselves that is based on awareness of our nature and what is suitable for it. Non-rational creatures simply follow their natural tendencies and conform to their nature in that way. Rational creatures are aware of the natural law, in so far as they can become aware of their nature and of what it requires; this is how they exercise foresight for themselves. Aquinas claims, then, that in reflecting on the final good, the will, the passions, and so on, we discover our nature and what is suitable for it, and thereby discover the law of our nature.

Aquinas has therefore pursued his reductive treatment of moral theory in his discussion of natural law. Reflexion on rational agency is the rational basis for understanding not only happiness and the virtues, but also the requirements of natural law. A proper understanding of natural law reveals its requirements in the features of rational agency that we have already understood through the earlier inquiries in the Prima Secundae.

This is an informative, even a controversial, claim if it is intended to rule out other explanations or interpretations of what we learn about in the ethical reflexion of the Prima Secundae. It conflicts with Nietzsche's view that our ethical views, and the psychological views connected with them, express an illusion about ourselves.[52] Aquinas also rejects the view that our ethical views simply reflect our preference for this conception of ourselves, and do not tell us anything further about how we really are. In claiming that we conform to natural law, we claim to know something about how we are, and to express this in our ethical choices. Hence the virtues we recognize are appropriate for the sort of creature that we are; they are not simply expressions of one among many views of ourselves.

Aquinas already asserts this connexion between nature and rational desire at the beginning of the Prima Secundae; his formal criteria for happiness anticipate his claims about natural law. He argues that our ultimate end is not the satisfaction of our desires, but the perfection of ourselves; we aim at what we value as the perfection of our nature. In the discussion of natural law, Aquinas adds that our aiming at our perfection is not completely misguided. In conceiving ourselves as rational agents who aim at our perfection we correctly grasp our own nature.[53]

If this is what Aquinas means in invoking natural law, he imposes a constraint on acceptable moral systems. Our nature does not determine that one specific system rather than another is the right one. To find the right one for people at a particular time or place, we must consider not only the fact that we are rational agents of a certain sort, but also the

---

[51] Quoted above n32.   [52] See Nietzsche, *TI* vii 1 = PN 501.
[53] On Aquinas' naturalism see Finnis, *Aq*, ch. 7, esp. 88, 101–2.

fact that we are in particular conditions that may distinguish us from people at other times or places. Still, our nature imposes some moral constraints that we must recognize if we are to explain how different circumstances matter. We may decide, for instance, that in some circumstances we ought to ration food and in others we ought to ration water. Natural law requires neither rationing of food nor rationing of water; but we need to refer to a natural need for food and drink if we are to justify rationing in particular circumstances, by appeal to some principle requiring equitable distribution of resources needed to meet basic needs.

310. The First Principle of Natural Law

Natural law does not present a new kind of moral consideration, lying outside deliberation about happiness. On the contrary, the presence of natural law in human beings consists in their being rational agents pursuing their final good. When Aquinas tells us that the precept that good is to be pursued and evil avoided is the first principle of natural law, he means that we regard other principles as correct in so far as they prescribe actions that promote the final good, and that if we knew they did not promote the final good, we would no longer regard these actions as required.

The natural law prescribes the actions of all the virtues, in so far as it prescribes action in accordance with nature.[54] What is natural for human beings is what accords with their nature as rational beings. This is the sort of action towards which human beings have a natural inclination, which they form because of a natural judgment or 'natural criterion of reason' (*SG* iii 129).[55] Our reason for obeying the natural law is not that God orders us to obey it, as though we were regarding it simply as a divine command based on no further reason. It is, as Butler says, the law of our nature; it would be suitable for our nature whether or not God commanded us to do it. We can confirm that our natural inclinations lead us to what is suitable for our nature, by comparing their tendencies with an account of human nature. This is what Aquinas does in the *Summa*.[56]

---

[54] 'If we speak of virtuous actions in so far as they are virtuous, in this way all virtuous actions belong to the law of nature. For it has been said that everything to which a human being is inclined in accordance with his nature belongs to the law of nature. Moreover, everything is naturally inclined to the activity that is suitable for it in accordance with its form, as fire, for instance, is inclined to heating. Hence, since rational animal is the form proper to a human being, every human being has a natural inclination towards action in accordance with reason. And this is action in accordance with virtue' (1-2 q94 a3).

[55] The passage is quoted in full in n39. On this account of rightness see §334; Suarez, *Bon.* ii.2.11 = 295a.

[56] 'All things have present in them naturally principles by which they not only can carry out their characteristic actions, but by which they make them appropriate (convenientes) to their end, whether they are actions that follow on a thing from the nature of its genus, or they follow from the nature of its species. . . . But because a human being, among the other animals, has cognition of the character (ratio) of the end and the proportion of the action to end, that is why the natural conception placed in him to direct (dirigatur) him towards acting appropriately is called natural law (lex) or natural right (ius) . . . The natural law, therefore, is nothing other than the conception naturally placed in a human being, by which he is directed towards acting appropriately in the actions characteristic of him, whether they belong to him from the nature of the genus (e.g., generating, eating, and so on), or from the nature of his species (e.g., reasoning, and so on). For everything that makes an action inappropriate to the end that nature aims at in an action is said to be against the law of nature. For an action may be inappropriate to the principal or to the secondary end; and this may happen in two ways. (1) In one way, from something that altogether impedes the end, as too much or too little eating impedes bodily health, as the principal end of eating, and impedes fitness for getting on with one's work, which is the secondary end. (2) In another way, from something that makes the attainment of the primary or secondary end difficult or less suitable,

The role of our natural inclinations, however, is not purely epistemic; they do not simply inform us about what is suitable for our nature, but they actually fulfil our nature. When we reflect on the actions we do by natural inclination, we discover that they include the rational activities that direct other inclinations. By natural inclination we exercise foresight for ourselves; this is the participation in divine providence that defines rational agents.[57]

How much knowledge of natural law is contained or implied in the knowledge that belongs to every rational agent? Aquinas claims that natural inclination leads us not only to the first principle, that good is to be pursued and evil avoided, but also to some more definite principles. He divides these secondary principles into four groups: (1) The highest precepts. (2) Precepts (such as those in the Decalogue) easily reached from the highest precepts. (3) Subordinate precepts requiring more reflexion, derived as conclusions from premisses. (4) Precepts derived as determinations rather than conclusions.

311. Natural Inclinations and the Highest Precepts of Natural Law

The highest precepts are immediately derived from the first principle, in accordance with the order of natural inclinations: 'Therefore, according to the order of natural inclinations is the order of precepts of the law of nature' (1-2 q94 a2). Different natural inclinations rest on different aspects of our nature. (a) The inclination that results in precepts about self-preservation rests on the nature we share with all other natural substances. (b) The inclination that results in precepts about the satisfaction and control of bodily appetites rests on the nature we share with other animals. (c) The inclination that results in precepts about social life rests on our nature as rational animals (q94 a2; a4; q95 a4).

It is not easy, however, to see how much content Aquinas wants to attribute to the common and first principles of natural law.[58] Sometimes they appear to be very general

---

e.g., excessive eating, in so far as it happens at a time when it ought not to. If, therefore, an action is inappropriate to an end, as altogether prohibiting the principal end, it is directly prohibited through the law of nature by the first precepts of the law of nature, which are in matters of action as common conceptions are in theoretical matters. If, on the other hand, it is unsuitable to an end of some secondary sort, or even to a primary end, as making the attainment of the end difficult or less suitable, it is prohibited not by the first precepts of the law of nature, but by the second, which are derived from the first, just as conclusions in theoretical matters gain their credibility from principles known through themselves' (4Sent. d33 q1 a1 = P vii 967a).

[57] The essential connexion between being a rational agent and grasping the natural law is revealed in Aquinas' explanation of why no one, not even ourselves, teaches us the natural law: 'Those who attain to works of virtue without an external instructor or legislator are said to be a law to themselves; "When the Gentiles, who have not the law, do naturally the things that belong to the law, . . . they are a law to themselves". Therefore he also who acquires knowledge through himself ought to be called his own teacher' (Ver. q11 a2 obj 5). (On the passage from Romans see n4 above.) But he rejects the suggestion, on the ground that A cannot teach A unless the aspect of A that teaches is distinguishable from the aspect of A that is taught. In the case of the natural law, A could teach A only if both the teaching A and the taught A were a rational agent. Since any rational agent must already grasp the natural law, and thereby be a law to himself, no agent who is a law to himself can be taught the natural law: 'A law in matters of action has the same character as a principle has in matters of speculation, but not the same character as a teacher. Hence it does not follow that if someone is a law to himself, he can be a teacher to himself' (Ver. q11 a2 ad5).

[58] These principles '. . . need no further publication than that they are written in natural reason as known through themselves, such as that one ought to do evil to no human being, and others of this sort' (q100 a3).

and formal, prescribing that (for instance) we act in accordance with reason, but leaving it for further inquiry to decide what is involved in acting in accordance with reason.[59] But sometimes they seem to have more definite content. Aquinas claims that a prohibition on killing is derived from the prohibition on harming, which in turn is derived from the unreasonableness of harming (q95 a2). The principle from which the specific precepts are derived is the principle about human nature and especially about the naturally social character of human beings (q95 a4).

Aquinas seems to mean that the principle of acting in accordance with reason is most directly derived from the principle that good is to be done and evil avoided, and that the principle of not harming is derived from the principle of acting in accordance with reason. The principle of not harming seems to have some definite content that is absent from the principle of acting in accordance with reason. Aquinas seems to rely on a connexion between the rational and the social nature of human beings.

We may grasp his argument better if we recall that he does not simply appeal to needs, desires, and sentiments that human beings share. He appeals to the rational agency that we share. Morality, as he understands it, is the application of rational agency to the different aspects of human life. The application of rational agency proceeds through one's conception of one's final good. The appeal to human nature does not rely on a conception of happiness as the fulfilment of one's desires. Aquinas argues that this is a mistaken conception of happiness, because my ultimate end as a rational agent is not simply the satisfaction of my desires. I pursue my perfection, in so far as I seek to satisfy the desires that are worth satisfying. I do not want my ultimate ends to be things that I simply happen to prefer.

This makes a difference to our understanding of the appeal to 'natural inclinations'. If we appeal to all unlearnt impulses or desires in anyone, some of these seem inappropriate to provide a moral norm or standard. Even if we appeal to the impulses that are statistically more widespread in the human species, we still seem to commit ourselves to morally doubtful conclusions.[60] Aquinas believes that natural and widespread impulses are to be shaped and redirected by the training that forms moral virtues; he could not reasonably take untrained natural impulses to set goals for morality.

Aquinas' claims about natural inclinations need to be interpreted in the light of his conception of agency. He thinks of human nature as essentially rational, and therefore as requiring the application of rational agency to choices.[61] His argument from natural inclinations appeals to these aspects of rational agency.

---

[59] 'All hold this to be right and true, that one should act in accordance with reason. Now from this principle it follows as an appropriate conclusion, that deposits are to be returned, and this indeed is true in most cases; but it is possible for it to happen in a particular case that it would be harmful, and therefore unreasonable, if deposits were returned, if, for instance someone asked for <something to be returned> in order to attack his country' (q94 a4). Cf. 2-2 q47 a7: 'And this end is presented (praestitutus) to a human being in accordance with natural reason; for natural reason prescribes to each person that he should act in accordance with reason'. This is apparently a reference to synderesis; cf. q47 a6 ad1. See §317.

[60] For an example of a morally questionable appeal to nature see 2-2 q154 a11.

[61] As Aquinas makes clear in speaking of the 'order' of natural inclinations (q94 a2), the application of rational agency does not disregard the aspects of human beings that make them living organisms and make them animals.

312. Rational Agency and Social Nature

If we rely on Aquinas' claims about rational agency, we can understand his claims about our inclination towards society.[62] We might think he refers to a natural desire for social life, and that the various principles of justice and so on seek to achieve this natural desire. This would be an insecure starting point.[63] For we might infer that the strength of my desire for the end determines the weight of my reason to pursue the means to the end, so that people who care less about social life have less reason to care about the good of others.

This is not Aquinas' argument. He believes that a rational agent's perfection requires social life in which one is concerned about the good of others in the same way as one's own. Can we understand this in the light of Aquinas' claims about perfection?

In Aquinas' view, we cannot be free in relation to our ends unless we can regard them as matters for deliberation as opposed to mere preference. This sort of freedom is valuable to us, because our ends seem to matter to us for some reason beyond the mere fact that we prefer them; that is why we aim at perfection. Once we recognize that we care about perfection, not simply about the satisfaction of preferences, we also notice that my preferring this end—its being my end in particular—is not a sufficient reason for pursuing it. There must also be something to be said for it beyond the fact that I care about it.[64] In this sense my desire for my happiness turns out not to be entirely self-centred, once I understand that happiness requires reasons that go beyond my preferences.

The demand for reasons going beyond my preferences affects my adoption of one end over another, by accepting one conception of happiness over another. But it also affects my relations to other rational agents. To find a reason for preferring one end to another is to find a good that is good antecedently to my desiring it; my desire rests on an external reason that does not depend on my desires. External reasons are good reasons not because they seem good to me, but because they are good reasons that must seem good to a qualified judge who does not share my initial desires. This is how reason-based ends differ from preference-based ends.

In caring about my own perfection, and not simply about the satisfaction of my own preferences, I have to recognize other rational agents as agents who can recognize a good reason for preferring one end over another. Aquinas is right to suppose that my natural inclination—properly understood—towards my own good as a rational agent also implies an inclination towards social life. I have to respect the judgments of others to some degree, since I regard their judgments as being possibly relevant to my decisions about the ends it would be best for me to pursue. This kind of respect for others places us in a rational community with them.

---

[62] 'Thirdly, a human being has a tendency towards a good in accordance with the nature of reason, which is proper to him. Thus he has a natural tendency towards grasping the truth about God, and towards living in society. And on this ground the things that refer to this sort of tendency belong to the natural law; for instance, to avoid ignorance, not to offend those he ought to interact with, and other things of this sort that refer to this' (q94 a2). At the end of the first sentence the antecedent of 'which' might be 'tendency', 'nature', or 'reason'.

[63] The insecurity of appeals to natural desires becomes clear in Pufendorf's attack on appeals to natural sociability at *JNG* vii 1.3.

[64] See *2Sent.* d3 q4 a1 ad2 = P vi 427a; Finnis, *Aq.* 111.

One might object that this sort of respect for other people's judgment falls short of the sort of respect for their needs and interests that is necessary for a 'natural inclination to live in society' (as Aquinas puts it). It seems quite possible to respect another person's judgment, and even to regard it as a source of insight into one's own good, while being entirely indifferent to the other person's interests.

We might answer that the two forms of respect are distinct, but connected. I have more reason to respect and to trust another person's judgment if we treat each other with mutual respect. If I depend on you, and you treat me purely as your instrument, I have some reason to give you the sorts of answers that you will want to hear; you are more likely to hear my honest opinion if I am not entirely dependent on your favour. We are more likely to recognize other people's views as counting for something in their own right if we all recognize one another as counting for something in our own right.[65]

This argument for connecting two forms of respect concedes that my planning for my own life on the basis of my judgments about my good is quite independent of what other people do. If we reject this concession, we can strengthen the argument for connecting a rational community with a moral community. For more of my life is subject to rational agency if I care about others for their own sakes, not simply as means to the satisfaction of my preferences. Non-instrumental concern for others promotes my own perfection, as Aquinas conceives it, since they are rational agents with whom I can deliberate about what ends are worth pursuing.

If my concern for others is purely instrumental, they have no reason to believe that any plans of mine involving them count for anything more than my preferences about them; my plans for them do not necessarily define ends that they have any reason to care about for themselves. But if we are concerned about one another for our own sakes, our lives can all embody ends that we all recognize as worth pursuing for some reason apart from our preferences. In that case, my life is not guided simply by my preferences; it is guided by preferences grounded in reasons that can be recognized as such by all rational agents. If I simply regard other people as means to achieving my aims, I can give no reason for them to prefer my aims to theirs, and so we have reason to cooperate only as long as our aims happen to coincide. When I care about others for their own sakes, however, we are capable of sharing deliberations that take account of reasons that we can all accept. Hence the conclusions of our deliberation have a rational claim on us all.

These arguments about the inclination to society go beyond anything that Aquinas explicitly defends. But they indicate how one might connect his claims about natural law with his conception of rational agency. Moreover, they are relevant to the claims that he presents more fully in his arguments for friendship and justice.[66]

The claims about inclinations and nature show that Aquinas' claims about the basis of natural law in human nature do not rely on an empirical survey of prevalent human desires. They rely on distinctive features of his conception of rational agents and their ultimate end. This is the conception that we need to keep in mind in examining his attempts to derive precepts of natural law from the basic principles.

---

[65] Cf. Hegel's views on different sorts of recognition, discussed by Neuhouser, *FHST*, ch. 3.
[66] See §337.

313. Derived Principles of Natural Law

The awareness of our nature that is embodied in our natural inclinations allows us to form more specific precepts that tell us what is required by the inclination to society. Given the specific needs of a human society, we can see why we need the precepts of the Decalogue.[67] The precept against killing is derived from the precept against harming (q95 a2), and the law of nations—i.e., the laws and institutions found universally in different nations—is derived from the law of nature 'by means of a conclusion that is not very far removed from the principles' (q95 a4 ad1). The principle from which the specific precepts are derived is the principle about human nature and especially about the naturally social character of human beings. The needs of a human community explain the provisions for property, exchange, and so on that are found, in one form or another, in different human societies.[68]

Aquinas contrasts the precepts of the Decalogue with the common principles from which they are derived. The Decalogue itself does not state the common principles, but states the most general guides to action that can be derived from them.[69] The common principles provide the first level of natural law, and the Decalogue the second level. The precepts of the law of nations also belong to the second level. They are less obvious than the precept against killing, but they are more obvious than those that 'by the diligent inquiry of wise people (sapientes) are found to accord with reason' (q100 a3). Reflexion on the needs of a human community tells us that (e.g.) every community needs to assure some protection, security, and support for human social life, but it does not tell us exactly how these aims are to be fulfilled in specific circumstances.

When we add more specific detail, we can reach a third level of precepts. In contrast to the precepts of the Decalogue, precepts at the third level demand more reflexion if we are to see that they are required by natural law (q100 a1, 3). The non-obvious consequences of the common principles include some important areas of morality. Aquinas has to explain why the Decalogue does not include duties to oneself, but confines itself to duties to God and to one's neighbour. He offers different explanations: (1) The requirements of natural law are obscured by sin in the case of precepts about loving others, but not in the case of precepts of self-love. (2) True self-love is included in the love of God and one's neighbour. (3) Everyone easily recognizes that we have duties (debita) to God and our neighbour, but not everyone easily recognizes that we have duties to ourselves; 'for at first sight it appears that everyone is free in those matters that refer to himself' (q100 a5 ad1; 2-2 q122 a1).

---

[67] 'For some things in human actions are so explicit that immediately, with slight consideration, they can be approved or rejected through those common and first principles.... For there are some things that the natural reason of any human being at all at once through itself judges to be things to be done or not to be done, such as Honour your father and your mother, and Do not kill, Do not steal' (q100 a1).

[68] '... it belongs to the character (ratio) of human law, to be derived from the law of nature, as is clear from what has been said. On this basis positive right (ius) is divided into the right of nations and civil right—namely, on the basis of the two ways in which something may be derived from the law of nature, as stated above. For to the right of nations belong those things that are derived from the law of nature as conclusions from principles—such as just purchases, sales, and other things of this sort, without which human beings cannot live together. This concerns the law of nature, because a human being is naturally a social animal, as is proved in *Politics* i' (q95 a4). Aquinas' account of the law of nations is discussed and modified by Suarez, *Leg.* ii 20.2.

[69] As Aquinas puts it, the Decalogue contains the common principles in the sense in which an immediate conclusion contains its premisses (q100 a3).

Since the Decalogue includes only precepts that are easily recognized,[70] it does not include precepts of self-love.[71]

To accept precepts at this third level, people need instruction from the wise, and so these precepts are excluded from the list in the Decalogue. The reference to the wise (sapientes) suggests that we recognize that we have duties of self-love (as opposed to self-regarding reasons for it) only through the sort of 'diligent inquiry' that traces the more remote consequences of the common principles of natural law.

Precepts at the fourth level are reached less directly from the natural law. They are not derived from the first principles as conclusions from premisses, but are 'determinations' rather than 'derivations', because they specify one among a number of possible ways of fulfilling a requirement of natural law. The natural law requires, for instance, that wrongdoers should be punished, but it does not require that they should receive this or that punishment. When we lay down a specific punishment, we 'determine' a requirement of natural law, by stating a specific way, not itself required by natural law, of fulfilling the generic requirement of natural law (1-2 q95 a2; a4 ad1).

Aquinas sharply distinguishes this fourth group of precepts from the third. People do not agree without reflexion that the natural law requires us to recognize duties of self-love. But once we reflect appropriately, we see that these are required by the natural law; they are not optional or alterable. In reflecting about punishment or about taxation, by contrast, we will not (Aquinas assumes) reach the conclusion that imprisonment for five years is the only just punishment for a specific type of offence, or that direct rather than indirect taxation is always uniquely just.

The fourth group of precepts belongs to civil, not to natural law (q95 a4 ad1). The first group belongs to natural law. It is less clear what Aquinas believes about the second and third groups. He distinguishes the law of nations from natural law while claiming that it is derived from natural law.[72] But he does not seem to take this view of duties to oneself; they do not seem to be any less a requirement of natural law simply because they are not obviously required by it. Perhaps Aquinas believes that all of these precepts belong to natural law, in the sense that they can be justified by derivation, simple or complicated, from the first principles of natural law.

Does Aquinas' division of the different precepts derived from the common principles give us a clear idea of how the subordinate principles are to be derived, by easy inference or diligent inquiry? He suggests that the different basic inclinations of human nature indicate to us that we need provisions for the preservation of life, for relations between men and women and parents and children, and for our relations to a community and to God (q94 a2). From these, he suggests, we can understand why we need the different provisions that are embodied in the precepts derived from natural law.[73]

The sort of argument, then, that is needed to discover what is required by natural law seems similar to the sort of argument that is needed to show that one or another state of character is a virtue; the results of each type of inquiry ought to overlap. They cannot coincide

---

[70] Cf. 2-2 q56 a1; 1-2 q100 a3.
[71] On duties to oneself see Butler, D6.
[72] Aquinas discusses the question further in 2-2 q57 a3.
[73] Contrast Scotus' introduction of the divine will in formulating these principles, §384.

exactly, since Aquinas' discussion of the precepts derived from natural law is concerned with duties (debita) that are owed by one person to another person or to the community or to God; a search for these precepts will not necessarily include everything that is included in the virtues in quite the same order. Aquinas remarks, for instance, that self-regarding precepts are more difficult to recognize as duties, but our awareness of them is less dimmed by sin than is the awareness of other-regarding precepts. We more readily recognize them as the source of virtues if we are arguing from the ultimate end to the virtuous character.

314. Dispensations and Exceptions

This division of precepts of the natural law helps Aquinas to resolve an apparent difficulty for his view that natural law is independent of divine commands. Any Christian moralist has to explain cases where God has apparently given 'dispensations' from obedience to the natural law. On God's orders, Abraham prepared to kill Isaac, the Israelites plundered the Egyptians, and Hosea married a prostitute. In these cases God appears to have permitted or even instructed someone to violate a moral law. These cases appear to be dispensations from the natural law, since God seems to gives permission to break the natural law.[74] Are these really dispensations, and do they show that God is sovereign over the natural law?

We need to distinguish dispensation, which creates an exemption from a rule, from moral reflexion, which discovers an exception to a generalization. A dispensation creates an exception simply by declaring it, whereas the discovery of an exception depends on deliberation and argument, rather than an act of declaration. Only a properly constituted authority can dispense from a rule, whereas anyone in principle can discover an exception; the truth of the discovery of an exception does not depend on who discovered it, but the validity of a dispensation depends on who dispenses. If the regulations of a university require a professor to return from a leave of absence after at most two years, university officials may still dispense her from this requirement, if, for instance, she holds some public office. In doing this they do not alter the regulation. The professor would not have created a valid exemption without dispensation by the appropriate authority; reasoning about the point of the regulation and the value of disregarding it would not have not have shown that the regulation did not hold in all cases. Whether or not the officials acted wisely, the dispensation is valid if they are empowered to dispense from this regulation. But if we are to find a genuine exception to a generalization, we need to deliberate wisely, and it does not matter who finds it.

Aquinas agrees that God has the power to dispense from some laws, since positive law allows dispensation. God granted the Hebrews polygamy, concubinage, and divorce through a dispensation from the usual requirements of divine law (SG iii 125 §2986). A dispensation for a particular case does not change the law, and does not alter the fact that the law is violated; the law remains the same, but in this case the violation is permitted. These dispensations all dispense from the requirements of divine positive law.

---

[74] On the treatment of dispensations before Aquinas see Lottin, PM ii 99–100. Peter Lombard, 3Sent. d37 c.5 defends the plunder of the Egyptians by claiming that it was not theft, because it fulfilled a divine command. He cites Augustine, in Exod. 39; Faust. 71.

But if we go further, and ascribe to God the power of dispensation from natural law, we destroy Aquinas' account of the rightness of natural law. If God can dispense from natural moral law, God must be sovereign over it. If his giving permission to violate the law makes it all right to violate it, the wrongness of violating the law in other cases must be the fact that it involves disobedience to a command. If wrongness consisted in something more than disobedience to God, God's permission to do the action could not change the action from being wrong to being right.[75] If his dispensation makes the action right, it must have been wrong only because God prohibited it (malum quia prohibitum).

Aquinas believes that we are committed to these false conclusions about natural law and the will of God if we allow that God dispenses people from obedience to the natural law.[76] God did not dispense Abraham from obedience to the natural law, since God did not instruct Abraham to violate the natural law. If God told Abraham to prepare to sacrifice Isaac, Abraham's obedience did not violate the natural law, even though he would have violated it if he had prepared to sacrifice Isaac without God's instruction (1-2 q100 a8 ad3).[77]

The alleged 'dispensations', therefore, do not exercise God's sovereign will, but manifest God's wisdom. Since God understands the natural law better than we do, God is right in instructing us to act in ways that in other circumstances would be morally wrong. The lower precepts of the natural law cannot be stated in generalizations that hold without exception and that we can immediately apply to practice without further moral reflection. The generalizations that we formulate and legitimately rely on may none the less have exceptions. Sometimes we can discover these exceptions for ourselves, but sometimes we ought to rely on God to reveal them to us. It was not up to Abraham to decide for himself when he ought to prepare to kill an innocent person. But when we have reason to believe we have been given God's instructions about a particular case, we have reason to believe that the generalization we normally accept has an exception, since God's instructions are infallibly correct.

In denying that these exceptional cases are genuine dispensations, Aquinas makes it clear that he identifies the natural law with the truths grasped by God's wisdom, not with commands coming from God's legislative will. The fact that God commands the observance of the natural law gives us a reason to observe it, distinct from the reason derived from the

[75] On apparent 'change' in secondary precepts see 1-2 q94 a4; *in EN* v lec. 12; *3Sent.* d37 q1 a3 sol. = P vii 425b.

[76] On dispensations see *3Sent.* d37 q1 a4 = P vii 436–7. On Scotus' treatment in *3Sent.* d37 see §383. Cajetan comments in ad 1-2 q100 a8 = L vii 216–17. See Boler, 'Exceptions'.

[77] 'Now the precepts of the Decalogue contain the very aim (intentio) of the legislator, namely God. For the precepts of the first table, which direct us to God, contain the very direction (ordo) to the common and final good, which is God. And the precepts of the second table contain the very direction of justice that is to be observed among human beings, namely that nothing that ought not to be done (indebitum) should be done to anyone, and that what is owed (debitum) should be rendered to each . . . . Consequently the precepts of the Decalogue are altogether indispensable' (1-2 q100 a8). 'Consequently when the children of Israel, by God's command, took away the spoils of the Egyptians, this was not theft, because it was owed to them, according to God's judgment. Similarly, when Abraham consented to kill his son, he did not consent to murder, because it was required (debitum) by the command of God, who is lord of life and death, that his son should be killed. . . . In this way, therefore, the precepts of the Decalogue, as far as concerns the character of justice that they contain, are unchangeable. But as far as concerns some determination by application to individual actions—for instance, that this or that is murder, theft or adultery, or not—this is changeable' (1-2 q100 a8 ad3). On the immutability of the natural law see also 1-2 q94 a5 ad2; 2-2 q64 a6 ad1; q104 a4 ad2; q154 a2 ad2. Aquinas' position is discussed at length by Suarez, *Leg.* ii 15.16–28. Suarez argues that in each case of an apparent dispensation, the subject-matter or the circumstances differ, so that the action that would otherwise be a theft is not a theft (see esp. his helpful example of annulling, rather than dispensing from, a promise, §27).

fact that it is the law suitable for our nature. Suitability to our nature gives both God and us the basic reason for acceptance of the natural law.

315. Misunderstandings of Natural Law

Later moralists, both inside and outside mediaeval Aristotelianism, continue the discussion of natural law, and many of them continue the discussion of questions raised by Aquinas, To approach this later debate on natural law, it is useful to draw some preliminary conclusions about Aquinas' position.

We have found so far that Aquinas is not a 'natural law moralist', since he does not try to explain morality from some prior conception of law.[78] His view about the connexion of moral principles to natural law does not imply that ethics should be cast in legal form—that, for instance, the actions required by each of the virtues can be fully expressed in a set of rules that are determinate enough to serve as guides for action applicable to particular cases. Aquinas believes that some specific legal precepts can be defended by appeal to natural law, but he does not commit himself to the further claim that a definite set of such precepts specifies the entire content of the virtues.

According to Aquinas, natural law does not introduce a new understanding of the nature of moral obligation, or some attempt to explain moral requirements as a type of legal requirements.[79] One might reasonably interpret Aquinas in these ways, if one simply noticed his use of legal terms in his discussion of natural law. But if one also attends to his application of these legal terms to the natural law, one sees the error in such an interpretation. For he argues that the demands of the virtues are precepts of natural law. To see this, we have to expand our conception of law; Aquinas does not expect us to apply our previous conception of a law to morality. In this respect his account of natural law is reductive.

Aquinas' appeal to natural law is therefore important and controversial; it claims that our basic ethical principles must correspond to the requirements of our nature, and that we have some idea of what these requirements are. It does not, however, imply that we ought to learn to be virtuous by learning a set of rules and applying them to action. Nor does it imply that the right moral system is ultimately deontological, resting on a set of principles requiring types of action or states of character without reference to any further goal.

If the introduction of natural law had these implications, it would depart sharply from an Aristotelian approach to ethics, and we might seek historical explanations of such a departure. We might, for instance, appeal to the influence of ways of thinking inspired by the Decalogue. Such an explanation may explain why other people attach importance to natural law, but it is irrelevant to Aquinas. His appeal to natural law does not imply any deviation from the fundamentally teleological aspects of Aristotelian ethics. His explanation of law and natural law seeks to show that the Aristotelian framework can readily incorporate reasonable claims about natural law.

One might suppose that a conception of morality as law binding rational agents as such is sharply opposed to the teleological and eudaemonist conception of agency and morality

---

[78] See §302.
[79] See Anscombe, 'Modern', discussed at §114.

that we normally attribute to Aristotle.[80] But Aquinas does not see any opposition; for he believes that his eudaemonist discussion of the final good explains to us the principles that he introduces in his discussion of natural law.

---

[80] Schneewind, *IA* 20: 'But Thomas departs from Aristotle in holding that the laws of the virtues can be formulated and used in practical reasoning. There are laws containing precepts for all the virtues and thus providing rational guidance where we need it (1-2 q65 a3; cf. 1-2 q94 a3). Thomas does not invoke the Aristotelian insight of the virtuous agent as our final guide. For him, the virtues are basically habits of obedience to laws.' See also 287: '. . . St Thomas subordinated the virtues to the laws of nature'. Schneewind may intend to claim both (i) that Aquinas' attitude to the virtues is deontological, whereas Aristotle's is teleological, and (ii) that he accepts general rules, whereas Aristotle is a particularist. Or he may intend (ii) alone.

22

AQUINAS: PRACTICAL REASON AND PRUDENCE

316. Virtue, Will, and Practical Reason

Examination of Aquinas' account of natural law brings us back to some questions about practical reason that faced us in our discussion of the virtues and vices. He suggests that the content of the subordinate principles of the natural law has to be discovered by reasoning that leads us to the whole content of the virtues. His account of the virtues accords a similar role to practical reason. He claims that virtues belong to passions that conform to reason, and hence conform to a good will. Since practical reason directs the passions, it should fix the appropriate ends of action.

The account of virtue that accords primacy to will and practical reason fits into Aquinas' claims about the will. He argues that it is distinctive of rational agents to choose freely, by deliberation in the light of the ultimate end. If the moral virtues manifest this freedom, they include an appropriate place for deliberation and practical reason. If the characteristics that distinguish the virtuous person from the vicious could not be traced to deliberation and will, we would not be exercising our freedom in forming our moral character.

Is Aquinas entitled to the claims that he makes for practical reason in his account of virtue and passion? We have already noticed a difficulty.[1] The most obvious exercise of practical reason is deliberation; deliberation is confined to means, and does not extend to ends; hence prudence, the deliberative virtue of practical intellect, is also concerned with means, and not with ends.

Questions about the scope of prudence take us back to our discussion of Aristotle. If we suppose that, in Aristotle's view, pre-rational habituation of the non-rational parts gives us virtue of character, which determines our ends, we attribute to him an anti-rationalist view that subordinates prudence to a non-rational grasp of ends.[2] But Aristotle's claim that

---

[1] See §288.

[2] This pre-rational habituation is only part of what Aristotle has in mind when he speaks of *ethismos*, which also includes the development of prudence. See §87. Bradley, *ATHG* 237–9, holds that an anti-rationalist interpretation of Aristotle is correct, at least 'if we choose to remain within the limits set by the texts and not to read between the lines' (238), and so he finds a sharp contrast with Aquinas' position.

deliberation and prudence are confined to means to ends does not support an anti-rationalist view. Aquinas, following Aristotle, takes 'means to ends' (ea quae sunt ad finem) to include parts and constituents of ends. We can deliberate about which ends to pursue by asking how they contribute to a more ultimate end. Hence we can elect the virtues, and the actions expressing them, so as to choose them for their own sakes.

These claims about deliberation do not resolve all the difficulties about practical reason and prudence. How can deliberation reach the conclusions that the virtuous person reaches? Since instrumental deliberation rests on causal reasoning, we can understand how such deliberation is correct or incorrect. Deliberation about constituents is not so easy to understand. We can illustrate it by giving simple examples—deliberating about what would constitute a good meal or an enjoyable holiday—but we might doubt whether such examples show that deliberation has the scope Aquinas claims for it. In these simple examples, we need some fairly clear idea of what would be a good meal or an enjoyable holiday, in order to deliberate about its constituents. But in the case that interests Aquinas, our initial idea of the ultimate end does not seem clear enough for us to find its constituents by deliberation. We want our conception of the ultimate end presupposed by deliberation to be definite enough to provide a starting point for deliberation, and also to be indefinite enough to preserve freedom. But if it is definite enough for deliberation to start, must it not be definite enough to introduce some element in our character that is beyond our deliberative control?

In Aquinas' view, deliberation begins from an appropriate conception of the ultimate end. This conception is clear enough for the virtuous person to get the right answer about the constituents of the end, but it is also indefinite enough to leave the choice of virtuous ends in our control. Does he offer a plausible defence of this view?

In clarifying Aquinas' views on these questions, we will also clarify his views on the rational character of the will. Aquinas conceives the will as rational desire. In asserting the primacy of the will against the passions, he asserts the primacy of rational against irrational desire; but he does not intend to assert the primacy of reason over desire. A proper conception of the will must include both a cognitive and a desiring element; and we must neither assume that all rational desire is simply the product of instrumental reasoning directed towards a non-rational desire nor reduce the desire in rational desire to a mere product or epiphenomenon of practical reason. He claims that the will is, on the one hand, rational desire and, on the other, rational by participation in reason.

Aquinas, then, does not want to reduce will to practical reason, or to suggest that practical reason motivates without desire. This extreme rationalist position would reduce virtue to knowledge, as Socrates did (ST 1-2 q58 a2). In opposing this extreme rationalist view, Aquinas urges that something needs to be added to knowledge if we are to explain the role of practical reason in a human being's action.

The anti-rationalist position of Hutcheson and Hume claims that the different specific ends people pursue reflect their different desires, inclinations, and attitudes, and must ultimately be explained by these, rather than by their different rational beliefs about anything.[3] Anti-rationalists might agree with Aquinas' claim that reason is needed to grasp ultimate ends;

---

[3] See Hutcheson, IMS 123.

but they must interpret this to mean that we need reason to recognize what in fact we pursue as our ultimate end. This function for reason is simply the task of recognizing a fact about the actual structure and tendency of our desires; it does not require the will to be moved towards this end by any sort of reason.

It would be just about possible to interpret Aquinas as a sort of anti-rationalist, if we focussed exclusively on his claims about our grasp of the ultimate end; for he agrees that we do not have any choice about whether to prescribe the pursuit of this to the will. We must consider whether this aspect of his view implies a severe restriction on the scope of practical reason.

317. Universal Conscience and the Ultimate End

The functions of deliberation depend on a non-deliberative grasp of principles, parallel to the function of theoretical intellect in grasping principles. Theoretical intellect grasps the principles of theoretical sciences intuitively, without any further inferential justification; and Aquinas believes that this intuitive grasp of principles has a practical non-deliberative counterpart. The correct ends for human life are fixed (determinati, 2-2 q47 a15), and are the objects of our natural inclination (1-2 q51 a1; q63 a1; *Ver.* q18 a7 ad7), but grasped by practical reason. This practical reason that grasps the end is different from the practical reason that follows the desire for the end and finds means to that end. Only the second sort of practical reason belongs to prudence.[4] These two functions of practical reason deal, respectively, with universal and particular principles.[5]

This division between two roles of practical reason has no explicit Aristotelian support, but it is a reasonable expansion of Aristotle. For we need some account of how we can form the ends that are characteristic of the virtuous person. To answer this question, Aquinas introduces synderesis ('universal conscience'), which is the specific disposition of practical reason that grasps the first principles.[6] He claims that these principles are the first principles of natural law.

Aquinas inherits a conception of synderesis originally from Jerome. Discussions of Jerome treat synderesis as a universal grasp of basic moral principles that is present in us all, no matter how bad we become. It explains why even bad people retain their capacity to recognize the wrongness of what they are doing.[7] Aquinas tries to explain this capacity

---

[4] '. . . reason, in so far as it grasps the end, precedes desire for the end (cf. q12 a1 ad1, 3), but desire for the end precedes reason reasoning towards electing the things that are towards the end, which belongs to prudence' (1-2 q58 a5 ad1).

[5] 'About the universal principles of things to be done a human being is rightly disposed through the natural understanding of principles, through which a human being cognizes that nothing bad is to be done, or also (vel etiam) through some practical science. But this is not enough for reasoning correctly about particulars' (1-2 q58 a5). Cajetan ad loc (= L vi 378 §viii) takes 'or also' to introduce prudence as scientia, contrasted with intellectus of the principles.

[6] 'Synderesis' should perhaps be translated 'observance'; see Lampe, *PGL* s.v. *suntêrêsis*, §2. Synderesis is a topic of discussion in mediaeval philosophy independent of reflexion on Aristotle; Aquinas is the first writer to connect the discussion systematically with Aristotle. See Lottin, *PM* ii 103; Potts, *CMP* 10; Crowe, *CPNL* 123–7 (who argues against reading 'synderesis' in Jerome).

[7] Jerome introduces synderesis in his discussion of *Ezekiel* 1:5–10. He mentions that many people take the face of the eagle to represent a fourth part of the soul that is superior to the other three Platonic parts. It displays 'sparks as of the appearance of shining bronze' (scintillae quasi aspectus aeris candentis, 1:7). Jerome identifies the sparks with *synteresis*,

through an Aristotelian account of practical reason. He follows his predecessors in citing Aristotle's claim that all intellect is correct (*DA* 433a26; *in DA* iii 15 §§826–7).[8] Since Aristotle could not reasonably claim that every exercise of practical intellect is correct, he must, in Aquinas' view, be thinking of practical intellect applied to ultimate principles.[9] This is where he needs an infallible grasp of principles. In the theoretical sciences, the truth of conclusions derived from the principles depends on the correctness of our grasp of principles. Equally, we must grasp the principles of practical reason.[10] The practical principles that guide our natural inclination are naturally known, as the first principles of theoretical sciences are (1-2 q63 a1; 2-2 q47 a6). The special faculty that grasps ultimate practical principles is synderesis (1a q79 a12).

Aquinas, therefore, identifies synderesis with the Aristotelian intellect that grasps first principles.[11] He believes that Aristotle himself recognizes this function for practical intellect. Synderesis is always correct because it grasps the ultimate first principles, and we cannot be mistaken about them. Hence it can fulfil its function—as described by Jerome on Cain—of 'protesting against evil' (remurmurare malo).

Earlier writers use 'conscientia' to apply indifferently to our grasp of ultimate principles and to our grasp of what we should do in this or that particular situation. Aquinas

a capacity, present even in bad people, to grasp the rightness and wrongness of particular actions: '. . . that spark of conscience (scintilla conscientiae) which was not extinguished in the breast of Cain after he was turned out of Paradise, and by which we discern that we sin, when we are overcome by pleasures or frenzy and sometimes even deceived by a likeness of reason itself' (Jerome, *in Ezech.* 1.7). Jerome believes that conscience is not effective in everyone; he cites *Jeremiah* 3:3, 'Yet you have the forehead of a whore; you refuse to be ashamed'. But he treats it as a moral capacity superior even to reason. Jerome's comment becomes part of mediaeval discussion on conscience because Peter Lombard cites it among authorities for the view that a human being naturally wills good; he takes Jerome to refer to 'the superior spark of reason' (*3Sent.* d39). Aquinas refers to Jerome at *Ver.* q16 a1 obj1; a3 sc2.

  [8] For earlier evidence see Lottin, *PM* ii 132, 167. Aquinas' predecessors cite this claim without trying to integrate universal conscience into an account of Aristotle on practical reason, but Aquinas tries to show how Aristotle's outlook includes universal conscience.

  [9] Aristotle himself probably does not recognize a role for non-inferential 'understanding' (*nous*) in grasping ultimate practical principles. One might appeal to *EN* 1143a35–b5 to argue that he recognizes such a role. Aquinas, however, wisely avoids this interpretation of the passage; see *in EN* vi 9 §§1247–55.

  [10] 'And so, in human actions also, in order for some correctness in them to be possible, it is necessary for there to be some permanent principle that has unchangeable correctness, a principle by reference to which all actions are examined, so that this permanent principle resists everything evil and assents to everything good. And this principle is synderesis, whose task it is to protest against evil and to tend towards good' (*Ver.* q16 a2).

  [11] '. . . so also in practical reason some things preexist as principles naturally known; and of this sort are the ends of the moral virtues, because the end in things to be done is related as the principle is in theoretical matters, as was said above. [See 2-2 q23 a7 ad2; 1-2 q57 a4.] Some things are in practical reason as conclusions; this is the character of the things towards the end, which we arrive at from the ends themselves. These are the concern of prudence, applying universal principles to particular conclusions about things to be done. And thus it does not belong to prudence to fix the end for the moral virtues, but only to arrange about the means to the end' (2-2 q47 a6). 'What fixes the end for the moral virtues is the natural reason which is called universal conscience' (q47 a6 ad1). 'And so, just as in theoretical reason there are innate principles of demonstrations, so also in practical reason there are innate ends that are connatural to a human being. And so about these <principle> sthere is no state of possession that is acquired or infused, but one that is natural, as universal conscience is, in whose place the Philosopher places understanding in matters of action. . . . [P]rudence is in practical reason in so far as it treats of things that are towards the end. But because the natural tendency towards an end comes from the one who constitutes (praestituente) nature, who assigns this sort of direction to nature, for that reason the natural tendency of the will towards the end is not from reason, unless in accord with a natural communication, by which it results that desire joined with reason tends naturally to conforming itself to reason as standard (regulae). And from this it results that the will tends naturally towards the end that is naturally placed in reason' (*3Sent* d33 q2 a4 sol.4 = P vii 365a). Aquinas says nothing in support of this interpretation of Aristotle in his commentary on the relevant part of the *EN*.

believes that this broad use of 'conscientia' is confusing. We should confine it to our grasp of particulars, and use 'synderesis' for our grasp of the ultimate principles. To capture Aquinas' distinction, we may render 'synderesis' by 'universal conscience' and 'conscientia' by 'particular conscience'. The distinction helps to clarify Jerome's view. When Jerome says that conscience can be overcome, he refers to the failure of particular conscience to recognize that a particular action, or a specific type of action, is wrong. The spark of conscience that is not extinguished in anyone is universal conscience.[12]

Practical intellect, exercised in universal conscience, is prior to the desire for the end, since apprehension precedes desire (1-2 q58 a5 ad1); but the desire for the end precedes the election of the means, which concerns prudence. Virtue aims at the right end not because of prudence, but because of universal conscience. The truths that concern universal conscience are sharply contrasted with those that concern prudence; for the right ends of human life are 'fixed' or 'definite' (2-2 q47 a15), whereas the means to these ends are not fixed, and hence are subject to the deliberative virtue of prudence.[13]

How should we connect this moral insight belonging to universal conscience with the moral convictions that we form through the moral virtues? If universal conscience is a source of moral principles independent of the moral virtues, Aquinas seems to recognize two distinct, and possibly conflicting, sources of moral principles. The moral virtues have a eudaemonist focus; the right actions depend on the different ways in which the will ought to control the passions for the ultimate good of the agent. If universal conscience is a separate source of moral principles, it may lack this eudaemonist focus.

Moreover, Aquinas' doctrine of universal conscience may well appear to require a strongly rationalist and non-deliberative interpretation or reconstruction of Aristotle's views on practical reason.[14] The rational understanding that belongs to universal conscience is non-deliberative, and so is distinct from the understanding that belongs to prudence. Aquinas' appeal to an analogy with theoretical demonstration suggests that he may be substituting a deductive for a deliberative account of practical reason. If he does this, he takes practical reason to be analogous to theoretical reason in ways that Aristotle does not seem to contemplate. Unlike Aristotle, he appeals to self-evident basic ethical principles and to derivative principles that are (apparently) to be deduced from them.

If he attributes this role to universal conscience, Aquinas correspondingly reduces the role of deliberation in practical reason. The only function that Aristotle explicitly attributes to practical reason is deliberation, but it has often been supposed that this cannot be the only function he has in mind. Aquinas may be influenced by this argument: (1) Deliberation is about means to ends and has to assume some initial grasp of ends. (2) This initial grasp of ends must be a function of practical reason. (3) Hence it must be intuitive rather than deliberative. (4) Hence it must consist in a grasp of self-evident principles. We need to see whether Aquinas' remarks on universal conscience imply this strongly foundationalist and demonstrative picture of practical reason.

---

[12] See 2Sent d39 q3 a1 = P vi 740a; Ver. q17 a2 = M 331a.

[13] See 2-2 q47 a15: sed ea quae sunt ad finem in rebus humanis non sunt determinata.

[14] On synderesis and Aristotelian practical intellect cf. Bradley, ATHG 240. He finds a sharp contrast between Aristotle and Aquinas partly because he holds an anti-rationalist view of Aristotle on desire and practical reason. See §89.

318. How Universal Conscience Grasps Natural Law

To see where Aquinas stands on these questions, we may consider his views on the relation of universal conscience to natural law. We saw that he follows St Paul in taking human beings to be a law to themselves, because of their universal knowledge of natural law. He also agrees with St Paul in attributing this universal knowledge to conscience, but he tries to be more precise.

The sources that he discusses use 'conscientia' (or the underlying Greek *suneidêsis*) indiscriminately. To clarify their views, he needs to say whether a given remark refers to particular or to universal conscience. When Damascene describes conscience as the law of our intellect (*Ver.* q17 a1 sc1), Aquinas applies the description to universal rather than particular conscience.[15] Similarly, he takes St Paul's remarks on conscience to mean that universal conscience grasps the natural law, whereas particular conscience applies the principles of the natural law to actions.[16]

This connexion of the natural law with universal conscience helps to explain how rational agents necessarily grasp the natural law. For universal conscience differs from particular conscience in being infallible and inextinguishable.[17] The source of moral error is not the loss or corruption of universal conscience, but the errors we make in applying it in the exercise of particular conscience. The first principle of natural law is grasped infallibly and inextinguishably by everyone.

It is difficult to say how many of the precepts of natural law are within the proper scope of universal conscience. On the one hand, universal conscience is infallible in everyone. On the other hand, it protests at evil-doing, as it does in Cain. But these two features are difficult to reconcile. For if it is infallible, it cannot include any of the mistakes that lead the bad person astray; hence its principles need to be very general and schematic. But if it protests, it must include precepts that are specific enough to expose the bad person's errors.[18]

Universal conscience does not extend to precepts of natural law at the lower levels.[19] The fourth class, determinations of natural law, are not requirements of natural law itself. The third class, consisting of the less obvious derived precepts, are not first principles of natural law, whereas universal conscience is confined to first principles.

It is difficult to decide whether universal conscience grasps all the precepts at the first and second levels. Precepts at the second level, including the Decalogue, are obvious consequences of the principles of natural law, but they are not the most obvious precepts of all, since they are derived from precepts prohibiting harm.[20] But Aquinas sometimes seems to imply that universal conscience does not grasp precepts at either of these levels. Some people do not accept them; if they fell within the scope of universal conscience, then,

---

[15] 'It should be said that conscience is the law of our intellect because it is the judgment of reason, derived from natural law', *Ver.* q17 a1 ad sc1. See also a2 ad4; *ST* 1a q79 a13.

[16] 'One is said to be conscious to oneself through the natural law in the way of speaking in which one is said to consider in accordance with principles, but [one is said to be conscious to oneself] through conscience in the way of speaking in which one is said to consider by the very act of consideration' (*Ver.* q17 a1 ad sc2; cf. a2 ad6).

[17] See *Ver.* q16 a2, quoted in n10 above.

[18] On the extent of infallible moral knowledge see *in DA* iii 15 §826; *in EN* v 12 §1018; *2Sent.* d24 q2 a3.

[19] See §314.

[20] 'The precepts of the Decalogue are first precepts of law, and precepts to which natural reason assents at once as most obvious' (2-2 q122 a1). See Finnis, *NLNR* 51.

apparently, universal conscience would be mistaken in these people, and would not be infallible, as Aquinas claims it is. People's grasp of the natural law does not always lead them to the right conclusions, even on simple moral questions.[21] That is why the written law is needed to correct the natural law.

To explain the extent of error, Aquinas distinguishes the common first principles, which are always valid and always recognized by everyone, from the secondary precepts, which have exceptions and are not always recognized by everyone. The common first principle of acting in accordance with reason is always valid and always recognized, and hence never lost through error. The precept of returning deposits follows from this common first principle as a precept valid for most cases; but it has some exceptions, and people can be in error about it.[22] Passions or bad habits or a bad natural condition may distort one's grasp of a secondary precept; the Germans, for instance, found nothing wrong in theft 'even though it is expressly contrary to the law of nature' (1-2 q94 a4).[23] In these cases, apparently, we go wrong because we do not accept a principle, not because we fail to see how our principle applies to this case.

Aquinas suggests that the destructible precepts are those that have exceptions. The rule of restoring deposits has genuine exceptions, and we need to reason about the cases in which it ought not to be followed (q94 a4). Since there is room for such reasoning, there is also room for us to mislead ourselves into thinking the principle is never valid, or that the exceptions are so numerous that we need not restore deposits except when it suits us. The true belief that the precept has exceptions gives an opening for the sophistical and self-serving reasoning (explicit or implicit) that challenges the precept even on the occasions when it should be observed.

319. Why Universal Conscience is Indestructible

To clarify Aquinas' claims about the scope of universal conscience, we may examine his claim about indestructibility. Acceptance of the very first principle, that good is to be done and evil avoided, is not a merely anthropological or psychological fact, but a defining feature of a rational agent. Similarly, someone who did not accept any principle of acting in accord with reason would be unwilling to consider an action with reference to what is good all things considered; and someone who did not consider actions from this point of view would not be a rational agent at all.

The indestructible principles, then, seem to be those that are necessary for being a rational agent open to moral evaluation. These are indestructible in a rational agent, because their destruction would transform a rational agent into something else. If we became entirely indifferent to questions about the overall goodness of her actions, we would no longer be agents open to moral assessment. However vicious a rational agent becomes, some principles cannot be destroyed in him. An agent in whom they were destroyed would no longer be morally vicious, but would display some non-moral type of badness that would not

---

[21] '...the law of nature in some people's hearts, as it concerns some matters, is corrupted to the extent that they regard as good things that are naturally bad' (q94 a5 ad1).

[22] Scotus exploits these exceptions to argue for divine dispensations. See §379.   [23] Cf. q94 a6; q99 a2 ad2.

reflect a bad state of character. Since universal conscience grasps this universal aspect of the natural law, it cannot be destroyed, even in vicious people.[24] It does not grasp the precepts of the Decalogue. The wrongness of theft is obvious not to all those who think about it, but only to those whose thought is free of corrupting influences (such as those that affected Caesar's Germans). The precepts that are obvious to everyone who thinks about them are the higher precepts about acting according to reason and (perhaps) about refraining from harm. These are the principles whose acceptance is a condition of being a rational agent.

Aquinas has a good reason, therefore, for believing that universal conscience is infallible and indestructible in everyone. His belief does not rest on optimism about the moral sensitivity of every human being; it rests on conditions for rational agency. These are the same conditions that Aquinas develops and clarifies in his account of the will, of responsibility, and of the virtues. Rational agents, as he understands them, have an indestructible grasp of these conditions. His account of universal conscience does not introduce a new claim about human moral knowledge; he simply returns to the basic characteristics of a rational will.

This explanation of indestructibility supports Aquinas' view that universal conscience grasps the first principles of natural law. The awareness of natural law is also indestructible; everyone has some grasp of it, just by being a rational agent. He does not believe that the indestructibility of the natural law is merely contingently connected to being a rational agent. Since he takes the connexion to be necessary, he believes it is captured in the teleological character of rational agency.

But this austere conception of universal conscience faces an objection. Universal conscience protests at evil-doing, but the precepts that it grasps seem too schematic to protest at anything. Could Cain not have accepted all the highest principles of the natural law, and still have claimed to be justified on this occasion in killing Abel? If universal conscience is indestructible in rational agents because it is necessary for rational agency, it is present even in rational agents who make the wickedest conceivable choices. It can protest against these choices only if they violate the conditions of rational agency; but Cain's choice seems to be compatible with being a rational agent.

Aquinas might reply that if Cain is a rational agent, he has some regard for human society and for other rational agents. He does not believe in general that other people should simply be treated either as mere resources for securing his ends or as mere obstacles in his way. But he thinks he is allowed to make an exception to his general attitude because of his rivalry with Abel, even though he could not justify this exception if he were challenged. Evildoers do not really act on the basis of a considered conception that connects their action with the ultimate practical principles they accept. On the contrary, they fail to act on their ultimate principles, and their failure is to be explained by the bad influences—passion, custom, and so on—that Aquinas mentions. Cain killed Abel because he resented Abel's success, and

---

[24] 'And in this way it is impossible for universal conscience to be destroyed in the universal case, but it is extinguished in a particular case whenever someone sins in election. For the power of appetite or of some other passion so absorbs reason that in election universal conscience does not apply the universal judgment to the particular action. But this does not extinguish universal conscience without qualification, but in a particular respect' (*Ver.* q16 a3). 'He is indeed corrupted about the principles of things to be done, not indeed in the universal, but in the particular thing to be done—namely, in so far as reason is abased through the state of vice, so that he does not apply the universal judgment in electing its particular thing to be done' (*Ver.* q16 a3 ad3).

failed to subdue his sinful desire (*Gen.* 4:7).[25] He did not attempt to justify what he had done; he did not even admit he had done it.[26] Cain acted on the good presented to him by passion, not on the good implied by his ultimate convictions or assumptions about good and evil.

The vicious person accepts the correct principles grasped by universal conscience. His error is the result, as Aquinas says, of 'the custom of sinning'.[27] The error is 'about particulars', in the sense that it is about specific and determinate ends; but it is not confined, as incontinence is, to particular occasions (1-2 q77 a2). The vicious person is wrong about the specific ends that are worth pursuing. His convictions do not result from a serious effort to reach a rational conception of the good from the ultimate practical principles grasped by universal conscience; they result from ignoring these principles and their implications, because at the moment some particular goods seem immediately attractive.

This description clarifies the protesting function of universal conscience. The vicious person does not always recognize that his action violates the ultimate practical principles he accepts; but he accepts principles whose clear implications forbid the vicious actions he chooses. The 'protest' of universal conscience is silent; the vicious person would see his error if he considered the clear implications of the ultimate principles he accepts. Like Cain, the vicious person does not try to justify his actions by reference to ultimate practical principles. He does not, for instance, believe he has some good reason that he can defend to other people for stealing or killing, and he does not deny that human society requires a prohibition on killing or stealing; he simply does not face these questions when he forms a conception of the good under the influence of his passions.

Even the vicious person, therefore, grasps the common first principles. Some of the principles embodied in the Decalogue are obvious consequences of the common first principles, and people naturally recognize them as consequences, but not everyone consistently accepts them. Those who do not accept them are diverted from the normal and natural course of reasoning because their reason is depraved 'from passion, or from bad customs or from a bad natural state' (q94 a4). The common principles cannot be destroyed from human hearts in their universal character, but the natural law can be destroyed 'in a particular action to be done (operabili), in so far as reason is impeded from applying a common principle to a particular action to be done, because of appetite or some other passion' (q94 a6).[28]

We noticed earlier that Aquinas' appeal to universal conscience and natural law might be taken to suggest a strongly deductive picture of practical reason, filling a gap in Aristotle's account by appeal to ultimate principles intuitively known, from which other practical principles are reached by deduction. We can now see, however, that this would be a mistaken interpretation of Aquinas; the principles grasped by universal conscience are necessary features of rational agency. They lack the sort of moral content that would allow us to say that we grasp basic moral principles by intuition and deduction. If Aquinas had claimed

---

[25] 'But if <you act> badly, sin will at once be at the door; but its desire will be under you, and you will master it' (*Gen.* 4:7 Vulg.).

[26] See *Gen.* 4:9; 'I do not know; am I my brother's keeper?'   [27] See 1-2 q99 a2 ad2; *Mal.* q3 a12 = M 516a.

[28] Both of these deficiencies, in applying the most common principles and in recognizing the principles derived from them, make it appropriate for divine law to enjoin on us even the principles that we can know by reason (1-2 q99 a2 ad2). The divine law need not cover the principles that are not obscured by sin, but it must cover those that are obscured by sin, even if these principles are obvious to anyone who reflects clearly without being biased by a tendency to sin (1-2 q100 a5 ad1; 2-2 q22 a1 ad1).

that, for instance, we know the precepts of the Decalogue by intuition and can therefore treat them as ethical axioms, he would be adding an important claim to Aristotle that would turn Aristotle's theory in a definitely intuitionist direction. This, however, is not Aquinas' view of the Decalogue; for he suggests that our tendency to draw mistaken conclusions from the most common principles is the reason why God revealed the Decalogue to us (q99 a2 ad2). If he had supposed that we have non-inferential knowledge of principles at the level of the Decalogue, he would not have given this explanation of our tendency to error.

Since universal conscience is infallible and indestructible, it does not grasp the specific end that guides the virtuous person. The end grasped by universal conscience is common to virtuous and vicious people, whereas the virtuous person has a more detailed conception of this end, ruling out the exceptions that vicious people allow themselves. Aquinas' claims about the proximate end of the virtuous and the vicious person show that the vicious person's error does not consist simply in his misdirected appetites; it also consists in deliberative error that prevents him from seeing that the virtuous person's end is the way to achieve happiness.

Something must mediate, therefore, between universal conscience and the virtuous end.[29] Since the natural law includes specific principles that are not within the scope of universal conscience, we need the intellectual virtue that grasps them. The prescription of universal conscience commits us to the further principle: 'It is reasonable to impose whatever control over appetite is needed for action in accordance with reason'. But this principle does not identify a specific and determinate type of control over appetite. To find the more specific principles that identify the right kinds of actions, we need to proceed 'by rational inquiry' (per rationis inquisitionem, 1-2 q94 a3). To see where the vicious person goes wrong, we need to examine the type of 'rational inquiry' that Aquinas introduces to discover the principles of the virtues.

320. How Prudence Discovers Ends

The intellectual virtue that allows us to engage in this rational inquiry successfully is prudence. If prudence is a deliberative virtue, the rational inquiry that takes us from the universal to the specifically virtuous end is deliberative inquiry. But this conclusion may surprise us if we remember that deliberation is restricted to discovering means to ends. If this restricted role for deliberation prevents it from discovering specific ends that embody

---

[29] 'For just as reason in theoretical matters is derived from principles known through themselves, the state possessing which is called understanding (intellectus), so also it is necessary that practical reason be derived from principles known through themselves, e.g., that what is bad is not to be done, that the precepts of God are to be obeyed, and so on for other cases; and the state possessing these is called universal conscience. For this reason I say that universal conscience is distinguished from practical reason not through the substance of the capacity, but through the state, which is in a certain way innate in our mind from the very light of the active intellect, in the same way as the state that possesses theoretical principles (e.g., that every whole is greater than its part, and so on) <is innate in our mind>' (2Sent. d24 q2 a3 = P vi 600b). 'This very thing that is being conformed to correct reason is the proper end of each moral virtue. For temperance aims at (intendit) this, namely that a human being should not deviate from reason because of appetites; and similarly <the aim of> bravery is that a human being should not deviate from the correct judgment of reason because of fear or rashness. And this end is fixed for a human being in accordance with natural reason; for natural reason instructs each person to act in accordance with reason' (2-2 q47 a7).

universal ends, some non-deliberative function of prudence is needed for the formation of the specifically virtuous end.[30]

To see what function Aquinas intends for prudence, we should see how he describes the inquiry that discovers the virtuous end. The vicious person has only the 'prudence of the flesh' that is mentioned by St Paul, whereas the virtuous person has genuine prudence, the 'prudence of the spirit'.[31] Since genuine prudence 'arranges' the different ways in which the different virtues achieve the mean that consists in acting in accord with reason, prudence finds the virtuous end.[32]

The specific end of the virtuous person is the proximate as opposed to the ultimate end of virtue. The proximate end is an object of election, in so far as it is chosen as a way to realize the ultimate end. Since Aristotle claims that virtue makes the end right, Aquinas says that aiming at the correct end is an act of moral virtue 'principally'. But since the aiming is a result of the correct election, it must be a result of deliberation, which is the basis of election. Since prudence is the deliberative virtue, correct aiming is an act of prudence 'originally', since it results from the exercise of prudence. Prudence does not simply find ways to achieve the virtuous end in specific types of cases; it also discovers the virtuous end by deliberation, and thereby fixes the end for virtue.[33] Deliberation finds 'the things towards' the universal end of acting in accordance with reason. If we find the way to achieve the universal end, we have

[30] This argument may influence Westberg, RPR 165–7.

[31] Rm. 8:6 (Vulg.), 'for the prudence of the flesh (prudentia carnis: Gk *phronêma sarkos*) is death'. See 2-2 q47 a13.

[32] '. . . prudence is correct reason about matters for action, as the Philosopher says in *Ethics* VI (c.4). Now correct reason about things to be done presupposes one thing, and produces three things. For it presupposes the end, which counts as (sicut) the principle in things to be done, just as theoretical reason presupposes principles from which it demonstrates. But correct reason in matters of action produces three things: First, it deliberates correctly; secondly it judges correctly about the results of deliberation; thirdly, it prescribes (praecipit) correctly and steadily (constanter) what has been reached by deliberation. And so for the prudence of the flesh it is required that someone presupposes as the end what is pleasing to the flesh, and that he deliberates about, and judges about, and prescribes, the things that are appropriate for this end . . . Prudence of the spirit is spoken of, in accordance with what has been said, when someone, having presupposed the end of spiritual good, deliberates, judges, and prescribes the things that are appropriately directed to this end' (*in Rm.* 8:1 = P xiii 76b). The role ascribed to prudence here applies to the acquired virtues, as opposed to the infused virtues.

[33] '. . . For the perfection of a moral virtue three things are necessary. The first is the presentation of the end. The second is the tendency towards the end that has been presented. The third is election of the things towards the end. Now the proximate end of human life is the good of reason in common; hence Dionysius says that human evil is to be against reason. That is why the aim in all moral virtues is to lead passions and actions to the correctness of reason. Now correctness of reason is natural; hence the presentation of the end belongs to natural reason and precedes prudence, just as the understanding of principles precedes scientific knowledge (scientiam). That is why the Philosopher says, in Ethics VI, that prudence has as its principles the ends of the virtues. But this good of reason is determined in so far as a mean in actions and passions is constituted by the right (debitam) proportion of circumstances, which prudence brings about. And so the mean of moral virtue, as is said in Ethics II, is in accord with correct reason, which is prudence; and so in a certain way prudence presents the end to the moral virtues, and its action is mixed in their actions. But the tendency towards that end belongs to moral virtue which consents to the good of reason in the natural way (per modum naturae); this tendency towards the end is called election, in so far as the proximate end is directed towards the ultimate end. And that is why the Philosopher says, in Ethics II, that moral virtue makes the election correct. But the discernment of the things by which we can achieve this good of reason, in actions and in passions, is an act of prudence; hence the presentation of the end precedes the act of prudence and of moral virtue; but the tendency towards the end, or correct election of the proximate end, is an act of moral virtue principally, but of prudence originally. Hence the Philosopher says that correctness of election belongs to the other virtues from prudence, just as correctness in natural aiming comes from divine wisdom directing nature. And in accord with this the action of prudence is also mixed in the actions of the other virtues. For just as the natural tendency <towards an end> comes from natural reason, so also the tendency of moral virtue comes from prudence; but election is of the things towards the end, in so far as election involves (importat) a precept of reason about pursuing these things' (*3Sent.* d33 q2 a3 = P vii 362a).

found the distinctive end of the virtuous person.[34] Neither virtue nor prudence presents (praestituere) the universal end, but prudence finds the things 'towards' it.[35] It presents the specifically virtuous end as a result of deliberation about how to realize the universal end presented by universal conscience.[36]

Some of Aquinas' successors mark the different roles of prudence by identifying two different type of prudence. 'Universal' prudence takes us from the universal end to the specifically virtuous end. It begins from the precept of acting in accordance with reason and reaches the conclusion that we should (for instance) modify our tendency to fear so that we are ready to face danger in the right causes. From this deliberation we conclude that we should cultivate bravery. 'Particular' prudence takes us from the specifically virtuous end to the right actions. It assumes that bravery is a virtue, and considers what it would be brave to do in these circumstances.[37] Though Aquinas himself does not explicitly distinguish universal from particular prudence, he recognizes the two different tasks for prudence that underlie this division. He attributes to prudence the scope that is assumed by those who speak of the two types of prudence.

Prudence, therefore, directs all the moral virtues.[38] This directing does not extend simply to the choice of means to the ends of the different virtues; this is the task of particular prudence. It also includes the fixing or 'presenting' (praestituere) or 'determining' (determinare) of the end. The specific determination that he mentions is the determination of the mean that constitutes moral virtue; this determination is a task for universal prudence.[39] Prudence discovers the right proximate end, a specific sort of mean, by reflexion on the common end. The presentation of the proximate end precedes the discovery of the right action by particular prudence, but it does not precede every operation of prudence; it presupposes that universal prudence has discovered the proximate end by reflexion on the ultimate end.[40]

---

[34] 'But in what way and through what things a human being in acting is to reach the mean of reason—this belongs to the arrangement [dispositionem; v.l. 'rationem'] made by prudence. For, granted that reaching the mean is the end of moral virtue, still the mean is found by the right arrangement of the things that are towards the end' (2-2 q47 a7).

[35] 'The end does not belong to the moral virtues as themselves presenting the end, but because they tend towards the end that is presented by natural reason. They are helped to do this through prudence, which prepares the way for them, by arranging (disponendo) the things that are towards the end. Hence the remaining possibility is that prudence is nobler than the moral virtues and sets them in motion. But universal conscience sets prudence in motion, just as understanding of principles sets science in motion' (2-2 q47 a6 ad3).

[36] On prudence and the Decalogue see 2-2 q56 a1.

[37] Evidence of this development is traced by Lottin, PM iv 551–626. He mentions James of Viterbo (561); Henry of Ghent, Quodl. v 17; xii q14; Godfrey of Fontaines, Quodl. ii 11; the Paris MAs (626).

[38] 'Prudence directs the moral virtues not only in electing the things towards the end, but also in presenting the end. For the end of each moral virtue is to attain the mean in its proper matter; and this mean is determined in accord with the correct reason of prudence' (1-2 q66 a3 ad3). See also 1-2 q21 a2 ad2; q58 a2 ad4; 2-2 q119 a3 ad3.

[39] Hughes, BF xxiii 209n, seeks to explain why this claim is not in conflict with the passages on prudence as concerned with means (1-2 q57 a4; 2-2 q47 a6): 'Prudence presupposes a right attitude, appetitus, to moral ends, then prescribes where these are to be found here and now'. This answer seems to underestimate the role that Aquinas has in mind in this passage (which is not simply concerned with finding the mean here and now), and fails to ask how the 'right attitude' can be formed without some prior contribution by prudence. One might have looked for clarification of Aquinas' remark about fixing the end in his comments on Aristotle's claim that prudence is the 'true apprehension (hupolêpsis) of the end', EN 1142b33. But he reproduces the passage without comment at in EN vi 8 §1233. See §324n1.

[40] '. . . it is necessary that through reason, which prudence perfects and makes correct, the end should be presented (praestituere) to the other virtues—not only the common end, but also the proximate end, which is to attain the mean in the proper subject-matter <of a virtue>. Now a mean is determined in accordance with correct reason, as is said in Ethics II. Secondly, through correct reason comes the tendency of the virtues towards their proper end, which is aiming at the end in acquired virtues, in so far as from actions regulated by reason the state of virtue causing the aim just mentioned is

This account of the prudent person's deliberation explains the division of labour that is implied in the claim that virtue grasps the end and prudence finds the means. While this division of labour implies two distinct roles, it does not imply that either is prior to or independent of the other. On the contrary, the grasp of the end that is proper to virtue is the product of the grasp of the means that is proper to universal prudence. For the 'means' grasped by universal prudence specify the schematic ultimate end, and so they are suitable ends for the virtuous person. While a virtuous person acts because of the good that is characteristic of his specific virtue, he also pursues the ultimate end. The good specific to a virtue is its proximate end, and universal prudence discovers this by reference to the ultimate end (2-2 q123 a7).[41]

We need not suppose, then, that universal prudence reaches the specifically virtuous end from the universal end by some non-deliberative process. Aquinas' account of the ultimate end, deliberation, and election explains how prudence discovers a specific end by deliberation. He relies on a function of deliberation that he needs in his argument about freedom, happiness, and the virtues.

Our necessary desire for the ultimate end does not severely restrict the scope of practical reason. The desire that is presupposed is schematic; it aims at an end with a certain structure, but leaves the discovery of the content to further rational reflexion. The schematic, structural desire for the ultimate end is not distinctive of virtue, since it is common to all rational agents, and is not subject to their will; it is necessary for rational and free agency. Similarly, universal conscience is not a non-deliberative capacity for reaching the ends of the virtuous person. For universal conscience is common to virtuous and vicious people; it recognizes the common end of acting in accord with reason, but it does not specify this common end as the virtuous end.

Nor does Aquinas fill any gaps in his account of deliberation by appeal to natural law. He does not appeal to our innate awareness of general moral principles in order to explain how we reach the ends distinctive of the virtues. The first principle of natural law is the general form of rational agency that belongs to universal conscience. To reach more specific principles, we need rational inquiry, which is the task of deliberation and prudence. Different conceptions of the good result from different views about goods that are 'means' to the ultimate end. Happiness is 'constituted' of these goods and 'consists' in them.[42] In finding the means to the ultimate end we find the proximate end for the virtues.

This conclusion fits Aquinas' general views about rational agency and will, and the view of freedom that rests on his conception of agency. Freedom and virtue require rational agents who aim at a conception of the ultimate end; for deliberation would not be essentially comparative and essentially focussed on the overall good unless it were based on desires with the appropriate structure. But this structure still leaves it open to agents to fix the more determinate ends they will pursue. Rational agents fix these ends by their rational capacities, in contrast to non-rational agents who are 'determined to one end'.

---

brought about; and with reference to this, prudence is said to be the mother of the virtues. Thirdly, through prudence the way is made correct for each virtue, which tends towards <the correct> end in so far as through deliberation and election the useful is separated from the harmful in relation to the end of the virtue; and with reference to this, prudence is said to be the mediator and guardian of the virtues' (*3Sent.* d33 q2 a5 sol. = P vii 366a).

[41] Cf. *in EN* iii 15 §549.   [42] See 1-2 q1 a5 ad1; a6 ad2.

Aquinas uses this point to reconcile Aristotle's belief that election is confined to means with his claim that virtue makes the election right. An objector argues that in making the election right virtue must itself elect, and that since what virtue makes right is the end, it must be possible to elect ends, and not only means (1-2 q13 a3 obj1). In reply Aquinas allows that virtue elects, and that ends are subject to election, but he repeats that only means can be elected. The ends that virtue grasps are subject to election because they are directed towards the ultimate end.[43] Since we can elect ends that are directed towards the ultimate end (q13 a3 ad2), we can elect virtues through deliberation. Since our necessary pursuit of happiness does not make us aware of what happiness actually consists in, we can acquire merit by following the right view of what happiness consists in.[44]

These passages on deliberation and happiness explain how universal prudence takes us from the universal end grasped by natural reason to the specifically virtuous end. Prudence considers those things by which one achieves happiness;[45] to consider this question adequately, it must deliberate about different possible conceptions of happiness.

Just as Aristotle sometimes obscures the central role of deliberation in his account of prudence and the virtues, Aquinas sometimes obscures it too, though he clarifies it more than Aristotle does. His Aristotelian claims about virtue grasping the end, and his non-Aristotelian claims about natural law and universal conscience, might understandably encourage us to assign a more limited role to deliberation and to prudence than we have found in Aquinas. But the extended role that we have found fits his account of will, happiness, and virtue. This role helps to explain features of morality through features of rational agency.

321. How Prudence Forms the Virtuous Motive

Since prudence discovers the specifically virtuous end, it is needed for the correct election involved in acting virtuously. Prudence ensures the right motive for the action; for the prudent person's deliberation about happiness results in the right determinate conception of happiness, and this conception forms the end of the virtuous person's actions. Aquinas follows Aristotle not only in claiming that prudence requires the moral virtues (1-2 q57 a4; q58 a3; a5), but also in claiming that they require prudence (q57 a5; q58 a4). His reason for the second claim is Aristotelian. Moral virtue requires not only the right action, but also the right way of doing it. The right way of doing it must proceed from reason, not only from impulse or passion (q57 a5);[46] to proceed from reason it must proceed from correct election.

If correct election were concerned only with relatively low-level, technical choices, it would not be an obviously necessary condition for virtue. To say that virtue requires the right election would be to claim that agents who know the right sorts of things to pursue, but just lack the causal information needed to find them, cannot be virtuous. But this is not what Aquinas means. When he claims that virtue requires correct election, as opposed to

---

[43] '... the ends proper to the virtues are directed towards happiness as the ultimate end; and in this way there can be election of them' (q13 a3 ad1).

[44] See *Ver.* q22 a7, quoted at §273.   [45] ea quibus pervenitur ad felicitatem, 1-2 q66 a5 ad2.

[46] On this condition see §285.

impulse or passion, he means that reason produces the appropriate motive for choosing the virtuous action.[47] If we are guided by prudence, we do the generous action, say, for the right reason, and not simply because we have a generous impulse (q24 a3 ad1; q77 a6 ad2). The distinctive feature of the right reason is not the fact that it rests on correct causal information, but the fact that the person acting on the right reason cares about the appropriate aspect of the virtuous action (cf. q65 a1; q19 a7 ad2). Those who do the generous action from the right motive are not generous because they believe that the generous action will have precisely this effect on the other person, but because they act on their settled conviction about the value of this sort of action. Their conviction expresses the agent's conception of the ends worth pursuing, not simply her views about the most effective way to reach the ends she has set herself. That is why prudence is necessary for the perfection of the reason that is involved in election, and so necessary for moral virtue (q58 a4 ad1). The correct election of the virtuous person rests on a true conception of the ends worth pursuing, and prudence forms this conception.

This conclusion reconciles Aquinas' views about virtue with his views about freedom, responsibility, and practical reason. He believes that we are free to be either virtuous or vicious and are responsible for being one or the other. In his view, freedom belongs to the will in so far as it is capable of acting on the results of deliberation about alternatives.[48] This deliberation about alternatives cannot be applied to the ultimate end itself, since we are not free to accept or reject it. Nor can it be applied to the principles grasped by universal conscience, since we are not free to accept or reject these if they are indestructible in rational agents. Neither of these apparent restrictions on freedom, however, is a real restriction; each specifies the conditions for being a rational agent, which are also the conditions for being free.

If the determinate principles characteristic of the moral virtues were grasped by universal conscience, we would not be free to accept or reject them. Aquinas, however, believes that we are free to choose between virtue and vice, and therefore to choose the distinctive end of virtue or vice. His account of freedom implies that these ends are open to deliberation. If they are within the scope of prudence, then they are open to deliberation, and hence open to our free choice.

This implication of Aquinas' views on freedom shows how his different claims support one another if the specifically virtuous end is reached by deliberation, and how they threaten one another if he accepts some other account of how we reach the specifically virtuous end. Both an anti-rationalist account, attributing the right ends to the training of non-rational passions, and a non-deliberative rationalist account, attributing them to intuitive knowledge of principles, make it difficult to see how Aquinas' claims about the will, freedom, virtue, and practical reason cohere in the way he intends them to.[49] If the right ends are discovered by prudence, deliberating from the universal end and reaching the specifically virtuous end, Aquinas' position is coherent and intelligible.

---

[47] '. . . the motion of virtue has its origin in reason and its terminus in desire, in so far as it is moved by reason. That is why in the definition of moral virtue it is said, in *Ethics* ii, that it is "a state involving election, consisting in a mean that is determined by reason, as the wise person will determine it".' (1-2 q59 a1). The Latin version uses 'sapiens' to translate *phronimos* here, but Aquinas takes it to refer to prudence (*in EN* ii 7 §323).

[48] See §286.   [49] On mortal v. venial sin see §297.

322. Objections to Aquinas' View

Ought Aquinas to have assigned such a broad role to prudence? We may wonder whether universal and particular prudence are inseparable aspects of a single virtue or separable virtues. We might suppose that someone could be good at one of these deliberative tasks and bad at the other, so that the two virtues must be separable. We might even doubt whether universal prudence is a virtue of a moral agent at all. It seems to belong to a moral theorist who is considering what states of character are virtues and how to produce them; these are the questions that both Aristotle and Aquinas answer. But the ability to find the right answers at this high level does not seem to guarantee the ability or the experience that we need to find answers about what to do in particular situations. Equally, we might suppose that a virtuous person who has the right ends and knows what to do about them in particular situations could nonetheless lack the knowledge that would answer the theorist's questions.

This issue about the universal prudence of the moral theorist and the particular prudence of the virtuous agent already arises for the reader of Aristotle. The *Ethics* is a work of political science, political science is the same state as prudence, and prudence is deliberative. The theorist who writes the *Ethics* seems to display the same deliberative virtue that the virtuous agent displays in deciding what to do here and now.[50]

To defend his belief in the unity of prudence, Aquinas needs to show that the higher-level deliberation fixing the specifically virtuous end makes a morally significant difference to the action or motive of the virtuous person. If he is right, we must be able to see that something relevant to the moral evaluation of the action or agent depends on the presence or absence of universal prudence. We might hope to find morally relevant effects of universal prudence if we examine Aquinas' detailed discussions of individual virtues of character. Universal prudence matters in virtuous agents, if these agents are not allowed simply to take the specifically virtuous end for granted, but must also have some conception of why it is the right end to accept. If Aquinas describes this conception in any detail, he will also make it clear what sort of deliberation leads us from the universal end to the specifically virtuous end.

323. Natural Law, Universal Conscience, and Prudence

We may now review Aquinas' discussion of natural law, universal conscience, and practical reason, to see how they affect his theory. Both natural law and universal conscience are mandatory topics of discussion for him, since they are recognized by moralists who do not accept his Aristotelian assumptions and framework.[51] If he had no room for them within an Aristotelian account, he would have acknowledged the failure of an Aristotelian account to capture these recognized aspects of morality and moral understanding.

He reaffirms his Aristotelian account. The roles of universal conscience and of natural law fit his view that the central element in the Aristotelian position is the account of a rational agent as necessarily pursuing a final good and deliberating about its composition. Universal conscience is not a source of moral principles unavailable to a rational agent who tries to

---

[50] On this issue in Aristotle see §98.　　[51] See §301.

deliberate about the means to happiness; it makes us rational agents who have a conception of a final good that is open to deliberation. Similarly, the first principle of natural law does not add a further constraint on the deliberation of a rational agent about his own good; it simply expresses a necessary feature of this rational agent. The subordinate principles of natural law are reached by deliberation about happiness, and therefore they are the proper concern of prudence.

If we agree with Aquinas on these points, we agree that true moral principles are the conclusions of a rational agent's correct deliberation about her own happiness. Deliberation about happiness is essential to free rational agents. The principles that such agents implicitly accept in being concerned with their own happiness are strong enough to vindicate the moral virtues, as Aquinas conceives them.

Though this position is Aristotelian, Aquinas has no explicit Aristotelian precedent for his claim that deliberation about happiness is an essential feature of a rational agent and of a free agent. In his explanation of claims about rational agency and freedom through features of deliberation about happiness, he extends and develops Aristotelian claims, though not in an un-Aristotelian direction. The central role that Aquinas attributes to deliberation about happiness requires him to assign a large role to prudence. He emphasizes those remarks in Aristotle that favour a wider role for prudence over those that favour a narrower role.

In contrast to this Aristotelian and eudaemonist position, claims about universal conscience and natural law might seem to force Aquinas in a different direction. But he argues that they do not. All reasonable claims about moral insight derived from these sources can be understood, in his view, within the deliberative account of practical reason. This deliberative account expresses Aquinas' reductive claim that there is nothing more to the understanding of morality than the understanding of rational agency. His views on practical reason, prudence, universal conscience, and natural law, all support the reductive claim.

23

AQUINAS: THE CANON
OF THE VIRTUES

324. The Unity of Prudence

How much can we learn from universal prudence, as Aquinas conceives it? In his view, universal conscience grasps the common principles of natural law, but it does not specify the virtues that fulfill the natural law. It recognizes that good is to be done and evil avoided, and that we achieve the good in acting in accordance with reason. But we need further rational inquiry to discover that the precept of acting in accordance with reason requires the cardinal virtues. This inquiry is the task of universal prudence, which reaches the specifically virtuous end by deliberation in the light of the ultimate end.

Since we are rational agents who also have passions, we need virtues that conform our passions to our wills and conform both passions and wills to a true conception of the ultimate end. Since we aim at our perfection, and not simply at the maximum coherent satisfaction of our desires, virtue does not consist in guiding our passions by a conception of the good that aims at the satisfaction of these same passions.

Aquinas' claims about prudence commit him to a further claim about the general character of a virtue. He believes that universal prudence (reaching the specifically virtuous end by deliberation from the ultimate end) is the same virtue as particular prudence (reaching the virtuous action by deliberation from the specifically virtuous end). Hence he believes in the 'vertical unity' of universal and particular prudence. Moreover, he believes that the same prudence is needed for each of the virtues of character, so that he believes in the 'horizontal unity' of prudence. Virtuous people have the right conception of the end for the sake of which they do their different virtuous actions; the right conception of this end, as Aristotle insists, is prudence (*EN* 1142b31–3).[1]

Since prudence is horizontally and vertically unified, it is concerned with 'the whole of human life' (*in EN* vi 4 §1163), and the end it grasps is 'the common end of all of human life' (*in EN* vi 8 §1233). We must grasp this common end to form the right conception of

---

[1] In *in EN* vi 8 §1233 Aquinas clearly takes 'the end' to be the antecedent 'of which prudence is the true apprehension' in *EN* 1142b33. Some interpreters of Aristotle suppose, implausibly, that the antecedent is 'what is expedient towards the end'.

the end that guides practical reasoning (*EN* 1144a31–6; cf. *in EN* vi 10 §1273–4). Aquinas attributes belief in this common end to Aristotle, and takes it to underlie Aristotle's belief in the unity of prudence.[2] Since all the virtues aim at this common end, they need a horizontally and vertically unified prudence to tell them how to achieve their aim. The unity of prudence, therefore, is not a merely generic unity that would allow the existence of mutually independent species.

325. The Reciprocity of the Virtues

These claims about the unity of prudence imply that discovery of the virtues requires prudence. Aquinas therefore affirms one part of the traditional belief in the reciprocity of the virtues (RV).[3] The virtues are connected in so far as they are all about passions and actions that are connected to one another (*ST* 1-2 q65 a1 ad3; *Virt. Card.* a2 ad4). A stronger connexion is their connexion with the common end of human life; the correct conception of this single common end is required for every virtue.[4]

This aspect of RV follows from Aquinas' conception of the ultimate end. His initial conception is purely formal, in the sense that it does not yet specify some definite way of life or traits of character. But it imposes a non-trivial structure on ends and on deliberation. To pursue a final good is to seek to combine different ends in some mutually-supporting system that achieves the perfection of the agent. The traits and actions required by each virtue must contribute to this system of ends. This aspect of RV, therefore, follows from Aquinas' basic claims about rational agency. The relation between prudence and the perfection of the passions secures the other half of RV, the necessity of virtue for prudence (1-2 q58 a5).[5] We need our passions perfected if we are to focus steadily and without distraction on the right end.

In committing himself to RV, Aquinas implies that each virtue relies on the same universal and particular prudence in the virtuous agent and that the specific perfection of the passions required by each virtue is necessary for prudence. Some of Aquinas' predecessors and successors reject RV;[6] Scotus and Ockham argue against it at length. Some aspects

---

[2] 'He says "being one", because, if there were different prudences concerned with the matters of different moral virtues, just as there are different kinds of artifacts, it would be quite possible for one moral virtue to exist without another, each of them having a prudence corresponding to it. But this cannot be the case, because the principles of prudence are the same for the whole matter of morals, so that everything is derived from the standard of reason. And that is why because of the unity of prudence all the moral virtues are connected with one another' (*in EN* vi 11 §1288).

[3] On RV see §12 (Socrates); §49 (Plato); §116 (Aristotle); §185 (Stoics). It becomes a topic of discussion in mediaeval ethics because of Augustine; see §229. Some predecessors of Aquinas who discuss this issue are cited by Lottin, *PM* iii 209–23.

[4] See *3Sent.* d36 q1 a1 = P vii 415b: 'For each virtue operates because of the good of virtue. Hence if one aims at the good of virtue, as is appropriate for the virtuous person, one does not turn one's aim away from that end. Hence the Philosopher says that the wasteful person, who spends without concern for the good, easily turns away to any evil.' Cf. ad2, ad3. Lottin, *PM* iii 233. This is how Godfrey of Fontaines defends the unity of prudence and argues from it for RV. See Lottin, *PM* iv 590; 600.

[5] Discussed in §316.

[6] Some moralists accept RV in the case of infused moral virtues; when charity is infused by divine grace, the other virtues are infused at the same time. But this feature of the infused virtues makes it seem more plausible to deny RV in the case of the acquired virtues. See Lombard, *3Sent.* d36 c1; Bonaventure, *3Sent.* d36 a1 q1 (affirming the connexion for the infused virtues); q3 (denying it for the acquired virtues) = OO iii 790–9; Aquinas, *3Sent.* d36 q1 a2 = P vii 416.

of Aquinas' defence are better postponed until we have examined the objections; but a preliminary discussion will help us to follow the later debate.

326. Objections to the Reciprocity of the Virtues

According to RV, a perfectly virtuous agent would have all the virtues. But the very idea of such an agent may seem to rest on a misunderstanding of the character of the virtues.[7] It is difficult to see how the virtues of a Greek hoplite could co-exist with those of a mediaeval monk and with those of a twenty-first century social worker. But RV appears no more plausible if it is applied only to the virtues recognized at a particular time; why should every set of virtues in every society and culture be linked in the way required by RV?

In any case, RV seems to conflict with fairly obvious facts. The best people we can think of, from our own time or other times, do not seem to exemplify all the virtues. Perhaps they would have had less of the virtues they had if they had also tried to form other virtues. The idea that everyone should ideally display all the same 'required' virtues may seem both unrealistic and unattractive; perhaps the varieties and imperfections of different people's moral characters actually add appealing diversity to human life.

These objections to RV are especially compelling if the virtues are remedial conditions that counteract different specific tendencies for things to go wrong. If we suffer from our proclivity to excessive fear and excessive pleasure, we need bravery to counteract one proclivity and temperance to counteract the other. If we tend to take a biased view of other people's claims, we need justice. If we tend to be indifferent to the needs of others, we need benevolence.[8] The judgments that shape our conception of the virtues are judgments about the different things that can go wrong.

This remedial conception of the virtues conflicts with the conception of perfect virtue that supports RV. If different virtues counteract different dangers, they may be separable and may conflict, just as different medicines prescribed for different diseases may have conflicting effects.[9] If the virtues are piecemeal remedies for specific dangers and threats, the complete development of each virtue may not incorporate the other virtues. If we acquire different virtues, we may have to choose between conflicting goods, so that we face an inevitable loss whatever we choose.[10]

If different virtues apply conflicting remedies to different flaws, one person ought not to aim at them all. And so Aristotle's assumption that we cannot have too much of a virtue appears to ignore a remedial view. Even if a single person can or should cultivate all the virtues, they may not be internally related in a perfectly virtuous person. Perhaps the demands of justice or honesty should not incorporate the demands of generosity or kindness.

---

[7] See Strawson, 'Social' 27–9; Flanagan, VMP 10–11f.

[8] This view is developed by Warnock, OM, ch. 6; he rejects RV, 87. Foot, VV 10, also accepts a remedial view, and rejects RV, 17.

[9] Aquinas remarks that 'a medicine that would be adapted to one disease would be harmful to the second . . . and what would be a suitable medicine for one sin might provide an incentive to the second' (ST Suppl. q9 a2).

[10] '. . . so far from forming a unity in the sense that Aristotle and Aquinas believed they did, the virtues actually conflict with each other: which is to say that if someone has one of them he inevitably fails to have some other' (Foot, 'Dilemma' 57).

To see whether these are well-founded objections to RV, we need to consider whether Aquinas has good reasons for insisting that each virtue incorporates prudence. He takes universal prudence to grasp a set of principles that express the requirements of all the virtues.[11]

327. From the Ultimate End to the Cardinal Virtues

To show that prudence is unified, Aquinas needs to show that universal prudence, deliberating from the universal end, discovers the specific ends of each of the virtues, and that these ends are connected in such a way that understanding of one requires understanding of the others in their relation to the ultimate good.

Has Aquinas given deliberation too large a task, and too indefinite a starting point? We might agree that agents such as us need passions and wills guided by reason and virtue if they are to pursue their good correctly, but we might still have no clear view about what the virtues are—whether, for instance, they include the control of appetites or the formation of rational plans for the maximum satisfaction of appetites. As Aquinas remarks, we might agree that the human good requires us to act in accordance with reason, but still not agree that acting in accordance with reason requires temperance and bravery, as he understands them. It seems still more obvious that we might agree about acting in accordance with reason, but deny that such action includes action for the good of others that does not provide some antecedently-desired good for ourselves.

If our deliberation is to reach a definite result, do we perhaps need some principles, accepted apart from deliberation, that constrain the process of deliberation and introduce some definite moral content? Scotus and Ockham derive these further principles from the revealed will of God.[12] Others might derive them from some definite social facts, or collective preferences, or contingent psychological traits, that apply to some group of actual human beings but cannot be derived from Aquinas' general claims about rational agency. Any of these attempts to constrain deliberation rejects Aquinas' attempt to explain the virtues by reference to rational agency.

Aquinas believes that deliberation about one's ultimate end yields not only an account of virtue, but also a sufficiently detailed account of the virtues. Deliberation shows that the moral precepts of the Decalogue are required by the virtues, and that we have reason to care about the interests of other people for their own sakes. The considerations he has appealed to so far seem to him to support a detailed account of the virtues.

This detailed account is mostly presented in the Secunda Secundae. This Part discusses a bewildering variety of virtues and vices. Moreover, it clearly belongs to moral theology more than to moral philosophy, since it presupposes the supernatural additions (infused virtues, and so on) to the acquired moral virtues. Still, its main structure and aims are fairly clear; it tries to answer some of the questions about the virtues that we might ask when we reflect on the ultimate end, prudence, and deliberation.

---

[11] *in EN* vi 11 §1288, quoted in n2.

[12] Ockham agrees with Aquinas in recognizing non-positive and positive elements of morality. But he takes the positive elements to include higher principles that Aquinas regards as non-positive. See §395.

The main argument rests on Aquinas' claim that the matter of morality is derived from the four distinct cardinal virtues.[13] In his view, the various traits that we recognize as virtues are either aspects or applications of the cardinal virtues. They have a definite structure that shows how they meet some general requirements of rational agency.[14]

328. The Nature of a Cardinal Virtue

The cardinal virtues express the 'perfect character of virtue, which requires correctness of desire' (1-2 q61 a1). They are not necessary for every virtuous action, since not all virtuous action requires correct desire, and a mere capacity to perform some virtuous action does not imply the possession of a cardinal virtue. Aquinas' distinction between virtuous action and acting virtuously supports his claim that prudence is necessary for being a virtuous person (cf. q56 a3; q57 a5), and hence supports his defence of the reciprocity of the virtues.

To act virtuously, according to Aquinas, we must act on the cardinal virtues, no matter what special virtue we display in a particular action. Some virtues are cardinal (*cardinales*, from *cardo*, 'hinge') because they are those 'in which the moral life turns and is founded in a certain way'. The moral life is founded on them because that is the life proper to a human being, in contrast to a non-rational animal or an angel; this is the life of practical reason, the 'active life, which consists in the exercise of moral virtues'. Aquinas infers the generic features of such a life from Aristotle's account of acting virtuously (*EN* ii 4; *Virt. Card.* a1).[15] Aristotle's demand for knowledge introduces prudence;[16] his demand for correct election for the right end introduces justice; and his demand for firm and unshakeable election introduces temperance and bravery (2-2 q123 a11). Prudence is relevant because it provides the appropriate prescriptive (*praeceptiva*) knowledge, justice because it directs a person's actions to the right end, temperance and bravery because they produce the appropriate control (*moderatio*) and firmness.

These claims do not fit the passage in Aristotle that Aquinas cites, but they fit Aristotle's intentions in his account of virtue as a whole. The reference to prudence fits Aristotle's remark that the mean must be determined by the reason by which the prudent person would determine it. The demand for the right end fits Aristotle's claim that we need the right election. Firmness and control fit his demand for a firm and unchanging state. Firmness and constancy depend on the condition of our non-rational desires and passions; if they are misdirected, they will make us waver even if we make the correct (in some ways) election on occasions where strong passions are not involved.

We discover the virtues by examining the 'formal principle', which is the good of reason. This consists, first of all, in consideration by reason itself, and, secondly, in the direction of

---

[13] See *3Sent.* d33 q2 a1 sol.4 = P vii 359ab.

[14] Jordan, 'Scientia' 91–5, discusses the organization of *ST* 2–2, and emphasizes Aquinas' innovation in making the cardinal virtues the principle of organization.

[15] He cites *Proverbs* 26:14 ('As a door turns on its hinge, so does an idler in his bed') as his Scriptural authority for the term 'cardinal', and he cites Ambrose as his patristic authority for the use of 'cardinal' for the canon of four virtues. See *Card.* a1; *ST* 1-2 q61 a1 sc; *3Sent.* d33 q2 a1 sol.2 = P vii 358b.

[16] Aquinas' interpretation does not fit; Aristotle seems to be demanding simply the sort of knowledge that is necessary for voluntariness. Aquinas recognizes this point about the passage in 2-2 q58 a1. At *in EN* ii 4 §283 he does not introduce his own interpretation of the demand for knowledge.

other things by reason. These other things are actions and passions; the passions are those that can turn us away in bad directions or prevent us from going in good directions. We need prudence (for consideration by reason), justice (for right action), and temperance and bravery (for the proper regulation of potentially distracting and inhibiting passions). The same conclusion results if we consider the subject of the different aspects of the right formal principle. One subject has to be the rational part, of which prudence is the virtue. Another has to be the part that is rational by participation, and this is divided into the will, the spirited part, and the appetitive part (1-2 q61 a2).[17]

The cardinal virtues, therefore, are generic and pervasive; we do not need to look for particular occasions on which we are exercising prudence or temperance, say, as opposed to some other virtue. This feature seems to distinguish them from a virtue such as generosity or wit; if we are not in the right situation, we cannot display wit, but if we are in any situation that calls for any of the virtues, the appropriate action displays the formal principles of the different cardinal virtues (cf. 2-2 q123 a11; q141 a7).

Aquinas' view that the cardinal virtues mark pervasive features of all virtuous action is defensible by appeal to Aristotle; but it is more characteristic of Stoicism.[18] The Stoics claim that in every virtuous action we act in accordance with each of the cardinal virtues, even though we exercise some specific virtue in a way in which we do not exercise all the others. Aquinas argues that the four virtues are different specific virtues, so that we exercise temperance (e.g.) on particular occasions on which we do not (in the same way) exercise other virtues as well. This emphasis on the different occasions for the exercise of the four virtues is more clearly Aristotelian than Stoic, though the Stoics also admit that not all of the virtues are always exercised in the same way.

329. 'Principal' Displays of the Cardinal Virtues

Aquinas claims that the cardinal status of these four virtues supports and justifies the Aristotelian view that they are different specific virtues displayed in distinct ranges of action. The goodness of the pervasive virtues is displayed 'principally' or 'especially' in different ranges of action.[19] Whenever we act virtuously, we must display the appropriate firmness, but we especially display it in facing the danger of death; hence it is appropriately displayed in bravery, which is the virtue concerned with facing this danger. A similar argument applies to temperance. The claim that these are special or 'principal' displays of the relevant pervasive virtues supports the claim that these are distinct virtues with their own range of actions.

[17] For objections to this classification see §290.
[18] Ambrose relies on the Stoic division in *Off*. He argues that the saints of the Old Testament display the cardinal virtues: 'What duty (officium) belonging to the principal virtues was lacking in these men?' (i 115). In his view, the types of duties originate (nacsuntur) in the four virtues (116). He uses Stoic arguments to show that each of the cardinal virtues deals with questions that can be answered only by appeal to the other cardinal virtues (i 126–9). See Davidson, ad i 115. On the treatment of the cardinal virtues in early Christian writers and in mediaeval writers before Aquinas see Lottin, *PM* iii, ch. 12 (see esp. 154). The four virtues are mentioned in *Wisdom* 8:7 (referring to wisdom): 'And if anyone loves justice, her labours are virtues; for she teaches temperance and prudence, justice and bravery, and nothing is more useful in life for human beings than these'. On *4 Macc*. see §203.
[19] See 1-2 q61 a3; 2–2 q123 a11; 141 a7; *Virt. Card*. a1.

These are 'special' or 'principal' displays in two ways: (1) These are cases in which it is especially difficult to display the pervasive virtue of (say) bravery, because the danger of death is especially likely to impede us from following the right course of action. (2) These are cases in which it is especially important to display the pervasive virtue; our moral lives will go to pieces if we cannot manage to exercise firmness in this area.

These two points sometimes pick out the same actions; the difficulty and importance of restraining certain fears may partly explain why we need a virtue that restrains them. But the most difficult actions are not always the most important. A gymnast may show a principal or outstanding degree of physical agility in doing something that is especially difficult, but it may not be important for other people to cultivate precisely this degree of agility. Similarly, we may not all need the firmness of the people who face death in battle bravely, if most us need not face that situation; perhaps we ought to cultivate firmness in sticking to our convictions on the appropriate occasions, if that trait affects much more of most people's lives.

Aquinas does not always separate these two types of 'principal' exercise of the virtues. Sometimes he mentions difficulty (2-2 q123 a11), but sometimes he has importance in mind. He argues that prudence, rather than other virtues of practical intellect, is cardinal, because it makes the decisive difference to our action (*Virt. Card.* a1 = M 815a). In the case of the pleasures of touch, which concern temperance, he mentions that desires for these pleasures are strong (2-2 q141 a4) and that they involve the necessities of life (q141 a5); these two facts give two reasons for taking temperance to be a cardinal virtue.[20]

The case of justice highlights the issue about difficulty and importance. It seems to be more difficult to exercise virtue when we have to consider the interests of others than when we have to consider only ourselves. On this ground, pursuit of the right end may be said to be 'principally' shown in other-directed action. Is such action also a 'principal' manifestation in the other sense, that it is especially important? That depends on whether concern for the good of others is especially important; we apparently need to be convinced on this point before we can be convinced that justice, as Aquinas understands it, is really a cardinal virtue.

Aquinas has good reason to treat the cardinal virtues, in the broad sense, as pervasive features of acting virtuously. He also has good reason to recognize some cardinal virtues in his narrower sense, as specific virtues with their different range of actions; for some specific ranges of actions may be more relevant than others to achieving the pervasive virtues. In agreeing with Aquinas on this point we need not also agree that he has the right account of what the cardinal virtues (in the narrow sense) are.

Indeed, we need not even agree that the same things are cardinal virtues in all times and places. Perhaps bravery, understood as firmness in facing death in battle, was once a cardinal virtue, but ceased to be one as circumstances changed. If we reach this conclusion, we recognize one merit of Aquinas' account: he offers us a reasonable basis for deciding whether a virtue is really cardinal, and therefore a reasonable basis for disagreeing with his conclusion about the cardinal status of a particular trait.

---

[20] '...on the one hand, because such pleasures are more natural to us, and therefore it is more difficult to refrain from them and to restrain appetite for them; on the other hand, because their objects are more necessary for the present life' (2-2 q141 a7).

330. The Range of a Cardinal Virtue[21]

Aquinas attributes a wide scope to each cardinal virtue. Bravery, for instance, is concerned with fears and confidence, but more specifically with the fear of death, not simply because it is difficult not to be moved by the fear of death, but also because love of one's own life is natural (2-2 q123 a4 ad2). Since the love of life is natural, it is both difficult and important to control one's fear of death; hence this is a 'principal' exercise of bravery in both senses.

Aquinas agrees with Aristotle's claim that bravery is properly concerned with the danger of death in war, not with all danger of death equally. He distinguishes those dangers that result from our pursuing a good from those that happen to us whether or not we are pursuing a good, and he argues that dangers of the first sort are especially appropriate concerns of a virtue. The danger of death resulting from illness or storms or robbers or (Aquinas might have added) earthquakes or road accidents 'do not seem to threaten someone directly because of the fact that he is pursuing some good' (2-2 q123 a5). They happen to us anyhow, and we do not avoid them by becoming less active in the pursuit of goods. We expose ourselves, however, to the danger of death in war precisely because we 'defend the common good through a just war'; we would be less exposed if we failed to defend the common good in this way. This is a good reason for claiming that we need a state of character that is not deterred from active pursuit of the relevant good by the danger of death in war; for (Aquinas assumes) the fact that we expose ourselves to this danger is not a sufficient reason to give up the pursuit.

Once we see Aquinas' reasons for picking out the danger of death in war as a special concern of bravery, we can see why other dangers might also be relevant. Even the dangers he initially dismissed may be proper concerns of bravery in the right circumstances. We may face the danger of death from disease if we continue to visit a friend who suffers from an infectious disease, and we may face danger from shipwreck or robbers if we 'pursue some pious undertaking' (e.g., a pilgrimage). In training people to face the danger of death in war bravely, we should also train them to see the same reasons for facing the danger of shipwreck or illness. Death in war, therefore, need not be the exclusive or primary focus of bravery. It is a 'principal' case because it illustrates the type of danger that is the primary focus of bravery, and why it is primary; but other types of danger may also be relevant to bravery.

If Aquinas believes that bravery embraces all the dangers that might wrongly deter us from the appropriate pursuit of good, is his conception unrealistically broad? Some people might be good at facing one sort of danger without being good at facing others. Are we to deny that someone is brave if he is completely fearless in war, but weak and vacillating if it will cost him something to stick to his convictions? Someone might display both characteristics in the same area. A general, for instance, might be unafraid of the danger of death in battle, but might still be afraid to change his strategy, because he is afraid to admit he has failed and to expose himself to criticism and humiliation.[22] Does he display one sort of bravery and

---

[21] On Green and Aquinas on Aristotelian virtues see §113; Green, *PE* §253. On Aquinas' treatment of bravery see Walsh in BF xlii, Appx. Ambrose argues for a broad conception of bravery in *Off.* i 175–209. He rejects the view that bravery belongs primarily to aggressive war. He mentions not only the warriors of the Old Testament but also the Christian martyrs.

[22] Cf. Hector's fear of Polydamas' reproaches, *Iliad* xxii 98–110.

lack another? Or does his fear show that he is not brave? Perhaps we cannot expect firmness in facing every sort of danger that might threaten our pursuit of a good.

Aquinas might reasonably reply that his discussion of the cardinal virtues is not meant to describe features of every virtuous action, but to describe necessary conditions of acting virtuously—the sort of action that proceeds from a virtuous character. Perhaps we could be trained to face one sort of danger without being trained to face others that are equally important for the pursuit of the good. But if we did not see the point of resisting all the dangers that would wrongly impede us in the pursuit of the good, we would not see the point of bravery, and we would not be brave.

The demand that a brave person should see the point of brave action and bravery clarifies and supports Aquinas' belief in the horizontal and vertical unity of prudence. To see what dangers ought to be faced, and hence to see the point of facing this or that danger, we need to connect facing danger with the human good, and thereby to connect the specifically virtuous end with the universal end of human beings. Universal prudence grasps this connexion, and shows why the ends promoted by bravery are promoted by other virtues as well.

If Aquinas is right, people who see the point of resisting all these dangers may still be better at resisting some than at resisting others. Even if we have been trained to resist all sorts of dangers, we may be more used to some than to others. Unfamiliar dangers may produce the 'sudden motions' of passion that are especially difficult to resist.[23] Even if we have the appropriate virtue, we may need to get used to the sound of gunfire in a battle, or to the sight of blood in a hospital, before we can face the situation appropriately. Aquinas' claims about the extent of bravery do not imply that brave people can resist every sort of danger the first time they encounter it.

Aquinas' argument about facing danger in war makes it easier to recognize bravery in cases that Aristotle does not even contemplate. Martyrdom, for instance, is an expression (actus) of bravery (2-2 q124 a2). From Aristotle's point of view, it might appear inferior to death in battle, since it is rather passive, and does not involve the active prosecution of one's ends that Aristotle regards as characteristic of brave actions; hence it seems to belong with death in a shipwreck, which is not a primary concern of bravery (EN 1115a35–b6). But Aquinas' account of why bravery is a virtue shows that active prosecution is not necessary. After the remark that in shipwrecks and so on death is not fine (kalon, 1115b4–6), Aquinas suggests that it is brave and praiseworthy to face death when something good results from one's death.[24] Martyrdom meets this condition for bravery. Martyrs pursue the good by resisting danger; since the good they pursue in this case is the supreme good, their resistance to danger expresses bravery.

This example shows how Aquinas' account of a cardinal virtue helps him towards an appropriately flexible account of the scope of each virtue. His belief that bravery is a cardinal virtue and that it requires these specific actions rests on his conception of the human good and of the actions needed to achieve it. If we find some error at these points in his position, we may take a different view about which virtues are cardinal, and what actions they require. His appeals to universal prudence give us the means to endorse or to correct his views. It is

---

[23] On sudden motions see §§253, 289.

[24] 'neque ex morte aliquid bonum sequitur' (sc. in shipwrecks, etc.), in EN iii 14 §542. 'Bonum' renders kalon; see §332 below.

reasonable to draw the lines between the virtues where he draws them, and to single out some actions as principal exercises of the virtues. If his account needs to be corrected, he shows us how to correct it.

331. Subordinate Virtues

Aquinas believes that other recognized virtues can be classified as either integral or subjective or potential parts of the cardinal virtues.[25] The integral parts 'must concur to produce a perfect act of that virtue' (2-2 q48 a1), and so are aspects of the virtue, inseparable from it in the way that beams and foundations are inseparable from a house. The subjective parts are species of the virtue—for instance, the types of prudence that are displayed in different areas (2-2 q48 a1). The potential parts are 'annexed virtues that are directed towards some secondary acts or materials, as not having the whole power of the principal virtue' (q48 a1). They apply the virtue to areas that are less difficult than the areas of the primary exercises of the virtues.

Aquinas' description of these potential parts assumes that the cardinal virtues are pervasive features of acting virtuously. Though the potential parts of each cardinal virtue are less difficult to exercise than the principal cardinal virtue itself, they are inseparable from the principal virtue; we cannot have magnanimity, for instance, without bravery. The circumstances in which magnanimity maintains firmness are less difficult than those in which bravery maintains firmness, but since they require the same sort of firmness for the same reasons, magnanimity is a part of bravery.[26]

By organizing the virtues around the cardinal virtues, Aquinas argues that the virtues do not conflict, and especially that recognized 'pagan' virtues do not conflict with 'Christian' virtues. His treatment of magnanimity and humility illustrates his strategy. Once we see the relation of these subordinate virtues to their cardinal virtues, we see that they do not conflict. Magnanimity strengthens us in the pursuit of appropriately great actions, while humility restrains us from the distractions that would result from illusions about our own importance; hence we need both magnanimity and humility to pursue the right ends without distraction.[27]

If we object to magnanimity because it includes contempt for others, Aquinas answers that this contempt is contempt for the evil aims of others. Such contempt prevents the magnanimous person from accepting or acquiescing in the evil projects of others, and so he needs it if he is to be independent enough to stick to the right course of action. This contempt for others is not opposed to humility; for we can honour other people in so far as they display the gifts of God, and we can recognize our own failure to use the gifts we have received from God.[28] Determination to use our gifts for great results, and rejection of the

---

[25] 2-2 q48 a1; cf. q79; q80; q128; q143.

[26] '. . . magnanimity agrees with bravery in so far as it confirms the mind about something difficult. But it falls short of bravery in this point, that it confirms the mind in something about which it is easier to preserve this firmness' (2-2 q129 a5).

[27] 'That is why a double virtue is necessary in relation to desire for a difficult good. One is needed to control (temperare) and to restrain the mind from an uncontrolled (immoderate) pursuit of high objects; and this belongs to the virtue of humility. The other is needed to strengthen the mind against despair, and urge it on after great things in accordance with correct reason; and this is magnanimity' (2-2 q161 a1).

[28] Humility does not require false modesty. Aquinas (if he is the author of the prayer) prays that he will be 'humilem sine fictione', P xxiv 242a.

evil aims of others that would impede the proper use of our gifts and theirs, are two aspects of magnanimity.[29] In recognizing our own failure to use all our gifts, and in appreciating the gifts shown by others, we display aspects of humility.[30] Neither magnanimity nor humility can do its proper work without the other.

Humility also prevents a false sense of self-importance. This is why it does not always reject the sorts of actions that would sometimes show a lack of self-respect. Sometimes 'abject' services are required by charity, and in these cases a person without false self-importance will not refuse to do them.[31] Hence it is not abject to belong to a mendicant religious order, even though it would be abject to beg from others simply from disinclination to support oneself (SG iii 135).[32] Humble people do not refuse the abject course of action in the right circumstances, though they do not accept it indiscriminately.

The connexion between magnanimity and humility answers some objections to RV. We might well cite these two virtues to show why virtues sometimes conflict, and why traits required by one impede traits required by another. Aquinas answers that this appearance of conflict may mislead us about the relation between the two virtues. We can see that they do not conflict once we understand the circumstances in which contempt for others or belief in our own unworthiness is appropriate; for the two virtues have the same aim, and do not conflict, but complement each other. Recognition of the connexion between the virtues involves universal prudence, since it refers to the universal end promoted by the specific ends of the different virtues.

This example suggests how the cardinal virtues, as Aquinas understands them, make the other virtues intelligible. The subordinate virtues promote or facilitate or protect the goods pursued by the cardinal virtues. This arrangement of the subordinate virtues allows Aquinas' theory to be flexible. Different circumstances might produce different threats to the goods pursued by the cardinal virtues, so that the same subordinate virtues might have different contents, or different traits might actually become subordinate virtues. Aquinas' account shows why in different circumstances a particular subordinate virtue needs to be cultivated.

---

[29] Cf. 2-2 q21 a1 sc.

[30] 'In a human being one finds something great, which he possesses through the gift of God, and something defective, which belongs to him from the weakness of nature. Magnanimity, therefore, makes a human being think himself worthy of great things from consideration of the gifts he possesses from God. For instance, if he has great virtue of mind, magnanimity makes him pursue perfect works of virtue . . . Humility, however, makes a human being think little of himself from consideration of his own deficiency. Similarly, magnanimity despises others in so far as they fall short of God's gifts; for it does not think so much of others as to do anything inappropriate for their sake. But humility honours others and thinks them superior, inasmuch as it looks upon something of God's gifts in them. . . . And in this way it is evident that magnanimity and humility are not contraries, though they seem to aim towards contraries, because they proceed in accordance with different considerations' (2-2 q129 a3 ad4). The attitude that Aquinas describes here is endorsed by Paul at Rm. 12:3; '. . . not to think of yourself more highly than you ought to think, but to think with sober judgment (sôphronein)'.

[31] 'It is not, therefore, characteristic of humility, but of stupidity, if one accepts whatever is abject, but <it is characteristic of humility> if one does not refuse because of its abjectness what is necessary to do because of virtue. For instance, if charity demands that one carry out some abject task for one's neighbours, because of his humility one does not refuse to do this' (SG iii 135 §3097).

[32] MacIntyre, DRA xi, mentions this aspect of humility (in 'a prayer composed by Aquinas in which he asks God to grant that he may happily share with those in need what he has, while humbly asking for what he needs from those who have') in order to contrast Aquinas' outlook with Aristotle's views on magnanimity ('a prayer that in effect, though not by Aquinas's own intention, asks that we may not share some of the attitudes of Aristotle's megalopsychos'). He develops this contrast later (127). He may be referring to the prayer (of dubious authorship) in P xxiv 241b (da bonum quod non habeo ab habentibus humiliter quaerere).

Prudence and temperance, for instance, do not always require saving money for tomorrow. If the rate of inflation is high, someone who merely saves impoverishes himself, and would be better advised to take a less conservative attitude to short-term financial risk. In these circumstances the attitude conventionally recognized as 'prudent' may be ill-advised; but the virtue of prudence is not ill-advised. On the contrary, prudence advises a less conservative attitude to risk in these circumstances. The virtue of prudence, as Aquinas understands it, helps us to see why one subordinate virtue ought to be replaced by another.

His theory explains not only why certain traits are virtuous at a particular time, but also why it would be reasonable for subordinate virtues to change over time, within the constraints of the same cardinal virtues. He includes some details about the specific traits and actions required of virtuous people, and about the social roles and institutions that support these requirements. If we reject these details, we do not necessarily reject Aquinas' theory of the virtues. If he relies on some subordinate social or psychological assumption that either was always false or is no longer true, an objection to the details may not undermine the theory.[33] Once we understand the theoretical aspects of his account of the virtues, we can distinguish the acceptable from the unacceptable conclusions. If Aquinas' theory of the virtues works, it ought to allow us to argue effectively about the content and application of the virtues; if we can use his theory to give good reasons for rejecting his conclusions, we have vindicated the most important parts of his theory.

This point is relevant not only for the philosophical assessment of Aquinas' theory but also for understanding its historical fortunes. It was criticized, not surprisingly, for the particular description of rules and requirements that reflect its historical circumstances.[34] But the rejection of Aquinas' specific virtues does not justify the rejection of his theory of the cardinal virtues and subordinate virtues, and the way he tries to derive these from his conception of rational agency. We need to consider more closely whether the historically influential criticisms of Aquinas go beyond criticism of relatively superficial details that do not affect the main theoretical issues.

332. Moral Goodness in Latin Sources

We may accept Aquinas' claim that prudence, bravery, and temperance underlie any action that we can take to proceed from a moral virtue. But this is not enough to show that deliberative prudence supports the moral virtues, as he conceives them. For he takes the virtues to aim not at every sort of good, but at the morally good (1-2 q18). This requires conformity with reason (q18 a5; a8; a9; a9 ad2; *Mal.* q7 a6).[35] Reason directs actions to the common end of human life (q21 a2 ad2). This common end requires concern for the good of others, and hence for justice (q21 a3). Hence a morally good action is praiseworthy, in so far

---

[33] Aquinas' discussion of usury in 2-2 q78 offers an example of such assumptions. He qualifies the general prohibition with the conditions set out in a2–3. The development of discussions of usury in moral theology is described by Jonsen and Toulmin, *AC*, ch. 9 It is summarized by Davis, *MPT* ii 373–7, who mentions 'extrinsic titles' that justify the taking of interest on a loan (e.g., loss sustained by the lender, or real and unusual risk incurred by the lender).

[34] For Machiavelli's objections to the Christian character of the virtues that Aquinas describes see §407. Hume expresses rather similar objections in speaking of the 'monkish' virtues, *Inq.* ix 3.

[35] On good and moral good see Bradley, *ATHG* 277.

as it is in the power of the will; it is correct (rectus), in so far as it is directed to the appropriate end; and it is meritorious, in so far as it conforms to justice in relation to another (q21 a3).

We might reasonably expect Aquinas to say more about the general character of moral goodness. In particular we might expect an Aristotelian theory to recognize Aristotle's claim that the moral virtues are distinguished by their concern for the fine (kalon). Aquinas' treatment of this claim connects Aristotelian and Stoic treatments of the fine with modern views on moral goodness and rightness, and so it deserves some discussion. But the connexion is not as simple as we might expect it to be, and we need to trace some of the details.

Latin writers on Stoicism follow Cicero in translating 'kalon' by 'honestum' in moral contexts.[36] Ambrose, for instance, follows Cicero in distinguishing the honestum from the useful (Off. i 27–8), and in believing that, properly understood, the honestum and the useful coincide (ii 28; iii 9, 13, 44, 52, 60, 63); we achieve what is genuinely useful if and only if considerations of the honestum outweigh (praeponderare) all others (iii 66). The honestum is the general character shared by the four cardinal virtues (e.g., i 175, 182, 191, 210–11, 258; ii 1), and the source of all duties (ii 22). Ambrose implicitly distinguishes the honestum from beauty, for which he uses 'pulchrum' (i 83), but he recognizes that the honestum has a beauty of its own (iii 57). He connects the honestum with the seemly and appropriate (decorum) (i 219; iii 52, 54, 88, 118), and with what accords with nature (iii 28).[37] In his view, the Scriptures agree with the philosophers in claiming that only what is honestum is good (ii 8, 18; iii 29, 37,[38] 84–91, 96–9, 125–6).

But though Ambrose follows Cicero in using 'honestum' for the Greek 'kalon', to mark moral goodness, not all translators agree with him. The translators of the Vulgate render 'kalon' by 'bonum'.[39] One might defend their decision by observing that Ambrose uses 'honestum' to refer to the good that matters most from the moral and religious point of view; in calling something 'honestum' we recognize it as the most important good. At any rate, whatever may have been the reasons for the translation adopted by the Vulgate, their choice may have influenced the translators of Aristotle's Ethics; for in almost all

---

[36] See §180. [37] He justifies the connexion with nature by saying that God made all things 'very good', iii 28.

[38] On Ambrose's discussion of Gyges' ring see §50.

[39] Vulg. OT has 'bonum' where LXX has 'kalon'. The effects of its rendering of NT passages are still visible in English versions. Rheims, being a translation of Vulg., uses 'good' in these passages, and the AV follows it. Jesus tells the disciples to let their light shine before men so that 'men may see your good works and glorify your Father who is in heaven' (Mt. 5:16). Paul finds that 'when I would do good, evil is present with me' (Rm. 7:21). He tells the Galatians not to be 'weary in well-doing' (Gal. 6:9 NRSV: 'doing what is right'). In all these cases, and in many others, the Latin renders 'kalon' by 'bonum', and many English versions follow it. They do not always do this. Paul tells the Romans not to return evil for evil, but to take thought for things that are kala in the sight of everyone (Rm. 12:17). Vulg., as usual, has 'bona', but AV recognizes 'kala', and renders 'Provide things honest in the sight of all men', following the English practice of using 'honest' to render 'kalon'. See Empson, SCW 185–6. He mentions cases where earlier English versions have 'honest' and AV replaces it. The practice of Vulg. is even more surprising when one notices that it occasionally uses 'honestum', but not to translate 'kalon'. When Paul urges the Romans to cast away the works of darkness and put on the armour of light, he tells them to walk 'euschêmonôs', 'decently' as in the day. Here Vulg. translates by 'honeste', and Rheims and AV have 'honestly' (Rm. 13:13). The use of 'honestum' here is quite reasonable; but it would be at least as reasonable in many of the passages where 'bonum' renders 'kalon'. Vulg. shows why translators of Aristotle seeking help with Greek philosophical vocabulary might understandably suppose that 'bonum', rather than 'honestum', is the appropriate rendering of 'kalon', and that therefore no distinction needs to be drawn between the agathon and the kalon. They also follow Vulg. in using 'honestum' to render 'euschêmon' (see Aquinas, in EN, iv.16 §859, commenting on §608, which uses 'honestas' to render 'euschêmosunê' in 1128a25).

the places in the *Ethics* where Aristotle uses 'kalon', the mediaeval Latin translators use 'bonum'.[40]

This translation creates more difficulties for readers of Aristotle than for readers of the Bible, because Aristotle sometimes tries to distinguish features of the *kalon* from features of other sorts of goods.[41] The mediaeval translation conceals some of Aristotle's distinctive claims about the *kalon* from Aquinas. Aristotle often remarks that action for the sake of the *kalon* is characteristic of the virtuous person. In these passages the Latin version says that the virtuous person acts for the sake of the good (e.g., *EN* 1116a28; b3; Aquinas, *in EN* iii 9, §§373, 375). Since everyone acts for the sake of the good, the Latin version changes an apparently distinctive feature of the virtuous person into a feature that virtuous and non-virtuous people share. Aquinas often follows the Latin version in using 'bonum' where Aristotle has 'kalon', and so he misses the fact that Aristotle is saying something about the *kalon*.[42]

Often, however, the translation fails to conceal Aristotle's point from Aquinas. For he often recognizes that Aristotle is talking about the honestum. In these passages Aristotle uses 'kalon', but the Latin (as usual) has 'bonum'. Aquinas paraphrases Aristotle's remarks about the *kalon* by speaking of the honestum. These places are less numerous than the places where he simply uses 'bonum', but they are numerous enough to require some explanation.[43] Consideration of the context in Aristotle suggests to Aquinas that Aristotle is speaking of the honestum. The suggestion cannot come entirely from Aristotle, if Aquinas does not know that Aristotle uses 'kalon' in these passages. Probably, then, he relies on some conception of the honestum that he finds in a non-Aristotelian source.

---

[40] See, e.g., 1094b15, 1099a27, 1100b27, 30, 1104b31, 1110b15, 1114b6, 1115a30, b23, 1116a11, b3, 1117a8, 1120a27, 1122b6, 1168a33, 1169a6–b1. At 1099a22 and 1123b8 the translation used by Aquinas has 'pulchrum'. The earlier translations are in *Aristoteles Latinus* xxvi 1–3 (see the Greek–Latin index in fasc. 5). Sometimes 'honestus' is used for 'sôphrôn' (e.g., 1102b30) and once 'honestas' renders 'epieikeia' (1121b14). Mercken, *GCNEA* i 64, remarks that Grosseteste seeks 'to find for each Greek word a corresponding one in Latin'. Just as Grosseteste fails to provide a distinctive equivalent for 'kalon' in his translation of the *Ethics*, he fails to provide one in his translation of the Greek commentaries of Eustratius and others (edited by Mercken). The same practice in translating 'kalon' is followed outside the *Ethics*; see, e.g., Aquinas, *in Met.* xii 7 §2522. Perhaps Grosseteste was influenced by his Greek-speaking informants, since 'kalon' in later Greek has a broader use than in Classical and Hellenistic Greek.

[41] The choice of 'bonum' to render 'kalon' in Aristotle's *Ethics* is defensible, but also questionable. The translator has to weigh three maxims for a good translation: (a) Use the same Latin word to render the same Greek word. (b) Use different Latin words to render different Greek words. (c) Use a Latin word that provides a plausible rendering of a given Greek term in a particular context. Latin translators could follow the first two maxims if they always used 'honestum' for 'kalon' and always used 'bonum' for 'agathon'. This practice, however, would violate the third maxim, because 'honestum' is an unnatural and misleading rendering when 'kalon' refers to beauty. The mediaeval Latin translators decide to use one term 'bonum', which does not appear as unnatural as 'honestum' would appear in passages that refer to beauty. Their choice violates the second maxim, since it fails to distinguish 'kalon' from 'agathon' in contexts where one ought to distinguish them. Renaissance translators deal with Aristotle's different uses of 'kalon' by using 'pulchrum' and 'honestum' according to the apparent force of 'kalon' in different passages, and so violate the first maxim. For Lambinus' decisions see, e.g., his renderings of 1116a28, b3, 1120a12, 23–4.

[42] When Aristotle says that even in adversity the *kalon* 'shines through' (*EN* 1100b30), Aquinas says that the good shines even in misfortune (*in EN* i 16 §195). When Aristotle says that virtuous actions are *kalon*, and done for the sake of the *kalon* (*EN* 1120a23–4), Aquinas makes the boring remark that they are good and done for the sake of the good (*in EN* iv 2 §666). In many other places he does not know that 'bonum' conceals occurrences of 'kalon'.

[43] Aquinas probably does not rely on definite information about the Greek text, obtained from someone who had consulted it directly. If he had such information, why does he not use it in places where it would have been relevant? Had he known that Aristotle said that virtuous actions are *kalon* and done for the sake of the *kalon*, he would have had good reason to introduce the honestum into his paraphrase of the relevant passage (*in EN* §666 on 1120a23–4; see n42); but he does not introduce it here.

The most probable immediate source is Albert's commentary on the *Ethics*; for Albert also lacks direct access to the Greek, but still takes Aristotle to discuss the honestum.[44] Albert takes his conception of the honestum from Stoic sources, and applies it to Aristotle. He accepts Cicero's account of the honestum as what attracts us by its own power, apart from any further utility, and so he infers that it most deserves to be called good without qualification (simpliciter); for it does not appeal to us simply because it is useful for satisfying some prior desire.[45] For the same reason it is the only unqualified good, in contrast to the goods of fortune that in some circumstances are bad (*SE* v 2 = 314.22–34). Since it is the unqualified good, the honestum rather than the pleasant is the basis of choiceworthiness, and so our desire for it is rational rather than appetitive (non per modum concupiscentiae, sed per modum amicitiae, *SE* x 2 = 713.11–15). Hence the honestum is not the same in essence as the pleasant, though it always involves pleasure (*SE* x 2 = 713.37–44). All virtue, therefore, has as its object this one kind of good, the honestum.[46]

Since Albert notices that Cicero finds the honestum especially in the best form of friendship (*SE* viii 3 = 601.29–58),[47] he takes Aristotle's conception of the friendship of virtue to involve the honestum (*SE* viii 1 = 592.61–9). Cicero contrasts concern for the honestum with exclusive concern for one's own advantage;[48] Albert connects this contrast with Aristotle's contrast between friendship for utility or pleasure and friendship that involves concern for the other for the other's own sake.[49] The connexion between the honestum and unselfish action also explains why justice involves the honestum. In Albert's view, 'everything just, in so far as it is just, is also honestum'.[50] These remarks on the honestum in the 'questions' section of the commentary explain Albert's judgment that in various places Aristotle refers to the honestum.[51]

---

[44] The commentary *Super Ethica* (cited as *SE*, from Albert, *OO* xiv.1–2) is taken by its editors to be the one that Aquinas is said to have helped to edit. See Preface to xiv 1, pp. v–vi. On the influence of Albert on Aquinas' commentary see Gauthier, *EN* i 1, 122–3; L xlvii 1, 235–57; Bourke 'Ethics'; Doig, *APCE* 24–33 and ch. 2. Albert includes both a 'literal exposition' and a series of 'questions' that discuss philosophical issues raised by the text, but not necessarily discussed by Aristotle. Aquinas includes only the literal exposition, without the questions; one might say that the 'questions' section of his commentary appears in the *Summa*. (See Gauthier, *EN* i. 1, 131.) Albert's questions make clear the assumptions about the honestum that guide him in mentioning it at various places in his literal exposition. Passages where both Albert and Aquinas mention the honestum include 65.22 on 1104b31 (Aquinas §273); 282.53–4 on 1127a6 (§827); 594.96 on 1155a29 (§1544); 647.37 on 1162b35 (§1737); 684.61 on 1168a10 (§1848); 688.54 on 1169a–b1 (§1881). Passages where Aquinas mentions it and Albert does not mention it include 1094b14 (Aquinas §33); 1115a12 (§533); 1121b9–10 (§695); 1122b6 (§714); 1126b29 (§§824–5); 1168a33 (§1857); 1175b29 (§2051); 1176b8 (§2070).

[45] See *SE* i 9 = 50.66–8, from Cic. *Inv.* ii 157. See also *De bono in genere* q5 a1 ad2 = *OO* xxviii 72.51: the honestum is 'what is sought because of itself' (cf. 33.15–18, 62.22–30); *De prudentia* q1 a3 ad5 = xxviii 230.72–4: the honestum is 'what attracts us by its power and draws us by its proper and natural worthiness that it presents'.

[46] *De bono in genere*, q5 a1 ad1 = *OO* xxviii 71.73. Cf. Cic. *Inv.* ii 159.   [47] Cic. *Amic.* 44.

[48] Cicero acknowledges that the two types of concern sometimes coincide; *Inv.* ii 157.

[49] This is why he believes that the actions Aristotle discusses in his account of good self-love must be honestum actions; he calls them first 'bonae operationes', but then 'honestae operationes' (*SE* ix 10 = 688.40–55).

[50] See *De iustitia* q2 a1 ad8 = *OO* xxviii 282–79–85. Cf. Cic. *Amic.* 51. At 281.8–11 Albert ascribes to Cicero the account of law (lex) as 'written right (ius) prescribing the honestum and prohibiting the contrary'. On the sources of this definition see note to *OO* xxviii 46.69–47.2.

[51] In his other commentary, the *Ethica* (= *Opera*, ed. Borgnet, vii), Albert does not provide the same explicit discussion of the honestum. But some of his remarks show that he presupposes the sort of view that he develops explicitly in *Super Ethica*.. He treats the division of goods into the honestum, utile, and delectabile as familiar (i 3.6 = 38a). He does not mention the honestum at the point where Aristotle introduces the threefold division in Book ii (ii 8 = 162). But he introduces the honestum prominently into the discussion of friendship. See viii 1 = 518a: 'Further, not only is friendship about things necessary for life—for in that case it would only be useful—but it is also a good in its own right and

333. The Honestum in Aquinas' Commentary

Albert's comments help us to see why Aquinas believes that Aristotle discusses the honestum. Aquinas does not detect a reference to the honestum in every place where Aristotle speaks of the *kalon*; often he follows the Latin version in using 'bonum'.[52] But nearly every place where he uses 'honestum' marks an occurrence of '*kalon*', and he captures the main points of Aristotle's use of '*kalon*'. He relies on (i) the contrast between good and pleasant, (ii) claims about praiseworthiness, and (iii) claims about disinterestedness. When he detects a mention of the honestum, he seems to have one of these three features in mind. We may illustrate his reasoning by surveying some places in his commentary on the *Ethics* where he speaks of the honestum.

Aristotle remarks that fine and just things (*kala kai dikaia*) that are the concern of political science are subject to difference and variation, so that some people think they are conventional, and not natural (*EN* 1094b14–16). Aristotle replies that goods also display the same variation. Since the Latin version renders '*kala*' by '*bona*', it suggests that Aristotle first makes an observation about good and just things, and then proceeds to make an observation about good things treated as a separate class.[53] A commentator might find this curiously repetitive. But Aquinas avoids attributing this repetition to Aristotle by recognizing that the first lot of *bona* are 'virtuous actions, which he here calls just' (*in EN* §33). When he comments on difference and variation, he says: 'For some things which by some are counted just and right (honesta) are by some <counted> unjust and wrong' (§33). Since Aquinas' 'just and right' reverses the order of the Greek phrase '*kala kai dikaia*' used by Aristotle, he probably does not intend it as a translation of Aristotle, but as an explanation of the type of good and just things that he has in mind. Aristotle's reference to political science may have suggested to Aquinas that Aristotle has morally right actions in mind. Aristotle's use of '*kalon*' in this passage confirms Aquinas' judgment.[54]

Aristotle distinguishes three objects of choice that the virtuous person gets right and others get wrong: the *kalon*, the advantageous (*sumpheron*), and the pleasant (*hêdu*) (1104b30–1). The Latin, as usual, uses 'bonum' for '*kalon*', and uses 'malum' to render '*aischron*' (though it sometimes uses 'turpe', the normal opposite to 'honestum'). Aquinas, however, glosses

honestum. A sign of this is the fact that it is proper to the good to be praiseworthy. For we praise friend-lovers, that is to say, lovers of deliberative friendship; so that friend-loving seems to all to have the character of honestum goods, and is loved in its own right.' Cf. viii 2 = 519b: 'The honestum good and the pleasant good are ends, but the honestum is an end in relation to reason, whereas pleasure <is an end> in relation to sense, or in relation to nature generally'. The best kind of friendship is founded on the honestum (ix 3.2 = 588b). The two commentaries are discussed by Dunbabin, 'Albertus'.

[52] Nor does every mention of the honestum in Aquinas' commentary correspond to a mention of the *kalon* by Aristotle. For one exception see *in EN* §1552, discussed below.

[53] See 'Talem autem quendam errorem habent et bona . . .' *in EN* §16.

[54] Next he comes to Aristotle's claim that good things display the same sort of variation as we find in fine and just things. He reads it (as the Latin suggests) as a claim about good things displaying the same sort of variation as we find in good and just things. He infers that the second occurrence of '*bona*' refers to a subset of goods, and so he suggests that Aristotle refers to external goods ('bona exteriora', §34). He is probably wrong about this; the second example of goods that Aristotle offers is bravery (1094b19), which is not a merely external good. Aquinas deals with this difficulty by suggesting that 'bravery' here simply refers to bodily strength ('fortitudo corporalis', §34). Here he follows Albert and Eustratius (20.29–21.14). Since Eustratius already had the same idea when he read the Greek text, we cannot attribute Aquinas' exegesis simply to his reliance on the Latin. None the less, had he known where Aristotle uses '*kalon*' rather than '*agathon*', he might have thought differently about the remark on goods.

'bonum' by 'honestum' ('bonum, id est honestum', §273). To explain Aristotle's claim that the *kalon* is pleasant, Aquinas suggests that the honestum is pleasant in so far as it is in accord with reason ('secundum quod est conveniens rationi', §275).

The fact that Aristotle, as rendered into Latin, mentions three objects of choice of which the good is only one might suggest to a reader that 'good' refers to a subset of goods and not to all goods (since all objects of choice are goods in some way); in that case, it would be easy to infer that the relevant subset of goods are the honesta. In Book viii Aristotle mentions the good (*agathon*), the pleasant, and the advantageous as objects of love (*philêta*), and, after dismissing the advantageous as a merely instrumental object, identifies the good and the pleasant as the ends that are objects of love (1155b18–21). The division in Book ii appears to be parallel to that in Book viii, except that Book ii has '*kalon*' instead of '*agathon*'.

Aquinas sees the possible relevance of this passage in Book viii. For when he comes to comment on it, he explains it just as he explains the passage in Book ii, supposing that where the Latin text has 'bonum', Aristotle actually has the honestum in mind (§1552, per se bonum, id est honestum). Aquinas' suggestion that Aristotle is thinking of the honestum gives us some reason to attribute to him the argument that we have already noticed—that if Aristotle treats the good as only one object of desire, he must have in mind some proper subset of goods.

In the first five chapters of Book iii Aristotle several times mentions the *kalon*.[55] In all of these passages the Latin has 'bonum', and Aquinas follows it. In some passages the Latin uses 'turpe' (usually the opposite of 'honestum') as the opposite of 'bonum', so that a reader might suspect that the honestum is involved. Even here Aquinas does not take the hint offered by 'turpe'.[56] But sometimes he recognizes that Aristotle uses 'turpe' to refer to vicious behaviour. To illustrate Aristotle's claim that some things are so shameful (turpe) that we should refuse to do them at any price, he cites St Laurence, who endured being roasted on the gridiron rather than sacrifice to idols (§395).[57]

The section of the *Ethics* that discusses the particular virtues often refers to the special connexion between virtue, acting virtuously, and acting for the sake of the *kalon*. Aquinas misses several of these references.[58] But sometimes he captures them. Aristotle says that there are some things we ought to fear, and fearing them is *kalon*, while not fearing them is *aischron* (1115a12–13). Aquinas comments that in some cases fear is honestum (§533). The

---

[55] See *EN* 1110a21; b9; 1112b17; 1113b9; 1114b7.

[56] See *in EN* §§388–9, 393, 403–4, on 1110a4–8, 19–22, b9–15. Perhaps Aquinas fails to take the hint because he does not suppose that in this discussion 'turpe' always refers to moral wrongness. This is clear from his interpretation of Aristotle's remark that people are sometimes praised for 'enduring something *aischron* or painful as the price of great and *kala* things' (*EN* 1110a19–22). Aquinas does not take Aristotle to mean that people are praised for doing something vicious to promote some good; the 'shameful' (turpe) things he has in mind, according to Aquinas, involve humiliation rather than sin (*in EN* §393). Since he believes that Aristotle does not intend 'turpe' to refer to moral wrongness, he misses the hint that Aristotle is also referring to the honestum.

[57] Aquinas overlooks some interpretative issues that would arise for him if he had been aware of Aristotle's use of '*kalon*'. In his discussion of deliberation, for instance, Aristotle remarks that when several means to our end are open, we look for the 'easiest and finest (*kallista*)' means (1112b16–17). In using 'finest' here, Aristotle may well intend to point out that we must use moral criteria, as well as criteria of mere efficiency, in identifying possible means. This possibility does not strike Aquinas.

[58] Aristotle says it is characteristic of virtue to do good rather than receive it and to do *kalon* actions rather than to refrain from *aischron* actions (1120a12–13). Though the Latin uses 'turpe' rather than 'malum' where the Greek has '*aischron*', Aquinas says nothing about the honestum in this context (see §661). Similarly, he simply follows the Latin in other remarks about the *kalon*.

context helps him, since Aristotle goes on to say that the person with these appropriate fears is decent and has the proper sort of shame (*epieikês kai aidêmôn*). When Aristotle says brave people act for the sake of the *kalon*, Aquinas realizes that he does not simply intend the uninformative claim that they act for the sake of the good, but must mean that they act for some more specific end peculiar to their virtue (1115b23; §§549–50).[59]

Aristotle sometimes remarks that attention to the *kalon* is the hallmark of the virtues (see above on §661); the magnificent person, for instance, spends money for the sake of the *kalon*, because that is common to the virtues (1122b6–7). In Aquinas' paraphrase this person spends 'for the sake of the bonum honestum as an end; for acting for the sake of good is common to all the virtues'. The 'for ...' clause makes it clear that Aquinas takes Aristotle to have mentioned the bonum. He does not explain why he introduces the honestum.

Aristotle mentions the *kalon* several times in discussing friendship.[60] When he says friendship is not only necessary, but also *kalon* (1155a29), Aquinas comments that it is something good, that is to say, praiseworthy and honestum (§1544). He clearly supposes that the text he is explaining has 'bonum'; but Aristotle's remark about praiseworthiness suggests to him that the honestum is the relevant good. Similarly, when Aristotle remarks that people wish *kalon* things, but decide on advantageous things (1162b35), Aquinas takes him to say that people approve honestum things (§1737). Aristotle's example of something *kalon* is A's doing a good turn for B without expectation of return from B; his example of something advantageous is receiving a good turn from another. Aquinas notices that the first example illustrates the honestum. For the same reason, he mentions the honestum in his discussion of Aristotle's remark that the benefactor's action is *kalon* for the benefactor, but merely advantageous for the beneficiary (1168a9–12; §§1848–50).

Aquinas marks Aristotle's comment that the good person is normally supposed to act because of the *kalon*, and not for his own sake (1168a33–5). As before, the contrast between acting for the *kalon* and acting for one's own advantage suggests to Aquinas that the honestum is being discussed (§1857).[61] Similarly, when Aristotle says the virtuous person seeks to gain the *kalon* in preference to 'contested' goods (1169a20–5), Aquinas infers that Aristotle refers to the honestum (§§1878, 1881).[62] When Aristotle says that some appetites (*epithumiai*) for *kalon* things are praiseworthy, Aquinas mentions the honestum (1175b29 §2051); the reference to praiseworthiness gives him the clue. Similarly, Aristotle's contrast between the *kalon*, which is choiceworthy in itself, and pleasant amusement suggests to Aquinas that the honestum is relevant (1176b8 §2070).

---

[59] He does not mention the honestum here. But he mentions it in his discussion of the lower grades of bravery (§564). In the discussion of generosity, Aquinas passes over occurrences of *kalon* without comment, except when he remarks that extravagant people decline towards pleasure because they do not direct their lives to the bonum honestum (1121b9–10; §695). Perhaps he introduces the honestum because Aristotle mentions the good and the pleasant as the two possible aims of one's life. As before, Aquinas assumes that when Aristotle refers to pleasure and to good as ends, he has in mind some specific type of good (since pleasure is also a good, and pursued for the sake of the good); the non-instrumental good contrasted with pleasure is the honestum.

[60] When Aristotle says friendship promotes *kalon* actions (1155a15), Aquinas simply speaks of good actions (§1540).

[61] In two further places that mention the *kalon* Aquinas says nothing about the honestum (1169a6 §1873; 1169a8 §1874). This is surprising; for the first passage contains the contrast between the *kalon* and the advantageous, which usually prompts Aquinas to mention the honestum, and in the second passage Aristotle claims that when everyone strains to achieve the *kalon*, the common good is advanced.

[62] In Book x Aquinas sometimes accepts the 'bonum' of the Latin version without further comment (1179a5, 11; §§2129–30).

In these passages of his commentary, Aquinas speaks of the honestum where the context suggests that Aristotle speaks of, or alludes to, one of the three features of the honestum. He ascribes these features to the honestum on the strength of Albert's commentary. He relies, through Albert, on Ambrose and Cicero, and so ultimately on Stoic sources. Aristotle does not clearly express the conception of the *kalon* that the Stoics formulate, but the Stoic conception fits his claims. According to Albert and Aquinas, the honestum is good without qualification (simpliciter); its goodness does not consist in its being the object of a desire. That is why it attracts us by its own character.[63] It involves disinterested concern, as opposed to concern that is guided by one's own advantage. For these reasons, it is praiseworthy, and not simply advantageous.

This interpretation of Aristotle is supported by evidence that Aquinas is unaware of. In the contexts where he thinks Aristotle refers to the honestum, Aristotle actually uses '*kalon*', though the Latin versions use 'bonum'. We ought not to be surprised by the correspondence between Aristotle's Greek and Aquinas' exposition. For the Stoic assumptions about the *kalon* that underlie Aquinas' claims about the honestum also match Aristotle's claims about the *kalon*. Aquinas' success in identifying Aristotle's uses of '*kalon*' on the basis of Stoic views about the honestum suggests that the Stoic views fit the Aristotelian position as well.

334. The Honestum in the *Summa*

Aquinas' treatment of the honestum in his commentary on the *Ethics* provides a starting point for examining his remarks in the *Summa*. Though he does not explicitly introduce the honestum into his explicit discussion of moral goodness (1-2 qq18–21), it has an important place in his conception of the virtues and of moral goodness.

He divides the good in general into the pleasant, the useful, and the honestum, citing Ambrose as his authority.[64] He recognizes that the division seems to be proper to the human good, but takes it to be applicable to good in general, if the honestum is identified with what is desired for its own sake.[65] Elsewhere, he comments on the relation between the honestum and the useful, explaining that everything honestum is also useful, except for the ultimate end.[66]

At the beginning of the Prima Secundae, Aquinas takes for granted this notion of the honestum as the non-instrumental good (1-2 q8 a2 ad2; q8 a3, ad sc). He speaks of the honestum on the assumption that it is moral goodness. In the discussion of the passions, he insists that the honestum is good in accordance with reason (q34 a2 ad1). The passions

---

[63] See §2070: virtuous actions are 'good in their own right and honesta, so that some also say that honestas is what draws us by its own power and attracts us by its own worthiness'.

[64] Ambrose, *Off.* i 27. See §332 above.

[65] 'This division seems to be proper to human good. But if we consider the character of good from a higher and more universal point of view, we shall find that this division belongs to good in so far as it is good. . . . What is desired (appetitur) as the last thing, completely ending the motion of desire, as a thing towards which, in its own right, desire (appetitus) tends, is called honestum, because what is called honestum is what is desired (desiderare) in itself' (1a q5 a6).

[66] 'Among goods, however, is found what is good without qualification and in its own right, as honesta goods are, which are desired as ends for their own sake, even though they lead to something else, because in all honesta usefulness coincides with honestas, except in the ultimate <good>, which is the end of ends, which is to be desired (cupere) only for itself' (*2Sent.* d21 q1 a3).

are relevant to moral virtue, in so far as they can be regulated by the rule of reason, which is the root of the honestum good.[67] In saying that the honestum has the character of the praiseworthy and the meritorious (q39 a2 obj2), he refers back to the discussion of moral goodness (q21 a2), without suggesting that any further explanation is needed. He assumes—even though he did not say so in his discussion of moral goodness—that the features of moral goodness belong to the honestum.

In the Secunda Secundae he assumes that the virtues involve the honestum. Friendship has the character of the praiseworthy and honestum only in so far as it is 'founded on the honestas of the virtues', hence only in the best kind of friendship (2-2 q23 a3 ad1). The duty (debitum) of honestas extends to the requirements of the virtues in general, going beyond the demands of strict justice (q102 a2 ad2; q106 a1 ad2; a4 ad1; q114 a2).[68] This honestas of virtue involves unselfishness; it is especially displayed in benefiting another, in contrast to the merely useful good of gaining a benefit for oneself (q26 a12). This remark occurs in a discussion of Aristotle's chapter on benefactors and beneficiaries (*EN* ix 7), where Aquinas' commentary introduces a reference to the honestum. Aristotle claims that virtuous people prefer the *kalon* even at the cost of their life (1169a25–6); Aquinas follows him (with a modification), claiming (without specific reference to Aristotle) that the honestum is to be preferred even at the cost of one's bodily life (2-2 q110 a2).

After these brief references to the honestum, Aquinas discusses it more explicitly quite late in the Secunda Secundae, when he considers honestas as a part of temperance (q143 a1). He relies on a remark by Cicero that connects the honestum with the fitting (decorum, *prepon*), and connects the fitting with (among other things) temperance, because the temperate person does what is fitting for a human being, as opposed to a non-rational creature (Cic. *Off.* i 93–4).[69] Aquinas follows Cicero to this extent (2-2 q141 a2 obj3 ad3).[70]

The connexion of the honestum with temperance leads him to consider the honestum in general. He confirms its connexion with virtue as a whole (q145 a1); the virtues are honestum because they are ends in themselves though not the ultimate end (q145 a1 ad1).[71] It is characteristic of the honestum to direct all human affairs in accord with reason; this is what makes it 'fitting' (decorum) (q145 a2). What is ordered in accordance with reason is thereby naturally fitting for a human being (q145 a3); temperance is especially honestum because it prevents actions that are especially base (*turpe*) by being contrary to rational nature (q141 a8 ad1). The features that Aquinas attributes to the honestum are those he previously attributed to the morally good.[72]

For this account of the honestum Aquinas relies on Stoic sources, and especially on Cicero. On this point the *Summa* is similar to the commentary on the *Ethics*. His attitude to

---

[67] 'Now every honestum good proceeds from these two things, namely from correctness of reason and of will' (q39 a2). 'All the passions of the soul ought to be regulated in accordance with the rule (or "standard", regula) of reason, which (sc. rule? reason?) is the root of the honestum good' (q39 a2 ad1).

[68] On debitum see §320.   [69] On the decorum see §332 above on Ambrose.

[70] On temperance and the honestum see Albert, *De Temperantia* q4 a4 = *OO* xxviii 192.81, 193.3–7.

[71] Cajetan comments that Aquinas speaks differently of the honestum in 1a q5 a6 from how he speaks in 2-2. In the Prima Pars he takes honestum, utile, and delectabile to divide the good exhaustively. Here, however, he speaks more narrowly, with special reference to morals; 'et ideo honestum concidit hic cum virtute seu virtuoso' (ad 2-2 q145 a1 = L x 147, also quoted in M).

[72] See also 2-2 q110 a2 (the honestas of virtue); Supp. q49 a2 ad6 (the correct use of something useful is the basis of honestas).

Stoic sources is critical, however. He rejects the Stoic doctrine that the honestum is the only good. He agrees that it is the principal human good, because it belongs to reason, which is principal in a human being; but since it is not the only human good, sorrow can reasonably be directed to the loss of non-moral goods (3a q15 a6 ad2).

Aquinas, therefore, treats honestas as moral goodness, a good that is discovered by reason, specifying what fits rational nature, and not only good for the individual, but also meritorious because of its contribution to the common good maintained by justice. In the *Summa*, no less than in the commentary on the *Ethics*, Aquinas' conception of the honestum forms his Aristotelian account of moral goodness.

These points about the role of the honestum in Aquinas' theory are clear to Suarez. As we will see, he recognizes the cumulative importance of Aquinas' scattered remarks, and presents a connected account of moral rightness (honestas) as fitness to rational nature.[73] He has good reason to claim that he is making Aquinas clear and explicit, not adding a new element to Aquinas' position. The position that can reasonably be ascribed to Aquinas can no less reasonably be ascribed to Aristotle as well.[74]

These details on Aquinas' treatment of the honestum should help us to see what he commits himself to in his claims about the deliberative aspects of prudence. Once we see that he is committed to an account of moral virtue that gives this central place to the impartial, rational outlook concerned with the common good, we can ask more precise questions about his description of prudence and its relation to the moral virtues. We need to see whether he can argue that prudence forms a conception of the ultimate end from which deliberation leads us to the honestum.

335. Justice

The virtues as a whole, including the self-regarding virtues, aim at the honestum primarily because they require justice; for the impartial outlook aiming at the honestum is characteristic of justice.[75] Aquinas suggests that justice is especially concerned with actions rather than passions, and that it belongs to the will in contrast to non-rational desire. He is right to claim that acting virtuously requires a contribution by the will as well as the passions. But why should this contribution belong to a distinct virtue, and why should this virtue be justice? We might suppose that bravery and temperance themselves require a rightly-directed will that the virtuous person's passions obey. Apparently we can make this clear without mentioning justice.

This objection takes us back to Aquinas' puzzling claim that bravery and temperance belong to the non-rational parts and justice belongs to the will.[76] We may agree that it is not the function of justice to correct and modify any particular set of non-rational desires, whereas this is the function of bravery and temperance. But we can agree about this difference while still insisting that bravery and temperance also engage the will. So far, then, Aquinas has no sufficient reason for making justice a cardinal virtue.

---

[73] See Suarez, *Bon.* ii. 2.11 = 295a.   [74] See §116.
[75] See §320 on debitum. Sometimes the debitum honesti is contrasted with the debitum iustitiae.
[76] See §290.

Why should our pursuit of our ultimate end, which is our own happiness, involve a virtue that is directed towards the good of others? Aquinas does not answer this question when he discusses whether justice is a virtue.[77] He simply assumes that justice correctly directs (rectificat) human actions, and that therefore it makes a human being good. We do not learn much more from his reasons for thinking that right (ius) is the object of justice (2-2 q57 a1). He assumes that justice involves some 'work that is equalized (adaequatum) to another in accordance with some way of being equal' (q57 a2). But the basis for this claim about the connexion between right direction and equality is not clear.

Aquinas is right to suppose that the cardinal virtues must include some provision for 'co-ordinating' the actions of different human beings (q58 a8).[78] But some sorts of co-ordination might appear to result from my successful manipulation of other people for my own advantage. This is not the sort of co-ordination on the basis of equality that Aquinas has in mind. What would support the more precise claims he makes about the content of justice?

He claims that human beings are naturally social, and that their social inclination underlies the common principles of natural law (1-2 q94 a2).[79] But Aquinas does not describe the inclination in much detail.[80] In particular, he does not make it clear how a bare inclination towards society supports a demand to treat others on some basis of equality. This lack of detail in Aquinas corresponds to a similar gap in Aristotle, who also fails to explain fully why the other-regarding virtue of justice must be included among the virtues that are necessary for an agent's happiness.[81]

336. Friendship

At this stage in Aristotle's argument, we appealed to his discussion of friendship. Does Aquinas' treatment of friendship give us any similar help? At first sight, it is different from Aristotle's treatment; he treats friendship as one of the two types of love, and he treats love as the primary passion.[82] But he does not really treat friendship as a species of passion; for he distinguishes the love belonging to friendship from the love belonging to appetite.[83] The love

[77] 'A human being's action is made good by meeting the standard (regula) of reason, in accordance with which human actions are made correct. Hence, since justice makes human actions correct, it is clear that it makes the action of a human being good' (2-2 q58 a3). Cf. *2Sent.* d27 a3 ad3 = P vi 633b; *in EN* v 2 §908.

[78] 'Whatever can be corrected through reason is the matter for moral virtue, which is defined through correct reason . . . Now through reason one can correct the internal passions of the soul, and the external actions, and also the external things that a human being can use. But through external actions and external things, by which human beings can have a common life (communicare), one looks for the proper direction (ordinatio) of one human being to another . . . And that is why, since justice is directed to another person, it is . . . only about external actions and things, . . . in so far as one human being is co-ordinated with another (alteri coordinatur) in accordance with them' (2-2 q58 a8). Cf. *3Sent.* d33 q1 a1 sol.3 ad3 = P vii 350b.

[79] See §311. Cf. *SG* iii 128–9, partly quoted at §307n39.

[80] The commentary on Aristotle's *Politics* i 1 (= P xxi 371a) is also brief on this point.

[81] On egoism see Finnis, *Aq.* 111, citing *2Sent.* d3 q4 a1 ad2 = P vi 427a (we do not love something because it is ours but because it is good; for good is per se the object of will); *ST* 2-2 q31 a2 ad2 (the human nature of sinners has a claim on us apart from their fault); q64 a6 (we ought to love the nature that God has made).

[82] In *Rhetoric* ii 4 Aristotle treats love or friendliness (philia) as a passion, but he makes no such claim about friendship in his discussion in the *Ethics*.

[83] '. . . the movement of love tends towards two things: towards the good that one wills to someone (to oneself or to another) and towards that to which one wills good. Therefore one has appetitive love towards the good that one wills

of friendship is intellectual love, belonging to the will, in contrast to sensory love, belonging to the sensory appetite.[84] Intellectual love, resulting from the recognition of the good pursued by the will, is not a passion, though it has the same name as the passion of love (q26 a2). This sort of love is 'dilection', the product of election rather than passion (q26 a3; cf. 1a q60 a3).

Aquinas argues that this different relation to reason and election is connected with a difference in the objects of love (1-2 q26 a4; cf. 2–2 q23 a1). Amicable love for another person is love of the person in his own right (secundum se), whereas love of the other for the sake of some further benefit to oneself is purely appetitive love (1-2 q27 a3). In amicable love we do not look for any further result for ourselves, and in this respect the object of love can be an ultimate object.[85] This does not make it the ultimate end, but it is an ultimate end in the sense that it is not simply directed towards a further end of ours.[86] If we do not wish good to the other person himself, but want his good for our sake, that is appetitive love rather than amicable love.[87]

The basis for this amicable love is some similarity between oneself and the other.[88] This recognition of similarity is also described as an 'apprehension of unity', in which one recognizes the other as 'another oneself' (alius ipse),[89] and achieves the 'intimacy' (inhaesio)

to another, and amicable love towards the one to whom one wills good. Now the members of this division are related as primary and secondary: for whatever is loved with amicable love is loved without qualification (simpliciter) and in its own right (per se), but whatever is loved with appetitive love is loved, not without qualification and in its own right, but for something else. . . . Consequently the love with which a thing is loved, that it may have some good, is love without qualification, whereas while the love with which a thing is loved so that it may be another's good is love in a certain respect (secundum quid)' (1-2 q26 a4).

[84] 'Love is something belonging to desire, since good is the object of both. Hence the division of love corresponds to the division of desires. . . . there is . . . desire following an apprehension in the subject of the desire, but from necessity and not from free judgment. This is the character of sensory desire in non-rational animals. In human beings, however, it has some share in freedom, to the extent that it obeys reason. Again, there is another desire following an apprehension in the subject of the desire in accordance with free judgment. And this is the rational or intellectual desire, which is called will' (1-2 q26 a1).

[85] 'The object of love is of two sorts. One is the sort that is loved in the manner of goodwill, whenever we wish someone's good because of himself, as when we love friends even if nothing has to come about from them for us. Another is the sort that is loved with appetitive love; and this is good that is in us or it is loved because some good in us arises from it, as when we love pleasure or we love wine to the extent that it produces pleasure. Now whatever is loved with appetitive love cannot be an ultimate object of love, since it is referred to the good of another—the one who has the appetite; but what is loved with the love of goodwill can be an ultimate object of love' (4Sent d49 q1 a2 sol.1 ad3 = P vii 1188a).

[86] 'Loving someone because of himself can be understood in two ways. One is the way in which something is loved as ultimate end; and in this way only God is to be loved because of himself. Another is the way in which we love someone to whom we will good, as comes about in morally right (honesta) friendship, but not the way <in which we love> a good that we will for ourselves, as comes about in pleasant or advantageous friendship, in which we love the friend as a good of ours—not because we desire advantage or pleasure for the friend, but because from the friend we desire advantage and pleasure for ourselves, just as we love other things that are pleasant and advantageous for us, such as food or clothes. But when we love someone because of virtue, we will good to him, not for ourselves [or: not him for ourselves?]; and this especially arises in the friendship of charity' (Car. a8 ad16).

[87] 'According to the Philosopher, not just any love has the character of friendship, but the love that is with goodwill—that is to way, when we love someone in such a way that we will good to him. If, however, we do not will good to the things we love, but we will their good for ourselves, in the way in which we are said to love wine, or a horse, or anything of that sort, it is not amicable love, but a sort of appetitive love. For it would be absurd to speak of having friendship for wine or for a horse' (2-2 q23 a1).

[88] 'For from the very fact that two are similar, as having one form, they are in a way one in that form: thus two human beings are one thing in the species of humanity, and two white human beings are one thing in whiteness. Hence the affection of one tends towards the other, as being one with him, and he wills good to him as to himself' (1-2 q27 a3).

[89] 'Now since love is of two kinds, appetitive love and amicable love, each of these arises from a kind of apprehension of the oneness of the beloved with the lover. For when we love a thing, as having an appetite for it, we apprehend it as

that seeks to know the other as one knows oneself. Since this amicable love is directed to features of the other person, apart from one's own previous needs, it produces 'ecstasy', taking one's concern outside oneself. Appetitive love involves a concern for something outside oneself, but only in relation to oneself and what one lacks. Amicable love takes one more radically outside oneself, in making one concerned for the other person in his own right,[90] so that it remains in the object, whereas appetitive love turns back to oneself.[91] In this respect amicable love values its object apart from its relation to oneself. Hence one loves the good for its own sake, not because it is one's own good.[92] Whereas appetitive love draws external things into ourselves, in so far as we fit them to our antecedent concerns, amicable love draws us towards external things, by fitting our concerns to other people's concerns.[93]

Since amicable love is directed towards other people in their own right, it is 'complete' or 'perfect' love, whereas appetitive love is imperfect.[94] We perfectly love another person when we want his good; for our love is directed entirely towards him. We love him imperfectly when we want his good for some further end to which our love is primarily directed.[95] In amicable love, therefore, we love the other person 'as ourselves', not because

belonging to our well-being. Similarly, when one loves another with amicable love, one wills good to him, just as one wills good to oneself, and that is why one apprehends him as another oneself—that is to say, in so far as one wills good to him as to oneself. That is why a friend is said to be "another oneself".' (1-2 q28 a1).

[90] As far as the desiring part is concerned, one is said to undergo ecstasy, when one's desire is carried towards something else, going out from oneself in a way. . . . [This] ecstasy is caused . . . by amicable love, without qualification, but by appetitive love not without qualification, but in a certain respect. For in appetitive love the lover is carried out of himself in a certain way—namely, to the extent that, when he is not content to enjoy the good that he has, he seeks to enjoy something outside himself. But since he seeks to have this external good for himself, he does not go outside himself without qualification, but this movement remains within him in its end. But in amicable love one's affection goes out from oneself without qualification because he wills and does good to his friend, as having concern and foresight for the friend because of the friend himself' (1-2 q28 a3).

[91] 'One can tend towards the good of a thing in two ways. One is the way in which one refers the good of that thing to another . . . as someone loves wine to the extent that he wishes for the sweetness of the wine, and he delights in this because he enjoys it, not because the wine itself has it. This is the love that some call appetitive love. But this love does not stop with the thing that is said to be love, but is turned back to the subject for which the good of the thing loved is desired. In another way love is carried towards the good of a thing so that it stops at the thing itself, to the extent that one is satisfied that what has a good has it, and one wishes for it a good that it lacks. And this is the love of goodwill, which is the beginning of friendship, as the Philosopher says' (3Sent d29 q1 a3 = P vii 318a).

[92] 'Nature is said to be turned to itself, because one always loves one's own good. But it is not necessary that one's aim comes to rest in the fact that it is one's own, but in the fact that it is good. But unless something were good for oneself in some way, either in reality or in appearance, one would never love it. But one does not love it because it is one's own, but because it is good; for good is in its own right the object of will' (2Sent d3 q4 ad2 = P vi 427a).

[93] 'In appetitive love, we draw to ourselves things that are external to us, since we love other things with this love to the extent that they are useful or pleasant to us. But in amicable love it is the other way round, because we draw ourselves to things that are outside us; because we are related to the people whom we love with this love as we are related to ourselves, sharing ourselves in a way with them. And so in amicable love similarity is the cause of love; for we do not love someone in this way except to the extent that we are one with him, and similarity is a sort of unity' (in Ioann. 15.4 = P x 570b).

[94] 'Now love is of two kinds, one incomplete, and the other complete. It is incomplete love of a thing, when one loves a thing not so that one wills good to it in itself, but so that one wills its good for oneself. Some people call this appetite, as when we love wine, wanting to enjoy its sweetness, or when we love a human being because of our own advantage or pleasure. But another kind of love is complete love, by which the good of someone in himself is loved, as when by loving someone I will that he himself have a good, even if nothing comes to me from it. This is said to be amicable love, by which someone is loved in his own right; that is why it is called complete friendship, as is said in Ethics VIII' (Spe a3c).

[95] 'Complete love is that by which someone is loved in his own right, as the one for whom one wills good, in the way in which a human being loves his friend. Incomplete love is that by which one loves something not in its own right, but so that he may obtain that good for himself, in the way in which a human being loves the thing he has an appetite for' (2-2 q17 a8).

we love him as much as we love ourselves, but because we love him as someone similar to ourselves.[96]

This description of love is clearer than Aristotle's on some points. Aquinas explains more clearly why friendship for another for the other's own sake is the only complete form of friendship. In his view, it is the only one that proceeds from the love of friendship, which is intellectual rather than appetitive love. The lower two types of Aristotelian friendship lack 'the character of genuine friendship',[97] because they rest on purely appetitive love. In non-amicable love our concern does not go completely outside ourselves, because we want to have some external good for ourselves.[98] Purely appetitive love does not reach its conclusion (terminus) with the good of what we love, but turns back to ourselves (3Sent d29 q1 a3). In this respect Aquinas does not distinguish our acquisitive love for wine or other possessions from the lower types of friendship for persons.

We might legitimately criticize him for failing to recognize the respects in which the lower types of friendship are not purely possessive. He seems to assume without warrant that appetitive love is always acquisitive; but it need not be so, except in the formal sense in which (according to Aquinas) every sort of desire aims at some sort of good for oneself. This sort of self-direction does not imply selfishness.

Aquinas could perhaps concede this point without damage to his main argument. In appetitive love we are constrained by affections and inclinations that both begin and sustain love. Recognition of goodness in the other (person or thing) depends on belief in its correspondence with some prior preference of mine; if the preference changes, the reason for loving the other disappears. Intellectual love, by contrast, responds to the recognition of some value that we recognize as a good reason to continue our preference; we suppose that if our preference were to go away but the value that we recognize did not go away, that would be a sign of error in our preference.

This contrast between appetitive and intellectual love helps to explain why intellectual love is needed for the love of friendship. Aquinas identifies a distinctive type of concern for other people, and for some non-personal objects; we have a reason for this concern that does not depend on our antecedent inclination, and we would think our inclination mistaken if it went away while the reason remained unchanged. For these purposes it is more important to ask what sustains the relevant concern than to ask what originates it. Some non-rational preference or attraction may provoke concern for this person rather than that one. But the type of friendship that results depends on the sort of concern that sustains it.

Aquinas' contrast between amicable and appetitive love anticipates Kant's contrast between acting on duty and acting on other motives.[99] Kant's main point is not that all

---

[96] 'The expression "as himself" can in one way qualify the knowledge and the love on the side of the one known and loved. In this way one angel knows another as himself, because he knows the other to be even as he knows himself to be. In another way the expression can qualify the knowledge and the love on the side of the knower and lover. In this way one angel does not know another as himself, because he knows himself through his essence, and the other not through the other's essence. Similarly he does not love another as himself, because he loves himself through his own will; but he does not love another through the other's will' (1a q60 a4 ad1). 'One is required to love one's neighbour as oneself, not however as much as oneself. Because of this it does not follow that all neighbours are to be loved to an equal degree' (Car. a9 ad9). Aquinas' views on degrees of love are discussed by Steel, 'Preferential'.

[97] . . . deficit a ratione verae amicitiae, 1-2 q26 a4 ad3.   [98] . . . affectio in fine infra ipsum concluditur, 1-2 q28 a3.

[99] Kant, G. 397.

motives other than the motive of duty are selfish. The two people he contrasts with the person acting out of duty are the trader who does the honest thing for the sake of his business and the philanthropist who acts out of his generous sentiments. The action of the philanthropist lacks moral worth not because it is selfish, but because his reason for doing the generous action rests ultimately on his generous impulses; if he lacked them, he would have lost his reason for these actions. Kant is primarily concerned with the distinction that Aquinas draws in his account of intellectual love.

This account of the love of friendship shows that Aquinas is closer to Aristotle's account of the best kind of friendship than to modern conceptions of friendship. We might well find it surprising to be told that genuine friendship depends on the recognition of value and not on our inclination, preference, or caprice. But Aquinas' view of the love of friendship makes it a more suitable basis for the sort of moral concern that might be defended by appeal to the judgments of prudence.

The appeal to similarity and to union is still not very informative. Aquinas implies that I recognize in another the same features calling for love that I recognize in myself when I have the proper sort of self-love for myself (cf. 1a q60 a3–4). He also seems to suggest, however, that some further type of union is involved besides mere similarity; hence he speaks of the union that results from membership in a family or a political community (1a q60 a4).

These different features of friendship should explain why we care about others for their own sake. They rest on Aquinas' claim that everyone seeks his own perfection. As we have seen, this involves the application of intellectual love to our desires and aims. The desire for perfection differs from the desire for the systematic satisfaction of my desires; it does not take my current desires for granted, but criticizes them to see whether they really fulfil my capacities as a rational agent. This criticism shows us that we perfect ourselves only in so far as we regard other people as valuable in their own right and not simply as means to aims that we can pursue without attributing such value to others.

This argument does not yet make it clear why pursuit of my own perfection requires concern for the good of others for their own sake. Aquinas' view of intellectual love shows why it is possible to care about the good of another person apart from any antecedent inclination of mine. But it does not yet seem to show why such concern for another person is required by reason.

To find the appropriate argument, it is helpful to consider the connexion between intellectual love, concern for one's own perfection, and interaction with others. Intellectual love causes us to aim at our perfection rather than the mere satisfaction of our desires. Equally, concern for our perfection causes us to act on intellectual love. For we seek our perfection as rational agents, and our rational agency consists in acting on intellectual love; as rational agents we pursue ends that we see some good reason for pursuing apart from our antecedent inclinations.

In seeking our own perfection as rational agents, we have reason to co-operate with other rational agents. When Aquinas speaks of 'sharing' (communicatio) with another person, he especially refers to the sharing of rational activity. As Aristotle sees, this shared activity includes common deliberation about what to do. Aquinas' emphasis on intellectual love adds a further element of sharing. In recognizing another as a rational agent, I recognize her as being moved by intellectual love. I therefore take her views on the merits of different actions to be worth considering, since she at least assesses actions by some estimate of their value. If her views are worth considering, I have reason to share in common deliberation about value with the other person.

This conclusion may seem relevant to 'respecting' (as we say) a person's opinion, in the sense of thinking it worth some consideration. But such respect seems to fall short of concern for persons and their welfare. Can we bring Aquinas' claims about rational agency any closer to the attitudes proper to friendship?

He might plausibly reject any sharp division between respect for a person's opinion as a co-operator in practical reasoning and respect for a person as deserving concern for her welfare in her own right. If we are mutually concerned for each other's welfare, we have more reason to trust each other's opinion about the good. Since my advice to you aims at your good, you have reason to take it seriously; similarly, I have reason to listen to your advice, which aims at my good. Each of us has reason to believe that our joint advice to ourselves aims at our common good.

This argument suggests why Aquinas has a good reason for resting his claims about friendship on the apparently rather austere basis of intellectual love and external reasons. In his view, we cannot recognize ourselves as rational agents, moved by intellectual love to seek our own perfection, without being committed to friendship for rational agents as such.

The argument from intellectual love to friendship is basically the same as the argument for society that Aquinas offers in the context of natural law. He claims that as rational agents we have a natural inclination towards society. Once we try to amplify this claim, we find that he appeals to the connexion between rational agency and concern for other people as participants in rational agency. The basic connexion between rational agency and co-operation with others underlies Aquinas' arguments both about friendship and about justice.

337. Friendship as a Basis for Justice

This account of friendship clarifies Aquinas' claim that a human being is naturally political. This claim does not mean simply that human beings have naturally social instincts or preferences; for in that case the value of social ties would depend (as far as this argument goes) on their satisfying these preferences. Aquinas means that the good of others is a proper concern of intellectual love; the appropriate sort of community fulfils the rational demand for perfection.

It is difficult to find a clear argument in Aquinas that connects intellectual love, concern for the good of others, human beings as naturally political, and the demands of justice.[100] Moreover, the argument we have just attributed to him may appear to give an unwelcome result. Is a defence of friendship not too narrow for a defence of justice? The demands of justice extend to people for whom we lack the sort of concern that is characteristic of friendship.

---

[100] For further passages on the naturally political nature of human beings see BF xxxviii, App.1. Some of the passages in 2–2 that add some detail to the general claims in 1–2 are 2–2 q26 a3; q47 a10 ad2; q58 a5; a9 ad3; q64 a2; q65 a1; q114 a1 ad2.

This objection overlooks Aquinas' description of the basis of the love of friendship. In claiming that it involves the recognition of similarity and the recognition of value connected with this similarity, he allows the possibility of variations in the closeness of friendship. Since we can recognize relevant sorts of similarity in many people, Aquinas has defined an ethical relation that extends more broadly than friendship as we might naturally conceive it. Hence he speaks of love between citizens as the love that belongs to civic virtue, involving the sharing of right (honesta) actions.[101] His account of the love of friendship and its connexion to similarity is meant to explain the relation between citizens as well as the relation between closer friends (cf. *Div. Nom.* 4.9 = P xv 314a). We are entitled, then, to appeal to Aquinas' claims about friendship in order to understand his views about fellow-citizens.

We can connect friendship more closely with justice through the claim that justice involves the recognition of equality and the appropriate treatment of people as equals (2-2 q57 a1–2). When we recognize the relevant sort of equality, and treat people in accordance with it, we assign to each person what is his own.[102] Not all recognition of similarity involves recognition of equality (1a q60 a4 ad1), but recognition of equality involves the recognition of some aspect of similarity. In the case of distributive justice, the recognition of equality includes A's recognition of the equality of B and C, when A has to divide something between B and C. In the case of corrective justice, recognition of equality includes A's recognition of the equal right or equal claim of B and C. Recognition of the second sort of equality is especially important when we are trying to see how a virtue that concerns the good of others can fit into the outlook of a rational agent who is concerned with his own good.

If Aquinas is right to claim that recognition of the right sort of similarity is the basis for the love of friendship, he has a reason to believe that the sort of co-ordination required by justice (2-2 q58 a8) requires recognition of equality and concern for benefiting others. If we knew nothing of his views on the basis of friendship, we might object to Aquinas' claim by arguing that the appropriate sort of co-ordination is the sort that allows me to exploit other people to fulfil my antecedent inclinations, without any independent concern for their good. He can answer this objection by appeal to his account of friendship. If we are concerned for our own perfection, and we see that we cannot engage in the activities that perfect our own rational agency if we do not pursue the good of other people for their own sakes, we will not suppose that the right sort of co-ordination must be (as far as we can manage) purely exploitative.

338. The Aims of Justice

This argument suggests a possible defence of Aquinas' puzzling claim that justice differs from the other cardinal virtues in belonging to the will and in dealing with actions rather than passions. These features of justice are part of his reason for regarding justice as a distinct cardinal virtue. Earlier we rejected his grounds for believing that bravery and temperance

---

[101] See 1a q60 a4; *3Sent.* d29 q1 a6 = P vii 321a.

[102] '...the matter of justice is an external action in so far as either it or the thing we use through it is made proportionate to some other person towards whom we are directed (ordinamur) by justice. Now each person's own is what is owed (debitum) to him according to equality of proportion. Therefore the proper act of justice is nothing else than to render to each what is his own' (2-2 q58 a11).

belong to the passions rather than the will.[103] We might still agree, however, that justice differs from bravery and temperance in not being concerned with a specific passion or range of passions. The passions must be perfected in a just person, since different sorts of misdirected passions may cloud or distort a will that aims at just action; but no specific passion is connected to justice in the way fear is connected to bravery. The aim of justice is not to perfect any passions, but to turn the will in the right direction. We may be surprised to hear that the right direction of the will turns it towards the good of others; for we might expect that the special virtue of the will would direct it to the agent's own good.[104]

It is easier to agree with Aquinas if we see the connexion that he intends between concern for our perfection and concern for the good of others. When we choose on the basis of reason and deliberation, we act on will in contrast to passion. Aquinas believes that when we take this point of view, we can see why we need to be concerned for the good of others. If we were simply concerned with orderly satisfaction of our current desires, then we would have no desire-independent reason to care about the good of others for their own sake; but when we pass beyond satisfaction to perfection, we see the reasons for accepting justice. Aquinas has a reasonable defence of his view that the appropriate perfection of the will results in the virtue that also embodies the appropriate concern for the good of others.

This argument for connecting justice with the will applies to justice quite generally, but Aquinas believes that it applies in different ways to different types of justice. He follows Aristotle in distinguishing general from special or partial ('particularis') justice. General justice and virtue as a whole imply each other, though they differ in definition; special justice is co-ordinate with the other special virtues, and extends only over part of the area of general justice (2-2 q58 a6–7).

Aristotle's basis for distinguishing these two types of justice is not clear. Aquinas distinguishes them along lines that are not explicitly marked by Aristotle, though they have an Aristotelian basis. While both types of justice are concerned with our relations to other people, general justice is properly concerned with directing different people's actions towards a common good, whereas special justice is concerned with the relations of one individual to another.[105]

In Aquinas' view, general justice 'directs the actions of all the virtues towards a common good' (2-2 q58 a6). He does not mean that we could have all the virtues without directing them towards a common good; he means that if we had them to the extent that is possible without direction towards a common good, we would not have all the virtues. This description of general justice fits Aristotle's claim that general justice prescribes the actions of the other virtues with a view to the good of the political community (EN 1129b17–19).[106]

Special justice differs from general because it is properly concerned not with the common good, but with directing an individual's actions in relation to another particular individual (ad alteram singularem personam, 2-2 q58 a7).[107] Aquinas considers whether this distinct virtue is superfluous because general justice already embraces concern for the good of other people. He answers that general justice considers the good of individuals only mediately,

---

[103] See §290.   [104] On justice and the will see Scotus' discussion of the two affections, §363.
[105] On general justice see Finnis, *Aq.* 118.   [106] See §117. Aquinas introduces the common good at *in EN* v 2 §912.
[107] Aquinas introduces this aspect of special justice (ad aliquam personam privatam) at *in EN* v 3 §918, without explicit support in the text of Aristotle.

and that therefore it is necessary for some other virtue to consider the good of individuals immediately (2-2 q58 a7 ad1).[108] He connects this division with the division between public and private law (ius; 1-2 q60 a3).[109]

This division fits Aristotle, in so far as Aristotle's divisions of special justice seem to be especially concerned with relations (for instance, distribution, rectification, and exchange) that involve claims by individuals on one another. Aristotle also marks out special from general justice by claiming that special justice is properly concerned with equality (*EN* 1129a31–b1) and with ensuring that each person has his 'own' or his 'due' (*ta hautou*, 1132b16–20). Aquinas, however, takes concern with equality and with one's due to be a feature of justice as a whole, of general no less than of special justice. Nor does he rely on Aristotle's claim that special justice and injustice are concerned only with external goods.[110] Instead, he appeals to the distinction between a concern for individuals and a concern for the common good.

In support of Aristotle and Aquinas, we may notice that some provisions of justice seem to be concerned with facts about individuals—what someone has done, who has paid what, what agreements have been made, and so on—rather than with facts about the common good. By contrast, the requirement that citizens perform military service seems to refer directly to a common good, not to what this or that individual has done; the fact that it is a common good, rather than a good for this particular individual or group, seems to explain, at least in part, why it is just to require service from individuals. The different conditions that show why a requirement is just seem to suggest that the division between facts about individuals and facts about the common good is relevant.

Sometimes, however, both sorts of questions about justice seem to arise about the same action or policy. Even if the requirement of military service or taxation rests on the common good, its imposition on particular individuals raises questions of special justice; unfair benefits and burdens are imposed, for instance, if some people are exempted from service or taxation for inappropriate reasons. From one point of view, this unfairness does not affect the common good. If, for instance, the rich are allowed to avoid military service by paying for substitutes, the substitutes might be equally effective soldiers; similarly, the state might raise as much money by inequitable as by equitable taxation. If this is against the common good precisely because it is unjust, the requirements of special justice constrain the content of general justice. The constraints might also go the other way. Punishments for the crimes of an individual may be affected by considerations of the common good; we may consider whether, for instance, someone is a danger to society or whether a particular sort of punishment is likely to deter other people.

These questions are prominent in later arguments about justice. Aquinas does not discuss them. He does not suggest, for instance, that general justice could achieve the common

---

[108] 'Legal justice certainly directs someone sufficiently in things related to another—as far as the common good is concerned, immediately, but as far as the good of an individual person is concerned, mediately. And so there needs to be some particular justice to direct someone immediately towards the good of another particular person' (2-2 q58 a7 ad1).

[109] This distinction is briefly discussed by Nicholas, *IRL* 207–8. He remarks that the distinction in Roman law between crimes (public law) and delicts (private law) does not correspond exactly to the distinction between crimes and torts. But he draws a distinction that helps to explain Aquinas' claims: '. . . the distinction is between an act which endangers the order or the security of the state, and one which is an infringement of an individual's rights . . . .'

[110] He mentions this aspect of special justice at *in EN* v 3 §919.

good by ignoring the legitimate claims of individuals. He takes it for granted that general justice considers the good of individuals mediately (2-2 q58 a7 ad1), and he does not suggest that the common good might conflict with the good of this or that particular individual.

Some of his remarks about justice, however, suggest how a conflict might arise. The good of each individual and the common good would not coincide if the common good were calculated by aggregation of the gains and losses to individuals; for in that case a course of action might promote the common good, but harm particular individuals. Aquinas appeals to 'utility' in arguing for the justice of laws and institutions.[111] He does not go into detail about how utility is to be assessed or how it affects justice, but he suggests a basis for claims about general justice that potentially conflicts with the good of each individual.

A further potential conflict appears if the common good is taken to be the good of a society in contrast to the individuals composing it. The difference becomes clear if we think of a society as having an interest in its own survival across generations; this might require a sacrifice of the interests of individuals who are required to harm themselves in order to defend this state from dissolution and absorption into another state. This would be an application of the analogy of part and whole, which Aquinas sometimes uses for the relation of state to individual.[112] The whole has an interest in its survival that sometimes may require it to destroy a part; similarly (we may say) the state as a whole has an interest in its survival that may require harm to individuals.

We would reach a close coincidence between the common good and the good of individuals if we insisted that, contrary to the previous suggestion, the common good must be what is best for everyone. Each individual would have a strong 'veto' over every course of action proposed in the name of the common good, so that if x is proposed as promoting the common good, but A can show that A benefits more from y than from x, then A has shown that x does not promote the common good.

If Aquinas allows this strong veto to individuals, he is entitled to assume that nothing promoting the common good can violate individual goods. But a veto seems to impose unreasonable restrictions on the pursuit of the common good. Institutions and requirements such as military service, taxation, observance of traffic laws, and so on, do not seem to allow individuals the sort of veto that they would allow if they observed Aquinas' constraint, so interpreted.

But Aquinas does not endorse a strong veto; he does not assert that general justice mediately pursues what is best for each individual, but only that it mediately pursues individual good. This condition might be satisfied if pursuit of the common good requires benefit to each individual, but not necessarily greater benefit than would have been achieved in some other way. Perhaps x benefits both A and B, but A would have benefited more from y, which would have harmed B, and B would have benefited more from z, which would have harmed A. In that case, x promotes the common good of A and B, and so is to be preferred over y and z, even though both y and z would have been better for someone. In this case, we may say that A and B have a weak veto though not a strong veto.[113]

---

[111] See, e.g., 2-2 q64 a3, ad3; q77 a1. [112] On whole and part see n100 above.

[113] This weak veto, in turn, might be understood to require (a) a basic minimum for both A and B, or (b) a reasonable degree of equality between A and B.

This suggestion that the good of individuals imposes a weak veto on the common good, gives Aquinas a plausible claim about justice. For we often suppose that a course of action is unjust if it imposes an unreasonable degree of sacrifice on particular people, even if it also confers a large benefit on a larger number. A weak veto embodies a conception of 'one's own' or 'one's right' (ius suum).[114] Some rights guarantee the protection of certain goods for each individual against the demands of others. A weak veto seems to embody a reasonable guarantee. It may still be too demanding; for we may suppose that many just and beneficial policies make some people worse off than they were before. Such policies might be rejected as unjust only if they impose an unreasonable degree of harm. In deciding what would be an unreasonable degree of harm, we decide what should be guaranteed to individuals as their right.

339. Eudaemonism and Justice

In trying to understand some of these aspects of justice, we seem to raise a more general difficulty for the overall structure of Aquinas' conception of the virtues. Though a weak veto for individuals might seem to do better than a strong veto in capturing an aspect of justice, it might seem to be too weak for the demands of Aquinas' general theory. Since he accepts eudaemonism, he seems to assume that the will aims at the overall good for oneself. How, then, can a rational and informed will accept a course of action that fails to secure what seems best overall for oneself? If individuals have only a weak veto on the common good, they may be required to forgo what seems better for themselves and to accept the just course of action that protects them against unacceptable harm but fails to secure what is best for them. Given Aquinas' eudaemonism, must he not insist on a strong veto? But if he does that, he seems to demand more than it is reasonable to demand in the just pursuit of the common good.

This objection affects the unity of prudence, and hence affects RV. Aquinas believes we can reach the specific end pursued by justice, by deliberation from the universal end of one's own good. If the requirements of justice do not always seem to promote one's own good, how can we justify them by deliberation that refers ultimately to one's own good?

Aquinas might answer by distinguishing the eudaemonist basis of pursuit of a common good from the basis of policies that advance a common good. His eudaemonism requires us to satisfy ourselves that we are better off participating in a society pursuing a common good than we would be without it. We must rely on Aquinas' claim that human beings are naturally political, and on the defence of this claim that rests on his account of friendship. That account supports the claim that one's ultimate good requires participation in a common good, and hence membership of a society that pursues it.

Individuals, therefore, have a strong veto on the existence of a political community, and it is unjust to force them into a community that makes them worse off than they would be under any other arrangement open to them. They also have a strong veto on the effect of the community on their lives as a whole; if they are forced to have a worse life within the community than they would have under any other arrangement open to them,

---

[114] Some related issues about rights are discussed by Tuck, NRT, ch. 1.

the community fails a eudaemonist constraint.[115] Aquinas might reasonably argue that a community does not really pursue a common good unless it meets this constraint.

But an individual need not have a strong veto over every action taken by the community in the pursuit of the common good. For Aquinas' eudaemonism does not necessarily apply eudaemonist reasoning to every question. We have already seen a limit on eudaemonist reasoning in Aristotle's conception of action for the sake of the fine (*kalon*). Virtuous agents who recognize that a situation requires virtuous action act virtuously, without further reflexion on the implications for their own happiness. But the choice of virtuous action depends on deliberation about happiness; for this deliberation shows, according to Aristotle, that we promote our happiness by taking the virtuous person's attitude, which sometimes rejects eudaemonistic deliberation.[116]

Aquinas takes over this limit on eudaemonist reasoning, since he incorporates Aristotle's views about the fine in his own conception of the morally right (honestum). He argues that the brave person acts for the sake of the good of his proper state of character, or 'to express a likeness of his state in his action' (2-2 q123 a7). This aim does not conflict with the claim (quoted from Augustine) that the virtues aim at happiness; happiness is the ultimate end, but the end proper to the virtue is the proximate end.[117] Prudence arranges actions to aim at the ultimate end,[118] but brave people do not focus directly on this end in particular actions; they aim to act appropriately for their state of character.[119] Eudaemonist deliberation justifies the cultivation of bravery as a virtue, but it does not replace the normal reflexions of the brave person facing a particular choice.

We have already noticed that Aquinas distinguishes the ultimate from the proximate end, in explaining how prudence does and does not set the end for virtue. Prudence does not set the ultimate end, but it sets the proximate end by deliberation on the content of the ultimate end. This is the deliberation that belongs to universal prudence reaching the properly virtuous end. The deliberation of particular prudence takes the virtuous end for granted and reaches conclusions about the appropriate actions.

The deliberation of universal prudence has a teleological and eudaemonist form, since it starts from the ultimate end. But the deliberations of particular prudence need not have this form. Once we have concluded that we ought to pursue a specific proximate end for the sake of the ultimate good, we may not need to keep referring to the ultimate good. Indeed, reflexion on the nature of the particular end may convince us that we ought not to refer explicitly to the ultimate good in all circumstances.

It is plausible to suppose that when we form the proximate ends proper to friendship and justice, we will limit reflexion on the ultimate good. For we may find that we can achieve these proximate ends only if we pursue them for their own sake without further reflexion on their effects. This conclusion does not conflict with Aquinas' eudaemonism.

This understanding of the universal and the specific end of virtue explains how Aquinas' eudaemonist outlook both controls the content of justice and marks out an area that is

---

[115] Plato raises this question at R.520. See §62.   [116] See §112.

[117] This is relevant to Aquinas' answer to questions about pagan virtue. See §356.

[118] In 'in agibilibus per prudentiam disponuntur actus humani' (q123 a7) Aquinas distinguishes the concern of prudence for the ultimate end from the concern of bravery for the proximate end.

[119] 'intendit enim agere secundum convenientiam sui habitus', q123 a7.

not directly subject to eudaemonist considerations. If the existence of a community that promotes the happiness of individuals requires them to suspend eudaemonist deliberation in some cases, and to be guided simply by the considerations proper to justice, eudaemonist considerations do not imply a strong veto for each individual on pursuit of the common good.

Later theorists recognize the importance of accepting practices that restrict appeals to the sort of deliberation that justifies acceptance of the practice. Aquinas does not emphasize the importance of such restrictions when he discusses justice. But his account of rational action allows such restrictions; he recognizes that 'the power of the first aim' (virtus primae intentionis) remains in actions that do not themselves proceed, on that occasion, directly from reflexion about the end we are aiming at.[120]

Aquinas does not develop his position in the detail that would be necessary for us to see what he thinks it is committed to, or how he thinks it can answer objections. Study of his views on justice is useful partly because they raise many of the issues that concern later theorists, and in particular because he combines several claims—especially those about the common good and about individual rights—that have tended to mark out sharply different conceptions of justice. His position has resources to answer the questions that arise as a result of more detailed examination of justice.

340. Commands and Counsels

RV commits Aquinas to the recognition of virtues that are required for everyone; these virtues are derived from the precepts of natural law, which direct natural human inclinations for one's own good and the good of others. He faces a complication, however, when he needs to make room for some of the specific demands of Christianity, and especially those that are held to justify the outlook of religious orders. These demands seem to create a difficulty, because they require religious (i.e., the members of these orders) to withdraw from the ordinary self-regarding and other-regarding obligations that go with the different virtues, in order to devote themselves to prayer and special discipline.

The moral basis of the religious life is not simply a question for Aquinas in his specific time and circumstances. It also requires us to ask when it is permissible to pursue some aim or aspiration that withdraws us from the ordinary obligations of a member of society, in order to achieve some good that we take to be especially important, in circumstances where we know that most people will not be attracted to this aim.

The obligations that constitute the way of life of a religious order (monks, nuns, or friars) separate some people from the obligations imposed on the rest of their society. Members of these orders are exempt from some of the requirements imposed on ordinary citizens, and they are subject to special obligations that cannot be imposed on everyone. Indeed, the observance of some obligations of the religious life (e.g., virginity) seems to depend on the assumption that other people will not observe them.[121]

---

[120] See §248. Aquinas' remarks on bravery (just quoted) suggest how his views about 'virtual intention' might clarify his account of the virtuous state of character.

[121] Aquinas' explanation in *SG* iii 130 cites *Matt.* 19:21; 1*Cor.* 7:23, 32–3; *Heb.* 12:17; *Cant.* 8:7; *Matt.* 13:45–6; *Phil.* 3:7–8.

Aquinas faces a difficulty, since he admits that these special obligations do not specify the demands of virtue and justice.[122] He takes them to rest on 'counsels of perfection', as opposed to 'precepts of necessity'. They are not prescribed as necessary for achieving the ultimate end, and hence they are not necessary parts of the virtues; but they are advised as the best way of reaching the end. This claim may puzzle us. If the counsels identify better or easier means to achieve the end that everyone wants, why do they not apply to everyone? For surely good deliberation picks the best and easiest means? Should we not abandon a merely possible means if a better and easier one is available, given the difficulty of the merely possible means and the value of the end being pursued?

Aquinas gives two reasons for not requiring everyone to follow this route: (1) Not everyone is capable of following it; as St Paul suggests, it might be better to be unmarried and free of lust, but since this is not possible for most people, it is better for them to marry than to burn.[123] If it is not possible for everyone, it would be self-defeating to impose this conduct on everyone. (2) The 'reasonable order' of human beings requires most people not to take the road of the counsels but to take the ordinary road.

If the second point were true, but the first false, some people might be compelled to undertake special burdens, since they would be required to undertake difficult tasks that they would like to avoid. Sometimes people have supposed that Plato's rulers must undertake special burdens of this sort.[124] Aquinas does not believe that the counsels force this issue on us. For if most people would not in any case want to follow the counsels, and would not be capable of it, it is not unfair if some people withdraw from ordinary roles and tasks. Those who withdraw do not impose unfair burdens on people who would like to be monks or friars but are needed to maintain the reasonable order of society; for the number of people who are capable of the religious life is small enough to make it unnecessary to select among equally qualified candidates.

To justify this claim that most people neither can nor want to take up the religious life, Aquinas might appeal to the fact that religious—from one point of view—abandon some of the basic human concerns prescribed by natural law because of human nature. This is part of the ground for objecting to voluntary poverty (SG iii 131). Self-preservation, reproduction, and concern for others are all abandoned to the extent that the ordinary means for securing them are rejected. Aquinas needs to argue that they are not entirely abandoned; the religious assure themselves that all these functions can be handled 'by proxy', since they are taken care of by other people's deliberation. Other people must carry out these basic provisions of natural law. The religious assume that society takes care of the things that they set aside, and in particular that other people exercise charity by supporting the religious.

---

[122] 'But this is not necessary to a human being for justice in such a way that justice cannot be without it; for virtue and justice are not destroyed if a human being uses bodily and earthly things in accordance with reasonable order. And for that reason the kinds of advice given by divine law of this kind are called counsels, and not precepts, in so far as a human being is exhorted to lay aside less good things for the sake of better things' (SG iii 130). 'Things that belong to excellence come under counsels of perfection rather than under precepts of necessity. That is why precepts were not to be given about magnificence and magnanimity, but rather counsels' (2-2 q140 a2 ad1).

[123] 'I wish that all were as I myself am. But each has his own special gift from God, one having one kind and another a different kind. To the unmarried and the widows I say that it is well for them to remain unmarried as I am. But if they are not practicing self-control, they should marry. For it is better to marry than to be aflame with passion' (1Cor. 7:7–9). Aquinas comments in ST Suppl. q42 a3 ad4.

[124] See §62.

Is this an unfair expectation? If what other people are required to do is simply what nature makes appropriate for them and is not an unwelcome burden in comparison with the religious life, it is not unfair if the religious live in a way that presupposes that other people will continue with the natural functions. Other people are reluctant to give up the life according to nature for the withdrawn life; and there is no reason to tell them that they must overcome their reluctance. Indeed, it would be disastrous if they all did overcome it.

Moreover, the fact that religious orders withdraw from some aspects of society does not make them socially useless parasites. Aquinas defends voluntary poverty by arguing that a religious undertakes it in order to be more useful to other people in other ways.[125] On this ground, he defends friars, who teach and engage with others, in comparison with monks who withdraw more completely. In his view, complete separation from society is not necessary in order to devote oneself to the contemplative life. Teaching immerses friars in the everyday world less than ordinary occupations and social roles would immerse them. In their partly withdrawn way of life, they devote less anxiety (sollicitudo) to securing the basic means of life; hence the idea of abandoning ordinary pursuits in order to take some of them up again is not as pointless as it sounds.

But even if, from the human point of view, the religious option involves no unfairness to the ordinary people and imposes no special burden on them, does it involve some unfairness from the divine point of view? For if the counsels of perfection are really divine advice about the best way to salvation, do they not give some people an easier route to salvation than other people have? Worldly cares are presumably to be avoided because they introduce temptations, opportunities to abandon one's ultimate good. Is it not unfair for one sort of person to face these temptations that other people can avoid?

One might answer that this is not a special difficulty about the religious life. Even if it were always true that religious are exposed to less dangerous temptations than those that confront other people, they would not necessarily gain an unfair advantage just by being religious. They simply exemplify the more general point that different people face different temptations and dangers. Someone like Trollope's Dr Grantly is not free of dangers in his life as a Christian minister, but he has a relatively easy time fulfilling his vocation to some degree, just as a soldier in peacetime has a relatively easy career as a competent soldier. Dietrich Bonhöffer faced more severe temptations and dangers as a Christian minister, and displayed a degree of heroic virtue that Dr Grantly would never display, even if he were better than he is.[126] Similarly, a general who commands an army in wartime in difficult and dangerous situations has an opportunity to display greatness, and to suffer humiliating

---

[125] 'Hence the one who through voluntary poverty removes from himself the capacity to help others in temporal goods, in order to acquire spiritual goods through which he can help others more usefully, does not act against the good of human society . . .' (SG iii 134).

[126] See Trollope's description of Dr Grantly: 'He was a moral man, believing the precepts which he taught, and believing also that he acted up to them; though we cannot say that he would give his coat to the man who took his cloak, or that he was prepared to forgive his brother even seven times' (W, ch. 2). On another generally sympathetic character Trollope comments: 'Mr Harding's warmest admirers cannot say that he was ever an industrious man; the circumstances of his life have not called on him to be so; and yet he can hardly be called an idler' (ch. 1). Bonhöffer describes the moral predicament of Germans in 1943 in the Prologue to LPP: 'The great masquerade of evil has played havoc with all our ethical concepts. For evil to appear disguised as light, charity, historical necessity, or social justice is quite bewildering to anyone brought up on our traditional ethical concepts . . .' (4). On the attempt to live a life of private virtue that might be reasonable in more normal circumstances he comments: 'Here and there people flee from public altercation into the

failure, that the peacetime general never has. If the Stoics are right to say that a virtuous person acts reasonably in accordance with the circumstances, and that reasonableness includes a disposition to act rightly in counterfactual as well as actual circumstances, the facts about different circumstances do not necessarily introduce unfairness.[127] Hence they do not create any special moral or theological objection to the religious life.

People who are incapable of the religious life cannot reasonably complain that they are not allowed to share in it, provided that their incapacity does not result in their being treated unfairly. Similarly, if some people are capable of the religious life, but are required to renounce it for the sake of the common good (because society needs them as farmers, or plumbers, or politicians), they have no reason to complain, provided that they are not unfairly penalized because they have remained in situations where they cannot follow the counsels of perfection. The demands of RV and the requirements of friendship and justice do not necessarily conflict with the ways of life recommended by the counsels of perfection.[128]

341. Self-Love, Sin, and Virtue

We have noticed that this discussion of the virtues, and especially of friendship and justice, raises a question, for Aquinas no less than for Aristotle, about the primary and fundamental character of one's desire for one's own happiness. Aquinas follows Aristotle in maintaining the primacy of self-love. He rejects the view that self-love needs to be limited by some other affection, and he examines the Scriptural and Augustinian arguments that appear to raise moral objections to self-love, in order to show that they do not support justified objections to self-love, correctly understood.

Aquinas believes that we ought to love God more than ourselves, and hence that we should not take states of ourselves to be the most important end to achieve.[129] He compares the subordination of self-love to the love of God with the subordination of concern for one's own advantage to the common good. The love of God is not separate, any more than concern for the common good is, from one's pursuit of one's own happiness. We come to love God as the common source of all goodness because we are concerned about our own

sanctuary of private virtuousness. But anyone who does this must shut his mouth and his eyes to the injustice around him' (5).

[127] The view that virtue requires an appropriate attitude to a variety of circumstances, as opposed to one definite way of life, is explored by Taylor, *SS*, ch. 13, esp. 222–4 (who discusses this view as a form of opposition to a specifically religious way of life).

[128] I say 'do not necessarily conflict' in order to acknowledge that in some particular situations (e.g., conditions of scarcity or emergency) there may be no room for the withdrawal required by the religious life. Machiavelli might be taken to claim that he lived in such conditions of emergency; see §409.

[129] 'Natural love is founded on the sharing of natural goods given to us by God. By this natural love not only a human being, in the unimpaired condition of his nature, but also every single creature, each in its own way, loves God above all things, and even more than itself, because each part naturally loves the common good of the whole more than its own particular good. This is clear from what they do; for each part has its principal inclination towards common action for the benefit (*utilitas*) of the whole. This is also evident in civic virtues, in accordance with which citizens sometimes accept damage even to their own property and persons for the sake of the common good. Hence this is found to be true much more in the friendship of charity, which is founded on the sharing of the gifts of grace. For this reason a human being ought, out of charity, to love God, who is the common good of all, more than himself, because happiness is in God as in the common and original principle of all who can share in happiness' (2-2 q26 a3).

good (1-2 q2 a8). Hence we could love God above everything by our uncorrupted natural abilities without grace; we need grace only because of the corruption resulting from sin.[130]

Overriding love of God does not require us to renounce self-love; for self-love does not require us to care less about the love of God. Aquinas agrees with Aristotle in claiming that vicious people have misguided self-love, but have no more self-love than virtuous people have.[131] Vicious people have the 'prudence of the flesh', which rests on a false conception of themselves. This is not a type of genuine prudence, but an impostor, because it does not include a grasp of the correct end.[132] Similarly, vicious people do not love themselves more than virtuous people love themselves; they have the wrong conception of the self who is appropriately loved.

In one way the love of God or the common good limits self-love, but in another way it does not. To see the difference, we may recall Aquinas' division between the universal and the specific end of the virtuous person, and the corresponding roles of universal and particular prudence. The universal end is one's own happiness; inquiry about this discovers the particular end that happiness consists in. Understanding of the particular end may show us that when we act on it we should not ask whether our action promotes the universal end. In our practical thought as a whole, self-love is not limited; for we are always following

---

[130] 'Now in natural things, everything which, as such, naturally belongs to another, is principally, and more strongly inclined towards what it belongs to than towards itself. . . . And since reason imitates nature, we find the same inclination in the civic virtues; for it is characteristic of a virtuous citizen to expose himself to the danger of death for the safety of the whole commonwealth. . . . And so, since God himself is the universal good, and under this good angels, human beings, and all creatures are included, because every creature naturally, in accordance with what it is, belongs to God, it follows that by natural love angel and human being alike loves God more and more principally than himself. Otherwise, if either of them naturally loved self more than God, it would follow that natural love would be perverse, and that it would not be perfected but destroyed through charity' (1a q60 a5). '. . . in the state of unimpaired nature a human being referred the love of himself to the love of the God as to its end, and similarly the love of all other things. And so he loved God more than himself and above all things. But in the state of corrupt nature man falls short of this as far as the desire of his rational will goes; for because of the corruption of nature it follows its private good, unless it is healed through God's grace' (1-2 q109 a3).

[131] 'Properly speaking, it is impossible for someone to hate himself. For everything naturally desires good, nor can anyone desire anything for himself, except under the character of good: for "evil is outside the scope of the will", as Dionysius says. . . . Now to love someone is to will good to him. . . . Hence it is necessary for someone to love himself, and impossible to hate himself, properly speaking' (1-2 q29 a4). 'Now the fact that someone desires a temporal good misdirectedly results from his loving himself misdirectedly; for to will some good to someone is to love him. Therefore it is evident that misdirected love of oneself is the cause of every sin' (1-2 q77 a4). 'Properly directed self-love is required (debitus) and natural, so in such a way that one desires an appropriate good for oneself. But misdirected self-love, which leads to contempt of God, is taken to be the cause of sin, according to Augustine' (1-2 q77 a4 ad1). 'A human being loves himself in this, that he wills his excellence; for loving oneself is the same as willing good to oneself. Hence it amounts to the same to take arrogance or self-love to be a beginning of all sin' (1-2 q84 a2 ad3).

'Love of self is common to all, in one way; in another way it is proper to the good; in a third way, it is proper to the bad. For it is common to all for each one to love what he thinks himself to be. Now a human being is said to be something, in two ways. First, in accordance with his substance and nature; and in accordance with this all take it to be a common good to be what they are, that is, composed of a soul and body. And in this way all, both good and bad, love themselves, in so far as they love their own preservation. Secondly, a human being is said to be something in accordance with some principal characteristic, as the principal one in a state is spoken of as being the state, so that what the principal ones do, the state is said to do. In this way, all do not regard themselves as what they are. For the rational mind is principal in a human being, and the sensory and corporeal nature is secondary. . . . Now the good regard their rational nature . . . as principal in them, and hence in accordance with this they regard themselves as what they are. Bad people, however, regard their sensory and bodily nature . . . as principal in themselves. Hence, since they do not recognize (cognoscentes) themselves correctly, they do not truly love themselves, but they love what they suppose themselves to be. But the good, since they recognize themselves truly, truly love themselves' (2-2 q25 a7). Aquinas continues with a paraphrase of EN ix 4.

[132] Aquinas discusses prudence of the flesh (based on Rm. 8:6, Vulg.) at 2-2 q47 a13. Contrast Luther, who identifies it with self-love without qualification. See §416.

our judgment about our own happiness. But in our actions in pursuit of the particular end, self-love is limited; for we discover—by deliberation about our happiness—that we ought not to be deliberating directly about happiness when we pursue the particular end.

Aquinas believes, therefore, that when Satan sinned against God, he did not sin simply in so far as he was moved by self-love and treated his own happiness as his ultimate end. In these respects he did not sin at all. His sin resulted from misdirected self-love, not from self-love itself. Though self-love is the source of all sin (amor sui principium peccati, 1-2 q77 a4; 2–2 q25 a7), it does not lead us into error by causing us to care too much about our own happiness. We fall into error only if we assign the supreme place to ourselves in pursuing the relevant particular end. We make a mistake if we believe that our own happiness depends entirely on ourselves and that it does not require subordination to the will of God. This mistake expresses the outlook of arrogance (superbia). Hence it would be more exact to say that arrogance is the source of the sin of Satan (1a q63 a1–2, a4).[133] The claim that self-love is the source of every sin is true only in so far as arrogance is a form of misguided self-love.[134]

The sin of Satan rests on an error about the nature and sources of his happiness, and so on an excessive desire for some condition of himself to the exclusion of anything else. He manifests his error in his failure to direct his own perfection towards a higher end (SG iii 109 §2846). But this does not mean that he cares too much about his own happiness as opposed to some other ultimate end; it means that he is wrong to suppose that concern for his happiness justifies exclusive self-love. His particular end ought to have included a correct view about his subordination to God; he ought not to have been so absorbed in himself and his concerns.

This general treatment of self-love fits Aquinas' discussion of friendship and justice. In both cases, the rational will does not have to step outside its desire for happiness. We ought to choose on the basis of beliefs about our perfection. In his view, correct beliefs about perfection support the practice of all the cardinal virtues, including those aspects that require concern for the good of others.

342. Success of the Argument for the Virtues

We have seen how Aquinas explains his conception of the free and rational will, and uses this conception to identify the virtues of a rational agent. Since the freedom of the will depends on deliberation about the good, the virtues that embody the good use of free will result from this deliberation. To show that this is the right way to understand the virtues, Aquinas

[133] 'In spiritual goods there can be no sin while someone has an affection towards them, unless regulation by the superior is not maintained in such an affection. And this is the sin of arrogance, not to be subject to a superior where one ought to be. Hence the first sin of the angel can be nothing other than arrogance' (1a q63 a2).

[134] 'The sin of arrogance may be considered in two ways. First ∴ it is a special sin, because it has a special object: for it is misdirected desire of one's own excellence. . . . Secondly, it may be considered as having a certain overflowing into other sins. In this way . . . all sins can arise from arrogance, in two ways. First, properly, to the extent that other sins are directed towards the end of arrogance . . . Secondly, indirectly and as though accidentally, by removing something that prohibits, namely to the extent that through arrogance a human being despises the divine law through which he is prohibited from sinning. . . . But one should notice that it belongs to this generic character of arrogance that all the vices can sometimes arise from arrogance, but it does not belong to it that all the vices always arise from arrogance' (2-2 q162 a2). Cf. 1–2 q84 a2.

argues that universal prudence reaches the specifically virtuous ends by deliberating about how to achieve the universal end of the agent's ultimate good.

At two points in the description of the virtues, Aquinas might appear to deviate from this line of argument, by introducing moral content that cannot be reached by deliberation about the universal end: (1) His list of specific virtues of character might appear to require some views about their content that cannot be derived from reflexion on rational agency; we might expect that such views would be derived from our knowledge of the natural law. (2) His appeal to the first principles of natural law grasped by universal conscience might appear to imply that we have knowledge of moral principles that are independent of an individual rational will's pursuit of its ultimate end.

At both points, however, Aquinas adheres to his main purpose of deriving moral content from deliberation about the universal end. Our grasp of natural law does not yield general moral principles known independently of eudaemonistic grounds. The natural law is the 'law of our nature'; our nature is the sort of rational agency that Aquinas describes; and so an appeal to natural law does not lead us away from rational agency, but leads us back to it.

Aquinas' view of the will and the passions shows why we need the cardinal virtues, both as pervasive features of virtuous action and as distinct traits of character. If we were not subject to passions, we would not need the virtues that are concerned with their proper direction. If we did not have a will that aims at perfection, we would not know, without appeal to some further standard, what the proper direction of the passions consists in. If, for instance, our ultimate end were simply the orderly satisfaction of our first-order desires, whatever they might be, the specific end to be pursued by the virtues would depend on the nature of our first-order desires. Since, however, our ultimate end is our perfection as rational agents, specific desires are open to criticism and reform in the light of this end.

We might concede that this argument explains why some self-regarding conditions are virtues, but still deny that it will account for other-regarding virtues. This objection leads us to Aquinas' description and defence of friendship and justice. He argues that his account of rational agency answers this objection. He believes that if we recognize a virtue of the rational will that co-ordinates one's actions with those of other people, we ought to value friendship, to recognize the appropriate sort of equality, and to participate in a society aiming at a common good.

The arguments supporting Aquinas' conception of the different cardinal and subordinate virtues support his view that universal prudence reaches the specifically virtuous ends, and that the deliberation proper to universal prudence is part of a virtue of character. For the scope and connexions of the virtues are determined by their effect on one another and by their contribution to the ultimate end. We must understand this contribution if we are to understand why bravery sometimes requires active resistance, sometimes passive acceptance, and why both pride and humility are appropriate for different aspects of oneself and for different comparisons of oneself with others. In specifying the requirements of the different virtues, Aquinas argues from the ultimate end of agents who pursue their own perfection as rational agents with wills, and therefore pursue the good of others as part of their own good.

24

AQUINAS: SIN AND GRACE

---

343. Questions for Aquinas

Apart from the questions about sin and vice that arise for the moral philosopher, Aquinas faces special questions that arise from Christian moral theology. For the Christian moralist, sin is a pervasive feature of human life. The division between vicious people and other people does not mean that only vicious people are subject to the perversion of the will that produces sin. Christian doctrine implies that everyone is marked by original sin, which has some causal influence on actual sin. Even in the regenerate the influence of original sin does not disappear. Baptismal regeneration releases them from some effects of original sin, but not from actual sin. Though divine grace helps them, it does not cancel the effects of sin altogether.

These doctrines require Aquinas to explain how sin can be as pervasive as Christianity says it is, if Aristotle is right about virtue and vice. They raise a question about the voluntariness of sin, and therefore of virtue and vice. Aquinas argues that we are free and responsible agents in our choice between virtue and vice, and between virtuous and vicious actions. In forming our rational conception of ways to achieve happiness, and in consenting or refusing consent to the influence of our passions, we exercise freedom. Aquinas has to show that our most important choices are not mere reactions to the influence of irresistible passions 'submerging' and 'binding' the rational will; our outlook cannot be so warped as to deprive us of choice between good and bad characters and actions.

We might doubt this position if we reflect on ordinary facts about environment, heredity, upbringing, and culture. But these sorts of apparently interfering causal influences seem less severe threats than the threat arising from the Christian doctrine of original sin. This doctrine seems to imply that we are irresistibly inclined to error quite independently of any choice of ours.[1] To solve the theological problem, Aquinas has to show that his account of freewill leaves room for the appropriate degree of freewill despite the influence of original sin.

---

[1] See e.g. Articles §10 on free will. Cf. *West. Conf.* 6.4–5: 'From this original corruption, whereby we are utterly indisposed, disabled, and made opposite to all good, and wholly inclined to all evil, do proceed all actual transgressions. This corruption of nature, during this life, doth remain in those that are regenerated; and although it be through Christ pardoned and mortified, yet both itself, and all the motions thereof, are truly and properly sin.'

Doubts about freewill raise difficulties not only for Aquinas, but also for the Christian moralist generally. If original sin and divine grace play a primary causal role in making us sinful, vicious, or virtuous, we do not seem to be responsible, praiseworthy, and blameworthy for our virtue and vice. The Christian moralist cannot simply accept this consequence. For the Christian position maintains that sin deserves punishment; without blame and liability to punishment, there would be nothing to forgive.

The pervasiveness of sin implies a correspondingly pervasive role for God on the positive side. Since the acquired moral virtues do not remove sin, we need something else to remove it. We depend on divine grace, working in several ways. It releases us through baptism from some of the effects of original sin. It disposes us to turn to God; it infuses theological and moral virtues in us; and it gives us perseverance to remain in them. Once we recognize the extent of divine intervention, we may well conclude that the acquired moral virtues become insignificant. The infusion of divine grace is not a reward for having acquired the moral virtues by ourselves; why, then, should these virtues have a central place in the pursuit of the ultimate end? The crucial steps seem to proceed from divine grace.

Questions about the connexion between vice, sin, grace, and virtue are not simply questions for someone who agrees with Aquinas' Aristotelian starting point. They also arise in trying to find a coherent statement of the Christian position on sin, grace, and responsibility. We need to see whether Aquinas' Aristotelian theory makes it easier or more difficult to find this coherent statement of the Christian position.

At first sight, Aristotelian assumptions raise doubts about the Christian position. For Aristotle recognizes the possibility of becoming virtuous by our own efforts and through our own will. If we agree with him, we seem to raise difficulties for the Christian belief in the ubiquity of sin; this is why Luther believes that the incorporation of Aristotelian ethics is a fatal dilution of the Christian conception of human nature.[2] If Aquinas is to avoid this objection, he needs to describe sin in such a way that it does not imply an Aristotelian vice, but can be present in someone who has the acquired moral virtues.

Aquinas' views on the roles of original sin, grace, and human merit are complex. On the one hand, he seems to affirm the possibility of being virtuous by our own efforts; and so, if God approves human virtues (which he should, because of his relation to the natural law), our acquired virtues seem to be a source of merit. On the other hand, Aristotle's conditions for voluntariness leave Aquinas with more scope than another theory would allow him for attributing a large causal role to external influences—either original sin or divine grace—while insisting that an action or state of character is up to us and that we are responsible for it. He has a possible basis for reconciling our responsibility for our actions with Christian doctrines about grace and merit.

These questions are relevant not only for the student of Aquinas' theology, but also for the student of some aspects of his moral philosophy. (1) We may reasonably be interested in the coherence of his overall position. If his explanation of central concepts in morality and moral psychology does not fit the Christian doctrines that use these concepts, some aspect of his position needs to be revised. (2) If Aristotelian moral philosophy does not fit Christian theology, the project of 'baptizing' Aristotle does not succeed; Christianity not

---

[2] See §411n5.

only introduces new moral beliefs but also demands a new theoretical framework to explain them. This view about Christianity is one part of Luther's case against the 'Aristotelian church'.[3] If it is right, it supports the belief in a sharp discontinuity in the history of moral philosophy. (3) Comparison between Aristotelian and Christian views may also help us to decide about their soundness. If the two positions conflict, they cannot both be right. Whether or not we accept the Christian position because it is Christian, we may believe that, as Kant argues, it embodies some reasonable moral assumptions.[4] If these are incompatible with Aristotle, they point to errors in the Aristotelian position. Conversely, we may believe that the superiority of Aristotelian ethics reveals some moral errors in Christianity. If the two positions agree in the way that Aquinas believes they agree, it does not follow that they are both true, but we will not face the objections that arise from a conflict between them.

344. The External Causes of Sin

Aquinas relies on his conception of responsibility and freedom to defend the common assumption that we act freely and responsibly both in sinning and in acting virtuously. We are not victims of passions or of ignorance that we are not responsible for; it is in our power to acquire the virtues. Hence we are responsible for sin no less than for virtuous action.

The common assumption about responsibility faces two objections that arise from God's role in the production of sin: (1) God seems to be responsible, as creator and first cause, for the existence of sin.[5] (2) God has willed all human beings to be subject to original sin.

The second objection casts doubt on a possible answer to the first. For we might argue that God has created us with freewill, and that we have no one but ourselves to blame for our sins. But the doctrine of original sin seems to imply a closer connexion between God and sin; for God seems to have willed us to have an innate tendency to sin. If we claim that Adam was free because he was capable of choosing without any antecedent bias one way or the other, we make it difficult to see how we can be free; for original sin seems to give us an antecedent bias towards sin. If this sort of bias undermines our responsibility for sinning, Aquinas' claims about sin and freewill are inconsistent.

His account of freewill, therefore, needs to leave room for original sin and for divine grace. Augustine's controversies with the Pelagians show the difficulties raised by Christian theology for a philosophical account of freedom.[6] Pelagius' position tries to limit the role of divine grace so that it does not threaten human freedom; God does not determine the human will, but responds to the free actions that we undertake without being determined one way or the other by our sinful nature or by irresistible divine grace. We might take Pelagius to rely on assumptions about freedom that underlie an incompatibilist account. Augustine's answer to him seems to concede that if Pelagius is right about freewill, the right account of divine grace excludes freewill. Augustine, however, does not believe that divine grace really excludes freewill, since he also rejects Pelagius' conception of freedom.

---

[3] See §411.   [4] See Kant, *Religion*, Parts 1–2.

[5] See 1a q19 a9. Cf. *West. Conf.* 5.4: 'the sinfulness thereof [sc. of the sin of Adam and Eve] proceedeth only from the creature, and not from God; who being most holy and righteous, neither is nor can be the author or approver of sin'.

[6] See §225.

He affirms that some sort of freedom is necessary for the sort of responsibility that Christian doctrine attributes to human beings both for their sins and for their merits.[7]

Aquinas approaches the dispute between Augustine and Pelagius with a more explicit account of freewill and responsibility. He claims to have shown that, in the respects necessary for freedom, the human will is not determined, but is capable of going in both directions as a result of deliberation. We have found that he does not commit himself to an incompatibilist account of freedom. We ought to be able to confirm or to refute this account of his views on freedom once we see how he applies them to questions about grace and sin.

345. Sin and Causal Responsibility

Aquinas argues that God is not the cause of sin, because sin is a deviation from the order that is directed to God as the end, whereas God inclines everything to turn towards himself as the end. The sin is to be attributed to the sinful will, not to God himself (*ST* 1-2 q79 a1–2; 1a q49 a2). This answer may seem unsatisfactory, as Aquinas sees, given that God creates human beings with wills that are liable to sin (1-2 q79 a1 obj3). Aquinas needs to show that his claims about responsibility for sin take account of this fact.

God's primary aim in creation is the good of the whole universe (1a q49 a2), and in order to achieve the perfect good of the whole he permits some defects in particular things (1a q22 a2 ad2). It is part of God's providence that some creatures capable of falling sometimes actually fall (1a q49 a2). The defects in particular creatures are the result of God's concern for the good of the whole universe, and so he causes them 'consequently, and as though by accident' (1a q49 a2). Aquinas does not mean that they need not have happened, or that God's choices did not make them inevitable. He means that they are by-products of the aim that God achieves directly.[8]

This causal role might suggest that God is responsible for sin by permitting it. The pilot is the cause of the shipwreck because he is absent from his post and fails to do what would have prevented the shipwreck (cf. 1a q49 a2 obj3). We might analyse this causal role counterfactually; the pilot causes the shipwreck because if he had been present and piloting the ship, the shipwreck would not have happened, and so he made the crucial difference between the shipwreck's happening and not happening. If this analysis is applied to God, God seems to be the cause of sin. For God could have prevented sin, either by not creating the particular sort of free and imperfect will that is liable to sin and is required to sin sometimes for the sake of the whole universe, or by providing the help that would prevent the sin.[9]

Aquinas, however, adds a further clause to the counterfactual analysis; the pilot ought to have been piloting the ship at the time when he was not (potens et debens gubernare, 1-2 q79 a1). The absence of the pilot was not the cause of the shipwreck if the crew foolishly put to sea before the pilot was expected to come on board, even though he would have piloted

---

[7] See §225n64.   [8] Some relevant problems are discussed by Kretzmann; see §307n42.

[9] 'For it happens that God does not provide help to some people to avoid sin, and that if he provided this help, they would not sin' (1-2 q79 a1).

the ship and the ship would have avoided the rocks, if he had come on board earlier. Such examples suggest that the merely counterfactual test allows too many things to count as causes. It not only gives the wrong answer about the pilot's responsibility, but also allows many other inappropriate candidates to be causes. If, for instance, the sailor at the wheel had happened to be better at piloting, the wreck would have been avoided; but his ignorance is not the cause of the wreck, unless there is some reason to expect him to be a better pilot, or to expect a better pilot to be at the wheel.

These examples suggest that our causal judgments assume some background of standing normal conditions. The absence of the pilot causes the shipwreck on the assumption that the crew behaves normally, the ship has no hole in the side, the winds are not irresistibly strong, and so on. Given these presumptions of normality, the absence of the pilot is the crucial deviation from normality that explains what went wrong in this particular case. In Aquinas' view, our assumptions about the standing conditions must include assumptions about what can reasonably be expected not only from a purely predictive point of view, but also from an evaluative point of view. If it would not be reasonable to expect the pilot to be on board, his absence cannot be cited as the cause of the shipwreck. In this case our expectation is moral, not predictive; if he ought to be on board, but more often than not he is drinking in the pub when the ship sails, his absence is still the cause of the shipwreck. Aquinas, therefore, has some reason to claim that sometimes a moral judgment reasonably influences our causal judgment, because the relevant moral facts determine the causal facts.[10]

This analysis of causal judgments about the pilot is important for Aquinas' argument. To decide whether God is the cause of sin, we cannot simply ask whether there would have been no sin if God had wanted to prevent sin. We must also consider whether God ought to have intervened to prevent sin. Aquinas argues that the answer to this question is No. In God's providence and concern for the good of the whole universe (cf. 1a q49 a2 ad3), God creates creatures with freewill who are capable of sinning and will sometimes sin; God did nothing wrong in creating them or in allowing them to sin.

A similar reply deals with the objection that God sometimes turns people's will to evil.[11] Even if A's action could have prevented something happening to B, it does not follow that A caused what happens to B. If the dentist had kidnapped me and filled my tooth against my will, my tooth would not have fallen out; but she does not cause my tooth to fall out by not kidnapping me. But if she failed to do something she ought to have done to take care of my teeth, she might be the cause of my tooth falling out.

If some of the relevant causal judgments depend on judgments about whether an agent who failed to intervene ought to have intervened, we cannot first decide whether God is the cause of sin, and then use our conclusion on this point to decide whether he treats us fairly or not. We must first decide whether God treats us fairly, and then we can say what he causes.

---

[10] On some cases where judgments about recklessness influence judgments about causation see Hart and Honoré, CL 143–5.

[11] 'God is said . . . to incline wills towards evil, not by acting or by moving them, but rather by deserting or not impeding, just as if someone were not to give a hand to someone falling and were said to be the cause of that person's fall. God, however, brings it about from a just judgment that he does not provide help to some people to prevent them from falling' (Mal. q3 a1 ad1).

346. God and Human Freewill

This evaluative element in some causal judgments underlies Aquinas' account of the role of God in the production of actual sin as well as original sin. Aquinas argues that since God has created us with freewill, God is not responsible for our acts of sin, even though God plays a crucial causal role in bringing them about. The effects of an inferior cause can be attributed (reducere) to a superior cause as long as they follow the direction of the superior cause, but cannot be attributed to the superior cause if they violate its direction. If servants violate their master's instructions, their error cannot be attributed to him; similarly, the error of a freewill that violates God's instructions cannot be attributed to God (1-2 q79 a1 ad3).

We might object that if the master knows his servants are about to make an error and fails to correct them, he is still the cause of the error, since they would not have made the error if he had not left them alone. In Aquinas' view, this objection is sound only if the master could reasonably be expected to intervene to prevent the servant's error. If Aquinas' claims about God's providence are accepted, the crucial condition about reasonable expectation fails when we consider God's relation to our freewill.

On this basis Aquinas tries to show how God's will is the cause of the act of sin even though it is not the cause of sin (q79 a2). He admits that the cause of the act of sin is the movement of the freewill, and that God is the cause of every movement (q79 a2 sc). To make his position consistent Aquinas distinguishes two claims: (1) God is the cause of the act of sin in so far as it is an act of freewill. (2) God is the cause of the sinful character of the act of sin. Since he affirms (1), but denies (2), he claims that his recognition of divine causality does not make God the cause of sin. When we walk with a limp, the fact that we move at all results from our 'motive power'; if we did not decide to walk, we would not walk with a limp. But our limping instead of walking normally is the effect of the condition of our leg, not of our motive power. Similarly, God is the cause of our moving ourselves to action, and therefore is the cause of all our actions, including sinful actions, but God is not the cause of their sinfulness.

This is a satisfactory resolution only if we accept Aquinas' distinction between primary and secondary causes.[12] In claiming that the freewill is the cause of its motion, Aquinas intends a modest claim, that 'a human being moves himself to action through freewill' (1a q83 a1 ad3). This claim does not imply that human beings are the first causes of their actions, so that the motion of the free will has no external first cause. Motion resulting from freewill is the natural form of motion for rational agents, just as other sorts of motion are natural for other creatures. In creating us to be moved by reason and deliberation, God has given us freewill (cf. 1-2 q9 a6).

Aquinas does not say or imply that God gives us freewill only if he creates us so that there is no external cause of any of the movements of our freewill. He implies that we have freewill even if God is the first cause of a necessitating sequence that ends with our sinful action. Aquinas denies that God is the cause of our sin not because he denies that

---

[12] See §270. *West. Conf.* 5.2 relies on a similar claim about freedom and secondary causes: 'Although in relation to the foreknowledge and decree of God, the first cause, all things come to pass immutably and infallibly, yet, by the same providence, he ordereth them to fall out according to the nature of second causes, either necessarily, freely, or contingently'.

God's action necessitates our sin, but because he thinks it is not reasonable to expect God to prevent our sinning. He relies on his interpretation of the analogy with the pilot.[13]

This reconciliation of God's causal role with human freedom rests on a compatibilist account of freedom. Specifically, it rests on Aquinas' claims that all the facts about freedom are included in the facts about the human will and its deliberative pursuit of the ultimate good. If he had accepted an incompatibilist account of freedom, his concessions about divine causality would raise serious difficulties about the reality of human freedom. His moral psychology fits his theology.[14]

347. How God Causes Sin

Aquinas admits that in an important sense God is the cause of blindness and hardness of heart (1-2 q79 a3), and that these actions express God's predestination, either election or reprobation (1-2 q79 a4).[15] But this causal role does not make God the cause of sin, because God does not arbitrarily choose to blind or to harden someone. The sun does not shine into the house if we pull the curtains[16] to block it out; similarly, Aquinas suggests, it is up to us to present an obstacle to illumination by divine grace.[17] But he recognizes that this comparison is not completely accurate. In the case of the sun and the light, the sun does not withdraw the light by its own judgment; the cause of the withdrawal is the person who closes the curtain. God, however, withdraws grace by his own judgment (proprio iudicio), and so he, as well as the person who creates the obstacle, is a cause of the person's blindness or hardness of heart.

In recognizing that God withdraws grace by his own judgment, Aquinas implies that God does not face an obstacle that he cannot remove. God sees that he could intervene effectively, but he chooses not to; and so he bears some causal responsibility for the hardening of hearts. Indeed, if the purely counterfactual test for causation were adequate, God would be the cause; for our presenting the obstacle to God would not result in the hardening of our hearts if God chose to intervene with his grace to enlighten us. Aquinas, however, prefers to say that both God and the sinner are causes of the hardening of the sinner's heart, since the freewills of two agents play an indispensable role in producing the result. The sinner's presenting the obstacle is indispensable, though it would not have been indispensable if God had decided differently. Though God could have chosen to withdraw grace from anyone he pleased, he chooses in fact to withdraw it only from those who present an obstacle;[18] he would not have withdrawn it if the sinner had not presented the obstacle. None the less—as Aquinas points out in qualifying the comparison with the sun—God's withdrawal of grace is not an automatic result triggered by the sinner's presenting the obstacle; it is God's decision to respond in this way.

To see how large a causal role Aquinas has assigned to God, we should combine this claim about the withdrawal of grace with the previous points about primary and secondary

---

[13] This point was introduced in §270.   [14] On compatibilism see §§264, 270.

[15] Relevant issues are discussed by Stump, 'Sanctification' 227–34.

[16] Aquinas speaks of closing the windows, which makes the same point, given the sort of window he was familiar with.

[17] Cf. 1-2 q79 a3.   [18] Hence withdrawal of grace is a punishment for sin; 1-2 q87 a2.

causes. God's providence and predestination initiate a sequence of sufficient conditions that result in the creation of free agents with different kinds of wills; and Aquinas allows the necessitation (in the sense of a sequence of sufficient conditions) of the choices and actions of particular agents.[19] This is the result of God's predestination operating, so to speak, in advance. God also operates, so to speak, at the same time as the sinner chooses rightly or wrongly, by illuminating or blinding, and so ensures that the sinner will or will not persist in sin. God, therefore, contributes both to our initial sins and to our persistence in sin.

Aquinas believes that these divine causal contributions to sin fit his account of how human agents are responsible for their sins. If the will is moved by considerations that make it open to rational criticism, praise, and blame, we are responsible for actions produced by the will. Aquinas' account implies that it does not matter how we came to be in the condition in which we are moved by such considerations; in particular it does not matter whether or not we are responsible for being in this condition. Responsibility and freedom depend on the will as proximate cause. They do not depend on our views about the ultimate cause, and God's causal contribution does not cancel them.

From an incompatibilist point of view, this is a serious flaw. For Aquinas seems to allow the possibility that God creates a series of sufficient causal conditions for sin; if God does this, we cannot, on incompatiblist assumptions, be responsible for our sins. This doubt seems equally pressing if the series of sufficient conditions results from natural processes independent of God. Incompatibilists believe that the type of necessitation involved in causal determination excludes the capacity for choosing opposites that is characteristic of freedom. Aquinas, however, assumes that the relevant capacity allows a compatibilist analysis.[20]

348. Original Sin

Aquinas faces a further objection besides the one that arises from belief in God as omnipotent creator. He supposes that if God leaves us with the sort of will that has the relevant rational capacities, we are responsible for actions that proceed from the will. Another Christian doctrine, however, seems to suggest that God does not leave us with the right sort of will. If we have original sin, one source of sin is not voluntary, but an inevitable feature of human nature (given the sin of Adam). Aquinas recognizes that as a result of the sin of Adam, 'human nature is corrupted (vitiata) to the extent that we are all prone (proclives) to sin' (1-2 q80 a4). He believes there would still be sin without original sin, but he clearly believes that original sin plays an important role in the production of sin.

He suggests that the devil could be regarded as the cause of sin, in the way in which someone who dried out the wood was the cause of the burning of the wood. He implies that the effects of original sin are not by themselves sufficient for actual sin. But he leaves open the question whether they make sin inevitable.[21] In an environment where very few people drop matches, no other sparks fly, and so on, drying out a piece of wood may not result in

---

[19] The compatibility of Aquinas' position with causal necessitation is affirmed vigorously by Banez. See §418.

[20] Hume accepts compatibilism, but does not believe that it removes objections to predestination. See *IHU* viii (last para.).

[21] Cf. *Articles* §9; see §418n97.

a fire. But if we dry it out in a place where people habitually make campfires, its being dry may well be taken to be the cause of the fire, and even (in the circumstances) to make the fire inevitable.

Aquinas denies that original sin is transmitted because some corrupt element is transmitted in generation, and specifically in the semen of the father. Such a view would make original sin a hereditary defect parallel to an inherited disease such as haemophilia. Aquinas objects that this explanation does not show how original sin could be a source of culpability; it seems to exclude anything blameworthy (q81 a1). He therefore rejects the view that Adam sinned, and passed the fault in him on to us through generation.

In his view, Adam sinned, and generated us, so that we share the blame for his sin. We share the fault of Adam not through something transmitted in our generation, but simply by being his descendants.[22] Aquinas appeals to the solidarity of the human race, treated as a 'collective' (collegium, *Mal.* q4 a1). Membership in a collective allows us to attribute to each member the actions taken on behalf of the collective. Aquinas believes that this solidarity is similar enough to the solidarity of a single organism to justify the transference of the guilt of Adam to us. If my hand carries out a murder, the murder is voluntary, not by the will of the hand, but by the will of the soul that moves the hand, and it can be imputed to the hand because of its connexion with the whole body (1-2 q81 a1c §4). Aquinas suggests that the generative relation of Adam to the rest of the human race implicates the rest of us in his sin just as the will of the soul implicates the hand in the murder.

This analogy seems to collapse just where Aquinas relies on it. In the case of the single organism the hand is not a responsible agent in its own right, and so no question arises about the division of responsibility between it and the will that moves it. If my hand really did have a will of its own, and we knew that it had protested against, or failed to support, the decision of the will, we might doubt whether it would be just to punish the hand as well as the rest of the person. Could God not have chosen not to punish us for the sin of Adam?

Aquinas tries another illustration. He recognizes (following a passage in Aristotle) that someone is not properly reproached for his hereditary defects; but he argues that someone can properly be reproached 'in so far as he is traced back to some origin' (q81 a1 ad5). He suggests that someone shares the disgrace of his family as a result of the fault of his ancestors. This illustration, however, does not make Aquinas' view more plausible. For he has to say it is just to punish descendants for the crimes of their ancestors, even if the descendants are completely ignorant of them, or repudiate them, or try to make amends for them.

We need not deny that descent has some relevance to what we should take responsibility for. Sovereign states and other bodies undertake responsibilities that outlast the life of any particular person or generation; if, for instance, Britain undertook to offer citizenship to emigrants from some other country, a later generation are not free to withdraw the offer simply on the ground that they are not the actual people who made it. Perhaps it is no more unreasonable for a later generation to take responsibility for some of the harm done by their ancestors, and to do something towards undoing the harm or compensating the victims. But it is difficult to see how anything reasonable in these claims about taking responsibility

---

[22] See esp. q82 a1 ad2. Original sin 'has the character of blameworthiness (culpa), to the extent that it is derived from our first parent'.

for something could be used to show that we are justly punished for the sin of Adam simply because we are his descendants.

349. The Effects of Original Sin

We need to accept Aquinas' belief in collective inherited responsibility if we are to agree with him in believing that we are justly punished for the sin of Adam and that we need baptism to free us from the guilt that we contract simply by being descendants of Adam. But even if we do not agree with these aspects of his view, we may agree with him about the presence of original sin in us, and we can still ask whether his belief in its presence fits his claims about the freedom of the human will.

In claiming that original sin belongs to us because of the sin of Adam, Aquinas means to say that it is not a necessary feature of human nature. Human nature does not exclude the formation of a human being from human flesh, outside the historical connexion with Adam, who would have no original sin (q81 a4). Original sin is a fact about the human beings who actually exist, but not about all possible human beings.

In actual human beings original sin causes the privation of original justice. Original justice in Adam was the appropriate harmony in his soul that turned him firmly towards God and away from concentration on the particular goods pursued by different parts of his soul (q82 a1c, ad1; cf. *Mal.* q4 a1). Original justice is not a natural feature of human beings; God created Adam with freewill and the capacity for virtue, simply by creating a human being; but original justice was a gift from God distinct from the act of creating a human being, and God gave it to Adam as a gift to be passed on to his descendants.[23] Adam lost this gift by sinning through his freewill, and he lost it on the same terms as those on which it had been given, as a gift to him and to his descendants.[24] He sinned in so far as he turned away from God to a created good (*Mal.* q4 a2); the effect of his sin in us is the loss of the original justice that we would have had if he had not sinned.

Even if we do not agree that responsibility and guilt are transmitted, Aquinas might still be right about the possible transmission of original justice. Original justice or its privation need not be transmitted genetically or by a separate act of God for each new person; it could be transmitted historically and culturally. Without any further intervention by God, earlier generations with original justice could bring up later generations in surroundings favourable to justice. In fact, however, the effects of sin are transmitted, and they explain why later generations grow up as they do, among people and institutions resulting from earlier generations who have turned away from original justice.

If Aquinas identifies original sin in us with the privation of original justice, it is not the total corruption that would make us psychologically incapable of avoiding sin. Admittedly, once original justice is lost, the human mind and will are no longer subject to God (1-2 q82 a2; a3). Since we now lack the firm state of character that maintains the appropriate order

---

[23] *Mal.* q4 a1: 'This gift had been given to the first human being, not only as an individual person, but also as a sort of principle of the whole of human nature, so that from him it would be transmitted to his descendants through the origin'.

[24] *Mal.* q4 a1: 'And when this gift had been received, the first human being by sinning through freewill lost the gift on the same terms (eo tenore) as those on which it had been given—that is to say, for himself and for all his descendants'.

among our different impulses and desires, we are prone to commit sin. But we keep the capacity to avoid sin, in so far as we have freewill in relation to the impulses leading to sin; Aquinas' account of original sin does not deny us freewill. Considerations leading us towards sin attract us more than they would if we had original justice. Since we lack the order that turns us towards God, particular goods that distract us from God attract us more than they otherwise would (q82 a3); they appeal to the inferior part of the soul that can 'cloud and distract reason' (q82 a3 ad3). But clouding and distracting are not the same as 'binding' reason. The passions move us only in so far as the will consents to them; attention to the relevant considerations of overall good changes our minds about consenting to the passions. Original sin does not undermine our responsibility for actual sins.[25]

Baptism removes some, though not all, the effects of original sin.[26] We retain the 'fuel' of sin in the non-rational parts of the soul, and so we retain some tendency towards sin.[27] In baptism, however, we receive grace and virtue to overcome the disorder in the non-rational desires (3a q69 a4). The baptized person still has the appetites that make us prone to evil and make it difficult to act correctly, but baptism reduces these appetites, 'so that a person may not be overcome by them' (q69 a4 ad3), and it is easier to avoid evil and to choose right action.

The difference between the unbaptized and the baptized person seems to be that in the unbaptized person the rational part of the soul is not well enough ordered to avoid finding the suggestions of the inferior part attractive enough to be obeyed. This is partly a fault in the rational part, and partly a result of the strength of the impulses in the non-rational part. Baptism makes a difference to both causes of sin; it supplies grace and virtue to the rational part, and makes the desires of the non-rational part less insistent, so that the rational part both has less to overcome and has more resources for overcoming it.

350. Natural and Supernatural Good

Though Aquinas insists that the corruption of human nature that consists in the loss of original justice still leaves us with freewill, he also believes that our capacity for virtue is limited, and that its limits reveal our need of divine grace.[28] If we had been untouched by original sin, we would be capable, without any further divine grace, of (1) performing particular good actions, (2) achieving the acquired virtues of character, and (3) achieving the good proper to the acquired virtues,[29] though we would be incapable, without further help of divine grace, of (4) achieving our supernatural good.

---

[25] For Luther's and Melanchthon's views on the effect of original sin see §§415, 418.

[26] 'Original sin is removed by baptism in respect of guilt (reatu), in so far as the soul recovers grace, as far as concerns the mind. Original sin remains, however, in respect of actuality (actu), as far as concerns the fuel (fomes), which is the disorder of the inferior parts of the soul and of the body itself.' (1-2 q81 a3 ad1).

[27] 'It belongs to the very character of the fuel that it inclines us towards evil or makes a difficulty in the way of the good' (3a q27 a3).

[28] *Articles* §10; see §419.

[29] 'But in the undamaged condition of nature, as far as sufficiency of active virtue is concerned, a human being was able through his natural powers to will and to achieve in action the good proportionate to human nature, which is the character of the good of <i.e., achieved by> acquired virtue . . .' (1-2 q109 a2).

In our actual state, affected by original sin and its results, we are still capable of particular good actions. Aquinas describes these as 'works leading to some good proper to the nature (connaturale) of a human being' (1-2 q109 a5); he cites Augustine's examples of tilling the fields, drinking, eating, and having friends (q109 a2, a5). We are still incapable of the supernatural good. The difference between our sinful state and the state of original justice appears at the third stage, in our inability to achieve the human good.[30] Though we can achieve the acquired virtues, we cannot achieve the good that they aim at. Since acquired virtue does not require the absence of sin, we can achieve acquired virtue even if we cannot avoid sin. Without grace we are capable of avoiding sin on a particular occasion, but not capable of avoiding it altogether; our misguided passions and intellect present us with false suggestions that we sometimes accept (q109 a8).[31] In the original condition of uncorrupted nature we were able to fulfil the commands of the law without grace, as far as concerns the 'substance of the actions', but in our corrupt condition we cannot fulfil them (q109 a4).[32]

The difference between the particular good actions prescribed by the acquired virtues and the ultimate good aimed at by these virtues helps to explain the places where Aquinas seems to say that we can achieve a good proper to our nature without grace.[33] We are capable of acquired political virtue by our natural ability without divine grace, and this allows us to achieve a 'proportionate' good through the particular actions prescribed by the acquired virtues.[34] By achieving the proportionate good, we take a step towards achieving the good that is proper to human nature, but we cannot achieve that whole human good by our natural ability.[35]

351. The Need for Grace

If we need grace to achieve both the natural and the supernatural good, why, and at what stage, do we need it? We might suggest that even if we cannot achieve the supernatural good by our natural abilities, we can still exercise these abilities to take the necessary steps towards receiving grace. Aquinas asks (1) whether we can prepare ourselves for grace without first receiving grace, (2) whether we can rise from sin without grace, and (3) whether, once we have received grace, we can do good works without further grace. By answering No to all these questions, he shows the different ways in which grace is necessary.

[30] 'In the state of corrupt nature, a human being even falls short of this <good> that he is capable of in accordance with his nature, so as to be unable to achieve (implere) the whole good of this sort through his natural abilities' (q109 a2, following quotation in n29).

[31] Cf. Melanchthon, §418.   [32] On Luther's discussion of the 'substance of the action' see §415.

[33] '<A> good that is proportionate to human nature, a human being is capable of achieving (implere) though freewill' (Ver. q24 a14). 'To <a> good that is proper to human nature, a human being is capable <of attaining> through freewill, but <attaining to a> meritorious good is above his nature' (q24 a14 ad4).

[34] 'The good of political virtue is commensurate with human nature. And hence, without the help of grace making him acceptable the will of a human being is capable of tending towards that good, though admittedly not without the help of God' (2-2 q136 a3 ad2).

[35] In in 2Cor. iii 1 = P xiii 512b Aquinas explains how Paul affirms the necessity of divine grace without denying free will: 'But so that he does not seem to be doing away with freewill by saying this, he says "by us, as though out of us", as though he were to say: I can indeed do something, which belongs to freewill, but the fact that I do it is not out of me but from God, who confers this very ability (posse)'.

To prepare ourselves to receive grace, we would have to turn away from sin by turning towards God, in the sense specific to a just person, who is eager to hold fast to God (cupiunt adhaerere, q109 a6). Since, in our sinful condition, we lack this direction to God, we cannot turn ourselves towards God by our natural abilities; hence we cannot prepare ourselves, without grace, to receive grace.[36] God alone is the cause of grace (q112 a1); though preparation of the human being is needed for the reception of grace, this preparation is the work of God.[37] We cannot, therefore, treat grace as simply a response to some effort or attitude that is independent of grace.[38]

To emphasize the fact that divine grace is not a response to human effort, Aquinas insists that the first grace that turns us to God cannot be merited. No one can merit the first grace of justification for himself (q114 a5), and no one can by his natural powers merit the sort of happiness that consists in eternal life (q114 a2c, ad1). Grace and justification are not a fitting response to someone who does what he can to prepare himself for them (q112 a3), in the way that punishment is a fitting response to crime. On the contrary, 'the gift of grace exceeds all preparation of human virtue' (q112 a3). In 'operating grace', the first grace that God gives, God does not respond to any preparation independent of grace; any preparation is itself the result of operating grace.[39]

These assertions about the necessity of grace independently of any human preparation might suggest that Aquinas takes grace to replace freewill. But he disagrees. Though he denies that we can prepare ourselves for grace without having received grace, he believes we must prepare ourselves.[40] Preparation includes turning ourselves towards God through freewill; but freewill cannot turn to God unless God himself turns it (q109 a6 ad1).

Since turning to God is an act of freewill, we are responsible for remaining in sin and presenting an obstacle to grace (SG iii 159).[41] If we exist in sin without grace, we cannot avoid sin in general, even though we can avoid it on each particular occasion. Hence 'it will not be entirely in one's power to present no obstacle to grace' (iii 160). God's withholding grace consists in his not removing this obstacle that we present (160). A person's sins can be imputed to him even if they result from his inability not to sin; for he has acquired this

---

[36] 'A human being cannot prepare himself for receiving the light of grace, unless through the gracious (gratuitum) help of God internally moving him' (q109 a6).

[37] 'No preparation is needed on the side of the human being, as though preceding the divine help. Rather, whatever preparation there can be in a human being is from the help of God who is moving the soul towards good. And on this account even the good movement of the freewill by which someone is prepared for receiving the gift of grace is the action of the freewill moved by God . . . It is principally from God moving the freewill' (q112 a2). 'It is clear, however, that what belongs to grace is the effect of predestination; and this cannot be taken to be the reason of predestination, since it is included under predestination. . . . Now what comes from freewill is not distinguished from what comes from predestination, just as what comes from a secondary cause is not distinguished from what comes from a first cause; for divine providence produces effects through the action of secondary causes . . . Hence also what is through freewill is from predestination. . . . Whatsoever is in a human being directing him towards salvation is all included under the effect of predestination; even the preparation for grace; for neither does this come about except through divine help . . .' (1a q23 a5).

[38] See also SG iii 149. Aquinas' views are discussed by Stump, Aq., ch. 13.

[39] 'In that effect in which our mind is moved and does not initiate motion, and God alone initiates the motion, the activity (operatio) is attributed to God; and in accordance with this we speak of operating grace' (1-2 q111 a2).

[40] 'It belongs to a human being to prepare his soul, because he does this through freewill. And yet he does not do this without the help of God moving him and drawing him to God' (1-2 q109 a6 ad4).

[41] '. . . before a human being's reason, in which mortal sin is, is restored by justifying grace, he can avoid individual mortal sins, and avoid them for a time, since it is not necessary for him to be always actually sinning. But to remain for a long time without mortal sin cannot happen' (1-2 q109 a8).

inability by previous sin. Even if he cannot avoid sin altogether, he can avoid it on this occasion, so that it is fairly imputed to him. This complex analysis is intended to show that God is not the cause of sin for anyone (162), but none the less exercises predestination and reprobation (163).

Turning to God has to be an act of freewill, because otherwise it would not be a genuine human action. Similarly, a movement of freewill is needed for the justification of sinners (1-2 q113 a3), because movement according to freewill is the natural form of movement for rational agents (as opposed to young children, q113 a3 ad1). Justification requires a movement of the mind to turn it towards God; and the first such movement is the movement of faith, which has to be an act of freewill (q113 a4).[42] When God infuses grace, God at the same time moves the freewill to accept grace (q113 a3).[43] Aquinas asserts a role for freewill, but not independently of the grace of God. A person's faith is not a contribution distinct from God's, and therefore does not constitute merit or some substitute for merit, independent of, and antecedent to, God's grace. Grace is the mover of the free will.[44]

If we hold an indeterminist view of freewill, Aquinas' claims may appear inconsistent. According to an indeterminist view, it would be self-contradictory to claim that God could initiate causally sufficient conditions for an action of the freewill; God could only initiate a series that includes an undetermined movement of the freewill. Since Aquinas does not insist that acceptance of divine grace depends on some undetermined movement, he seems not to rely on an indeterminist view of freewill.

In Aquinas' view, God moves us by our freewill in the way that is natural for human beings, by presenting us with an apparent good.[45] God presents us with a good that is so clearly the best available good that, given our beliefs and desires, we see no reasonable alternative to pursuing it. God does not interfere with our wills; we could still reject the option that God presents, if we were to concentrate on some other aspect of it (as we can do with all non-final goods).[46] But if God knows our beliefs and desires, God can present us with an option that we will not reject.

God is similar, in this respect, to causes of sin that are outside the will. The passions, for instance, may present a particular course of action as being so attractive that, given the sort of person we are, we will choose that course of action; but the will assents to this course of action as a result of deliberation, in an act of freewill. God has a greater influence over us than our passions have; for God can infallibly determine how good an option will appear to us to be, in the light of our beliefs and desires, and therefore God can determine whether we choose it or not. But God's causal role still allows us to be moved by our freewill.

---

[42] Conversio; cf. 1-2 q5 a5 ad1.

[43] For this role of grace see BCP, Collect for Easter: ' We humbly beseech thee, that as by thy special grace preventing us thou dost put into our minds good desires, so by thy continual help we may bring the same to good effect'. This is translated from the Roman Missal: 'vota nostra, quae praeveniendo aspiras, etiam adiuvando prosequere'.

[44] '. . . the virtues, through which the powers <of the soul> are moved to action, flow into the powers of the soul from grace itself. And in this respect grace is compared to the will as the mover to the moved, which is the comparison of a rider to the horse—but not as an accident to a subject'. (1-2 q110 a4 ad1).

[45] 'For the gift of justifying grace especially orders a human being towards <a> good, which is the object of will, and hence a human being is moved towards it through the movement of the will, which is the movement of freewill' (1-2 q113 a3 ad2).

[46] cf. q13 a6 ad3.

352. Grace, Freewill, and Merit

Though our turning to God is an action of freewill, it is not independent of grace; and so God does not respond to it by giving us grace. On the contrary, our freely turning to God is an effect of grace. Hence we do not merit God's justifying grace. God's grace moves us towards the condition of justice, by forgiving our sins and infusing grace. It is not simply an action of God, but also produces a qualitative change in us, by making us worthy of eternal life (q113 a2).[47] But this justifying grace does not actually make us just people.[48] Justification is a movement towards the condition of justice (in statum iustitiae), but the end of this particular movement is not our being just, but our having our sins forgiven (q113 a6).[49] Justification happens at an instant (q113 a7), but it does not make further, non-instantaneous progress impossible or irrelevant.

Before justification merit is irrelevant, but after the first grace of justification it has a place. God gives us a start without merit, but it is up to us whether we take the further steps; if we take them, we have obtained merit as a basis for reward. Action on freewill is the basis of any merit (q114 a1c, ad1); since actions resulting from grace are also the products of freewill, Aquinas claims that they can have merit. But in allowing a place for merit, he does not mean that a human being acts independently of divine grace in achieving eternal life. He rejects such a division of contributions (q114 a5 ad1, on Augustine's error). Any meritorious action depends on our having received the first grace of justification, and its continuation depends on further grace.

Moreover, the fact that actions have merit at all depends on God's direction. In an ordinary case of merit, A's action merits B's reward if and only if B's reward is proportional to A's action; if B gave a smaller reward to A than A merited, B would be underestimating the degree of benefit that A has done to B and would be trying to escape with doing a smaller benefit to A. This way of measuring merit cannot be applied to the relations between God and human beings. It must be up to God to decide what the appropriate measure of merit is to be.[50] Since human actions have merit only 'from the presupposition of divine ordering', God does not owe any reward to us; he owes this treatment of our actions only to himself (q114 a1 ad3).[51]

Aquinas distinguishes the 'condign' merit of desert from the 'congruous' merit of suitability. Our meritorious actions do not deserve eternal life 'in accordance with the substance of the action', as products of our own freewill, but they are capable of being suitable.[52] 'In accordance with their substance' they are building a house, ending a war, helping a person in need, and so on. None of these, considered as such, could entitle us to

---

[47] For opposition to this see §420.

[48] See q113 a1, ad statum iustitiae; a5, in statum iustitiae, . . . accedat ad iustitiam; a8 ad1, adeptionis iustitiae. These should be given an ingressive rather than a perfective interpretation.

[49] See Cajetan's note ad loc. (quoted in M).

[50] 'Now the way and measure of virtue for a human being is from God. And therefore a human being's merit in relation to God cannot exist unless in accordance with a presupposition of divine ordering; namely, in such a way that a human being receives by his own activity a sort of reward <for the action> for which God also assigned him a power of acting' (q114 a1).

[51] On God's debita to himself, see §303.

[52] '. . . it seems appropriate that if a human being acts in accordance with his power (virtutem) God should reward him in accordance with the excellence of his (sc. God's) power (suae virtutis)' (q114 a3). The translation of 'suae virtutis' follows M, which refers to God's generosity.

demand eternal life as a reward. As actions of our freewill, they do not entitle us to eternal life, because our willing of them is still imperfect, and still not entirely free from sin. If human beings do what they can, it is appropriate to reward them in proportion to their actions, even though they have no right to claim the reward that God offers out of divine generosity.

But these meritorious actions also have the merit of desert, in so far as they proceed from the grace of the Holy Spirit, as the results of God's choice to give us the grace that leads us to eternal life.[53] The reward, consisting in eternal life, is not an expression of God's generosity in doing something that God has not undertaken to do, but it is a reward that God has promised to give. Since the actions are the effects of the grace that God has given us to lead us to eternal life, they are the effects of God's promise to give us eternal life, and so they deserve eternal life. God's own actions through grace constitute a claim on God, even though our actions, considered simply as ours, do not.

When we look at our actions in accordance with their substance and as products of freewill, Aquinas means us to abstract from the fact that they are the products of divine grace; in abstraction from that fact, they have only congruous merit. But when we look at our actions as proceeding from the grace of the Holy Spirit, we ought not to abstract from the fact that they also proceed from freewill; for human actions have no genuine merit unless they are the products of freewill. Since the actions inspired by the Holy Spirit have the merit of desert, they result from freewill. The Holy Spirit infuses charity, since what we do out of love is more voluntary than anything else, and voluntariness is the basis of merit.[54] The fact that we depend on the grace of God for inspiration by the Holy Spirit, and the fact that intervention by the Holy Spirit is effective, do not remove freewill. If the Holy Spirit initiates the right sort of deliberation and election in us, our actions are the product of freewill and therefore can claim merit.

Does this intervention by the Holy Spirit undermine Aquinas' claim that we are self-determining in the sense relevant to freedom? If a neuro-surgeon controls me so effectively that I seem to myself to be deliberating as I normally would, the surgeon, not me, seems to control my action, and so I do not seem to be free. Does Aquinas' view imply that such unobserved intervention results in free action?

Intuitive reactions to these cases may not refute his claims about the Holy Spirit. The neuro-surgeon is assumed to manipulate our mental activities in ways that interfere with the normal processes of practical reason and deliberation; perhaps he programmes me to favour one candidate in an election, even though, without his intervention, I would still have been convinced by my previous reasons for preferring the other candidate. But if the neuro-surgeon simply presents me with very convincing arguments—convincing to someone with the outlook I have already formed—for favouring one candidate, he has not manipulated me, since he has contributed to the normal rational process, and has not circumvented it or interfered with it. This description of the neuro-surgeon removes

---

[53] 'For in this way the value (valor) of the merit depends on the power (virtus) of the Holy Spirit moving us into eternal life.... Moreover, the worth (pretium) of the action depends on the worthiness (dignitas) of the grace through which a human being, being made a partaker of the divine nature, is adopted as a son of God, to whom is owed the inheritance by the very right of adoption' (q114 a3).

[54] '...in so far as the character of merit requires that it should be voluntary, merit is attributed primarily to charity' (q114 a4 fin.).

the point of calling him a surgeon—someone who can interfere and manipulate purely physiologically and not rationally.

To understand the operations of the Holy Spirit, we need to think of rational intervention, not of the sort of interference that undermines the normal causal role of reasons in deliberation and action. If the Holy Spirit simply makes it clear what the rationally preferable course of action is, it does not interfere with our free will, even if its intervention is always effective; for it is not effective by extra-rational means.

In all these arguments Aquinas affirms that freewill is central in sin, grace, and merit. He denies that God is the cause of sin, but he does not deny that we are causally determined to sin as a result of God's will. Justification requires an act of freewill, and the result of justification is meritorious free action; but both the act of freewill in justification and the merit of our free action depend on divine grace. He affirms the role that Christian doctrine attributes to the will of God in relation both to sin and to justification, while still affirming that we are responsible both for our sinful and for our virtuous actions.

In Aquinas' view, the conception of the will and of freedom that is needed to explain these Christian claims is also the conception that is needed to make sense of rational agency. If we understand how the will is free in relation to the passions, and how we can act freely and responsibly in choosing virtuous action and in turning away from it, we also have the right theoretical basis for understanding the theological claims about sin and grace. Aquinas has defended his moral psychology and ethics from a Christian point of view, and he has defended Christian doctrine from a philosophical point of view.

His defence does not seem completely successful. He does not seem to have vindicated the justice of God in punishing us for the sin of our ancestor. He has a better defence, however, of the justice of God in allowing the descendants of Adam to lack original justice and to be deformed by original sin. God would apparently be treating us unfairly if he held us responsible for actions that we did under the influence of some condition that deprived us of freewill; Christian theology would undermine the presupposition of freedom that seems to be basic for morality. Aquinas argues against this objection to Christian dogma, by explaining why it does not require the denial of freewill and does not make the pursuit of the moral virtues pointless.[55]

Aquinas' conception makes freewill and responsibility co-exist with a large role for external determination. If his conception is wrong, he is also wrong to suppose that sound moral philosophy can be combined with Christian theology in the way he describes. In the 16th and 17th centuries, questions about his position resulted in the disputes between Calvinists and Arminians (in the reformed churches), and between supporters of Banez and of Molina (among Roman Catholics).[56]

353. Infused Virtue

These views on original sin and grace underlie Aquinas' account of the infused virtues and their relation to the acquired virtues. We need infused virtues because of the nature of

---

[55] Cf. Melanchthon on the 'philosophical virtues', §417n59.   [56] See §418.

happiness. One sort of happiness is proportionate to human nature, which human beings are capable of achieving through principles of their own nature. Another sort is a happiness exceeding human nature, which a human being can achieve only by divine power, by some sort of sharing in divinity. Aquinas believes, as Aristotle does, that 'through a virtue a human being is perfected for the acts by which he is directed towards happiness'; and so, since there are two kinds of happiness, two kinds of virtues direct us towards them. Since the second kind of happiness is beyond human ability, the virtue that directs us towards it is also beyond our ability, and hence is infused in us by the grace of God (1-2 q62 a1). This kind of virtue supports Augustine's claim that 'the whole life of unbelievers is sin, and nothing is good without the highest good' (q63 a2 obj1). Aquinas believes Augustine's claim is false of the acquired virtues, but true of the infused virtues (q55 a4).[57]

The three primary infused virtues are the theological virtues of faith, hope, and charity. They turn us towards supernatural happiness in so far as they turn us immediately to God. Since supernatural happiness is our complete and unqualified ultimate good, the virtues that are infused with charity are the only complete and unqualified virtues; for moral virtue requires prudence, and complete prudence has to be directed towards the right ultimate end, which is set by charity (1-2 q65 a2; 2–2 q23 a7).

With this infused charity all the moral virtues are infused (1-2 q65 a3). We need infused moral virtues (q63 a3) to perfect us in relation to the different spheres of the moral virtues, so that we achieve the right order in relation to God (q63 a3 ad2). The supernatural end to which the theological virtues direct us also demands exercises of the moral virtues that we recognize as necessary to achieve this end.[58] Infused temperance makes us abstain from bodily pleasures to a degree that is not necessary for the ordinary acquired virtue of temperance. The infused virtue of generosity makes us go further in benefiting other people than someone with merely acquired generosity could be expected to go. This is the outlook described in the Beatitudes (q63 a2).

The infused virtues differ from the acquired virtues in the place they give the will. The acquired virtues are states leading to actions that constitute 'the good use of freewill', and they are acquired by habituation and training that involve choice by the will. We seem to have no similar role in the production of infused virtue.[59] Does this mean that Aquinas makes freewill unimportant? If we are passive in relation to the infused virtues, supernatural happiness may appear to be outside our control altogether. Aquinas sometimes emphasizes the primacy of the will in the moral virtues; he understands them as the states formed by rational agents who correctly deliberate about the ways to secure the ultimate end and who make the correct election as the result of deliberation. But this emphasis on the will applies only to the acquired moral virtues. We need to decide whether the infused moral virtues reduce the importance of the acquired moral virtues so drastically that the acquired virtues have no important role to play in happiness.

---

[57] On pagan virtue see §356 below.

[58] Human nature provides the principles from which we acquire the acquired virtues, but the theological virtues provide a different set of principles: 'Hence it is necessary that to these theological virtues there should correspond other states divinely caused in us that are related to the theological virtues in the way in which the moral and intellectual virtues are related to the natural principles of the virtues' (q63 a3; cf. *Virt.* a10).

[59] '...but it is caused in us only through divine action (operatio). And that is why Augustine, defining this kind of virtue, included in his definition of virtue "which God brings about (operatur) in us without us"' (q63 a2).

We might think that the acquired virtues are related to the infused virtues in the way that making soup from scratch is related to opening a tin of soup (or eating the contents of a tin of soup without having to open it); if the tinned soup is equally cheap, nutritious, tasty, and so on, then there seems to be no point in bothering to make soup ourselves, unless we happen to enjoy that sort of thing as a recreation. But Aquinas does not intend this to be the relation between the acquired and the infused virtues. He does not take grace to cancel free will; the operation of grace ensures that our free will leads us in a particular direction, not that we go in that direction independently of free will. Similarly, when God infuses charity in us, the Holy Spirit does not operate without our free will. Since love is a voluntary motion, it has its principle in the human will; it consists in some 'habitual form' that is the source of voluntary action (2-2 q23 a2).

The Holy Spirit is not limited in its operation by the previous state of the human will; hence it does not presuppose the acquired virtues in anyone who is to receive the infused virtues (q24 a3). But in initiating our voluntary action, it also initiates our voluntary approval of the outlook of the moral virtues. Infusion of divine grace causes us to see that other actions besides those we would have approved of otherwise are required by the moral virtues.

The description of the infused virtues helps to explain the degree to which human beings by their natural capacities can achieve happiness. Human beings can make clothes and find other defences to compensate for lack of natural bodily defences; similarly, he says, though a human being lacks the natural capacity to acquire happiness, he has freewill 'by which he is capable of being turned towards God who makes him happy' (1-2 q5 a5 ad1). Since a human being has to turn towards God by freewill, and since he exercises the infused virtues by freewill (q68 a3 ad2), the right direction of the will in the acquisition of moral virtues is not irrelevant to the infusion of the infused virtues. The acquired moral virtues are not needed to prepare us for infused virtues,[60] but they are an appropriate way to direct the will towards the ends that are included in the ends of the infused virtues. 'The good use of freewill' that Aquinas takes to be central in his account of the acquired moral virtues is central in the account of the infused virtues as well.

The acquired and the infused virtues have the same matter. Temperance seeks the mean in the enjoyment of physical pleasures; as we discover further ends that are promoted by restraint in this enjoyment, we discover further reasons for restraint. If, for instance, an athlete needs to eat a lighter meal to stay in training or a scholar needs to eat a lighter meal to keep a clear head, they discover different applications for temperance. This is why the infused moral virtues are still called by the names of the acquired moral virtues, even though they differ in species, because of their different objects (1-2 q63 a4; Virt. a10 ad8).

---

[60] 'The virtue in accordance with which God gives his gifts to each one, is a disposition or previous preparation or attempt (conatus) of the one who receives grace. But the Holy Spirit also precedes (praevenit) this disposition or attempt, by moving a human being's mind either more or less, in accordance with his [sc. the Holy Spirit's] will' (2-2 q24 a3 ad1).

354. How the Infused Virtues Perfect the Acquired Virtues

In his exposition of the Beatitudes Aquinas claims that the infused virtues are the perfections of the acquired virtues.[61] His claim might puzzle us; for we might suspect that the pursuit of supernatural happiness will require us to modify, even to abandon, the states of character that belong to the acquired virtues. Aquinas admits that sometimes the states of character we have acquired may make it more difficult to practise the infused virtues (q65 a3 ad2); why, then, will we not become indifferent or positively hostile to the acquired virtues if we practise the infused virtues? Infused temperance practises a degree of asceticism about bodily appetites that goes beyond the requirements of acquired temperance. Why not say that in relation to Aristotle's Doctrine of the Mean this ascetic outlook goes too far in the direction of deficiency, and so does not really count as the virtue?

Aquinas does not believe the infused virtues, leading us to follow the divine law, conflict with the virtues that we can vindicate by reference to the natural law. He relies on the primacy of charity among the infused virtues. Charity is not only the love of God, but also the love of other people, in so far as they are 'in God' (2-2 q25 a1), or in so far as something of God is in them (q25 a1 ad1). Love for God extends to all rational creatures in so far as they are God's creation and participate in his rational nature. This is why it extends to strangers, enemies, and evil people. Since charity extends an individual's concern more widely than the acquired moral virtues extend it, charity introduces new moral demands. But the point of view of the acquired moral virtues shows us that the demands of charity are reasonable; for it shows us that it is reasonable to love God's creation if we love God. Hence we can see how the infused virtues extend the outlook of the acquired virtues, and do not supplant it with a completely different outlook.

Even from outside the theological perspective, we can see, in Aquinas' view, why the infused virtues are perfections of the acquired virtues. If we have the acquired virtues, we can see what their perfection would be like, but we recognize that we lack it. We ought to be able to see that the degree of justice that we are capable of is the most that can be reasonably expected within human limits, but that a more complete justice would be preferable; and then we ought to see that the infused virtue of justice is preferable in the relevant ways. This is how the person who 'hungers and thirsts after justice' (*Matt.* 5:6) differs from the person who is just within the limits that can ordinarily be expected in a human being.

The particular end of the acquired virtues is 'genuinely good, as being capable of being directed, as far as it is in itself, towards the principal good'. There can be a genuine virtue, if it is directed towards a genuine particular good, though it is imperfect if it is not directed towards the ultimate good (2-2 q23 a7). Aquinas suggests that charity makes a difference in so far as it directs the good pursued by the acquired virtues towards a supernatural good.

The continuity of the infused with the acquired virtues affects the plausibility of Aquinas' theory as a whole. If he could not show that the infused virtues express more fully the outlook of the acquired virtues, it would be difficult for him to show that they are the

---

[61] 'A virtue withdraws a human being from following the irascible passions, in accordance with the standard of reason, so that one does not exceed in them. But a gift withdraws him in a more excellent way, so that, in accordance with the divine will, one is entirely undisturbed by them' (q69 a3). Aquinas continues with parallel remarks about virtues controlling the appetitive passions and about virtues concerned with the good of others.

exercise of the same free will that is moved by deliberation about the final good to form the states of character that constitute the acquired virtues. If the infused virtues were entirely discontinuous, how could the same processes of deliberation that support the acquired virtues support the infused virtues? It would be reasonable to conclude that infusion by-passes freewill, or that the acquired virtues are not genuine virtues at all, or both.

If we deny that the acquired virtues are genuine virtues, we separate 'secular' from 'Christian' morality. Eudaemonist reasoning seems to lead to the cultivation of the Christian virtues, while secular morality may be regarded simply as a device to protect us from death and violence. Such a division between different areas of morality has Augustinian precedents.[62] Aquinas rejects this division; he agrees that there are distinctively Christian virtues, but he insists that the acquired virtues are genuine virtues too, and that the Christian virtues are developments of, not alternatives to, the virtues that perfect human nature in relation to its natural end.

355. Sin and Infused Virtues

Sometimes Aquinas emphasizes the similarity between acquired and infused virtues. Though infused virtues are not acquired by practice and habituation, they are relatively stable states; they are capable of increase and decrease, and they can be lost. On other points he contrasts infused with acquired virtues; but some of his contrasts are open to question.

He believes that the presence of an acquired virtue is consistent with sin, because the error implied by one sin is consistent with the presence of the aims and patterns of choice that constitute an acquired virtue. Infused virtues, however, are destroyed by just one mortal sin, because they are not acquired by gradual practice. Charity depends on an infusion by God, who infuses it in the way that the sun infuses light into the air. The infusion of light is stopped at once, if some obstacle is put in the way; similarly, the infusion of charity is stopped at once, and the state is lost (2-2 q24 a12). St Peter actually lost charity when he denied Christ, but quickly recovered it (q24 a12 ad2; cf. obj2). Whereas the other infused virtues remain in an unformed state as a result of a mortal sin contrary to them, we cannot say this about charity, since it is the ultimate form of the virtues (q23 a8 ad1; q24 a12 ad5).

This comparison assumes that the infusion of charity must be like the infusion of light, which is absent if any barrier is put in the way.[63] But if we compared it with the infusion of electrical current, we need not say that it is absent if its normal effects are blocked; electricity is still coming into the house even if I pull all the plugs out and do not use any of it; and water is still present in a pipe even if I keep the tap turned off. The mere claim that charity is infused directly by God does not seem to require Aquinas' comparison rather than one of these other comparisons.

His real objection to the compatibility of charity with mortal sin seems to come from his claim that charity is the ultimate form of the virtues. Charity co-ordinates all the other virtues for the right end (cf. q23 a7–8), by fixing our attention on the ultimate end through the love of God. If we turn away from God, as we do in a mortal sin, we must lack the virtue that

---

[62] See §228.   [63] On light and on obstacles to divine grace cf. 1-2 q79 a3.

fixes our attention on the ultimate end, since our attention is not in fact steadily fixed on the ultimate end. Charity is the very virtue whose presence is intended to exclude the sort of lapse that is characteristic of mortal sin; and so we cannot have charity if we commit mortal sin.

This point does not justify Aquinas' division between the acquired and the infused virtues. The acquired virtue of justice requires attention to (say) the common good; and so a grave act of injustice implies that our attention is not in fact fixed where it ought to be. Still, as Aquinas agrees, a sin does not completely destroy the virtuous state that forbids it; an otherwise just person who does an unjust action does not suddenly become an unjust person. Similarly, even though God directly infuses the infused virtues, St Peter did not become indistinguishable from that of a hardened sinner the moment he denied Christ.

These objections to Aquinas are relevant to an evaluation of his conception of the infused virtues. To the extent that he contrasts them with the acquired virtues, he suggests that their infused character marks a contrast with the normal relation of a state and its exercise to the will of the agent. In the case of the acquired virtues, he believes that the possession of a virtue still leaves the will liable to error, but he takes an infused virtue to exclude this sort of error. If the contrast he draws is open to doubt, perhaps he should allow a closer parallel than he recognizes between acquired and infused virtues. Perhaps the two types of virtue are even more closely connected than he allows.

356. Defence of Pagan Virtue

Aquinas' conception of charity and the acquired virtues explains why sinful people can have virtues, and why these virtues are not abolished by charity. When Aquinas asks whether it is possible to have virtues without the theological virtue of charity, he refers specifically to Augustine's attack on pagan virtue (1-2 q63 a2; q65 a2; 2–2 q23 a7; *Virt. Comm.* a9). He argues that we can acquire genuine virtues without theological virtues, though they are imperfect virtues; they rest on a conception of happiness that is correct as far as it goes, though it is a conception only of imperfect happiness (1-2 q5 a5).

According to this argument, Augustine's teleological criterion is right, if it is understood as the moderately strict criterion requiring the virtuous person to have the correct specific end.[64] In Aquinas' view, the acquired moral virtues aim at an end that pagans are capable of aiming at; if pagans do the appropriate actions, and do them for the sake of this end, they have genuine virtues. The absence of the higher end does not imply the absence of the lower, and hence it does not imply the absence of the goodness appropriate to the lower end.[65]

Aquinas' division of virtues and ends supports, but also restricts, Augustine's claim that actions lacking charity are sinful because they lack charity.[66] Aquinas adds that this is not the

---

[64] See §230.

[65] *2Sent.* d41 q1 a2 = P vi 755b: 'Hence, although this goodness, in accordance with which an action is called meritorious, is removed from the actions of unbelievers, none the less there remains another sort of goodness or civil virtue, either from the circumstance or from the kind. And therefore it is not necessary that every action of theirs is bad, but only that it has a goodness that falls short; just as, though a horse falls short of the rationality that a human being has, it is not therefore bad, but it has goodness that falls short of the goodness of a human being.' The views of Aquinas and some predecessors and successors on the acquired virtues are discussed by Lottin, *EM*, chs. 2–3.

[66] Augustine, *c. Iul.* iv 3.

only aspect of such actions that deserves moral evaluation; they should also be evaluated with reference to their more immediate ends (*Virt. Card* a2).[67] If the actions of agents who lack the infused virtue of charity proceed from an acquired virtue, their goodness is limited, but genuine.[68] In this respect, they do not sin,[69] and their action does not constitute demerit before God.[70]

These two aspects of the virtuous actions of a virtuous pagan clarify a point that Augustine leaves obscure. If the agent does not believe in God, he does not love God for God's sake, does not acknowledge his dependence on God, and so on. But these errors do not remove the goodness of his actions or of his character. The presence of the motive appropriate to the relevant virtue (together with the appropriate action) implies the presence of the virtue.[71] Pagan virtues are genuine virtues because they aim at some particular praiseworthy end.[72] A genuine virtue cannot aim at a genuine good that one uses for a bad end; it must also use goods for a good end. Measured by this standard, the acquired virtues are the appropriate, though imperfect, formation of the free will in ways that make it suitable for being directed by grace towards the supernatural ultimate good.

When Aquinas distinguishes perfect from imperfect happiness, and tries to connect two distinct kinds of virtue with these two types of happiness, he goes beyond Augustine's explicit remarks. But he clarifies an aspect of pagan virtue that Augustine implicitly recognizes, since Augustine also recognizes that pagan virtues identify some genuine elements of happiness.[73]

[67] Aquinas replies to objections derived from Augustine: 'An unbeliever having intercourse with his wife does not sin, if he does it for the good of offspring, or renders what is due to the fidelity by which he is bound to his wife, since this is an act of justice and temperance, which observes the due circumstances in pleasures of touch; just as he does not sin in doing other actions of civil virtues. Nor is it said that all the life of unbelievers is sin because they sin in every action whatever, but because they cannot be freed from the slavery of sin through their action' (*4Sent*. d39 q1 a2 ad5 = P vii 1025b).

[68] 'There can be another act of someone lacking charity, not in so far as he lacks charity, but in so far as he has some other gift of God, either faith or hope, or, indeed, some good of nature, which is not entirely removed through sin, as has been said above. And in this way there can be without charity an act that is good in its kind, but not perfectly good, because it lacks the necessary direction towards the ultimate end' (2-2 q23 a7 ad1). 'As has been said above' refers to 2-2 q10 a4; cf. 1-2 q85 a2.

[69] *in Rm*. 14:23: 'But in an unbeliever there is a good of nature together with unbelief. And therefore, when an unbeliever does something good on the instruction of reason, not by referring it to a bad end, he does not sin.'

[70] *Mal*. q2 a5 ad7: 'Hence someone who, not having charity, honours his parents, does not merit eternal life, but does not incur demerit either.'

[71] See 2-2 q123 a7 obj2: 'Augustine says (*De Trin*. xiii 8): "We love virtues for the sake of happiness alone, and yet some dare to seek to persuade us <to love them> in such a way", (namely by saying that the virtues are to be desired because of themselves) "that we do not love happiness itself. If they do this, we will even cease to love them, whenever we do not love that because of which alone we loved them". But bravery is a virtue. Therefore the act of bravery is to be referred not to bravery but to happiness. . . . [Reply in corpus:] . . . as his proximate end, the brave person aims at expressing in action a likeness of his state; for he aims at acting in accord with what is appropriate for his state. But his remote end is happiness or God.' Cf. Augustine's discussion of this text in §231.

[72] 'If, however, we take virtue in so far as it is directed towards some particular end, in this way some virtue can be spoken of without charity, to the extent that it is directed to some particular good. But if this particular good is not a true, but an apparent good, the virtue that is directed to this good, will also not be a true virtue, but a false likeness of a virtue. . . . If, however, this particular good is a true good, for instance the preservation of the state, or the like, it will indeed be a true virtue, but an imperfect virtue, unless it is referred to the final and perfect good. And according to this, a true virtue simpliciter cannot be without charity' (2-2 q23 a7). I have omitted Aquinas' quotation from Augustine; see §230n106.

[73] Contrast Kent's comparison of Aquinas with Augustine, *VW* 27: 'Aquinas argued that only supernatural virtues are virtues *simpliciter*, that those virtues alone direct one to the ultimate end, that they alone are perfect virtues. To that extent he followed Augustine's teachings. Yet he broke with Augustine in arguing that natural virtues are true virtues even in the absence of charity and other supernatural virtues.' On Aquinas and Augustine cf. Lottin, *EM* 98–9.

But does Aquinas take proper account of Augustine's objections to the pagans?[74] Augustine urges that the good conduct of the miser, who aims at a good immediate end for the sake of a bad ultimate end, is insufficient for a virtue. But Aquinas also argues that pagan virtues aim at a correct, though incomplete, conception of the ultimate end; that is why he speaks of imperfect happiness (1-2 q5 a5).[75] Imperfect happiness is not simply a particular good; someone who aims at it, and correctly (though incompletely) grasps its composition, is not like Augustine's miser, but aims (within limits) at the right ultimate end.[76]

One sort of Augustinian might answer Aquinas by appeal to an extremely strict teleological criterion, and might argue that pagans who are wrong about the ultimate end have no virtue at all.[77] According to this view, one's conception of the ultimate end is fundamental. If we think of the ultimate end as a foundation, it is reasonable to suppose that effects of error about it will be pervasive. If the foundation of a tower leans, the tower will lean, however good the upper parts may be. Similarly, if pagans are wrong about the ultimate end, they set out in the wrong direction, and so cannot have any virtues.

Aquinas' conception of pagan virtue reverses the relation of foundation and superstructure. We may build a leaning tower if we begin with a straight foundation, and add a leaning superstructure. In his view, failure to pursue the right ultimate end does not entirely warp the direction of one's will.[78] Though pagans do the right action for an incorrect end, they also do the right action for a correct end.[79]

This explanation of Augustine's remarks on pagan virtue removes a reason for believing that secular and Christian morality are sharply separate. According to Aquinas, Christian moral reflexion should not denounce the acquired virtues as misguided or irrelevant, but

---

[74] See Baius' criticism of Aquinas, quoted at §417.

[75] See 1-2 q65 a2: 'Moral virtues, in so far as they work good as directed to an end that does not exceed the natural capacity of a human being, can be acquired through human works. And acquired in that way, they can be without charity, even as they were in many of the Gentiles.' Cf. q63 a2.

[76] The question that arises about the misuse of the intellectual virtues also seems to arise about the acquired and the infused virtues. Cf. §291. Since acquired virtues can be present in a state of sin (not properly acknowledging one's limitations and one's dependence on God, as Augustine argues), they are—in a way—subordinate to the sinful disposition that 'misuses' them by failure to recognize God's role in their acquisition.

[77] Ockham does not go this far, but he argues that since Christians perform virtuous actions for the honour of God, their end in performing such actions is different from the end of a pagan who performs the same actions. Since different ends define different virtues, the virtues of pagans and of Christians differ specifically, not just numerically (4Sent. q5 = P vii 58.5–23; Quaest. var. q7 a4 = P viii 402.634–403.652).

[78] 2-2 q10 a4 ad2–3: 'Faith directs one's aim in relation to the supernatural last end: but even the light of natural reason can direct one's aim in relation to a connatural good. [ad 3] Unbelief does not so wholly ruin natural reason in unbelievers that it prevents some cognition of the truth from remaining in them, through which they are able to do some work that is good in its kind.' This distinction between the incorrect and the correct end of the pagans seems to be overlooked in Ockham's discussion of pagan virtue at 4Sent. q5 = OT vii 58.5–23. He argues against the view that the virtues of pagans are 'eiusdem rationis' (53.19–27) as the virtues of Christians. He has no difficulty in showing that there is one end they do not share, in so far as the Christian acts 'because of God' and 'because God has prescribed' (58.11). But he does not discuss the possibility that Christians and pagans also have the same end in so far as they aim at virtue and human happiness. His view is more complicated at Q var. q7 a2 = OT viii 335.115–337.167. Here he mentions different degrees (gradus) of virtue. He recognizes one stage at which the virtuous person chooses the right action precisely because it is required by right reason (335.132–6). A person with heroic virtue acts in addition (praeter hoc) for the love of God (335.137–336.142). Since heroic virtue adds an additional end to the end of the virtuous person not moved by the love of God, Ockham is in a position to accept Aquinas' account of pagan virtue. Indeed, he considers such an account favourably at Dial. i 6.77 On the degrees of virtue see King, 'Theory' 233–5; Wood, OV 208–15.

[79] I have not considered the difference between an incomplete conception of the ultimate end and a correct conception of the imperfect ultimate end. See further Bradley, ATHG, ch. 8; Shanley, 'Pagan virtue'.

should defend the Christian point of view from the principles that we already accept if we take the point of view of the acquired virtues. Aquinas' views on this question did not convince all his successors; a more extreme 'Augustinian' view was revived during and after the Reformation. But his discussion suggests that this extreme Augustinian view may not be the authentically Christian or the authentically Augustinian outlook.

25

SCOTUS: WILL, FREEDOM,
AND REASON

---

357. Alternatives to Aquinas

Aquinas intends his position to be (1) faithful to Aristotle, (2) philosophically plausible, and (3) theologically adequate.[1] Scotus and Ockham share Aquinas' aims, but believe they can improve on his position. First, they argue that their position, as opposed to Aquinas' position, is really supported by Aristotle, or at least fits Aristotle no less well than the Thomist position fits it. In particular, Scotus' discussion of Aristotle on rational capacities and of the relation of virtue to the rational and non-rational parts raises legitimate questions about the soundness of Aquinas' interpretation.

Secondly, Scotus and Ockham sometimes doubt whether the position that Aquinas finds in Aristotle is true, and they are reluctant to attribute a false view to Aristotle if a true view can be attributed to him with equal plausibility.[2] But they do not follow Aristotle uncritically. One of Scotus' major departures from Aquinas—the belief in the primary and irreducible affections of the will for the advantageous and for the just—is introduced without any appeal to Aristotelian authority.

Thirdly, Scotus and Ockham argue that Christian doctrine conflicts with some of Aquinas' major doctrines, especially on human freedom and divine grace. If Aquinas' position is closer to Aristotle, but it conflicts with Christian doctrine, Aristotelian moral philosophy cannot be reconciled with Christian faith.

Some of these mediaeval criticisms of Aquinas underlie objections to the Aristotelian outlook that are sometimes regarded as distinctively modern. If we go straight from Aquinas to Hobbes, we may be struck by some rather sharp contrasts, and we may attribute these

---

[1] On these aims see §235.

[2] Wolter, 'Potency' 165, cites a comment by Scotus on his attitude to Aristotle: 'Regarding the meaning (intentio) of these philosophers, Aristotle and Avicenna, I do not want to attribute more absurd things to them than the things they themselves say, or the things that necessarily follow from the things they say. And from the things they say I want to take the most reasonable understanding (intellectus) I can' (*1Sent.* d8 q5 = OO v 2, 810 = *Ord.* i d8 = V iv 294 §250). The text in V differs from OO. In citations from Scotus 'OO' refers to Wadding's edition of Scotus' *Opera Omnia*, the only fairly complete edition. 'W' refers to Wolter, *DSWM*, the only extensive selection of relevant texts and translations (sometimes unreliable). 'V' refers to the incomplete Vatican edition. 'OP' refers to the incomplete St Bonaventure edition (consulted for *QM*). On texts and editions of Scotus see Williams, *CCDS* 6–13.

contrasts to the difference between a mediaeval outlook and a distinctively modern outlook raising questions that could not have arisen within a mediaeval framework. If, however, we find that the 'modern' views are either present in or anticipated by Aquinas' mediaeval critics, we will be less inclined to mark a sharp division between mediaeval and modern outlooks.

We might suppose, for instance, that modern views differ from mediaeval views in not taking Aristotelian eudaemonism for granted. Hobbes argues that there is no supreme good of the sort that the old moral philosophers accepted. Butler argues that the principle of self-love is not supreme, but is subordinate to conscience.[3] But these objections to the Aristotelian view are not modern innovations. Scotus raises them both. It should be worth our while, therefore, to see why he raises these objections and how he defends them.

358. Early Critics of Aquinas

It may be helpful to consider Scotus' views in the context of other objections to Aquinas, and especially to Aquinas' moderate intellectualist doctrine of the will. This doctrine is a basic element in his account of freewill, of the will and the ultimate good, and of the relation between practical reason and virtue. Aquinas believes that his doctrine shows how human actions are free and not necessitated, and how the freedom he accords to the will guarantees freewill and responsibility.

His view provoked disagreement. In 1270, while Aquinas was probably composing the Prima Secundae, Stephen Tempier, the bishop of Paris, condemned thirteen theses, including two theses about will and freewill that might plausibly be ascribed to Aquinas.[4] One of them maintains that the human will wills or elects by necessity; the other claims that freewill is a passive capacity that is moved necessarily by the object of desire.[5] In the Summa Aquinas rejects these theses about necessity, on the strength of his views about deliberation and about the capacity of the will to alter our attention.[6]

The Summa, however, did not reassure everyone. In 1277, just after the death of Aquinas, Bishop Tempier again condemned a list of philosophical theses incompatible with Christian orthodoxy.[7] This time he condemned 219 theses, including several that Aquinas seems to accept. One of the condemned theses is the intellectualist claim that the will is determined by reason, but is none the less free.[8] Tempier did not name Aquinas, and one might argue that this thesis does not capture Aquinas' position.[9]

---

[3] See Hobbes, L11.1; Butler, S ii 16.

[4] See Torrell, Aq. 146–7 (on the date of the Prima Secundae); 191 (on the condemnation of 1270).

[5] See Props. 3, 9; in Aquinas, SG = M iii 492–3.

[6] Torrell, Aq. 225, says that in the commentary on De Int. Aquinas 'alludes to the errors of the moderni on free will (i 14)'. He presumably refers to i 14 sub fin. (= P xviii 36), where Aquinas discusses the claim that the will cannot fail to desire what appears good, and therefore is moved by necessity.

[7] On Tempier see Korolec, 'Free will' 637; Piché, CP 159–82; Hissette, Enquête 230–63; Torrell, Aq. 299–303.

[8] 'That the will necessarily follows what is firmly believed by reason, and that it cannot refrain from what reason prescribes. For this necessitation is not force, but the nature of the will.' (Prop. 163; see Piché, CP 128) Cf. Props. 158–60, 164. Prop. 129 is closely related to intellectualism. It appears to condemn Aquinas' account of incontinence, which Prop. 163 may allude to in 'firmly believed'. See §295.

[9] Lottin, PM i 280, argues that, though Prop. 163 probably aimed at Aquinas, it does not accurately capture his views. See also Torrell, Aq. 244–5. Torrell, 299–302, is confident that Aquinas was an implicit target of the condemnation. This claim is defended by Wippel, '1277'.

After the death of Aquinas, both Franciscans and fellow-Dominicans attacked him. An early Franciscan opponent, William de la Mare, compiled a 'Correctory of Brother Thomas', to warn readers against his errors.[10] A Franciscan chapter general of 1282 prohibited the reading of the *Summa* except by readers with understanding,[11] and in copies that had the Correctory copied in the text. On the other side, some of the Dominican chapters general denounced detractors of the works of Aquinas, and reaffirmed his authority.[12]

The Correctory concentrates on the intellectualism that was condemned in 1277.[13] It asserts that the condemned thesis about the will being determined by the intellect follows from Aquinas' explanation of freedom through reason (a7). The discussion of happiness and the will supports the primacy of the will against Aquinas' emphasis on intellect. William attacks Aquinas for claiming that a human being is in control of his actions because he has deliberation about them (a6), that a human being determines himself through reason to willing one thing or another (a7), that command is an act of reason (a8), and that reason is the cause of freedom (a10). In all these cases, William objects that Aquinas undermines freedom by subjecting the will to necessitation by the intellect. One Thomist critic implicitly admits that the objection is damaging if it is true; for his defence of Aquinas underestimates the role that Aquinas actually assigns to reason in explaining freedom.[14]

Is the condemned thesis a fair summary of Aquinas' position? One critic, Henry of Ghent, believes it is, and criticizes Aquinas' view on that basis. He ascribes to 'certain people' (98.90) the view that the will is determined by judgment in the way in which natural desire in non-rational animals is determined by their cognition (98.02–03).[15] One supporter of Aquinas, Godfrey of Fontaines, does not deny that Aquinas holds the thesis, but argues instead that the thesis should not have been condemned.[16] Eventually Godfrey was vindicated. Aquinas was canonized in July 1323, and in early 1325 the Bishop of Paris rescinded the condemnation of 1277, in so far as it might be taken to apply to Aquinas' position.[17] The rescission, however,

---

[10] On William de la Mare's 'Correctorium fratris Thomae' and the replies written by Thomists see Glorieux, *Correctorium* vii–x; Kent, *VW* 81–4; Stadter, *PMMF* 239–44.

[11] The text in Fussenberger, 'Definitiones' 139, has 'rationabiliter intelligentes', with the variant reading 'notabiliter intelligentes'.

[12] See Reichert, *Monumenta* 199.1–11 (for the year 1278); 204.19–25 (for 1279); 235.1–9 (for 1286).

[13] The discussion of Aquinas' moral philosophy in the Correctory is selective. In its treatment of the Prima Secundae it discusses happiness and the will, but it passes from Question 17 (a10) to Question 88, and then to 110 (a12); hence it omits Aquinas' main treatment of the virtues and of the natural law.

[14] William's objections and the replies of a Thomist are in Glorieux, *Correctorium* 230–40. The Thomist's attempt to explain away Aquinas' views is hasty: 'I am always amazed by the way in which these people twist Thomas' words into their own false construction, when he himself in his whole discussion teaches the opposite. Hence this fairy-tale deserves no answer' (233).

[15] See Henry, *Quodl.* 1 q16 (ed. Macken, 98.90–101.57). See Prop. 159, quoted in §389n12. His view is discussed by Wippel, '1277', 256n68. Stone, 'Freedom', offers a survey of Henry's views on will and action.

[16] See Godfrey, *Quodl.* 12 q5, p. 102. Godfrey says that this and others among the condemned theses seem (videntur, p. 102, last para) to have been taken from Aquinas' writings. He also insists that some of the condemned theses do not seem to be false (non est multum manifestum quod sint erronei, p. 103, para 3). He does not say that the thesis about the will and the intellect is both Aquinas' view and not clearly false, but he does not say that it misrepresents Aquinas either.

[17] 'If in the past any of our predecessors of blessed memory as bishops of Paris condemned as erroneous certain articles, by a sentence of excommunication, and expressly prohibited them, for fear that people understanding them badly would fall into error, among which articles some were asserted by some people to touch on the teaching of blessed Thomas Aquinas:—by the firm opinion of those present, we entirely annul the aforesaid condemnation of the articles and the sentence of excommunication, to the extent that they touch on, or are asserted to touch on, the teaching of the aforesaid blessed Thomas, without thereby either approving or rejecting the articles themselves, but freely leaving them to discussion in the schools' (Denifle and Chatelain, *CUP* ii §838, for the year 1325). On the rescission see Torrell, *Aq.* 324.

neither identifies any theses that had been taken to represent Aquinas' views nor asserts that he did or did not hold any of the theses.

Aquinas' attitude to the condemned thesis depends on his account of the influence of the will on the intellect. The will may move us to act against a conclusion of reason, if we choose to attend to more attractive aspects of the option that we have just rejected, so that we change our minds and come to prefer the option previously rejected. But this role for the will does not modify Aquinas' intellectualism; the effects of the will on the intellect still depend on the apparent good, and hence on the intellect.

Moreover, even if Aquinas' views about the influence of will on intellect implied the rejection of intellectualism, it would not follow that the condemned thesis misrepresents him. The condemned thesis does not refer to the operations of the will that influence intellect by causing us to change our minds after forming an initial impression of the goodness of some object; for while we are subject to these operations that make us eventually prefer y to x, we do not firmly believe that x is better. The condemned thesis says only that the will necessarily follows what is firmly believed by reason; 'firmly' excludes the operations of the will that make us change our minds. Even if Aquinas held that the will's influence on deliberation is undetermined by reason, he still holds that the will necessarily follows the firmly-held conclusion of reason, and hence he holds the condemned thesis.[18]

The critics reject the claim that determination of the will by the firm belief of reason is not a case of force (coactio), but simply the nature of the will. They imply that such determination forces the will, and therefore takes away freewill.[19] Another condemned thesis claims that the will of a human being is necessitated by its cognition, just as the desire of a non-rational animal is (Prop. 159). The critics would be wrong to ascribe this thesis to Aquinas if they meant that he makes the relation of human cognition to human willing just the same as the relation of an animal's perception to its sensory desire. But they are right if they mean that without a cognitive change the will cannot change.

The critics infer that 'after the conclusion has been reached about something to be done, the will does not remain free' (Prop. 158). Their claim would be false, if it means that we cannot reconsider conclusions we have reached, but it is true if it means that we are not free to will not to act on a conclusion without seeing any reason to object to it. The critics suppose, then, that we are forced and not free in our action unless our action proceeds from a will that is free to change its direction independently of any cognitive change.

The implicit view of the critics is the explicit position of Henry of Ghent, one of the commissioners who drew up the condemnation. He argues that the will has the appropriate sort of freedom only if it is not determined by the apparent good presented by intellect. In

---

[18] Lottin, Hissette, and Wippel (see nn8–9) hold that the thesis does not express Aquinas' view; they do not give enough weight to 'firmly'. They assume that the role of will in directing our attention proves that Aquinas does not hold the view.

[19] It is perhaps confusing to suggest that the objector is opposing 'determinism' (as Hissette claims, Enquête 225, speaking of 'déterminisme psychologique', which he takes to be evidently incompatible with the Christian conception of liberty). Determinism may be irrelevant for two reasons: (1) It is not clear that if the will is undetermined by reason it is not determined by anything; hence the objector does not rule out all forms of determinism. (2) Even if Aquinas were to allow the operations of will in influencing intellect to be undetermined, this would not make it false that the will necessarily follows the firm belief of reason. We need not suppose that the objector takes indeterminism to be necessary or sufficient for the absence of force.

his view, the intellect simply presents the apparent good, and the will is free to accept or to reject it.[20] If we said only that the will is free to prefer an apparently greater good to an apparently lesser good, we would make the will inappropriately dependent on the intellect. Without voluntarist freedom the will is forced.

Henry has good reason to assume that Aquinas holds the position that he rejects.[21] According to Aquinas, we are free because we can deliberate well and badly, and can attend rightly or wrongly to different aspects of different options open to us; hence it is reasonable to assess our actions by the standards that are involved in praising and blaming. Henry argues that Aquinas' defence of freedom is inadequate, and hence the condemnation of the intellectualist position is justified.

Henry's defence of the condemnation of 1277 shows that Aquinas' intellectualism appeared to conflict with Christian doctrine because it appeared to preclude freewill. If the critics are right, they not only undermine Aquinas' views on the will, but also raise doubts about his conception of the final good, and about its role in moral theory; for his moral theory rests on his conception of rational agency, and hence on his conception of the will.

Scotus formulates the anti-intellectualist objections clearly, and presents a voluntarist account of the will. He also explores some of the implications of voluntarism for freewill, for the virtues, and for the theological issues that Aquinas tries to understand within his conception of the will. He argues for both voluntarism and rationalism. On the one hand, he denies that the will is determined by intellect. On the other hand, he maintains a sharp division between the rational will and the non-rational passions. He maintains voluntarism to defend freedom, but maintains rationalism to maintain the primacy of reason over passion in determining virtuous action.

To show that his voluntarism is consistent with his rationalism, Scotus needs to show that the will is rational even though it is not determined, as the intellectualist supposes, by reason. If he shows this, he also needs to show that the rational character of the will allows voluntarism about freewill. Some disputes among interpreters of Scotus reflect disagreement about the relative importance of the voluntarist and the rationalist strands in his position. It is perhaps less important to decide where exactly Scotus stands than to see where his arguments against Aquinas might lead.[22]

Some of Aquinas' critics argue that his position is an unstable combination of conflicting elements. In particular, he tries to combine Aristotelian eudaemonism and intellectualism with the Christian and Augustinian views on will and freedom. The solution offered by the critics abandons eudaemonism and intellectualism in order to maintain freedom. But, as we will see, the critics' solution may be less stable than Aquinas' position.

The view of Scotus as a sharp critic of Aquinas may be criticized for attributing too extreme a position to him. Similar objections have been raised against attempts to draw a sharp contrast between Aquinas' intellectualism in ethics and the voluntarism attributed to Ockham and his successors as well as to Scotus. Whether or not these objections are

---

[20] See Henry, *Quodl.* 9 q5 = Macken 121.27–122.50 (tr. Teske, 51–2).

[21] He paraphrases Aquinas, *Mal.* q6 at *Quodl.* 9 = 120.14–16 Macken (tr. Teske, 50–1).

[22] Some critics believe it is misleading or unhelpful to describe Scotus as a voluntarist, or even to be preoccupied with the question of whether he is a voluntarist: 'Thanks to the serious research advanced by notable scholars, this question no longer preoccupies us' (Ingham, 'Moral order' 127, with references).

justified, it is none the less useful to consider the arguments that might be used to support a strongly voluntarist reaction to Aquinas. Even if they lead to a more extreme voluntarist conclusion than Scotus himself accepts, the arguments have been thought to justify a strongly voluntarist conclusion, and this feature of them has made them both historically and philosophically important and influential.[23]

359. The Character of the Will

To explain his conception of the will, Scotus exploits Aquinas' interpretation of Aristotle. In *EN* i 13 Aristotle distinguishes the rational part of the soul from the 'desiring' part that is capable of obedience to reason and is rational by participation. Aquinas takes this division to divide intellect from every form of desire, including will, and so he includes will among the states of the soul that are rational only by participation (*ST* 1-2 q56 a6 ad2).[24] Scotus endorses Aquinas' conclusion that the will is rational not essentially, but by participation (*3Sent.* d33 q1 schol. = *OO* vii 2, 697 = W 322–4). According to Scotus, this means that the will, like the passions, does not necessarily follow the judgment of reason.

This is not Aquinas' interpretation of 'by participation'. In his view, the will is necessarily and essentially rational; it is rational by participation only because it is rational derivatively, because of its relation to intellect. Scotus, however, argues that 'by participation' implies that the will is neither essentially nor necessarily rational. He maintains that unless we agree that the will does not necessarily follow intellect, we deny freewill.

His conception of freedom sets out from another point of agreement with Aquinas. Freewill depends on the capacity of the will to go in either of two directions. Aquinas derives this capacity of the will from the capacity of deliberating reason to go in either of two directions (1-2 q6 a2 ad2). Scotus agrees that freedom involves the capacity for opposites, but he does not agree with Aquinas' attempt to trace this capacity to deliberation.

Aquinas connects the capacity for opposites with deliberation because he takes it to be confined to election of means to the ultimate end, which are the concern of deliberation. Since it is not in our power not to pursue the ultimate end, our will is determined to follow the course of action that appears, as a result of deliberation, to promote the ultimate end.[25] We are free in being determined by the result of our deliberation about the good. If we did not necessarily pursue the final good, we would not be applying reason to our desires, and hence we would not be acting on our wills.

This pursuit of the final good requires external reasons. If there were no external reasons, we could discover what promotes happiness only by reference to our non-rational desires, and the will would be ultimately non-rational. Our discovery that x is better than y would always be open to revision as a result of our simply coming to prefer ends to which y is a

---

[23] Wolter, *PTJDS*, chs. 7–9, argues that the voluntarist elements in Scotus' position have been exaggerated. A strongly voluntarist account of Scotus is defended by Williams, *MPJDS*, who is criticized by Vos et al., *DSDL* 58–62. Cross, *DS*, ch. 7, maintains a voluntarist account of Scotus' moral psychology, but a less voluntarist account of his ethics.

[24] See §257 for further discussion of this passage in the *EN*.

[25] This claim needs some qualifications: (1) It does not exclude the possibility of reconsidering our deliberation. (2) It does not allow for cases where a non-rational impulse deprives us of the use of reason. See §253.

means over ends to which x is a means. Aquinas, however, believes that we can change our mind about the merits of x and y only if we concentrate on aspects of y that make y seem better to us (cf. 1-2 q13 a6).

Since Aquinas' views on freedom are so closely connected with his eudaemonism, Scotus disagrees on both counts. He argues that eudaemonism not only excludes freedom but also conflicts with obvious truths about rational action. He has three main arguments against eudaemonism: (1) Psychological: facts of experience show that we sometimes fail to pursue what we believe to promote our happiness. (2) Moral: the eudaemonist position conflicts with facts about the moral virtues and the motives of the virtuous person. (3) Metaphysical (libertarian): the eudaemonist position implies that the will is not free, because we are not free to reject happiness, or to choose contrary to what we believe to promote it. Though these arguments raise distinct issues, they are difficult to keep apart; in particular, Scotus' views about rationality and freedom influence his objections to eudaemonism on psychological and moral grounds.

360. Psychological Objections to Eudaemonism

In Scotus' view, the will is partly a natural desire; to this extent, it 'necessarily and perpetually and above all (summe) desires happiness' both in general and in a particular case (4Sent. d49 q10 schol = OO x 506 §3 = W 184). Because of this natural desire, the will never rejects something precisely because it promotes happiness and never wills anything precisely because it leads to unhappiness (4Sent. d49 q10 = OO x 514 §10 = W 192). But since the will is also a free desire, it cannot be necessarily determined to will any end, even happiness.[26] Our pursuit of happiness, therefore, is natural only in a loose sense, because the will often freely chooses to follow its natural inclination to happiness (4Sent. d49 q10 = OO x 513 §6 = W 190).

If the will necessarily pursued happiness, it would follow that whenever I believed both x and y were open to me and that x rather than y would promote my happiness, I would choose x rather than y. But Scotus replies that sometimes we are aware that x rather than y promotes happiness, but we can simply choose to pursue neither x nor y. If we suspend further action, we choose to be indifferent towards happiness.[27]

Even when we act, we do not always act with a view to happiness, and hence we do not necessarily will happiness.[28] Since we aim at particular ends without reference to happiness, and we do not always stop to think about how they bear on happiness, eudaemonism is

---

[26] '...the will contingently wills the end and happiness, both in general and in particular, although in most cases it seeks happiness in general, and also in particular when the intellect has no prior doubt that happiness consists in this particular thing' (4Sent. d49 q10 = OO x 513 §6 = W 188–90).

[27] '...it can suspend itself from every act, when happiness is shown to it. Hence, for any object, the will is capable of neither willing nor rejecting it, and of suspending itself from any act in a particular case about this or that object. And this anyone can experience in himself, when someone offers him some good, even if <the other> were to show him a good as a good to be considered and willed; he is capable of turning away from this, and of eliciting no act of will about it' (4Sent. d49 q10 = OO x 514 §10 = W 194).

[28] '...if the will necessarily willed happiness, it would determine [determinabit] the intellect to consider about happiness always, which is false' (4Sent. d49 q10 = OO x 513 §5 = W 188).

false. In such cases, we choose 'negatively' not to pursue happiness, because we have a good reason for pursuing something without considering happiness. In other cases, we choose 'contrarily' not to pursue happiness, because we recognize that our action is contrary to happiness, but we still choose to do it.[29]

361. Defences of Eudaemonism

Scotus treats his arguments against eudaemonism as appeals to obvious facts of common observation that a eudaemonist cannot describe or explain. But Aquinas does not say that we consciously think about happiness whenever we act. He claims that in many cases the 'power of the first aim' (virtus primae intentionis) remains in the pursuit of subordinate ends (ST 1-2 q1 a6 ad3).[30] We 'consider' happiness only in so far as we are guided by our conception of the ultimate end; we need not have it in mind all the time. In reply to Scotus Aquinas might reasonably claim that if we hold our particular aims open to scrutiny and revision in the light of our other aims, even though we do not scrutinize them on a particular occasion, we still rely on a conception of happiness. Even if we will to act contrary to our conception of happiness, we act (according to Aquinas) on the consent of the will, and hence we assume that our conception of the good allows us to act on this particular impulse. Given the influence that Aquinas ascribes to our conception of the good, cases where we do not consider it or we act against it do not seem to present decisive objections.

Cajetan's defence of Aquinas against Scotus rests on an apparently more controversial aspect of Aquinas' doctrine. According to Cajetan, if we refrain from pursuing happiness 'negatively', we assume that our action fits our ultimate end, because we do not stop to consider the question; this is what happens in the thoughtless pleasures that are venial sins. If we choose contrary to our conception of happiness, Cajetan argues that we must actually have formed a different conception of our ultimate end, and a mistaken one. If we did not change our conception of happiness, we would desire the contrary of our full perfection, and such a desire is impossible.[31]

Cajetan's answer to Scotus depends on his assumption that no one can desire the contrary of his full perfection. Perfection is the aspect of happiness that requires more than mere comprehensive satisfaction of our actual desires; in appealing to perfection we take our

---

[29] Even if one recognizes that fornication cannot be directed towards happiness, one may choose it none the less, without directing it towards happiness (4Sent. d49 q10 = OO x 540 §15 = W 194–6). It is not clear whether Scotus regards this second case as a case of incontinence, or as a case where the agent sees overriding reason to choose F while still believing that F is contrary to his happiness. If he thinks it is a case of incontinence, Scotus rejects Aquinas' explanation of incontinence by appeal to ignorance. If he thinks it is not a case of incontinence, Scotus disagrees even more deeply with Aquinas' view of rational choice. He should apparently allow both cases.

[30] See §248.

[31] 'For let us speak of the ultimate end taken formally. We say that nothing can be desired except this end itself or something for the sake of this end . . . No one can desire the contrary of his full perfection. For whatever one desires, one desires it so that one may have some perfection, even though he desires contrary to the sort of thing that is the ultimate end (as is evidently the case in someone who sins mortally), and apart from it (as is evidently the case in someone who sins venially)' (Cajetan ad Aquinas, ST 1-2 q1 a6 = L vi 15). When he says that the sinner 'desires contrary to the sort of thing that is the ultimate end', Cajetan means that the sinner is acting in accordance with his own conception of the ultimate end, though not in accordance with the correct conception.

desires to be open to criticism by reference to what we take to be a correct conception of ourselves.[32] When Cajetan claims that all our desire aims at some perfection, perhaps he relies on Aquinas' view that we will something on the basis of external reasons that we take to be mutually supporting. If we act on our will, and not on our non-rational desire, we rely on assumptions about external reasons that involve perfection.

Cajetan's objection, therefore, is stronger than it initially appears.[33] If voluntarists cut the link between will and the rational comparison that refers to a final good, do they not cut the link between will and practical reason? If they do that, how does the will differ from a passion? Scotus needs to show not only that we can ignore or reject happiness in our choices, but also that these choices are expressions of the will rather than of some other desire. He would not secure his main point if we were to concede only that some of our desires are immune to 'global' considerations of comprehensiveness and perfection. For Aquinas recognizes such desires; they result from passions so strong and disordered that 'reason is totally bound'; they 'submerge' reason so that they move us irrespective of our rational aims and plans.[34]

Scotus argues not that some desires are independent of the desire for happiness, but that the will is independent of it. Will differs from passion in being rational desire, and hence in being responsive to critical evaluation of one's desires and their objects. Aquinas claims that will is thoroughly rational desire because it responds to the global criticism that our conception of happiness applies to particular objects of desire. This conception of will underlies Cajetan's objection to Scotus. Scotus does not explain why the agent who prefers a particular good over his conception of the ultimate good acts not on a passion, but on a rational desire that belongs to the will. Hence he does not refute eudaemonism.

Scotus describes the will as 'free desire' (liber appetitus), and so denies that it is determined by the antecedent strength of one's non-rational desire—in this case the desire for happiness. Aquinas agrees that the will is free by not being determined by the strength of non-rational desires; he takes this freedom to require the will to respond to the rational evaluation of desires. But the choices that we recognize, according to Scotus, as contrary to our conception of our ultimate end seem to be determined by the antecedent strength of our particular desires. If the 'free desire' identified with the will does not rest on evaluation of our desires, how does it differ from a passion? Scotus' argument to show that we can desire objects contrary to happiness does not show that we can will them.

362. The Conflict between Eudaemonism and Freedom

Scotus replies that eudaemonist claims exclude freewill. Aquinas tries to secure freewill by arguing that though we pursue happiness necessarily, we do not pursue particular goods necessarily. Our freedom consists, then, in the fact that our deliberation compares alternatives and fixes on one of them. But Scotus claims that this account of freedom rests

[32] See §274.   [33] Cf. Godfrey in §390.

[34] We might even argue that Aquinas is wrong to deny that incontinence is a case of binding; and so we might understand Scotus' example of choosing contrary to our conception of happiness as a case of incontinence that involves the binding of reason by non-rational passion. Such an argument would not secure Scotus' main aim. See §253.

on two inconsistent claims: (1) We all necessarily desire happiness when it is apprehended universally. (2) We do not necessarily desire it when it is apprehended in a particular case. While the first claim implies that we are necessitated to prefer what apparently promotes happiness, the second claim implies that we are not (*4Sent.* d49 q10 = OO x 505–6, 512–13 = W 184–8).

This objection raises questions about Aquinas' account of the influence of the will on deliberation. He believes it is in our power to fix on the alternative that we will pursue. He even believes that we are free not to pursue the option that initially seems best; if we focus on the bad aspects of x and the good aspects of y, we may change our initial view that x is better than y. Since it is up to us what we attend to, our choice and our action are in our power.

A voluntarist might infer that it is up to us to focus on whatever aspects of a subordinate good we please, independently of our conception of the good. But, according to Aquinas, I can will to stop deliberating or to ignore some features of an action in favour of others only if I believe it is better to direct my deliberation and attention in these ways. Our other beliefs determine what we look for and what we discover. If we cannot persuade ourselves, in the light of our beliefs, that a particular good is not on the whole desirable, we are necessitated (in his view) to choose it. From Aquinas' point of view, this sort of necessitation does not threaten freewill, but preserves it.

From the voluntarist point of view, however, this intellectualist conception of the role of the will excludes freedom. Scotus argues that if the will is not free not to pursue the final good, it is not free not to pursue subordinate goods. We lack freedom in relation to the final good (according to Aquinas) because our will depends on our conception of the good; if, then, our will equally depends on our conception of subordinate goods, it equally lacks freedom in relation to these subordinate goods.

This argument is cogent only if Scotus has given the right account of how we lack freedom in relation to the final good. In Aquinas' view, lack of freedom does not result from the dependence of our will on our conception of the good; he believes we would lack freedom only if we were incapable of recognizing and of acting on alternatives. In relation to subordinate goods we have the relevant capacity for recognition and action. Aquinas argues that we can ascribe this capacity to ourselves without denying the dependence of will on intellect.[35]

Even if Aquinas claimed that the will is independent of intellect in forming our deliberation about subordinate goods, he would still have to agree that it depends on intellect once we

---

[35] It may be useful to distinguish two claims: (1) It is not necessary that (when we recognize x as promoting the ultimate end, we desire x). (2) In cases where we recognize x as promoting the ultimate end, it is not necessary that we desire x. (1) denies the necessity of the connexion between recognizing x as good (i.e., as promoting happiness) and desiring x. Scotus is right to say that if we accept (1), we can no longer maintain eudaemonism. (2), however, denies the necessity of desiring x, but not because it denies the necessity of desiring x once we recognize it as good. We might accept (2) if we accept the necessity of desiring happiness, but reject any necessary connexion between desiring happiness and desiring x. Acceptance of (2) rather than (1) seems to underlie Aquinas' argument for denying the necessity of pursuing a non-ultimate good. For, in his view, every non-ultimate good can be looked at from some point of view that would make it appear not good; we must deliberate correctly if we are to look at it from the right point of view (1-2 q10 a2; q13 a6). Aquinas believes that our general desire for the ultimate end does not necessitate us, independently of our deliberation, to recognize one or another particular good as a means to the ultimate end. But he does not deny that we are determined to pursue something as a means to the ultimate end once we recognize it as such and do not change our mind.

have definitely made up our minds; when we have a firm belief about what is better, we have no alternative but to follow it. This is the claim that Tempier's commission took to be incompatible with freewill, and Scotus agrees with the commission. But why should Aquinas agree? In his view, freewill gives a reasonable basis for praise and blame, and we have a reasonable basis in the antecedents of a human action, as he describes them. We need to go further into Scotus' position to see why he believes that Aquinas' account cannot justify praise and blame.

The disputes about happiness identify the main points of disagreement between Aquinas and Scotus about how the will is a free and rational desire. From the voluntarist point of view, Aquinas' conditions for freedom are inadequate, because they imply that the will is determined by our natural desire for happiness and our beliefs about what promote it. Scotus believes that the will is not free unless it is free in relation to our natural desires. From Aquinas' point of view, however, the voluntarist conception of freedom is self-defeating; since it rejects determination by the ultimate end, it rejects determination by reason, and hence prevents the will from being free in relation to non-rational desires.

One might conclude that Aquinas is right about rationality, but Scotus is right about freedom, so that our initial belief in the will as a free rational desire is incoherent. In order to settle the issue in favour of Scotus, we must be able to understand how a will that has the degree of freedom required by voluntarism is also rational.

363. Moral Objections to Eudaemonism: The Two Affections of the Will[36]

To answer the eudaemonist objection that he cannot attribute both rationality and freedom to a will detached from eudaemonist global reasoning, Scotus appeals to the two primary affections that Anselm ascribes to the will: the affection for advantage and the affection for justice.[37] If we had only the will to happiness, we could not be blamed for pursuing happiness through unjust means; for if we believed that these unjust means promoted happiness, we could not avoid pursuing them (Anselm, *De Casu Diaboli* 13). In order to be open to praise and blame for acting justly and unjustly, we must have a will to justice that is independent of the will to happiness.[38] The affection for justice causes us to will something that is not directed towards ourselves. It manifests freedom in the will, because an agent who is capable of choosing the just rather than the advantageous is not necessitated by nature to pursue only his own advantage.[39]

---

[36] On the two affections see Boler, 'Transcending'.

[37] For Anselm's distinction see *3Sent.* d26 q1 = OO vii 2, 635 §17 = W 178; *2Sent.* d6 q2 = OO vi 1, 537 §5 = W 464; Wolter, 'Native freedom' 149–50; Visser and Williams, 'Freedom'; Delahaye, 'Morale'. Cf. §280n46.

[38] '...it is necessary that God make both wills come together in him [sc. Satan], so that he would both will to be happy and will justly. In this way justice being added would control the will for happiness in such a way that it would both restrain the excess of the will and would not cut off the power of exceeding' (Anselm, *De Casu* 14).

[39] If we pursued everything with a view only to advantage, we would not have a free will; we would only have a 'natural desire belonging to an intellectual nature' just as a non-rational animal has a 'natural desire belonging to a sensory nature' (*2Sent.* d39 q2 = OO vi 2, 1021 §5 = W 202).

We might recognize these two affections without rejecting eudaemonism. Aristotle contrasts the choice of the fine with the choice of the advantageous, meaning that in choosing the fine I forgo some advantage for myself.[40] Similarly, the Stoics contrast the useful (utile) with the fine (honestum), and Aquinas takes over the contrast.[41] A eudaemonist claims that both of these affections are expressions of our pursuit of happiness, and that someone with a correct conception of his own happiness will prefer the just over the merely advantageous. Aquinas agrees that justice has some special connexion with the will because it requires an agent to consider other people's advantage, and not merely her own; he does not regard this as an objection to eudaemonism.[42]

Anselm suggests a further argument against eudaemonism besides this argument from responsibility. He describes a just person as one who 'preserves correctness of will not because of anything else, in so far as he is to be called just, than the correctness itself' (De Veritate 12). The clause 'not because of anything else than the correctness itself' might be taken to mean that the just person regards correctness of will as worth preserving even if no further benefit results from it. This is what Aristotle means in saying that the virtuous person acts for the sake of the fine itself. But Anselm might intend a further and more restrictive claim, that the just person cannot value correctness of will for anything other than itself, and hence cannot value it for the sake of happiness.[43] He maintains that we are not just if we will the action we ought to will only because we are led to it by force or by external reward.[44] But he does not make it clear whether the prospect of happiness is necessarily an external reward that excludes choosing correctness of will for its own sake. If the prospect of happiness counts as an external reward, the just person does not always choose for the sake of happiness.

Scotus accepts this restrictive claim. He takes the existence of an affection for justice to refute eudaemonism, because he identifies the pursuit of happiness with the pursuit of advantage (3Sent. d27 q1 = OO vii.2, 651 §12 = W 434). If our happiness were our supreme end, we would not be free to choose justice over our own advantage, and we would not be free to love God above everything. Hence the appropriate sort of love for God subordinates self-love to the love of God, and so subordinates our desire for our happiness to the love of God.[45]

Scotus rejects the 'refined' eudaemonism that tries to reconcile apparently self-sacrificing action with the primacy of one's pursuit of one's own happiness. He argues that brave people who sacrifice their lives will the non-existence of themselves and their virtue for the good of the community; they act for the sake of the community, not for the sake of their

---

[40] See, e.g., EN 1162b34–1163a1; §§106–7. [41] See §§180, 332. [42] See §339.

[43] See Delahaye, 'Morale' 406, on De Veritate: 'La finalité morale s'exprime en termes de justice, non pas en termes de béatitude'.

[44] '...someone who wills what he ought to will only if he is forced to, or when induced by an external reward, does not preserve correctness for its own sake, but preserves it only for the sake of something else—if he can be said to preserve it at all' (De Veritate 12).

[45] 'Everyone who loves out of charity loves himself as directed towards the infinite good, because he loves the act or state by which he tends towards that good, and in this respect his love tends towards another, because his act is towards God as its principal object, and then he has charity to himself not as the final object, but as a proximate object directed towards the final and first object which is distinct from himself' (3Sent. d29 q1 supp = OO vii 2, 667 §4 = W 456).

own virtue.[46] It must be possible, therefore, for virtuous people to choose the common good while recognizing that it conflicts with their own happiness.

This example is similar in one respect to Scotus' earlier example of the person who chooses 'contrarily' against happiness; it reflects the deliberate choice of a course of action that is contrary to one's own happiness. But in the earlier case, we objected that Scotus does not show that the choice against happiness really proceeds from the will, because he does not show that it proceeds from rational desire. In the present case, he answers that objection. For he assumes that if we are moved by justice, or bravery, or the love of God, we take it to be best all things considered; what we have best reason to do does not necessarily promote our own happiness. Familiar assumptions about morality show, in his view, that choice with a view to one's happiness is not the only sort of rational choice that can be ascribed to the will. The eudaemonist position is indefensible, if it fails to make room for the non-self referential character of the choices required by morality.[47]

364. Freedom Identified with the Affection for Justice

Scotus identifies this affection for justice with the innate freedom of the will.[48] If the will were merely an intellectual desire focussed on happiness, it would not be free; hence the free will is not bound to the pursuit of happiness.[49] We have a natural tendency to pursue our own happiness (identified with our self-confined advantage); freedom not to follow this natural tendency is a necessary condition of having the affection for justice.

Such freedom, however, seems to be insufficient for justice. Scotus accepts Anselm's account of justice as 'correctness of will maintained for its own sake' (4Sent. d46 q1 = OO x 238 §2 = W 240).[50] In speaking of justice he refers to what is right and reasonable from an impartial point of view distinct from one's own preferences. Why should innate freedom of the will involve an affection for some impartial standard of rightness?

Perhaps Scotus means that the virtuous person who freely rejects his happiness is free because he is not simply moved by the strength of some inclination, but is moved by some rational appraisal of the options open to him. Scotus suggests that rational appraisal is embodied in the outlook of justice. If we are considering our own advantage against some action for the sake of some different end, we need to compare the two actions by some

---

[46] 'The Philosopher maintains in Ethics iii that the person with the bravery of a citizen in accordance with correct reason ought to expose himself to death for the good of the commonwealth. But the philosopher would not suppose that such a person would have any reward after this life . . . And so, setting aside all future reward, this is in accord with right reason, that every person with the bravery of a citizen should will his own non-existence to prevent the perishing of the good of the commonwealth. Now according to correct reason, the divine good and the good of the community (politicum) are to be loved more than the good of some individual. Therefore a given person, in accordance with correct reason, ought to will his own non-existence because of the divine good' (3Sent. d27 q1 = OO vii 2, 652 §13 = W 436).

[47] On Scotus' rejection of eudaemonism see Williams, 'Happiness'; 425–45; Cross, DS 85–9.

[48] 'Justice can be understood either as infused (which is called "gratuitous") or as acquired (which is called "moral") or as innate (which is the very freedom of the will)' (2Sent. d6 q2 = OO vi 1, 539 §8 = W 468). Scotus identifies the affection for justice with 'the innate freedom of the will, in accordance with which it is capable of willing some good not directed towards itself' (3Sent. d26 q1 = OO vii 2, 635 §17 = W 178).

[49] 'In this way, therefore, it is clear that a free will is not bound in every way to will happiness, in the way in which it would will it if it were only an intellectual desire without freedom' (2Sent. d6 q2 = OO vi 1, 540 §9 = W 470).

[50] Cf. Anselm, De Veritate 12 (quoted above, n44); Lottin, PM i 13.

standard that shows us how far it is reasonable to pursue our own advantage and how far it is reasonable to pursue the other end. This standard estimates different ends by reference to some impartial conception of what deserves to be chosen. Attachment to this impartial standard is the affection for justice. Hence the affection for justice is not a natural affection that we freely chose to follow; it is the expression of freedom.

Scotus seems to believe, then, that the affection for justice, not the desire for one's own happiness, is the standard for the evaluation of our natural inclinations. Aquinas says that we have freewill in so far as we act on deliberation about our own happiness, but Scotus argues that we have freewill in so far as we act on deliberation about justice.[51] The freedom of a rational will is displayed in the recognition of some impartial standard of rightness.[52]

This defence of Scotus' claims about freedom and the affection for justice helps to explain a disagreement with Aquinas over the status of the desire for happiness. For Aquinas, it is not a contingent fact that a rational will desires the ultimate good identified with happiness; a correct explication of the desire for happiness also explicates a rational will. Aquinas thinks it is essential to a rational will to assess the comparative merits of different actions; and he identifies this comparative assessment with assessment in the light of an ultimate end. An agent who was incapable of this comparative assessment would not be a free agent at all.

In contrast to Aquinas, Scotus treats the pursuit of happiness as a contingent feature of a rational will. It is a necessary and natural feature of a human will, but it is not essential to its being a rational will. In Aquinas' view, we no longer have a rational will if we do not have a will that decides in the light of an ultimate end. Scotus, however, argues that impartiality is essential to a rational will. The rational point of view identifies and considers the actual merits of different courses of action, and sets aside the particular inclinations of the various 'interested parties'. Ordinary inter-personal justice may be understood as the application of this attitude to inter-personal questions, but the attitude applies to cases where the 'interested parties' are aspects of one person, rather than different people.[53]

This aspect of the affection for justice is also an aspect of the desire for happiness, as Aquinas understands it. The pursuit of happiness requires global and systematic practical reasoning. But it also includes aiming at perfection; this aim rests on a conception of the merits of different options, not simply on how they fit into the agent's preferences. This aspect of Aquinas' position is strongly and appropriately emphasized in Scotus' claims about the affection for justice.

365. Sin and Self-Love

This comparison between Aquinas and Scotus might suggest that they emphasize distinct, but perhaps complementary, aspects of the rational will. Aquinas insists that its outlook is

---

[51] If he means this, the difference between him and Aquinas might not be very great. The difference would be that Aquinas emphasizes the desire for happiness as our starting point, whereas Scotus emphasizes the application of an impartial standard as the conclusion that we reach.

[52] To show that we are capable of not pursuing our own advantage, it is sufficient to cite disinterested actions. But these do not show that we have freewill, if that is a property of a rational will.

[53] On reason and impartiality see Cumberland, *LN*, i 30; Berkeley, *PO* 7.

global and systematic, whereas Scotus insists that it is impartial. But Scotus also believes that eudaemonism is mistaken, because it would sometimes be wrong to choose happiness over justice. Since the choice of happiness is sometimes blameworthy, it must be the free choice of evil; since the will is free to refuse it, the will cannot be determined to pursue happiness. When Lucifer asserts himself against God, he does not act out of love of God, which cannot be excessive; hence, he does not act on the affection for justice, which would require the love of God above all else. He must, then, be acting on excessive affection for the advantageous, which Scotus identifies with desire for one's own happiness.[54] The city of the devil rests on 'love of self that goes as far as contempt of God' (2Sent. d6 q2 = OO vi 1, 535 §4 = W 464); Lucifer ought to have preferred justice over his own advantage, but he sinned by preferring his own advantage.[55] If he sinned, he must have chosen freely between his own advantage and justice. Lucifer sins in so far as he pursues his own happiness, but, according to the eudaemonist, he has no choice about whether to pursue his own happiness. Hence the eudaemonist has to say that Lucifer does not act freely, and that we cannot fairly blame him.

This example does not refute eudaemonism. Aquinas agrees that Lucifer's sin is excessive love of himself to the exclusion of others. Self-love is excessive in someone who focusses on himself to the exclusion of other things and people; but this exclusive focus rests on a mistake about one's own happiness.[56] Aquinas agrees that the affection for justice and the love of God ought to override self-absorbed self-love, but he distinguishes this sort of self-love from the desire for happiness.

Is it worthwhile to defend Aquinas' position in this way? Why should we insist that the affection for justice and the love of God are really the expression of the desire for one's own happiness? Such a defence seems to force us into a misleadingly self-centred way of describing desires that do not really put self-love above everything.

Aquinas might answer by appeal to Scotus' belief that in pursuing the demands of justice and charity we pursue what is best all things considered. To justify this belief, we need to explain why we should care about the requirements of justice and charity in relation to other appropriate objects of concern, including self-regarding goods. Aquinas defends non-self-regarding concerns by appeal to the sort of good that we also pursue in the pursuit of self-regarding goods. Concern for our own good leads us to impartial love for another person, for the common good of a community, and for God as including all the good that we find partly realized in other things (ST 2-2 q26 a3; Car. a4 ad2 = M 764a). A self-regarding starting point shows why we have good reason to take an impartial attitude to some goods.

This progress from self-regarding to impartial concern does not reduce non-self-regarding concern to self-regarding concern. But it shows how our self-regarding concerns pursue an end that we achieve more fully in impartial concerns. If we connect our actions to a systematic ultimate end, we can show (according to Aquinas) that the aims of impartial

---

[54] See 2Sent. d6 q2 = OO vi 1,537 §5 = W 464: 'the greatest advantage is one's complete happiness'.

[55] Scotus' quotation is inexact. Augustine actually speaks of the earthly city, not the city of the devil, as the one that is guided by excessive self-love (CD xiv 28a). Augustine also speaks of the earthly city with its angels as founded on self-love (xiv 13–14). He agrees with Scotus in saying that the basis of Lucifer's sin is excessive self-love. But he does not commit himself to Scotus' view that Lucifer is moved by desire for his happiness rather than some other desire. See §226; O'Donovan, PSLSA, ch. 2.

[56] On Aquinas' view see §341.

concerns are not completely separate from the aims of self-regarding concerns. If Scotus agrees that it is reasonable to look for this sort of connexion, he accepts one of Aquinas' claims about happiness as the ultimate end.

These questions about the implication of eudaemonism are relevant to Scotus' argument to show that some rational choices are not directed to one's happiness. He argues as follows: (1) The desire for happiness is directed towards oneself. (2) Virtuous people's choice is not directed towards themselves. (3) But their choice is rational. (4) Therefore, some rational choice is not directed towards oneself. (5) Therefore, it is not directed towards one's own happiness.[57] The argument depends on the claim that some choices are or are not 'directed to oneself' (ordinatum ad se). If Scotus is right, eudaemonism is incompatible with admitted facts about the virtuous person's rational choices (stated in (2) and (3)).

'Directed towards oneself' seems to have different senses in Scotus' argument. The virtues forbid the self-centred attitude that takes one's own interest to be more important than anyone else's, or takes the interests of others to be purely instrumental to one's own. According to Aristotle and Aquinas, however, this self-centred attitude is not required by the desire for one's own happiness. To desire one's own happiness is to aim at some feature of oneself in contrast to other people; but it does not imply that one cares less about others than about oneself.

The first step of Scotus' argument is true, therefore, if 'directed towards oneself' refers to the self-referential character of the desire for happiness. But the second step is false, if it refers to the same thing. The second step is true if 'directed towards oneself' means 'self-centred'; but if it means the same in the first step, that step is false. The conclusion damages eudaemonism only if 'directed towards oneself' means 'self-referential'; but it does not follow from the first two steps if they are both true.

This reply does not show that a eudaemonist can justify the non-self-centred attitude of the virtues within the self-referential outlook of the desire for one's own happiness. But it suggests that this question about justification is at least worth asking. If Scotus were right, it would not be worth asking, because the eudaemonist would be attempting an impossible task.

366. Sin and Freedom

In Scotus' view, eudaemonism distorts the relation between the pursuit of happiness and the affection for justice. The sin of Lucifer is a genuine sin only because we are capable of moderating our desire for happiness, and are required to moderate it. Lucifer could have freely chosen to moderate his affection for advantage, but he freely chooses not to moderate it.

According to this picture, the will has two affections, for advantage and for justice, and freedom consists in our choosing between them. But how are we to reconcile this picture with Scotus' claim that the freedom of the will is its affection for justice? (2Sent d6 q2 = 00

---

[57] 'The affection for justice is nobler than the affection for the advantageous, where "justice" is understood not only as acquired and infused justice, but as innate justice, which is the inborn freedom in accordance with which one can will something not directed towards oneself' (3Sent. d26 q1 = OO vii 2, 635 §17 = W 178).

vi.1, 539 §8 = W 468)?[58] Scotus explains that if the will simply had an affection for advantage, it would be simply a natural rational desire, and would not be free. The affection for justice is freedom, because it is the primary controller of the affection for advantage.[59]

But what are we to say about the will of Lucifer who chooses his own happiness freely but inappropriately? If his freedom consists in his affection for justice, apparently he acts on his affection for justice. In that case, he believes that justice supports his self-assertion, because the divine law imposes unreasonable limits on his happiness. God requires Lucifer to find his own happiness in loving God rather than in loving himself without God, to achieve it at the time God wills, and to achieve it by merit (*2Sent* d6 q2 = 00 vi.1, 540 §9 = W 470); perhaps Lucifer thinks these are unreasonable restraints on him. He exercises freedom, therefore, in so far as he compares God's demands on him with some impartial standard of reasonable action, and concludes that it is unreasonable for him to sacrifice his happiness to God's demands. This explanation traces Lucifer's sin to an error about the justice of the limits that God imposes on Lucifer's happiness. It is similar, therefore, to the eudaemonist explanation, in so far as it appeals to error, but it differs about the content of the error.

But if Scotus agrees with the eudaemonist even to this extent, can he maintain his objection to eudaemonism? He rejects the eudaemonist explanation not only because of its broad conception of one's own happiness, but also because it traces Lucifer's sin to his false belief about the means to happiness. If his choice resulted from this false belief, his intellectual error would not convict him of sin, because such errors are not subject to freewill.[60] If Lucifer acts on some rational standard that he mistakenly supposes to justify his self-assertion, his mistake explains his sin. Ignorance resulting in misapplication of a rational standard should deprive him of freedom in precisely the way in which, according to Scotus, the pursuit of happiness would deprive us of freedom, if Aquinas were right about the status of happiness. Scotus' argument about ignorance and freedom seems to undermine his account of how Lucifer sins freely.

We might answer that it is too simple to assert that ignorance and error exclude freedom by excluding praise and blame. Sometimes ignorance and error are blameworthy; and if Lucifer's ignorance is blameworthy, it does not exempt him from blame and praise. But if Scotus relies on this defence to show that Lucifer sins freely, the eudaemonist may also rely on it. Whether it is difficult or easy to identify the relevant kind of ignorance, Scotus and the eudaemonist seem to face the same task.

If, then, Scotus sticks to his objection about ignorance and responsibility, he should not say that Lucifer's free choice of his own happiness is a result of his affection for justice. Instead he should say that the choice is the result of his preference for following his natural desire for happiness over the affection for justice, and that this preference is to be ascribed to the free will. Lucifer compares the requirements of justice and the requirements of his own advantage, and chooses to follow his own advantage, by the free exercise of his rational will, but not because he misapplies some rational principle.

---

[58] Quoted in n48.

[59] '. . . that affection for justice, I say, is the inborn freedom of the will, because it is itself the primary controller of such an affection [sc. for advantage]' (*2Sent.* d6 q2 sch. = OO vi 1, 540 §8 = W 468–9).

[60] See *2Sent.* d6 q2 = OO vi 1, 539 §8 = W 468: nec imputaretur sibi ad peccatum. Hume uses the same sort of argument to show that false judgments cannot be the source of immorality: *T* iii 1.1 §12.

According to this view, freedom is not identical to the affection for justice; for Lucifer's will is free and he acts freely even though he rejects the affection for justice and the rational standard that it follows. Scotus' rejection of explanations appealing to ignorance implies that a free will could be fully informed about the implications of any rational standard and could still refuse to follow that standard. The affection for justice makes freewill possible, since an agent without such an affection could not reject happiness; but it is not identical to the freedom of the will. The will is no less free in rejecting than in accepting the affection for justice.

But how can Lucifer's sin, understood as a rejection of the affection for justice, express the choice of his will rather than his passion? Scotus' argument about freedom and ignorance excludes any explanation that refers to Lucifer's mistaken belief about what is best. Hence his choice depends on some motive that does not respond to a judgment about what is best. The passions are motives of this sort, but Scotus argues that Lucifer acts on his will rather than his passions. What is the difference? Scotus complains that when Aquinas seeks to make the will rational, he deprives it of freedom; but when Scotus wants to make the will free, he deprives it of rationality. Admittedly, Scotus does not believe that the will is insensitive to the greater good; he recognizes that it is difficult to reject the conclusion of practical reason.[61] Still, he believes we can reject this conclusion, on the basis of some reason that we acknowledge to be inferior. We might, therefore, wonder why this is an act of the will rather than a passion.

367. Eudaemonism, Intellectualism, and Voluntarism

Scotus' claims about the two affections and about freedom attack Aquinas' eudaemonism and intellectualism. Against eudaemonism Scotus argues that a free rational will chooses by reference to an impartial rational standard that is distinct from, and not subordinate to, one's own happiness. His objection to eudaemonism would be plausible if Aquinas treated the desire for happiness as a self-confined natural impulse; but Aquinas treats the desire for happiness as a necessary characteristic of a free and rational will, not as an impulse that restricts the freedom of a rational will.

But even if Scotus' argument against eudaemonism fails, his positive claim that a free will is rational and impartial may be a viable alternative to eudaemonism. We might, then, understand him as a non-eudaemonist intellectualist who assigns to the affection for justice the place that Aquinas assigns to the desire for happiness. Scotus might be right to take some impartial perspective as the defining feature of a rational will. Aquinas believes that this impartial perspective can be fitted into a broadly eudaemonistic perspective; but the reverse procedure might appear equally plausible, or even more plausible.[62]

---

[61] Bonansea, 'Voluntarism' 99, cites *2Sent.* d6 q2 = OO vi 1, 540 §8: 'In so far as the will is simply intellectual desire, it would be inclined actually above all to the highest intelligible good . . . But in so far as it is free it can restrain itself in eliciting an act, so as not to follow that inclination, neither as regards the substance of the act nor as regards the intention to which the capacity is naturally inclined.' Bonansea adds *Rep. Par.* ii d39 q2 = OO xi 1, 406 §5: 'It is difficult for the will not to incline to what is prescribed finally by practical reason, but it is not impossible'.

[62] To pursue this line of inquiry is to see some of the reasons that might support Butler's belief that conscience is the supreme principle in a rational agent.

It is difficult, however, to combine this intellectualist position with Scotus' other main attack on eudaemonism. He argues that if the will were not free to reject happiness, it would not be free, since it could not choose between opposites in this respect. A parallel argument shows that the will must be free to reject justice. While Scotus sometimes identifies the freedom of the will with the affection for justice, he cannot identify the two if he also maintains his broader objection to eudaemonism. Freedom seems to require the ability to reject justice no less than the ability to reject happiness.

This voluntarist aspect of Scotus' position dissolves any special connexion between freedom and the affection for justice.[63] Disinterested malice, for instance, seems to express freedom in a choice that rejects both happiness and justice. If you harm me or someone or something I care about, I may want you to suffer even if I recognize that I will gain nothing and that it is quite unjust for you to suffer (if what you did was completely justifiable or excusable). Scotus should apparently agree that a free will can make such choices.[64] He cannot identify the affection for justice with the innate freedom of the will, if disinterested malice expresses innate freedom.

Scotus could maintain a consistently voluntarist position by abandoning his claim that freedom of the will consists in the affection for justice. But then he would also abandon his reason for believing that a free will is also a rational will. On the one hand, he contrasts the free will with dependence on natural inclination, but on the other hand, he contrasts it with dependence on the greater good. The first contrast gives us a reason to reject the second; for the relevant contrast between the rational will and non-rational inclination requires the will to be responsive to value in a way that is excluded by the second contrast.

We would free his position from conflict if we were to deny any connexion between the doctrine of the two affections and voluntarism.[65] We might take the doctrine of the two affections as a part of Scotus' moral theory, not as part of his theory of the will and its freedom. In that case, we could affirm that the will is equally free whichever of the two affections guides it, and that the affection for the just is morally better, but not a fuller expression of freedom. Perhaps Scotus is confused in identifying freedom with the affection for justice.

We should not conclude so readily, however, that he is confused. For if we deny the identification of freedom with the affection for justice, we make it more difficult to separate the will from the passions. If the impartial attitude of the affection for the just is the outlook of reason, the free and rational will acts primarily through the affection for the just. But if the will is equally expressed through the rejection of happiness for something worse, through the affection for advantage, and through the affection for the just, what makes the will a rational capacity? It is not easy to defend Scotus' belief that the will is rational without his claim that the affection for the just most fully expresses the free will. We might even decide that his claims about freedom and the affection for the just are plausible apart from his voluntarism.[66]

[63] For a more sympathetic account of Scotus on freedom and justice cf. Adams, 'Will' 252–4.

[64] Scotus might say that malicious action of this sort really manifests my desire for revenge, and so it is self-regarding after all; but if he is willing to allow a eudaemonist explanation in this case, it is difficult to see why he is entitled to resist a parallel explanation of behaviour that he takes to rest on the affection for justice.

[65] Boler, for instance, in 'Transcending', treats the doctrine of the two affections as primarily an aspect of Scotus' moral theory.

[66] A similar conclusion may emerge from consideration of similar questions about Kant's position.

368. A Dualism of Practical Reason?

Scotus' attack on eudaemonism shows that he does not take the supremacy of self-interest for granted, and that he does not treat this as the only principle of practical reason. On this point, he rejects the main tradition of ancient and mediaeval ethics.[67] In modern moral philosophy Butler rejects this primacy of self-love. Sidgwick recognizes the importance of the question raised by Butler, and discusses it in his account of practical reason. Since Scotus anticipates Butler and Sidgwick, it is helpful to anticipate some of the questions that they raise.[68]

One of Sidgwick's claims about Butler raises a worthwhile question about Scotus as well. Since Butler rejects the primacy of self-love, we may say that he accepts a 'duality' of practical reason, marked by the irreducible principles of self-love and conscience. Sidgwick also claims that Butler recognizes a 'dualism' of practical reason; not only are there two irreducible principles, but neither is subordinate to the other or to any third principle. But Butler does not seem to treat his duality as a dualism. He maintains that self-love and conscience are distinct superior principles, but conscience is supreme. He therefore denies that they are equally ultimate principles.

Where does Scotus stand on this question? Does he regard the affection for advantage and the affection for justice as two ultimate and equal principles, or does he take the affection for justice to be superior? A non-eudaemonist intellectualist interpretation of his account of the will suggests that the affection for justice is the supreme principle. If the will is a rational capacity, and the two affections of the will are two aspects of the application of practical reason to our actions, perhaps they express the same general principle. In deliberating with a view to our own happiness, we impose the appropriate rational order on our desires with reference to our own good; in deliberating with a view to justice, we impose the appropriate rational order on the desires of the different people affected. Deliberation with reference to happiness imperfectly embodies practical reason for only one person's desires, whereas deliberation with reference to justice embodies it more fully.

This interpretation of Scotus fits the intellectualist version of his doctrine of freedom. But it does not account for all of his position. The most plausible argument for the supremacy of justice treats the affection for justice as a higher level of the sort of rational order that is present in the desire for happiness. If we find this rational order in the desire for happiness, it is plausible to treat the desire for happiness as a necessary structural feature of a rational agent. But this structural conception of the desire for happiness is Aquinas' conception. Scotus does not treat the desire for happiness, as Aquinas does, as a rational order in desires. On the contrary, he tends to treat the desire for happiness as though it were a desire for some specific object, or some specific bias in our desires, that is not an essential feature of a rational agent.

Scotus' conception of happiness is consistent with the supremacy of the affection for justice, but it deprives him of a plausible argument for it. If we doubt whether practical reason involves the impartial outlook of justice, we can remove this doubt by noticing that

---

[67] The Cyrenaics are his only predecessors; they reject eudaemonism for quite different reasons. See §§31–2.
[68] See Sidgwick, *ME* 197–8.

we acknowledge a similar, though partial, outlook in rational self-love. Butler, Reid, and Sidgwick see this parallel between the outlooks of prudence and of impartial morality. The parallel gives a good reason for taking the affection for justice to be superior to the desire for happiness. But this reason is not available to Scotus, given his conception of happiness. In trying to maintain the rationality of the affection for justice without allowing the rationality of the desire for happiness, he weakens his case for the supremacy of justice. Kant faces a similar difficulty for similar reasons.

Even apart from his views on happiness, Scotus' views about freedom make it difficult for him to maintain the superiority of the affection for justice. For he believes that freedom requires the capacity both to follow the affection for justice and to reject it. Lucifer exercises this capacity by rejecting justice in favour of his own advantage. This position is consistent with the supremacy of the affection for justice; for we might say that justice is rationally supreme, resting on the best reasons, and that Lucifer exercises his freedom by rejecting action based on the best reasons. But it is difficult for Scotus to defend this view, if he also believes that the free will is essentially rational, and hence that Lucifer made a rational choice in favour of self-interest. The essential rationality of the free will makes it plausible to affirm a dualism, not merely a duality, of practical reason, so that neither the affection for advantage nor the affection for justice is superior. According to this dualist position, deliberation with a view to happiness does not rest on a principle that also underlies deliberation with a view to justice. The two kinds of deliberation rest on fundamentally different aims and assumptions that cannot be rationally subordinated to each other. Though Sidgwick's description of the dualism of practical reason may not fit Butler, it may fit Scotus.

This conclusion reveals a question about the non-eudaemonist intellectualism that Scotus sometimes seems to accept (when he identifies freedom with the affection for justice, or with innate justice). If we accept the argument from prudence to justice, relying on impartial reason, we may be less tempted to reject eudaemonism; for the impartial aspects of the affection for justice do not (for the reasons we have considered) require us to abandon the supremacy of the desire for happiness.

A similar question may face Butler.[69] His argument to show that self-love is a superior principle with authority over particular passions seems to presuppose a structural conception; self-love does not pursue some specific object co-ordinate with the objects of the other desires and competing with them, but it pursues some more abstract object that is partly constituted by the satisfaction of particular passions. This conception of self-love fits the Aristotelian conception of the desire for happiness, and also fits Butler's conception of the role of conscience in inter-personal relations. But this Aristotelian conception of self-love may make us less inclined to deny the supremacy (properly understood) of self-love.

Butler has a more plausible argument against the supremacy of self-love if he relies on the hedonist conception that he sometimes accepts. This conception partly corresponds to Scotus' view of the affection for advantage as a purely natural feature of a human being, rather than an essential feature of a rational agent. But this conception also carries a cost for Butler; for it does not include the abstract and structural conception that displays the continuity between self-love and conscience.

---

[69] For Butler's account of the superiority of self-love see, e.g., S ii 11–13.

Perhaps, then, Sidgwick's claims about Butler point to an important question about both Butler and Scotus. Perhaps Butler's most plausible argument for the supremacy of conscience rests on a conception of self-love that makes it less plausible to deny the supremacy of self-love. Similarly, perhaps Scotus' conception of the pursuit of justice as the fullest manifestation of freedom and practical reason is most plausible in the light of an account of happiness that Scotus rejects. This does not imply that either Scotus or Butler ought to be a dualist, believing in two equally ultimate principles. It may imply that they are wrong to reject the eudaemonist assumptions that they reject.

This conclusion may not do justice to the case for maintaining a duality of practical reason without a dualism. Perhaps the acceptance of Aquinas' conception of the desire for happiness does not justify us in accepting the supremacy of happiness, once we consider the claims of impartial justice to express human freedom. The non-eudaemonist intellectualist interpretation of Scotus anticipates a Kantian argument for connecting freedom with practical reason. This argument raises difficulties for Kant that are parallel to some of the difficulties that we have found in trying to make room for Scotus' voluntarism. Both Scotus and Kant may be better off with a more intellectualist conception of freedom than the one that they tend to accept.

369. Will as Rational Capacity

From an intellectualist point of view, therefore, Scotus' view that freedom requires the freedom to reject the rational standards both of happiness and of justice seems to be his fatal error. Intellectualism without eudaemonism would be an intelligible and consistent position; why does Scotus insist on his further claim about freedom?

His answer depends on his view about the defining characteristic of the will. In his view, the will differs essentially from other desires in being an Aristotelian rational capacity (potentia rationalis; QM ix q15 = OO iv 796b = W 144), and hence a capacity for opposites.[70] Will, rather than intellect, matches Aristotle's conception of a capacity for opposites; hence Aristotle even 'hints' (innuit) that his conception of a rational capacity applies strictly to nothing except the will (QM ix 15 schol. 3 = OO iv 799b–800a §§9–11 = W 160–4).

According to Aquinas, however, Aristotle believes that rational capacities are actualized in ways that are subject to will and election, and that the will itself is not a rational capacity (1-2 q55 a1).[71] Aristotle cites sciences and crafts as his examples of capacities for opposites (Met. 1046b2–3, 6–8). He even distinguishes desire and decision from the capacities that he describes as capacities for opposites (1048a10–11). These remarks support Aquinas, and Scotus recognizes this objection to his own view (QM ix q15 = OO iv 797a §3 = W 148; 'Secundo, quia . . .'). Still, he believes that Aristotle's account of rational capacities does not fit intellect, which is not capable of opposites in its own right.[72] Once intellect is determined

---

[70] He agrees, therefore, with Henry of Ghent's claim that 'the will in a human being is called a rational capacity because it is capable of opposites' (Summa a36 q5, sol., Bad. 237B (p.124, Wilson), quoted by Wolter, 'Potency' 164n9).

[71] Cf. §285.

[72] 'Reason is not determinative, since it is of opposites with respect to which it cannot determine itself, and much less something other than itself' (QM ix 15 schol. 3 = OO iv 799b §9 = W 160).

to one effect, it no longer has the other in its power; and so it is no longer a capacity for opposites.

This argument assumes a strong sense of 'capacity for opposites', so that a subject has this capacity only if nothing external to the capacity itself ever determines it to one of the opposites. But the assumption is doubtful. We might say that a car can travel at either under or over 100 km/h, but when I press the accelerator hard enough, it is determined to travel at over 100 km/h; it is no longer able to travel at under 100 km/h at that very time in those very circumstances. If Aristotle attributes such a capacity to intellect, he can say that we are capable of believing either that the earth is round or that the earth is flat, until we find strong evidence for its being round; this evidence determines us to believe that it is round. Similarly, the doctor's knowledge makes her capable of healing and of poisoning, until she decides to heal; then she is determined to heal.

But in this sense non-rational capacities also seem to be capacities for opposites. The capacity of water to heat or to cool whatever is placed in it is capable of opposite actualizations before it is determined to one of the opposites. If we throw an ice cube into water at 20 degrees C, the ice cube will be warmed; if we throw a red-hot poker in, the poker will be cooled.[73] Since Aristotle claims that rational capacities differ from non-rational in being capacities for opposites, he cannot mean that x has a capacity for opposites by being capable of F and not F before being determined to F. Scotus infers that Aristotle intends rational capacities to be capable of opposites in Scotus' strong sense.[74] Intellect, therefore, is not a rational capacity (since it is not capable of opposites in the strong sense implying absence of external determination); only will is a rational capacity.

This argument is open to question if Aristotle believes that intellect has a capacity for opposites that distinguishes it from non-rational capacities but does not imply absence of external determination. And in fact Scotus acknowledges such a capacity: intellect has a special relation to opposites because of its representative character; it includes awareness of the relevant opposites.[75] Medical knowledge gives us awareness both of sickness and of health and of a rational basis for preferring one over the other; this is a difference between its relation to opposites and the relation of non-rational capacities to opposites.

Aquinas relies on this conception of a rational capacity to show how action caused by the will results from the exercise of a capacity for opposites. He argues that rational agents are moved by their will as a result of rational comparison.[76] This comparison requires both awareness of the possibility of opposite actions and consideration of their merits. In acting on such a comparison we realize a capacity for opposites; since we compare and evaluate these opposites, our capacity is different from that of a non-rational agent.

Scotus objects that if this were sufficient for a rational capacity, the possession of the rational capacity for F and the opposite of F would be insufficient for doing F and for doing

---

[73] Scotus cites this example from Boethius (quoted in OP iv 693) on Aristotle, *De Int.* 21b10.

[74] 'If it is said that a rational capacity is capable of opposites unless it is determined to one of them, in which case it is not [capable of both], it follows from this that there is no difference between opposed rational and irrational capacities as far as concerns this point, of being capable of opposites' (*QM* ix 15 schol. 3 = OO iv 800 §12 = W 166).

[75] 'A form that is grasped by intellect, as a science is, is a principle for assimilating to opposites by an intentional similitude, just as the science itself is a virtual similitude of opposites that are cognized, since one contrary includes the privation of the other' (*QM* ix 15 = OO iv 797a, §2 = W 148).

[76] See §245.

the opposite of F, even if the external conditions are suitable for one or the other; for if we know how to cure and how to poison, but we do not choose to do one or the other, we will do neither. Scotus takes this consequence to refute the claim that awareness of opposites gives us a capacity for opposites, because he assumes that x is not really the capacity for F if something external to x is needed to cause F.

This demanding conception of a capacity, however, does not seem to be Aristotle's; for, in his view, rational capacities need something else in the agent, and not just suitable external conditions, if they are to be actualized.[77] Hence he accepts the consequence that Scotus regards as unacceptable. That is why he denies, as Aquinas sees, that the will is a rational capacity. For rational capacities need something further to determine them in one direction or the other, but since the will determines the direction in which we apply a rational capacity; it is not itself a rational capacity.

These features of Aristotle's account cast doubt on Scotus' claims that intellect does not meet Aristotle's condition for rational capacities, and that only will meets this condition. But even if Aristotle had identified will with a rational capacity, he would not have implied that, as Scotus claims, nothing external can determine the will; for he does not believe that rational capacities cannot be determined by anything external to them. If Scotus were right, Aristotle would have claimed that if we have a capacity for opposites, then we must be able to do not-F at every time before we do F, and that nothing before actually doing F provides a sufficient condition for our doing F. This would be an indeterminist conception of the relevant sort of capacity. In claiming that Aristotle attributes an indeterminist capacity for opposites to us, Scotus ascribes indeterminism to Aristotle. In claiming that only the will satisfies the appropriate conditions for being a capacity for opposites, he accepts indeterminism in his own right. His argument fails, since we can apparently draw the distinctions that Aristotle draws without committing ourselves to indeterminism.

370. Rational Capacity and Contingency

But even if Scotus is wrong about *Metaphysics* ix, he still has a reason to believe that Aristotle needs Scotus' conception of the will. For Scotus argues that a will with the strong capacity for opposites (i.e., the capacity to actualize either one without external determination) is needed if our action is to be contingent.[78] Aristotle insists (in *De Interpretatione* 9) that some events happen contingently; hence (Scotus infers) he accepts Scotus' conception of rational capacity as involving this strong ability to do opposites.

Scotus assumes: (1) If my doing F is contingent, then when I choose to do F I am capable of refraining from F. (2) If I have this capacity when I choose to do F, then nothing prior

---

[77] 'Something else, then, namely desire or decision, must control the action; for when the agent has an overriding desire for one alternative, that is how it will act, whenever it is in the conditions suitable for its potentiality and meets the thing that is acted on. Necessarily, then, when anything with a rational potentiality desires to act in a way for which it has a potentiality, and it is in the conditions suitable for the potentiality, it acts' (Ar. *Met.* 1048a10–15).

[78] '... unless <a rational capacity> were capable of opposites when it is determined in actuality—that is, at that very moment in which <it decides> for that one—no effect that actualizes <it> would be actually contingent' (QM ix 15 schol. 3 = OO iv 800a §12 = W 166).

to my choosing to do F determines my choosing to do F.[79] Both assumptions are open to doubt. We might question the first assumption by claiming that my doing F is contingent even if my choosing to do F removes my capacity to refrain from F. But even if we accept Scotus' first assumption, we might question the second. Even if I have some capacity to refrain from F when I do F, it is not clear why this capacity excludes prior determination to do F. If there are antecedent sufficient conditions determining me to choose F rather than not F, my choosing F is necessitated; but Aristotle does not infer that it is necessary. In his discussion of the Sea Battle he denies that past truth necessitates a future event, but he does not infer that contingent human choices and actions have no sufficient causal conditions.[80] He does not rely on the strong conception of rational capacity that Scotus attributes to him, and he does not treat the will as such a capacity.[81]

Still, Scotus may have identified a serious difficulty in Aristotle and in Aquinas. Perhaps the distinctions Aristotle draws are too weak to support his claims about contingency. He believes that something about the contingency of human choices and actions justifies us in taking them to be open to praise, blame, and moral evaluation. Scotus claims that we cannot find the relevant sort of contingency in human choices unless we identify the will with a rational capacity, as he conceives it.

371. Voluntarism and Indeterminism

Scotus maintains, against Aquinas' intellectualism, that the belief that x is better than y does not determine the will to choose x rather than y. If anything external to the will determined the will, it would exclude freewill; for it would imply that the will itself is not a capacity for opposites, since something external to it would determine which opposite would be realized.

This argument helps us to see how Scotus' position goes beyond the simple rejection of intellectualism. If I freely choose between x and y, my choice (according to the anti-intellectualist) is not determined by my conception of the merits of x and y, since that would be determination by an appearance that lies outside the will; but my choice may still be determined by how the will is. If we attribute this sort of freedom to the will, we might still accept a determinist (or compatibilist) account of the formation of the will. Voluntarism, therefore, does not include incompatibilism, and so does not require indeterminism.

But this version of voluntarism may well seem unattractive. It is difficult to see why appearances and considerations should be the only external determinants that exclude free will. Compatibilist voluntarism, however, allows our beliefs, values, and choices, to be

---

[79] '. . . I say that the will can be moved to an act with no determination to the act previously understood in it, in such a way that the first determination in time and nature is in the positing of the act, and that if then it is supposed that it is capable of nothing unless previously determined, that is false' (QM ix 15 = OO iv 801a §13 = OP 696 = W 168). I follow the text of OO and OP rather than W.

[80] Some readers have claimed to find it in *Met*. vi 3, but it is difficult to convince ourselves that he accepts it there if we are not already persuaded that Aristotle accepts indeterminism. For references see Kirwan, *Met*. 222–5. Aquinas explains the chapter through his doctrine of different types of causes in *in Met*. vi 3 §§1215–22.

[81] On Scotus' view that he agrees with Aristotle see Wolter, 'Potency' 177–8. On earlier Franciscan disagreements with Aristotelian views see Stadter, *PMMF* 4–6, 79–80, 124, 136, 182, 210–11.

determined by a sequence of sufficient conditions that goes back outside us, indeed to events long before we were born.

Scotus might reasonably claim to offer a more plausible version of voluntarism. In his view determination of the will by considerations external to it is to be rejected not because the determinants are intellectual, but because they are external to the will. His belief in self-determination rests on his belief that the will is a rational capacity, capable by itself of going in opposite directions.

Scotus' defence of voluntarism, therefore, commits him to indeterminism. If something prior to my willing now to raise my arm determined my willing this now, my will would not now be a rational capacity that determines itself to opposite effects. His strong claim about the will as a rational capacity commits him to both voluntarism and indeterminism.

Just as voluntarism without indeterminism is consistent but unattractive, Aquinas' intellectualism makes compatibilism attractive. The determination of will by intellect is compatible with indeterminism about freewill; perhaps the will is determined by the intellect, but we act freely only if the conclusion of the intellect is not causally necessitated.[82] This view, however, is unstable. Aquinas suggests that we have freewill because we deliberate about alternatives, and the result of our deliberation affects our choice and action. This is his explanation of the intuitions that suggest that freedom requires some ability to do otherwise. If his explanation is correct, these intuitions do not require incompatibilism; hence we undermine one argument to show that the ability to do otherwise must include an indeterministic process.

Aquinas' intellectualism, therefore, supports compatibilism, and Scotus' voluntarism supports indeterminism. These are not the only consistent combinations; later discussions of freewill try other combinations.[83] But Aquinas and Scotus have good reasons for believing that they are more plausible than the other consistent combinations would be.[84]

---

[82] On incompatibilist intellectualism see §270n62.

[83] Hobbes, e.g., defends both compatibilism and anti-intellectualism against Bramhall.

[84] The issue about determination leads to another dispute between Aquinas and Scotus. Aquinas' account of human freedom in relation to external causal influences depends heavily on his distinctions among types of causes. Provided that the proximate cause is in the will responding in the right way to the merits of the situation, the fact that the will's response is itself the product of external causal influences does not seem to him to compromise human freedom; it simply has to be connected to human action by the right sort of causal chain. Aquinas relies on this distinction to argue that external causal influences such as the passions, human nature, external events, the Devil, and God do not threaten human freedom. See §270. Scotus is dissatisfied with Aquinas' solution, because he rejects Aquinas' distinction among causes. See Adams, WO ii 1117–30.

26

SCOTUS: VIRTUE
AND PRACTICAL REASON

372. Passion, Will, and Virtue

Scotus believes that since freedom depends on will rather than intellect, and since virtuous action is (as Augustine says) the good use of freewill, the will is also the subject of the moral virtues. If the moral virtues belonged to the passions or to the intellect, they would not be subject to freewill, and so we would not be open to praise or blame for being virtuous or vicious.

If the will is the subject of the moral virtues, Aristotle and Aquinas are wrong to make the passions the subjects. Scotus rejects Aristotle's view that (as Averroes remarks) assigns the virtues to the sensory appetite rather than to the will (*3Sent. d33* q1 = OO vii 2, 696 §1 = W 318). This is also the view of Aquinas (*ST* 1–2 q56 a4). Such a view seems to leave out the essential role of the will.

Though he rejects the view that he ascribes to Aristotle, Scotus also believes that Aristotle sometimes treats the will as the subject of the virtues. He mentions some plausible Aristotelian reasons: (1) Virtue is a state involving election, which is a product of the will. (2) Virtue is the origin of praiseworthy actions, which must proceed from the will. Scotus assumes that voluntary actions and states depend on the will, and that states and actions are praiseworthy in so far as they are voluntary. (3) The object of virtue is the right (or 'fine'; bonum honestum), which is the intrinsic object of the will (*3Sent. d33* q1 = OO vii 2, 696 §2 = W 320). Aristotle connects the pursuit of the right with the rational part (e.g. *EN* 1169a3–6). Since he insists that the virtuous person elects what is right for its own sake, he seems to attribute the characteristically virtuous attitude to the will.

These are good reasons for treating the will as essential to moral virtue. They rest so firmly on Aristotelian principles that neither Aristotle nor Aquinas could reasonably reject them. Scotus is justified in claiming that Aristotle's explicit account does not reflect the importance of the will in virtue. Moreover, Aquinas does not completely correct Aristotle. On the one hand, he agrees that the subject of a state that is to be called a virtue without qualification is the will or some other capacity in so far as it is moved by the will (1-2 q56 a3);[1] hence a virtue must be either in the will itself or in some capacity that is moved by the will. On the other hand, he denies that the will is the subject of bravery and temperance. He allows only that it is the subject of virtues aiming at some external good, directed towards God or one's neighbour (q56 a6c; ad3).

Some of Scotus' arguments expose this internal difficulty in Aquinas. He does not rely on voluntarist claims about the will that Aquinas rejects, but he explains why Aquinas' views about the will should make the will a subject of the moral virtues (*3Sent.* d33 q1 = OO vii 2, 702 §13 = W 332). Scotus argues that every moral virtue requires a good habituated state in the will no less than in the sensory desires. Since Aquinas gives inadequate reasons for assigning some of the virtues to the passions and some to the will,[2] he should amend his view so as to give a larger role to will, in contrast to passion, in the moral virtues.

373. Intellect, Will, and Virtue

Some of Scotus' other objections to Aquinas, however, are more strongly voluntaristic. He rejects not only passions but also intellect as the subject of the moral virtues. Aquinas agrees with him in denying that intellect is the subject, but Scotus draws a more extreme conclusion from this point. He believes that if we place virtue in the intellect, we make vice a matter of ignorance, so that virtue and vice will not be open to praise and blame. Against this position, he defends the view that he attributes to Augustine, ascribing virtues to the direction of an agent's 'love', and therefore to the will.[3]

He argues, therefore, against the view that virtue consists in correct reason.[4] If this view were right, the will would be passive in relation to the intellect; hence (Scotus infers) we would not be blameworthy, since our errors could be traced back to cognitive mistake or ignorance.[5] If a mistaken choice of the will results from ignorance of the good, the will did not choose freely, and therefore we cannot be blamed for the choice. Since we are praised and blamed for virtue and vice, virtue and vice must belong fundamentally to a will that does not necessarily follow practical reason. If the will necessarily followed practical reason, it would not warrant praise or blame, and so would not be the subject of virtue and vice.

The view that Scotus attributes to his opponents is more extreme than Aquinas' view. Aquinas does not claim that knowledge is all that is needed for virtue. He argues that we must also be turned towards the right ends, and that therefore virtue requires a good state of the passions (1-2 q56 a4 ad4). Since the passions present some goods to us in an especially attractive way, we can be diverted from our conviction about what is best by the particular attractions offered by the passions. Since Aquinas does not suggest that every error is purely cognitive, he does not hold a purely intellectualist view of virtue.

---

[1] See §290.   [2] Walter of Bruges criticizes Aquinas on this point. See Kent, *VW* 66.

[3] On Augustine see §218.

[4] He denies that 'it suffices <for virtue> that reason presents <the object> correctly, and therefore virtue is needed in reason, not in the will' (*3Sent.* d33 q1 schol. = OO vii 2, 698 §5 = W 324).

[5] '...then reason would have to go wrong first in presenting <the object> before the will elected badly, and thus there would be an error in the intellect before the first sin of the will. This is unreasonable; for in that case the punishment would precede the crime' (*3Sent.* d33 q1 schol. = OO vii 2, 698 §5 = W 324–6). This proposition (si ratio recta, et voluntas recta) about the primacy of intellect was condemned in 1277. See Prop. 130 (Piché, *CP* 118).

None the less, if we have a clear and firm grasp of the greater good, that greater good, according to Aquinas, is what we choose. Since Aquinas believes that the will follows the intellect's conception of the good, he believes that in this respect the intellect is prior to will, so that in this respect the will is not primary in moral virtue. If the true grasp of the good is the source of virtue, failure to be virtuous must result from an imperfect grasp of it. In Aquinas' view, the imperfect grasp is not always the result of ignorance; in some cases, the will is 'clouded' by the passions, though it is not forced to consent to them. Even when our imperfect grasp of the end results from ignorance, we may be responsible, since the ignorance may be culpable.[6]

From a voluntarist point of view, these attempts to hold us responsible for our imperfect grasp of the end are unsatisfactory. First, we may ask why the will consents to the erroneous suggestions of the passions. Its error in consenting must apparently be explained either by ignorance or by negligence. But negligence must be explained by ignorance or by the influence of passions, which we are still trying to understand. Moreover, ignorance itself does not merit blame; if it is to be blameworthy, the ignorance must be the result of some blameworthy omission or negligence; but what makes this blameworthy? If we appeal to the passions again, we seem to be embarked on an infinite and vicious regress.

We embark on this regress if we assume that responsibility is to be explained wholly by reference to the causation of the state or action, and that this causation must involve the transmission of responsibility from some subject that is more fundamentally responsible. Eventually we need to describe fundamental responsibility.[7] Aquinas disappoints us here, since the causal sequences he traces for us seem to leave us with our original question about fundamental responsibility still unanswered. Dissatisfaction with this result leads naturally into a voluntarist account of fundamental responsibility.

This is Scotus' account. He argues that passion and ignorance are not sources of blameworthy error, and that only the will is fundamentally responsible. An erring will need not be misled by the attractiveness of some object of the passions, and it need not be ignorant. Even if it is fully informed about the better, it may none the less choose the worse. This fundamental level of responsibility neither allows nor needs further explanation.

The difficulties that face a voluntarist account of the will, however, also cast doubt on this fundamental responsibility. If we cannot stop with ignorance or passion because we still need an explanation of our ignorance or of our consent to the passion, we equally seem to need some explanation of the choice made by the will. But voluntarism seems to preclude any explanation of the choice. If the appeal to ignorance or passion is unsatisfactory, the appeal to the will, as conceived by a voluntarist, seems equally unsatisfactory.

Aquinas, therefore, ought not to agree that the cause of responsible action is something that we are more fundamentally responsible for. He ought to argue that we look for the sort of causal origin that will make it appropriate and fair to praise and to blame the agent. Praise and blame look forward, since they seek to modify the agent. They also look backwards, since they presuppose that the agent was open to praise and blame in choosing to behave one way or another, and therefore that he could reasonably have been expected to take account of these consequences when he decided what to do.[8]

---

[6] See §262.   [7] See Strawson, FB 48–50.

[8] This retrospective aspect of praise and blame distinguishes them from the mere attempt to change someone's behaviour in the future; it is also needed to justify the infliction of punishment in cases where future reform is not to be expected.

Aquinas' description of the influence of the passions and of the role of the will supports the claim that agents are open to the influence of praise and blame, and so are justifiably praised or blamed for choosing one way or the other. Praise and blame appeal to the agent as being rational and capable of modifying his choices as a result of considering what is best all things considered. If we recognize the influence of passions, and also recognize the decisive role of the will, we can modify our actions by consideration of the overall good. We need not be most fundamentally responsible for the action or state that causes us to be deliberately ignorant or negligent; it is only necessary to show that when we are in this state we are open to the sorts of rational considerations that belong to praise and blame.

This defence of Aquinas raises doubts about Scotus' specifically voluntarist reasons for believing that the will is the subject of virtue. Even if virtue is praiseworthy, knowledge and ignorance may be a basis of responsibility. And even if a firm and clear conviction of what is best necessarily results in the corresponding action, the will may still be a subject of virtue.

Scotus' basic disagreement with Aquinas, therefore, is not about whether the will is the subject of the moral virtues, but about the sense in which we should understand this claim. If we were to agree that the will is the subject of these virtues, but we maintained Aquinas' intellectualist conception of the will, Scotus would still believe that we had failed to explain how we exercise our freewill in virtue and vice, and therefore how we are responsible for our actions and characters.

374. Universal Conscience

Since, therefore, Scotus believes that the subject of moral virtue is the will, understood as the voluntarist understands it, he rejects those aspects of Aquinas' account of the virtues that rest on assumptions derived from Aquinas' intellectualism and eudaemonism. These assumptions are prominent at different places in Aquinas' doctrine of practical reason. The ultimate principles of practical reason, grasped by universal conscience, refer to the final good and what is required of a rational agent who pursues it. The principles grasped by universal conscience necessarily move the will once they are grasped, since they show us what is required for our happiness. The subordinate principles of natural law are not grasped by universal conscience and do not necessarily move the will, because some people do not recognize their connexion with happiness. These people go wrong because negligence, ignorance, passion, or bad upbringing makes them unaware of, or inattentive to, the connexion between (say) the different precepts of the Decalogue and the ultimate end.

Since Scotus rejects the conception of the will that underlies Aquinas' doctrine of practical reason, he rejects Aquinas' account of the relation between universal conscience, prudence, and motivation. In his view, the recognition of a connexion between a particular action (or state of character) and one's ultimate good is not sufficient for the choice of that action; we are free to reject happiness either for something better or for something worse. Hence the explanation for failure to follow the requirements of the moral law cannot simply be failure to see the connexion between these requirements and one's own happiness; it must also be possible to exercise one's freewill in rejecting happiness. Nor can recognition of the connexion between a particular action and one's own happiness be the appropriate motive for the virtuous person's choice of that action; that motive is inappropriate for those virtues that require us to be moved by the affection for the just.

Scotus, therefore, alters Aquinas' claims to fit a voluntarist position. Intellect grasps the first principles of morality, but they do not necessarily move the will, since the will is free and is not necessarily moved in one or the other direction by what intellect discovers (*2Sent.* d39 q2 = OO vi. 2, 1018–19 §3 = W 200–2). An undetermined choice of the will is needed to determine whether it will follow our natural inclination to justice.

Universal conscience tells us what is just. In doing what it tells us, we follow our affection for justice rather than our affection for advantage (*2Sent.* d39 q2 = OO vi 2, 1021 §5 = W 202 [ad 2]). This answer is similar to Scotus' treatment of the desire for happiness. He admits that we have a natural inclination towards happiness (*4Sent.* q49 d10 = OO x 513 §6 = W 190), and agrees that most of the time the will chooses to follow this; but he denies that the will necessarily pursues happiness, and insists that it freely chooses whether or not to follow our natural inclination.[9]

According to this strongly voluntarist view, the will freely chooses between the affection for justice and the affection for advantage; once it has chosen justice, it follows the demands of the natural law. The will is not moved by the thought that it is more reasonable to follow the inclination towards justice or the inclination towards advantage; for if that were the basis of the will's choice, it would remain passive towards reason, contrary to Scotus' view.[10]

Scotus' anti-intellectualism gives a clear reason for separating the cognitive from the motive aspects of prudence. Neither Aristotle nor Aquinas treats the operations of prudence as simply theoretical reasoning that may or may not move the agent. Prudence includes a motivational aspect because it begins its deliberation from the agent's desire for happiness, and discovers ways to fulfil that desire. From Aquinas' point of view, someone who grasps all the precepts of prudence but does not act on them has failed to grasp clearly and steadily the connexion between these actions and his own happiness. Scotus denies this link between prudence and motivation, whether prudence tells us about what is required for happiness or about what is required for justice. The information that it gives us must leave the will free to choose one way or another.

Since Scotus applies his voluntarism to practical reason and prudence, he separates the cognitive from the motive element in moral virtues more than Aquinas ever does. If the virtuous person has a good will, and chooses the right actions for the right reasons, will, as opposed to intellect, is the primary element of virtue. Aquinas is not forced into this choice; since both the virtuous and the vicious person aim at happiness, the difference between them reflects their different conceptions of happiness. But if Scotus is right, the virtuous and the vicious person may have the same conception of happiness.

---

[9] Sometimes Scotus, as we have seen, affirms a necessary connexion between the freedom of the will and its affection for justice. In that case, the free will must choose in accordance with the impartial norms of justice. But such a view makes it difficult to maintain that universal conscience belongs entirely to the intellect and has no necessary effect on the will. For if universal conscience discovers what is just by discovering the first principles of natural law, it seems to determine the free will that is determined by the norms of justice.

[10] Cf. §393.

375. Practical Reason and Prudence[11]

Scotus' doubts about Aquinas' eudaemonism, and hence about Aquinas' conception of practical reason and prudence, influence his treatment of the reciprocity of the virtues (RV), and of the horizontal and vertical unity of prudence. In his view, different virtues embody independent ways in which the will can be correct, and independent aspects of prudence belong to the different virtues. Prudence is vertically unified because the prudence belonging to each virtue includes both universal and particular prudence; but it is horizontally divided among the different virtues.

To show that prudence is vertically unified, Scotus assumes that virtue requires not only the acceptance, but also the election, of a specific end. In electing things for their own sakes we are electing them as ends (or as constituents of them). Since election rests on deliberation, the correct election of an end must rest on some deliberative virtue. This deliberative virtue is prudence.[12] Scotus might reasonably connect this claim about grasping the end with Aristotle's conception of a moral virtue as an elective state (*hexis prohairetikê*). The virtuous state is distinguished from others by its tendency to elect specific things for their own sakes. He might reasonably argue that Aristotle's description of a virtue presupposes deliberation resulting in the choice of ends.

A second argument for the vertical unity of prudence rests on the unity of each virtue. This unity depends on the unity of the end 'towards the election of which it primarily inclines us' (*3Sent.* d36 = OO vii 2, 813 §18 = W 408). If there were no prudence prescribing the election of this end, there would be no single end for the virtue to elect. This argument presupposes that virtue involves election of things for their own sakes, and so involves a distinctive pattern of deliberation. This distinctive pattern requires a distinct end, and therefore requires universal prudence.

While Scotus argues on these grounds that virtue is inseparable from both universal and particular prudence, and so defends the vertical unity of prudence, he denies the horizontal unity of prudence, and so denies RV. He claims that Aristotle's account implies the separability of the virtues, because both correct action and correct judgment about the subject-matter of one virtue can be present by themselves, without correct action or judgment on the other virtues.[13] The different virtues are similar to different senses; each may work perfectly well without the others.[14] The state of a perfectly

---

[11] See §394; Adams, 'Connection'. 375

[12] 'Moral virtue always, by a certain natural direction, follows some sort of prudence; now from the election of a particular end, say chastity, a moral virtue is generated. And so some sort of prudence precedes that election' (*3Sent.* d36 = OO vii 2, 813 §18 = W 408).

[13] 'The character of a virtuous act or state needs nothing except conformity to right reason, which is evident from the first chapter of the second book of the Ethics: "A virtue is a state that elects, existing in a mean, determined as a wise person will determine it." But without any agreement of virtues concurring in the same agent, it is possible for there to be such conformity, of state no less than act, to right reason in accordance with which one elects. What is assumed is evident; for one does not elect rightly about the matter of temperance except by right reason preceding and prescribing about such-and-such an object of election; but it is possible for the correct prescription of one virtue to precede without any prescription of reason about the matter of a second virtue' (*3Sent.* d36 = OO vii 2, 787 §5 = W 384).

[14] 'One is not . . . a moral person without qualification unless one has all the virtues, just as one is not a perceiver [sentiens] without qualification unless one has all the senses. But one is none the less perfectly temperate, even if one is less perfectly moral, just as one is not less perfect as a seer or hearer even if one is less perfect as a perceiver' (*3Sent.* d36 = OO vii 2, 793 §9 = W 388).

virtuous person's character is not unified, but simply a conjunction of the different specific virtues.[15]

Even if we allow that the virtues ought to co-operate, we need not accept RV. Perhaps the actions and motives appropriate for each virtue depend partly on the other virtues, so that the virtues do not tread on each other's toes. But we might know enough to avoid conflict with the other virtues even if we lacked the other virtues. If I am painting a room and you are going to polish the floor, I may know that I ought not to splash paint all over the floor because it will make your work more difficult, but I may not know how to polish the floor. Similarly, we may need some principles of universal prudence if our different virtues are to co-operate; but it does not follow that we need universal prudence.

376. The Unity of Prudence: Aquinas against Scotus

Aquinas implicitly rejects both horizontal and vertical separation, in explaining why we need prudence. Virtue requires both doing good actions and acting well (bene operari, ST 1-2 q57 a5), but we do not act well if we depend entirely on other people's deliberation; 'one's own action is not yet completely perfected as far as concerns reason that directs and desire that sets us in motion' (q57 a5 ad2). If we deliberate for ourselves about how to fulfil the specifically virtuous end, but we rely on other people's deliberation to form the specifically virtuous end, our reason and desire are not completely perfected.

Aquinas assumes that virtuous agents can see how different virtues interact, and how they together promote the final good. The requirements of justice, for instance, determine which situations and goals require us to face danger, and so they influence brave people's conception of why they ought to face this danger but not that one. Moreover, the requirements of justice preserve a human community with a specific form of social life that promotes the human good; hence the requirements of justice ought to determine some requirements of bravery.

If Aquinas is right about this, he has an answer to Scotus. Though Scotus points out that some motivational and deliberative aspects of virtue fall short of RV, the aspects that he recognizes do not satisfy Aquinas' demand for perfected desire and reason. Agents who lack universal prudence cannot grasp why these actions are really brave, or why co-operation with other virtues requires these actions; and so, since their own deliberation does not grasp these things, they have to rely on the deliberation of others.

Is Aquinas right, or does his argument about the importance of one's own deliberation and the perfection of one's own reason rest on an absurdly demanding conception of perfect virtue?[16] If he is right, we have less than a complete virtue if we do not see the point of the virtue and the actions it requires, and we do not see how it ought to co-operate with the other virtues. In the Secunda Secundae Aquinas illustrates his claims in his discussion

---

[15] This analogy with the senses might fit virtuous motives as well as virtuous actions. Even if we agree that each virtue requires the right motive, we need not agree that we have the motive appropriate for one virtue if and only if we have the motive appropriate for each of the others. And so, even if we need prudence to give us the right motive for each virtue, we need separable aspects of prudence for the different virtues.

[16] See §§98, 322.

of such virtues as bravery, magnificence, and magnanimity (2-2 qq 123–35).[17] Many of the objections he answers rest on a narrow conception of these virtues. He rejects this narrow conception by an appeal to wider moral principles. These principles explain why a martyr can be as brave as a soldier, and why magnanimity does not conflict with humility (2-2 q129 a3 ad4). We need universal prudence if we are to understand what a particular virtue requires; if we have too narrow a conception of the virtue, we have the virtue imperfectly.[18]

Scotus, therefore, seems to overlook some requirements that are included in the virtues. We do not face these requirements on every occasion; that is why we recognize everyday virtuous acts, and take the virtue of the agent for granted, without demanding everything that Aquinas demands of the virtuous agent. But we should not attend only to easy and everyday cases; states of character are revealed by difficult and testing situations.[19] In these situations Aquinas' requirements are relevant, and the opponents of RV demand too little.[20]

377. Eudaemonism and the Unity of Prudence

Universal prudence, according to Aquinas, aims at achieving the ultimate good, and so must be horizontally unified.[21] Scotus, by contrast, recognizes no common end for all the virtues or for every branch of prudence. For, in his view, the will aims either at the advantageous, if it follows our natural inclination, or at the just, if it exercises its freedom. Since some of the moral virtues aim at the agent's own advantage, and some aim at the advantage of others, some appeal to our affection for advantage, and others appeal to our affection for the just. Scotus recognizes no comprehensive end regulating our tendency to follow these two affections; the will has no further reason for following the affection for the just in some cases and the affection for advantage in other cases.

[17] See §331.

[18] Some more modern examples support Aquinas. The sense of honour that leads some characters in nineteenth-century novels to suppose that insults need to be avenged by duelling, or that gambling debts have to be paid first, or that different standards of fidelity apply to husbands and wives, turn out to rest on misunderstandings of the nature and point of different virtues and their relation. More recently, the assumption that concern for fairness and justice requires exclusive attention to merits and qualifications, narrowly conceived, can be challenged in various ways; one reasonable challenge argues that the assumption rests on a misconception of the nature of the relevant virtues and of their connexion to other virtues and principles. These examples suggest that it is difficult to divide the concerns of particular prudence from those of universal prudence, or the concerns of the moral agent from those of the moral theorist. Aquinas' suggestion that virtuous agents need universal prudence to carry out the correct deliberation does not betray any exaggeration, or any tendency to confuse the agent with the theorist. It would be exaggerated to suggest that a virtuous agent must be able to construct the sort of theory that Aristotle or Aquinas constructs; but it is not exaggerated to suggest that a virtuous agent must grasp (perhaps without formulating) the sorts of considerations that concern the theorist. Aquinas' own discussion of the virtues illustrates this role for universal prudence in influencing the outlook of agents on their virtues.

[19] See Aristotle, EN 1130a1–2; Aquinas, in EN v 2 §909.

[20] We can defend RV against some objections that appeal to historical and psychological counter-examples. To say that virtuous agents must grasp the relations of a particular virtue to other virtues, and must guide their actions by their grasp of those relations, is not to claim that they must display all the virtues to an equal degree, or that their situations require the actions characteristic of all the virtues. People may 'specialize' in different virtues; social and psychological facts may make specialization mandatory or desirable. But we can be specialized in one virtue without ignoring the claims of other virtues; and the demand for virtuous agents to attend to the claims of the different virtues is the central demand that supports RV. RV is exacting, and we cannot take it for granted that even the people conventionally regarded as exemplars of the virtues have actually fulfilled it; but it is neither unrealistic nor unreasonable.

[21] See §324.

Since Scotus rejects eudaemonism, he loses some reasons that convince Aquinas of RV. Aquinas believes that reference to some single comprehensive end is necessary for rational willing. Since Scotus rejects any such condition on rational willing, he denies that the virtuous person's deliberation would be defective if it did not refer to a comprehensive end; and so he has no reason to insist on RV.

If we agree with Aquinas on universal prudence, and accept his suggestion that the aims of the different virtues are connected and mutually supportive, we accept the main assumptions about practical reason that underlie his belief in an ultimate end. Indeed, his belief in an ultimate end simply extends this picture of the virtuous person's reasoning to rational action in general.[22]

Equally, Scotus' view about the connexion between eudaemonism and the reciprocity of the virtues is intelligible in the light of his views about freewill. For if the virtuous person has to see some connexion between the self-regarding and the other-regarding virtues in the light of some end that makes them all reasonable, a will that refuses to choose all or some of them fails to see something that makes them reasonable objects of choice. But this explanation of wrong choice by reference to ignorance is the very sort of explanation that Scotus rejects as inconsistent with the freedom of the will. We may welcome this consequence of Scotus' voluntarism. Alternatively, we may decide that it casts doubt on his account of a free and rational will.

378. Knowledge of Natural Law

Scotus disagrees with Aquinas not only on the connexion between practical reason, prudence, and motivation, but also on the nature of the principles grasped by practical reason. In agreement with Aquinas, he recognizes a natural law that we grasp by natural reason, and he believes that God prescribes the observance of this natural law. But he differs from Aquinas about the extent of the natural law, and about its relation to the will of God. He is less optimistic about the practical guidance we can derive from the higher principles of natural law.

According to Scotus, natural law is relevant to our moral knowledge in three ways: (1) We know that some moral principle is true from its terms, so that it is a first principle corresponding to a first principle of demonstration in theoretical science. (2) A principle follows evidently from a first principle. (3) A principle is said to belong to natural law by extension if it is a practical truth concordant (consonum) with the principles or conclusions of natural law, 'in so far as it is immediately known to all to agree (convenire) with such a law' (4Sent. d17 = OO ix 296–7 §3 = W 262).

We do not need any special revelation to know natural law; it is known by 'natural light'. On this basis we can know all three classes of truths about natural law, and hence we can know, for instance, that monogamy rather than bigamy accords with natural law (4Sent. d33 q1 = OO ix 706 §7 = W 294). Similarly, we can know by the natural light that a guilty person must be judged, because this accords with natural law (4Sent. d17 = OO ix 298 §7 = W 266). Scotus allows that paternal authority is just by natural law, but he denies that

---

[22] See §§271–3.

political authority can claim any title in natural law; it rests on the agreement and choice of the community (*4Sent*. d15 q2 = OO ix 156 §6 = W 314). It seems to follow that political life is not justified by the natural law.

As Scotus explains the natural law, its highest principles do not proceed from the sovereign will of God. Scotus reports other people's view that principles belonging to the law of nature 'possess necessary truth; therefore God cannot make them false' (*3Sent*. d37 = OO vii 2, 857 §1 = W 270).[23] He agrees with this view as far as concerns the first two types of principles; for he agrees that God's intellect by itself, apart from God's will, recognizes principles of the first two types.[24] If, therefore, all the precepts of the Decalogue were of these two types, God's will would not be free to reject them; God would have practical knowledge of moral principles whose rightness is independent of God's will.[25]

Scotus, however, claims that the precepts of the second table of the Decalogue, containing duties towards our neighbour, belong to the third class of principles. Unlike principles in the second class, they do not follow evidently from the first principles. Though they 'agree' with the natural law, they are not required by it.[26] In opposition to the view of Aquinas that all the moral precepts of the Decalogue belong to the natural law, [27] Scotus claims that the second table does not belong to it in the strictest sense. Its precepts are not necessary for achieving the end that is pursued in the natural law.[28]

Gabriel Biel elaborates Scotus' views about the relation of the second table to the natural law. He maintains that it is not strictly part of the natural law, because, as Scotus maintains, it is not necessary for reaching the ultimate end (*3Sent* d37 a2 concl. 3 = W & H 636 M 2). In Biel's view, these precepts are only part of natural law 'construed broadly' (*large accepta*).[29] He follows Scotus in relying on 'consonance' to explain the relation of these precepts to the natural law.[30]

---

[23] These people infer that 'the things that are commanded <in natural law> are not good only because they are commanded, but, on the contrary, it is because they are good in their own right (*secundum se*) that they are commanded' (*3Sent*. d37 = OO vii 2, 878 §2 = W 272).

[24] For any principles of these first two types it would follow that 'God's will would be necessarily determined without qualification about objects of will other than himself' (*3Sent*. d37 = OO vii 2, 879 §4 = W 274).

[25] *3Sent*. d37 q1 sch. = OO vii 2, 879 §4 = W 274. See n41 below.

[26] 'Things are said to belong to the law of nature in another way, because they are highly consonant with that law, even though they do not follow necessarily from the practical first principles that are known from their terms and are necessarily known by every apprehending intellect. And in this way it is certain that all the precepts of the second table as well <as the first> belong to the law of nature, because their rightness is very much consonant with the practical first principles that are necessarily known' (*3Sent*. d37 = OO vii 2, 898 §8 = W 278).

[27] For Aquinas' view see *ST* 1-2 q100 a1, described by Scotus *3Sent*. d37 = OO vii 2, 877–8 §2 = W 272. Cf. §309.

[28] 'For in the things prescribed in it [sc. the second table] there is no goodness that is necessary for <achieving> the goodness of the ultimate end; nor in the things prohibited in it is there evil necessarily turning us away from the ultimate end. Rather, if that good were not prescribed, the ultimate end could <still> be achieved and loved. And if that evil were not prohibited, the achieving of the ultimate end would <still> be consistent with it.' (*3Sent*. d37 = OO vii 2, 898 §5 = W 276). Scotus' views on the natural law are discussed by Crowe, *CPNL*, ch. 7.

[29] 'But that they belong to the law of nature, as commonly construed, is clear because they are highly consonant with that law, even though they do not follow from the first practical principles, which are known from their terms to every understanding and are necessary. For the first precept <of the second table>, the one about honouring one's parents, is highly consonant with this principle: benefits are to be repaid to a benefactor. The other precepts, the negative ones, are consonant with this one: one's neighbour is not to be unjustly condemned' (Biel, *3Sent*. d37 a2 = W&H 637 M 17–21). See Oberman, *HMT* 94. Suarez criticizes Scotus' view at *Leg*. ii 15.6–12. See also Cajetan ad 1-2 q100 a8.

[30] On 'valde consonans' cf. Suarez, *Leg*. ii 19.9, who takes it to mean 'suitable' ('utilem et consentaneum ipsi naturae') rather than 'consistent'.

Scotus and Biel differ from Aquinas on this point. In Aquinas' view, prudence discovers by rational inquiry that principles at this level are required by the law of nature. Even though prudence can discover such principles, the Decalogue was issued because some of them are difficult to discover, partly because of the ingrained tendency to sin. A divine command is needed to make them clear to everyone. Scotus might reasonably point out that Aquinas does not give a very clear account of how prudence discovers these principles. His disagreement about the second table of the Decalogue may rest partly on doubts about Aquinas' claims on behalf of prudence, and especially universal prudence.

379. Divine Commands and Natural Law

If Scotus is right, we cannot reach the precepts of the second table of the Decalogue by deliberation about means to the ultimate end. Greater insight into the requirements of the natural law and greater knowledge of the circumstances of human life cannot close the gap between the principles of natural law and requirements at the level of the second table.[31]

Scotus infers that the precepts of the second table are aspects of divine positive law expressing commands of God. A peaceful social life does not require a positive law prescribing private property, because we could achieve a peaceful social life by other means.[32] God specifies the natural law, not through practical knowledge of what it requires, but through a free choice of how it is to be applied.

This treatment of the moral principles of the Decalogue leaves room for dispensations.[33] Scotus agrees with Aquinas' view that the provisions of the natural law itself are indispensable. But he believes that the second table of the Decalogue goes beyond the natural law, strictly speaking, and that its precepts are dispensable. Contrary to Aquinas, Abraham's willingness to sacrifice Isaac is not justified by the natural law, but is permissible only because of a dispensation; God decides that Abraham need not obey the moral principle that we are usually required to obey. Though Abraham's intended action is murder, God does not require him to refrain from intending murder in this case. Since the specific prohibition on intending murder is not required by the natural law, but is a command of God, intending murder is wrong only because it violates a command of God. If, therefore, God commands us to commit a murder, he makes murder permissible in this case.[34] God is free to dispense from the general rules because they are the result of God's choice.

---

[31] Scotus' views on the natural law were among the 'rash opinions' of his that were attacked by a 'doctorum theologiae multitudo' (according to Du Plessis d'Argentré). Scotus (with Biel and Almain) is taken to claim that 'the things prohibited in the second table of the Decalogue (including lying) are not bad in their own right'. His critics maintain that all injustice against one's neighbour is immutably bad 'propter ipsam rationem connexi cum sapientia Dei et iustitia' (*Iohannis Duns Scoti temerariae opiniones*, §10, in Du Plessis, *CJNE* i. 289–90). See Oberman, *DR* 207.

[32] 'And this is how it is perhaps in all cases of positive rights (iuribus positivis), because, granted that there is some one principle that is the foundation in establishing all these laws or rights (leges sive iura), still the positive laws do not follow necessarily without qualification from that principle; rather, they clarify (declarant) that principle or explain it (explicant) as far as it applies to certain particular cases; and these explanations are very much in accord with the universal first principle' (*3Sent.* d37 Schol. §190 = OO vii 2, 898–9 = W 280).

[33] On the difference between dispensations and exceptions see §314.

[34] 'What belongs secondarily to the law of nature is what is regularly consonant with the law of nature spoken of in the primary way. About the first [type of precept of natural law] no dispensation applies, and therefore its opposite seems to be invariably a mortal sin. About the second a dispensation applies in a case in which the opposite seems to be commonly consonant with the law of nature' (*4Sent.* d33 q1 = OO ix 706 §7 = W 294).

Biel is less permissive than Scotus. He argues that though God could dispense from the precepts of the second table, God chooses not to dispense from them, because their consonance with natural law makes them so close to it.[35] Though Biel does not allow actual dispensations, he agrees with Scotus that God is free to dispense from these precepts, because God is sovereign over them.[36]

This affirmation of God's power of dispensation differs from Aquinas' appeal to God's insight into the requirements of the natural law. Aquinas denies that the natural law is dispensable. Since it prescribes what suits human nature, God cannot want to violate it or to permit others to violate it. He can, however, act on his understanding of why the natural law requires Abraham to be ready to sacrifice Isaac. In Scotus' view, God is not bound by any requirement of the natural law. Since he imposed the prohibition on murder, he is also free to dispense from it.

380. Natural Law and the Will of God

The objections to Aquinas that we have considered so far do not rely on voluntarism. Even if we agreed with Aquinas' conception of the will, we might share Scotus' doubts about the derivation of specific precepts from the higher principles of natural law. These doubts arise from Aquinas' claim that if we consider 'the law of our nature', and what is naturally suitable for creatures with our nature, we can find some rational basis for accepting some specific moral and social precepts over others.

In appealing to natural law as the source of such precepts, Aquinas maintains the demand for external reasons that we have found to be central in his conception of freedom. If we appeal to natural law, we appeal to some reason that rests on what we are and what is suitable for us. This reason is external to what particular rational agents want, and so we exercise freedom in examining our desires in relation to this external reason. Aquinas' intellectualist conception of freedom imposes conditions that he seeks to satisfy through his conception of practical reason and natural law.

If we accepted this intellectualist conception of freedom, and rejected Aquinas' optimism about deriving precepts from the higher principles of natural law, we would have to recognize that our freedom is limited at this level, or else we would have to find some rational standard distinct from our nature. To recognize that some appeal to something other than our nature must enter at this stage, however, is compatible with accepting the rest of Aquinas' conception of the will.

But a voluntarist must reject Aquinas' account of the relation of God's will to the natural law. If we suppose that God creates the world, defines the natural law, and speaks through the prophets and the Scriptures, because God recognizes that this is best, we seem to deprive God of freewill, as the voluntarist understands it. Some of the reasons for this voluntarist

---

[35] 'Though God as legislator could, without qualification, dispense by relaxation of the precept, in relation to the observance of the precepts of the second table, still God does not dispense in this way in fact, because of their great closeness to the law of nature properly so called' (*3Sent.* d37 a2 concl. 5 = W&H 637 N 1–5).

[36] Among later Scotists Poncius, *PMSCI* 366, affirms the possibility and the actuality of dispensations. He argues that Abraham and so on really violated the natural law.

objection apply to God in the same way as they apply to human wills; just as we are free not to observe the natural law even if practical reason prescribes it to us, God must also be free not to observe it.

Other reasons for the voluntarist objection apply particularly to God. God differs from a human agent in being omnipotent. Intellectualists and voluntarists agree about this, but they do not agree on the relevant conditions for omnipotence. From a voluntarist point of view, an intellectualist conception of God's will limits God's power. If God responds to external reasons in the same way as we do, their influence on God seems to limit divine power. The doctrine of divine omnipotence seems to support a voluntarist account of the freedom of the divine will.

381. God's Justice

Some of Scotus' disagreements with Aquinas' views on practical reason are closely connected with these voluntarist claims about God. If he agreed with Aquinas about the derivation of practical precepts, while still maintaining voluntarism, the results would be unwelcome. The principles of the natural law, according to Aquinas, support the precepts of justice, because they show that the precepts of justice are best all things considered; but, according to the voluntarist, God is free to reject what is best all things considered; hence God is free to violate the precepts of justice. Since it is possible for God to do what he is free to do, it is possible for God to violate the precepts of justice.

Scotus rejects this conclusion; for he agrees with Anselm's claim that only what God wills is just and what God does not will is not just (*4Sent.* d46 q1 §8 = OO x 252 §8 = W 246). Anselm does not affirm a voluntarist interpretation of this claim. On the contrary, he argues that since God is just, and it is just to give both the good and the bad what they deserve, God must give both the good and the bad what they deserve. Similarly, he argues that God's justice must give rise to mercy because that is just.[37] Scotus agrees that Anselm's claim about God's necessarily willing what is just expresses a necessary truth about God's will.

If Anselm is right, and Aquinas is right about the natural basis of precepts of justice, God is not free to violate the precepts of justice. A voluntarist, however, cannot accept Aquinas' explanation of how God necessarily wills what is just. Aquinas makes knowledge of justice part of God's nature, so that from the voluntarist point of view, God is not free, since the choice of moral principles is not left entirely to God's will.

Scotus, therefore, interprets Anselm's claim so that it fits voluntarism. He treats justice as the result of God's choice, undetermined by any knowledge of what is best.[38] Just as the

---

[37] Anselm, *Proslogion* 11: 'For the one who rewards the merits of both the good and the bad is more just than the one who rewards the merits of the good alone. It is just, therefore, in relation to (secundum) you, just and benevolent God, both when you punish and when you spare. . . . For only what you will is just, and what you do not will is not just. In this way therefore your mercy arises from your justice, because it is just for you to be good in such a way that you are good in sparing.'

[38] 'The divine will is not inclined determinately through anything within itself towards any secondary object in such a way that it would be inconsistent for it to incline to the opposite object to that one, because just as the divine will can will the opposite without contradiction, so it can will it justly; otherwise it could without qualification will something and not will it justly, which is inappropriate' (*4Sent.* d46 q1 §8 = OO x 252 §8 = W 246).

legal is defined by the decision of the legislator, the just is defined by the decision of God the legislator. This is why God cannot act unjustly and cannot instruct us to violate justice.[39]

God's relation to justice is different, therefore, from the relation of a human will to justice. Scotus believes (in some of his comments, at least) that we have freewill because we are capable of rejecting the affection for justice. God, however, is incapable of rejecting it; his freedom consists in following the affection for justice. Scotus sometimes implies that this is true of human wills as well, though he cannot easily reconcile this claim with his voluntarism.[40] But he affirms unequivocally that the divine will is necessarily just. In the divine will, however, adherence to the affection for justice does not constrain the content of the willing as it does in a human will; for Scotus believes that whatever God freely wills is just in so far as God wills it. A human will guided by an affection for justice is guided by impartial rational standards, but God acts justly whatever standard God follows or violates.

These claims about divine and human justice form a consistent position. A human will follows justice by following an impartial rational standard because that is the standard that God has chosen to follow. But since God's choice establishes impartial rationality as the standard of justice, God's own will cannot be related to it in the same way as a human will.

We may find it difficult to reconcile this account of justice with our belief that justice essentially has some more definite content. According to Scotus, if God had chosen to treat human beings completely capriciously, without reference to their merits, their desert, or their nature, that treatment would have been just. Our belief that treatment in accordance with one's nature is just reflects our knowledge of the secondary principle of justice that rests on God's undetermined choice. God retains the power to alter secondary principles and to replace them with others that would be equally just (1Sent. d44 q1 sch. = OO v 2, 1368–9 §§1–2 = W 256).[41] Our beliefs about the content of justice do not tell us what justice requires in all possible worlds; they tell us only about the situation that is maintained by God's 'directed' (or 'ordered', ordinata) power, not about the situations that are possible within God's unqualified (absoluta) power.[42]

If we supposed that it would be unjust for God to treat us in ways that conflict with our nature, we would be assuming that God has a duty (debitum) towards us. But Scotus denies that God has any duties towards us. Since God does not owe (debere) us anything, God cannot violate any duty.[43] The fact that God treats us in accordance with our nature is an expression of God's generosity, but it does not fulfil God's duty of justice, since God has no such duty.[44] God is not bound to do anything except to love his own goodness. Treatment in accordance with one's nature is recognized as just by the creature; but God makes it just

---

[39] This issue returns in Shaftesbury's criticism of voluntarism. See Sens. Comm. 3.4 = Char. i 123 = 57 K.

[40] See §364.

[41] 'If, before the act of divine will, the divine understanding could have such knowledge, it would have it purely naturally and necessarily, because all knowledge that precedes the act of will is purely natural, and through its essence, as is the purely natural character (ratio) of understanding. Of necessity therefore it would know that this is to be done, and then the <divine> will, to which <the understanding> presents it, could not fail to will it, because in that case it could fail to be correct, because a will that can disagree with practical reason can fail to be correct' (1Sent. d38 q1 schol §2 = OO v 2, 1286) The text at V vi 305 is slightly different.

[42] On potentia ordinata v. absoluta see §396.   [43] On debitum and obligatio in Aquinas see §303.

[44] 'He owes something to creatures out of his generosity, to share among them what their nature demands; for this demand in them is taken as something just, as a sort of secondary object of that [primary] justice. Still in truth nothing is both determinately just and outside God, except in a qualified way, namely with this modification, as far as a creature is

out of generosity, having chosen to treat creatures in accordance with their nature. It was God's free choice, independent of any antecedent requirements of justice, to create us and to treat us in accordance with our nature. If God had chosen differently, God would have been no less good and no less just; for what counts as just is the result of God's choice.

Scotus, therefore, rejects Aquinas' views about practical reason and natural law. If practical reason were able to derive specific precepts of justice from natural law, the content of justice would be fixed (to this extent) by natural reason, and if God chose to follow different precepts, God would choose to violate justice, contrary to Anselm's principle. Scotus denies that practical reason can find precepts of justice, because he denies that we can argue from the higher principles to specific precepts. The content of precepts of justice depends on the free choice of God.

We can now understand the connexion between Scotus' voluntarism and his doubts about practical reason. While he could have maintained a consistent voluntarist position together with Aquinas' views on practical reason, such a view would have required him to maintain that it is possible for God to violate justice. To maintain a version of voluntarism that denies this possibility, he needs to limit the scope of prudence.

382. Consonance with Natural Law

Has Scotus reached a satisfactory conclusion about the ways in which God's commands determine the content of precepts of justice? In his view, secondary principles, including the precepts of justice, are not required by the higher principles of natural law. Hence he claims that the precepts of the second table of the Decalogue are not necessarily connected with the final good.[45] What does he mean?

We might take him to mean that the natural law never requires (for instance) truthfulness rather than lying, so that, even if all the circumstances of a given action are taken into account, lying is never contrary to the higher precept requiring love of God and one's neighbour. On this view, both truthfulness and lying are equally consistent with natural law, just as driving on the right and on the left are equally consistent with it. It is up to God to decide whether truthfulness is to be prescribed as a general rule, just as it is up to a legislator to decide on the rule of the road. Equally, it is up to God to dispense from that general rule in particular cases, just as a legislator might choose to allow some vehicles (such as bicycles or trams) to travel on the opposite side to other vehicles.

But this interpretation does not fit Scotus' claim that some specific secondary principles are 'highly consonant' with the primary principles of natural law. In saying that some rules are highly consonant with natural law, he seems to mean that their observance promotes

concerned. What is just without qualification is only what is related to the primary justice, because, that is to say, it has actually been willed by the divine will' (*4Sent* d46 q1 = OO x 253 §12 = W 252–4).

[45] 'The reasons (*rationes*) of the things that are prescribed or prohibited there are not unqualifiedly necessary practical principles or unqualifiedly necessary conclusions. For in the things prescribed there is no goodness necessary towards the goodness of the ultimate end, turning us towards the ultimate end, nor in the things prohibited is there badness necessarily turning us away from the ultimate end. Rather, if that good thing were not prescribed, the ultimate end could be loved and achieved, and if that bad thing were not prohibited, the acquiring of the ultimate good would be compatible with (*staret cum*) it' (*3Sent.* d37 q1 = OO vii 2, 898 §5 = W 276).

its aims better than other action would. Hence the prohibitions of lying and stealing are not simply consistent with natural law, but very much in accord with it (*3Sent*. d37 = OO vii2, 899 §8 = W 280). The requirements of the natural law show that truthfulness rather than lying is generally, though not always, more in accordance with it.

Scotus, therefore, concedes something to those who take the secondary principles to be independent of God's legislative will. For the fact that truthfulness is more consonant with the primary principles of natural law is not a result of God's legislation. The primary principles are not fixed by God's free choice, and their content, rather than God's choice, determines what is more or less consonant with them. Scotus sees a role for God's choice, however, in the fact that these rules should not always be observed. They are highly consonant, but not required, because sometimes we ought not to follow them. In claiming that some rules derived from the common principles of natural law should not always be observed, Scotus agrees with Aquinas (*ST* 1-2 q94 a4).[46] He infers that on the occasions when we ought not to observe the highly consonant rules, God freely dispenses us from their observance. Hence, in his view, the secondary principles are not required by natural law, but are fixed by God's choice.

But this is a puzzling conclusion. Scotus seems to argue that if a given secondary principle is not required by natural law, it depends on God's free choice and God can dispense us from observing it. But how can it be up to God to choose the secondary principles, if some courses of action are especially consonant with nature and the higher principles? Scotus concedes that even though the correct secondary principles do not follow necessarily from the higher principles, rational inquiry can discover their special consonance with the higher principles. In that case God should have practical knowledge of the secondary principles, contrary to Scotus' view. Since practical reason can establish them, God could not reject them without willing injustice.

If some secondary principles are especially consonant with the higher principles, the fact that they have exceptions may not help Scotus. He assumes that exceptions are dispensations, depending on the authoritative legislative will of God, rather than exceptions discoverable by practical reason.[47] But it is difficult to agree with him. If we can discover by practical reason that a general rule is consonant with the law of nature, we should also be able to discover by practical reason the exceptions to the general rule that are consonant with the primary aim of the rule. If natural law is necessarily connected to the human good, the principles about the human good that tell us what is usually in accord with natural law should also tell us that the usual provisions have exceptions and why these are reasonable exceptions to make. When Aristotle discusses equity, he suggests that exceptions to a generalization are to be justified by the principles underlying the generalization (Aristotle, *EN* 1137b11–24).[48]

But if Scotus were to say this, he could not claim that God exercises freedom in dispensing us from the natural law; he would have to claim that God's superior practical knowledge sees appropriate grounds for recognizing exceptions to general rules.[49] If breaking this promise

---

[46] See §318.   [47] See §§314, §379.

[48] See also Suarez on the difference between the principle and the formulations of it, *Leg.* ii 13.6.

[49] Wolter's account of dispensations, *DSWM* 26–7, seems to explain them by appeal to God's practical knowledge; that is why 'they are something the human mind did figure out, or might have, if emotions did not blind one's reason' (26). Boler, 'Psychology' 44–56 discusses Scotus' claims about commands and dispensations in detail.

here and now is more consonant with the natural law than keeping this promise would be, God's permission to break this promise does not dispense us from the natural law; for it is based on the wise recognition that the natural law supports breaking rather than keeping this promise. If God is not free to reject natural law, God is not free to reject the rule that is more in accordance, either in general or in a particular case, with natural law. The second table of the Decalogue, then, does not consist of laws that God is free to change or to dispense us from in particular cases; it is guided by aims and principles that are independent of God's legislation.

In that case, the admission that correct precepts of justice are especially consonant with natural law creates serious difficulties for Scotus.[50] It would be easier for him to defend his claims about the role of God's free choice if he held that both monogamy and polygamy, both respect for human life and committing murder, are equally consonant with the primary principles. If he took this view, he could say that only God's legislation makes respect for human life more consonant with the natural law. He would then reconcile his views about the natural law with his claim that God is free to do anything that does not involve a contradiction and that everything God is free to do would be right and just if he were to choose to do it.[51]

Perhaps the conflicting tendencies in Scotus' claims about secondary principles can be explained by an ambiguity in his claim that observance of these principles is not necessary for achieving the final good. This claim might mean two things: (1) We can achieve the final good even if we violate these rules in every case. (2) We can achieve the final good even if we violate them in some cases. The second claim, but not the first, allows us to believe that the rules are highly consonant with natural law. The first claim, but not the second, allows us to believe that God exercises free choice in prescribing the observance of these rules and in dispensing us from it.

Since some of Scotus' claims seem to depend on the first interpretation of his claim about non-necessity and some seem to depend on the second, and since the two interpretations are incompatible, his position seems to be unstable. The claims about consonance moderate his voluntarism. But if they conflict with the voluntarist claims he accepts, they suggest that his version of voluntarism is difficult to maintain.

383. Biel on Consonance and Dispensations

Some of the difficulties in Scotus' position become clearer if we consider Biel's efforts to explain what we know in knowing that a subordinate precept is 'consonant' with natural law. Biel includes among things 'naturally known' as part of natural law both the necessary consequences of the principles and the non-necessary consequences that are 'very consonant'

---

[50] Contrast Wolter, *DSWM* 24, 59, 71. It is not clear that the position he ascribes to Scotus is consistent.

[51] On the second table of the Decalogue see Prentice, 'Contingent', who explains the non-necessity of the second table by arguing that these precepts are not strictly necessary in all circumstances for achieving the ultimate end. But it is difficult to see what this means. It would be relatively simple to argue that God could have placed us in circumstances where we could have done without private property. But this would only show that, given the nature of the human good, different arrangements are required in different circumstances. That does not necessarily increase divine freedom in dispensing from the requirements of the second table.

(multum consona) with the principles, and therefore form subordinate precepts. Private property, for instance, is not necessary for a political community, since people might maintain peace even if they had everything in common. But private property 'is highly consonant' with peaceful living among individuals with human weaknesses. For such people take better care of private assets than of public, and are prone to struggle for the possession of public assets (*3Sent.* d37 q1 a1 not. 2 F = 631.1–15).

If this is Biel's conception of what is consonant with the principles of natural law, consonance is more than consistency. A consonant precept also tends to promote the end prescribed by the principle. Private property is not simply one means to secure peace; it is usually the best way, though in some circumstances some other arrangement might be as good or better.

It is difficult to see how principles that are consonant with natural law in this sense are dispensable. In the usual circumstances, private property (let us suppose) advances peace better than common possession would. In those circumstances, then, the abandonment of private property would violate natural law, by frustrating the end of the precept. Similarly, the precepts against murder and theft do not seem to be dispensable in most cases. But in the circumstances where the observance of these precepts would violate the end of the relevant higher principles, we ought not to avoid murder and theft; murder or theft seems to be not only allowed but even required by natural law. It is only in the circumstances where the observance and the violation of the rule equally fulfil natural law that both observance and violation of the rule might reasonably be permitted. But in such circumstances we do not seem to need anyone's permission; we only need the reasonable belief that both actions are permissible.

Given Biel's conception of the subordinate principles as highly consonant with the higher principles, it is reasonable for him to understand dispensations more narrowly than Scotus understands them. The only two types of dispensation that he allows are the revocation of a law and its clarification (631 G 1–4) He rejects dispensations that would give permission to violate a precept without revoking it. This last kind of dispensation is the kind that Scotus and Ockham seem to allow; hence Biel does not seem to agree with them about what dispensations are possible.

Even within the range of dispensations that he allows Biel is quite restrictive. He argues that the precepts of the second table are not part of natural law in a strict sense, but only in a broad sense (636–7, M 1–21). They do not follow necessarily, or from the meaning of the terms, or from the principles that strictly belong to natural law, but are said to belong to natural law because of their consonance with the higher principles (637 M 17–21). Biel claims that these principles are dispensable, in the sense that God could dispense us from their observance; he mentions Abraham's willingness to kill Isaac and Hosea's marrying a prostitute as examples to prove that God has the relevant power. None the less, he argues, these precepts are not in fact subject to dispensation, because God does not exercise his power to dispense from them. God refrains from actual dispensation because these principles are consonant with the strict law of nature (637 N 1–4).

This is a puzzling conclusion. It would be intelligible if Biel were to deny that God dispenses from these precepts in the sense that Biel mentions and sets aside—giving permission to violate them, while leaving them standing. It is also reasonable for him to reject dispensations in the first sense he allows, by revoking the precept altogether. But it is more difficult to see why he rejects dispensations of the sort that clarify the import of the law and the intention of the legislator. The general consonance of the precept with natural law does not seem a good reason for refusing to point out that in these circumstances observance of the precept does not promote the end of the higher precept. In such cases, we might suppose, we are not simply allowed, but even required, to point out that observance of the precept does not promote the end of a higher precept. Perhaps Biel has a more indirect argument in mind, claiming that because of the general benefit of following a rule we ought not to weaken respect for it by violating it even on the occasions when violation would have better results. But he offers no such argument for rejecting dispensations.

Biel's reflexions on dispensations are instructive. He agrees with Scotus and Ockham in allowing possible dispensations from precepts that belong to natural law only by being consonant with its higher principles. But he finds their arguments for actual dispensations unsatisfactory, and so confines himself to claims about possible dispensation. He is also dissatisfied with their account of a dispensation, and rejects the possibility of dispensations that give permission to violate a precept that one recognizes as correct. But after he has narrowed his conception of dispensation, it becomes difficult to see why he rejects actual dispensation.

384. The Extent of God's Freedom

Some of the difficulties that Scotus raises are clearer if we distinguish different things that might or might not be subject to the will of God. Three claims deserve to be considered: (1) Avoiding murder and theft is usually, though not always, good for creatures with our nature. (2) Avoiding murder and theft is usually, though not always, in accordance with natural law. (3) It is usually, though not always, right, to follow the natural law. Different types of voluntarism result from giving God power over the truth or falsity of these three claims.[52]

Scotus does not take God to have power over the first claim. He does not suggest that God's free choice determines what is good for creatures with our nature. When God decided to create two things, no further choice was needed to make more than one thing; God could not both have created two things and refrained from creating more than one thing. This limitation follows from God's lack of freedom to make contradictions true. Similarly, then, although it was God's choice to create human beings, no further choice was needed about what would be good for them. In creating beings with human nature, God created creatures for whom specific things are good.

If God were free in relation to these sorts of choices, Scotus would have to choose between some unappealing explanations of God's freedom. Could there be, without contradiction, creatures with the same nature but different goods? Or could there be, without contradiction,

---

[52] Cf. Wolter, *DSWM* 23–5.

the same creatures with different natures? Or, even if these things are self-contradictory, could God none the less have made them true? Scotus does not seem to be tempted to answer Yes to any of these questions. If he were tempted in any of these directions, he would face serious difficulties about goods, natures, and species, or about the extent of God's power.

If Scotus claims that God's will determines whether the natural law accords with what is good for creatures with our nature, he affirms that the natural law might not have been connected with our good. This claim would be difficult to accept; what would be natural about natural law if it were not connected with what is good for creatures with our nature? Scotus seems to believe that the rules derived from natural law depend on what is good for creatures with our nature. We consider our good in asking which rules are highly consonant with natural law, and the answer to this question depends on practical reason, not on the divine will.

Apparently, then, the most plausible way for Scotus to affirm divine freedom is to maintain that, though natural law makes peace rather than war good for human beings, God is free to violate natural law. Though God cannot (in the sense explained) change natural law, God can, on this view, violate it by ordering us to lie, cheat, steal, and so on indiscriminately. But Scotus rejects this view; he affirms that whatever God wills is just, and therefore in accordance with the natural law, even if it is not in accord with the usual provisions of the natural law.

Scotus does not claim that God is free to change the usual provisions of the natural law, but that God is free to dispense us from them. Hence he allows a necessary connexion, not subject to God's will, between the requirements of the human good and the usual provisions of natural law, but he denies that this necessary connexion eliminates God's power over the natural law. This solution faces the difficulties about consonance that we have noticed.

The same difficulties cast doubt on Scotus' explanation of the view that necessarily whatever God wills is just. In the actual world justice accords with our nature. But the precepts of justice depend on God's will. Hence there is a possible world in which God chooses to treat us in ways that violate our nature, and chooses to command us to treat one another in such ways. In this possible world, such violations of our nature are just, since whatever God wills is just. Moreover, in this possible world, people who understand human nature and justice know what treatment accords with human nature, but do not believe that this treatment is just.

This combination of views is open to doubt. Our knowledge that justice requires treating people in accordance with what is naturally appropriate seems to be similar to our knowledge that temperance requires the proper control of desires for physical pleasure, and that bravery requires the proper control of fear. Scotus does not suggest that God could decide that temperance requires unrestrained indulgence, bravery requires unrestrained fear, friendship requires indifference to the interests of others, and so on. He might say that these suggestions would be self-contradictory, and that God cannot make self-contradictions true. But his claim about justice seems no less self-contradictory than these claims about the other virtues would be.

Scotus might answer this objection by claiming that he is not speaking of justice as simply one virtue among others, but using 'just' to refer to rightness in general. This answer does not seem to fit everything he says; for when he begins the discussion of divine justice, he refers to the Aristotelian virtue. But when he says that whatever God wills is just, he may identify justice with rightness (rectum) generally. He seems to distinguish this sort of justice from the type of justice that prescribes treatment appropriate to the subject.[53] Perhaps he means that if God exercised unqualified power differently, God would act rightly in prescribing intemperance rather than temperance and in prescribing injustice rather than justice.

The difficulty that Scotus faces here results from his voluntarist conception of God's omnipotence, combined with the ethical demand for God to act justly. To make his position consistent, he has to interpret justice as simply the product of God's exercise of unqualified power in preferring one type of requirement over another. But normally he believes that the natural law imposes certain restrictions on the content of acceptable precepts; this is why only some precepts are consonant with natural law. Since these are the precepts that God commands us to observe, the right principles have some content that is not simply the product of God's choice. But once we make this clear, Scotus' claims about God's freedom in relation to the precepts of justice are difficult to accept.

385. God's Promises and God's Generosity

Scotus argues that God's freedom in relation to precepts of justice does not make God arbitrary or capricious; God's goodwill is reliable even though it is not necessary. God's generosity explains how God reliably benefits us even though God is free not to benefit us. When God created us, God freely undertook to follow natural law, which seems to express the same impartial norms as those that appeal to our affection for justice. God undertakes this by making a promise like the promise to Noah (*Gen.* 9:12–17).

But how can we rely on God's undertaking, unless God accepts the principles of right and justice underlying the keeping of promises? But if God already accepts these, must they not already have guided God in creation? If God reliably accepts them, God reliably follows the affection for justice. But it is not necessary that God follows the affection for justice, since God is free; hence God's preference for the affection for justice must result from God's free choice. A choice in favour of the precepts of justice does not seem any less arbitrary if it is supported by a promise.[54] We might suppose that, in Scotus' view, God is necessarily guided by an affection for justice, since it is necessary that whatever he wills is just. But this necessary truth, if understood to fit Scotus' voluntarism, does not commit God to any

---

[53] 'The claim that <the divine will> cannot sometimes act against the second <sort of justice> does not seem defensible (probable) because whatever does not include a contradiction is something that <the divine will> is capable without qualification of doing, and thus of willing. But it cannot will anything that it could not will correctly (recte) because God's will is the primary rule; and so whatever does not include a contradiction God can be understood to will. And so since this secondary justice determines to something whose opposite does not include a contradiction, God can will and will rightly, and act against this secondary justice' (*4Sent.* d46 q1 = OO x 241 §6 = W 244).

[54] A similar question arises for Hobbesian people making a covenant in the state of nature. Cudworth raises this question, supposing that Hobbes faces the difficulties faced by theological voluntarism. See Cudworth, *EIM* i 1.4 = H13.

definite content for justice; in particular, it does not commit him to the aspect of justice that requires the keeping of promises. The objection that God's promises are unreliable still seems to be unanswered.

Biel also combines voluntarism about the will of God with claims about God's generosity and mercy.[55] In justifying us God does not owe us anything. God's treatment of us manifests divine mercy (misericordia), expressing God's indescribable righteousness (ineffabilis iustitia), and not responding to our goodness. Biel relies on the Christian doctrine that God does not justify us because God sees that we are good,[56] but seems to draw the unwarranted conclusion that God does not justify us because God sees that it is the best thing to do.

Truths about divine mercy and generosity do not seem to support voluntarism. Generous people do more, for the right reasons, than justice demands, or they demand less, for the right reasons, than justice allows them to demand. But if they act for the right reasons, they are not indifferent to justice.[57] If, for instance, A threatens harm to an innocent victim B, it is not generous of C to refrain from harming A, if harming A is the only way to prevent harm to B; and if A wants to buy C's gun to harm B, it is not generous of C to give A the gun as a free gift. If we were to call C generous in these cases, we would normally say it was 'misplaced' generosity, to separate it from the virtue of generosity.

If, then, Scotus believes that God is not bound by obligations of justice, but acts out of generosity, he should not ascribe to God a motive independent of justice. He should show that God acts on principles that do even more for us than can be demanded by justice, but in harmony with, and not contrary to, the aims of justice. If, then, God is necessarily generous, God is necessarily guided by the aims of justice. But being necessarily generous seems no less incompatible with divine freedom (as a voluntarist conceives it) than being necessarily just would be. Hence God cannot be necessarily generous, if God is free.

According to Christian doctrine, some of God's actions towards human beings are not owed to them in strict justice, but express God's readiness to do more for us than God could be expected to do in strict justice. But God's willingness to go beyond strict requirements does not mean that God is not guided by what is best all things considered; on the contrary, if an intellectualist is right, God sees that the generous treatment of human beings is better than the merely just treatment of them, and God sees that this generous treatment does not violate the aims of justice, but fulfils them. Attempts to support voluntarism through appeals to the Christian doctrine of divine mercy do not seem to succeed. They do not seem to remove the doubts that Scotus' voluntarism raises about divine goodness. We do not make the voluntarist account of divine freedom any more intelligible by trying to connect it with generosity; it is no more appropriate for generosity than for any other virtue.

---

[55] 'For neither is it because something is good or just that God wills it, but it is because God wills it that it is thereby good and just. For the divine will does not depend on our goodness, but our goodness depends on the divine will, and nothing is good except because God has accepted it as such' (Biel, *Can. Miss. Exp.*, Lect. 23E [= O&C i 212]). See Oberman, *HMT* 96–7. For Luther's view see §411.

[56] On justification see §351.   [57] Cf. Aquinas, *ST* 2-2 q117 a5.

27

OCKHAM

386. Approaches to Ockham

Ockham has become notorious for holding views that, from a later philosophical perspective, have appeared to undermine the Aristotelian outlook that is expounded by Aquinas.[1] This is true in ethics as in other areas of philosophy. Such an approach to Ockham is open to question. Ockham does not affirm the radical consequences that other people draw from him. Moreover, it is not obvious that Aquinas always presents the best account or defence of Aristotle; his opponents may intend to offer a better defence of Aristotle rather than abandon an Aristotelian outlook. It is not always easy to decide what Aristotle means, or how to give Aristotelian answers to questions that arise for his theory. Scotus and Ockham disagree with Aquinas' answers to these questions, but they often believe that Aquinas is wrong about Aristotle as well as about the truth.

Still, it may be reasonable to examine aspects of Scotus or Ockham that suggest more extreme conclusions than they draw. Some aspects of their position may commit them to more than they recognize, and on this point later philosophy may sometimes be a good guide to the interpretation of earlier philosophers. We have illustrated this point in Scotus, especially on freedom and on the natural law. His claims about freedom, the will, and the affection for justice express both a more intellectualist tendency (identifying freedom with the rational affection for justice) and a more voluntarist tendency (identifying freedom with the undetermined capacity to choose either advantage or justice). Similarly, he treats God as partly sovereign over the natural law, but denies that God alters the natural law randomly or arbitrarily; hence he claims that the precepts of the second table of the Decalogue are 'highly consonant' with the natural law, though not required by it. On these and related points, Ockham develops a more strongly voluntarist position; it is useful to see how he answers some questions that Scotus appears to leave unsettled.

Ockham believes he rejects the insufficiently Aristotelian elements in Aquinas and others. He believes, for instance, that Aristotle's rejection of Platonic Forms supports the metaphysical priority of the particular, and that the views of Aquinas and Scotus on universals concede too much to an un-Aristotelian Platonic realism.[2] In moral philosophy

---

[1] See Freddoso in Ockham, *QQ* i, pp. xix–xxi.   [2] See Freddoso in *QQ* p. xx; Adams, *WO*, ch. 2.

Ockham agrees with Scotus' view that Aquinas' intellectualism and eudaemonism conflict with the freedom and contingency of human action. Since Aristotle insists on these features of human action, a plausible defence of Aristotle should, in Ockham's view, reject Aquinas' position. Similarly, Ockham gives Aristotelian reasons for rejecting Aquinas' claims about virtue, practical reason, and prudence.

387. How to Reject Happiness

Ockham rejects eudaemonism, because he agrees with Scotus in believing that we do not necessarily will happiness. Some of his arguments appeal to experience; they might persuade us without reference to any controversial doctrine about freewill. He argues, for instance, that in some circumstances we might believe we cannot achieve happiness, and therefore might cease to will to be happy. Similarly, if we will not to exist, we thereby also will not to be happy.[3] Since it is possible in these ways not to will happiness, we do not necessarily will happiness.[4]

The eudaemonist position would be open to this objection if it claimed that we always will happiness in a sense of 'will' that implies we always believe happiness is possible for us. In this sense I do not will to lift a sack that I believe weighs a ton, though I might wish I could lift it. But this is not the sense of 'will' that is relevant to the eudaemonist thesis. As Aristotle says, we can wish (*boulesthai*; '*velle*' in the Latin version) even for things that we believe to be impossible and for things that are not up to us (*EN* 1111b20–30), and this is the attitude that, according to the eudaemonist, we take towards happiness as an end.

This attitude to happiness does not imply that our desire for it is empty, or practically irrelevant. We might wish we could be invulnerable to disease or immortal, but our wish might make no difference, since there is nothing we can reasonably do about it. We can, however, act in ways that bring us closer to happiness, even if we cannot ensure our happiness. That is why our pursuit of happiness guides our actions even when we think happiness is not open to us; for even in these cases we try to get closer to happiness. This defence answers Ockham's first example.

A similar defence answers his second example, of willing our own non-existence. If, for instance, I choose to suffer death rather than betray people who count on me, I recognize that I would be worse off as a traitor than I would be if I were dead. The suggestion that I would be better off dead is initially paradoxical, but not unintelligible; it implies that I would be so much worse off if I remained alive as a coward that I ought to prefer non-existence to such a life.[5]

These ways of dealing with Ockham's alleged counter-examples will not convince anyone who does not find eudaemonism plausible in other respects. But if we are convinced by

---

[3] 'I say first that the will . . . can reject (nolle) the ultimate end whether it is shown in general or in particular. . . . What the intellect can dictate is to be rejected can be rejected. This is evident in itself. But the intellect can believe that there is no ultimate end or happiness, and consequently can dictate that the ultimate end or happiness is to be rejected. Secondly, whoever can will the antecedent can will a consequent that he believes to be a consequent. But one can will not to exist, therefore he can reject existence, therefore he can reject the happiness that he believes to follow on his existing' (*4Sent.* q16 = OT vii 350.5–14).

[4] On rejection of happiness cf. Adams, 'Will' 257–62; Heinaman, 'Rationality'.   [5] Cf. Plato, *La.* 195c7–d3.

the theoretical reasons for accepting Aquinas' version of eudaemonism, we need not be dissuaded by these objections.

388. Does Eudaemonism Exclude Freedom?

Ockham also argues against eudaemonism on the ground that the will is a free capacity and can therefore receive two contrary actualities (*4Sent.* q16 = OT vii 350.17). If the will is free, then, in Ockham's view, it must be free to refuse happiness; hence we cannot will the ultimate end naturally, unless 'naturally' means simply that we most commonly do it (*1Sent.* d1 q6 = OT i 507.9–16). If the will is free, it can refuse happiness, both in general and in particular, because otherwise it would lose the indifference needed for freedom (*1Sent.* d1 q6 = OT i 501–2; *4Sent.* q16 = OT vii 350–3).[6]

Aquinas maintains that the will is not free in relation to the pursuit of the ultimate end, but is free in relation to the pursuit of subordinate ends, because it has the capacity for contrary actualities in relation to these ends. Ockham rejects this defence of freedom because he rejects Aquinas' account of how the will is free in relation to subordinate ends. From Ockham's point of view, Aquinas' position implies that the choice of the will is determined by the judgment of intellect about means to the final good. If this determination does not ensure freewill, Aquinas does not allow us freedom.

Even if Aquinas showed that the will is in some way indifferent in relation to means, he would not meet Ockham's conditions for indifference. We recognize freedom and contingency, in Ockham's view, if we regard human beings as being in control of (or 'masters of', *domini*) their actions.[7] Control and power over one's actions comes from freewill,[8] which involves indifference and contingency.[9] Hence it requires metaphysical indeterminism.[10] Admitted facts about freedom require us to have powers that are indeterministically actualized; no past conditions determine the actualization of these powers in one way or the other.

Ockham, therefore, demands more than Aquinas' conditions for contingency and freedom. Though Aquinas agrees that control requires contingency, he does not interpret contingency in Ockham's strict sense, which assumes Scotus' conception of a rational capacity. Scotus argues that the will is free to choose either of two opposite courses of action, and that therefore nothing outside the will determines our choice; hence the greater apparent good does not determine the will. Ockham follows Scotus on this point.

This claim about freedom raises a question about Ockham's views on how we know we are free. He argues that any attempt to prove the reality of freedom must rely on some

---

[6] Cf. Scotus, *1Sent.* d1 q4 schol. = OO v 1, 209 §3 = d1 pars 2 q2, V ii 66–7 §§91–2.

[7] He discusses, for instance, Damascene's remark that non-rational agents are acted on as opposed to acting. On Damascene see §243n40.

[8] See Aquinas, *in Met.* ix 2 §1787: 'For only the rational part of the soul is in control (*domina*) of its action, and in this it differs from inanimate things'.

[9] 'Those things that have freewill have control and power over their actions; but this requires indifference and contingency' (*1Sent.* d1 q6 = OT i 502.10–15).

[10] [Freedom:] 'I can cause and not cause the same effect, there being no difference anywhere else outside that capacity' (*Quodl.* i q16 a1 = OT ix 87.12–15). [The contingent:] 'what produces a given effect, and, with nothing changed either on its own part or on the part of anything else, has it in its power equally to produce or not to produce, because from its own nature it is determined to neither' (*1Sent.* d1 q6 = OT i 501.8–11).

premiss less known, or no better known, than the conclusion, but none the less our freedom can be grasped (cognosci) evidently through experience, through the fact that a person experiences that whenever reason dictates (dictet) something, the will is still able to will or not to will or to reject it (*Quodl.* i 16 = OT ix 88.25–8).

This appeal to experience may show that we can conceive opposites and choose between them. But might we not explain this capacity through Aquinas' appeals to the role of deliberation? Aquinas does not guarantee the precise sort of contingency that Scotus and Ockham have in mind; but we might doubt whether we experience this sort of contingency in our deliberation and choice. It is not clear that experience gives us certain knowledge of undetermined choice.

389. Moderate v. Extreme Voluntarism

On these points Ockham agrees with Scotus. But he goes further than Scotus in rejecting a connexion between will and reason. Though Scotus rejects the dependence of will on intellect, he takes the will to involve a rational capacity, and hence a certain kind of rational preference. Hence he attributes to the will both an affection for advantage and an affection for justice, and he sometimes identifies the freedom of the will with the affection for justice. This identification raises difficulties. If freedom consists in acting from the affection for justice, it seems to consist in a certain kind of determination, not in the absence of determination. If, however, the will is equally free in acting on either of its main affections, it is not clear why freedom is expressed in acting on one rather than on the other.

Ockham does not follow Scotus in treating the will as essentially rational; nor does he connect freedom with the affection for justice. Instead, he emphasizes indifference, contingency, and self-determination. His claims about freedom and capacity exclude an intellectualist account of the will—both in its eudaemonist version and in Scotus' version that identifies the freedom of the will with the affection for justice. An intellectualist account implies that the will does not meet the strong conditions for a rational capacity; for it implies that the will is determined by the conception of the overall good (happiness or justice) as it appears to the intellect, and therefore by something outside itself. But—Ockham replies—in an agent with freewill, the will is self-determining; if it were not, its choices would be necessitated by something outside it. According to Ockham, Scotus' claims about the self-determining character of the will conflict with the primacy that Scotus assigns to the affection for justice. Ockham asserts the independence of the will from reason and makes reason simply the servant of the will.

According to Henry of Ghent, this is the only sense in which reason has a 'directive' function. Just as a servant directs his master by carrying a light to show him how to go where he wants to, reason directs the will, and since the will is the master, it can withdraw reason from its enlightening function when it wants to.[11] The demotion of reason to the 'guiding'

---

[11] 'To the fifth point, that what directs is superior to what is directed, it must be said that something can direct in two ways. First, by authority, as a master directs a servant. He is superior. In this way the will directs the intellect. Second, by providing a service, as a servant directs a master, by holding a lamp before him at night, so that the master does not

role of a servant expresses the difference between Scotus and Ockham, on the one hand, and Aquinas, on the other. The difference is obscured by Scotus' claims about the affection for justice, but it is clear once Ockham discards these claims.

This demotion of reason fits the voluntarist attempt to explain how action on the will differs from action on the passions. Whereas external or internal stimuli determine the passions, nothing determines the will; even considerations presented by the intellect cannot determine it. The intellectualist position makes the will too much like the passions, by taking it to be determined by an external stimulus.

This objection to intellectualism underlies some criticisms of Aquinas' position. Tempier, for instance, condemned any belief in the necessitation of the will by the apparent good.[12] If we free the will from this sort of necessitation, we may claim to have done what Aquinas failed to do, by identifying the distinctively human form of choice and action.

390. Difficulties for Voluntarism

Once Ockham makes clear the implications of voluntarism, he also invites criticisms. Voluntarists set out to explain phenomena that they believe Aquinas' intellectualism fails to explain; but one may doubt whether they really explain these phenomena.

Freedom is supposed to provide appropriate grounds for praise and blame; hence Scotus complains that an intellectualist account makes sin non-blameworthy by reducing it to cognitive error. To see whether the voluntarist position does any better, we may consider the choice that faces the will when it gets advice from reason. Voluntarists do not allow the will to choose in the light of the apparent overall good; for if that determines it, practical reason determines it. But if it decides by something other than the overall good, does it not choose non-rationally, as we would choose on the basis of a passion? And if we conclude that it cannot decide on the basis of any considerations at all, do we not introduce a degree of randomness and irrationality that makes us wonder why we should care so much about having freewill?

Such questions raise doubts about voluntarism. It tries to capture the difference between the free and rational will and the non-rational passions. But a degree of freedom that excludes intellectualism also seems to exclude a genuinely rational will. In that case, how are praise and blame appropriate? For if the will is not necessarily moved by rational considerations, it does not seem to respond to the considerations that are mentioned in praise and blame.

This objection may seem unfair. For we might argue, on behalf of the voluntarist, that if the will is not necessarily moved by reason, but usually follows reason, it still seems fair to expect us to respond to the right considerations; claims about responsibility do not seem to

---

stumble. Such a director is inferior. And this is the way in which the intellect directs the will. Hence the will can withdraw the intellect from directing and understanding whenever it wills, as a master can withdraw a servant' (Henry of Ghent, *Quodl. quodl.* i q14, ad 5am f 17vb = Lottin, *PM* i 275). 'It must be said therefore without qualification that, when a good and a better thing have been proposed, the will can elect a less good thing' (q16 f21va = Lottin 277). Here Henry follows Tempier's condemnation of rationalism (prop. 163, quoted in §358). See §403.

[12] 'That the will of a human being is necessitated by his cognition, just as the desire of a non-rational animal is' (Prop. 159 in Piché, *CP* 126). Cf. Prop. 164.

need a necessary connexion. This reply does not entirely answer the objection, however. Any choice that is an appropriate basis for praise and blame should be appropriately connected to the right reasons; an arbitrary or capricious choice of the right course of action does not warrant praise, and such a choice of the wrong course does not seem to justify the blame that would apply to a non-arbitrary choice. According to the intellectualist, non-arbitrary choice of the right or wrong action is determined by the right or wrong reasons. What can the voluntarist say? If recognition of the right reasons leaves us no less free to choose the wrong action, and we are no more determined by the right reasons when we choose correctly than when we choose arbitrarily, how does correct choice differ from arbitrary choice of the right action?

Godfrey of Fontaines supports this objection by arguing that 'one is less able to maintain freewill by claiming that the will moves itself immediately than by claiming that it is moved by an object'.[13] Since voluntarism makes all choices equally undetermined by considerations adduced by reason, it cannot draw the appropriate distinction between deliberate and impulsive ('sudden') actions, and cannot explain why the distinction matters.[14] We would normally say that deliberate actions are caused by deliberation, and respond to the reasons presented in deliberation, whereas impulsive actions are not determined by consideration of the comparative weight of reasons on each side. Voluntarists, however, cannot draw the distinction in this way, and cannot say how the good will responds to the right considerations; for, in their view, all free actions are equally undetermined by the considerations revealed by deliberation.

If this is a fair objection to voluntarism, Aquinas' position may seem more attractive. His intellectualism would restrict our freedom to an unwelcome degree if he did not allow such a wide scope for deliberation and rational comparison of alternatives.[15] If, for instance, we necessarily pursued not only some conception of an ultimate end, but a rather precisely specified ultimate end, then some important choices that we take to be in our control would not be in our control and we would be less free than we think we are. Aquinas, however, is not open to this objection; in his view, we are free to pursue or to reject specific conceptions of an ultimate end, and our deliberation determines the specific ends we pursue. His intellectualism is more plausible given the wide scope that he attributes to deliberation.

Aquinas, then, has a reasonable reply to voluntarism. He argues that freewill consists in the operation of the will that results in free election, and that we are capable of free election.

---

[13] Godfrey of Fontaines, *Quodl.* xv q4b 26. Korolec, *CHLMP* 637, mentions other opponents of voluntarism.

[14] 'The third reason is of this sort: The position that cannot preserve the freewill in the second act more than in the first, and <cannot preserve it> in a deliberate act more than in a sudden one, is less able to preserve freewill than a position that can do this. But that position that proposes that a human being has freewill precisely because the will is in no case moved by anything else, but moves itself immediately, cannot preserve freewill in the first act any more than in the second, or in a deliberate act any more than in a sudden one; for in all cases without distinction the will moves itself. But that other position, which proposes that a human being has no freewill except through the fact that by the mediation of the deliberation of reason a human being moves himself towards secondary objects of will, is more able to preserve mastery of one's act and freedom of the act in the second act than in the first one, and in a deliberate act more than in a sudden one. . . . And from this same point it follows, as was said above, that all acquiescence, however sudden, in things that are mortal sins in their genus would be a mortal sin' (Godfrey, *Quodl.* xiv q4b 28). A position similar to Godfrey's is defended by one of the 'Averroist' commentaries on Aristotle's *Ethics* discussed by Gauthier, 'Commentaires' 199.

[15] See §270.

If he makes the will subject to the appearance of the greater good, that does not refute his account.

391. Developments of Voluntarism

Even though the objections presented by Godfrey of Fontaines are serious, they do not necessarily require a return to intellectualism. They might suggest that a voluntarist should abandon the remaining element of intellectualism that remains in Scotus and Ockham. They separate will from passion by treating the will as a rational capacity, and they connect the rationality of the will with freedom and responsibility. Ockham rejects the connexion that Scotus sees between freewill and the affection for justice, but he still connects freedom with reason. Though he rejects intellectualism, and even abandons the elements of intellectualism in Scotus' position, he still (according to our previous distinctions) maintains rationalism rather than anti-rationalism, in so far as he distinguishes the rational will from the non-rational passions.[16] But the difficulty that Ockham faces in explaining the rationality of the will may raise doubts about his separation of will from passions.

Some of the later history of reflexions on reason and will suggests how one might separate will, freedom, and reason, and why it is difficult to separate them. Voluntarism is one element in the Kantian conception of the will. But Kant does not give up the connexion between the will and practical reason. The voluntarist aspects of his position conflict with the intellectualist aspects. He returns to Scotus' belief that the affection for justice is somehow constitutive of, not simply one possible manifestation of, the freedom of the will; and so some of the objections to Scotus seem to fit Kant as well. A thorough attempt to separate the freedom from the rationality of the will appears only in Schopenhauer and in existentialist views about radical freedom.[17]

Ockham does not accept any of the later views that abandon the essential rationality of the will and rely exclusively on self-determination. But it is relevant to compare these later views with his view. For if they are the most plausible attempts to develop the voluntarist side of Scotus and Ockham, they show how one might defend the voluntarist position.

Ockham claims to account for our intuitive knowledge of our freedom. But he seems to undermine some of our further intuitive beliefs about the will and agency. For it now becomes difficult to see why self-determination by the will should be either necessary or sufficient for rational agency. Ockham begins, as Aquinas does, by seeking to give an account of the distinctive features of rational agents who have control over their actions. But even if self-determination, as Ockham understands it, ensures control, as he understands it, it does not seem to ensure rational agency. If a voluntarist tries to answer this objection by adding some further condition satisfied by rational agents, we may wonder whether the 'further' condition does not capture rational agency by itself without any appeal to self-determination by the will.

This doubt about voluntarism might suggest an anti-rationalist solution. Voluntarist arguments may convince us that an intellectualist conception makes the will no more

---

[16] On intellectualism v. rationalism see §256.
[17] See Schopenhauer, *EFW* 41. On existentialism, see Olafson, *PP*, chs. 1–2.

free than the passions, since it implies that both are externally determined. Intellectualist arguments may convince us that a voluntarist conception of the will also blurs the distinction between will and passion, since it does not make will essentially rational. We might respond by rejecting the division between will and passion. If the mere fact that an action is self-determined (according to the voluntarist conception) does not make it morally more significant, we may infer that the contrast between the will and the non-rational impulses is not morally significant either. Hence we might as well say that the will is a sort of passion, or that reason is the servant of the passions no less than of the will.

This is the anti-rationalist ('sentimentalist') conclusion of Hobbes and Hume. In their view, freedom consists simply in internal determination; they see no relevant distinction between the will and the 'sentiments' or 'passions' as sources of the internal determination. They reject both an indeterminist and an intellectualist account of freedom.[18] Though they accept the voluntarist criticisms of intellectualism far enough to believe that determination by intellect is not freedom, they do not regard voluntarism as an adequate alternative. Against both intellectualists and voluntarists, they conclude that the will is a passion.

Hence Hume's sentimentalist maxim (in which he follows Locke and Hobbes) that 'reason is and ought to be the slave of the passions' is an intelligible outcome of Henry of Ghent's claim that reason is the servant of the will. Voluntarism opposes sentimentalism in asserting a sharp distinction between the passions and the will; but the voluntarist claim about the subordination of reason might well appear more plausible than the voluntarist account of the difference between the will and the passions. Hume's sentimentalist conception of the will and practical reason is therefore an indirect result of voluntarist criticism of Aquinas.[19] But it is not clear that arguments for voluntarism and sentimentalism justify the rejection of Aquinas' view.

392. Virtue and Passion

Ockham not only believes that Aquinas gives an inadequate account of the freedom of the will, but he also believes that the free will should have a more prominent part than Aquinas allows it in an account of the moral virtues. He supports Scotus' objections to the role that Aquinas assigns to the passions. He rejects Aquinas' view that virtue must belong to the sensory part because the sensory part has to be perfected (3Sent. q11 = OT vi 352). He agrees with Scotus in placing virtue in the will (354), because only a condition of the will is properly a virtue (358). Since the will is the basis of praise and blame, it must be the subject of virtue.[20] Ockham argues that the will has to have a causal role in the formation of a virtue sufficient to justify praise and blame.[21]

---

[18] See Hobbes, L6.53; Cudworth, F c.5, 167H; Hutcheson, IMS 165–6. On Locke's hesitations about sentimentalism see E ii 21.47.

[19] Similarly, Reid's reply to Hume is a partial, though not total, return to Aquinas' position. See, e.g., EAP 534H.

[20] 'The only state that is properly virtue is the one whose act is the only one that is virtuous. But only the act of the will is virtuous. Proof: Only the act of will is praiseworthy or blameworthy; hence only it is virtuous; hence only the state produced from such an act is virtue. This is confirmed by the Philosopher in Ethics III, where he says that no act is blameworthy unless it is in our power. For no one faults a person blind by nature for being blind. But if he is blind by his own sin, then he is at fault' (3Sent. q11 = OT vi 366.1–9).

[21] Cf. Quodl. ii q16 = OT ix 182.19–25; Freppert, BMWO 49.

This argument shows only that the will must be one subject of virtue, and that any other subject of it must be closely enough connected to the will to make the virtue as a whole praiseworthy. But this conclusion does not conflict with the basic elements of Aquinas' position. Nor does it justify Ockham's further claim that the will is the only subject of virtue, so that the passions cannot also be a subject.

Ockham claims that his view is consistent with Aristotle. According to Ockham, Aristotle's frequent remarks that the virtues of character are in the non-rational part mean that these virtues are in the will, not that they are in the passions; the will is a 'non-rational' part because it is rational only by participation (*3Sent.* q11 = OT vi 368.14–21).[22]

But even if Aristotle treats the will as non-rational in this sense, his remarks about the role of the non-rational part of the soul in virtue do not seem to fit the will. For he explains his claim that the moral virtues are in the non-rational part by discussing the training of passions, pleasure, and pain. He refers to this aspect of the non-rational part (contrary to Ockham's view) when he takes moral virtue to be virtue of the non-rational part.

In treating the will as a subject of moral virtue, Ockham draws attention to a feature of the will that is insufficiently recognized in Aquinas' account of virtue. The arguments that Ockham and Scotus present show that Aquinas should make the will a subject of every moral virtue. But they do not undermine Aquinas' arguments for making the passions a subject of some virtues. Consideration of all these arguments should lead us to deny that each moral virtue must have just one subject. These claims of Ockham's about the importance of the will in virtue are not necessarily voluntaristic. We could accept them even if we accepted Aquinas' view that the will is determined by one's conception of the good. We have argued that Aquinas should accept these conclusions, given his conception of the will. We have no further reason, so far, to suppose that a true account of the virtues rests on a voluntarist conception of the will.

393. Correct Reason and Will

As we have understood Scotus, he holds an externalist view about the relation between the grasp of moral principles and motivation. This raises a difficulty for his claim that prudence makes an action morally good. Ockham exploits this difficulty, in his discussion of the sense in which virtue involves acting in accordance with correct reason.[23] As elsewhere, he revises Scotus' position so as to give the free will a more prominent place.

The primacy of the will implies that a morally good action cannot simply be an action conforming to correct reason. If God were to cause my will to conform to correct reason, but my will remained completely passive (*voluntate nihil agente*) in this process, this act would be neither virtuous nor deserving (*3Sent.* q11 = OT vi 389.18–22). Only the act of the will conforming to correct reason is primarily good or bad, because this is primarily imputable to the agent (vi 390.3–4).

To evaluate Ockham's argument, we need to see what it means for God to cause my will to conform to correct reason. God might induce purely external conformity, by causing

---

[22] In applying this formula to the will Ockham follows Aquinas' questionable account of *EN* i 13. See §257.
[23] See Freppert, *BMWO* 59–68.

a series of random thoughts in a 'Random Good Samaritan' to conclude with an equally random choice to take the injured stranger to the inn. This choice is not praiseworthy and does not engage the will actively. Alternatively, God might cause an 'Intellectualist Good Samaritan' to notice all the features of the injured stranger and his situation that justify helping him, so that the Samaritan's will is engaged by the greater good of helping the stranger. In the second case, an intellectualist does not admit that the Samaritan's will does nothing; the conformity of the will to right reason is not purely external, but includes a correct response. This sort of conformity to correct reason seems—to an intellectualist—to be imputable to the agent.

Ockham seems to believe that neither the Random nor the Intellectualist Good Samaritan has genuine virtue; for in neither case would the will be 'active' in the sense that is needed for imputability. In denying that the will of the Intellectualist Good Samaritan is active he relies on a voluntarist account of the conditions for activity of the will and for imputability of an action to an agent. If the will necessarily conformed to correct reason, virtuous action would not be in the power of the will, because the will would be unable to prevent action on correct reason. Since one's will does not necessarily conform to one's correct reason, correct reason itself cannot ensure virtue, but may be present in either a virtuous or a vicious agent. An agent who chooses to act for a bad end may have correct reason but freely choose to disregard it; hence correct reason is not the primary cause of virtuous action (Q. var. q7 a3 = OT viii 364.534–48). Virtuous action needs both actual prudence and the activity of the will (Q. var. q8 = OT viii 417.189–418.2).

Virtue, then, seems to consist in a choice by the will to act in accordance with the provisions of correct reason. This choice is not in accordance, or in conflict, with correct reason, but is undetermined by reason.[24] If we are virtuous, or even continent, we need not only the appropriate dictate of correct reason, but also the undetermined free choice of the will.

These views conflict with Aquinas' view about the role of prudence in virtue. He claims that universal prudence grasps the components of happiness, and thereby fixes (praestituere) the end for the moral virtues.[25] Given this conception of universal prudence, and given Aquinas' conception of the will and its relation to the good, prudence is responsible for the distinctively virtuous condition of the will. Since the will aims necessarily at the ultimate good, and since prudence discovers the constitution of this good, the will of a prudent person necessarily pursues the distinctively virtuous end that prudence has discovered. We can distinguish the cognitive contribution of prudence from the motive contribution of the will; but, given Aquinas' eudaemonism, the right direction of the will follows from the discovery of the constitution of the ultimate end. Since prudence is necessary and sufficient for virtue, the virtuous person differs cognitively from the incontinent, continent, and vicious person.

Scotus rejects this role for prudence, since he takes the will to be independent of practical reason. In his view, neither the affection for advantage nor the affection for justice determines the will; whatever we take to be the content of practical principles grasped by prudence, no will necessarily accepts them once it is aware of them. But Ockham believes that Scotus

---

[24] '... Correct reason dictates the contrary of what is desired by sensory desire. And the will from its freedom does not will what sensory desire desires, but what is dictated by correct reason...' (Q. var. q6 a10 = OT viii 272.11–13).
[25] See §320.

does not go far enough in pursuing the implications of his voluntarism.[26] Ockham agrees that prudence accords with correct reason, so that prudence is a partial efficient cause of the virtuous action. It is not the whole efficient cause, however, because virtue requires an independent act of willing in accordance with the dictates of correct reason. Since this is an act of a will that is free to reject any dictate of reason, it does not result from attention to a decisive practical consideration; for if there were such a consideration, its decisiveness would limit the freedom of the will. No consideration, therefore, moves the will reliably.

Ockham offers one answer to a difficulty that faces Aristotle's claims about the relation between prudence and virtue of character. When Aristotle claims that virtue makes the end right and prudence the means, we might take this in an anti-rationalist sense, so as to imply that correctly-oriented passions make the end right.[27] Ockham approaches this anti-rationalist interpretation, though he does not completely accept it. He takes Aristotle's references to a non-rational part to indicate the role of will, and so he infers that an act of will, independent of reason, is essential to virtue. Ockham does not deny that virtue is more reasonable than vice; in Hutcheson's terms, he grants that we have justifying reasons in favour of virtue rather than vice.[28] But he denies that these justifying reasons supply the virtuous person with decisive motivating reasons.

Ockham's development of Scotus' voluntarism about prudence and virtue results in his claim about the motivation of the virtuous person. This cannot be the general desire for the good, since that belongs to every will. It must be a choice, not determined by any further reasons, to accept the conclusions reached by correct reason. In this respect, it must be a choice beyond the scope of practical reason.

394. Separability of the Virtues

Ockham goes further than Scotus goes in rejecting Aquinas' belief in the reciprocity of the virtues and in the unity of prudence.[29] His views on prudence reflect the role that he attributes to the will in each virtue. He denies that the different virtues aim at any unified good, since he does not believe that they all aim at happiness. He has no reason, therefore, to believe that the same deliberative knowledge is required to grasp the relations and connexions of the different ends of the virtues in a single conception of happiness.

Once we admit these differences in the ends of different virtues, we have no reason to recognize prudence as a horizontally unified science of the good. Moreover, if the will is not determined by the conclusions of prudence, we lose one of Aquinas' reasons for accepting the necessary connexion of the different virtues. Since the prescriptions of prudence belonging to the different virtues belong to distinct sciences, a will assenting to the conclusions of prudence for one virtue may not assent to its conclusions for another virtue.

Ockham therefore claims that different virtues have independent desires and aims. Even if we are intemperate to some degree, we may still have the will (velle) to carry out the actions required by justice (Q. var. q7 a3 = OT viii 346.115–23). If, for instance, we suppose that justice requires us to aim at the common good, we can have this aim while still having

---

[26] See §§383–4.   [27] See §89.   [28] See Hutcheson, IMS 121.   [29] On Scotus see §375.

some tendency to intemperance.[30] In such cases we are not so intemperate that we would be willing to damage the common good for the sake of our intemperate desires, but we are intemperate enough to indulge our intemperate desires when we do not seem to harm the common good.

For similar reasons, Ockham believes we can have correct reason about the subject-matter of one virtue (for instance, temperance) and not about the subject-matter of another (for instance, generosity). Hence he agrees with Scotus in rejecting the horizontal unity of prudence (*Q. var.* q6 a10 = OT viii 284.290–285.303). The virtues are connected in so far as they all accept certain universal principles such as 'everything right (*honestum*) is to be done', 'everything good is to be loved', and 'everything prescribed by correct reason is to be done' (*Q. var.* q7 a3 = OT viii 347.141–52). But to reach a practical conclusion from these general principles we need the different types of prudence that are acquired by experience in the different areas of the different virtues.[31] Prudence in the proper sense has to be both about particulars and acquired by experience, and so there is a different prudence for each virtue (*Q. var.* q6 a10 = OT viii 282.233–41).

This division of prudence seems to conflict with Aristotle's view that there is one prudence for many virtues (*3Sent.* q12 a4 = OT vi 406.5–10).[32] Ockham replies that there are different prudences for the principles and for the conclusions, and in fact prudence is most properly about particular things that we can do (*3Sent.* q12 = OT vi 419.17–18). Hence the horizontal unity that Aristotle attributes to prudence is a purely generic unity that allows different and independent species of prudence to belong to different virtues. In this treatment of prudence Ockham agrees with Scotus, who argues that 'different things to be done require different prudences' (*3Sent.* q36 = OO vii 2, 823 §22 = W 410), so that prudence is a genus embracing the specific prudences belonging to the different virtues.[33]

Contrary to Scotus, however, the prudence that is needed for a given virtue does not include any universal prudence, and so prudence is not vertically unified. In Ockham's view, only a loose and improper use of 'prudence' allows prudence to grasp universal principles reached through experience.[34] Prudence in the proper sense is confined to particulars (*Q. var.* q6 a10 = OT viii 282.249); it is 'immediate directive knowledge acquired only through experience with respect to something that can be done' (*Q. var.* q7 a2 = OT viii 331.20–6). It is exemplified in the knowledge that this angry person is to be pacified by gentle words (*Q. var.* q7 a2 = OT viii 331.20–6;[35] cf. q6 a10 = OT viii 281.225–282.232).

Ockham, therefore, disagrees with Scotus' view that any application of moral science to action is an exercise of prudence.[36] In his view, an exercise of prudence involves a singular

---

[30] Ockham takes prudence to be necessary for each virtuous action. See Freppert, *BMWO* 53.

[31] 'The <different forms of> knowledge are prudences that are directive in different virtuous actions' (*Q. var.* q7 a3 = OT viii 347.149–50).

[32] The editors of OT suggest that Ockham is referring to *EN* 1140a25–7. A more appropriate passage is 1145a1–2.

[33] Ockham concedes that when one virtue is sufficiently perfected, it inclines us towards the primary expression (*actus*) of another virtue (*Q. var.* q7 a3 = OT viii 347–8); he also allows that the virtues share their common principles (*3Sent.* q12 = OT vi 425–6). But he insists that each virtue requires its own prudence derived from the experience that is necessary for that virtue and unnecessary for other virtues.

[34] Cf. *Q. var.* q7 a2 = OT viii 330.1–13.

[35] Cf. *1Sent.* Prol. q11 = OT i 319.25–321.9; q12 = OT i 359.16–360.16; *Quodl.* 2 q14 a3 = OT ix 177.30–178.50. Strictly speaking, prudence is the grasp of the 'minimum universale', which the craftsman (*artifex*) has.

[36] Scotus, *Ord.*, Prol. 5, q1–2 = V i 227–8 §351 = Prol. q4 schol. = OO v 1, 163 §41.

proposition acquired by experience (*Q. var.* q6 a10 = OT viii 283.252–80). The virtues do not aim at any single good, and so they are not essentially connected. While they may share some general principles, the sharing of these general principles is not essential to each of the specific virtues.

It is easy to quote passages from Aristotle on Ockham's side. Aristotle often insists that prudence requires grasp of particulars if it is to be genuinely practical knowledge (e.g., *EN* 1141b21–2; 1142a23–30; 1143b2–5). One might argue, in support of Ockham, that Aquinas and his successors introduce a conception of universal prudence with no solid support in Aristotle. But we have seen that Aquinas' conception of prudence rests on a plausible interpretation of Aristotle's doctrine of practical reason. Aquinas sees that Aristotle's eudaemonism requires the expansive conception of prudence that is not prominent in Aristotle's own remarks on prudence. Though Ockham relies on one genuine element in Aristotle, the doctrines of Aquinas that he rejects are central Aristotelian doctrines.

395. Non-positive v. Positive Morality

Aquinas' account of practical reason influences his treatment of two elements of Christian moral theology that have no explicit place in Aristotelian ethics: the belief in universal conscience and the doctrine of natural law as an expression of the eternal divine law. Aquinas fits these Christian elements into his Aristotelian theory, by identifying universal conscience with the constitutive elements of practical reason, and by taking the precepts of natural law to be discovered by practical reason deliberating about the human good that is grasped, in schematic form, by universal conscience. Aquinas infers that the content of natural law is a matter of practical knowledge, and specifically of deliberation. It is not an expression of divine positive law that is created by God's willing it to be so. It expresses divine reason, since it embodies the principles on which God creates the natural world and human beings in it.

Scotus and Ockham agree with Aquinas in recognizing moral principles grasped by natural reason. According to Scotus, these constitute the principles of natural law, properly so called, which are not subject to God's will or dispensation. But their content is restricted, since the second table of the Decalogue cannot be derived from them. Since Scotus restricts the content of natural law properly so called, he expands the area of divine positive law, and so restricts the deliberative task of practical reason; deliberative prudence cannot discover the second table from the precepts of practical reason. But this apparently clear division is obscured, as we have seen, by Scotus' claim that the principles of the second table are 'highly consonant' with natural law in the strict sense.

Similar questions arise about Ockham. He recognizes both a non-positive part of moral science and a positive part (*Quodl.* ii q14 a2 = OT ix 177.18). He does not follow Scotus in regarding the whole second table as positive, and so he seems to be less voluntarist than Scotus. But it is difficult to understand the extent of non-positive morality and its relation to the divine will.[37]

---

[37] Non-positive morality: King, 'Theory' 228.

Non-positive moral science directs human actions without any precept of a superior. It is demonstrative because its first principles are grasped (notis, 177.25–6) through themselves or known (scitis) through experience, and it derives its conclusions necessarily from these. Principles known through themselves include 'Everything right (honestum) is to be done' (ix 177.26); 'The will ought to conform itself to correct reason'; and 'Every blameworthy evil is to be avoided'. As an example of a principle known through experience Ockham mentions 'Any angry person on such an occasion is to be mollified and calmed by gentle words'; this can be known only by experience of calming particular angry people by gentle words (Q. var. q6 a10 = OT viii 282.228).[38]

Positive moral science contains human and divine laws, which oblige (obligant, ix 177.21) us to pursue or avoid things that are good or bad only because they are ordered or prohibited by a superior to whom it belongs to legislate. This part of moral science is not demonstrative.

Principles of non-positive morality are not specific precepts at the level of the second table of the Decalogue. But they are not all as tautologous or analytic as 'The will ought to conform itself to correct reason' seems to be. They also include 'One should benefit a benefactor'.[39] Hence Ockham seems to allow more content than Scotus allows to natural law in the strict sense.[40] Aristotle's Ethics discusses principles of non-positive morality,[41] but Ockham does not say whether these principles are the whole, or only a part, of the Ethics. His views do not suggest that non-positive morality includes the sort of detail that we find in the Ethics; he does not seem to share Aquinas' confidence in the competence of rational inquiry and deliberation to reach specific precepts of justice.[42]

Ockham implies, therefore, that at least some of our moral knowledge—both of general principles and of particular prescriptions for action—is epistemically independent of any beliefs about the legislative will of God. But he also denies that the principles of correct reason are independent of God's legislative will.[43] Since the divine will is prior to correct reason, virtue is in accord with correct reason 'as long as the divine command stands' (stante praecepto divino) or as long as the present order stands.[44]

What sort of priority does Ockham ascribe to the divine will? We might take him to mean that though the requirements of correct reason are independent of God's will, God is free to endorse or to reject them. If God were to reject them, and to demand that we act contrary to correct reason, virtue would not be in accord with correct reason. That is why—we might

[38] For these examples cf. Q. var. q7 a2 = OT viii 330.11–13.

[39] See Q. var. q6 a10 = OT viii 281.219–282.232 (omni benefactori est benefaciendum). Ockham argues (viii 283.252–284.280, against Scotus) that this knowledge, combined with the recognition that this person is a benefactor, can direct our action, so that in this case prudence is not required for directing action.

[40] See §378.

[41] In Quodl. ii q14 a2 = OT ix 177.24–8, Ockham mentions principles known through themselves and known through experience, 'such as that everything right (honestum) is to be done and everything wrong is to be avoided, and <principles> of this sort, about which Aristotle speaks in moral philosophy'.

[42] On non-positive and positive morality see Clark, 'Voluntarism'. He suggests that Ockham's basic principle relies on right reason, which requires the love of God, and that the will of God gives all further content to morality. But the example of the benefactor suggests that Clark may exaggerate the emptiness of non-positive morality. See also Adams, 'Naturalist?'; 'Structure'.

[43] See McGrade, 'Omnipotence' 274–9 (a more moderate interpretation of Ockham's position); Clark, 'Right reason'.

[44] See Quodl. iii q14 = OT ix 255.43–5; cf. Q. var. q7 a3 = OT viii 363.515; Q. var. q7 a4 = OT viii 394.440–2. On directed and unqualified divine power see §396 below.

suppose—Ockham believes that the accord between virtue and correct reason holds only as long as the divine command (accepting the conclusions of correct reason) stands.

But this is not Ockham's view. For he also seems to believe that two facts depend on the divine will, both (1) the fact that virtue agrees with correct reason, and (2) the fact that correct reason requires the specific actions it requires.[45] The fact that God wills an action makes it true that the action conforms to correct reason. Ockham does not simply hold, as Aquinas holds, that the divine will and correct reason necessarily agree; he also holds that correct reason prescribes a given action only because God wills it. God cannot reject the dictates of correct reason, but this does not mean that God's freedom is limited by the requirements of correct reason; on the contrary, whatever God wills thereby becomes a dictate of correct reason. Our intuitive knowledge of the requirements of correct reason reflects God's prior willing that has made it true that correct reason requires this action rather than another.[46]

This view of correct reason supports Ockham's view of dispensations. If God's will fixes the requirements of correct reason, it seems to be within God's power to change them. Since the fact that correct reason accepts a principle does not show that it is not dependent on the divine will, all the precepts of the Decalogue are dispensable.[47] Ockham, therefore, goes further than Scotus, who makes only the second table of the Decalogue dispensable. God could make hatred of God meritorious, even though the love of God is—given what God has actually willed—required by correct reason.

This dependence of correct reason on the prior will of God makes it difficult to understand what content we are to attribute to correct reason. Ockham's position would be intelligible if we found that some synthetic practical principles appeared irresistibly to us as fundamentally reasonable, even though we could not say what is reasonable about them. One might say that they seem basically reasonable but not further justifiable, because they record the results of God's antecedent acts of will that have constituted these principles as reasonable. If, however, we follow Aquinas in supposing that the basic principles of morality can be discovered by the appropriate sort of deliberation on the human good, it is difficult to see how correct reason and morality, so understood, could simply express God's antecedent will; they seem to reflect distinct facts about human nature, which do not depend on the divine legislative will.

It is rather difficult, then, to see what Ockham means about the relation between the divine will and correct reason. He seems to treat correct reason as a source of non-positive morality in a purely epistemic sense; though we grasp these moral principles without any explicit reference to the divine legislative will, our knowledge of their content does not capture their metaphysical status. Though we can know them without reference to divine legislation, in fact they depend on divine legislation. This claim that correct reason depends

---

[45] Ockham takes this view when he asks whether there is some cause of predestination in the predestined (1Sent. d41 q1 = OT iv 597.19–598.4). He denies that something must cause God's will to conform to correct reason: 'It can be said that every correct will conforms to correct reason. But it does not always conform to a prior correct reason that shows the cause why the will ought to will this. Rather, by the very fact that the divine will wills this, correct reason dictates that it is to be willed' (1Sent. d41 = OT iv 610.1–5). This passage is discussed by Oakley, 'Natural law'. See also Kilcullen, 'Natural law and will'; Clark, 'Right reason'.

[46] Cf. Scotus' treatment of Anselm's maxim, §381.

[47] See Suarez, Leg. ii 15.3, relying on Ockham, 2Sent. q15 ad 3 = OT v 352.

on the divine legislative will seems to require a rather impoverished conception of the content of correct reason. If this is what he means, his departure from Aquinas is more radical than it might initially have seemed if we attended simply to the prominence of Ockham's remarks on correct reason.

None the less, since he believes that we can grasp some important elements of morality by correct reason, Ockham is justified in endorsing a conception of natural law.[48] Though he discusses it in his political writings, rather than a moral context, his remarks on it are not surprising. Indeed, it would be plausible to identify the basic principles of natural law with the basic principles of non-positive morality, as he understands it. These are principles that we know because we are rational agents, not because we recognize any specific divine precepts.

396. Divine Freedom and Divine Justice

If we agree that moral principles—both positive and non-positive—depend on divine legislation, a further question arises about the relation of the divine will to this legislation. Is God free to change this divine legislation or not? Ockham's conception of divine freedom prevents him from agreeing that morality consists of principles that God cannot change. He is dissatisfied with Aquinas' argument to show that God acts freely and not from necessity (Aquinas, *Pot.* q1 a5; q3 a15), because he thinks Aquinas sets the standards for freedom too low.[49] In Ockham's view, Aquinas shows only that God acts through his intellect and will, but this is insufficient to show that he acts freely.[50] Ockham cites Aquinas' own remark that action through intellect and will is not necessarily free action.[51]

Aquinas argues that his conception of freedom answers this objection. In his view, God does not act out of a necessity of his nature, but is self-determining.[52] He understands necessity as 'mere' necessity, to be contrasted with acting for an end of one's own. In saying that God does not act out of mere necessity, he does not concede that it is possible for God not to act for the end for which God acts; on the contrary, he affirms that God cannot fail to act for the sake of God's goodness.[53] God's non-necessary choice is reflected in the fact that more than one good ordering of creatures would have been consistent with God's essential

---

[48] Ockham's views on natural law are rather loosely connected to his moral theory in general. But his discussion of the first two types of natural law ('absolute' v. 'with some condition') fits his conception of non-positive morality. The main passage is *Dial.* iii, Tract 2, 10, translated in Ockham, *LFM* 261. For further details see Crowe, *CPNL* 201–5; Offler, 'Modes'; McGrade, *PTWO* 177–85.

[49] See Pegis, 'Necessity'; Freppert, *BMWO* 105.

[50] See *2Sent.* q3–4 = OT v 52.14–53.3; q3–4 = OT v 55.15–56.5; *1Sent.* d43 q1 = OT iv 625.8–626.19.

[51] See Aquinas, *ST* 1a q60 a2 (natural dilectio involves intellect and will but is not free); 1-2 q1 a2; *Pot.* q10 a2 ad4, 5.

[52] '. . . whatever acts out of necessity by nature (ex necessitate natura), it is impossible for it to be an acting principle, since the end would be determined for it by something else. And so it is clear that it is impossible for God to act out of necessity of nature' (Aquinas, *Pot.* q1 a5c = M 19a).

[53] 'The natural end of the divine will . . . is its goodness, which it cannot not will. But creatures are not commensurate with this end in such a way that without these the divine goodness could not be revealed; and it is this revealing that God aims at from creatures. For just as the divine goodness is revealed through the things that now are and through the ordering of these things, so also it can be revealed through other creatures and creatures ordered in another way. . . .' (*Pot.* q1 a5c = M 19b).

goodness. God does not act necessarily; God chooses one of these good options, when it is open to God to choose one of the other good options.[54]

This answer does not satisfy Ockham. In his view, God must be free to reject all the various good options; no constraint requiring God to choose among the good options is consistent with divine freedom. God was free to choose some other set of laws than the ones God actually chose, and therefore God is free to alter those already chosen. The decision not to alter them is an expression of God's 'directed' or 'ordered' (ordinata) power; this is God's power directed in the way God has freely chosen to direct it. This directed power is distinct from God's 'unqualified' or 'absolute' (absoluta) power.[55] Hence the fact that it is not within God's directed power to change a given law simply means that God has directed his power so as to leave this law unchanged; it still remains within God's unqualified power to change the law. God has the unqualified power to cause A without causing B unless A and B are identical (so that it would be self-contradictory for something to be A without being B) (2Sent. q15 = OT v 342.8–21). Hence God's power extends to doing everything that can be done without a contradiction or blameworthy evil.[56] Only God's currently-directed power would be violated if God were to change the current order to another order. When Ockham says that certain principles are stable 'given that the divine command stands', he means that they are stable from the point of view of God's directed power, but it is still within God's unqualified power to change them.[57]

In the light of these views about morality and divine freedom, Ockham defends his version of Anselm's claim that what God wills is necessarily just and right. God is not obliged to do anything, because God is no one's debtor. Even if a human being is obliged to do x and would act wrongly by doing not-x, God is not obliged to do x and would not act wrongly by doing not-x (Q. var. q8 = OT viii 434.573–436.607). For sin consists not only in a specific sort of action, but also in the fact that the action violates an obligation. Since God cannot be obliged, God cannot sin.[58] Similarly, punishment is owed to any human being only because this is how God has ordered it.[59] Since God is not obliged to do anything, and therefore is not obliged to do anything other than what God does, Anselm is right to believe that God cannot act unjustly. A human will needs some rule to direct it to act rightly, because it does

---

[54] On divine freedom and creation see Aquinas, §§307, 347.

[55] On potentia absoluta and potentia ordinata see §381; Aquinas, ST 1a q25 a3 ad1; Scotus, 1Sent. d44 = OO v 2, 1368 §2 = W 256 (with Wolter's introduction, 56–7); Ockham, Quodl. vi q6 = OT ix 604.14–16; 1Sent. d20 = OT iv 36.4–10; Adams, WO ii 1186–207; Wood, OV 22–5. Aspects of the historical influence of the distinction are explored by Oakley, 'Absolute'.

[56] 'omne quod non includit contradictionem nec malum culpae potest fieri a Deo solo', 2Sent. q15 = OT v 342.19–21.

[57] For 'given that the divine command stands' see n45 above.

[58] 'For one does not call a sin, as has been said, anything other than some act of commission <that a human being is obliged not to do> or of omission <of an action> that a human being is obliged to do. . . . But God cannot be obliged to do any act, and therefore, by the very fact that God wills this, it is just to be done. . . . It is obligation, therefore, that makes someone a sinner or not a sinner' (4Sent. q10–11 = OT vii 198.4–13). On God's debts and obligations see Adams, 'Will' 264–5.

[59] '. . . for, just as God creates any creature out of his mere will (mera voluntate), so also by his mere will he is able to do whatever pleases him about his creature. For just as, if someone were always to love God and were to do all works accepted by God, God could annihilate him without doing <him?> any wrong (sine aliqua iniuria), so also he can give him, after such works, not eternal life but eternal punishment without doing <him> wrong. And the reason is that God is no one's debtor, but whatever he does for us, he does out of mere grace. That is why, by the very fact that God does something, it is done justly. For it is clear that Christ never sinned, and yet was most severely punished even unto death' (4Sent. q5 = OT vii 55.11–21). Cf. 4Sent. q11 = OT vii 225.19–226.5; Holopainen, WOTFE 134.

not act rightly of itself. The divine will, by contrast, needs nothing to direct it, because it is itself the primary directive rule, and cannot act badly (*Q. var.* q8 = OT viii 410.19–23).

Ockham seems to assume a strictly positive conception of obligation and of right and wrong. Apart from principles that cannot be denied without self-contradiction, all right and wrong is the creation of someone's will. Hence nothing that God chooses to do, whatever it might be, could be wrong.[60] Right and wrong presuppose the imposition of a debt or obligation by an imposer who is distinct from the debtor or the person obliged.[61]

397. Questions about God's Justice

Ockham's claims about the necessary conditions for obligation and sin seem to require a voluntarist interpretation of his claims about non-positive morality. His claims about the connexion between obligation and imposition seem to require him to deny that the principles of non-positive morality have any content that is independent of God's legislative will. If they had independent content, some things that are always morally right might not be obligatory until God chooses them. But Ockham does not seem to allow the possibility that in some circumstances non-positive morality might be possibly right but non-obligatory; he expresses moral principles with gerundives ('right actions are to be done' etc.), which he normally uses to express obligations.

His claims about God's freedom from obligations and duties seem to rest on a narrow use of 'obligation' and 'duty' (or 'debt', debitum).[62] We might disagree with him on several grounds: (1) We might agree that obligations and duties are the same, but deny that obligation requires imposition.[63] (2) We might agree that obligations and duties are the same, and agree that obligations are imposed or incurred by voluntary action. On this view, non-obligatory actions might create obligations or duties. We might believe that while people have no obligation to become parents, or spouses, or monks, they incur obligations once they enter into these conditions. Similarly, then, though God was not obliged to create us, God might incur an obligation towards us by creating us; once God created us, perhaps some things that would not otherwise have been wrong for God to do became wrong. (3) We might agree with Ockham's assumption that obligation requires not mere imposition, but imposition by a superior. But then we might follow Suarez in separating obligations from duties and maintain that God has duties, though no obligations, towards us.[64] (4) Even if we agree with Ockham that obligations and duties are the same and that they all require imposition by a superior, we might believe that some right and wrong action is independent of obligation and duty.

To agree with Ockham, then, we must reject all of these views, and agree that obligations imposed by a superior exhaust the content of the morally right and wrong. It is not clear

---

[60] 'A human being never sins except because he is required (tenetur) to do what he does not do or because he does what he ought (debet) not to do. By this account a human being is made a debtor (debitor). God, however, is required to do nothing and is not obliged as a debtor, and for that reason he cannot do what he ought (debet) not to do and cannot not do what he ought to do' (*2Sent.* q15 = OT v 343.17–22).

[61] See Aquinas on God and debitum; *ST* 1a q21 a1.

[62] Ockham does not seem to distinguish debitum from obligatio.

[63] Perhaps Aquinas accepts this view. See §303.   [64] On obligationes v debita see Suarez, *Leg.* ii 9.4.

why we should agree on this general point about obligation and morality, since the four other views seem at least as plausible, from the moral point of view, as Ockham's view. We seem to have a reason to accept his views about obligation only if we already accept Ockham's views on divine freedom. In this case, then, his views on freedom seem to be the basis of his views on morality.

But even if we agree that all right and wrong action by one agent presupposes a debt or obligation imposed by another agent, Ockham still has not vindicated Anselm's claim. For even if he has shown that it is impossible for God to act wrongly or unjustly, given God's freedom from imposed obligations, it does not follow that everything God does is just and right. Why should we not say instead that what God does is neither right nor wrong?

It is not clear how Ockham answers this question. Though he claims that wrongness requires the violation of an imposed obligation, he does not say that rightness requires the fulfilment of an imposed obligation. But it is difficult to see why rightness and wrongness should differ in their relation to imposed obligations. If Ockham claims that God's will, simply by being God's will, is just, he apparently ought to say that whatever violates or opposes God's will is unjust, whether or not God has laid any obligation on us to obey his will.[65] But if he takes wrongness to presuppose an imposed obligation, he apparently ought to say the same about rightness.

Perhaps Ockham is not clear about the relation between two claims that he seems to accept: (1) What is right is what accords with God's will. (2) What is right is what is imposed by the will of a superior. If we consider which human actions are right, both claims imply that God's legislative will determines what it is right for us to do. But if we consider God's actions, the two claims have different implications; for the first implies that what God does is right, whereas the second implies that it is neither right nor wrong. Ockham's claims about obligation, rightness, and wrongness commit him to the view of some later voluntarists, that God's actions are neither just nor unjust, because they are above any imposition of obligation.[66] He should not agree, therefore, with Anselm's view that God's actions are necessarily just.

398. Conflicts within Morality

These claims about the dependence of morality on God's will do not cancel the difference between non-positive and positive morality. If we consider God's unqualified power, even non-positive morality is—according to one of Ockham's explanations, at any rate—a product of God's freely willing one content rather than another for the principles of correct reason. But once God has willed that content, we can consider morality with reference to God's directed power; with this condition assumed, we can know by correct reason, without reference to any further act of divine legislation, that some actions are right and others are wrong, and we can also count on God to act and prescribe in accordance with the principles we grasp by correct reason.

---

[65] As Ockham sees, this point requires some qualification, to take account of the fact that God wills that we not will our parents' death, even though God wills that our parents will die (*Q. var.* q8 = OT viii 434.573–435.583).

[66] Cf. Locke, discussed by Price, *RPQM* 43.

Though the content of non-positive morality known to correct reason is fixed, in relation to God's directed power, non-positive morality may still conflict with divine positive morality. For apparently God might freely choose to violate a precept of non-positive morality, or might instruct us to violate it. Scotus does not acknowledge this possibility; the only dispensations he mentions are dispensations from divine positive law. Ockham, however, acknowledges the possibility of a conflict. God's unqualified power extends to everything that does not involve a contradiction, and (according to Ockham) it is not self-contradictory to deny that theft and adultery are sometimes right; hence God could (by his unqualified power) command us to commit adultery, so that adultery would be right.[67] In the extreme case, God could make it right to hate God.[68]

On the strength of this claim, Suarez takes Ockham to hold that no action is bad except in so far as it is prohibited by God, and no action could not become good if it were prescribed by God, and conversely.[69] Ockham relies on God's freedom from obligation, and on the fact that God's will, exercising unqualified power, fixes the content of non-positive morality. Non-positive morality does not consist entirely of analytic truths that would be immutable even within God's unqualified power (because God could not make them false without self-contradiction). It consists of substantive principles that contain obligations resulting from the divine will. Hence non-positive morality is mutable within God's unqualified power.

It is therefore logically possible for God to give us a command that we could not obey. In Ockham's view, we obey God's commands because we follow the precept of non-positive morality that enjoins the love for God. In following this precept we follow the law that accords with the will of God, and it is not within God's directed power to change it. But God could, as far as God's unqualified power goes, change loving God from being right to being wrong. God might command us not to love God; we could not be moved to obey this command unless we loved God, but if we loved God we would not be obeying this command. Hence we could not obey God's command not to love God (*Quodl.* iii 14 = OT ix 256.74–257.94).[70]

This argument presupposes that the only motive for obeying God that we need to consider is love for God. Ockham is not considering obedience out of 'servile' fear of God's power to harm us,[71] but obedience on moral grounds, and hence obedience based on the love of God. On this assumption, God can give us a command that we cannot fulfil—not because God

---

[67] 'On another point I say that, granted that hatred, theft, adultery, have a bad circumstance attached to them, and so do similar things in the common law, in so far as they are done by someone who by a divine precept is obliged to the contrary; still, as far as concerns the unqualified being of such actions, they can be done by God without any bad circumstance attached. And they can even be done meritoriously by a traveller <in this life>, if they were to fall under a divine precept, just as now in fact their opposites fall under a divine precept' (*2Sent.* q15 ad3 = OT v 352.3–9).

[68] 'God is not obliged to cause any action, and therefore he can cause any action at all without any blameworthy evil (*malum culpae*), and similarly <he can cause> its opposite. And for that reason, just as he can cause entirely an act of loving without moral goodness or badness (because moral goodness and badness connote that the agent is obliged to that act or to its opposite), so also he can cause entirely an act of hating God without any moral badness for the same reason, because he is not obliged to cause any act' (*2Sent.* q15 ad4 = OT v 353.11–18). Ockham uses 'connote' (connotare) for a secondary or indirect signification; see Adams, *WO* i 147–8.

[69] 'nullum esse actum malum, nisi quatenus a Deo prohibitus est, et qui non possit fieri bonus si a Deo praecipiatur, et e converso', Suarez, *Leg.* ii 6.4.

[70] Cf. *Quodl.* iii 15 = ix 260 fin.   [71] On servile fear see Aquinas, *ST* 2-2 q7 a1.

commands us to do something self-contradictory in itself, but because our obedience to any command of God presupposes a motive that is prohibited by this particular command.[72]

Ockham describes this possibility in order to show what his position implies about the will of God, not because he believes that God does or will command us not to love God. He takes divine freedom to exclude any conception of God that makes God's choices depend on God's understanding of what is best. Though Ockham accepts the Anselmian principle about God's justice, he accepts it in the attenuated sense that regards justice as simply a product of God's choice.

399. God and Morality: Versions of Voluntarism

Neither Scotus nor Ockham is an unqualified voluntarist about morality and the divine will. The qualifications are especially clear in Scotus. He attributes to God an affection for justice that is the mark of divine freedom no less than of human freedom. This affection for justice ensures the truth of the Anselmian principle that necessarily God wills what is just. Moreover, not all the principles of morality are products of God's choice, since the higher principles of natural law (including the first table of the Decalogue) are discoverable by natural reason as principles about natural suitability. The positive laws that God imposes on us (including the second table of the Decalogue) also manifest the affection for justice, since they are highly consonant with the higher principles of natural law. Ockham also recognizes the rational and just aspects of the divine will. He does not follow Scotus in connecting the affection for justice with freedom, but he recognizes a non-positive area of morality, and believes that God endorses it.

It is not easy to combine God's acceptance of justice with God's freedom, as Scotus conceives it. If he is right about freedom, God's preference for justice and for the principles of natural law is a preference of God's self-determining will that chooses between justice and injustice, but not on the basis of goodness or rightness. To maintain the Anselmian maxim, Scotus has to treat justice as simply the product of God's choice. Similarly, Ockham believes that God's legislative will is necessarily rational; it is not guided by rational principles, but creates them. Human moral judgment, however, is guided by reason; facts about moral rightness and wrongness are accessible to human reason, and virtue consists in willing in accordance with correct reason. Ockham does not share the scepticism of later writers who deny any special connexion between practical reason and morality.

The position of Scotus and Ockham is often taken to be an important influence on the direction taken by later moral philosophy. Sometimes it is taken to be the origin of 'divine command' conceptions of morality defended during and after the Reformation.[73] This is not simply the view of historians in the nineteenth century or later. Cudworth defends eternal and immutable morality, as he conceives it, both against the positivism that he traces back to Protagoras and against the theological voluntarism that he attributes to Ockham, other

---

[72] See Adams 'Structure' 27–31; *WO* ii 1273–8 (on divine power). According to Oberman, *HMT* 94–5, Biel rejects Ockham's account of God's command to hate him. The evidence cited for this claim about Biel is insufficient; see *3Sent.* d37 a2 concl 3 = 636L W&H. Gregory of Rimini argues against Ockham at *1Sent.* d42–4 q1 a2 = 384–7 T&M.

[73] See §§411, 421–2.

mediaeval theologians, 'modern' theologians, and Descartes. From Cudworth's point of view, the mediaeval voluntarists abandon the view that morality has rational foundations. Cudworth does not invent this assessment of voluntarism; he relies on the critique of Ockham by Suarez, who cannot be accused of ignorance of Scholasticism or of raising anachronistic questions.[74]

This assessment of Scotus and Ockham may not be correct, since they may not accept all the views that later critics, or later followers, connect with voluntarism. They both understand morality as conformity to correct reason.[75] Is this a reason for rejecting the criticisms presented by Suarez and Cudworth?

Ockham maintains: (1) Moral virtue is in accord with correct reason. (2) Correct reason grasps the principles of non-positive morality. (3) Non-positive morality consists of obligations. (4) All obligations are imposed by God. (5) God's will does not follow any independent principles of morality. These claims are consistent, but they force Ockham into an awkward position. He has to claim that the content of correct reason itself is the product of a choice made by the free will of God independently of any antecedent principles of right. But this way of safeguarding the freedom of the divine will makes it difficult to see what is rational about the principles accepted by correct reason. We cannot say that some specific aim or character constitutes their rationality, since that would constrain God's choice of what to count as correct reason.

Ockham seems to be committed, therefore, to saying that it is logically possible for God to have made correct reason require cruelty, self-destruction, injustice, neglect of the future for the sake of the present, and so on. If this is indeed a consequence of his position, we might reasonably conclude that the appeal to correct reason has lost the sense that it has in Aquinas, and really amounts to nothing more than the claim that God has put some specific convictions into us.

Ockham seems to imply that it is up to God to choose what the natural law will be. He thereby denies any necessary connexion between the nature of a creature, the good of that creature, and the natural law applying to that creature. If the creature's nature fixes its good, but God is free to vary the natural law so that it does not conform to a creature's nature, apparently God is free to prescribe laws that conflict with the creature's good. Ockham does not claim that the principles of justice are unconnected with the good of human beings, or that God is free to impose new principles of justice that are unconnected with human good; but it is difficult to see how he can avoid such a claim, if he admits that the nature of human beings fixes their good.

He might, therefore, reply that the nature of a creature does not fix its good, and that God is free to change a creature's good together with changes in the natural law. This denial of a necessary connexion between human nature and the human good ought not to appeal to Scotus; for belief in such a necessary connexion seems to underlie his account of the affection for advantage. He accepts the Aristotelian view that facts about a creature's nature, rather than the creature's preferences or divine preferences, fix its good. As long as we maintain this connexion between a creature's nature and its good, we cannot make its good depend

---

[74] See Cudworth, *EIM* i 1.5 = H14.
[75] See Wolter, *DSWM* 16–29; Adams 'Structure'; Bonansea, 'Voluntarism' 95–6.

on the divine legislative will. Ockham does not explicitly reject Scotus' claims about nature and good, but his position might be more defensible if he rejected them.

A thoroughly voluntarist position, eliminating the possibility of conflict between nature and the will of God, might seek to make the human good depend on God's will, without completely severing it from human nature. Ordinary legislators support their commands with sanctions. If God does this too, God can attach pleasure to the fulfilment of divine commands and pain to the violation of them. Since we naturally aim at pleasure and avoid pain, God can change the natural law without changing this aspect of our nature.

This penal conception of our reason for obeying natural law would not avoid a conflict between God's commands and our nature, if our nature made other things non-instrumentally good for us apart from pleasure. If, then, we want to maintain the penal account of natural law, we are well advised to accept a hedonist account of the good. Hence Hobbes combines a penal account of natural law with hedonism. In his view, the laws of nature, apart from divine commands, are not really laws, but counsels of prudence prescribing means to our pleasure. As divine commands they are laws combined with sanctions appealing to pain and pleasure. The appropriate connexion with human nature relies on a hedonist conception of the good.[76]

This more extreme voluntarist position is not the logical outcome of Scotus' and Ockham's qualified voluntarism. From the extreme voluntarist point of view, Scotus and Ockham create difficulties for themselves by failing to reject Aristotelian assumptions about the connexion between natural law, the human good, and facts about human nature. These assumptions open the prospect of conflict between human nature, the human good, and the will of God. Ockham accepts the possibility of such conflict. If we take it to be morally and theologically unacceptable, we will discard the Aristotelian assumptions. This is not the only possible conclusion, however. Perhaps we should accept the possible conflicts resulting from Scotus' and Ockham's position, or we should prefer Aquinas' position over voluntarism.

A different sort of voluntarist response to the difficulties faced by Scotus and Ockham might deny that divine legislation fixes the human good, and confine it to the fixing of moral rightness and wrongness. According to this view, facts about human nature and human good are fixed by the existence of human beings in their natural environment, but they are separate from moral rightness and wrongness until God commands the observance of principles promoting the human good. According to this view, the will of God is sovereign over whether the natural law is really law; without the divine command, it would not be natural law, but simply a set of principles. This conception of law relies on Ockham's narrow conception of obligation, making obligation depend on imposition by the will of another, and taking law to imply obligation.[77]

This version of voluntarism avoids the difficulty that arises for Ockham, since it does not fix the content of correct reason by acts of divine free choice, but allows the content of correct reason to be fixed by human nature and human good. But this advantage is costly; if we separate the content of correct reason from the strictly moral principles that require divine imposition, we sever the connexion that Ockham preserves between correct reason and morality. This element of anti-intellectualism takes a step beyond Scotus and Ockham, though one can see why reflexion on the difficulties in their position might support this step.

---

[76] See Hobbes, L. 15.41.   [77] Different versions of this view are defended by Suarez and Pufendorf.

400. Voluntarism, Morality, and Reasons

We have now discussed the aspects of voluntarism that are intended to maintain divine freedom against the restrictions (as Scotus and Ockham suppose) that would follow from acceptance of Aquinas' view. Similarly, voluntarists intend to safeguard human freedom in relation to God and morality. In their view, God does not present us with principles that are rationally compelling for us, so that we would be acting irrationally if we rejected them. Instead, Scotus argues that God presents the natural law as a series of requirements of justice; we will have a reason to follow them if we choose to follow our affection towards justice, but we have no overriding reason to choose to follow this affection rather than some other.

If facts about human nature do not provide external reasons, the voluntarist loses Aquinas' account of the basis of ethics in natural reason. The voluntarist's alternative basis consists in principles that provide internal reasons for agents who already have the relevant sorts of affections and have made the appropriate sorts of undetermined choices. If we choose to follow our affection towards our own advantage, self-interested principles give us internal reasons; if we choose to follow our affection towards justice, other principles provide internal reasons.

If all reasons are internal, we can solve difficulties about divine commands and ethics that might seem to arise otherwise. A believer in external reasons must apparently recognize at least the logical possibility of a conflict between divine commands and rational principles of morality; for why, we might ask, should God not order us to do one thing while rational morality orders us to do another? If we are thorough voluntarists at the human as well as the divine level, we can remove this difficulty. God cannot command us to act contrary to external reasons, if there are none. The right way to describe a conflict between God's commands and some other principle is to say that some other affection of ours prompts us to do x, but God commands us to do y. It is then up to us to choose whether to follow the affections that incline us to obey God (love of God, fear of divine punishment) or to follow our other affections. None of these courses of action is externally more reasonable than another; which it is reasonable for us to follow depends on our undetermined choice to follow one or another affection.

These voluntarist views help us to understand some of Hobbes's assumptions. If there are no external reasons, reasons and obligations rest on some affection and some choice. If our basic affection aims at self-preservation, any obligation must ultimately appeal to that affection; hence it must appeal to our desire for self-preservation either directly or indirectly (through a sanction for violation). Since God and human legislators impose a sanction for the violation of their commands, their commands provide us with obligations.[78]

Hobbesian assumptions about motivation and affection do not follow from a voluntarist position. But the starting point of the Hobbesian argument, assuming the unintelligibility of external reasons, may well appear arbitrary and unjustified unless we are already convinced by voluntarist arguments against Aquinas' version of intellectualism.

[78] For this sort of view see Tuck, NRT, ch. 4, on Selden.

28

MACHIAVELLI

---

401. Questions about Moral Philosophy

In some ways Machiavelli is not a very suitable source if we are looking for serious philosophical criticism of Aquinas. His main interests and abilities lie in politics and history, and he is neither a deep nor a systematic philosophical thinker. Still, these very features of his views make it even more useful to examine them; for he shows how specific practical problems and attitudes may suggest objections to the Christian assumptions embodied in Aquinas' system. Machiavelli intends to challenge the Christian conception of the place of the Christian virtues in social and political life. But he also raises a broader question that he does not intend: what counts as an adequate theory of the virtues? Machiavelli sets out some demands that the Christian conception does not satisfy; but it is not obvious that any other conception of the virtues can satisfy his demands.[1]

Aquinas intends his account of the ultimate end and the moral virtues to embrace different sorts of practical situations and demands. The virtues satisfy the demands of (i) self-interest; (ii) morality; (iii) the common good of a community; (iv) a human being's approach to the vision of God. Machiavelli rejects Aquinas' system by arguing that no one set of virtues can satisfy all four sorts of demands.

Aquinas believes that the virtues contribute to a person's own interest because they require the regulation of passion by practical reason, and because the particular sort of regulation they require is appropriate for a human being's social and political nature. The kinds of demands and restrictions imposed on us by the requirements of morality do not conflict with the good of the individual human being; on the contrary, they fulfil it.

The second and third demands on the virtues are not sharply distinct; for Aquinas, following Aristotle, identifies the requirements of social morality with the common good of some community, small or large. But it is useful to see that two distinct conditions have to be satisfied. Aquinas connects them closely because he does not believe that we can determine

---

[1] Burd, *Il Principe* xiv, remarks: 'It is no paradox to say that *The Prince*, though in many ways immoral, has been none the less of indirect service to morality. . . . [It] has the significance which belongs to the works of all authors who have questioned, not in a spirit of selfishness or from indifference, but from a reasoned conviction, the commonly accepted codes of morality. Such writings serve, by contrast, for a perpetual reminder that the ultimate sanction of morality is, for the non-religious mind at any rate, the suicidal nature of immorality . . .'

the good of the community by some non-moral standard, and then subordinate morality to this goal. The community whose good is to be promoted must itself be formed on principles suitable for the nature of the individuals belonging to it; this is one consequence of the Aristotelian claim that the state is a natural association. Principles derived from the moral virtues partly determine what counts as the good of a community.

The virtues are to satisfy the fourth demand because the pursuit of a comprehensive good in this life is the appropriate preliminary to the vision of God in the next life; Aquinas' conception of the final good prevents him from saying that if we want the vision of God, we ought to renounce the world altogether. He has to appeal to his specific analysis of the virtues to show that the moral virtues needed for social life do not conflict with the Christian virtues. The kinds of bravery and magnanimity that are appropriate to a citizen do not conflict with the humility required of a Christian.

Machiavelli offers a powerful objection to Aquinas because he casts serious doubt on whether any one set of virtues can really satisfy all the four sorts of demands that Aquinas recognizes as legitimate. It is useful to consider his grounds for scepticism.

402. Civic Virtues

Machiavelli and Aquinas share one of their starting points. For Machiavelli follows Greek and Roman political theory in placing a high value on the virtues of the citizen and on the demands of civic life. He is concerned with the fortunes of a city-state that has to struggle to maintain its political independence and its civic harmony; and to this extent the problems he faces are similar to those that face Thucydides, Plato, and Aristotle. Even though his major work is a series of discourses on Livy, his situation and experience are closer to those of the Greek historians and political theorists than to the actual situation of Livy, who looks back on Rome's existence as a city-state from the rather different perspective of the early Empire under Augustus.

Some of Machiavelli's priorities are also similar to those of Greek political thinkers. He aims at a city's independence from external control and at its internal cohesion. He sees that factions tend to form, especially around powerful and ambitious individuals, and the deeper division between the rich and the poor tends to divide the citizens along more permanent lines. The citizens rightly want to preserve their liberty, including both freedom from external domination and freedom to choose the rulers they prefer. Most people, in Machiavelli's view, want freedom from interference by the state so that they can ensure security for themselves in their private lives (D i 16.8); but citizens with the right sort of civic spirit seem to want such freedom for its own sake (cf. ii 23.4).

The sovereign 'republic' governed by its citizens[2] (or some of them) is not the only sort of state that Machiavelli knows. He also discusses monarchies, and indeed The Prince is a book of advice for autocratic rulers. But he makes it clear that he prefers a republic. In the Discourses

---

[2] 'Free government'; D i 18.1. I cite D by the chapters and sections in Walker, and P by chapters and pages in Atkinson. I usually follow Walker's translation of D (severely criticized by Whitfield, DM 231–7) and Atkinson's translation of P. I cite Walker's edition as 'W'. Walker is forthright about the point of view from which he considers his subject: '. . . scholarship in the broad sense should place a man's stature against the background of really great thinkers, indeed against the background of common human judgment and of Christian perception, and, as judged from this standpoint, many of Machiavelli's principles, principles which are basic to his outlook and his theory, stand universally condemned' (i 8).

he is mainly concerned with republics, and clearly thinks it is desirable to maintain a republic in good condition if it is already healthy. He thinks it is a more difficult task to introduce a republic among people who have been used to absolute rule, or to restore a republic that has been 'corrupted' (D i 49); corruption is easy, and the danger is always present (i 42). The welfare of the state is always precarious; Machiavelli tries to protect it by giving advice about the sorts of dangers that may arise, and by suggesting ways to counteract them.

The aims of a republic, and the threats that it faces in trying to achieve these aims, determine Machiavelli's conception of a citizen's virtue. A good state maintains virtue in its citizens, and the only way to reform a state is to introduce laws and institutions that encourage the development of virtue. The virtue of a citizen is the set of characteristics that promotes the preservation of the republican state. The primary characteristic is willingness to make sacrifices for the common good. A secondary characteristic is a desire for glory, which is the most reliable motive leading to public spirit (cf. i 43). This desire is secondary in civic virtue because it needs to be restrained and controlled by the demands of the public interest; if it is necessary to sacrifice glory in order to preserve the state, that sacrifice should be made.[3]

Machiavelli does not always speak of virtue in exactly this way. He uses the term univocally[4] for the qualities that are most appropriate for achieving a given end; but since he considers different ends in different contexts, the qualities he includes under 'virtue' may differ also. He speaks of virtue not only in a civic, but also in a military context; the virtue of a general or a soldier is the appropriate sort of military efficiency rather than efficiency in promoting the common good of a state.[5] Civic virtue includes the appropriate degree of military virtue; and no doubt a good soldier must be ready to do his part in the whole army he belongs to. But still the two sorts of virtue may not be identical; it is clear and familiar to Machiavelli that an efficient and successful general may not be devoted to the common good of his state, and indeed may often be a threat to it.[6] A ruler may even be successful in maintaining his power and ensuring stability in the state; but if he behaves as Agathocles did, he cannot win glory and cannot count as having virtue (P 8). Machiavelli's use of 'virtue' for these two different, though related, sets of qualities raises no special difficulty; it is no less natural than the use of 'good' in 'good politician', 'good citizen', and 'good general'; but we have to be careful to see what sort of virtue he is referring to on each occasion.

403. Civic v. Christian Virtue

In the light of his conception of virtue, Machiavelli thinks he can show that the Christian virtues conflict with civic and military virtue. The Christian attitude to the world tends to develop the wrong traits of character and to impede the development of the right ones.[7]

---

[3] 'For when on the decision to be taken wholly depends the safety of one's country, no attention should be paid either to justice or injustice, to kindness or cruelty, or to its being praiseworthy or ignominious' (iii 41.2). W ad loc. points out that the historical examples cited by Machiavelli do not show that either the Romans or the French agree with his general principle.

[4] On 'virtue' see W i 99–102; Skinner, FMPT i 138; 'Virtù' 163; Plamenatz, 'Virtù;'. On contemporary uses of 'virtue', compared with Machiavelli's use, see Skinner, FMPT i 125–6.

[5] See W i 100–2. [6] See D i 10.6; P19 (on Severus); P7 (on Cesare Borgia).

[7] 'For our religion, having taught us the truth and the true way of life leads us to ascribe less esteem to worldly honour' (D ii 2.6).

The cultivation of 'humility, abnegation, and contempt for mundane things' as the highest human good weakens the proper civic attachment to 'magnanimity, bodily strength, and everything else that tends to make men very bold' (D ii 2.6). Christianity demands strength in suffering rather than strength in action.[8]

It is not clear, however, that Machiavelli regards these harmful effects as necessary results of Christianity. For he suggests that the apparent conflict between the Christian virtues and active civic virtue may result from a misunderstanding of Christianity.[9] Unfortunately he does not try to reconcile this suggestion with his previous remarks. It would be strange if he meant that Christianity does not encourage the virtues of humility and detachment from the concerns of the world; for he is correct in saying that it does not place a person's highest good in worldly success. But he may mean that the cultivation of the Christian outlook need not conflict with a proper civic spirit, because Christian principles allow[10] loyalty to one's community and vigour in promoting its welfare.

This is an important concession by Machiavelli. For even the less 'monkish' form of Christianity that he recognizes does not regard loyalty to the state as an individual's overriding goal. He does not suggest that 'civic Christianity' would regard every action necessary for the defence of the state as morally legitimate and beyond criticism. If he concedes this, he also concedes that the appropriate civic virtue need not include an unreserved commitment to the preservation of the state.

It is doubtful, however, whether Machiavelli consistently intends to allow that civic virtue requires only the Christian's limited loyalty to the state. For his usual view implies a much deeper objection to Christian morality. His position is summed up in the claim that 'it is good to defend one's country in whatever way it is done, whether it entail ignominy or glory' (iii 41.1). Machiavelli illustrates this extreme principle with some relatively innocuous examples that might be consistent with a more moderate principle; he mentions the use of tricks and stratagems in war[11] and the acceptance of humiliating terms of peace. But he accepts the extreme principle without restriction, as a defence of actions that are not merely humiliating but clearly immoral. Any action taken by a ruler organizing a republic is justified if its effects are good enough.[12]

---

[8] 'This pattern of life, therefore, appears to have made the world weak, and to have handed it over as a prey to the wicked, who run it successfully and securely since they are well aware that the generality of men, with paradise for their goal, consider how best to bear, rather than how best to avenge, their injuries' (ii 2.7).

[9] 'But though it looks as if the world were become effeminate and as if heaven were powerless, this undoubtedly is due rather to the pusillanimity of those who have interpreted our religion in terms of laissez faire [or 'inactivity'; ozio], not in terms of virtue. For, had they borne in mind that religion permits us to exalt and defend the fatherland, they would have seen that it also wishes us to love and honour it, and to train ourselves to be such that we may defend it' (ii 2.7). W ad loc. cites Aquinas' comments on the bad effects of tyranny, Reg. Princ. i 3 = M 5a: 'Moreover it is natural that when people are brought up under fear, they decline into a servile outlook, and become pusillanimous towards every manly and demanding (strenuum) activity'. Aquinas blames tyranny for the outlook that Machiavelli blames on Christianity.

[10] In the passage just quoted from W, Machiavelli says only 'allows' rather than 'enjoins'. W translates 'permette', but some texts read 'promette' (preferred by Rinaldi, O, and glossed 'invita a').

[11] On these W ii 204 cites Aquinas, ST 2-2 q40 a3. Aquinas argues that attempts to deceive the enemy by lying or breaking promises are impermissible and contrary to the 'iura bellorum' that should always be observed. But stratagems (insidiae) that may mislead the enemy are permissible.

[12] 'Nor will any reasonable man blame him for taking any action, however extraordinary, which may be of service in the organizing of a kingdom or the constituting of a republic. It is a sound maxim that reprehensible actions may be justified by their effects, and that when the effect is good, as it was in the case of Romulus, it always justifies the action' (i 9.2). W ad loc. cites examples given in iii 3–4.

This general principle explains Machiavelli's conviction that the recognized moral virtues do not suit a ruler who tries to do what has to be done for the sake of the state. In discussing the qualities that a ruler should cultivate, he rejects the usual advice of moralists who urge rulers to cultivate the moral virtues.[13] Such advice is inapplicable to the real world, where a ruler has to be willing to act immorally on the right occasions, if he is to maintain his position.[14] This instruction to any ruler who wants to maintain his power follows from Machiavelli's separation of civic virtue from moral virtue. He rejects the advice of moralists because he assumes that the overriding aim is the safety of the state or the ruler; moral principles conflicting with this aim are irrelevant.

We might, then, suppose that Machiavelli accepts Augustine's contrast between pagan and Christian virtue, but draws the opposite conclusion from it. If Augustine treats pagan virtues as 'splendid vices' and insists that genuine moral virtue is based on Christian faith, Machiavelli agrees with him on both points. He disagrees with Augustine in preferring the splendid vices of pagans to the Christian virtues, because he believes that the arrogance and self-assertion that Augustine finds in the pagan outlook are desirable traits.

404. Machiavellian Virtue v. Moral Virtue

We have found, however, that Augustine does not hold this view of pagan virtue, and that he is right not to hold it.[15] The virtues advocated by pagan moralists are not forms of self-assertion or arrogance; they include concern for the interests of others for their own sake. Machiavelli's division between the pagan and the Christian outlook does not fit the views of pagan moralists.

We can confirm this claim by considering the example of Romulus' murder of Remus. Machiavelli cites this incident to show that ruthlessness is sometimes necessary (i 9.2; Livy i 7.1–2). In this case it was immoral and vicious for Romulus to do what he did, but it was necessary for the preservation of his own rule and for the preservation of the state; hence it was justified, though not morally justified. Machiavelli admits that the traits of character he advises a ruler to acquire will appear deplorable and vicious from the moral point of view, not simply from the Christian point of view.[16]

Cicero mentions this incident as an apparent example of a conflict between the right (honestum) and the expedient (Off. iii 40–1). He assumes that it would be wrong to prefer the expedient over the right (nam id quidem improbum est, 40). He argues that in some cases reflexion on a particular case shows that the expedient course of action that seemed

[13] For the usual advice to a prince see the selections from Pontano and Platina in Kraye, CTRPT ii, chs. 5–6.

[14] 'Many writers have conceived of republics and princedoms which have never in fact been seen or known to exist. Since there is so great a discrepancy between how one lives and how one ought to live, whoever forsakes what is done for what ought to be done is learning his ruin rather than his preservation. For a man who wants to practise goodness in all situations is inevitably ruined, among so many men who are not good. Hence a prince who wishes to retain his power must learn to be able not to be good, and to use, or not to use, that ability according to necessity' (P 15, 255–7).

[15] See §228.

[16] 'I know everyone will admit that it would be most laudable for a prince to be endowed with all the qualities mentioned above, those that are considered good. But since he is unable to possess them, or comply with them, entirely because of human conditions which do not permit it—he must be prudent enough to know how to escape the infamy of those vices that do cost him his power' (P 15, 257–9).

unjust is not really unjust (Collatinus, 40);[17] but he rejects this defence of Romulus' conduct, and concludes that what Romulus did was wrong (41).

Cicero qualifies his judgment by remarking that Romulus did not simply assert the claims of expediency over morality; he cited the incident of Remus' jumping over the walls as an aggressive action that deserved punishment. Even if we think Romulus was justified, we need not agree that his action was clearly immoral, and hence we need not agree that it clearly illustrates the separation of the expedient from the right.

Machiavelli's brusque rejection of Cicero's argument shows that his attack on Christian morality is misleading. He attacks morality on a broader front, and repudiates the values of Cicero no less than those of Christian moralists. His focus on Christian values has misled interpreters who have supposed that he advocates the Classical, civic virtues against the other-worldly, Christian virtues.[18] This contrast is misleading because Machiavelli's outlook conflicts with the views of pagan moralists, who agree with Christians in denying that an appeal to the expedient can justify violation of justice.

It is not entirely misleading to connect Machiavelli's views with Classical antiquity. His conception of the ruler who values strength and self-assertion, and of the citizen or soldier who values glory, fits some aspects of the Homeric outlook. This outlook never entirely faded from Greek and Roman life and thought. Machiavelli's contrast between the active and aggressive pagan outlook and Christian humility anticipates Nietzsche's contrast between the Hellenic and the Jewish outlooks.[19] But while he captures the self-assertive aspect of Greek and Roman thought, he conveys the false impression that this is the dominant character of pagan moral theory. To suggest that principles for the moral restraint of self-assertion are the invention of Christians, or of philosophers out of touch with ordinary morality, is to distort the apparent facts. Since Machiavelli distorts history in this way, he makes his own position seem more attractive than it ought to seem.

Cicero offers a further comment on morality and expediency that corrects any over-simplified contrast between the 'pagan' and the 'Christian' ideals. After his judgment that Romulus was wrong to murder Remus, he adds that it would be unreasonable to require complete self-sacrifice, and that self-assertion without injury to other people is legitimate. He endorses Chrysippus' comparison with a race, in which competition is legitimate, but tripping up the other runners is prohibited.[20] Neither Cicero nor Chrysippus maintains that it is always wrong to harm anyone else; the successful competitor harms the losers, by winning

---

[17] See *D* i 28.3; iii 5.1; Livy ii 2.7.

[18] For a misleading contrast between Machiavelli and Christian morality see Berlin, 'Originality' 45: '. . . what he institutes is . . . a differentiation between two incompatible ideals of life, and therefore two moralities. One is the morality of the pagan world: its values are courage, vigour, fortitude in adversity, public achievement, order, discipline, happiness, strength, justice, above all assertion of one's proper claims and the knowledge and power needed to secure their satisfaction . . . These seem to Machiavelli the best hours of mankind and, Renaissance humanist that he is, he wishes to restore them. Against this moral universe . . . stands in the first and foremost place, Christian morality.' The conflict between Machiavelli and Cicero is appropriately emphasized by W ii 278; Skinner, *M*36–47; *FMPT* i 128–35 (on Machiavelli's rejection of traditional, and not only Christian, conceptions of the virtues). It is underestimated by Colish, 'Cicero and Machiavelli'.

[19] See Nietzsche, *GM* i 7.

[20] 'Someone who is running a race ought to strain and strive as hard as he can to win; but he ought not at all to trip up another competitor or to push him aside with his hand. So also in life, it is not unfair for each person to seek for himself what is appropriate for his use, but it is not right for him to snatch from someone else' (*Off.* iii 42 = SVF iii 689) Cf. §182n45.

at their expense. But Chrysippus implies that competition and self-assertion are subject to some constraints of justice, so that legitimate competition should not injure others, even if it harms them.

The constraints accepted by Cicero and Chrysippus do not offer very definite guidance in practice. They do not say, for instance, whether two states at war are engaged in legitimate competition or illegitimate aggression. But they are not practically empty either; for they imply that exclusive concern for one's own interest without reference to the interests and legitimate claims of others does not sufficiently justify one's action. If Chrysippus had been our only ancient source for this moral constraint on self-assertion and competition, we might have treated it as a Stoic paradox that was out of step with common morality. But Cicero does not treat it as a Stoic paradox; he treats it as being obviously right and not very controversial, a maxim that he expects to find broad acceptance. This is the elementary moral restraint, accepted by both pagan and Christian moralists, that Machiavelli thinks must be rejected.

For this reason we should not take Machiavelli at face value when he appears to be defending pagan virtue against Christian virtues. His advice to rulers is incompatible with the civic virtue that is recognized as a support of the Classical city-state, no less than with the Christian virtues that he accuses of undermining civic virtue. In both cases Machiavelli rejects any moral restraints on the end that he regards as overriding. Why does he suppose that the end he favours has this overriding status?

405. Civic Virtue and its End

It is difficult to see what Machiavelli's argument is. Some clarification is useful, not for the sake of finding out what he really means, but for the sake of a better understanding of some recurrent ambiguities in many people's presentation of the issues. For in this case too we can find a more extreme and a more moderate defence of his position.

If certain virtues and moral restraints are to be rejected because they conflict with specific ends, they must have less value than the ends that they conflict with; if this were not so, the conflict might equally give us a reason for rejecting the ends. Why does Machiavelli believe that the moral virtues must always give way in case of a conflict? His extreme defence requires him to claim that some particular end is more important than the moral virtues; his more moderate defence does not require this claim.

According to the extreme defence, Machiavelli means: 'If we have the correct view of what is worth pursuing in life, we will see that the preservation of the state is a more important end than any other end or any combination of other values; and so it is irrational to observe any other principle that conflicts with this end'. This is the most reasonable interpretation of Machiavelli's favourable remarks about Roman civic virtue. The Romans (in Machiavelli's image of them) take the preservation of the state to be the supreme end, and subordinate every other end and value to this one; because they organize their lives on this principle, they have civic virtue, and deserve praise for it.

Why, then, does Machiavelli believe that the preservation of the state should be the overriding end? He could certainly find widespread support in Classical theorists for the view that civic life is the best form of life, or one of the best forms of life, for a human being, or that life in a state is necessary for other goods that make life worth living. We might even concede to him that if we face a choice between the preservation of this state and an irrevocable relapse into the disorganized, fragmented, insecure way of life that would result from the non-existence of any state, we ought to preserve the state at all costs. But any such concession clearly falls far short of the conclusion that Machiavelli needs. For he appeals to civic virtue to show that we ought to prefer the preservation of this particular state, as an independent political entity with this particular form of government, over anything else, whatever the moral cost might be. Nothing we have said seems to support this extreme claim.

Greek and Roman theory and practice seem to reject the extreme claim. Throughout Greek history groups within a city were willing to compromise its political independence in order to change the constitution; both sides did this in Athens at the end of the Peloponnesian War, and Polybius defends those who preferred Macedonian control over the degree of independence that allowed pro-Spartan oligarchies to rule.[21] These are not exactly cases of a conflict between the preservation of the state and the observance of moral principles; but they show that the end Machiavelli regards as overriding is at least not self-evidently overriding. His appeal to antiquity does not support his claim that unconditional loyalty to Athens or Florence is more reasonable than, say, loyalty to Athens or Florence with this constitution and this way of life following these moral principles. If the price of preserving the state is the violation of a principle that partly defines the object of our loyalty, then it is not clear that we always ought to preserve the state.

This objection to Machiavelli does not dispose of all the reasons that might be offered for choosing immoral means to the preservation of the state on particular occasions. But at least it casts doubt on his claim that we ought to pay any moral cost, however steep, because the mere preservation of the state, irrespective of its character or constitution, is the supreme end. The fact that his supreme end violates morality does not show that it needs no defence; and he offers no defence of it.

Perhaps, then, he does not intend the extreme claim that the preservation of the state is the supreme end. A more moderate defence of his position might set out from the assumption that all virtues, moral principles, and other values derive their value for an agent from the agent's choice of some ultimate end. If the ultimate end is the source of all other values, we cannot appeal to any of them to defend the choice of an ultimate end. If, then, we choose the preservation of the state as our ultimate end, we cannot appeal to the moral virtues, whose value for us is entirely derived from our choice of ultimate end, to justify moral restraints on our pursuit of this ultimate end. Hence we should be willing to violate the moral virtues for the sake of this ultimate end.

406. Instrumental Practical Reason

This defence has an advantage over the extreme defence, since it does not require Machiavelli to explain why the supreme end he picks is the best one to choose. He no longer has to pronounce on this question. He is free to say that neither the Christian nor the civic ideal

---

[21] Polybius xviii 14.

(understood as entirely devoted to the preservation of the state) is more rational than the other. In that case, he has nothing to say against us if we choose the outlook of the moral virtues, but he warns us that we had better recognize the price we must pay. Since he is not willing to pay the price, he prefers to subordinate morality to the preservation of the state. He is not claiming that the moralists are wrong, but simply warning us that if we listen to them, we may find the results disagreeable.

This second interpretation of Machiavelli's position makes it easier to understand why he sometimes offers his advice in a conditional form that might allow him to deny that he advocates immorality. In the *Prince* he often remarks that he is not saying whether monarchy is a desirable form of government, whether someone ought to have set up a particular regime, or whether a particular regime ought to survive. He confines himself to saying what a ruler has to do if he wants to survive, and what will affect his reputation in different ways. He need not concern himself with questions about whether there ought to be any such rulers or whether they ought, all things considered, to act in the ways he describes.[22]

It is more difficult to make this interpretation fit the *Discourses*, however; Machiavelli does not seem to be neutral on the question whether the unconditional preservation of the state is the supreme end, or whether civic virtue should be cultivated. But perhaps his partisan position can be reconciled with a refusal to evaluate ends. He might consistently admit that he is offering no reason for preferring the end that he prefers, but, since he prefers it, he advocates the course of action needed to advance it.

If this is the right interpretation of Machiavelli, it is easier to see why he does not offer any justification of his preferred ultimate end. If he thinks that justification has to proceed by reference to some more ultimate end, he has a reason for denying that the choice of one or another ultimate end can itself be justified. On this point he anticipates an argument of Hume's. The Humean argument might be taken to develop one aspect of a voluntarist treatment of will and reason. When Henry of Ghent maintains the subordination of intellect to will, he suggests that intellect is limited to the role of counsellor or guide along the path that the will chooses.[23]

One aspect of this argument is Aristotelian, and not exclusively voluntarist; for it is a standard Aristotelian view that—in some sense—the ultimate end provides the justification for other ends, and is not itself justified. But Aquinas does not infer that a choice between different conceptions of the ultimate end cannot be justified. The ultimate end that Aquinas takes as the starting point for further justification is the human good, identified with happiness; he believes that this can be specified enough to justify one conception of the ultimate end over another.

This is the point at which Machiavelli disagrees. Though he gives no reason for disagreeing with Aquinas, he identifies a point where Aquinas' position especially needs defence. Aquinas assumes that our views about worthwhile ultimate ends can be reconciled and explained in the light of his conception of happiness; if he is wrong about this, but still accepts a teleological pattern of justification, the questions raised by Machiavelli become more pressing.

But even if we think Machiavelli has raised a reasonable question, we need not follow him to his conclusion. For even if we find it difficult to say why one ultimate end is preferable to another, we ought to find it even more difficult to believe that it is never more reasonable

---

[22] On advice and generalizations see W i 69–73.   [23] See §389.

to prefer one over another. It seems possible to form trivial and silly conceptions of what is ultimately worthwhile; and Machiavelli does not try to persuade us that these are just as reasonable as any other conception. Once we admit this, we may well be surprised by the suggestion that we should take the unconditional preservation of the state as our ultimate end. If we separate unconditional loyalty to this state from loyalty to a certain kind of state, it does not seem a particularly reasonable end, given the costs that it is likely to involve.

It is still less obvious why a ruler should take the preservation of his own power as the ultimate end. Why should we not suppose that he has a mistaken conception of what is most important? Since he stands to lose heavily if he is driven from power, we may suspect that he exaggerates the importance of his staying in power. Machiavelli makes his conception of the overriding end seem more attractive and plausible because he tries to connect it with the Classical ideals of civic virtue; but the connexion breaks down at the very point where he needs it to prove his case. Once he departs from pagan as well as Christian morality, he removes one crucial support for his claim that there are worthwhile ultimate ends for which the Christian virtues have to be sacrificed.

One might argue that it does not matter if Machiavelli has no rational defence for the overriding end that he favours; for perhaps he can show that it is our natural and inevitable end, and that we will take the necessary means to it once we see that they are necessary for that end. This is the basis of Hobbes's argument for some of Machiavelli's conclusions about the paramount importance of the preservation of the state.[24] But it is difficult to argue that preservation of the state or of the present regime in the state corresponds to any natural and inevitable end of human motives. To show that it is connected with any such end, we need to show that the preservation of the present regime is necessary for reliable and secure self-preservation. Hobbes tries to find arguments to support this conclusion. His difficulty in finding such arguments suggests that Machiavelli's position is difficult to defend.

But even if we reject Machiavelli's argument to show that there is some conflict in principle between the Christian virtues and the appropriate sort of loyalty to the appropriate sort of state, we have not necessarily disposed of his objections to moral constraints on the preservation of the state. Many of the considerations he appeals to could be used in support of a different argument. We might argue that, in the actual circumstances we face, any moral system that allows overriding importance either to Christian or to pagan moral virtues must also face conflicts. Even if we do not demand unconditional loyalty, we may find, for instance, that the preservation of a just state seems to require resort to immoral means. Lenin and Trotsky came to this conclusion in their defence of the Bolshevik Revolution. They were not concerned with the territorial integrity of the former Russian empire for its own sake, but they believed that they could not preserve or construct a just society without resort to apparent immorality.

The existence of such conflicts need not result from a confrontation between two opposed ideals; it may turn out that one and the same ideal pursues aims that are not incompatible in principle, but turn out to result in serious conflicts when we try to realize them in the actual circumstances. The discovery of these conflicts, if they are serious and widespread enough, will show us that we cannot rely on our moral ideal for the sort of guidance that we might reasonably expect; and then we may want to consider whether our moral ideal needs to be revised.

[24] See Hobbes, L13.14.

This way of using Machiavelli's argument does not count as an interpretation of it; for he clearly intends a more radical criticism of morality than would follow from the exposure of internal conflict. But this more moderate use of his arguments may result in a more damaging criticism of the ideals connected with morality. We should therefore look more closely at Machiavelli's reasons for thinking that we will often have compelling reasons for rejecting the normal constraints of morality.

407. Morality and Circumstances

Aristotelian ethics relies on some assumptions not only about human nature—the sort of creature a human being is—but also about what human beings are like in actual circumstances. It also relies on assumptions about other external circumstances—the material resources available, the different kinds of dangers and threats presented by the external world and by other societies. In the *Politics* Aristotle makes it clear how important these assumptions are in arguments to show that particular virtues are to be cultivated in one or another set of circumstances.[25] The ideal state, in which the Aristotelian virtues can be fully developed, needs the right sort of people, with the right sorts of occupations, and therefore in the right sorts of material circumstances.

Aristotle insists that the conditions taken for granted by a political theorist should not be totally unrealistic; they should not assume that human beings are omniscient or free of their normal tendencies to vice, or that they can achieve physical security and comfort without any effort. But though our assumptions should not be unrealistic to this degree, Aristotle allows them to be quite demanding; the description of the ideal state and of the virtues of its citizens is not meant to present an attainable ideal for all of us in our ordinary circumstances.

Aquinas' conception of the virtues is intended to make them less dependent on favourable circumstances than they appear to be in Aristotle's account.[26] Still, Aquinas must make some assumption about reasonably favourable circumstances; these are the circumstances in which the actions normally characteristic of the virtues can be expected to have the results that make them appropriate expressions of the virtues.

Magnanimity, for instance, requires people to accept gracefully the honours they receive for virtuous actions; this requirement presupposes circumstances in which people will be honoured for the appropriate actions. Justice requires us to keep promises; this requirement presupposes circumstances in which we trust other people enough to keep promises. The virtues that involve reference to other people and to external circumstances have to rely on presuppositions about people and circumstances, if they are to give us definite advice about what to do. In metaphysical terms, virtues impose a certain form on the actions and circumstances that provide their matter; the characteristics of the matter affect the sort of form that can be imposed on it, and the means that allow the form to be imposed.[27]

---

[25] See, e.g., *Pol.* vii 4–7.

[26] Aquinas' accounts of bravery and magnanimity, e.g., make these virtues applicable in conditions where the corresponding Aristotelian virtues would not apply. See §331.

[27] Machiavelli uses the contrast between matter and form at i 18.5.

Machiavelli's arguments are relevant to this feature of a moral theory, since they tend to reject the presuppositions that normally underlie the moral virtues. Machiavelli's remarks about human nature suggest that we cannot rely on other people as much we would have to if the virtues were to have their 'normal' application. People do not in general behave like rational agents. Even if they live in a sound and uncorrupted republic, they are not content with what they have, but are always looking for novelty, and begin to seek domination over other states.[28] Hence prosperity and success lead to corruption; and when people are corrupted, they are even more unreliable (e.g., D iii 8.5–6).

Corruption arises gradually, especially from inequality (i 17.5). It is difficult to reverse, since any reversal requires re-education; and once corruption has happened, strong action is needed to restore the state to its original sound condition. Restoration requires either the elimination of small defects before they become too serious, or removal of the large defects after they have become apparent. But Machiavelli thinks neither of these courses of actions is very likely. Before the defects have become serious, they are likely to be unnoticed or ignored; and after they have become serious enough to be noticed, it is too late to do anything about them by normal 'constitutional' methods, since these normal methods will also have been corrupted (i 18.5).

At this point extraordinary means are needed to remove corruption and to restore the state to its original soundness. But Machiavelli thinks this is unlikely to work out satisfactorily.[29] The sort of person who is likely to be willing to seize power in a corrupt republic is not usually the sort of person who might be expected to remove its corruption.

In Machiavelli's view, then, the circumstances of a republic are always precarious. In favourable external conditions, people's desire for novelty and domination tends to begin the processes leading to corruption; and in unfavourable conditions the corruption is difficult to remove. The Greek view that we should establish the best constitution, and then make sure by legislation and moral education that it does not collapse, does not fit Machiavelli's view of the actual circumstances. He does not believe that the right legislation and moral education will produce the moral characters and the forms of political and social life that will maintain the best constitution. On the contrary, he believes that states find it difficult to restrain their tendency to corruption. 'Normal' political behaviour, in which we can reasonably assume that the state will survive in its present form or in a better form, has no place in Machiavelli's account of the relation between human beings and their social environment.

408. Adaptation to Circumstances

In the light of these views, Machiavelli forms a conception of virtue that is quite different from the moral virtues recognized by the moralists he opposes. External conditions, summed

---

[28] See i 37.1; ii, Pref.7 (where W cites Polybius vi 57); iii 21.2 ('. . . men are fond of novelty; so much so that it is often those who are prosperous who desire it than those who are in evil plight'); P 3, 103.

[29] 'Hence it is necessary to resort to extraordinary methods, such as the use of force and an appeal to arms, and, before doing anything, to become a prince in the state, so that one can dispose it as one thinks fit. But, to reconstitute political life in a state presupposes a good man, whereas to have recourse to violence in order to make oneself prince in a republic supposes a bad man. Hence very rarely will there be found a good man ready to use bad methods in order to make himself prince, though with a good end in view, nor yet a bad man who, having become a prince, is ready to do the right things and to whose mind it will occur to use well that authority which he has acquired by bad means' (i 18.5–6).

up by Machiavelli under the head of 'Fortune', interfere with everyone's plans; but he does not think we should just resign ourselves to frustration by fortune. On the contrary, part of virtue is the capacity to plan effectively for the results of fortune, so that they will not ruin our plans completely; for though we cannot control it, we can to some extent foresee it, and adapt ourselves to it when it happens.[30] For this reason Machiavelli argues that virtue as well as fortune played a large role in the rise of Rome (ii 1–2).

From his remarks about fortune Machiavelli infers that virtue consists in being prepared for fortune. The Stoics might agree with him, but not exactly in the sense that he has in mind.[31] In his view, virtue, and especially prudence, consists in the ability to adapt ourselves to fortune. To this extent his conception of prudence is closer to the one that is most familiar to us than to an Aristotelian conception. Machiavelli remarks that in the wars that the Romans won 'it will be seen that in them, mingled with fortune, was virtue and prudence of a very high order' (ii 1.4). The prudent person does not care about loss of honour or dignity if the dishonourable course is the most efficient way to deal with present circumstances (i 38.2). Someone who refuses to change his character to fit the demands of the circumstances is bound to come off worst (iii 9). The Romans showed their prudence in so far as they dealt with fortune actively, by anticipating it and adjusting to it.[32] But most people cling irrationally to tactics that have succeeded in the past, so that they cannot deal with new circumstances.[33]

Machiavelli's advice to be adaptable might be interpreted in more than one way. Some sort of adaptability is reasonable; if we care enough about our ends, it is foolish not to think about ways to secure them in different circumstances. Totally inflexible people simply show that they are too lazy or too unconcerned to think about ways to promote their ends. But some circumstances make it more difficult to promote some ends than others, and in these cases we face a choice between failure and adaptation. It is not clear in this case why Machiavelli should always advise adaptation. Some of our goals consist in trying to achieve particular results, while other goals consist in acting in particular ways. If the first sort of goal conflicts with the second, it is not clear why the second should always give way. In advising complete adaptability Machiavelli seems to assume that every other aim should give way to the aim of achieving what we can in the circumstances.

Once we accept Machiavelli's conception of the ends to be aimed at, and of the circumstances in which we have to aim at them, his view that virtue differs from the recognized moral virtues becomes easier to understand. However admirable it may be for rulers to keep their word, they must, in the prevailing conditions, be ready to break it. They

---

[30] '[Fortune] shows her power in places where no virtue has been directed (ordinate) towards resisting her; she directs her onslaught to those places where embankments and dams have not been constructed to retain her' (P 25, 363).

[31] Skinner, M25–7, presents a somewhat misleading contrast between Classical moralists (who think fortune favours the brave and whom Machiavelli follows) and Christians (especially Boethius, who think of fortune as indifferent to human aims). The 'Christian' conception is also Stoic, and therefore Classical.

[32] 'Nor were they ever satisfied with what is constantly on the lips of current sages, "reap the benefit of time", but rather they reaped the benefit of their virtue and prudence' (P 3, 117). The Romans displayed the prudence that 'consists in knowing how to recognize the character of the obstacles and in choosing the lesser evil as good' (P 21, 339).

[33] 'Nor is there a man prudent enough to know how to adjust to all this; either he is incapable of deviating from what nature inclines him to do, or else, since he has always flourished by keeping to one path, he is unable to persuade himself to leave it . . . Yet if nature were to change with the times and circumstances, fortune would not change' (P 25, 367).

must resort to both force and fraud when the occasion demands them.[34] In advocating force and fraud, the tactics of the lion and the fox, Machiavelli alludes again to Cicero's condemnation of such tactics. When Cicero mentions these two ways of committing injustice, he remarks that 'both are most foreign to a human being, but fraud deserves greater hatred' (*Off.* i 41).[35]

409. Exceptions to Morality?

Machiavelli's argument for the legitimacy and appropriateness of fraud is not completely clear; in fact he seems to rely on two arguments, whose combination makes his claim seem less immoral than he intends it to be. He argues: (1) We have to take account of the fact that other people are dishonest and cannot be relied on; and so we have to be prepared to forestall their dishonest behaviour. (2) Considerations of efficiency often suggest that we should break promises; we should make and break them simply on grounds of self-interest.

If we accept the first argument, we have some reason to reject the second. We may reasonably cite other people's wickedness as a moral defence of our behaviour. Machiavelli points out that the circumstances in which a promise is made reasonably affect one's obligation to keep it (*D* iii 42), so that, for instance, a promise extracted by force may be regarded as non-binding. He might appear to be arguing for limits on our moral obligation to keep promises. But if we think we need to make a moral case for breaking our promises, we do not suppose that expediency is all that matters; hence we will reject Machiavelli's second argument, which appeals exclusively to expediency.

If, however, we accept Machiavelli's second argument, it is not clear why his advice would be invalid, as he says it would be, if other people were just and reliable. When most people keep their promises, the advantage to be gained by a false promise is often greater, since people will be readier to believe that you will keep your promise and will be taken off guard if you break it. The second argument makes it irrelevant to ask whether I am violating a promise to an honest person who is morally entitled to rely on me.

Apparently, then, Machiavelli's reliance on these two argument reveals some confusion of thought about the relation of morality and expediency. Each argument seems to undermine the other. But their combination may none the less appear to help his case. For if we confusedly suppose that the moral considerations he offers justify the unscrupulous policy he advocates, we may overlook the immoral character of his policy.

We will perhaps move more readily from Machiavelli's first claim to his second if we believe that the demands of morality are entirely abrogated whenever we cannot count on their reciprocal observance. This might be thought either to support, or to follow from, the view that morality consists in the observance of mutually recognized rules, and therefore requires the existence of stable social institutions enforcing compliance and reciprocity.

---

[34] 'Hence a prudent ruler cannot and should not respect his word, when such respect works to his disadvantage and when the occasions that made him promise no longer exist. And if all men were good, this precept would not be good; but since they are bad and do not respect their own promise to you, you need not respect your promise to them either' (P 18, 281).

[35] W i 104 discusses Machiavelli and the relevant senses of 'fraud'.

This is Hobbes's view of morality.[36] But it is not clear that we should accept it; certainly a defender of such a view cannot take it for granted that all moral obligations are cancelled towards those who violate moral obligations. It is reasonable to say that we have different moral obligations in these cases; but that admission does not force us into acceptance of Machiavelli's second argument.

He might mislead both himself and us because of another obscurity in his advice. Many of his examples suggest that he is advocating this policy: (1) Disregard ordinary constraints of morality when the survival of the state depends on disregarding them.[37] This policy applies to many of the incidents that Machiavelli records from Roman history, when the Romans thought they had their backs to the wall and that extraordinary means were needed. But his policy on promises is rather different: (2) Take account only of instrumental considerations in deciding what to do for the preservation of the state.

The second policy implies, but the first does not, that one should never be willing to pay any price in efficiency in order to follow the requirements of morality. Machiavelli suggests, however, that we ought to endorse it if we endorse the first policy. Perhaps some of the ordinary rules of morality are suspended if we face genuine emergencies. As he argues, considerations of glory and honour may be secondary to the safety of the state, if our survival depends on it (cf. *D* iii 41). But if this is so, the adoption of extraordinary means in emergencies is consistent with acceptance of the moral virtues; for the moral virtues leave room for these extraordinary means. Machiavelli seems to argue that since extraordinary means are morally acceptable in emergencies, we ought to disregard morality altogether in all circumstances. The argument is not only unconvincing but also inconsistent; for if we think it matters to find moral grounds or permission for extraordinary means in emergencies, we cannot consistently suppose that moral considerations never matter.

Perhaps this conflict in his argument is less evident to Machiavelli because he does not see any sharp distinction between ordinary and extraordinary circumstances. Given the inherent defects in human nature, and the ever-present danger of corruption, every situation is an emergency in which the prudent politician must be ready to use measures that (from the moral point of view) might be regarded as extraordinary. We cannot count on finding circumstances in which it is safe to follow the ordinary moral rules prescribing the conduct typical of the different virtues.

The demand for extraordinary means assumes that any middle course is disastrous. We might be tempted to conclude from Machiavelli's arguments that we need to be prepared to compromise—that on the whole we should follow the recognized moral virtues, but we should be ready to depart from them in an emergency, to the minimum degree that seems necessary to resolve the immediate difficulty. But Machiavelli believes that this effort to incorporate his advice into a more respectable and traditional framework is bound to get the worst of both worlds. A strictly moralistic course of action, indifferent to worldly success or civic considerations, is at any rate consistent; we know where we are with such people, and we will keep them out of public life. But if we adopt immoral means only reluctantly and in

---

[36] Hobbes draws this sharp distinction between the state of nature and the commonwealth at *L* 15.40.
[37] Cicero endorses a restricted version of this principle: 'For them [sc. consuls exercising military command in the field] let the safety of the people be the supreme law' (*Leg.* iii 8). See W ii 207.

small doses, they will not have the proper effect; too little severity today will only make the situation worse and require more severity tomorrow.

He argues, therefore, that we ought to set out on the immoral course whole-heartedly and without any half-measures. We cannot hope to keep a republic exactly in the right condition; and so it is better to be frankly aggressive and to pursue expansion in the hope of maintaining the status quo (i 6.10).[38] We face a clear choice between the moral virtues and the unscrupulous outlook; and his warnings about the dangers of corruption in a republic imply that any politician will have to be prepared to 'enter on the path of wrong doing'. Though Machiavelli speaks as though he is giving advice only to people who want to be tyrants, the principles underlying his advice support a much broader rejection of morality.

He defends his advice by arguing that people who have listened to their moral objections to ruthless measures have made things worse than they would have made them if they had frankly and whole-heartedly disregarded moral scruples. The scrupulous policies of Soderini, whose excessive mildness and reluctance to use harsh measures caused his overthrow, show why it is a mistake to shrink from immorality (iii 3.2; cf. i 52.2). Soderini failed to adapt himself as he should have to circumstances (iii 9.5; cf. iii 30.4). The foolish people who try to practise the ordinary moral virtues, even in cases where the overriding end requires immoral means, defeat all of their ends. Instead of condemning ourselves to such failures, we ought to make up our mind about which ends we are going to take to be primary.

Even if Machiavelli were right to claim that 'extraordinary' measures should be more ordinary than we suppose, he hardly shows that extreme situations occur so often that the moral principles applying to non-extreme situations are inapplicable to practice. Moreover, the more convincing he makes his case to show that normal moral restrictions should be suspended, the more he undermines his case to show that expediency is all that matters. For the most convincing case for suspension of ordinary moral restraints will draw attention to the prohibitive moral cost of sticking to ordinary restraints. The more strongly we can demonstrate the prohibitive moral cost, the more we support the moral principles in the light of which we assess moral costs. If Machiavelli simply argued that sometimes morality involves some sacrifice of advantage, he would hardly make a convincing case for the immoral course of action. He has a much stronger case if he appeals to moral cost; but that appeal does not show that moral considerations are irrelevant; on the contrary, it acknowledges that they are relevant.

410. The Strength of Machiavelli's Objections to Morality

Machiavelli's case against the moral virtues seems to generalize hastily from a few examples.[39] He does not consider the broader consequences of the tactics that he advocates. In inter-state relations mutual distrust is no less damaging to the interests of each state than naive

---

[38] 'Such methods are exceedingly cruel, and are repugnant to any form of life (vivere), not only Christian, but also human. It behooves, therefore, every man to shun them, and to prefer rather to live as a private citizen than as a king with such ruin of human beings. None the less, the sort of man who is unwilling to take up this first course of well doing, if he wants to hold what he has, he must enter on the path of wrong doing. Actually, however, most men prefer to steer a middle course, which is very harmful; for they know not how to be wholly good nor yet wholly bad . . .' (i 26.3; cf. i 30.2; ii 23.2). On Machiavelli's use of 'vivere' for social and political life see Rinaldi ad loc., n19.

[39] W i 102–14 criticizes some of Machiavelli's claims.

trustfulness would be. Machiavelli has something in common with many people who suggest that the moral virtues do not pay; he offers arguments for his own side that are much less rigorous than those he demands from his opponents. If one concedes that there are cases of the sort Machiavelli describes, it is equally necessary to consider the destructive effects of ruthlessness within a society and of deception in relations between societies.

It is doubtful in the end whether Machiavelli actually leaves himself with a more coherent outlook than the one he rejects. In his view, the only consistent course of action for advocates of the Christian virtues is to retire to a monastery; their efforts to combine Christian virtues with civic virtues result in a half-hearted and dangerous attitude to the needs of states and citizens. But his own position seems to contain an internal conflict at least as serious as the one he alleges in his opponents' views. For the tactics he recommends to political leaders seem to conflict with his admiration for civic virtue. He recognizes that a sound republic depends on general confidence in the observance of laws; but he advises rulers to disregard these laws whenever it is to get rid of their opponents. As an advocate of civic virtue he advocates loyalty by citizens to rulers whom they have no reason to trust; in expecting them to be loyal to a community, he is indifferent to the character and behaviour of the rulers of the community. As he recognizes, the sort of person who is willing to take the measures needed for effective government is not likely to be the sort of person who inspires trust.

But even if Machiavelli's own position is incoherent, he might still have found serious objections to the moral outlook that he criticizes. Suppose it is true that in a significant number of cases the preservation of a state requires measures that would normally be rejected as immoral. What should the defender of the moral virtues say in reply? Three main types of answers might be considered: (1) Morality, as normally understood, is supreme, and the price has to be paid. If survival ever requires killing of the innocent, it requires something that is absolutely wrong, and we must forgo survival. (2) Morality is not supreme; when these issues are at stake, it does not apply, and it should not restrain us from taking the prudent course of action. (3) Morality is supreme, but it does not require us to pay the extreme price; it can explain why what would ordinarily be impermissible is required or permitted in these extreme cases.

The only possibility that Machiavelli really considers is the first. He assumes that the defender of the Christian virtues is obliged to condemn all emergency measures, and thereby is obliged to admit that the Christian virtues are not a promising option for anyone who has some concern about social and political life. Machiavelli has a rather loose conception of an emergency; he tends to confuse genuine emergencies with cases where nothing more than the survival of a particular government is at stake. Still, we may concede for the sake of argument that there are cases like the one faced by Soderini, where the survival of a free community depends on the adoption of measures that would normally be rejected. How should Machiavelli's moralist opponents respond?

Moralists who reject extraordinary means in principle seem to set themselves against concern for social and political life. But then what, we may ask, is the point of their system of virtues? The other-worldly answer that Machiavelli envisages is one consistent answer. But it is not available to Aquinas; for he thinks the moral virtues are not simply a preparation for the afterlife, but contain the right principles for the organization of social life that recognizes a human being's political nature. An extreme world-renouncing view seems to threaten the social character of Aquinas' moral outlook.

Does this make it difficult to defend the first answer to Machiavelli's objections? This question depends partly on how often the situations described by Machiavelli arise. Defenders of the first answer, holding that some measures are absolutely wrong whatever the cost, point out legitimately that the cases where an action is both clearly immoral and clearly required by circumstances are difficult to identify in actual conditions. Machiavelli's examples seem similar to the artificial examples in which the deliberate killing of one innocent person is both necessary and sufficient for saving the lives of many other innocents. Even though Machiavelli's examples are historical rather than fictional, they are similar to fictional examples in failing to consider the possibility of other measures that would not be open to the same moral objections.[40]

But though this defence shows that the first answer may not have the extreme and costly consequences that might appear to result from it, we may doubt whether it entirely answers Machiavelli. If morality refuses to acknowledge the possibility of emergencies in which extreme measures are needed to defend those social relations that are necessary for the embodiment of the moral virtues in social life, morality seems to undermine its own necessary conditions.[41] A supporter of Aquinas' conception of social morality has some reason to reject the sort of absolutism that allows no room for emergencies.

The second answer to Machiavelli's objections might appeal, in different forms, to Luther and to Hobbes. For each of them, for different reasons, tries to withdraw some of the moral virtues from any competition with the outlook that Machiavelli advocates. From Luther's Augustinian point of view—or at least from one of Luther's points of view, corresponding to one Augustinian point of view—the Christian virtues are other-worldly, and do not apply to secular rulers in secular situations. Different standards apply to secular rulers, and they are allowed to operate independently of moral scrutiny from the Christian point of view.[42] From Hobbes's point of view, the virtues are relevant only when the essential background of peace and stability is assured; and this is the background that concerns Machiavelli. Hobbes's account of morality relieves Machiavelli from any need to admit that the measures he advocates are immoral; they are simply beyond moral evaluation.

The third answer would no doubt appear to Machiavelli to be the sort of unsatisfactory compromise that he condemns. But the very considerations that make his examples seem attractive support the third answer. If we are moved by any of Machiavelli's examples, it is not because we recognize some conflict between moral considerations and some totally different kind of consideration. That might be our reaction to a conflict between the demands of morality and those of art or culture or religion. Whatever questions are raised by these sorts of conflicts, they do not seem relevant to the present issue. If we agree with Machiavelli

[40] Geach, V 114–16, discusses related issues, suggesting that it is not clear how often immoral means are the only effective ones.

[41] Rawls, TJ 217, recognizes circumstances where liberty may reasonably be limited for the sake of forming conditions for the fuller exercise of liberty.

[42] This concession from the Christian point of view does not lead directly to Machiavelli's conclusion; for Christians who hold this view still assume that the secular moral virtues will guide secular life. But it may be easier from this point of view to regard secular morality as simply a means to the ends of secular life, rather than forming the ends against which it can be evaluated.

that extreme measures are sometimes necessary, we recognize that people's survival and welfare are involved; and indeed if someone failed to take extreme measures, we might well think he was open to moral condemnation for sacrificing the lives and welfare of the people who could have been saved. The very fact that absolutist theories try to justify failure to bring about a great good at the cost of some moral evil shows that we are powerfully impressed by the moral force of the argument for extraordinary measures. If we are really moved by moral considerations here, then it seems that we ought to be able to articulate these considerations within our general view of the moral virtues.

The mere acceptance of this solution does not imply that an account of the virtues can easily be adjusted to suit Machiavelli's objections. If the kinds of cases that concern him arise very often, then any attempt to take account of them might result in principles and policies very different from those that Aquinas connects with the moral virtues. But here we should recall the limits of Machiavelli's argument. The fact that in some cases some moral considerations have to be sacrificed to others does not show that no moral consideration ever has anything more than an instrumental role. A reasonable view of which elements in Machiavelli's case are plausible makes it easier to see how his opponents' position can be defended.

We ought to conclude, then, that Machiavelli presents no devastating objection in principle to the account of the virtues and of human welfare that is defended by Aquinas. His arguments and examples might appear to show that the Christian virtues are irrelevant or harmful in social and political life; but this appearance is deceptive.

29

THE REFORMATION
AND SCHOLASTIC MORAL
PHILOSOPHY

411. Objections to Scholasticism

Modern moral philosophy developed especially in England, Scotland, and Germany, in areas where the Reformation was widely accepted, in its Lutheran, or Calvinist, or Anglican forms. Since mediaeval moral philosophers were also theologians, expounding the doctrines and practices of the mediaeval Latin Church, and since the Reformers rejected some of these doctrines and practices, it is worth considering whether the religious and theological disputes connected with the Reformation affect prevalent attitudes to mediaeval moral philosophy.[1]

We may recall some of Aquinas' views about the relation of theology and moral philosophy: (1) His theology explains why it is worthwhile to engage in moral philosophy. God's wisdom reveals itself in the natural law, and in the system of moral virtues that we can construct on the basis of what we know in the natural law. The Christian doctrine of God and creation, as Aquinas understands it, justifies us in supposing that God has created us with the capacity to find the truth about the world and about ourselves by rational inquiry. Aristotle's ethics is the system that results from the most successful use so far of our capacity for rational inquiry. Hence, we have reason to suppose that it shows us the truth, and that it reveals to us part of the mind of God. (2) Aquinas' theology not only makes room for moral philosophy, based on reason without revelation; it also relies on the conclusions of moral philosophy. The virtues that result from the infusion of divine grace do not require us to reject or to abandon the acquired virtues. They build on the acquired virtues, and perfect them, even though they also go beyond them in aiming at an ultimate end beyond anything that we can conceive or realize through the acquired virtues.[2] Part of the reason for supposing that the infused virtues are genuine virtues is the fact that they

---

[1] 'The Reformers' include Luther, Melanchthon, Calvin, and confessional documents of various dates (including the Augsburg Confession (1530), the Westminster Confession (1647), and the English Articles (1553, 1563)). Schaff, *CC* iii, prints these documents.

[2] See §353.

fit the acquired virtues in these ways.[3] (3) Aquinas discusses the nature of sin, free will, divine grace, justification, faith, and good works. His views on these questions are closely connected with views about the role of the institutional Church in (for instance) the grace conferred in baptism and the Eucharist, the functions of confession and repentance, and the relation of the monastic to the secular way of life.

Though we have seen that Aquinas' successors do not agree with him about everything, the summary we have given applies fairly well to later Scholasticism as well, and suggests a starting point for comparison with the Reformers. It is easy to see that the Reformers reject Scholastic views in the third set of questions, about the Christian doctrine of salvation, and about its institutional implications for the life and discipline of the Church. Disputes on these questions are elaborated in the Reformers' confessions of faith and the responses produced by the Council of Trent.

These disputes are connected with disputes on the first and second sets of questions. Luther and Calvin assert that the Scholastics are mistaken in their views about the acquired moral virtues and their relation to the moral demands of the Christian faith. These Scholastic errors are connected to errors about freewill. The Reformers oppose these errors through their distinctive doctrines of predestination, election, grace, and faith.

Luther and Calvin advocate the study of Scripture without the overlay of Scholastic doctrine. Luther sometimes suggests that this doctrine is not only unhelpful, but positively misleading in the search for a true understanding of Scripture.[4] He charges that the Scholastics have replaced the genuine Church with a 'Thomist or Aristotelian Church'.[5] One of his early works, the 'Disputation against the Scholastic theologians', is a long list of Scholastic theses he rejects.[6] Calvin conveys the same judgment in constantly referring to the Scholastics as 'sophists'.[7] Neither Luther nor Calvin rejects the use of post-Biblical authorities to understand Christian doctrine. They often cite Augustine with approval, and criticize some Scholastics for misunderstanding him.[8]

---

[3] See Aquinas, *ST* 1-2 q65 a2–3.

[4] 'Indeed, I believe that I owe this duty to the Lord of crying out against philosophy and turning men to Holy Scripture. For, perhaps, if someone else who had not been through it all were to do it, he would either be scared to do it or he would not be believed. But I have been in the grind of these studies for, lo, these many years, and am worn out by it, and, on the basis of long experience, I have come to be persuaded that it is a vain study doomed to perdition' (Luther, *Rm.* 8:19 = Pauck 236).

[5] See *Babylonian Captivity* = *Works* xxxi = Dillenberger 265–6. Luther is discussing the doctrine of transubstantiation, which he ascribes to Aquinas' misunderstanding of Aristotle's doctrine of substance and accident. He concludes: 'I feel we ought to be sorry for so great a man, not only for drawing his views from Aristotle in matters of faith, but also for attempting to found them upon a man whom he did not understand, thus building an unfortunate superstructure on an unfortunate foundation'.

[6] See C v 320–6 = *Works* xxxi 9–16. Some of his comments on Aristotle: (41) 'Almost the entire *Ethics* of Aristotle is the worst enemy of grace. (42) It is an error to maintain that Aristotle's doctrine concerning happiness does not contradict Catholic doctrine. (43) It is an error to say: without Aristotle no one becomes a theologian. (44) On the contrary, no one becomes a theologian unless he does it without Aristotle.'

[7] See, e.g., *Inst.* i 16.3, with McNeill's note (200n5).

[8] 'Now let us hear Augustine speaking in his own words, lest the Pelagians of our own age, that is, the Sophists of the Sorbonne, according to their custom, charge that all antiquity is against us' (Calvin, *Inst.* ii 3.13). 'Moreover, they unjustly set the fathers against us (I mean the ancient writers of a better age of the church) as if in them they had supporters of their own impiety. If the contest were to be determined by the authority of these fathers, the tide of victory—to put it very modestly—would turn to our side' (*Inst.*, Pref. §4). 'Obviously, he [sc. Peter Lombard] intended to follow Augustine's opinion, but he follows it at a distance and even departs considerably from the right imitation of it. ... The schools have gone continually from bad to worse until, in headlong ruin, they have plunged into a sort of Pelagianism'

Though the Reformers attack Scholasticism, it is not always easy to see what these attacks imply about Aquinas. They normally have in mind the views of later Scholastics. Calvin sometimes discusses the 'sounder Schoolmen', who are less seriously wrong than the later Scholastics.[9] His division between Scholastics deserves to be taken seriously. For on some critical questions in moral psychology and the foundations of morality, the later Scholastics disagree sharply with Aquinas. Hence, some of the Reformers' objections to the Scholastics may not constitute objections to Aquinas.[10] We need to compare the views of the Reformers with Aquinas' actual position, not simply with the Scholastic position as they interpret it.

The Reformers' views on questions in moral philosophy are secondary to their theological arguments. Neither Luther nor Calvin offers the detailed discussion that we find in Aquinas or Scotus. Melanchthon, however, provides an outline of his moral philosophy in a short textbook. Though this material does not amount to a detailed discussion or critique of Scholastic ethics, it gives us enough to ask our main question: does the theological position of the Reformers require a departure from Scholastic moral philosophy?

412. Natural law

The Reformers accept the Scholastic belief in natural law as a source of our basic knowledge of moral principles.[11] They rely on St Paul's remark that the Gentiles without the Mosaic law are a law to themselves. According to Augustine and his successors, St Paul affirms a natural law known independently of revelation.[12] Calvin, agreeing with Aquinas, takes the Decalogue to make clear the requirements of the natural law, which are known independently of revelation. He appeals to St Paul in his support.[13] We know the principles

---

(iii 11.15). In iii 15.7 Calvin distinguishes the later sophists from Lombard, 'their Pythagoras', who is sound and sober in comparison with them.

[9] After a discussion of Peter Lombard on operating and co-operating grace, he adds: 'I chose to note these two points in passing that you, my reader, may see how far I disagree with the sounder Schoolmen (sanioribus Scholasticis). I differ with the more recent Sophists to an even greater extent, as they are further removed from antiquity' (ii 2.6). In iv 17.14 he suggests that Lombard and others try to explain away the extreme statements by the Papacy on transubstantiation.

[10] Luther's conception of the Scholastic position is largely, but not entirely, derived from Biel (but see n5 above, on transubstantiation). On Calvin's knowledge of Aquinas see Wendel, *Calvin* 126–7. Barth, *TJC* 22 comments on Luther's and Calvin's neglect of Aquinas: '[They] avoided the man in whom they must have recognized, even if he was not then the most widely read author, and whom they ought to have fought as their most dangerous opponent, the true genius of the Catholic Middle Ages. I refer to Thomas Aquinas. . . . The reformers engaged in close combat with late scholastics of the age of decline, about whom we say nothing today, when all the time behind these, and biding his time, stood their main adversary Thomas . . . How could it be possible that in the first half of the 17th century a Lutheran theologian from Strassburg could write a book entitled *Thomas Aquinas veritatis evangelicae confessor!'*

[11] Cf. *West. Conf.* 19.1–2: ' God gave to Adam a law, as a covenant of works, by which he bound (obligavit) him and all his posterity to personal, entire, exact, and perpetual obedience; promised life upon the fulfilling, and threatened death upon the breach of it; and endued him with power and ability to keep it. This law, after his fall, continued to be a perfect rule of righteousness; and, as such, was delivered by God upon Mount Sinai in ten commandments, and written in two tables; the first four commandments containing our duty toward God, and the other six our duty to man. . . .'

[12] The views of the Reformers are summarized by McNeill in 'Reformers' and 'Luther'. He suggests that Zwingli is the most inclined to treat St Paul's remarks on the natural law as simply a reference to especially good pagans who received special grace. See §226 (on Ambrosiaster).

[13] 'For he proves that ignorance is put forward in vain by the Gentiles, since by their deeds they declared themselves to have no small rule of righteousness; for no people did ever at any time so abhor from humanity, that they did not keep themselves within some laws. Since, therefore, all the Gentiles voluntarily, and without any [external] supervisor

of natural law through conscience, and so we cannot plead ignorance of morality as an excuse for our errors.[14] We need the Decalogue to remind us of the requirements of the natural law, but we do not depend on it for our grasp of these requirements.[15]

This description of the natural law gives it an epistemological function independent of the will of God; Ockham accepts this epistemological function, while claiming that it is metaphysically dependent on the will of God.[16] According to Aquinas, the natural law is not only known naturally without revelation, but is also appropriate for human beings with their nature; hence it is the basis of 'intrinsic rightness' (as Suarez puts it), so that morality is not the result of divine imposition, but of facts about human beings. Ockham rejects this view, arguing that the provisions of natural law are the result of divine imposition, and subject to dispensation.[17] It is not clear how the Reformers understand the metaphysical status of the natural law.

Luther sometimes adopts a voluntarist position close to Ockham's. He follows Ockham and Biel in arguing that God's mercy and generosity require the voluntarist conception of the relation between his will and the moral law. Luther argues that if God acted as he does because he sees it is good, then his action is required of him, and he is bound to act as he does. But the Christian doctrine of God's grace and God's love imply that God is not bound to act as he does. His treatment of us is not owed to us in justice, as a response to our merits, but an expression of his mercy and grace. This argument leads Luther into a sharp contrast between the divine and the human will and between divine and human love. God does not love something because it is an appropriate object of love; on the contrary, God makes something lovable by loving it.[18]

(monitore), are inclined to make laws unto themselves, it is out of all question that there are naturally grafted in the minds of all men certain conceptions of justice and uprightness, which the Greeks call *prolêpseis*. They have, therefore, law without law, because, even though they have not the written law of Moses, they are by no means devoid of the knowledge of right and equity; for otherwise they could not discern between vice and virtue . . . He has opposed nature to the written law, meaning that there appeared in the Gentiles a natural light of justice, which supplied the place of the law by which the Jews are taught, so that they were a law to themselves.' (Calvin, *ad Rm.* 2:14).

Luther, *ad Rm.* ad loc. mentions Augustine's two interpretations, and prefers the second.

[14] '. . . natural law is that apprehension of the conscience which distinguishes sufficiently between just and unjust, and which deprives men of the excuse of ignorance, while it proves them guilty by their own testimony' (*Inst.* ii 2.22). Cf. *West. Conf.* 4.2: ' After God had made all other creatures, he created man, male and female, with reasonable and immortal souls, endued with knowledge, righteousness, and true holiness after his own image, having the law of God written in their hearts, and power to fulfil it; and yet under a possibility of transgressing, being left to the liberty of their own will, which was subject unto change. Besides this law written in their hearts, they received a command not to eat of the tree of the knowledge of good and evil; which while they kept were happy in their communion with God, and had dominion over the creatures.' On this difference between the natural law and the command not to eat the apple see §307n45.

[15] 'If the Gentiles by nature have law righteousness (*legis iustitiam*) engraved upon their minds, we surely cannot say they are utterly blind as to the conduct of life. There is nothing more common than for a man to be sufficiently instructed in a right standard of conduct by natural law (of which the apostle is here speaking)' (*Inst.* ii 2.22). 'Now that inward law, which we have above described as written, even engraved, upon the hearts of all, in a sense asserts the very same things that are to be learned from the two Tables. For our conscience does not allow us to sleep a perpetual insensible sleep without being an inner witness and monitor of what we owe God, without holding before us the difference between good and evil, and thus accusing us when we fail in our duty' (*Inst.* ii 8.1). For further references see McNeill's note ad loc.

[16] See §395.   [17] See §395.

[18] *Heidelberg Disputation* = C v 391.30 = *Works* xxxi §28: 'Divine love does not find but creates its object of love. Human love of a human being comes into being through its object of love. The second part is clear and accepted by all philosophers and theologians. For the object of love is its cause, assuming, in agreement with Aristotle, that every

This attempt to connect a voluntarist conception of God's will with the Christian doctrine of God's grace and mercy seems to rest on the confusion that we have found in Biel. The argument seems to assume that if God does not recognize a requirement based on justice, he cannot act on the belief that what he does is the best thing to do, or is appropriate to the nature of the recipient. But this assumption rests on the further questionable assumption that only a voluntarist can give an account of mercy and generosity.

Calvin's position in the dispute between naturalism and voluntarism is less evident. One might expect him to favour voluntarism, given his emphasis on the sovereignty of God. Moreover, some of his remarks on the inscrutability of God's decrees might be taken in a voluntarist sense. This interpretation, however, is too hasty. His description of the natural law as the law of God is indecisive.[19] He takes a more definite position, however, in rejecting the doctrine of God's unqualified power. He denies that God is 'without law' (exlegem).[20] God's will is free of all vice, 'the highest rule of perfection, and the law of all laws'. Hence 'whatever God wills must be accounted just from the very fact that he wills it' (iii 23.2).

This Anselmian formula allows, but does not require, a voluntarist interpretation. Calvin invokes it in his discussion of predestination, in order to answer those who demand to be given a reason that explains to them why God elected those who were elected rather than others. Calvin's denial that we can understand these decrees of God does not commit him to the general claim that rightness is wholly dependent on God's will. In his view, we can reasonably be confident that what God wills is right, even though we cannot always know why it is right; he does not deny that God's willing conforms to standards of rightness that are not wholly dependent on it. Hence he rejects the doctrine of God's unqualified power, antecedent to any standard of right.[21]

Melanchthon expresses the most definite commitment to metaphysical naturalism. It is because moral philosophy relies on facts about human nature that its principles are certain, even though some more specific rules may be merely plausible. For this reason, sceptical doubt about the principles is excluded.[22] When he begins his exposition of ethics,

---

capacity of the soul is passive and material and acts by receiving . . . The first part is clear, because the love of God living in a human being loves sinners, evil people, fools, and weaklings in order to make them just, good, wise and strong. . . . For sinners are beautiful (pulchri) because they are loved, not loved because they are beautiful.'

[19] *Inst.* iv 20.16.

[20] 'But we do not give any countenance to absolute power, which, as being profane, should rightly be hateful to us. We do not imagine a God outside law who is a law to himself (non fingimus Deum exlegem qui sibi ipsi lex est). For, as Plato says, human beings oppressed by appetites need law; but the will of God is not only pure of all vice, but the highest rule of perfection, and indeed the law of all laws' (iii 23.2). Battles translates 'qui sibi ipsi lex est' as part of the view that Calvin repudiates, whereas Beveridge translates it as part of Calvin's view (Wendel, *Calvin* 127–9, agrees with him). Battles' rendering is more probable. Calvin seems to contrast the view that God has no inherent law but gives it to himself (sibi lex est), with the view that he has an inherent law in his will ('the law of all laws'). Wendel incautiously cites this passage as evidence of Calvin's agreement with Scotus on God and the natural law. Schneewind, *IA* 32n, treats it as evidence of Calvin's voluntarism about the natural law.

[21] *Inst.* i 17.2: '. . . let our law of soberness and modesty be to assent to his supreme command, that his will may be for us the sole rule of justice, and the most just cause of all things. Not, indeed, that absolute will of which the Sophists babble, separating his justice from his power by an impious and profane division—but providence, that governing principle of all things, from which flows nothing but right (rectum), though the reasons have been hidden from us.' McNeill ad loc. quotes parallel passages.

[22] 'But here we must take note that philosophy is not every opinion of everyone, but certain items of knowledge, which are demonstrations, or else the parts of them, i.e., principles or conclusions. For just as in other arts there are principles and demonstrations that cannot be mistaken, so also in moral philosophy there are certain practical principles,

Melanchthon repeats that we must begin from human nature, because we must begin from the ultimate end for a human being.[23] In these ways, he treats natural law as the law of human nature, and hence treats moral philosophy as a study of the good that is determined by human nature.

413. Dispensations from Natural Law?

This connexion between natural law and human nature also settles some questions about the relation of natural law to the divine will and especially to divine freedom. In claiming that natural law is a law of human nature, Melanchthon implies that, even if we had this nature without being created by God, we would still have rational principles guiding our actions and character. He also implies that by creating us with this nature and this knowledge, God did not have to do anything else to give us rational principles for guiding our action. If the natural law is the law of our nature, some actions are rationally and morally significant for us apart from the legislative will of God. If, however, our knowledge of natural law were simply (as Ockham supposes) our natural knowledge of God's legislative will, we would have no reason to follow it distinct from any reason we had to follow God's legislative will.

If natural law depends on facts, distinct from God's legislative will, about human nature, how is it related to morality and to the legislative will of God? If God were to require us to violate natural law, would that be a case in which it would be right to violate natural law, or would it be a case in which God would require us to act wrongly? This counterfactual question raises the general question about divine dispensations.

Melanchthon's view on this question rests on his account of the immutability of natural law. He argues that natural right (ius[24] naturae) is always immutable (PME 210.7), but he explains this claim in ways that take account of apparent mutability.

First, he argues, using Plato's example in *Republic* i, that a lower principle must be interpreted in the light of a higher, so that the principle of returning deposits must be qualified by reference to the principle of not harming someone who is not inflicting harm. Such examples show that a law of nature is immutable, given its place in the order of laws of nature.[25] Sometimes one law has to be limited by another because of human sin. The law of nature prescribes that everything should be available for common use; but, because of human sin, common use would allow harm to innocent people; and so the principle of not

---

and from them secure demonstrations result. And just as the arts are an exposition (explicatio) of nature, so also demonstrations in moral philosophy are an exposition of human nature. ... We must therefore reject the Academics, who remove the reputation of certainty from the arts. Rather, philosophy sometimes accepts, just as medicine does, creditable (probabiles) arguments, and it is for the expert to judge how far they hold; for those that conflict with the principles are to be altogether repudiated' (PME 158.32–159.6).

[23] 'Now the first question is about the end, because, just as natural philosophy looks for the other causes of a human being, so moral philosophy properly considers the end of a human being. Therefore in order to grasp the nature of a human being we need moral philosophy, because the complete grasp of anything, in so far as it can be achieved, requires a search for all the causes. Next, the learned person must consider at this point, that moral philosophy arises from nature, because the search for a cause belongs primarily to the natural philosophers' (PME 163.19–27). Melanchthon's teleology is a major topic omitted from Kusukawa, TNP, chs. 4–5.

[24] He defines ius as a facultas, 207.34.

[25] 'Thus, the law of nature is immutable in such a way that each item of knowledge is maintained in its proper place and order' (210.17–19).

harming the innocent makes private property preferable in our actual circumstances. In this sense, private property belongs to natural right.[26]

A second division among requirements of natural right distinguishes those that cannot be violated without a complete corruption of human nature. These include not harming the innocent, the responsibility of parents to bring up children, and the keeping of honest agreements. These are genuine practical principles, or conclusions necessarily derived from them.[27] Other principles are in accordance with nature, but may be violated without a complete corruption and ruin of human nature. In our present state of sin, it is sometimes better to permit them, and to concentrate on preventing the violations of the higher principles.[28]

This is Melanchthon's explanation of some of the so-called 'dispensations' from the natural law that are described in the Old Testament. In his view, they are not genuine dispensations. God tolerated polygamy in Israel because it was not a breach of the higher principles of natural right. Melanchthon gives two explanations: (1) Since God is the author of nature, natural right is also in his power. (2) In contrast to the principles of natural knowledge, our assent to moral principles is weakened because of sin and the corruption of our nature.[29] These explanations are meant to show why the Israelites allowed polygamy.[30] The second is fairly easy to understand. The first is more puzzling, since it suggests that God has power over natural right, and therefore can dispense from its observance. If that is what Melanchthon means, he aligns himself with Scotus in believing that these are genuine dispensations, and hence exercises of God's will as legislator.

But Melanchthon does not seem to regard God as dispensing from the natural law. If I am dispensed from observing the law, then the law remains in force and applies to me, but I have no obligation to keep it because the legislator has given me permission not to keep it. Melanchthon seems to have a different view, that God in his role as judge remits any punishment, and in his role as overseer permits the Israelites to go on with this practice. The sense in which God has power over natural right is not the power to change it or to dispense from the obligation to keep it, but the power to refrain from enforcing it with sanctions.

Melanchthon does not commit himself, therefore, to the voluntarist account of dispensations endorsed by Scotus and Ockham. He does not deal with all the cases discussed in the dispute about dispensations; the commands to Abraham and Hosea, for instance, do not seem to fit the pattern he suggests. Nor is it clear whether he takes God to have been free, as Ockham believes, to prescribe some other set of laws that would not have been appropriate for human nature.

[26] 'So also it is the law of nature to use things in common. But because this law now, in corrupt nature, conflicts with the higher law to harm no one, reason now teaches the one who has harmed no one to distinguish areas of ownership (dominia), because under the pretext of the law about common use, many in this corruption of nature would be moved by unjust appetites to harm others' (210.21–7).

[27] 'For the wreckage and destruction of human nature would immediately follow, if everyone were allowed, whenever he felt like it, to attack the fortunes or bodies of others' (211.1–4).

[28] See Suarez, *Leg.* ii 20.3 on toleration of behaviour prohibited by natural law.

[29] 'For since God alone is the founder of nature, even the law of nature is in his power alone. Moreover, the following must be added. Though moral principles are secure, just as natural principles are, that heavy things are borne downwards, and so on, still assent to moral principles is less secure, because of the corruption of nature. For because they do not obey nature enough, assent becomes less secure, and the items of knowledge themselves are less clear, and we easily assent to imaginings that are contrary to them' (211.21–8).

[30] Cf. Suarez on prostitution etc., *Leg.* ii 20.3.

Melanchthon makes no basic innovation in Scholastic views of natural law. He does not maintain the most strongly voluntarist Scholastic view. In his claims about human nature and the ultimate end for human beings, he is still influenced by Aristotelian assumptions.

414. Hooker on Natural Law

Melanchthon's predominantly naturalist account of natural law may be compared with Hooker's unequivocally naturalist position. Hooker defends the principles of the Reformation (as he understands them) against a more extreme voluntarist position that rejects natural reason as a moral authority and demands direct warrant from Scripture, and he uses his doctrine of natural law to defend natural reason in morality. He faces opponents who appeal directly to the will of God, as revealed in Scripture, as authority for church order, and hence (in their view) for a presbyterian rather than an episcopal polity.

Hooker does not try to resolve this issue about government by arguing for the unique Scriptural authority of episcopacy. Instead he argues that God acts in accord with natural law, which is not a product of God's purely legislative will.[31] Since the principles of natural law are the basic principles of practical reason, we have access to them through our practical reason. When God does not legislate specifically on a particular question, he leaves us free to settle it through our practical reason, guided by the principles of natural law. One such question is the question about the government of the Church, which we ought to settle by consideration of what is just and expedient for particular places at particular times.

Hooker begins this argument by accepting the naturalist view that the principles of natural law constitute moral requirements antecedent to any legislative act of God. Hooker agrees with Aquinas on the natural law and natural reason. In his view, God's intellect grasps the principles of natural law, apart from any act of will or command. This view of the role of reason and will in natural law is close to the position later defended by Vasquez, and lacks the voluntarist elements (however limited these may be) found in Suarez.[32]

To explain why he speaks of a natural law that God does not legislate, Hooker distinguishes two senses of 'law'. In the narrower sense law requires imposition by superior authority, but in an 'enlarged' sense it requires only a rule by which actions are framed. The natural law and the eternal law are laws in the enlarged sense. Their existence does not imply that anyone imposes them on anyone; it requires only the appropriate sort of fact to constitute a rule, canon, or norm.[33]

---

[31] 'They err therefore who think that of the will of God to do this or that there is no reason besides his will' (*LEP* i 2.5 = Keble i 203). Hooker cites *Eph.* 1:11 on God's 'counsel' (*boulē*).

[32] For Suarez's narrower conception of law see *Leg.* i 12.4.

[33] 'I am not ignorant that by "law eternal" the learned for the most part do understand the order, not which God hath eternally purposed himself in all his works to observe, but rather that which with himself he hath set down as expedient to be kept by all his creatures according to the several conditions wherewith he hath endued them. They who thus are accustomed to speak apply the name of Law unto that only rule of working which superior authority imposeth; whereas we somewhat more enlarging the sense thereof term any kind of rule or canon whereby actions are framed, a law.' (*LEP* i 3.1). For more evidence of Hooker's naturalist attitude to natural law, as the expression of the divine intellect, see i 2.2 ('The being of God is a kind of law to his working: for that perfection which God is giveth perfection to that he doth') 5.1–2; 8.4; ('A law therefore generally taken, is a directive rule unto goodness of operation') 8.8; 12.3; 14.4; ('. . . so our own words also, when we extol the complete sufficiency of the whole entire body of the Scripture, must . . . be

This appeal to reason and natural law, understood as a rule rather than as a product of legislative will, influences Hooker's ecclesiology as well as his moral philosophy. In controversies about the episcopal government of the Church, he rejects the position of his Puritan opponents, that a specific form of church government must be justified directly from the Scriptures as having divine authority. In his view, episcopacy is justified by appeal to natural reason, and that should be sufficient warrant for it.[34] We should not suppose that God directs us only through laws revealed in Scripture; God also directs us through the natural law and through practical reason drawing conclusions from the natural law.[35]

Hooker not only rejects an extreme Protestant position on the sources of authority in church and state, but also rejects an extreme voluntarist position on divine commands and morality. His argument helps us to understand the significance of the Reformation for the doctrine of natural law. While voluntarism was defended before the Reformation, the particular emphasis of the Reformers on the sovereignty of God and the sufficiency of Scripture as a rule of doctrine and life might easily suggest a voluntarist conclusion. Luther draws this conclusion in his early work.[36] Hooker's opponents are Calvinists who draw the same conclusion. But though the views of the Reformers might suggest this conclusion, they do not require it. Melanchthon rejects it and Hooker argues strongly against it. If one objects that they are too moderate to count as authentic exponents of the Reformers' position, Calvin's position is even more significant; for though he might be expected to find voluntarism congenial to his general position, he does not endorse it. The later Calvinists, such as those whom Cudworth attacks for their voluntarism, go beyond Calvin's position.[37] The sympathetic attitude to naturalism that we find in Culverwell is a plausible development of Calvin's position.[38]

415. The Effects of Sin

Belief in a natural moral law implies belief in moral principles prescribing actions suitable for human nature and known by natural reason. These principles provide a standard for measuring one's actions. Since, according to Aquinas, natural law requires the cultivation of the virtues of character, we observe natural law by forming the Aristotelian virtues. If we acquire these virtues, we should be able, in reasonably favourable external conditions, to achieve the natural good for human beings.

Aquinas examines our capacity to achieve the virtues and the natural human good, in the light of Christian doctrines of sin, and of the necessity of grace (ST 1-2 q109). He maintains

understood with this caution, that the benefit of nature's light be not thought excluded as unnecessary, because the necessity of a diviner light is magnified') 16.2.

[34] See e.g. vii 14.3. Hooker's moderation on this point does not satisfy his editor Keble. See Keble's elaborate discussion, lxvii–lxxv.

[35] 'For as they [sc. our opponents] rightly maintain that God must be glorified in all things, and that the actions of men cannot tend unto his glory unless they be framed after his law; so it is their error to think that the only law which God hath appointed unto men in that behalf is the sacred Scripture . . . yea, those men which have no written law of God to show what is good or evil, carry written in their hearts the universal law of mankind, the Law of Reason, whereby they judge as by a rule which God hath given unto all men for that purpose. . . . So that in moral actions, divine law helpeth exceedingly the law of reason to guide man's life; but in supernatural it alone guideth' (i 16.5).

[36] See n18 on the *Heidelberg Disputation*.   [37] See Cudworth, *EIM* i 1.5 = H15.

[38] See Culverwell, *LN*, ch. 6 = G&M 55.

(q109 a2) that we can both will and do good without grace in the state of sin, even though we cannot attain our natural good in the state of sin.[39] According to the Reformers, this concession to human beings in the state of sin underestimates the effects of original sin.[40] But it is not so easy to see where they disagree with Aquinas, or what difference their disagreement makes.

Sometimes Luther expresses his disagreement with the Scholastics by rejecting their claim that 'as far as the substance of the act is concerned', we can fulfil the law even in the state of sin. This contrast may be somewhat misleading. In rejecting the Scholastic view, Luther does not mean to deny that on particular occasions we can do the very action required by the moral law, if this is understood in a purely behavioural sense. In this sense, both the person who cares about justice and the person who simply wants to avoid getting caught may do what justice requires, as far as the substance of the act is concerned.

In speaking of the substance of the act, however, neither Luther nor the Scholastics have in mind this purely external sense.[41] When Aquinas speaks of 'the substance of the works (opera)' (e.g., 1-2 q109 a4), he does not refer simply to behaviour. He speaks of 'just and brave actions and the other works of the virtues' so that they include the virtues themselves; for he believes that even in the condition of sin we can acquire the moral virtues (q109 a2). Luther disagrees on this point; he often rejects Aristotle's claim that we become good by doing good actions.[42] He seems to deny that we can achieve the acquired virtues, as Aquinas understands them.

In Luther's view, the Scholastic pursuit of the moral virtues conflicts with St Paul's view that 'through the law comes the consciousness of sin'.[43] In trying to keep the moral law, we realize that we cannot keep it by our own efforts, and this realization makes us aware of our need of divine grace. The belief that we can acquire the moral virtues prevents us from recognizing our incapacity to keep the law.

This objection by itself is not convincing. Aquinas does not claim that we can keep the law by our own efforts; he does not even claim that we can do all the works of the law (q109 a4). The virtues that we can acquire, in his view, are not those that fulfil the divine law, but only those that are suitable for human nature without the further help of divine grace. It would

---

[39] See §350.

[40] See *West. Conf.* 9.1–3: ' God hath endued the will of man with that natural liberty, that it is neither forced, nor by any absolute necessity of nature determined to good or evil. Man, in his state of innocency, had freedom and power to will and to do that which is good and well-pleasing to God; but yet mutably, so that he might fall from it. Man, by his Fall into a state of sin, hath wholly lost all ability of will to any spiritual good accompanying salvation; so as a natural man, being altogether averse from that good, and dead in sin, is not able, by his own strength, to convert himself, or to prepare himself thereunto.' On original justice in Aquinas see §349; Abercrombie, *OJ* 60–72.

[41] 'It may be, then, that they mean by "substance of the deed" an external action. But they do not do this at all; they have reference also to an internal action. For they subsume under "substance of the deed" a work that is done for the sake of God from the heart by an act of the will that is naturally educed. Fools that they are, they do not notice that the will, even if it could, would never do what the law prescribes. For it resists the good, and inclines towards evil. . . . For as long as it is reluctant towards the law, it is turned away from it and thus does not fulfil it. Consequently, it needs grace to make it willing and cheerful towards the law' (*Rm.* 4:7 = Pauck 133–4). See also *Rm.* 8:1–4 = Pauck 218.

[42] See *Rm.* 1:17 = Pauck 18: 'The righteousness of God must be distinguished from the righteousness of men which comes from works—as Aristotle clearly indicates . . . According to him, righteousness follows upon and flows from actions. But, according to God, righteousness precedes works and works result from it.' Cf. *Rm.* 8:3 = Pauck 228: 'Works and actions do not produce virtue, as Aristotle says, but virtues determine actions, as Christ teaches'.

[43] See *Rm* 3:20 = Pauck 106.

be possible, indeed appropriate, for virtuous people, by the standards of the moral virtues, to be acutely aware of their sinfulness and of their incapacity to keep the divine law.[44]

Luther rejects this position because he believes the aim of acquiring the moral virtues is more deeply misguided. Sometimes he suggests that the virtues, as Aristotle conceives them, are not the source of praiseworthy actions, since no action can be praiseworthy in the state of sin.[45] His argument is Augustinian, in so far as he claims there is something lacking in the motives of even the best of us without divine grace. His view about what is lacking reflects his disagreement with the Scholastics about the effects of original sin.

According to the Scholastics, the primary effect is in the 'fuel' (fomes)[46] in the appetitive part of the soul. This makes our desires misdirected by lacking the proper direction towards God that they all had in the condition of original justice. Aquinas does not mean that the rational part is still completely correct, and that our fault can be confined to the non-rational part. The rational part is clouded, and hence liable to be misled, by misdirected passions, and it lacks the basic direction towards God that would make all the other genuine goods clear to it.

Aquinas' view is optimistic, however, in so far as he believes that original sin does not inevitably turn the will to a wholly perverted conception of the ultimate end. Without divine grace, we cannot conceive our supernatural end, and without original justice we cannot even keep an adequate conception of our natural end constantly in mind. But we are capable of forming a conception that, even if inadequate, is correct, because it contains the components of contemplation and virtuous activity. If the will forms this conception of the end, we are capable of acting on it far enough to form the states of character that constitute the moral virtues. Since we have universal conscience (synderesis) to grasp the first principles, and we have prudence, to take us from first principles to the specifically virtuous end, we are capable of acquiring the virtues.[47]

On this point, Luther disagrees. For he believes that our conception of our ultimate end, in the state of sin, is basically and inevitably misguided; he denies that universal conscience gives us a true grasp of the ultimate end.[48]

---

[44] See §§350, 356.

[45] *Rm.* 9:6–9 = Pauck 266: 'So then, why does man take pride in his merits and good works? They cannot in any way please God because they *are* good and meritorious, but only because God has elected from eternity that they would please him. We do the good only on the basis of gratitude, because our works do not make us good, but our goodness, or, rather, the goodness of God makes us good and our actions as well. For what we do is not good in itself, but only because God reckons it to be so . . . It is therefore wrong to define virtue in the way of Aristotle: It makes us perfect and produces laudable acts only in the sense that it makes us perfect and causes our acts to be praiseworthy before men and in our own eyes. Before God this is abominable, and the opposite would please him much more.'

[46] Luther speaks of the fomes at *Rm* 4:7 = Pauck 126: '. . . sin itself is that passion (fuel) and concupiscence, or that inclination towards evil and resistance against the good which is meant in the statement, "I had not known that concupiscence is sin" ' (*Rm.* 7:7).

[47] To this degree Aquinas maintains the principle that the keeping of a law is practicable. See (against the 'heretics') Suarez, *Leg.* i 9.18 (referring to the Council of Trent).

[48] See *Rm.* 4:7 = Pauck 130: 'They [sc. the Scholastic theologians] said . . . that when the will is subject to synteresis, it is, only slightly to be sure, "inclined toward the good". And this tiny motion towards God (of which man is naturally capable) they imagine to be an act of loving God above everything!' Cf. 8:1–4 = Pauck 218: 'Thus philosophy stinks in our nostrils, as if reason could plead at all times for the best, and we tell tall tales about the law of nature. Now it is true that everyone knows the law of nature and that reason pleads for the best. But what best? It pleads for that which is best, not according to God's standards, but according to ours, in other words: it pleads for an evil kind of good. For it seeks itself and its own in all things but not in God. . . . it knows only its own good or what is good, honourable, and useful for

416. Objections to Self-Love

Luther is pessimistic about our prospects for acquiring virtues because he believes that our motives and aims in the state of sin are basically corrupted by self-love.[49] The commandment to love our neighbour as ourselves does not, according to Luther, include a command to love ourselves. On the contrary, it condemns the love of ourselves, and instructs us to turn the attention and love that we now sinfully turn towards ourselves, until it becomes the love of our neighbour instead of ourselves.[50]

Like Scotus, Luther takes self-love to be a natural attitude that has to be abandoned if we are to love God as our ultimate end. In contrast to Scotus, he assumes that self-love is in itself bad, and that in a genuinely virtuous person it would have to be renounced in favour of the love of God. He also rejects Scotus' view that we are capable, in the state of sin, both of self-love and of the love of God, and hence capable of rejecting self-love as our ultimate end. In assuming the inevitable supremacy of self-love in the state of sin, he agrees with eudaemonists against Scotus. In assuming that the love of God requires the renunciation of self-love, he agrees with, and goes beyond, Scotus against the eudaemonism of Aquinas.

Calvin agrees with Luther's view that we are not commanded to love ourselves; he denounces the primacy of self-love as a fiction of the 'Sophists'.[51] But he does not suggest

itself, but not what is good for God and for others. Therefore it knows and wills mainly a good that is a particular good, indeed, that is good only for the individual self.' On Luther's treatment of synteresis see Rupp, *RG* 150–3.

[49] '. . . these words will appear strange and even foolish to those who regard themselves as holy and who love God with a covetous love, i.e., for the sake of their own salvation and eternal rest, and for the purpose of avoiding hell, in other words: not for God's sake but for their own sake. They are the ones who babble that ordered love begins with itself and that everyone must first of all wish his own salvation and then his neighbour's as his own. . . . But as a matter of fact, to be blessed means to seek in everything God's will and his glory, and to want nothing for oneself, neither here nor in the life to come' (*Rm.* 9:3 = Pauck 262). See also *Rm.* 8:5–13 = Pauck 224: 'The "prudence of the flesh" chooses what is to selfish advantage and it avoids what is harmful to the self. Moreover, it rejects the common good and chooses what harms the common spirit. This is the prudence that directs the flesh, i.e. concupiscence and self-will. It enjoys only itself, and uses everyone else, even God; it seeks itself and its own interests in everything . . . Good is only what is good for him and bad only what is bad for him.' Luther alludes to Augustine's division between usus and fruitio; see §231n122.

On the ordo caritatis see Scotus *3Sent.* d29 schol. = OO vii 2, 667; Biel *3Sent* d29 a2 = 523C–528H (W&H).

[50] Luther argues against the view that ordered love begins with oneself and extends to one's neighbour: 'It does not seem to me to be a solid understanding of the commandment "You shall love your neighbour" if one interprets it in terms of the notion that in view of the fact that the commandment itself says "as yourself", the one who loves is the model according to which he loves his neighbour. For one derives the following conclusion from this: You must love yourself first and according to the pattern of this self-love of yours you must also love your neighbour. . . . I believe . . . that by this commandment "as yourself" man is not commanded to love himself but he is shown the wicked love with which in fact he loves himself; in other words, it says to him: You are wholly bent in on yourself and versed in self-love, and you will not be straightened out and made upright unless you cease entirely to love yourself and, forgetting yourself, love only your neighbour. . . . we are commanded to have the same eagerness for the love of others as for self-love. . . . what is commanded (namely, the love of the neighbour) is based on what is prohibited (namely, self-love)' (*Rm.* 15:2 = Pauck 407–8).

[51] 'Let us therefore hold, that our life will be framed in best accordance with the will of God, and the requirements of his Law, when it is, in every respect, most fruitful for our brothers. But in the whole Law, there is not one syllable which lays down a rule as to what man is to do or avoid for the advantage of his own flesh. Indeed, since men are naturally prone to excessive self-love, which they always retain, however far they depart from the truth, there was no need of a law to inflame a love already present in excess. Hence it is perfectly plain that the observance of the Commandments consists not in the love of ourselves, but in the love of God and our neighbour; and that the one who leads the best and holiest life is the one who as little as possible lives and is concerned for himself; and that no one lives worse or more wrongly than the one who lives and is concerned only for himself, and considers and seeks only what is his own. Indeed, to express more clearly how strongly we should be inclined to love our neighbour, the Lord has referred to self-love as the rule (regula), because he could refer to no stronger or more intense feeling. And the force of the way of speaking

that self-love is itself a result of sin, or that the moral law condemns self-love; it condemns only excessive self-love. The persistence of self-love is not a reason for condemning human beings in their natural and sinful state; nor does the moral law require the renunciation of self-love.

The primacy of self-love guarantees, for Luther, that we cannot acquire the moral virtues, if these are taken to require the choice of virtuous action for its own sake. If we choose them for the sake of pleasure, or to avoid punishment, or in the hope of glory, then, Luther assumes, we cannot be genuinely virtuous.[52] But if we deny that we are moved by either of these motives, that is also boastful vainglory.[53] For if we are pleased to do good works, we lay ourselves open to subtle self-deception about our moral condition; we are acting for our delight and inward satisfaction, not out of the love of God.[54] In all these cases our good action is really 'passive', because fear and desire force us to do what we would not do voluntarily.[55]

Luther's attack on the motives of allegedly virtuous people combines two charges: (1) Because of original sin, we are subject to self-assertion, arrogance, and delusions of perfection that may corrupt our motives even when we do virtuous actions. (2) If we are moved primarily by self-love, we are inevitably dominated by self-assertion, arrogance, and so on. If the second charge is correct, then we cannot consistently both be psychological eudaemonists and take the moral virtues to be attainable.

This attack does not imply that the philosophers' conception of moral virtue is mistaken. On the contrary, Luther seems to take it for granted that virtue requires the pursuit of virtuous action for its own sake; on the basis of this assumption he argues that the aspiration to virtue of character is misguided, once we acknowledge the dominance of self-love in the state of sin. He does not seem to endorse one objection that might be attributed to Augustine—that the pagan philosophers' conception of moral virtue is itself flawed.[56]

Aquinas could accept—though he does not accept—Luther's first charge without any basic damage to his Aristotelian conception of virtue and happiness. If arrogance and self-satisfaction are more widespread and pervasive than Aquinas believes they are, then it

must be carefully considered. For he does not (as some sophists have stupidly dreamed) assign the first place to self-love (*philautia*), and the second to charity. He rather transfers to others the affection of love that we feel for ourselves. Hence the Apostle declares, that charity "does not seek its own," (*1Cor.* 13:5). Nor is the Sophists' argument worth a straw, that the thing regulated (regulatum) is always inferior to its rule (regula). The Lord did not make self-love the rule, as if love towards others was subordinate to it; but whereas, through natural depravity the feeling used to stay within ourselves, he shows that it ought to be diffused to another, so that we should be prepared to do good to our neighbour with no less eagerness, ardour, and concern, than to ourselves' (Calvin, *Inst.* ii 8.54). Contrast Aquinas' explanation of the omission of self-love from the Decalogue, §313.

[52] 'Even though they do good works outwardly, they do them either because they fear punishment or because they love riches or glory or some other created good, but not willingly and gladly (non voluntate et hilaritate)' (*Rm.* 3:9 = Pauck 86).

[53] A human being 'cannot but seek his own and love himself above everything. That is the sum and substance of all his faults' (*Rm.* 3:10 = Pauck 88–9).

[54] 'Inasmuch as the love of spiritual values is honourable and good, it very often becomes an end in itself, so that these values are not placed in relation to God and referred to him. And so we pursue them not because they are pleasing to God but because they give us delight and inward satisfaction, and also because we thereby earn the plaudits of men; in other words: we pursue them not for God's sake but for our own' (*Rm.* 3:21 = Pauck 112–13).

[55] 'And thus they do the good not actively but (if I may say so) passively (non faciunt, sed potius . . . faciuntur); i.e., fear and desire force them to do the good that they would not do voluntarily. But people who seek God do the good gratuitously and joyfully and only for God's sake, and not in order to obtain some created good either spiritual or corporeal' (*Rm.* 3:12 = Pauck 93).

[56] See §§229–30.

is more difficult than Aquinas supposes it is to acquire the moral virtues. It is the second charge that attacks Aquinas' basic principles. For it relies on Scotus' view that the supremacy of self-love prevents the appropriate love of virtue for its own sake and the appropriate love of God for his own sake. In his treatment of self-love, arrogance, and the sin of Lucifer, Aquinas answers this objection to the supremacy of self-love.

Luther's objection to self-love is more extreme and more strident than Scotus' objection. It is also more disputable. If self-love is understood as the desire for happiness, as Aquinas understands it, it does not necessarily conflict with the love of God above everything else; for Aquinas believes he can show that our happiness consists in the self-forgetful love of God, just as it consists partly in the self-forgetful love of our neighbour.

417. Pagan Virtue

These reflexions on the condition of human beings in the state of sin lead the Reformers back to Augustine's attack on the pagan virtues. They do not seem to be satisfied with Aquinas' attempt to reconcile Augustine's position with the acknowledgment of genuine moral virtues independent of Christian faith. Augustine's remarks inspire later Christian attacks on pagan virtues. Such attacks were ascribed to Jan Hus, and condemned as heretical by the Council of Konstanz in 1415.[57]

Luther argues that since all the alleged virtues of pagans rest on self-love, they are really vices and not virtues.[58] Melanchthon suggests that when the Scholastics recognize pagan virtues, they are really allowing justification by works, not recognizing the necessity of grace and faith.[59] Calvin's position is more qualified, and closer to Augustine's. He suggests that the fault of pagans is that they do not refer their actions to the appropriate end, the service of God; they are open to this objection even if they are not vicious, measured by non-theological standards.[60]

Attacks on Aquinas were not confined to the Reformers. On the Roman side, Michael Baius discusses these issues at length in *De Virtutibus Impiorum*, where he often appeals

---

[57] D §1216.

[58] 'No one loves justice, except Christ alone. All others love either money or pleasure or honour, or, despising these, love glory at any rate, or, if they are the best of all, love themselves above justice. . . . Therefore, since love of oneself remains, it is quite impossible for a human being to love, speak, or do justice, even though he may simulate all these things. It follows that the virtues of all philosophers, indeed of all human beings, whether jurists or theologians, are virtues in appearance, but really vices' (Luther, *Heb.* 1:9 = C v 347.8–18 = *Works* xxix 119). Further passages are quoted by Rupp, *RG* 203–5.

[59] Melanchthon, *LC* 21–2 = Pauck 33–4: 'And our sophists are not yet ashamed to teach righteousness of works, satisfactions, and philosophical virtues. Let us grant that there was some kind of constancy in Socrates, chastity in Xenocrates, temperance in Zeno. Still, because they were in impure minds—indeed, because these shadows of virtues arose by love of oneself (amore sui) from selfishness (philautia), they ought not to be counted as true virtues, but as vices. . . . what do most philosophers teach, even the best of them, except trust and love of ourselves?' Chemnitz defends a hostile view of pagan virtue against Trent at *ECT* i 387–405 (Topic 6).

[60] Calvin discusses *c. Iul.* at some length in *Inst.* iii 14.3. He does not actually claim that pagan virtues are really vices. He comes close to saying so: 'Therefore, since by the very impurity of the heart these <good works> have been corrupted as from their origin, they ought no more to be reckoned among virtues than the vices that commonly deceive on account of their affinity and likeness to virtue. . . . He [sc. Augustine] therefore affirms that all Fabricii, Scipiones, and Catones in their illustrious achievements have sinned in that, since they lacked the light of faith, they did not refer them to the end to which they ought to have referred them.'

to Augustine. The Pope condemned his views in 1567.[61] The Jansenists revived similar views, with the same Augustinian inspiration;[62] the Pope condemned them in 1690.[63] Baius' objection seems to be similar to Calvin's rather than Luther's; he appeals to the absence of the right end (serving God) rather than the presence of the wrong end (self-love) to explain why pagan virtues are spurious.[64]

The Council of Trent presents the official Roman reaction to these views. It rejects the view that all the actions of pagans, whatever their reason or motive, are really sins and deserve the hatred of God.[65] The English Articles are more cautious than Luther and Baius and simply say that the works of unbelievers have the 'nature' or 'character' of sin.[66]

[61] Pius V, 1567, *Errores Michaeli Baii* = D §1925: 'All the actions of unbelievers are sins, and the virtues of philosophers are vices'. §1933: 'Everything that a sinner, or slave of sin, does is sin'. §1937: 'Anyone who acknowledges any natural good, that is to say, any good that takes its origin from natural powers alone, agrees with Pelagius'. On this ground Baius supports Ambrosiaster's interpretation of Paul's remarks on the Gentiles in *Rm.* 2; he argues that those who accept a 'natural law' interpretation of these remarks endorse Pelagianism (§1992). These are the Pope's descriptions of Baius' views, not quotations from Baius.

[62] Knox, *E*209, explains the connexion between Jansenism and objections to pagan virtue: 'If you believe in the Fall as a shattering blow that unmade man to his very essence, . . . you begin to suspect common human virtues; you trace ulterior motives in them, and write them down as "natural", useless in God's sight'. At 219 he discusses the Jansenist use of the Augustinian division: 'either by charity or by cupidity'. See Augustine, §230n113. Wang, *SAVP* 33–5, discusses this disjunction, and its role in the controversy arising from the Jansenist-inclined Synod of Pistoia (D §§2623–4).

Abercrombie, *OJ* 87–92, 125–8, summarizes the views of Baius and Jansen. In his long, tedious, and polemical *Augustinus* Jansen presents an extreme version of Augustine's case against pagan virtue, relying especially on Augustine's polemic against Julian (see §230). In his view, Augustine allows only the right *officium* and nothing more to pagans. He tries to show (ii 162) that Aquinas really agrees with his view that any genuine virtue must refer all one's actions to God as their end As an example of someone who tries to evade Augustine's plain meaning, Jansen attacks Suarez, *De Gratia* i 7.19–20 = OO vii 399, who interprets Augustine along the lines we have attributed to Aquinas; see §356.

[63] The Pope ascribes these views to Baius: 'It is necessary for an unbeliever to sin in every work. Anyone who hates a sin simply because of its wrongness and inappropriateness to nature, without any reference to the offence against God, truly sins' (D §§2308–9).

[64] 'St Thomas . . . thinks they are virtues because they are referred to some particular genuine good, which can be referred to the universal good, even if these states are found in those who are ignorant of the one true God because of blindness, or who despise him because of arrogance. However, these are clearly similar to the one of whom the Psalmist says: "The fool has said in his heart, There is no God". Here one must especially wonder how St Thomas thought this possible reference of a proximate end to the universal good could be enough to constitute a virtue, given that the same possible reference belongs also to that particular good that the impious seek above the universal good and in explicit contempt of it. . . . A human being is made, and is required, to love God with all his might and to serve him alone; now anyone who lives in accord with virtue does what he is required to and what he is made for; therefore, anyone who does not serve God and seeks to do the duties belonging to the virtues not because of something else but for their own sakes, does not live in accord with virtue' (Baius, *Virt. Imp.* 4 = p. 65). The omitted passage includes a quotation from *c. Iul.* iv 3.

Gregory of Rimini also presents an Augustinian attack on pagan virtue: 'And for that reason one must say the following about the pagans and unqualifiedly faithless who are said to have practised such things: Granted that they did things of the sort that were good in their genus and in accordance with duty (ex officio), as Augustine puts it, still they did not do these things ultimately because of God, and for that reason neither did they do them finally because of the end they ought to have done them for, and thus they did not do them virtuously, but badly and viciously . . .' (*2Sent.* d26–8 q1 98N (p.73 ed Marcolino et al.)). He refers to Augustine, *c. Iul.* iv 3.22. See Leff, *GR* 176; Trinkaus, *IL* 74.

[65] 'If any one says that all the things done before justification, in whatever way they may be done, are truly sins, or merit the hatred of God . . . let him be anathema' (D §1557).

[66] 'Works done before the grace of Christ, and the inspiration of the Spirit, are not pleasing to God, forasmuch as they spring not of faith in Jesu Christ, neither do they make men meet to receive grace, or (as the School-authors say) deserve grace of congruity: yea rather, for that they are not done as God hath willed and commanded them to be done, we doubt not but they have the nature of sin' (*Articles* §13). The Irish Articles of 1615 have 'we doubt not but they are sinful' (§26 = Schaff, *CC* iii 531). 'Have the nature of sin' corresponds to 'peccati rationem habere' in the Latin version, which one might be more inclined to render 'have the character of sin'. This Article is not on exactly the same question as the passage from Trent just quoted. For even though the Article is entitled 'Of works before justification', it actually

758

The Westminster Confession takes a similar view, that the works of unbelievers are sinful in so far as they lack the appropriate motive.[67]

Aquinas' interpretation of Augustine is consistent both with the position of the Council of Trent, that not every aspect of all works before justification is truly sinful, and with the view of the English Articles, that 'forasmuch' as these works are the works of pagans, they have the nature of sin, and cannot even deserve grace by congruity.[68] The Council of Trent and the Articles mention the two aspects of pagan virtue that Aquinas distinguishes; he also agrees with the Articles that works before justification do not deserve grace even by congruity.[69]

Among these different views about pagan virtues, the most radical is Luther's attack based on claims about self-love. He draws on Augustine's description of the outlook of the 'earthly city' as the self-love that goes as far as contempt of God. This description might be taken to imply a sharp contrast between self-love and the love of God; this is how Scotus takes it.

Such a contrast, however, raises a difficulty for Augustine, who also recognizes the basic and universal character of the desire for one's own happiness.[70] He might appear to be committed to all these claims: (1) The desire for one's own happiness is basic and universal in human beings. (2) The desire for one's own happiness is a manifestation of self-love. (3) To love God above all things requires the abandonment of self-love. (4) The Christian is required to love God above all things. Since Aquinas accepts (2), he rejects (3), and claims that Augustine rejects it; in his view, Augustine condemns only misguided self-love. Scotus accepts (3), and therefore denies (1).

Luther accepts all four of these claims, applied to human beings in the state of sin without grace, and so he infers that we cannot fulfil the requirement of loving God above all things in that state. But he suggests that even if we cannot fulfil the law in our state of sin, because of self-love, we can at least recognize and lament our inability to fulfil it; he sometimes regards this as the appropriate preparation for the reception of grace.[71] He seems to expose a difficulty in his position. For his unqualified claims about the pervasiveness of self-love seem to imply that self-love must underlie even our sorrow at our failure to keep the law; and so even this sorrow must be no less sinful than all our efforts to keep the law.

The strong claims about self-love, selfishness, and arrogance support Luther's claim that all actions in the state of sin without grace are sinful because of their motives. But we do not need to accept these strong claims if we are to say more generally, as the English Articles say, that actions in the state of sin 'have the character of sin', in so far as they are not appropriately directed towards God.[72]

---

mentions works 'before the grace of Christ', which are not the same (since some works that are not before the grace of Christ are before justification).

[67] 'Works done by unregenerate men, although for the matter of them they may be things which God commands, and of good use both to themselves and others; yet, because they proceed not from a heart purified by faith; nor are done in a right manner, according to the Word; nor to a right end, the glory of God; they are therefore sinful and cannot please God, or make a man meet to receive grace from God. And yet their neglect of them is more sinful and displeasing unto God' (*West. Conf.* 16.7).

[68] See the passages just quoted in n66.   [69] See *ST* 1-2 q109 a6; q114 a5; §§350–2.

[70] See Augustine, §231n121.

[71] 'Their works are good, not when they put their trust in them, but when they do them in preparation for justification, confident that they will be made righteous through it alone' (*Rm.* 3:21–2 = Pauck 108).

[72] See *Articles* §13 (n66 above).

Even if Luther were right in his strong claims about self-love, he would not be entitled to infer that the Scholastic pursuit of the moral virtues is entirely misguided. He would be right to say that the Scholastics are wrong to suppose that the moral virtues, as they understand them, really move us to act virtuously for its own sake; they cannot, then, meet the Scholastics' own standards for being genuine virtues. They might still, however, be states preferable to their opposites, in so far as they move us to the right actions on the basis of motives that, however sinful, are none the less preferable to the motives characteristic of the vices.

Luther could avoid this qualified endorsement of the moral virtues, if he denied that the actions and motives they encourage are preferable to their opposites. He does not deny this, however, and he has good reason not to deny it. For he acknowledges that, even in the state of sin, we are bound by the natural law, that we acknowledge it, and are capable of fulfilling it to some degree. Neither St Paul nor Luther suggests that observance of the natural law consists simply in behavioural conformity to it; the observers of the law are supposed to have a trained and sensitive conscience as well.[73] Once this is conceded, the virtues of character must be worth cultivating, even if all that we can achieve in the state of sin is a state of character that is irreparably flawed by self-love.

But it is not clear in any case why we ought to agree with Luther's claim that pagans are so dominated by inappropriate self-love that they are incapable of the degree of unselfish motivation that is needed for moral virtue. If we appeal to eudaemonist arguments to show that they are dominated by self-love, we have not shown that this self-love is inappropriate; even if we agree that (as Calvin claims) we are excessively prone to inappropriate self-love, we may believe we are capable of overcoming it far enough to acquire the moral virtues. Luther's most extreme claims may appear to depend on a shift between self-love in general (universal, but not inappropriate) and selfish self-love (inappropriate if taken to excess, but not universally dominant). If we fail to distinguish the two, we may agree too hastily with this claim that self-love is both universally dominant and inappropriate.

If we reject Luther's extreme position, the claim that the works of unbelievers are sinful need not conflict with the claim that unbelievers can acquire genuine virtues. Aquinas agrees with the Augustinian and Calvinist claim that in failing to pursue a supernatural end, unbelievers sin; but this claim is consistent with acknowledging that they can have genuine virtues that are focussed on moral rightness (honestas). This position is set out clearly by Gonet, a later Thomist, who argues that the moral virtues are directed towards the moral good, which is a genuine good, though not a complete good (verum bonum, sed non perfectum).[74]

---

[73] Rm. 2:15: 'They show that what the law requires is written on their hearts, while their conscience also bears witness and their conflicting thoughts accuse or perhaps excuse them'.

[74] In MT Trac. iv, ch. 6, Gonet discusses the question 'Can there be moral virtues without charity?' because modern (recentiores) writers have said No, and have appealed to Augustine, c. Iul. iv 3, and to De nupt. et concup. 3–4. He answers (iv 6.8, p. 212) that these passages refer to perfect virtues that lead to eternal life, and that Augustine (Ep. 130) also recognizes real but imperfect virtues. Aquinas takes the same view, that the acquired virtues are genuine virtues because they focus on the honestum: ' From what has been said you will understand that there are three kinds of virtue. Some are not true virtues, but only apparent, because they are not directed to true good, but to apparent, [e.g., the 'prudence' of the miser]. Others are true virtues, but not perfect, because they are directed to true good, but not to perfect good; for they are directed to good as right (bonum honestum), which has not got the character of the ultimate end, but only of an intermediate end; the acquired moral virtues are of this kind' (iv 6.13, p. 212).

These areas of agreement and disagreement about the works of unbelievers also help us to understand the dispute about whether it is possible for us to keep the moral law in the state of nature. Luther and Calvin believe it is impossible; Calvin recognizes that his view 'is commonly looked upon as a most absurd opinion' (*Inst.* ii 7.5), but he takes it to be obviously true none the less. He argues that no one has succeeded in loving God completely, and that no one has ever been free of sensory appetite (concupiscentia).[75]

On the other side, Suarez rejects the heretics' view that we cannot keep the law in the state of sin. He argues that God does not require what is impossible, but God requires the keeping of the law (*Leg.* i 9.17–18). This raises complex questions about different views of freedom, which Calvin discusses at length (*Inst.* ii 5). But the opposition between the two views is not quite as sharp as it first appears. Aquinas agrees with Calvin that in the state of sin we cannot fulfil the whole law, because we cannot completely fulfil the commandment to love God (*ST* 1-2 q109 a4). It is possible for us to fulfil the law only because it is possible to act with the help of God (q109 a4 ad2).

The impossibility of fulfilling the law would be much more serious if we agreed that every action that is not done out of the love of God is sin, and therefore violates the natural law. Suarez opposes this view, which he ascribes to Baius and to the Lutherans (*Leg.* ii 11.6–7). Baius appeals, as Luther does in such contexts, to Augustine.[76] But if we do not accept the extreme view about self-love, we need not accept this indiscriminate condemnation of the works of unbelievers. Nor is it necessary for Calvin's argument about the necessity of grace for justification.

A summary account that ignores the details of the complex and polemical arguments on each side inevitably over-simplifies the issues and exaggerates the extent of agreement. But it may none the less be useful for our main purpose. Apart from Luther's exaggerated claims about self-love, the arguments of the Reformers do not show that the Scholastics were wasting their time in advocating the Aristotelian virtues of character. To refute the Scholastics on this point, the Reformers would have had to show that they had seriously misunderstood the demands of the natural law and the states of character needed to fulfil these demands. But the arguments about the effects of original sin do not show that the Scholastics were wrong on these points.

One might, however, draw a conclusion more hostile to the Scholastics from these questions about the motives of allegedly virtuous pagans. If one accepts the extreme Lutheran claims about self-love and its corrupting effects, one might infer that it is a mistake to connect the natural law with the cultivation of the virtues. If we grant that genuine virtue is impossible without the transformation resulting from divine grace, we might decide that natural reason has nothing to do with this 'genuine' virtue, and that we can abandon genuine virtue to the theologians. Hence we might prefer to confine the natural law to prescriptions for action, without reference to motives. Even if these actions are worthless, from the

---

[75] 'By impossible I mean that which never was, and, being prevented by the direction and decree of God, never will be. I say, that if we go back to the remotest period, we shall not find a single saint who, clothed with a mortal body, ever reached the goal of love so as to love the Lord with all his heart, and soul, and mind, and strength. And again I say there has been no one who has not been weighed down by appetite. Who will answer this?' (*Inst.* ii 7.5).

[76] The relevant passage from Baius is quoted by Perena ad loc.

theological point of view, without divine grace, they are still useful for the good of society; perhaps these are the real concern of natural law.

This reduced conception of natural law is a Hobbesian conception; the dismissal of genuine virtue is Mandeville's reaction to disputes about virtues and motives.[77] Such a conclusion does not express the views of the Reformers. Their central views about the effects of original sin, and about grace and justification, do not undermine the pursuit and cultivation of the moral virtues, as Aquinas understands them.

418. Sin and Freewill

The Reformers believe that the Scholastics over-estimate the role of freewill in human beings in the state of original sin. Luther sometimes asserts that freewill remains 'in name alone' in the state of sin.[78] The Council of Trent condemns this formulation,[79] though it affirms that freewill was weakened by original sin.[80] The Augsburg Confession takes a more moderate position than Luther's extreme view, claiming that freewill extends to 'civil justice' and to 'things subject to reason'.[81]

It is sometimes difficult to see what the disputes are about because of some obscurities in claims about freewill. Melanchthon recognizes three sorts of freedom: (1) Power over external actions; it depends on our choice whether we act one way or the other. (2) Contingency of our actions in relation to external causes, both natural and divine. (3) Independence of will from the passions.[82] According to Melanchthon, we clearly have

[77] See Hobbes, L15.40; Mandeville, FB i 56–7.

[78] 'After <original> sin freewill is present in name alone, and as long as it does what is up to it, it sins mortally. After <original> sin free will is capable of good as a subjective capacity, but of evil always as an active capacity' (Luther, Heid. Disp. 13–14 = C v 378 = Works xxxi 48–9 = Dillenberger 502).

[79] Canon 5 on Justification: 'If anyone says that after the sin of Adam human freewill is lost and extinguished, or says that it is a thing in name only, in fact a name without any <corresponding> reality, and a fiction that Satan introduced into the Church, let him be anathema' (D §1555).

[80] '. . . in them [sc. the Jews] freewill was not at all extinguished, though admittedly it was weakened in its powers and bent down' (D §1521).

[81] 'Of freewill they [sc. the Lutherans] teach that man's will has some liberty to choose civil righteousness, and to work things subject to reason. But it has no power, without the Holy Spirit, to work the righteousness of God, that is, spiritual righteousness; . . . but this righteousness is wrought in the heart when the Holy Spirit is received through the Word. . . . [A quotation from Augustine follows.] They condemn the Pelagians and others, who teach that without the Holy Spirit, by the power of nature alone, we are able to love God above all things' (Aug. Conf. 18). Melanchthon expands this claim by distinguishing the roles of reason and faith: 'Nor, indeed, do we deny liberty to the human will. The human will has liberty in the choice of works and things which reason comprehends by itself. It can to a certain extent render civil righteousness or the righteousness of works; it can speak of God, offer to God a certain service by an outward work, obey magistrates, parents; in the choice of an outward work it can restrain the hands from murder, from adultery, from theft. Since there is left in human nature reason and judgment concerning objects subjected to the senses, choice between these things, the liberty and power to render civil righteousness, are also left. . . . But . . . human hearts without the Holy Spirit are without the fear of God; without trust toward God, they do not believe that they are heard, forgiven, helped, and preserved by God. Therefore they are godless. . . . Therefore, although we concede to free will the liberty and power to perform the outward works of the Law, yet we do not ascribe to free will these spiritual matters, namely, truly to fear God, truly to believe God, truly to be confident and hold that God regards us, hears us, forgives us, etc. . . . Therefore such a distribution is of advantage in which civil righteousness is ascribed to the free will and spiritual righteousness to the governing of the Holy Spirit in the regenerate' (Apol. Aug. Conf. 18). On civil righteousness see Maurer, HCAC 89–101.

[82] For (1) see LC 13.2 = Pauck 27. For (2) see 11.17 = Pauck 24–5. For (3) see 13.11 = Pauck 27.

the first sort of freedom; we can experience it in our actions. But it is not enough for the freewill that the Scholastics affirm. We lack the second type of freedom, since nothing is contingent in relation to the will of God. We also lack the third type of freedom. Since the second and third types of freedom are essential for the truth of the Scholastic claims, we must reject these Scholastic claims.[83]

In arguing against Erasmus, Luther agrees that we have the first type of freedom, but denies that we have the second type.[84] To claim the second kind of freedom, we must, in Luther's view, deny the sovereignty and efficacy of the will of God, as we know of it through the Scriptures.[85] Luther rejects the view of providence and predestination that makes it depend on God's foreknowledge of what will happen independently of God's will. If God's providence simply rested on foreknowledge of what we will do freely, our sinning or avoiding sin would be up to us, and we would not depend on divine grace to escape from sin. Since we have Scriptural authority to show that we are absolutely dependent on divine grace, we cannot have freewill to act independently of God in the state of sin, and God's providence cannot rest simply on foreknowledge. We cannot restrict God's role to foreknowledge. We must also allow, according to Luther, that God begins a causal chain that, given God's initial will, inevitably results in one or another action of ours. This is God's predestination.[86]

Luther and Erasmus agree that if God initiates a causal chain in which each previous condition is sufficient for a specific successor, and in which the whole chain is sufficient for my action, I lack freewill. Since Luther is convinced of the truth of predestination through such a causal chain of sufficient conditions, he believes he must deny freewill; the mere fact that our choice to do A rather than B is among the conditions determining our doing A rather than B does not ensure that our doing A rather than B is an exercise of freewill. Since Erasmus is convinced that it would be unjust of God to condemn us for actions that we are not free not to do, he believes he must deny predestination, as Luther understands it.

We can find a role for predestination without denying freewill, as Luther and Erasmus understand it, if we adopt a Molinist solution.[87] According to this view, predestination is an act of the divine will, not simply the product of God's foreknowledge of what we will do independently of him. But it rests on a special kind of divine knowledge. God knows not only the laws of nature and the actual future. He also knows the counterfactual futures; this is his 'middle knowledge'.

God knows, for instance, what I would freely do in different circumstances. He knows that if I were offered a bribe of §10, I would not sell state secrets to the enemy, but if I were offered §10m, and threatened with the death of my family, I would sell the secrets. He also knows the circumstances in which an enemy agent would offer me the small bribe, and those in which he would offer me the large bribe and present me with this threat. Both

---

[83] When Chemnitz states what he takes to be the 'chief point at issue' about freewill, he does not go as far as Luther in denying contingency; see *ECT* i 420–7. At 426–7 he accuses Trent of obscuring the issues by its condemnation of Pelagianism.

[84] Luther discusses Erasmus' account of freewill in *SA* Part 3 = C iii 150–6 = *BW*, tr. Packer and Johnson), 137–43.

[85] See *SA* = C iii 150–93 = *BW* 137–89.

[86] Calvin discusses freewill at length in *Inst.* ii 2. At ii 3.5, he distinguishes necessity from compulsion (coactio), as Luther does at *SA* = C iii 125 = *BW* 102.

[87] See Freddoso's helpful edition of Molina's *Concordia*. The controversy is discussed by Farrelly, *PGFW*. Molina sets out from Aquinas' discussion of non-actual possibles in *ST* 1a q14 a9.

my decisions and the enemy's decisions are free; the antecedents and circumstances do not provide sufficient conditions.

If God knows all this, and wants me to sell the secrets, God arranges the second set of circumstances. Hence my selling the secrets is the result of God's will, not simply of God's foreknowledge; for God chooses to put me in these circumstances rather than in any of those in which God knows I would not sell the secrets. None the less, it does not threaten my freedom, because God's choice of the circumstances rests on knowledge of what I would freely do in different circumstances.

The Molinist appeal to middle knowledge as the basis of predestination identifies a role for predestination within an incompatibilist conception of freewill. A compatibilist might also attribute knowledge of counterfactual futures to God, but such knowledge would play no special role in a defence of freewill. The special role in a defence of freewill relies on the claim that God's middle knowledge is of what I would do in different circumstances, without being determined to do it. If each set of circumstances and antecedent conditions provided sufficient conditions for one or another action by me, middle knowledge would be irrelevant.

The Molinist solution does not fit the Reformers' conception of predestination and divine grace. If we remain free to avoid sin in the state without grace, then we do not depend on God's grace; both sin and virtue are in our power and independent of God. This is why Luther insists that the proper recognition of divine sovereignty and divine grace requires the rejection of freewill. The form of predestination that rests on middle knowledge falls short of the form of predestination that Luther takes to be required by Christian doctrine.

One might argue, in any case, that the Molinist position fails to do all that might be expected of it. One reason for insisting on freewill, conceived as excluding determinism, is the belief that if we allow God's choices to initiate a causal chain of conditions sufficient for sin, we make God the author of sin, and hence responsible both for the sin and for the condemnation of the sinners whom God chooses not to save. Middle knowledge may seem to avoid this objection, since sinners would not sin without having made the undetermined choice to sin; hence, they, and not God, are responsible.

To be content with this answer, however, we must ignore the fact that God chooses to confront sinners with circumstances in which God knows they will sin. God could have confronted them with different circumstances in which they would have freely chosen not to sin. If, then, Judas would not have sinned without God's predestination, and since God's predestination ensures that Judas will sin, by ensuring the circumstances in which—as God knows—he will sin, God seems to bear responsibility for Judas's sinning, even if Judas himself also bears responsibility for it.

These arguments between Erasmus, the Reformers, and the Molinists proceed on assumptions that are shared by Scotus and Ockham, who also believe that if the will is determined by antecedent external conditions, we lack freewill.[88] But Aquinas does not seem to accept these assumptions, since his account of the relation between human freedom and divine foreknowledge and predestination does not depend on the denial of determinism. In his view, contingency requires secondary causes operating in the way proper to their nature; it does not require any gap in sufficient conditions. Human wills are secondary causes

---

[88] See §371.

operating properly when they are moved by the greater apparent good; if our actions are caused by our wills moved by the greater apparent good, we act freely, no matter how it comes about that the greater apparent good is presented to us in this way.

According to Aquinas, then, we are responsible for our sinful actions because we choose them as a result of will and election. We, and not God, are the causes of our sins because God does nothing wrong in failing to prevent them.[89] This all remains true even though God's will initiates a set of sufficient conditions for our sinful action. This is the position that Banez ascribes to Aquinas and defends in opposition to the Molinist solution.[90]

Aquinas' position, as defended by Banez, maintains the claims about freewill that Luther opposes, but it does not weaken the claims about predestination that Luther supports. It is not surprising, then, that Banez's position was attacked as being too close to that of the Reformers. The Banezians and the Molinists agreed on a series of agreed statements on freewill and predestination, to distinguish them both from Pelagians and Calvinists.[91] But their agreement concealed a disagreement about the nature of freewill. Aquinas maintains his combination of views because he maintains a weaker condition for freewill than the one that Luther and Erasmus share. Hence, the conditions that appear to Luther to exclude freewill may not exclude it, if we accept Aquinas' conception.

If this is true, Luther has a reason for rejecting the Tridentine formulations about freewill if he accepts an indeterminist conception of freewill. But his Scriptural reasons for denying freewill are reasons for affirming predestination, and may not require the denial of freewill as Aquinas understands it.

On this issue, then, the conflict between the Reformers and the Scholastics may be less sharp than it initially appears. Luther's primary dispute is with the position of Scotus, Ockham, and Biel on freewill; this is the position that Erasmus defends. The debate between Luther and Erasmus neglects the conception of freewill that goes back to the Stoics and to Aristotle. This is also Aquinas' conception of freewill.

On the division between the will and the passions, the opposition between Melanchthon and Aquinas is sharper. Melanchthon opposes Aquinas on both historical and philosophical grounds: (1) He believes that the division between will and passion is un-Biblical. In the Scriptures, the source of motivation and action is the 'heart', without further distinction.[92] (2) The division between will and passion conceals the fact that we necessarily follow our strongest passion. In suggesting that it is up to us to resist our passions, the Scholastic position commits itself to a Pelagian position about our freedom in the face of sin.[93]

---

[89] See §345.

[90] Banez presents his view in *SC* ad 1a q19 a8 = 425–35; ad q23 a5 = 506–59. Freddoso, *DF* 24–8 differentiates the Banezian view from simple compatibilism about freewill and determinism.

[91] In 1607 Pope Paul V forbade the opposing sides to accuse each other of heresy. See D §1997; Farrelly, *PGFW* 147–8.

[92] '...philosophy gradually crept into Christianity, and the impious doctrine about freewill was accepted... The term "freewill" was used, a term most foreign to the divine writings, and to the sense and judgment of the Spirit, and a term by which we see holy men have often been offended. The equally harmful term "reason" was added from Plato's philosophy. For just as we in these later ages of the Church have embraced Aristotle in place of Christ, so immediately after the beginning of the Church Christian doctrine was weakened through Platonic philosophy' (*LC* = *MWA* ii 1, 8.32–9.2 = Pauck 23). It would have been better to follow the Scriptural doctrine that God judges hearts, and to avoid the Aristotelian notion of the will (15.22–31 = Pauck 29).

[93] According to Melanchthon the crucial division separates the cognitive power from what we can indifferently call 'will', 'affection', or 'desire' (9.13–14 = Pauck 23). He rejects an intellectualist account of the will: 'For just as a tyrant

Melanchthon's historical argument is open to question. While the Aristotelian distinction is not constant or explicit in the Scriptures, it does not seem alien to Paul's remarks about willing and doing, or about the contrast between appetites and mind.[94] Moreover, if it is anachronistic to apply the Scholastic division to the Scriptures, it is no less anachronistic to apply Melanchthon's anti-rationalist thesis about action on the strongest affection to them.

The more important objection to the Scholastic division is the second, resting on philosophical and theological argument. Melanchthon suggests that if the will is capable of rejecting and restraining the suggestions of the passions, it is in our power to refrain from sin, and hence—contrary to fact—we do not depend wholly on divine grace to free us from sin. [95] The Scholastics do not see what is wrong with the claims of pagans to genuine virtue, because they do not see that confidence in our capacity to achieve virtue is simply the arrogance that excludes the appropriate sort of trust in God. According to Melanchthon, the Scholastics are open to Augustine's objections to pagan pretensions to virtue.[96]

This would be a fair objection, if the Scholastic division implied a voluntarist conception of the will. According to this conception, the will cannot be determined, and hence cannot be determined to sin, by anything external to it. Aquinas' intellectualist conception of the will, however, is not committed to this claim about external determination. If sinful action is attractive enough to our non-rational desires and to our intellect, it may present an irresistibly attractive apparent greater good to our will, so that our will is determined to pursue the sinful course of action. We are free to avoid a sinful action on a particular occasion, because our acting or not acting depends on the consent of our will.[97] But if the sinful action is so attractive to our will that the will must recognize it as the greater good, then it is impossible for us not to choose the sinful action. This sort of impossibility is consistent with Aquinas' division between will and passion, and with his claim that the will is not necessarily moved by the passions. Aquinas offers this explanation of our inability to refrain from sin (1-2 q109 a8).[98]

On this issue, then, we ought to reach the conclusion that we reached on the issue about predestination. The Reformers have a good reason, from within their own theological perspective, for criticizing the Scholastics who are also voluntarists. They have no equally

---

is in a republic, so is the will in a human being, and just as the senate is subjected to the tyrant, so is cognition to the will, so that, although cognition gives good advice, still the will rejects it and is carried off by its affection . . . ' (9.24–8 = Pauck 24). In some cases where the Scholastics think will rather than affection controls us, Melanchthon suggests that we are really controlled by the stronger affection, and in other cases we act against affection because of pretence (per simulationem, 14.1 = Pauck 28), 'as when someone behaves in a friendly, affable, and polite way, perhaps for no certain reason, towards one whom he sincerely hates and wishes harm to'. This sort of pretence encourages the Scholastics to recognize a distinct faculty of will: 'And this <apparent freedom> is that will that the stupid scholastics have imagined for us, namely a power such that however you may be affected it can still direct and control the affection. . . . However you may be affected, they ascribe to the will a power of eliciting, as they put it, good actions' (14.8–13 = Pauck 28).

[94] See §212.   [95] See *LC* 21.31–22.16 = Pauck 34, quoted at n59 above.

[96] You pretend that you do not deny original sin, and yet you teach that a human being by his own powers can do something good' (*LC* 24.5–7).

[97] Articles §9 describes the pervasive effect of sin without explicit denial of freewill: 'Original sin consisteth not in the following of Adam (as the Pelagains do vainly talk), but it is the fault and corruption of the nature of every man, that naturally is engendered of the offspring of Adam; whereby man is very far gone from original righteousness, and is of his own nature inclined to evil, so that the flesh lusteth always contrary to the spirit; and therefore in every person born into the world, it deserveth God's wrath and damnation'.

[98] See §350. In *LC* 26.19–24 Melanchthon attacks the 'sophists' who identify the flesh with sensory desire. Articles §9 mentions this and other views of 'flesh' without deciding between them.

good reason for rejecting the views of the Scholastics who are intellectualists. Their claims about predestination and sin rule out human freedom as Scotus, Ockham, and Biel understand it. But they do not rule out freedom as Aquinas understands it, and they do not conflict with Aquinas' moral psychology.

419. Justification, Grace, and Faith

The Reformers emphasize our inability to avoid sin and the sovereign predestination of God, in order to explain the Pauline doctrine of justification. They follow Paul and Augustine in taking justification to be the work of God's grace and generosity, working through faith, and not a human achievement or a response by God to human merits, resulting from voluntary and meritorious actions that require a favourable response from God. Emphasis on human achievements and merits independent of God appears to them to fall into the Pelagian heresy that Augustine exposes and rejects.

The Pelagian position is heretical, if it claims that virtuous actions by themselves merit the divine reward of eternal life. Such a claim makes it difficult to understand the Scriptural emphasis on grace and faith as opposed to works and merits. It is more difficult, however, to reject the (so-called) 'Semi-Pelagian' view that justification requires God's grace and cannot be achieved by human merit, but God's grace is itself a response to human effort.[99] Though this effort does not merit eternal life, it is still a human contribution, independent of divine grace, that prepares us for divine grace. We might conceive this preparation as the faith to which God responds, or we might conceive faith as a gift of grace, given in response to appropriate human endeavour.

Though Luther's *Lectures on Romans* sometimes seem to recognize the possibility of 'preparation' as a human achievement,[100] he normally rejects this view of preparation. He argues that God's grace forgives us our sins, and thereby justifies us. It does not reward us for having refrained from sin as far as possible. It does not even reward us for recognizing and lamenting our inability to avoid sin; for that would itself be a human achievement limiting the operation of divine grace.[101]

Luther attacks a doctrine of preparation that can be found in Ockham and Biel.[102] But it is not so clear how far his attack affects Aquinas' position. For Aquinas denies that we can merit the grace of justification, either by condign or by congruous merit, independently of

---

[99] Some of the relevant issues are discussed by McGrath, *ID* §7.

[100] *Rm.* 2:12 = Pauck 51: '. . . people who by some good action toward God, according to the measure of their natural ability, earned grace which then directed them farther—not as if grace were given to them in recognition of such a merit, because then it would not have been grace, but because they thus prepared themselves for receiving it as a free gift'. On preparation see Rupp, *RG* 185.

[101] The Articles reject a doctrine of preparation, understood as our own efforts independent of divine grace. See §10: 'The condition of Man after the fall of Adam is such that he cannot turn, and prepare himself, by his own natural strength and good works, to faith and calling upon God: Wherefore we have no power to do good works pleasant and acceptable to God, without the grace of God by Christ preventing us, that we may have a good will, and working with us when we have that good will'. In 'by his own natural strength and good works', and 'without the grace of God. . .', the Article explains the sense in which it rejects a doctrine of preparation, and the sense in which it denies a role to freewill. The Article is headed 'Of Free-Will', but it does not deny that we have freewill in the condition of sin.

[102] See McGrath, *ID* §§20–1.

grace (*ST* 1-2 q109 a6; q112 a2).[103] Luther has no reason to reject Aquinas' views on this issue about justification. Might he, however, reasonably reject Aquinas' claim that preparation for grace and turning to God are acts of freewill rather than acts of God operating independently of our freewill? If we accept a voluntarist and indeterminist conception of freedom, Aquinas' claims about preparation and turning to God imply that, despite his views on merit, he believes that justification depends on some human action that is independent of divine grace.

Aquinas does not believe this, however, since he does not rely on a voluntarist and indeterminist conception of freedom. In his view, God's grace moves us in the way that human beings are characteristically moved, and hence it moves us through freewill. God moves us by presenting a good for us to consider and act on, even if God infallibly determines us. Aquinas considers the doctrine of preparation that Luther rejects, according to which a human being's unaided efforts ensure a divine response.[104] He rejects this doctrine, since he denies that preparation precedes grace and is the effect of a human being's unaided efforts.[105] He believes none the less that justification requires preparation that is an act of human freewill.

Luther might object that Aquinas' emphasis on freewill in preparation and turning to God is inconsistent with his claim that preparation and turning to God are the effects of God's grace rather than of unaided human effort. But the charge of inconsistency is unjustified. In the light of Aquinas' conception of freewill, the roles of divine grace and human freewill are consistent. The role that Aquinas allows to freewill does not imply Semi-Pelagianism. Though the Council of Trent is less unambiguous than Aquinas is on this point, it does not disagree with Aquinas on the sufficiency of divine grace for justification.[106] Though both

---

[103] See §352. The Articles also reject congruous merit before justification. See §13: 'Works done before the grace of Christ, and the inspiration of the Spirit, are not pleasing to God, forasmuch as they spring not of faith in Jesu Christ, neither do they make men meet to receive grace, or (as the School-authors say) deserve grace of congruity: yea rather, for that they are not done as God hath willed and commanded them to be done, we doubt not but they have the nature of sin'.

[104] 'It would seem that grace is necessarily given to whoever prepares himself for grace, or to whoever does what he can, because, on *Rm.* 5:1, "Being justified . . . by faith, let us have peace," etc. the gloss says: "God welcomes whoever flies to Him, otherwise there would be injustice with Him." But it is impossible for injustice to be with God. Therefore it is impossible for God not to welcome whoever flies to Him. Hence he receives grace of necessity' (*ST* 1-2 q112 a3 obj1). This view is rejected by Luther on *Rm.* 14:1 = Pauck 391. Pauck cites this passage from Aquinas, not remarking that it is a view that Aquinas rejects. Luther's view and its antecedents are explored by Oberman, *DR*, ch. 4, esp. 97–9.

[105] 'This gloss is speaking of one who flees to God by a meritorious act of his freewill that has already been informed through grace; for if he did not receive this <meritorious act>, it would be against the justice that God himself established. Or if it is referred to a movement of freewill before grace, it is speaking in the sense that a human being's flight to God is through a divine motion, and that it is just for this motion not to fail' (*ST* 1-2 q112 a3 ad1).

[106] The Council discusses the beginnings of justification in its Decree on Justification, ch. 5 = D §1525: 'While God touches the human heart through the illumination of the Holy Spirit, neither does a human being do nothing at all when he receives that inspiration (since he is also capable of rejecting it), nor, however, is he capable of moving himself towards justice in the sight of God by his own free will without the grace of God'. The context shows that the last phrase means that we move ourselves by our own free will with the grace of God. Cf. Canons 1–4 = D §1551–4. Can. 4 rejects the view that human freewill 'cannot dissent, if he were to will to (si velit), but like some inanimate object does nothing at all, but is in a purely passive condition'. The 'si velit' here introduces ambiguity. For if it is true that if God chooses, then a person will not want to reject grace, God's grace is sufficient for justification even though 'si velit' is true. It is not clear, then, that Luther or Calvin needs to maintain the view that is condemned here, if he wants to maintain the sufficiency of grace. Similarly, Can. 9 (§1559) condemns the view that we are justified by faith alone, 'in such a way as to understand that nothing else is needed to co-operate for gaining the grace of justification, and that it is in no way necessary for him to be prepared and disposed by the movement of his own will'. The Council does not make it clear whether divine grace is sufficient for the movement of one's own will.

Aquinas and the Council emphasize the importance of freewill, they do not treat the role of freewill as involving a role for unaided human effort.[107]

It is clearer that Luther disagrees with Aquinas about whether justification requires both an act of divine grace and an act of the human being who is justified. Sometimes the Reformers state their view of justification by claiming that it is entirely God's action and that human beings are simply recipients. On this view, justification is entirely passive; the 'effect' on the recipient is a mere 'Cambridge' change.[108] If A kills B's wife C, then A makes B a widower, and if A marries C, then A makes C's brother B into A's brother-in-law. But in both cases what 'happens' to B is entirely reducible to what A does and what happens to C. Similarly, one might understand the Reformers' doctrine of justification as a purely forensic action. If it consists simply in God's forgiving sinners, and 'justifying' or 'acquitting' them by remitting the punishment that would otherwise fall on them, then it is a one-sided transaction. Nothing happens to sinners beyond the fact that God chooses to pronounce them innocent.[109] Aquinas is wrong, then, to claim that justification requires a movement of a sinner's freewill in turning to God. Even if this turning to God is itself an effect of God's grace, Aquinas is mistaken, from the purely forensic point of view, in ascribing any real change or any real action to the sinner. He is wrong, that is to say, in treating justification as though it were really making just (iustum facere) rather than simply 'reckoning just', in a sense that does not imply being just.[110]

Some of Luther's remarks certainly suggest a purely forensic and one-sided view of justification. It is less clear that this could be the Reformers' consistent position. To see the issues that arise in trying to settle this question, we may turn to further areas of disagreement with the Scholastic view.

420. Grace and Virtue

As Aquinas understands grace, it begins a qualitative change in the justified sinner. When grace is infused, we also receive the infused moral virtues. Since these virtues are superior to the acquired moral virtues, the infusion of grace ensures that we become better than we were. In our unjustified state, we could not fulfil the 'works of the law', the moral demands of rational morality and the further demands imposed by the Gospel. With the help of grace, however, we can avoid the distorting effects of original sin, and so we can now fulfil the demands that we previously could not fulfil.

Some of Luther's remarks appear to oppose this view. In being justified, we do not cease to be sinners.[111] This is a natural conclusion from a purely forensic conception of justification

---

[107] The Council's emphasis on freewill is endorsed by Ignatius Loyola, *SE* §17: '... we ought not to speak so lengthily and emphatically about grace that we generate a poison harmful to freedom of the will. Hence one may speak about faith and grace as much as possible, with God's help, for the greater praise of his divine majesty; but not in such ways or manners, especially in times as dangerous as our own, that works and free will are impaired or thought worthless.'

[108] On active and passive states see §245.

[109] The Council of Trent affirms that justification is God's work, but still more than a mere Cambridge change in us: 'for the justice that is said to be ours, because we are justified through its being inherent in us, that same justice is God's, because it is infused in us by God through the merit of Christ' (ch. 16 = D §1547). Similarly, it condemns the view that justifying grace is only the favour of God, to the exclusion of infused charity (Can. 11 = D §1561).

[110] On justification and making just in St Paul see §§209–10.

[111] 'Iustus et peccator simul': *Rm.* 7:25 = Pauck 127: '... he is at the same time both a sinner and righteous, a sinner in fact but righteous by virtue of the reckoning and the certain promise of God that he will redeem him from sin. . .' Cf. McGrath, *ID* 199. Related remarks by Luther are cited by Rupp, *RG* 175–80: Maurer, *HCAC* 328–30.

that makes it simply an action of God without any further change in the justified person. If this is the whole of Luther's position, justification consists in being forgiven the sins that are not forgiven in the unjustified sinner. According to this view, we would have no reason to expect the justified person to sin any less often than the unjustified.

Since Luther rejects this conclusion, he cannot believe that justification, forensically conceived, is the only effect of divine grace. Following St Paul, he rejects the suggestion that it is all right to continue in sin once we recognize that we are forgiven and justified.[112] He argues that, on the contrary, good works are required of a justified sinner, and that the justified sinner will want to perform them; as Luther says, they are 'fruits' of faith and justification.[113]

This claim is consistent with a purely forensic view of justification, if we distinguish justifying grace from sanctifying grace. Even if justification itself consists only in forgiveness, and therefore does not by itself make us just, still, God makes sanctifying grace follow justifying grace, and sanctification involves the capacity for the good works that are the fruit of justification. If this is what Luther means, his claim that grace does not involve a qualitative change in the sinner must be confined to justifying grace. Infusion, as Aquinas understands it, is not an aspect of justification, but of sanctification (as Luther conceives them).[114]

Apparently, then, the Reformers have no reason to reject belief in infused moral virtues. Still, they do not recognize any such virtues. Why do they reject them? One possible reason is relatively superficial. Aquinas has a rather extreme conception of the conditions for the presence of an infused virtue; he takes it to be incompatible with any mortal sin. This does not mean that the person with infused moral virtues is guaranteed not to fall into mortal sin; it means that once we fall into mortal sin, we lose all our infused virtues, and on repenting of it, we get them all back. This is what happened to St Peter; in denying Christ he lost all his infused virtues, and in repenting of his betrayal, he got them all back.

One might conclude that Aquinas has an unreasonably demanding conception of the life resulting from justification. Since the Reformers maintain that justifying and sanctifying grace do not eliminate sin, they might reasonably deny that justification results in the infusion of virtues whose presence is incompatible with sin, and so they might reasonably reject Aquinas' conception of infused virtues.

If, then, we were to relax Aquinas' standards for infused virtues, so that both the acquired and the infused virtues allow the presence of sin, would the Reformers have a good reason

---

[112] See *Rm.* 6:1 (§210n89). Trent condemns the view that the Decalogue does not bind Christians (Can. 19 = D §1569). *West. Conf.* agrees with Trent: 'The moral law doth forever bind all, as well justified persons as others, to the obedience thereof; and that not only in regard of the matter (vi materiae) contained in it, but also in respect of the authority of God the Creator who gave it. Neither doth Christ in the gospel any way dissolve, but much strengthen, this obligation (vinculum)' (19.5).

[113] On fruits of faith see *Aug. Conf.* Art. 6: '. . . that faith ought (debeat) to bring forth good fruits, and that they should (oporteat) do good works, commanded by God, because of the will of God, not so that we may be confident that we merit justification in the sight of God through these works'. Art. 20 repeats this point about works. See McGrath, *ID* 203–4. Other passages are cited by Maurer, *HCAC* 369–71.

Trent condemns the view that even for the justified it is impossible to keep the commandments of God (Can. 18 = D §1568). It affirms that good works are not merely the fruits and signs of justification, and that the justice received is conserved and increased (Can. 24 = D §1574). The *Articles* describe good works as fruits of faith, but do not endorse the view, condemned by Trent, that they are nothing more. See §12: 'Albeit that good works, which are the fruits of faith, and follow after justification, cannot put away our sins, and endure the severity of God's judgment, yet are they pleasing and acceptable to God in Christ, and do spring out necessarily of a true and lively faith; insomuch that by them a lively faith may be evidently known as a tree discerned by the fruit'.

[114] Calvin discusses sin and sanctification in *Inst.* iii 3.10–14.

to believe in infused virtues? An answer to this question partly depends on whether they agree with Aquinas on the relation of the infused to the acquired virtues. Aquinas takes them to increase the acquired virtues, and to fulfil their demands more completely. But if we think of the 'fruits of justification' as simply actions that fulfil God's commands, but are not necessarily connected to the actions enjoined by the acquired virtues, we reject Aquinas' view of the infused virtues.

The Council of Trent distinguishes the Roman from the Reformed view by claiming that good works after justification are more than simply fruits of justification (Canon 24). The point of this claim is to make these good works sources of merit. In so far as genuine virtues might also be regarded as sources of merit, the dispute about merit might also affect different people's judgment about whether good works after justification really proceed from infused virtues.

The belief that good works are sources of merit might easily be regarded as a semi-Pelagian position. Even if we deny that good works before justification merit eternal life, we might argue that two essential roles are left for freewill acting independently of divine grace. We might regard preparation for reception of grace as an action of freewill, and we might regard good works as a response of human freedom to the help given by divine grace in justification. This second role for freewill conflicts with the Reformers' treatment of good works as nothing more than fruits of justification.

From the Tridentine point of view, then, the Reformers seem to deny the essential role of human freewill in co-operating with divine grace. From the Reformers' point of view, the Tridentine position seems to re-assert the insufficiency of divine grace, and to treat God's action as the required response to human merit.

Aquinas denies that human beings by their natural capacities can acquire either condign or congruous merit before justification. But he maintains that good works after justification have congruous merit, as the products of human freewill, and condign merit, as the actions of the Holy Spirit (ST 1-2 q114 a3).[115] He recognizes a crucial role for freewill in these good works after justification. But he does not argue that since these works are the products of freewill, they are the products of human choice independent of divine grace. His conception of freewill does not commit him to this claim about independence. In the light of Aquinas' conception of the will, we can understand how we are capable of forming the acquired virtues in a state of sin, and how we receive the infused virtues in a state of grace, without losing the freedom that is characteristic of the will.

421. Natural Law and Ethics

If we accept a Lutheran or Calvinist view of grace, justification, and sanctification, what role is left for morality and moral philosophy? One might argue that in the Christian life ordinary morality has been superseded, because the Christian is not under law, but under

---

[115] See §352. The Roman Missal expresses this view in the Collect for Pentecost 12: '. . . Deus, de cuius munere venit, ut tibi a fidelibus tuis digne et laudabiliter serviatur'. BCP for Trinity 13 has 'of whose only gift it cometh that thy faithful people do unto thee true and laudable service'. The reference to condign merit is obscured by the substitution of 'true' for 'digne', but not entirely removed (since 'laudable' is retained).

grace (*Rm.* 6:14), and the law is given only for sinners (*1 Tim.* 1:9). In some places Luther suggests that Christians are not bound by law, because 'the righteous does of himself all and more than all that the laws demand'.[116] This claim provokes objections from the Roman side. Suarez devotes a chapter of *De Legibus*, Book i to a refutation of the Lutheran view (as he understands it) that the righteous are not subject to the law (i 18–19).[117] But whatever Luther holds on this question, Calvin asserts that the Christian is bound by the moral law (*Inst.* ii 7.12–15).

The positive role of the moral law explains why Melanchthon emphasizes the natural law in his exposition of moral philosophy. His justification for doing this appears in his treatment of the 'righteousness of reason' in the *Apology for the Augsburg Confession*. In this work he follows Luther in denying that we can merit God's favour or forgiveness by the righteousness of reason and 'civil works'. If these works were all we need, Roman theologians would be justified in their practice (as he describes it) of teaching Aristotle's ethics in place of the Gospel; 'for Aristotle wrote so well on natural ethics that nothing further needs to be added' (*Apol. Aug. Conf*, Art. 2).[118] The Roman theologians are wrong, because the righteousness of reason does not make us independent of divine grace. But that does not make the righteousness of reason valueless. It is required both by natural reason and by divine command.[119] Hence Luther's critique of the law and 'righteousness of works' does not imply the rejection of moral philosophy. Natural law is the subject-matter of moral philosophy, as distinct from the Gospel.[120]

Since natural law is not the Gospel, we cannot achieve our ultimate end of knowing God by following the natural law, as prescribed by moral philosophy. Still, moral philosophy is a part of the divine law, in so far as it can be discovered by reason. Even though awareness of it is obscured by sin, it is not completely lost, and it is worth our while to clarify it (*PME* 158.12–24). Melanchthon takes up some of the main topics of Aristotle's *Ethics*—the ultimate end, the virtues, and the voluntary. He expands Aristotle's treatment of justice, including a discussion of particular cases of right and wrong, Biblical, Classical, and contemporary. He concludes with a discussion of some particular virtues and duties, including friendship. He lays less emphasis than Aquinas lays on the individual virtues of character, and more emphasis on the requirements of justice and right. But he does not suggest any basic change in the structure of an Aristotelian moral theory. He discusses moral philosophy and natural

---

[116] Luther, *Temporal Authority* = *Works* xlv 89 = Dillenberger 369.

[117] See Skinner, *FPMT* ii 139. See also Suarez, *De bonitate*, iii 1 = *OO* iv 305b. He attacks Luther's claim that all the actions of a human being are sins, even though they are not imputed to the faithful.

[118] This is the passage that Leibniz presumably has in mind in saying that in this work Luther 'allowed a favourable mention of Aristotle and his *Ethics*' (*Theod.* Prelim. Diss §12 = Huggard 81).

[119] 'We for our part maintain that God requires the righteousness of reason. Because of God's command, honourable works commanded in the Decalogue should be performed, according to *Galatians* 3:24 and *1 Timothy* 1:19 . . . To some extent reason can produce this righteousness by its own strength, though it is often overwhelmed by its natural weakness and by the devil, who draws it to open crimes. We freely give this righteousness of reason its due credit; for our corrupt nature has no greater good than this, as Aristotle correctly says, 'Neither the evening nor the morning star is more beautiful than righteousness'. . . . Nevertheless, it ought not to be praised at the expense of Christ' (*Apol. Aug. Conf.* Art. 4). On Melanchthon's attitude to moral philosophy see Kusukawa, *TNP* 64–72.

[120] 'Moral philosophy is that part of divine law that prescribes about external actions' (*PME* 157.7). 'For this is the firm and especial merit (*laus*) of moral philosophy, to understand what is truly a part of divine law. . . ' (157.16). For Leibniz's praise of Melanchthon see Leibniz, *Theod.* Prelim. Diss. §12 = G vi 57 = Huggard 81.

law because he wants to make it clear how the knowledge available to the moral philosopher differs from the proper concern of the theologian.[121]

One aspect of Melanchthon's conception of the natural law and moral philosophy may appear to separate him from Aquinas. He sometimes takes moral philosophy to be concerned specifically with external actions, in contrast with the Gospel, which is concerned with the 'perfect obedience of the heart'.[122] This claim seems difficult to reconcile with Melanchthon's Aristotelian view that moral philosophy is about the virtues, understood as states of character, including states of the will,[123] and therefore not simply about right external behaviour. A virtue requires right judgment, which must guide the will.[124] Given this conception of virtue, Melanchthon cannot consistently claim that moral philosophy is concerned only with external actions, if external actions are mere patterns of behaviour as distinct from their causes in will, judgment, and character.

His view is consistent, however, if the contrast between 'external actions' and 'the obedience of the heart' refers to the difference between the motives of people in the state of sin and the motives of people under grace. In a sinful condition, even virtuous states of character, as measured by moral philosophy, are merely 'external', in so far as they do not proceed from the love of God above everything. If this is what Melanchthon means, his claim about external actions tries to reconcile Aristotelian moral virtues with Luther's extreme Augustinian view that we are totally incapable of genuine virtue when we are in the state of sin. The use of 'external actions' for Aristotelian virtues does not convey this point very well; it would have been better to contrast the motives that are possible without grace with those that become possible under grace, rather than to speak of external and internal. But once we understand Melanchthon's use of 'external', his position is a reasonable clarification or modification of Luther's claim about the possibility of virtue in the state of sin.

422. Implications

Even this superficial survey of some of the issues relevant to moral philosophy that were discussed by the Reformers and their opponents may help to explain some of the different effects of the Reformation. Some elements in the views of the Reformers initiate some significant changes in approach to moral philosophy; but other elements support the outlook of Scholastic naturalism.

---

[121] 'Thus far we have set out preliminaries about this area of learning, so that it may be distinguished from the Gospel, and so that we can understand how far it is to be approved, and what benefits it has' (163.16–18).

[122] 'For the divine law was stamped on the minds of human beings, but it was darkened in this weakness of nature, so that we cannot sufficiently grasp those precepts, and what they order us to hold about the will of God, and what they prescribe about the perfect obedience of the heart. But there remains judgment about right (honestis) external actions, and this arises in us; it is itself the law of nature and a part of divine law. (158.13–19). And properly instructed philosophy is inherently and truly the clarification of natural law. And so, just as the pious are allowed to rely on the law of God or the law of nature, so also they are allowed to rely on moral philosophy, which applies to external practices (mores)' (160.14–17).

[123] 'Virtue is a state that inclines the will towards obedience to correct reason' (174.30–1).

[124] 'For so that there will be some definite rule of virtue, the will is to be directed by the judgment of the mind. And that judgment is the knowledge of natural law and of divine law and of all learning that has firm grounds taken from natural and divine law, or is the clarification of natural and divine law' (175.23–8).

Hobbes's views on moral philosophy and on Christianity reflect the views of some Reformers.[125] He believes that human nature in its own right is not fulfilled by morality, and that morality has to be imposed on human beings to restrain their self-seeking tendencies. This imposed morality concerns civil obligation in which the civil authorities are supreme. God is free in relation to the moral law and freely chooses to impose it on us, for reasons that do not concern us; reflexion on the Scriptures reveals the commands of God, and these commands require our subjection to the civil authorities. Each one of these claims could be defended from some tendency in the thought of the Reformers, and especially of Luther.

Hobbes did not have to turn to the Reformers to find such views. He develops the outlook of mediaeval voluntarists, derived from a one-sided reading of Augustine's two cities. But since the Reformers make this outlook especially prominent, their influence explains some of Hobbes's attitudes. Hobbes has some support for his claim that he expounds Christian teaching from the point of view of the Reformation.

None the less, Christians had good reason to reject Hobbes's views on morality and on Christianity. For though Hobbes's views draw on some elements in the Reformation, they conflict with the considered views of (for instance) Luther, Melanchthon, Calvin, and Hooker. For different reasons and to different degrees, these all take Aristotelian ethics to be basically sound. They do not believe that morality is simply a device for securing mutually beneficial patterns of action among self-seeking individuals. They believe, as Aquinas believes, that moral thought and action should cultivate the moral virtues that fulfil rational nature. This aspect of the outlook of the Reformers is a defence, not a rejection, of Scholastic naturalism.

[125] See Grove, WFSAD 26.

BIBLIOGRAPHY

ABERCROMBIE, N. J., *The Origins of Jansenism*. OUP, 1936.

ACKRILL, J. L., 'Aristotle on *eudaimonia*', in *EPA*, ch. 11. From *Proceedings of the British Academy* 60 (1974), 339–59.

_____ *Essays on Plato and Aristotle*. OUP, 1997.

ACKROYD, P. R., and Evans, C. F. (eds.), *The Cambridge History of the Bible* i. CUP, 1970.

ADAM, J. (ed.), *The Republic of Plato*, 2 vols. CUP, 1902.

ADAMS, M. M., 'Ockham on will, nature, and morality', in Spade, *CCO*, ch. 11.

_____ 'Scotus and Ockham on the connection of the virtues', in L. Honnefelder, R. Wood, and M. Dreyer (eds.), *John Dunn Scotus: Metaphysics and Ethics*. Leiden: Brill, 1996, 499–522.

_____ 'The structure of Ockham's moral theory', *FS* 46 (1986), 1–35.

_____ *William Ockham*, 2 vols. Notre Dame, Ind.: UNDP, 1987.

_____ 'William Ockham: voluntarist or naturalist?', in J. F. Wippel (ed.), *Studies in Medieval Philosophy*. CUAP, 1987, ch. 10.

ALBERIGO, J., et al. (eds.), *Conciliorum Oecumenicorum Decreta, 3rd edn*. Bologna: Instituto per le Scienze Religiose, 1973.

ALBERTUS MAGNUS, *De bono in genere, De iustitia, De prudentia*, and *De temperantia*, in *Opera Omnia*, xxviii.

_____ *Opera Omnia*. Münster: Aschendorff, 1951–.

_____ *Super Ethica*, in *Opera Omnia*, xiv.

ALCINOUS, *Didascalicus. Alcinoos: Enseignement des doctrines de Platon*, tr. P. Louis, ed. J. Whittaker. Paris: Les Belles Lettres, 1990.

ALEXANDER of APHRODISIAS, *De Anima* = *CAG* Supp. ii 1.

_____ *De Anima Mantissa* = *CAG* Supp. ii 1.

_____ *De Fato* = *CAG* Supp. ii 2. Tr. and ed. R. W. Sharples. London Duckworth, 1983.

_____ *Dubia et Solutiones* = *CAG* Supp. ii 2.

_____ *in Aristotelis Topica* = *CAG* ii.

_____ *Quaestiones* = *CAG* Supp. ii 2.

ALGRA, K., et al. (eds.), *The Cambridge History of Hellenistic Philosophy*. CUP, 1999.

AMBROSE, *De Officiis*, 2 vols., ed. I. J. Davidson. OUP, 2001.

AMBROSIASTER, *Commentarius in Epistulas Paulinas*, ed. H. J. Vogels. Vienna: Hoelder-Pichler-Tempsky, 1966 (= *CSEL* lxxxi.1).

ANDERSON, G. W., 'Canonical and non-canonical', in Ackroyd and Evans, *CHB* i, ch. 6.

ANNAS, J., *An Introduction to Plato's Republic*. OUP, 1981.

_____ 'Doing without objective values', in Everson, *ECAT*, ch. 8.

_____ *Platonic Ethics, Old and New*. Ithaca, NY: Cornell UP, 1999.

_____ 'Prudence and morality in ancient and modern ethics', *Ethics* 105 (1995), 241–57.

_____ 'The Hellenistic versions of Aristotle's ethics', *Monist* 73 (1990), 80–96.

_____ *The Morality of Happiness*. OUP, 1993.

ANONYMUS, *in Platonis Theaetetum*; in *Corpus dei Papiri*, Part 3.

ANSCOMBE, G. E. M., *Intention, 2nd edn*. Oxford: Blackwell, 1963 (1st edn. 1957).

ANSCOMBE, G. E. M., 'Modern moral philosophy', in *Collected Philosophical Papers, iii: Ethics, Religion, and Politics*. Minneapolis: University of Minnesota Press, 1981, ch. 4. From *Phil.* 33 (1958), 1–19.

—— 'Thought and Action in Aristotle' in *CP* i, ch. 7.

ANSELM, *Opera Omnia* i, ed. F. S. Schmitt. Seckau, 1938. Includes *De Casu Diaboli, De Veritate, Proslogion*.

—— *The Major Works*, ed. B. Davies and G. R. Evans (various translators). OUP, 1998.

AQUINAS, *Compendium Theologiae*, in *Opuscula Theologica*, ed. R. A. Verardo. Turin: Marietti, 1954.

—— *De Caritate*, in *QD*.

—— *De Divinis Nominibus*, in *P* xv.

—— *De Malo*, in *QD*.

—— *De Potentia*, in *QD*.

—— *De Regimine Principum*, 2nd edn., ed. J. Mathis. Marietti: Turin, 1948.

—— *De spe*, in *QD*

—— *De Veritate* (Cited as *Ver*), in *QD*.

—— *De Virtutibus Cardinalibus*, in *QD*.

—— *De Virtutibus in Communi*, in *QD*.

—— *Expositio et Lectura super Epistulas Pauli Apostoli*, 8th edn., 2 vols., ed. R. Cai. Turin: Marietti, 1953.

—— *in Aristotelis De Anima*, ed. A. M. Pirotta. Turin: Marietti, 1936.

—— *In Aristotelis De Caelo*, in *P* xix.

—— *in Aristotelis Metaphysica*, ed. M. R. Cathala and R. M. Spiazzi. Turin: Marietti, 1950.

—— *in Aristotelis Perihermeneias*, in *P* xviii.

—— *In Decem Libros Ethicorum Aristotelis ad Nicomachum Expositio*, 3rd edn., ed. R. M. Spiazzi. Turin: Marietti, 1964.

—— *In Epistulam ad Romanos*, in *Expositio*, ed. Cai.

—— *In Evangelium Ioannis*, in *P* x.

—— *in Iob*, *P* xiv.

—— *in Primam Epistulam ad Timotheum*, in *Expositio*, ed. Cai.

—— *In Secundam Epistulam ad Corinthos*, in *Expositio*, ed. Cai.

—— *Opera Omnia*, editio Leonina. Rome: Typographia Polyglotta, 1882–(incomplete).

—— *Opera Omnia*, 25 vols. Parma: Fiaccadori, 1852–68.

—— *Quaestiones Disputatae*, 2 vols., ed. R. Spiazzi et al. Turin: Marietti, 1949.

—— *Quaestiones Quodlibetales*, in *P* ix.

—— *Scriptum super Sententiis*, in *P* vi–vii.

—— *Sententia Libri Ethicorum*, Leonine ed. xlvii–xlviii., ed. R.-A. Gauthier. 1969.

—— *Summa contra Gentiles*, 3 vols., ed. P. Marc et al. Turin: Marietti, 1967.

AQUINAS, *Summa Theologiae*, Blackfriars edn., 60 vols., T. Gilby and T. C. O'Brian (general eds.). London: Eyre and Spottiswoode, 1964–73. Vols. cited: xix (ed. E. D'Arcy); xxii (ed. A. J. P. Kenny); xxiii (ed. W. D. Hughes); xxv (ed. J. Fearon); xxxviii (ed. M. Lefébure); xlii (ed. P. G. Walsh).

ARISTOTLE, *Analytica Priora*. OCT.

—— *Analytica Posteriora*. OCT.

—— *De Caelo*. OCT.

—— *De Interpretatione*. OCT.

—— *De Partibus Animalium*. Loeb.

—— *Ethica Eudemia*. OCT.

—— *Ethica Nicomachea*. OCT.

—— *Magna Moralia*. BT.

—— *Metaphysics*. OCT.

—— *Physics*. OCT.

Bibliography

_____ *Politics*. OCT.

_____ *Rhetoric*. OCT.

_____ *Topics*. OCT.

ARPALY, N., *Unprincipled Virtue*. OUP, 2003.

ASPASIUS, in *Ethica Nicomachea, CAG* xix.

ATHENAEUS, *Deipnosophistae*. BT.

Augsburg Confession, in Schaff, *CC* iii.

AUGUSTINE, *Confessiones*. OO i.

_____ *Contra Academicos*. OO i.

_____ *Contra duas Epistulas Pelagianorum*. OO x.

_____ *Contra Faustum Manichaeum*. OO viii.

_____ *Contra Iulianum*. OO x.

_____ *Contra Secundinum Manichaeum*. OO viii.

_____ *De 83 Diversis Quaestionibus*. OO vi.

_____ *De Beata Vita*. OO i.

_____ *De Civitate Dei*, 2 vols., ed. J. E. C. Welldon. London: SPCK, 1924.

_____ *De Continentia*. OO vi.

_____ *De Doctrina Christiana*. OO iii.

_____ *De duabus Animis*. OO viii.

_____ *De Libero Arbitrio* OO. i.

_____ *De Moribus Ecclesiae Catholicae et de Moribus Manichaeorum*. OO i.

_____ *De Nuptiis et Concupiscentia*. OO x.

_____ *De Spiritu et Littera*. OO x.

_____ *De Trinitate*. OO viii.

_____ *De Vera Religione*. OO i.

_____ *Enarrationes in Psalmos*. OO iv.

_____ *Epistulae*. OO ii.

_____ *Expositio 84 Propositionum ex Epistula ad Romanos*. OO iii.

_____ *In Evangelium Ioannis*. OO iii.

_____ *Opera Omnia*, Benedictine edn., 11 vols. Paris: Gaume, 1836–9.

_____ *Retractationes*. OO i.

_____ *Sermones*. OO v.

AULUS GELLIUS, *Noctes Atticae*. OCT.

BAILEY: *see* Epicurus.

BAIUS, M., *De Virtutibus Impiorum*, in *Michaeli Baii Opera*. Cologne: Egmont, 1696.

BANEZ, D., *Scholastica Commentaria in Primam Partem Summae Theologicae S. Thomae Aquinatis i*, ed. L. Urbano. Madrid: Editorial FEDA, 1934.

BARBEYRAC, J., 'An historical and critical account of the science of morality', tr. Carew, in S. Pufendorf, *Of the Law of Nature and Nations, 4th edn.*, tr. B. Kennett. London: Walthoe, 1729.

BARNES, J., 'The beliefs of a Pyrrhonist', in Burnyeat and Frede, *OS*, ch. 3.

_____ *The Toils of Scepticism*. CUP, 1990.

BARR, J., *Biblical Faith and Natural Theology*. OUP, 1993.

BARTH, K., *The Theology of John Calvin*, tr. G. W. Bromiley. Grand Rapids, Mich.: Eerdmans, 1995.

BARTON, J., *Ethics and the Old Testament, 2nd edn*. London: SCM Press, 2002.

BAYLE, P., *Historical and Critical Dictionary: Selections*, tr. R. H. Popkin. Indianapolis: Bobbs-Merrill, 1965.

BERKELEY, G., *Alciphron*, in *Works*, 9 vols., ed. A. A. Luce and T. E. Jessup. London: Nelson, 1948–1964, vol. iii.

BERKELEY, G., 'Passive obedience', in *works*, vols., ed. A. A. Luce and T. E. Jessup: London:–Nelson, 1948–1964, vi. 1–50.

BERLIN, I., 'The originality of Machiavelli', in H. Hardy (ed.), *Against the Current*. OUP, 1981, 25–79.

BETT, R., *Pyrrho, His Antecedents, and His Legacy*. OUP, 2000.

—— tr. and ed., *Sextus Empiricus Against the Ethicists*. OUP, 1997.

BIBLE. *The Holy Bible: translated from the Latin Vulgate and diligently compared with other editions in divers languages*. Rheims, 1582 (NT); Douai, 1609 (OT).

BIBLE. *Biblia Sacra iuxta Vulgatam Versionem, 3rd edn.*, ed. R. Weber et al. Stuttgart: Deutsche Bibelgeschell-schaft, 1983.

BIBLE. *Septuaginta, id est Vetus Testamentum Graece iuxta LXX interpretes*, ed. A. Rahlfs. Stuttgart: Deutsche Bibelgeschellschaft, 1979.

BIBLE, 'Authorized Version'. *The Holy Bible . . . Translated out of the Original Tongues and with the Former Translations Diligently Compared and Revised by His Majesty's Special Command*. London: 1611.

BIBLE. *The Holy Bible, . . . with the Apocryphal/Deuterocanonical Books, New Revised Standard Version*. OUP, 1989.

BIEL, G., *Canonis missae expositio*, 4 vols., ed. H. A. Oberman and W. J. Courtenay. Wiesbaden: Steiner, 1963.

—— *Collectorium circa quattuor libros Sententiarum*, 4 vols., ed. W. Werbeck and U. Hoffman. Tübingen: Mohr, 1979.

BOBONICH, C. J., *Plato's Utopia Recast: his later ethics and politics*. OUP, 2002.

BOBZIEN, S., *Determinism, Fate, and Stoic Philosophy*. OUP, 1998.

BOETHIUS, *Commentaria in Aristotelis De Interpretatione*. BT.

BOLER, J., 'Aquinas on exceptions in natural law', in MacDonald and Stump, *AMT*, 161–92.

—— 'The moral psychology of Duns Scotus: some preliminary questions', *FS* 50 (1990), 31–56.

—— 'Transcending the natural: Duns Scotus on the two affections of the will', *ACPQ* 67 (1993), 109–26.

BONANSEA, B. M., 'Duns Scotus' voluntarism', in J. K. Ryan (ed.), *John Duns Scotus 1265–1965*. CUAP, 1965, ch. 5.

BONAVENTURE, *Opera Omnia*, 10 vols. Quaracchi: Collegium S. Bonaventurae, 1882–1902.

BONHÖFFER, D., *Letters and Papers from Prison: Enlarged Edition*, ed. E. Bethge. London: SCM Press, 1971.

BONITZ, H., *Index Aristotelicus*. Berlin: Reimer, 1870 (= *Aristotelis Opera*, ed. I. Bekker, vol. 5).

Book of Common Prayer and Administration of the Sacraments and Other Rites and Ceremonies of the Church according to the Use of the Church of England (1662).

BOSANQUET, B., *A Companion to Plato's Republic, 2nd edn*. London: Rivingtons, 1906.

BOURKE, V. J., 'The *Nicomachean Ethics* and Thomas Aquinas', in A. A. Maurer et al. (eds.), *Thomas Aquinas 1274–1974: Commemorative Studies*, 2 vols. Toronto: Pontifical Institute of Mediaeval Studies, 1974, i 239–59.

BRADLEY, D. J. M., *Aquinas on the Twofold Human Good*. CUAP, 1997.

BRANDT, R. B., *A Theory of the Good and the Right*. OUP, 1979.

BRINK, D. O., 'Rational egoism, self, and others', in O. Flanagan and A. O. Rorty (eds.), *Identity, Character, and Morality*. Cambridge, Mass.: MIT Press, 1990, ch. 15.

BRITTAIN, C. F., 'Attention deficit in Plotinus and Augustine: psychological problems in Christian and Platonist theories of the grades of virtue', *PBACAP* 18 (2003), 223–63.

BROAD, C. D., 'Certain features in Moore's ethical doctrines', in Schilpp, P. A. (ed.), *The Philosophy of G. E. Moore*. Evanston, Ill.: Northwestern UP, 1942, ch. 1.

—— 'Egoism as a theory of human motives', in D. R. Cheney (ed.), *Broad's Critical Essays in Moral Philosophy*. London: Allen and Unwin, 1971, ch. 11.

BROADIE, S. W., *Ethics with Aristotle*. OUP, 1991.

BRUNSCHWIG, J., 'On a book title by Chrysippus', *OSAP* supp. (1991), 81–95.

—— 'The conjunctive model', in *Papers in Hellenistic Philosophy*. CUP, 1994, ch. 5.

_____ 'The cradle argument in Epicureanism and Stoicism', in Schofield and Striker, *NN*, ch. 5.

BURNABY, J., *Amor Dei: a study of the religion of St Augustine*. London: Hodder & Stoughton, 1938.

BURNYEAT, M., 'Can the sceptic live his scepticism?', in Burnyeat and Frede, *OS*, ch. 2. From M. Schofield, M. Burnyeat, and J. Barnes (eds.), *Doubt and Dogmatism*. OUP, 1980, 20–53.

_____ 'The sceptic in his place and time', in Burnyeat and Frede, *OS*, ch. 4. From R. Rorty, J. B. Schneewind, and Q. Skinner, *Philosophy in History: Essays on the Historiography of Philosophy*. CUP, 1984, ch. 10.

_____ and Frede, M. (eds.), *The Original Sceptics: a controversy*. Indianapolis: Hackett, 1997.

BUTLER, J., *Sermons* and *Dissertation on Virtue*, in *The Works of Bishop Butler*, 2 vols., ed. J. H. Bernard. London: Macmillan, 1900.

BYRNE, B., *Romans*. Collegeville, Minn.: Liturgical Press, 1996.

CAJETAN (Tomasso de Vio), Commentary on Aquinas, *Summae Theologiae*, printed in L.

CALVIN, J., *Commentarius in Epistolam Pauli ad Romanos*, ed. T. H. L. Parker. Leiden: Brill, 1981. Tr. H. Beveridge. Edinburgh: Calvin Translation Society, 1844.

_____ *Institutes of the Christian Religion*, 2 vols., tr. F. L. Battles, ed. J. T. McNeill. London: SCM, 1960.

_____ *Institutes of the Christian Religion*, tr. H. Beveridge. Edinburgh: Calvin Translation Society, 1845.

_____ *Ioannis Calvini Opera Selecta*, 5 vols., ed. P. Barth and W. Niessel. Munich: Kaiser, 1952–9.

CARONE, G. R., 'Plato's Stoic view of Motivation', in R. Salles (ed.), *Metaphysics Soul, and Ethics in Ancient Thought*, OUP, 2005, ch. 14.

CHARLES, D., 'Aristotle on well-being and intellectual contemplation', *SPAS* 73 (1999), 205–23.

_____ 'Aristotle: ontology and moral reasoning', *OSAP* 4 (1986), 119–44.

_____ *Aristotle's Philosophy of Action*. London: Duckworth, 1984.

CHARLESWORTH, J. H. (ed.), *The Old Testament Pseudepigrapha*, 2 vols. Garden City, NY: Doubleday, 1985.

CHEMNITZ, M., *Examination of the Council of Trent*, 2 vols., tr. F. Kramer. St Louis, Mo.: Concordia, 1971.

CHENU, M. D., *Toward Understanding St Thomas*. Chicago: Regnery, 1964.

CHERNISS, H. F. (ed. and tr.), *Plutarch's Moralia*, xiii 2. HUP, 1976.

_____ 'The sources of evil according to Plato', in Vlastos, *Plato ii*, ch. 16. From *Proceedings of the American Philosophical Society* 98 (1954), 23–30.

CHIESARA, M. L., *Aristocles of Messene*. OUP, 2001.

CHRYSOSTOM, John, *Commentaria in Epistulam ad Romanos*, in *PG* lx.

CICERO, *Academica*. BT.

_____ *Brutus*. BT.

_____ *De Amicitia*. BT.

_____ *De Finibus Bonorum et Malorum*. OCT.

_____ *De Inventione*. BT.

_____ *De Legibus*. BT.

_____ *De Natura Deorum*. BT.

_____ *De Officiis*. OCT.

_____ *De Re Publica*. BT.

_____ *Epistulae ad Familiares*. OCT.

_____ *Paradoxa Stoicorum*. BT.

_____ *Pro Murena*. OCT.

_____ *Tusculanae Disputationes*. BT.

CLARK, D. W., 'Voluntarism and rationalism in the ethics of William of Ockham', *FS* 31 (1971), 72–87.

_____ 'William of Ockham on right reason', *Speculum* 48 (1973), 13–36.

CLARK, S., *A Discourse concerning the Unchargeable Obligations of Natural Religion, and the Truth and Certainly of the Christion Revolution*, in *The Works of Samuel Clarke*, 4 vols., ed. B. Hoadly, London: Knapton, 1738 (repr. Bristol: Thoemmes, 2002), vol. ii.

CLEMENT of ALEXANDRIA, *Stromata*, 2nd edn., ed. O. Stählin et al. Berlin: Akademie Verlag, 1970 (repr. 1985).

CLEMENT, *Quis Dives Salvetur?*, ed. G. W. Butterworth (Loeb). HUP, 1919.

COHEN, S. M., 'Socrates on the definition of piety', in G. Vlastos (ed.), *The Philosophy of Socrates*. Garden City, NY: Anchor Books, 1971, ch. 8. From *JHP* 9 (1971), 1–13.

COLISH, M. L., 'Cicero and Machiavelli', *Sixteenth Century Journal* 9 (1978), 81–93.

—— *The Stoic Tradition From Antiquity to the Early Middle Ages*, 2 vols. Leiden: Brill, 1985.

Commentaria in Aristotelem Graeca. 23 vols. + *Supplementum Aristotelicum*, 3 vols. Berlin: Reimer, 1882–1907.

COOPER, J. M., 'Aristotle on the forms of friendship', in *RE*, ch. 14. From *Review of Metaphysics* 30 (1977), 619–48.

—— 'Eudaemonism, the appeal to nature, and "moral duty" in Stoicism', in *RE*, ch. 20. From S. Engstrom and J. Whiting (eds.), *Rethinking Duty and Happiness: Aristotle, Kant, and the Stoics*. CUP, 1996, ch. 9.

—— 'Friendship and the good in Aristotle', in *RE* ch. 15. From *PR*, 86 (1977), 290–315.

—— 'Greek Philosophers on Euthanasia and Suicide, in *RE*, ch. 23. From B. A. Brody (ed.), *Suicide and Euthanasia*. Dordrecht: Kluwar Academic, 1989, 9–38.

—— 'Justus Lipsius and the revival of Stoicism in late sixteenth-century Europe', in N. Brender and L. Krasnoff (eds.), *New Essays on the History of Autonomy*. CUP, 2004, ch. 1.

—— 'Pleasure and desire in Epicurus', in *RE*, ch. 22.

—— 'Political animals and civic friendship', in *RE*, ch. 16.

—— 'Poseidonius on emotions', in *RE*, ch. 21.

—— *Reason and Emotion*. PUP, 1999.

—— *Reason and the Human Good in Aristotle*. HUP, 1975.

—— 'Reason, moral virtue, and moral value', in *RE*, ch. 11. From M. Frede and G. Striker (eds.), *Rationality in Greek Thought*. OUP, 1996, ch. 3.

Corpus dei Papiri Filosofici Greci e Latini. Florence: Olschki. Part 1, vol. 1(1), 1989. Part 1, vol. 1(2), 1992. Part 3, 1995.

CRANFIELD, C. E. B., *Romans*. Edinburgh: T&T Clark, 1975.

CROSS, R., *Duns Scotus*. OUP, 1999.

CROWE, M. B., *The Changing Profile of the Natural Law*. The Hague: Nijhoff, 1977.

CUDWORTH, R., *A Treatise of Freewill*. *See* following entry.

—— *A Treatise concerning Eternal and Immutable Morality, with a Treatise of Freewill*, ed. S. Hutton. CUP, 1996.

CULVERWELL, N., *An Elegant and Learned Discourse of the Light of Nature* (cited as *LN*), ed. R. A. Greene and H. MacCallum. Toronto: U. of Toronto Press, 1971 (repr. Indianapolis: Liberty Fund, 2001; Orig. Pub. London, 1652).

CUMBERLAND, Richard, *De Legibus Naturae*. London: Nathanael Hooke, 1672; tr. John Maxwell, London: J.Knapten, 1727.

CUMMINS, R., 'Functional explanation', *JP* 72 (1975), 741–65.

DAHL, N. O., 'Plato's defence of justice', in Fine, *Plato ii*, ch. 8. From *Philosophy and Phenomenologica Research* 51 (1991), 809–34.

—— *Practical Reason, Aristotle, and Weakness of the Will*. Minneapolis: U of Minnesota Press, 1984.

DAMASCENUS, IOANNES, *Expositio Fidei*, ed. B. Kotter. Berlin: De Gruyter, 1973.

DARWALL, S. L., *The British Moralists and the Internal 'Ought'*. CUP, 1995.

DAVIES, W. D., and Allison, D. C., *The Gospel according to St Matthew*, 3 vols. Edinburgh: T&T Clark, 1988–97.

DAVIS, H., *Moral and Pastoral Theology, 5th edn*, 4 vols. London: Sheed and Ward, 1946.

DE SOUSA, R. B., *The Rationality of Emotion*. Cambridge, Mass.: MIT Press, 1987.

DELAHAYE, P., 'Quelques aspects de la morale de Saint Anselme', in *Spicilegium Beccense*. Paris: Vrin, 1959, 401–22.

DENIFLE, H., and CHATELAIN, E. (eds.), *Chartularium Universitatis Parisinensis*. Paris: Delalain, 1896.

DENZIGER, H., and SCHÖNMETZER, A. (eds.), *Enchiridion Symbolorum, 36th edn.* Freiburg: Herder, 1976. Cited as 'Denz.' or 'D'.

DIELS, H. and KRANZ, W., (eds.), *Fragmente der Vorsokratiker, 6th edn.,* 3 vols. Berlin: Weidmann, 1952.

DILLON, J. M., *The Middle Platonists.* London: Duckworth, 1977.

DIO CHRYSOSTOM, *Orationes.* BT.

DIODORUS SICULUS, *Bibliotheca Historica.* BT.

DIOGENES LAERTIUS, *Vitae Philosophorum.* OCT.

DOIG, J. C., *Aquinas' Philosophical Commentary on the Ethics.* Dordrecht: Kluwer, 2001.

DONAGAN, A., *Theory of Morality.* Chicago: U of Chicago Press, 1977.

―――― 'Thomas Aquinas on human action', in Kretzmann et al., *CHLMP,* ch. 33.

DRIVER, S. R., *Deuteronomy.* Edinburgh: T&T Clark, 1895.

DU PLESSIS D'ARGENTRÉ, C. (ed.), *Collectio Judiciorum de Novis Erroribus qui . . . in Ecclesia Proscripti sunt et Notati,* 3 vols. Paris: Cailleau, 1728–36.

DUNBABIN, J., 'The Two Commentaries of Albertus Magnus on the *Nicomachean Ethics*', *RTAM* 30 (1963), 232–250.

DWORKIN, R. M., 'Hard cases', in *Taking Rights Seriously.* HUP, 1977, ch. 4.

DYBIKOWSKI, J. C., 'Is Aristotelian *eudaimonia* happiness?', *Dialogue* 20 (1981), 185–200.

EMPSON, W., *The Structure of Complex Words, 3rd edn.* London: Chatto and Windus, 1977.

ENGBERG-PEDERSON, T., *Aristotle's Theory of Moral Insight.* OUP, 1983.

―――― 'Discovering the good', in Schofield and Striker, *NN,* ch. 6.

English Articles, in *BCP* and Schaff, *CC* iii. Cited as 'Articles'.

EPICTETUS, *Dissertationes* and *Enchiridion.* BT.

EPICURUS, *Epicuro: Opere, 2nd edn,* ed. G. Arrighetti. Turin: Einaudi, 1973. Includes *On Nature; Sententiae Vaticanae: Kuriai Doxai.*

―――― *The Extant Remains,* C. Bailey, ed. and tr. OUP, 1926.

EUSEBIUS, *Praeparatio Evangelica, 2nd edn.,* 2 vols., ed. K. Mras. Berlin: Akademie, 1982.

EUSTRATIUS, *in EN, CAG* xx.

EVERSON, S. E. (ed.), *Ethics: Companions to Ancient Thought.* CUP, 1998.

―――― 'Introduction: virtue and morality', in *ECAT,* 1–26.

FARRELLY, M. J., *Predestination, Grace, and Free Will.* London: Burns & Oates, 1964.

FINE, G. (ed.), *Plato ii.* OUP, 1999.

―――― 'Sceptical dogmata; *Outlines of Pyrrhonism* I 13', *Methexis* 13 (2000), 81–105.

FINNIS, J. M., *Aquinas: Moral, Political, and Legal Theory.* OUP, 1998.

―――― *Natural Law and Natural Rights.* OUP, 1980.

FLANAGAN, O., *Varieties of Moral Personality.* HUP, 1991.

FOOT, P. R., 'Moral beliefs', in *Virtues and Vices,* Oxford: Blackwell, 1978.

―――― 'Moral realism and moral dilemma', in *Moral Dilemmas.* OUP, 2002, ch. 3. From *JP* 80 (1983), 379–98.

―――― *Natural Goodness.* OUP, 2001.

―――― *Virtues and Vices.* Oxford: Blackwell, 1978.

FOSTER, M. B., 'A mistake of Plato's in the *Republic*', *Mind* 46 (1937), 386–93.

―――― 'Some implications of a passage in Plato's *Republic*', *Philosophy* 11 (1936), 301–8.

―――― *The Political Philosophies of Plato and Hegel.* OUP, 1935.

FRANKENA, W. K., 'The concept of morality', in G. Wallace and A. D. M. Walker (eds.), *The Definition of Morality.* London: Methuen, 1970, ch. 9.

FRANKFURT, H. G., 'Freedom of the will and the concept of a person', in *The Importance of What We Care About.* CUP, 1988, ch. 2. From *JP* 68 (1971), 5–20.

FREDE, M., 'On the Stoic conception of the good', in K. Ierodiakonou (ed.), *Topics in Stoic Philosophy*. OUP, 1999, ch. 3.

FREPPERT, L., *The Basis of Morality according to William of Ockham*. Chicago: Franciscan Herald Press, 1988.

FURLEY, D. J., 'Nothing to us?', in Schofield and Striker, *NN*, ch. 3.

——— *Two Studies in the Greek Atomists*. PUP, 1967.

FUSSENBERGER, G. (ed.), 'Definitiones capitulae generalis Argentinae', *Archivum Franciscanum Historicum 26* (1933), 127–40.

GALEN, *De Placitis Hippocratis et Platonis*, 3 vols., ed. and tr. P. H. De Lacy. Berlin: Akademie-Verlag, 1978–81.

GALLAGHER, D., 'Thomas Aquinas on the will as rational appetite', *JHP* 29 (1991), 559–84.

GAUTHIER, R.-A., 'Saint Maxime le Confesseur et la psychologie de l'acte humain', *RTAM* 21 (1954), 51–100.

——— 'Trois commentaires "averroistes" sur l'Ethique à Nicomaque', *Archives d'histoire doctrinale et litteraire du Moyen Age* 22–3 (1947–8), 187–336.

GAUTHIER, *SLE; see* Aquinas.

——— and Jolif, J.-Y. (eds.), *L'Ethique à Nicomaque*, 2nd edn., 4 vols. Louvain: Publications universitaires de Louvain, 1970.

GEACH, P. T., *The Virtues*. CUP, 1977.

GERSON, L. P., *Aristotle and other Platonists*. Ithaca, NY: Cornell UP, 2005.

——— *Plotinus*. London: Routledge, 1994.

GIANNANTONI, G., *I Cirenaici*. Florence: Sansoni, 1958.

——— *Socraticorum Reliquiae*, 4 vols. Naples: Ateneo, 1983.

GLORIEUX, P. (ed.), *Le correctorium corruptorii 'Quare'*, *Bibliothèque Thomiste* 9 (1927).

GODFREY of FONTAINES, *Les Quodlibet*, 5 vols., ed. M. de Wulf et al. Louvain: Institut Superieure de Philosophie, 1904–37.

GODWIN, W., *Enquiry concerning Political Justice*, 3rd edn., ed. F. E. L. Priestly, 3 vols. Toronto: U. of Toronto Press, 1946 (orig. pub. London, 1798).

GONET, J. B., *Manuale Thomistarum, seu Totius Theologiae Brevis Cursus*. Antwerp, 1745.

GOSLING, J. C. B., *Plato's Philebus*. OUP, 1975.

——— and Taylor, C. C. W., *The Greeks on Pleasure*. OUP, 1982.

GOULET-CAZÉ, M.-O., *L'Ascèse Cynique*, Paris: Vrin, 1996.

GRAF, T., *De subiecto psychico gratiae et virtutum, pars prima: de subjecto virtutum cardinalium*, 2 vols. Rome: Herder, 1934.

GRANT, A., *The Ethics of Aristotle*, 4th edn, 2 vols. London: Longmans, 1885.

Greek New Testament, 3rd edn., corrected, ed. K. Aland et al. United Bible Societies, 1983.

GREEN, T. H., *Prolegomena to Ethics*. OUP, 1883.

GREENWOOD, L. H. G. (ed.), *Aristotle, Nicomachean Ethics Book Six*. CUP, 1909.

GREGORY of RIMINI, *Gregorii Ariminensis OESA Lectura super primum et secundum Sententiarum*, 7 vols., ed. A. D. Trapp and V. Marcolino. Berlin: De Gruyter, 1981–7.

——— 'Natural law, God, religion, and human fulfillment', *American Journal of Jurisprudence* 46 (2001), 3–36.

——— 'The first principle of practical reason', in A. J. P. Kenny (ed.), *Aquinas: a Collection of Critical Essays*. London: Macmillan, 1970, 340–82.

GROTE, G., *History of Greece*, 2nd edn., 10 vols. London: John Murray, 1851.

——— *Plato and the other Companions of Sokrates*, 2nd edn., 4 vols. London: Murray, 1888 (1st edn., 1865).

GROTIUS, H., *De iure belli et pacis*, 3 vols., ed. and tr. W. Whewell. CUP, 1853 (1st edn. , 1625).

GROVE, H., *Wisdom: the first spring of action in the Deity*, 2nd edn. London: Fenner, 1742.

GUTHRIE, W. K. C., *History of Greek Philosophy*, 6 vols. CUP, 1962–81.

HARE, R. M., *Freedom and Reason*. OUP, 1963.

HART, H. L. A., and HONORÉ, A. M., *Causation in the Law*. OUP, 1959.

HEGEL, G. W. F., *Lectures on the History of Philosophy*, 3 vols., tr. E. S. Haldane and F. H. Simson. London: Kegan Paul, 1892.

――*Philosophy of Right*, tr. T. M. Knox. OUP, 1942.

HEINAMAN, R. E. (ed.), *Aristotle and Moral Realism*. London: UCL Press, 1995.

HEINAMAN, R. E., 'Rationality, eudaimonia, and kakodaimonia in Aristotle', *Phr.* 38 (1993), 31–56.

HELIODORUS, *in EN*, CAG xix.

HENRY of GHENT, *Quodlibet I*, ed. R. Macken. Leuven: Leuven UP, 1979.

――*Quodlibet IX*, ed. R. Macken. Leuven: Leuven UP, 1983.

――*Quodlibetal Questions on Free Will*, tr. R. J. Teske. Milwaukee: Marquette UP, 1993.

――*Summa (Quaestiones Ordinariae)*, art. *xxxv–xl*, ed. G. A. Wilson. Leuven: Leuven UP, 1994.

HERMAN, B., *The Practice of Moral Judgment*. HUP, 1993.

HERODOTUS, *Historiae*. OCT.

HISSETTE, R., *Enquête sur les 219 articles condamnés à Paris le 7 mars 1277*. Louvain: Publications Universitaires, 1977.

HOBBES, T., *Leviathan*, ed. E. M. Curley, Indianapolis: Hachelt, 1994 (1st pub. London, 1651).

HOISTAD, R., *Cynic Hero and Cynic King*. Lund: Bloms, 1948.

HOLDEN, H. A. (ed.), *Cicero: De Officiis, 6th edn.* CUP, 1886.

HOLOPAINEN, T. M., *William Ockham's Theory of the Foundations of Ethics*. Helsinki: Luther-Agricola-Society, 1991.

HOMER, *Odyssey*. OCT.

HOOKER, R., *The Laws of Ecclesiastical Polity*, in *The Works of Richard Hooker, 7th edn.*, 3 vols., ed. J. Keble. OUP, 1888.

HOPKINS, J., and RICHARDSON, H. (eds. and tr.), [Anselm] *Truth, Freedom, and Evil: three philosophical dialogues*. New York: Harper & Row, 1967.

HUDSON, S. D., *Human Character and Morality*. London: Routledge and Kegan Paul, 1986.

Hume, D., *A Treatise of Human Nature*, ed. D. F. Norton and M. J. Norton. OUP, 2000 (1st pub. London, 1739–40).

――*Inquiry concerning the Human Understanding* and *Inquiry concerning the Principles of Morals, 2nd edn.*, ed. L. A. Selby-Bigge. OUP, 1902.

HURSTHOUSE, R., *On Virtue Ethics*. OUP, 1999.

――'The virtuous agent's reasons: a reply to Bernard Williams', in Heinaman, *AMR*, 24–33.

HUTCHESON, F. *Illustrations on the Moral Sense*, ed. B. Peach. Cambridge, Mass.: Harvard UP, 1971. From *An Essay on the Nature and Conduct of the Passions and Affections with illustrations on the Moral Science*, 3rd edn. London: A. Ward et al., 1742 (1st edn. 1728).

IGNATIUS LOYOLA, *Spiritual Exercises: Rules for thinking with the Church*, in G. E.. Ganss (ed.), *Ignatius of Loyola: the Spiritual exercises and selected works*. NY: Paulist, 1991.

INGHAM, M. E., 'Scotus and the moral order', *ACPQ* 67 (1993), 127–50.

INWOOD, B., 'Goal and target in Stoicism', *JP* 83 (1986), 547–56.

――'Hierocles: theory and argument', *OSAP* 2 (1984), 151–83.

――'Seneca and psychological dualism', in *Reading Seneca*. OUP, 2005, ch. 2. From J. Brunschwig and M. Nussbaum (eds.), *Passions and Perceptions*. CUP, 1993, ch. 6.

IRWIN, T. H., *Aristotle's First Principles*. OUP, 1988.

――'Ethics as an inexact science: Aristotle's ambitions for moral theory', in B. Hooker and M. Little (eds.), *Moral Particularism*. OUP, 2000, ch. 5.

――(tr. and ed.), *Nicomachean Ethics, 2nd edn.* Indianapolis: Hackett, 1999.

――*Plato's Ethics*. OUP, 1995.

IRWIN, T. H., 'Stoic and Aristotelian conceptions of happiness', in Schofield and Striker, *NN*, ch. 8.

JAFFA, H. V., *Thomism and Aristotelianism*. Chicago: U of Chicago Press, 1952.

JANSEN, C., *Augustinus, seu doctrina Sancti Augustini de humanae naturae sanitate, aegritudine, medicina …* Rouen: Berthelin, 1652.

JEROME, *Commentaria in Ezechielem*, in *PL* xxv.

JONES, A. H. M., 'The Hellenistic age', *Past and Present* 27 (1964), 3–22.

JONSEN, A. R., and Toulmin, S. E., *The Abuse of Casuistry: a history of moral reasoning*. UCP, 1988.

JORDAN, M. D., 'Ideals of scientia moralis', in MacDonald and Stump, *AMT*, 79–97.

JOSEPHUS, *Antiquitates Judaicae*. Loeb.

JUSTIN MARTYR, *First Apology*, in *PG* vi.

KANT, I., *Groundwork of the Metaphysics of Morals* (cited as G) and *Critique of Practical Reason* (cited as *KpV*), in *Kant: Practical Philosophy*, tr. M. J. Gregor. CUP, 1996.

_____ *Religion and Rational Theology*, tr. and ed. A. W. wood and G. di. Giovanni, CUP, 1996.

KENNY, A. J. P., 'Aquinas on Aristotelian happiness', in MacDonald and Stump, *AMT*, 15–27.

_____ *Aristotle on the Perfect Life*. OUP, 1992.

_____ *The Aristotelian Ethics*. OUP, 1978.

KENT, B. D., 'Transitory vice', *JHP* 27 (1989), 199–223.

_____ *Virtues of the Will*. CUAP, 1995.

KIDD, I., 'Poseidonius on emotion', in A. A. Long (ed.), *Problems in Stoicism*. London: Athlone, 1971, ch. 9.

KILCULLEN, J., 'Natural law and will in Ockham', in K. Haakonssen and U. Thiel (eds.), *Reason, Will, and Nature* (*History of Philosophy Yearbook* 1). Canberra, 1993, 1–25.

KINDSTRAND, J. F. (ed.), *Bion of Borysthenes*. Stockholm: Uppsala, 1976.

KING, P., 'Aquinas on the passions', in MacDonald and Stump, *AMT*, 101–32.

_____ 'Ockham's ethical theory' in Spade, *CCO*, ch. 10.

KIRK, K. E., *Some Principles of Moral Theology*. London: Longmans, 1920.

_____ *The Vision of God*, 2nd edn. London: Longmans, 1932.

KIRWAN, C. A. (ed.), *Aristotle: Metaphysics IV, V, VI*, 2nd edn. OUP, 1992.

KITTEL, G. (ed.), *Theological Dictionary of the New Testament*, 10 vols. Grand Rapids, Michi: Eerdmans, 1965–76.

KNOX, R. A., *Enthusiasm*. OUP, 1950.

KNUUTTILA, S., *Emotions in Ancient and Mediaeval Philosophy*. OUP, 2004.

KOROLEC, J. B., 'Free will and free choice', in Kretzmann et al., *CHLMP*, ch. 32.

KORSGAARD, C. M., *The Sources of Normativity*. CUP, 1996.

_____ 'In defence of the grand end', *Ethics* 103 (1993), 361–374.

_____ 'Reason and justice in the *Republic*', in E. N. Lee, A. P. D. Mourelatos, and R. M. Rorty (eds.), *Exegesis and Argument*. Assen: Van Gorcum, 1973, ch. 11.

_____ 'Return to the cave', in Fine, *Plato* ii, ch. 9.

_____ ''Two conceptions of happiness'', *PR* 88 (1979), 167–97.

KRAUT, R. *Aristotle on the Human Good*. PUP, 1989.

KRAYE, J., (ed.), *Cambridge Translations of Renaissance Philosophical Texts*, 2 vols. CUP, 1997.

KRETZMANN, N., 'A general problem of creation', in MacDonald, *BG*, ch. 8.

_____ 'A particular problem of creation', in MacDonald, *BG*, ch. 9.

_____ 'Goodness, knowledge, and indeterminacy in the philosophy of Thomas Aquinas', *JP* 80 (1983), 631–49.

_____ *The Metaphysics of Creation*. OUP, 1999.

_____ *The Metaphysics of Theism*. OUP, 1997.

_____ Kenny, A., and Pinborg, J. (eds.), *Cambridge History of Later Mediaeval Philosophy*. CUP, 1982.

_____ and STUMP, E. S., 'Being and goodness', in MacDonald, *BG*, ch. 4.

KUSAKAWA, S., *The Transformation of Natural Philosophy: the case of Philip Melanchthon*. CUP, 1995.

LACTANTIUS, *Divinae Institutiones*, ed. S. Brandt. Vienna: Tempsky, 1890 (= *CSEL* xix 1).

LAMBINUS, D. (tr.), *Ethica Nicomachea*, in *Aristotelis Opera*, iii, ed. I. Bekker. Berlin: Reimer, 1870.

LAMPE, G. W. H. (ed.), *A Patristic Greek Lexicon*. OUP, 1961.

LAWRENCE, G. L., 'Aristotle on the ideal life', *PR* 102 (1993), 1–34.

LEAR, G. R., *Happy Lives and the Highest Good*. PUP, 2004.

LEAR, J. D., *Aristotle: the desire to understand*. CUP, 1988.

LEFF, G., *Gregory of Rimini*. Manchester: Manchester UP, 1961.

LEIBNIZ, G. W., *Theodicy*, tr. E. M. Huggard. London: Routledge, 1951.

LESSES, G., 'Virtue and fortune in Stoic moral theory', *OSAP* 7 (1989), 95–127.

LIGHTFOOT, J. B., *St Paul's Epistle to the Philippians*, 6th edn. CUP, 1881.

LILLA, S. R. C., *Clement of Alexandria*. OUP, 1971.

LIPSIUS, J., *De Constantia*. Antwerp: Plantin, 1515 (repr. Hildesheim: Olms, 2002; also repr. in *Opera Omnia*, v).

_____ *Manuductio ad Stoicam Philosophiam, 2nd edn.*, Antwerp: Plantin, 1510 (repr. in *Opera Omnia*, v).

_____ *Opera Omnia*, 7 vols., Antwerp: Plantin, 1614.

LOCKE, J., *An Essay concerning Human Understanding*, ed. P. H. Nidditch. OUP, 1975.

LOMBARD, PETER, *Sententiae, 3rd edn.*, 2 vols., ed. Collegium S. Bonaventurae. Grottaferrata: Editiones Collegii S Bonaventurae ad Claras Aquas, 1971.

LONG, A. A., *Epictetus: a Stoic and Socratic guide to life*. OUP, 2002.

_____ 'Socrates and Hellenistic philosophy', in *Stoic Studies*. CUP, 1996, ch. 1. From *CQ* 38 (1988), 150–71.

_____ 'Stoic psychology,' in Algra et al., *CHHP*, ch. 17.

_____ 'The Socratic legacy', in Algra et al., *CHHP*, 19.

_____ and Sedley, D. N., *The Hellenistic Philosophers*, 2 vols. CUP, 1987.

LOTTIN, O., *Etudes de Morale*. Gembloux: Duculot, 1961.

_____ *Psychologie et morale aux XIIe et XIIIe siècles*, 6 vols. Louvain and Gembloux, 1942–60.

LUCRETIUS, *De Rerum Natura*. OCT.

LUTHER, M., *De Servo Arbitrio* (cited in *SA*), tr. in *The Bondage of the Will*, tr. J. I. Packer and O. R. Johnson. London James Clarke, 1957.

_____ *Lectures on Romans*, tr. and ed. W. Pauck. London: SCM Press, 1961.

_____ *Luthers Werke in Auswahl, 6th edn.*, 8 vols., ed. O. Clemen. Berlin: De Gruyter, 1966. Cited as 'C'.

_____ *Luther's Works*, 56 vols., ed. J. Pelikan and H. T. Lehmann. St Louis: Concordia, 1955–76. Cited as 'Works'.

_____ *Selections*, ed. J. Dillenberger. Garden City, NY: Doubleday, 1961.

_____ *The Bondage of the Will*, tr. J. I. Packer and O. R. Johnson. London: James Clarke, 1957.

MABBOTT, J. D., 'Is Plato's *Republic* utilitarian?' in Vlastos (ed.), *Plato* ii, ch. 4.

McCABE, M. M., 'Extend or identify: two Stoic accounts of altruism', in R. Salles (ed.), *Metaphysics, Soul, and Ethics in Ancient Thought*. OUP, 2005, ch. 16.

MacDONALD, S. C., 'Aquinas' libertarian account of free will', *Revue Internationale de Philosophie* 52 (1998), 309–28.

_____ *Being and Goodness*. Ithaca, NY: Cornell UP, 1991.

_____ 'The relation between being and goodness', in MacDonald, *BG* 1–28.

_____ 'Ultimate ends in practical reasoning: Aquinas' Aristotelian moral psychology and Anscombe's fallacy', *PR* 100 (1991), 31–66.

_____ and Stump, E. S. (eds.), *Aquinas' Moral Theory*. Ithaca, NY: Cornell UP, 1999.

McDowell, J. H., 'Are moral requirements hypothetical imperatives?', in *MVR*, ch. 4. From *SPAS* 52 (1978), 15–29.

——— 'Comments on "Some rational aspects of incontinence"', *Southern Journal of Philosophy* 27 (1989) supp. 89–102.

——— 'Might there be external reasons?', in *MVR*, ch. 5. From J. E. J. Altham and R. Harrison (eds.), *World, Mind, and Ethics: essays on the ethical philosophy of Bernard Williams*. CUP, 1995, 387–98.

——— *Mind, Value, and Reality*. HUP, 1998.

——— 'Some issues in Aristotle's moral psychology', in *MVR*, ch. 3. From *Monist* 62 (1979), 331–50.

——— 'The role of eudaimonia in Aristotle's Ethics', in *MVR*, ch. 1. From *Proceedings of the African Classical Associations* 15 (1980), 1–14.

——— 'Two sorts of naturalism', in *MVR*, ch. 9. From R. Hursthouse, G. Lawrence, and W. Quinn (eds.), *Virtues and Reason: Philippa Foot and moral theory*. OUP, 1995, ch. 6.

Mace, C. A., 'Emotions and the category of passivity', *PAS* 62 (1961–2), 135–42.

McGrade, A. S., 'Natural law and moral omnipotence', in Spade, *CCO*, ch. 12.

——— *The Political Thought of William Ockham*. CUP, 1974.

McGrath, A. E., *Iustitia Dei*, 2nd edn. CUP, 1998.

Machiavelli, N., *Discourses*, 2 vols., ed. and tr. L. J. Walker. London: RKP, 1950.

——— *Il Principe*, ed. L. A. Burd. OUP, 1891.

——— *Opere*, vols. 1–2, ed. R. Rinaldi. Turin: Unione Tipografico-Editrice Torinese, 1999.

——— *The Prince*, ed. and tr. J. B. Atkinson. Indianapolis: Bobbs-Merrill, 1976.

Mac Intyre, A. C. *After Virtue*. London: Duckworth, 1981.

——— *Dependent Rational Animals*. Chicago: Open Court Press, 1999.

——— *Whose Justice? Which Rationality?* London: Duckworth, 1988.

Mackie, J. L., *Ethics: Inventing Right and Wrong*. Harmondsworth: Penguin, 1977.

McNeill, J. T., 'Natural law in the theology of the Reformers', *Journal of Religion* 26 (1946), 168–82.

——— 'Natural law in the thought of Luther', *Church History* 10 (1941), 211–27.

McTighe, K., 'Socrates on desire for the good and the involuntariness of wrongdoing', in H. H. Benson (ed.), *Essays on the Philosophy of Socrates*. OUP, 1992, ch. 15. From *Phr.* 29 (1984), 193–236.

Mandeville, Bernard, *The Fable of the Boes*, ed. F. B. Kayr, OUP, 1924.

Mannebach, E., *Aristippi et Cyrenaicorum Fragmenta*. Leiden: Brill, 1961.

Marcus Aurelius, *Meditations*, 2 vols., ed. A. S. L. Farquharson. OUP, 1944.

Martens, J. W., 'Romans 2:14–16: a Stoic reading', *New Testament Studies* 40 (1994), 55–67.

Marx, K., and Engels, F., *The German Ideology*, ed. C. J. Arthur. NY: International Publishers, 1970.

Mates, B., *Stoic Logic*, 2nd edn. UCP, 1961.

Maurer, W., *Historical Commentary on the Augsburg Confession*, tr. H. G. Anderson. Philadelphia: Fortress, 1986.

Mausbach, J., *Die Ethik des Hl. Augustins*, 2 vols. Freiburg: Herder, 1909.

Maximus Confessor, *PG* xci.

Melanchthon, P., *Apology for the Augsburg Confession*, in *Die Symbolischen Bücher der Evangelisch-Lutherischen Kirche*, ed. J. F. Müller. Gütersloh: Bertelsmann, 1876. Tr. in T. G. Tappert (ed.), *The Book of Concord*. Philadelphia: Fortress Press, 1959.

——— *Loci Communes* (1521), in *MWA*, ii. 1. Tr. W. Pauck, in *Melanchthon and Bucer*, London: SCM Press 1969.

——— *Melanchthons Werke in Auswahl*, 7 vols., ed. R. Stupperich. Gütersloh: Bertelsmann, 1951–75.

——— *Philosophiae moralis epitome* (1546), in *MWA* iii.

Mercer, C., 'Leibniz, Aristotle, and ethical knowledge', in R. Pozzo (ed.), *The Impact of Aristotelianism on Modern Philosophy*. CUAP, 2004, ch. 5.

Mercken, H. P. F., *The Greek Commentaries on the Nicomachean Ethics of Aristotle*, i. Leiden: Brill, 1973.

Meyer, S. S., 'Aristotle, teleology, and reduction', *PR* 101 (1992), 791–825.

_____ 'Moral responsibility: Aristotle and after', in Everson, *ECAT*, ch. 9.

MILL, J. S., *Collected Works*, 33 vols., J. M. Robson (gen. ed.). Toronto: U of Toronto Press, 1963–91. Includes *An Examination of Sir William Hamilton's Philosophy*, in vol. ix, and *Utilitarianism* and 'Nature', in vol. x.

MITSIS, P. T., *Epicurus' Ethical Theory*. Ithaca, NY: Cornell UP, 1988.

_____ 'Epicurus on death and the duration of life', *Proceedings of the Boston Area Colloquium in AP* 4 (1989), 303–322.

MOLINA, LUIS de, *On Divine Foreknowledge: Part IV of the Concordia*, tr. A. J. Freddoso. Ithaca, NY: Cornell UP, 1988.

MONTAIGNE, M., *Essais*, 3 vols., ed. M. Rat. Paris: Garnier, 1952.

Moo, D. J., *Romans*. Grand Rapids, Mich.: Eerdmanns, 1996.

MOORE, G. E., *Principia Ethica, 2nd edn.*, ed. T. W. Baldwin. CUP, 1993 (1st edn., 1903).

MOREAU, J., *La construction de L'idéalisme platonicien*. Paris: Boivin & Cie., 1939.

MURPHY, N. R., *The Interpretation of Plato's Republic*. OUP, 1951.

NAGEL, T., *The View from Nowhere*. OUP, 1986.

NEMESIUS, *De Natura Hominis*. BT.

NEUHOUSES, F. W., *Foundations of Hegel's Social Theory*, Cambridge, Mas.: Harvard UP, 2000.

NICHOLAS, B., *Introduction to Roman Law*. OUP, 1962.

NIETZSCHE, F., *On the Genealogy of Morality*, ed. K. Ansell-Pearson. CUP, 1994.

_____ *Twilight of the Idots*, in W. Kaufmann (ed. and tr.), *The Portable Nietesche*. Harmondsworth, penguin, 1976, 436–564.

NUSSBAUM, M. C., *The Therapy of Desire*. PUP, 1994.

OAKLEY, F., 'Mediaeval theories of natural law: William of Ockham and the significance of the voluntarist tradition', in *Natural Law, Conciliarism, and Consent*. London: Variorum, 1984, ch. 15. From *Natural Law Forum* 6 (1961), 65–83.

_____ 'The absolute and ordained power of God in Sixteenth- and Seventeenth-century theology', *Journal of the History of Ideas* 59 (1998), 437–61.

OBBINK, D., *Philodemus on Piety, Part 1*. OUP, 1996.

OBERMAN, H. A., 'Duns Scotus, nominalism, and the Council of Trent', in *DR*, ch. 9. From J. Ryan and B. M. Bonansea (eds.), *Scotus 1265–1965*. CUAP, 1965, 311–44.

_____ *The Dawn of the Reformation*. Edinburgh: T&T Clark, 1986.

_____ *The Harvest of Medieval Theology: Gabriel Biel and the late medieval nominalism*. HUP, 1963.

OCKHAM, W., *A Letter to the Friars Minor and Other Writings*, tr. J. Kilcullen, ed. J. Killcullen and A. S. McGrade. CUP, 1995.

_____ *Dialogus*, ed. J. Kilcullen et al. British Academy, forthcoming (draft at 'www.britac.ac.uk').

_____ *Opera Theologica et Philosophica*, 17 vols. St Bonaventure: Franciscan Institute, 1974–88.

_____ *Quodlibetal Questions*, 2 vols., tr. A. J. Freddoso and F. E. Kelly. New Haven, Conn.: Yale UP, 1991.

O'Donovan, O. M. T., *The Problem of Self-Love in St Augustine*. New Haven, Conn.: Yale UP, 1980.

_____ 'Usus and fruitio in Augustine, De Doctrina Christiana I', *Journal of Theological Studies* 33 (1982), 361–97.

OFFLER, H.S., 'Three modes of natural law in Ockham', *Franciscan Studies* 37 (1977), 207–18.

OLAFSON, F., *Principles and Persons: an ethical interpretation of existentialism*. Baltimore: Johns Hopkins Press, 1967.

OLIVI, Petrus Johannes, *Quaestiones in Secundum Librum Sententiarum*, 3 vols., ed. B. Jansen. Quaracchi: Coll. S. Bonaventurae, 1924.

787

ORIGEN, *Commentaria in Evangelium secundum Matthaeum. PG* xiii.

—— *Contra Celsum*, 5 vols., ed. M. Bonnet. Paris: Cerf, 1967.

—— *De Principiis*, 5 vols., ed. H. Crouzel and M. Simonetti. Paris: Cerf, 1978.

Oxford Latin Dictionary, ed. P. G. W. Glare. OUP, 1982.

PARFIT, D. A., *Reasons and Persons*. OUP, 1984.

PASNAU, R. A., *Thomas Aquinas on Human Nature*. CUP, 2002.

Patrologiae Graecae Cursus Completus, 161 vols., ed. J.-P. Migne. Paris: Migne, 1857–66.

Patrologiae Latinae Cursus Completus, 221 vols., ed. J.-P. Migne. Paris: Migne, 1844–55.

PEGIS, A. C., 'Necessity and liberty: an historical note on St Thomas Aquinas', *New Scholasticism* 15 (1941), 18–45.

PENNER, T., 'Desire and power in Socrates', *Aperion* 24 (1991), 147–201.

—— 'Thought and desire in Plato', in Vlastos, *Plato* ii, ch. 6.

PETERS, R. S., 'Emotions and the category of passivity', *PAS* 62 (1961–2), 117–34.

PHILO, *Works*, tr. F. H. Colson and G. H. Whitaker. Loeb. Works cited: *De Posteritate Cain* (vol. ii); *De Cherubim* (ii); *De Ebrietate* (iii); *Quis Rerum Divinarum Heres* (iv); *Legum Allegoriae* (i); *De Plantatione* (iii).

PHOTIUS, *Bibliotheca*, 9 vols., ed. R. Henry. Paris: Les Belles Lettres, 1959–91.

PICHÉ, D., *La condamnation parisienne de 1277*. Paris: Vrin, 1999.

PLAMENATZ, J. P., 'In search of Machiavellian Virtù', in A. Parel (ed.), *The Political Calculus: essays on Machiavelli's philosophy*. Toronto: U of Toronto Press, 1972, ch. 7.

PLATO, OCT. Works cited: *Apology, Charmides; Clitopho; Crito; Euthydemus; Euthyphro; Gorgias; Hippias Major; Laches; Laws; Meno; Phaedo; Phaedrus; Philebus; Protagoras; Republic; Symposium; Theaetetus; Timaeus.*

PLOTINUS, *Enneades*. OCT.

PLUTARCH, *Moralia*, Loeb. Works cited: *Adversus Colotem* (vol. xiv); *De Communibus Notitiis* (xiii); *Non Posse Suaviter Vivere secundum Epicurum* (xiv); *De Sera Numinis Vindicta* (vii); *De Stoicorum Repugnantiis* (xiii); *De Tranquillitate Animi* (vi); *De Virtute Morali* (vi).

POLYBIUS, *Historiae*. BT.

PONCIUS, JOANNES, *Philosophiae ad mentem Scoti cursus integer*. Lyons: Huguetan & Barbier, 1722.

PORPHYRY, *De Abstinentia*, 3 vols., tr. and ed. J. Bouffartigue et al. Paris: Les Belles Lettres, 1977–95.

POSEIDONIUS, *Fragments*, 4 vols., ed. L. Edelstein, and I. G. Kidd. CUP, 1972–99. Cited as EK'.

POTTS, T. C., *Conscience in Mediaeval Philosophy*. CUP, 1980.

PRENTICE, R., 'The contingent element governing the natural law on the last seven precepts of the Decalogue, according to Duns Scotus', *Antonianum* 42 (1967), 259–92.

PRICE, A. W., *Love and Friendship in Plato and Aristotle*. OUP, 1989.

PRICE, H. H., *Perception, 2nd edn*. London: Methuen, 1950.

PRICE, R., *A Review of the Principal Questions in Morals, corrected and enlarged 3rd edn. repr.*, ed. D. D. Raphael. OUP, 1974 (orig. 3rd edn., 1787; 1st edn., 1758).

PRICHARD, H. A., *Moral Obligation and Duty and Interest*. OUP, 1968 (*Moral Obligation*, orig. 1949; *Duty and Interest*, orig. 1928).

PRIOR, A. N., *Logic and the Basis of Ethics*. OUP, 1949.

PUFENDORF, S., *De iure naturae et gentinum*, 3rd edn. Amsterdam: Hoogenhuysen, 1688 (1st edn., Lund, 1672).

—— *De iure naturae et gentinm*, tr. C. H. Oldfather and W. A. Oldfather, OUP, 1934.

QUASTEN, J., et al., *Patrology*, English translation 4 vols. Westminster, Md.: Christian Classics, 1986 (orig. pub. 1950–78).

RANKIN, O. S., 'Ecclesiastes' in *The Interpreter's Bible*, 12 vols., ed. G. A. Buttrick. Nashville: Abingdon Press, 1956, vol. v.

RAWLS, J., *A Theory of Justice, 2nd edn*. HUP, 1999 (1st edn., 1971).

_____ 'Outline of a decision procedure for ethics', *PR* 60 (1951), 177–97. Repr. in *Collected Papers*, ed. S. Freeman. HUP, 1999, ch. 1.

_____ *Political Liberalism*, 2nd edn. New York: Columbia UP, 1996 (1st edn., 1993).

REICHERT, B. M. (ed.), *Monumenta Ordinis Fratrum Praedicatorum* iii. Rome: Generalita, 1898.

REID, T., *Essays on the Active Powers of the Human Mind*, in *Works*, 6th edn., 2 vols., ed. W. Hamilton. Edinburgh: Maclachlan and Stewart, 1863.

RIST, J. M., *Epicurus: an introduction*. CUP, 1972.

ROGERS, K., 'Aristotle's conception of *to kalon*', *AP* 13 (1993), 355–71.

ROMAN MISSAL = *Missale Romanum ex Decreto Sacrosancti Concilii Tridentini*. Rome, 1570.

ROSS, W. D., *Aristotle*. London: Methuen, 1923.

_____ *The Right and the Good*. OUP, 1930.

_____ 'The Socratic Problem', *Proceedings of the Classical Association* 30 (1933), 7–24. Repr. in Patzer, A. (ed.), *Der historische Sokrates*. Darmstadt: Wissenschaftliche Buchgesellschaft, 1987, 225–39.

RUPP, E. G. (ed.), *Luther and Erasmus: Free Will and Salvation*. London: SCM, 1969.

_____ *The Righteousness of God: Luther studies*. London: Hodder & Stoughton, 1953.

SAARINEN, R., *Weakness of the Will in Mediaeval Thought*. Leiden: Brill, 1994.

SACHS, D., 'A fallacy in Plato's *Republic*?', in Vlastos, *Plato* ii, ch. 2.

SANDAY, W., and Headlam, A. C., *The Epistle to the Romans*, 3rd edn. Edinburgh: T&T Clark, 1897.

SANDERSON, ROBERT, *De Obligatione Conscientiae*. W. Whewell, tr. and ed. CUP, 1851 (orig. 1647).

SANTAS, G., *Socrates: Philosophy in Plato's Early Dialogues*. London: RKP, 1979.

SCHAFF, P., *The Creeds of Christendom*, 6th edn., 3 vols. New York: Harper & Row, 1931.

SCHMITT, C. B., and Skinner, Q. (eds.), *The Cambridge History of Renaissance Philosophy*. CUP, 1988.

SCHNEEWIND, J. B. (ed.), *Moral Philosophy from Montaigne to Kant*, 2nd edn.: CUP, 2003.

_____ *The Invention of Autonomy*. CUP, 1997.

SCHOFIELD, M., *Saving the City*. London: Routledge, 1999.

_____ 'Social and political thought', in Algra et al., *CHHP*, ch. 22.

_____ 'The syllogisms of Zeno of Citium', *Phr.* 28 (1983), 31–58.

_____ 'Who were *hoi duschereis* in Plato, *Philebus* 44a ff?', *Museum Helveticum* 28 (1971), 2–20, 181.

_____ and Striker, G., (eds.), *The Norms of Nature: studies in Hellenistic ethics*. CUP, 1986.

SCHOPENHAUER, A., *Essay on the Freedom of the will*, tr. K. Kolenda.

_____ A., *The Will as World and Representation*, 2 vols., tr. E. F. J. Payne, New York: Dover, 1966.

SCOTT, D. J., 'Aristotle on well-being and intellectual contemplation', *SPAS* 73 (1999), 225–42.

SCOTT, R. B. Y. (tr. and ed.), *Proverbs and Ecclesiastes*. Garden City, NY: Doubleday, 1965.

SCOTUS, DUNS, *Duns Scotus on the Will and Morality*, tr. A. B. Wolter. CUAP, 1986. Cited as W.

_____ *Opera Omnia*, 12 vols., ed. L. Wadding. Lyons: Durand, 1639 (repr. Hildesheim: Olms, 1968). Cited as OO.

_____ *Opera Omnia*, ed. C. Balic. Civitas Vaticana: Typis Polyglottis Vaticanis, 1950–. Cited as V.

_____ *Opera Philosophica*, 4 vols. St Bonaventure: Franciscan Institute, 1997–2004. Cited as OP.

_____ *Quaestiones subtilissimae in Metaphysica Aristotelis* = OP iii–iv. Cited as QM.

SEDLEY, D. N., 'The ideal of godlikeness', in Fine, *Plato* ii, ch. 14.

SEGVIC, H., 'No one errs willingly: the meaning of Socratic intellectualism', *OSAP*. 19 (2000), 1–45.

SENECA, *Dialogi*. OCT. Cited: *De Beata Vita*; *De Benficiis*; *De Clementia*; *De Ira*, *De Otio*.

_____ *Epistulae Morales*. OCT.

SEXTUS EMPIRICUS, *Adversus Mathematicos*. BT. Cited as '*M*'.

_____ *Pyrrhoneae Hypotyposes*. BT. Cited as '*P*'.

SHAFTESBURY, ANTHONY ASHLEY, LORD, *Characteristics*, ed. L. E. Klein, CUP, 1999.

SHAKESPEARE, WILLIAM, *Hamlet*, ed. H. Jenkins. London: Methuen, 1982.

SHAKESPEARE, WILLIAM, *Othello*, ed. M. R. Ridley. London: Methuen, 1962.

SHANLEY, B. J., 'Aquinas on pagan virtue', *Thomist* 63 (1999), 553–77.

SHARVY, R., '*Euthyphro* 9d–11b: analysis and definition in Plato and others', *Nous* 6 (1972), 119–37.

SHERMAN, N., *The Fabric of Character: Aristotle's theory of virtue*. OUP, 1989.

SHOREY, P., 'Plato's ethics', in G. Vlastos (ed.), *Plato: a collection of critical essays, ii*. Garden City, NY : Anchor Books, 1971, ch. 1.

SIDGWICK, H., *Outlines of the History of Ethics, 3rd edn.*, London: Macmillan, 1892.

—— *The Ethics of Green, Spencer, and Martineau*. London: Macmillan, 1902.

—— *The Methods of Ethics, 7th edn.*, London: Macmillan, 1907.

SIMPLICIUS, *in Aristotelis Categorias*. *CAG* viii.

—— *in Epiceti Enchiridion*, ed. I. Hadot. Leiden: Brill, 1996.

SKINNER, Q. R. D., *Machiavelli*. OUP, 1981.

—— 'Machiavelli on virtù and liberty', in *Visions of Politics*, 3 vols. CUP, 2002, ii. ch. 6.

—— *The Foundations of Modern Political Theory*, 2 vols. CUP, 1978.

SLINGS, S. R., *Critical Notes on Plato's Politeia*. Leiden: Brill, 2005.

SMITH, A., *The Theory of Moral Sentiments, 6th edn.*, ed. D. D. Raphael and A. L. Macfie. OUP, 1976 (orig. pub. 1790; 1st edn., 1759).

SMITH, M., *The Moral Problem*. Oxford: Blackwell, 1994.

SORABJI, R. R. K., *Animal Minds and Human Morals: the origin of the Western debate*. London: Duckworth, 1993.

—— 'Aristotle on the role of intellect in virtue', in A. O. Rorty (ed.), *Essays on Aristotle's Ethics*. UCP, 1980, ch. 12. From *SPAS* n.s. 74 (1973–4), 107–29.

—— *Emotion and Peace of Mind*. OUP, 2000.

SPADE, P. V. (ed.), *Cambridge Companion to Ockham*. CUP, 1999.

SPARKS, H. F. D., 'Jerome as biblical scholar', in Ackroyd and Evans, *CHB* i, 510–41.

SPINOZA, B., *Ethics*, in *Collected Works of Spinoza*, i, tr. E. M. Curley. Princeton: PUP, 1985.

STADTER, E., *Psychologie und Metaphysik der menschlichen Freiheit*. Munich: F. Schöningh, 1971.

STEEL, C., 'Thomas Aquinas on preferential love', in T. A. F. Kelly and P. W. Rosemann (eds.), *Amor Amicitiae*. Leuven: Peeters, 2004, 437–58.

STEWART, Z., 'Democritus and the Cynics', *Harvard Studies in Classical Philology* 63 (1958) 179–91.

STOBAEUS, *Anthologia*, 5 vols., ed. C. Wachsmuth and O. Hense. Berlin: Weidmann, 1884–1912.

—— *Eclogae*, in *Anthologia*.

STONE, M. W. F., 'Henry of Ghent on freedom and human action', in *Henry of Ghent and the Transformation of Scholastic Thought*, ed. G. Guldentops and C. Steel. Leuven: Leuven UP, 2003, 201–25.

STRAWSON, G., *Freedom and Belief*. OUP, 1986.

STRAWSON, P. F., 'Social morality and individual ideal', in *Freedom and Resentment and Other Essays*. London: Methuen, 1974, ch. 2. From *Philosophy* 36 (1961), 1–17.

STRIKER, G., 'Antipater, or the art of living', in *EHEE*, ch. 14. From Schofield and Striker, *NN*, ch. 7.

—— 'Ataraxia: happiness as tranquillity', in *EHEE*, ch. 9. From *Monist* 73 (1989), 97–110.

—— *Essays on Hellenistic Epistemology and Ethics*. CUP, 1996.

—— 'Following nature: a study in Stoic ethics', in *EHEE*, ch. 12. From *OSAP* 9 (1991), 1–73.

—— 'Plato's Socrates and the Stoics', in *EHEE*, ch. 15. From Vander Waerdt, *SM*, ch. 9.

—— 'The role of oikeiôsis in Stoic ethics', in *EHEE*, ch. 13. From *OSAP* 1 (1983), 145–67.

STUMP, E. S., *Aquinas*. London: Routledge, 2003.

—— 'Sanctification, hardening of the heart, and Frankfurt's concept of free will', *JP* 85 (1988), 395–420.

SUAREZ, F., *De bonitate*, in *Opera Omnia*, 28 vols., ed. C. Berton. Paris: Vivès, 1866, vol. iv.

—— *Tractatus de Legibus ac Deo Legislatore*, 8 vols., ed. and tr. L. Perena et al. Madrid: Consejo Superior de Investigaciones Cientificas, 1971–81.

Bibliography

TARRANT, H., 'The Hippias Major and Socratic theories of pleasure', in Vander Waerdt, *SM*, ch. 4.

TAYLOR, A. E., *A Commentary on Plato's Timaeus*. OUP, 1928.

TAYLOR, C. C. W., 'Hellenistic ethics' (review of Schofield and Striker, *NN*), *OSAP* 5 (1987), 235–45.

―――― (tr and ed.), *Plato's Protagoras, Revised Edition*. OUP, 1991.

―――― 'Pleasure, knowledge, and sensation in Democritus', *Phr.* 12 (1967), 6–27.

―――― *The Atomists Leucippus and Democritus: fragments*. Toronto: University of Toronto Press, 1999.

TAYLOR, CHARLES., *Sources of the Self*. HUP, 1989.

―――― 'What is human agency?', in *Human Agency and Language*, i. CUP, 1985, ch. 1. From T. Mischel (ed.), *The Self*. Oxford: Blackwell, 1977, 103–35.

TE SELLE, E., *Augustine the Theologian*. New York: Herder, 1970.

TERTULLIAN, *Adversus Marcionem, PL* ii.

TORRELL, J. P., *Saint Thomas Aquinas* i (*The Person and his Work*). CUAP, 1996.

TRINKAUS, C. E., *In Our Image and Likeness: humanity and divinity in Italian humanist thought*. Chicago: U of Chicago Press, 1970.

TROLLOPE, A., *The Warden*. London: Longman, 1855.

TSOUNA-McKIRAHAN, V., 'Is there an exception to Greek eudaemonism?', in M. Canto-Sperber and P. Pellegrin (eds.), *Le style de la pensée*. Paris: Les belles letters, 2002, 464–89.

―――― 'Socratic origins of Cynics and Cyrenaics', in Vander Waerdt, *SM*, ch. 14.

―――― *The Epistemology of the Cyrenaic School*. CUP, 1998.

TUCK, R., *Natural Rights Theories: their origin and development*. CUP, 1979.

URBAN, L. W., 'A revolution in Anglican moral theology', *Anglican Theological Review* 53 (1971), 5–20.

USENER, H., *Epicurea*. Leipzig: Teubner, 1887. Cited as 'U'.

VANDER WAERDT, P. A. (ed.), *The Socratic Movement*. Ithaca, NY: Cornell UP, 1994.

Vasquez, Gabriel, *Commentaria at Disputatieries in Priman Secundae Sancti Thornae*, 2 vols. ngolstadt, 1606.

VERSENYI, L. G., *Socratic Humanism*. New Haven: Yale UP, 1963.

VISSER, S., and WILLIAMS, T., 'Anselm's account of freedom', *Canadian J, Conn. of Philosophy* 31 (2001), 221–44.

VLASTOS, G., 'Justice and happiness in the *Republic*', in *PS*, ch. 5. From *Plato* ii, ch. 5.

―――― (ed.), *Plato ii*. Garden City, NY: Doubleday, 1971.

―――― *Platonic Studies*. PUP, 1981.

―――― *Socrates: Ironist and Moral Philosopher*. Ithaca, NY: Cornell UP, 1991.

―――― 'Socrates on acrasia', *Phoenix* 23 (1969), 71–88. Repr. in D. W. Graham (ed.), *Studies in Greek Philosophy*, 2 vols. PUP, 1993–5, ii, ch. 5.

―――― *Socratic Studies*. CUP, 1994.

―――― 'The unity of the virtues in the *Protagoras*', *Review of Metaphysics* 25 (1972), 415–58. Repr. in *PS*, ch. 4.

VON ARNIM, H. (ed.), *Stoicorum Veterum Fragmenta*, 4 vols. Leipzig: Teubner, 1903–24. Cited as '*SVF*'.

VON WRIGHT, G. H., *The Varieties of Goodness*. London: Routledge, 1963.

VOS, A., et al. (eds.), *Duns Scotus on Divine Love*. Aldershot: Ashgate, 2003.

WALSH, J., 'Buridan on the connexion of the virtues', *JHP* 24 (1986), 453–82.

WANG TCH'ANG-TCHE, J., *Saint Augustin et les vertus des paiens*. Paris: Beauchesne, 1938.

WARNER, M., 'Love, self, and Plato's *Symposium*', *Philosophical Quarterly* 29 (1979), 329–39.

WARNOCK, G. J., *The Object of Morality*. London: Methuen, 1971.

WATERLAND, D., 'Remarks upon Dr Clarke's exposition of the Church Catechism', in *Works*, ed. W. van Mildert, ii vols. Oxford: 1823, v 375–430.

WEINFELD, M., *Deuteronomy 1–11*. New York: Doubleday, 1991.

WENDEL, F., *Calvin: Origin and Development of his Religious Thought*. London: Collins, 1963.

WESTBERG, D., *Right Practical Reason: Aristotle, action, and prudence in Aquinas*. OUP, 1994.

Westminster Confession, in Schaff, *CC iii*.

Wetzel, J., *Augustine and the Limits of Virtue*. CUP, 1992.

White, N.P., *A Companion to Plato's Republic*. Indianapolis: Hackett, 1979.

―――― *Individual and Conflict in Greek Ethics*. OUP, 2002.

―――― 'Rational prudence in Plato's *Gorgias*', in D. J. O'Meara (ed.), *Platonic Investigations*. CUAP, 1985, ch. 6.

Whitfield, J. H., *Discourses on Machiavelli*. Cambridge: Heffer, 1969.

Whiting, J. E., 'Aristotle's function argument: a defence', *AP* 8 (1988), 33–48.

―――― 'Friends and future selves', *PR* 95 (1986), 547–80.

Whittaker, J., *see* Alcinous.

Wieland, G., 'Aristotle's *Ethics*: reception and interpretation', in Kretzmann et al., *CHLMP*, ch. 34.

―――― 'Happiness: the perfection of man', in Kretzmann et al., *CHLMP*, ch. 35.

Wiggins, D. R. P., 'Deliberation and practical reason', in *NVT*, ch. 6. From *PAS* 76 (1975–6), 29–51.

―――― *Needs, Values, Truth*. Oxford: Blackwell, 1987.

―――― 'Weakness of will, commensurability, and the objects of deliberation and desire', in *NVT*, ch. 7. From *PAS* 79 (1978), 251–77.

Williams, B. A. O., 'Acting as the virtuous person acts', in Heinaman, *AMR*, 13–23.

―――― *Ethics and the Limits of Philosophy*. HUP, 1985.

―――― 'Internal and external reasons', in *ML*, ch. 8.

―――― 'Moral luck' in *ML*, ch. 2.

―――― 'Persons, character, and morality', in *ML*, ch.1.

―――― *Moral Luck*. CUP, 1981.

―――― *Shame and Necessity*. UCP, 1993.

―――― 'Voluntary acts and responsible agents', in *Making Sense of Humanity*. CUP, 1995, ch. 2.

Williams, N. P., *The Ideas of the Fall and of Original Sin*. London: Longmans, Green, 1927.

Williams, T. (ed.), *Cambridge Companion to Duns Scotus*. CUP, 2003.

―――― 'How Scotus separates morality from happiness', *American Catholic Philosophical Assoc.* 69 (1995), 425–45.

―――― 'The Moral Philosophy of John Duns Scotuss'. Doctoral Dissertation, U. Notre Dame, 1994.

Wippel, J. F., 'Thomas Aquinas and the condemnation of 1277', *Modern Schoolman* 72 (1994–5), 233–72.

Wittgenstein, L., *The Blue and Brown Books*. Oxford: Blackwell, 1958.

Wittmann, M., *Die Ethik des hl. Thomas von Aquin*. Munich: Hüber, 1933.

Wolf, S., 'Self-interest and interest in selves', *Ethics* 96 (1986), 704–20.

Wolter, A. B., 'Duns Scotus on the will as rational potency', in *PTJDS*, ch. 8.

―――― 'Native freedom of the will as a key to the ethics of Scotus', in *PTJDS*, ch. 7.

―――― *The Philosophical Theology of John Duns Scotus*. Ithaca, NY: Cornell UP, 1990.

Wood, A. W., *Karl Marx*. London: RKP, 1981.

Wood, R., *Ockham on the Virtues*. West Lafayette, Ind.: Purdue UP, 1997.

Xenophon, OCT. Cited: *Memorabilia; Symposium*.

Zeller, E., *Die Philosophie der Griechen in ihrer geschichtliche Entwicklung*, 5th edn., 6 vols. Leipzig: Reisland, 1920–3.

INDEX

The numbers refer to sections, not to pages.
Authors who are cited or quoted simply as sources (e.g., Stobaeus) are not indexed.
Italics indicate a cross-reference.
Bold type cross-refers to a more articulated entry.